P9-DOF-531
3 0379 10053 2862

Dictionary of the Middle Ages

AMERICAN COUNCIL OF LEARNED SOCIETIES

The American Council of Learned Societies, organized in 1919 for the purpose of advancing the study of the humanities and of the humanistic aspects of the social sciences, is a nonprofit federation comprising forty-six national scholarly groups. The Council represents the humanities in the United States in the International Union of Academies, provides fellowships and grants-in-aid, supports research-and-planning conferences and symposia, and sponsors special projects and scholarly publications.

MEMBER ORGANIZATIONS

AMERICAN PHILOSOPHICAL SOCIETY, 1743
AMERICAN ACADEMY OF ARTS AND SCIENCES, 1780
AMERICAN ANTIQUARIAN SOCIETY, 1812
AMERICAN ORIENTAL SOCIETY, 1842
AMERICAN NUMISMATIC SOCIETY, 1858
AMERICAN PHILOLOGICAL ASSOCIATION, 1869
ARCHAEOLOGICAL INSTITUTE OF AMERICA, 1879
SOCIETY OF BIBLICAL LITERATURE, 1880
MODERN LANGUAGE ASSOCIATION OF AMERICA, 1883
AMERICAN HISTORICAL ASSOCIATION, 1884
AMERICAN ECONOMIC ASSOCIATION, 1885
AMERICAN FOLKLORE SOCIETY, 1888
AMERICAN DIALECT SOCIETY, 1889
AMERICAN PSYCHOLOGICAL ASSOCIATION, 1892
ASSOCIATION OF AMERICAN LAW SCHOOLS, 1900
AMERICAN PHILOSOPHICAL ASSOCIATION, 1901
AMERICAN ANTHROPOLOGICAL ASSOCIATION, 1902
AMERICAN POLITICAL SCIENCE ASSOCIATION, 1903
BIBLIOGRAPHICAL SOCIETY OF AMERICA, 1904
ASSOCIATION OF AMERICAN GEOGRAPHERS, 1904
HISPANIC SOCIETY OF AMERICA, 1904
AMERICAN SOCIOLOGICAL ASSOCIATION, 1905
AMERICAN SOCIETY OF INTERNATIONAL LAW, 1906
ORGANIZATION OF AMERICAN HISTORIANS, 1907
AMERICAN ACADEMY OF RELIGION, 1909
COLLEGE ART ASSOCIATION OF AMERICA, 1912
HISTORY OF SCIENCE SOCIETY, 1924
LINGUISTIC SOCIETY OF AMERICA, 1924
MEDIAEVAL ACADEMY OF AMERICA, 1925
AMERICAN MUSICOLOGICAL SOCIETY, 1934
SOCIETY OF ARCHITECTURAL HISTORIANS, 1940
ECONOMIC HISTORY ASSOCIATION, 1940
ASSOCIATION FOR ASIAN STUDIES, 1941
AMERICAN SOCIETY FOR AESTHETICS, 1942
AMERICAN ASSOCIATION FOR THE ADVANCEMENT OF SLAVIC STUDIES, 1948
METAPHYSICAL SOCIETY OF AMERICA, 1950
AMERICAN STUDIES ASSOCIATION, 1950
RENAISSANCE SOCIETY OF AMERICA, 1954
SOCIETY FOR ETHNOMUSICOLOGY, 1955
AMERICAN SOCIETY FOR LEGAL HISTORY, 1956
AMERICAN SOCIETY FOR THEATRE RESEARCH, 1956
SOCIETY FOR THE HISTORY OF TECHNOLOGY, 1958
AMERICAN COMPARATIVE LITERATURE ASSOCIATION, 1960
MIDDLE EAST STUDIES ASSOCIATION OF NORTH AMERICA, 1966
AMERICAN SOCIETY FOR EIGHTEENTH-CENTURY STUDIES, 1969
ASSOCIATION FOR JEWISH STUDIES, 1969

Detail from the Bayeux Tapestry (1066–1083). Harold, the future king of England, is captured by Count Guy when his ship is blown ashore near St. Valéry. NATIONAL GEOGRAPHIC SOCIETY

Dictionary of the Middle Ages

JOSEPH R. STRAYER, *EDITOR IN CHIEF*

Volume 2

AUGUSTINUS TRIUMPHUS—BYZANTINE LITERATURE

CHARLES SCRIBNER'S SONS • NEW YORK

Library of Congress Cataloging in Publication Data
Main entry under title: (revised)

Dictionary of the Middle Ages.

Includes bibliographies.
1. Middle Ages—Dictionaries. I. Strayer, Joseph Reese, 1904–1987.

D114.D5 1982 909.07'03'21 82-5904
ISBN 0-684-16760-3 (v. 1) ISBN 0-684-18169-X (v. 7)
ISBN 0-684-17022-1 (v. 2) ISBN 0-684-18274-2 (v. 8)
ISBN 0-684-17023-X (v. 3) ISBN 0-684-18275-0 (v. 9)
ISBN 0-684-17024-8 (v. 4) ISBN 0-684-18276-9 (v. 10)
ISBN 0-684-18161-4 (v. 5) ISBN 0-684-18277-7 (v. 11)
ISBN 0-684-18168-1 (v. 6) ISBN 0-684-18278-5 (v. 12)

7 9 11 13 15 17 19 Q/C 20 18 16 14 12 10 8 6

PRINTED IN THE UNITED STATES OF AMERICA.

The *Dictionary of the Middle Ages* has been produced with
support from the National Endowment for the Humanities.

The paper in this book meets the guidelines for
permanence and durability of the Committee on
Production Guidelines for Book Longevity of the
Council on Library Resources.

Maps prepared by Joseph Stonehill.

Dictionary of the Middle Ages

AMERICAN COUNCIL OF LEARNED SOCIETIES

The American Council of Learned Societies, organized in 1919 for the purpose of advancing the study of the humanities and of the humanistic aspects of the social sciences, is a nonprofit federation comprising forty-six national scholarly groups. The Council represents the humanities in the United States in the International Union of Academies, provides fellowships and grants-in-aid, supports research-and-planning conferences and symposia, and sponsors special projects and scholarly publications.

MEMBER ORGANIZATIONS

AMERICAN PHILOSOPHICAL SOCIETY, 1743
AMERICAN ACADEMY OF ARTS AND SCIENCES, 1780
AMERICAN ANTIQUARIAN SOCIETY, 1812
AMERICAN ORIENTAL SOCIETY, 1842
AMERICAN NUMISMATIC SOCIETY, 1858
AMERICAN PHILOLOGICAL ASSOCIATION, 1869
ARCHAEOLOGICAL INSTITUTE OF AMERICA, 1879
SOCIETY OF BIBLICAL LITERATURE, 1880
MODERN LANGUAGE ASSOCIATION OF AMERICA, 1883
AMERICAN HISTORICAL ASSOCIATION, 1884
AMERICAN ECONOMIC ASSOCIATION, 1885
AMERICAN FOLKLORE SOCIETY, 1888
AMERICAN DIALECT SOCIETY, 1889
AMERICAN PSYCHOLOGICAL ASSOCIATION, 1892
ASSOCIATION OF AMERICAN LAW SCHOOLS, 1900
AMERICAN PHILOSOPHICAL ASSOCIATION, 1901
AMERICAN ANTHROPOLOGICAL ASSOCIATION, 1902
AMERICAN POLITICAL SCIENCE ASSOCIATION, 1903
BIBLIOGRAPHICAL SOCIETY OF AMERICA, 1904
ASSOCIATION OF AMERICAN GEOGRAPHERS, 1904
HISPANIC SOCIETY OF AMERICA, 1904
AMERICAN SOCIOLOGICAL ASSOCIATION, 1905
AMERICAN SOCIETY OF INTERNATIONAL LAW, 1906
ORGANIZATION OF AMERICAN HISTORIANS, 1907
AMERICAN ACADEMY OF RELIGION, 1909
COLLEGE ART ASSOCIATION OF AMERICA, 1912
HISTORY OF SCIENCE SOCIETY, 1924
LINGUISTIC SOCIETY OF AMERICA, 1924
MEDIAEVAL ACADEMY OF AMERICA, 1925
AMERICAN MUSICOLOGICAL SOCIETY, 1934
SOCIETY OF ARCHITECTURAL HISTORIANS, 1940
ECONOMIC HISTORY ASSOCIATION, 1940
ASSOCIATION FOR ASIAN STUDIES, 1941
AMERICAN SOCIETY FOR AESTHETICS, 1942
AMERICAN ASSOCIATION FOR THE ADVANCEMENT OF SLAVIC STUDIES, 1948
METAPHYSICAL SOCIETY OF AMERICA, 1950
AMERICAN STUDIES ASSOCIATION, 1950
RENAISSANCE SOCIETY OF AMERICA, 1954
SOCIETY FOR ETHNOMUSICOLOGY, 1955
AMERICAN SOCIETY FOR LEGAL HISTORY, 1956
AMERICAN SOCIETY FOR THEATRE RESEARCH, 1956
SOCIETY FOR THE HISTORY OF TECHNOLOGY, 1958
AMERICAN COMPARATIVE LITERATURE ASSOCIATION, 1960
MIDDLE EAST STUDIES ASSOCIATION OF NORTH AMERICA, 1966
AMERICAN SOCIETY FOR EIGHTEENTH-CENTURY STUDIES, 1969
ASSOCIATION FOR JEWISH STUDIES, 1969

Editorial Board

Advisory Committee

Editorial Staff

Contributors to Volume 2

DOROTHY AFRICA
BANSENCHAS

GUSTAVE ALEF
University of Oregon
BOYAR

JAMES W. ALEXANDER
University of Georgia
BECKET, THOMAS, ST.

THEODORE M. ANDERSSON
Stanford University
BANDAMANNA SAGA; BJARNAR SAGA HÍTDŒLAKAPPA; BRYNHILD

ANI ATAMIAN
Columbia University
ĀYĀS

JERE L. BACHARACH
University of Washington, Seattle
ʿAZĪZ BIʾLLĀH NIZĀR ABŪ MANṢŪR, AL-

BERNARD S. BACHRACH
University of Minnesota
BURGUNDIANS

JULIE O. BADIEE
Western Maryland College
BAḤR AL-MUḤĪT

J. M. BAK
University of British Columbia
BANAT; BANUS; BUDA

DEIRDRE BAKER
University of Toronto, Centre for Medieval Studies
AVIANUS

PHILIP J. BANKS
BARCELONA

FRANK G. BANTA
Indiana University
BERTHOLD VON REGENSBURG

JOHN W. BARKER
University of Wisconsin, Madison
BYZANTINE EMPIRE: HISTORY (1204–1453)

CARL F. BARNES, JR.
Oakland University
BARGEBOARD; BAR TRACERY; BERNARD OF SOISSONS; BRUNSBERG, H(E)INRICH VON; BURGHAUSEN, HANNS VON

ÜLKÜ Ü. BATES
Hunter College, City University of New York
BEDESTAN

FRANZ H. BÄUML
University of California, Los Angeles
BITEROLF UND DIETLEIB

HUGO BEKKER
Ohio State University
BRANT, SEBASTIAN

HANS BEKKER-NIELSEN
University of Odense
BISHOPS' SAGAS

ADELAIDE BENNETT
Princeton University
AVILA BIBLE, MASTER OF THE; BRAILES, WILLIAM DE

DALE L. BISHOP
Columbia University
AVESTA; BUNDAHISHN

CURTIS BLAYLOCK
University of Illinois
BASQUES

THOMAS W. BLOMQUIST
Northern Illinois University
BANKING, EUROPEAN

JONATHAN M. BLOOM
Harvard University
AZHAR, AL-; BĀDGĪR; BADR AL-JAMĀLĪ

HELEN BORELAND
Westfield College, University of London
BERCEO, GONZALO DE

DIANE BORNSTEIN
Queens College, City University of New York
BETROTHAL

CALVIN M. BOWER
University of Notre Dame
BOETHIUS, ANICIUS MANLIUS SEVERINUS

WILLIAM M. BOWSKY
University of California, Davis
BERNARDINO OF SIENA, ST.

CHARLES M. BRAND
Bryn Mawr College
BYZANTINE EMPIRE: HISTORY (1025–1204)

YURI BREGEL
Indiana University
BUKHARA

MICHAEL BRETT
University of London, School of African and Oriental Studies
BERBERS

CONTRIBUTORS TO VOLUME 2

S. KENT BROWN
Brigham Young University
AUTOCEPHALOS

ROBERT BROWNING
BELISARIOS; BYZANTINE LITERATURE

LESLIE BRUBAKER
Wheaton College
BALDACHIN; BALL-FLOWER; BAPTISM OF CHRIST; BAS-DE-PAGE; BAPTISTERY; BASILICA; BAY SYSTEM; BAYEUX TAPESTRY; BEATUS MANUSCRIPTS; BEMA; BENEDICTIONAL; BENNO OF OSNABRÜCK; BERKELEY, WILLIAM; BERNARD OF SANTIAGO; BIDUINO; BLACHERNITISSA; BOSS; BOTTEGA; BRATTISHING; BREVIARY OF ALARIC; BROUN, ROBERT; BUTTRESS

ROBERT G. CALKINS
Cornell University
BATAILLE, NICHOLAS; BIBLE MORALISÉE; BIBLIA PAUPERUM; BONDOL, JEAN; BOUCICAUT MASTER; BOURDICHON, JEAN; BROEDERLAM, MELCHIOR

ANTHONY K. CASSELL
University of Illinois
BOCCACCIO, GIOVANNI

JAMES E. CATHEY
University of Massachusetts, Amherst
BERSERKS

PETER CHARANIS
Rutgers University
BYZANTINE EMPIRE: ECONOMIC LIFE AND SOCIAL STRUCTURE

COLIN CHASE
University of Toronto, Centre for Medieval Studies
BEOWULF

FREDRIC L. CHEYETTE
Amherst College
BASTIDE; BEAUMANOIR, PHILIPPE DE

WANDA CIŻEWSKI
Pontifical Institute of Medieval Studies, Toronto
BIBLICAL INTERPRETATION

SIDNEY L. COHEN
Louisiana State University
BIRKA; BRACTEATES

LAWRENCE I. CONRAD
Princeton University
BEIRUT

ROBIN CORMACK
Courtauld Institute
BYZANTINE ART

NOEL COULSON
University of London, School of African and Oriental Studies
BLOOD MONEY, ISLAMIC LAW

WILLIAM J. COURTENAY
University of Wisconsin
BIEL, GABRIEL

EUGENE L. COX
Wellesley College
BURGUNDY, COUNTY OF; BURGUNDY, DUCHY OF

WILLIAM CRAWFORD
University of Toronto, Centre for Medieval Studies
AUSPICIUS OF TOUL; AUXILIUS

ANTHONY CUTLER
Pennsylvania State University
BYZANTINE MINOR ARTS

G. P. CUTTINO
Emory University
BORDEAUX

ABRAHAM DAVID
Hebrew University of Jerusalem
BENJAMIN OF TUDELA

PETER F. DEMBOWSKI
University of Chicago
BIOGRAPHY, SECULAR

GEORGE T. DENNIS
BALDWIN I OF THE LATIN EMPIRE

JEAN DESHUSSES, O.S.B.
Abbaye d'Hautecombe, Saint Pierre de Curtille
BENEDICT OF ANIANE

WACHTANG DJOBADZE
California State University at Los Angeles
BAGRAT'S CATHEDRAL; BANA; BEKᶜA OPIZARI; BETANIA; BITSHVINTA (PITSUNDA); BOLNISI SEON

FRED M. DONNER
Yale University
BADR, BATTLE OF

KATHERINE FISCHER DREW
Rice University
BARBARIANS, INVASIONS OF

ANDREW S. EHRENKREUTZ
University of Michigan
AYYUBIDS

E. ROZANNE ELDER
Western Michigan University
BERNARD OF CLAIRVAUX, ST.

STEPHEN R. ELL
University of Chicago
BARBERS, BARBER-SURGEONS; BEDLAM; BIOLOGY

MARCY J. EPSTEIN
Pontifical Institute of Medieval Studies, Toronto
BALLADE; BALLATA

STEVEN EPSTEIN
Harvard University
BRUNI, LEONARDO

CLAUDE EVANS
University of Toronto
BRETON LITERATURE; BRITTANY, CELTIC

THEODORE EVERGATES
Western Maryland College
BAN, BANALITÉ

ANN E. FARKAS
BASMENOYE DELO

T. S. FAUNCE
Princeton University
BODEL, JEAN

PAUL J. FEDWICK
Pontifical Institute of Medieval Studies, Toronto
BASIL THE GREAT OF CAESAREA, ST.

PAULA SUTTER FICHTNER
Brooklyn College, City University of New York
BAVARIA

RICHARD S. FIELD
Yale University
BLOCK BOOK; BOIS PROTAT

JOHN V. A. FINE, JR.
University of Michigan
BOGOMILISM; BORIS; BOSNIA; BOSNIAN CHURCH; BULGARIA

CONTRIBUTORS TO VOLUME 2

RUTH H. FIRESTONE
University of Missouri, Columbia
BUCH VON BERN, DAS

DAVID C. FOWLER
University of Washington, Seattle
BALLADS, MIDDLE ENGLISH; BIBLE, OLD AND MIDDLE ENGLISH

ROBERTA FRANK
University of Toronto, Centre for Medieval Studies
BJARNI KOLBEINSSON; BRAGI BODDASON THE OLD

JOHN B. FREED
Illinois State University
AUSTRIA; BABENBERG FAMILY; BILLUNGS; BRANDENBURG; BURGUNDY, KINGDOM OF

EDWARD FRUEH
Columbia University
BRUNO OF MAGDEBURG

KLAUS GAMBER
Liturgiewissenschaftliches Institut, Regensburg
BENEVENTAN RITE

NINA G. GARSOÏAN
Columbia University
AVARAYR; AZAT; BDEŠχ

ADELHEID M. GEALT
Indiana University
AVANZO, JACOPO; BARNA DA SIENA; BARONZIO, GIOVANNI; BARTOLINO DA NOVARA; BARTOLO DI FREDI; BENEDETTO ANTELAMI; BERLINGHIERI, BONAVENTURA; BERNARDO DA VENEZIA; BERTUCCIO; BONINO DA CAMPIONE; BONNANO DA PISA; BRAILES, WILLIAM DE; BRUNELLESCHI, FILIPPO; BUON, GIOVANNI AND BARTOLOMEO; BUSCHETO OF PISA

D. J. GEANAKOPLOS
Yale University
BESSARION

PATRICK GEARY
University of Florida
BEATIFICATION

PETER B. GOLDEN
Rutgers University
AVARS; AZERBAIJAN; BATU; BĀYĀZID I, YILDIRIM

DAVID GOLDFRANK
Georgetown University
BOGOLIUBSKII, ANDREI

ROBERT S. GOTTFRIED
Rutgers University
BLACK DEATH; BOROUGH (ENGLAND–WALES)

ARYEH GRABOIS
Haifa University
BIBLE

JAMES GRAHAM-CAMPBELL
University of London
BORRE STYLE

EDWARD GRANT
Indiana University
BURIDAN, JEAN

T. E. GREGORY
Ohio State University
BYZANTINE EMPIRE: HISTORY (330–1025)

JAMES GRIER
University of Toronto, Centre for Medieval Studies
BENEDICAMUS DOMINO

JOHN L. GRIGSBY
Washington University, St. Louis
BALLETTE; BLONDEL DE NESLE

MINNETTE GRUNMANN-GAUDET
University of Western Ontario
BERTRAND DE BAR-SUR-AUBE

LAWRENCE GUSHEE
University of Illinois
AUGUSTINUS TRIUMPHUS; AURELIAN OF RÉÔME

PIERRE-MARIE GY, O.P.
Couvent Saint-Jacques, Paris
BENEDICTIONAL; BENEDICTIONS

JEREMIAH M. G. HACKETT
Pontifical Institute of Medieval Studies, Toronto
BACON, ROGER

NATHALIE HANLET
Columbia University
BRUNO OF SEGNI, ST.

JACK R. HARLAN
University of Illinois
BREAD

RALPH S. HATTOX
Princeton University
BEVERAGES, ISLAMIC

R. H. HELMHOLZ
Washington University, St. Louis
BLASPHEMY

HEATHER HENDERSON
University of Toronto, Centre for Medieval Studies
AURAICEPT NA NÉCES

SCOTT H. HENDRIX
Lutheran Theological Southern Seminary
BRETHREN OF THE COMMON LIFE

JOHN HENNIG
AVE MARIA

ROBERT H. HEWSEN
Glassboro State College
AYRARAT; BARDHAᶜA; BAYLAḲĀN; BERKRI

BENNETT D. HILL
University of Illinois
BENEDICTINES

JOHN H. HILL
BALDWIN I OF JERUSALEM; BOHEMOND I, PRINCE OF ANTIOCH

DAVID HOOK
University of London
AUTO DE LOS REYES MAGOS

JOHN HOWE
Texas Tech University
BRUNO OF QUERFURT, ST.

PETER HUENINK
Vassar College
BERNWARD

LUCY-ANNE HUNT
University of Birmingham
AXUMITE ART

PAUL R. HYAMS
University of Oxford
BLOOD LIBEL

J. K. HYDE
University of Manchester
BOLOGNA, UNIVERSITY OF

W. T. H. JACKSON
Columbia University
BEAST EPIC; BERENGARII IMPERATORIS GESTA; BURCHARD OF WORMS

CONTRIBUTORS TO VOLUME 2

C. STEPHEN JAEGER
Bryn Mawr College
BLIGGER VON STEINACH

MICHAEL JEFFREYS
University of Sidney
BYZANTINE LITERATURE: POPULAR; BYZANTINE POETIC FORMS

JAMES J. JOHN
Cornell University
BULL, PAPAL

CHARLES W. JONES
University of California, Berkeley
BEDE

MICHAEL JONES
University of Nottingham
BRITTANY, DUCHY

CHRISTIANE L. JOOST-GAUGIER
New Mexico State University
BELLINI, JACOPO

WILLIAM CHESTER JORDAN
Princeton University
BAILIFF; BAILLI; BANKING, JEWISH, IN EUROPE; BARON; BLANCHE OF CASTILE; BUTLER

WALTER EMIL KAEGI, JR.
University of Chicago
BYZANTINE EMPIRE: BUREAUCRACY

HOWARD KAMINSKY
Florida International University
BABYLONIAN CAPTIVITY

TRUDY S. KAWAMI
BISHAPUR

SUSAN ANN KEEFE
BAPTISM

DOUGLAS KELLY
University of Wisconsin, Madison
BENOÎT DE SAINTE-MAURE

THOMAS E. KELLY
Purdue University
BESTIAIRE D'AMOUR

MARILYN KAY KENNEY
University of Toronto, Centre for Medieval Studies
BANGOR (WALES); BERWICK, TREATY OF

JULIUS KIRSHNER
University of Chicago
BALDUS; BARTOLO DA SASSOFERRATO

M. JEAN KITCHEL
University of St. Thomas, Houston
BURLEY, WALTER

JOHN KLASSEN
Trinity Western College
BOHEMIA-MORAVIA

JAMES E. KNIRK
University of Wisconsin, Madison
BRETA SQGUR

BERND KRATZ
University of Kentucky
BERTHOLD VON HOLLE; BRUDER HANS

MICHAEL KWATERA, O.S.B.
St. John's Abbey
BOOK OF HOURS; BREVIARY

JACOB LASSNER
Wayne State University
BAGHDAD; BARMAKIDS

LOUIS J. LEKAI
BIBLE, CISTERCIAN

ROBERT E. LERNER
Northwestern University
BEGUINES AND BEGHARDS; BEGUINS

ROY F. LESLIE
University of Victoria
BRUT, THE

ARCHIBALD R. LEWIS
University of Massachusetts
BARRELS

JOHN LINDOW
University of California, Berkeley
BALDR; BALDRS DRAUMAR

DONALD P. LITTLE
McGill University
BARQŪQ

MICHAEL P. LONG
University of Wisconsin, Madison
BELLS

JAMES F. LYDON
University of Dublin
BURGH, DE

BRYCE LYON
Brown University
BALDWIN I OF FLANDERS; BARONS' WAR; BRUGES

JOHN M. McCULLOH
Kansas State University
BRANDEUM

DAVID R. McLINTOCK
University of London
BAPTISMAL VOWS, OLD HIGH GERMAN/OLD SAXON; BIBLICAL POETRY, GERMAN

GEORGE P. MAJESKA
University of Maryland
BOCHKA

KRIKOR H. MAKSOUDIAN
Columbia University
BAGRATIDS (BAGRATUNI), ARMENIAN; BIBLE, ARMENIAN

FEDWA MALTI-DOUGLAS
University of Texas at Austin
BIOGRAPHY, ISLAMIC

SHAUN E. MARMON
Princeton University
BAB AL-MANDAB; BAḤRAYN, AL-; BAṬṬŪṬA, IBN; BAYBARS AL-BUNDUQDĀRĪ

H. SALVADOR MARTÍNEZ
New York University
¡AY, IHERUSALEM!

JOAQUÍN MARTÍNEZ-PIZARRO
Oberlin College
BJARKAMÁL

E. ANN MATTER
University of Pennsylvania
AUTPERTUS, AMBROSIUS

BRIAN MERRILEES
University of Toronto
BLANCHEFLOUR ET FLORENCE; BOEVE (BEUVES) DE HAUMTONE

JOHN MEYENDORFF
Fordham University
AZYMES; BARLAAM OF CALABRIA; BYZANTINE CHURCH

MARK D. MEYERSON
University of Toronto, Centre for Medieval Studies
BENZO OF ALBA; BERNORINUS; BERTHARIUS; BOVO II OF CORVEY

ANNE M. MORGANSTERN
Ohio State University
BAERZE, JACQUES DE; BEAUNEVEU, ANDRÉ

CONTRIBUTORS TO VOLUME 2

ROY PARVIZ MOTTAHEDEH
Princeton University
BUYIDS

ROBERT MULTHAUF
Smithsonian Institution
BREWING

M. K. NELLIS
Clarkson College
BEAUTY AIDS, COSMETICS

JOHN W. NESBITT
BESANT

HELMUT NICKEL
Metropolitan Museum of Art, New York
BOW AND ARROW/CROSSBOW

TIMOTHY B. NOONE
University of Toronto, Centre for Medieval Studies
AVITUS, ST.

TORE S. NYBERG
University of Odense
BIRGITTA, ST.

W. A. ODDY
The British Museum
BRONZE AND BRASS

THOMAS H. OHLGREN
Purdue University
BARD

NICHOLAS OIKONOMIDES
University of Montreal
AUTOCRATOR; BASILEUS; BASILICS

PÁDRAIG P. Ó NÉILL
University of North Carolina, Chapel Hill
BIBLE, GLOSSES AND COMMENTARIES (IRISH); BOOKS, LITURGICAL (CELTIC); BRIGIT (BRIGID), ST.

ANGELO PAREDI
Biblioteca Ambrosiana
BUCENTAUR

CLAUDE J. PEIFER, O.S.B.
St. Bede Abbey
BENEDICT BISCOP, ST.; BENEDICT OF NURSIA, ST.

CHARLES PELLAT
BASRA

ELIZABETH WILSON POE
Tulane University
BERNART DE VENTADORN; BERTRAN DE BORN

E. J. POLAK
Queensborough Community College, City University of New York
BONCOMPAGNO (BUONCOMPAGNO) OF SIGNA

JAMES M. POWELL
Syracuse University
BONIFACE, ST.

WADĀD AL-QĀḌĪ
American University of Beirut
BALĀDHURĪ, ABŪ ḤASAN AḤMĀD IBN YAHYA IBN JĀBIR AL-

J. F. QUINN
Pontifical Institute of Medieval Studies, Toronto
BONAVENTURE, ST.

ROGER E. REYNOLDS
Pontifical Institute of Medieval Studies, Toronto
BANGOR, RITE OF; BLESSED VIRGIN MARY, LITTLE OFFICE OF

I. S. ROBINSON
University of Dublin
BERNOLD OF CONSTANCE

H. ROE
University of Toronto, Centre for Medieval Studies
BARDIC GRAMMARS (IRISH, WELSH)

EDWARD H. ROESNER
New York University
BAMBERG MANUSCRIPT

LINDA ROSE
BAR HEBRAEUS; BARDAS CAESAR; BARI; BONIFACE OF MONTFERRAT; BOSPORUS; BRUSA

CHARLES STANLEY ROSS
Purdue University
BARBOUR, JOHN

BERYL ROWLAND
York University
BESTIARY

TEOFILO F. RUIZ
Brooklyn College, City University of New York
AVIZ, ORDER OF

JAMES R. RUSSELL
Columbia University
BAHRĀM V GŌR; BAHRĀM VI ČŌBĒN

RAYMOND C. ST-JACQUES
University of Ottawa
BIBLE, FRENCH

GEORGE SALIBA
Columbia University
BĪRŪNĪ, MUḤAMMAD IBN AḤMAD ABŪ' L-RAYḤĀN AL-

CHRISTOPHER SANDERS
University of Copenhagen
BEVERS SAGA

T. A. SANDQUIST
University of Toronto
BRACTON, HENRY DE

ELLEN C. SCHWARTZ
Eastern Michigan University
BULGARIAN ART AND ARCHITECTURE

STANFORD J. SHAW
University of California, Los Angeles
BĀYAZĪD II

LEAH SHOPKOW
University of Toronto, Centre for Medieval Studies
AYNARD OF ST. ÈVRE; BRAULIO OF SARAGOSSA, ST.

GIULIO SILANO
AZO

JAMES SNYDER
Bryn Mawr College
BERMEJO, BARTOLOMÉ; BERRUGUETE, PEDRO; BERTRAM, MEISTER; BORRASSÁ, LUIS; BOUTS, DIRK

ROBERT SOMERVILLE
Columbia University
BERENGAR OF TOURS

PRISCILLA SOUCEK
New York University, Institute of Fine Arts
BĀB; BĀDIYA; BAWWĀB, IBN AL-

SUSAN SPECTORSKY
Queens College, City University of New York
BUKHĀRĪ, AL-

CONTRIBUTORS TO VOLUME 2

JERRY STANNARD
University of Kansas
BOTANY

ALAIN J. STOCLET
University of Toronto, Centre for Medieval Studies
BENEDICTINE RULE

JOSEPH R. STRAYER
Princeton University
AUSCULTA FILI; AVIGNON; BANNERET; BENEFICE, ECCLESIASTICAL; BENEFICE, LAY; BRICK; BRITTON; BULGARUS; BURGUNDIO OF PISA

RONALD G. SUNY
University of Michigan
AZNAURI; BAGRATIDS (BAGRATUNI), GEORGIAN

DONALD W. SUTHERLAND
University of Iowa
BOROUGH-ENGLISH; BURGAGE TENURE

EDWARD A. SYNAN
Pontifical Institute of Medieval Studies, Toronto
BRUNO OF WÜRZBURG, ST.; BRUNO THE CARTHUSIAN, ST.

CLAIBORNE W. THOMPSON
BÓSA SAGA OK HERRAUÐS

R. W. THOMSON
Harvard University
BALAVARIANI

DAVID R. TOWNSEND
University of Toronto, Centre for Medieval Studies
BAUDRI OF BOURGUEIL; BEBO OF BAMBERG

WARREN T. TREADGOLD
Stanford University
BARDAS PHOKAS; BARDAS SKLEROS; BASIL I THE MACEDONIAN; BASIL II "KILLER OF BULGARS"

AVRAM L. UDOVITCH
Princeton University
BANKING, ISLAMIC

WILLIAM L. URBAN
Monmouth College
BALTIC COUNTRIES/BALTS

GEORGES VAJDA
Centre National de la Recherche Scientifique, Paris
BAḤYA BEN JOSEPH IBN PAQUDA

JOHN VAN ENGEN
University of Notre Dame
BENEDICTUS LEVITA

PHILIPPE VERDIER
Cleveland Museum of Art
BOUCHER, GUILLAUME

CHARLES VERLINDEN
AZORES; BLACKS

ROSALIE VERMETTE
Indiana University
BARLAAM AND JOSAPHAT

EVELYN BIRGE VITZ
New York University
BIOGRAPHY, FRENCH

MUHAMMAD ISA WALEY
The British Library
BURĀQ

DAVID A. WALSH
University of Rochester
BARISANUS OF TRANI

JAMES A. WEISHEIPL
Pontifical Institute of Medieval Studies, Toronto
BRADWARDINE, THOMAS

HAIJO JAN WESTRA
University of Calgary
BERNARD OF CHARTRES; BERNARD SILVESTER

ESTELLE WHELAN
New York Univeristy
AYYUBID ART AND ARCHITECTURE; AZULEJO; BADR AL-DĪN LUʾLUʾ; BARBOTINE; BAYT; BLAZON

JOHN WILLIAMS
University of Pittsburgh
BAÇÓ, JAIME; BASSA, FERRER

MARTHA WOLFF
National Gallery of Art
BURIN

KLAUS W. WOLLENWEBER
Memorial University of Newfoundland
BAUERNHOCHZEIT, DIE; BUSSARD, DER

CHARLES T. WOOD
Dartmouth College
BONIFACE VIII, POPE

ABIGAIL ANN YOUNG
University of Toronto, Centre for Medieval Studies
AURELIANUS, AMBROSIUS

JAROLD K. ZEMAN
Acadia University
BOHEMIAN BRETHREN

RONALD EDWARD ZUPKO
Marquette University
BARREL; BOISSEAU; BOLL; BUSHEL

Dictionary of the Middle Ages

Dictionary of the Middle Ages

AUGUSTINUS TRIUMPHUS—BYZANTINE LITERATURE

AUGUSTINUS TRIUMPHUS (**Augustine of Ancona,** *ca.* 1275–1328), Augustinian friar, teacher, and author, was born in Ancona. The errors in many earlier biographical accounts (the name Triumphus, a birth date of 1243, supposed acquaintance with Thomas Aquinas) stem from his adoption as ancestor by G. B. Trionfo at the end of the sixteenth century. Augustine's first documented appearance is as lector at Padua in 1297 or 1298. He was then sent by his order to Paris for the study of theology, returning around 1305 to Padua, where he taught for nearly a decade. He went to Paris again and became a master of theology in 1315, as well as regent of his order's studium generale.

After stays in Padua and Venice, Augustine settled in Naples in 1321 as regent of the studium there, also becoming chaplain and counselor to King Robert of Naples and his son Charles. Although Augustine had made plans to return to Ancona, perhaps due to failing health, death overtook him in Naples in April 1328.

In matters of philosophy and theology Augustine is generally understood as a follower of Giles of Rome (Aegidius Romanus) and thus of Thomas Aquinas. Despite strong and developed positions concerning predestination and the Immaculate Conception, Augustine was chiefly influential in his writing supporting the sovereignty of the pope over monarchs in temporal matters; his *Summa de ecclesiastica potestate* was warmly regarded by John XXII in 1326 and was very widely distributed in manuscript and printed editions, with no fewer than five incunabula. His position was that the pope, as the vicar of Christ, had authority in both spiritual and temporal affairs; this authority came directly from God and was delegated by the pope to secular rulers. Thus the Donation of Constantine was only a restoration by the emperor to the pope of usurped powers.

The *Summa* was the culmination of an interest in questions of authority and governance that had been evident at the outset of Augustine's career in treatises defending Boniface VIII against the accusations of Philip IV the Fair *(. . . contra articulos inventos ad diffamandum Bonifacium VIII),* denying to the French king the right of adjudging the Knights Templar heretics *(. . . super facto Templariorum),* and subordinating the college of cardinals to the pope *(De potestate collegii mortuo papa).*

The extreme interest of historians in these works so closely entangled in the most inflamed political issues of the fourteenth century has meant that our grasp, both bibliographical and interpretative, of his other writing remains rather primitive. The definitive canon is yet to be established. Although Augustine's tombstone (no longer extant) mentioned thirty-six volumes of his works, Ministeri accepts only twenty-seven as authentic, dividing them more or less evenly between philosophical, theological, scriptural, and political writings. A modern critical evaluation of his work as a whole and its influence appears to be wanting.

BIBLIOGRAPHY

Bibliographies may be found in Willigis Eckermann's survey, in *Theologische Realenzyklopädie,* IV (1979), 744; and in the *Bibliographie historique de l'Ordre de Saint-Augustin 1945–1975.* Also consult B. Ministeri, "De Augustini de Ancona vita et operibus," in *Analecta Augustiniana,* 22 (1951–1952).

LAWRENCE GUSHEE

[See also **Boniface VIII; John XXII; Papacy; Philip IV the Fair.**]

AURAICEPT NA NÉCES. The Irish "Scholars' Primer" is sometimes described as the first grammar written in a European vernacular. It is not organized as a systematic treatise, but amounts to an anthology of pre-Norman Irish scholarship on language. The oldest part of the text, an Old Irish tract on ogham (eighth century?), forms only a tiny portion of the whole, which is in Middle Irish and Early Modern Irish. Both major recensions of the *Auraicept na nÉces* consist mainly of successive layers of gloss and commentary. Judging from the language of this commentary, the text was studied actively, and thus augmented, into the twelfth century.

The *Auraicept* grammarians cite both "Latinists" (Donatus and Priscian, for example) and "Féne," experts in Irish learning, as authorities. At certain points they also employ two sets of grammatical terms, one consisting of Latin loan-words and calques, found in monastic products such as the St. Gall glosses on Priscian, and the other of equivalents recognized as Irish. Whatever the milieu in which the *Auraicept* was produced, it is clear that its students drew on the work of the monastic schools, in which Latin grammar formed the core of the curriculum, and applied techniques and schemata derived from these studies to native historical, legal, and literary learning. The commentators' reliance on etymology as a means of explication reflects the influence of Isidore of Seville, and many of the outwardly puzzling aspects of the presentation of grammatical material are to be understood as attempts to adapt descriptive categories and techniques used in Latin grammars to the Irish language.

Twelfth-century changes in political and ecclesiastical organization undermined the "mixed" scholarly milieu that had produced the *Auraicept,* but it retained its prestige as a canonical tract in the later secular bardic schools, and was widely circulated in manuscripts of the fourteenth century and later.

BIBLIOGRAPHY

Edition. George Calder, ed., *Auraicept na n-Eces* (1917).

Secondary Works. O. J. Bergin, "The Native Irish Grammarian," in *Proceedings of the British Academy,* **24** (1938); and Brian Ó Cuív, "Linguistic Terminology in the Mediaeval Irish Bardic Tracts," in *Transactions of the Philological Society* (1965).

HEATHER HENDERSON

[See also **Bardic Grammars; Irish Literature; Ogham; Virgil the Grammarian.**]

AURELIAN OF RÉÔME (Aurelianus Reomensis) (*fl.* 840–850), at one time a member of the Benedictine community of Moutiers-Saint-Jean in Burgundy, wrote the first treatise on plainchant, usually titled *Musica disciplina.* This is his only known work; and nothing more is known of his life. The most original and detailed sections of the work are those on the ecclesiastical modes and on the recitation formulas and the means of connecting them with antiphons. The section on the modes offers important evidence, both theoretical and anecdotal, of connections between Byzantine and Carolingian church music. Aurelian also presents a compendium of musical learning drawn from Boethius, Cassiodorus, and Isidore of Seville and, in the final chapter, from contemporary sources.

BIBLIOGRAPHY

Musica disciplina, edited by L. Gushee, was published as Corpus Scriptorum de Musica no. 21 (1975).

LAWRENCE GUSHEE

[See also **Music, Liturgical; Musical Treatises (General Overview).**]

AURELIANUS, AMBROSIUS (*fl.* first half of fifth century), was a Romano-British military leader. For knowledge of him we are indebted chiefly to Gildas (sixth century) and to earlier traditions handed down by Nennius (ninth century).

From Gildas we know that Ambrosius was of Roman ancestry, that his parents had "worn the purple," that he was sober-minded, and that he had living descendants in Gildas' day. Most important, we learn that he led the British to victory over the Saxons at an unnamed place when the Saxons turned to plunder after being hired by the "proud tyrant" of Britain—doubtless King Vortigern, who took over after the official Roman withdrawal.

Bede adds nothing to Gildas' account when he recapitulates Ambrosius' deeds, but Nennius adds several new details that muddle the tradition somewhat. He makes him the king of all kings of the British and he represents Vortigern as acting partially out of fear of Ambrosius when he hires the Saxons to fight against the Picts and the Scots. We can only suppose that Nennius thought that Ambrosius, rather than Vortigern, was the high king, and that Vortigern was a subsidiary monarch.

As a Roman of senatorial rank or descended from those with imperial pretensions (hence Gildas' reference to purple, which connotes royalty to Bede and Nennius), Ambrosius is remembered by Nennius only in the strange story of Vortigern's tower. Vortigern attempts to build a fortress, but its foundations crumble in the night; a fatherless boy is found for the sacrifice necessary to dedicate the new structure. But he prophesies, showing Vortigern a pool below the tower in which a white dragon (the British) overcomes a red dragon (the Saxons). The boy says that his name is Ambrosius and that his father was a Roman consul. Thus Nennius creates a double character out of Gildas' probably historical Ambrosius: a British high king and the prophetic child of Celtic myth. But he knows of no military victory by either over the Saxons. Instead, the military hero of the British, for Nennius, is Arthur.

All the later mentions of Ambrosius are tied to the Arthurian legend and are based on Nennius or Gildas. The prophetic child of Vortigern's tower becomes Ambrosius Merlin, the Merlin of Arthurian romance, in Geoffrey of Monmouth and Orderic Vitalis. Only William of Malmesbury, in *De gestis regum Anglorum,* recalls the warrior of Gildas. He makes Ambrosius a Roman and Vortigern's successor on the throne, and Arthur his commander in chief. Thereafter, it is Ambrosius Merlin who is remembered, not Ambrosius Aurelianus.

Modern historical research and archaeology have done little to increase our knowledge of Ambrosius. We have learned a great deal about his times, all of which suggests that a Romano-British military commander of high rank is by no means an unlikely figure. But no coins, inscriptions, or other physical remains have been discovered. So the two key questions remain: who was Ambrosius, and what did he do?

Modern research indicates that there were two parties in fifth-century Britain: a pro-British party, led by Vortigern (whose name is a British title meaning "high king") and probably Pelagian in sympathy, and a pro-Roman party, Catholic in sympathy. Ambrosius is thought to have led the latter, thus explaining the hint of hostility between Ambrosius and Vortigern in Nennius. It is interesting to note that the original title of both Ambrosius and Arthur is *dux,* a Roman rank.

What Ambrosius did is less clear, but the current consensus is that under his leadership the British returned to late Roman methods of combat, using heavy cavalry, which enabled them to throw back the Saxon invaders for a time. Perhaps the greatest mystery about Ambrosius, however, is why he never captured the romantic imagination as did his shadowy successor, Arthur.

BIBLIOGRAPHY

See *Bede's Ecclesiastical History,* Bertram Colgrave and R. A. B. Mynors, eds. (1969); *Gildae Sapientis de excidio et conquestu Britanniae,* Theodor Mommsen, ed. (1898), 1–85; *Historia Britonum cum additamentis Nennii,* Theodor Mommsen, ed. (1898), 111–222; William of Malmesbury, *De gestis regum Anglorum libri quinque. Historiae novellae libri tres,* William Stubbs, ed., 2 vols. (1887–1889). Also see E. K. Chambers, *Arthur of Britain* (1927); Robin G. Collingwood and J. N. L. Myres, *Roman Britain and the English Settlements* (1937); Sheppard Frere, *Brittania* (1967); and John Francis Haverfield, *The Romanization of Roman Britain,* 4th ed., rev. Sir George MacDonald (1923). For more detail concerning the political climate of late Roman Britain, see J. H. Ward, "Vortigern and the End of Roman Britain," in *Britannia,* 3 (1972). For a description of a villa attributed to Aurelianus, see S. Applebaum, "Some Observations on the Economy of the Roman Villa at Bignor, Sussex," in *Britannia,* 6 (1975).

ABIGAIL ANN YOUNG

[See also **Arthurian Literature; Bede (St.); England, Anglo-Saxon; Gildas; Nennius (Historia Brittonum).**]

AURICEPT NA NECES. See **Auraicept na nÉces.**

AUSCULTA FILI, papal bull of Boniface VIII against Philip the Fair (Philip IV), king of France (1285–1314). Philip had angered the pope by arresting a French bishop as a traitor on very scant evidence. Since Philip did not make amends (although he did release the bishop), Boniface called a council of French prelates to consider Philip's misdeeds and to propose measures that would reform the policies of the French government. This decision was announced to Philip in the bull *Ausculta fili,* 5 December 1301. In the bull, Boniface emphatically asserted his superiority over all kings and over Philip in particular, and announced that the council he was calling was to provide for the good government and welfare of France. The bull infuriated Philip, who set in motion the summoning of the assemblies to denounce Boniface, the attempt to call a Church council to depose Boniface, and finally the expedition of Guillaume de Nogaret to Italy to arrest the pope at Anagni in 1303.

BIBLIOGRAPHY

Georges Aigard, *Phillippe le Bel et le Saint-Siège* (1936); Joseph R. Strayer, *The Reign of Philip the Fair* (1980). Simon Vigor, *Histoire du différend d'entre le pape Boniface VIII et Philippe le Bel, roy de France,* Pierre Dupuy, ed. and trans. (1655), gives the text of the bull on pp. 48–52. It was erased from the papal registers by order of Pope Clement V.

JOSEPH R. STRAYER

[See also **Boniface VIII; Nogaret, Guillaume de; Philip IV the Fair.**]

AUSPICIUS OF TOUL, saint and fifth bishop of Toul (*ca.* 470–487), and a contemporary of Sidonius Apollinaris, was the author of a Latin verse letter to Arbogast, the Frankish comes at Trier, in which he praises Arbogast and then urges him to shun cupidity and avarice and show respect for Iamblichus, bishop of Trier. The verse form of the letter is the earliest rhythmical imitation of the "Ambrosian" stanza, and as such it has held an important place in the controversy over the origins and development of rhythmical Latin verse.

BIBLIOGRAPHY

W. Meyer, "Die rythmischen Jamben des Auspicius," in *Nachrichten von der Königlichen Gesellschaft der Wissenschaften zu Göttingen: Philologisch-historische Klasse* (1906), 192–229. The best edition of the text is found here. The first half of the poem is printed in *The Oxford Book of Medieval Latin Verse,* edited by F. J. E. Raby (1959), 45–46.

F. J. E. Raby, *A History of Christian Latin Poetry from the Beginnings to the Close of the Middle Ages,* 2nd ed. (1953), 82–83. The bibliography on Auspicius and the development of rhythmical Latin verse is extensive.

WILLIAM CRAWFORD

[See also **Latin Meter.**]

AUSTIN FRIARS. See **Augustinian Friars.**

AUSTRIA. Most of the territory of modern Austria belonged to the Roman provinces of Noricum and Pannonia. When the Romans withdrew in the fifth century, the wealthier inhabitants accompanied them; but pockets of the Christianized and Romanized, Illyrian-Celtic population survived, especially in the western Alpine valleys, until the tenth century, when they were finally Germanized. The former Roman military settlements, including Vienna, continued to be inhabited; and some of the Christian cultic centers, such as the monastery of St. Peter's at Salzburg, appear to have weathered the collapse of the empire. Various tribes, including the Huns, Ostrogoths, and Lombards, passed through the country during the period of migrations.

The Bavarians, an amalgamation of smaller Germanic tribes, settled in the Alpine foothills and in the Danube Valley at the beginning of the sixth century. The Avars and Slavs appeared in the second half of the century, and occupied the territory east of the Tauern and the Traun. The Alpine Slavs submitted to Bavarian rule in the eighth century, and the Enns formed the border between the Avars and Bavarians in the Danube Valley. St. Rupert, a former bishop of Worms, who came to Salzburg in 696, labored among the surviving Christians and began mission work among the Slavs. St. Boniface established the actual bishopric of Salzburg in 739. Monasteries, such as Kremsmünster in Upper Austria, founded by Duke Tassilo III in 777, became centers for the propagation of the faith.

Charlemagne deposed Tassilo in 788 and assumed direct control of Bavaria, which had been under nominal Frankish hegemony since the sixth century. He continued the Bavarian dukes' battle against the Avars, who finally submitted in 803. The newly conquered territory, which was linked with the neighboring Traungau, underwent several administrative reorganizations. It was divided into a mark along the Danube, stretching from the Enns to the Wienerwald; Upper Pannonia, the territory between the Wienerwald and the Raba; Lower Pannonia, which extended to the southeast as far as the confluence of the Danube and the Drava; and the Carantanian mark, roughly the present-day Austrian provinces of Carinthia and Styria. The Frankish counts and the Slavic princes reported to the prefect of the east.

At Charlemagne's request Pope Leo III elevated Salzburg to the rank of an archbishopric in 798, and it assumed the primary responsibility for the conversion of the pagans. The patron saints of Vienna's

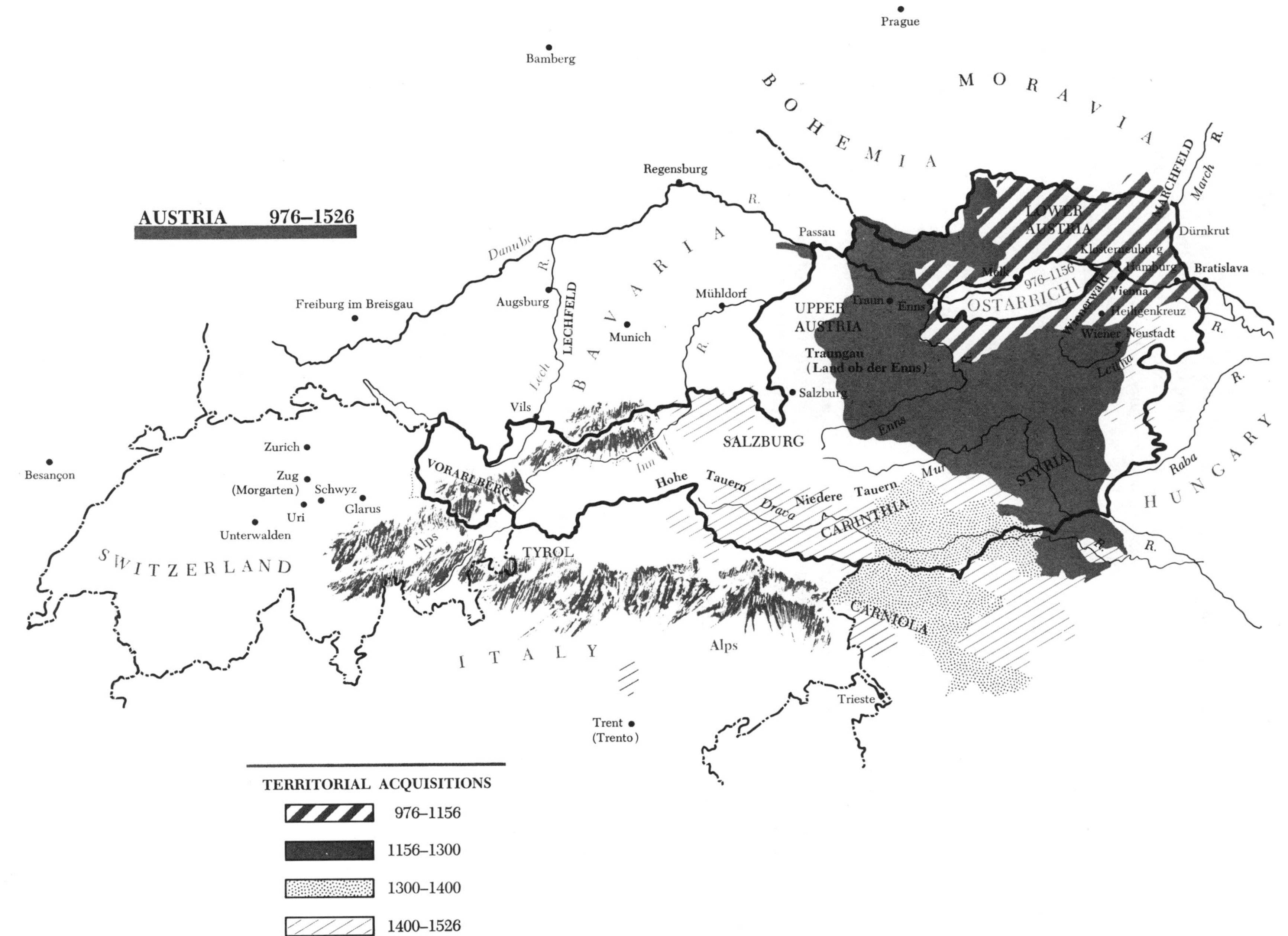
AUSTRIA 976–1526
Prague
Bamberg
BOHEMIA
MORAVIA
MARCHFELD
March R.
Regensburg
R.
Passau
LOWER AUSTRIA
Dürnkrut
Klosterneuburg
Hainburg
Bratislava
Melk
976–1156
OSTARRICHI
Wienerwald
Vienna
Heiligenkreuz
Wiener Neustadt
Leitha
Danube
R.
Freiburg im Breisgau
Augsburg
LECHFELD
BAVARIA
Munich
Mühldorf
R.
Traun
Enns
UPPER AUSTRIA
Traungau
(Land ob der Enns)
Salzburg
Lech
Vils
SALZBURG
Enns
Inn
Mur
STYRIA
Raba
HUNGARY
R.
R.
R.
Besançon
Zurich
Zug
(Morgarten)
Schwyz
Glarus
Uri
Unterwalden
SWITZERLAND
VORARLBERG
Alps
TYROL
Hohe Tauern
Niedere Tauern
Drava
CARINTHIA
CARNIOLA
ITALY
Alps
Trieste
Trent
(Trento)
TERRITORIAL ACQUISITIONS
976–1156
1156–1300
1300–1400
1400–1526

AUSTRIA

two oldest churches, St. Peter's and St. Rupert's, are a reminder of Salzburg's missionary activities in the ninth century. The Danubian counties were eventually assigned to the diocese of Passau, while Carantania as far as the Drava belonged to Salzburg. This remained the basic diocesan organization until the fifteenth century.

Carolingian rule east of the Enns collapsed in 907, when a Bavarian army under the leadership of Margrave Luitpold, the eastern prefect and the actual ruler of Bavaria during the minority of Louis the Child, was annihilated by the Magyars at Bratislava. There was, nevertheless, considerable continuity between the Carolingian and Ottonian periods. The Bavarian bishoprics and abbeys, which the Carolingians had richly endowed with property in the colonial lands, retained their claims; and the important noble families in southeastern Germany were the descendants of the Carolingian counts in the marks.

Otto the Great's defeat of the Magyars on the Lechfeld, south of Augsburg, in 955 opened up the Danubian mark once again to German penetration. A Margrave Burchard is first mentioned around 970, but he was deposed in 976 for joining the revolt of his wife's nephew, Duke Henry the Wrangler of Bavaria, and was replaced by Leopold I (976–994), who established his residence at Melk. The selection of the first Babenberg margrave in 976 is usually described as marking the birth of Austria. Bishop Otto of Freising (1138–1158), the son of Leopold III, traced his family's ancestry to a Frankish count named Adalbert, who was executed in 906 and whose chief residence had been Bamberg, from which the surname Babenberg is derived. Modern scholars are inclined, however, to link the Babenbergs, on account of their characteristic first name Leopold (Luitpold), to the Luitpoldingians, the tenth-century dukes of Bavaria, who were the descendants of the Luitpold killed at Bratislava. The Babenbergs governed the mark and the later duchy for 270 years.

The early Babenbergs were engaged in almost constant warfare with the Poles, Czechs, and Magyars along the mark's ill-defined northern and eastern boundaries. The German kings, who often retained the duchy of Bavaria for themselves in the eleventh century, undertook several campaigns in the mark. Henry III and Margrave Adalbert (1018–1055) defeated the Magyars in 1043 and fixed the mark's eastern border along the March and Leitha; this remained the Austro-Hungarian border until 1918. The mark was first called Ostarrichi, the modern Österreich, in 996; the Latin designation Austria appeared in the second quarter of the twelfth century. Large-scale land reclamation and German settlement began around 1050. The Babenbergs gained comparatively little from these advances because the kings were reluctant to increase the margraves' power by enfeoffing them with land from the royal domain.

Like so many other German princes, the Babenbergs benefited from the turmoil of the Investiture Conflict. Through the marriage of Leopold III (margrave 1095–1136) to King Henry V's sister Agnes, the widow of Duke Frederick I of Swabia, they became the kinsmen of both the Salians and the Hohenstaufen, and gained control of the royal domain in the mark. At the same time Leopold remained on friendly terms with such ardent reformers as Archbishop Conrad I of Salzburg (1106–1147), who promoted the spread of the Hirsau customs and the Augustinian canons in the Alpine lands. The margrave himself founded the collegiate church of Klosterneuburg and the Cistercian abbey of Heiligenkreuz. Leopold was canonized in 1485, and has been the patron saint of Lower Austria since 1663.

When Conrad III became king in 1138, he relied heavily on his Babenberg half brothers. He enfeoffed Leopold IV (1136–1141) and Henry II (1141–1177) with the Welfs' Bavarian duchy, thus embroiling them in the Hohenstaufen-Welf feud. Frederick Barbarossa terminated the strife in 1156 by restoring Bavaria to his Welf cousin Henry the Lion, and compensated his Babenberg uncle by separating the mark from Bavaria and elevating it to the rank of a duchy.

At the same time the emperor conferred on Henry II Jasomirgott the so-called Lesser Privilege *(Privilegium minus)*, which made the duchy inheritable in both the male and the female lines, granted the duke and his wife the right to select their heir if they had no children, required the duke to attend only imperial diets held in Bavaria and to participate only in campaigns in neighboring territories, and recognized the duke's judicial supremacy in the duchy. It was a crucial step in the duchy's evolution into a sovereign principality and in Austria's eventual separation from Germany. Vienna became the new duke's chief residence.

In 1192, Henry's son Leopold V (1177–1194) acquired Styria in accordance with an agreement that he had reached with its childless duke, Otakar IV, in 1186. The nucleus of Styria was the mark in the Mur

AUSTRIA

Valley, which had been linked with four other counties in the eleventh century. This complex, which took its name from the Otakars' ancestral castle of Steyr in the Traungau, had been elevated to a duchy in 1180. It was a valuable acquisition, since the Otakars had already eliminated most of their noble rivals and were the advocates of most of the ecclesiastical foundations in the duchy. Among the princes only the Premyslids in Bohemia surpassed the Babenbergs in wealth after the union of Austria and Styria. Leopold V is best remembered in English-speaking countries for capturing Richard Lion-Heart as he was returning from the Third Crusade. The duke used his share of the ransom money to build Wiener Neustadt in his newly acquired Styrian domains.

The reign of Leopold VI (1194–1230), who succeeded his brother Frederick I (1194–1198) as the duke of Austria, was the golden age of medieval Austria. Most of the noble families in the duchy had died out by the beginning of the thirteenth century, and the Babenbergs had acquired their lordships and advocacies through inheritance and purchase. Leopold promoted the development of the Austrian and Styrian towns. He granted Vienna valuable trading privileges and a municipal charter, enlarged the city to its medieval town limits, and tried to make it into the episcopal see of a new Austrian bishopric. Walther von der Vogelweide and the unknown author of the *Nibelungenlied* spent time at his court. Leopold himself gained an international reputation as a chivalrous knight by participating in both the Albigensian and the Fifth Crusades.

Leopold's son Frederick II (1230–1246), nicknamed "the Quarrelsome," saw himself as a virtually independent ruler. He quickly antagonized his ministerials, various churches, and the neighboring princes. In 1236, when he failed to appear at an imperial diet to answer their charges, he was outlawed as a contumacious vassal, and Emperor Frederick II took possession of the duchies as vacant imperial fiefs. The duke was able to regain his lands, however, because the other princes resented this increase in Hohenstaufen power and because the emperor needed his support after being excommunicated in 1239. The final step in their reconciliation was a proposal in 1245 that the emperor should marry the childless duke's niece Gertrude and that Austria should be elevated to the rank of a kingdom in return; the plan foundered because Gertrude refused to agree. It was during Frederick's reign that the Traungau was separated from Styria and attached to Austria as the *Land ob der Enns,* the nucleus of the modern Austrian province of Upper Austria. Frederick, the last male Babenberg, died fighting the Magyars in 1246.

The disposition of the Babenberg inheritance was the central issue dividing Germany during the interregnum. The emperor claimed the duchies as vacant imperial fiefs, while Innocent IV recognized Gertrude's rights. After the emperor's death (1250), Ottokar II of Bohemia seized Austria in 1251 and tried to legitimize his actions by marrying Margaret, the elderly sister of the last duke. The Bohemian king subsequently added to his domains Styria (1260); Carinthia, whose duke, the last of the Spanheims, had died without a lay heir in 1269; and Carniola, where both the Babenbergs and the Spanheims had possessed rights. It was the first time that the Austrian and Bohemian lands that were to form the heart of the Danubian monarchy had been united.

Ottokar had no legal right to his acquisitions and was, therefore, opposed to the election of a new German king who might call him to account. He refused to pay homage to Rudolf I of Habsburg, who had obtained the crown in 1273, and was consequently outlawed as a contumacious vassal. Supported by the neighboring princes and by the Austrian and Styrian ministerials and towns, Rudolf was able to occupy the duchies without a fight in 1276; Ottokar was forced to surrender the territories. When Ottokar tried to regain his lost domains, he was defeated and killed in a battle fought near Dürnkrut on the Marchfeld, northeast of Vienna, on 26 August 1278. Rudolf enfeoffed his sons Albrecht and Rudolf with Austria and Styria in 1282, the legal beginning of 636 years of Habsburg rule.

Albrecht I (duke 1282, king 1298–1308) was regarded as a foreigner in Austria, and he encountered considerable internal opposition. The princes refused to elect him as king after his father's death in 1291, and he obtained the crown in 1298 only after defeating Adolf of Nassau at Göllheim. Albrecht was murdered in 1308 by his nephew, whom he had cheated of his share of the family inheritance. Albrecht's son Frederick the Fair (1308–1330) was chosen king in the double election of 1314, but he was decisively defeated by his rival Louis the Bavarian at Mühldorf in 1322. The Habsburgs' hopes of obtaining the crown were ended for a century.

Supported by the Habsburgs' rivals for the throne, the forest cantons of Schwyz, Uri, and Unterwalden united in 1291 and secured their independence by defeating Frederick's brother Leopold I (*d.* 1326) at Morgarten in 1315. During Frederick's rule the Habsburgs began to be identified with Austria rather than with their Swiss domains, as is attested by the appearance of the phrase *dominium Austriae* ("the lordship of Austria") to describe the dynasty, the family's princely authority, and the complex of territories the house governed.

The Habsburg line was continued by Frederick's brother Albrecht II (1330–1358). Although he was unable to stop the imperial city of Zurich from joining the Swiss Confederation (1351), he prevented his own canton of Glarus and the city of Zug from doing so. Albrecht's greatest achievement was the acquisition of Carinthia. His grandfather had enfeoffed Count Meinhard II of Tyrol, his most loyal supporter, with Carinthia in 1286, and had also pledged Carniola to him. Since Meinhard's granddaughter Margarete Maultasch, the heiress to her family's lands, was married to a son of King John of Bohemia, Emperor Louis the Bavarian, who had allied with the Habsburgs against the Luxemburgs, refused to recognize her rights to Carinthia and granted the duchy to Albrecht in 1335. Carniola also submitted to Albrecht's rule. Margarete retained only the Tyrol.

Albrecht's son Rudolf IV (1358–1365), who was nicknamed "the Founder" for building the Gothic nave of St. Stephen's in Vienna, believed that the Habsburgs were Germany's rightful royal dynasty. He was especially incensed that the Golden Bull of 1356, issued by his father-in-law Charles IV, excluded them from the rank and prerogatives of electors. To secure comparable rights for the Habsburgs, Rudolf forged five documents, most notably the Greater Privilege *(Privilegium maius),* an expanded version of Barbarossa's 1156 privilege. The Habsburgs' archducal title first appears in this document. This further diminution of the Habsburgs' obligations to the *Reich* gained legal validity when Emperor Frederick III (with the consent of the electors) confirmed it in 1453.

These blatant forgeries; the reconstruction of St. Stephen's, which the duke hoped would serve as the cathedral of a Viennese bishopric; and the founding of the University of Vienna in 1365 were undertaken in emulation of Charles IV, who had procured Prague's elevation to metropolitan status, rebuilt St. Vitus' Cathedral, and founded the University of Prague. Rudolf also persuaded Margarete Maultasch to surrender the Tyrol to the Habsburgs in 1363. The advocacies of the bishoprics of Trent and Bressanone formed the basis of the Tyrolese count's sovereignty.

After Rudolf's death his brothers Albrecht III (1365–1395) and Leopold III (1365–1386) assumed the joint governance of the family lands and made some further acquisitions: Freiburg im Breisgau (1368), the lordship of Montfort-Feldkirch in Vorarlberg (1375), and Trieste (1382). They divided their domains, however, in 1379. Albrecht obtained Austria above and below the Enns, while the remaining territories passed to Leopold. Some attempt was made to assure the continued cooperation of the two branches of the family and to preserve the nominal unity of the Habsburg domains, but the history of the period 1379–1490 was filled with dynastic strife. The estates profited from this discord and the Habsburgs' financial needs, assuming a major role in the governance of the principalities.

The dukes of the Austrian Albrechtine line tended to be short-lived. Albrecht III, who was the real founder of the University of Vienna, was succeeded by his son Albrecht IV (1395–1404) and grandson Albrecht V (1404–1439). After a tumultuous minority, Albrecht V married Elizabeth, the daughter of Emperor Sigismund, the Luxemburg king of Germany, Bohemia, and Hungary, and became embroiled in the battle against the Hussites. The northern part of the duchy of Austria suffered greatly during the fighting. As Albrecht II, the duke succeeded Sigismund in 1438 as king of Germany, Bohemia, and Hungary. Thereafter, except for the years 1742–1745, a Habsburg wore the German crown until the end of the Holy Roman Empire in 1806. Albrecht's second cousin, Emperor Frederick III, the Austrian estates, and Count Ulrich of Celje fought for power in Austria during the long minority of Albrecht's son Ladislaus Posthumus (1440–1457). George of Poděbrad and John Hunyadi governed Bohemia and Hungary, respectively, in Ladislaus' name. After his premature death George and John's son Matthias Corvinus assumed the crowns of St. Wenceslaus and St. Stephen, respectively.

Leopold III, the founder of the Leopoldine line, was killed by the Swiss at Sempach in 1386. After the death of his two oldest sons, the surviving brothers, Ernest (1402–1424) and Frederick IV (1406–1439), divided their father's lands. Ernest obtained Styria, Carinthia, and Carniola; Frederick received the Tyrol and the Habsburgs' remaining territories in southwestern Germany. Frederick's support of the antipope John XXIII cost the Habsburgs most of their remaining Swiss possessions, including their ancestral castle (1415). His son Sigismund (*d.* 1496), who assumed personal control of the Tyrol only in 1446, abdicated in favor of his cousin Maximilian in 1490.

Ernest's son Frederick V (*b.* 1415, duke of Inner Austria 1424), better known as Emperor Frederick III (1452–1493), obtained the German crown in 1440. He served as the guardian of Ladislaus Posthumus, the nominal king of Bohemia and Hungary and duke of Austria. After Ladislaus' death in 1457, Frederick was forced to share the governance of Austria with his younger brother Albrecht VI (1458–1463). Frederick was unable to maintain order in the duchy or to stop the Turkish raids in Carniola, Carinthia, and Styria. However, in 1469 he obtained the pope's consent for the establishment of a bishopric in Vienna. In 1485, Matthias Corvinus occupied most of Lower Austria, including Vienna, and held it until his death in 1490. In spite of his failures, Frederick had the utmost confidence in the destiny of his dynasty, as can be seen by his famous device, *A.E.I.O.U.* It meant, in both Latin and German, "All the world is subject to Austria." The marriages of Frederick's son Maximilian to Mary of Brugundy in 1477, and of his grandson Philip I the Fair to Joanna the Mad of Spain in 1496, nearly turned this idle boast into reality during the reign of his great-grandson Charles V.

BIBLIOGRAPHY

Hugo Hantsch, *Die Geschichte Österreichs bis 1648,* 5th ed. (1969); Karl Lechner, "Die Babenberger: Markgrafen und Herzoge von Österreich 976–1246," in *Veröffentlichungen des Instituts für österreichische Geschichtsforschung,* **23** (1976); Alexander W. A. Leeper, *A History of Medieval Austria* (1941); Erich Zöllner, *Geschichte Österreichs: Von den Anfängen bis zur Gegenwart,* 4th ed. (1970).

JOHN B. FREED

[See also **Avars; Babenberg Family; Bavaria; Carolingians and Carolingian Empire.**]

AUTO DE LOS REYES MAGOS, the sole surviving vernacular religious play from Castile predating the fifteenth century, copied onto two leaves at the end of a thirteenth-century theological manuscript. Of uncertain date, but usually assigned to the second half of the twelfth century, this short Epiphany play has generally been held to be a mere fragment; but it may in fact be complete. In it the three Magi ponder the significance of the star and agree to seek the newborn king together and to verify his divinity by means of three gifts, his choice of which will reveal his true nature. They visit Herod, who, once alone, gives vent to his fury and summons his sages. The latter quarrel, one finding no scriptural authority for the advent of the Messiah, another accusing the first (and by implication all Jews) of failure to appreciate the prophecies of Jeremiah.

The text of the *Auto* cannot be said to have been definitively established, but this has not prevented literary appreciation. There is a striking use of *figura,* and the quarrel between the Jewish sages surely reflects the medieval traditions of Ecclesia, Synagoga, and Concordia. Though firmly rooted in the tradition of the *Ordo stellae,* the *Auto* is in many details markedly original.

BIBLIOGRAPHY

The most widely used text is that of Ramón Menéndez Pidal, "Disputa del alma y el cuerpo y Auto de los reyes magos," in *Revista de archivos, bibliotecas y museos,* 3rd ser. **4** (1900); alternative readings are given by A. M. Espinosa, "Notes on the Versification of *El Misterio de los Reyes Magos,*" in *Romanic Review,* **6** (1915).

Textual problems are discussed in Ricardo Senabre, "Observaciones sobre el texto del *Auto de los reyes magos,*" in *Estudios ofrecidos a Emilio Alarcos Llorach,* I (1977), 417–432. The language of the play is dealt with in Rafael Lapesa, "Sobre el *Auto de los reyes magos:* Sus rimas anómalas y el posible orígen de su autor," in *De la Edad Media a nuestros días* (1967), 37–47; and in J. M. Sola-Solé, "El *Auto de los reyes magos:* ¿Impacto gascón o mozárabe?" in *Romance Philology,* **29** (1975–1976).

Literary studies include D. W. Foster, "Figural Interpretation and the *Auto de los Reyes Magos,*" in *Romanic Review,* **58** (1967); David Hook and A. D. Deyermond, "El problema de la terminación del *Auto de los reyes magos,*" in *Anuario de estudios medievales* (in press); B. W. Wardropper, "The Dramatic Texture of the *Auto de los Reyes Magos,*" in *Modern Language Notes,* **70** (1955).

Winifred Sturdevant, *The Misterio de los Reyes Magos: Its Position in the Development of the Medieval Legend of the Three Kings* (1927; repr. 1973); and J. M. Regueiro, "El *Auto de los reyes magos* y el teatro litúrgico medieval," in *Hispanic Review,* **45** (1977).

DAVID HOOK

[See also **Ecclesia and Synagoga; Spanish Drama.**]

AUTOCEPHALOS (Greek, αὐτοκέφαλος; "autonomous, independent"), a designation referring to a bishop independent of patriarchal and metropolitan jurisdiction. In the early Church this status characterized the bishops of Cyprus, officially from at least 431 (Council of Ephesus, canon vii), as well as the bishops of Armenia and the archbishops of Sinai. For limited periods a similar independent standing was enjoyed by the prelates of Prima Justiniana in Illyria (initiated in the sixth century) and by those of Lower and Upper Georgia (eighth and eleventh centuries, respectively), Bulgaria (tenth century), and Serbia (thirteenth century). There is evidence that the bishops of Britain, before 597, and those of Ravenna once possessed such independence.

Whereas in the West, among Catholics, the term "autocephalos" became imbued with the meaning of schismatic, the Orthodox East employed the word altogether differently. From the time of Justinian (527–565) the Church was conceived as a "pentarchy" in which the patriarch of Rome, then primus inter pares, was followed in importance by the bishops of Constantinople, Alexandria, Antioch, and Jerusalem. But with the subsequent cleavage between East and West, the patriarch of Constantinople replaced the bishop of Rome and received the title "archbishop of Constantinople–New Rome and ecumenical patriarch." As early as the Council of Chalcedon (451), he was granted the rights to serve as the final court of appeals from the other Eastern churches (canons 9 and 17) and to direct the missionary efforts in "barbarous" lands (canon 28). In addition, although possessing no real ecclesiastical authority over the other Oriental patriarchs, except that brought by the spread and duration of the Ottoman Empire, the ecumenical patriarch has been accorded de jure the prerogative to exercise "the right of initiative" among other eastern sees in matters of common concern. After the patriarchate of Moscow (established in 1589) was accorded fifth place in the hierarchy of the eastern sees, and owing to the decline of Ottoman rule, the modern period has seen a burgeoning number of national churches that share the Orthodox communion but whose bishops meet regularly in synods to conduct their own internal affairs. These, too, are called autocephalos in recognition of their independent integrality.

BIBLIOGRAPHY

Maximos Christopoulos, *The Oecumenical Patriarchate in the Orthodox Church: A Study in the History and Canons of the Church,* Analecta Vlatadon no. 24 (1976); John Hackett, *A History of the Orthodox Church of Cyprus* (1901), 16–19, 247–260; Jean Meyendorff, *The Orthodox Church* (1962), 65–66, 142–182; William Ainger Wigram, "Episcopacy in the Eastern Orthodox Church," in Claude Jenkins and Kenneth Donald Mackenzie, eds., *Episcopacy Ancient and Modern* (1930), 305–320.

S. KENT BROWN

[See also **Byzantine Church.**]

AUTOCRATOR, official title of the Byzantine emperor; its Latin equivalent is *moderator.* With the development of the system of coemperors from the eighth century on, the title autocrator was used to indicate the sole or the main emperor, and was added to his official signature in the eleventh century. The autocrator wielded real power, and alone had the right to sign administrative orders with the menologion (that is, to write with purple ink the month and the indiction at which the document was issued). He did not bear any insignia that would distinguish him from his coemperors; and he wielded his absolute powers from the moment he was acclaimed as autocrator by the army, the Senate, and the people. During the Palaeologan period (1261–1453) he alone received the crown from the hands of the patriarch of Constantinople. He also received the oath of allegiance of the army, the civil servants, the Church (from the ninth century), and all the subjects of the empire (from the eighth century), who were thus personally and directly bound to their sovereign.

BIBLIOGRAPHY

Louis Bréhier, "L'origine des titres impériaux à Bysance," in *Byzantinische Zeitschrift,* **15** (1906); and *Les institutions de l'empire byzantin* (1949), 1–88; John Bury, *The Constitution of the Later Roman Empire* (1909), repr. in *Selected Essays of J. B. Bury* (1930); Aikaterine Christophilopoulou, *Ekloge, anagoreusis kai stepsis tou Byzantinou autokratoros* (1956); and "He antibasileia eis to Byzantion," in *Symmeikta,* **2** (1970); André Grabar, *L'empereur dans l'art byzantin* (1936); Ernst Kornemann, *Doppelprinzipat und Reichsteilung im Imperium Romanum* (1930); Nicolas Svoronos, "Le serment de fidelité à l'empereur byzantin et sa signification constitutionelle," in *Revue des études byzantines,* **9** (1951); Otto Treitinger, *Die oströmische Kaiser- und Reichsidee nach ihrer Gestaltung im höfischen Zeremoniell* (1938).

NICHOLAS OIKONOMIDES

[See also **Basileus; Byzantine Empire; Despot; Roman Empire, Late.**]

AUTPERTUS, AMBROSIUS (*d.* 784), Benedictine theologian and exegete, was born in Provence. On a trip to Italy in 754, he visited the monastery of San Vincenzo on the Volturno near Benevento, where he entered the religious life. Autpertus was ordained a priest and became renowned for his learning, piety, and inspired preaching. In 777 he was elected abbot by the Frankish monks of his community; but a faction of Lombard monks backed an Italian candidate instead, causing him to abdicate in December 778. In 781 another abbot of San Vincenzo was accused of disloyalty to Charlemagne. The case was submitted to Pope Adrian I, and Autpertus was summoned to Rome for the hearing. He died on the way, and his body was returned to San Vincenzo.

Autpertus' best-known work is the *Expositionis in apocalypsin,* an extensive commentary that relies heavily on the sixth-century African author Primasius. A decidedly ecclesiological interpretation of the Apocalypse, it was widely circulated in the Middle Ages. He has been shown to be the author of the *Conflictus vitiorum atque virtutum,* an allegory inspired by the *Psychomachia* of Prudentius, attributed by medieval scribes to various of the Fathers, especially Augustine and Ambrose. A prayer to the Trinity, *Oratio summa et incomprehensibilis natura,* summarizes the message of the *Conflictus.* His *Vita Paldonis, Tatonis, et Tasonis* is the story of the foundation of San Vincenzo by three royal brothers. Also extant are sermons on cupidity, the Transfiguration, and the Purification and Assumption of the Virgin Mary. Contemporary sources ascribe to Autpertus commentaries on Leviticus, the Psalms, and the Song of Songs, but these have not been identified.

BIBLIOGRAPHY

Texts. Expositionis in Apocalypsin, Robert Weber, ed. (1975); *Conflictus vitiorum atque virtutum,* in *Patrologia latina,* XL, 1091–1106, LXXXI, 615–624, and LXXXIII, 1131–1144; *Oratio summa et incomprehensibilis natura,* from the *Chronicon Vulturnense,* Vincenzo Federici, ed., in *Fonti per la storia d'Italia,* **58** (1925), 3–15; *Vita Paldonis, Tatonis, et Tasonis,* Georg Waitz, ed., in *Monumenta Germaniae historica, Script. rer. Lang.,* 546–555, and *Patrologia latina,* LXXXIX, 1319–1322; his sermons are in *Patrologia latina,* XXXIX, 2129–2134, and LXXXIX, 1277–1320.

Studies. Sebastiano Bovo, "Le fonti del commento di Ambrogio Autperto sull'Apocalisse," in *Studia Anselmiana,* **27–28** (1951), 372–403; Jean Leclercq, "La prière au sujet des vices et des vertus," in *Studia Anselmiana,* **31** (1953), 3–17; Claudio Leonardi, "Spiritualità di Ambrogio Autperto," in *Studi medievalia,* 3rd ser., **9** (1968), 1–13; Heinrich Weisweiler, "Das frühe Marienbild der Westkirche unter dem Einfluss des Dogmas von Chalcedon: Ambrosius Autpertus und sein Kreis," in *Scholastik,* **28** (1953), 505–513; Jacques Winandy, *Ambroise Autpert, moine et théologien* (1953); "La contemplation à l'école des Pères. Ambroise Autpert," in *La vie spirituelle,* **82** (1950), 147–157; "L'oeuvre littéraire d'Ambroise Autpert," in *Revue bénédictine,* **60** (1950), 93–119.

E. ANN MATTER

[See also **Exegesis, Latin.**]

AUXILIUS (*fl.* 891–912), a priest of uncertain (though probably Frankish) origin, was the author of tracts defending the legality of the election of Pope Formosus (891–896) and the validity of the Holy Orders conferred by him. Auxilius, himself ordained by Formosus, wrote in response to the reenactment by Pope Sergius III (904–911) of the decrees of the "cadaveric synod" of 897, which declared the decrees of Formosus invalid and required those who had been ordained by him to submit to reordination or cease the exercise of their offices on pain of excommunication.

BIBLIOGRAPHY

Auxilius' writings include *Infensor et defensor,* in *Patrologia latina,* J. P. Migne, ed., CXXIX, 1073–1102; and *De ordinationibus a Formoso papa factis, ibid.,* 1059–1074; E. Dümmler, *Auxilius und Vulgarius* (1866), includes texts of Auxilius' *In defensionem sacrae ordinationis papae Formosi,* pp. 59–95, and *Libellus in defensionem Stephani episcopi,* pp. 96–105.

See also D. Pop, *La défense du pape Formose* (1933). A thorough review of the political and theological questions raised in the Formosan controversy.

WILLIAM CRAWFORD

[See also **Papacy, Origins and Development of.**]

AVANZO, JACOPO, Paduan[?] painter, active second half of fourteenth century; associated with Altichiero for work on the chapel of S. Giacomo (now S. Felice) and the oratory of S. Giorgio, in the Santo, Padua (documented 1377–1384). These documents do not mention Avanzo. His association with the frescoes is based on fifteenth-century sources and his identity remains problematic. He may be the artist who signed the crucifixion panel now in the Colonna Gallery, Rome: "Jacobus de ava(n)ciis de fononia f."

BIBLIOGRAPHY

Hanno W. Kruft, *Altichiero und Avanzo, Untersuchungen zur oberitalienischen Malerei des ausgehenden Trecento* (1966); Gian Lorenzo Mellini, *Altichiero e Jacopo Avanzi* (1965).

ADELHEID M. GEALT

AVARAYR, a plain in southeastern Armenia. It was the site of the famous battle fought on 26 May 451 between the Armenian nobility headed by the *sparapet* Vardan Mamikonean and the Sasanian army attempting to reimpose Zoroastrianism on the country. Despite the annihilation of the Armenian army, Christianity survived in Armenia, the autonomy of which was soon recognized by the Persians. Vardan and his companions are still commemorated as martyrs by the Armenian church.

BIBLIOGRAPHY

Sirarpie Der Nersessian, *The Armenians* (1969), 31–32; and René Grousset, *Histoire de l'Arménie des origines à 1071* (1947), 202–206.

NINA G. GARSOÏAN

[See also **Vardan Mamikonean.**]

AVARS, an Altaic tribal confederation that formed a state centered in present-day Hungary (*ca.* 567–*ca.* 803) and played an important role in Byzantine, Slavic, and Frankish affairs. Attempts have been made to connect them with either the Abar/Apar (Chinese, Juan-juan), a Mongol-speaking tribal union of Mongolia (*ca.* 400–522/555), or the Hephthalites of Afghanistan-western Turkestan, both of whose states were destroyed by the Turks. The Byzantine historian Theophylaktos Simokattes, our major source, terms the European Avars, who arrived in the Caspian-Pontic steppes in 558, "Pseudoavars" and notes, as proof for his assertion, that they actually consisted of the tribes Ouar and Khounni. Chinese sources, however, identify the Ouar (Avar) and Khounni (Hun, Hsiung-nu) as constituent elements of the Juan-juan and Ephthalite unions. Moreover, when the Turks appeared in Europe, they stated, in a series of ambassadorial exchanges with Byzantium, that they had come in pursuit of their "slaves" the Avars, clearly indicating that Juan-juan or Hephthalite elements had fled to the West.

Once settled in the Roman province of Pannonia, the ethnic composition of the Avars (whose union also included Oghuric Protobulgarians, Slavs, Germans, and possibly Ugrian ethnic units) underwent further changes. New, Asiatic elements entered the region about 670, replacing the old ruling strata. The sparse linguistic relics of Avaric point to either Mongol or Turkic origins.

After the Avars' arrival in 558, Byzantium sought to use these newcomers to police the other Pontic-steppe nomads. Having brought the Kutrigurs and Antes under control, the Avars began to concentrate in "Scythia Minor" (Dobruja) about 562. Although their initial attack on the Frankish king Sigebert in Thuringia was unsuccessful, they later (565) defeated him. In 567, in alliance with the Lombards, they destroyed the Gepids. The Lombards, now wary of their "allies," in 568 migrated to Italy, leaving Pannonia to the Avars. This westward orientation coincided with the appearance of the Turks (568), who contested Avar control of the Pontic steppes. Moreover, Byzantium, hoping to use the Turks against Persia and fearful of the Avar presence so close to its borders, had become increasingly hostile since the accession of Justin II (565–578).

By the 580's the Avars, led by the Khaghan Bayan, began a series of raids on the Balkans together with their Slavic subjects and allies (Slavic raids here had begun several decades earlier). Under Avar pressure many Slavic expeditions ended in settlement, leading to the subsequent slavicization of much of the Balkans. A culminating point in this ongoing Avar-Byzantine conflict was the joint Avar-Persian assault on Constantinople in 626. Its failure, accompanied by Byzantine-supported breakaways of the Slavs (such as Samo's state in northern Bohemia, in the 620's) and Bulgars (the Magna Bulgaria state of Kubrat, about 635), gave the first evidence of the Avar decline. Warfare with Byzantium was reduced to a less grandiose scale. Ultimately, however, it was the expanding Carolingian state, following a series of Frankish victories over the Avars in 791, 795, and 796, that ended their status as a major power. Avar remnants lingered on, and were later absorbed by the Hungarians.

Some scholars credit the Avars with introducing the stirrup and saber to Europe.

BIBLIOGRAPHY

An extensive bibliography of Avar studies is in Arnulf Kollautz, *Bibliographie der historischen und archäologischen Veröffentlichungen zur Awarenzeit Mitteleuropas und des Fernen Ostens* (1965). Important and useful bibliographies are in Kollautz' "Die Awaren. Die Schichtung in einer Nomadenherrschaft," in *Saeculum,* 5 (1954); and in the work he wrote with Hisayuki Miyakawa, *Geschichte und Kultur eines völkerwanderungszeitlichen Nomadenvolkes,* 2 vols. (1970), esp. II, 319–337. See also Alexander Avenarius, *Die Awaren in Europa* (1974); and Károly Czeglédy, *Nomád népek vándorlása napkelettől napnyugatig* (1969).

PETER B. GOLDEN

[See also **Austria; Bulgaria; Huns; Lombards, Kingdom of; Theophylaktos Simokattes.**]

AVE MARIA. Owing to its repetition in devotions, such as the Angelus and, in particular, the Rosary, the Ave Maria is the prayer most frequently said by Roman Catholics. Its complete wording—*Ave, Maria, gratia plena, Dominus tecum; benedicta tu in mulieribus, et benedictus fructus ventris tui. Sancta Maria, mater Dei, ora pro nobis peccatoribus, nunc et in hora mortis nostrae. Amen*—was the result of a process extending over more than a thousand years.

It cannot be stated with certainty when the words of Luke 1:28 and 1:42 were first used as a prayer to Mary. Their combination, apparently common in the Eastern Church in the fifth century (Syriac ritual attributed to Severus, patriarch of Antioch), was used by St. John Damascene and St. Andrew of Crete. Liturgical use is recorded on Egyptian ostraca of the early seventh century and in the liturgies of St. James, St. Mark, St. Basil, and the Ethiopian liturgy of the Twelve Apostles.

In the West the earliest records are the Gregorian offertory for the fourth Sunday of Advent, which uses *in mulieribus* (as Luke 1:28), while the corresponding transitorium for the sixth Sunday of Advent in the Ambrosian liturgy has *inter mulieres* (Luke 1:42), as does an inscription in Santa Maria Antiqua in Rome (about 700). The attribution of Elizabeth's words (Luke 1:42) to the Angel Gabriel (as in the Gospel of Pseudo-Matthew and in a ninth-century hymn, expressly justified by Peter of Celle, and in the *Mariale* of St. Albert the Great) promoted their combination with Luke 1:28.

From the middle of the eleventh century, this combination became a separate devotional formula, largely as a ramification of the Officium parvum B.M.V. (for instance, in British Museum MSS Cotton Tib. A3 and Add. 21,927), where Luke 1:28 is the invitatorium to Psalm 94 at Matins and Luke 1:42 is a versicle and response at Lauds.

Repetition became a special feature of this paraliturgical devotion. In 1090, Countess Ada of Hennegau recited the Ave sixty times every day. In the same district, fifty years later, a monk named Aybert said it—in analogy to the daily recitation of the entire Psalter as recommended by St. John Cassian and as practiced in Irish monasticism—150 times (as was done in the Rosary) every day, with 100 genuflections and 50 prostrations. In the late-twelfth-century Oxford Corpus Christi MS 402, nuns are told that at the recitation of Pater Noster and Ave Maria, they are to genuflect or incline profoundly. The connection between the Pater Noster and the Ave, basically the most familiar Catholic devotions, was expressly recommended by a Würzburg synod in 1283. St. Margaret of Hungary is said to have recited on certain days no fewer than 1,000 Aves with as many prostrations, and a similar devotion was observed by a Cistercian nun, Ida of Louvain, before 1300.

From the end of the twelfth century, the Ave became a prayer generally recommended to the laity as a substitute for the Officium parvum B.M.V. In 1198, Odo of Sully, bishop of Paris, told his clergy to exhort the people to say *Orationem Dominicam et Credo et Salutationem B.M.V.* (the combination that was then to form the beginning of the Rosary recitation); at Béziers it was ordered in 1246 that children attaining the age of seven should be taught *Salutationem B.M.V., Pater noster, et Credo* (note the difference in the order of these texts). In a corresponding ruling for the laity in general by synods in Germany and England in 1287, it was explicitly said that the salutation was the Ave Maria. In 1247 at Le Mans, a synod prescribed that the children should learn those basic texts by heart *si fieri potest;* there are other records of difficulties encountered by the laity with the Latin texts, in particular the Ave.

Tradition says that Urban IV added to the basic Ave the name of Jesus (Luke 1:31); up to 1568 the Ave frequently ended with the words *Jesus Christus. Amen.*

The second part of the Ave was formed gradually between the thirteenth and fifteenth centuries. A comparison of the various vernacular versions in particular shows that there was a tendency to conclude with the reference to "us sinners," the appeal for help at the hour of death through which the Ave Maria has been a most significant expression of existential consciousness. The addition of the words *ora pro nobis peccatoribus* was recorded in 1444 by St. Bernardine of Siena, and that of the words *nunc et in hora mortis* in the breviary of the Mercedarians (printed at Paris in 1514). The complete and final text was first printed in the breviary of the Camaldolese Order (Venice, 1514); the breviarium reformed by Pius V in 1568 was the first official book of the Roman Church to contain it.

BIBLIOGRAPHY

See P. G. Grosjean, ed., *Familiar Prayers* (1953), 90–144; G. Jaquemet, "Ave Maria," in *Catholicisme hier, aujourd'hui et demain,* I (1948), 1110f.; J. A. Jungmann, "Ave Maria," in *Lexikon für Theologie und Kirche* I² (1957), 1141.

JOHN HENNIG

[See also **Rosary.**]

AVERROËS. See **Rushd, Ibn.**

AVESTA, the sacred scripture of the Zoroastrians, followers of the teachings of Zoroaster (Zarathustra), the prophet of ancient Iran. Its language, called Avestan because it is attested only in the Avesta itself, is one of the Old Iranian languages, which constitute one branch of the Indo-Iranian, or Aryan, language family within Indo-European. In the Avesta itself one can distinguish two stages or dialects of Avestan, commonly referred to as Gathic and Younger Avestan. The latter designation may be somewhat misleading, since contents of some of the Younger Avestan texts are quite ancient, and the essential differences may be dialectal as well as diachronic.

The word "Avesta" itself is derived from Middle Persian *abestāg,* which may mean "compilation" or "authoritative writing." One frequently encounters in the Middle Persian Zoroastrian texts the phrase *abestāg ud zand* ("the Avesta and its interpretation"). This in fact reflects the form in which texts of the Avesta were transmitted, with the Avestan text interspersed with Middle Persian translation and commentary. This juxtaposition of the terms *abestāg* and *zand* led early Western scholars of Zoroastrianism to refer to the scriptures as the Zend-Avesta.

The Avesta is a collection of sacred compositions, some of which can be attributed to the prophet Zarathustra himself. Although there is much controversy over when Zarathustra lived, it is probably safe to assume that he preached in eastern Iran at least ten centuries before the birth of Christ. The teachings of Zarathustra, called the *Gāthās,* "hymns," constitute the most ancient section of the Avesta, and are placed at the heart of the *Yasna,* or liturgy for the sacrifice.

During the centuries following Zarathustra other compositions in the Avestan language joined the *Gāthās* as authoritative teachings and liturgy for the Zoroastrian community. These compositions were finally collected and written down during the period of the Sasanians, who ruled over the Iranian empire from 226 to 651. Various traditions credit a Parthian, Vologases, or the Sasanian Ardashir I or his son Shapur I with the collection of the Avesta, which, according to Zoroastrian tradition, had been dispersed following Alexander's conquest of the Achaemenid Empire. Although an earlier written form may have existed, the Avesta was only written down in its own Avestan script during the sixth century by Zoroastrian priests who had worked out an appropriate elaboration of the consonantal Pahlavi script used in Zoroastrian Middle Persian texts.

A ninth-century Middle Persian work, the *Dēnkarṭ,* provides a summary of the extant Avesta. The Avesta, it points out, contained twenty-one *nasks,* one of which had been lost and another of which had been transmitted only in its *sada* form, that is, without its Middle Persian translation. The other nineteen *nasks* are described in the *Dēnkarṭ.* Of these *nasks* only one has survived in its entirety: the *Vendīdād,* "the law against the demons." The other surviving sections of the Avesta are for the most part liturgical compilations that do not constitute *nasks* in themselves.

Of prime importance in the Avesta is the *Yasna,* or "sacrifice." Composed of texts of varying antiquity, the *Yasna* is so arranged as to accompany the performance of the central Zoroastrian rite, the Haoma sacrifice. The *Yasna* contains seventy-two chapters, called *Hā* or *Hāiti,* which include prayers of invocation, a hymn to the god Haoma, the confession of faith, the four most sacred prayers and exegeses, the *Gāthās* of Zarathustra, and hymns to various divinities whose protection of the sacrifice is invoked. In the midst of the seventeen *Gāthās* is placed the *Yasna Haptānghaiti,* "the *Yasna* of the seven chapters," a section only slightly less ancient than the *Gāthās* and written in the same archaic Gathic dialect.

Of special interest to Zoroastrians and historians of religion alike are the *Gāthās,* since they represent our only evidence of Zarathustra's own contribution to the Iranian religious tradition. Unfortunately, the vocabulary and syntax of the *Gāthās* have presented serious obstacles to translators, as any review of attempted translations will attest. Although the *Gāthās* were transmitted with an accompanying Middle Persian translation, it seems clear that the Sasanian-era scholars who provided it had no clear idea of the meaning of these sacred but seemingly impenetrable texts. The *Gāthās* do yield, however, the major themes of Zarathustra's teaching: the cosmic conflict between truth and the lie, the goodness of Ahura Mazda's creation, the necessity of choice between good and evil, and reward and retribution in the afterlife.

The *Yašts,* "hymns of praise," form a second major section of the Avesta. These compositions, transmitted orally over the centuries by their priest-poet reciters, are directed to the various divinities, *yazatas,* of the Zoroastrian pantheon. Of particular interest are the so-called "great" *Yašts* to Ardvī Sūrā Anāhitā, the goddess of the waters; to Mithra, the god of contract; to Tishtrya, who brings the rains; to Verethraghna, the god of victory; and to the *fravashis,* the souls of the righteous. The *Yašts* are of great interest because of the legendary and mythological material they contain as well as their poetic form.

The *Vendīdād,* a book of twenty-two chapters, represents a still later stage of Avestan composition. Although its legal strictures are couched in the formula of Zarathustra's directing questions to Ahura Mazda, the grammatical irregularities of the text suggest that it was composed when priests had only a rudimentary knowledge of Avestan, and that based primarily upon rote repetition from more ancient Avesta passages. The *Vendīdād,* more properly called the *Vīdēvdād,* concerns itself largely with the avoidance of impurity. A major theme is the proper means of the disposal of corpses.

In addition to these major books, there are other liturgical collections or prayer books: *Vīsprad, Niyāyishes, Gāhs, Sīrōzas,* and *Afrinagāns,* and other fragments. Of the latter category the most interesting are the *Nērangistān,* "book of charms," and the *Hādhōkht Nask,* which contains a fascinating account of the fate of the soul after death.

BIBLIOGRAPHY

Mary Boyce, *A History of Zoroastrianism,* I (1975), 3, and *Zoroastrians: Their Religious Beliefs and Practices* (1979), 113–114, 134–138; Ilya Gershevitch, ed. and trans., *The Avestan Hymn to Mithra* (1959), 3–49; A. V. Williams Jackson, *An Avesta Grammar in Comparison with Sanskrit* (1892), xi–xxxiii.

DALE L. BISHOP

[See also **Dēnkarṭ; Gāthās; Yašts; Zoroastrianism.**]

AVIANUS is known for a collection of fables which he compiled from the previous collections of Phaedrus and Babrius. These he versified in elegiac distich and ornamented with a wealth of Vergilian diction. The collection was dedicated to the author's friend Theodosius Macrobius, the grammarian, around 400. Nothing is known of the author himself, although his works enjoyed great popularity from the Carolingian era, when they were introduced for educational purposes, until as late as the eighteenth century.

BIBLIOGRAPHY

Adolph Goldschmidt, *An Early Manuscript of the Aesop Fables of Avianus and Related Manuscripts* (1947); Léopold Hervieux, *Les fabulistes latins,* III: *Avianus et ses anciens imitateurs* (1894); Kenneth McKenzie and William A. Oldfather, *Ysopet-Avionnet: The Latin and French Texts* (1919).

DEIRDRE BAKER

[See also **Fables.**]

AVICEBROL. See **Solomon Ben Judah Ibn Gabirol.**

AVICENNA. See **Sīnā, Ibn.**

AVIGNON, a city on the east bank of the lower Rhône, lay in the midst of the Comtat Venaissin. The county was officially ceded to the papacy in 1229, at the end of the Albigensian Crusades, but the pope took possession only in 1274. Avignon, however, remained a possession of the counts of Provence, who were also kings of Naples, until 1348, when it was sold to Pope Clement VI by Joanna I. This sale merely recognized the fact that the pope had long had effective control of the city.

Incessant war and violence in Rome and the Papal States and the election of a French pope, Clement V

(1305), led to the choice of Avignon as a papal residence in 1309. The city was technically in the Empire, not in France, but France lay just across the river and seemed to guarantee the security lacking in Italy. That security was somewhat diminished when the Hundred Years War began (1337) and roving bands of mercenaries threatened the city, but it was easier to defend Avignon than Rome. The city was enclosed in a strongly built wall, and the papal palace was also a fortress. The popes talked of going back to Rome, but remained in Avignon until 1377. Gregory XI then returned to Rome, but had almost decided to go back to Avignon when he died in 1378. The cardinals, under pressure from the Roman populace, elected an Italian pope (Urban VI), but soon repented of their choice, and elected a French pope (the antipope Clement VII), who fled to Avignon. Thus began the Great Schism (1378–1417), with one pope in Rome and another in Avignon. It was ended by the Council of Constance (1414–1418), which elected a universally recognized pope. The last Avignonese pope (Benedict XIII) fled to Spain, and Avignon was never again a papal residence, though it remained a papal possession until the French Revolution.

Fourteenth-century Avignon had a reputation for luxury and corruption. Luxurious it was: the papal palace was well furnished and decorated with frescoes by such well-known painters as Simone Martini. Cardinals and other high officials lived like princes. The luxury also attracted a group of very capable artists, writers, and scholars to Avignon. As for corruption, the old sources of papal revenue (gifts of pilgrims to Rome, income from the Papal States, tenths paid by the clergy) had been cut off or had to be shared with lay rulers: this at a time when increased centralization meant that all important ecclesiastical offices were filled by, and all important canon law cases decided by, the papal curia. Nothing could be done in Avignon without money, and the lines between legitimate fees, presents to expedite appointments and legal decisions, and outright bribery could not easily be drawn. The return of the papacy to Rome ended neither the luxury nor the corruption. In many ways the Avignonese papacy was a forerunner of the Renaissance papacy at Rome.

BIBLIOGRAPHY

G. Mollat, *The Popes of Avignon,* J. Leve, trans. (1963).

JOSEPH R. STRAYER

[See also **Antipope; Babylonian Captivity; Schism, Great.**]

AVIGNON SCHOOL. See **Ars Subtilior.**

AVILA BIBLE, MASTER OF THE. Of Umbro-Roman origin, he illuminated three giant Bibles, including one formerly in the Cathedral of Avila (Madrid, Biblioteca Nacional, MS Vitrina 15); a frontispiece to Odo's *Commentary on Psalms;* and a Passional in the second and third quarters of the twelfth century. Five more manuscripts may be associated with his Romanesque style.

BIBLIOGRAPHY

Edward B. Garrison, *Studies in the History of Mediaeval Italian Painting,* 4 vols. (1953–1962); Knut Berg, *Studies in Tuscan Twelfth-Century Illumination* (1968); C. R. Dodwell, *Painting in Europe: 800 to 1200* (1971).

ADELAIDE BENNETT

[See also **Manuscript Illumination.**]

AVITUS, ST. (*d. ca.* 530), abbot of Micy, was born in Auvergne, France, and entered monastic life at the abbey of Ménat, near Clermont, between 485 and 490. He broke away from the cenobitic life and traveled throughout the Loire Valley with Carileffus, a fellow monk, before settling near the abbey of Micy, where he built a hermitage. Following the death around 520 of Maximinus, the abbot of Micy, the monks chose Avitus as his successor.

The earliest and most accurate life of Avitus, dating from the ninth century, is in the *Monumenta Germaniae historica;* those lives dating from the twelfth century and later tend to confuse him with another monk.

BIBLIOGRAPHY

Monumenta Germaniae historica: Scriptorum rerum Merovingicarum, III, Bruno Krusch, ed. (1896, repr. 1977), 380–385; C. Belmon, in *Dictionnaire d'histoire et de géographie ecclésiastiques,* V (1931), 1204–1205.

TIMOTHY B. NOONE

AVIZ, ORDER OF, military order founded by Afonso Henriquez, king of Portugal (1143–1185), in 1147, although its foundation has also been attributed to Coimbran knights or to northern crusaders

AXUMITE ART

thrown ashore as they traveled to the East. The order was known originally as the *Novo ordem* (New Order) until around 1211, when King Afonso II (1211–1223) rewarded its knights in Evora with lands in Aviz; he requested in return for his grant that the knights build a fortress there, from which the military order took its name around 1215. Like its better-known counterparts in Spain (Orders of Santiago, Calatrava, and Alcántara), or those in the East, the Order of Aviz was organized as a monastic community. The knights followed the Benedictine rule with the reforms implemented at Cîteaux and other Cistercian houses. For almost a century after 1147 the Order of Aviz functioned as an offshoot of the Spanish military order of Calatrava under the same papal bull of confirmation granted to Calatrava by Alexander III in 1164.

With houses in Coimbra, Evora (which they helped capture in 1165), Passou, and elsewhere, the Order of Aviz played an important role in defending and advancing the southern frontiers of Portugal against Islam. However, since after 1248 Portugal no longer had a frontier with any Muslim kingdom, the importance of the order diminished. In 1385, when its military role was already becoming redundant within Portugal, its master, John (João, King Pedro I's bastard son) used the order as a springboard to gain the Portuguese crown. He thus became the founder of a new dynasty—that of Aviz. In 1551 the order was annexed to the crown, following the early example of the Spanish kings, and membership became after that date a ceremonial and honorific title.

BIBLIOGRAPHY

Derek W. Lomax, *Las órdenes militares en la península ibérica durante la edad media* (1976).

TEOFILO F. RUIZ

[See also **Military Orders.**]

AXUMITE ART. The kingdom of Axum, ancestor of Ethiopia, was founded in the first century A.D. and survived until the overthrow of its last king in the late tenth century. Centered on the northern Ethiopian highlands, its boundaries extended into southwest Arabia to the east and the Nile Valley in the west. It remained relatively immune to outside influences, and resisted Islamic invasions. One link was forged with Egypt and Syria in the mid fourth century with its conversion to Christianity and subsequent placing of the Ethiopian church under the ecclesiastical jurisdiction of the Monophysite church of Alexandria.

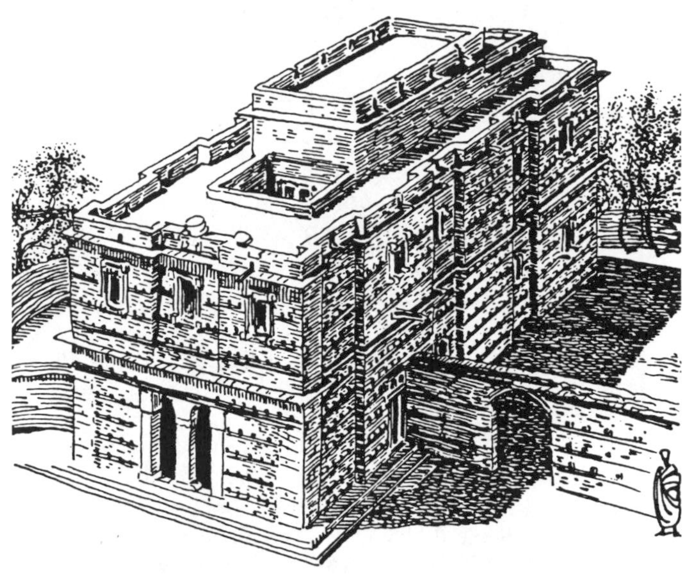

Perspective view, Principal Church at Debra Damo as it was in 1906, and remained up to 1945. FROM DAVID BUXTON, *The Abyssinians.* COURTESY OF THAMES AND HUDSON

Information about the art and architecture of Axum may be culled from archaeological, epigraphic, and numismatic evidence. Commemorative giant granite stelae up to 100 feet high, some decorated with bands imitating windowed stories and surmounted by rounded, indented headpieces, were erected. Recent excavations suggest the stelae date from the Christian Axumite period, although several nearby tombs or catacombs are pre-Christian. One tomb constructed of brick horseshoe arches can be related to Christian Syrian architecture of the fourth to sixth centuries. Finds of glass vessels point to trade connections with the Mediterranean, and of ceramics with the Nile Valley.

Monumental palaces at Axum and Matara of up to forty square meters were built on podiums, with entrance stairways, and possibly had one or more upper stories. Characteristic building features were the alternating recessed and projecting wall surfaces and built-up corner towers. Similar features survive in ecclesiastical architecture in the monastic church of Debra Damo, of rectangular plan, parts of which may date from the tenth to eleventh centuries and embody elements of Axumite masonry and wood construction, notably in the monolithic columns of the nave, supporting lintel beams, and the window

 ¡AY, IHERUSALEM!

and door frames of horizontal timbers fitted into masonry walls. The dome over the altar is constructed of curved timbers and the wooden sanctuary arch is carved with a geometric cross design, while the coffering of the narthex roof consists of panels with animal decoration. Similar features are found in rock-cut churches elsewhere, preceding the famous rock-cut churches of Lalibela.

BIBLIOGRAPHY

David Buxton, *The Abyssinians* (1970); N. Chittick, "Excavations at Aksum, 1973–4: A Preliminary Report," in *Azania,* **9** (1974); *Deutsche Aksum Expedition,* Enno Littmann, Daniel Krencker, and Theodor von Lüpke, eds., 4 vols. in 2 (1913); Ugo Monneret de Villard, *Aksum* (1938); S. Munro-Hay, "MḤDYS and Ebana, Kings of Aksum: Some Problems of Dating and Identity," in *Azania,* **14** (1979); Edward Ullendorff, *The Ethiopians* (1960); E. A. Wallis Budge, *A History of Ethiopia, Nubia and Abyssinia* (1928, repr. 1966).

LUCY-ANNE HUNT

[See also **Abyssinia.**]

¡AY, IHERUSALEM! This *planctus* for the fall of Jerusalem is one of the most recent discoveries in medieval Spanish letters. It was found, together with two other small poems, in the Archivo Histórico Nacional of Madrid by the librarian María del Carmen Pescador del Hoyo, who also published them. According to Eugenio Asensio, it was composed between the fall of Jerusalem (1244) and the fall of St. John of Acre (1291), more precisely between 1272 and 1276, during the pontificate of Gregory X and in connection with the second Council of Lyons, which was convened by the pope on 7 May 1274, to collect funds for a new crusade to recapture the holy city of Jerusalem. "¡Ay, Iherusalem!" would have had the same purpose: "poner vn canto / en el Conçilio santo / de Iherusalem." Despite the poor transmission of the text, the date of composition can be confirmed by comparison of the language and vocabulary of the poem with those of other authors and works of the thirteenth century, such as Gonzalo de Berceo, the *Libro de Alexandre,* the *Poema de Fernán González,* and the *Primera crónica general.*

It is a crusade song, a hybrid genre common to all European literatures, which combines elements of lyric and of historical narrative, generally taken from papal bulls, clerical sermons, and letters. The poet of "¡Ay, Iherusalem!" apparently drew on several historical sources for its composition: a letter of Guillaume of Châteauneuf, master of the Hospitalaries (he is personified in the first stanza), a letter of Robert, patriarch of Jerusalem (mentioned in stanza 9), and other oral and written material. Of course, this historical material is manipulated according to the requirements of poetic fiction.

"¡Ay, Iherusalem!" comprises 110 lines grouped into 22 stanzas of 5 lines each. The first two lines are dodecasyllabic *pareados* and the last three are hexasyllabic, of which the first two are *aconsonantados* and the third works like an *estribillo.*

Elegiac in tone, "¡Ay, Iherusalem!" combines learned and popular elements. Although we do not know the author's identity, he was certainly familiar with both church jargon and its poetic manifestations (*prosas,* or poetic compositions; the *consistorio;* the *altar de Syón; vestimentas,* or liturgical robes; and so on), and the topics, formulas, and techniques of the jongleurs (such as the use of *moro* for *perro, siete años e medio, carta con letras de sangre*). It is the learned aspect that dominates in the poem, however, not only in the sophisticated system of versification but also in some of its rhetorical features. As Asensio has pointed out, the medieval Latin poems almost invariably had an exordium that not only provided the listener with the argument of the composition but also set forth its moral or sentimental tone. While in the "Carmen Campidoctoris," a Latin song in praise of the Cid, the exordium of the first five stanzas invites the listener to enjoy, and in the "Plantus de obitu Karoli" a feeling of sadness is conveyed by the constant repetition of "Heu mihi misero," in our poem, also a *planctus,* the same feeling of sadness, desolation, and loss is conveyed by the *estribillo, "¡Ay Iherusalem!"*

BIBLIOGRAPHY

María del Carmen Pescador del Hoyo, "Tres nuevos poemas medievales," in *Nueva revista de filología hispánica,* **14** (1960); Eugenio Asensio, "*¡Ay, Iherusalem!* Planto narrativo del siglo XIII," *ibid.,* repr. in *Poética y realidad en el cancionero peninsular de la Edad Media,* 2nd ed. (1970); Henk de Vries, "Un conjunto estructural: el 'Poema tríptico del nombre de Dios en la ley' (Tres nuevos poemas medievales, NRFH, XIV, 1960)," in *Boletín de la Real Academia Española,* **51** (1971).

H. SALVADOR MARTÍNEZ

[See also **Planctus.**]

AYALA, PEDRO LÓPEZ DE. See **López de Ayala, Pero.**

ĀYĀS, also known as Aias, Aigai, Ajazzo, Lajassi, Laisso, Lajazzo, Aiazzi, and (today) as Yumurtalik in Turkey, was the major port of Cilician Armenia. Located on the Mediterranean, on the Gulf of İskenderun (Alexandretta), near the mouth of the Ceyhan River, Āyās was part of the royal demesne of the kings of Cilicia. Since it was situated along the ancient trade route to Persia, India, and China, it was an important entrepôt for the eastern Mediterranean during the reign of Leo I/II. After the fall of Acre to the Mamluks in 1291, Āyās became the principal Christian port in the Levant for trade between Europe and the Near and Far East. It is not known who was responsible for expansion of the port facilities and buildings of the city, but Alishan attributes these accomplishments to Constantine, the father of King Het^{c}um I of Cilicia.

In 1322, Āyās was sacked by the Mamluks; the twin fortresses protecting the port were destroyed, and its officials were required to pay half of all port and customs duties to their captors. A contribution from Pope John XXII in 1331 aided in rebuilding some of the fortifications. In 1336 two Mamluk officials were murdered, bringing severe reprisals upon the town. Soon after there was another Mamluk raid, and the population was spared only upon agreement to raze every fortification in the city. Āyās was briefly held in 1367 by Peter I of Cyprus, who burned much of the city, but it was thereafter in Mamluk hands.

Āyās was a cosmopolitan city, a trading center for merchants from the city-states of Italy, Byzantium, Catalonia, Marseilles, Egypt, and the lands of the Dānishmendids and the Tatars. It became particularly popular as a meeting place for Muslim and Christian merchants during a period of papal prohibition of Christian merchants' trading in Muslim ports. Generous commercial privileges were granted to the Venetians and the Genoese by Leo I/II, and were renewed by Het^{c}um I and Leo II/III.

Āyās was a strongly protected port with both a mainland and an island castle, the latter built in about 1282 and used as a refuge during raids until it was destroyed in 1322. The city was also the site of an Armenian archbishopric by the mid thirteenth century.

BIBLIOGRAPHY

Ghevont Alishan, *L'Armeno-Veneto,* 2 vols. (1893); and *Sissouan, ou l'Arméno-Cilicie* (1899); Wilhelm von Heyd, *Histoire du commerce du Levant au moyen-âge,* 2 vols. (1885–1886, repr. 1959); Francesco Balducci Pegolotti, "La pratica della mercatura," in Giovanni Francesco Pagnini della Ventura, *Della decima et di varie altre gravezze imposte dal comune di Firenze,* III (1766, repr. 1967)—Pegolotti visited Cilicia in 1335 and recorded valuable information on Cilicia's rates of duty and on the trade routes to and from Āyās.

ANI P. ATAMIAN

[See also **Cilicia; Het^{c}um I; Leo I/II of Armenia; Mamluk Dynasty.**]

AYNARD OF ST. ÈVRE. The little that is known about Aynard, a monk at the monastery of St. Èvre in Toul, comes from the introduction to his *Liber glossarum* (Metz, Archives Communales, MS 500), composed in 969 for the education of the monks. The work is a glossary that provides both definitions and synonyms for words, and also makes distinctions between similar terms. It draws on a variety of sources: Jerome (for Hebrew), Nonius, Servius, the commentaries of Remigius of Auxerre, Isidore of Seville, Paul the Deacon's reworking of Festus, and a variety of unidentified glossaries, including a Greek glossary of some kind.

BIBLIOGRAPHY

Georg Goetz, *Corpus glossariorum latinorum,* V (1894), xxxiv–xxxvi, 615–620 (excerpt from the *Liber glossarum*); Maximilian Manitius, *Geschichte der lateinischen Literatur des Mittelalters,* II (1923).

LEAH SHOPKOW

AYRARAT (province; Assyrian *Urartu,* Hebrew *Ararat,* both used for the whole of Armenia; Greek *Alarodioi* for the population), the central portion of Greater Armenia located in the plain of the Araks River. The origin of the name is uncertain, but it is not used by any classical authors and it seems to have been a purely local designation for the royal domains of the Arsacid house of Armenia and probably of the Orontid and Artaxiad dynasties before it. As such, its classical equivalent is probably the *Araxenon Pedion* ("Araxene Plain") found in Strabo (11.14.4).

In the anonymous *Armenian Geography (Ašxarhac^{c}oyc^{c})* of the seventh century, Ayrarat is depicted as a vast territory including twenty-two districts comprising the whole of east-central Armenia (*ca.* 39,030 sq. km. = 15,066 sq. mi.). This, however, is much larger than the original royal demesne of the Armenian kings, which appears to have consisted of only ten districts covering 28,155 sq. km. (= 10,867 sq. mi.). Since the House of Bagratuni was almost certainly a branch of the Orontid royal house, it seems that their principality in Ayrarat emerged under the Artaxiad dynasty. The Artaxiad kings, apparently unable to dislodge the Bagratunis, must have granted them as an appanage the land subsequently known as Bagravand, which previously had probably been a part of Erasxajor. Under Trdat/Tiridates II (*ca.* 216–238) of the Arsacid dynasty, further districts were granted to important families; and by the fourth century, the remaining lands of Erasxajor had been granted to the House of Kamsarakan, a branch of the Arsacids. The ceding of these territories to various princely houses did not necessarily imply their loss to royal control, for the rulers of these principalities, like all Armenian noblemen, remained direct vassals of the crown. This was certainly true of the Bagratunis, the head of whom held the position of *t^{c}agadir* (coronant) at the Arsacid court.

After the fall of the Arsacid monarchy in 428 the various principalities within the former royal domains went their separate ways, while Erasxajor, now the Kamsarakan principality of Aršarunik^{c}, broke up into several smaller principalities, each held by a branch of the Kamsarakan house. The eastern lands of the old royal domains apparently remained under the jurisdiction of the *marzpans,* the Persian governors-general of Armenia, after the fall of the monarchy.

At the Byzantine-Persian partition of Armenia in 591, however, a new imperial province was created in east-central Armenia, which because of its relatively low elevation was known as Lower Armenia (37,480 sq. km. = 14,467 sq. mi.). Besides nucleal lands of the old royal domains in the east, this new Byzantine province included the principalities of Bagravand, Aršarunik^{c}, and a number of other principalities of the previous century. Taken together these lands correspond closely to the greater Ayrarat depicted in the *Armenian Geography,* except that its author includes in Ayrarat the land of Ostan Hayoc^{c} ("Capital of the Armenians," i.e., the district surrounding the capital cities of Artašat and Dwin).

The two centuries of Arab rule in Armenia saw the rise of the Bagratunis to a preeminent position among the surviving Armenian princes, and in about 884 they achieved recognition from both the caliph and the Byzantine emperor as dependent rulers in central Armenia. This new kingdom included all the former districts of Ayrarat and most of eastern Armenia as well. Annexed by the Byzantines in 1046, it was conquered by the Seljuk Turks in 1065, after which the term "Ayrarat" began to fall out of use. In the *Geography* of Vardan Vardapet (thirteenth century), Ayrarat covers a much more limited area. Seized by the Georgians in the twelfth century, overrun by the Mongols in the thirteenth, and under Turkoman rule in the fourteenth and fifteenth, the former Ayrarat was partitioned by Ottoman Turkey and Safavid Iran in 1512 and again in 1639.

Ayrarat in its broadest sense included the richest and most fertile regions of Armenia. All of her major capitals were located here along with several other cities and towns, as well as several dozen monasteries and over sixty fortresses. In addition, the main roads connecting Iran to Anatolia and Caucasia, and Mesopotamia to Caucasia passed through Ayrarat, which from earliest times became a thoroughfare for foreign invaders, military expeditions, and international trade.

BIBLIOGRAPHY

Nikolai Adontz, *Armenia in the Period of Justinian,* Nina G. Garsoïan, ed. and trans. (1970), 179–180, 236–241; Ghevont M. Alishan, *Ayrarat bnašxarh Hayastaneayc'* (1890); S. T. Eremyan, *Hayastanĕ ĕst "Ašxarhac'oyc'"-i* (1963), 35, 118; T. X. Hakobyan, *Hayastani patmakan ašxarhagrut'iwn,* 2nd ed. (1968), 121–158; Heinrich Hübschmann, *Die altarmenischen Ortsnamen* (1904, repr. 1969), 278–283, 361–366.

ROBERT H. HEWSEN

[See also **Armenia (Geography); Armenian Muslim Emirates; Aršacids/Arsakuni; Bagratids/Bagratuni; Kamsarakans.**]

AYYUBID ART AND ARCHITECTURE

AYYUBID ART AND ARCHITECTURE were produced primarily in Syria, Palestine, and Egypt between 1169 and 1260. The period was characterized by the elaboration of themes introduced by the Ayyubids' Turkish predecessors, and it provided the foundation for the material culture of the Mamluk

AYYUBID ART AND ARCHITECTURE

Tabouret. 12th–13th century. Hexagonal, six stump feet. Rakka, Syria. FREER GALLERY OF ART, SMITHSONIAN INSTITUTION, WASHINGTON, D.C.

Empire that followed; it is therefore frequently considered to be transitional. Although this judgment is factually correct, it does not do justice to the unique contributions of the Ayyubid patrons and to the artistic creativity that distinguished their rule.

The Ayyubid princes were particularly active in the construction of fortifications, largely in response to the threat posed by the Crusaders in the Near East. Beginning with Saladin's reconstruction of the Cairo city walls and his establishment of a citadel overlooking the city, the Ayyubids were responsible for a whole series of such structures, notably at Damascus, Aleppo, and Āmid (in northern Mesopotamia), as well as at a number of smaller cities and frontier sites.

One consequence of their control of such vast domains was the widespread diffusion of previously localized architectural practices. For example, the machicoulis had been known in Syria since Umayyad times and had perhaps first been adapted to defensive use in the twelfth century by the Crusaders at Sahyūn; but it was Saladin's brother al-Malik al-ᶜĀdil Sayf al-Dīn who brought it to the Cairo citadel before 1207–1208. On the other hand, the technique of thrusting column shafts perpendicularly into a defensive wall in order to bond the stone revetment more firmly to the rubble core had been known in Fatimid Cairo since the late eleventh century; it was introduced into Syria and northern Mesopotamia by the Ayyubids, under whom it was elaborated to include multiple courses.

In Syria a large number of mausoleum complexes, of a type initiated by the Zankid Nūr al-Dīn, were sponsored by the Ayyubids and their followers. The typical complex consisted of a *madrasah* built around a central courtyard with an elegant lobed-marble ablutions basin. Surrounding this courtyard would be an *eyvan,* living quarters, and, on the *qiblah* side, a sanctuary with a central dome. Usually the founder's mausoleum was a separate domed chamber entered from the passage from street to courtyard. The best-known surviving Ayyubid examples are al-ᶜĀdiliyya (now much altered) and al-Māridāniyya in Damascus and al-Firdaws in Aleppo. Such buildings were quite austere on the exterior, where ornamentation was largely limited to the portals; usually hooded with elongated *muqarnas* semidomes; and often framed in stone masonry of alternating colors *(ablaq),* an old Syrian technique.

The interior of the sanctuary was usually both rich and sober in its decoration. Stucco frames and arches articulated the wall surfaces, emphasizing the main building lines. Each wall might be adorned with a single painted or carved stucco medallion enclosing a clearly organized axial or radial arabesque design, both spacious and monumental in effect. Such designs could be echoed in the stucco frameworks of stained-glass windows and in wood. The wooden *minbar,* doors, lintels, and cenotaphs were more often, however, composed of strapwork enclosing polygonal pieces of carved ivory. Further color might be provided by a *miḥrāb* framed in polychrome stone intarsia strapwork.

In Damascus the typical mausoleum was distinguished by a double drum supporting the dome, clearly articulating on the exterior the two interior zones of transition—octagonal and sixteen-sided.

As for Egypt, the main impact of Ayyubid architectural ideas was not felt there before the reign of al-Malik al-Ṣāliḥ Najm al-Dīn (1240–1249). It was he who introduced the *madrasah* to Cairo, where, in contrast to Syrian practice, it was characterized by two or more *eyvans,* reflecting a typical Egyptian

Basin. Ayyubid period (1239–1249). Brass, richly inlaid with silver. FREER GALLERY OF ART, SMITHSONIAN INSTITUTION, WASHINGTON, D.C.

house plan. Stone gradually supplanted brick as the favored building material, and, in the famed mausoleum of the Abbasid caliphs, completed before 1242, the stucco decorations and stained-glass windows reflect Syrian taste. Only after al-Sālih's death, however, did his widow add a tomb chamber to his *madrasah,* thus establishing the first mausoleum complex in Egypt.

Nine brass objects inlaid with silver and inscribed to various Ayyubid princes and dignitaries survive; the earliest is an ewer dated 1232, now in the Freer Gallery of Art, Washington, D.C. This group forms the nucleus of a larger body of related works. A few of these objects bear signatures of craftsmen with the *nisbah* al-Mawṣilī ("of Mosul"). Furthermore, most of them show stylistic connections with contemporary inlaid metalwork made at Mosul and with manuscript illustrations from the same milieu, demonstrating once again, as in the adoption of the mausoleum complex, the continuity between the material culture of the Zankids and the Ayyubids. Thirteen of the Syrian inlaid brasses include Christian scenes, often misunderstood and combined with Islamic motifs in unexpected ways; they constitute one of the leading unsolved puzzles of medieval Islamic art.

Painted and lustered ceramics in a variety of shapes and designs were manufactured at several Syrian sites during the Ayyubid period. They were frequently enhanced with sgraffiato or relief, either molded or carved. Such ceramics have been found at al-Raqqah (whence the generic label "Raqqah ware"), Baalbek, Hama, and al-Ruṣāfah. Besides vessels and tiles, the Syrian workshops produced quantities of ceramic stands and taborets.

In Ayyubid domains manuscript illustration has so far been attributed only to Aleppo. The miniatures are notable for their dependence on Byzantine models, particularly in the persistence of "Hellenistic" fold patterns and of compositions borrowed from manuscripts of the Macedonian renaissance and the later monastic scriptoria. The earliest dated example is a copy of al-Harīrī's *Maqāmāt* finished in 1222, now in Paris (Bibliothèque Nationale, MS ar. 6094). The entire group, however, shows strong affinities with a Coptic manuscript in the same library (MS copte 13), which was copied in 1180 at Damietta in the Egyptian delta.

BIBLIOGRAPHY

Esin Atil, *Art of the Arab World* (1975); K. A. C. Creswell, *The Muslim Architecture of Egypt,* II (1959); Richard Ettinghausen, *Arab Painting* (1962); Ernst J. Grube, "Raqqa-Keramik in der Sammlung des Metropolitan Museum in New York," in *Kunst des Orients,* 4 (1965); D. S. Rice, "Studies in Islamic Metalwork—II," in *Bulletin of the School of Oriental and African Studies,* 15 (1953); Jean Sauvaget, *Alep,* 2 vols. (1941); Jean Sauvaget and M. Écochard, *Les monuments ayyoubides de Damas,* 3 vols. (1938–1948); L. T. Schneider, "The Freer Canteen," in *Ars Orientalis,* 9 (1973).

ESTELLE WHELAN

AYYUBIDS, a twelfth- and thirteenth-century dynastic regime, several generations of which dominated religious, political, and military developments in Egypt, Syria, upper Mesopotamia, and the Yemen. Although founded by Saladin (*ca.* 1137–1193), the dynastic establishment derived its name from his Kurdish father Āyyūb ibn Shadhi (*d.* 1173). The latter, along with his brother Shirkuh (*d.* 1169) and other Kurdish relatives and supporters, rose to prominence in the service of the famous anti-Crusader leaders Zengi (*d.* 1146) and Nūr al-Dīn (*d.* 1174) to lay foundations for the spectacular career of his sons and their descendants.

The inception of the Ayyubid regime took place between 1164 and 1174. During that decade Saladin participated with distinction in three expeditions of Syrian warriors, commanded by Shirkuh and aimed at the promotion of Nūr al-Dīn's interests in Fatimid Egypt. In March 1169, following the victorious conclusion of the third expedition and the sudden death of its leader, Saladin emerged as commander of the expedition and as vizier of the Fatimid caliphate. In subsequent years, he succeeded in building up strong land and naval forces, in winning several engagements with the Crusaders, and in promoting his father, brothers, and Kurdish supporters to positions of authority in Egypt. In 1171, after abolishing the Fatimid caliphate and suppressing its Shiite Ismaili establishment, Saladin extended his influence westward by sending a military expedition to Tripoli and Tunis. In 1174 he sent his brother Shams al-Dawla southward to achieve a successful conquest of the Yemen. This growing power of the Ayyubid master in Egypt, and his reluctance to cooperate in the anti-Crusader campaigns of Nūr al-Dīn, brought the two leaders to the brink of a military confrontation, averted in May 1174 by the death of the Syrian suzerain.

During the following twelve years Saladin, though ostensibly committed to the ideal of the Holy War (*jihād),* concentrated on a successful expansion of his authority in Syria and upper Mesopotamia, achieving his goals by means of diplomacy and vigorous military campaigns. Assisted by his brothers and relatives, as well as by Kurdish, Turkish, Arab, and Persian military commanders, diplomats, and writers, Saladin found himself by 1186 in direct control over Egypt, all of Moslem Syria, and the Yemen, and in indirect authority over Mosul, its dependencies, and several districts in upper Mesopotamia. On 2 October 1187, having inflicted a crushing defeat on the Crusaders at Ḥattīn, Saladin reached the apogee of his career by liberating Jerusalem from Christian domination.

Although he gained a lasting international fame and enhanced the popularity of his nascent regime, Saladin's hopes of exterminating the Crusaders were frustrated by the Third Crusade (1189–1191). By the end of the famous confrontation in 1191 at Acre, Saladin, having deployed tremendous manpower and both financial and logistic resources, found his army demoralized, his navy destroyed, and Acre with its elite garrison recaptured by the Crusaders. On 2 September 1192, the conqueror of Jerusalem was compelled to sign a compromise armistice agreement with Richard the Lionhearted, which gave a new lease on life to the kingdom of the Crusaders. Truncated though this kingdom became, it was to outlive Saladin's dynastic legacy except for the Hama and Ḥiṣn Kaifa branches. An embittered and humiliated Saladin returned to his beloved Damascus to die there on 4 March 1193.

Although Saladin organized the political and territorial structure of the Ayyubid state, his hopes of perpetuating the supremacy of his house did not materialize. By 1202 the tenuous political dominance of Saladin's sons was lost to his experienced and dynamic brother, al-ᶜĀdil. Thereafter, the Ayyubid establishment was dominated by the house of al-ᶜĀdil. Only in 1250 did al-Nāṣir Yūsuf of Aleppo recover the leadership over Syria for the house of Saladin. Ten years later, however, the great-grandson of the dynasty's founder surrendered to the Mongols. His ignominious death at the hands of Hulagu marked the end of Ayyubid rule.

While the dynastic legacy of Saladin comprised numerous principalities, only a few of them were focal points of the colorful Ayyubid history. The Ayyubids of the Yemen (1174–1229) reintroduced Sunni (orthodox) Islam to that area. Although they maintained close political, economic, and institutional links with the Ayyubid regime in Egypt, they also entertained ambitious ideas: Muᶜizz al-Dīn (1197–1202), for example, assumed the title of caliph. The Yemeni branch of the Ayyubids ended in 1229, when Ṣalāḥ al-Dīn (1215–1229) conceded the province to the Rasulids.

The Ayyubid principality of Aleppo (1193–1260) was the only major territorial unit that remained in the hands of Saladin's descendants. Despite incessant struggles for power, only in 1250 were their ambitions fulfilled, when al-Nāsir Yūsuf established himself in Damascus and for ten years enjoyed control of a united Muslim Syria. In 1257, he attained the highest honor of being formally invested by the caliph of Baghdad with the office of sultan—an empty gesture, since within the following three years both

AYYUBIDS

the caliph and the Ayyubid sultan were exterminated by the Mongols.

The possession of neither the Yemen and Aleppo, nor the Ayyubid principalities of Homs (1193–1264), Hama (1193–1342), Diyar Mudar (Edessa, Harran: 1193–1259), Diyarbakir (Mayyafariqin: 1193–1260), Diyarbakir (Amida and Hisn Kaifa: 1232–1523), Transjordan (1193–1262), Baalbek (1193–1260), Banyas (1218–1260), and Bosra (1193–1246) gave as much prestige and power as had the mastery over Egypt and Damascus. Egypt's territorial compactness and resources constituted important ingredients of the political longevity of the great Ayyubid sultans of Cairo, al-ᶜĀdil (1200–1218) and his son al-Kāmil (1218–1238). The latter is best known for his victory over the Fifth Crusade (1218–1221), his magnanimous attitude toward the proselytizing mission of St. Francis of Assisi, and his diplomatic coup with Frederick II, involving the cession of Jerusalem, Bethlehem, and Nazareth to the Holy Roman emperor, thus avoiding bloodshed (1228/1229).

Because of the Egyptian economic and military power, the sultans of Cairo generated integrative influence over the remaining Ayyubid principalities. A key role in these tendencies was played by Damascus. Unification of the two regions by the sultans of Egypt meant internal peace for the Ayyubid establishment, as under Saladin, al-ᶜĀdil, and al-Ṣāliḥ ibn Ayyūb (1245–1249). No serious challenge to the authority of the sultan could be attempted without the political, military, and economic participation of Damascus. Thus, as R. Stephen Humphreys remarks, "the incessant conflicts between the sultan and the princes almost always took the form of a war between Damascus and Cairo" (*From Saladin to the Mongols,* p. 13).

The internal rivalry benefited the Crusaders, who on two occasions (1229 and 1244) successfully negotiated their recovery of Jerusalem. Consumed by the long decades of fratricidal struggle, the decadent Ayyubid leadership not only failed to resist the Mongol invasion of Mesopotamia and Syria (1258–1260) but succumbed to a coup d'etat staged in Egypt by the commanders of their Mamluk troops (1250). During the following decade, despite some futile efforts of the Ayyubid epigones, the legacy of Saladin was replaced by a new Islamic power, the Mamluk sultanate of Egypt and Syria.

The main factors in the rise of the Ayyubids had been their family solidarity, their persistent pursuit of political aggrandizement, and their dedication to the *jihād.* When family conflicts replaced family unity and when Jerusalem became an object of diplomatic trade-offs between the successors of Saladin and the Crusaders, then the Ayyubid establishment was doomed to collapse.

Despite their turbulent career, the Ayyubids performed a significant role in the history of the medieval Middle East. At the time of the disintegration of the Fatimid caliphate and of the Seljukid successor states, the Ayyubids evolved a political, military, and economic system with the unity of Egypt and Syria as its guiding principle. Although they were accorded the official status of sultans only in exceptional instances, they contributed to the acceptance of the institution of the sultanate in the Syro-Egyptian political life.

While initially the Ayyubids benefited from the support of their immediate and extended family, in the closing decades their rule largely depended on the size and quality of their armed forces as well as on the loyalty of their commanders. The composition of the Ayyubid army likewise underwent an evolution. Originally warriors consisted of divers ethnic, professional, and tribal groups; but toward the end of the Ayyubid regime, the military was essentially made up of several well-trained Mamluk cavalry regiments, which depended on Transcaucasian slave markets for the supply of manpower. During the Third Crusade, Ayyubid naval policy ended disastrously when Saladin's challenge to Christian supremacy at sea culminated in a nearly total destruction of his fleet. Later on, rather than confront the Crusaders at sea, the Ayyubid leadership limited its naval concern to the destruction of coastal towns and fortresses that might be targets of Christian amphibious attacks.

The elite in the highly hierarchic civil, religious, bureaucratic, and educational apparatus constituted another pillar of the Ayyubid state system. Ayyubid accomplishment in the suppression of heterodoxy in Egypt and the Yemen and their zeal and generosity in the renovation, expansion, and endowment of places of worship, mosques, mausoleums, shrines, and colleges *(madrasa)* enhanced the positive relationship between the government and theological institutions, and created a stimulating intellectual environment in which Cairo was transformed from the capital of Ismaili Islam to the center of Islamic orthodoxy.

To secure a strong economic basis for their state, the Ayyubids expanded and refined the institution of the feudal grants *(iqta^ca)*, a system inherited from earlier regimes. These *iqta*ᶜ*a* allotments, centrally distributed in return for precisely defined military or administrative services, were often scattered geographically to prevent accumulation of economic and territorial power in the hands of individual beneficiaries. Likewise, a proportion of land revenue was put aside to provide for the needs of the ruler and his court, the royal army, and the civil service. Another part of the revenue was assigned, sometimes in perpetuity, to support theological, medical, or charitable institutions.

Compelled by ever-increasing military expenditure, the Ayyubids resorted to fiscal policies that accelerated the decline of medieval Egypt and Syria. Many factors crippled the vitality of the once prosperous Egyptian economy: proliferation of noncanonical taxes *(mukūs);* critical debasements of coinage; elimination of non-Moslems from the Red Sea trade zone; and preemptive interference with the activities of indigenous import and export merchants. All these political, military, social, religious, and economic practices paved the way for both the coming and the nature of the Mamluk sultanate. A direct product of the Ayyubid regime, the Mamluks exterminated the Crusaders and successfully defended Syria and Egypt against the onslaughts of the Mongols.

Of all their diversified architectural legacy it is the mountain fortress of Cairo, begun by Saladin and completed by al-Kāmil, that has always elicited public admiration and awe. Similarly it is the fame of their struggle against the Crusaders—above all the liberation of Jerusalem of 1187—that has been remembered by posterity. This fame contributed to the flourishing of historiography in Mamluk Egypt and to the glamorous popularity of Saladin among modern Western historians and romancers.

BIBLIOGRAPHY

Andrew S. Ehrenkreutz, *Saladin* (1972); Francesco Gabrieli, *Arab Historians of the Crusades* (1969), with bibliography; Hamilton A. R. Gibb, "The Achievement of Saladin," in *Studies on the Civilization of Islam* (1962); Hans L. Gottschalk, *Al-Malik al-Kamil von Egypten und seine Zeit* (1958); R. Stephen Humphreys, *From Saladin to the Mongols: The Ayyubids of Damascus, 1193–1260* (1977); and Stanley Lane-Poole, *Saladin and the Fall of the Kingdom of Jerusalem* (1898).

ANDREW S. EHRENKREUTZ

[See also **Ayyubid Art and Architecture; Fatimids; Hulagu; Mamluks; Richard I, the Lionhearted; Saladin.**]

AZAT (from Pahlavi *azat,* "free"), third class of medieval Armenian society attested from the earliest fifth-century sources. The *azat* formed the lowest level of the nobility, inferior to the princely *naχarar* but free from monetary or servile obligations, personally inviolable before the law, and consequently wholly distinct from the nonnoble population, which is occasionally referred to as *an-azat* (non*azat*, unfree). The Armenian *azatk*ᶜ were the etymological and sociological equivalents of the Sasanian *āzātān*, who are listed as the lowest class of the free nobility in the Hājjīābād inscription of King Shapur I (241–272?), and of the Georgian *aznauri,* although they never provided the support for the crown against the dynasts found in Georgia.

In the opinion of Cyril Toumanoff, the early medieval *azatk*ᶜ were probably the descendants of small family and clan heads of tribal times who had failed to achieve sovereign status. As distinct from the *sepuh* who were the junior members of princely *naχarar* families, the *azatk*ᶜ formed a separate class subordinate to the dynasts whom they served. In composition the *azat* clan may have been somewhat mixed, including occasional déclassé princely cadets, some allodialists, and conditional feudal landholders or *χostakdar* held to specific services. Their main duty as well as privilege was serving in the cavalry of their overlord, thus making of them a clearly identifiable equestrian class, but they also seem to have had some judicial rights. In the later latinized state of Cilician Armenia the equestrian character of the Armenian *azat* led to their identification with Western knights with whom they shared many of the duties and privileges.

BIBLIOGRAPHY

Nicolas Adontz, *Armenia in the Period of Justinian,* Nina G. Garsoïan, ed. and trans. (1970), 337–338, 342–343; Hakob Manandyan, *The Trade and Cities of Armenia in Relation to Ancient World Trade,* Nina G. Garsoïan, trans. (1965), 70–71, 175; Cyril Toumanoff, *Studies in Christian Caucasian History* (1963), 40, n. 14; 93–94, n. 137; 123–124, n. 215; 126–127, n. 216.

NINA G. GARSOÏAN

[See also **Aznauri; Naχarar.**]

AZERBAIJAN, the name of a region currently encompassing two provinces of northwestern Iran

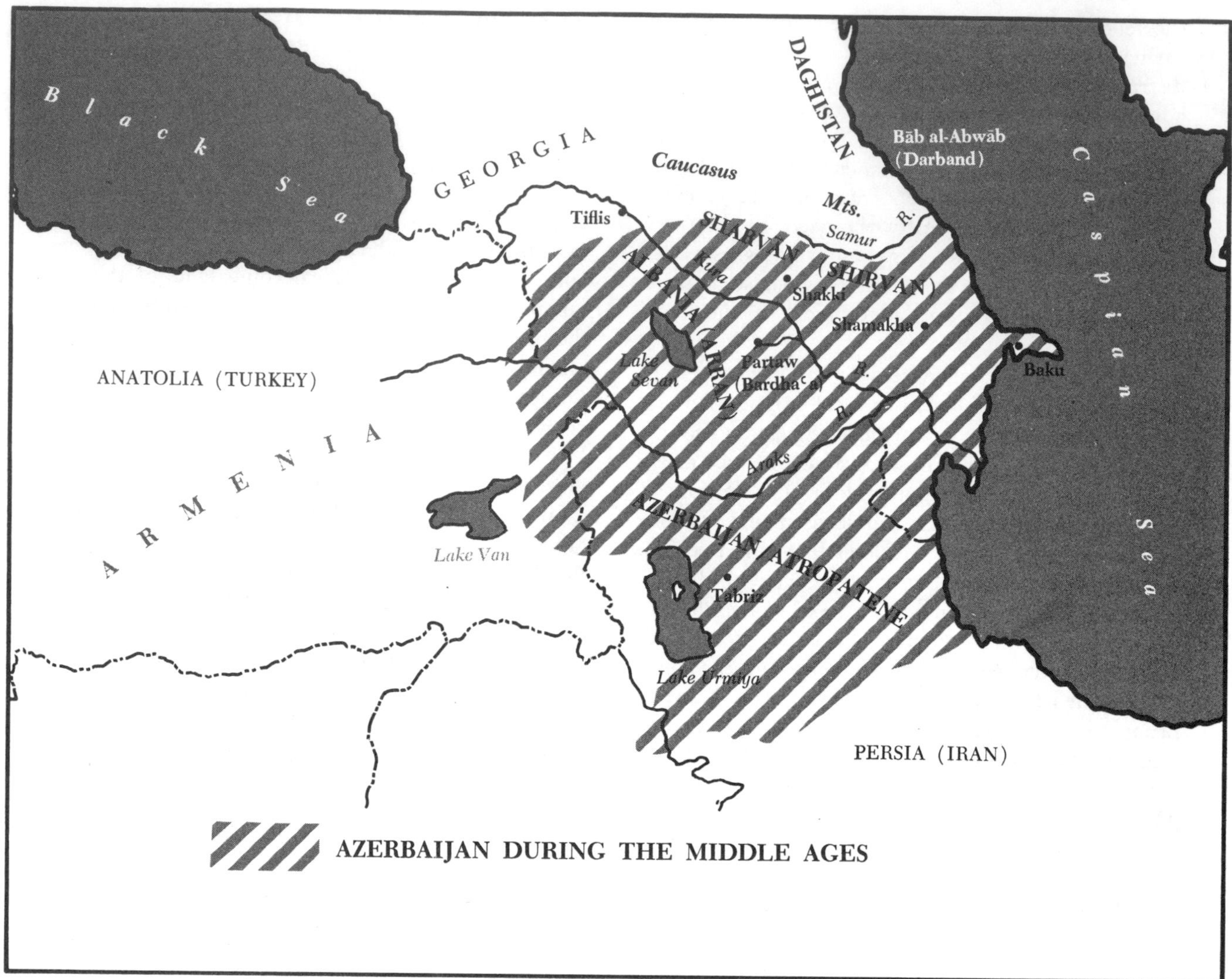

(East and West Azerbaijan) and the Azerbaijan S.S.R. in Transcaucasia. Historically it consisted of several distinct areas that collectively came to be called "Azerbaijan" by the late Middle Ages. Shirvan/Sharvān was the territory in the eastern Caucasus between the Araks and Samur rivers (present-day Northern Soviet Azerbaijan). It included the cities of Baku, Shamakha, Shakki, and sometimes the region of Darband/Bāb al-Abwāb, located beyond the Samur. Albania (Armenian, Aluan; Georgian, Rani; Arabic, Arrān) consisted of the lands between the Kura and Araks rivers (present-day Southern Soviet Azerbaijan). The principal city was Pērōzāpāt/Partaw/Bardhaᶜa/Barda.

Azerbaijan (from Arabic Ādharbayjān, Persian Ādharbādhagān, Middle Persian Āturpātākān; Armenian, Atrpatakan; Georgian, Adarbadagani; Greek, 'Αδαρβιγάνων or 'Ατροπατήνη, allegedly so named after the Achaemenid governor of Media) coincided with the classical Media Minor or Media Atropatene (present-day Iranian Azerbaijan) in northwestern Iran. The principal city was Tabrīz.

The population of the northern areas was of Paleocaucasian stock related to the non-Turkic peoples of Dagestan. The ancient Albanian language survives in those areas today in only a few villages. The people of the southern and Caspian coastal lands were largely Iranian or iranized. Today the entire region is predominantly Turkic-speaking.

In Sasanid times (*ca.* 224–651), Azerbaijan/Atropatene, an important military and cultic center, was a province of the Persian Empire. Zoroastrianism/Mazdaism, the state religion of the Sasanids, was native to its Iranian population. Albania was a largely recalcitrant vassal state, open to profound Armenian Christian influences. Azerbaijan/Atropatene was brought into the Arabian caliphate in 639–643, but Albania became a battlefield for a prolonged Arab-Khazar war that subsided only after 737. The Persian *limes* system was taken over by the Arabs, who were strongly concentrated in Darband/Bāb al-Abwāb, while Albania, increasingly fragmented into local dynastic holdings, maintained a quasi-independent, but tributary, status. The Albanian Mihrānid ruling house was extinguished about 822 and local princes became the dominant political force, often at the expense of the Abbasid caliphs.

By the late ninth century the centrifugal tendencies evident throughout Transcaucasia found expression in a series of dynasties of Turkic and Iranian (Kurdish, Daylamite, and other) origins: Sājids, Musāfirids, and Rawwādids in Azerbaijan/Atropatene (tenth–eleventh centuries): Yazīdids (861–1027) in Shirvan; and Shaddādids (951–1174) in Armenia and Arrān. This "Iranian intermezzo" was ended with the arrival of the Seljuks in the mid eleventh century. Seljuk hegemony brought about the massive settlement of Turkic tribesmen in Azerbaijan, resulting ultimately in its turkicization. When Seljuk rule weakened during the twelfth century, the atabeg Ildenizid dynasty became the most powerful force in Azerbaijan (1136–1225). It was swept away by the Khwārizmshāh Jalāl al-Dīn (1220–1231) and by the Mongols, who followed soon after.

Under Ilkhānid rule (1256–1353) Arrān and Azerbaijan were consolidated and the process of islamicization and turkicization was completed. In the anarchy that accompanied the collapse of the Ilkhānids, the Jalāyirids (1336–1432) attempted to assume the mantle of Genghis Khan in Azerbaijan, but were fatally undermined by the invasions of Tamerlane (*d.* 1405) and strife with the Turkoman confederation of the Qara Qoyunlu (1380–1468). The latter was subsequently conquered by a rival confederation, the Aq Qoyunlu (1378–1508). That group, however, was challenged by the rising Ottoman state and the Shiᶜa movement of the Safawids, which was largely supported by heterodox tribesmen in Azerbaijan and Anatolia. The Safawids (1501–1732) took control of Azerbaijan in 1501 and went on to conquer all of Iran, where they established Shiᶜa Islam as the state religion.

BIBLIOGRAPHY

Sources. Munajjimbāshī (Münejjimbashī), Jāmiᶜ adduwal, which contains the *Taᶜrīkh al-bāb*—see Vladimir F. Minorsky, *Studies in Caucasian History* (1953), and *A History of Sharvān and Darband in the 10th–11th Centuries* (1958); Movsēs Dasxuranç̣i (Movsēs Kałankatuaç̣i), *Movsisi Kałankatuaçwoy ałuaniç patmutᶜiwn ašxarhi,* Mkrtich Ēmin, ed. (1860, repr. 1912); and *The History of the Caucasian Albanians by Movsēs Dasxuranç̣i,* C. J. F. Dowsett, trans. (1961).

Secondary Literature. Ali Ashraf Alizade, *Sotsialno-ekonomicheskaya i politicheskaya istoria Azerbaidzhana XIII–XIV vv.* (1956); Vasily Bartold, *Mesto prikaspyskikh oblastey v istorii musulmanskogo mira* (1925), repr. in his *Sochinenia,* II, pt. 1 (1963); *Kratky obzor istorii Azerbaydzhana* (1925), repr. in his *Sochinenia,* II, pt. 1 (1963); and "Turetsky epos i Kavkaz," in *Yazyk i literatura,* 5 (1930), repr. in his *Sochinenia,* V (1968); and Zia M. Bunyatov, *Azerbaydzhan v VII–IX vv.* (1965).

PETER B. GOLDEN

[See also **Albania (Caucasian); Aq Qoyunlu/White Sheep; Sasanian Dynasty; Seljuks; Shirvan; Tabrīz.**]

AZHAR, AL-. Located in the heart of medieval Cairo, al-Azhar is one of the most venerable mosques, and the principal religious university, in the Islamic world. Today it consists of dozens of structures added over the centuries to a core begun in 970, immediately after the Ismaili Fatimid dynasty conquered Egypt and established its capital there. Known originally as Jāmiᶜ al-Qāhira ("The Congregational Mosque of Cairo"), by the year 1000 the mosque had gained its epithet *al-Azhar* ("the radiant"), usually understood to be an allusion to Fāṭima al-Zuhrāᵓ, the daughter of the prophet Muḥammad.

After its foundation the mosque became a center for the teaching of Ismaili doctrine, and as such is often considered to be the first "university" in the Islamic world. The fall of the Fatimids in 1171 marked the end of its role as a center of Ismaili learning. Under Ayyubid rule the mosque was neglected. In the middle of the thirteenth century, the Mamluk sultan Baybars reendowed and restored it as a center for Sunni religious studies. As such, its influence grew steadily, aided by the preeminent cultural role Cairo began to play after the fall of Baghdad to the Mongols in 1258. Throughout the succeeding centuries al-Azhar continued to grow under the patronage of Mamluk and Ottoman rulers.

The original Fatimid mosque was a rectangular enclosure, roughly 85 by 69 meters, of which one-third formed the hypostyle prayer hall. The walls were built of brick, covered with carved and inscribed stucco on the interior. The flat roof was made of wood. Although some elements of the plan and construction are traceable to earlier mosques in Egypt, many features were directly inspired by earlier Fatimid mosques in North Africa. The Fatimid caliph al-Ḥāfiẓ (1131–1146) added porticoes around the courtyard, and the Mamluk sultans and emirs added minarets, new entrances, and madrasahs, to such an extent that the exterior of the Fatimid foundation is totally surrounded by later additions.

BIBLIOGRAPHY

K. A. C. Creswell, *The Muslim Architecture of Egypt,* I (1952), 36–64, 254–257.

JONATHAN M. BLOOM

[See also **Schools, Islamic.**]

ᶜAZĪZ BIᵓLLĀH NIZĀR ABŪ MANṢŪR, AL-, fifth Fatimid caliph and first to rule entirely from Egypt, was born in Mahdia (Tunisia) on 10 May 955. He became caliph upon the death of his father, al-Muᶜizz, in December 975, but his position was not secure until the official proclamation on 9 August 976. The caliph died suddenly of a kidney ailment on 14 October 996 at Bilbeis, while leading a military expedition into Syria against the Byzantines. He was succeeded by his eleven-year-old son al-Ḥākim.

His reign was marked by relative peace, with almost all military activity limited to the Syrian front. Al-ᶜAzīz created a new-style Fatimid army that was multiracial and composed of military slaves as well as elements of the original army. The latter was composed primarily of North African Kutāma Berbers who served as cavalry. The new army had both infantry that included Persians from Dailam, Iran, and cavalry that included Central Asian Turks. Special quarters were built in Cairo for the racially separated cavalry and infantry units. Sub-Saharan African military slaves also were acquired by al-ᶜAzīz. Only the demise of the dynasty at the hands of Saladin almost two centuries later ended the military organization introduced into the Fatimid state by al-ᶜAzīz.

This Fatimid caliph's reign was noted for its excellent administration, fair treatment of minorities, and economic prosperity. For most of his reign Ibn Killis, a convert from Judaism, served brilliantly as chief administrator. The Fatimid ruler also relied upon Jews and Christians as administrators, and these minorities generally fared well during his reign. One exception took place in Cairo in 996. Christians were blamed for destroying part of the Fatimid fleet anchored nearby, and in the ensuing riots more than 100 Christians, including merchants from Amalfi, Italy, were killed. This incident and less serious ones did not disrupt the trade that flourished between Egypt and Europe, Persia, India, Yemen, and the Byzantine Empire.

Al-ᶜAzīz expanded the usual role of the Fatimid caliph as an Ismaili Shiite leader. He banned some Sunni practices, established the tenth of Muḥarram in Egypt as an official day of mourning, and made personal appearances every Friday during Ramadan. The caliph was the first to appoint Ismaili judges in many parts of his realm, which ranged from Egypt to Tunisia, the Hejaz, Palestine, and occasionally central and even northern Syria.

Very little is known about al-ᶜAzīz's personal life. It is said he had red hair and blue eyes. One of his wives was a Christian whose brothers were appointed Melchite patriarchs of Jerusalem and Cairo-Fusṭāt. Another woman, a Muslim, was probably the mother of al-Ḥākim. Al-ᶜAzīz was an active and wealthy patron, indulging himself in the acquisition of precious jewels, expensive textiles, and exotic foods and animals. His wealth was also used to support construction of a new royal residence in greater Cairo, a mosque for his mother in the Karafa cemetery, and the foundations for a large mosque known as al-Ḥākim's Mosque.

BIBLIOGRAPHY

The best summary in English is in *Encyclopedia of Islam,* 2nd ed. (1960). The value of al-Maqrīzī's *Ittiᶜaz al-Hunafā'bi-Akhbār al-A'imma al-Fātimiyīn al-Khulafā',* Jamāl al-Dīn al-Shayyāl, ed. (1967), vol. I cannot be overestimated as it contains fragments of the lost contemporary Fatimid source Ibn Zūlāq; Yaacov Lev, "A political Study of Egypt and Syria under the Early Fatimida 358/968–386/996" (unpublished Ph.D.), and forthcoming articles by Yaacov Lev based on his Ph.D. in press at *Studia Islamica.*

JERE L. BACHARACH

[See also **Egypt, Islamic; Fatimids; Ḥākim, al-.**]

AZNAURI (plural *aznaurni*), a Georgian petty nobleman, a landholder or warrior, parallel to the *azat* nobility of Armenia. The term dates from at least the fifth century and corresponds to Strabo's earlier description of the "third class" in Iberian society. It was at first applied to all nobles, regardless of status, but in the later Middle Ages a clearer distinction was made between the *tavadi* and *mtavari* (dynastic princes), and the *aznaurni* (dependent gentry). The vassal gentry were much more subject to their lord's will than were French vassals. From the fifteenth century on, the Georgian *aznauri* was considered a *gma* (slave) of his lord and was bound more closely to his lord than was his lord to the king.

BIBLIOGRAPHY

William E. D. Allen, *A History of the Georgian People,* 2nd ed. (1971); Georges Charachidzé, *Introduction à l'étude de la féodalité géorgienne (Le code de Georges le Brillant)* (1971); Cyril Toumanoff, "La noblesse géorgienne: Sa genèse et sa structure," in *Rivista Araldica,* 59, no. 9 (1956), and *Studies in Christian Caucasian History* (1963).

RONALD G. SUNY

[See also **Azat; Feudalism.**]

AZO (*ca.* 1150–1230) was one of the last and greatest of the Bolognese jurists known as the Glossators. He was probably born at Bologna, and was the leading teacher of civil law there for more than thirty years. It was under him that the Bolognese school achieved its apogee in both achievement and fame.

Azo had apparently been the disciple of Johannes Bassianus, and became the link through whom the doctrines of the school of Bulgarus became accepted by the following generation and entered into the *Glossa ordinaria* to the *Corpus juris civilis.* His most important work was his *summa* of the *Corpus,* a systematic exposition of the civil law based on the first nine books of the *Codex* and on the *Institutiones* of Justinian. The *summa,* composed between 1208 and 1210, became the definitive work of its type. This work was ideally close to that of Accursius, Azo's greatest disciple and the compiler of the *Glossa ordinaria.* It is not surprising, therefore, that Accursius saw fit to include a vast portion of his master's glosses in his masterpiece; about a third of the pre-Accursian attributed glosses in that work bear Azo's siglum, or signature. Among Azo's other famous disciples were Roffud of Benevento, Martinus of Fano, and Johannes Teutonicus; both directly and through his pupils, then, Azo greatly influenced both civil and canon law.

Although Azo's other works enjoyed a less felicitous destiny than his *summa,* they remain noteworthy. His last work was a *lectura* on the *Codex*—that is, his lectures on the *Codex* as collected by one of his students. It contains references to his *summa, Brocardica aurea,* glosses on the *Digest* of the *Corpus,* and *consilia.* He also published some *quaestiones* and *distinctiones,* which remain unedited.

BIBLIOGRAPHY

Hermann Kantorowicz, with William W. Buckland, *Studies in the Glossators of the Roman Law* (1938, repr. with addenda and corrigenda 1969), 41, 44–45, and *passim.*

GIULIO SILANO

[See also **Bulgarus; Corpus Juris Civilis; Glossators.**]

AZORES. The Azores appear, with Italian names, in Abraham Cresques' Catalan Atlas of 1375. They had been discovered shortly before, by Genoese navigators in the service of Portugal, under the command of Admiral Lanzarote Pessagno. In 1439, King Alfonso V gave his uncle, Henry the Navigator, permission to settle seven uninhabited islands (Henry had already landed some sheep there). In 1443 the king decreed that settlers on the islands would have a five-year exemption from tithes and from export taxes on goods sent to Portugal.

The Azores were so remote from Portugal that foreign settlers were encouraged to go there. In 1450, Jacob van Brugge, a Fleming, was given permission by Prince Henry to colonize the island of Terceira and to hold it as a fief (capitania). Colonization of São Miguel was begun by criminals sentenced to exile, but after the death of Henry the Navigator (1460), more and more reliance was placed on Flemish settlers. Jacob van Brugge, who had married a Portuguese woman, was, like most of the other Flemish leaders, a seaman. He was lost at sea in 1474, probably while exploring the ocean to the west.

Another Fleming who settled in the Azores was William van der Haegen, the founder of the still-existing da Silveira family (a Portuguese translation of his name). William was active on São Jorge, Faial, and Terceira. Later he was made capitan (governor) of Flores and Corvo. He grew woad (a dyestuff) there, and exported it to Flanders on his own ships. Josse de Hurtere, who came from the region of Bruges, settled in the Azores at the invitation of Prince Ferdinand, heir of Henry the Navigator. He

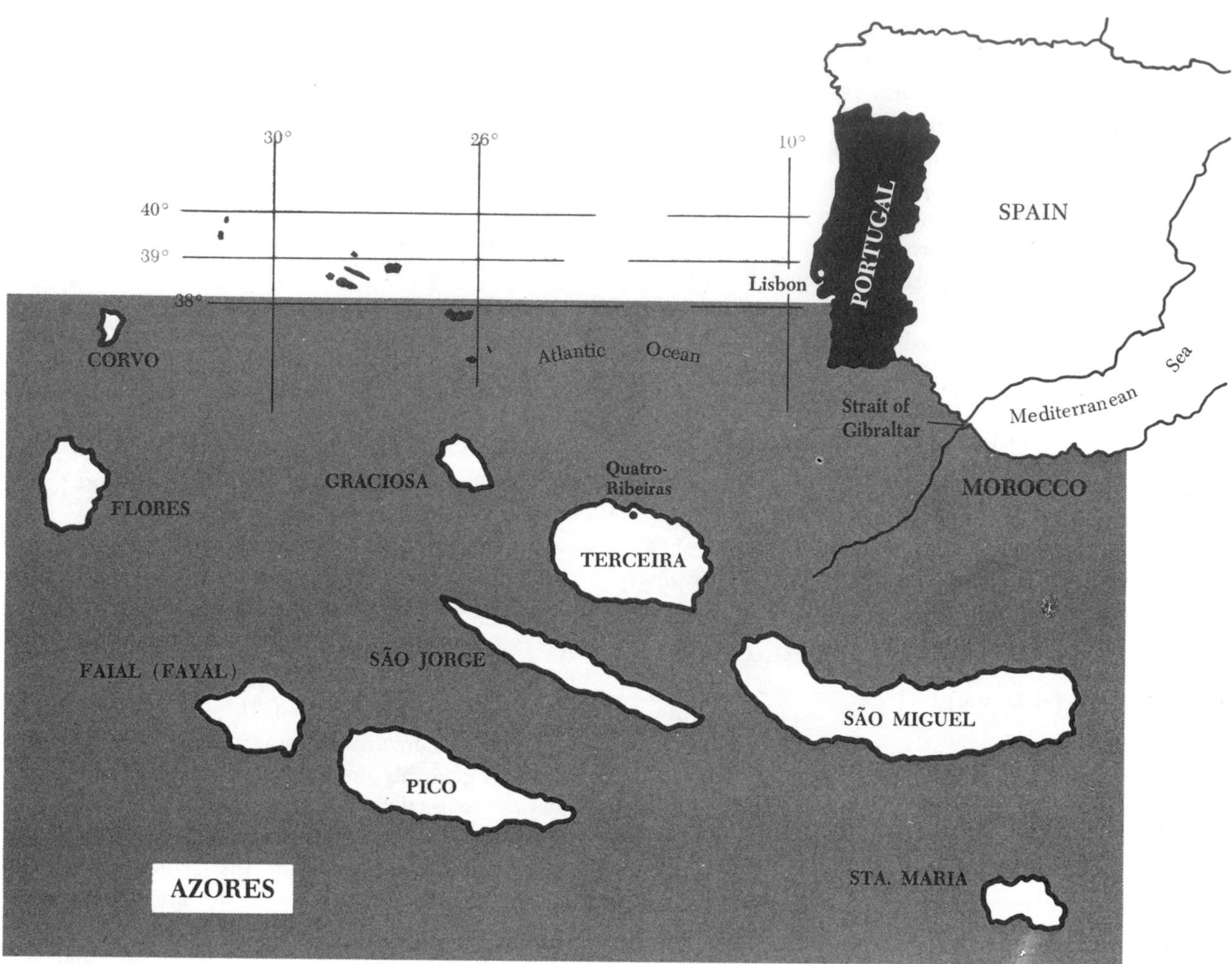

was capitan of Faial and Pico, and traded with Flanders by way of England. When he died about 1495, his eldest son succeeded him as capitan. The Hurtere family (Dutra in Portuguese) was related by marriage to the Cortereal family, who had explored Newfoundland. Two of the Dutra-Cortereal family were capitans of Faial and Pico. Many of the Flemish partners of the Hurtere family are known because they established families in the Azores.

The most famous of the Flemish capitans in the Azores was Ferdinand van Olmen, who had a holding called Quatro Ribeiras, irrigated by the Ribeira dos Flamengos (Flemish River). In 1487 he was asked by King John II to seek a route to the Indies; during the voyage he died at sea, somewhere between Iceland and Newfoundland. Gaspar, Miguel, and Vasqueanes Cortereal attempted a similar voyage early in the sixteenth century.

BIBLIOGRAPHY

Jules Mees, *Histoire de la découverte des Îles Açores et de l'origine de leur dénomination d'Îlles flamandes* (1901); Charles Verlinden, "Formes féodales et domaniales de la colonisation portugaise dans la zone atlantique aux XIVe et XVe siècles et spécialement sous Henri le Navigateur," in *Revista portuguesa de historia,* **9** (1961); *The Beginnings of Modern Colonization* (1970), 181–191; "La découverte des archipels de la 'Méditerranée atlantique' (Canaries, Madères, Açores) et la navigation astronomique primitive," in *Revista portuguesa de historia,* **16** (1978).

CHARLES VERLINDEN

[See also **Exploration by Western Europeans; Portugal, History.**]

AZULEJO (Spanish, from *azul,* perhaps derived from Persian *lāzhuvard,* "lapis lazuli," through Ar-

Azulejo (tile), 16th Century, Seville. COURTESY OF THE HISPANIC SOCIETY OF AMERICA

abic *lāzuward*), a glazed ceramic tile forming part of a decorative revetment or pavement. The term *azulejo* had apparently been reassimilated into Arabic as *al-zulayj* ("tile") by the second quarter of the thirteenth century. Although a band of polychrome glazed tiles appears at the springing of the dome before the mihrab at the Great Mosque of Córdoba (961–968), such tiles seem to have been reintroduced from the Near East only during the Almohad period (1130–1269). They remained popular in Spain and western North Africa well into the sixteenth century.

Azulejos are relatively large, regularly shaped ceramic pieces with designs in one or more colors, sometimes also with relief. They are generally distinguished from tile mosaic, which is composed of numerous small ceramic shapes cut from large monochrome slabs and fitted together to form polychrome patterns. By the fifteenth century *azulejos* had begun to supplant true tile mosaic.

Surprisingly, in view of the supposed origin of the term *azulejo,* cobalt blue played only a relatively small part in western Islamic tile decoration. Black, white, green, brown, yellow, and turquoise were much more common.

BIBLIOGRAPHY

Ars Hispaniae, III (1951), 313, figs. 170, 173; M. Asín Palacios, "Enmiendas a las etimologías árabes del 'Diccionario de la Lengua' de la Real Academia Española," in *al-Andalus,* 9 (1944), 25; Reinhart Dozy and W. H. Engelmann, *Glossaire des mots espagnols et portugais dérivés de l'arabe,* 2nd ed. (1869), 229; Alice W. Frothingham, *Catalogue of Hispano-Moresque Pottery in the Collection of the Hispanic Society of America* (1936); Guillermo J. de Osma y Scull, *Azulejos sevillanos del siglo XIII* (1902).

ESTELLE WHELAN

[See also **Islamic Art.**]

AZYMES (Greek ἄζυμα), "unleavened bread" required for the Jewish Passover meal. In some Christian traditions—particularly the Armenian and the Latin—unleavened bread is used in the Eucharist, whereas most Eastern Christians use ordinary leavened bread. From the eleventh to the fifteenth centuries, the issue of eucharistic bread was a matter of controversy between Byzantines and Latins. The Orthodox Byzantines accused the Latins of innovating because the New Testament accounts of the Last Supper use the word *artos,* which normally means leavened bread (Matt. 26:26; Mark 14:22; Luke 22:19; 1 Cor. 11:24), and because unleavened bread—flat and tasteless—hardly suggests the symbolic significance of the "bread of life." Furthermore, Greek anti-Latin polemicists maintained that the use of unleavened bread implied the revival of Apollinarianism, which maintained that Christ was devoid of a human soul; their argument indicated that the yeast in the bread symbolized the life-giving quality of the soul.

In spite of some childish and uncharitable overtones, the controversy reveals an important difference in eucharistic theology: the Greeks viewed the eucharistic food as the "type" of authentic humanity, assumed by Christ, rather than as a purely divine "transubstantiated" element of his divinity. The argument was first made in anti-Latin pamphlets by Niketas Stethatos (eleventh century). It was used in a letter from Leo of Ohrid to John of Trani that was a contributing factor to the schism of 1054, and was later developed by innumerable polemicists. The Latin defense consisted in pointing out the historical fact of Christ's celebrating of the Passover meal in accordance with Jewish practice and, therefore, presumably using unleavened bread, and also in referring to Paul's use of the "azymes" as a symbol of new life (1 Cor. 5:6–8).

BIBLIOGRAPHY

J. H. Erickson, "Leavened and Unleavened: Some Theological Implications of the Schism of 1054," in *St. Vladimir's Theological Quarterly,* **14** (1970).

JOHN MEYENDORFF

[See also **Eucharist; Schisms, Eastern-Western Church.**]

BAARLAM. See **Barlaam.**

BĀB, Arabic term signifying door, gate, or entrance, and used in architectural terminology for monumental entrances of a defensive or ornamental nature. Defensive entrances with projecting towers and recessed doorways were used in Umayyad "desert palaces" *(bādiya),* and similar gates protected royal quarters in Baghdad (762–765) and Cairo (1087–1092). These gates were often given symbolic or commemorative names, and had ceremonial as well as defensive purposes. Some early mosque gateways in North Africa and Egypt appear to have been modeled on Roman triumphal arches.

PRISCILLA SOUCEK

[See also **Islamic Architectures.**]

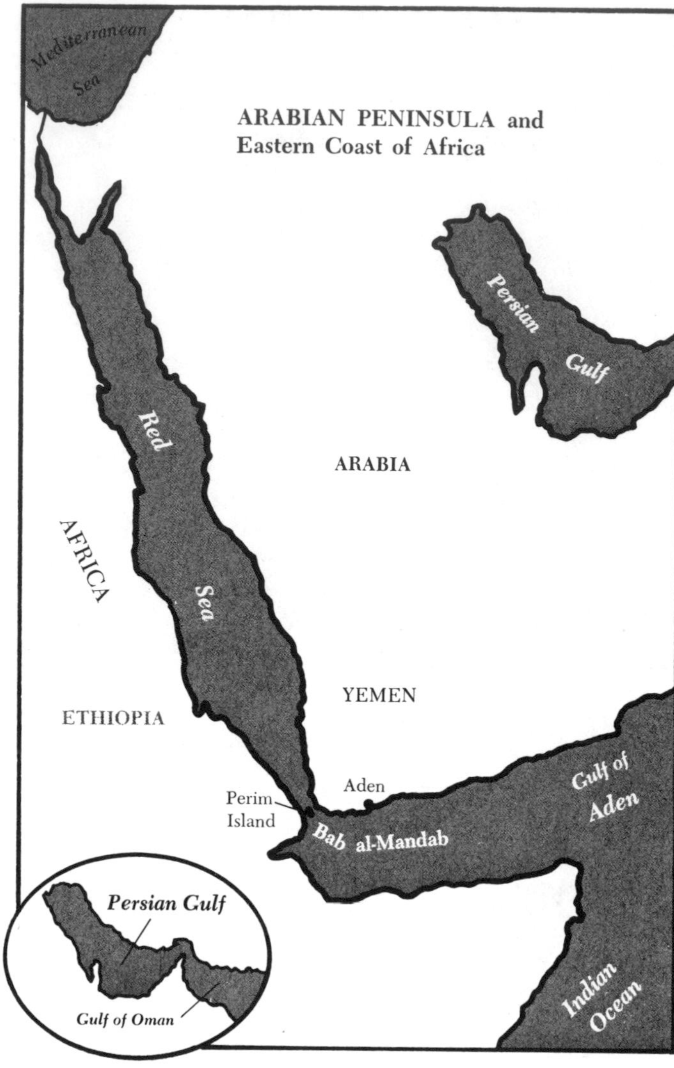

BAB AL-MANDAB. The straits of Bab al-Mandab, passageway from the Red Sea to the Gulf of Aden and the Indian Ocean, lie between the southwest corner of the Arabian Peninsula and the eastern coast of Africa. An extinct volcanic island, Perim (Mayyūn to Arabic-speakers), lies some one and one-half miles off the Arabian shore and divides Bab al-Mandab into two straits of unequal size. Large Strait, on the African side, deep and approximately nine miles wide, is used by most of today's maritime traffic. Small Strait, one and one-quarter miles wide and between five and sixteen fathoms deep, is used by light craft, but submerged rocks off the eastern shore of Perim make sailing conditions quite hazardous.

During the Middle Ages the name Bab al-Mandab applied not only to the straits but also to a point or cape on the Arabian coast nearby. The tenth-century Muslim geographer al-Hamdānī mentions "al-Mandab" among the towns on the Arabian coast belonging to the tribe of Banū Majīd and "Bab al-Mandab" among the capes in the Gulf of Aden "known for danger and difficulty" (*Al-Hamdānis Geographie der Arabischen halbinsel,* David H. Müller, ed. [1884], vol. 1, p. 53). And a twelfth-century Jewish merchant in Aden, writing to a colleague in India, informs the latter that "the bigger ship, however, arrived near Berbera where its captain got into trouble with it until it was thrust against Bab al-Mandeb, where it foundered. The pepper was lost completely; God did not save anything of it" (trans. in Solomon D. Goitein, *Letters of Medieval Jewish Traders* [1973], 189).

Medieval sources frequently allude to the navigational difficulties encountered in and around the straits of Bab al-Mandab. The combination of currents caused by the wind and very irregular tidal currents often results in a treacherous and unpredictable current within the straits—one that could easily pull a sail-powered vessel off course and onto the rocks. In order to overcome the force of the current, the medieval pilot would have had to rely upon a steady wind blowing with his craft. The early Muslim geographer and traveler al-Muqaddasī describes Bab al-Mandab as "a difficult strait that can be crossed only when the wind is up and blowing with great force" (*Aḥsan al-taqāsīm fī maᶜrifat al-aqālīm,* Michael J. de Goeje, ed. [1906], 12; compare French trans. by André Miquel, *La meilleure repartition pour la connaissance des provinces* [1963]; 34, 302). Despite the potential dangers in and around Bab al-Mandab, the straits must have handled a fairly large volume of maritime traffic in the Middle Ages—particularly during the period of the Fatimid dynasty in Egypt (969–1171), when the Red Sea replaced the Persian Gulf as the main trade route from India to the Mediterranean.

The thirteenth-century Muslim geographer Yāqūt al-Rūmī derived the name "Bab al-Mandab" from the Arabic verb *nadaba* ("to mourn for the dead")—hence "Bab al-Mandab," "Gate *(bāb)* of the Place of Mourning for the Dead." This name, according to Yāqūt, originally applied to a legendary mountain that had occupied the site of the straits and served as a land bridge between Arabia and Africa. Bab al-Mandab also figures in the legends surrounding the supposed invasion of southern Arabia by the Ethiopian king Abraha in the year of the prophet Muḥammad's birth.

BIBLIOGRAPHY

Given in text. See also G. Rentz, "Bab al-Mandab," in *Encyclopedia of Islam,* 2nd ed., and the bibliography given therein; U.S. Hydrographic Office, *Sailing Directions for the Red Sea and the Gulf of Aden,* 4th ed. (1962).

S. E. MARMON

[See also **Arabia; Fatimids; Geography and Cartography, Islamic; Muqaddasī.**]

BABENBERG FAMILY. The Babenbergs were the creators of medieval Austria. Otto of Freising believed that his family was descended from the Old Babenbergs, who were defeated in the first decade of the tenth century in a struggle for control of Franconia; but modern scholars have linked the Babenbergs to the Luitpoldingians, the tenth-century dukes of Bavaria. Otto II enfeoffed Leopold (Luitpold) I (976–994), the first Babenberg margrave, with the former Carolingian mark along the Danube in 976, the birthdate of Austria.

Through the marriage of St. Leopold III (1095–1136) to the daughter of Henry IV, the Babenbergs became the kinsmen of the Salians and the Hohenstaufen. King Conrad III granted Bavaria to his half brothers Leopold IV (1136–1141) and Henry II (1141–1177), but Frederick Barbarossa returned Bavaria to the Welfs in 1156 and compensated his uncle Henry by separating Austria from Bavaria and making it a duchy. Henry's son, Leopold V (1177–1194), acquired Styria in 1192. The reign of Leopold VI (1194–1230), who succeeded his brother Frederick I (1194–1198) as the duke of Austria, was the golden age of medieval Austria. When the last male Babenberg, Frederick II (1230–1246), died, Austria and Styria were the most developed German principalities; they provided the material basis for the Habsburgs' later preeminence.

BIBLIOGRAPHY

Karl Lechner, *Die Babenberger: Markgrafen und Herzöge von Österreich, 976–1246* (1976); Andreas von Meiller, ed., *Regesten zur Geschichte der Markgrafen und Herzöge Oesterreichs aus dem Hause Babenberg* (1850); Oskar Freiherr von Mitis, comp., Heinrich Fichtenau and Erich Zöllner, eds., *Urkundenbuch zur Geschichte der Babenberger in Österreich,* 4 vols. (1950–1968).

JOHN B. FREED

[See also **Austria; Otto of Freising.**]

BABYLONIAN CAPTIVITY, a term widely used by modern writers to designate the Avignon papacy. The removal of the papacy from Rome, its French character, and its general subordination to the French royal house are thereby made to seem analogous to the deportation of many Jews to Babylon by Nebuchadnezzar in the sixth century B.C. (see Jeremiah 52:15–30); this episode was referred to as the "captivity" of the Jews in, for example, Ezra (1 Esdras) 2:1. The phrase is so well established that it is used without much thought, but the analogy is superficial and in any case is irrelevant to what modern scholarship sees as the true import of the Avignon period of papal history.

The original, abusive designation of papal Avignon as Babylon was the work of Petrarch, whose career as a clerical intellectual began in Avignon under the patronage of the Italian cardinal Giovanni Colonna. Petrarch's dislike of the vices and importunities of the court city combined with his Italian resentment of French predominance to inspire him with hatred. His sense of exile led him to quote Psalm 137 (Vulgate 136), "By the Rivers of Babylon," with the comment that the Rhone was the river of the new Babylon.

The image of Babylon in Revelation 17 as a scarlet, bejeweled woman sitting on a scarlet beast, "having a golden cup in her hand full of abominations and filthiness of her fornication," and bearing on her forehead the legend "Mystery, Babylon the Great, the mother of harlots and abominations of the earth" was taken by Petrarch as an apt symbol of papal Avignon, with its riches and carnal indulgence. Although this image of Babylon was commonly understood as standing for pagan Rome, and the name Babylon was applied by the medieval West to both Baghdad and Cairo, Petrarch saw no reason not to add Avignon to the semantic field, while identifying Christian Rome with Babylon's antitype, the Holy City of Jerusalem. In this he shared for a time Cola di Rienzi's Joachimite fantasies of a regenerated world centered in a Rome restored to its former glory.

In fact, the Avignon period of papal history marked the highest point the popes would reach in centralizing and routinizing their governance of the European Church. The benefit of this system to the great mass of Europe's clerics was considerable, for it made possible a wider access to church benefices. At the same time, however, it antagonized local patrons whose rights of collation were overridden, while the flow of money into the papal treasury from fees, annates, and *servicia,* along with bribery at all levels, seemed evidence of both greed and venality, to say nothing of the other vices that the money helped to support. And the overwhelmingly French character of the Avignon papacy, with its seven French popes and almost entirely French cardinalate, readily provoked criticism from non-French quarters. Thus Petrarch's Europe-wide correspondence brought his denunciations of "Babylon" to quarters ready to receive them. John Wycliffe would later refer to papal Avignon as a "nest of simony," and the Good Parliament of 1376 complained of "that sinful city of Avignon."

We do not, though, find "Babylonian Captivity" used as a slogan in the fourteenth century. It appears in 1520 in Martin Luther's Latin treatise *De captivitate Babylonica ecclesiae praeludium* (The Babylonian Captivity of the Church), which referred not to Avignon but to the entire medieval period of Roman Christianity, with its doctrine of salvation by works and its alleged deformations of the sacraments. Luther had read some of Petrarch's most savagely anti-Avignon letters in the *Epistolae sine nomine* (Book Without a Name), and perhaps drew his Babylonian metaphor from that source. Whoever was the first modern scholar to take Luther's term and combine it with Petrarch's quite different reference, he created a durable Protestant image of the Avignon papacy that made it the beginning of the decline of the medieval Church into worldliness, moral corruption, and fiscality. The ensuing Great Schism and conciliar movement thus seemed only inevitable reactions; the Italianized Renaissance papacy seemed to be Babylon renewed; and Europe seemed ready for Protestantism. "Babylonian Captivity" as a term for the Avignon papacy is therefore to be eschewed by historians who do not wish to imply this Protestant construction of late medieval Church history.

BIBLIOGRAPHY

Alexander Flick, *The Decline of the Medieval Church,* 2 vols. (1930), is the best example in English of the Protestant historiography that uses "Babylonian Captivity" to bring the Avignon papacy into a picture of secular decline of the Church. The text of *Petrarch's Book Without a Name,* Norman Zacour, trans. (1973), and Zacour's introduction give most of Petrarch's Avignon-Babylon imagery; this edition also lists further readings. For the more sober modern view see Johannes Haller, *Papsttum und Kirchenreform* (1903), 22–153; Guillaume Mollat, *The Popes at Avignon 1305–1378,* Janet Love, trans. (1963); Bernard Guillemain, *La cour pontificale d'Avignon, 1309–1376: Étude d'une société* (1966); Yves Renouard, *The Avignon Papacy 1305–1403,* Denis Bethell, trans. (1970).

HOWARD KAMINSKY

[See also **Papacy; Petrarch; Provisions; Schism, Great.**]

BAÇÓ, JAIME, called Jacomart, a painter at Valencia, was born before 1417 and died in 1461. He was named court painter by Alfonso V of Aragon, who ordered him to Naples in 1440. No works that are surely his survive from this sojourn. In 1451 he was back in Valencia, where he headed a successful shop that produced altarpieces. Specific works are attributed to him by deduction. As with other painters of this period and region, these works display the influence of Flemish painting. His placid style is marked by a liberal use of gold and elaborately patterned draperies and tile floors.

BIBLIOGRAPHY

Elias Tormo y Monzó, *Jacomart y el arte hispano-flamenco cuatrocentista* (1913). See also Chandler R. Post, *A History of Spanish Painting,* VI, 1 (1935), 14–49.

JOHN WILLIAMS

BACON, ROGER, English Franciscan, master of arts at the University of Paris, and experimentalist, was born at Ilchester, Somerset, *ca.* 1213, and died *ca.* 1291. Bacon came from a family of minor nobility. He studied the liberal arts at Oxford, but received his degree in arts from either Oxford or the University of Paris before 1239. As regent master of the Arts Faculty at Paris, he was one of the first to lecture on the forbidden books of Aristotle, and did so "longer than any other master," until at least 1247. His early Scholastic writings belong to this period.

Scholars disagree about the chronology of Bacon after the year 1247. It is suggested by Crowley and Easton that he probably had become a member of the Franciscan order by 1257. From his later writings it can be seen that he was a teacher of mathematics, perspective, and philosophy at the *studium* of the Franciscans at Paris sometime between 1257 and 1266. In 1266–1268, under the express order of Pope Clement IV, he produced the *Opus maius,* the *Opus minus,* and the *Opus tertium.* We know from the *Compendium studii philosophiae,* which was written in 1271–1272, that Bacon was still writing controversial works. His opinions were condemned by the master general of the Franciscan order, Jerome of Ascoli (later Pope Nicholas IV), sometime between November 1277 and Pentecost, 1279.

This condemnation of the opinions of Bacon, who is referred to as "sacrae theologiae magistri," has been widely misunderstood by Bacon scholars, most of whom have interpreted the crucial passage in the condemnation to mean not only that Bacon's opinions were condemned but also that in 1278, Bacon was put in prison by Jerome of Ascoli. The text, however, simply states that the opinions of Bacon, who had been imprisoned, were to be condemned on account of "aliquas novitates suspectas." The reference to an imprisonment of Bacon by his order must, then, refer to an earlier imprisonment.

There is no agreement among Bacon scholars about the content of these "certain suspect novelties." They disagree on the authenticity of the report in the *Chronicle of the Twenty-four Generals,* which claims that Bacon's opinions were condemned in 1278 by Jerome of Ascoli. Little and Crowley both argue that Bacon's ideas on astrology, with their implications that heavenly bodies affect terrestrial life, were the main suspect novelties. But Thorndike argues that Bacon's views on astrology were not unique; he claims that they were no different from those held by, for example, Albertus Magnus. A scholar such as Easton views Bacon's interest in Joachimite prophecy as being a part, at least, of the suspect novelties. It is likely that Bacon's great interest in astrology, alchemy, prophecy, prediction of the future, and his strong polemic on the state of education and religious life led to his condemnation. If, as Crowley claims, Bacon was the object of St. Bonaventure's criticism of those who practiced alchemy, studied the secrets of nature, and believed in an illicit form of astrology, then a similar criticism by Jerome of Ascoli may have taken place.

According to the *Compendium studii theologiae,* Bacon was alive in 1292, the year during which he wrote that work. Scholars generally assume that Bacon died after that date. Such, then, is the meager information that we have on the "Doctor mirabilis." There is a great paucity of information about all but a few facts of his chronology, most of which have to be deduced from Bacon's own works.

BACON'S EARLY THOUGHT

During his time as regent master at Paris, Bacon studied Aristotle with the aid of Neoplatonic sources. His view of the hylomorphic composition of all creatures, both spiritual and corporeal, is similar to that of his teacher Robert Kilwardby. The *Fons vitae* of Avicebron (Ibn Gabirol), the *Liber sufficientiae* of Avicenna (Ibn Sīnā), and the anonymous *Liber de causis* are, next to Aristotle, the main sources of his early philosophy. The overall influence of these works ensured that the philosophy of Aristotle would be interpreted in a Neoplatonic manner.

This early thought of Bacon is important in that it is a good example of the work of a young Parisian

BACON

master of arts about 1239–1247. Our source for this work is the student notes contained in MS Amiens 406. A brief description of the contents of the manuscript is given in works by M. Cousin, M. Charles, and Robert Steele. The only adequate study of the doctrine in this early work is that of Crowley.

It has been recognized for some time that the early Bacon was an eclectic thinker who was nevertheless fully committed to the doctrine of universal hylomorphism. In Crowley's judgment Bacon's treatment of this subject shows no great advance in respect to the works of other teachers and contemporaries, such as Hugh of St. Cher, Richard Rufus, and Richard Fishacre.

The teaching on being became very important in thirteenth-century philosophy, especially in the work of Thomas Aquinas—see his early but seminal *De ente et essentia* ("On Being and Essence"). Speculation on being as a question in metaphysics was shaped by many traditional sources. Before the introduction of Aristotle's *Metaphysics* in the thirteenth-century universities, St. Augustine and Boethius were the main influences.

The influence of Boethius' seminal *De hebdomadibus* is evident in a number of Bacon's early statements on the question of being. The distinction between *ens* (being) and *esse* (to be) concerns the difference between beings or entities and that being by which they are entities. In terms of medieval ontology, God is seen as Creative Being, and creatures as created beings. For some teachers, including Aquinas, the Boethian distinction between *ens* and *esse* refers to the composition of individual substantial being and the *esse* that gives them being. Bacon, unlike these other teachers, does not distinguish between *esse* and God's illuminating presence in created things. In his later work, especially *Opus maius,* book II, Bacon claims that God is the agent intellect. God, then, is the original light that illumines all created beings and sustains them in their being. That by which a being is a being *(quo est)*, Bacon interpreted as form *(forma)*, and what a thing is, as *ens.* The fundamental structures of change in created things are seen in terms of a primary relation of matter and form.

No satisfactory study of Bacon's metaphysics exists. Some categorize him as a Franciscan Augustinian, not a follower of Aristotle. There are Augustinian elements in Bacon, such as his teaching on divine illumination. But, in his early work, Bacon sees himself as an interpreter of Aristotle. Even though his theory of hylomorphism is eclectic and has a close resemblance to Franciscan teaching, Bacon is convinced that he is being faithful to Aristotle. Despite the Augustinian elements in Bacon's theories, it would be erroneous to label him "an Augustinian," as distinct from "an Aristotelian," thinker. In his early work Bacon is eclectic in his theory of being, his hylomorphic theory, and his theory of the soul. As Crowley puts it, "His system was developed independently of St. Augustine's teachings or writings. He does not appeal to the authority of St. Augustine in support of universal hylomorphism, and as we shall see, his whole doctrine of the soul shows the same independence."

Already in these early Scholastic lectures, Bacon directed criticism against the common teaching of some teachers. He argued against the notion of a negative unity of matter, a position later defended by Aquinas. Bacon favored a positive unity of matter. Indeed, prime matter for Bacon was coextensive with finitude or contingency and was its source. For other Scholastics prime matter was limited to the world of material things. Also in opposition to a common teaching, Bacon refused to admit the notion of negative numerical unity of matter. Crowley points out the close correspondence on this point between Bacon and the other Franciscan teachers, especially those of the Oxford School.

On the question of forms, Bacon admits neither an extrinsic origin alone nor an intrinsic origin alone. Thus the external agent gives no more than the impulse or virtue that arouses the active potency in matter. Bacon argues for a unity of form, but it is a unity of composition and not of simplicity. On this point his teaching corresponds to that of St. Bonaventure.

Bacon's notion of soul owes much to the pseudo-Augustinian work *De spiritu et animae.* He set out to interpret Aristotle's teaching on the soul, but in treating soul as a spiritual substance, Bacon seems to have misunderstood the genuine Aristotelian doctrine of the soul. There are many passages suggesting that the body is the prison house of the soul, something ignoble that is an obstruction to the action of the soul. From his doctrine of the soul, it is evident that he held a doctrine of the plurality of forms.

In his early Scholastic works, then, Bacon held the commonly accepted doctrine on the composite unity of the human soul that was taught at Oxford in the Franciscan school. The problem of the plurality of forms was a cause of disagreement, but the disagreement was not one between Franciscans and Dominicans. Rather, it was a disagreement between

BACON

philosophers and English theologians, on the one hand, and the theologians of the Paris schools, on the other.

BACON'S LATER THOUGHT

Bacon's later thought is contained in the works that were written between about 1265 and 1292. These writings belong to diverse genres, and they exhibit much repetition; whole sections are repeated verbatim. It is better, therefore, to present a summary of the main work, the *Opus maius.* I will follow that discussion with a summary of some of the main genres, and their importance in his work.

All of Bacon's later work is concerned with a proposed reform of education and society whose basic model is found in the *Opus maius.* Bacon's fundamental complaint about the learning of his time was that the "boy-theologians" of the Franciscans and the Dominicans had neglected the study of secular subjects in the universities and in the *studia* as a result of their early induction into the religious life. According to Bacon the philosophy of Aristotle was badly misunderstood by teachers like Albertus Magnus and Aquinas; and the whole mob of philosophers at Paris, especially the theologians, neglected the sciences. There is, therefore, a large polemical element in Bacon's later thought. This element, together with a scientific and experimental concern, makes his later work very different from the earlier Scholastic lectures.

Bacon's later thought is unmistakably practical in its basic direction. Indeed, for him the overall goal of science and philosophy is the moral perfection of the individual and society. The way to this goal was the educational program. He aimed at the reformation of the Christian commonwealth *(respublica christiana)* by means of education, and he saw this reformation as also a reform of theology. The goal and overall object of his thought is clearly theological, so the picture of Bacon as a scientific rationalist before his time is not an accurate one.

Bacon was concerned with the unity of knowledge. By means of authority, reason, and experience, man can come to know the unity of knowledge. All knowledge of nature and the properties of things, and of the Holy Scripture, leads to the knowledge of God. Bacon thus stands in the Franciscan tradition with its return of the arts to theology *(reductio artium ad theologiam).* Philosophy and learning are justified insofar as they are useful *(utile)* for knowledge of God. In and of themselves they are but a relative good. Yet much of the polemic of Bacon's later works—most notably the three opera, the *Compendium studii philosophiae,* and the *Compendium studii theologiae*—consists in showing that without philosophy and learning in their due place, one cannot have a worthwhile theology.

In 1266, when Bacon received the order from Pope Clement IV to present a summary of his thoughts on the reform of education, he attempted to write a major synthesis of the learning of his time. He sought to write a summa but ended up with a work, the *Opus maius,* that was a *scriptum preambulatum* to such a summa. In all of his writings after this time—that is, after 1266–1267—Bacon repeats basically the same set of ideas. The difference in the later works is that they contain many additions, subtractions, and extensions of his thought. But there is very little that is substantially new in them. A review, then, of the main ideas of the *Opus maius* is in order.

In part I of the *Opus maius,* the four main obstacles to human and divine wisdom are set forth: "submission to faulty and unworthy authority, influence of custom, popular prejudice, and the concealment of our own ignorance accompanied by an ostentatious display of our own wisdom." Bacon gives a list of classical sources to argue that there is an esoteric wisdom that is not to be had by the common teacher or student. To achieve that wisdom, one has to overcome the obstacles to truth.

In part II, Bacon shows the close relationship between philosophy and theology. All the wisdom of philosophy is reducible to divine wisdom because philosophy, too, has been revealed to man by God. Thus Bacon argues that God revealed the truths of philosophy to the patriarchs and the prophets in the Old Testament. The philosophers, especially the Greeks, received this wisdom from the Hebrew teachers. Part II also attempts to establish Aristotle as the most suitable philosopher for the Christian teacher, even though St. Augustine is quoted with approval.

Part III concerns the use and necessity of grammar for learning. Bacon evidently reworked and repeated this part in many later works. With its later repetitions it is an important source for our knowledge of the study of Latin and other languages at Paris in Bacon's time. Bacon's interest here in the study of languages was based on a belief about the transmission of wisdom; he believed that all knowledge came to the Latin-speaking members of his own times from other languages. Hence it was imperative for a scholar to know Hebrew, Greek, and

BACON

Arabic. The evidence for this attitude of Bacon's can be seen in his Greek and Hebrew grammars. Bacon also showed a theoretical interest in the logic of language. In part III, and again in his later works, he presents a short treatise on signification in language, *De signis.*

Part IV of the *Opus maius* is concerned with the relationship between mathematics and theology. The first section relates the study of mathematics to that of physical causes. Knowledge of physical causes, especially of the efficient or generating causes, and the material causes is had through the power of geometry. This theory of the propagation of force along straight lines is taken from Grosseteste's theory that all multiplication of force or power occurs according to lines, angles, or figures. This section of part IV is expanded in the treatise *De multiplicatione specierum* (On the Multiplication of Species), which Bacon sent to the pope with the *Opus Maius.*

The motive for Bacon's great interest in geometry seems to have been his belief that knowledge of the heavens would yield knowledge of events on earth, and he saw mathematics as the means that would provide the understanding of the influences of the stars and heavenly bodies. He also put forward a very strong argument on the nature of mathematics: that the other categories, such as place, time, quality, and relation, are reducible to the category of quantity. Without quantity they cannot be known. Even heavenly bodies are known through quantity, as is evident from astronomy. To summarize in Bacon's own words: "Therefore all the categories depend on a knowledge of quantity of which mathematics treats, and therefore the whole excellence of logic depends on mathematics."

In the second section of part IV of the *Opus maius,* Bacon set out to give an apology for the uses of mathematics in matters of divinity *(Mathematicae in divinis utilitas).* He takes up a topic here that he had already discussed in his commentary on the pseudo-Aristotelian *Secretum secretorum*: the distinction that must be made between magic and mathematics. In both works Bacon argues that many people confuse a false mathematics with true mathematics, such as geometry and astronomy. The argument is an important one, in that it involves the status of judicial astronomy. In other words, can one predict future events on the basis of a knowledge of astronomy?

According to Bacon false mathematics implies a necessity in things. Free will would have to be denied, and many Christian mysteries would have to be associated with magic. Bacon argues strongly that this kind of mathematics was condemned not only by the Church Fathers but also by the preeminent astronomers and philosophers such as Ptolemy, Haly (al-Majūsī), and Avicenna. Nevertheless, he claims that a reading of the houses and constellations in astrology can be used to gain knowledge of the future. And in the case of the birth of Christ, he is prepared to argue, on the basis of the work of Abū Ma^cshar, that the event was predicted by the pagan astrologers.

By an application of mathematics to theology, then, Bacon means that one can use mathematical knowledge to shed light on some religious matters. For example, knowledge of the heavens in mathematics can shed light on many scriptural references to the heavens. It also allows a scholar to verify the truths of biblical geography, to clarify the chronology of the Scriptures: everything from the construction of the calendar to the date of Creation to the age of the patriarchs could be calculated with some accuracy.

Bacon concludes part IV of the *Opus maius* with a note on the correction of the calendar and a short excursus on the geography of the world. He depends on ancient sources for his knowledge, but he does show an interest in the travels of his contemporary William Rubruck. Bacon thinks that the application of mathematics to geography will lead to a better knowledge of longitude and latitude, and that people will gain a better understanding of the dimensions of the world. Bacon's interest, however, is spurred on by his great concern with the coming of the Antichrist. He thinks that mathematics in geography may be able to tell us something about the date of that event.

Perhaps the most important practical aspects of this part are Bacon's advocacy of mathematics in education and his forthright criticism of magic. Astronomy is not to be confused with a nonmathematical natural superstition that leads to geomancy, necromancy, and other forms of magic. His criticism of magic is, therefore, a great apologia of mathematics and of science.

Part V of the *Opus maius, De perspectiva,* is concerned with the theory of vision or optical science. Bacon was not unique in his treatment of optics; similar information is found in John Peckham and Witelo. The importance of Bacon is that he attempted to synthesize all the traditions of optical teaching before his time. It is evident that his teaching in this part of the *Opus maius* must be related to other parts of his work: *De multiplicatione specierum; De speculis comburentis;* and the optical material in parts IV and VI of *Opus maius,* the *Opus tertium,* and part I of *Communia naturalium.*

A dominant influence here is the work of Robert Grosseteste. In both of their systems, optics is at the center of natural philosophy. In the *Opus tertium* Bacon argues that *perspectiva* is the key to the whole machine of the world, and that it is taught only at Oxford. But while he may have acquired his initial interest in *perspectiva* through the influence of Grosseteste's work at Oxford, he did in fact come under the influence of others, including Bartholomeus Anglicus and Albertus Magnus. We know that Bacon did not regard the account of *perspectiva* by Albertus Magnus as satisfactory.

The main points of Bacon's synthesis of optical teaching are taken from the work of Alhazen (Ibn al-Haytham). Following Alhazen, Bacon shows that a visual pyramid is formed that has its base on the visible object and its apex at the center of the curvature of the cornea. Vision occurs as soon as this pyramid of radiation enters the observer's eye and its rays are arranged on the surface of the anterior glacial humor. At this point the species are refracted in such a way that they do not intersect. In all of this, Bacon follows Alhazen closely.

Bacon, however, places the teaching of Alhazen in the context of the learning of his own time, and attempts to give an overall philosophical synthesis of optics *(De perspectiva)* within the unity of knowledge. Thus, he is doing much more than giving an account of optics; he is giving a philosophical account of the place of optics in the whole scheme of knowledge. For example, his theory of the multiplication of species attempts to draw together the conflicting teachings of natural philosophers, mathematicians, and philosophical psychologists. Bacon's treatment of species provides one example of the way he used his early training in philosophy to interpret a problem in natural science.

Bacon used the Neoplatonic metaphysics of light to interpret the notion of species, which he sees as the natural effect of any agent; it is not just a material emanation. Species produces its own likeness, and there is a generation that is multiplied through the medium of light. By means of the agent, the potentiality of matter is drawn forth. In the end the term "species" covers almost every activity of light, image, and phantasm. Vision, Bacon explains, is the synthesis of a species entering the eye from the object and the productive power of the eye grasping the species. The visual power is not just a recipient of a species from the object; it is also an active agent.

Bacon's teaching seems to have had some influence on two other optical writers of the thirteenth century, Peckham and Witelo. Peckham's optical teaching is presented in the form of a synthesis that could be used in the schools. And even though Bacon wrote his work for the pope, he seems to have intended it as a synthesis that could be used for teaching purposes.

Apart from giving a new synthesis to the teaching of optics, which he regarded as the fundamental physical science, Bacon made some contributions of his own. For the eye in its relationships to refracting media, he provided models and rules for plane surfaces and for the properties of convex and concave spherical surfaces. He saw all these physical and optical laws as the common laws of a universal nature *(leges communes naturae).* This notion of science as having to do with natural laws was an important emphasis in Bacon's work, and it aimed to direct science away from superstition and magic and toward actual laws of nature. In a practical sense the assimilation by Bacon of the work of Euclid, Ptolemy, al-Kindī, and Alhazen in optics or *perspectiva* is evidence for Bacon's claim that his *scientia* was more important than that taught to the common run of scholars in his own time.

In part VI of the *Opus maius,* Bacon continues his reflections on *perspectiva* and gives an account of how one sees a rainbow. The whole direction of part VI is toward formulating a notion of an experimental science or method of discovery *(scientia experimentalis).* According to Bacon, purely theoretical knowledge *(argumentatio)* does not give a sufficient account of experience. He intended his formulation of *scientia experimentalis* as a kind of *logica practica* that would have the same relation to practical matters of experience and experiment as logic has to theory in philosophy. Bacon's new method of experience was intended as a doctrine and as an instrument of knowledge. It was meant to perform three tasks: the certification of the conclusions of deductive reasoning in the sciences by means of experience; the addition of new sciences to existing knowledge; and the examination of nature for possible use in the technology of war or peace. In all of this, one of his main sources was the *Secretum secretorum,* a work that Bacon believed had come from the Stagirite.

Scholars have debated whether Bacon's notion of

experimental method is comparable with modern scientific method. Any answer to this question must not be anachronistic. Within the limitations of the science of his time, Bacon's formulation of an experimental method was valid. Its importance lies in the fact that, unlike some other experimentalists, he saw the importance of some methodic connection between mathematics and experiential testing and observation. For example, his application of a mathematical notion of proportions foreshadowed later medieval medical theory. Bacon's importance, here as in optics, lies in the fact that he attempted a synthesis of existing knowledge with a view to its practical presentation in the schools. He was correct in arguing that the schools overemphasized the traditional philosophical disciplines to the detriment of scientific concerns.

Part VII of the *Opus maius* is concerned with moral philosophy, which differs from the sciences treated in the first six parts in that it is essentially a practical science. Called "moral science" by Aristotle, and "civil science" by others, it is concerned with the rights of citizens and states. It sets down the rules and obligations of life. For Bacon this science is nobler than all the other branches of philosophy. When united with Christian revelation, moral philosophy becomes the end and purpose of the other sciences in the Christian commonwealth. Bacon argues that God revealed wisdom to the philosophers and legislators among the pagans, and that this truth corresponds to the moral truth that was revealed to the patriarchs and the prophets.

Eternal happiness, the coming of the Antichrist, and the moral life are treated here. By far the largest part of this section is taken up with the teachings of Seneca and Cicero on the moral life. Bacon was excited at having found some of the moral works of Seneca, especially *De ira.* Through most of part VII, Bacon gives an account of this teaching on moral self-perfection. He is primarily concerned with virtues and vices as they affect the individual and his salvation.

In the concluding part of the *Opus maius,* Bacon is concerned with the just and honorable direction of the Christian commonwealth. With contemporaries like Grosseteste and Adam de Marsh, he shared the ideal of moral and religious reform of society through education. Moral philosophy, which for Bacon was "the end of all branches of philosophy," had to do with the laws governing the direction of society. In this part of his work, Bacon displays his high regard for the moral teachings of Seneca and Cicero, and puts them on a level with Christian morality.

When one compares the philosophy of Bacon, as found in his later work, with that of his contemporaries, one finds that in Bacon the practical objectives of learning and philosophy are given primacy of place. Philosophy is not seen as an end in itself; it is, rather, a way of preparing for the practical end of leading a good and just life.

THE WORKS OF ROGER BACON: OVERVIEW

A great diversity of genres exists in the writings of Bacon. One work may contain many different styles of presentation and exposition: polemic, text exposition, and scientific explanation, for example. The following is a brief account of this diversity of style.

In Bacon's early work, written between 1239 and 1247, one finds his *questiones* on the works of Aristotle and the pseudo-Aristotelian works, together with *questiones* on the *Liber de causis.* These *questiones* do not differ in style or kind from the work of other young masters of arts at the time. Sometimes they consist merely of brief explanations; at other times there is a longer and formal exposition of a problem.

Most of Bacon's later work seems to be an extension of his plan for a great synthesis of knowledge. The parts of that synthesis that were achieved are written in diverse styles. Following is a list of the styles found in the later work.

(1) *Commentary.* A good example is Bacon's own edition of the pseudo-Aristotelian *Secretum secretorum.*

(2) *Polemic.* One finds examples of polemic on the urgent needs of the times throughout the three opera, in the introductions to the more formal scientific works, and in the compendia of philosophy and theology. One work stands out as an altogether polemical work: the *Compendium studii philosophiae.*

(3) *Synthesis.* The three opera are intended as a synthesis of knowledge. Polemic is generally avoided in the *Opus maius,* although the *Opus minus* and the *Opus tertium* contain many polemical passages within sections intended as expositions of educational and scientific questions.

(4) *Scientific and philosophical exposition.* The *Communia naturalium,* typical of this style, is straightforward exposition of the nature of the sciences. Polemic is restricted to the beginning of the work.

(5) *Treatises on specific subjects.* These usually consist of short letters. Examples are Bacon's short treatises on medicine, and his letter on the secret works of nature and the futility of magic.

BACON'S OVERALL IMPORTANCE

Bacon is a good example of an early thirteenth-century commentator on Aristotle at the University of Paris. As an experimentalist, he exemplified Grosseteste's new program for education. His immediate influence at Oxford is not directly evident. He did have an indirect influence there through the propagation of his ideas in the anonymous *Summa philosophiae,* possibly written by one of his students. At the University of Paris, to judge from the popularity of his later scientific works such as the *Communia naturalium,* Bacon did exert a scientific influence. Such influence can also be traced in *perspectiva* through the works of his contemporaries Peckham and Witelo. After 1278, Bacon's experimental works appear to have had little influence, except, perhaps, among some Franciscan spirituals such as Raymond Gaufredi and others.

Bacon's interest in language study was important in leading to serious provision for the study of Hebrew and Arabic. In that way, he prepared the way for a teacher such as Raymond Lull. While Bacon's *Opus maius* was known to later scholars such as Cardinal Pierre d'Ailly in the fifteenth century, much of his work was forgotten. The rediscovery of Bacon's work by Elizabethan bibliophiles and savants such as John Dee and John Shelden, among others, led to a great renewal of interest in Bacon's scientific and mathematical works. The image of Bacon as an early modern scientist before his time became prevalent. So too did the modern image of Bacon as a modern scientist.

BIBLIOGRAPHY

Original Works. A complete critical edition of Bacon's works is still lacking. Single works have been edited, and some have appeared in a number of editions.

Opus maius, S. Jebb, ed. (1733; 1750); *Opus maius,* J. H. Bridges, ed., 3 vols. (1897–1900; repr. 1964). Bridges' edition contains all parts of the *Opus maius* and a text of *De multiplicatione specierum.* Part VII of the *Opus maius* has been critically edited by E. Massa, in *Rogeri Baconi moralis philosophia* (1953).

Opus minus, Opus tertium, Compendium studii philosophiae, Epistola de secretis operibus . . . are edited by J. S. Brewer in *Fr. Rogeri Bacon opera quaedam hactenus inedita* (1859). A prefatory letter to the *Opus minus,* which some scholars have seen as prefatory also to the *Opus maius,* is edited by F. A. Gasquet, "An Unpublished Fragment of Roger Bacon," in *English Historical Review,* **12** (1897). A heretofore unknown section of pt. III of *Opus maius* has been edited by K. M. Fredborg, Lauge Nielsen, and Jan Pinborg, "Opus maius: De signis," in *Traditio,* **34** (1978).

Parts of the *Opus tertium* have also appeared in *Un fragment inédit de l'Opus tertium de Roger Bacon,* Pierre Duhem, ed. (1909); and *Part of the Opus tertium of Roger Bacon,* A. G. Little, ed. (1912).

Other works by Bacon are *The Greek Grammar of Roger Bacon and a Fragment of His Hebrew Grammar,* E. Nolan and S. A. Hirsch, eds. (1902); *Fratris Rogeri Baconi Compendium studii theologii,* H. Rashdall, ed. (1911); and S. H. Thomson, "An Unnoticed Treatise of Roger Bacon on Time and Motion," in *Isis,* **27** (1937).

Much of Bacon's work is in *Opera hactenus inedita Rogeri Baconi,* R. Steele, ed. (unless otherwise stated), 16 fasc. (1905–1940): (1) *Metaphysica: De viciis contractis in studio theologie* (1905); (2–4) *Communia naturalium* (1905–1913); (5) *Secretum secretorum cum glossis et notulis* (1920); (6) *Computus* (1926); (7) *Questiones supra undecim prime philosophie Aristotelis (Metaphysica, XII)*; (8) *Questiones supra libros quatuor Physicorum Aristotelis,* F. M. Delorme, ed. (1928); (9) *De retardatione accidentium senectutis cum aliis opusculis de rebus medicinalibus,* A. G. Little and E. Withington, eds. (1928); (10) *Questiones supra libros prime philosophie Aristotelis (Metaphysica, I, II, V–X)* (1930); (11) *Questiones altere supra libros prime philosophie Aristotelis (Metaphysica I–IV)* and *Questiones supra De plantis* (1932); (12) *Questiones supra Librum de causis* (1935); (13) *Questiones supra libros octo Physicorum Aristotelis,* F. M. Delorme, ed. (1935); (14) *Liber De sensu et sensato, Summa de sophismatibus et distinctionibus* (1937); (15) *Summa grammatica, Summule dialectices* (1940); (16) *Communia mathematica* (1940).

Secondary Works. The first modern monograph is Émile Charles, *Roger Bacon, sa vie, ses ouvrages, ses doctrines d'après des textes inédits* (1861). Modern critical monographs are Franco Alessio, *Mito e scienza in Ruggiero Bacone* (1967); Theodore Crowley, *Roger Bacon: The Problem of the Soul in His Philosophical Commentaries* (1950); Stewart C. Easton, *Roger Bacon and His Search for a Universal Science* (1952).

Studies of particular topics are Raoul Carton, *L'expérience physique chez Roger Bacon, L'expérience mystique de l'illumination intérieure chez Roger Bacon,* and *La synthèse doctrinale de Roger Bacon,* nos. 2, 3, and 5 in the series Études de Philosophie Médiévale (1924); A. C. Crombie, *Robert Grosseteste and the Origins of Experimental Science 1100–1700* (1969); Pierre Duhem, *Le système du monde* (1916–1958): III, 260–277, 411–442; V, 375–411, VIII, 121–168; Jeremiah M. G. Hackett, "The Attitude of Roger Bacon to the *Scientia* of Albertus Magnus," in James A. Weisheipl, ed., *Albertus Magnus and the Sciences: Commemorative Essays 1980* (1980); A. G. Molland, "Roger Bacon as Magician," in *Traditio,* **30** (1974); E. Schlund, "Petrus Peregrinus von Maricourt: Sein Leben und Seine Schriften," in *Archivum Franciscanum historicum,* **4** (911); Lynn Thorndike, "Roger Bacon and Experimental Method in the Middle Ages," in *Philosophical Review,* **23**, no. 3 (1914); "The True Roger Bacon," in *American Historical Review,* **21**, no. 3 (1916); and *A History of Magic and Experimental Science,* II (1929), 616–691; Charles B. Vandewalle, *Roger Bacon dans l'histoire de la philologie* (1929).

JEREMIAH M. G. HACKETT

[See also **Aristotle in the Middle Ages; Astrology/Astronomy; Franciscans; Grosseteste, Robert; Mathematics; Optics; Oxford, University of; Paris, University of; Philosophy/Theology, Western European.**]

BĀDGĪR is the Persian term for a wind catcher, a device used in many regions of the Islamic world to collect cooler and cleaner air above the roof and direct it down into a room or underground cistern. There are two main types of wind catcher: the unidirectional and the omnidirectional. The unidirectional, found in regions where the prevailing wind is constantly from one direction, such as Pakistan and Egypt (where it is known as a *malqaf*), consists of a scooplike timber, brick, or metal inlet on a roof that deflects the prevailing wind into a conduit built in the interior walls of a structure. A simple house might have one wind catcher; a larger house might have one or more for each principal room.

The omnidirectional wind catcher is common in regions where the prevailing wind changes direction seasonally or diurnally. It is a square tower with an X configuration of interior planes creating four passages leading down into the space to be cooled. With someone's selective opening and closing of the passages, the *bādgīr* collects and accelerates the breezes on the windward side while simultaneously exhausting warmer, stale air on the leeward side.

While some wind catchers in rural areas of the Gulf are made of cloth, most in Iran are built of brick; for example, hundreds of brick *bādgīr*s punctuate the skylines of Yazd and Kermān, cities on the edge of the torrid central Iranian desert. The introduction of European styles of construction in the Islamic world has pushed these traditional systems of cooling into disfavor, but architects have recently begun to rediscover the possibilities of such passive cooling systems.

JONATHAN M. BLOOM

BĀDIYA, an Arabic term used in the Umayyad period to designate a rural residence. Normally it consisted of a dwelling surrounded by a defensive wall and cultivated fields or orchards. Often described by modern scholars as "desert palaces," most were located in the steppe regions of greater Syria, where irrigation or conservation of rain made some agriculture possible. Those erected for the Umayyads or their high officals often had baths and residences richly decorated with wall paintings, stucco carving, or mosaics.

PRISCILLA SOUCEK

[See also **Islamic Architecture.**]

BADR, BATTLE OF. Badr, a village in western Arabia, southwest of Medina, was the site of the first major encounter between followers of Muḥammad and his chief opponents, the non-Muslims of his hometown of Mecca. After Muḥammad and his Meccan followers had made their hegira from Mecca to Medina in 622, they found themselves in difficult circumstances because they had little property and no immediate means of earning a living. The Prophet seems therefore to have embarked on a policy of raiding in the hope of securing booty. This policy resulted in hostilities against the Ḳuraysh tribe of Mecca.

About two months later (March 624) the Prophet learned that a large Ḳuraysh caravan, led by Abū Sufyān ibn Ḥarb, was returning from Gaza to Mecca. He therefore gathered a force of about 300 followers, doubtless hoping to plunder the caravan with little opposition. Abū Sufyān, however, fearing an ambush by the Muslims, requested Meccan troops to escort the caravan in the vicinity of Medina. The Meccans dispatched a force, said to number 900 or 1,000 men, under the leadership of Abū Jahl, chief of the powerful Ḳuraysh clan of Makhzūm. Not all members of the force were eager for a confrontation with Muḥammad, however, and when Abū Sufyān sent word that he had successfully evaded the Muslims by making a detour, two clans decided to return to Mecca. The rest of Abū Jahl's force was persuaded to go on to encounter the Muslims, in order to avoid losing face by appearing to withdraw before a group that they greatly outnumbered. They therefore advanced, and pitched camp near Badr.

In the meantime, Muḥammad and his force had reached Badr. They blocked all the wells there save one, around which they grouped on favorable terrain. The Meccans were thereby forced either to make a humiliating withdrawal for lack of water or to advance and engage the Muslims from a disadvantageous position. They chose the latter option, with disastrous results. The actual course of the battle cannot be satisfactorily disengaged from the large mass of imaginative detail embroidered around it, but it is clear that after a number of single combats, the Meccans were routed in a general engagement. The Meccans reportedly had between forty-five and seventy men killed and a similar number captured, with some important leaders (including Abū Jahl) among the slain. The Muslims, by comparison, suffered only about fifteen casualties.

The battle of Badr brought immediate economic relief to the victorious Muslims, in the form of booty and ransom for captives, but it also had other consequences of more lasting importance. It simultaneously undermined the prestige of the Ḳuraysh of Mecca, hitherto the most powerful group in western Arabia, and greatly augmented that of Muḥammad, thus helping to increase his position and influence among other west Arabian groups. It also greatly strengthened Muḥammad's position in Medina by making the Muslims surer that God was on their side and by helping to bring those with ambivalent feeling toward the Prophet into the Muslim camp.

Indeed, the victory at Badr provided such a significant boost to Muḥammad's prestige and power that we must consider it a critical factor in the ultimate success of his political consolidation. Even the Meccans' defeat of the Muslims a year later in the battle of Uḥud could not totally erase the political effects of Badr, which had raised Muḥammad from a nonentity to a figure to be reckoned with in west Arabian politics.

Several verses of the Koran, notably parts of sura 8, "The Spoils" *(al-Anfāl)*, are considered by Muslim commentators to refer to the battle of Badr, although the text itself contains only one explicit reference to the battle (3.123). As the Islamic community grew during and after Muḥammad's lifetime, participation on the Muslim side in the battle of Badr came increasingly to be viewed as a badge of special merit, signifying early and staunch allegiance to Islam and to the Prophet.

BIBLIOGRAPHY

Ibn Hishām, *Sīra, Das Leben Muhammeds,* Ferdinand Wüstenfeld, ed. (1858–1860), 427 ff., also translated by Alfred Guillaume as *The Life of Muhammad* (1955), 289 ff.; al-Ṭabarī, *Annales* (1879–1901), i, 1284 ff.; al-Wāqidī, *Kitāb al-maghāzī* (1966), 19 ff.; William Montgomery Watt, *Muhammad at Medina* (1956), 10–13; and, as editor, *Bell's Introduction to the Qurᵓān* (1970).

FRED M. DONNER

[See also **Abū Sufyān; Arabia; Ḳuraysh; Muḥammad.**]

BADR AL-DĪN LUᵓLUᵓ, ruler of Mosul, 1211–1259. He began his career as a *mamlūk* of the sixth Zankid ruler, Arslānshāh I (1193–1211), who appointed him *atābik,* or regent, for his minor son, Masᶜūd II (1211–1218). Badr al-Dīn continued in the same capacity, as effective ruler of Mosul, during the reigns of Masᶜūd's sons Arslānshāh II and Mahmūd. With the death of the latter in 1234, the Mosul branch of the Zankid house came to an end; Badr al-Dīn assumed sovereignty in his own name and was recognized as the legitimate ruler by the caliph.

An able statesman, he managed, through a complex and shifting network of alliances with various Ayyubid and Seljukid princes, both to maintain the independence of Mosul and to absorb the smaller principalities of Sinjār and Jazīrat ibn ᶜUmar, thus extending his territorial boundaries west to the Khabur River. Furthermore, his conciliation of Mankū Khān helped to stave off the Mongol invasion of Mosul until 1262, three years after his death. Current knowledge of his diplomacy comes largely from coin inscriptions.

Badr al-Dīn was also important as a patron. At Mosul he restored the city wall, built a palace (Qarā Saray), and built or restored the shrines of Imām Yaḥyā and ᶜAwn al-Dīn; his beautiful carved wooden cenotaph for the latter is still preserved. Most of these buildings are of brick, with doorways and other elements of the gray-blue local stone. They generally bear flowing cursive inscriptions and spacious floral arabesques in multiple systems superimposed on one another at different levels of relief. Human figures and fantastic creatures were also carved in relief. Outside Mosul a bridge at ᶜArabān on the Khabur River and a ruined caravansary east of Sinjār also survive.

Five silver-inlaid bronze vessels identified as having come from Badr al-Dīn's court are in European collections. They are characterized by figural decoration, usually organized in medallions, and elegant floral motifs comparable to those in contemporary architectural ornament.

Of seven surviving volumes of a copy of the *Kitāb al-Aghānī (The Book of Songs)* from the second decade of the thirteenth century, several contain frontispieces of princes in varied courtly settings; painted inscriptions on their sleeve bands read "Badr al-Dīn Luʾluʾ ibn ʿAbdallāh," the appropriate version of his name in the period before his assumption of sovereignty.

BIBLIOGRAPHY

The best short article on Badr al-Dīn is "Luʾluʾ," in *Encyclopedia of Islam,* III (1936); Max van Berchem, "Monuments et inscriptions de l'atabek Luʾluʾ de Mossoul," in *Orientalische Studien Theodor Nöldeke,* I (1906); D. S. Rice, "The Brasses of Badr al-Dīn Luʾluʾ," in *Bulletin of the School of Oriental and African Studies,* **13** (1950); and "The Aghānī Miniatures and Religious Painting in Islam," in *Burlington Magazine,* **95** (1953); Friedrich Sarre and Ernst Herzfeld, *Archäologische Reise im Euphrat- und Tigris-Gebiet,* II (1920), 238–270; S. Stern, "A New Volume of the Illustrated Aghānī Manuscript," in *Ars orientalis,* **2** (1957).

ESTELLE WHELAN

[See also **Islamic Art; Mosul.**]

BADR AL-JAMĀLĪ (*ca.* 1010–*ca.* 1093), commander of the armies and vizier of the Fatimid caliphate in Egypt during the last quarter of the eleventh century, was single-handedly responsible for the rejuvenation of Fatimid power during the long caliphate of al-Mustanṣir (1036–1094). Badr was an Armenian slave of a Syrian emir, Jamāl al-Dawla ibn ʿAmmār, from whom he derived his name al-Jamālī. Twice appointed governor of Damascus, Badr earned a reputation for toughness toward both the Seljuk Turks and the Syrian army. As the Seljuk threat to the Fatimid state increased, internal tensions mounted in Egypt: a severe famine had depleted the country's resources; the military forces were divided—the Turkish guard fought the Sudani troops, while both demanded payment from the caliph. In 1073, to restore order in Egypt, al-Mustanṣir summoned Badr from Acre, where he had commanded the army. Badr murdered the Turkish guard, subdued rebellion in the Nile Delta, and reestablished Fatimid power in Upper Egypt, where Arab tribes and Nubians had made incursions. In return for these services, the caliph named him commander of the armies, chief preacher, chief justice, and vizier. For the next twenty years Badr was the de facto ruler of Egypt, but he was unable to consolidate Fatimid power in Syria as he had done in Egypt. His vizierate instituted a change in Fatimid organization: the next—and final—century of Fatimid rule was characterized by weak caliphs under the control of powerful and ambitious viziers.

In Egypt, Badr was a great builder: the most notable of his works are the walls of Cairo and three of their gates (Bāb Zuwayla, Bāb al-Futūḥ, and Bāb al-Naṣr), which still stand; the Mashhad al-Juyūshī, a commemorative structure on the Muqaṭṭam hills overlooking Cairo; and minarets in upper Egypt.

BIBLIOGRAPHY

Gaston Wiet, *Matériaux pour un Corpus inscriptionum arabicarum, Iᵉ partie: Egypte,* II (1929–1930), 132–160; K. A. C. Creswell, *The Muslim Architecture of Egypt,* I (1952), 146–219.

JONATHAN M. BLOOM

[See also **Cairo; Fatimids.**]

BAERZE, JACQUES DE. Flemish wood-carver active at Dendermonde from before 1390 until at least 1398. With Melchior Broederlam he made two large altarpieces, ordered by the duke of Burgundy for the chartreuse at Champmol near Dijon: one commemorated the life of Christ; the other, the lives of saints and martyrs. The altarpieces are now at Dijon, in the Musée des Beaux-Arts.

BIBLIOGRAPHY

D. M. Hinkey, "*The Dijon Altarpiece* by Melchior Broederlam and Jacques de Baerze: A Study of Its Iconographic Integrity" (Ph.D. diss., University of California, Los Angeles, 1976).

ANNE M. MORGANSTERN

[See also **Broederlam, Melchior.**]

BAGH. See **Gardens, Islamic.**

BAGHDAD, the major administrative center of the Abbasid caliphate and the capital of modern Iraq. It was originally situated along the junction of the Tigris River and the Ṣarāt Canal. The city was founded in 762 by the second Abbasid caliph, al-Manṣūr. Pre-

BAGHDAD

viously the Abbasid rulers had established the center of their administration at a number of sites in Iraq, each of which was called al-Hāshimiyyah. It would appear that the Abbasids preferred to build their administrative complexes near established urban centers, but they always left a discreet distance between the area reserved for the government and military and that for the urban population. In such fashion they hoped to provide for security while availing themselves of goods and services nearby. The pattern seems to have been employed at Baghdad as well.

Al-Manṣūr's decision to seek a new location for still another administrative center was conditioned by security needs. His current administrative center was situated in the general vicinity of Al-Kufa, a city known for its residual support of Alid causes. After a lengthy search along the course of the Tigris as far north as Mosul, he decided to construct a palace complex at the junction of the Tigris and the Ṣarāt Canal. A considerable body of lore explains this decision. Careful analysis of this literature indicates a combination of tales, some of which contain the echo of historical truth. It appears that al-Manṣūr decided on this particular location because of strategic and geographic advantages. The Ṣarāt was deep enough to accommodate commercial traffic, so that the caliph was able to utilize two major river systems which the Ṣarāt connected: the Tigris and the Euphrates. Moreover, it was situated astride the major overland highways. Baghdad thus became the commercial as well as the geographical center of the newly established Abbasid regime.

The site of the palace complex was surrounded by three bodies of water: the Tigris, the Ṣarāt, and a canal that branched off the Ṣarāt, later called Khandaq Tahir. The Tigris was a wide, undulating river that could not be forded. Throughout the history of the city, movement across the Tigris was funneled onto a series of pontoon bridges that could be cut from their moorings. The other canals similarly served as natural barriers in time of attack.

The first major structure to be erected was the famous Round City, called Madīnat al-Salām (City of Peace). It was built on the site of an old hamlet called Baghdad, and that name was subsequently applied to the entire urban area, although the name Baghdad was also used to specify a more narrowly defined place. Before the founding of the Abbasid city, the general area featured a number of villages that were divided among four administrative districts on both sides of the Tigris: Qaṭrabbul, Bādūrayā, Nahr Buq, and Kalwādhā. There was a small market area known as the Tuesday Market on both sides of the river.

The construction of a major edifice required an organized and highly efficient set of work procedures. Construction did not begin until a large labor force had been assembled, and it took four years more for all the major elements of the Round City to be completed, thus allowing the caliph to move there from his old capital at al-Hāshimiyyah. Thousands, if not tens of thousands, of workers—the skilled and unskilled laborers, the artisans from the outlying districts—and the military all required housing and access to established markets for services, as well as an industrial complex for the production of building materials. Baghdad therefore assumed a quality of permanence even before the Round City was completed.

In time the urban area grew around the original walls of the Round City and developed into a sprawling complex of interdependent elements, each containing its own markets, mosques, and cemeteries, and giving rise as well to local loyalties. The area south of the Ṣarāt Canal, which contained the Tuesday Market, developed into the great commercial suburb of Karkh, and was inhabited by the general populace. The area north of the Ṣarāt was originally intended for the government and the army.

The Round City was not a conventional city, for it contained no economic infrastructure whatsoever. To the contrary, strict precautions were taken to limit access by the general populace. It was, strictly speaking, an enormous palace complex that housed the residence and mosque of the caliph, the residences of his younger children, the agencies of government, and residences for the government bureaucracy that staffed these agencies. The size of the Round City (450 hectares) was unprecedented. Though only a palace, it was, in fact, larger than any settlement on the Diyala Plains, the vast hinterland of Baghdad.

The very size of the palace complex, and the large and exclusive population it contained, made it difficult to provide services and supplies from the nearby markets. As a result distributive outlets were permitted within the walls. Following a riot in the market arcades, the merchants who had been permitted into the city were removed; however, the caliph was aware that his original plan for exclusive government and private sectors had to be compromised. Toward the end of his rule, al-Manṣūr moved to a more modest residence, al-Khuld, situated outside the Round City along the Tigris.

BAGHDAD

The caliph had previously begun construction of a second palace complex on the east bank of the river. It was completed by his son and successor, al-Mahdī, in 776. The new area, called al-Ruṣāfah or ʿAskar al-Mahdī, was originally intended to be a second major military camp; however, it also contained a combination of magnificent palace and Friday mosque that was to serve as the residence of the heir apparent. The Khuld palace was thus situated between two major walled edifices and amid large concentrations of military forces. Moreover, the caliph could easily cross the river by way of pontoon bridges protected by the chief of police. Although al-Manṣūr no longer enjoyed the security of an elaborate protective wall, he was still situated near the pulse of government, at some distance from the general populace, with large and accessible security forces nearby.

When al-Mahdī came to power, he resided in the palace built expressly for him. Unlike the Round City, which was partly chosen for its advantageous location near the Tuesday Market, al-Ruṣāfah's situation was determined primarily by its strategic location opposite the Round City and the upper west bank. This created two problems: a lack of water and a need for services because there was no major market area nearby. Since the absence of either would have seriously compromised the function of the administrative center, al-Mahdī extended feeder channels from a canal north of the city and established a market near the Main Bridge that was called the Thirst Market.

Every industrial and commercial enterprise was established there, so that it was like Karkh, the market suburb of the west bank. In time two large private neighborhoods were developed nearby: Bāb al-Ṭāq, which was near the Main Bridge, and al-Mukharrim, which extended south along the river. Regulations designed to prevent overcrowding were put into effect. It appears that an ambitious program of suburban development begun by al-Manṣūr shortly before his death had led to a major expansion of the markets, and resulted in congested living conditions.

Al-Hādī, who succeeded his father as caliph in 785, ruled for a year before his mysterious death. He was succeeded by his brother, the legendary Hārūn al-Rashīd, who returned to the Khuld palace. The reign of al-Rashīd is generally considered the zenith of growth in Baghdad. The city then reached its limits in surface area and population. Surprisingly, the caliph had no monumental structures erected, but several magnificent palaces were built for his subordinates. For undisclosed reasons al-Rashīd grew disenchanted with Baghdad. Toward the end of his reign, he frequently stayed at al-Rafiqah, a regional center that was allegedly built by al-Manṣūr on a plan similar to that of the Round City. Al-Rashīd's death in 809 brought his son al-Amīn to power, and almost immediately plunged the Islamic state into a debilitating civil war. A second son, the heir apparent, al-Maʾmūn, dispatched an army that marched on the capital and laid siege to it. The chronicles describe in graphic terms widespread devastation and suffering, as the defenders fought valiantly behind fixed positions. A closer examination of these texts reveals, however, that the damage was grossly overestimated, and that shortly after the conflict ended, the major structures that had been damaged were all repaired and in use once again.

The death of al-Amīn while trying to escape from Baghdad resulted in the ascendancy of al-Maʾmūn, who remained in Khorāsān rather than risk entering the city in the wake of the previous hostilities. When he finally did settle in the city, it was in a modest east bank palace. Moreover, al-Maʾmūn never quite felt comfortable in Baghdad; he was more often than not a visitor, preferring to spend his time in Khorāsān. When al-Maʾmūn died in 883, he was succeeded by a third brother, al-Muʿtaṣim. The latter, following precedent, relied heavily on military contingents recruited from among Turkish captives. The unruly behavior of the Turks resulted in several altercations, causing al-Muʿtaṣim to leave the city altogether. He then founded a rival capital at Samarra, some sixty miles up the Tigris. The caliphate remained there until 892, when al-Muʿtaḍid returned to Baghdad and built the first of a series of caliphal palaces that were collectively called the Dār al-Khilāfah.

The new caliphal enceinte, which was situated in the southeast section of the urban area, is described in great detail. The sources speak of magnificent residences, exquisitely appointed and featuring unusual elements, including a zoological garden and fantastic mechanical devices. This tremendous architectural achievement was the last major caliphal effort at construction. With the declining fortunes of the caliphate, the city began to shrink in size and population. Beginning with the Buyid hegemony in 945, the caliphs were increasingly reduced to figureheads. The Buyids, indeed, went so far as to build a major group of palaces in the northeast section of the city that was intended to rival the splendid residence of their patrons. This construction was more than offset, however, by the breakdown of order and the decline of some neighborhoods.

The chronicles describing the events of the tenth and eleventh centuries indicate a pattern of religious conflict, economic dislocation, and widespread decay. The replacement of the Buyids by the Seljuks in 1055 did not alter this pattern, despite some construction on the east bank. When Hulegu the Mongol conquered Baghdad in 1258, effectively bringing an end to the Abbasid regime, he conquered a hollow shell of a once proud city. The great geographer Yāqūt (died 1229) describes a series of truncated neighborhoods at some distance from one another, where at one time there had been a continous line of settlement. This pattern continued until modern times.

The physical and human dimensions of the medieval city are difficult to gauge. The sources give exact figures for the surface area in varying metrological systems. If one accepts these figures as accurate, the city would have covered approximately seven thousand hectares. This would make Baghdad five times larger than tenth-century Constantinople and thirteen times larger than Ctesiphon, hitherto the largest city known on the Diyala Plains. Although the figure also reflects the so-called suburban districts of Baghdad, there is reason to believe that the greater city was densely populated.

To what extent can the human resources be expressed in real figures? Some local histories contain chapters dealing with the statistics of the city. While there is no hint of any census, various crude efforts were made to calculate the population, usually by the use of multipliers based on such factors as the consumption of foodstuffs, men having specialized occupations, and the number of houses and baths. The figures obtained from this method are, however, unreliable. In modern Baghdad the density of occupation in the oldest neighborhoods is about two hundred per hectare, which agrees with the most conservative estimates for the population of medieval Constantinople. The physical and human dimensions of medieval Baghdad must have been vast by any standard of measurement; however, the greater urban area did not represent a single city, but a series of urban settlements collectively known as Baghdad.

BIBLIOGRAPHY

Arabica, 9 (1962), special issue dedicated to the anniversary of the city's founding; Jacob Lassner, *The Topography of Baghdad in the Early Middle Ages: Text and Studies* (1970); Guy Le Strange, *Baghdad During the Abbasid Caliphate* (1900); Georges Salmon, *L'introduction topographique à l'histoire de Bagdâdh* (1904); Maximilian Streck, *Die alte Landschaft Babylonien* (1900).

JACOB LASSNER

[See also **Abbasids; Hārūn al-Rashīd; Mahdī, al-; Manṣūr, al-.**]

BAGRAT'S CATHEDRAL was built at Kutaisi by the first king of unified Georgia, Bagrat III. Completion of the construction of the cathedral, which, like that at Oški, is a triconch, early in the eleventh century is indicated by a contemporary inscription on the floor dated 1003. The cathedral is built of evenly cut and smoothly finished yellowish sandstone. The galleries for the king and members of the court are located on the west arm. The exterior walls and southern porch are sumptuously decorated with sculptures of plant and animal motifs. On the western wall is a relief depicting the ascension of Elias. A large part of the cathedral was destroyed in 1691 by invading Turks.

BIBLIOGRAPHY

W. Tsindtsadze, *Bagratis tadzari* (1964), 14–18.

W. DJOBADZE

[See also **Georgian Art and Architecture.**]

BAGRATIDS (BAGRATUNI), ARMENIAN. The Bagratids (Bagratuni in Armenian) were one of the major feudal families in Armenia. Their importance in Armenian history grew during the seventh and eighth centuries. In the late ninth century, they divided into two major and a number of minor branches, and established themselves on the royal and princely thrones of Armenia, Georgia, and Albania.

The origins of the Bagratids are subject to a great deal of discussion. The anonymous seventh-century *Primary History* of Armenia states that they were the descendants of Hayk, the eponymous ancestor of the Armenian people. Beginning in the late eighth century, both Armenian and Georgian sources derived Bagratid genealogy from Jewish ancestry. In the ninth century the Bagratid claim became more pretentious, singling out King David as the primogenitor of the family. According to modern scholars, this change in the family tradition was due to a quest for legitimacy.

The clue to the true origin of the Bagratids is thought to be contained in the family name Bagratuni. With the elimination of the Urartian–Armenian suffix *-uni,* the stem Bagrat or Bagarat is left, which seems to derive from the Old Persian *Bagadāta* ("God-given"). Nikolai Adontz, who was the first to study Armenian feudalism, thought that the family was of Iranian, specifically of Median, origin. Cyril Toumanoff has tried to establish their link with the Iranian Orontid dynasty that ruled Armenia under the Achaemenids and the Seleucids.

Very little is known about the early history of the Bagratids. The family first appears in the fourth century. The fifth-century Armenian historian P^{c}awstos Buzand knew them as the hereditary coronants of the Armenian Arsacid kings, and used their gentilitial title *aspet.* These *aspets* of Armenia are also mentioned by Agat^{c}angełos, another fifth-century Armenian historian. Their ancestral territory, or alodium, was Sper, in northwestern Armenia. According to the Armenian Arsacid throne list (the *gahnamak*), in rank of importance they occupied the second place after the princes of Siwnik^{c}.

After the fall of the Armenian Arsacid dynasty in 428, the Bagratids slowly began to emerge as a major house. Sahak Bagratuni held the governorship *(marzpanate)* of Persarmenia in 481/482. The former Arsacid district of Kogovit and its center, Daroynk^{c}, passed into their hands, and in the sixth century they may also have acquired the district of Bagrewand in central Armenia. In the late sixth and early seventh centuries, Bagratid princes were in the service of both Byzantium and Iran. Most famous among them was Smbat Bagratuni, the viceroy of Hyrcania.

From 618 to 712, under successive Sasanian, Byzantine, and Arab rule, the position of prince of Armenia alternated between the Bagratid and Mamikonean princes. The rivalry between the two families continued until the elimination of the Mamikoneans in the third quarter of the eighth century. The circumspect pro-Arab policy of Prince Ašot the Blind was chiefly responsible for the deliverance of the Bagratids from the massive Arab purges of the 770's, which annihilated most of the lesser and major feudal houses in Armenia. Subsequently, under the powerful and able princes Ašot Msaker, Bagarat Bagratuni, and Smbat the Confessor, the Bagratids succeeded in achieving political solidarity, which paved the way for Ašot the Great to establish the kingdom of Bagratid Armenia in 884, and allowed the other branches of the family to rule over Georgia and Albania.

Among the Bagratid possessions were the princedoms of Tarōn, Tayk^{c}, Mokk^{c}, Arc^{c}ax, and P^{c}aṛisos, and the kingdoms of Ani, Kars, Lori-Joraget, Georgia, and Albania. As a result of the Byzantine expansionism and the Seljuk raids, the Albanian and Armenian Bagratid states and their dynastic lines disappeared between 1050 and 1150.

BIBLIOGRAPHY

Joseph Markwart, "Die Genealogie der Bagratiden und das Zeitalter des Mar Abas und Ps. Moses Xorenaci," in *Caucasica,* **6/2** (1930); Nikolai Adontz, "Bagratuneac^{c} p^{c}aṙk^{c}a" [The Glory of the Bagratids], in *Patmakan usumnasirut^{c}iwnner* (1948), 49–156; Cyril Toumanoff, "The Orontids of Armenia," in *Studies in Christian Caucasian History* (1963), 306–354.

KRIKOR H. MAKSOUDIAN

[See also **Ašot I the Great.**]

BAGRATIDS (BAGRATUNI), GEORGIAN. Descended from the Orontids and originally the rulers of Sper, an area on the western periphery of Armenia and Georgia, the Bagratid family rose to rule as princes and kings in both Armenia and Georgia. Armed with a family tradition of Davidic descent, the Bagratids first achieved preeminence in Armenia, through Arab patronage, with the elevation of Ašot II to prince of Armenia (686–690). Although the Bagratids of Armenia in time became kings (*ca.* 884–886), they never managed to forge a unified state as would their cousins in Georgia. At the end of the eighth century Adarnase, prince of Eruševi-Artani, sought refuge in Iberia; and as the family acquired new territories in Georgia, the caliph appointed Adarnase's son, Ašot I the Great, as prince of Iberia (813–830). The Byzantine emperor named him curopalate. In 888 the Iberian monarchy was restored by Adarnase IV (888–923), and Bagratid kings continued to rule Georgia until the Russian annexations of the early nineteenth century.

The rise of the Bagratids to preeminence among noble families in Georgia was aided by Arab policy in two ways. The harsh repression of Georgian noble resistance to Arab rule in the late eighth century led to the extinction of many prominent families, among them the royal dynasties of the Guaramids and Chosroids. Second, the caliph began to depend on the Bagratids to keep order in Caucasia, which was threatened by Arab separatists. Though facing opposition from other dynastic princes, the Georgian Bagratids managed to survive as rulers of Iberia in the ninth century even as the hold of the caliphate over Caucasia weakened.

Through the manipulations of the Bagratid prince of Tao, David the Great, his adopted son Bagrat was placed on the throne of Abkhazeti (Abkhazia) in western Georgia (978). When Bagrat's biological father, Gurgeni of Iberia, died in 1008, Bagrat III became the first king of a united Georgia (Sakartvelo). As the fortunes of the Armenian Bagratids suffered from the twin blows of Seljuk invasions and Byzantine aggrandizements, those of the Georgian Bagratids rose to a glorious zenith in the late eleventh and twelfth centuries. In the reigns of David II (IV) the Builder (1089–1125) and Tamara (1184–1212), Georgia united around the monarch, held off the Turks, and established a multinational empire, the most powerful state in Caucasia.

Decline followed the Mongol invasions of the early thirteenth century, and the Georgian kingdom fragmented into semi-independent principalities *(samtavro)*. The Bagratids ruled with the sanction of the Mongols through the fourteenth century. Georgia was briefly reunited under Alexander I (1412–1442), but then in the last quarter of the fifteenth century it again splintered into three major parts—Kakheti, Kartli, and Imereti—and Bagratids sat on all three thrones. From then until the end of the Georgian kingdoms, the Bagratid monarchs of eastern Georgia (Kartli and Kakheti) usually ruled either with the acquiescence or under the direct control of Persian overlords, while their cousins in western Georgia (Imereti) lived under similar influence from the Ottoman Empire.

BIBLIOGRAPHY

N. A. Berdzenishvili, V. D. Dondua, M. K. Dumbadze, G. A. Melikishvili, and Sh. A. Meskhia, *Istoriia Grúzii, I: S drevneishikh vremen do 60-x godov XIX veka* (1962); A. Gugushvili, "The Chronological-Genealogical Table of the Kings of Georgia," in *Georgica,* **1**, nos. 2–3 (1936); E. Taqaishvili, "Georgian Chronology and the Beginnings of Bagratid Rule in Georgia," in *Georgica,* **1** (1935); Cyril Toumanoff, *Studies in Christian Caucasian History* (1963).

RONALD SUNY

[See also **David II (IV); David of Tao; Georgia, Political History; Tamar.**]

BAḤR AL-MUḤĪT ("the encircling sea") was the name Muslim geographers gave to the great world ocean. Envisioned as a continuous body of water encircling the continents, it was thought to be the source of most of the world's smaller seas. The concept of a circumambient world ocean originally came from the Greeks, and was transmitted to the Muslims by translations of Greek geographical works into Arabic. The *baḥr al-muḥīt* was sometimes called the Green Sea or the Sea of Darkness, and was especially identified with the Atlantic Ocean beyond the Canary Islands.

BIBLIOGRAPHY

Ḥudūd al-ᶜAlam, *A Persian Geography,* Victor Minorsky, trans. (1937), 51–56; George Kimble, *Geography in the Middle Ages* (1968), 54–61.

JULIE O. BADIEE

[See also **Geography and Cartography, Islamic.**]

BAHRĀM V GŌR (420–438), Sasanian king, son of Yazdagird I, after whose death Bahrām led an Arab army to the gates of Ctesiphon to claim his crown from nobles who had placed his cousin Xusrō (Xosrau) on the throne. As king he was noted for feasting, for hunting, for archery, and for a reorganization of the court musicians. Bahrām ruled his Christian subjects with a stern hand: a policy of persecution was initiated by his prime minister, Mihrnerseh, and continued by the latter during the reign of Yazdagird II. In 428, Bahrām deposed Artašēs V, the last Arsacid king of Armenia, and appointed a Persian as governor. (The Middle Persian term *marzbān* is attested during his reign for the first time.) Bahrām attempted, unsuccessfully, to establish the Nestorian church in Armenia as a counterweight to the influence of Orthodox Byzantium.

Surnamed *gōr* (Pahlavi "wild ass" or "onager"), apparently for his petulant character, Bahrām was killed while hunting, when his horse stumbled and he fell into a pit (New Persian *gōr*). The episode, with a pun on *gōr*, may be mythological, for it resembles the Armenian epic legend of king Artawazd, killed on the hunt when his horse fell into an abyss on Mount Ararat.

BIBLIOGRAPHY

Sources. Al-Ṭabarī, *Annales,* M. J. de Goeje, ed., trans. by Theodor Nöldeke as *Geschichte der Perser und Araber zur Zeit der Sasaniden* (1879); Movsēs Xorenac^{c}i, *Patmut^{c}iwn Hayoc^{c}*, M. Abełean and S. Yarut^{c}iwnean, eds. (1913), trans. by R. W. Thomson as *History of the Armenians* (1978).

Studies. Arthur E. Christensen, *L'Iran sous les Sassanides,* 2nd ed. (1944); R. Ettinghausen, "Bahram Gur's Hunting Feats or the Problem of Identification," in *Iran* (London), 17 (1979).

J. R. RUSSELL

[See also **Sasanian Dynasty.**]

BAHRĀM VI ČŌBĒN, anti-Sasanian usurper of the throne of Persia (590–591). According to citations by al-Ṭabarī and others of the lost Sasanian royal chronicle, the *Xwadāy Nāmag,* the Iranian region suffered attacks from the Byzantines and Arabs in the west and the Turks in the east in 589, when Bahrām is first mentioned as the commander of the Sasanian forces in the Oxus region appointed by King Hormizd IV. Bahrām, whose surname may mean "possessing a javelin" or "the wooden," is referred to by Dīnawarī as the royal governor in Azerbaijan; Mas^{c}ūdī terms him *marzbān* of the region. The Byzantine historian Theophylactus Simokattēs reports that Bahrām was a member of the noble Mihrān house, a branch of the Arsacid dynasty (deposed by Ardešīr I), and that he achieved renown for his successful campaign against the Turks on the eastern frontier of Persia.

Bahrām, apparently encouraged by his victory and the popularity it brought him, overthrew Hormizd IV, but the latter's son, Xusrō (Xosrau) II Abarwēz, regained the throne with the help of the forces of the Byzantine emperor Maurice, whose daughter Maria he married. Bahrām had hoped, it seems, to reestablish the Arsacids on the Iranian throne and, according to the seventh-century Armenian historian Sebēos, had even offered to restore to the Armenians the lands their own Arsacid kings had ruled long ago. Most of the Armenian nobles sided instead with Xusrō II and his Byzantine allies, and Armenian forces under Mušeł joined the latter to defeat Bahrām near Ganzak in Azerbaijan.

The Sasanian house was regarded by the Zoroastrian priesthood as endowed with the glory of the semilegendary Kayanian dynasty, and Bahrām was branded as a heretic for his challenge to the king's legitimacy, but Xusrō may have been disliked by others for his alliance with the infidel Greeks, and it has been suggested that Bahrām is cast as the redemptive hero Bahrām Warzāwand ("having miraculous power") in some Persian eschatological texts.

The rebellion of Bahrām is related in the *Shāhnāma* of Firdawsī; and a Middle Persian romance, the *Bahrām Čōbēn Nāmag,* was rendered into Arabic by Jabala ibn-Sālim, according to the *Fihrist* of al-Nadim. According to the Armenian historian Movsēs Kałankatuac^{c}i, Bahrām's descendants settled in Caucasian Albania, and J̌uanšēr was descended from them.

BIBLIOGRAPHY

Sources. Movsēs Kałankatuac^{c}i, *Patmut^{c}iwn Ałuanic^{c} Ašxarhi,* J. Emin, ed. (1860), trans. by C. J. F. Dowsett as *The History of the Caucasian Albanians by Movsēs Dasxuranc^{c}i* (1961); Sebēos, *Patmut^{c}iwn,* G. V. Abgarean, ed. (1979), trans. by F. Macler as *Histoire d'Héraclius par l'évêque Sébêos* (1904); Theophylactus Simokattēs, *Historiae,* C. de Boor, ed. (1887); al-Ṭabarī, *Annales,* M. J. de Goeje, ed., trans. by Theodor Nöldeke as *Geschichte der Perser und Araber zur Zeit der Sasaniden* (1879).

Studies. Nikolai Adontz and Nina G. Garsoïan, *Armenia in the Period of Justinian* (1970); Arthur E. Christensen, *L'Iran sous les Sassanides,* 2nd ed. (1944); K. Czeglédy, "Bahrām Čōbīn and the Persian Apocalyptic Literature," in *Acta orientalia* (Budapest), 8, no. 1 (1958).

J. R. RUSSELL

[See also **Armenia, History of; Sasanian Dynasty; Xosrau.**]

BAḤRAYN, AL-. During the early centuries of Islam, the name "Al-Baḥrayn" applied to the coastal area on the mainland of eastern Arabia that is now known as Al-Hasa and forms part of the territory of Saudi Arabia. The modern island state of Bahrain (official spelling) was known as Uwāl or Awāl to medieval Muslim authors until, at some indeterminate date, the designation of the mainland was transferred to the offshore island. An informant as late as the traveler Ibn Baṭṭūṭa (*d.* 1377), however, seems to apply the name "Al-Baḥrayn" to both the mainland and the island.

Al-Baḥrayn was famous in early Islamic history as a refuge for dissident elements within the Muslim community and a potential power base for anti-Abbasid activity. First the Khawārij in the seventh century, and then the Qarmaṭians in the tenth century, used Al-Baḥrayn as their home territory, from which they struck at the authority of the central government. The Qarmaṭians even went so far as to steal the Black Stone from Mecca and transport it to Al-Baḥrayn—an act of sacrilege that horrified the orthodox Muslim community. The Shiite Qarmaṭians finally suffered defeat in 1077 at the hands of the ᶜUyūnids, an indigenous Bedouin dynasty backed by the formidable power of the Seljuks, the self-styled defenders of orthodoxy.

The island of Uwāl (Al-Baḥrayn) remained temporarily under the control of the ᶜUyūnids but changed hands several times during the twelfth and thirteenth centuries. The island, now known more commonly as Al-Baḥrayn, boasted a prosperous pearl fishery that impressed both Ibn Baṭṭūṭa and the earlier Jewish traveler Benjamin of Tudela. Benjamin reported the existence of a large Jewish community in Al-Baḥrayn, and at the time of his visit a Jewish official controlled the pearl fishery. (The medieval Al-Baḥrayn/Uwāl was the "pearlry" of the Middle East, and Baḥraynī divers still claim their precious harvest from the ocean floor.) Ibn Baṭṭūṭa particularly noted the fine gardens, date groves, and pomegranate trees.

During the mid fifteenth century the Bedouin dynasty of the Jabrids maintained control of both the island and the mainland of Al-Baḥrayn/Al-Hasa, and suppressed the still-strong Shiite element while favoring the Mālikī legal school. The most famous member of this dynasty, Ajwad ibn Zāmil, became proverbial for the splendor of his court. The following century, however, witnessed the eighty-year domination of Al-Baḥrayn by the Portuguese, followed by the nominal suzerainty of the Persians until 1783, when the House of Khalīfa came to power.

BIBLIOGRAPHY

The above article has largely been based on G. Rentz and W. E. Mulligan's excellent article "al-Baḥrayn" in *Encyclopedia of Islam,* 2nd ed.; and W. Madelung, "Karmaṭī," *ibid.* See also Elkan Adler, ed., *Jewish Travellers* (1930), 57–58; Ibn Baṭṭūṭa, *Travels* A.D. *1325–1354,* H. A. R. Gibb, trans. (1962), II, 408–409.

S. E. MARMON

[See also **Karamans.**]

BAḤYA BEN JOSEPH IBN PAQUDA (*fl. ca.* 1080), Spanish rabbi active at Saragossa. His surviving work consists primarily of an Arabic guide to the interior life, *al-Hidāya ᵓilā farāᵓiḍ al-qulūb,* which in its Hebrew translation *(Ḥovot ha-Levavot)* became a classic of Jewish spirituality. Although it was greatly inspired, as the author acknowledges, by Muslim ascetic works (and also by Neoplatonism and the Muᶜtazilite kalam), this "treatise on the duties of the heart" remains a fundamentally Jewish work in that it postulates the Hebrew scriptures as a rule of life, both temporal and spiritual.

Aside from an initial outline of basic theology ("On the Unity of God") and a teleological account of the physical universe and of human psychology ("Consideration of Creatures"), the work is essentially a spiritual journey, the stages of which are submission to God; the double warning of reason and revelation; surrender to God; sincerity of worship; humility; repentance; examination of conscience; asceticism; and finally the pure love of God, which results in closeness to God but not, properly speaking, in mystical union, which would involve the annihilation of the human self.

BIBLIOGRAPHY

Baḥya ben Joseph, *The Book of Directions to the Duties of the Heart,* Menahem Mansoor, trans. (1973), with bibliography. See also Alexander Altman, "The Religion of the Thinkers: Free Will and Predestination in Saadia, Bahya and Maimonides," in Solomon D. Goitein, ed., *Religion in a Religious Age* (1974); Georges Vajda, "Les études de philosophie juive du Moyen Age depuis la synthèse de Julius Guttmann," in *Hebrew Union College Annual,* **43** (1972).

GEORGES VAJDA

BAILIFF, a subordinate administrator serving both the English central government and private individuals. Bailiffs ought not to be confused with the great Continental "baillis," though books in English sometimes use the term "bailiffs" for these officials—indeed, at one point Magna Carta employs the word in the very wide sense of any royal official of whatever rank (cap. 38). That bailiffs in the restricted sense of the term sometimes made pretense of greater powers, such as adjudicating felonies (Magna Carta, cap. 24), goes without saying, but these pretensions were regarded as illegal.

We might call any number of subordinate Continental officials bailiffs. Some very nearly bore the name, for example, the *bayles* of southern France. This article, though, treats the English medieval bailiff, whose history and role is an example of a spectrum of low-level functionaries.

As "staff" subordinates of sheriffs, English bailiffs carried out routine tasks of administration: execution of writs, giving seisin of contested lands to victorious litigants, arranging deodands, seizing chattels of felons, choosing jurors. Bailiffs also were employed as "hundred reeves"—that is, as general administrators of the districts known as hundreds and as presiding officers of their courts (which had very limited jurisdiction). The bailiffs frequently held these positions as farms, and since many of the hundreds were in private hands, they exercised their public powers in the name of individual barons.

Bailiffs also administered or helped administer towns (boroughs). Appointments originally seem to have been made by the king, but the growth of municipal self-government in the twelfth and thirteenth centuries encouraged burgesses to buy the privilege of electing bailiffs from among their own ranks.

In another restricted sense, we may refer to manorial bailiffs—reeves charged with exacting their lords' rights and income from their estates. They might stand in (be attorneys) for their lords in certain types of civil cases in the common law. In the early thirteenth century an action developed in the royal courts whereby a lord could bring suit against his bailiff, forcing him to give information on his activities. The development of this action and its frequency of use in the later thirteenth century (confirmed by statutes in 1267 and 1285) suggest the increasing sophistication of agricultural administration in line with the emergence of "improving" landlords in English agriculture during the same period.

BIBLIOGRAPHY

Bryce Lyon, *A Constitutional and Legal History of Medieval England,* 2nd ed. (1980), 532; William McKechnie, *Magna Carta,* 2nd ed. (1914), 316–317, 369–375, 431; Frederick Pollock and Frederic Maitland, *History of English Law,* 2nd ed. (1898), I, 557, 647, 656–658; II, 221. See also, among original records, the *Roll and Writ File of the Berkshire Eyre of 1248,* Michael Clanchy, ed., Selden Society, vol. 90 (1972–1973), on the duties and problems of the medieval English bailiff.

WILLIAM CHESTER JORDAN

[See also **Bailli.**]

BAILLI. During the Middle Ages the word "bailli" denoted a provincial administrator in northern France. Although the word was used both of comital administrators in Flanders with similar competence and of administrative assistants in England with very different competence, it was the French official who had the deepest and longest-lasting influence on medieval government. Scholars often distinguish two categories of baillis in French history, the "petty" and the "grand."

The petty baillis go back perhaps as far as the end of the reign of Louis VII (1137–1180), and may have been modeled somewhat on the English sheriff and itinerant justice. They competed, as it were, with the *prévôts,* a class of royal collectors of domain revenue, who had emerged in the eleventh century and had steadily taken on "governmental" functions. For important reasons, especially the tendency of the office to become hereditary, many towns with resident *prévôts* began to encounter additional government agents in the course of the twelfth century. These were the petty baillis.

Originally traveling inspectors of the *prévôts,* the petty baillis represented the royal court, although technically they may not have been members of it (in contradistinction to the earliest English itinerant justices). Eventually, because of continuing accretions to the royal domain, the difficulties of long-distance travel, and the government's uneven supervision of them, many petty baillis took up residence in principal towns alongside *prévôts.* However, they continued to administer justice on circuit.

In those towns with two agents, the petty bailli—ordinarily a salaried official—was concerned primarily with justice and the fines of justice, the accounting of variable occasional income such as that from the royal forests and temporal regalia (the revenue incident to royal administration of vacant benefices), and so forth. The *prévôt,* on the other hand, was a farmer of royal revenues. His duties extended to judicial matters, but his competence was limited, more or less, to causes involving the rights, privileges, and obligations touching the revenues encompassed by the farm. From the *prévôt*'s court there was, no doubt, resort to the petty bailli. (This follows from the supervisory functions of the petty bailli.) In the banlieues of towns with both a petty bailli and a *prévôt,* the former tended to become more important than the latter, and in some instances his income was supplemented by a farm of royal revenues in the suburbs. There were other royal agents in the provinces, most of whom were revenue farmers of low status, but the pillars of royal administration in Francia in the late twelfth century were the petty baillis and the *prévôts.*

BAILLI

The conquest of Normandy by Philip Augustus in 1202–1204 transformed the situation. In Normandy before the conquest, there were baillis recognizably similar to the petty baillis of Francia. But there was an important distinction: the Norman baillis, though itinerant with respect to their administration of justice, were regional officials in a way that the baillis of Francia had never been. Their competence was defined not by special royal commissions but by routine appointment to geographical administrative units *(bailliages)* that were composed of a specific and territorially determined number of viscounties. The latter were comparable with the areas in which individual *prévôts* of Francia collected revenue. (The Normans also had itinerant justices, properly so called; but this aspect of judicial administration was suppressed soon after the conquest.)

In Normandy, Philip permitted the regional baillis, replaced by his own men, to increase their competence. They became, in conventional scholarly language, "grand baillis." The new men were given their posts almost as semimilitary commissions. Their temporary function as military governors in a battlefront province prepared the way for the office of bailli to be regarded as an omnicompetent dignity—over justice, police power, finance. The number of these regional bailliages or grand bailliages was fixed at eight, and ultimately reduced to six, for all of Normandy.

Rapidly this idea of the omnicompetence of a regional bailli spread to Francia. A select handful of the existing petty baillis of the old royal domain were elevated to grand baillis. There can be no doubt that some petty baillis remained petty baillis, but their status seems to have been reduced to that of the *prévôts.* The grand baillis were the true supervisors whose courts were the courts of appeal for all lesser royal jurisdictions in the bailliages. As there were new accretions to the domain (Languedoc, the county of Mâcon), the grand bailliage form of administration was imposed. Terminology varied, however; the grand bailli in the south was called the seneschal, and in Auvergne, for a time, the constable. But whatever the terminology, the pattern was Norman as modified by Philip Augustus.

Socially the baillis were chosen from the petty nobility or knightly class (this was less consistently true for Languedoc). Geographically they were selected from families with roots in the old royal domain. Ordinarily, in other words, Normans were not chosen to be baillis in their own province, nor, in the early thirteenth century, were southerners the preferred administrators of the south. To prevent the growth of ties with the administered population, baillis were forbidden to hold property in their bailliages or to integrate their families by marriage into local society. They were transferred fairly regularly (about every five years). It must be added, however, that enforcement of these and similar procedures was inconsistent. Consequently, analysis of "movements" (changes in the rate of transfer or suspension) of baillis has been used as a fundamental indicator of the success or lack of success of French royal government.

The grand baillis in Normandy submitted their financial accounts twice yearly to the Norman Exchequer. The grand baillis of Francia and the seneschals of Languedoc submitted theirs thrice yearly to the king's council at Paris. The officials also served these institutions as advisers. Pay for a bailli was very high. Depending on the strategic and economic importance of his district, the salary range ran from about 300 to 700 French pounds yearly in the thirteenth century, sums that must have exceeded the income of most nobles in France.

In the later Middle Ages the competence of the grand bailli was lessened as fiscal and judicial functions tended to be taken over by trained experts, and constitutional functions by local representative institutions. The office became increasingly honorific; new officials gradually displaced the grand bailli even though the title and many emoluments remained as sinecures.

BIBLIOGRAPHY

A comprehensive treatment of the bailli and the relationship of this official to the French administration is in Ferdinand Lot and Robert Fawtier, *Histoire des institutions françaises au moyen âge,* II (1958), 144–158 and elsewhere. A briefer but more up-to-date treatment is James Fesler, "French Field Administration: The Beginnings," in *Comparative Studies in Society and History,* 5 (1962–1963). Both of these syntheses are largely based on the magisterial work of Léopold Delisle in *Recueil des historiens des Gaules et de la France,* **24** (1904) and of Henri Stein in the *Annales de la Société historique du Gâtinais,* **20, 21, 32, 34** (1902, 1903, 1914, 1918–1919). Intensive studies of individual regions and their administration include: Joseph R. Strayer, *The Administration of Normandy under Saint Louis* (1932); Henri Waquet, *Le Bailliage de Vermandois aux xiiie et xive siècles* (1919).

WILLIAM CHESTER JORDAN

[See also **Law, French; Normans and Normandy; Philip II Augustus.**]

BALĀDHURĪ, ABŪ ḤASAN AḤMĀD IBN YAHYA IBN JĀBIR AL- (*d.* 892), one of the greatest Arab historians of the ninth century, was a man of great learning, a genealogist, and a poet. Little is known about his life, but we do know that his paternal grandfather, Jābir, was a secretary of the governor of Egypt, al-Khaṣīb. This grandfather must have been responsible for Aḥmād's name "al-Balādhurī," for it is related that he ate too much of the seed of *balādhur* (*Semecarpus anacardium,* marking nut), became mentally deranged, and died.

Balādhurī was born probably in the first decade of the ninth century. He lived and studied mainly in Baghdad, although he did travel to Damascus, Emesa, and Antioch to pursue his studies. In Baghdad he was on good terms with several caliphs, viziers, and secretaries, especially with the caliph al-Mutawakkil, whose boon companion he was. He was a sharp-tongued poet, especially gifted in panegyric. He knew Persian well: it is reported that he translated into Arabic poetry the important prose political testament of the Persian king Ardashir. Balādhurī's fame, however, rests on the two books that show his knowledge, reliability, and critical spirit:

Futūḥ al-Buldān ("History of the Muslim Conquests") is a record of the wars of the prophet Muḥammad; the campaigns of the early caliphs against the apostates in Arabia; and the Muslim conquests of Syria, northern Iraq (Jazira), Armenia, Egypt, North Africa, Iraq, and Persia. The historical information is extremely valuable. Of unique value are Balādhurī's accounts of the administration of the early Muslim state, including the change from Greek and Persian to Arabic as the official language, the development of the Arabic script, the use of signet rings, and questions of taxation, coinage, and currency. This book has been published several times in Europe and the Arab world, and has been translated into English and German.

Ansāb al-Ashrāf ("Genealogies of the nobles among the Arabs") is a large, valuable book on pre-Islamic and early Muslim culture and history up to the caliphate of the Abbasids. Organized according to genealogy, it begins with the life of the prophet Muḥammad and concentrates thereafter on the tribe of Ḳuraysh, the Prophet's tribe, beginning with the Alids and going on to the Abbasids, then to the rest of the Banū Hāshim and the Banū ᶜAbd Shams, in which section the Umayyads occupy a prominent position. The rest of the clans of Ḳuraysh and other branches of Muḍar follow, along with the clans of Qays. The historical information that Balādhurī records in the biographies is often unique, the pre-Islamic data being particularly valuable. Though some attempts have been made to edit this text, the work is not yet complete.

BIBLIOGRAPHY

For a biography of Balādhurī, see R. Tajaddud, ed., *Ibn al-Nadīm, Al-Fihrist* (1971), 125–126. An English ed. of the *Futūḥ al-Buldān* is in P. K. Hitti and F. C. Murgotten, *The Origins of the Islamic State* (1916; 1924). A German ed. of the *Ansāb al-Ashrāf* is in preparation.

WADĀD AL-QĀḌĪ

[See also **Historigraphy, Islamic.**]

BALAVARIANI is the Georgian title for the story of Barlaam and Josaphat (or Joasaph), which had a vast popularity in both Eastern and Western literature. This legend is ultimately based on Indian stories concerning the Buddha. By the early ninth century an Arabic book of *Balavar and Būdasaf* was in circulation, and from it the Georgian Christian adaptation of the story was derived. The exact time and place of translation are not known, but translations from Arabic into Georgian were frequent in the eighth and ninth centuries, especially by the Georgian monks in Palestine. A Greek translation was made from the Georgian about 1000 by Euthymius of Iviron on Mount Athos. From the Greek, incorrectly attributed to John of Damascus, the Western versions derive.

Two recensions of the Georgian version are known. The longer is the more ancient, probably from the ninth century; the shorter recension is a later abbreviation. The Georgian does not have the heavy theological elaboration that characterizes the Greek version; indeed, the Christian overtones are almost incidental in the Georgian, which does not include the *Apology of Aristides* that was later incorporated into the Greek version.

The *Balavariani* tells the story of King Abenes of India, who did not wish his son Iodasaph (Josaphat) to know about death, disease, or poverty. But from the teaching of Balavar, here presented as a Christian monk, Iodasaph eventually learned that the things of this world are transitory and that true felicity lies in the spiritual life. Balavar's instruction is imparted through a series of fables, of which the first—that of the caskets—is best known in English from Shakespeare's *Merchant of Venice.* Eventually Barlaam and Josaphat entered the roster of Christian saints.

BIBLIOGRAPHY

Robert L. Wolff, "The Apology of Aristides—A Re-examination," in *Harvard Theological Review,* **30** (1937); and "Barlaam and Ioasaph," *ibid.,* **32** (1939).

R. W. THOMSON

[See also **Barlaam and Josaphat; Georgian Literature.**]

BALDACHIN (from the Italian *Baldacco,* Baghdad, the source of some materials used in its construction) is a canopy supported at each corner by a pole and carried in processions, or a permanent structure derived from such a canopy. Baldachins were used to cover sacred objects, especially altars.

LESLIE BRUBAKER

BALDR (or Balder), in Scandinavian mythology the son of Odin, foremost of the gods, and Frigg, Odin's wife. The older poetry—skaldic and Eddic—mentions him frequently, and allusive references to his story abound; one short Eddic poem, *Baldrs draumar,* is devoted exclusively to a prophetic recounting of his fate. As so often, however, *Snorra Edda* provides the fullest account of the myth, one apparently based squarely on the older poetry but differing greatly from the version in book III of the *Gesta Danorum* of Saxo Grammaticus.

According to Snorri, Baldr was the fairest and best of the gods. He suffered disquieting dreams, so in council the gods decided that Frigg should take oaths from all things, great and small, not to harm Baldr. Thereafter the gods took sport in throwing weapons at the invincible god. Loki, however, was jealous, and, disguised as an old woman, he learned from Frigg that no oath had been taken from mistletoe because Frigg had thought it insignificant. Loki plucked the mistletoe and gave it to Baldr's blind half brother, Hǫðr, suggesting that he, too, join in the sport. Baldr was struck dead by the blow, and the gods were overcome with grief.

Frigg dispatched Hermóðr, another of Odin's sons, to the world of the dead to plead for Baldr, as an elaborate funeral was held. All the gods were in attendance, but none could launch the funeral ship. Finally a giantess was summoned, and the ship was set afloat. Baldr's wife, Nanna, died of grief and was put aboard beside her husband. Then the ship was set afire. As Thor consecrated the fire with his hammer, he kicked a dwarf into the flames. Meanwhile, Hermóðr rode dark approaches, leaped the gate, and spoke with Hel, the goddess of the dead. She agreed to release Baldr if all creation would weep for him. The condition was very nearly met, but one old hag refused to weep. She was thought to be Loki.

Saxo makes Hotherus (Hǫðr) not the half brother of Balderus (Baldr) but his mortal enemy, married to Nanna. Hotherus kills Balderus as part of an ordinary military battle between their two armies. To what extent this represents east Scandinavian tradition as opposed to Saxo's euhemerism is unknown.

Although interpretation of the myth of Baldr has a long history, no consensus has been reached. Currently in disfavor are Frazer's notion that worldwide ritual patterns are reflected, Baldr personifying oak, and Kauffmann's suggestion of a heroicized royal sacrifice. Earlier in the twentieth century, scholars tended toward the idea of a borrowing of either the Christ story (Bugge, Krohn) or the Near Eastern dying god (Neckel), while more recent scholars have sought a native basis, in Germanic initiation ritual (de Vries) or ancient Indo-European tradition (Dumézil). There appear to be elements of truth in all these attempts at interpretation, and the story is almost certainly multifaceted. Even if one is inclined to accept native traditions as the best explanation of the story in all its aspects and details, one is left with such fundamental problems as Loki's absence from some versions of the story and the role of the mistletoe—a plant not native to Iceland. Thus, although the god Baldr was apparently not widely worshiped, his myth has remained one of the most enigmatic within Scandinavian mythology.

BALDRS DRAUMAR

BIBLIOGRAPHY

Sophus Bugge, *Studier over de nordiske gude- og heltesagns oprindelse* (1881–1889), also in German: *Studien über die Entstehung der nordischen Götter- und Heldensagen* (1889); Jan de Vries, "Der Mythos von Balders Tod," in *Arkiv för Nordisk Filologi,* 70 (1955); Georges Dumézil, *Loki* (1948), also in German (1959); "Høtherus et Balderus," in *Beiträge zur Geschichte der deutschen Sprache und Literatur,* 83 (1961–1962); and "Balderiana minora," in *Indo-Iranica: Mélanges présentés à Georg Morgenstierne* (1964); Sir James George Frazer, *Balder the Beautiful,* The Golden Bough, VII, 3rd ed. (1913); Friedrich Kauffmann, *Balder: Mythus und Sage* (1902); Kaarle Krohn, "Lemminkäinens Tod < Christi > Balders Tod," in *Finnisch-ugrische Forschungen,* 5 (1905); Gustav Neckel, *Die Überlieferungen vom Gotte Balder* (1920).

JOHN LINDOW

[See also **Baldrs Draumar; Eddic Poetry; Saxo Grammaticus; Scandinavian Mythology; Snorra Edda.**]

BALDRS DRAUMAR (Baldr's dreams) is an Eddic poem prophetically describing the fate of the god Baldr. The only vellum containing the poem is the Icelandic fragment AM 748 I 4° (1300–1325), which also contains all or part of six other Eddic lays and is otherwise devoted to rhetoric and poetics. *Baldrs draumar* is quite short—only fourteen strophes—and some scholars have regarded it as incomplete, but it forms a unified whole.

The poem begins by telling how all the gods had met in council, for Baldr was beset by terrifying dreams. (Snorri, too, begins his account of the Baldr story with these dreams.) Odin sets off for the world of the dead. After passing a hellhound, he arrives and, by means of magic charms, awakens a dead prophetess. Identifying himself as Vegtamr ("Road-accustomed")—whence the title *Vegtamskviða* ("Lay of Vegtamr") in later paper manuscripts—he asks for whom the hall of the dead has been decorated. On learning that Baldr is expected there, he asks who will be Baldr's slayer; the seeress tells him that Hǫðr is to kill Baldr. The third question concerns the identity of Baldr's avenger. The prophetess answers that Odin will sire a son on Rindr, a giantess; when he is one day old, uncombed and unwashed, that son will avenge Baldr. Finally Odin asks what appears to be a riddle—it remains obscure—concerning some weeping maidens. At this the seeress recognizes Odin. She will not again be raised until Loki gets free at Ragnarok.

Baldrs draumar shows similarities with other Eddic lays. The opening strophe is virtually identical to strophe 14 of the burlesque *Þrymskviða,* and strophe 3 is quite similar to several passages in that poem. The figure of the dead seeress, soaked with rain and snow and dew, has reminded some observers of the dead Helgi Hundingsbani, particularly as portrayed in *Helgakviða Hundingsbana* II, strophe 44; and the final, unanswerable question leading to an epiphany is similar to the ending of *Vafþrúðnismál*—where, indeed, the head riddle concerns Baldr's death. There is, however, probably no need to think of direct relationship among the poems. The similarities with *Þrymskviða* appear to be the result of formulaic language. The romantic portrayal of the dead Helgi shares nothing with that of the seeress, save the motifs of damp and dew; but dew is mythically associated with the world tree and is frequently the base word in kennings for blood. Finally, the head riddle followed by epiphany is part of a type scene of the common Norse story pattern of the contest of wisdom.

More striking are the similarities with *Vǫluspá.* Besides being recounted by a seeress, *Vǫluspá* is concerned with Baldr's fate, and parts of strophes 32 and 33 closely resemble strophe 11 of *Baldrs draumar.* Although some scholars have found the notion of a direct literary relationship to be unavoidable, one might also conclude that both poems are products of a fairly stable Icelandic Baldr tradition.

Much of the scholarship on the poem concerns the traditional problem of dating. Earlier scholars tended to date the poem to the pagan period, before 1000, but recent consensus would, somewhat tentatively, assign it to the later twelfth century.

The somber mood of *Baldrs draumar* made it popular with romantic poets. It was rendered into English by Thomas Gray ("The Descent of Odin," 1768) and into German by Herder (1772).

BIBLIOGRAPHY

Baldrs draumar may be studied in the facsimile edition of Elias Wessén, *Fragments of the Elder and Younger Edda: AM 748 I and II 4°* (1945); and in the edition of the Poetic Edda by Gustav Neckel, *Edda: Die Lieder des Codex Regius nebst verwandten Denkmälern,* I, *Text,* 4th ed. by Hans Kuhn (1962). Useful commentary is in Richard C. Boer, *Die Edda mit historisch-kritischen Commentar,* II (1922), 343–347; Franz Rolf Schröder, "Die eddischen 'Balders Träume,'" in *Germanisch-romanische Monatsschrift,* 45 (1964); Einar Ól. Sveinsson, *Íslenzkar bók-*

menntir í fornöld, I (1962), 284–287; and Jan de Vries, *Altnordische Literaturgeschichte,* II (1967), 101–104.

JOHN LINDOW

[See also **Baldr; Eddic Poetry; Scandinavian Mythology; Snorra Edda.**]

BALDUS, also known as Baldo degli Ubaldi da Perugia (1327–1400), was a civilian (teacher of civil law) and canonist of prodigious learning, energy, and originality. He was among the most celebrated and influential academic jurists of the latter Middle Ages. He was also the most prominent descendant of a renowned Perugian family. His father, Francesco, was a professor of medicine; his brothers, Angelo and Piero (the latter a canonist), were admired by their contemporaries as outstanding jurists; and his son Francesco, though not as important as his father and uncles in the annals of Italian jurisprudence, had an excellent reputation for his commentaries on Justinian's *Corpus iuris civilis.*

It is not possible to state with certainty where, when, and with whom Baldus studied. The tradition that he received his doctoral insignia at the University of Perugia in 1344, and that in the same year, at the precocious age of twenty-four, he participated with Bartolo da Sassoferrato in a public disputation at the University of Bologna, is erroneous. According to Baldus' own testimony, his mentors included Federico Petrucci, Francesco Tigrini, and Bartolo. He may have taught at the universities of Perugia and Pisa in the 1350's. It is certain that he was present at the University of Florence between 1358 and 1364; at the University of Perugia during almost the whole period between 1364 and 1376; at the University of Bologna in 1370; at the University of Padua between 1376 and 1379; again at the University of Perugia between 1380 and 1390; and at the University of Pavia from 1390 until his death in 1400. Among his many disciples were Giovanni da Imola, Pietro d'Ancarano, Paolo da Castro, Cardinal Francesco Zabarella, and Pope Gregory XI.

Baldus' writings encompassed the three major branches of legal science: civil, canon, and feudal. Among his most significant works are commentaries on various parts of the *Corpus iuris civilis,* on the first three books of the *Gregorian Decretals,* and on the *Libri feudorum.* His extensive examinations of a specific law or topic, such as the syndication of officials, statutes and jurisdiction, and the Peace of Constance, were published in monographic form. Baldus' career, which spanned a full half-century, was not confined to the university. He held numerous public offices, serving, for example, as vicar-general of the bishop of Todi and as judge, legate, and counselor of Perugia. Ecclesiastical and municipal officials, corporate bodies such as guilds, and individuals constantly solicited Baldus' professional opinion. The several thousand legal opinions *(consilia)* rendered by Baldus represent a virtually inexhaustible treasure of information on the private, public, and criminal life of the inhabitants of central and northern Italy in the second half of the fourteenth century.

The ideas and doctrines of Baldus have never been systematically studied, and thus cannot be easily summarized. His works, which are voluminous and dialectically complex, are filled with thousands of cross-references and apparent contradictions. Without the benefit of modern editions, Baldus' work is difficult to use, and there remains uncertainty that he actually was the author of every commentary and opinion attributed to him. There is no doubt, however, that his doctrines and opinions continued to be cited as authoritative and as precedents in the sixteenth and seventeenth centuries by theologians and jurists such as Jean Bodin.

BIBLIOGRAPHY

Various printed editions of Baldus' commentaries, tracts, and *consilia* are listed by Enrico Besta, *Fonti: Legislatione e scienze giuridica dalla caduta dell'Impero Romano al secolo decimoquinto (–decimosesto),* 2 vols. (1923–1925), I, pt. 2, 855ff. A partial listing of manuscripts attributed to Baldus is found in Gero Dolezalek, *Verzeichnis der Handschriften zum römischen Recht bis 1600,* III (1972), *s.v.* "Baldus." The most important collection of materials relating to Baldus' life is *L'opera di Baldo per cura dell'Università di Perugia* (1901). A convenient list of important books and articles published before 1969 is found in Helmut Coing, ed., *Handbuch der Quellen und Literatur der neueren europäischen Privatrechtsgeschichte,* I: *Mittelalter (1100–1500)* (1973), 273.

For recent publications on Baldus, consult Giuseppe Ermini, *Storia dell'Università di Perugia,* I (1971), 146–152; Julius Kirshner, "'Ars imitatur naturam': A Consilium of Baldus on Naturalization in Florence," in *Viator,* 5 (1974); "Between Nature and Culture: An Opinion of Baldus of Perugia on Venetian Citizenship as Second Nature," in *The Journal of Medieval and Renaissance Studies,* 9 (Fall 1979); and "Two Fourteenth-Century Opinions on Dowries, Paraphernalia, and Non-Dotal Goods," in *Bulletin of*

Medieval Canon Law, n.s., 9 (1979); Domenico Maffei, *La donazione di Costantino nei giuristi medievali* (1964), 191ff.; J. A. Wahl, "Baldus de Ubaldis and the Foundations of the Nation-State," in *Manuscripta,* **21,** no. 2 (1977); and "Immortality and Inalienability: Baldus de Ubaldis," in *Medieval Studies,* **32** (1970).

JULIUS KIRSHNER

[See also **Bartolo da Sassoferrato; Corpus Juris Civilis.**]

BALDWIN I OF FLANDERS, the first known count of Flanders (862–879). Soon after his appointment Baldwin, known as Iron Arm, carried off and married Judith, daughter of Charles the Bald. Infuriated, Charles forced his bishops to excommunicate the couple, and attempted to seize them. Pope Nicholas I, however, recognized the marriage. When Baldwin returned from Rome, his threat to ally with the Vikings persuaded Charles to make peace. The excommunication was lifted, the couple was formally married at Auxerre, and Baldwin was confirmed in his authority as count.

In 864, when the Vikings attacked Flanders, Baldwin defended himself from a fortified point at Bruges and drove them from the country. Successful in repulsing ensuing raids, he died in 879, just as Flanders was bracing itself for another invasion. Triumphant against this threat was Baldwin's son and successor, Baldwin II (879–918).

Baldwin I Iron Arm typified the officials in charge of the Carolingian counties, duchies, and marches during the second half of the ninth century, when the Carolingian Empire was disintegrating. Generally a loyal and efficient representative of the royal power, he nevertheless usurped local authority and seized more land, setting a precedent for his successors, who established a county virtually independent of the Carolingians and their Capetian successors.

BIBLIOGRAPHY

The most useful works on Baldwin are Henri Pirenne, *Histoire de Belgique,* 5th rev. ed. (1929), I, 56–59; Jan Dhondt, *Korte Geschiedenis van het Ontstaan van het Graafschap Vlaanderen* (1943); François L. Ganshof, *La Flandre sous les premiers comtes* (1949) and *La Belgique carolingienne* (1958).

BRYCE LYON

[See also **Flanders, Low Countries.**]

BALDWIN I OF JERUSALEM, brother of Godfrey of Bouillon and founder of the kingdom of Jerusalem. A leader of the First Crusade, Baldwin captured Edessa in 1098. Two years later, following the death of Godfrey, he was crowned at Bethlehem as the first king of the Crusaders' state. Campaigns against rival princes continued until 1107, after which he turned his efforts to an offensive against the Muslim seaports. By 1112 he had gained most of the coastal towns. Eventually his domain extended as far south as ᶜAqaba, and he even campaigned in Egypt, where he died at Al-ᶜArish in 1118. Baldwin found Jerusalem a weak and helpless state, and left it strong and powerful. He gave a semblance of unity to the Latin states and brought a kind of peace to a world of religious turmoil.

BIBLIOGRAPHY

Foucher de Chartres, *A History of the Expedition to Jerusalem, 1095–1127,* Harold S. Fink, ed., and Frances Rita Ryan, trans. (1969); John C. Andressohn, *The Ancestry and Life of Godfrey of Bouillon* (1947); Jean Richard, *Le royaume latin de Jerusalem* (1953); Steven Runciman, *A History of the Crusades,* I (1951), 146, 325–336; William B. Stevenson, *The Crusaders in the East* (1907), 59–66.

JOHN H. HILL

[See also **Crusades and Crusader States to 1199.**]

BALDWIN I OF THE LATIN EMPIRE (1172–*ca.* 1205), ninth count of that name in Flanders and the sixth in Hainaut. Regarded as pious, charitable, and morally irreproachable, he also had the reputation of being a strong and a just ruler. In 1186 he married Marie, the daughter of Count Henry of Champagne. On 23 February 1200, Baldwin took the cross, and in April 1202 set out on the Fourth Crusade, leaving his wife as regent in Flanders.

After the capture and sack of Constantinople in April 1204, and some intrigue, he was elected first Latin emperor on 9 May, and a week later was solemnly crowned in Hagia Sophia following the Byzantine ceremonial. He then distributed fiefs to his followers and tried to consolidate his position around the capital. While warring against the Bulgarians, Baldwin was captured and imprisoned at Tirnovo, where he died.

BIBLIOGRAPHY

Robert L. Wolff, "Baldwin of Flanders and Hainaut, First Latin Emperor of Constantinople: His Life, Death, and Resurrection, 1172–1225," in *Speculum,* **27** (1952).

GEORGE T. DENNIS

[See also **Latin Empire of Constantinople.**]

BALLADE, one of the *formes fixes* for French lyric song of the fourteenth and fifteenth centuries. The term is probably derived from the Provençal *balar* and the Italian *ballare* ("to dance"). The poetic form consists of three or more stanzas with identical rhyme and metric schemes, ending with a consistent refrain of one or two lines. The musical form follows the pattern *AAB:* the initial melodic section is repeated, then followed by a contrasting melodic section that includes the refrain.

The ballade probably originated with thirteenth-century refrain forms found occasionally among the chansons of the trouvères. Its earliest appearances as a distinct form occur among the monophonic songs of Jehan de l'Escurel (*d.* 1304). The form came to be associated in the fourteenth century with polyphonic musical settings, largely through the prolific works of Guillaume de Machaut (*ca.* 1300–1377), who standardized the ballade to include three stanzas, each bearing a single-line refrain. The first statement of the *A* section of music typically ends with an open cadence; the second statement, with a closed one (*ouvert-clos* structure). The music is usually written for one voice (typically tenor or countertenor) counterpointed by two or three instruments; thus, the polyphonic setting preserves the expressive tone of its monophonic antecedents.

The successors of Guillaume de Machaut—the *ars subtilior* composers of Avignon, Navarre, Foix, and Barcelona—retained his structures while adding rhythmic complexities to the contrapuntal texture. In the fifteenth century the "Burgundian school" of Binchois, Busnois, and Dufay simplified the rhythmic structures of lyric song, placing more emphasis on harmonic effects and on smooth, conjunct melodies.

The ballade also appears as a literary form without music, written by such poets as Froissart, Deschamps, Christine de Pisan, Charles d'Orléans, and Villon in France, and by Gower and Chaucer in England. Ballade texts are predominantly love songs, although several examples of ceremonial and laudatory texts are known.

BIBLIOGRAPHY

Willi Apel, *French Secular Compositions of the Late Fourteenth Century* (1970–1971); and "Rondeaux, Ballades, and Virelais in French Thirteenth-Century Songs," in *Journal of the American Musicological Society,* 7 (1954); Leo Schrade, ed., *Polyphonic Music of the Fourteenth Century,* II–III (1956), on works of Guillaume de Machaut; G. Reaney, "Fourteenth-Century Harmony and the Ballade, Rondeau, and Virelai of Guillaume de Machaut," in *Musica disciplina,* 7 (1953).

MARCY J. EPSTEIN

[See also **Ars Subtilior; Charles d'Orléans; Chaucer, Geoffrey; Christine de Pisan; Deschamps, Eustache; Froissart, Jean; Gower, John; Machaut, Guillaume de; Rondeau; Villon, François; Virelai.**]

BALLADS, MIDDLE ENGLISH. The canon of balladry as created by Francis J. Child in his five-volume *English and Scottish Popular Ballads* consists of 305 numbered texts that establish our modern definition of the ballad as "a traditional narrative song." It is uncertain which of his texts can be classified as "Middle English ballads." Fewer than a dozen were recorded by 1500, though there is a possibility of medieval origin for certain ballads not recorded until later.

By far the earliest ballad (if indeed it is one) is "Judas" (Child's number 23), preserved in a manuscript of the mid thirteenth century. Thereafter comes a gap of two centuries before we encounter any more ballads. This gap could be fortuitous, but it is more likely that the birth of the ballad simply did not come until the mid fifteenth century, when the decline of the minstrel profession (brought about by a loss of patronage from the great families now involved in the Wars of the Roses) led to a convergence of minstrelsy and an existing folk-song tradition to produce, eventually, the popular ballad as we now know it.

The earliest of the fifteenth-century ballads is "Inter diabolus et virgo" (1), a version of Child's first ballad that he did not discover until later (see V, p.

283). In it the devil and a maid engage in a riddling contest. Then come "Robin Hood and the Monk" (119), "St. Stephen and Herod" (22), "Robin and Gandeleyn" (115), "I Have a Young Sister" (see 46; it survives to this day as "I Gave My Love a Cherry"), "Robin Hood and the Potter" (121), and "The King and the Barker" (273, Appendix I). The earliest printed text, probably issued from the press of William Caxton about 1500, is "A Gest of Robyn Hode" (117); it was followed almost immediately by "Adam Bell, Clim of the Clough, and William of Cloudesly" (116), printed by Wynkyn de Worde about 1505. There is, finally, the so-called *Corpus Christi* carol, apparently unknown to Child, preserved in the commonplace book of Richard Hill.

Four ballads recorded in the sixteenth century appear to be of medieval origin: "Crow and Pie" (111); "The Hunting of the Cheviot" or "Chevy Chase" (162) and "The Battle of Otterburn" (161), both recalling a border battle of August 1388; and "King John and the Bishop" (45), probably not contemporary with the historical King John, but perhaps based on a medieval popular tale. Among the forty-five ballads of the Percy Folio manuscript (*ca.* 1650) the following may be medieval: "The Maid and the Palmer" (21); "Robin Hood and Guy of Gisborne" (118); six ballads traceable to medieval romance—"The Boy and the Mantle" (29), "King Arthur and King Cornwall" (30), "The Marriage of Sir Gawain" (31), "Sir Aldingar" (59), "Sir Cawline" (61), and "The Lord of Lorn and the False Steward" (271); and, perhaps most impressive of all, "Child Waters" (63), reminiscent of Chaucer's "Clerk's Tale" of patient Griselda.

Eighteenth-century songbooks yield more examples: "Gil Brenton" (5), "Sheath and Knife" (16C), "The Lass of Roch Royal" (76), and "The Gipsy Laddie" (200), the last perhaps a parody of *Sir Orfeo.* The manuscripts of David Herd (1732–1810) include several items possibly of medieval origin: "The Wee Wee Man" (38), "Tam Lin" (39), "Clerk Colvill" (42), "The Grey Cock" (248), and "Clerk Saunders" (69A–77B). Child's most prolific informant, Anna Gordon Brown (1747–1810), in 1783 copied out a text of "Young Beichan" (53), a ballad on the legendary life of Gilbert Becket, father of the twelfth-century archbishop and martyr, and, some seventeen years later, in response to a request from Sir Walter Scott, contributed the first known version of "Thomas Rymer" (37), ultimately derived from the fourteenth-century romance *Thomas of Erceldoune.*

Nineteenth-century collectors identified a few additional texts of considerable antiquity, most of which found their way into Child's edition: four carols or religious songs—"The Cherry Tree Carol" (54), "The Carnal and the Crane" (55), "Dives and Lazarus" (56), and "The Unquiet Grave" (78)—as well as "The Bitter Withy," "The Holy Well," "Sweet Jesus," "Gloria Tibi Domini," and perhaps the "Boar's Head Carol," along with "The Bold Fisherman." All of these had escaped Child's net. The ballad "Hind Horn" (17) of course derives ultimately from the medieval romance *King Horn,* but it is hard to say whether it had a continuous oral history. The most interesting nineteenth-century recovery is "King Orfeo" (19), first recorded in the Shetlands and published in 1880. The recent discovery of a fragmentary Scottish version strengthens the possibility that this haunting ballad is a true relic of the Middle Ages.

BIBLIOGRAPHY

David Buchan, *The Ballad and the Folk* (1972); *The English and Scottish Popular Ballads,* Francis J. Child, ed., 5 vols. (1882–1898, repr. 1965); David C. Fowler, *A Literary History of the Popular Ballad* (1968); Albert B. Friedman, *The Ballad Revival* (1961); *A Manual of the Writings in Middle English, 1050–1500,* Albert E. Hartung and Burke Severs, eds., VI (1980), esp. "XV Ballads," by David C. Fowler, 1753–1808, 2019–2070 (bibliography); *The Traditional Tunes of the Child Ballads,* Bertrand H. Bronson, ed., 4 vols. (1959–1972); D. K. Wilgus, *Anglo-American Folksong Scholarship since 1898* (1959).

DAVID C. FOWLER

[See also **Middle English Literature; Music, Popular.**]

BALLATA, Italian lyric song form of the thirteenth through fifteenth centuries; derived from songs intended for dancing, as distinguished from the canzona. The text is strophic, with a refrain at the beginning and end of each stanza. The musical form is schematized as *AbbaA:* refrain *(ripresa)* set to first section of music, two verses *(piedi)* set to second section of music, one verse *(volta)* set to first section, refrain. The refrain was originally sung by a chorus of dancers, and the verses by a soloist who led the dance; in the fourteenth century the form was apparently in use as a solo art song. The ballata is identical in structure to the French virelai, although the two forms differ in musical style.

Trecento ballate were categorized by poetic theorists according to the number of lines in the *ri-*

presa: the *ballata minima* or *piccola* (one line, seven or eleven/twelve syllables); *ballata minore* (two lines); *ballata mezzana* (three lines); and *ballata grande* (four lines). The musical settings of *ballate* were typically monophonic until the mid trecento, when they were also written for one voice with an instrument or second voice supplying a countermelody. Monophonic settings appear among the works of Gherardello da Firenze, Lorenzo da Firenze, and Niccolò da Perugia. The polyphonic form was developed principally in Florence and the North between 1360 and 1400, by Francesco Landini, Andreas de Florentia, Bartolino da Padova, Ciconia, and others. Among the numerous ballate by Landini (*d.* 1397), the early works tend to be strictly Italianate (florid melodic style, both voices texted). Later examples show the influence of the French ars nova style (*ouvert-clos* cadences, musical rhyme, syllabic setting of text, one voice texted).

The fifteenth-century ballata seems to have evolved into a purely literary form, like the French *formes fixes* of the same period. Texts are typically love songs, sometimes philosophical aphorisms.

BIBLIOGRAPHY

Ettore Li Gotti, *La poesia musicale italiana del secolo XIV* (1944); Nino Pirrotta, ed., *The Music of Fourteenth-century Italy* (1967); and *Polyphonic Music of the Fourteenth Century,* IV, Leo Schrade, ed. (1958), works of Landini; and VI–XI, W. Thomas Marrocco, ed. (1967–1977), of Italian secular music.

MARCY J. EPSTEIN

[See also **Ars Nova; Landini, Francesco; Virelai.**]

BALLETTE. The *ballette,* originally a dance song, is associated with *rondets, rondels de carole,* rondeaux, and virelais. It corresponds to the Provençal *ballada,* and announces the late French ballade. Though its form remained unfixed until the fourteenth century, it normally contained three strophes *(couplets)* of four to six lines in rhyme or assonance, with the refrain heading the poem repeated after each strophe.

BIBLIOGRAPHY

Jean Frappier, *La poésie lyrique en France aux XIIe et XIIIe siècles* (1949), 22–23, with bibliography; Friedrich Gennrich, *Rondeaux, Virelais, und Balladen aus dem Ende des XII, dem XIII, und dem ersten Drittel des XIV Jahrhunderts* (1921); Théodore Gérold, *La musique au moyen âge* (1932), 147; Nico van den Boogaard, *Rondeaux et refrains du XIIe au début du XIVe siècle* (1969); Paul Zumthor, *Essai de poétique médiévale* (1972), 246, 249, with important bibliography.

JOHN L. GRIGSBY

[See also **Ballade.**]

BALL-FLOWER, a sculptured spherical, three-petaled flower shape enclosing a small ball. It was used decoratively, usually as part of a series set in a concave molding, and was especially popular in English Decorated Gothic architecture during the early fourteenth century.

LESLIE BRUBAKER

BALTIC COUNTRIES/BALTS. The term "Balt" denotes a linguistic group found along the southeastern shore of the Baltic Sea and the rivers that flow into it. Those Baltic peoples also shared a religious and cultural heritage that was noticeably distinct from their Scandinavian, Finno-Ugric, and Slavic neighbors. The term, invented in 1845 by Georg Nesselman, is in common use among linguists and ethnologists. "Aistian" is a common variant, deriving from Tacitus' *Aestiorum gentes.* As usually applied, "Balt" refers only to the ancestors of the modern Latvians and Lithuanians, and to the Old Prussians. However, the Estonians and other Finno-Ugric peoples shared many aspects of the culture, the religion, and the historical experience of the Balts.

The Baltic peoples first came to notice because the amber found on their shores was in great demand among ancient civilizations. Although next to nothing is known about the "amber routes," the contents of countless tombs reveal that amber did travel from the North to the more advanced cultures in the South. However, ancient scholars were unable to discover anything worth reporting about the far northern regions, and the Baltic shores remained shrouded in myth. The earliest useful account is Tacitus' *Germania* (A.D. 98):

> They worship the mother of the gods: as an emblem of that superstition they wear the figures of wild boars: this boar takes the place of arms or of any other protection, and guarantees to the votary of the goddess a mind at rest even in the midst of foes. They use swords rarely, clubs frequently. Grain and other products of the earth they cultivate with a patience out of keeping

BALTIC COUNTRIES/BALTS

> with the lethargy customary to Germans; nay, they ransack the sea also, and are the only people who gather in the shallows and on the shore itself the amber, which they call in their tongue "glaesum."
>
> Nor have they, being barbarians, inquired or learned what substance or process produces it: nay, it lay there long among the rest of the flotsam and jetsam of the sea, until Roman luxury gave it a name. To the natives it is useless: it is gathered crude; is forwarded to Rome unshaped: they are astonished to be paid for it.

Almost a thousand years later, little more was known. The chronicler Adam of Bremen wrote:

> Of these islands the largest, the one called Courland, takes eight days to traverse. The people, exceedingly bloodthirsty because of their stubborn devotion to idolatry, are shunned by everybody. Gold is very plentiful there, the horses are of the best; all the houses are full of pagan soothsayers, diviners, and necromancers, who are even arrayed in a monastic habit. Oracular responses are sought there from all parts of the world, especially by Spaniards and Greeks. . . . We were told, moreover, that there are in this sea many other islands, of which a large one is called Estland. It is not smaller than the one of which we have previously spoken. Its people, too, are utterly ignorant of the God of the Christians. They adore dragons and birds and also sacrifice to them live men whom they buy from the merchants. . . . [Sambia] is inhabited by the Sembi or Prussians, a most humane people, who go out to help those who are in peril at sea or who are attacked by pirates. Gold and silver they hold in very slight esteem. They have an abundance of strange furs, the odor of which has inoculated our world with the deadly poison of pride. But these furs they regard, indeed, as dung, to our shame, I believe, for right or wrong we hanker after a martenskin robe as much as for supreme happiness. Therefore, they offer their very precious marten furs for the woolen garments called faldones. Many praiseworthy things could be said about these peoples with respect to their morals, if only they had the faith of Christ whose missionaries they cruelly persecute. . . . They take the meat of their draft animals for food and use their milk and blood as drink so freely that they are said to become intoxicated. These men are blue of color, ruddy of face, and long-haired. Living, moreover, in inaccessible swamps, they will not endure a master among them.

These rudimentary accounts a thousand years apart reveal the astounding ignorance of the western Europeans regarding Baltic peoples. Since written sources are so poor, scholars are forced to rely very heavily on archaeology to describe the cultures of the region and the great changes they underwent in this millennium.

The indirect contact with the Roman world had issued in the "Golden Age" of the Balts, a time of prosperity and technological development that lasted from the second to the fifth centuries. This development became the basis for a more orderly political life centered in fortified hilltop villages and rude castles. Presumably the clan-oriented social organization reached full development at this time, and the "seniores" of the clans ruled as chiefs or petty kings.

After the fifth century and the decline of the Roman Empire, the economy and society of the Baltic peoples reflected the changed pattern of international trade and the greater need for defense against outside enemies. The Vikings in particular represented a threat, for those hardy adventurers were capturing slaves and selling them in the markets of southern Russia. To ward them off, the Baltic tribes chose chiefs who directed regional defense from strong earthen and wooden forts. The Baltic peoples developed a reputation for being inhospitable and dangerous.

Coin hoards give proof of the Viking presence. While the 7,000 dirhams found in Baltic cemeteries do not compare with the 40,000 unearthed on Gotland, they represent important evidence that the Vikings did not pass through the Baltic lands, but used the waterways around the periphery, and that the traffic was especially strong in the mid ninth century, then declined until the early tenth century. Aside from short-lived Viking settlements in Kurland (Courland), there was apparently no direct rule over any of the native peoples.

The Anglo-Saxon author of the *Vita sancti Anscharii* (876) and Rimbert described large towns in Kurland: 7,000 warriors living in "Saeborg" and 15,000 in "Apulia." While archaeologists have not fully excavated those sites, other towns reveal evidence of trade with Scandinavia and a considerable local commercial production. The amount of silver found is remarkable—in itself proof of exchange, since silver is not mined locally.

This was not a passive commerce. By the middle of the eleventh century, Kurish pirates were raiding Danish settlements; and archaeologists have found Kurish weapons and ornaments along all the Baltic's western coasts, especially on Gotland, the center of Baltic and Scandinavian trade. Simultaneously they have noted Viking motifs entering Baltic ornamentation and adorning Baltic weapons. Their excavations have revealed such a high standard of living combined with a strong artistic sense that some eth-

nologists call the tenth to the twelfth centuries "the second golden age."

Metallurgy, clothing, glass, and pottery became town industries; simultaneously the potter's wheel and millstones replaced the older technologies. The three-field system may have come into limited use in farming, and peas and beans became common. Tools were both more sturdy and more graceful. And silver bars became such a practical currency that they were used well into the Christian era. Horses were highly

BALTIC COUNTRIES/BALTS

prized, and so honored that special cemeteries were made for them.

Almost all fortifications were enlarged and strengthened in this period; the settlements consisted of a strong log-and-earth refuge and a lightly protected village. This construction must have reflected concern about the advancing Danish kings, Russian princes, and Polish dukes. Moreover, German merchants were visiting the river tribes and contesting control of the seas with native pirates and traders. Although the military threats were short-lived, the impact of the direct trade may be judged by the effectiveness of Christian embargoes imposed on individual tribes: by 1200 the native peoples were dependent on imports of cloth, metal, and food. The Baltic warriors' reaction to the threats from the west was to retaliate, attacking their enemies in Poland, Pomerania, and across the Baltic Sea.

This border warfare became closely tied to religion. The Baltic pagans naturally found churches to be especially worthwhile targets for raids, and they took delight in desecrating altars, icons, and other holy objects, and in carrying off the silver, the coins, and the priests (for ransom). The long lines of prisoners and cattle herded away by gloating victors were described in many chronicles of the era. The Christians saw the pagans as a dangerous foe whose conquest and conversion were urgently needed.

Although the Baltic tribes preferred to attack foreigners, they did not hesitate to raid one another. The Lithuanians and Estonians made themselves feared and hated for their brutal incursions to collect slaves and booty.

The Baltic religious practices of this era were complex. The chronicler Peter of Dusburg wrote: "They took erroneously all creations for gods, such as the sun, the moon, and the stars, thunder, birds, and even animals and so on right down to the toads. They had forests, fields, and sacred waters in which no one was allowed to cut down trees, plow, or fish." The worship of the sun, fire, and weather gods was most prominent.

Christian missionaries tended to dismiss the pagan theology, and concentrated on eradicating bigamy, infanticide, and ritual drinking bouts. Later, not trusting native Christians to pass on a true account of the faith, the Church relied on foreign priests who could communicate only the most superficial and superstitious aspects of Christianity.

Christianization came very slowly. The first converts were probably made by Slavic princes, who occupied the southern borderlands in the eleventh century. About 1040, Yaroslav of Kiev subjugated the Sudovians (or Sudavians) and founded Nowogródek (Novogrudok) among the Lithuanians. These territories were later loosely ruled by the Volhynian princes, who encouraged some Slavic immigration and proselytization. From Polotsk the Russians required the chiefs of the Daugava (western Dvina) Valley to pay tribute and become converts to the Orthodox Church. The degree of conversion, however, was not great, and traditional paganism remained almost unaffected.

The Roman Church also made early efforts at missions, but with even less success. Hardly had the Poles been converted (*ca.* 966) than Western missionaries entered Prussia. Adalbert of Prague was martyred there in 997, and Bruno of Querfurt in 1009. Later the archbishops of Hamburg-Bremen followed their Scandinavian successes with missions to Estonia. One in 1143 apparently failed, and subsequent efforts did no better until the 1180's, when an Augustinian friar from Segeberg accompanied merchants to the mouth of the Daugava River and there established a thriving mission. In 1186 this friar, Meinhard, was named bishop of Uxküll (Ikskile). His successors were bishops of Riga (founded 1201).

Meinhard's difficulties with the local converts were directly connected to taxes and tithes. He had built a castle to protect his flock from attack by the stronger neighboring tribes and had garrisoned it with mercenaries. The Livs, both converts and pagans, had promised to reimburse him with taxes, but later refused to pay anything. In desperation Meinhard called on Christian princes for help, and their expeditions soon became crusades.

Under Bishop Albert (1199–1229) these crusades became such a success that castles were built and cities were founded; and then a crusading order, the Brothers of the Sword (Fratres Militae Christi), was created to garrison the fortresses and carry the war to the tribes that remained pagan. As these German crusaders came into the regions subject to the Russians, they did not hesitate to see the Orthodox Church as a heretic organization; they supplanted the handful of priests and tax collectors, and defeated the armies that attempted to drive them away. Livonia became a crusader state, governed by bishops, abbots, semi-independent cities, and a military religious order.

The arrival of crusaders presented a new problem to the Baltic tribes, but they did not quickly recognize it, mistakenly identifying the newcomers as seekers of booty and tribute. That they made this

BALTIC COUNTRIES/BALTS

error is understandable, because some of the first crusading ventures were nothing more than raids: the Swedes who came in support of Bishop Meinhard in 1196 landed in the wrong province, then sailed home after ravaging the countryside for three days and collecting tribute. Similarly, the Poles and Pomeranians who invaded Culm (Chetmno) and Pogesania early in the thirteenth century were simply imperialists intent on expanding their domains.

The crusading movement, however, had a different dynamic nature. It was not to be distracted by disputes over inheritances, marriage alliances, or the difficulty of the task. Skilled warriors were coming from hitherto unconceived distances to fight on behalf of bishops and crusading orders they hardly knew; and they went home, without riches or booty, to encourage others to emulate them. Secular rulers could not have hired mercenaries of such capability, nor have rewarded their vassals sufficiently to persuade them to persevere in the wars. The only gains were spiritual or (in the case of the numerous merchants) some profit from trade. The crusaders kept coming, expending blood and treasure to bring Christ to the pagans. Their numbers, equipment, and commitment enabled them to wear down the militarily backward Baltic peoples.

The response to the newcomers varied. Most tribes remained neutral until attacked, and some attacked their endangered kinsmen from the rear, using the opportunity to seek revenge for past insults. A few even welcomed the Westerners. When the Livs allied themselves with the crusaders, that tribe, once despised and raided by everyone, became powerful and respected. Their chiefs were rewarded with booty, slaves, and prestige; and their principal chief, Caupo, was taken to Rome for an audience with the pope. For a century Liv warriors were supporters of the Christian cause, exercising an important voice in military affairs and proudly lording it over traditional rivals; Liv peasants had light taxes and few labor duties.

The neighboring Lettgallians (or Latgalians) resisted longer, but came over to the crusaders when they discovered that the newcomers would aid them against the dreaded Estonian raiding parties. The Kurs also yielded quickly, succumbing to famine rather than conquest, and surrendering their political independence for food brought from Germany.

The Estonians alone resisted to the last. Militarily dominant in the north, they saw nothing to gain from the new religion. But they could not resist the German knights and the entire strength of the Livs and Lettgallians, much less the Scandinavian, German, and Slavic vassals that King Waldemar II of Denmark summoned to Reval (Talinn) in 1219. Although apparently beaten, the Estonians did not accept the defeat as final. They rebelled in 1223, capturing several castles belonging to the Brothers of the Sword and the Danes, and they fought on until 1227.

Realizing that even then the Estonians were not reconciled to their fate, the papal legate, William of Modena, called in secular nobles from northern Germany to rule them—a practice not necessary in Livonia. This mistrust was proved correct in 1343, when the Estonians rose in a terrible and desperate insurrection, slaughtered every Christian man, woman, and child they could find, and called on Russians and Lithuanians to aid them. When that rising was suppressed in blood (1345), the crusaders disarmed the Estonians and made many into serfs. In any case, from the beginning most Estonians had to pay double taxes as a penalty for apostasy, and were required to perform heavy labor duties. In 1346 the Danish king sold Estonia to the Teutonic Order.

The Semgallians (or Semigallians) sought a crusader alliance against their Samogitian neighbors and, despite several changes of heart, generally remained loyal to the Christians until the battle of the Saule in 1236. That decisive engagement in Samogitia destroyed both the Brothers of the Sword Order and hopes of conquering all the Baltic coastal provinces immediately. Independence, however, did not suit the Semgallian needs, and by 1240 they were again seeking Christian aid against the Samogitians. Thereafter they were subject to the city of Riga, the archbishop of Riga, and the Teutonic Knights (who had absorbed the Brothers of the Sword). Their duties were among the most favorable granted to a native people, equivalent to those performed by the Livs.

This state of affairs lasted until 1259, when the Teutonic Knights suffered a military defeat and levied an emergency tax on all their subjects. The Semgallians refused to pay it, and bade the crusaders depart peacefully. The latter went, but returned with armies. From 1260 to 1289 Semgallia was a battleground. At length the tribes abandoned the country, or surrendered and allowed themselves to be resettled in the northern reaches of their land. Heavy taxes and duties were imposed, and the southern areas became a border wilderness.

As the northern Baltic peoples were suffering defeat, so were the southern ones. The crusader ad-

BALTIC COUNTRIES/BALTS

vance along the Baltic shores could be said to predate the Crusade of 1147, in which Danes and Germans had crushed the Mecklenburg and Pomeranian pagans. The *Drang nach dem Osten* ("Push to the East") was an old movement, one supported by Holy Roman emperors and Saxon dukes, but in 1147 it took on a new momentum and was supplemented by a permanent settlement of German farmers and burghers. Soon this immigration passed the limits of German political control, as Polish and Pomeranian dukes invited pioneers to farm the swamps and forests of their underpopulated lands. In the late twelfth century these dukes were moving east, leading the way with armies while settling immigrants on their western territories.

The eastward thrust of the Poles and Pomeranians hit the Prussians at the westernmost bend of the Vistula River, in Culm, and then in Pogesania, Pomesania, and Galindia. Although at first driven back with heavy losses, the Poles later established a foothold in Culm, the Pomeranians claimed coastal Pogesania, and the heavy fighting in Galindia resulted in the virtual destruction of the native settlements there.

The Prussian reaction to this pressure was isolated retaliation, each tribe making war individually. Soon the Prussian warriors were devastating the nearest parts of the Masovian and Kujavian duchies in Poland, and making inroads in Pomerania.

The Christian responses to this were diverse: paying tribute, sending missionaries, and seeking the aid of crusading orders. The payment of tribute was difficult, since Poland was not a country rich in coinage, and there were too many chiefs to pay off all of them effectively. Missionary activity came without significant planning. The martyrdom of earlier missionaries had not been forgotten when a Cistercian monk named Christian was sent from the monastery at Lekno in 1207 to ransom prisoners from Sambia. He discovered that some Prussians were receptive to proselytization, and soon he was authorized to organize missionary work. In 1215 he was named bishop of Prussia.

Despite his numerous conversions, however, Bishop Christian did not win over the majority of any tribe; and the initial wave of baptism was followed by stagnation and even ebb. Just as had happened in Livonia, the missionaries found it easier to persuade individuals to accept the cross than to pay the tithe; and they found it almost impossible to bring all the people to accept doctrines that flew in the face of native custom. The hard-core pagans were unwilling to abandon bigamy, exposure of female children, cremation of the dead, and the superstitious reverence for forest and sky gods—much less to pay taxes. Bishop Christian eventually sought military aid from Poland and Pomerania, which was a mistake: he had to go into exile with the retreating crusaders.

The last remedy against Prussian attack was to call in crusading orders. Hardly a major order did not send some knights, and Duke Konrad of Masovia founded an order of his own, the Dobriner Order, which had ties to the Brothers of the Sword in Livonia; of these, only a relatively new and unimportant order, the Teutonic Knights, proved effective. In 1230 they established a foothold in Culm, and by 1234 they had moved down the Vistula River, conquering parts of Pomesania and Pogesania with the aid of numerous Polish and Pomeranian crusaders. A handful of crusaders came from the Holy Roman Empire, but they were not especially significant until civil war broke out in Poland after the Mongol invasion of 1240–1241. After the Polish withdrawal from the conflict, Prussia became the responsibility of the Teutonic Order, which in the next decades shifted its main effort from the Holy Land to the Baltic.

The "converted" Prussians rose in rebellion in 1242, offering to become subjects of the duke of Pomerania if he would aid them. That began a desperate war that ended in the Treaty of Christburg (1249). Imposed by a papal legate rather than negotiated, the treaty is a basic source of knowledge about the habits of the natives and the excesses of the early crusaders. In effect, the Prussian warriors were guaranteed full security of their rights and estates as long as they were outwardly Christian and fought alongside the Teutonic Knights against the enemies of the Church. The lower classes were protected from manorialization and serfdom as long as they acknowledged the Christian faith, paid specified taxes and the tithe, and served in the militia.

The expedition of King Ottokar of Bohemia completed the conquest of the maritime Prussians in 1254, when his army overawed the militant Sambians (or Samlanders). (The crusaders named the principal castle of Sambia Königsberg in his memory.) The Teutonic Knights then moved across the Nemunas (Neman) to attack the Samogitians, who practically annihilated crusading armies in 1259 and 1260. In the latter year they inflicted the crushing loss at Durben, where the crusaders were unable to persuade their native allies to agree on the division

BALTIC COUNTRIES/BALTS

of booty before the battle. The Kurs subsequently pulled out of the battle line, leaving the Livonian and Prussian forces in an untenable position. Many knights and most of the loyal native warriors fell.

The insurrection of 1260 followed. The Nattangians (or Natangians), Warmians, and Bartians were first in the field, capturing some castles and isolating others; later the rising spread into the eastern provinces, into Sambia, and into Livonia. The Teutonic Order, which relied heavily on native warriors to fill the ranks of its armies, was hard pressed to maintain itself until crusading armies from the Holy Roman Empire came to the rescue. In 1283 the Sudovians, the last tribe to maintain its independence, divided into two parts, one surrendering and accepting resettlement, the other going into permanent exile in Lithuania.

Now the only Baltic people to remain independent were the Lithuanians, and they were under attack from Germans, Poles, Russians, and Tatars. Their ability to resist was strong, however, because of their fortunate geographical situation, their relative unity and numbers, and their superior leadership; moreover, after the Tatar invasion, some northern and western Russians placed themselves under Lithuanian protection. This gave prestige and wealth to the foremost Lithuanian chief, Mindaugas (Mindoug) who made himself supreme over his rivals in the mid thirteenth century. Although he converted to Christianity briefly, he lapsed to paganism after the battle of Durben.

A new dynasty was founded at the beginning of the fourteenth century by Vitus; and his successor, Gedimin, ruled one of the largest states in Europe. Gedimin's sons, Kęstutis (Kiestut) and Algirdas (Olgierd) divided Lithuania into eastern and western regions as a "diarchy," Kęstutis being responsible for fighting the Teutonic Knights and Algirdas for fighting Russia. Kęstutis was generally on the defensive, resisting crusaders who came from Germany, Bohemia, Austria, France, and Britain to strike into Samogitia from Prussia and Livonia. That situation lasted until Jogaila, Algirdas' son, became king of Poland and combined with Vytautas, Kęstutis' son, to defeat the Teutonic Knights at Tannenberg in 1410. Subsequently the Lithuanians were the junior partners in a combined Polish-Lithuanian state. They accepted Western Christianity and slowly lost their close ties with their Russian subjects.

The Baltic lands became a part of the Western economy, exporting grain, furs, and beeswax to the Hanseatic cities. Some natives drifted into the towns as artisans and laborers, and were partly assimilated into the north German culture of the burghers and gentry. The vast majority of the natives, however, knew little about the Western culture beyond the payment of taxes, the administration of justice, and the rudiments of the Christian religion. They benefited from the strong government, the maintenance of law and order, and the protection from foreign invasion, but they did not benefit as much as did their German rulers.

The thirteenth century had proved decisive for Baltic history. Only the Lithuanians had retained their political independence, their pagan religion, and major aspects of their ancient way of life. The Kurs, Semgallians, Livs, and Lettgallians began melting together to become Latvians. The Prussians ultimately disappeared, becoming culturally and linguistically Germans and Poles. The Estonians remained essentially unchanged. All suffered the loss of land and liberty, although historians are far from agreeing on the timing or the extent of the process.

The spread of serfdom proceeded at an uneven pace. The earliest treaties with the native people indicate that the Christian rulers imposed only relatively light duties on the converts—often only four days' work in the fields annually, work on fortifications, light taxes, and military service. The Teutonic Knights apparently did not seek to herd the allied tribes onto manors and teach them the more successful farming techniques of the West. They had attempted that in the first years of the conquest, and had learned from the rebellions not to repeat the mistake. They saw that the only way to modernize the economy and to assure themselves of a loyal peasantry was to attract immigrants from north Germany, Poland, and Pomerania. Ultimately this policy made the natives a minority in Prussia, although it had practically no effect in the more distant and colder Livonia.

The status of the Prussians declined greatly during the Thirteen Year War (1454–1466). This great conflict brought Polish armies and German mercenaries into the country, and disrupted the stable society that had characterized the governance of the crusading order. The Teutonic Knights needed money or lands to pay their mercenaries, and consequently they could not protect their vassals and peasants as they had in the past. The native nobility became absorbed into the German gentry; the peasants were forced onto the new manors and eventually were amalgamated into the German and Polish population as day laborers and serfs.

In Livonia serfdom probably spread through the introduction of prisoners of war onto manors or vacant lands. Unfortunately, source materials are poor and contradictory. All that can be said with certainty is that serfdom was well established by the sixteenth century, and that most of the peasants remaining free lost their rights during the terrible Livonian War (1557–1583), when Russians, Swedes, Danes, and Poles fought over the land. The peasants were sacrificed to reward the mercenary soldiers with estates.

Dominant over the coastal Baltic peoples was a Germanic culture that had twin roots—in the Hanseatic cities and in the petty nobles and gentry that owned the estates, filled the government offices, and served as military officers. The Germans generally excluded natives from all important offices and occupations. Nevertheless, such was the attraction of this Western culture and Western religion that the Latvians and Estonians were later able to resist russification effectively.

In the interior, particularly in Lithuania, Polish models predominated. The Roman Catholic church, so long resisted as a threat to national existence, became the most important institution in preserving national identity.

BIBLIOGRAPHY

Sources. Adam of Bremen, *History of the Archbishops of Hamburg-Bremen,* Francis Tschan, trans. (1959), 197–199; Henricus Lettus, *The Chronicle of Henry of Livonia,* James Brundage, trans. (1961); *The Livonian Rhymed Chronicle,* Jerry Smith and William Urban, trans. (1977); Wilhelm Mannhardt, *Letto-Preussische Götterlehre* (1936); Tacitus, *Germania,* William Peterson, trans. (1914), 328–329. The chronicles are collected in *Scriptores rerum Prussicarum,* 6 vols. (1965–1968). Documents are found in Georg von Bunge *et al.*, eds., *Liv-, Est-, und Kurlaendisches Urkundenbuch,* 17 vols. (1967–); and Rudolf Philippi *et al.*, eds., *Preussisches Urkundenbuch* (begun in 1961).

Studies. Friedrich Benninghoven, *Der Orden der Schwertbrueder* (1965); Eric Christiansen, *The Northern Crusades* (1980); Marija Gimbutas, *The Balts* (1963); Edgar Johnson, "The German Crusade on the Baltic," in Kenneth Setton, ed., *A History of the Crusades,* III (1975), 545–585; Thomas S. Noonan, "Pre-970 Dirham Hoards from Estonia and Latvia," in *Journal of Baltic Studies,* 8 (1977), and 9 (1978); and "The Nature of Medieval Russian–Estonian Relations, 850–1015," in Arvids Ziedonis, Jr., William Winter, and Mardi Valgemäe, eds., *Baltic History* (1974), 13–20; William Schmalstieg, *Studies in Old Prussian* (1976); Arnolds Spekke, *History of Latvia* (1951); Marian Tumler, *Der Deutsche Orden; Werden, Wachsen, und Wirkung bis 1400* (1955); William Urban, *The Baltic Crusade* (1975), *The Prussian Crusade* (1980), and *The Livonian Crusade* (1981).

WILLIAM L. URBAN

[See also **Chivalry, Orders of; Crusades, Political; Lithuania.**]

BAMBERG MANUSCRIPT (Lit. 115), a music manuscript copied about 1300, is of uncertain origin, but probably was written west of the Rhine. The main body of the manuscript contains one hundred motets, copied in alphabetical order. All are double motets, with different texts in each of the upper parts, and all but one are for three voices. Forty-four have two Latin texts—an unusually high proportion of Latin double motets, probably reflecting the repertory as it circulated in regions somewhat peripheral to the mainstream of motet cultivation. Forty-seven use two French texts; and nine have texts in both Latin and French. Despite the seeming homogeneity of the repertory, the works come from a wide variety of backgrounds that span virtually the entire early history of the motet—from clausulae with text added to the upper voice, to works based on French songs, to compositions by Adam de la Halle.

Few of the motets are entirely unique. Some may be of peripheral origin, especially those in which the upper parts move in phrases of equal length and rhythmic contour, reminiscent of the conductus motet; these betray a conservative style that seems to have lingered in an area somewhat removed from the mainstream of compositional development. The motets are followed by a conductus and seven remarkable clausulae, all created in a progressive idiom. Of the clausulae no fewer than six are hockets, and five are unique to the Bamberg manuscript. Five are settings of the "in seculum" portion of the plainchant gradual *Haec dies, Confitemini: In seculum longum,* attributed by the theorist Anonymous IV to "a certain Spaniard," and widely circulated in different forms; *In seculum breve,* a rhythmic transformation of the polyphonic fabric of the preceding hocket and ascribed by Anonymous IV to "a Parisian"; *In seculum viellatoris,* not a hocket, its rubric ("the *In seculum* of the vielle player") prompting speculation about thirteenth-century performance practices; and *In seculum d'Amiens longum,* a hocket apparently associated with Amiens and followed by *In seculum d'Amiens breve,* another example of the transfor-

BAN, BANALITÉ

mation of the rhythmic substance of a polyphonic composition.

BIBLIOGRAPHY

Gordon A. Anderson, "Notre Dame Latin Double Motets, *ca.* 1215–1250," in *Musica disciplina,* 25 (1971); "The Notation of the Bamberg and Las Huelgas Manuscripts," *ibid.,* 32 (1978); and *idem,* ed., *Compositions of the Bamberg Manuscript: Bamberg, Staatsbibliothek, lit. 115 (olim Ed. IV. 6)* (1977); Pierre Aubry, *Cent motets du XIIIe siècle,* 3 vols. (1908); Friedrich Ludwig, *Repertorium organorum recentioris et motetorum vetustissimi stili,* I, pt. 2 (1978), 472–504; Ernest H. Sanders, "Peripheral Polyphony of the Thirteenth Century," in *Journal of the American Musicological Society,* 17 (1964).

EDWARD H. ROESNER

[See also **Motet; Motet Manuscripts.**]

BAN, BANALITÉ. Ban *(bannus)* was the royal power to command and punish, mentioned as early as the fifth century in the Germanic law codes. According to Carolingian capitularies of the late eighth and early ninth centuries, the ban encompassed three areas of public law: protection of the defenseless (churches, widows, minors, orphans); jurisdiction over crimes of violence (arson, rape, assault); and the military obligation of all freemen. Decentralization of government in the ninth and tenth centuries resulted in the delegation of the ban to royal officials (counts) and to prelates who exercised royal authority within immunized ecclesiastical lands. In the western half of the Carolingian Empire (France, Belgium), from the late tenth century, the ban often devolved to castellans, either by delegation or by usurpation from the counts, and to other powerful landlords who imposed protection on weak monasteries and thereby usurped the ban within ecclesiastical immunities.

Texts from the eleventh and twelfth centuries refer to the ban as an unrestricted territorial authority, usually associated with the exercise of justice, in the hands of the great landed aristocracy and some prelates. But the term *bannus* in that sense was gradually displaced by other terms (*districtus* and *potestas* in northern France and Belgium, *mandamentum* in southern France and Catalonia), and came to denote an economic monopoly imposed by landlords on tenants. The four most common *banalités* (the French term by which they are generally referred) were the obligations to grind grain at the landlord's mill (usually a water mill), to bake bread at his oven, to press grapes at his wine press, and to respect his exclusive right to sell wine during prescribed periods. Banal monopolies were not imposed uniformly in any region but varied widely, depending on landlords and local conditions, although banal mills were prevalent in the grain-producing regions of the north and banal ovens were common in the south.

Payments for the use of banal facilities were exacted in kind, as a percentage of items processed (grain, wine, loaves of bread), and thus were indexed to the volume of tenant agricultural production and to commodity prices, both of which rose steadily through the thirteenth century. The exact contribution of banal revenues to a landlord's annual income is impossible to determine, but they could be significant economic resources at a time when tenurial rents were fixed by custom at relatively low levels. Banal revenues were often assigned in whole or in part as fiefs to knights.

Opinions differ as to the origin and evolution of the *banalités.* Most regional monographs and all secondary studies now follow the thesis of Georges Duby, according to which the counts and castellans transformed the ban (political and military power) into a nonlanded type of lordship (banal lordship) over all inhabitants within range of a castle, and created a new set of exactions, including protection and head taxes, and the *banalités.* An alternate explanation, yet to be adequately documented, argues that banal monopolies derived ultimately from landlordship and were imposed as a consequence of peasant tenure, not residence.

BIBLIOGRAPHY

The various meanings of *bannus* are indicated (in English) in *Mediae Latinitatis Lexicon Minus,* J. F. Niermeyer, ed. (1976). A summary of theses about the evolution of the ban and the origin of *banalités* is C. Van de Kieft, "Gruit en ban," in *Tijdscrift voor Geschiedenis,* 77 (1964), translated as "Monopole de vente du 'gruit' et droit de ban," in *Acta historiae Neerlandica,* 1 (1966). General treatments are Georges Duby, *Rural Economy and Country Life in the Medieval West* (1962), Cynthia Postan, trans. (1968), 187–189, 205, 224–231; Robert Fossier, *Histoire sociale de l'Occident médiéval* (1970), 195–201; Guy Fourquin, *Lordship and Feudalism in the Middle Ages,* Iris and A. L. Lytton Sells, trans. (1976), 36–37, 46–54, 169–172.

THEODORE EVERGATES

[See also **Feudalism; Law, French, in North; Law, French, in South.**]

BANA, an aisled tetraconch in the ancient Georgian province of Tao (now in Turkey). This imposing cathedral built of ashlar is now a ruin. Before its destruction by the Turks in the nineteenth century, it was visited and described by Karl Koch. The structure is the same type as Zuart^{c}noc^{c} and the Syrian tetraconchs. Above the ambulatory are a gallery that opens inward and, between the crossarms, four three-story rectangular compartments that serve to support the dome. The columns in the conchs have highly transformed Ionic and Corinthian capitals. The exterior walls of the cathedral are adorned with continuous, shallow blind arcades, and carvings of stylized pomegranate motifs fill the spandrels. The diameter of the masonry dome was about ten meters.

According to an eleventh-century chronicle the cathedral was built in 881–923 by Kvirike Baneli, who became the first bishop of Bana.

BIBLIOGRAPHY

E. Takaīshvili, "Bana," in *Materialy po Arkheologii Kavkaza,* **12** (1909), 88–117.

W. Djobadze

[See also **Georgian Art and Architecture.**]

BANAT, the general term applied to any of the frontier territories of the kingdom of Hungary, each governed by a banus, south of the border along the Sava River and the Carpathian Mountains. Most of them were under pressure from—and occasionally lost to—Bosnia, Serbia, Wallachia, and other states. The most important banats, that of Macsó (Machoviensis, Mačva), between the Drina and Morava Rivers, and that of Severin, stretching to the Lower Danube (in 1247–1260 granted to the Knights Hospitalers; in 1429–1432, to the Teutonic Knights), were important outposts of defense until their conquest by the Ottoman Empire (1496, 1521–1524). The banat of Jajca (Jajce), established in 1464, stood until 1528.

BIBLIOGRAPHY

I. C. Filitti, "Banatul Olteniei si Craioveştii" ["The banat of Oltenia and the Craioveştii family"], in *Arhiva Olteniei,* **11** (1932); *Monumenta Hungariae historica,* pt. I, *Diplomataria,* XXXI, XXXIII, XXXVI, XL, esp. XL on the banat of Jajce: Lajos Thallóczy et al., eds., *Codex diplomaticus partium regno Hungariae,* 4 vols. (1903–1915); Frigyes Pesthy, "A macsói bánok" [The bani of Macsó], in *Századok,* **9** (1875); and *A Szörényi bánság és Szörény vármegye története* [History of the banat of Severin and the county of Szörény], 3 vols. (1877–1878), esp. III.

J. M. Bak

[See also **Banus; Hungary.**]

BANDAMANNA SAGA ("Saga of the Confederate Chieftains") is one of the most skillfully composed of the Icelandic family sagas and the only full-blown comedy. It tells the story of a young man, Oddr, who lives in disharmony with his father, Ófeigr, and leaves home to win fame and fortune in the shipping business. Once resettled in Iceland, he ignores his father, but enters into a friendship with the ne'er-do-well Óspakr. Before setting out on a new trading venture, he leaves his property and chieftainship in Óspakr's custody. On his return, Óspakr's true nature emerges when he tries to withhold the chieftainship. Oddr repossesses it by force, and the two part on chilly terms.

When Oddr soon afterward loses forty sheep, suspicion falls on Óspakr. Oddr's friend Váli attempts to settle the matter quietly, and is killed by Óspakr. Oddr institutes legal proceedings, but his power and prosperity have given rise to envy and his case is disallowed on a technicality. His father, now old, shows up in the nick of time, and bribes the jury to reconsider the case and declare Óspakr an outlaw. The rival chieftains are angered and band together, eight strong, to prosecute Oddr for bribery, but Ófeigr once more intervenes to detach two of the chieftains from the conspiracy (with renewed bribery and the promise of an advantageous marriage) and play the decision into their hands. They keep their part of the bargain by imposing a risible fine on Oddr and responding to the outraged protests of their confederates insult for insult. The saga concludes with the ample rewarding of the two venal chieftains, a happy reconciliation between Oddr and his father, and the death of the outlawed Óspakr.

The development of character and comic dialogue in *Bandamanna saga* is unsurpassed. The sharp-witted and sharp-tongued old father, the brilliantly successful but naive son, the villain, the faithful friend, and the assemblage of fatuous chieftains are all drawn with deft strokes. In particular the dialogue scenes in which Ófeigr subtly cajoles the jury and the two corrupt chieftains by expounding an irresistible morality of self-interest are among the most famous in saga literature. The humor in the saga is almost entirely at the expense of the greedy chieftains, and the author has therefore been credited with a distinctly antiaristocratic bias. These social overtones add much to the richness of the text.

Bandamanna saga is preserved in two medieval manuscripts—AM 132, fol. (Mǫðruvallabók), from the middle of the fourteenth century, and Gl. kgl. sml. 2845, 4° (Konungsbók), from the fifteenth century—that represent differing redactions. *M* is about one-fifth longer, and the texts never correspond exactly for more than two lines. Hallvard Magerøy has studied the problem closely and has resolved the priorities in favor of *M*. *K* is an abbreviation. The polished art of the saga suggests a date in the second half of the thirteenth century, during the full flowering of the genre. The story is set in the eleventh century (later than most family sagas), but no historical basis for the account is known to us aside from references to the quarrel between Oddr and Óspakr in *Eyrbyggja saga* and *Grettis saga*.

BIBLIOGRAPHY

Edition. Guðni Jónsson, ed., *Grettis saga Ásmundarsonar; Bandamanna saga* (1936), 293–363.

Translations. Hermann Pálsson, trans., *The Confederates and Hen-Thorir* (1975), 43–90; M. H. Scargill and Margaret Schlauch, trans., *Three Icelandic Sagas* (1950), 55–93.

Criticism. Hallvard Magerøy, *Studiar i Bandamanna saga* (1957).

THEODORE M. ANDERSSON

[See also **Eyrbyggja Saga; Grettis Saga Asmundarsonar; Sagas, Legendary.**]

BANGOR (WALES). St. Deiniol or Daniel (*d.* 584) founded a monastic community at Bangor in Arfon, Gwynedd, during the mid to late sixth century. According to tradition, St. Dyfrig (Dubricius) consecrated Deiniol as Bangor's first bishop. Deiniol is said to have been succeeded by his son Deiniolen, who was supposedly brought up at the neighboring monastery of Bangor Iscoed, which was destroyed by Æthelfrith in 616. The next known bishop of Bangor was Elfoddw (or Elfodd, *fl.* 768–809), who was also bishop of the establishments of Abergele Rhos and Caergybi. The *Annales Cambriae* credit Elfoddw with bringing Gwynedd into conformity with Rome by means of his Easter reforms. Nennius, who compiled at least part of the *Historia Brittonum,* was Elfoddw's disciple and probable successor. From this time on, Bangor was known as one of the chief bishoprics in Wales.

Originally Bangor's jurisdiction, like that of other Celtic bishoprics, was not based upon a territorial see. Rather, its bishop held authority over the monastery of St. Deiniol, its daughter foundations, and any other churches that chose to include themselves under his sway. With the Norman conquest, however, Bangor was reorganized as a diocese encompassing the territory of Gwynedd and under the jurisdiction of Canterbury. But before this change could be accomplished, a long and bitter struggle ensued.

The last bishop of Bangor before Norman interference was Revedun, who was consecrated by Bishop Sulien (1072/1073–1078, 1080–1085) of St. David's. In 1092 a Breton, Hervé (Hervey), was appointed bishop by William II and consecrated by Thomas of York. Hervé did not stay long in Bangor, and the see remained vacant until 1120, when a Welsh candidate nominated by Gruffydd ap Cynan was consecrated at Canterbury. Gruffydd's son Owain Gwynedd continued the fight, first by unsuccessfully resisting the Norman nominee, Meurig. After Meurig's death in 1161, Owain extracted an oath from the canons that they would elect no bishop against his will, and kept the see vacant until his candidate Arthur of Bardsey was elected bishop and consecrated in Ireland (1166), against the commands of the archbishop of Canterbury, Thomas Becket, who was in exile. Owain's fight, culminating in the election of Gwion, 22 May 1177, gave Bangor a measure of independence until the conquest by Edward I in 1284.

BIBLIOGRAPHY

For a history of Bangor, see James Conway Davies, ed., *Episcopal Acts and Cognate Documents Relating to Welsh Dioceses 1066–1272,* I (1946), 30–37, 76–101; II (1948–1949), 415–491. See also John E. Lloyd, *A History of Wales from the Earliest Times to the Edwardian Conquest,* 3rd ed. (1939), I, 175, 192–193; II, 448–449, 455, 481–484, 521. For a summary of St. Deiniol's life, see Sabine Baring-Gould and John Fisher, *Lives of the British Saints* (1908), II, 323–331.

MARILYN KAY KENNEY

[See also **Celtic Church; Wales, Early History.**]

BANGOR, RITE OF. There is substantial disagreement among historians as to the existence of a distinct liturgical use in the Welsh diocese of Bangor during the Middle Ages. According to an introduction to the Book of Common Prayer in the sixteenth century, there was in England such a use along with those of Sarum and Hereford, yet the meager extant manuscript evidence indicates at best a slight variation on the Sarum.

From the period antedating the Norman Conquest there no longer seem to exist liturgical books or descriptions of a peculiar liturgical use in Bangor. With the coming of the Norman bishop Hervey (*d.* 1131) to Bangor, it is probable that the Roman rite, perhaps in a form not greatly different from that used in Sarum, would have replaced an old Celtic or Insular use.

Often the Bangor use has been attributed to Bishop Anian (1267–1305), who rebuilt the cathedral after the conquest of Wales by the English and who baptized the future King Edward II. But there is, aside from a single pontifical, almost no surviving manuscript evidence to indicate what liturgical use he instituted.

In the nineteenth century the distinguished liturgiologist William Maskell discovered what he took to be manuscripts of a missal and a pontifical used in Bangor, and he attempted to isolate those aspects of liturgical practice he considered peculiar to Bangor.

Among those in the missal were variations in several of the Mass prayers and minor changes in the rubrics. But close inspection reveals that most of these "peculiarities" are minor variations on the Sarum rite and that many can be found in other extant Sarum books. Moreover, there is serious doubt that the late English missal Maskell examined was for use in Bangor.

Maskell's pontifical of Bangor was written about 1291 for Bishop Anian. It was twice lost, once in the fifteenth century and once during the Civil War, but about 1700, thanks to Bishop Humphreys, it found its way back to Bangor, where it now belongs to the Cathedral Library and is kept at the University College of North Wales. The contents of the pontifical are very similar to those of other contemporary English pontificals, and where they differ, it is primarily in the omission, not the alteration, of ceremonies.

The historian is thus reduced to speculation about the use of Bangor. It is probable that Bangor, like any diocese, had its own liturgical peculiarities. As a diocese on the periphery of English ecclesiastical life, its practices may well have been the subject of special comment. However, whether these practices were different enough from those of the English dioceses to make of them a separate use is a question still unanswered.

BIBLIOGRAPHY

William Maskell, *Monumenta ritualia ecclesiae anglicanae*, I (1846), cxv–cxviii; and *The Ancient Liturgy of the Church of England* (1882), cliv–140; Archdale A. King, *Liturgies of the Past* (1959), 369–373; John Brückmann, "Latin Manuscript Pontificals and Benedictionals in England and Wales," in *Traditio*, 29 (1973), 402–403, 452.

ROGER E. REYNOLDS

[See also **Sarum Rite.**]

BANKING, EUROPEAN. European banking originated in twelfth-century Italy, and throughout the Middle Ages Italians and Italian technique played a critical role in the development of credit institutions that are today considered a part of modern banking.

The decline of Roman civilization and the establishment of Germanic successor states brought in their wake a falling off of economic activity in the western part of the old empire. Population dwindled, cities decayed, and trade, commerce, and industry stagnated in an increasingly agricultural world. Mercantile ventures did not cease in the early Middle Ages; coins continued to circulate and credit transactions were frequent.

However, the relatively scanty references to credit that survive from the period indicate that lending was occasional and destined to satisfy immediate consumption needs. Such trade as existed was in the hands of foreigners—Jews, Syrians, and Greeks, who distributed luxury wares from the East to a small, aristocratic clientele. Only the moneyers who had a close connection with the few producing mints could be categorized as consistent providers of credit. The West between the sixth and the late tenth centuries was a relatively underdeveloped area in comparison with Byzantium or the Islamic world. In a society devoid of commerce and industry there is little opportunity for professional moneymen and no need for organized credit institutions.

The economic recovery of western Europe began in the tenth century. The primary factor in this re-

BANKING, EUROPEAN

covery was population growth. At just what time the pattern of low population, low consumption, and low production was broken is not certain, although the consequences of demographic expansion are clearly in evidence by the late tenth century. The maritime cities of Italy provide the earliest examples of commercial expansion. Venice, Amalfi, Gaeta, and Naples were followed by Genoa and Pisa in strengthening their ties with Constantinople. By the eleventh century the interior towns of the Italian peninsula also experienced the effects of population growth, which produced increased investment in trade, industry, and mercantile activity. From Italy the "commercial revolution" radiated outward to ultramontane Europe. Until the early fourteenth century, commercial and industrial expansion provided the foundation upon which medieval banking developed.

The earliest evidence of medieval banking comes from Genoese notarial materials of the mid and late twelfth century. In maritime Genoa *cambitor* ("changer") and *bancherius,* a term derived from the *banchus* ("table") at which the banker did his business, were synonymous. The oldest Genoese notarial cartulary, that of John the Scribe, covering the years 1155–1164, suggests that the changers had not yet begun the expansion of their operations into the fields of credit, deposit, and transfer banking that were to become integral components of the changers' art in the Middle Ages.

The *bancherii* named in the contracts redacted by John conducted their affairs in much the same way as other businessmen: their obligations were simple purchase-sale contracts, investments in overseas trade, real estate deals, and the like. There is nothing in the mid-twelfth-century sources to indicate that the Genoese *bancherii* were anything but mere money changers.

The last quarter of the twelfth century marks the period of expansion of the changers' activities into banking proper. The notarial contracts pertaining to the business of some twenty Genoese *bancherii* reveal that changers were granting loans to and accepting deposits from their clients. The Genoese changers received deposits upon which they promised to return a fixed interest rate, apparently in the neighborhood of 10 percent per year. In a second type of deposit, the Genoese bankers agreed to share with the investor profits earned on the deposited capital. In 1186 one Andreas, servant of the great Fieschi family, handed over £7 to Rubeus *bancherius,* who promised to return the capital fifteen days after demand, adding that "if God should give me any profit on these pounds, I will give you as much of it as seems best to me." This kind of flexible arrangement between banker and depositor survived into the fifteenth century as the deposit *a discrezione;* its longevity was due perhaps to the ecclesiastical prohibition on the taking of interest (usury). But it is also true that despite the greater risk inherent in the deposit *a discrezione,* the possibility of larger profits led investors to prefer this type of agreement and ensured its continued use.

Although specific interest rates are seldom mentioned in medieval banking contracts, there can be no doubt that bankers paid and charged interest on deposits and loans. In the strictest sense, canon law defined any return on a straight loan *(mutuum)* greater than the amount advanced as usurious and sinful. As a practical matter, however, canon lawyers and moral philosophers developed a more accommodating position in regard to lending. In the life of the marketplace a conventional rate of about 10 percent was paid on deposits and around 20 percent interest was charged on loans without attracting the ire of ecclesiastical authorities. Thus, in 1190 the Genoese *bancherius* Bernardus promised to pay 10 percent per annum on £11 Genoese deposited with his bank, payable on eight days' notice. In the small Tuscan town of San Gimignano, the communal statutes permitted a return of 10 to 20 percent on credit transactions. The usury doctrine of the Church was not a serious detriment to the development of credit institutions in the Middle Ages.

In addition to operating as deposit bankers, by 1200 the Genoese *bancherii* were allowing their customers to make in-bank payments by transfer of debits and credits from the account of one client to that of another. At the same time interbank arrangements permitted a client of one bank to settle accounts with a colleague who was a client of a second bank by means of a simple oral order of transfer. Early Genoese bankers also invested directly in commerical ventures, a practice followed by successive generations of exchange bankers.

A similar grafting of deposit and transfer functions onto simple manual exchange took place throughout most of western Europe in the course of the Middle Ages. During the fourteenth and fifteenth centuries exchange banks existed in all the major trading centers, including Genoa, Milan, Florence, Pisa, Siena, Lucca, Palermo, Naples, and Ven-

BANKING, EUROPEAN

ice in Italy; Barcelona and Valencia in Spain; Bruges in Flanders; and Frankfurt am Main and Strassburg in Germany. Only in the less economically advanced areas—Scandinavia, the Baltic region, and the Hanse towns of northern Germany—did fully developed exchange banking fail to develop.

In England the Crown effectively controlled the flow of coin and bullion, and forbade private exchange banks. Merchants were required to bring foreign coins to the Royal Exchanger in the Tower of London, and tables under the auspices of the Royal Exchanger were set up in English ports for the convenience of merchants or travelers needing to change money. In medieval England banking remained in the hands of foreigners—Italians and, to a lesser degree, Catalans.

Wherever exchange banks existed, the bankers dealt with their customers from behind wooden tables *(tavole)* or benches, normally covered with some type of cloth, upon which rested the ledger, coin purse, scales, and other accoutrements of the changers' business.

The changers located their places of business close to one another. In thirteenth-century Lucca, for example, the changers' *(campsores)* tables actually butted against each other in the square fronting the Cathedral of S. Martin, and their permanent offices *(apothece)* were ranged nearby. In Venice the changers operated from the Rialto Bridge. Most private bankers in Genoa congregated near the Piazza Bianchi, the heart of the business district. Florentine exchangers set up in the Mercato Vecchio, the Mercato Nuovo, or near Or San Michele, all within a short distance of each other. In Bruges some of the changers' stalls were located on St. Peter's Bridge next to the Waterhalle (also called the New Cloth Hall), while others were situated in the arcade of that late-thirteenth-century building. The exchange bankers of Barcelona operated near the harbor, in the square called the Canvis de la Mar as well as in the adjoining streets Canvis Vells ("old exchange") and Canvis Nous ("new exchange"), until the *Lonja* ("exchange") was completed in 1392 to house them. Such physical grouping of banks was the logical consequence of the changers' reliance upon oral rather than written orders of transfer; proximity meant that interbank transactions could be carried out with maximum dispatch.

Money changers worked with their own capital, sometimes pooled with that of colleagues or close relatives through short-term partnership agreements, and with their customers' funds held on deposit. They accepted both time and demand deposits, although plainly preferring the former. The exchange banks of fourteenth-century Bruges, for example, paid no interest on demand deposits. Time deposits permitted the banker to gauge his rollover of capital, and thus to maintain a lower fractional reserve than would have been possible if a large portion of his funds had been subject to withdrawal on demand. In fourteenth-century Bruges, in the exchange bank run by Guillaume Ruyelle, 30 percent of the deposit liabilities were held in reserve. The ratio must have varied from place to place and bank to bank, according to specific conditions. Yet, whatever the bankers' policies in this regard, failure of private exchange banks was chronic in the Middle Ages.

Money changers deployed their capital in the form of loans, although it was common practice for bankers to invest heavily in commercial ventures as well as banking. The exchange bankers dealt with a varied clientele. In Lucca, for instance, they made many small, short-term loans, secured by pledges of grain or wine, to the peasantry of the surrounding countryside. In the city small borrowers also put up pledges in the form of clothing, utensils, and tools as security on loans. In this respect the Lucchese changers verged upon the territory of the pawnbroker. This type of petty moneylending transferred credit at a very modest level, yet in the aggregate it was of considerable economic and social consequence.

In economic terms, however, the most important contribution of the exchange banks was in the creation of commercial credit and in the clearance of clients' obligations by book transfer. As noted above, at the close of the twelfth century, bankers in Genoa engaged in clearing operations. By the thirteenth century clearance was apparently a standard function of exchange banking throughout the Mediterranean region. Only in the fourteenth century did northern money changers adopt the techniques of deposit and transfer banking pioneered and carried across the Alps by the Italians. It is most likely, although there is no direct proof, that Flemings who encountered Italian bankers at the fairs of Champagne, or in the industrial centers of Flanders where Italians had settled, imitated the more sophisticated banking operations used in Italy. Changers at Lille around 1300 seem not to have progressed beyond simple money changing, and there is no reason to think the situation was not the same at Bruges.

By the middle of the fourteenth century, however, the surviving books of the Bruges exchange bankers

BANKING, EUROPEAN

show that they kept accounts with one another for clearance purposes. It was thus a routine matter for a merchant to pay a debt by assignment in bank. As the Bruges ledgers indicate, merchant A buying goods from merchant B could pay his obligation by simply ordering his banker to open a credit in favor of merchant B. If merchant B then wished the funds transferred to his own bank, he only had to order merchant A's banker to transfer the amount to his account with the second banker. This system appears to have been highly organized in Bruges, and provided an inestimable service to the mercantile community. It facilitated settlement of debt without payment in specie. To the extent that bank deposits were transferable, they functioned as substitute money. This fact was recognized in Venice, and no doubt in other cities, where fifteenth-century sources refer to *contadi di banco* and *moneta di banco,* literally meaning "bank money," to describe transferable deposits.

In the above example the order to transfer would have been conveyed orally by the principals. Written orders *(polizze)* similar to the modern check were not used until the fourteenth century, and then only sporadically. Such a system resting upon oral orders was able to function because throughout Europe the written entry in a banker's ledger was accepted as proof of the transaction and book entries were afforded full legal faith.

In addition to transfer, exchange bankers created credit by permitting certain of their clients to overdraw their accounts. Wherever the sources provide information on the workings of the money changers, loans arising out of overdrafts appear commonplace. In fourteenth-century Bruges overdrafts apparently were permitted rather liberally. The money changer Collard de Marke, for instance, in December 1368 had thirteen debit balances on his books that exceeded £50 groat or more, accounting for some 57.3 percent of his total aggregate loans. The remaining 42.7 percent of his loans by overdraft derived from 102 small transactions.

Another service related to their primary function as professional handlers of money was the charge that exchange bankers received from public authorities to retire worn, clipped, or otherwise mutilated coins, to distribute new issues and call in old ones, and to deliver bullion to the mint. Changers also dealt extensively in jewelry, probably as a result of taking in such items as pledges against loans. Venetian bankers of the late fifteenth century made extensive advances against the security of jewels. In Florence one type of bank, termed *banchi a minuto,* sold jewelry on credit, extended loans secured by jewels, carried out exchange transactions, and dealt in bullion. The *banchi a minuto* were as much jewelry shops as they were banks.

The money changers seem to have had a more or less universal penchant for investing a portion of their banks' assets directly in commerce as well as in banking operations. In Genoa, Florence, Venice, and Barcelona this pattern often ended in disaster. Overextension of their resources in risky mercantile undertakings was one factor in the high mortality rate among medieval exchange banks.

The tendency for private exchange banks to end in failure led to the first experiments in public banks. The earliest of these, the Taula de Canvi de Barcelona ("Exchange Bank of Barcelona"), opened under municipal auspices on 20 January 1401. Private bankers had for some time acted as fiscal agents for the city of Barcelona and the Generalitat of Catalonia, the financial branch of the Cortes. They had also served as agents in paying the royal army, and had advanced considerable amounts to the Crown and other government agencies. The public bank in Barcelona was founded in a period of economic crisis in Catalonia that caused a wave of failures in the private banking sector. The Taula, as a single entity, continued to perform the same services for the city of Barcelona and the Generalitat that the private bankers had earlier done collectively. The new institution acted as the fiscal agent for these public bodies. It received surplus taxes, lent money to the city at moderate rates of about 5 percent, and received and administered the savings of citizens. Loans to private individuals were, however, forbidden. Until prohibited by the municipality in 1437, private changers kept their surplus funds at the Taula, which thus acted briefly as a kind of central bank. Despite periodic crises the Taula de Canvi enjoyed a continuous existence until 1853, when it was absorbed into the Bank of Spain.

The attempt to experiment with a public bank in Genoa was less successful than in Barcelona. In 1408 the Casa di San Giorgio opened its doors, but stayed in business only until 1444. As with the Taula, loans to private individuals were forbidden. Credit was extended, however, to the tax farmers and others on security of shares *(loca)* in the public debt. Also as in Barcelona, private bankers opened accounts with the public bank. Yet, in spite of a considerable volume of business, the Casa di San Giorgio faced a number of crises during which it was forced to suspend spe-

BANKING, EUROPEAN

cie payment. Finally, confronted with what they considered a ruinous government mandate to hold down the rising rate of the gold florin in order to halt the depreciation of the Genoese currency, the Protectors of the Casa di San Giorgio voted to give up their charter and liquidate the bank. Not until 1586 was a second attempt made to found a public bank in Genoa. Public banking revived only in the sixteenth century with the founding of public banks in Palermo, Naples, Venice, Genoa, and other commercial centers around 1575.

Along with money changing, pawnbroking developed in the course of the central Middle Ages to supply local credit needs. Although merchants from Cahors, a town in southwestern France, may have been among the first to practice pawnbroking, the field was dominated by Italians, initially by men from Chieri and Asti in Piedmont, who were later joined by Lombards and Tuscans. Collectively they were all called "Lombards" or "Cahorsins" in northern Europe, pejorative terms used synonymously to mean usurers. Between 1240 and 1340 pawnbrokers established shops in the cities and towns in an area that included Dauphiné, Savoy, the Comté, Burgundy, Champagne, Lorraine, the Rhineland, Brabant, Flanders, Artois, the Île de France, and part of Normandy.

Pawnbrokers operated under licenses granted by municipal authorities and feudal lords that exempted them from the restrictions of the usury laws. It would seem that these licensed usurers charged in the neighborhood of 43 percent interest. In Italy money changers may have provided the services of a pawnshop, lending money against the security of pledges. In the later Middle Ages, Italian pawnbroking became increasingly concentrated in the hands of Jews. Despite the unpopularity of the Lombards, their services were a necessary evil, for they provided consumer credit to borrowers unable to secure funds elsewhere.

Exchange banking and pawnbroking were primarily local in scope. International banking—that is, dealing in bills of exchange as well as credit extension—was the preserve of large-scale, Italian mercantile banking companies. These organizations developed in all the major trading centers of northern Italy in the course of the thirteenth century. Centrally directed from a home office in the city of origin and represented in the principal commercial centers of western Europe by partners, factors, and correspondents, these enterprises created a Europe-wide Italian banking network that determined the structure of international banking until well into the modern era.

The Italian mercantile banking companies evolved out of family partnerships, and they retained a decidedly familial character throughout their existence. The Bonsignori company of Siena, for example, grew out of the early activities of Orlando and Bonifazio Bonsignori as papal bankers *(campsores domini papae)* during the pontificate of Innocent IV. Following the death of Bonifazio in 1255, Orlando formed an expanded partnership with his nephews and other Sienese merchants from beyond the immediate family circle. By 1289 the *Gran Tavola dei Bonsignori* ("Company of the Sons of Bonsignore" or "Great Bank of the Bonsignori") numbered some twenty-two partners, four sons of Orlando and eighteen other merchants, sons or relatives of the original partners. But despite the inclusion of outsiders, the Bonsignori retained control of the company until the 1290's, when the crisis that led to the company's failure forced reorganization.

The Ricciardi company of Lucca, which vied with the Bonsignori as the most powerful international firm in the late thirteenth century, evolved from similarly obscure origins in a partnership, formed in the early 1240's, consisting of two Ricciardi and, apparently, an outsider. By 1247 a new partnership, now formally styled Societas Ricciardorum, counted at least thirteen partners and was represented at the papal curia, Genoa, the fairs of Champagne, and in England. In 1286 there were nineteen known *socii*—although this figure is probably too small—of the company and an unknown number of employees operating on the firm's behalf throughout Europe. The Bonsignori and Ricciardi were the most important of the first generation of Italian international companies in terms of the structure and scale of their operations. Companies from Florence, Pistoia, Milan, and other Italian cities carried on business in exactly the same fashion.

Legally the companies were unlimited partnerships, although by the end of the thirteenth century, they had acquired a quasi-corporate identity symbolized by the company style and company seal. The life span of any given enterprise consisted of a series of consecutive terminal partnerships. The admission of new and the withdrawal of old partners, or the distribution of profits, was an occasion for ending one partnership and organizing another. However, the assets and liabilities of one specific partnership were carried over on the books of its successor. As far as third parties were concerned, because of the princi-

BANKING, EUROPEAN

ple of unlimited liability, they need only have known that they were dealing at any given moment with a bona fide representative of the company in order to be assured of full legal guarantees.

The merchant bankers worked with their own funds and to some extent with the monies of outside investors. Each partner conferred a given sum to the *corpo,* or partnership capital, on which each earned a prorated share of the profits. Some partners were permitted to contribute their labor instead of cash, and their efforts were rewarded with a percentage of the organization's earnings. Regular partners were also allowed to invest over and above their commitment to the *corpo* by placing funds *sopra corpo,* a deposit arrangement that earned in the neighborhood of 8 percent paid out before the general distribution of profits. Additional capital flowed to the companies in the form of deposits *a discrezione* placed by outside investors. These investors received a share of the profits as assigned by the managing partners.

Until the mid fourteenth century the Italian companies were centrally organized. The Bonsignori, the Ricciardi, and the Bardi and Peruzzi of Florence, for example, were each organized as one juridical entity. Branches abroad were not legally independent units. The banking crisis of the mid fourteenth century, marked by the crash around 1345 of the Bardi, Peruzzi, and Acciaiuoli companies of Florence, led to the abandonment of the centralized form of organization in favor of the more flexible decentralized type.

Examples of decentralized organization are the combinations of independent partnerships set up late in the fourteenth century by Francesco Datini of Prato and in the fifteenth century by the Medici of Florence. These organizations consisted of a separate partnership for the main office and each of the branches located abroad. Thus, the Medici enterprise was a combination of quasi-independent partnerships. In 1458 the Medici family members of the bank were partners in eleven different enterprises, including a cloth manufacturing firm and a silk manufactory as well as the branches in Venice, Bruges, London, Avignon, Milan, Geneva, and a bank in Florence. The only common link between these independent entities was that the Medici family controlled the affairs of each subordinate enterprise. The great advantage of this kind of organization was that if one partnership experienced difficulty, its problems need not have directly affected the other subsidiaries.

From their inception in the thirteenth century, the Italian companies combined trade with banking, but in general the larger enterprises tended to favor finance over commerce. Although the two areas were intimately related in the overall business of the companies, and profits came indiscriminately from both, it is possible here to examine in detail only the banking side of the Italian companies' affairs.

International banking consisted principally of foreign exchange dealings and large-scale money lending. In these undertakings the Italian merchant bankers were assisted by the support of the papacy. From at least 1232, and perhaps earlier, the Roman curia relied increasingly upon Italian merchants to satisfy its fiscal needs, particularly in transfer and lending. Although the papacy continued to employ the Templars and Hospitalers for shipment or transference of funds (especially to the Holy Land) and as depositories of papal funds throughout the thirteenth century, these functions fell increasingly into the hands of the Italian merchant bankers. After the mid thirteenth century the Italian companies transferred papal income from throughout Europe to the camera, acted as depositories for papal funds, exchanged money, extended credit to ecclesiastics, and frequently lent money to the camera itself. Particularly important was the Italians' role as papal depositories, for it allowed them the use of considerable cash sums for their own purposes. The Ricciardi of Lucca held some 80,000 gold florins of papal monies during the pontificate of Boniface VIII, and the pope's demand for repayment was one of the major factors in the company's fall in the first years of the fourteenth century. The crash of the Bonsignori cost the papacy 64,000 florins in lost deposits.

Italian merchant bankers also performed similar services for secular rulers. Through loans they financed a large share of the expenses of Louis IX's crusade. Charles of Anjou utilized Florentine, Sienese, and Lucchese firms to finance his regime in southern Italy. And Italian companies, principally the Ricciardi, the Frescobaldi, the Bardi, and the Peruzzi, served successively as fiscal agents to the English Crown. Loans to princes, however, were fraught with danger, and usually proved fatal to those companies that overextended their capital resources by continually granting credits to secular rulers. Such policies were major factors in the demise of the Ricciardi and the celebrated failures of the Bardi and Peruzzi in 1345.

A primary banking function of the Italian houses throughout the Middle Ages was the transfer of as-

BANKING, EUROPEAN

sets from place to place by means of the exchange contract *(cambium)*. However, foreign exchange transactions were credit as well as transfer operations, since they involved payment in another place, usually in a different currency, at some time in the future. In the late twelfth and thirteenth centuries, exchange dealings were effected by a notarial contract, the *instrumentum ex causa cambii,* and from the fourteenth century on by the less formal holograph letter of exchange. The former was technically a promise to pay; the latter, an order to pay. However, from the late twelfth century the mechanics of the *cambium* transaction remained essentially the same, regardless of legal forms.

A *cambium,* in order to be completed, involved the participation of four parties, two to strike the original contract and two to carry it out. The deliverer, in effect a lender, handed over to the taker, or borrower, a given sum of money, for which he received a bill of exchange guaranteeing payment at a designated place and time in an equivalent amount of a foreign currency. The transaction was concluded abroad when the deliverer's agent, the payee, collected the bill from the payer, the agent of the taker. Final collection in a foreign place was, however, inevitably at some time in the future, and the taker thus enjoyed the use of the original sum until payment was made. To compensate the deliverer, interest was built into the rates of exchange.

The banker investing in bills of exchange could not be certain of his profit until he had reconverted his foreign credits into local currency. This could be done by importing merchandise or specie that could be sold on the local market, but usually the merchant bankers made their returns in bills. Thus, to complete an exchange transaction two bills were required: one to transfer funds from place A to place B, and a second to bring them back to place A. Sometimes three bills were involved, as when credit moved, for example, from Italy to Bruges, from Bruges to Barcelona, and from Barcelona back to Italy. Such a circuitous route for credit was not uncommon; from around 1400, Flanders had an unfavorable balance of trade with Italy but a favorable one with Catalonia.

In the late twelfth and thirteenth centuries merchant bankers drew and remitted bills of exchange, with settlement normally specified at one of the six great Champagne fairs. Around the turn of the thirteenth century, Italian companies began to bypass the fairs, thus contributing to the decline of Champagne as a financial center, in favor of establishing branches in the commercial and financial centers of the north. Bills payable on sight were then negotiated directly between the banking places of Europe. Regular money markets existed in fourteenth- and fifteenth-century Bologna, Florence, Genoa, Lucca, Milan, Naples, Palermo, Pisa, Siena, Venice, and the ambulatory papal curia in Italy; Avignon, Montpellier, and Paris in France; Barcelona, Valencia, and Palma de Mallorca in Spain; Bruges in Flanders; and London in England. In the same period the fairs of Geneva, and after 1465 of Lyons, functioned as clearing centers. No banking places existed east of the Rhine, although about 1500 the fairs of Frankfurt am Main were emerging as centers of international banking.

The Italian companies operating in the constricted economy of postplague Europe worked on a smaller scale than their predecessors. Individual merchants and small firms having fewer than ten members seem to have been the rule. After 1350 only the Medici bank of Florence approached the size of the Bardi, the Peruzzi, and the Acciaiuoli companies of the 1330's. In 1469 it had a staff of sixty and branches in Avignon, Bruges, Geneva, London, Rome, and Venice. Where no branch existed, the Medici and other companies worked through correspondents through whom they could draw and remit their bills.

The failure of the Medici bank toward the end of the fifteenth century closed out an era in the history of banking. Although Italians continued in banking in later centuries, their dominance of international commerce and finance was broken. Within a few years before and after 1500, the center of gravity of international finance began to shift northward. By 1520 Italian bankers held only a secondary position in European money markets.

BIBLIOGRAPHY

Georges Bigwood, *Le régime juridique et économique du commerce de l'argent dans la Belgique du Moyen-Âge,* 2 vols. (1921–1922); Center for Medieval and Renaissance Studies, University of California, Los Angeles, *The Dawn of Modern Banking* (1979); Carlo Cipolla, *Studi di storia della moneta,* I, *I movimenti dei cambi in Italia del secolo XIII al XIV* (1948); Raymond de Roover, *Money, Banking and Credit in Mediaeval Bruges* (1948); *L'évolution de la lettre de change, XIVe–XVIIIe siècles* (1953); "The Organization of Trade," in *The Cambridge Economic History of Europe,* III (1963); *The Rise and Decline of the Medici Bank: 1397–1494* (1966); *The Bruges Money Market Around 1400, with a Statistical Supplement by Hyman Sardy* (1968); and *Business, Banking and Economic Thought in Late Medieval and Early Modern Europe,* Julius Kirschner, ed. (1974); John Gilchrist, *The Church and Economic Activity in the Middle Ages* (1969); Richard Kaeuper, *Bankers to the Crown: The Ricciardi of Lucca and Edward I* (1973).

F. Lane, "Venetian Bankers, 1496–1533," in *Journal of Political Economy,* **45** (1937); and "Investment and Usury," in *Explorations in Economic History,* 2nd ser., **2** (1964); Robert Lopez, "The Trade of Medieval Europe: The South," in *The Cambridge Economic History of Europe,* II (1952); and *La prima crisi della banca di Genova (1250–1259)* (1956); Robert Lopez and Irving Raymond, *Medieval Trade in the Mediterranean World* (1955); Federigo Melis, *Note di storia della banca pisana nel trecento* (1955); John Noonan, *The Scholastic Analysis of Usury* (1957); Léon Poliakov, *Jewish Bankers and the Holy See from the Thirteenth to the Seventeenth Century,* Miriam Kochan, trans. (1977); Yves Renouard, *Les relations des papes d'Avignon et des compagnies bancaires de 1316 à 1378* (1941); Armando Sapori, *La crisi delle compagnie mercantili dei Peruzzi* (1926); and *Studi di storia economica (secoli XIII–XIV–XV),* 3rd ed., 3 vols. (1955–1967); André Sayous, "Les transformations des méthodes commerciales dans l'Italie médiévale," in *Annales d'histoire économique et sociale,* **1** (1929); Abbot P. Usher, *The Early History of Deposit Banking in Mediterranean Europe,* I (1943).

THOMAS J. BLOMQUIST

[See also **Banking, Jewish, in Europe; Exchequer; Lombards (Bankers); Mints and Money, Western European; Trade, Western European; Usury.**]

BANKING, ISLAMIC. In the medieval Islamic world, banking was tied primarily to the needs of commerce and fiscal administration. Its methods and constraints were comparable, but by no means identical, with those in western Europe. These differences partly explain the fact that in the vast domains of Islam during the Middle Ages, one encounters bankers and one encounters ramified banking activities, but one does not encounter banks. There were no institutions whose specialized and exclusive concern was dealing in money.

Islam, like Christianity, prohibits usurious transactions including, of course, interest-bearing loans. The general term for usury is *ribā,* a practice sharply denounced in the Koran and in all subsequent Islamic religious writings. In Islamic religious law *(sharīᶜa, fiqh)* the prohibition is absolute and covers a broader range of commercial and economic exchanges than does the Christian concept of usury. In Islamic law, usury is defined as any unjustified increase in capital for which no compensation is given. Not only does this exclude interest-bearing cash loans, it also makes illicit many speculative transactions and certain forms of delayed payment. Engaging in usurious transactions or enjoying any gains generated by them is absolutely prohibited to a Muslim regardless of whether these exchanges take place with another Muslim or with a nonbeliever. By contrast, members of religious minorities within the medieval Islamic realm were not constrained from pursuing usurious transactions with people outside their own faith. Nevertheless, interest-bearing loans were neither widespread nor very important in medieval Islamic trade. The strict Islamic prohibition against usury does not seem to have inhibited either trade or banking activities. The availability of numerous other licit commercial techniques played the same economic role as interest-bearing loans in financing trade and exchange and so made the significant use of loans unnecessary.

A great variety of credit arrangements were known and practiced in the medieval Islamic world. Made necessary by the lively regional and international trade of the Middle East, they constituted the essential components of banking activity.

Buying and selling on credit was an accepted and widespread commercial practice. The eleventh-century legal scholar Sarakhsi declared that "selling on credit is an absolute feature of trade." Similar assertions are found in other medieval Islamic sources. Credit sales—deferred payments for goods bought and advance payments for future delivery—were not only considered fully legitimate forms of commercial conduct but also were viewed as indispensable to successful and profitable trading. Sarakhsi expressed this view explicitly and crisply: "We hold that selling for credit is part of the practice of merchants and that it is the most conducive means for the achievement of the investors' goal which is profit. In most cases, profit can be achieved only by selling for credit and not selling for cash."

Islamic commercial law, besides outlining methods of dealing for credit, also provides for instruments of credit such as the *ḥawāla* and the *suftaja.* The *ḥawāla* was the payment of a debt through the transfer of a claim, and the *suftaja* a letter of credit or bill of exchange. From as early as the eighth century, these techniques made possible the transfer of large sums of money over considerable distances without the use of any specie. The *suftaja,* always, and the *ḥawāla,* usually, occurred as a written obligation and were thus the first and most important forms of commercial credit papers in the medieval Near East.

Day-to-day commercial practice as depicted in surviving commercial documents, particularly those of the Cairo Geniza from the eleventh through the thirteenth centuries, confirms the extensive use of these credit techniques. Virtually every business letter or contract contains a reference to some form of credit, and exchange on all levels was normally conducted on a credit basis. Immediate cash payments were rare and were usually rewarded by a standard discount of 2 percent to 4 percent. In commerce, credit was normally granted for a two-month period. Without this kind of credit, one twelfth-century Egyptian writer commented, commerce would come to a complete standstill. Many petty transactions of daily domestic life were also executed on a credit basis.

Considering the profusion of credit transactions and the variety of gold and silver coins in simultaneous circulation, it is no surprise that we encounter an elaborate system of banking and money exchange to accommodate the various needs of trade and government. The practices that arose in response can, for the purposes of analysis, be divided into two major categories: money changing and merchant banking. Their functions frequently overlapped.

Exchange, the central feature of the money market, was performed "manually" rather than through written instruments. The money market was neither highly structured nor, with some intermittent exceptions, subject to any consistent governmental regulation. The exchange rate between various currencies was governed by their intrinsic value and, secondarily, by the demand at any given moment for a particular type of coin. This demand was in turn determined by the requirements of commerce and of administration.

Profits from exchange operations derived not only from shrewd currency speculation based on an intimate acquaintance with the money market but also from a fixed commission charged for each exchange transacted.

Money-changing operations were by no means restricted to the money changers. Almost every merchant dabbled in them, and for many, especially those involved in long-distance trade, it was a major part of their activities.

Many middle-level and grand merchants also engaged in a variety of protobanking activities, but there was no specialization. Such activities went hand in hand with regular commercial operations and were invariably subsidiary to more traditional aspects of trade such as buying, selling, exporting, and importing. Indeed, a merchant's banking activities were simply an extension of his commercial operations, one more service and skill that he would be expected to possess. To some extent, most merchants actually served as their own bankers. Every aspect of their credit and banking operation—money changing, issuing letters of credit, accepting deposits, acting as a clearinghouse for payments—can be linked directly to their commercial endeavors.

BIBLIOGRAPHY

Walter J. Fischel, "The Origin of Banking in Medieval Islam," in *Journal of the Royal Asiatic Society* (1933); and *Jews in the Economic and Political Life of Medieval Islam* (1937); Solomon D. Goitein, "Bankers' Accounts from the Eleventh Century, A.D.," in *Journal of the Economic and Social History of the Orient,* 9 (1966); and *A Mediterranean Society,* I (1967), 229–266; Sobhi Labib, "Geld und Kredit, Studien zur Wirtschaftsgeschichte Aegyptens im Mittelalter," in *Journal of the Economic and Social History of the Orient,* 2 (1959); A. L. Udovitch, "Bankers Without Banks: Commerce, Banking, and Society in the Islamic World of the Middle Ages," in *The Dawn of Modern Banking* (1979), 255–273.

A. L. Udovitch

BANKING, JEWISH, IN EUROPE. The banking activities of the Jews in medieval Europe concentrated on lending at interest and pawnbroking. The Jews' customers, at least for the purpose of this article, were Christians. This division (Jewish creditors/Christian borrowers) was fairly firm even though Jews occasionally joined with Christians in joint credit ventures and in a few instances "fronted" for Christians unwilling to bear the public opprobrium of "usury." Scriptural proscriptions, of course, forbade lending at interest within the Jewish community as well as within the Christian, but theory was one thing and practice another. The proscriptions either were openly defied or were modified in response to commercial needs, or ways were developed to disguise interest payments. Certainly, usurious credit transactions were a way of life among Christians; more work needs to be done on their extent within Jewish communities.

Jewish lending to Christians varied with time, with region, and with the competition of Christian lenders for the same market. In England the fundamental business of Jews was lending at interest from the time of their coming to the island (*ca.* 1100) until

BANKING, JEWISH, IN EUROPE

their expulsion in 1290. Living under the protection of the king, many engaged in lending on a lavish scale, often taking real property as pledges. So extensive were their interests that a sophisticated treasury developed from the royal Exchequer both to monitor and to adjudicate their affairs. The level of complexity of their credit transactions and the formalization of these transactions in a type of contract known as a "starr" probably helped to shape the English common law of gage. The reign of King John (1199–1216) was a watershed for the Jews of England. Heavy arbitrary taxation went a long way toward ruining them, and the increasing anti-Jewish fervor of the governing class during John's reign and the next half-century forced Edward I to expel them. Their role as a source for royal and baronial loans was taken up by Italian companies that had been in competition with them for decades.

On the Continent the situation was more complex. It is not certain when, if ever, the primary occupation of the Jews became money lending. Particularly in southern Europe they were an organic part of a cosmopolitan culture. They were landholders, agriculturalists, artisans, physicians, and governmental officials. Nonetheless, by the twelfth century a large portion of Jewish activity was concentrated in commerce either primarily or incidentally connected with the traffic in loans.

The variety of lending was enormous. The Jews were involved in papal finance as well as the market in small consumption loans. Great barons borrowed on their lands, while townsmen and peasants pawned coats, cheap jewelry, coverlets, and cups. Competition from Christian entrepreneurs for the same markets was real. Originally competition at the elite level came from the monastic lenders (until the papacy cracked down in the twelfth and thirteenth centuries); later, lay Christian lenders succeeded to the role. Always, of course, taverners and wealthy widows serviced the small loan market in (friendly) competition with Jewish creditors.

Most Jews lent as individual men or women (the proportion of Jewish women lenders was often about half) or as (married) couples. Companies—if the word be permitted—were usually small. When big loans were at issue, individuals or small companies tended to cluster together to raise the capital. These consortia on rare occasions persisted over long periods.

The traffic in loans at interest was frequently legal, and even when illegal was frequently tolerated by the authorities. Legal rates of interest differed, but two common figures were 43⅓ percent and 86⅔ percent per year (the equivalent of two or four pennies per pound per week). Short-term rates sometimes appear lower, but also sometimes much higher, than the official rates. Seemingly high rates may be misleading, however, especially with regard to consumption or distress loans. The townsman who borrowed six pennies to pay an unexpected tax and who promised to repay one shilling (twelve pennies) was obviously not being squeezed so terribly as the 100 percent rate might suggest. To be sure, some borrowers claimed that they had to pay interest as high—in the aggregate—as 1,000 percent or more on small loans, but they may have had extraordinarily long terms for repayment or have been exaggerating for their own benefit. In 1306 the poor of Paris protested the expulsion of French Jews because they feared that Christian usurers would charge more for the same services.

Not everywhere and not at all times was lending at interest legal. Under Louis IX of France (1226–1270) the crown sought to eradicate it—successfully when the object of the royal wrath was Jewish lenders, less successfully (though hardly less energetically) when the transgressors were Christians. The increasing fervor of anti-Jewish polemic encouraged, and was encouraged by, this attack throughout Europe. Needless to say, the achievement of the aggressive antiusury, anti-Jewish authorities varied considerably. Expulsion, the ultimate weapon, was most effectively employed in England, France, and eventually Spain. Particularist Germany and divided Italy were less susceptible to clear, consistent policies of this sort.

Present-day scholarship on Jewish banking in Europe is more oriented toward its historical sociology than its financial aspects. Researchers are attempting to identify (more carefully than hitherto) the social status of borrowers, the impact of distress loans from Jews on the collective mentality of the borrowers, the relationship of the market in loans to outbreaks of anti-Jewish violence, and the role of women in lending and borrowing. They systematically analyze the starrs and the English records of the Jews' Exchequer, the judicial decisions of special royal commissioners in France, the contemporary minutes of urban courts in Germany, and the almost embarrassingly rich notarial archives throughout southern Europe. Through such research a convincing picture of Jewish-Christian financial exchange should emerge, which will be an important contribution to our modern understanding of Jewish-Christian relations.

BIBLIOGRAPHY

Richard Emery, *The Jews of Perpignan in the Thirteenth Century* (1959); Paul Hyams, "The Jewish Minority in Medieval England," in *Journal of Jewish Studies,* **25** (1974); Stuart Jenks, "Judenverschuldung und Verfolgung von Juden im 14. Jahrhundert: Franken bis 1349," in *Vierteljahrsschrift für Sozial- und Wirtschaftsgeschichte,* **65** (1978); William Chester Jordan, "Jews on Top: Women and the Availability of Consumption Loans in Northern France in the Mid-Thirteenth Century," in *Journal of Jewish Studies,* **29** (1978); Vivian Lipman, *The Jews of Medieval Norwich* (1967); Gerard Nahon, "Le crédit et les juifs dans la France du XIIIe siècle," in *Annales: ESC,* **24** (1969); Léon Poliakov, *Jewish Bankers and the Holy See from the Thirteenth to the Seventeenth Century,* Miriam Kochan, trans. (1977); Joseph Shatzmiller, *Recherches sur la communauté juive de Manosque* (1973).

WILLIAM CHESTER JORDAN

[See also **Banking, European; Jews in Europe; Usury.**]

BANNERET (or knight-banneret), a knight who brought to the army, or was given command of, other knights and their retinues. As a sign of his rank he carried a rectangular banner; an ordinary knight carried a triangular banner. The number of men commanded by a banneret varied according to his reputation, his resources, and the wishes of the army commander, who was usually a great lord and often a king. In France at the end of the thirteenth century, a banneret's company seems to have been reckoned at about twenty men—two or three ordinary knights; a few squires; and the rest ordinary soldiers, bowmen, and men-at-arms. In England a banneret commanded a larger force, but it is impossible to say what the normal quota was. A banneret was often a member of the king's household and as such was not always easily distinguished from a baron.

A banneret should be carefully distinguished from a baronet. The latter was a title, invented by the Stuart kings of England, that conveyed a hereditary knighthood. A banneret was a fighting man; a baronet was a courtier.

BIBLIOGRAPHY

Robert Fawtier, ed., *Comptes royaux,* II (1954), nos. 27022–27050; Ferdinand Lot, *L'art militaire et les armées au moyen âge,* I (1946); Michael Prestwich, *War, Politics and Finance Under Edward I* (1972), 42–71; James F. Willard and William A. Morris, eds., *The English Government at Work,* I (1940), 336–337.

JOSEPH R. STRAYER

[See also **Knights and Knight Service.**]

BANSENCHAS (Tales of women) briefly catalogs prominent women. It is clearly a product of early Irish scholarship and not gleanings from folktales collected by a medieval redactor. Seven surviving manuscripts contain versions of the *Bansenchas,* the earliest being a twelfth-century copy. The seven vary considerably in form and content.

There is a metrical version and a prose version, and in each the arrangement of the *Bansenchas* is chronological. It begins with Eve and other biblical matriarchs. The roster continues with women from classical Greek mythology and Homeric literature. Only Creusa, Dido, and Lavinia are taken from Vergil. The rest of the roster is exclusively Irish.

The Irish women in the *Bansenchas* are both literary and historical figures. They come from the *Leabar Gabálá Érenn* (Book of the taking of Ireland), the king cycles, heroic tales, and various annals. The latest datable entry takes the list into the late twelfth century. None of the entries is very extensive, but many contain brief allusions to the person's literary or historical context. Above all, the concern of the *Bansenchas* is to render a genealogical, matriarchal, and dynastic recounting of history.

BIBLIOGRAPHY

Margaret (Maighréad) C. Dobbs, ed., "The Ban-Shenchus," in *Revue celtique,* **47** (1930); **48** (1931); **49** (1932). Also see Muireann ní Bhrolcháin, "An Bansheanchas Filiochta," M.A. thesis, University College Dublin (1977); Marlyn E. McGrath Lewis, "An Examination of the Historical Portions of the BanSenchas," Ph.D. thesis, Harvard University (1978).

DOROTHY AFRICA

[See also **Irish Literature; Historical Compositions.**]

BANUS (Hungarian, *bân;* Serbo-Croatian, *ban*), originally a high officer of the kingdom of Croatia; after 1100 a deputy of the king of Hungary in Croatia, Dalmatia, or Slavonia (between the Drava and Sava rivers), or a governor of a southern frontier area

BAPTISM

(banat). These offices, sometimes combined and mostly augmented by additional territories of the hinterland, secured for their holders baronial status and considerable income and military power. Rulers or powerful leaders in South Slav states, such as Bosnia, also had the title banus.

BIBLIOGRAPHY

Anton Hellmar, *Series banorum Dalmatiae, Croatiae, Sclavoniae* (1747); Vjekoslav Klaić, "Hrvatski bani za Arpadovica (1102–1301)" [Bans of Croatia under the Árpáds], in *Vjesnik Kr. Hrvatsko-slavonsko-dalmatinskog zemljskog arkiva,* **1** (1899); and "Hrvatski hercezi i bani za Karla Roberta i Ljudevita I (1301–1382)" [Bans and dukes of Croatia under Charles Robert and Louis I], in *Rad Jugoslavenske akademije znanosti i umjetnosti,* **142** (1900).

J. M. BAK

[See also **Banat; Croatia.**]

BAPTISM can be defined in two ways: the sacramental action of an exterior washing of the body, signifying a spiritual cleansing, administered under a prescribed form of words; or a sacramental rite of initiation to Christian life through a sequence of ceremonies relating to the stages of catechumenate, prebaptism, baptism, and postbaptism.

THE RITE

The primary sources for the rite of baptism in the Middle Ages are the Ordinals, sacramentaries, pontificals, and missals containing the procedure and prayers for the ceremony. The baptismal rites in the liturgical books from Rome, Gaul, Milan, Spain, and Ireland possess certain distinct characteristics that have traditionally been used to classify all the Western baptismal rites as Roman, Gallican (Frankish), Milanese (Ambrosian), Spanish (Mozarabic), or Celtic. The origins of these rites are very obscure, but it is known that their formation was interdependent. By the twelfth century the Roman rite had supplanted local rites of baptism in all the churches of the West except Milan. The Roman rite was based on an *ordo,* or procedure, for baptism in the Romano-Germanic pontifical, a liturgical book compiled in the mid tenth century in Germany from older sources. The baptismal *ordo* of this influential pontifical has many similarities with the Gallican, Spanish, Celtic, and Milanese rites. Below, this *ordo* will be used to outline the sequence of ceremonies of baptism because in its general structure, with a few allowances that will be mentioned, it describes all the variant regional rites of the early Middle Ages and because it served as the basis for the Roman rite almost universally adopted by the West from the twelfth century.

The main rite of baptism is for infants, with supplementary rites for the sick and for pagan converts. The following series of four ceremonies is celebrated at one liturgy in immediate sequence: (1) ceremonies of the catechumen—renunciation of Satan and profession of faith, exsufflation ("blowing out" the devil), signing of the cross on the infant and laying on of hands, placement of salt on the tongue of the infant, a series of exorcisms with signings and laying on of hands; (2) prebaptism ceremonies—exorcism, touching of the nose and ears of the infant with saliva and the pronouncement "effeta," touching of breast and shoulder blades with exorcised oil (accompanied by a threefold renunciation of Satan), blessing of the baptismal water; (3) ceremonies of baptism—the questions "What is your name? Do you wish to be baptized?" and triple immersion in the water of the font with the words "I baptize you in the name of the Father and of the Son and of the Holy Spirit"; (4) postbaptism ceremonies—immediate presbyterial anointing of the head of the infant with chrism, donning of a white vestment, Mass with first reception of the Eucharist, confirmation with chrism on the forehead, if a bishop is present to perform this.

The older Roman *ordo* for baptism (sections 6, 7) extended the catechumenate ceremonies over a period before Easter, with biweekly meetings for the instruction and exorcism of the catechumens. At the most important of these meetings, the catechumens were first given the words of the Creed and the Lord's Prayer, and were introduced to the four Gospels. In the Gallican, Milanese, Spanish, and Celtic rites there was only one postbaptismal anointing. In Milan, Gaul, and Ireland there was a foot-washing ceremony, the *pedilavium,* after the postbaptismal anointing. In Ireland the Stowe Missal (*ca.* 800) included a signing of the neophyte's right hand before the *pedilavium.* In Spain, before baptism the infants were led over a hair rug as a symbol of their penitential attitude, salt was optional, and there was only a single immersion in the font. At the beginning of the Middle Ages, baptism was not considered sacramentally complete in the Roman rite without the Eucharist and episcopal confirmation. By the twelfth century the Lord's body was generally not given to infants, and confirmation was a separate sacrament. In all other respects the baptismal *ordo* of the tenth-century Romano-Germanic pontifical describes the liturgy of baptism that predominated throughout the medieval West from the twelfth century.

INTERPRETATION OF BAPTISM

Liturgical commentaries, canonical collections, and conciliar legislation are the main sources for medieval interpretation of baptism. In its entirety the baptismal literature of the sixth through eleventh centuries, especially rich during the Carolingian period, shows that in many small details liturgical practice and its theological explanation were subject to a remarkable degree of variation.

A famous letter sent by Charlemagne to his archbishops at the beginning of the ninth century, asking them how they observed and explained the rite of baptism, and the answers received by the emperor have provided notable examples of the early medieval method of explaining baptism. Following the sequence in the *ordo,* each ceremony was explained typologically from events in Scripture. For example, the catechumenate stage was compared to the Jewish people, who had received a baptism of repentance from John the Baptist; exorcism, to Jesus' expelling the evil spirits from the demoniacs (Matt. 8:28–34); salt, to Lot's wife, who was turned into a pillar of salt (Gen. 19:26); touching of the nose and ears with saliva, to Jesus' opening the ears and mouth of the deaf-mute (Mark 7:31–35); postbaptismal chrismation, to the anointing of priests and kings in the Old Testament; the white vestment worn daily through the Easter octave, to the people robed in white about the throne of God in the Apocalypse (Rev. 7:13–17) and to Christ's Transfiguration (Matt. 17:2).

Such explanations were not uniform; nor, when they referred to the institution, necessity, matter, and form of the sacrament, did the expositors succeed in providing a definitive and complete theology of baptism. With the appearance in the twelfth century of the Scholastic writers such as Hugh of St. Victor, Peter Abelard, Bernard of Clairvaux, and Peter Lombard, the thoughts of the previous centuries began to be systematized and summarized, although an exhaustive theology of the sacrament still awaited the thirteenth century with such figures as Alexander of Hales, Bonaventure, Albertus Magnus, and Thomas Aquinas.

INSTITUTION AND NECESSITY

Baptism was necessary for entrance into the kingdom of heaven on the basis of Christ's words: "Unless a man be born again of water and the Spirit, he cannot enter the kingdom of God" (John 3:5) and "If I do not wash you, you can have no part with me" (John 13:8). No unanimity was reached as to whether the institution of the sacrament began at the time of Christ's own baptism, or with his words to Nicodemus (John 3:5), or when he commissioned his apostles to go out and baptize all nations (Matt. 28:19). It was believed that some could be saved without the sacramental rite by a baptism of blood (martyrdom) or a baptism of desire, although there was no firm agreement on the nature or validity of a baptism of desire.

MATTER

Water alone, and no other form of liquid, was required for valid baptism. In the Old Testament prefigurations of Christian baptism, water was always the essential symbol. It signified the generative, salvific, and healing power of the future sacrament in such instances as the Spirit's moving over the waters in the creation story of Genesis, the four rivers of Paradise, the Flood and Noah's ark, the passage of the Israelites through the Red Sea, the water produced by Moses from the rock in the desert, and the healing of Naaman the Syrian in the River Jordan. Water was also part of the institution of baptism in the New Testament. The water and blood that flowed from Christ's side on the cross were symbolic of baptism and the Eucharist, the two fundamental sacraments of the future Church.

FORM

The form of baptism was "In the name of the Father and of the Son and of the Holy Spirit." Canon law maintained that omissions or mispronunciations of the formula did not affect the validity of the sacrament if the minister had the correct intention. The interspersion or the separation of the words of the formula with the application of water, and a triple or only a single administration of water were two legitimate options variously favored during the Middle Ages. Also, full immersion, infusion (partial immersion with water poured over the head), and aspersion (sprinkling) were all diversely employed without canonical restriction. Full immersion became rare beginning in the twelfth century with the practice of baptizing delicate newborns.

EFFECTS

The effects of baptism were described according to the theology of St. Paul (Rom. 6) as a total incorporation into Christ by dying with him in the waters of the font, a symbol of Christ's tomb, and rising with him to a new eternal life through participation in his resurrected body, the Church, and the sacrament of the Eucharist. According to St. Paul (Eph. 4:22–24), baptism was a putting off of the old sinful person when entering naked into the font, and a clothing in a new self, symbolized in the donning of a white robe immediately upon arising from the font. In John (3:3–7) baptism was explained as a rebirth through living water and the Spirit. Here the font was the womb by which the Church produced her offspring. The two aspects of death and new life in the waters of baptism remained the essence of the medieval theology of the sacrament. The newly baptized was cleansed from all sin, both original sin and the guilt and punishment due for any sins committed prior to baptism; and through baptism he or she became a member of Christ's Church. This character, or identification, was permanent and made the repetition of baptism impossible.

MINISTER

Baptism administered by any person with the necessary matter, form, and intention was valid, although there were instances of objection to its administration by women, Jews, pagans, and (especially) unworthy priests. In normal conditions, in an ecclesiastical setting, the minister was by law of no lower clerical grade than priest. In areas where the Roman rite was influential, either the bishop presided over the entire ceremony of baptism, or the priest baptized and the final confirmation was delayed until the bishop visited his diocese. This delay eventually brought about the theology that explained confirmation as a separate sacrament.

RECIPIENT

Infant baptism was the normal procedure during the entire Middle Ages. Only in areas still under conversion did the Church deal with a significant number of adult candidates. Infant baptism and sponsorship were justified by the accounts of Jesus' healing persons through the faith of another, such as the daughter of the Syro-Phoenician woman, who was healed because of the faith of her mother (Mark 7:24–30). The Church, as the new mother of those being reborn in the womb of the baptismal waters, supplied the necessary faith for the infants. If the recipients were old enough to respond to the interrogations of faith, instruction had to precede their baptism. During the Carolingian period, when fervent missionary activity introduced a large number of adult heathens to Christianity, certain aspects of the elaborate catechumenate of antiquity were again prescribed in the rites for baptism, and numerous clerical manuals provided priests with a program of instruction for catechumens. Carolingian legislation ordered that the people were to be instructed in a language that they understood, although the actual extent of delivery of baptismal instruction in the vernacular is not known.

TIME OF BAPTISM

Until the twelfth century canon law permitted the celebration of baptism only on the vigils of Easter and Pentecost except when there was imminent danger of death. However, the frequency with which this restriction was repeated and the need to forbid explicitly occasions such as the Epiphany, the Nativity, and the feasts of the Apostles are only two indications that the law was not strictly observed. The significance of baptism for the catechumens was impressively conveyed when the sacrament of their initiation was celebrated integrally with the passion, death, and resurrection of Christ in the liturgy of the Paschal triduum.

For this reason, and also because Lent offered an opportunity for preparation, the Church sought to maintain the connection between baptism and Easter, or at least Pentecost, which commemorates the descent of the Holy Spirit upon the Apostles. In the eleventh century local legislation began to insist that infants be baptized as soon after birth as possible, because of the fear of early death. By the end of the Middle Ages this practice was general, and the sacrament lost its liturgical association with the solemn rites of Easter and Pentecost.

PLACE OF BAPTISM

Some separate baptistery buildings, especially in cathedral cities, survived from late antiquity and were still used on the solemn feasts for baptism, but normally the medieval rite took place at a font erected within the church. In rural areas specific churches were designated as baptismal churches. By the ninth century these were fairly abundant in the more settled districts. Before the tenth century the font of the rural parish or mission church was often a simple wooden barrel or vat that could be set up temporarily. A fixed location for the font in the church was not defined by law, although archaeological evidence has shown that the rear or portal area was the most usual place for baptism.

BAPTISMAL SPONSORSHIP

In the Roman *ordo* of baptism, sponsors brought the catechumens to a series of scrutinies in the weeks before Easter. At these meetings the sponsors (as well as the ministers) made a sign of the cross on the infants and participated in a Eucharistic celebration for their godchildren, who could not yet attend this part of the Mass. At baptism they received the infants immediately from the font. At confirmation sponsors held the infants in crooks of their right arms or, if the neophytes were older, they stood on the feet of their sponsor.

A canon repeated in Burchard of Worms's *Decretum* 4.24 (section 11) stated that the sponsor should be the same person for catechumenate, baptism, and confirmation, although this was not the Roman custom. The sponsor could not be the natural parent of the child. Carolingian legislation repeatedly admonished parents and sponsors to undertake the religious education of the child. No one could be a sponsor until he or she could demonstrate a knowledge of the Creed and the Lord's Prayer. In the ninth century a reason given for restricting baptism to Easter was so that sponsors could be instructed in the faith, the meaning of baptism, and their future duties in the preceding weeks of Lent, which were traditionally geared to a special consideration of those preparing for baptism during the Paschal vigil. It is not known to what extent sponsors actually fulfilled the role of religious instructors in the Middle Ages. In royal circles sponsoring a child was viewed as a great dignity and, like marriage, was sometimes given an important political function.

BIBLIOGRAPHY

Sources. Michel Andrieu, *Les ordines romani du haut Moyen-Âge,* II–V (1931–1961), *ordos* 11, 15, 23–33, 50; Cyrille Vogel and Reinhard Elze, eds., *Le pontifical romano-germanique du dixième siècle,* II (1963), 155–164; E. C. Whitaker, *Documents of the Baptismal Liturgy,* 2nd ed. (1970).

Studies. T. C. Akeley, *Christian Initiation in Spain c. 300–1100* (1967); Jean Danielou, "Le symbolisme des rites baptismaux," in *Deux vivant,* I (1945); Egon Färber, "Der Ort der Taufspendung," in *Archiv für Liturgiewissenschaft,* 13 (1971); John D. C. Fisher, *Christian Initiation: Baptism in the Medieval West* (1965); Robert M. Grant, "Development of the Christian Catechumenate," in *Made, Not Born* (1976); Burkhard Neunhauser, *Taufe und Firmung* (1956), esp. 79–96; Clement F. Rogers, *Baptism and Christian Archaeology* (1903).

Illustrations. Myrtilla Avery, *The Exultet Rolls of South Italy,* II (1936).

SUSAN ANN KEEFE

[See also **Baptismal Vows, Old High German / Old Saxon; Baptistery.**]

BAPTISM OF CHRIST in the Jordan by John the Baptist is recounted in Matthew 3:13–17, Mark 1:9–11, and Luke 3:21–22. During his baptism Christ's divinity was revealed; Christ's baptism is also significant as the prototype of all baptisms.

Early representations of the baptism of Christ are preserved in the Roman catacombs and on sarcophagi: Christ was shown as a nude youth standing in the Jordan, with John the Baptist, dressed as a philosopher, to one side. The dove of the Holy Spirit was almost always included; and two trees, one withered and one with leaves, were often depicted to illustrate the Baptist's sermon on repentance.

The first preserved image depicting Christ nimbed as he is baptized dates from around 500 (Arian Baptistery of Santo Spirito, Ravenna). During the Carolingian period Christ was occasionally shown in a loincloth rather than nude, but the loincloth was not commonly represented until the eleventh century; landscape was rarely shown before the thirteenth. From the Carolingian period on, representations included angels; sometimes the hand of God or clouds symbolizing heaven were shown. In the fourteenth century the change in the Latin Church from baptism by immersion to baptism by infusion was reflected in depictions of Christ's baptism.

Byzantine representations of the Baptism of Christ are preserved from the sixth century. Christ was usually shown in water to his waist; a hand of God, sending forth the dove, was almost always included; and Christ was frequently attended by angels and apostles. Middle Byzantine images of the baptism (for instance, at Hosios Lukas) normally showed attending angels, a personification of the Jordan, apostles, and the dove. As in certain Western representations, a tree felled by an ax was sometimes included to illustrate the Baptist's sermon. Many Byzantine images also represented the column topped by a cross that was erected by pilgrims on the site of Christ's baptism.

BIBLIOGRAPHY

Gertrud Schiller, *Iconography of Christian Art,* Janet Seligmann, trans., I (1971), 127–143.

LESLIE BRUBAKER

[See also **Byzantine Art; Early Christian Art; Iconography.**]

BAPTISMAL VOWS, OLD HIGH GERMAN/ OLD SAXON. In addition to the *Merseburg charms,* a ninth-century Merseburg manuscript contains a text setting out the questions to be asked, and the answers required of, a candidate for baptism. Another version is known from a seventeenth-century transcription of a text in a Speyer manuscript now lost. Before confessing the articles of the faith, the candidate is asked whether he or she renounces evil spirits and "all sacrifices and offerings and gods that heathen men have for sacrifices and offerings and gods."

A ninth-century Vatican manuscript preserves a similar text in Old Saxon, in which the candidate is asked whether he or she renounces the devil and all sacrifice to the devil. On being asked further whether he or she renounces "all the works of the devil," the candidate is required to reply that he or she renounces "all the works and words of the devil, Thunaer and Uuoden and Saxnot, and all the evil spirits that are their companions." Aside from the second Merseburg charm this is the only early German text to mention Wodan, and the only one—aside, perhaps, from a charm against epilepsy—to mention the god of thunder, though "Thonar et Waten" are both mentioned in the Latin *Versus Pauli diaconi (Monumenta Germaniae historica; Poetae latini aevi Carolini,* I, no. xiv). Saxnot, doubtless a tribal god of the Saxons, is mentioned nowhere else.

Another Saxon formula was transcribed in the seventeenth century from a manuscript now lost. In this the candidate is asked whether he or she renounces all heathen practices and all heathen sacrifices and (*gelpon*[?]) festivities "that heathen men had for sacrifices and offerings." The past tense may indicate the passing of pagan cults. The text ends like an exorcism with the instruction "Suffla in faciem et dic hanc orationem: Exi ab eo immunde spiritus et redde honorem deo vivo et vero" (Blow in his face and say this prayer: Go out of him, unclean spirit, and render honor to the true and living God).

The Vatican formula probably dates from the late eighth century, when the Saxons were still heathen or only recently converted. From High German and Old English features in its spelling, we may deduce that it was composed, with the aid of a High German model, by an Anglo-Saxon missionary working among the Saxons.

BIBLIOGRAPHY

J. Knight Bostock, *A Handbook on Old High German Literature,* 2nd ed. (1976), 109–111.

DAVID R. MCLINTOCK

[See also **Baptism.**]

BAPTISTERY, the building or chamber set apart for the sacrament of baptism and containing a pool or font for the immersion or infusion of the initiate. During the third century baptisteries became common adjuncts to churches. Most early baptisteries were square or rectangular rooms attached to the church (as at Aquileia) or to the atrium (St. Mary, Ephesus); the earliest extant Christian baptistery, at Dura Europos (before 256) was simply a rectangular room incorporated in a *domus ecclesia.* Some early baptisteries had vaulted ceilings; some included apses. By the middle of the fourth century, an octagonal plan was introduced. The centralized ground plan recalls Roman mausolea and may have been selected for baptisteries because the initiate symboli-

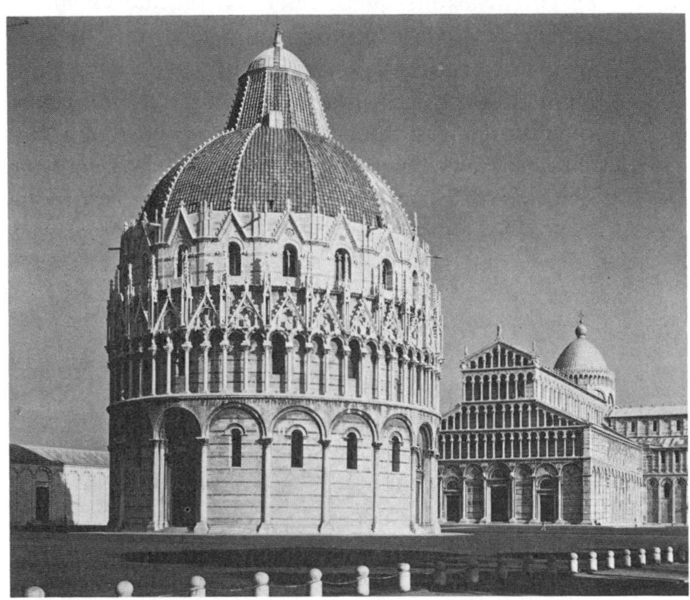

Baptistery and Cathedral. Pisa. 11th-12th Centuries. SEF/EDITORIAL PHOTOCOLOR ARCHIVES

BARBARIANS, INVASIONS OF

cally died and was reborn into Christianity through the sacrament of baptism. The eight-sided plan may have been chosen because, in Ambrosian number symbolism, eight was the number associated with regeneration, salvation, and resurrection. The central octagon could be surrounded by a square ambulatory (Riva San Vitale, Switzerland) or an octagonal one (Arian Baptistery, Ravenna) or pierced by niches (Orthodox Baptistery, Ravenna). Early baptisteries were often richly decorated with stucco, mosaics, and marble revetments. Outside of Italy changes in the baptismal ritual made the separate baptistery obsolete after the ninth century, and fonts were introduced into the church proper for the sacrament. Italian baptisteries, retaining the central plan, continued to be constructed throughout the Middle Ages.

BIBLIOGRAPHY

Kenneth J. Conant, *Carolingian and Romanesque Architecture,* 2nd ed. (1974), 380; Richard Krautheimer, "Introduction to an 'Iconography of Mediaeval Architecture,'" in *Journal of the Warburg and Courtauld Institutes,* 5 (1942); and *Early Christian and Byzantine Architecture,* rev. ed. (1975).

LESLIE BRUBAKER

[See also **Architecture, Liturgical Aspects; Early Christian and Byzantine Architecture.**]

BARBARIANS, INVASIONS OF. The term "barbarian invasions" here refers to the movement of various Germanic peoples into the Roman Empire from the third to the seventh centuries (German, *Völkerwanderung*). The Germanic people first came to the attention of the more advanced Mediterranean world in the middle of the first millennium B.C. They were then located in northern Europe, living in an area that extended from the lower part of the Scandinavian peninsula south and west through Jutland and east along the southern coast of the Baltic Sea.

About 500 B.C. the Germans began to move. It is not known why: perhaps the climate became cooler and damper; perhaps the seas rose and flooded part of the land that they had occupied; perhaps overpopulation strained the food supply. In any event, some of the German peoples slowly moved south and east, and others moved southwest into an area recently vacated by Celtic groups. An advance wave moving southwest brought the Germans into contact with Rome. Two groups of these people, known in Roman records as the Teutones and the Cimbri, pushed into southeastern Gaul and northern Italy, causing great consternation and fear until the popular general Marius was sent north to check them. Marius defeated the Teutones at Aquae Sextiae (Aix-en-Provence) in 102 B.C., and the Cimbri at Vercellae (Vercelli) in 101. These two peoples thereafter retreated north.

Although the Germans discontinued their invasion so far south, they continued to press toward the west whenever Celtic pressure relaxed sufficiently to permit this. There were, thus, a few Germanic groups in Gaul at the time of Caesar's conquest, and Caesar had to defeat the German leader Ariovistus as well as the Celtic Gauls.

One result of Caesar's conquest of Gaul was to push the advance units of the Germans back east of the Rhine. A military victory over the Germans, followed by a rapid crossing of the Rhine (55 B.C.) and a brief campaign east of the river to impress the Germans with the might of Roman arms, established the Rhine as a boundary between the Roman world and the Germanic peoples. Not that the Rhine was designed to be a permanent frontier, for efforts were made during the reigns of Augustus and Tiberius to push the Roman frontier east to the Elbe, thereby shortening the boundary that was then the Rhine-Danube line. Failure to conquer Germany left a point of weakness in the angle formed by the upper courses of the Rhine and Danube, a salient that was later strengthened by the creation of a special fortified *limes* (the *agri decumates*) between the headwaters of the two rivers.

The Rhine-Danube line, extended by Trajan to incorporate the province of Dacia north of the Danube, was the boundary between the Roman and Germanic worlds from the first to the third centuries of the Christian era. During that time extensive contacts were established between the two peoples. Roman traders connected the two worlds, and individual Germans penetrated Roman territory, where demand for labor already existed, and increased rapidly from the third century on.

This contact between the Roman and Germanic worlds undoubtedly caused changes in German society. Peoples who had not shown much political organization now began to amalgamate into tribes or nations under the leadership of individuals variously called *duces, iudices,* or *reges.* There is no way to understand the development of kingship among the Germanic people except to recognize that the model provided by Rome undoubtedly played some part. By the time the great migrations of the fourth and fifth centuries began, most of the Germanic peoples were led by kings, and most of these kings held positions that had become hereditary in a particular royal family.

Also, most of the Germanic peoples continued to reflect an earlier organization into family groups held loosely together, especially in time of war, by a military leader with the title of *dux*. Germanic political-familial organization was further complicated (and effective union made more difficult) by the existence among the Germans of an extrafamilial, extratribal organization known as the comitatus, a group of warriors who had associated themselves with a military leader by mutual oaths of loyalty. His personal military following strengthened the position of the king, but political rivals or nobles with strong retinues of their own threatened effective royal power.

The important point is that the Germanic groups that entered the empire were not well-defined nations held together by recognized political relationships; they were groups of tribes and subtribes that had come together in the period immediately preceding the invasions, and the emergence of a tribal leader or king had been quite recent. They were loose confederations of families of varying background, brought together by proximity of dwelling place and the common purpose of moving into the tempting land of the Roman Empire.

Our information about Germanic institutions before the third-century invasions comes largely from Caesar's *Gallic Wars* and Tacitus' *Germania*, with some additional information from Strabo, Pliny the Elder, and Ptolemy. Caesar, in the middle of the first century B.C., wrote largely from firsthand military contact with the Germans; Tacitus, at the end of the first century of the Christian era, gathered his information while staying along the Rhine frontier.

The accounts given by these two Roman writers are considerably at variance with one another. Neither is especially reliable, and there seems little point in assuming that Caesar was correct when he described what amounts to the holding of land in common among the Germanic people. Conversely, we need not necessarily accept Tacitus' account, which indicates that at least some of the Germans were beginning to accumulate private property by the time he was writing. But both writers may be correct, in which case a fundamental change had taken place between the first century B.C. and the end of the first century of the Christian era in the Germanic attitude toward property. According to E. A. Thompson, the Germans practiced communal possession of property in the earlier time, but under Roman influence recognized private property by the later. Once private property was recognized, a few individuals or families inevitably accumulated more than the others, and a kind of aristocracy of wealth resulted.

However we interpret the evidence, it is clear that the Germans were not nomadic by the first centuries of the Christian era. They were settled agriculturists whose farming expertise may not have been much better than the slash-and-burn technique. It is clear that a certain amount of Germanic movement is explained by the need to move on, from time to time, to find fresh soil.

The first great invasions came in the third century. For the most part these were not movements of entire peoples looking for new homes, but raiding expeditions made possible by the Roman civil wars that lasted from 235 to 284, during which time the frontiers were often abandoned as one army after another left its post to participate in the game of emperor-making. A group of peoples referred to as Franks crossed the Rhine frontier, passed through Gaul, and may have penetrated as far south as Tarragona in Spain, plundering and burning as they went. Once the Roman military organization was turned against them, the Franks retreated to the lower Rhine area, leaving behind a heavily damaged Gaul where some of the fields had passed out of production and would remain so for a long time, and where many of the towns had to build walls as protection against future raids.

In central Europe, from the area just north of the Rhine-Danube *limes*, another conglomerate of Germanic people called the Alamanni took advantage of the weakened defenses to cross the frontier and head toward Italy. They plundered northern Italy and even threatened the city of Rome itself; in 271 the Emperor Aurelian found it necessary to erect a new wall for protection—the first wall built around Rome since the fourth century B.C.

In eastern Europe the Goths poured across the undefended Danube frontier, ravaged the Balkan peninsula, crossed to Asia Minor, and created havoc there before returning north of the Danube and the Black Sea (although a few Goths sailed the Mediterranean, raided islands, passed through the Straits of Gibraltar, and presumably linked up with related Goths in the Baltic Sea area).

The third-century invasions were a serious blow to Rome but did not cause the loss of any territory

BARBARIANS, INVASIONS OF

to the Germans, with the exception of the province of Dacia, north of the Danube, abandoned to the Goths. Contacts between Germans and Romans now became more frequent. Increasingly the Roman authorities found it difficult to raise enough military recruits within the empire, and both individuals and groups of Germans were peacefully admitted to the empire for the purpose of enlistment. As the Germans learned more about the internal weaknesses of the empire, they renewed their testing of the frontier defenses; throughout the fourth century the Romans were forced to maintain and bolster their border garrisons in order to avoid further serious loss of territory.

The barbarian invasions of the empire began in earnest in the late fourth and early fifth centuries. Although there were a number of long-standing reasons for the invasions—the attraction of life within the empire, where agriculture seemed easier and more productive than in Germany; population pressure; the weakness of Roman defenses; the hope of finding a new homeland—the single immediate cause was the appearance of invaders from Asia, the Huns.

Nothing about the Huns is certain except that they appeared in the area north of the Black Sea just before 375, when they defeated the Ostrogoths, absorbed some of them into a loose confederation, and then turned west toward the Visigoths, who in terror applied for permission to cross the Danube into Roman territory. The main body of the Ostrogoths remained under Hunnish domination for the next three-quarters of a century, but in the meanwhile the continued westward movement of the Huns pushed a number of other Germanic peoples against the Roman frontier.

THE VISIGOTHS

It is usually assumed that about the time of the birth of Christ, the Goths were living in southern Scandinavia and upper Jutland. In the second century the Goths began to move south and east, and by the third century they dominated an area centered in the Dnieper valley. This migration had been accomplished in scattered groups, but during the fourth century there began a general coalescence into two major groups, a more eastern one (Ostrogoths) and a western one (Visigoths), although these groupings were not so firm that individuals and families could not pass back and forth with ease from one to the other.

The western Goths pushed into the area north of the Danube and, about 271, Aurelian conceded Dacia to them. Peace with Rome was confirmed by treaty in the early fourth century, and a number of Roman influences, including Christianity, penetrated Visigothic life. In 341 an Arian bishop, Ulfilas, of Roman-Gothic descent, was appointed for the Goths; as a result of his work, the groundwork was laid whereby the Visigoths later became Arian Christians, and Gothic became a written language. (Ulfilas devised an alphabet and script based on Greek, and translated the New Testament into the Gothic language.)

After the Ostrogoths had been defeated and reduced to servitude by the Huns in 375, the Visigoths requested permission to cross the Danube into Roman territory. An agreement was reached and the main body of the Visigoths under the leadership of Fritigern crossed the river, although a smaller group joined with some Ostrogoths and, under the leadership of the Visigoth Athanaric, settled in the Carpathian Mountains and in Moldavia.

The Visigoths who crossed the Danube were soon in conflict with the East Roman authorities over food and land. An increasingly tense situation led finally to war between the Visigoths under Fritigern, now called king, and the East Roman army under the command of the emperor Valens. A battle from which the Visigoths emerged victorious and in which Valens was killed took place at Adrianople in 378.

After Adrianople the Visigoths wandered through the Balkan peninsula for some years, attempting to force the cession of land from the new emperor, Theodosius I. During this trying period the Visigothic kingship became a stronger institution and the Visigothic menace more serious. Agreements were repeatedly made and broken as the Visigoths tried to secure better land and the Romans tried to contain the Visigothic menace.

By 397 the Visigoths were led by a king named Alaric and had settled in Epirus. Still dissatisfied, Alaric led the Visigoths into Italy in 401. The Western Roman Empire (now under the emperor Honorius) was unable to organize resistance in the face of internal jealousies, and even though troops were recalled from the Rhine frontier (thus opening that border to further Germanic invasion), the Visigoths entered Italy and, failing to secure acceptable terms or adequate food, sacked Rome in 410.

The sack of Rome created consternation in the Roman world and brought Romans in general to full comprehension of the German threat. That "Eternal

BARBARIANS, INVASIONS OF

Rome," beloved of the gods, could be so treated must indicate divine displeasure. Although the pagan cults had been outlawed since 392, paganism remained strong, especially among members of the senatorial order. Pagans blamed desertion of the old gods for the disaster, and in response to this charge, Augustine wrote his *City of God* as the great Christian apologetic of late antiquity.

From Rome the Visigoths continued south (carrying with them the emperor's sister, Galla Placidia, whom they had seized as a hostage), evidently expecting to cross to the agriculturally rich provinces of North Africa. The death of Alaric, however, combined with too few ships, turned the Visigoths around. Now led by Ataulf, brother-in-law of Alaric, they moved north once again through Italy and into southern Gaul. Here, in 418, after years of continued negotiation with the West Roman authorities, the Visigoths returned Galla Placidia and were recognized as federate allies *(foederati)* of the empire.

The Visigoths were settled in Aquitaine in accordance with a system of hospitality that became usual in Rome's handling of barbarian *foederati.* The hospitality was between a Roman host and a barbarian guest (and involved a sharing of revenues or lands, or both). In return for the support thus received, the barbarians assumed responsibility for the defense of the province. It was a system that usually worked well because there had been a general decline in population since the third century, and the land could easily absorb the new Germanic settlers. (None of the barbarian groups that entered the empire was very large.) The system also worked because the barbarians were eager to make it work. Accordingly, defense now rested with the barbarian army while much of the administration continued as before, with the difference that the Roman civil service was now responsible to a Germanic "king" rather than to a Roman provincial governor.

It was in response to an Ibero-Roman request for defense that the Visigoths pushed across the Pyrenees later in the fifth century. Eventually the Visigoths lost most of Aquitaine to the Franks (in 507) while retaining Spain and Septimania (the Mediterranean coast of France east to the Rhone).

The Visigothic kingdom lasted until its overthrow by Moors in 711. In the meantime, after a period of initial friction between Germanic Visigoths and provincial Romans, primarily over religion, the Visigoths abandoned their Arianism and, upon their acceptance of Catholicism, a fusion of the two peoples gradually took place. The new society thus created owed much to its Roman heritage in law and education, but in politics and military life it owed much to its Germanic heritage. In the long run the Visigoths failed to create a strong state under royal leadership because of the Germanic tradition of loyalty to a personal lord rather than to the king. This, rather than the superior strength of the Moors, allowed Spain to become part of the Islamic world for the next four centuries.

VANDALS, SUEVES, AND BURGUNDIANS

The denuding of the Rhine frontier of its troops, in a futile effort to protect Italy from the Visigoths, allowed a number of other barbarian peoples to cross. Among these were the Vandals, first noted by Pliny in the first century of the Christian era as a large body of Germanic peoples living on the southern shore of the Baltic Sea. In the second century several groups of Vandals moved south and, unable to penetrate Dacia, turned west toward the Pannonian plain (just north of the Danube), where they remained until the fourth century. Here they were in contact with the imperial *limes* and subject to some Roman influences, and here they may have been converted to Arian Christianity through the influence of the Visigoths.

Under pressure from the Huns, the Vandals moved farther west; by 406 they were at the Rhine when that frontier was denuded of its defense. The Vandals (together with a smaller group of Germanic people, the Sueves) crossed Gaul and settled temporarily in Spain. But the Visigoths, now allies of Rome, undertook a number of campaigns against the Vandals in defense of the Roman provincials in Spain; as a result of the Visigothic threat, the Vandals looked farther afield for a place of permanent settlement. In 429, under their king Genseric (or Gaiseric), they crossed the Straits of Gibraltar into northern Africa, where they easily overthrew the Roman administration. Six years later the Romans accepted the Vandals as federate allies of the empire.

By the middle of the fifth century, the Vandals not only controlled the North African coast west from Tunisia, but had moved into the islands of the western Mediterranean. In 455, failing to secure from the Western emperor a favorable response to the terms they demanded for African and Sicilian wheat, the Vandals sacked the city of Rome.

The Vandal kingdom lasted until its overthrow by the East Roman (Byzantine) army under Justinian's general Belisarius in 530. It left little influence behind because the Vandals, unlike most of the other

BARBARIANS, INVASIONS OF

Germans who settled on Roman territory, looked upon the land and resources of Africa as wealth to be exploited by its conquerors, not to be shared with the Roman population. We are left with the impression that the Vandals made little effort to conciliate the Roman provincial part of their population and that little progress was made, during the life of the kingdom, toward amalgamation. But this picture may be too grim, for we have little written information from Vandal Africa except from those disaffected from Vandal rule—for example, all members of the Church hierarchy, alienated by the Arianism of their barbarian overlords. At any rate, the Vandals received no support from Roman provincials when the Byzantine armies appeared.

In the meantime the Sueves, who had shared in the temporary Vandal exploitation of Spain, retreated northwestward when the Visigoths occupied the rest of the peninsula. An independent Suevian state lasted until 585, when it was incorporated into the Visigothic kingdom.

At about the same time that the Suevians and Vandals crossed the Rhine, another conglomerate Germanic group, the Burgundians, also crossed. The Burgundians are first identified in the first century of the Christian era in the Baltic area, probably as part of the larger grouping then called Vandal. They moved west in the third century, and settled just beyond the *limes* of the *agri decumates* between the headwaters of the Rhine and Danube rivers. Here, for a century and a half, they were in close economic and cultural contact with Rome, and here they may have been converted to Arianism through the influence of the Vandals and Visigoths.

In 406 the Burgundians did not penetrate very deeply into Roman Gaul. Instead, they established a kingdom in the middle Rhineland (partly in Gaul and partly in Germany), and were accepted by Rome as federate allies.

This Burgundian kingdom did not last very long, however, since its tendency to expand more deeply into Gaul brought reaction from the Roman defenders (now released from the Visigothic threat). About 435 the Burgundians were defeated and partially destroyed by Huns in the employ of the Roman general Aëtius. The remainder of the Burgundian people then moved south, and in 443 was allowed by Rome to establish a second federate kingdom in the region around the western end of Lake Geneva. From this area the kingdom gradually expanded west and south to fill most of the Rhone Valley from Lake Geneva to the Mediterranean. The kingdom's lack of effective consolidation under a single king is reflected in the fact that there were three capitals—Geneva, Lyons, and Vienne—and when a king left more than one heir, a different king might rule at each capital.

The Burgundians were settled in southeastern Gaul by a system of hospitality similar to that followed for the Visigoths in Aquitaine. They were in an area that was highly Romanized, and they inherited a responsible civil service. As a result, Burgundian rule caused fewer difficulties for the Roman population than was the case in most of the other barbarian kingdoms (with the possible exception of the Ostrogothic). This kingdom reached the height of its importance under the leadership of King Gundobad (474–516), whose efforts to reconcile the Germanic and Roman parts of his population culminated, following Visigothic precedent, in the issuance of two law codes, one for each of his peoples (the *Lex Burgundionum* for the Burgundians and the *Lex Romana Burgundionum* for the Romans). The Burgundian kingdom lasted until 535, when it was incorporated into an expanding Frankish kingdom, although its particularist traditions continued strong and Burgundy, with its own laws and customs, remained an identifiable area within the Frankish superstructure.

THE OSTROGOTHS

After the Huns had defeated the Ostrogoths in 375, they continued west, pushing the main body of the Visigoths across the Danube and absorbing the remainder and other Germanic groups as they advanced toward Pannonia. Eventually a large but poorly coordinated Hunnish empire stretched from the eastern Alps to the Black Sea. Attila became king of the Huns in 434. Under Attila's leadership the Huns became an important factor in the struggle between Rome and its Germanic invaders.

The Roman general Aëtius, who had once been a hostage among the Huns, often used Huns as allies or mercenaries in his army. By 451, however, cooperation between Romans and Huns had become difficult, and the Huns began pushing into Gaul. This Hunnish threat brought into the field a Roman army made up of contingents from the federate allies (Visigoths, Burgundians, and Franks). At the battle of the Catalaunian Fields (sometimes called Châlons) in the region of Champagne in 451, Attila and his Huns were defeated by the allies under the leadership of the Visigothic king Theodoric I (who died in the battle). Defeated but far from destroyed, the Huns

BARBARIANS, INVASIONS OF

retreated east of the Rhine, and in the following year moved into Italy, capturing many cities before turning toward Rome. As the Huns approached the city, Pope Leo I came out to meet them, and for whatever reason—the entreaties of Leo, the threat of divine wrath, or the illness of Attila—the Huns withdrew. Attila died in 453, and almost immediately the Hunnish empire disintegrated, the conquered peoples taking advantage of the situation to break away. By 454 the Hunnish menace had all but disappeared.

Freed from Hunnish control, a group of Ostrogoths led by King Valamir received permission from the East Roman emperor Marcian to settle in Pannonia. A nephew of Valamir's, seven-year-old Theodoric son of Thiudmir, was shortly thereafter sent to Constantinople to serve as a hostage for the good behavior of the Ostrogoths. This Theodoric remained at the imperial court from 461 until 470.

Meanwhile, another group of Ostrogoths under Theodoric son of Triarius settled in Illyria as federate allies of the Eastern Empire. Imperial policy tended to play the two groups of Goths off against one another, and as a result neither was very strong. In 471, Theodoric son of Thiudmir succeeded to the leadership of his group of Ostrogoths, and for ten years the emperor Zeno manipulated a struggle between the two Ostrogothic Theodorics. In 481, Theodoric son of Triarius was killed in battle. His followers and some of his people then joined Theodoric son of Thiudmir, and gradually a single, larger, and stronger Ostrogothic grouping developed.

As Ostrogothic power grew, it became a more serious threat to Zeno, who, to solve that problem and an Italian problem, commissioned Theodoric and his Ostrogoths in 488 to go to Italy to overthrow Odoacer. The latter had been ruling Italy since 476, when, as *magister militum* (commander) of the Roman army (and thus a potential "emperor maker"), he had deposed the emperor Romulus Augustulus. Instead of naming a new emperor, Odoacer accepted election as king by his followers and sent notice to the Eastern emperor that he himself was now ruling Italy in the name of the emperor at Constantinople. Although Odoacer was a German, his "kingdom" is not counted as one of the barbarian kingdoms because his position was based not on leadership of his people but on his role as *magister militum* in the Roman army. The year 476 is important as marking the end of the Western Roman Empire, for from this date the rulers of the Germanic kingdoms ceased to act in the name of the Western emperor and became independent kings. Nonetheless, in theory the date has no significance because, in Eastern eyes, the empire remained a whole over which the Eastern emperor now exercised all imperial authority.

But Odoacer did not rule a dependent Germanic kingdom, and although he had been recognized with the title patrician, the Eastern emperor evidently regarded him as a threat. A too powerful Odoacer might assume the imperial title for himself. Therefore, to get the Ostrogoths out of the Balkans and to get Odoacer out of Italy, Zeno urged the Ostrogoths to go west. In 489 the Ostrogoths crossed into Italy, and between 489 and 493 they defeated Odoacer, occupied the northern part of the peninsula, and eliminated Odoacer and his chief supporters.

In spite of pursuing very unscrupulous tactics in consolidating the Ostrogoths under his control and in getting rid of Odoacer, Theodoric proved to be one of the more enlightened of the barbarian kings. He succeeded in establishing a state that at least nominally recognized the overlordship of Constantinople but that was in fact independent. It was a state marked by very considerable cooperation between Goths and Romans, because Theodoric pointedly respected Roman law and Roman customs, and retained much of the Roman administrative system and many of its trained personnel (including Cassiodorus and Boethius). A Gothic aristocracy emerged, based for the most part on military leadership during the many years of wandering in the Danube area and in the Balkan peninsula, and gradually came to adopt the habits of the Roman aristocracy. With time it seemed almost certain that a fusion of the two societies would take place.

But the Ostrogothic success was the success of one man, Theodoric, and when he died in 526, disaster soon followed. The ethnic differences between Goths and Romans were exasperated by religious differences. So long as the Catholic powers of the Mediterranean world were weak, the Romans of Italy accepted, albeit grudgingly, Theodoric's policy of toleration that accorded equal recognition to Arians and Catholics. But once there was an orthodox restoration in Constantinople and the Franks had adopted Roman Catholicism, friction over religion led to treason against the king.

Added to dissension over religion was an increasing tendency of local nobles to regard their positions as virtually independent of royal control (a problem that plagued all the barbarian kingdoms). In any event, the Ostrogothic realm was already deeply troubled when the Byzantine army, fresh from its

BARBARIANS, INVASIONS OF

overthrow of the Vandals, landed in Italy in 536. The Ostrogoths struggled long and hard, but by 552 Justinian could regard Italy as effectively restored to the empire—a restoration that was short-lived, inasmuch as a weakened Italy invited another barbarian invasion within a few years.

THE FRANKS

While Vandals and Sueves were heading south and the Burgundians were settling first in the middle Rhine area and later around Geneva, another Germanic people remained in approximately the same position it had occupied for some time. These were the Franks (divided into a number of groups ruled by dukes or kings), who in the early fifth century were living in the region of the lower Rhine, partly in Gaul and partly in Germany. Their position there had been confirmed in the mid fourth century by the emperor Julian the Apostate, who had made them federate allies of the empire, charged with protecting this part of the frontier.

The history of the Franks between the middle of the fourth century and the middle of the fifth century is obscure. This was a period of increasingly close contacts with the Romans of northern Gaul as the Franks fulfilled their responsibilities as federate allies. Military cooperation increased after the Huns had been defeated in 451, and the Roman defense of northern Gaul was abandoned to a field army stationed at Soissons, near Paris, under the command of a Roman named Aegidius (who was succeeded in this position by his son Syagrius). During this period the numerous Frankish peoples began to coalesce into two major groupings, the Salian Franks (the more westerly) and the Ripuarians (somewhat to the east and up the Rhine). Salian consolidation was accomplished under the leadership of the rulers of a family later known as the Merovingian (from the name of its mythical founder, Merovech). The first Merovingian king of whom we have clear historical proof is Childeric (*d.* 481). He was succeeded by his son Clovis, who eventually united all the Franks under his command. By 508 he succeeded in eliminating all the rival Frankish kings, many of whom had been close blood relations.

The Franks gradually expanded their territory. By 459 they had occupied Mainz and Trier; by 475, Metz and Toul. Their advance westward was temporarily checked by the Roman army of Syagrius stationed at Soissons (where after 476, Syagrius ruled over a territory no longer formally attached to the Western Empire, sometimes described as sub-Roman). This army was, however, defeated by the Franks in 486, and thereafter Frankish territory extended west and south to the Loire.

Clovis' conquests, extended by his sons, brought all of Gaul (with the exception of Brittany and Septimania) under Frankish control, and extended Frankish power to the east well beyond the Roman Rhine frontier. Although the Franks were in many ways less sympathetic to their Roman provincials than were some of the other barbarians—notably the Visigoths, Burgundians, and Ostrogoths—in the long run it was the Franks who established a lasting state. This success was due in no small degree to the fact that the Franks, under the leadership of Clovis, remained heathen until the early sixth century, when Clovis made the momentous decision in favor of Roman Catholicism rather than Arianism. The Catholic Franks thereafter enjoyed at least the neutrality, if not the active support, of the Catholic hierarchy in Gaul, a support that gave them a decided advantage in their conflicts with Visigoths and Burgundians.

ALAMANNI, BAVARIANS

The Alamanni are first mentioned in the early third century as living in the area of the *agri decumates* between the upper Danube and middle Rhine rivers. They invaded Italy several times during the mid third century, and Gaul during the fourth, but each time they were repulsed.

During the fourth and fifth centuries the Alamanni formed a fairly powerful and important confederation, but their status began to decline in the late fifth century under Frankish attack. They were defeated by Clovis at the close of the fifth century, and thereafter part of the Alamanni lived directly under Frankish rule in Alsace. Another part moved back toward the east, where they remained in the region of Lake Constance until brought under Frankish control by Charles Martel in the early eighth century.

The Bavarians, first mentioned in the mid sixth century by Jordanes, were then occupying the area still known as Bavaria in southern Germany. Although subject to Frankish pressure at most times, they retained a kind of autonomy under their Agilofing dukes, and normally cooperated with the Lombards in Italy. During the late seventh century the Bavarians became independent of the Franks. In 788 their continued independence under Duke Tas-

BARBARIANS, INVASIONS OF

silo III aroused the fury of Charlemagne, and Tassilo was forced to swear homage. Bavaria was incorporated in the Frankish kingdom.

THE LOMBARDS

The attempts of the East Roman emperor Justinian to restore the old boundaries of the Roman Empire were a tacit admission that, whatever the theory of continued imperial unity, the barbarian kingdoms were indeed independent of Roman control. Justinian's actions resulted in a rearrangement of the Western world. North Africa became part of the East Roman Empire; the Ostrogoths had been virtually eliminated; Italy, although temporarily ruled from Constantinople, had been ruined in the long, drawn-out wars between the Ostrogothic and Byzantine armies; and a small area in the southeastern part of the Iberian peninsula had been wrested from the Visigoths. From the five Germanic kingdoms that had been established as a result of the fifth-century invasions, only the kingdom of the Franks remained strong in Gaul, and a weakened although still vital Visigothic kingdom remained in Spain.

The destruction of the Ostrogothic kingdom left Italy in a very disorganized state. The Ostrogothic population had resisted conquest as long as possible, and was to a large extent wiped out in the process. Byzantine control of Italy brought Byzantine tax collectors, for Justinian needed money not only to pay for his Italian wars but also for renewed wars against Persia on the eastern frontier. But Italy was too devastated to pay, and restlessness in the face of a weak Byzantine garrison left the country open to another invasion. There had been contingents of Germanic Lombards in the Byzantine army that finally defeated the Ostrogoths; it was not long before the Lombards, realizing its weakness, invaded Italy.

The Lombards are first definitely located about 5 B.C., when they were defeated by Tiberius. At that time they were living along the lower Elbe River, and they were still there when Tacitus wrote. By A.D. 167 they had moved south, and were in contact with Roman Pannonia. They seem to have remained there until the late fifth century (489), when they moved into an area of lower Austria that had been abandoned by Rugians who followed Odoacer into Italy.

In the fifth and early sixth centuries the Lombards do not seem to have been regarded as a major people. In the early sixth century they moved into Pannonia, where some of them were probably converted to Arian Christianity. During this period the Lombard kingship grew stronger, and Lombards served from time to time in the East Roman army.

A number of Lombard mercenaries served with the Byzantine general Narses in the last campaigns against the Ostrogoths in Italy. This experience in Italy proved to be decisive for the future of the Lombards; wanting to avoid the Avars in Pannonia and realizing the weakness of Italy, the Lombard king Alboin led his people into Italy in 568.

The Lombard invasion of Italy was a curious migration of many small groups of Germanic peoples in addition to the Lombards proper. They apparently broke the *limes* of Friuli with little difficulty, took Aquileia (forcing the patriarch to take refuge on the little island of Grado), and moved into the Po Valley. By 572, when Pavia fell, nearly the entire Po Valley was Lombard. Meanwhile, other Lombards crossed the Apennines, occupied most of Tuscany, established the foundations of the future Lombard duchy of Spoleto north and east of Rome, and moved into the southern part of the peninsula (the future Lombard duchy of Benevento). Although the Byzantines retained Venice and Ravenna and their immediate hinterlands, Rome and a surrounding territory, Calabria, the Campanian coast, and Liguria around Genoa, the greater part of the Italian peninsula came under Lombard domination.

The early phases of the Lombard occupation were not promising for the future of a strong Lombard kingdom. The king who had led them into Italy was assassinated in 572, and his successor was killed in 574. Thereafter the Lombards elected no successor for ten years. Although the dukes, under the threat of Frankish attack, chose a new king in 584 and the kingship thereafter was a regular institution, this tension between the royal power and the ducal power always remained in Lombard Italy. The failure of the Lombard dukes to support their king led to conquest by the Franks in the late eighth century.

In its two centuries of existence, the Lombard kingdom moved a long way toward assimilation of Germans and Romans, despite the Lombard reputation for cruelty and the consistent efforts of the papacy to oppose the Lombard state. Building without an intact Roman civil service (which had disintegrated during the Ostrogothic-Byzantine wars), the Lombard kings nonetheless worked out an effective political and military organization in which the Germanic Lombards were undoubtedly the favored partners in the association but in which the Romans had a protected place that, as time went on, brought increasing participation in political and military life.

BARBARIANS, INVASIONS OF

Under Liutprand in the eighth century, it seemed for a time that the entire Italian peninsula might be consolidated into a single political entity. But although Liutprand's successors were far from incompetent, they faced two disturbing factors: an alliance between the papacy and the Franks and, simultaneously, the Lombard kings' inability to rely on the loyalty of the Lombard dukes. In 774 the Lombards were defeated by the Franks, and the greater part of Italy came under the rule of the Carolingians.

ANGLES, SAXONS, AND JUTES

The Germanic invasions of the Roman province of Britain followed a pattern somewhat different from that of the invasions of the continental provinces. On the Continent the Germans invaded territory that was defended (at least nominally) by Roman arms, and the Germans, when settled, were normally made partners in future defense in return for the cession of land. Hence, there was relatively little destruction of Roman property or institutions, with the result that in all the continental Germanic kingdoms there was a real fusion of Roman and Germanic elements. That the Germans did not necessarily prevail is indicated by the triumph of the Latin language in almost all the continental territory that had been part of the Roman Empire.

The situation was different in Britain. The Roman province of Britain had been abandoned by its Roman troops before the barbarian invasions of the island began. During the troubled fourth century, troops had occasionally been withdrawn from Britain to strengthen the Roman armies elsewhere, but such withdrawals were at least partially restored. The collapse of imperial authority in Gaul and Britain in the late fourth and early fifth centuries led the Romano-Britons to raise three imperial claimants in rapid succession. The last of these, Constantine III, looked to Gaul for a larger field of operation. He took the remaining Roman troops from Britain with him to Gaul, in a fruitless effort to gain the imperial throne. The troops did not return.

Therefore, after 407 the Romano-British provincials, in spite of repeated appeals to Rome, had to provide their own defense as best they could. But despite the helplessness of the island and the almost certain knowledge of this weakness among the continental Germans, the island of Britain was not seriously invaded from the Continent until the middle of the fifth century; the Picts and Scots from Scotland and Ireland seemed a greater danger. In fact, the first Germans to go to Britain seem to have been mercenaries engaged to strengthen British defenses against northern and western invaders.

A sub-Roman province that retained its Roman administrative system without formal connection with Rome held out in Britain until the middle of the sixth century, but by this time Germanic invaders, starting from the region of Kent in the southeast part of the island, had gradually pushed British resistance west, and the more Romanized part of the population retreated before the Germanic advance. By the mid sixth century a more or less permanent boundary between Germanic England and Celtic Britain was established, a boundary that left the "Celtic fringe"—Wales, Scotland, and Ireland—outside Anglo-Saxon control. In the area settled by the Germans, little Roman influence was left. Anglo-Saxon England was a Germanic area where Latin survived only as the language of education and the Church.

Tracing the barbarian invasions of Britain is difficult. According to Bede, who wrote in the early eighth century, there were three peoples involved: Angles, Saxons, and Jutes. The Angles, who had been living in southern Jutland, seem all to have migrated to Britain, although this movement extended over a very long period of time. The Saxons in the early fifth century were living along the North Sea coast just west of Jutland. Not all of the Saxons migrated to Britain. Part remained in Germany, moving slightly deeper into German territory (an area to be called Saxony) that was conquered by Charlemagne in the late eighth century. Only the fact that the customs and institutions of the people who settled in Kent differed somewhat from those of the peoples who settled the rest of England lends credence to the possibility that a third Germanic tribe was involved in the conquest of Britain. The Jutes cannot be traced back to a homeland on the Continent, although some scholars insist there is archaeological evidence indicating the area near the mouth of the Rhine is their place of origin.

Since the language and customs of the Angles and Saxons were closely related and the two peoples eventually merged with the people who settled in Kent, no attempt will be made here to trace in detail the establishment of Germanic settlements in England. Eventually, as the Romano-Celts withdrew westward, the Anglo-Saxons were able to set up independent states. Gradually seven kingdoms emerged. In the south, Kent, Sussex, and Wessex; farther to the north, Essex and East Anglia; and to the west and north, Mercia and Northumbria. Leadership passed from north to south and back again, but beginning with the new barbarian invasions from the north in the late eighth century, there was a tendency for the Anglo-Saxons to come together to resist the enemy. This process was slow and not continuous, but gradually the rulers of Wessex assumed leadership of the resistance to the Danes. By the tenth century all of Anglo-Saxon England was united under the kings of Wessex.

Anglo-Saxon England was the most Germanic state of the kingdoms created out of the former Western Roman Empire. Towns and villas vanished, Roman law disappeared, and Latin culture languished until revived by the Church. Even Christianity apparently disappeared with the retreat westward of the more Romanized Romano-Britons; Anglo-Saxon England was re-Christianized through the efforts of Roman missionaries under Augustine.

THE PLACE OF THE BARBARIAN INVASIONS IN THE "FALL" OF THE ROMAN EMPIRE

By the middle of the sixth century, all of the Western Roman Empire had given way to a number of Germanic kingdoms that had been established by invading barbarians. Were the invasions responsible for this imperial disintegration?

It cannot be denied, of course, that the barbarian invasions brought into the empire new groups of vigorous peoples, eager for land and willing to fight to get it. At the same time the native Roman population had come to rely on a distant Roman army to protect it, and had lost the ability or inclination to defend itself. So there is a very direct relationship between the arrival of the barbarians and the disappearance of Roman unity in the West.

But it may well have happened that the Western Roman Empire would have disintegrated even without the invasion of the Germans. The whole empire was in great trouble from the third century on, and had been held together thereafter only through the efforts of Diocletian and Constantine, who had kept the empire going by instituting the most rigid planning. This planning could be effective only if the state were absolute, and in the new regime the needs of the army for defense and of the civil service for administration bore so heavily on the population that everyone was to a degree enslaved to the state. Civil war was endemic in the empire from at least the third century on. It may well be, in fact, that the barbarian invasions, instead of causing the "fall" of the Roman Empire, instead permanently cut that empire into an eastern and a western part—and, by pulling them apart, created a situation in which the East Roman Empire could capitalize on its greater economic strength and survive until the fifteenth century.

BIBLIOGRAPHY

For general treatments of the barbarian invasions and for conditions within the late Roman Empire, J. B. Bury, *History of the Later Roman Empire from Theodosius I to the Death of Justinian* (1923) and *The Invasion of Europe by the Barbarians* (1928); A. H. M. Jones, *The Later Roman Empire, 264–602,* 2 vols. (1964); Ferdinand Lot, *The End of the Ancient World and the Beginnings of the Middle Ages* (1931) and *Les invasions germaniques* (1935); and Lucien Musset, *The Germanic Invasions* (1975).

On the early Germans and Germanic institutions, including treatment of the literary and archaeological evidence, see Émiliene Demougeot, *La formation de l'Europe et les invasions barbares,* 2 vols. (1969); Francis Owen, *The Germanic People* (1960); E. A. Thompson, *The Early Germans* (1965); and Malcolm Todd, *Everyday Life of the Barbarians* (1972).

For a treatment of Germanic agricultural settlement, especially in northeast Gaul, see Robert Latouche, *The Birth of Western Economy* (1961); and, for a study of the system of hospitality used by the Romans as a means of settling the Germans within the boundaries of the empire, Walter Goffart, *Barbarians and Romans A. D. 418–585* (1980). On early development of Ostrogothic institutions, see Thomas S. Burns, *The Ostrogoths* (1980).

KATHERINE FISCHER DREW

[See also **Alamanni; Anglo-Saxons; Burgundians; France; Germany; Huns; Italy and the Empire; Lombards; Odoacer; Ostrogoths; Roman Empire, Late; Theodoric the Ostrogoth; Vandals; Visigoths.**]

BARBERS, BARBER-SURGEONS. The precise origins and antecedents of the medieval barber-surgeons are unclear. In the high and late Middle Ages they held an established position in the hierarchy of medical practice. Situated between the university-trained physicians and surgeons on the one hand, and the rural practitioners and faith healers on the other, barber-surgeons provided much of the practical medical care then available, especially to persons of nonnoble status. But while this hierarchy seems clear in theory, it was never so in practice.

In this discussion surgery and barber-surgery, and even barber-surgery and medicine (what would now be called internal medicine), will not be separated in terms of their technical aspects. All medieval medi-

BARBERS, BARBER-SURGEONS

cal practitioners drew, to a greater or lesser extent, upon the same body of medical knowledge. Emphasis varied, but any systematic division of medical practice along the lines of the social and legal divisions of practitioners is artificial. For that reason the terms "physician" and "surgeon" will be used indifferently for any practitioner, although the social and legal implications of the different ranks of medical practitioners will be examined in their turn.

Barber-surgery was perceived as artisanal and was usually regulated by a guild. The barber-surgeon learned his trade by experience, rather than in a classroom. By the end of the Middle Ages, barber-surgeons had established themselves as an integral part of functioning medicine, with responsibilities toward government and other branches of the medical profession.

The early Middle Ages witnessed a medicine based in monasteries and elaborated by monks. In a few places, such as Visigothic Spain and Lombard Italy, lay physicians and surgeons persisted, but by 800 medicine was almost exclusively the province of clerics. To what extent practitioners of surgery existed apart from the religious setting is impossible to say. It has been suggested, however, that lay practitioners assisted monk-physicians with bloodier and technically more difficult procedures. The evidence for this contention is scanty.

Several forces combined to separate medicine from surgery in a formal sense and, to some extent, to separate all of medical practice from the clergy. In the first place, as class or status lines solidified, surgery was perceived as a manual occupation, and thus of low status. Second, canon law began to forbid the practice of medicine, and especially surgery, to many clerics, partly on the ground that clerics were forbidden to shed blood. Even the decisions regarding the critically ill patient could place a cleric in the position of causing death. That is not to say that the clergy suddenly ceased to practice medicine and surgery. Theodoric, one of the greatest medieval surgeons, became bishop of Cervia in 1266. Part of the practical intent of the prohibitions was probably to keep clerics at their spiritual duties and to afford fewer opportunities for traveling away from local parishes in order to undertake university training. Despite the uneven results of such prohibitions, the way was opened for lay practitioners.

To be sure, the eleventh through the thirteenth centuries also saw the establishment of formal medical training at universities. The school at Salerno was the earliest and most practically oriented. Roger of Salerno and Guido of Arezzo were the twelfth-century exponents of a rather practical surgery that enjoyed some favor at Montpellier in the thirteenth century. Other universities, notably Bologna and Paris, rejected the Salernitan tradition. In Bologna surgery became more theoretical as it drew on the works of the great Arab physicians. Although surgery always aimed at practical results, namely procedures that could actually be performed, classical and Islamic surgical texts taught operations so complex and risky that the vast majority of medieval surgeons could not attempt them. Knowledge of such procedures was nonetheless taught, divorcing knowledge from practice to some extent.

Legislation began to organize medicine more formally. In the early thirteenth century the training, qualification, and licensing of physicians were regulated in Sicily by Frederick II. In Paris medical instruction was available by 1213. By 1350 definite license and degree requirements had been established. Surgery was not taught during the thirteenth and fourteenth centuries. A statute of Paris forbade physicians to practice surgery, and surgeons wishing to become physicians had to renounce their former craft.

In Italy, by the fifteenth and sixteenth centuries, surgery was in general a lower-class, and medicine an upper-class, profession, according to Carlo Cipolla. This sharp distinction did not arise quickly, but was implicit in the universities' rejection of surgery and in surgery's stigma of manual labor. It is worth noting, though, that surgery could lead to considerable economic and social advancement. By its nature it is a practical craft, and a practitioner capable of producing desirable results could prosper. Thus, many exceptions to such class generalizations occurred.

Even had they embraced surgery, the universities could not have met the need for surgeons. In the fifteenth century Oxford and Cambridge together produced only seventy-five doctors of medicine. According to James Mustain, even allowing for foreigners, there were probably fewer than 100 university-trained physicians in England during that century.

Thus a definite need existed for surgeons. Trauma alone demanded persons with technical skills, as did dental problems and operable diseases. This need was met by a variety of surgeons, ranging from a few university-trained practitioners down to the many practically instructed barber-surgeons. The distinc-

BARBERS, BARBER-SURGEONS

tions between these groups, at least from 1200 to 1400, were rather hazy. Venice, for example, made no distinction.

Surgeons provided multiple services. Treatment of trauma was a major function. Reduction of fractures, amputation of mangled limbs, wound care, and repair of traumatic eviscerations fell to surgery. Even our limited knowledge of medieval skeletal remains suggests that trauma was a major cause of morbidity and mortality. Operable diseases that offered at least a chance of survival included hernias, cataracts, and urinary-tract stones. Barber-surgeons also performed dental extractions and gum surgery. Instrumentation was relatively simple, and a form of anesthesia using soporific sponges was available. These sponges were dipped in opium, mandrake, hemlock, and henbane, then dried. When dipped in hot water, their vapors could render a patient unconscious and with an increased threshold of pain. This was not, of course, true anesthesia, the absence of which precluded most peritoneal and thoracic surgery. Phlebotomy, or bloodletting, was also a specialty of the barber-surgeon. The functions of the modern barber—haircutting and shaving—were not neglected. It is not at all clear how the functions of barber and surgeon came to be combined. Perhaps they were simply complementary aspects of tending to physical needs in a manual way.

With the exception of phlebotomy, these services represented nearly all of what, by modern standards, could be considered the therapeutically effective modalities of the age. (By contrast, effective medical therapies were limited to basic nursing care and a very small number of efficacious drugs.) The level of skill, of course, varied tremendously, and expert practitioners were highly prized. In 1327, for example, the commune of Venice hired Pellegrino of Padua, who was a master of operating for the stone. In 1329, Venice rewarded three surgeons for their skill and devotion. One Maestro Pietro was found in 1330 to be practicing hernia repairs—quite well, it was noted—without a license. The commune shortly afterward sanctioned his practice. Rural districts could not hope to attract the elite of surgeons and physicians, and relied heavily on persons trained as barber-surgeons.

Like most tradesmen and artisans, the barber-surgeons organized themselves into guilds, ranging from relatively autonomous associations to state-regulated and semiofficial organizations, as in Venice. Usually guild membership involved inscription in the guild records, the swearing of an oath, the establishment of qualification, and the payment of a fee. In 1281 a law of the Grand Council of Venice forbade anyone's practicing medicine in the city without swearing an oath to the Giustizia Vecchia. The practice of surgery and dentistry was restricted to members of the guild of the *barbieri.* In Florence the guild was more autonomous, and controlled several occupations. Florentine barbers belonged to the Arte dei Medici e Speziali. The distinction of the barbers from the physicians *(medici)* was unclear. In the early fourteenth century few barbers matriculated in the guild (one member was called "physician and barber"). Between 1386 and 1444, however, 248 barbers matriculated, a number greater than that of the *medici.*

The London guild of barbers also included other occupations because, by a law of 1363, everyone plying a skilled trade had to belong to a guild, a situation resulting in some incongruous combinations. Candlemakers, for example, belonged to the barbers' guild.

Richard le Barber was the first master (1309) of London's guild of barber-surgeons to be charged with avoiding scandals and monitoring the moral behavior of the barbers. Two classes of barbers were recognized: simple barbers, who occupied themselves with dentistry and phlebotomy, and barber-surgeons, who performed surgical procedures. London barber-surgeons were often appointed porters of the city gates, in the hope that their medical skill would permit them to recognize and exclude lepers.

In York, according to Margaret Barnet, barber-surgeons greatly outnumbered physicians. The guild of barber-surgeons, like most, had an oath and tried to uphold standards. After 1614 the guild master held yearly dissections and anatomy lectures, which members were obliged to attend.

The guilds also fulfilled religious and social functions. In York the members performed a mystery play. In London members arranged Masses for their deceased colleagues. Most guilds held banquets and had meetings, which presumably helped alleviate boredom and provided a sense of community.

Oaths of these guilds were relatively simple, usually brief statements agreeing to abide by the rules of the guild and to be loyal to the city. Citizenship in the city or some equivalent thereof might be required. Guild regulations attempted to maintain a standard of work and to minimize friction among members. Sometimes fees were regulated, but medi-

BARBERS, BARBER-SURGEONS

eval medicine generally adopted a sliding scale. It was expected that the poor would be treated without charge and the rich charged enough to make up the difference.

For those who had plied their trade elsewhere, the guilds usually required an examination to determine competence before allowing them to practice in their new home. Apprentices were boarded and fed by their masters, and learned the skill by observation and supervised practice. The period of apprenticeship could be as long as eight years.

It is important to contrast this situation with the education of university-trained physicians. At universities physicians were taught philosophy (among other disciplines) along with medicine. Medicine itself was taught systematically and theoretically, with little practical experience. The result was a physician who was learned in a general way, and who was a master of discourse about disease. At his best such a physician could be a superb diagnostician and prognostician. His rhetorical skills were high, and these ought not to be underestimated in terms of their influence on a patient's morale. His therapeutic skills, however, were negligible. This contrast was recognized at the time. John R. Hale has commented that in the fifteenth century, the physician was often perceived as someone who charged a great deal but whose pomp failed to disguise his lack of success.

By contrast, the surgeon and barber-surgeon learned their trades by experience and were more practically oriented. Most therapeutic potential lay in their hands. While some were quite learned and wrote treatises, their intellectual stature was overshadowed by that of their university-trained counterparts. While the latter are more central to the intellectual history of medieval medicine, the barber-surgeons are central to the social, and to some extent the technical, history of medieval medicine.

Before leaving the subject of barber-surgeons, it is worthwhile to examine briefly their social position and relation to institutions. Although there were spectacular exceptions, barber-surgeons were of what we would now consider the urban lower class, little different from other artisans. Their earnings were usually meager, and rural practitioners often needed other sources of income. Rarely did they tend the noble or the wealthy merchant.

The duties of the barber-surgeons often left the medical domain for the legal. In Venice they were obliged to report criminals and suspicious wounds or illnesses. They might be called upon to testify in murder cases or to help in postmortem examinations. Physicians in Venice could be called upon to torture criminals.

Medical practitioners were sometimes employed outright by the government. This was particularly the case in the Italian city-states. Again to cite Venice, one of the most extensively studied cities, in the early fourteenth century, eleven physicians and seventeen surgeons were employed by the commune. It is typical of the social conceptions of the period that in general the *medici* received much higher wages. Physicians and surgeons served in the fleet and tried to control contagious disease in the city. When the office of the Provveditori alla Sanità was established in 1486, in an effort to safeguard public health, barbers came under its regulation.

Service under such magistracies could be quite onerous. Public health officers were obliged to impose restrictions on trade and social intercourse. Many citizens neither understood nor accepted such regulations, a situation that made the officials and their executors quite unpopular. Further, the practitioners themselves were exposed to contagious and terrifying diseases. In 1348, when plague struck Venice, most medical practitioners fled the city. One who remained to help combat the disease, Francesco of Rome, was honored by the commune for his loyalty. He replied that he preferred to die in Venice rather than live elsewhere.

Despite obvious rivalries and class distinctions, the various types of medieval medical practitioners did cooperate in many instances. In fourteenth-century Paris university physicians gave some instruction to barbers. In some places surgeons may have existed as a separate class of practitioner who instructed barber-surgeons. Physicians occasionally deigned to perform surgery, and were likely to be obliged to perform postmortem examinations. The University of Pisa maintained a chair of surgery until the end of the seventeenth century.

It is a well-known stereotype of medieval life that when medical school cadaver dissections were performed, a master read from a textbook (often Galen) while a barber-surgeon performed the actual dissection. This image, far from uniformly true, is suggestive of why medieval medicine made little technical progress. Theory and practice were the domains of different groups.

Moreover, people remained distrustful of earthly medicine. Throughout the Middle Ages many religious writers cautioned against placing faith in medicine, lest the hope for cure should distract one from repentance. Peter Cantor, for example, summed up this sentiment exactly when he wrote that a man on his deathbed might wish more ardently for the arrival of his physician than for that of his confessor. Preoccupation with bodily illness could imperil the soul. Barbers in particular were suspected of prolonging illness for personal gain. People were admonished not to call on medicine when God was needed. In the face of attitudes like these, it is a small wonder the barber-surgeon held a low status. As a practitioner he might interfere with God's work. As a laborer he worked with his hands. As a source of knowledge and theory, he could not compete with the physician. For us, however, he is best remembered as often the sole source of practical medical care.

BIBLIOGRAPHY

Margaret C. Barnet, "The Barber Surgeons of York," in *Medical History,* **63** (1979); Carlo M. Cipolla, *Public Health and the Medical Profession in the Renaissance* (1976), 74–77, 102; John R. Hale, *Renaissance Europe: The Individual in Society, 1480–1520* (1973), 103–104; Loren C. MacKinney, *Early Medieval Medicine with Special Reference to France and to Chartres* (1937); James K. Mustain, "A Rural Medical Practitioner in Fifteenth Century England," in *Bulletin of the History of Medicine,* **46** (1972); Charles H. Talbot, *Medicine in Medieval England* (1967), 88–124; and "Medicine," in *Science in the Middle Ages,* David C. Lindberg, ed. (1978), 391–428; Sidney Young, *Annals of the Barber-Surgeons of London* (1890), 22–39.

STEPHEN R. ELL

[See also **Guilds and Metiers; Medicine, History of.**]

BARBOTINE, ceramic clay of a consistency permitting it to be pressed through a tube, analogous to a pastry tube, as applied relief decoration on ceramic vessels and other pieces. The barbotine technique was used in Mesopotamia during the neo-Assyrian period and was subsequently adopted in other ancient civilizations. In the Middle Ages it was known throughout the Islamic world.

The technique, however, always remained particularly characteristic of Mesopotamia. It is found on glazed jars and other pieces excavated at Hira, as well as at Susa and Bīshāpūr in neighboring southwestern Iran; these pieces are from the Sasanian and early Islamic periods. Barbotine decoration reached its highest level of development, though, on unglazed water jars *(ḥabbs)* and related vessels from northern Mesopotamia and probably Syria. These often very large jars were made of porous clay and left unglazed, which permitted evaporation of their contents through the vessel walls, thus keeping the liquids cool. Their decoration is usually figural and rendered in a combination of barbotine, molded, and incised techniques, with occasional carving as well.

Barbotine Ware Jug, 1st Century A.D., METROPOLITAN MUSEUM OF ART

Gerald Reitlinger distinguishes three "styles" of decoration on these vessels, the first of which he dates between the ninth and twelfth centuries. In that group the human figures, birds, and animals are rendered almost diagrammatically, primarily in barbotine. In Reitlinger's other two stylistic groups, which fall in the twelfth to fourteenth centuries, the main figures are usually molded in varying levels of relief and are treated much more naturalistically. Barbotine, though lavishly used, is generally restricted to details and repeated abstract motifs serving as space fillers and borders. Particularly distinctive is a little humanoid creature entirely in barbotine, consisting of a shield-shaped head on a shield-shaped body, spindly legs, and extremely long, rubbery arms. This curious figure appears repeatedly on these later *ḥabbs*.

BIBLIOGRAPHY

Gerald Reitlinger, "Unglazed Relief Pottery from Northern Mesopotamia," in *Ars Islamica,* **15–16** (1951); Friedrich Sarre, "Islamische Tongefässe aus Mesopotamien," in *Jahrbuch der Königlichen Preuszischen Kunstsammlungen,* **26** (1905); and "Die Keramik im Euphrat- und Tigris-Gebiet," in *Archäologische Reise im Euphrat- und Tigris-Gebiet,* IV, Sarre and E. Herzfeld, eds. (1920).

ESTELLE WHELAN

[See also **Islamic Art.**]

BARBOUR, JOHN (1316?–1345), archdeacon of Aberdeen, was the author of *The Bruce* (*ca.* 1375), a historical romance celebrating Scotland's struggle for freedom. Barbour conflates Robert Bruce (crowned Robert I; *d.* 1329) with his grandfather, the sixth Robert the Bruce, who had unsuccessfully sought the Scottish crown at the end of the thirteenth century. The poem gives the impression of using eyewitness accounts, especially to describe the Battle of Bannockburn (1314), in which the chivalrous Bruce defeated Edward II. The second half includes the expedition to Ireland by Robert's brother, Edward the Bruce.

BIBLIOGRAPHY

The Bruce: An Epic Poem, Archibald A. H. Douglas, trans. (1964); A. M. Kinghorn, "Scottish Historiography in the Fourteenth Century: A New Introduction to Barbour's *Bruce,*" in *Studies in Scottish Literature,* **6** (1969); Bernice W. Kliman, "John Barbour and Rhetorical Tradition," in *Annuale mediaevale,* **18** (1977).

CHARLES STANLEY ROSS

[See also **Robert I; Scotland.**]

BARCELONA. The medieval history of Barcelona begins with the construction of the late Roman defenses, the 10.4 hectares of which sheltered the greater part of the inhabited area until the later tenth century. Both archaeological and literary evidence, particularly that of Ausonius, suggests a flourishing fourth-century economy, although Roman Barcino was still a minor city in comparison with the provincial capital of Tarragona.

The first steps in the change of roles between the two came in the fifth century, when Barcelona was used as a base by the Visigothic king Ataulf, who died there in 415, and by the usurper Sebastian. It fell to the forces of Euric in 472, and henceforth became something of a Visigothic royal center: a palace is recorded in 510–511, and Amalaric retreated to the city after defeat by Childebert. For the next two decades it can be considered a capital, a role later lost to Seville.

Information on human life in the Visigothic city is derived mainly from archaeology: the early Christian basilica and baptistery in one corner of the city, and an adjoining structure tentatively associated with the Visigothic palace, further remains of which are believed to have been found under the surviving royal palace. The importance of these structures lies in the indication of a change in the topographical pattern of antiquity, the forum area being abandoned in favor of what was to become the early medieval focus. The city maintained some administrative significance, as demonstrated by the *De fisco barcinonensi* (592), which shows it as the center of an area including the dioceses of Ampurias, Girona, Tarragona, and Egara (Terrassa); it also had a mint of significance in this period and later.

As elsewhere, the bishops played an increasing role in urban life: by far the outstanding early bishop was Pacianus (late fourth century), author of works that included a treatise against pagan practices. Later bishops are principally known from their presence at Church councils, the exceptions being the Arian Ugnus (*fl.* 589) and, later, Quiricus and Idalius, both men of letters. Apart from the basilica, partially under the existing cathedral, only one other church probably existed in the Visigothic period—that of SS. Just i Pastor. Much of the evidence comes from cemeteries around the city proper and also in its *territorium.* However, by the early seventh century burials took place within the walls, another transition to the medieval city. During this century it increasingly served as a fortress—for example, during the revolt of Paulus—a function it retained for several centuries.

Little can be said of the period of Arab occupation (*ca.* 717–801), even though Barcelona rather than Tarragona was the administrative center for the region. The strategic role of the defenses is apparent in Ermold the Black's poem on Louis the Pious. For most of the ninth and tenth centuries, Barcelona was a frontier bastion, and only in the tenth century did resettlement take place south of the Llobregat frontier. It fell to the Muslims in 852, and perhaps in 897–898, and to al-Manṣūr in 985. The citizens enjoyed privileges given by Charlemagne and confirmed in 844, and were overseen by the bishop and by the count of Barcelona, probably through his viscount. The inhabitants clustered around the residences of these three could hardly have numbered more than a thousand.

Some change can be seen in the mid tenth century with the emergence of a port and *villanova* beyond Montjuïc. Slightly later, suburban settlement appeared outside the northeast gate adjoining the market. Within the walls a new cathedral may have been erected, the Church of S. Miquel was established within the still-standing Roman baths, and the Church of S. Jaume was built in what had once been the forum. This renewal was partially the result of broadening contacts with Rome and the caliphate.

After the 985 attack there was a further phase of renewal: the gates were strengthened, the defenses were increasingly incorporated into private residences, the community of canons was reorganized and given buildings, and a hospital was founded. In the suburbs destroyed buildings were soon reconstructed, further growth occurring outside the Castell Vell gate and the northeast gate along the line of the Roman aqueducts. Much of this growth, however, was not the result of commerce but of an agricultural revolution taking place in the surrounding plain.

The struggles between the court and the nobility about 1025–1058 restricted urban expansion, but stimulated the emergence of safety zones *(sagreres)* around the parish churches of the *territorium;* these zones became villages that survived until incorporated into the modern city. Growth resumed in the 1050's, when a large number of new houses appeared. The Romanesque cathedral was consecrated in 1058, and the resultant street pattern of this part of the city dates from this period. A further *villanova* can be identified through the regular street and property pattern on both sides of the Carrer de Montcada (*ca.* 1080): the eastern limit of this zone was a channel carrying water to power the mills (Rec Comtal), and later to irrigate the surrounding horticultural plots. The suburb outside the northeast gate expanded toward the most important of the parish churches, S. Maria del Mar. Within the city walls the Jewish quarter, or *Call,* was defined, its inhabitants numbering some 300 in 1079. Between 3,000 and 4,000 people lived in the city.

Growth during the following half-century was more gradual, possibly being limited by the Almoravid attacks of 1114–1115. From that date, however, commerce began to play a greater role in the urban economy, and links with Genoa and Pisa became apparent; shipbuilding was carried out along the shore. The increasing significance of artisans is indicated by the appearance of workshops, particularly around the market.

A new spurt of growth occurred from about 1135, probably stimulated by increased immigration from both the surrounding *territorium* and most of the county. Some of those involved were noble; others were the forerunners of lines that later dominated urban society, gaining their wealth through agriculture, urban rents, control of artisans, commerce, and public office. Increasing specialization occurred in the market, with the appearance of a meat market (1186) and a cloth hall (1192); other manifestations of trade existed in residences for foreign merchants *(alfondecs)*, shipyards, and "Arab" baths (1160). About 1167, Benjamin of Tudela described Barcelona as "a small city and beautiful, lying upon the sea coast. Merchants come thither from all quarters with their wares, from Greece, from Pisa, Genoa, Sicily, Alexandria in Egypt, Palestine, Africa and all its coasts." By 1200 the settled area covered some 60 hectares, and there may have been 10,000 to 12,000 inhabitants.

In the thirteenth century Barcelona became the habitual residence of the court, and under James I the change from pan-Pyrenean to Mediterranean politics led to a century and a half of common interest with the citizens as a result of the latter's commercial connections with the rest of the Mediterranean. A class of *ciutadans honrats* emerged, and they came to predominate among the councillors, a post established by James I in 1249 to formalize the previous system of urban government by the vicars and an amorphous body of worthy men *(prohoms).* The number of councillors was eventually established as five, their authority being supported by another body of 100 (later 128) known as the Consell de Cent.

Parallel to the emergence of urban institutions, expansion took place in commerce, a new merchant class replacing the inactive oligarchy and profiting from the import of Eastern luxuries as well as local trade. Forty-seven cities, principally around the shores of the Mediterranean, came to have consular representatives from Barcelona, and the compilation of maritime law and custom (*Llibre del Consolat del Mar,* fourteenth century) became widely accepted.

A third social group was the professional classes, often including Jews, who were particularly close to the Crown until the later thirteenth century. A fourth group was the artisans; although trade group-

BARCELONA

ings are first mentioned in 1200, they had originated in the twelfth century, often in the guise of religious brotherhoods. Gradually, however, their organization and internal discipline became more controlled by the rules of the guild, or *gremi,* and the tendency to be grouped together, giving rise to the surviving streets with trade names, became greater. A total of 130 *gremis* are recorded, although a number of them are postmedieval.

Urban growth in the thirteenth century was marked by a number of areas of distinct, regular plan; the first was the coastal Ribera district, divided and sublet by the process of emphyteusis, or perpetual leases. A similar area consisted of the three parallel streets leading to the convent of S. Pere (1250's); further planned development occurred between the latter and the *villanova* of the 1080's, replacing the previous sporadic ribbon growth along the main thoroughfares. By the end of the century further development had taken place to the southwest, and the coastline had receded, giving space for yet another *villanova.*

The new religious foundations of the thirteenth century tended to mark the limits of this growth, with the Dominicans at S. Caterina (1223), the Franciscans on the coast (1230's), the Mercedarians nearby (1250's), and the Poor Clares at the other end of the coastal growth near the mouth of the Rec (1237), and the Junqueres convent at the northern limit of the city (1269). This was the approximate territory, covering some 130 hectares, within the defenses erected between 1260 and 1362, which did not extend south of the Rambles. Prosperity was indicated by the alterations of the Romanesque cathedral and its gradual conversion into a Gothic building, the first stage of which covered the period 1298–1397, and by the surviving urban houses of the wealthy, such as the Aguilar Palace with its wall paintings of the conquest of Majorca.

The first signs of social stress appeared in 1285 with the revolt of Berenguer Oller, although the general appearance of prosperity was maintained in spite of occasional bad years. At the time of the first population records (1359–1365), the population was perhaps some 33,000, although prior to the Black Death, it may have exceeded 40,000. The city had passed its medieval peak: the last areas of planned development, to the north of S. Clara, belong to the early fourteenth century; the rebuilding of the parish churches in Gothic style was a long process; and the number of religious houses was limited after 1370.

In spite of the slow progress after the mid fourteenth century, other modifications of a more general nature were made: the supply of piped water to public and private fountains; the paving of streets; the covering of streams so that they flowed through drains or sewers; the construction of squares. Toward the end of the century the construction of the cathedral was given new impetus, and for the first time municipal buildings, the commercial exchange *(llonja),* and the standing shipyards *(drassanes)* were erected. The latter were just south of the walled city, and were enclosed by an extension built after 1374. Besides the *drassanes,* this zone included the major hospital of Santa Creu (1401) and a number of religious foundations; settlement, however, was limited to the main cross streets, and most of the area was still occupied by horticultural land as late as the eighteenth century.

Nevertheless, the period after 1380 was generally one of decadence. Bad harvests and plagues weakened both the urban population and that of the rural neighborhood. The interests of the Crown and the oligarchy became increasingly divergent, and in 1386, Peter III endeavored to introduce lesser folk into the system of urban government. This was resisted and disturbances followed, culminating in the pogrom of 1391 in which the Jewish *Call* was sacked; the community disappeared definitively in 1401, although a number of *conversos* maintained Hebrew practices in secret.

With changing economic conditions throughout the Mediterranean, trade was disrupted and a depression was noticeable from about 1425. Valencia tended to gain trade benefits at the expense of Barcelona, which ceased to be the capital when the court moved to Naples. The social pressures increased, and resulted in the clash between the Busca and the Biga parties, representing the lesser folk and the oligarchy, respectively. The former were supported by the royal representative in their claims for increased political participation, currency devaluation, and protection against imports. They were in control in 1453–1460, then suffered a savage retaliation by the Biga in 1461. One of the major causes of the Civil War in Catalonia (1462–1472), was this originally local conflict.

The result was disastrous for all concerned, but with the restoration of peace, measures of protection were reinstated and attempts at reconstructing the economy were undertaken—for example, the resumption of cloth exports and the continuation of building of the protective breakwater for the harbor. Nevertheless, endemic piracy and the shift in the interests of the Iberian peninsula toward the Atlantic meant that Barcelona's former glory could not be recovered. Neither did it regain its place as capital, and the royal palace was ceded to the Castilian Inquisition, which devoted its activities to rooting out the *converso* elements, causing a further flight of economically powerful families. Population was still very much what it had been in the mid fourteenth century, fluctuating around 30,000.

The end of the fifteenth century and the early years of the following one saw some revival of fortune, with stone houses being erected and marveled at by foreign visitors, and the completion of unfinished monuments, as well as the introduction of new religious houses and a degree of monastic reform. Nevertheless, the topography of the city had changed little during the previous century, and was to remain essentially the same until the economic revival of the eighteenth century.

BIBLIOGRPHY

Of general histories, Francisco Carreras y Candí, *La ciutat de Barcelona* (n.d. [*ca.* 1916], repr. 1980); and Agustín Durán y Sanpere, ed., *Història de Barcelona,* I (1975), are the most useful. For monumental architecture, see Juan Ainaud, José Gudiol, and F. P. Verrié, *La ciudad de Barcelona,* 2 vols. (1947). A. Durán y Sanpere, *Barcelona i la seva història,* 3 vols. (1972–1975), is a collection of articles on a wide range of subjects.

Works dealing with specific aspects of Barcelona include Alberto Balil Illana, *Colonia Iulia Augusta Paterna Faventia Barcino* (1964); P. J. Banks, "The Topography of the City of Barcelona and Its Urban Context in Eastern Catalonia from the Third to the Twelfth Centuries" (Ph. D. dissertation, University of Nottingham, 1980); Carmen Batlle y Gallart, *La crisis social y económica de Barcelona a mediados del siglo XV,* 2 vols. (1973); Pierre Bonnassie, *La organización del trabajo en Barcelona a fines del siglo XV* (1975); Antonio Capmany y de Montpalau, *Memorias históricas sobre la marina, comercio y artes de la antigua ciudad de Barcelona,* 4 vols. (1779–1792), repr. 2 vols. in 3 (1961–1963); Claude Carrère, *Barcelone, centre économique à l'époque des difficultés, 1380–1462,* 2 vols. (1967); J. E. Ruiz Doménec, "The Urban Origins of Barcelona: Agricultural Revolution or Commercial Development?" in *Speculum,* 52 (1977); André Sayous, *Els mètodes comercials a la Barcelona medieval* (1975); and Jaime Vicens Vives, *Ferran II i la ciutat de Barcelona, 1479–1516,* 3 vols. (1936–1937).

PHILIP J. BANKS

[See also **Aragon, Crown of; Catalonia; Visigoths.**]

BARD. In modern usage the term "bard" (Irish: *bárd;* Scottish: *baird;* Welsh: *bardd*) simply means "poet." In historical terms, bards were the early poets of the Celtic peoples, wandering tribes of mixed heritage who inhabited most of western Europe as far east as Asia Minor. According to Posidonius of Apamea, the bards were one of the three learned classes of the Celts, the other two being the druids and the seers.

The bards composed, preserved, and performed songs in a variety of Celtic languages (Gaulish, Irish, Erse, Manx, Cornish, Welsh, and Breton) before the chieftain and his warriors. The earliest recorded description of bards dates from the first century B.C., when Diodorus Siculus observed: "Among the Gauls there are lyric poets called bards. They compose praises for some and satires on others and chant them to the accompaniment of a kind of lyre." The musical prowess of the bards is attested to by various sources, which include poems on harping: "O instrument of the gentle curve, loud-tongued one, crimson as hemlock, melodious harp that lulled us to sleep played by harmonious fingers."

The bardic songs, composed in alliterative, rhythmical, and formulaic verse, commemorated the past heroic deeds of gods and heroes, and eulogized the present accomplishments of their composers' aristocratic patrons. The following excerpt from a seventh-century Irish encomiastic poem describes the vengeance taken by Cathal for the death of his brother Raghallach: "He slew six men and fifty, he committed sixteen devastations. I had my share like another in the revenge of Raghallach, I have the gray beard in my hand of Maelbrigde, son of Mothlachan." In addition, the early bards, claiming to possess magical powers, used their poetry to instill highly valued qualities—honor and courage—into their listeners.

In Ireland before the Viking period, the bards were subordinated to another class of professional poets, the *fili,* but when the office of *fili* decayed, the bards assumed many of their duties. Like the *fili,* the bards underwent a rigorous period of training, lasting up to seven years, during which time they graduated through as many as sixteen grades. Each grade had its own prosody, subject matter, and intended audience, and a lower bard could not encroach on the poetic property of bards holding higher ranks. When a poet had progressed through all of the grades, he or she had learned 350 different types of versification, and could declaim 250 primary tales and 100 secondary ones.

In Wales the medieval court poets, the *gogynfeirdd* ("not so early bards"), a highly trained literary class, were an important segment of the social structure. The Law of Hywel Dda (940), for example, carefully defined their status, privileges, and benefits. Like the Irish poets, they attended bardic schools, but their profession was not hereditary, as in Ireland. The Welsh bardic order was divided into three grades: the *pencerdd* ("chief of song"), the *bardd teulu* ("bard of the king's retinue"), and the *cerddor* ("minstrel").

The Celtic bards were related in function to the Anglo-Saxon *scop* or *gleoman,* the Germanic *skop* or *spielmann,* the Icelandic and Scandinavian *skald,* the northern French *trouvère,* and the southern French *troubadour;* they were all living encyclopedias of genealogical, mythological, and historical lore, vital to the survival of traditional knowledge in their respective cultures.

BIBLIOGRAPHY

Myles Dillon, *Early Irish Literature* (1948), 171–189; Robin Flower, *The Irish Tradition* (1947), 67–106; Eleanor Knott and Gerard Murphy, *Early Irish Literature* (1966); Ceri W. Lewis, "The Court Poets: Their Function, Status and Craft," in A. O. H. Jarman and Gwilym R. Hughes, eds., *A Guide to Welsh Literature,* I (1976); John Lloyd-Jones, "The Court Poets of the Welsh Princes," in *Proceedings of the British Academy,* 34 (1948); E. C. Quiggin, "Prolegomena to the Study of the Later Irish Bards 1200–1500," in *Proceedings of the British Academy,* 5 (1911–1912); J. E. C. Williams, "The Court Poets in Medieval Ireland," in *Proceedings of the British Academy,* 57 (1971).

THOMAS H. OHLGREN

[See also **Bardic Grammars; Bardic Poetry; Celtic Literature; Irish Literature; Scottish Literature; Welsh Literature.**]

BARDAS CAESAR, Byzantine statesman, the uncle of Michael III and brother of Empress Theodora II. He conspired with Michael to oust Theodora, and became the effective head of state; hence his designation as Caesar. He is perhaps best known for organizing the university at the Magnaura Palace, which became an important center of secular learning and numbered the future patriarch Photius among its teachers. Study at the university was free, and the professors were paid by the government. Bardas became embroiled in a power struggle with Basil I the Macedonian, who had become Michael's favorite; during a campaign against Crete in 865, Bardas was killed by Basil, who then became coemperor with Michael.

BIBLIOGRAPHY

George Ostrogorsky, *History of the Byzantine State* (1957).

LINDA ROSE

[See also **Basil I the Macedonian; Byzantine Empire, 330–1025; Michael III; Theodora II.**]

BARDAS PHOKAS, Byzantine general and magnate. After the murder of his uncle Nikephoros II in 969, Phokas rebelled unsuccessfully against John I Tzimiskes. He was recalled from exile, and in 978–979 put down a rebellion by Bardas Skleros. Sent to combat another rebellion by Skleros in 987, Phokas first joined Skleros, then proclaimed himself emperor and assumed leadership of the revolt, which ended only after his death in 989.

BIBLIOGRAPHY

Gustave Schlumberger, *L'épopée byzantine,* I (1896), 59–75, 397–425, 546–572, 673–742, is the fullest account of Phokas' career. Also see George Ostrogorsky, *History of the Byzantine State,* rev. ed. (1969), 294, 298–299, 303–304; and I. Dujurić, "Porodica Foka" (The family of Phokas), in *Zbornik Radova Vizantološkog Instituta,* 17 (1976), with French summary.

WARREN T. TREADGOLD

[See also **Bardas Skleros; Byzantine Empire, 330–1025; John I Tzimiskes.**]

BARDAS SKLEROS, Byzantine general and magnate. In 969 he subdued Bardas Phokas' revolt against John I Tzimiskes, Skleros' brother-in-law. Skleros revolted against Basil II in 976 but was defeated by Phokas in 979. After going into exile at Baghdad, he rebelled again in 987, only to see his revolt taken over by Phokas. His last rebellion, in 989, ended with his submission to Basil.

BIBLIOGRAPHY

Gustave Schlumberger, *L'épopée byzantine,* I (1896), 59–75, 340–425, 437–445, 673–751, and II (1900), 12–26, is the fullest account of Skleros' career. Also see George Ostrogorsky, *History of the Byzantine State,* rev. ed. (1969), 294, 298–299, 303–304; Werner Seibt, *Die Skleroi* (1976), esp. 29–58.

WARREN T. TREADGOLD

[See also **Bardas Phokas; Basil II; Byzantine Empire, 330–1025; John I Tzimiskes.**]

BARDHA^{c}A (Armenian: Partaw), the capital of Caucasian Albania. Located on the lower course of the Terter River in the old Armenian principality of Utik^{c} (modern Azerbaijan S.S.R.), Bardha^{c}a was founded by the Albanian king Vač^{c}ē II (*ca.* 460), as a replacement for the earlier Albanian capital of Kabala. After 879 it became the usual residence of the Muslim governor of Armenia and Azerbaijan. Situated on the trade route from Iran to Tiflis and Dwin, Bardha^{c}a was by the tenth century the largest and most important commerical center of Caucasia. Praised by Arab geographers as a handsome city of adobe and brick, Bardha^{c}a possessed a large citadel, a fine mosque, a governor's palace, and extensive suburban markets. Suffering from internal problems even before its destruction by the Rus pirates in 944, Bardha^{c}a never recovered, and its importance passed to Ganjak (modern Kirovabad).

BIBLIOGRAPHY

H. A. Manandyan, *Trade and Cities of Armenia in Relation to Ancient World Trade,* Nina G. Garsoïan, trans. (1965); V. Minorsky, *A History of Sharvan and Darband* (1958); Moses of Kałankaytuk or Dasxuren, ed., *The History of the Caucasian Albanians by Movses Dasxuranc^{c}i,* C. J. F. Dowsett, trans. (1961).

ROBERT H. HEWSEN

[See also **Albania, Caucasian.**]

BARDIC GRAMMARS (Irish, Welsh). The bardic tradition ended in Ireland and Wales in the seventeenth century and lingered in Scotland until the eighteenth. The only descriptions of bardic schools—*Memoirs of the Right Honourable Marquis of Clanricarde* (1722) and Martin Martin's *A Description of the Western Islands of Scotland* (1703)—tell of students who are closeted in unlit, windowless cells and, according to Martin, "lie on their backs with a Stone upon their Belly," concentrating on the metrical and stylistic exercises set the evening before. Candles are brought in late in the day, so that the students may write out the results of their labors before the evening class. No account of a Welsh school survives, but it is clear that, as in Ireland, aspiring bards had always been apprenticed to established poets for varying lengths of time.

The earliest guides to the curriculum—the Irish *Scholars' Primer* (*Auraicept na nÉces,* George Calder, ed., 1917) and the Welsh *Gramadeg* of Einion Offeiriad or of Dafydd Ddu (G. J. Williams and E. J. Jones, eds., in *Gramadegau'r Penceirddiaid,* 1934)—are unreliable, but the essentials of instruction can be inferred from other sources. Great quantities of verse and hundreds of tales were memorized, and training in local history and genealogy was intensive. Close attention to details of meter, alliteration, and assonance, and the proper use of archaic poetic vocabulary and syntax, were essential to mastery of the poetic art.

The sources provide slight evidence for a native grammatical tradition in Ireland. Otherwise, such grammar as was taught in the schools was based on Donatus and Priscian. The origins of the bardic guild are unknown. Parallels with the Druidic schools described by Caesar (*Gallic War,* 6, 13–14) are obvious, and the Gaulish schools can, in turn, be connected with the Brahmanic schools of ancient India, raising the possibility of an Indo-Celtic learned tradition of great antiquity.

BIBLIOGRAPHY

Harold Idris Bell, *The Nature of Poetry as Conceived by the Welsh Bards* (1955); Nora K. Chadwick, *The Druids* (1966); David Greene, comp., *Irish Bardic Poetry* (1970); Eleanor Knott, ed., *A bhfuil aguinn dăr chum Tadhg Dall Ó Huiginn,* I (1922); Lambert McKenna, *Bardic Syntactical Tracts* (1944); John Ellis Caerwyn Williams, *The Poets of the Welsh Princes* (1978).

H. ROE

[See also **Auraicept na nÉces; Bard; Gramadegau'r Penceirddiaid; Irish Literature: Bardic Poetry; Scottish Literature, Gaelic; Welsh Literature: Poetry.**]

BARDIC POETRY. See **Irish Literature.**

BARGEBOARD, from medieval Latin *bargus* ("gallows"), one of two boards attached to or used in lieu

of a barge couple and affixed perpendicular to the end of a gable to prevent rain from seeping into the exposed ends of roofing boards. Medieval bargeboards frequently were richly carved or ornamented. The bargeboard is also called gableboard or vergeboard.

CARL F. BARNES, JR.

BAR HEBRAEUS (also known as Gregorius, Abu'l-Faraj, and Ibn al-ᶜIbrī), one of the greatest historians of the Middle Ages. Born in 1226 at Melitene, he was the son of a Christian physician who was either a convert from Judaism or of Jewish descent. He had a thorough education that included the study of Greek and Arabic, and was a scholar of theology and philosophy. Bar Hebraeus also practiced medicine. In 1243 the Mongol invasion drove him from Melitene, and the following year he went to Antioch, where he became a monk and was ordained a bishop at the age of twenty.

Bar Hebraeus was particularly interested in reviving Syriac language and literature and in bringing Muslim scholarship to the attention of Christians. To this end he wrote on Aristotelian thought as interpreted by Avicenna (Ibn Sīnā) and translated a work of Avicenna's into Syriac. Bar Hebraeus wrote treatises on astronomy and cosmography and on medicine, as well as a commentary on the Scriptures, but his most important work was his universal history, the *Chronography.*

This work is in three parts: a history of the world from Creation down to Bar Hebraeus' time; a history of the Church and especially of the patriarchs of Antioch and of the Monophysite branch of the Church down to 1285; and a history of the eastern Syrian church. In his work he made use of Syrian, Persian, and Arab historians such as Ibn al-Athīr for the Mongol period and Michael the Syrian, whose history of the area he continued to 1286. Some of Bar Hebraeus' material is clearly firsthand, which makes it especially valuable: he was metropolitan of Aleppo when the Mongols took that city in 1259–1260, and he appears to have been acquainted with members of the Mongol court. The *Chronography* was originally written in Syriac, but Bar Hebraeus made an Arabic version of the first part, which includes references to Muslim writers, just before his death in 1286.

BIBLIOGRAPHY

E. A. Wallis Budge, ed. and trans., *The Chronography of Gregory Abu'l Faraj* (1932).

LINDA ROSE

[See also **Athīr, Ibn al-; Historiography; Michael the Syrian; Sīnā, Ibn.**]

BARI, a fortified city and trading center in Apulia on the southeast coast of Italy. In 841 it was captured by a group of Muslim mercenaries hired by one of the rival claimants to the duchy of Lombardy, and for thirty years it was the seat of a Muslim pirate state. In 871 the Carolingian Louis II seized it with the help of a Byzantine fleet; and on Louis's death in 875, the inhabitants handed the city over to the Byzantines. Bari was the seat of the katepanate of Italy, created at the end of the tenth century. The Muslims raided Bari often, and in 1003 held the city briefly before it was retaken by a Venetian naval force. The Normans took it in 1071, ending Byzantine domination in southern Italy. The Byzantines recaptured it briefly in 1155, but in the following year the Norman William I retook Bari and ordered it razed.

BIBLIOGRAPHY

George Ostrogorsky, *History of the Byzantine State* (1957).

LINDA ROSE

[See also **Italy, Byzantine Areas; Italy and the Empire.**]

BARISANUS OF TRANI cast bronze doors for the cathedrals of Ravello, Trani, and Monreale. The works are composed of panels modeled in low relief from a set of molds probably designed for the Ravello composition, dated 1179, and modified for the later commissions. The upper registers, with Christ, the Virgin, the Baptist, Elijah, the Deposition, the Harrowing of Hell, and apostles, have a redemptive theme, while the lower panels, with equestrian saints and combat scenes as emblems of protection, complete the cosmic hierarchy initiated above. The style exhibits Byzantine elements but is basically linked with Campanian Romanesque sculptural tradition.

BIBLIOGRAPHY

A. Boeckler, *Die Bronzetüren des Bonanus von Pisa und des Barisanus von Trani,* Die frühmittelalterlichen Bronzetüren, IV (1953), 47–70; A. Grabar, review of Boeckler, in *Kunstkronik,* 7 (1954); D. Walsh, "The Iconography of the Bronze Doors of Barisanus of Trani," in *Gesta,* **21** (1982).

DAVID A. WALSH

BARLAAM AND JOSAPHAT. The legend of Barlaam and Josaphat (Joasaph) was one of the most popular hagiographic stories of the Middle Ages. In 1048 a Latin translation of the Greek version brought to the West a Christianized reworking of an Indian life of Buddha dating perhaps from the third century. The story tells of Josaphat, a young Indian prince locked away to prevent his prophesied conversion to Christianity, and of Barlaam, a monk who converts him. More than sixty versions, translations, or adaptations of the legend are recorded in European languages. Traditionally the Catholic church lists Barlaam and Josaphat among the saints whose feast day is 27 November.

BIBLIOGRAPHY

David Lang, trans., *The Balavariani (Barlaam and Josaphat): A Tale from the Christian East* (1966); Jean Sonet, *Le roman de Barlaam et Josaphat,* I (1949).

ROSALIE VERMETTE

[See also **Balavariani.**]

BARLAAM OF CALABRIA, born at Seminara around 1290, was an Italo-Greek monk who immigrated to Constantinople and, while teaching philosophy, became involved in a controversy with the Byzantine theologian Gregory Palamas on the issue of knowledge of God and theological methodology (1336–1338). Having gained the confidence of Byzantine imperial and ecclesiastical authorities, he was sent in 1339 to Avignon, where he undertook unsuccessful negotiations on church union with Pope Benedict XII. Upon his return his theological positions continued to be challenged by Palamas and his supporters, the Hesychast monks. He therefore attacked them, calling them "Messalians" and "people-having-their-souls-in-their-navels" (ὀμφάλο-ψυχοι), an allusion to psychosomatic methods of prayer used by the Hesychasts. On 10 June 1341, Barlaam was condemned by a council presided over by the patriarch John XIV Kalekas and was forced to apologize to the monks. On the next day he left Constantinople and spent the rest of his life in Italy, where he taught Greek to Petrarch and eventually was raised to the bishopric of Gerace. He died around 1348.

Defending the absolute unknowability of God, Barlaam initially fought Western Thomistic rationalism, but the claim of the Hesychast monks that communion with God is possible in the supernatural and mystical experience of the saints was equally unacceptable to him.

BIBLIOGRAPHY

John Meyendorff, *Byzantine Theology,* 2nd ed. (1979); Gerhard Podskalsky, *Theologie und Philosophie in Byzanz* (1977).

JOHN MEYENDORFF

[See also **Gregory Palamas; Hesychasm.**]

BARLEY. See **Grain Crops.**

BARMAKIDS, family of Iranian origin that served prominently in the administration of the early Abbasid caliphs. Their ancestor was reportedly the high priest of the Buddhist shrine at Nawbahār in Khorāsān. Following the Umayyad incursions into Khorāsān, the Barmakid family left their ancestral homeland for Iraq, and shortly thereafter presumably converted to Islam.

One of the family, Khālid ibn Barmak, became active in the eighth-century Abbasid revolutionary movement. Although he was not given a command post in the army once the Abbasids openly challenged the regime in power, he was, in keeping with his status as an Abbasid client, entrusted with a wide variety of sensitive administrative tasks. During the revolutionary campaigns Khālid distributed booty, and afterward he became paymaster of the army as well as the regime's primary tax collector. Eventually he exercised control over the entire government apparatus, becoming in effect the caliph's *wazīr,* or minister of state. Because of intrigues at court, he was removed from his position in Baghdad, but he proved very resilient and continued to serve his patrons in the provincial administration, where he had a distinguished career. He died during the reign of al-Mahdī in 781 or 782.

The career of Khālid set the pattern for other Barmakids: they were given sensitive administrative positions but, by and large, were kept at arm's length from the regular army. Khālid, and some of the later Barmakids, participated in various military campaigns, but they cannot be identified as members of the regular military establishment. Yaḥyā, the son of Khālid, achieved great fame for his victory over the Byzantines at Samālū, but this appears to have been a rather trivial expedition designed to give the future caliph (Hārūn al-Rashīd) experience in the field. Yaḥyā was accompanied by several of his relatives; it is most likely that the Barmakids were sent with the Abbasid prince in order to serve as his political tutors. Other accounts of the Barmakids in battle leave the impression that their function was primarily political.

In this sense the Barmakids were typical clients *(mawālī).* Their status was entirely dependent on the caliph they served. They had no recognizable constituency of their own. Whatever powers accrued to them were not derived from, and generally were not transferable to, their social class as a whole. The system was well suited to the conspiratorial outlook of the Abbasid sovereigns, who could isolate their clients without fear of antagonizing any well-defined political structure. Nevertheless, given their administrative talents, the Barmakids (and others like them) were allowed to create powerful client families within the state administration. These miniconstituencies were, however, very sensitive to changes within the ruling house.

The Barmakid family survived the first such major change. During the dispute between the caliph al-Hadi and his heir apparent Hārūn they apparently supported the latter. Only the fortuitous death of the caliph allowed the Barmakids to escape unscathed. Yaḥyā ibn Khālid was richly rewarded for his loyalty to Hārūn, and was subsequently appointed *wazīr,* a position he held for seventeen years.During this time he was ably seconded by his sons al-Faḍl and Ja^{c}far, each of whom held positions of prominence.

It was during this period that the influence of the Barmakids became most pronounced. Their power may have been derived, in part, from the caliph's aversion to the political and moral climate at the capital. Hārūn al-Rashīd had unoffcially moved his residence to a new administrative center that he developed adjacent to al-Raqqah, and had concentrated on foreign policy. Thus, the *wazīr* and his associates were left to administer affairs at Baghdad. In 803 the power of the Barmakids abruptly ended; the caliph, apparently without warning, had Ja^{c}far executed and the other members of the family imprisoned and deprived of their properties. Although the surviving family members were later released, they never again became prominent in affairs of state.

The cause of the fall of the Barmakids has remained an enigma, and it is doubtful that a satisfactory explanation can be produced from the available data. Several theories have been advanced. First, although the caliph was displeased with the moral climate at Baghdad, the Barmakids acquired a reputation as free spenders. Above all, they gave visual expression to their position by building a series of magnificent palaces. Ironically, the caliph had refrained from building a palace that could be identified with his rule. The point was not lost on advisers to Ja^{c}far ibn Khālid, who instructed him to hand over his opulent residence to the caliph's son ^{c}Abd Allāh (al-Ma$^{\supset}$mūn), lest al-Rashīd be displeased that his client required quarters that exceeded the caliph's needs.

Second, the "affair" between Ja^{c}far and the caliph's sister ^{c}Abbāsah. The caliph apparently enjoyed the company of both his client and his sister, but it was considered indiscreet for the three of them to meet privately. Al-Rashīd therefore married ^{c}Abbāsah to Ja^{c}far, but insisted that the marriage never be consummated. The caliph later found out not only that the two had cohabited but also that ^{c}Abbāsah had borne offspring. Ja^{c}far was subsequently imprisoned (along with his relatives) and executed.

Third, al-Faḍl ibn Yaḥyā's relationship to the Alids, particularly the Zaydids, was much too conciliatory to suit the caliph. This explanation fits well with al-Faḍl's exploits when he was the governor of

Khorāsān, during which period the provincial army made great gains against the Alids in Daylam and the non-Arab populations in Transoxiana. It is perhaps significant that in this last campaign al-Faḍl created a large client army of non-Arabs in Khorāsān. The number of troops (a half-million) is no doubt exaggerated, but the combination of these factors would seem to indicate that al-Faḍl had accumulated considerable power along with his conciliatory attitude to the Alids. He was the first and only of the Barmakid clients to have strong ties to a military apparatus. Still, four years elapsed between the time the caliph removed him as governor of Khorāsān and the family's fall from grace.

It is not unlikely that the caliph acted after a long accumulation of grievances against his clients, and not in response to a single act by any one of them.

BIBLIOGRAPHY

Lucien Bouvat, *Les Barmécides d'après les historiens arabes et persans* (1912); Dominique Sourdel, *Le vizirat ᶜabbaside de 749 à 936*, I (1959), 127–181; Hugh Kennedy, *The Early ᶜAbbasid Caliphate* (1981).

JACOB LASSNER

[See also **Abbasids; Hārūn al-Rashīd.**]

BARNA DA SIENA, a Sienese painter active in the 1350's, about whom little is known; his principal work is the fresco cycle depicting the life of Christ in the Collegiata of San Gimignano. A cut-down panel of *Madonna and Child with Donor* in the Museo Parrochiale di Arte Sacra, Asciano; a panel of *Christ Carrying the Cross,* in the Frick Collection, New York; and a *Mystical Marriage of St. Catherine,* in the Boston Museum of Fine Arts, are attributed to him. Influenced by Duccio and Simone Martini, Barna forged a highly personal style characterized by violent actions and emotions.

BIBLIOGRAPHY

Olga Nygren, *Barna da Siena* (1963); Sebastiana Delogu Ventroni, *Barna da Siena* (1972); Bruce Cole, *Sienese Painting from Its Origins to the Fifteenth Century* (1980), 187–189.

ADELHEID M. GEALT

BARON is a word with an uncertain etymology. Its earliest usage in medieval Latin made it a synonym for "man" or "paid warrior." Isidore of Seville falsely derived it from the Greek *barús,* meaning "heavy"; others have traced it to the Latin *bāro,* meaning "dunce." But there is no authoritative opinion.

At first glance, its definition is as confusing as its etymology, for "baron" in the Middle Ages meant many things: man (as opposed to woman), freeman, great nobleman, lesser nobleman, tenant, honored gentleman, and judge. All the meanings emanate naturally from the early sense of the baron as a warrior. The political environment of the early Middle Ages, which placed great emphasis on the warrior class as the governing class, gave dignity to the term "baron" much as it did to "knight" (old English *cniht,* originally meaning "youth" or "youthful warrior"). "Baron" tended to be regarded as a slightly more elevated term than "knight," but the distinction was never a very strict one until the early modern period.

Throughout western Europe the word "baron," therefore, took on specialized honorific senses. "Nobleman" is only the most obvious development: in England one speaks of greater and lesser barons. The fact that the warrior class subsisted from fiefs had the effect of imparting to the word "baron" the notion of tenant (often tenant in chief) in the feudal hierarchy; the nature of the baron's tenure gave rise to the phrase "by barony," which, in truth, hardly differed in meaning from "by knight's service." When one wanted to speak generally of great, though not necessarily the greatest, men (for example, Magna Carta 14 and 21), one employed the word "barons." Important personnel in government were called by the same name: pertinent here, for example, are the administrators and judges in the English king's financial service known as barons of the Exchequer.

BIBLIOGRAPHY

Frederick Pollock and Frederic Maitland, *History of English Law,* 2nd ed., I (1898), 240, 260, 279–280; John Round, *The King's Serjeants and Officers of State* (1911), 36–37.

WILLIAM CHESTER JORDAN

[See also **Knights and Knight Service; Nobility, Nobles.**]

BARONS' WAR, the civil war between Henry III of England (1216–1272) and a large group of his barons that took place between the late spring of 1263 and the late autumn of 1266. It was part of the constitutional crisis that wracked England from 1258 to 1267, a crisis caused by unpopular financial and political policies of the inept Henry III. Since 1258, when Henry had submitted to the demands of his barons at a great council at Oxford, he had been under their control, with England being governed by a small baronial council in accordance with the Provisions of Oxford (1258) and of Westminster (1259). As long as the barons remained united, there was little that the hapless Henry and his eldest son, the Lord Edward, could do. When eventually this unity cracked and some of the leading barons returned to the royal side, Henry and Edward made their bid to recapture power and to humble the baronial faction led by Simon de Montfort the Younger.

In late May 1263, Simon and his faction demanded a return to the Provisions of 1258 and 1259. When Henry refused, hostilities erupted. Although Edward was a talented fighter, the adherents of Simon, including the citizens of London, were too strong to subdue. Henry and Edward had to capitulate, agreeing in early September to abide by the order of things created in 1258 and 1259. There was no return to peace, however, because the humiliated Edward, determined to destroy the Montfortian party, continued unproductive political and military maneuvers throughout 1263, until both parties finally agreed to submit their differences to the arbitration of King Louis IX of France.

On 23 January 1264, when Louis rendered judgment in the Mise of Amiens against Simon and his party on every point, war resulted. The energetic Edward moved east from the Welsh border, joined forces with his father, and on 6 April 1264 they captured the town of Northampton and two of Simon's sons. It looked as though Edward might prevail, but Simon's control of London and the Tower enabled him to build up his forces and prepare to move against the royal army. After negotiations for peace again failed in early May, Simon, reinforced by the Londoners, marched toward Lewes in Sussex, where Henry and Edward had concentrated their strength. He attacked on the morning of 14 May. Edward and his knights defeated the Londoners, but Henry and his brother, Richard of Cornwall, were captured by Simon and their troops were completely routed. The Mise of Lewes gave Simon control over England. To ensure royal compliance, he took Edward and his cousin Henry of Almain, son of Richard of Cornwall, as hostages.

Even with victory and with Henry and Edward as prisoners, Simon could not secure his political objectives. There was widespread opposition to his cause, and the pope regarded him as a usurper. He had constantly to be in the field to enforce his will not only over the royal party but also over his own. On 28 May 1265 Edward escaped, making a dash to Ludlow near the Welsh border to join with royal forces and with the powerful Gilbert of Clare, earl of Gloucester, who had quarreled with Simon and defected.

Again there was war. Gathering an army in the Welsh march, Edward moved east into Worcestershire while Simon rallied his forces in the south and then moved north, taking Henry with him. On 4 August the armies met at Evesham. The fight quickly went against Simon and his followers, who fought in a circle around their royal prisoner. Among those slain were Simon and his eldest son, Henry. Simon's head was cut off and sent to the wife of Roger Mortimer, lord of Wigmore. The monks of Evesham buried his body.

Resistance to Henry III and Edward continued in the form of guerrilla warfare until the Dictum of Kenilworth (31 October 1266) brought equitable peace, the terms of which were defined more specifically by the Statute of Marlborough (1267).

BIBLIOGRAPHY

Two detailed and reliable studies on the struggle between Henry III and the barons are Ernest F. Jacob, *Studies in the Period of Baronial Reform and Rebellion, 1258–1267* (1925); and Reginald F. Treharne, *The Baronial Plan of Reform, 1258–1263* (1932). For a shorter account accompanied by valuable insights, see F. Maurice Powicke, *The Thirteenth Century, 1216–1307* (1953), 129–226. For the primary sources see Reginald F. Treharne, comp., *Documents of the Baronial Movement of Reform and Rebellion, 1258–1267,* I. J. Sanders, ed. (1973).

BRYCE LYON

[See also **Edward I of England; Henry III of England; Provisions of Oxford; Simon de Montfort the Younger.**]

BARONZIO, GIOVANNI (*fl. ca.* 1300, *d.* before 1362), Riminese painter. Knowledge of his style is based on his signed and dated (1345) polyptych *Madonna and Child with Saints* (now in the Galleria Nazionale, Urbino). Other attributions include the *Dormition* and *Crucifixion* diptych at the Kunstmuseum in Hamburg, the polyptych *Madonna and Child Enthroned with Saints and Angels* at Mercatello, and the frescoes in the chapel of S. Nicola at Tolentino (disputed). Baronzio based his style on knowledge of Giotto's forms. His vivacious, anecdotal narrative manner seems to have important links with Pietro Lorenzetti's fresco cycle at Assisi.

BIBLIOGRAPHY

Carlo Volpe, *La pittura riminese del Trecento* (1965), 41–43; Robert Oertel, *Early Italian Painting to 1400* (1968), 322.

ADELHEID M. GEALT

BARQŪQ, al-Sulṭān al-Malik al-Ẓāhir Sayf al-Dīn (*d.* 1399), founder of the Circassian dynasty of the Mamluk rulers of Egypt and Syria. He ruled twice as sultan: from November 1382 to June 1389, when he was deposed, and from February 1390 to June 1399. From the beginning of his career as a *mamlūk,* Barqūq was embroiled in conspiracy and strife. He was one of the *mamlūk*s imprisoned for the murder of their master, Commander in Chief of the Armies Ylbughā, in 1366, and was implicated in the execution of the sultan Sha^cban in 1377. During the next five years he served as one of the powerful emirs who controlled the two boy-sultans, al-Manṣūr ^cAlī and al-Ṣāliḥ Ḥājjī, and in 1382 succeeded in having the latter deposed and himself enthroned.

Factional strife did not end with Barqūq's accession; in 1383 the caliph and two emirs hatched an abortive plot to assassinate him, and in 1386, Barqūq began summarily to arrest emirs in Syria whom he distrusted. As a result the Syrian emirs rose in rebellion against him early in 1389, led by Ylbughā al-Nāṣirī, govenor of Aleppo, and Minṭāsh, governor of Melitene. An army sent against the Syrian rebels in March was defeated, and Ylbughā and Minṭāsh marched against Egypt in May. With the aid of artillery and desertions by Barqūq's supporters, they soon captured Cairo and imprisoned Barqūq at the fortress of Kerak in Palestine. Less than four months later he escaped from Kerak and, leading an army composed of his Mamluk supporters and Arab tribesmen, marched against Syria. By February of the following year, Barqūq had defeated an army led by Minṭāsh in Syria and had had himself reinstated as sultan in Cairo, thus beginning his second reign.

Barqūq finally eliminated Minṭāsh as a threat on his right flank in 1393, at which time a new and potentially far more dangerous enemy arose there: Tamerlane. Having captured Baghdad from the Jalāyirid sultan, who took refuge in Cairo, Tamerlane sent a threatening letter to Barqūq. In response, Barqūq led the Egyptian army to Syria, determined to meet Tamerlane on the battlefield. The latter chose to turn north, leaving Syria to the Mamluks and granting Barqūq a triumph by default. Except for an attempt on his life in 1398, the rest of Barqūq's reign seems to have been relatively quiet.

Internally his reign was characterized by innovations regarded as momentous in the history of Mamluk Egypt and Syria. The principal changes were a reduction in the size of the Mamluk army and replacement of the dominant Turkish element with slaves of his own stock, the Circassians. The former change undoubtedly was dictated by a weakened economy that made it impossible to support the army at a high level, and the latter was motivated by Barqūq's attempt to strengthen himself against rivals by recruiting a force bound to him through ethnic ties. However, the preference he showed to the Circassians and the abandonment of the customary system of military training and advancement by merit were important factors in the decline of the Mamluk state.

BIBLIOGRAPHY

David Ayalon, "The Circassians in the Mamlūk Kingdom," in *Journal of the American Oriental Society,* **69** (1949); Ibn Taghrī Birdī, *History of Egypt 1382–1469 A.D.,* I, William Popper, trans. (1954).

DONALD P. LITTLE

[See also **Circassians; Egypt, Islamic; Mamluk Dynasty; Mamluks; Syria; Tamerlane.**]

BARREL, a measure of capacity in England for both wet and dry products. London standards during the Middle Ages were the following: ale, butter, and soap, 32 gallons (about 1.48 hectoliters) or 4 ale firkins of 8 gallons each; beer, 36 gallons (about 1.66 hectoliters) or 4 beer firkins of 9 gallons each; coal, nearly 4 Winchester bushels (about 1.40 hectoliters); gunpowder, 1 hundredweight of 100 pounds (45.359 kilograms); herrings or eels, 30 gallons fully packed (about 1.14 hectoliters); salmon, and sometimes eels, 42 gallons (about 1.59 hectoliters); wine, generally

31.5 gallons (about 1.19 hectoliters). Numerous regional and local variations existed, however, for these and other products throughout the British Isles.

RONALD EDWARD ZUPKO

[See also **Weights and Measures, Western European.**]

BARRELS probably were invented in the Aegean–Black Sea area, where the fourth-century B.C. Cynic philosopher Diogenes, a native of Sinope, is said to have used one as a home. By Roman times they had become relatively common in Gaul, where they were used in transporting wine down the Rhone, and in the Adriatic, where large numbers were used in ports such as Aquilea by the time of Constantine. Probably by that time barrels also were widely used as containers in the Aegean–Black Sea region, for by Justinian's reign St. Nicholas of Myra, whose symbol was a tub or barrel, had a church dedicated to him in Constantinople.

As the Middle Ages progressed, barrels were used increasingly in place of pottery jars and amphorae to transport dry and liquid cargoes on the sea or along fluvial and terrestrial routes in both the Mediterranean area and the northern seas of Europe. They had two advantages: first, they weighed much less than pottery containers, and thus saved weight; second, they could be broken down and shipped unassembled, to save valuable cargo space, then be assembled in another port to hold liquid or dry cargoes on the return trip. Hence, the importance of what maritime historians have referred to as "the container revolution."

In northern European waters, except the Baltic, this revolution had probably been accomplished by late Carolingian times. It took place at a slower pace in the Mediterranean, where amphorae were used extensively until the Crusades, especially along Near Eastern shores, where timber was in short supply. Nevertheless, by the high Middle Ages most Mediterranean vessels from the Latin West had definitely switched to barrels as containers, so much so that in centers like Venice the capacity of a merchant ship was measured in terms of *bottes,* or barrels—a measurement that continued into early modern times.

In northern Europe the same measurement was used, especially during the twelfth and thirteenth centuries, when huge amounts of wine from southwestern France were shipped from Bordeaux to England and to northern European ports in large barrels known as tuns. Hence, the use of "tuns" or "tons" as a weight and a measurement of merchant ship capacity, or tonnage, that persists today.

BIBLIOGRAPHY

Bibliotheca sanctorum, IX (1879), 923–948; Margery James, *Studies in the Medieval Wine Trade* (1971); Frederic Lane, *Venice, a Maritime Republic* (1973), 379–380; Charles Singer et al., eds., *A History of Technology,* I (1962), 312–314.

ARCHIBALD R. LEWIS

[See also **Technology, Western.**]

BARREL VAULT. See **Vault, Types of.**

BARTOLINO DA NOVARA, military architect (*fl.* 1368; *d.* 1406–1410), built the notable and beautiful Castello Estense in Ferrara, commissioned by Nicolò II d'Este in 1385. Bartolino used a similar design for the Castello di Corte at Mantua, built between 1395 and 1406 for Francesco Gonzaga. In 1400, Bartolino was called to Milan to serve as an adviser on the cathedral, specifically concerning Jean Mignot's observations of structural inadequacies.

BIBLIOGRAPHY

Ulrich Thieme and Felix Becker, *Allgemeines Künstler Lexikon,* II (1908), 557; John White, *Art and Architecture in Italy, 1250–1400* (1966), 334, 347.

ADELHEID M. GEALT

BARTOLO, NANNI DI. See **Nanni di Bartolo.**

BARTOLO DA SASSOFERRATO (1313/1314–1357), the most celebrated and urbane jurist of the fourteenth and fifteenth centuries, began his life as a humble rustic. He was born at Venatura, a village near Sassoferrato in the territory of Ancona. His father was most likely a well-off peasant, but the lack of a surname suggests a modest social status. A brilliant, analytic, and roving mind, good fortune—he lived through the Black Death of 1348, which killed many of his contemporaries—and excellent training helped Bartolo to overcome his humble origins and to establish himself as the leading jurist in Italy and a leading citizen of Perugia at the time of his death.

His first teacher was a friar, Pietro d'Assisi, whose tutoring was so successful that at the age of fourteen, Bartolo entered the University of Perugia, where he studied with the great master Cino da Pistoia. Cino's lectures had a formative influence upon Bartolo. From them he learned the dialectical modes of argumentation developed at the University of Bologna and fashionable critical methods of exegesis imported from France, which he later employed in his commentaries on the civil law. The commentary consisted of several parts. First there was a literal rendition of a law. The jurist then subdivided the law into its component parts, summarized the content of the law, and presented practical cases in which it was relevant. He then offered important observations on the law, followed by a series of counterarguments. The commentary closed with a discussion of questions that might be occasioned by the law.

Bartolo continued his studies at Bologna, where he received a baccalaureate in 1333 and a doctorate in civil law in 1334. Among his professors at Bologna were Iacopo Bottrigari and Raniero Arsendi da Forlì. Bartolo's activities immediately after he received his doctorate are not firmly established. His often cited retreat to San Vittorio, a religious house in the vicinity of Bologna, did not occur, and is merely a legend arising from a corrupt manuscript tradition. It is certain that he held the office of assessor (legal expert) at Todi in 1336, and similar offices at Macerata in 1338 and at Pisa in 1339. He began his teaching career at the University of Pisa in 1339, lecturing on the *Digest.* After being called to the University of Perugia in 1343, he produced a vast body of work that filled eleven large folio volumes in the Venetian edition of 1602–1603.

Bartolo's writings include commentaries on all the principal divisions of Justinian's *Corpus juris civilis;* questions *(quaestiones)* that had been disputed in formal academic settings; and monographic tracts on public, private, criminal, and procedural law. Notable among the tracts are those devoted to contemporary political issues and institutions: "On the Government of the City-State" *(De regimine civitatis),* "On Tyranny" *(De tyrannia),* "On Guelphs and Ghibellines" *(De guelphis et gebellinis).* Two tracts, *Ad reprimendum* and *Qui sint rebelles,* are elaborate analyses of the constitutions of Emperor Henry VII, and concern the crime of lese majesty and rebellion. Bartolo's writings reflect an extraordinary knowledge of the *Corpus juris civilis,* the interpretations related to the Justinianic compilation, opinions and monographs of other jurists, canon law, customary law, feudal law, and the statutory law promulgated by city-states. This knowledge, combined with his mastery of dialectic, permitted Bartolo to arrive at hundreds of novel doctrines and constructions, though without modern critical editions of his work, it would be foolhardy to make extravagant claims on behalf of his originality.

What seems to distinguish Bartolo's jurisprudence from that of his predecessors, such as Cino da Pistoia, is that for Cino human laws were not self-sufficient, and the task of the jurist was to fit a law into a preconceived system guided by the abstract ideal of justice. The jurist performed his task by discovering the *ratio* or just quality of each law—that is, by gauging the law's conformity to natural reason, a metalegal postulate. Where Cino's universe tended to be abstract and immobile, and consequently impeded a full accommodation between the Roman law and contemporary practices, Bartolo's universe tended to be open-ended and flexible, responsive to the vexing problems generated by the economic, social, and political convulsions that beset Europe in the mid fourteenth century. He accomplished the accommodation between the Roman law and his society by "updating" the Justinianic compilation in the light of contemporary practice. At the same time he invoked the Roman law to justify, modify, or repress myriad practices that had no counterpart in the Justinianic compilation. This dual process is a defining feature of Bartolo's jurisprudence.

Among the most influential doctrines spawned by this process is Bartolo's teaching that the authority of a city-state *(civitas)* on affairs conducted within its jurisdiction is parallel to that of an emperor. In Bartolo's celebrated phrase the *civitas* is its own emperor *(civitas sibi princeps),* and does not recognize a superior. He endorsed the city-states' authority to promulgate statutes, to create new citizens, to impose taxes, and the like. Such statutes, he taught, must submit to the universal authority of the Roman law as interpreted by bona fide jurists.

Bartolo himself invoked this principle to defend the privileges and rights of individuals and corporate groups against the city-state; to restrict the operation of statutes in certain cases to persons and things under the jurisdiction of the city-state that enacted them; and to permit someone who had lost the right of the place from which he had been banished—a common phenomenon—to retain all the rights to which he was entitled under the "universal" Roman law. Exceedingly influential was his doctrine that a woman who marries a foreigner acquires citizenship in her husband's city, and while she ceases to be a citizen of her former city with respect to civic obligations and imposts, she remains a citizen there with respect to rights and privileges to which she is entitled.

The doctrines, methods, and jurisprudential perspective associated with the name of Bartolo, which were carried forward and modified by his intellectual heirs, most notably Baldus, were known as *Bartolismo.* His works were avidly read and reproduced, as witnessed by the thousands of manuscript copies and printed editions bearing the name of Bartolo that are in libraries throughout Europe. His opinions and doctrines were cited as authoritative by judicial officials in Spain and Germany as well as in Italy. Although Bartolo and his followers were attacked by fifteenth-century humanists for barbarizing the ancient Roman law, his preeminence was not diminished, and was expressed in the professional maxim that no one was a jurist who was not a Bartolist *(nemo jurista nisi sit Bartolista).*

BIBLIOGRAPHY

Editions of Bartolo's works in American libraries are listed in the *National Union Catalog* under Bartolus de Saxoferrato. For manuscripts, see Emanuele Casamassima, *Iter germanicum* (1971); and Antonio García y García, *Iter hispanicum* (1973).

On Bartolo's doctrines, see Ephraim Emerton, *Humanism and Tyranny* (1925), which must be read in conjunction with Diego Quaglioni's studies in *Pensiero politico:* "Per una edizione critica e un commento moderno del *Tractatus de regimine civitatis* di Bartolo da Sassoferrato," **9** (1976); "Intorno al testo del *Tractatus de tyrannia* di Bartolo da Sassoferrato," **10** (1977); and "Alcune osservazioni sul testo di due trattati Bartoliani: *De regimine civitatis* e *De guelphis et gebellinis,*" **12** (1979); Anna T. Sheedy, *Bartolus on Social Conditions in the Fourteenth Century* (1942); *Bartolo da Sassoferrato: Studi e documenti per il VI centenario,* 2 vols. (1962), published by the Università degli Studi di Perugia; and Cecil N. Sidney Woolf, *Bartolus of Sassoferrato* (1913).

See also Julius Kirshner, "*Civitas sibi faciat civem:* Bartolus of Sassoferrato's Doctrine on the Making of a Citizen," in *Speculum,* **48** (1973); and Walter Ullmann, "Bartolus on Customary Law," in *Juridical Review,* **52** (1940).

JULIUS KIRSHNER

[See also **Baldus; Cino da Pistoia; Corpus Juris Civilis; Law, Civil.**]

BARTOLO DI FREDI (*fl.* 1350's–1410), Sienese painter first recorded as the associate of Andrea Vanni. He is credited with the fresco cycle in the Collegiata of San Gimignano that depicts Old Testament scenes. Scholars also attribute to him the frescoes of the Birth and Death of the Virgin in the Church of San Agostino at San Gimignano. Principal panel paintings include the *Adoration of the Magi* (now in the Siena Pinacoteca), which must have inspired a later version by Gentile da Fabriano. Other important works are the *Madonna of Mercy* (1364), in Pienza; the dismembered polyptych of the *Coronation of the Virgin with Scenes from Her Life* (now at Montalcino and the Siena Pinacoteca) of 1380–1388; and an *Assumption of the Virgin* (now in the Museum of Fine Arts, Boston).

BIBLIOGRAPHY

Enzo Carli, *Bartoli di Fredi a Paganico* (1968); and "La data degli affreschi di Bartolo di Fredi a San Gimignano," in *Critica d'arte,* **8** (1949); Bruce Cole, *Sienese Painting from its Origins to the Fifteenth Century* (1980), 195–196; S. L. Faison, "Barna and Bartolo di Fredi," in *Art Bulletin,* **14** (1932).

ADELHEID M. GEALT

[See also **Vanni, Andrea.**]

BARTOLOMEO, MICHELOZZO DI. See **Michelozzo di Bartolomeo.**

BARTOLUS. See **Bartolo da Sassoferrato.**

BAR TRACERY (BAR BRANCH), patterns of interlocking stones composing window decoration or applied to solid masonry surfaces, as distinct from similiar designs cut into or through a single stone (plate tracery). First employed at Rheims in 1211, it is especially characteristic of the rayonnant and flamboyant styles in France and of the decorated and perpendicular in England. Bar tracery designs required full-size preliminary drawings or detailed, scaled working drawings. It is sometimes termed "branching tracery" because it appears to branch upward from mullions.

CARL F. BARNES, JR.

BAS-DE-PAGE ("bottom of the page"), a miniature in the rectangular space between the last line of text and the lower border of the page in a Western illuminated manuscript. The *bas-de-page* appeared at the end of the twelfth century in psalters (probably made in England) and quickly spread to other texts, especially the book of hours. The miniatures are often whimsical and unrelated to the accompanying text; but occasionally, as in the Bellville Breviary (*ca.* 1325), they sustain a narrative that continues from page to page and complements the text.

LESLIE BRUBAKER

[See also **Manuscript Illumination.**]

BASEL, COUNCIL OF. See **Councils, Western.**

BASIL I THE MACEDONIAN, Byzantine emperor (867–886). Born about 812 near Adrianople in the Macedonian theme, Basil came from a peasant family and had little or no education. Although the genealogy tracing his origin from the Armenian royal house of the Arsacids is an obvious forgery, Basil may have had Armenian blood. When he was an infant, he and his family were carried off, along with other Byzantine captives, by the Bulgarians who sacked Adrianople in 813.

Basil spent his youth in Bulgaria, from which he returned to the empire at the age of twenty-five, when the captives were rescued. Basil soon went to Constantinople and entered the service of the courtier Theophilitzes, with whom he traveled to the Peloponnesus. There Basil was befriended by Danelis, a wealthy widow. After he returned to Constantinople, his strength and horsemanship attracted the attention of Emperor Michael III, whose companion he became. Basil gradually rose in rank to the high office of *parakoimomenos.* He then persuaded Michael that Bardas Caesar was plotting against him. In 866, with the emperor's approval, Basil assassinated Bardas while they were on a military expedition, and replaced him as the main influence on Michael. Given the rank of coemperor, Basil contracted a nominal marriage with the emperor's mistress, Eudokia Ingerina. In 867 he had Michael killed, and became sole emperor.

Despite the unpromising means by which he had risen to power, Basil proved to be a highly competent ruler, and founded a dynasty that reigned until 1056. Michael III had brought the empire's finances to a state of crisis that by itself went far toward justifying his overthrow. By exacting partial repayment of Michael's gifts to his favorites, controlling expenditures, and reducing corruption among the tax collectors, Basil restored the empire's solvency. The state's wealth soon became sufficient to allow him to begin an extensive program of building and restoration, especially of churches. The most famous of his new buildings was the so-called Nea ("new church"), inaugurated in 880, which had great influence on subsequent church architecture. Basil's reign was a time of increased artistic and literary activity, with Photios the leading literary figure; the movement is often called the "Macedonian renaissance."

Basil's greatest administrative accomplishment was to begin a revision of the empire's laws based on the code of Justinian I and the *Ekloga* of Leo III, a task that was completed with the *Basilics* of Basil's successor, Leo VI. Two introductory legal works were finished during Basil's reign. The first, dating between 870 and 879, was the *Procheiron,* a textbook and reference work including a systematic selection of the laws most commonly applicable. The second work, dating after 879, was the *Epanagoge,* a revised and expanded version of the *Procheiron* that, translated into Slavonic, later had considerable influence in Russia.

One of Basil's first political acts was to force the abdication of Photios as patriarch of Constantinople and to restore the patriarch Ignatius, thus ending the empire's escalating conflict with the papacy. At the Fourth Council of Constantinople (869–870), Basil ended the Photian Schism with Rome and at the same time confirmed the jurisdiction of the patriarchate of Constantinople over the recently established Bulgarian church, which had earlier been under Roman jurisdiction. When Ignatius died in 877, Basil returned Photios to the patriarchate with the acquiescence of the papacy.

Under Basil, Byzantine cultural and political influence over the Balkans continued to spread. In 867 the Byzantine fleet raised an Arab siege of Ragusa (Dubrovnik); by 878, Basil had established the new theme of Dalmatia, thus furthering Byzantine control over the Dalmatian coast. Also during Basil's reign, Byzantine missionaries definitively converted the Serbs. In Asia Minor, Byzantine successes were more concrete. There, with the decline of the central power of the Abbasid caliphate, the principal enemies of the empire were the emir of Melitene and particularly his allies, the Paulician heretics led by Chrysocheir. Provoked by the increasing boldness of Paulician raids, which had reached as far as Ephesus, Basil fought a short but bitter war with the Paulicians that ended when a Byzantine force took their capital of Tephrike in 872, killing Chrysocheir and destroying their independence. Many Paulicians were converted to Orthodoxy and recruited into the Byzantine army.

This victory was followed by the capture of Sozopetra and Samosata, though an attack on Melitene failed (873). About 874 the Byzantines reconquered Cyprus, holding it for seven years before they were forced to restore the previous arrangement of sharing power with the Arabs. Byzantine possessions in south Italy were expanded by the acquisition of Bari in 875. Syracuse fell to the Arabs in 878, but the Byzantines counterattacked, recapturing Taormina in 880. In 885 an expedition led by Nikephoros Phokas (the grandfather of the later emperor Nikephoros II) made further gains in south Italy. Although the Mediterranean was still not free from Arab raiders, Byzantine naval power was plainly on the rise.

Basil's later years were saddened by the death of his eldest son, Constantine, in 879. Basil had never been fond of his new heir, the future Leo VI, who was probably not his son, but a son of Michael III by Eudokia Ingerina. In 882, Basil forced Leo to marry the saintly Theophano, and in 883 had Leo imprisoned for three years on suspicion of plotting against him. Basil died in 886, supposedly from a hunting accident, but under circumstances that suggest a plot by partisans of Leo. Although Basil's territorial conquests were modest in extent, his reign marked a substantial advance in the power and influence of the Byzantine state, a base on which his successors built in the following century.

BIBLIOGRAPHY

Albert Vogt, *Basile Ier* (1908), is the only book-length study. Also see R. Jenkins, "The Chronological Accuracy of the 'Logothete' for the Years A.D. 867–913," in *Dumbarton Oaks Papers,* **19** (1965); Cyril Mango, "Eudocia Ingerina, the Normans, and the Macedonian Dynasty," in *Zbornik Radova Vizantološkog Instituta,* **14–15** (1973); George Ostrogorsky, *History of the Byzantine State,* rev. ed. (1969), 233–241, with bibliography.

WARREN T. TREADGOLD

[See also **Bardas Caesar; Byzantine Empire, 330–1025; Epanagoge; Ignatius, Patriarch; Law, Byzantine; Leo VI the Wise; Michael III; Paulicians; Photian Council; Photios.**]

BASIL II "KILLER OF BULGARS," Byzantine emperor (976–1025). Born in 958 to Romanos II and the empress Theophano, Basil officially reigned with his younger brother, Constantine VIII, from Romanos' death in 963. Real power, however, was in the hands of Nikephoros II (963–969), and then of John I Tzimiskes (969–976), who acted as regents for the young emperors. Even after John's death Basil, although the nominal ruler, had less power than the eunuch Basil the Parakoimomenos. When Bardas Skleros rebelled between 976 and 979, he probably meant simply to replace the Parakoimomenos as the effective ruler, retaining Basil and Constantine as figureheads. In 985, however, Basil had the Parakoimomenos exiled, and assumed full power; Constantine was content to remain in the background.

Basil now faced a threat from the Bulgarians, who had rallied after their subjection by John I. Four princes (the Kometopouloi, or "sons of the count"), the chief of whom was Samuil, had founded a new Bulgarian state in Macedonia and western Bulgaria. In response to an offensive by Samuil against Thessaly in 985–986, Basil attacked Serdica (Sofia), but failed to take it; his retreating army was routed by the Bulgarians at the mountain pass southeast of Serdica called Trajan's Gate (986). The next year Bardas Skleros returned from exile in Baghdad and began another revolt. When Basil sent Bardas Phokas against him, Phokas joined Skleros in an agreement to partition the empire between them, then took over the rebellion entirely. Phokas had conquered all of Asia Minor by 988, when he prepared to attack Constantinople.

Basil, finding his resources inferior to those of Phokas, appealed to Prince Vladimir of Kiev, who agreed to send an auxiliary force and to convert to Christianity in return for Basil's sister Anna as his wife. At the battle of Abydos (989), aided by the Russians and by the sudden death of Phokas, Basil defeated the rebels, many of whom surrendered. The remainder, after brief resistance led by Skleros, submitted with their leader. Although Basil was reluctant to send Anna to Kiev, Vladimir persuaded him by occupying the Byzantine theme of Cherson in the Crimea. The marriage was celebrated (989); the Russians were converted and brought under the ecclesiastical and cultural influence of Byzantium; Cherson was returned; and the Varangian (Russian) force remained an important contingent of the Byzantine army.

Basil now planned the systematic subjection of Samuil's Bulgarians, who had been advancing in Thessaly. The emperor began campaigning against them in 990, and by 995 he had taken a considerable part of Macedonia from them. He was forced to interrupt the Bulgarian war, however, when a Fatimid army defeated the Byzantines near Antioch in 994. In 995, Basil quickly crossed the empire and secured the eastern frontier in a campaign that reached as far as Tripoli. His experience in the East convinced Basil that the magnates of Asia Minor, defeated in the revolts led by Skleros and Phokas, were still a threat to his authority. In 996 he promulgated an edict that forced them to restore unconditionally all lands they had acquired illegally since 922. Since the amount of land involved was very large and the edict was rigorously enforced, the effect was a massive transfer of land to smaller landholders, who were more easily taxed and controlled by the state.

This program of land redistribution occupied Basil until 998. In the meantime Samuil raided Greece, but was defeated by Basil's general Nikephoros Ouranos in 997. Then Samuil shifted his efforts toward the west, where he made important conquests, particularly the port of Dyrrhachium. In 997 or 998 he took the title of czar. Basil was diverted from a new campaign against Bulgaria in 998 by a new Arab victory over the Byzantines. In another successful campaign in the East, he not only forced the Fatimids to make peace but also annexed part of Armenia.

In 1001, Basil resumed his Bulgarian campaign, which this time he was able to pursue to the end. Selecting Philippopolis (modern Plovdiv) as his base, he cut off all Bulgarian territories east of Macedonia, and had them conquered by his generals. Basil then reconquered Thessaly and southern Macedonia. In 1002 he took the important fortified town of Vidin on the Danube after a long siege, which he did not raise despite a diversionary campaign by Samuil that sacked Adrianople. After the capture of Skopje in 1004 and of Dyrrhachium in 1005, Samuil's remaining domains were practically surrounded. Samuil was able to slow Basil's advance until 1014, when the main Bulgarian army was captured at Kleidion in the upper Strymon (Struma) valley.

Determined to break the Bulgarian resistance, Basil had the captives, who reportedly numbered 14,000, blinded, leaving one in each hundred with one eye to guide the rest back to Samuil. At the sight of his blinded army, Samuil suffered a fatal seizure. Under his heirs the resistance died down, and by about 1019 it was over. Basil established Byzantine authority over Bulgaria as completely as possible, incorporating Bulgarians into his army and dividing the new conquests into themes. In recognition of the primitive state of their economy, he allowed the Bulgarians to continue to pay their taxes in kind. Croatia and several petty Serbian states became vassals of Byzantium. After his victories in the Balkans, Basil conducted successful campaigns in the east between 1021 and 1023, annexing more of Armenia and Georgia. He was planning a campaign against Arab-held Sicily when he died in 1025.

Basil's reign saw the high point of middle Byzantine power. He left an empire that was not only vastly expanded in area but also remarkably securely held; its external enemies had been defeated, and internal opposition had been firmly put down. The army was strong, and the treasury was filled with a record gold reserve. Basil's only failure was in providing for the succession. Never married, he left the empire in the incompetent hands of Constantine VIII and his daughters.

BIBLIOGRAPHY

Gustave Schlumberger, *L'épopée byzantine,* I (1896), 327–777, and II (1900), is the most extensive treatment of Basil's reign. Also see George Ostrogorsky, *History of the Byzantine State,* rev. ed. (1969), 298–315; Steven Runciman, *A History of the First Bulgarian Empire* (1930), 217–261.

WARREN T. TREADGOLD

[See also **Bardas Phokas; Bardas Skleros; Bulgaria; John I Tzimiskes; Nikephoros II Phokas; Romanos II; Samuil of Bulgaria.**]

BASIL THE GREAT OF CAESAREA, ST. (*ca.* 330–379). Basil (Basileios) was born in Caesarea of Cappadocia (formerly Mazaca, now Kayseri, central Turkey). He became bishop of that city in 370 and died there. He was canonized and given the title "Great" soon afterward.

Basil came from a rich Christian family in which Hellenism and Christianity were both accepted. His father, Basil, was a sophist-rhetorician in Neocaesarea (Niksar), capital of Pontus Polemoniacus; his mother, Emmelia, was descended from a family of senators who suffered martyrdom in Cappadocia during the persecution under Maximinus in 306–313. His paternal grandmother, Macrina, a survivor of the persecution, introduced him to an evolved Origenism that had embedded itself in the liturgical tradition of the church of Neocaesarea through Greg-

BASIL THE GREAT

ory the Thaumaturgus (*ca.* 213–*ca.* 270); only later in life did Basil learn of the *homoousios* of Nicaea.

The acceptance of Hellenism as a propaideia of Christianity came through his father under whose guidance Basil commenced his general education (the *enkyklios paideia*). After his father's death in 345 or 346, Basil continued his humanistic education at Caesarea; then at Constantinople, where he heard Libanius; and finally at Athens. About 355 he returned home, taught rhetoric for a term, and then made the decision to become an ascetic. Despite his repeated claims to the contrary (see chiefly *Epistle* 223), his new vocation could not completely erase Basil's vast exposure to the classics. In fact, his writings clearly show a familiarity with Plato and Homer, and to a lesser extent with Aristotle, Plotinus, and the historians and rhetors; they also reveal degrees of acquaintance with rhetoric, mathematics, grammar, philosophy in its three branches (physics, ethics, dialectic), music, and medicine.

The type of asceticism that Basil embraced after his tour of the eremitic monastic settlements of Syria, Mesopotamia, Palestine, and Egypt was that advocated in his homeland by Eustathius of Sebaste (*ca.* 300–after 379). This community (cenobitic) type of asceticism was intended to be the extension of the first community of Jerusalem (see Acts 2:44; 4:32), closely rooted in and allied with the life of the local church. In 362, Basil abandoned his seclusion at the family villa of Annisa, accepting ordination as presbyter in Caesarea. After returning to Annisa for a short time, he settled in Caesarea, where he played a prominent role in the administration of that church, headed at the time by the inexperienced bishop Eusebius. In 369, when drought and famine struck the country, Basil "assembled in one place [his family property near Caesarea] those afflicted by the famine," among whom were Christians, Jews, and pagans. While the government did nothing, "he collected through contributions all kinds of food helpful for relieving famine" (Gregory of Nazianzus, *Oration* 43.35; cf. Gregory of Nyssa, *In laudem Basilii*). From this emergency center there developed in 372 a vast complex of buildings for the housing of travelers, the sick, orphans, and the poor. This early form of public charity was called "the Brand New City" and, after Basil's death, "the Basiliada."

After becoming bishop of Caesarea in 370, Basil continued to support his ascetic institutions. In that office he also vigorously pursued his ideal of deepening the sense of unity among the various Christian churches in the name of their common bond in Christ. Four times he appealed to the Western churches for support, on behalf of the Eastern bishops persecuted by Emperor Valens and in order to heal the schism of Antioch, where two orthodox bishops were disputing the see. Although during his lifetime Basil did not see most of his efforts crowned with success, his moderate views in matters of Trinitarian dogma prevailed at the Council of Constantinople (381), at which the consubstantiality of the Holy Spirit was officially introduced into the Christian Creed in terms very similar to those employed in Basil's treatise *De Spiritu Sancto.*

WRITINGS

Unlike Origen, whose tremendous knowledge lay buried in voluminous commentaries accessible to only a few experts, Basil endeavored to communicate his classical culture to the average person, thus enlarging the intellectual horizon of the inhabitants of Pontus and Cappadocia, long known for their intellectual stagnation and backwardness.

Philokalia. This anthology of the writings of Origen dealing with hermeneutics and the relationship between Hellenistic paideia and Christianity was composed at Annisa with the assistance of Gregory of Nazianzus.

Ascetica. The sermons and treatises are the product of Basil's addresses and visits to his brotherhoods. More a spiritual counselor than a legislator, Basil developed in his *Asceticons* (the earliest redaction, the *Asceticon 1* [CPG, 2876], and the enlarged editions, the *Asceticon 2* and *3* [CPG 2875]), a series of guidelines and principles of ascetic praxis centered on the commandment to love God and one's neighbors. Preserved are some 368 *erotapokriseis* ("questions-answers") and four prologi (CPG 2878, 2880, 2881, 2882; for the fifth see CPG 2883). Similar in nature to the *Asceticons* is the two-book *De baptismo* (CPG 2896). Certainly the work of greatest importance in understanding Basil's ascetic teaching is the *Regulae Morales* (CPG 2877), composed of eighty biblical rules, and in fact an anthology of some 1,553 verses extracted from the New Testament. This work from his mature years (370's) is preceded by two prologi, *De judicio Dei* (CPG 2885) and *De fide* (CPG 2886).

Liturgy. Apparently while a presbyter, Basil revised and expanded a eucharistic anaphora in use in Cappadocia. The Basilian anaphora (but probably none of the other prayers) is found in the modern

BASIL THE GREAT

Byzantine *Liturgy of St. Basil* (CPG 2905.2), which is paralleled by the oldest Syriac and Armenian versions (on which see Hieronymus Engberding, *Das eucharistische Hochgebet der Basileiosliturgie* [Münster 1931]).

Dogmatic treatises. The three-book *Contra Eunomium* (CPG 2837) is a word-by-word rebuttal of the *Apology* of Eunomius, the chief exponent of an extreme Arianism denying all similarity of nature (hence called Anomoeanism or Dissimilarianism) among the three hypostases of the Trinity. In another work, *De Spiritu Sancto ad Amphilochium* (CPG 2839), written between 373 and 375, Basil attacked the teaching of the Pneumatomachians ("fighters against the spirit"), another extreme wing of Arianism propounded notably by his former spiritual mentor and friend, Eustathius of Sebaste. In this work Basil never applies the term "God" to the Holy Spirit. However, his argumentation, based chiefly on the Bible and tradition, is so forceful that in 381 the Council of Constantinople proceeded, on the basis of his work, to promulgate the dogma of the divinity of the Holy Spirit.

Homilies. Of the close to 100 homilies attributed to Basil in the manuscripts, only forty are authentic (CPG 2836, 2845–2860, 2862–2866, 2868–2869, 2910, 2912–2914). The topics range from moral and ascetic to dogmatic and panegyrical.

Hexaemeron (CPG 2835). More than the nine surviving were planned as a commentary on Genesis 1–2. Despite an obvious pastoral and didactic purpose—giving his congregation a better understanding of the six days of creation—a great deal of the effort is devoted to a not always successful refutation of some of the cosmological theories of contemporary Greek science.

Epistles (CPG 2900). Preserved are 309 authentic letters, ranging from those addressed to Basil's intimate friends to those directed to high-ranking officials: governors, prefects, judges, generals, soldiers, bishops, presbyters. Written in an incomparably beautiful style, they reveal Basil at his best as a master of style, but most of all as a Christian leader concerned with problems affecting the church, society, and the less privileged.

Ad adolescentes, quomodo possint ex gentilium libris fructum capere ("To the Young on How to Derive Profit from the Reading of Pagan Literature") (CPG 2867). The basic theme of this work is that pagan literature, if read and studied with judgment, can serve as a propaideia of Christianity.

ISSUES

One of the most pressing problems confronting Basil was the relationship between asceticism (free charismatic bestowal of the Holy Spirit), on the one hand, and the Bible and the institutional (hierarchic) church, on the other. The tension came to a head in the 360's when a synod was held at Gangra to deal with the problem of insubordinate ascetics, mainly followers of Eustathius of Sebaste. Basil, who belonged to the ascetic milieu, deals (without acknowledging it) with the same issues as the synod (admission to the brotherhoods of married people, slaves, children), particularly in *Asceticon* 2 and 3 from the early 370's.

Basil's significance for the ascetic movement lies in his adoption of a church-oriented type of asceticism believed to be the extension of the early (church) community of Jerusalem; in giving to this corporate movement a biblical foundation justifying its existence on the basis of the commandments to love God and one's neighbors and of the common sharing *(koinōnia)* of the individual charismata of the Holy Spirit (the charisma as an element of cohesion as well as of differentiation); in supplying the movement with a much-needed philosophical justification: the social nature of humanity; and in combining the practice of austere evangelical asceticism with culture and love of learning. In sum, Basil reconciled the spirit and institution of charismatic asceticism with the life and patterns of the wider church and of society as a whole.

The second problem confronting Basil was the still-unresolved Arian controversy, which had severely divided the church over the preceding fifty years. During his lifetime this controversy initially (in the 360's) centered on the divinity of the Son (the Eunomians denying it), and later (in the 370's) shifted to that of the Holy Spirit (with the Pneumatomachians opposing it). Basil's most important contribution to Trinitarian theology was his establishment of the technical terms of the standard formulation. He distinguished *ousia* and *hypostasis,* which hitherto had been used as synonyms (for example, by the Council of Nicaea). *Ousia,* in his acceptation, denoted the common nature equally shared by Father, Son, and Holy Spirit; *hypostasis* was a mode of being (fatherhood, sonship, and sanctifying power, respectively) in which that *ousia* is manifested. Basil drew his main arguments from the Bible, but always as read and interpreted in light of the traditions of the churches, such as the liturgies and the baptismal formula. On the other hand, in refuting the subtleties (innovations) of the heretics, he did not hesitate to appeal to, and to introduce into theology, nonscriptural terms and distinctions such as *ousia* and *hypostasis.*

Basil is also relevant for the study of the relationship (in both theory and practice) of ecclesiastical institutions to those of the state, especially as regards initiatives in response to social and economic crises.

INFLUENCE

Since the early Middle Ages, Basil has been influential in matters of asceticism (monasticism), theology, liturgy, canon law, social initiatives, and the relationship between classical paganism and Christianity among peoples speaking Greek, Arabic, Armenian, Coptic, Ethiopic, Georgian, Latin, the Slavic languages, Syriac, and modern languages. Many of his works were translated into Syriac (beginning in the fifth century); Latin (*Asceticon 1,* by Rufinus in 397/398; five letters; nine homilies; *Hexaemeron,* by Eustathius *ca.* 400); Armenian (*Asceticon 2* and *3; Hexaemeron;* thirty-five homilies—all between the fifth and the eighth centuries); Coptic; Arabic (homilies and ascetica); Georgian (most works except the letters and the dogmatic treatises); and Old Church Slavonic (some homilies but mainly the *Asceticon 2* and *3*—two versions before the fifteenth century). After the fifteenth century, especially in the Latin West, most of Basil's works were also edited and translated into some of the vernacular tongues. In widest circulation was the address "To the Young on How to Derive Profit from Pagan Literature" translated by Leonardo Bruni (Aretinus) early in the 1400's.

Before the tenth century the *Liturgy of Basil* was the ordinary liturgy in almost all the Byzantine churches. It was also translated (although not used) three times into Latin before 1400. Basil's influence was also established by the quotations and excerpts from, and many references to, his works found from as early as the second half of the fourth century. His cult as a saint is documented in the annual liturgical commemoration of his death on 1 January (in the Latin church now on 2 January) and in the many icons depicting him as an ascetic and as a bishop of the church.

BIBLIOGRAPHY

Although several lives of Basil have been published (P. Allard, K. G. Bonis, P. C. Chrestou), the best is still that of Prudentius Maran, written in 1730, in *Patrologia graeca,* XXIX (1857), v–clxxvii. Maran's *vita* does not, however, entirely supersede that of Louis S. Le Nain de Tillemont, *Mémoires pour servir à l'histoire ecclésiastique des six premiers siècles,* IX (1703), 1–304, 628–691. For modern revisions of the chronology of the life and works of Basil, see Paul J. Fedwick, ed., *Basil of Caesarea: Christian, Humanist, Ascetic,* I (1981), 3–19; and Jean Gribomont, "Notes biographiques sur s. Basile," *ibid.,* 21–48.

Basil's works survive in some 6,000 manuscripts written in Greek, Arabic, Armenian, Coptic, Ethiopian, Georgian, Demotic Greek, Latin, Old Church Slavonic (Middle Bulgarian, Serbian, and Russian recensions), and Syriac. For a complete description of these manuscripts and also for all the translations, ancient quotations, editions, studies, spurious works, and the iconography of Basil, see Paul J. Fedwick, *Basil of Caesarea, 330–1985: A Critical Survey of the Direct and Indirect Tradition of His Writings* (in press).

For a preliminary assessment and discussion of the translations from before 1400, see Paul J. Fedwick, ed., *Basil of Caesarea,* II (1981), 439–532; and, for a select but extensive bibliography, *ibid.,* 627–699; and Paul J. Fedwick, *The Church and the Charisma of Leadership in Basil of Caesarea* (1979), 174–202. For an up-to-date list of all the authentic and dubious works, see *Basil of Caesarea,* I (1981), xix–xxix; and the *Clavis patrum graecorum,* Morits Geerard, ed., II (1974), nos. 2835–3005 (abbreviated above as CPG).

PAUL J. FEDWICK

[See also **Arians and Arianism; Byzantine Church; Councils, Ecumenical; Liturgy, Byzantine Church; Monasticism.**]

BASILEIA. See **Genesius.**

BASILEUS, title of the Byzantine emperor, first attested in an imperial document in 629; in Latin it was rendered by *imperator.* The use of the traditional title *augustus* decreased but never disappeared. The emperor also kept the title *despotes* until the twelfth century, when that term became an independent title, usually bestowed upon the sons-in-law or the sons of the emperor.

The standard title of the crowned empress was *basilis* or *basilissa*—or, more often, *augusta;* from the twelfth century on, *basilissa* apparently was reserved to the wives of *despotai.*

When there were two or more coemperors, the main one was called *autocrator.* This position also could be occupied by women (for instance, Irene, 797–802), who then adopted the masculine title *basileus.*

Although the ancient custom of elevation on a shield was abandoned by the beginning of the seventh century, the acclamation by senate, army, and people remained essential for accession to imperial power. From 457 a second essential act was the coronation, performed by the patriarch of Constantinople. To these acts the anointment was added in the second half of the twelfth century; in the thirteenth, elevation on a shield was revived, and was performed until the fifteenth century.

According to the Roman tradition, the rank of emperor was in principle elective. But in the seventh century the emperors started elevating to the throne one or more of their sons, who by becoming coemperors were ready to succeed their fathers. In the same century the idea of a collectively exercised sovereignty was still acceptable. But after the coup d'état of 681 the principle of a single supreme ruler was gradually established: he was eventually called *megas basileus* or *autocrator basileus,* and was acclaimed as such; his coemperors did not have the right to such acclamations.

During the Palaiologan period the coronation was reserved to the main emperor—or emperors—who personally elevated the simple *basileis* to the throne. If the emperor was a minor, the powers of regent were exerted by the senate (until the seventh century), by the empress mother, or by a high official or group of officials appointed by the previous emperor. Thus Byzantium had real dynasties, and from the seventh century the feeling of dynastic legitimacy grew constantly stronger, becoming fully recognized by the tenth century. The imperial power being considered an expression of the grace of God, any successful revolution was perceived as the expression of God's will. Consequently, the social origin of an emperor was not considered to have any great importance.

Before being crowned, the would-be emperor took a solemn oath affirming his orthodoxy, promising to maintain inviolate the decisions of the councils and the privileges of the Church, and to be a merciful and just sovereign to his people.

The emperor's insignia were the crown and the chlamys. In representations the emperors hold a scepter (often cruciform) in their right hand; in the left hand they hold the globe cruciger or the *akakia* (or *anexikakia,* a small silk purse full of dirt, to remind them of the vanity of this world). The purple color was reserved to the emperor alone: he wore purple garments and signed with purple ink.

The emperor was the only repository of sovereign power, which was descended from God. He was "crowned by God," "governed and guided by God"; he was called "divine" and "holy." He was the commander in chief of the army, the head of the administration, the supreme judge, and the sole lawgiver: a "living law," whose power was defined as an "authority bound by the law" *(ennomos epistasia).* He cared for the well-being of the Christian Church, defended the good doctrine, summoned the general councils, appointed (and, if necessary, deposed by force) the patriarch. But he was often obliged to yield to pressures from the Church, the importance of which grew constantly.

The emperor had ecumenical aspirations: the Christian world had to be ruled by one Christian sovereign, the Byzantine emperor, who also claimed to be the only legitimate heir of the Roman Empire—hence the Byzantine opposition to all Western rulers who assumed imperial powers (such as Charlemagne or the German emperors). A hierarchy of states was established in which the Christian rulers of western Europe, seen as deputies of the *basileus,* occupied a low rank.

BIBLIOGRAPHY

Louis Bréhier, "L'origine des titres impériaux à Bysance," in *Byzantinische Zeitschrift,* **15** (1906); and *Les institutions de l'empire byzantin* (1949), 1–88; John Bury, *The Constitution of the Later Roman Empire* (1909), repr. in *Selected Essays of J. B. Bury* (1930); Aikaterine Christophilopoulou, *Ekloge, anagoreusis kai stepsis tou Byzantinou autokratoros* (1956); and "He antibasileia eis to Byzantion," in *Symmeikta,* **2** (1970); André Grabar, *L'empereur dans l'art byzantin* (1936); Ernst Kornemann, *Doppelprinzipat und Reichsteilung im Imperium Romanum* (1930); Nicolas Svoronos, "Le serment de fidelité à l'empereur byzantin et sa signification constitutionelle," in *Revue des études byzantines,* **9** (1951); Otto Treitinger, *Die oströmische Kaiser- und Reichsidee nach ihrer Gestaltung im höfischen Zeremoniell* (1938).

NICHOLAS OIKONOMIDES

[See also **Autocrator; Byzantine Empire; Despot; Roman Empire, Late.**]

BASILICA, in Roman times, the building housing a court of justice or a commercial center; during the early Christian and medieval periods, a rectangular church plan with an apse and an entrance on opposite short ends, usually lighted by clerestory windows. The basilican plan was developed during the early Christian period from Roman models adapted to the liturgical needs of the Church.

Basilicas were often preceded by atria and narthexes, and the interior was usually divided by columns or piers into a wide central passage (nave) roofed with wooden beams and flanked by two or four lower aisles. Sometimes the apse was raised over a confessio or crypt, and a transept was occasionally inserted between the apse and the nave (as in Old St. Peter's, Rome). The interior wall elevation of the nave was two-part: a colonnade or an arcade with clerestory windows above. In northern Italy double basilicas were built during the early Christian period, with the two oblong buildings linked by a short transverse hall (as at Aquileia). Early Byzantine basilicas normally had low galleries over the aisles, and frequently lesser chambers flanked the apse; in the Holy Land the basilican plan was often joined with a martyrium. The simple basilican plan was comparatively rare in the East after the fourth century, but the domed basilica—with a dome rising from the central bay of the nave—was used throughout the early Byzantine period, especially in the fifth and sixth centuries (for instance, Hagia, Eirene, Constantinople). In the Latin West the basilican plan was used for churches throughout the medieval period, and was particularly popular from the Carolingian period on.

Early basilicas were not usually oriented, but medieval examples normally were planned along an east-west axis, with the apse at the eastern end and the entrance at the western end. During the medieval period atria were rare. Westworks—monumental facades between two towers—were introduced during the Carolingian period and remained popular north of the Alps. The double-ended basilica, with an apse at both short ends of the long axis, was known in the early Christian period and was revived in the ninth century (for example, at Fulda); the plan continued to be used in northern Europe (as at St. Michael's, Hildesheim). From the ninth century on, the Latin cross plan was increasingly common: transept arms were extended between the apse and nave and, in certain churches, a tower was raised above the crossing of the transept and the longitudinal axis of the nave.

The basilican plan was also elaborated in the later Middle Ages. Pilgrimage churches, built along the routes leading to Santiago de Compostella during the Romanesque period, extended the side aisles around the apse to form ambulatories, and small chapels containing altars and relics protruded from the transept arms and the apse. During the Romanesque and Gothic periods, the eastern end of the basilica was expanded: choirs were frequently added between the crossing and the apse, and, from the mid twelfth century on, the apse was elaborated into a chevet by the fusion of apse, ambulatory, and apsidal chapels. In English Gothic churches, a Lady Chapel was often appended to the eastern end of the church.

During the early Christian period the interior space of a basilica was simply divided into longitudinal sections (nave and aisles) terminated by an apse,

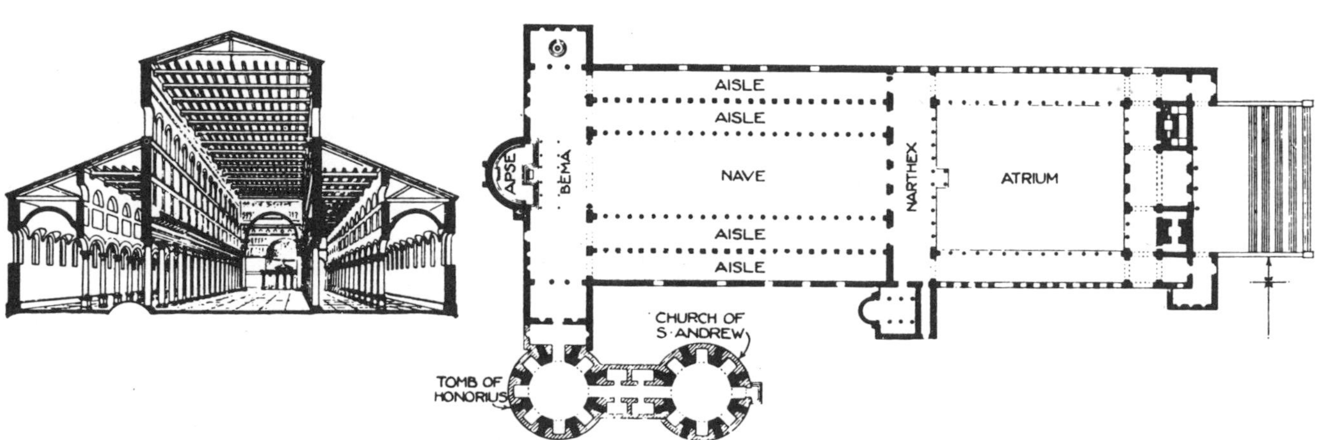

Transverse section and ground plan, Basilican Church of St. Peter, Rome. FROM SIR BANISTER FLETCHER, A HISTORY OF ARCHITECTURE

but from the Carolingian period on, the interior space began to be subdivided laterally into a series of regular and repeating units called bays. The modular bay system gave structural stability to the basilica, and allowed a decrease in wall surface area and an elaboration of the vaulting. In Romanesque basilicas the elevation of the nave wall was raised by the addition of a triforium, or gallery, between the arcade and the clerestory windows; in churches without clerestory lighting (such as St.-Sernin, at Toulouse) the triforium was placed between the arcade and the springing point of the vault. The three-part elevation (nave arcade, triforium, clerestory) was further refined during the Gothic period and, especially in the later twelfth century, a second gallery was sometimes added (as at Laon Cathedral).

Ceilings normally were vaulted, except in Cistercian churches. Early Romanesque churches usually had barrel-vaulted ceilings; light entered the basilica through gallery windows or through a relatively small clerestory. With the incorporation of groin vaulting in the nave ceiling, probably initiated by Norman architects (for instance, at Durham Cathedral, and at St. Étienne, Caen) in the second half of the eleventh century, the clerestory was greatly enlarged. The improvement in groin vaulting through the use of ribs during the Gothic period permitted greater height and larger openings in the nave walls of basilicas.

BIBLIOGRAPHY

Kenneth J. Conant, *Carolingian and Romanesque Architecture, 800–1200,* rev. ed. (1974); Paul Frankl, *Gothic Architecture,* D. Pevsner, trans. (1963); Richard Krautheimer, *Early Christian and Byzantine Architecture,* rev. ed. (1975).

LESLIE BRUBAKER

[See also **Gothic Architecture; Romanesque Architecture.**]

BASILICS, code of law in sixty books (hence the name *Hexekontabiblos*) grouped in six volumes (hence *Hexabiblos*), issued by the Byzantine emperor Leo VI (886–912) and prepared by a commission of lawyers under the supervision of the *protospatharios* Symbatios. The Basilics are the largest legal codification of the middle Byzantine period, and concern the civil, the public, the penal, and the canon law. Almost one-third of the text has not survived.

The main source of the Basilics was the Justinianic legislation: the *Codex,* the *Digest,* and, to a lesser extent, the *Institutes* and the *Novels* (of Justinian and of some of his successors). The *Procheiros Nomos* was also taken into consideration. The text of the Basilics often repeats the Justinianic administrative terminology (which disappeared in the tenth century), and is accompanied by numerous commentaries; the seventh- and eighth-century scholia to the Justinianic codifications are partly reproduced, and new scholia were added in the tenth through twelfth centuries. These commentaries are particularly important because they served to actualize the text of the code, which otherwise might have appeared outdated. Moreover, beginning in the tenth century a *Synopsis major* of the Basilics was constituted and continuously enriched with appendices containing new legislation. At the beginning of the twelfth century an index was made of the Basilics, known as the *Tipoukeitos* (perhaps from *ti pou keitai*).

BIBLIOGRAPHY

Editions. Basilicorum libri LX, D. C. G. E. Heimbach, ed., 6 vols. (1833–1870); *Basilika,* I. Zepos, ed., 5 vols. (1910–1912); *Basilicorum libri LX,* H. J. Scheltema et al., eds. (1953–).

Also see M. Kritou tou Patze, *Tipoukeitos, sive Librorum LX Basilicorum summarium,* C. Ferrini et al., eds., 5 vols. (1914–1957); Nicolas Svoronos, *Recherches sur la tradition juridique à Byzance: La Synopsis major des Basiliques et ses appendices* (1964).

NICHOLAS OIKONOMIDES

[See also **Corpus Juris Civilis; Law, Byzantine; Procheiros Nomos.**]

BASKET CAPITAL. See **Capital, Types of.**

BASMENOYE DELO is the mounting of precious metal that was often used to cover portions of Russian icons. In early times such coverings were attached to revered and treasured icons like the Mother of God of Vladimir, but on late icons the mounting was often an integral part of the object.

ANN E. FARKAS

[See also **Icon, Manufacture of.**]

BASQUES. The Basques inhabit a region about the size of Massachussetts on the Bay of Biscay, at the western end of the Pyrenees. The international boundary, fixed in 1512, divides them very unevenly: today possibly fewer than a hundred thousand Basques live in Labourd, Basse-Navarre, and Soule, while about ten times as many are in the Spanish provinces of Vizcaya, Álava, Guipúzcoa, and Navarre.

Wilhelm von Humboldt, who in the 1820's put Basque linguistics on a scientific footing, conjectured that Basques once dwelt over most of the Iberian Peninsula. Modern toponymic studies, however, indicate that the linguistic boundary has remained stable since the sixteenth century and that prior to that time only two significant contractions occurred: in the sixth and seventh centuries the eastern prong of Vasconia—including most of Navarre and parts of Saragossa, Huesca, and Lérida, as well as Andorra—was romanized; and after Alfonso VIII captured Vitoria in 1200, almost all of Álava and the western fringe of Vizcaya were castilianized.

Except for a few glosses and word lists, no Basque written records survive from before the mid sixteenth century. Consequently, we must resort to nonnative testimony or indirect evidence for a picture of Basque life in the Middle Ages.

The Romans established control over the Iberian Peninsula after the Second Punic War, but many tribes in the northern mountains retained their independence. The legions of Augustus temporarily vanquished the Cantabrians and Asturians, but these and the Basques resisted assimilation; and Diocletian pragmatically chose Navarre as a defensive buffer against the northern tribes. The arrival of the Visigoths in the early fifth century brought little change. Leovigild defeated the Basques and founded Vitoria (581) on their frontier; but the Visigoths, like the Romans, acknowledged Basque independence. The Arabs likewise made no determined effort to secure control over the mountain fastnesses.

When the Basques relinquished their native religion, they adopted a severely conservative style of Catholicism while clinging to many ancient superstitions, such as belief in witchcraft and the evil eye. Rural people held to their pagan rites until the eleventh century, but Pamplona had a Christian community and a bishop as early as the sixth century. During Charlemagne's Spanish campaign of 778, his forces subdued the Vascones and took their capital at Pamplona. Later, though, the Basques took revenge by annihilating the Frankish rear guard as it marched through the pass of Roncevaux. Legend has transformed those Basque Christians into Saracens and has made Count Roland into one of the great heroes of Western literature.

The Reconquest saw the rise of three neo-Basque kingdoms between León and the Frankish March in Catalonia. In the early ninth century Iñigo Arista founded the nucleus of the future kingdom of Navarre, which reached its apogee in the early eleventh century, when Sancho III exercised hegemony over the other Christian states of the peninsula. Sancho bequeathed Navarre to his eldest legitimate son, García; he left lands mostly in Aragon to Ramiro; and he willed Castile to his younger son, Ferdinand I, who promptly annexed León. The Castilians, under Ferdinand, later eliminated both García and Ramiro, and Navarre was temporarily divided between Castile and Aragon.

North of the Pyrenees, Labourd formed part of Gascony until the mid eleventh century, when with Aquitaine it passed to the counts of Poitiers. Shortly before, Sancho had attached Basse-Navarre to his domains. Soule had its own viscounts, who until the mid thirteenth century alternately recognized the suzerainty of kings of Navarre and dukes of Gascony. Through Henry II's marriage to Eleanor of Aquitaine, the English kings became masters of both Labourd and Soule until the mid fifteenth century.

Throughout the Middle Ages the majority of Basques held to their own customs and earned a reputation for barbarism. The Old Provençal *Song of St. Faith,* for example, depicts a villainous Basque beheading the saint while the Roman authorities burn her over a grill. Sancho III laid out his new route to Santiago in part to avoid the hazardous Basque country. Dangerous conditions there persisted well into the twelfth century, for in 1179 the Third Lateran Council accused the Basques and Navarrese of thievery and brigandage, and excommunicated them along with the Albigensians.

Basque legal institutions resemble Germanic more than Roman tradition. When the law began to be codified in the medieval *fueros* or *fors,* the Basques were granted exemption from military service and permitted extraordinarily free trade, even in such state monopolies as salt. The *fueros* also respected the Basque rule of primogeniture, regardless of the sex of the firstborn; thus landholdings remained intact through transmission to the eldest. Also, despite their role in the creation of the new monarchies, the Basques in their remote villgaes governed themselves through an elected council of landholders. They enjoyed an essentially republican form of government and developed few of the traits of feudalism.

BASRA

Vasconia's economy was based primarily on farming and raising livestock. The rich Cantabrian iron deposits were known already in Pliny's time, and fishing and shipping contributed to the prosperity of coastal towns. In the late Middle Ages, Bilbao became the main port for Castilian goods en route to northern Europe. It played an important role in the wool trade, but after the fifteenth century the demands of the Castilian textile industry sharply curtailed export volume. By then commerce with America provided a new challenge for Basque seamen.

BIBLIOGRAPHY

Julio Caro Baroja, *Estudios vascos* (1973); Rodney Gallop, *A Book of the Basques* (1930); Ramón Menéndez Pidal, "Sobre las vocales ibéricas ę y ǫ en los nombres toponímicos," in *Revista de filología española,* 5 (1918); Martín de Ugalde, *Síntesis de la historia del país vasco* (1974).

CURTIS BLAYLOCK

[See also **Fuero; Navarre.**]

BASRA (Bassora, Bassorah, al-Basrah; Balsora in medieval Europe), a town in southern Iraq. It was founded as a military encampment, on the site of an ancient Persian settlement, by a companion of the prophet Muḥammad during a campaign in the borderland between Arabia and Persia, probably in 638. At first the people of Basra dwelt in reed huts that could be rolled up and moved; thus, when the troops undertook military operations in Persia, they did not have to leave their families behind. After several fires occurred, reeds were replaced by crude, then by baked, bricks. Since the camp was about ten miles from the Tigris estuary, two main canals were dug to supply the population with drinking water. They made Basra an important port, and formed an island where gardens and groves were watered by a network of lesser canals. The early buildings of some importance were the Friday Mosque and the governor's house. The city was not walled until 771–772.

The original camp was divided into five sections assigned to contingents belonging to different Arab tribes. For some time those various elements kept their tribal identities, but the growing town attracted both Arabs and non-Arabs in increasing numbers, so that it became a melting pot. A feeling of common citizenship arose, and gradually obliterated tribal differences. Several important events occurred in Basra shortly after its foundation. In 656 there took place the famous "Battle of the Camel," in which Muslim forces fought other Muslims for the first time. During the following decades the city was affected by disturbances among its citizens and frequently threatened by foreign rebels, but it succeeded in retaining some autonomy under Umayyad rule.

Owing to the booty brought in by local warriors and the income from a fairly large area, Basra soon reached prominence within the Islamic world as an active port and emporium on the routes to Arabia, Syria, Persia, India, and the Far East. Although it is impossible to give an accurate population figure, 100,000 appears to be a reasonable number for the eighth century, which may be regarded as its heyday.

During this century Basra, a resort of poets, men of letters, and scholars, witnessed intense activity in both religious and intellectual matters. It was the cradle of Arabic grammar and literary prose, and of Islamic theology; in addition to the Prophet's traditions, many Basran scholars collected the poetical and historical traditions that were to form the nucleus of Arabic culture. Unfortunately, the rise of the Abbasid dynasty in 750, and the subsequent founding of Baghdad, struck a fatal blow to the southern metropolis; scholars and poets began to migrate to the new capital, and Basra became a mere provincial town. Moreover, it was seized by the Zanj in 871 and sacked by the Qarmatians in 923. Its plight was further worsened by the Mongol invasion, to such an extent that in the mid fourteenth century Ibn Baṭṭūṭa described the old city as being almost in ruins and containing mainly those parts that were near the site on which the modern city would be built. During the Ottoman period, which began in 1534, Basra played a modest economic role.

BIBLIOGRAPHY

Arabic sources have been used for the history of Basra to the mid ninth century by Charles Pellat, *Le milieu baṣrien et la formation de Ǧāḥiẓ* (1953). See also ᶜA. J. Nājī, "Basra 294–447/907–1055" (Ph.D. dissertation, University of London, 1970). For the ancient topography, see Ṣāliḥ Aḥmad al-ᶜAlī, "Khiṭaṭ al-Baṣra," in *Sumer,* 8 (1952); and Louis Massignon, "Explication du plan de Baṣra," in *West-östliche Abhandlungen R. Tschudi,* Fritz Mein, ed. (1954), repr. in Massignon's *Opera minora,* III (1963), 61–87.

For the social and economic institutions, see Ṣāliḥ Aḥmad al-ᶜAlī, *Al-Tanẓīmat al-ijtimāᶜiyya wa-l-iqtiṣādiyya fī l-Baṣra* (1953). On poetry during the Umayyad period, see ᶜAwn al-Sharīf Qāsim, *Shiᶜr al-Baṣra* (1972). See also Guy Le Strange, *The Lands of the Eastern Caliphate*

(1930); Paul Pelliot, *Notes on Marco Polo,* I (1959), 88–89; and Henry Yule, *The Book of Ser Marco Polo,* I (1921), 65.

CHARLES PELLAT

[See also **Iraq; Karamans; Zanj.**]

BASSA, FERRER (*d.* 1348), a Catalonian painter of altarpieces, murals, and manuscripts of whom the first certain record is from 1324. He is credited with introducing Italian artistic influences to Spain. The mural of the convent of Pedralbes in Barcelona (1345–1346) reveals his profound debt to Tuscan, especially Sienese, painting.

BIBLIOGRAPHY

Millard Meiss, "Italian Style in Catalonia and a Fourteenth Century Catalonian Workshop," in *Journal of the Walters Art Gallery,* 4 (1941); Manuel Trens, *Ferrer Bassa i les pintures de Pedralbes* (1936).

JOHN WILLIAMS

BASTIDE, in southwestern France in the thirteenth and fourteenth centuries, the name for a new free town; in Provence, from the thirteenth century on, the name for an isolated rural residence and farm. In both areas the word (from the Latin *bastida*) was originally used to designate a stronghold.

The prototype of the southwestern bastide was Montauban (Tarn-et-Garonne), created by Alphonse-Jourain, count of Toulouse, in 1144. Situated on a naturally defensible high point, it guarded the road to Toulouse, at the crossing of the Tarn River, from any threat by the duke of Aquitaine to the north. It was laid out on a grid plan (altered to conform to the site) with an open market square at the center. The count guaranteed the freedom of all comers, established the allotments *(casales)* for them to construct houses, and fixed low land rents *(cens).* Since the land on which the town was built belonged to the abbey of St.-Théodard, which already had a village nearby, the count's successor was induced to negotiate a colordship *(paréage)* with the abbot (1149). By the end of the century, the town had its own elected magistrates. So striking was Montauban to contemporaries that an epic poem, *Renaud de Montauban,* celebrated its foundation.

When, early in the thirteenth century, the creation of new towns resumed in southwestern France

Bastide of Carcassonne, view of the city walls. 12th century. SEF/ EDITORIAL PHOTOCOLOR ARCHIVES

after a half-century hiatus, the bastides commonly had the same characteristics as Montauban. Most were the creations of great princes—the counts of Toulouse, the kings of England (as dukes of Aquitaine) and France—or of nobles of slightly lesser rank, such as the counts of Foix. A few were established by princely officials, such as the Alaman family, for their own profit. They collaborated with minor lords or, most often, with ecclesiastical foundations (Cistercians, Premonstratensians, Templars, and Hospitalers) on whose lands the settlements were constructed, and the contracts of colordship served as the bastides' foundation charters.

Many bastides were strategically located on the frontiers of principalities, especially on both sides of the border between the county of Toulouse and the duchy of Aquitaine. Alphonse of Poitiers built seventeen in the Agenais alone between 1246 and 1271. To this activity kings Henry III and Edward I responded after 1263 with a massive establishment of plantations in the Bordelais and southern Perigord. The kings of France and England fought the "War of St.-Sardos" (1323–1325) over the foundation of a bastide.

The bastides' function, however, was more to attract population to the frontiers and to give the founder a political base through contracts of *paréage* than to constitute strongholds, for many were long unfortified or, like Villefranche-de-Rouergue (Aveyron), were built on indefensible sites. Bastide builders were equally interested in commerce, and chose locations on water and land routes in order to provide small market centers for the local economy and collection points for produce to be shipped long distances (from all of which they collected fees). The "boom" in English foundations in Gascony between 1263 and 1300 (77 out of 124 in the entire period to 1350) may have been connected to the expansion of the Bordelais wine trade. New names sometimes reflected vast ambitions: Cologne (Gers), Fleurance (Gers), Pavie (Gers), Grenade-sur-Garonne (Haute-Garonne).

The heart of the bastide was the public "square." Sometimes nothing more than a widening of the road along which houses were built (Najac [Aveyron]), or a few lots left vacant (Cordes [Tarn]), in fully planned foundations it was a rectangle or trapezoid, surrounded by a covered walk or arcade (surviving examples at Mirepoix [Ariège], Montauban), that contained the market and municipal offices, and sometimes a well, cistern, or fountain. The church was usually nearby. Town plans were occasionally irregular (La-Bastide-du-Levis [Tarn]) or circular (Fourcès [Gers]), but the majority—and best-known examples—were built on a grid plan with either one or two axes, modified as necessary to conform to the terrain (Montpazier [Dordogne], Carcassonne, Aigues-Mortes). They ranged in size from a few house plots to 3,000 (Grenade-sur-Garonne).

Sometimes a formal ritual commenced the plantation. The founder's officer erected a pole (*pal* or *pau*) where the center of the public square was to be, and suspended the founder's flag from it. (The "War of St.-Sardos" began when the lord of Montpezat hanged the royal herald from the *pal.*) Then the streets and lots were marked out. The officer announced the liberties the town would have, confirmed them with an oath, and handed over to a representative of the inhabitants a charter bearing the founder's seal. Inhabitants were often required to build on their lots within a specified time or else to pay a fine.

Some new inhabitants may have come from far away: Englishmen were residents in Gascon bastides. But most must have come from neighboring towns and villages, which occasionally were deserted as a result. *Paréages* included clauses prohibiting subjects of the colords from taking up residence in the new towns, and complaints against plantations flowed from neighboring lords and older towns to the courts of the kings of England and France. Foundations were fought with curses, excommunications, legal suits, sieges, and rival foundations. Some newcomers may have been landless or runaway peasants. It was important, however, to attract skilled artisans and merchants with capital. Liberties as good as or better than those of older towns were the main inducement, usually in imitation of other bastides: freedom from arbitrary taxes and servile obligations, protection of property, free disposition of land and chattels, fixed court fines, regulated fairs and markets, limited military service, no seignorial monopoly of mills and ovens, and an organized municipal government. While a few bastides became major towns (Montauban, Carcassonne, Aigues-Mortes), others failed: in Gascony one out of three sooner or later died.

The first of the Provençal bastides is mentioned in 1234. For long these were simple towers that controlled a territory within the lands of a village. Sometimes they gave birth to a tiny, ephemeral hamlet. In the thirteenth and fourteenth centuries their functions remained military and symbolic of power. In the fifteenth century they started to become centers of agricultural exploitation (especially by urban merchants and notaries), simultaneously farms and rural residences.

BIBLIOGRAPHY

Maurice Beresford, *New Towns of the Middle Ages* (1967), with bibliography; Pierre Chaplais, ed., *The War of Saint-Sardos, 1323–1325* (1954); Noël Coulet, "La naissance de la bastide provençale," in Charles Higounet, ed., *Géographie historique du village et de la maison rurale* (1980), 145–159; and "La bastide provençale au bas Moyen-Âge," in *Archeologia medievale* (1981); Charles Higounet, *Paysages et villages neufs du Moyen-Âge* (1975); and "Zur Siedlungsgeschichte Sudwest-frankreichs vom 11. bis zum 14. Jahrhundert," in *Vorträge und Forschungen,* **18** (1975), with bibliography; Pierre Lavedan and Jeanne Hugueney, *L'urbanisme au Moyen-Âge* (1974); J. P. Trabut-Cussac, "Bastides ou forteresses?" in *Le Moyen-Âge,* **60** (1954).

FREDRIC CHEVETTE

[See also **Feudalism; France; Urbanism, Western Europe.**]

BATA. See **Aelfric Bata.**

BATAILLE, NICHOLAS (*fl.* last quarter 14th c.). A renowned Parisian tapestry weaver, he wove the Apocalypse Tapestries, 1373–1379 (Angers, Musée des Tapisseries), for Louis of Anjou after designs by Jean Bondol. He also wove narrative and heraldic tapestries for other members of the French court.

BAṬṬŪṬA, IBN

BIBLIOGRAPHY

J. J. Marquet de Vasselot and Roger-Armand Weigert, *Bibliographie de la tapisserie, des tapis, et de la broderies en France* (1935), 42–43, 123–127; René Planchenault, *L'apocalypse d'Angers* (1966); Geneviève Souchal, *Les tapisseries de l'Apocalypse d'Angers* (1969); and *Masterpieces of Tapestry from the Fourteenth to the Sixteenth Century* (1973), 25–32.

ROBERT G. CALKINS

[See also **Bondol, Jean; Tapestry.**]

BATTLE AXE. See **Arms and Armor.**

BAṬṬŪṬA, IBN (1304–1368/1377), the greatest of the medieval "world travelers," was born at Tangier and, at the age of twenty-one, began a lifetime of travels and adventures that took him through most of the Muslim world, to sub-Saharan Africa, to India, and to China. The duration and geographical extent of his journeys surpass those of Marco Polo and Benjamin of Tudela. Ibn Baṭṭūṭa's account of his experiences, the famous *Riḥla,* stands out as an important source for our knowledge of much of the Middle East, Africa, and Asia in the fourteenth century, and as a major contribution to the travel-book genre of Arabic literature.

Shams al-Dīn Muḥammad ibn ᶜAbd Allah Ibn Baṭṭūṭa, the descendant of a family of qadis and religious scholars, set out from his birthplace in 1325, ostensibly to make the pilgrimage to Mecca and Medina. But, as he himself tells us, "I braced my resolution to quit all my dear ones, male and female, and forsook my home as birds forsake their nests." The desire to accomplish the pilgrimage, or hajj, a duty incumbent on all Muslims, soon turned into a passion for travel and exploration that impelled Ibn Baṭṭūṭa to lead a life of constant and practically uninterrupted travel for the next twenty-eight years. The skeletal chronology below will give some idea of the extent of Ibn Baṭṭūṭa's travels.

1325—Departure from North Africa and journey through what is now Morocco, Algeria, and Tunisia to Egypt. Ibn Baṭṭūṭa visited Alexandria and Cairo, traveled up the Nile to Luxor, crossed the desert to visit ᶜAydhāb, and then returned to Cairo, from whence he traveled to Syria through what is now Israel and Lebanon.

1326—Departure from Damascus and pilgrimage to Mecca; return journey through southern Iraq and southwestern Persia to Baghdad; visits to Mosul and Samarra and three more pilgrimages to Mecca and Medina (1327–1330).

1330—Travels through the Red Sea, South Arabia, and the coast of East Africa as far as Kilwa in modern Tanzania; return along the southern coast of Arabia and visits to Oman and the Persian Gulf. Ibn Baṭṭūṭa then made a fourth pilgrimage in 1332.

1332—Departure from Mecca and journey through Egypt, Syria, Asia Minor, the Crimea, and the Balkans (the territories of the Golden Horde), a visit to Constantinople, and further travels through southern Russia and central Asia to Afghanistan and India. Ibn Baṭṭūṭa reached the Indus valley in 1333 and spent almost ten years in India. He even served as the Maliki chief qadi of Delhi for an extended period. He left Delhi in 1342 and traveled through south India, the Maldives, Ceylon, Assam, and Bengal, and made a further journey through Malaysia and Indonesia to China.

1347—Return journey through Sumatra and Malabar to the Persian Gulf; more travels through Iraq, Syria, and Egypt; and a fifth pilgrimage.

1349—Departure from Alexandria for Tunis; visit to Granada in Muslim Spain; and a return to Morocco.

1352—Final journey. Ibn Baṭṭūṭa left from Sijilmasa in Morocco and traveled across the Sahara to visit the ancient kingdom of Mali in the area of the Niger River. He returned to Sijilmasa in 1353.

Ibn Baṭṭūṭa's travels in black Africa marked the end of his career as an explorer and adventurer. After his return to Sijilmasa, he spent the remainder of his life in North Africa. The Marīnid sultan of Fès, Abū ᶜInān, commissioned an Andalusian scholar, Ibn Juzayy, to record Ibn Baṭṭūṭa's experiences from the dictation of the traveler himself. The work was finished in 1357, and Ibn Baṭṭūṭa died in either 1368 or 1377, while serving as a qadi "in some town or another." After the conclusion of his final journey, the famous traveler seems to have settled into obscurity.

Some of the more fantastic descriptive passages in the *Riḥla* have occasioned skepticism from both medieval and modern readers. The consensus of modern scholars, however, is that the *Riḥla,* on the whole, is an important and generally trustworthy source for the history of most of the areas Ibn Baṭṭūṭa visited. The wealth of description of different lands and peoples, the information on everything from political events to types of cuisine, and the pronounced element of what we would call "human interest" make the record of Ibn Baṭṭūṭa's travels a still vibrant work of the genre with a great appeal for both the specialist and the general reader. Few sources provide us with as detailed an "everyday" description of the Muslim societies of the fourteenth century as that in the *Riḥla.*

The great historian Ibn Khaldūn tells an interesting anecdote about his own encounter with the famous traveler. He says that when Ibn Baṭṭūṭa returned to the Maghrib after his travels in India, many people considered his tales to be simple fabrications. Ibn Khaldūn, eager to discover the truth, discussed the matter with an official at the Marīnid court. The latter told him the story of a man who was imprisoned with his infant son. The boy grew up in prison and never saw the outside world. He asked his father one day to explain the origin of the meat they ate. His father described sheep, cattle, and camels repeatedly, but the unfortunate boy could only picture them as types of rats, since the rat was the only animal he had ever seen. Such was the predicament, Ibn Khaldūn concluded, of Ibn Baṭṭūṭa's incredulous auditors.

There is no doubt that Ibn Baṭṭūṭa occasionally embroidered his own experiences in the course of recounting his lifelong adventures. He also faithfully reported many popular legends and beliefs that were widely held in his time. Whatever his occasional slips in veracity, however, there is no doubt that he was, above all, a great and original observer and a reflector of his time.

BIBLIOGRAPHY

Voyages d'Ibn Batoutah, C. Defrémery and B. R. Sanguinetti, eds. and trans., 4 vols., 3rd ed. (1893–1895); *The Travels of Ibn Baṭṭūṭa,* H. A. R. Gibb, trans., 3 vols. (1958–1971); *Ibn Baṭṭūṭa in Black Africa,* Said Hamdun and Noel King, eds. and trans. (1975). See also Herman F. Janssens, *Ibn Batouta, le voyageur de l'Islam* (1948).

SHAUN E. MARMON

[See also **Benjamin of Tudela; Khaldūn, Ibn; Marco Polo; Travel and Transport.**]

BATU (Russian: *Batyi*) (*ca.* 1203–1255), founder of the Golden Horde. According to Turko-Mongolian custom, his father, Jochi (*d.* 1227), as oldest son of Genghis Khan, was given a loosely defined *ulus* (appanage) in the exposed periphery of the realm extending from western Siberia and Turkestan to the Volga. Upon the death of Jochi, it was Batu rather than his older brother Orda who received the westernmost territories. At the *quriltay* ("assembly of state") of 1235, Batu was given supreme command of the forces that undertook further conquests in the West.

Batu's general Sübüdey subdued Volga Bulgaria in 1236 while Möngke advanced against the Cuman-Kipchaks, who resisted until 1238. In late 1237 the Mongols moved on the northeastern Russ principalities, taking Ryazan in December 1237 and Vladimir in February 1238. In 1240 the Mongols pressed into southern Russ. Chernigov and Pereiaslavl' were ravaged, and Kiev fell, amid massive destruction, on 6 December 1240. Invasions of Poland and Hungary culminated in successive victories at Liegnitz (modern Legnica), Silesia, over Henry the Pious also known as Henry of Silesia (9 April 1241), who perished in flight, and over the Hungarians at Mohi (11 April 1241). Incursions into the western Balkans ensued.

Further conquests were cut short by the death of the Great Khan Ögedey (11 December 1241) and mounting disputes among the Genghisids. In the winter of 1242–1243, Batu returned to the Volga, where the vagaries of domestic Genghisid politics prompted the foundation of a more permanent political unit. Further impetus to this development was given by the election of his enemy Göyük (1246–1248) as supreme khan. Göyük's untimely death prevented warfare between the two. Batu now engineered the election of Möngke the Toluyid. In return for this support, he was given extensive autonomy. With his capital at Sarai, he was master of the Kipchak steppes and supreme overlord of Russ. In Mongol tradition he was called *sain* ("the good" or "the wise").

BIBLIOGRAPHY

ᶜAlā al-Dīn ᶜAṭā Malek Joveynī, *Taʾrīkh-i Jahān Gushā,* M. Qazvīnī, ed., 3 vols. (1912–1937), translated by John Andrew Boyle as *The History of the World-Conqueror,* 2 vols. (1958); A. N. Nasonov, *Mongoly i Rus* (1940); Rashīd al-Dīn Ṭabīb Faẓlallāh, *Jāmiᶜ al-tavārīkh,* I, *Taʾrīkh-i ghāzānī,* Edgar Blochet, ed., 2 vols. (1911); translated by John Andrew Boyle as *The Successors of Genghis Khan* (1971); Bertold Spuler, *Die Goldene Horde,* 2nd rev. ed. (1965).

PETER B. GOLDEN

[See also **Golden Horde; Mongols.**]

BAUDRI OF BOURGUEIL (1046–1130), a Benedictine monk, became abbot of Bourgueil in 1089 and archbishop of Dol in 1107; he held the latter office until his death, though temporarily suspended in 1120 by the papal legate. Baudri's career was colorful, frequently turbulent, and marked by associations with notable contemporaries. His *Historia Hierosolimitana,* an account of the First Crusade, enjoyed great popularity and influence, though it is for the most part only a reworking of an earlier and historically more valuable source. The *Itinerarium* offers an interesting description of visits to monastic houses in Normandy and England. Baudri's considerable body of verse displays the secular erudition one would expect of a product of the school of Angers; it evinces as well the contemporary revival of interest in the erotic lyric, addressed to persons of both sexes. Several hagiographical works are also extant.

BIBLIOGRAPHY

Editions. Patrologia latina, CLXII (1889), 1043–1058, and CLXVI (1894), 1049–1208; Phyllis Abrahams, *Les oeuvres poétiques de Baudri de Bourgueil* (1926). Louis Bréhier, "Baudri de Bourgeuil," in *Dictionnaire d'histoire et de géographie ecclésiastiques* (1932); John Boswell, *Christianity, Social Tolerance, and Homosexuality* (1980), 244–247. Additional bibliography is in Boswell's notes and in Martin McGuire and Hermigild Dressler, *Introduction to Medieval Latin Studies,* 2nd ed. (1977), 201.

DAVID R. TOWNSEND

[See also **Latin Literature.**]

BAUERNHOCHZEIT, DIE (The Peasants' Wedding) is the collective title now used for two closely related Middle High German verse tales *(Mären)* of the fourteenth century: *Meier Betz,* 417 lines, and *Metzen hochzit,* 680 lines long. The anonymous poem depicts in broad, at times coarse humor the wedding, in all its stages, of the peasant lad Betz (or Bärschi in the longer version; nicknames for Berthold or Bernhard) with Metzi (for Mechtild). At the betrothal before a council of relatives and elders, the dowry is fixed and the wedding set for the same evening. Following a raucous reception, the couple is put to bed (there are two differing accounts of the wedding night). The next morning, after mass, the traditional tussle of the younger men with the groom deteriorates into a brawl. The wedding feast is a gluttonous rout, many of the gifts are quite useless, and the dance soon turns into a bloody fight, which is finally suppressed by other villagers.

The *Märe* is preserved in three manuscripts. Of the shorter version, *H* (in Prague) and *S* (in Stuttgart), *H* is to be preferred; the longer version *Do* (in Donaueschingen) is a somewhat coarser elaboration. The dialect and certain coins mentioned *(Brisgöwer)* help to locate the poem in the Low Alemannic region, probably near Freiburg im Breisgau. An immediate source is not known, but the poem's bias against the uncouth peasantry places it in a tradition associated with Neidhart von Reuental (*ca.* 1210–1245). The farce depends largely on the accumulation of comic surnames (Peter Thirst, Meier Nosedrip, Broomstick) and on the parody of rural customs, dishes consumed at the feasts, table manners, wedding gifts, weapons used, and injuries sustained in the fighting. The poem's continuing popularity and influence is attested by the fifteenth-century epic comedy *Der Ring* by Heinrich Wittenwiler, and the Shrovetide plays.

BIBLIOGRAPHY

Hanns Fischer, *Studien zur deutschen Märendichtung* (1968), for complete list of manuscripts and bibliography; Edmund Weissner, *Der Bauernhochzeitsschwank, Meier Betz und Metzen hochzit* (1956), for edition, transmission, and history of the subject; and *idem,* "*Metzen hochzit* und Wittenwilers *Ring,*" in *Zeitschrift für deutsches Altertum,* 74 (1937), on the thirteenth- and early-fourteenth-century upper Rhenish currency called *Breisgauer Pfennige.*

KLAUS WOLLENWEBER

[See also **Mären; Middle High German Literature; Neidhart von Reuental; Wittenwiler, Henrich.**]

BAVARIA. From the early Middle Ages until the thirteenth century, the territory called Bavaria stretched from Bolzano and surrounding lands in the south to the Lech and the bend in the Regnitz River in the west, and to the Fichtelgebirge Mountains and the Upper Palatinate and the Bohemian Forest Mountains in the north and northeast. Toward the southeast lay a series of independently administered marches—in Eastern March, Carinthia, and Friuli. The core of Bavaria, though, was the Alpine forelands, of strategic and commercial importance because of their position on trade routes to Italy and to the southeast. By the beginning of the fourteenth century, Bavaria had been reduced to an area bounded roughly by the Lech in the west, the king-

BAVARIA

dom of Bohemia to the northeast, and the archbishopric of Salzburg and Habsburg holdings in Austria to the south and east.

Celts had occupied the banks of the Danube and their hinterlands in pre-Christian times. By the first century of the Christian era Rome had subjugated them and their territories up to that river. Dividing their conquests into two provinces, Raetia in the west and Noricum to the east, the Romans made Castra Regina (Regensburg) their administrative capital.

Roman rule of Noricum, the heartland of medieval Bavaria, collapsed in 488 under the pressure of Germanic migration—Alamannic tribes, Franks, and the Baiuvarii, after whom the territory was named. Though the settlement of the Bavarians probably began somewhere between 450 and 500, it is poorly documented; the first written records of these peoples and their customs are from the eighth century. By 800, though, they appear to have established themselves along the Danube from Regensburg to what is now Vienna in the east. They were

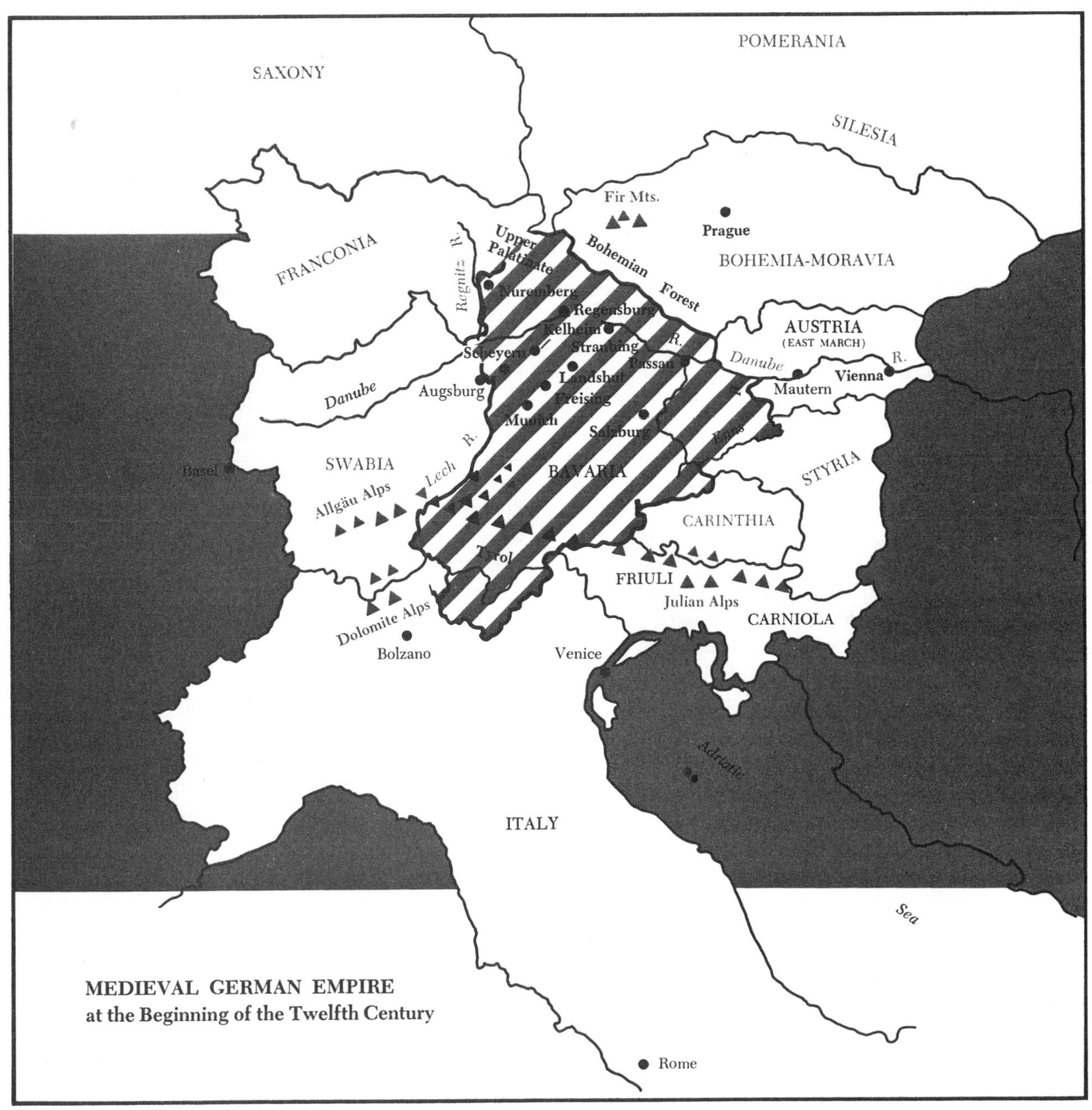

MEDIEVAL GERMAN EMPIRE
at the Beginning of the Twelfth Century

also found in thinner clusters to the south along the Enns and through other Alpine valleys, and to the west as far as the modern city of Regensburg.

Bavaria as a duchy in all likelihood owes its creation to the Merovingians, on whose territories it bordered. Although they represented the Frankish king, the dukes were hereditary from the beginning and were, at least in theory, the chief military and judicial figures in their lands. From around 555 to 788, the duchy was ruled by the Agilolfings, a dynasty of Frankish or Burgundian origin. In 788 Charlemagne deposed Tassilo III, the last of these rulers, but until that time they and their territory were largely independent of their Frankish overlords. It was a powerful landed aristocracy with its own judicial powers, who most effectively checked ducal prerogatives. Through their patronage of monasteries the nobles spread their influence even further. Church lands enjoyed a certain measure of juridical freedom.

As early as the fifth century a Christian mission came to the Danubian lands in the shadowy person of St. Severinus. Working from a monastery near Mautern, he and his followers engaged in charitable and other duties that replaced administrative functions no longer carried on by Rome. During the eighth century Christianity set down solid institutional roots in Bavaria. Irish-Frankish monks, notably St. Rupert in Salzburg, St. Emmeram in Regensburg, and St. Corbinian in Freising, founded houses that became centers of teaching and reform. In 738–739 the Anglo-Saxon St. Boniface organized the four major bishoprics of Salzburg, Regensburg, Passau, and Freising. Benedictine monasteries were scattered throughout Bavaria by 800. Some, such as Tegernsee, Benediktbeuern, and St. Emmeram's in Regensburg, became focal points of art and scholarship.

Following the partition and collapse of the Carolingian Empire in the ninth century, Bavaria changed hands many times until 1180. The later Carolingians, the Luitpoldingian dukes of Carinthia, the Ottonian and Salian imperial dynasties, the Swabian Welfs, and the Austrian Babenbergs ruled the duchy at one time or another. Despite the chaos that often accompanied these turnovers, the Bavarian dukes increased their powers, if not their territorial possessions. By the beginning of the tenth century they regularly participated in the elections of German kings. By 1077 they could demand that their nobility and clerical officials meet with them at court, ask for extraordinary revenues from them in times of territorial need, and arbitrate disputes among either the clergy or the nobility. They acquired the right of escheat in the duchy during the twelfth century, an especially advantageous development because major noble dynasties began to die out at that time.

The duchy also grew economically during this period. New lands were cleared for cultivation, a particularly difficult undertaking in Bavaria because most of its border areas were densely wooded. The population expanded; nobles, dukes, and clerical officials alike lured peasants into new areas with promises of immunity from dues and more favorable rights of possession and inheritance. The weakening of serfdom that followed these measures was especially noticeable in the southeast. New cities appeared, such as Munich, founded in 1158 by the Welf duke, Henry the Lion. However, it was not until the fourteenth century that it became an important economic center as a crossroads for the salt and wine trades. In general, the north of the duchy was more urban; the south, more agricultural.

The political outlines of modern Bavaria emerged from the struggle between its ambitious Welf dukes and the Hohenstaufen emperors of the twelfth century. Acquiring the duchy of Saxony in 1136, Duke Henry X the Proud fashioned a strip of Welf influence that slashed across the empire from the Baltic to the Adriatic. In 1139 Emperor Conrad III placed Henry under the imperial ban and installed the Babenberg margrave of the Eastern March as duke of Bavaria. In a reconciliation among Henry's son, Henry the Lion, Emperor Frederick Barbarossa, and the margrave-duke Henry II Jasomirgott, the Babenbergs renounced Bavaria in return for the so-called lesser privilege *(privilegium minus)* of 1156. This turned the Eastern March into an independent duchy, the core of modern Austria, and granted its dukes hereditary succession. Henry the Lion was made duke of both Bavaria and Saxony. Pursuing a virtually independent foreign policy, he fell into protracted conflict with Barbarossa once again. In 1180 the latter broke up the Welf holdings entirely, bestowing a much-reduced Bavaria on a loyal follower, Count Otto of Wittelsbach.

Descendants of one of Bavaria's great noble dynasties (the counts of Scheyern), the Wittelsbachs had lands throughout the duchy, though these holdings were concentrated in the northeast around Straubing and Kelheim. Though Otto I was the first of his house to hold the ducal title, it was his son, Louis I, who really entrenched his family's rule in Bavaria. He was aided in his endeavors by such measures as Frederick II's *statutum in favorem prin-*

cipum (statute in favor of the princes) of 1220 and 1231–1232, which gave Germany's princes sole control of courts, customs and coinage, and mines and cities in their lands. Louis founded the cities of Landshut (1204) and Straubing (1218).

Though the Wittelsbachs benefited financially from their rights over markets in these and other towns, their urban centers never reached the level of wealth and cultural importance of others throughout Germany, such as the neighboring imperial free cities of Augsburg and Regensberg. Indeed, relative capital poverty was one of the most serious limitations on the ambitions of the dukes of Bavaria, both in the later Middle Ages and in modern times. Perhaps it was because their resources were so pinched that the Wittelsbachs were, on the whole, tight administrators. They employed a ducal council with flexible membership as early as the thirteenth century. By the fourteenth century a more specialized one had appeared that exercised considerable sway in the affairs of the duchy. The ducal chancellery was the focus of the practical administration of the territory.

Bavaria rose to temporary pan-European stature in the first half of the fourteenth century under duke Louis IV, "the Bavarian." Undisputed German king after 1322, he was named emperor in Rome "by the Roman people." His court in Munich attracted such luminaries as Marsilius of Padua and William of Ockham, whose theories of the secular nature of imperial rule supported his own claims. But Louis's reign only masked a reversal of Wittelsbach fortunes that had begun after the middle of the thirteenth century. At the heart of the problem were dynastic territorial divisions, a common disruptive factor in many German ruling houses. The first of these divisions took place in 1255, creating Upper Bavaria, with its seat at Munich, and Lower Bavaria, with Landshut as its administrative center. In 1353 a separate duchy of Bavaria-Straubing was created. With the exception of the last, all these territories were rearranged by a division in 1392, establishing Bavaria-Ingolstadt, Bavaria-Munich, and Bavaria-Landshut. When the Straubing line died out in 1425, its lands were absorbed by the other three.

The negative consequences of this practice for the Bavarian dukes can be seen in the way they lost their rights to participate in imperial elections. Louis the Bavarian had been forced to come to some sort of partition arrangement with the sons of his older brother. This was hammered out in the Treaty of Pavia (1329), according to which Louis handed over the Palatinate and Upper Palatinate to his nephews. Though the electoral vote was supposed to alternate between the two branches of the house, the Wittelsbach counts Palatine quickly became allies of Emperor Charles IV after Louis's death, and the electoral privilege shifted to their branch of their house altogether. An even more diminished Bavaria was fully united once again under the rule of Duke Albert IV the Wise, who systematically pursued this goal. It was he who introduced primogeniture into the Wittelsbach Bavarian lands in 1506.

The beneficiaries in all of this were the Bavarian nobility, clergy, and cities, all of which the dukes throughout the centuries had been anxious to curb. Ever short of revenues in their diminished territories, the dukes became financial dependents of these groups and their representatives. This was especially true in the eastern part of Bavaria, where the lesser nobles were more numerous than in the south and west. The result was the elaboration of meetings of local estates, which by the end of the fourteenth century were already very assertive. A committee of the estates, for example, supervised the territorial division of 1392. Their voice in ducal government and their direction of it were not subtantially checked until the later sixteenth and the seventeenth centuries.

BIBLIOGRAPHY

Karl Bosl, *Geschichte Bayerns,* I (1952), a standard treatment of prehistory and the Middle Ages; *Bayerische Geschichte* (1971), an accessible overview of Bavaria from the Middle Ages to the present; and *Die Geschichte der Repräsentation in Bayern* (1974); Kurt Reindel, *Bayern im Mittelalter* (1970), anecdotal; Sigmund von Riezler, *Geschichte Baierns,* 8 vols. in 9 (1878–1914, repr. 1964), I–III; *Handbuch der bayerischen Geschichte,* Max Spindler, ed., I, 2nd ed. (1980), and II, corr. ed. (1977), the starting point for all research in the field; *Zur Geschichte der Bayern,* Karl Bosl, ed. (1965), scholarly essays on a variety of topics.

PAULA SUTTER FICHTNER

[See also **Babenberg Family; Germany; Henry the Lion; Holy Roman Empire; Wittelsbach Family.**]

BAWWĀB, IBN AL- ("Son of the Gatekeeper") (*d.* 1022), was the epithet used by the Iraqi calligrapher Abū ᵓl-Ḥasan ᶜAlī ibn Hilāl. Renowned for the disciplined fluidity of his script, he is remembered for perfecting the script used by an earlier Iraqi calligrapher, Ibn Muqla. In this hand, known as *khaṭṭ al-*

BĀYAZĪD I, YILDIRIM

mansūb (measured writing), the size and shape of all letters was carefully regulated by using the first letter, *alif*, as a module for the remainder. Said to have been skilled in illumination and bookbinding as well as calligraphy, Ibn al-Bawwāb served Buyid administrators in both Baghdad and Shīrāz. Later scribes collected specimens of his work and emulated his hand.

BIBLIOGRAPHY

David Storm Rice, *The Unique Ibn al-Bawwāb Manuscript in the Chester Beatty Library* (1955), 1–10.

PRISCILLA SOUCEK

[See also **Calligraphy; Paleography, Arabic and Persian.**]

BĀYAZĪD I, YILDIRIM (*d.* 1403?), Ottoman sultan. The rapidity with which he raced between the Balkans and Anatolia earned him the sobriquet Yildirim (Thunderbolt). His reign, marked by incessant military activity, also witnessed the rapid growth of military and administrative elements based on slave personnel (the *qul* system) recruited by the *devshirme* (tribute in children) and directly dependent on the sultan. It was this nucleus, committed to the House of Osman, that ultimately preserved and helped to rebuild the Ottoman realm following Tamerlane's victory at Ankara (1402). Some scholars have argued that these developments and the extensive conquests of Muslim lands in Anatolia are attributable to Christian and newly converted Muslim influences (Bāyazīd's mother and wife were Christians). This, however, seems unlikely, because there are numerous Muslim precedents for these institutional developments. Moreover, this policy culminated in the replacement of Christian vassal regimes with direct Ottoman government. Bāyazīd's status as ghāzī ("fighter for the faith") was unchallenged. Indeed, he attracted to his service Muslim elements fleeing Central Asia.

Bāyazīd followed an ambitious policy of expansion in Europe and Asia. In the Balkans he worked to extend and consolidate Ottoman holdings against formidable rivals: Venice and Hungary. In Anatolia he had to wage war against fellow Turkish Muslims. Although Bāyazīd was scrupulous to obtain a *fatwā* (legal judgment) justifying these campaigns, they were not wholeheartedly undertaken by his Turkoman ghāzīs. Therefore, Christian troops from his Balkan vassals were extensively used. His prolonged stay in either region usually resulted in the diminution of the Ottoman hold in the other; hence, the constant activity of his reign.

Bāyazīd took the reins of government from his dying father, Murād I, on the Field of Kosovo (15 June 1389). He immediately cemented ties with the vassal Serb state (by marital bonds) and then turned to the rebellious beys of Anatolia. Aided by the Byzantines and Serbs, he established Ottoman authority up to the borders of the Karamān state and annexed Qastamonu (1392). Bāyazīd was prevented from contemplated moves against the Sivas state of Burhān ad-Dīn by European complications. Byzantium, Bulgaria, and Serbia were restless vassals. Despite the energetic efforts of Evrenoz Bey in Greece and elsewhere, a larger Ottoman presence was required. Bāyazīd arrived, took the Bulgarian capital of Trnovo (1393), began a seven-year blockade of Constantinople (1394), campaigned in Danubian Europe, retook Nicopolis, and executed the Bulgarian king Shishman (1395). This produced a Venetian-Hungarian alliance and the Crusade of Nicopolis (1396), which ended in disaster for the Christian forces. Ottoman possession of the Balkans was now secure.

Karamān intrigues, however, brought Bāyazīd back to Anatolia, where he defeated and executed ᶜAlāᵓ al-Dīn Beg, the Karamānid prince, annexed his territory, and carried out extensive conquests in eastern Anatolia (1397–1398). This aroused the ire of Tamerlane, who considered this region his sphere. Insulting letters were exchanged and further provocations undertaken, especially by the arrogant Bāyazīd. The final confrontation took place outside Ankara (28 July 1402). Bāyazīd was defeated and captured. Subjected to repeated humiliations, he died in captivity.

BIBLIOGRAPHY

Die altosmanischen anonymen Chroniken, Friedrich Giese, ed., 2 vols. (1922–1925); Āşikpaşazade, *Tevariḫ-i āl-i ᶜOṣman, Aşiḳaşazade Tariḫi*, ᶜAlī Bey, ed. (1914); Peter Charanis, "The Strife Among the Palaeologi and the Ottoman Turks, 1370–1402," in *Byzantion*, **16** (1942); Dukas, *Istoria turco-bizantină*, Vasile Grecu, ed. (1958); translated by Harry J. Magoulias as *Decline and Fall of Byzantium to the Ottoman Turks* (1975).

PETER B. GOLDEN

[See also **Crusades of Later Middle Ages; Ghāzī; Nicopolis; Ottomans; Tamerlane.**]

BĀYAZĪD II

BĀYAZĪD II (*b.* 1447/1448; ruled 1481–1512). The reign of Bāyazīd II marked a transition between the periods of massive Ottoman conquest undertaken by Murād II and Mehmed II from the Danube to the Euphrates in the fifteenth century and those of Selīm I and Süleyman I into the Arab world and Hungary in the sixteenth century. Bāyazīd II consolidated the acquisitions of his predecessors and laid a firm foundation for the conquests that followed.

Bāyazīd's emphasis on internal development was imposed by conditions that arose during the rule of his father, Mehmed II. There was no clear rule of succession to the Ottoman throne, and his right to the sultanate was seriously challenged by his brother Jem Sultan. The latter, after unsuccessful efforts to secure rule of Anatolia with the help of Turkoman princes driven from their thrones by Mehmed, and with the financial assistance of the Mamluk Empire of Egypt and Syria (1481–1482), fled into impotent exile. He stayed first with the Knights Templar of Rhodes (1482–1484) and then with the pope at Rome, until he was carried off to France by Charles VIII (1495). He died en route, at Naples, possibly as the result of poisoning.

Through most of his reign, Bāyazīd concentrated on developing the administration of the lands conquered during previous reigns, tax farms *(iltizam)* and fiefs *(timar)* being the principal administrative units of government. Previous conquests had been financed by disruptive methods, such as confiscation of the properties of rich merchants and religious foundations, as well as by debasing the currency, actions that had created economic disorder and social and religious discontent. Bāyazīd remedied the worst results of these policies by restoring the confiscated properties and issuing new gold and silver coins of high quality. To place war and conquest on a foundation that would not disturb regular administration and economic structure, he established a special household tax *(avarız),* levied in peacetime and amassed in a war treasury to provide for the needs of campaigning armies. As a result, economic and commercial activity increased markedly, and the conquered territories were fully incorporated into the Ottoman administrative and financial systems.

As a result of the conquests of his predecessors, Bāyazīd faced powerful enemies and dangerous situations in both East and West. However, his concentration on internal development caused him to leave these problems unsettled, to be solved by his successors with force. In alliance with the Crimean Tatars, Bāyazīd defeated the threat of Stephen the Great of Wallachia and extended Ottoman rule and influence all the way around the western shores of the Black Sea (1484), in the process establishing a close Ottoman connection with the Tatars that was to provide a major source of fighting men, particularly in the centuries of Ottoman decline. Efforts of the Mamluk Empire of Egypt and Syria to extend its domain into Cilicia and eastern Anatolia led to a desultory Ottoman-Mamluk war (1485–1491) with no clear outcome; it was left to Selīm I to resolve the conflict by conquering the entire Mamluk Empire in 1516–1517. Venice encouraged Albanian opposition in the Balkans and Greece, as well as Turkoman and Timurid resistance in eastern Anatolia, in the hope of halting the Ottoman expansion across the Balkans. This led to an Ottoman-Venetian war (1497–1502) that culminated in extension of Ottoman naval power into the Aegean and the entry of the Ottomans into European diplomacy.

Finally, in the East, Bāyazīd faced the rise of the powerful new Safawid dynasty, with Şah Ismāᶜil leading a combined religious and military effort to conquer the states that had arisen in Persia since the time of Tamerlane and to send Muslim mystic preachers into Anatolia to appeal to the Turkoman nomads, who always resisted whoever ruled in Constantinople. Bāyazīd did little about this threat to Ottoman rule in the East, not only because of his preference for peace but also because of his own mystic proclivities. It was left to Selīm I to remedy the threat by a major campaign against the Safawids.

Bāyazīd's concentration on mystic contemplation in his later years led to a major dispute for power between the *devshirme* (tribute in children) Christian converts to Islam and the Turco-Muslim aristocracy who composed the Ottoman ruling class, with the former ultimately triumphing and putting Selīm I on the throne in 1512.

BIBLIOGRAPHY

İsmail Ertaylan, *Sultan Cem* (1951); Sydney N. Fisher, "Civil Strife in the Ottoman Empire, 1481–1503," in *Journal of Modern History,* 13 (1941); and *The Foreign Relations of Turkey, 1481–1512* (1948); Stanford J. Shaw, *History of the Ottoman Empire and Modern Turkey,* I (1976), 70–79; Selāhattin Tansel, *Sultan II. Bāyezitᵓ in Siyasī Hayati* (1966).

STANFORD J. SHAW

[See also **Mehmed II; Ottomans; Selīm I.**]

BAYBARS AL-BUNDUQDĀRĪ

BAYBARS AL-BUNDUQDĀRĪ (*ca.* 1223–1277), fourth Mamluk sultan of Egypt and one of the most successful military commanders of his time, was born in the Kipchak steppes of southern Russia during the turbulent period of the great Mongol conquests. Like many of his young Kipchak contemporaries, Baybars, a prisoner of war at the age of fourteen, was sold in the slave market of Sivas in Asia Minor to Syria-bound merchants around 1242. The current Ayyubid ruler of Egypt, al-Malik al-Ṣāliḥ ᶜAyyūb (1240–1249), had made a policy early on in his career of purchasing large numbers of young Turkish slaves, with the object of creating a highly trained and personally loyal military force. Al-Malik al-Ṣāliḥ eventually purchased or confiscated Baybars from his first master (an out-of-favor Ayyubid officer known as al-Bunduqdārī), and enrolled the promising young soldier in his elite Baḥriyya regiment after granting him his freedom.

When the troops of Louis IX landed at Damietta in 1249, the Baḥriyya launched a counterattack at the Battle of Al-Mansūra (1250), which culminated in a crushing defeat of the Franks and the capture of the French king. The ailing al-Malik al-Ṣālih did not live to see the victory of his elite Baḥriyya troops. Nor did he live to see Baybars, one of his favorites and by now a capable officer in his early twenties, fight bravely at Al-Mansūra and, shortly afterward, lead the assassination of his patron's son and successor, Tūrān-Shāh. The death of Tūrān-Shāh at the hands of his father's former slaves marks the end of the Ayyubid dynasty in Egypt and Syria, and the beginning of oligarchic rule by a Turkish (and later Circassian) military elite. The members of this elite were recruited, and their ranks constantly replenished, by means of a brisk slave trade that drew upon the human resources of the Eurasian steppes. Hence their sultans are known to modern scholars as the Mamluk, or "slave," dynasty, although their contemporary Muslim chroniclers simply referred to them as *dawlat al-atrāk* (the dynasty of the Turks).

Baybars soon became involved in the factional strife that followed the death of Tūrān-Shāh, and was eventually forced to flee from Cairo to Syria, where he lived for six years (1254–1260) as a mercenary adventurer. In the face of an impending Mongol invasion, however, Baybars accepted a reconciliation with the third Mamluk sultan, Quṭuz, and led the vanguard of the Egyptian army at the Battle of Ain Jalut in 1260. After the defeat of the Mongols, Baybars assassinated Quṭuz. His path now clear of rivals, the ambitious officer became sultan with the title al-Malik al-Ẓāhir (Triumphant King) in 1260, and immediately set about consolidating his power by an adroit combination of force and diplomacy.

Baybars' military victories against his two major enemies, the Franks and the Mongols, were due to his careful planning and foresight as well as to his talents as a field commander. The sultan relied heavily upon an extensive espionage network, and built a sophisticated postal relay system (the *barīd*) connecting Cairo with the outlying regions of Syria. During the seventeen years of his reign, Baybars reduced the Crusader possessions in Syria to an insignificant coastal strip. His recapture of Caesarea (1265), Safad (1266), Jaffa and Antioch (1268), and the famous fortress of the Hospitalers—Ḥiṣn al-Akrād (Krak des Chevaliers)—(1271), along with other victories, dealt the deathblow to the Crusader states. Baybars' troops also pushed the Mongols back beyond the eastern bank of the Euphrates, ravaged the kingdom of Armenia, reduced the Ismaili fortresses to a state of vassalage, and conquered Nubia. The victorious sultan died at Damascus, shortly after capturing Kayseri (Caesarea) in Asia Minor and defeating a combined Seljuk and Mongol army.

Baybars came to power by assassination, a method that was to prove fairly common among the Mamluk sultans. He succeeded, however, where his three predecessors and many later sultans failed, in that he maintained power despite the violent factionalism of an ambitious military elite. Baybars was undoubtedly a brilliant general and, as military despots go, he seems to have been a fair and able ruler. He has justly been termed the true founder of the Mamluk dynasty. The fact that the *Sīrat Baybars,* a semihistorical folk epic narrating the hero-sultan's adventures, was still recited in Egypt in the early part of the twentieth century points to the strong popular image that Baybars projected both to his contemporaries and to later generations.

BIBLIOGRAPHY

For Arabic sources, see the bibliography given in "Baybars I," in *Encyclopedia of Islam,* 2nd ed. The biography of Baybars by Abdul-Aziz Khowaiter, *Baibars the First* (1978), is an easily accessible recasting of Arabic sources, but the interpretative material should be viewed with caution.

SHAUN E. MARMON

[See also **Ayyubids; Crusades of Thirteenth Century; Krak des Chevaliers; Louis IX; Mamluk Dynasty.**]

BAYEUX TAPESTRY, an Anglo-Norman embroidery illustrating the life of King Harold until his defeat at the Battle of Hastings. The Bayeux Tapestry, though frayed at its ends and no longer fully preserved, is approximately nineteen and one-half inches high and over 231 feet long; the stitching is in eight colors of wool thread on linen. The embroidery was probably made in England between 1066 and 1083 for the Norman Odo, bishop of Bayeux and half-brother of William the Conqueror. On the main frieze, the story of Harold's life unfolds in vigorous linear style with very accurate details of costume and architecture. Bordering this are animal motifs, genre scenes, and fables, some of which are related to the events on the main panel. Because the narrative has little religious content and was conceived essentially as a story of betrayal and treachery (with Harold as the traitor), the Bayeux Tapestry has been called a secular *chanson de geste* in pictorial form. It has been in Bayeux since at least the late Middle Ages and is now displayed in the town hall.

BIBLIOGRAPHY

The Bayeux Tapestry, Frank Stenton, ed. (1957).

LESLIE BRUBAKER

[See also **Chansons de Geste; Normans and Normandy; Tapestry;** and Frontispiece, present volume.]

BAYLAKĀN (Armenian: *P^caytakaran*), an obscure but important city on the easternmost plain of ancient Armenia. Probably located on the site of the present village of Oren-Kala, about ten and a half miles (seventeen kilometers) west of the district center of Zhdanovsk in Soviet Azerbaijan, Baylakan is first mentioned in the fourth century, when it was the capital of P^caytakaran, the easternmost province of Arsacid Armenia and the launching place for the attempted usurpation of the Armenian throne by Sanatruk (or Sanēsan) Aršakuni in the 330's. Ravaged by a joint Armeno-Roman attack, P^caytakaran and its district, Hrak^ɔot-Perož or Ṛotĕstak, were taken from Armenia by the Persians in 387 and made a part of the province of Atrpatakan (Atropatenē/Azerbaijan), of which the city appears to have become the capital.

Baylaḳān prospered during the Arab period, when it lay on the important trade route linking Ardabīl with Tiflis via Vardan (Vardanakert) and Bardha^ca (Partaw). Excavations reveal that the town consisted of a rectangular enclosure of 96.33 acres (39 hectares) surrounded by walls erected in the fourth through seventh centuries, while the city was under direct Persian control. In the ninth century an adobe citadel with semicircular towers was constructed within the walls, which were subsequently allowed to fall into disrepair. According to Arab sources, Baylaḳān became the capital of Arrān after the destruction of Bardha^ca in 944, and Ibn Hawqal describes it as a fine city in the tenth century. Baylaḳān was destroyed by the Mongols in the thirteenth century, but was still a notable place two centuries later.

BIBLIOGRAPHY

R. H. Hewsen, "Caspiane: An Historical and Geographical Survey," in *Handes amsorya,* 83 (1973); Guy Le Strange, *Lands of the Eastern Caliphate* (1905, repr. 1966), 178, 179, 230; Hakob Manandyan, *O torgovle i gorodakh Armenii v svyazi s miravoy torgovley drevnikh vremen* (1945); translated by Nina Garsoïan as *The Trade and Cities of Armenia in Relation to Ancient World Trade* (1965), 164–166, 198; Aleksandr Mongait, *Archaeology in the U.S.S.R.* (1959), 254–256.

ROBERT H. HEWSEN

[See also **Armenia, Geography; Armenia, History.**]

BAY SYSTEM, the systematic subdivision of a building into equal or homogeneous parts by means of a pervasive skeleton of shafts and arches that both divide and connect the parts. A bay is one of the cellular modules of a building. The modular, geometric ground plan was introduced into Latin religious architecture during the Carolingian period (for example, in the monastery plan at St. Gall), and may have been influenced by northern European timber-frame domestic construction. By the Romanesque and Gothic periods the bay system was firmly established; the structural stability of the modular skeleton was one of the factors that allowed the increased height, elaborate vaulting, and decreased wall surface of Gothic cathedrals.

BIBLIOGRAPHY

Walter Horn, "On the Origins of the Medieval Bay System," in *Journal of the Society of Architectural Historians,* 17 (1958).

LESLIE BRUBAKER

[See also **Gothic Architecture; Romanesque Architecture.**]

BAYT (Arabic: "house"; plural, *buyūt*), a Near Eastern dwelling unit composed of several rooms flanking a larger space. The *bayt* was the basic element in the plan of most early Islamic palaces, where it was multiplied around series of courtyards.

Two types of *bayt* have been distinguished, both with roots in the ancient world. In Syria and Palestine a large central hall was flanked by at least two pairs of rooms. This type was found in the Roman governors' palace at Busra and persisted in the palatial residences of the later Umayyad period.

In Mesopotamia and Iran the central element was an *eyvān*. This arrangement was already known at the third-century Sasanian "palace" at Firuzabad and was multiplied many times in the Abbasid palaces at Ukhaydir and Samarra.

BIBLIOGRAPHY

Gertrude Bell, *Palace and Mosque at Ukhaiḍir* (1914), ch. 4; K. A. C. Creswell, *Early Islamic Architecture,* 2nd ed., I (1969), esp. pt. 2, 515–518; Ernst Herzfeld, *Geschichte der Stadt Samarra* (1948).

ESTELLE WHELAN

[See also **Eyvān; Islamic Art and Architecture.**]

BDEŠX or *bdeašχ* (Georgian: *pītiaχš* or *patiaχš;* Pahlavi *bītāχš;* Syriac: *ap̮taḫšā;* Greek: *πυτιάξης*, or *πιτιάξης*, or *βιτάξης*; *vitaxa*). The etymology is uncertain; most likely it is from the old Persian *pa[i]ti-aχši/a (head + rule), but the Sumerian *patesi* (governor or prince) and the Hittite *peda* + *ḫ̮aššu* (place + king) have also been proposed.

Bdešχ was the title given to the four viceroys governing the borders of early Christian Armenia, and probably goes back at least to Hellenistic times, although a number of questions relating to the *bdešχ*s are still disputed. They have been linked by some scholars to the four royal attendants of Tigranes the Great (95–56 B.C.) noted by Plutarch ("Life of Lucullus" 21.5), and are likely to have been at first local dynasts. Under the Armenian Arsacids they were the chief magnates of the realm, standing above the social hierarchy. The title was also known in Georgia and in Sasanian Iran, although the precise links of the latter to the Armenian office are not certain.

With occasional variations in name, the four Armenian *bdešχ*s are said to have ruled over the following: (1) Adiabene/Nor Širakan (Noširakan, Niχorakan, Mahkᶜert-tun) or the Median March in the southeast; (2) Sophenē/Copᶜkᶜ or the Syrian March in the southwest; (3) Arzanenē/Aɫjnikᶜ or the Arabian March in the south (also known as the "Great bdešχ"); (4) Gogarenē/Gugarkᶜ (Maskᶜ tᶜacᶜ Koɫmn) or the Iberian/Georgian March in the north. The title of *bdešχ* does not seem to have survived the Arsacid period in Armenia except for the *bdešχ* of Gugarkᶜ, who appear for a time in Georgia.

BIBLIOGRAPHY

Nicholas Adontz, *Armenia in the Period of Justinian,* Nina G. Garsoïan, ed. and trans. (1970), esp. 222–225; Josef Markwart, *Ērānšahr nach der Geographie des Ps. Moses χorenacᶜi* (1901), 165–179; B. Metzger, "A Greek and Aramaic Inscription Discovered at Armazi," in *Journal of Near Eastern Studies,* **15** (1956); Cyril Toumanoff, *Studies in Christian Caucasian History* (1963), esp. 154–192, 264–266.

NINA G. GARSOÏAN

[See also **Armenia, History.**]

BEAST EPIC, a narrative genre that describes the various encounters between the fox (Renard) and some other animal, usually a wolf (sometimes called Isengrim). Although similar to the animal fable, the beast epic is not a collection of fables and its morality is very different from that found in Aesop and his imitators. The episodes of the beast epic are meant to amuse, not to edify. The essential feature of the genre is the triumph of the cunning and totally amoral fox over the violent and stupid wolf. Many of the poems are simply a series of such confrontations and have no real narrative structure. Yet there is great consistency in the characterization of the various animals, even in works of different languages and centuries.

The genre is remarkably confined geographically. The extant examples are from the Low Countries, northern and eastern France, and north Germany (those in Middle English are adaptations of Dutch versions). The central incident in all early versions concerns the ailing King Lion, who summons his courtiers to find a cure. The wolf points out that the fox is absent and thus lacking in loyalty to his Lord. The fox, however, makes a belated appearance and declares that he can cure the king by wrapping him in the wolf's skin. The wolf thus pays with his hide for his crude attempt to discredit the fox.

This story is found in Greek versions of Aesop's

BEAST EPIC

fables but not in the medieval Latin versions of Aesop ascribed to "Romulus." It was certainly known in the ninth century, as evidenced by a short Latin verse version by Paulus Diaconus, although in it the bear, not the wolf, is the victim. This verse exhibits essential aspects of the beast epic—the selfishness of all the beasts in King Lion's court and the abuse of power by King Lion.

Other stories of encounters between lion and fox, some undoubtedly of popular origin but others recorded elsewhere in writing, were attached to the sick-lion story, forming the core of a number of longer works. The earliest of these is *Ecbasis captivi per tropologiam* ("Escape of a Captive Treated Allegorically") by a German monk at the monastery of St. Èvre in Toul. The date is a matter of much dispute; it may be *ca.* 940 or *ca.* 1030. This poem of 1,229 lines tells how a calf escapes from a farm and is captured by a wolf, who barricades himself in his cave to keep out the farm animals who come to rescue his victim. As he tells his allies, the otter and the hedgehog, the wolf is concerned only about the fox, who has tricked him in the past. It happens again. The fox lures the wolf out, and he is killed by the bull. The implication is clear: any monk (calf) who strays from his monastery (farmyard) is in danger from the devil (wolf). Yet all the interest is in the wolf's stories, which include the tale about the sick lion. Although this work contains many beast-epic episodes, it is too didactic-allegorical to be representative of the genre.

The poem *Ysengrimus* may well be the best example of the genre. Around 1150, Master Nivardus of Ghent wrote these 6,574 lines of distichs. His style is brilliant, his command of Latin remarkable. *Ysengrimus* could be called the decline and fall of the wolf; it begins with his sole triumph over the fox and then chronicles one incident after another in which Ysengrimus is insulted, befuddled, injured, and finally killed as a result of the fox's machinations. The sick-lion scene contains some remarkable characterization, not only of the lion, the fox, and the wolf, but also of the preaching ram, the meek hare, and the sly and vicious sow. Such novel elements as the fox's pilgrimage, the wolf's fishing expedition, and the wolf as monk later became staples of the beast epic. The identification of the wolf as monk reaffirms the anticlerical sentiment of the beast epic and its vicious satire of the religious establishment. There is no sympathy for any of the characters. Success comes to the cunning and amoral, failure to the stupid and weak. The good are good because they are too feeble to be anything else, the strong are evil because they are selfish and able to indulge themselves.

Ysengrimus does not appear to have directly influenced the vernacular beast epics. The French *Roman de Renard* uses the same subject matter but comprises a series of stories now called *branches,* works composed by different authors at different times. There is no long unified poem about the struggles between Renard and Isengrim, and any attempt to arrange the various *branches* as a continuous account would be artificial; it would involve starting with *branches* written later than those describing incidents in the body of the story.

The earliest extant *branche* (*branche* two according to Ernst Martin) is ascribed to Pierre de St.-Cloud and tells of Renard's adultery with Hersant, the she-wolf, and of his defeat by various animals. Other *branches,* probably written between 1179 and 1203, include the sick lion and wolf's fishing expedition and, most important, the judicial combat between Isengrim and Renard, which became central to many later beast epics.There is a strong element of antifeudal and antireligious satire in the *Roman de Renard* and also some jesting at the expense of the Arthurian romance, and considerable sympathy for the picaresque figure of the fox. The *Roman de Renard* established the word *renard* for "fox" in French, replacing the word *goupil.* Later imitations, such as *Renard le nouvel* (1288–1292) and *Renard le contrefait* (before 1342), perserve the same characterization of the animals.

The earliest extant beast epic in German is by Heinrich der Glîchezaere, an Alsatian, and was written around 1180. Of the original only about 685 lines survive, but an anonymous reworking of around 1240 survives entire. The work, totaling 2,266 rhyming lines, falls into three parts: the fox is tricked by various animals; he plays numerous painful tricks on Isengrim; and finally there is the sick-lion episode. Some of the animals' names are French (Pinte, Schantekler), others are German (Dieprecht, Diezelin).

Most of the thirteenth- and fourteenth-century beast epics were written in the Low Countries in Middle Dutch. The first extant work, usually called *Reinaert I (ca.* 2,350 lines), was written by a priest calling himself "Willem," thought to be Willem of Hulsterlo. It is based on the episode from the *Roman de Renard* in which Renard is charged before the lion with various crimes, including the murder of one of Schantekler the rooster's wives. The bear and then the cat suffer when sent to fetch Renard, and even his friend the badger has difficulties, but a confession made to him by the fox allows the author to recount several earlier adventures. Renard exculpates himself on the gallows with a totally fictional account of a plot against the lion by the bear and the wolf. This plot was to be financed by "Ermanrich's treasure," whose whereabouts Renard now promises to reveal. Cupidity and fear prevail; Renard is released and pretends to set out on a pilgrimage, so as to be absent when the lion finds out that he has been tricked.

This story, full of thrusts against feudal trials, the oppression by and cupidity of ruling nobles, and the obscurities of the law, appears in several manuscripts; it was translated into Latin by Baldwin around 1280. More than a century later, *Reinaert II,* an expanded version (*ca.* 7,800 lines), appeared. The additional material is collected from various popular sources, fables, and stories having little to do with Renard. But it includes incidents similar to those of *Reinaert I*—a trial, a treasure of a different kind, and Renard's escape with the help of the queen's friend the she-ape. The work ends with Renard's triumph over Isengrim in a judicial combat marked by a variety of low tricks. Renard becomes the king's greatest subject and his chancellor.

Reinaert II is a markedly didactic and satirical poem; the judicial combat is a savage parody of aristocratic justice. But the abundance of dreary moralizing contributes to its general inferiority to *Reinaert I.* Its importance is as a source for the much livelier Dutch prose versions printed at Gouda (1479) and Delft (1485). In 1481 Caxton printed an English translation of the Gouda edition. Hinrik von Alckmer was probably the author of a rhyming version in modernized language printed in Antwerp (1487), extant only as the "Culemann fragment." Here and in a reprint of the 1564 Delft version are prose explanations of the moral, illustrating its impact on contemporaries. From the rhyming Antwerp edition came the Low German *Reinke Vos,* printed at Lübeck (1498) and Rostock (1517). The explanations were retained, but in a 1539 Rostock reprint they take on a definitely Protestant tone. These Low German versions are lively and contain vivid portrayals of the animals. In these later Flemish and German versions it is made very clear that the society of the beasts reflects human society. The lion is ruler; and his "nobles," the bear, the wolf, and the fox are subordinate. Under the nobles are the priests, traders, and workers. Typically, only the priests are not frequently represented. The point of view is definitely bourgeois, reflecting the morality of this class and its discontent with an outmoded society.

The beast epic retained its popularity, as may be judged from numerous modernizations, especially the one by Goethe in 1794.

BIBLIOGRAPHY

Editions. Ecbasis cuiusdam captivi: Escape of a Certain Captive, Edwin H. Zeydel, ed. and trans. (1964); Nivardus of Ghent, *Ysengrimus,* Ernst Voigt, ed. (1884); *Le Roman de Renard,* Ernst Martin, ed., 3 vols. (1882–1887); *Le Roman de Renart,* Mario Roques, ed., branches II–XIX (1951–1963); Jacquemars Gielée, *Renart le nouvel,* Henri Roussel, ed. (1961); *Le Roman de Renard le contrefait,* Gaston Raynaud and Henri Lemaitre, eds. (1914); Heinrich der Glîchezaere, *Reinhart Fuchs,* Georg Baesecke, ed. (1926); *Reinaert: Willems Gedicht van den Vos Reinaerde und die Umarbeitung und Fortsetzung Reinaerts Histories,* Ernst Martin, ed. (1874); *Die Hystorie van Reynaert die Vos naar den druk van 1479 vergeleken met William Caxton Engelesche vertaling,* J. W. Muller, ed. (1892); *Reinke de Vos,* Friedrich Prien, ed. (1887); rev. ed., Albert Leitzmann and Karl Voretzsch, eds. (1925), the Low German version printed in Lübeck in 1498.

Translations. Reinke de Vos, T. J. Arnold, trans. (1954), a translation of Goethe's rendering of the Low German poem; *The History of Reynard the Fox,* D. B. Sands, ed. (1960); *Le Roman de Renart,* Jacques Haumont, trans. (1966).

Secondary literature. Robert Bossuat, *Le Roman de Renard* (1967), with a good bibliography; W. T. H. Jackson, *The Literature of the Middle Ages* (1960), ch. 10; Ernst Martin, "Zur Geschichte der Tiersage im Mittelalter," in *Prager deutsche Studien,* 8 (1908); Max Wehrli, "Vom Sinn des mittelalterlichen Tierepos," in *German Life and Letters,* n.s. **10** (1956–1957).

W. T. H. JACKSON

[See also **Allegory; Dutch Language and Literature; French Literature; German Allegory; Renard the Fox; Ysengrimus.**]

BEATIFICATION. The Middle Ages did not distinguish between the terms *beatus* and *sanctus* applied to persons who were the objects of popular cults. Thus, as a technical qualification, "beatification" is a postmedieval term. It refers to an intermediate sentence of the pope, made during the process of canonization, authorizing the cult of an individual yet not requiring it, or at least requiring it only of a particular diocese, region, nation, or religious institution.

Medieval analogies to beatification can be found in concessions, given first by metropolitans and later by popes; these permitted the veneration of individuals by particular communities without authorizing the elevation of the individual to public veneration as a saint. Examples cited by Stephan Kuttner include the decision of the archbishop of Metz (1149) to allow the bishop of Hildesheim to include Bernward among the saints, but not to authorize his translation or elevation; and that of Alexander III (1159) to permit the diocese of Grosseto to honor William of Grosseto with an office and, later, to determine his canonization.

Other analogies are the recognition by bishops of local, particular cults already existing within specific religious communities, families, and towns. Such recognitions did not prescribe veneration or pretend to canonize the individual, but simply authorized these cults. These practices continued until the reign of Urban VIII, who between 1625 and 1634 declared that the objects of cults that had developed in this manner (without previous ecclesiastical authorization) would have no chance of eventual recognition and canonization. Further, he established the official category of *beatus* and reserved beatification, like canonization, to the papacy.

Anachronistically, canonists seeking to establish the permanence of the papal prerogative of canonization have argued that the episcopal elevation, which into the late twelfth century constituted the normal form of canonization, was in fact only a beatification. Thus, some accounts of the history of canonization describe the process by which saints were recognized prior to the thirteenth century as beatification. However, as Kuttner has argued, the essential difference between beatification and canonization is not the opposition between universal (papal) and particular (episcopal) or between prescription (papal) and authorization (episcopal). Rather, the key difference is that beatification is an intermediate stage, not a definite sentence, in the process of canonization.

BIBLIOGRAPHY

Pierre Delooz, *Sociologie et canonisations* (1969); Nicole Herrmann-Mascard, *Les reliques des saints: Formation coutumière d'un droit* (1975), 74–105; Stephan Kuttner, "La réserve papale du droit de canonisation," in *Revue historique de droit français et étranger,* 4th ser. **17** (1938).

PATRICK GEARY

[See also **Canonization.**]

BEATUS MANUSCRIPTS. Beatus of Liébana, a Spanish monk, compiled a twelve-book *Commentary on the Apocalypse* (*ca.* 776) that consists of short passages from the Book of Revelation followed by various earlier writers' interpretations of the text as Christian allegory. It was probably first illustrated in the last quarter of the eighth century, although the earliest fragment of an illuminated Beatus manuscript (in the Silos Monastery, Spain) dates from the second half of the ninth century. More than twenty illustrated copies of the *Commentary,* dating from the tenth to the thirteenth century, are preserved, most of them Spanish; they are the most important sources for a knowledge of medieval Spanish painting.

Sixty miniatures, usually occupying a full page and sometimes spreading over two adjacent leaves, illustrate Beatus' text. They were almost certainly copied from an early illustrated Apocalypse manuscript rather than invented for the *Commentary,* but the scenes are not related to any other known cycle.

The miniatures in most of the Beatus manuscripts are painted in a characteristically colorful and flat style. Islamic influence is evident in the decorative patterns used and in some of the iconography. The Islamic cross-legged sitting posture is occasionally adopted for Christ, and Islamic architectural forms may be used in representations of either the Heavenly Jerusalem or evil Babylon.

Since Spanish Christians frequently equated the Muslims with the Apocalyptic forces of the Antichrist, some copies of Beatus' *Commentary* showed, for example, the Whore of Babylon in Islamic dress. The popularity of the illustrated *Commentary* in medieval Spain was probably due to the presence of the Muslim invaders, the Apocalypse and its exegeses providing a divine parallel to the contemporary political turmoil.

BIBLIOGRAPHY

Peter K. Klein, *Der altere Beatus-Kodex Vitr. 14-1 der Biblioteca Nacional zu Madrid,* 2 vols. (1976); John Williams, *Early Spanish Manuscript Illumination* (1977), 24–28.

LESLIE BRUBAKER

[See also **Apocalypse, Illustration of; Manuscript Illumination.**]

BEAUMANOIR, PHILIPPE DE (*ca.* 1250–1296), lawyer, poet, and royal official, came from a family of minor lords who held land from the abbey of St. Denis in the village of Remi near the city of Compiègne, north of Paris. A chronicler mentions a Pierre de Remin—probably his grandfather—at the Battle of Bouvines. His father, Philippe de Remin, was bailli of Gâtinais for Robert, count of Artois, and after the count's death was a member of the court of Mahaut, countess of Artois. About mid century the elder Philippe took the name of Beaumanoir after a stronghold he had built on his property at Remi. Philippe, the second son, was known as Philippe de Remi until his older brother Girard died (about 1279), at which time he too took the name of Beaumanoir. Sometime during his youth Philippe visited England and Scotland; a considerable knowledge of the island's geography appears in his poetry.

Beaumanoir began his public career when not yet thirty years of age, serving as bailli of Clermont from 1279 to 1282 for Robert, count of Clermont. At the same time he wrote his most important work, the *Coutumes de Beauvaisis,* which, except for some minor revisions, he completed in 1283. He served the king of France as seneschal of Poitou (1284–1287), seneschal of Saintonge (1287–1288, 1292), bailli of Vermandois (1289–1290), bailli of Touraine (1292), and bailli of Senlis (1292–1295). In 1289, King Philip IV sent him to Rome with the bishop of Auxerre to negotiate conflicts between the king and the cathedral chapter of Chartres, as well as one between the king and the bishop of Poitou in which he had been involved as seneschal.

Beaumanoir died at Moncel, near Senlis. He was buried next to his first wife, Saintisme, at the Dominican convent in Compiègne. His second wife, Mabille de Boves, was buried on his other side in 1304. Soon afterward Moncel was acquired by the king to establish a convent of Poor Clares. Of Beaumanoir's children, Marguerite married Guiard de Jouy, a royal usher-at-arms; Raoul de Remi, Beaumanoir's secretary and perhaps his son, became a notary and a canon of Soissons; Jean and Gilles de Remi, both canons of Noyon and also perhaps his sons, became royal clerks, the former serving as financial officer for Louis of Navarre before he became king, the latter as a royal notary from 1301 to 1321.

WORKS

The *Coutumes de Beauvaisis* is the longest and most significant work on customary law to survive from thirteenth-century France. In scope it matches the *Sachsenspiegel* of Eike von Repgow and the work *On the Laws and Customs of England* attributed to Henry of Bracton. It was written in the French of the Île-de-France, with a strong admixture of the dialect of Picardy. Widely copied during the two centuries following its composition, it survives in thirteen manuscripts; at least twenty-two others are known to have existed, as well as two fifteenth-century condensations.

Beaumanoir composed this work, he says, so that "those who desire to live in peace learn both how to defend themselves against those who easily assault them in pleas, and how to tell right from wrong as is used and accustomed in the country of Clermont-en-Beauvaisis." His more specific audience was the count and his council. The work begins with a lengthy disquisition on the office of bailli. This is followed by eight chapters on judicial procedure, one on the jurisdiction of the count of Clermont, and one on the jurisdiction of ecclesiastical courts. Only then does Beaumanoir turn to successions, inheritances, dowries and related questions, tenures and services, crimes, and obligations. The book concludes with a return to procedure.

The sources from which Beaumanoir drew his knowledge of the law were "the judgments made in our time in the county of Clermont, and clear usages peacefully used for a long time, and, in doubtful cases, the judgments made in neighboring castellanies and the law that is common to the whole kingdom of France." True to his promise, he cited in the course of the work more than a hundred different cases either as examples of rules or as precedents from which to draw rules. In this use of case law he resembled both Bracton and the canon lawyers, who had made court judgments a fundamental source of custom. When citing these cases, however, Beaumanoir neglected to mention either when or where they occurred, and the parties uniformly became "Jehan" and "Pierre," as if these real disputes were no different from those that law professors invented to help explain the texts of Roman and canon laws. He thus had not developed a strict concept of precedent, such as appeared in the fourteenth century.

Beaumanoir's understanding of canon law also appeared in his discussion of ecclesiastical courts and in his occasional comparison of the rules of custom with those of canon law. His knowledge of Roman law paralleled the degree of the infusion of its elements into northern French practice in the last decades of the thirteenth century. He discussed the renunciations of privileges that contractants might claim from Roman law, renunciations that notaries were then introducing into their forms of contracts; the annulment of real estate sales that were made for less than half the just value, a fraud the royal government was making justiciable in its courts; Roman prescription; Roman guardianship of minors; and many elements of written procedure using the inquest and allowing hierarchical appeal, all derived from Romano-canonical procedure. In a number of places he gave Romano-canonical equivalents for technical terms of customary law.

Between 1270 and 1280, Beaumanoir composed his poetical works: *La manekine,* a romance of 8,590 lines about a Hungarian princess who is forced to flee to England, where the king falls in love with her and various misfortunes ensue; *Jehan et Blonde,* a romance of 6,262 lines about the daughter of an English baron who is carried off by a young French squire; *Salu d'amours; Conte d'amours, Conte de fole largece; Lai d'amours; Ave Maria; Salut a refrains;* and two *Fatrasies.*

BIBLIOGRAPHY

Philippe de Beaumanoir, *Coutumes de Beauvaisis,* A. Salmon, ed., I, II (1899–1900), introduction and text; III (1974), *Commentaire historique et juridique* by Georges Hubrecht; Hermann Suchier, ed., *Oeuvres poétiques de Philippe de Remi, sire de Beaumanoir,* 2 vols. (1884–1885); André Sergène, "Le précédent judiciaire au moyen-âge," in *Revue historique de droit français et étranger,* 4th ser., 39 (1961).

FREDRIC CHEYETTE

[See also **Bracton, Henry; French Literature; Law, French.**]

BEAUNEVEU, ANDRÉ (*fl.* 1363–1404?), sculptor and painter from Valenciennes, active in Hainaut, Flanders, Paris, and Bourges. Beauneveu attracted the praise of Froissart and commissions from the most discerning patrons of his time: Charles V of France, for whom he made four royal tombs for St.-Denis; Louis de Mâle, count of Flanders; and Jean, duke of Berry, in whose service he is first mentioned in 1386. He served the duke as master of painting and sculpture from at least 1390 until his death. A series of prophets and apostles in the duke's psalter (Paris, Bibliothèque Nationale, MS fr. 13091) furnishes the basis for identifying fragments of his Bourges production that reflect his style in varying degrees, notably five statuettes of prophets and some large fragments of the stained glass windows from the Sainte-Chapelle.

BIBLIOGRAPHY

Millard Meiss, *French Painting in the Time of Jean de Berry,* I (1969), 135–140, 147–151; Paris, Galeries Nationales du Grand Palais, *Les fastes du gothique: Le siècle de Charles V* (1982), 153–155, 385–386, 429; Stephen K. Scher, "The Sculpture of André Beauneveu" (Ph.D. diss., Yale University, 1966); and "André Beauneveu and Claus Sluter," in *Gesta,* 7 (1968).

ANNE M. MORGANSTERN

BEAUTY AIDS, COSMETICS. Beauty aids may roughly be divided into two classes: cosmetic preparations—compositions applied to the body internally or externally to improve appearance in some way—and mechanical devices—tools or objects applied to remove unwanted material or to alter natural appearance. To the first class belong breath deodorizers; tooth-cleaning preparations; shampoos, soaps, and soap substitutes; hair bleaches and dyes; preparations for increasing the length or thickness of hair growth; preparations that soften and condition the skin or remove skin defects like blotches and warts; nail colorants and conditioners; even lice removers; as well as the conventional cosmetic makeup—rouge for cheeks and lips, eye liner and shadow, complexion base, powder, and perfume. To the second class belong the mirror; razor; scissors and tweezers; false teeth; toothpicks and cloths or twigs used as toothbrushes; false hair or padding that simulates hair; wigs; curling irons; hairpins; ornaments and tassels used to secure braids; braid cases and beard bags; and the quite complex group of hairnets, rolls, pads, and wire framework used as foundations for hairstyles.

The distinction between what is and what is not a beauty aid is not clear-cut, and information on the topic extends so widely that it must be limited. Dietary advice is often concerned with improving appearance. The mirror as symbol of Pride and as title *(speculum)* for encyclopedic surveys derives from its cosmetic use but is not really part of it. If perfumes are a beauty aid, are the small thirteenth-century openwork pomanders containing balls of musk or herbs that were carried to ward off illness also beauty aids? How closely related are the various types of cloth coverings for the hair of married women that are a central feature of medieval hairstyles—head-

Porcelain cosmetics box and cover, Chinese, 13th–14th century. VICTORIA AND ALBERT MUSEUM

rail, couvrechef, barbette, wimple, gorget, veil, coif? Is a handkerchief a beauty aid, or does it become one only when it passes into general enough use for Erasmus to caution small boys that it is rude to wipe one's nose with one's sleeve instead? In the same way the large number of ingredients in any one cosmetic formulation and the number and variety of formulas that exist for any one purpose make it impossible to discuss more than sample formulations and the main active ingredients.

Still another problem with this topic is documentation: lack of written evidence and difficulty in interpreting some of the evidence that exists. Elaborate beauty aids were extensively used in Egypt, Greece, and Rome; the conventional viewpoint has been that this knowledge was lost in the barbarian invasions and was brought back to Europe by the Crusaders. Certainly this was largely true of eastern perfumes, though isolated instances of their appearance in the West are recorded. But the Roman traditions of cosmetic practice passed directly to Byzantium and were maintained there with relatively few detectable changes in style; there may have been influence on the West in certain periods. It is unknown how much Roman customs had already affected the cosmetic practices of the barbarian groups, and what these practices were; or how many unrecorded preparations were passed down within a family, and from village herbalist to pupil. Some evidence comes from burials: Anglo-Saxon burials, for examle, contain bone combs, scissors, tweezers, knives, jeweled fillets, and small bronze rings for the hair. Other evidence comes from art and literature—sculpture, especially tomb effigies, and manuscript illumination. Just one example of the complexities involved is the question of whether the Anglo-Saxons colored their hair blue. Anglo-Saxon drawings represent hair primarily as blue, but also as green and orange: is it dyed or an artistic convention? There are also contemporary reports of blue-haired Saxons, but nothing that is clearly firsthand information and not perhaps derived from the drawings. A suitable blue dye with a history of use as body paint in early Britain—woad—was available, but we do not know if it was used.

In general, evidence for devices is clearer than the evidence for cosmetic formulations. Information on what manuscripts were available at a particular time and place is incomplete; there is no way to tell whether the more difficult and unpleasant recipes were actually used; and the role of home formulations is almost unknown. So there are wide gaps in what we know about the actual use of beauty aids, especially in the earlier Middle Ages. The criticisms of satirists and moralists, however, suggest that even before the Crusades, more attention was paid to appearance than they could approve.

COSMETIC PREPARATIONS

Perfume. Aromatic woods, gums, resins, and oils—frankincense; myrrh; cassia; spikenard; cedar and cypress wood; sesame, olive, and almond oils—were widely used for personal and religious purposes in the ancient world. Perfumes were a crucial part of public and private festivals as well as of a woman's toilette in Rome; their use passed to Byzantium,

BEAUTY AIDS, COSMETICS

where they also had a religious role as incense and in embalming.

Interest in perfumes was natural in Islam, developing in Arabia. Muḥammad placed perfumes third on his list of what his heart enjoyed most in the world, after children and women. In the Koran the floor of the Garden of Paradise is of wheat flour mixed with musk and saffron, and the houris are formed of pure musk. The next step in perfume development was Ibn Sīnā's (Avicenna's) development of distillation early in the eleventh century, using roses. Rosewater was brought back to Europe for washing hands before and after meals by the Crusaders. However, there are instances of earlier contact by the West with Eastern perfumes: incense and fragrant candles were used in the baptism of Clovis (496), and gifts of perfume sent to Charlemagne by Hārūn al-Rashīd started a court fashion at Aachen.

After the Crusades, use increased enormously; a perfumers' guild was chartered in France by Philip Augustus in 1190. Two more advances in formulation were made: small amounts of animal substances—musk, ambergris, civet, and castor—were found to act as fixatives; and alcoholic perfumes developed, probably in the fourteenth century. The legend is that the formula for the first of these, an alcoholic solution based on rosemary, was given to Queen Elizabeth of Hungary by a monk, and so was called Hungary Water. Carmelite Water (1379) was a toilet water intended to be inhaled to clear the mind and for bathing; it was used by the nuns of St. Just when caring for Charles V of France. It was based on balm, and included lemon peel, nutmeg, cloves, coriander seed, cinnamon, and angelica root.

Makeup. Almost every type of cosmetic known today had at least one representative in the late Roman Empire. But lack of understanding about how ingredients worked meant a large number of ingredients, some of which were distinctly peculiar, like a facial mask based on crocodile dung. These formulas, given by such writers as Pliny, Hippocrates, Galen, and Dioscorides, were transmitted wholesale through the Middle Ages. Lack of knowledge about toxicity could result in serious damage: Ovid comments on the loss of hair in attempts to bleach and dye it; and the white lead that remained a complexion base through the Middle Ages is very dangerous, explaining the number of formulations for treating red-spotted skin. Chalk, the other major whitener, was vulnerable to rain. A Roman woman had, besides base and perfume, rouge based on carmine, red lead, or fucus; soot or antimony preparations for darkening lids and lashes, applying eyebrows, and extending them across the forehead; various eye shadows including saffron; and probably a golden wig if not a German bleach. All of this was applied at home by skilled slaves. The thick coat of makeup was also characteristic of Byzantium and disapproved of by Christian moralists, who pointed out that it became difficult to weep for one's sins.

In medieval makeup, regional, class, and period distinctions are complex and necessary. The main difficulty is that extreme makeup was worn by two social classes—fashion leaders and prostitutes—but the distinctions vary from period to period. Empress Theodora of Byzantium, an expert on cosmetics, fitted both categories. So while white powder would indicate an upper-class woman in sixth-century Spain and a prostitute would wear a pink complexion base, in eleventh-century Britain prostitutes wore white base, sharing the general preference for a pale complexion. Rouge was less used by upper-class women, though Aldhelm mentions its use by Anglo-Saxon women; it varied from rose to orangish in color. Eye shadow in green, brown, or gray was used to some extent from the sixth to the fifteenth century; in fifteenth-century France crimson rouge and eye shadow marked the prostitute. The main revolution in appearance occurred in thirteenth-century Italy, where a "natural" look involved pinkish or flesh-colored base, fairly bright pink rouge, black eye liner, and sometimes colored eye shadow on the upper lid. In towns these products were obtained from the workshops of the cosmetic makers; outside, from wandering merchants. They were usually stored as powders, and used by mixing a small amount with saliva and applying the paste with a finger or a stick (for a line).

Other cosmetics. Breath deodorizers included rinses of water (Celsus, Pliny); cinquefoil (Pliny, an Anglo-Saxon herbal); dill, aniseed, and myrrh in white wine (Hippocrates); wild mint and pepper in wine (Guy de Chauliac, *d. ca.* 1370). In Chaucer's Miller's Tale, Absalon chews grain of paradise (cardamom) and licorice to sweeten his breath, then slips a "trewe-love," a sprig of either herb paris or clover, under his tongue before his courting expedition.

Dentifrices, when used, tended to come from the Arab physicians Abul Kasim and Ibn Sīnā. One of the simplest was a mixture of sal ammoniac and burned salt with half as much saccharine alum. Ibn Sīnā cautioned against very hard tooth powders, advising burned hartshorn; for removing tartar, he suggested dentifrices of meerschaum, salt, burned shells of

BEAUTY AIDS, COSMETICS

snails and oysters, sal ammoniac, burned gypsum, and verdigris with honey. Modern dentifrices still include calcium compounds and are carefully formulated for proper hardness. They would not, however, include honey or sugar, which were not yet recognized as decay-producing in the Middle Ages.

The thirteenth-century *L'ornement des dames* provides an interesting sampling of what types of cosmetics were in demand and how they were formulated. Makeup includes the white lead base, but an alternative formulation of wheat flour, egg white, cuttlefish bone powder, lard, and camphor is preferred. Rouge is based on brazilwood, also used to dye hair red. One facial mask combines ground peas and chickpeas with asses' milk; another, beef marrow with powdered aloes (astringent). The four recipes for pimples are astringent, including alum, absinthe, and wine lees. There are seven recipes for treatment of red spots on the face, including such items as ground black mustard, roots of snakeroot and lovage, and quicklime. There are also recipes for reddening or whitening the face, and curing red eyelids, discolored skin under the eyes, wrinkles, scurf, sunburn, and warts.

The bulk of the recipes, though, deal with hair: cures for falling hair (six), falling eyelashes, and falling eyebrows; ten ways to make hair longer or thicker; two depilatories; three ways to prevent hair from growing again; three dandruff cures; one treatment for premature whitening; and three methods each for killing lice generally and crab lice. Many of the hair stimulants are herbal: myrtle, feverfew, parsley, sage, cumin, mastic, bryony, acorns, willow bark; goat dung and burnt crow's eggs laid in May are perhaps the most unusual. Hair could be dyed blond (five ways), red, black/brown, or chestnut. One blond formula involves henbane and orpiment (yellow arsenic); another, soap, saffron, and alum. The black dye consists of iron rust, gallnuts, nut husks, and alum boiled in vinegar. The hair is gen-

Ivory mirror, front and back. Late 15th century. THE LOUVRE

BEAUTY AIDS, COSMETICS

erally shampooed with a lye wash, probably leached from wood ashes; soap, often made at home, was also used in shampooing and in some formulas. No mention is made of toilet waters other than barley water, or of any form of bathing. The worst formulation error is mercury (which is toxic).

MECHANICAL DEVICES

The medieval mirror *(speculum)* tended to be small, and was usually circular and made of polished metal, most frequently steel or silver. It fitted into a richly decorated case made of carved ivory, gold and silver, enamels, or ebony; a mirror worn on a girdle or as a necklace pendant often had a short handle and no case. Glass mirrors began to develop in the thirteenth century; a guild making very small convex mirrors existed at Nürnberg in 1373, but it was Venice that developed the larger flat mirror commercially. Mirrors become a major fashion item, fixed in sword hilts, carried in purses, concealed in silken cases by men.

The comb was much like the comb of classical times, made of wood, bone, or ivory with either a single or a double edge of teeth. Often a double-edged comb had one set of teeth coarser and further apart; one Anglo-Saxon comb has two carved guards protecting the teeth. The band between the sets of teeth usually had some decoration, but the single-edged comb often had a wide, ornately carved border. Frequency of use was another matter: an Anglo-Saxon complaint that the Danes were too attractive to women because they combed their hair daily and bathed every Saturday suggests that the Anglo-Saxons were less scrupulous, but by the early twelfth-century *Regimen of Health,* combing the hair was part of the regular morning routine. Decorative combs, however, rarely formed part of the finished hairstyle.

By the fifteenth century, razors were much like the ordinary straight razor in shape and materials; they could be personally owned and used, but barbers were widespread, attached to the public baths in Rome and Byzantium, and in the West to the "stews" reintroduced by the Crusaders, or to the monastery, court, or manor. In Byzantium the Roman preference for being clean-shaven persisted except in the ninth century, when a court fashion for a trimmed beard spread to other classes. In the West the church consistently disapproved of long hair for men, but its attitude toward beards varied and its disapproval tended to be disregarded. Even within the church there were problems over tonsure, head shaving for monks and nuns, and beards for monks and priests. When both styles were reasonably fashionable, young men tended to be clean-shaven and older ones bearded.

Bone comb, Viking, 8th–10th century. EDINBURGH MUSEUM OF ART

There is evidence that shaving was not done every day, but at intervals ranging from two days to two weeks, which accounts for the extent of January's bristles in Chaucer's Merchant's Tale. At two different periods men's haircuts required shaving: the hair was cut and shaved in back to ear level by the Normans at and shortly after the Conquest (seen in the Bayeux Tapestry) and in the widely worn fifteenth-century bowl cut. Razors are mentioned as essential to a lady's toilette in the thirteenth century, and from 1400 on, the fashionable high forehead style required shaving or plucking hair from the forehead, temples, and neck.

Scissors and tweezers were used widely even before the Crusades. Beards were trimmed, the longer ones often into two or three forked points. Aldhelm criticized seventh-century English nuns for cutting their nails into a fashionable talonlike shape. Eyebrows were plucked from about 1300 on; the Knight de la Tour Landry objects to it for his daughters (1346), and Alison in the Miller's Tale plucks hers, indicating that the fashion has reached the commons by Chaucer's time.

By far the greatest number and variety of devices

Frankish bronze tweezers, 5th–8th century. THE METROPOLITAN MUSEUM OF ART

dealt with hair. Curling irons were used on both hair and beard, more by men than by women because of the concealment of women's hair. In the twelfth century the beard was dressed with wax, parted, curled in a symmetrical pattern, and stowed for the night, carefully anointed, in a beard bag. Hairpins were straight shafts with carved heads, in wood, bone, ivory, or metal. Small, heavy ornaments or tassels fastened the ends of braids; ribbons and false hair could be woven into the braid. Braid cases were popular in the twelfth and fifteenth centuries, covering about half the length of the braid and bound in place with ribbon in a cross-gartered effect; the ends of the cases could be filled out with any sort of padding.

Fillets of cloth or metal were widely worn by both men and women, and girls might wear chaplets of flowers. In the thirteenth century married women's hair became visible; the braids were caught in coils at the side of the head in hairnets that become increasingly elaborate: of gold and silver wire set with gems, often cylindrical in shape and joined by a band over the head into a system called the crespine. In the very complex horned and cone-shaped hennin styles of the fourteenth and fifteenth centuries, any amount of framework, rolls, and padding was employed, including frameworks that stiffened the veil into patterns like the butterfly.

In dental science Arabs made the advances, but by the late Middle Ages in the West gold wire was used to attach loose or artifical (human, ivory, or bone) teeth to healthy ones. Irregular teeth could be filed down or sawed off, and tartar or coloration could be removed by scraping. Toothbrushes in the modern sense were not used: the teeth might be rubbed with a dentifrice on a soft cloth, a mallow root, or the flattened end of a twig. Giovanni of Arcoli (*d.* 1484) advised cleaning teeth after every meal with a thin piece of wood, not sharp-pointed or edged, preferably of a styptic wood like cypress, aloes, pine, or juniper, rinsing with wine steeped with sage, and rubbing on dentifrice once a day. Ordinary toothpicks were also known.

BIBLIOGRAPHY

Joyce Asser, *Historic Hairdressing* (1966), 22–51; Richard Corson, *Fashions in Hair: The First Five Thousand Years* (1980), 70–157; and *Fashions in Makeup from Ancient to Modern Times* (1972), 7–100; Roy Genders, *A History of Scent* (1972), 74–149; Vincenzo Guerini, *A History of Dentistry from the Most Ancient Times Until the End of the Eighteenth Century* (1909, repr. 1967), 67–160; Katherine Morris Lester and Bess Viola Oerke, *Accessories of Dress* (1940); Pascal P. Parente, ed. and trans., *The Regimen of Health of the Medical School of Salerno* (1967); Pierre Ruelle, ed. and trans., *L'ornement des dames* (1967); Florence E. Wall, "Historical Development of Cosmetics Industry," in *Cosmetics: Science and Technology,* 2nd ed., M. S. Balsam and Edward Sagarin, eds., III (1974), 38–161; Lawrence Wright, *Clean and Decent* (1967).

M. K. NELLIS

[See also **Costume; Ornement des Dames.**]

BEBO OF BAMBERG. A long letter of 1021 from Deacon Bebo to Emperor Henry II is extant in a manuscript of Jerome's commentary on Isaiah; Bebo had copied the book at the emperor's request. Another letter from Bebo to Henry, in a manuscript containing the last six books of Gregory's *Moralia,* indicates that Henry also commissioned this volume. The first letter complains of the usurpation of the prerogatives of deacons. It also gives firsthand details of the celebrations during Pope Benedict VIII's stay as Henry's guest in Bamberg at Easter of 1020.

BIBLIOGRAPHY

Editions. Siegfried Hirsch, *Jahrbücher des deutschen Reichs unter Heinrich II,* I (1862), 545–554 (see also Hirsch's introduction); Philipp Jaffé, *Bibliotheca rerum Germanicarum,* V (1869), 484–497.

See also Maximilianus Manitius, *Geschichte der lateinischen Literatur des Mittelalters,* II (1923), 706–708.

DAVID R. TOWNSEND

BECKET, THOMAS, SAINT (1118–1170). Thomas of London, born of knightly Norman parents, spent most of his adult career as an ecclesiastical official in the household of Archbishop Theobald of Canterbury before he became chancellor to King Henry II of England in 1155. One of the most important chancellors in medieval English history, Thomas made his office a great one. He accomplished this in part through tangible achievements, but probably in larger measure through his close association with Henry, whose delegated authority he exercised. Thomas' conduct as a field commander and military adviser to his king was demonstrated by his leadership in the campaign in Anjou and Maine (1156), and in the Toulouse foray (1159). Thomas also negotiated the marriage of Margaret of France, daughter of Louis VII, with Henry the Young King (1158). More mundanely, the chancellor served as an itinerant justice, supervised the work of the exchequer, carried on various judicial services, administered all vacant holdings in the king's hand, handled diplomatic contacts and received important visitors, and dispensed royal patronage. He was virtually the king's alter ego.

Henry, upon designating Thomas archbishop of Canterbury in 1162, had assumed that he would continue to be chancellor as well as primate of the Church in England. In this the king erred, and his old friend became a new enemy in short order. Thomas was a highly secular man in his interests when he was attached to Henry's court as chancellor; he enjoyed the active life, knightly pastimes, worldly power, ostentation in food, dress, and entertainment. He was an ambitious man to whom extremes both of position and of mood were characteristic.

Thomas brought to Canterbury the ability and efficiency that had made him a great chancellor; unfortunately, he also brought the meanspiritedness that had not been apparent when he held the chancellor's seals. As David Knowles and others have noted, he seems to have displayed whatever temperament his roles required of him: genial and worldly as chancellor, he became austere and obstinate as archbishop.

Thomas was enthroned as archbishop in August of 1162, and by January public conflict between the king and the archbishop had begun. While the clash of personalities was central to the dispute, there were also serious issues between the two men. Henry intended to gain virtual independence from the direct administrative authority of the pope (not, of course, in the theological and sacramental fields), in order to restore the quasi-autonomy that the English Church had enjoyed in the reigns of the Norman kings from 1066 to 1135, a privileged status that Henry thought had been badly compromised under King Stephen (1135–1154). Henry intended to be the head of the English Church in a political sense, and hoped for a cooperative ecclesiastical leadership from Thomas.

The initial issue leading to dispute between the two men was benefit of clergy, the canonical principle dictating that all clergy were to be impleaded of crimes in ecclesiastical rather than in royal courts; since Henry was strengthening and rationalizing English law and the royal court system, he demanded that clergy be impleaded in royal courts for such secular crimes as rape and murder (though they could be tried by the Church). The problem surfaced at the Council of Westminster (October 1163), after open squabbling between the two men over nonecclesiastical matters had poisoned their relations in July.

At Westminster, Henry claimed the right to punish clergy who had been tried, convicted, and degraded from their clerical status in Church courts. Thomas, supported by his bench of bishops, defied the king, arguing that clerks should not be summoned before a secular court for their initial plea, and that degradation was sufficient punishment for a guilty clergyman. The king, frustrated in his policy, did not accept his defeat with grace, and thenceforth a cleft appeared in the English episcopate; the leader of opposition to Becket was Gilbert Foliot, bishop of London, who had wanted to occupy the throne now held by Thomas.

Failing to gain the support of Pope Alexander III, and ruling a divided bench, Becket promised in December 1163 to observe Henry's program. The king should have been content with his victory, but instead he elected to commit the "ancient customs" to writing at the Council of Clarendon (January 1164). The Constitutions of Clarendon were a wide-ranging program of ecclesiastical and legal reform; they dealt with the jurisdiction of royal courts over nomination of parish priests, jurisdiction of laymen over archdeacons' courts, direct communication with Rome by Englishmen without previous royal consent, royal rights over episcopal and abbatial vacancies, and benefit of clergy. The king again demanded that clergy convicted of secular crimes in ecclesiastical courts be punished by royal authority after they were degraded from clerical status (as Thomas argued, this was contrary both to canon law and to recent English practice). The customs having been codified, the bishops united in their opposition to royal policy; but Thomas inexplicably surrendered to the royal position and urged his bishops to follow his example. When the pope criticized some of the Constitutions, Becket again reversed himself.

At the Council of Northampton, Henry strengthened his offensive, and when a compromise was refused by the king, Thomas fled to exile in France and appealed to the pope for support. Alexander III, like all great popes a man with refined political instincts, temporized, hoping to achieve compromise between two stubborn men to whom compromise was repugnant but whose theoretical and practical positions were in fact susceptible of accommodation (as events following Becket's murder would demonstrate). Thomas in exile increasingly displayed the negative side of his personality: confused and contradictory leadership, irresponsibility, extremism. He was largely responsible for the destruction of the unity of what Knowles judged the finest bench of bishops in the history of the English Church.

Thomas' letters display an unbecoming acrimony that drove his episcopal opponents to equally acerbic missives in response. All efforts at papal and other arbitration and mediation were met by Thomas' agreement, but always "saving the honor of God and of his order"—in effect no meaningful agreement at all, since he reserved to himself the interpretation of the agreements or even total escape from them. In 1169, Henry restored the archbishop to the royal grace, but when he refused the kiss of peace to Thomas at an archiepiscopal Mass, Thomas may have decided that the dispute could be resolved only by his own martyrdom—which, apparently, he now consciously pursued.

In June 1170, Archbishop Roger of York, assisted by half a dozen of his episcopal colleagues, crowned Henry the Young King (son of Henry II), deliberately usurping the prerogative of Canterbury. Becket reacted predictably and vigorously, as would any other man in his position defending his and his office's rights. Following the apparent reconciliation of king and primate in November 1170, Thomas, bound for England, excommunicated and suspended the bishops who had participated in the coronation, and repeated from the pulpit at Christmas Mass his excommunications of the archbishop of York and of the bishops of London and Salisbury.

The king, informed of this public act while in Normandy, reacted with rage, demanding why none would serve the royal purpose by removing what is gently translated as "this foul priest." When a king asks such a question, even in a fit of frustration, someone had best respond. Four men did, leaving the court to cross the Channel and answer the king's query. They murdered Thomas before his own high altar, spilling his brains across the pavement of the cathedral. The immediate result was public horror and Thomas' popular canonization, followed in February 1173 by papal canonization. In 1960, though, his feast day was removed from the ecclesiastical calendar.

The significance of the dispute has been muddied by modern literary and dramatic traditions, especially by the Becket plays of T. S. Eliot and of Jean Anouilh, but literary grace should not obscure historical objectivity. The clash of personalities was important, but the outcome of the dispute, while lacking the drama of the personal clashes, demonstrated that willingness to compromise so alien to Thomas. Neither the king nor the pope was obstinate following the dramatic climax of the quarrel, and both seemed anxious to see the problems resolved.

While Thomas, particularly in his dramatic demise, was successful in preventing Henry from carrying out his ecclesiastical policy to the fullest, the king could not have achieved all his goals in any case. Some, such as forbidding contact with Rome, were anachronistic and reactionary, looking to past rather than to present realities. Yet Henry in fact continued to guide the English Church as he wished, not stridently but through patient diplomacy and personal interventions, showing him at his best as a political animal. With Becket gone, problems at issue were reasonably adjudicated; the irritating factor had been removed. When one considers that archiepiscopal rank carried both a political and an ecclesiastical position, Thomas must be judged a failure. His own psychological problems contributed to this situation: his feelings of persecution, his reading of significance into situations that had none or little, his delusions of grandeur type him as a paranoid personality by the standards of the twelfth, as of the twentieth, century.

In the aftermath of the murder, the English Church was again on a fairly even keel; no fundamental problems of principle persisted to embitter relations between the king and the Church. The shifting grounds of the Becket controversy, which make it so hard to interpret, melted away, and Henry continued to control ecclesiastical elections, rewarding his supporters and ignoring (but not persecuting) his opponents in the recent unpleasantness. Compromise characterized royal-papal relations, neither the king nor the pope willing to drive their relations to extremes. The problem of benefit of clergy never again became very important, and the king kept virtually all his jurisdictional claims with regard to the Church and its personnel; he may have exercised them subtly, but he exercised them nonetheless, without causing scandal to the Church. In effect, Henry retained the essentials of his ecclesiastical policy: control of elections, some supervision of direct contacts with Rome, regalian rights during vacancies, and most jurisdictional claims.

BIBLIOGRAPHY

James W. Alexander, "The Becket Controversy in Recent Historiography," in *Journal of British Studies,* 9 (1970); Mary Cheney, *Roger Bishop of Worcester, 1164–1179* (1981); Anne Duggan, *Thomas Becket: A Textual History of His Letters* (1980); Raymonde Foreville, ed., *L'église et la royauté en Angleterre sous Henri II Plantagenet* (1943); *Thomas Becket: Actes de Colloque international de Sédières* (1975); and *Thomas Becket dans la tradition historique et hagiographique* (1981); David Knowles, *Thomas Becket* (1971); Beryl Smalley, *The Becket Conflict and the Schools* (1973); Wilfred L. Warren, *Henry II* (1973), 399–558.

JAMES W. ALEXANDER

[See also **Alexander III; Canterbury; Clarendon, Constitutions of; England, 1066–1216; Henry II.**]

BEDE (Latin: Baeda, Beda; 672/673–735), in later centuries "the Venerable," is commonly regarded as the most influential Western writer between Gregory the Great and the imperial coronation of Charlemagne. Some have called that period (604–800) the Age of Bede.

Bede appended the salient facts of his life to his *Ecclesiastical History:*

> I, Beda, *famulus Christi* and priest of the monastery of the blessed apostles St. Peter and St. Paul, which is at Wearmouth and Jarrow [Northumbria]... was born in the territory of that monastery. At the age of seven I was given to the most reverend abbot Benedict to be educated, and later to Ceolfrid. From that time I have lived my whole life in the habit of that monastery, directing all my energy to study of Scripture and, amid observance of the regular discipline and daily duty of chanting in church, ever happily applying myself to learning or teaching or writing. In the nineteenth year of my life I entered the diaconate, in the thirtieth the priesthood, both through the ministry of the very reverend bishop John [of Hexham], on the recommendation of abbot Ceolfrid. From the time I entered the priesthood to my fifty-ninth year of age I have devoted myself to briefly annotating Holy Scripture from the tracts of the venerable Fathers, as I and my associates needed, or even to producing these additional works in accord with their meaning and interpretation.

Then follow the titles of what he had composed to date.

These words and his extant writings, which include nearly all the listed works plus a few more, make clear that his chosen portion in life was to be a monastic schoolmaster; to that vocation all his learning, teaching, and writing applied. He evidently never traveled farther than seventy-five miles from Jarrow in an age when journeying to Rome and other holy places was common among insular clergy and nobility; but he lived at a center that had acquired much from all Christendom and from Teutonic ancestors.

EDUCATION

Abbot Benedict Biscop, who founded a cloister (Sunderland) at Wearmouth in 674 and a companion cloister at Jarrow two years after Bede became oblate, traveled extensively to Gaul and Italy, and studied at Lérins. In 669 he journeyed from Rome with the new archbishop of Canterbury, Theodore of Tarsus, and Hadrian, abbot of Niridanum, near Naples, both such masters of Greek that "even now there are students of theirs who know Latin and Greek as well as their native tongue" (*History* 4.2). Northumbria, evangelized by the Irish before the Synod of Whitby (664), turned its church toward Rome and transmitted the best of Irish schooling; the contentions between the two communions stimulated investigation and scholarship. From the Continent Biscop brought books, art, and artisans, and even Abbot John, the archanter of St. Peter's in Rome, to teach at Wearmouth. Theodore's library at Canterbury and Biscop's at Wearmouth-Jarrow became the strongest in Britain.

Bede's contemporaries maintained close ties with Gaul and with ancestral Germania through missions and travel. Bede especially admired his master and abbot, Ceolfrid, creator of the *Codex Amiatinus,* whose sole surviving composition, a letter to King Naiton (Nectan) the Pict, shows the "almost classical purity" of Bede's Latin. Ceolfrid's recorded acts indicate the Roman orthodoxy linked with democratic Christianity that characterize Bede. According to Alcuin, Bede would say, "I know that angels visit the congregation of brethren at the canonical hours, and what if they should not find me among the brethren? Would they not say, 'Where is Bede?'" He often acted as scribe, and was a close and discerning text critic. *Famulus Christi* (servant of Christ) was his phrase for the devout, honest monk.

WRITINGS

Bede composed his works in Augustinian *sermo humilis*—"sermons with simple diction but refined meaning" *(sermone simplici sed sensu subtili conposuit),* wrote Alcuin. Quentin speaks of Bede's "mosaic" method predominant in monastic exegesis and art of the time. He preferred quotations from his sources to paraphrases, but his eclectic selection and linking created a whole greater than the sum of the parts. Although he centered his exposition on images of individuals in action, Bede composed no epics or literature of entertainment. All he wrote had didactic and ethical purpose. He prefaced his *Ecclesiastical History* thus: "When history relates good things of good people the auditor is moved to follow the good; but when it reports evil things of bad people the devout and pious auditor or reader is equally eager, while avoiding what is harmful and evil, to follow after what he perceived to be good and acceptable to God."

Scriptural exegesis and homilies. The monastic schools were learning to place scriptural study at the apex of disciplinary education, as classical pagans had placed philosophy. More than half of Bede's works, often composed at the request of his bishop, Acca of Hexham, are of this kind. There are twenty-four titles in his list, largely verse-by-verse expositions of individual books. Very few have disappeared. Bede is predominantly but not slavishly Augustinian, and apparently had in his library more than half of Augustine's writings. *De doctrina christiana* (including the rules of Tyconius) and *De consensu evangelistarum* especially affected his critical approach. He also venerated Ambrose and Gregory the Great, founder of the English church. Jerome's translations of Scriptures and his commentaries on them were indispensable. Following these Fathers, Bede emphasized the Alexandrian form of allegorical interpretation, but how much to reveal reality and how much for didactic, mnemonic convenience is a question. Some of the commentaries (Genesis, Song of Songs, Catholic Epistles) were composed in layers, being added to in successive redactions.

Didactic works. A vocational curriculum had evolved in Western convents as a preparation for scriptural scholarship. It sharply contrasts with the Roman and Augustinian seven liberal arts, especially in its deemphasis of rhetoric and dialectic. For chant *(cantus),* which was central and elementary, instruction was wholly oral (written notation was not in common use), but for several other studies Bede prepared textbooks. *De orthographia* was for *notae*—that is, basic instruction in penmanship, spelling, and syntax; as soon as the oblates could master letters, they were apprenticed as scribes. *De locis sanctis* (On holy places)—the vocational form of geography—followed the information given by Arculf the pilgrim to the Irish at Iona. *De natura rerum,* modeled on the *Liber rotarum* of Isidore of Seville, treated elementary natural phenomena (the globular zones, earthquakes and tempests, planetary movements, pestilence). *De arte metrica* was devoted to versification as practiced by such Christian poets as Paulinus and Prudentius; Bede was the first to describe isosyllabic rhyme and rhythm as popularized by Christian hymnologists. *De schematibus et tropis* outlines imagery and figuration as found in the Bible.

A vocational study quickly finding favor was *computus,* the art of telling time, for time lay at the heart of monastic discipline, from the longs and shorts of scansion and chant through the daily hours, the seasonal plantings, the yearly feasts, to the chronology of Christian history and the ages and eternity of God's universe. The study was especially necessary in Northumbria, where the differences among the British, Irish, and English calendars were especially disruptive. In 703, Bede composed an elementary text, *De temporibus,* treating rules and formulas governing the Christian year, with a brief digest *(chronicon)* of world history, dependent on Eusebius and chronologically revised by reference to Jerome's text of scriptures and to Josephus.

Bede's unprecedented chronology, which refuted popular notions of the Second Coming and end of creation, led to a charge of "heretical" doctrine voiced at his bishop's see. The charge haunted the orthodox Bede thereafter, and in 725 he published a second, greatly enlarged, text on times that incorporated an extensive chronicle of world history confirming his calculated *annus mundi* (Year of Creation). That work unified the West in its conventions of time, such as the sequence of weekdays, beginnings of years, dates of movable feasts, the Christian era, and so forth. It contains what Duhem called the only original formulation of natural law for several centuries in the West—the tidal action called Establishment of Port.

Historical, biographical, and hagiographical works. Developing from his scholarship on times was Bede's study of history. The ancient ambiguity of *historia,* which yields both "story" and "history," was present in early Christian writing. It is observable in the Julian solar calendar, which underlies hagiography (the solar-cyclic cult of saints), and the Paschal tables, the lunar-cyclic sequence underlying historiography. The Hebrew-Christian doctrine of a calculable beginning and end of a created world determined that Christian historiography should emphasize chronography, periodicity, and modularity. On the other hand, its doctrine of the sanctity of the individual determined that hagiography should be essentially an ethical abstract of saintly traits. Bede created a martyrology: "the birthdays of the holy martyrs, in which I tried to record all I could discover, not only the day of martyrdom but the kind of contention and under whom as judge they overcame the world." The abundant entries reveal the rapid growth of the cult of saints. For individual cults Bede composed prose lives of Anastasius (lost) and Felix of Nola, and a prose and a verse life of Cuthbert of Lindisfarne. His *Lives of the Abbots of Wearmouth and Jarrow* is historiographic, but a hagiographic homily on the first abbot, Biscop, survives. As a chronographic historian Bede included chronicles in both works on times and as a recapitulation in his *Ecclesiastical History.*

The masterpiece most admired among British and modern readers is Bede's *Historia ecclesiastica gentis Anglorum,* published in 731. Not only is it the primary source of knowledge of the English church and peoples from the time of the Anglo-Saxon migration, but its humanitarian images and tested reliability more than warrant Bede's epithet, Father of English History. True, some few of his statements have been challenged, especially regarding the Gregorian mission, but not decisively refuted. Considering the sources available to him (which he conscientiously summarized in his preface), his interpretations are admirable. Stimulated especially by Albinus, archbishop of Canterbury, who furnished material from the south, and by King Ceolwulf, to whom he dedicated the work, Bede visualized a single English nation despite its several realms. Though intending to supplement Eusebius' fundamental *History,* he did not slavishly follow his model. Cassiodorus, Isidore, and Gregory of Tours had written histories of converted peoples, and more were to follow; but Bede the ethical teacher deemphasized the corporate acts of church and state in favor of individual choices. His excellence has been blamed for the dearth of historiography in Britain up to the Conquest.

Verses. Bede's Latin verse, which includes hymns, prayers, meditations, a life of St. Cuthbert, a eulogy of St. Audrey, and poems on Six Ages *(De sex aetatibus mundi)* and on Judgment Day, is more didactic than poetic. The books of hymns and epigrams that he listed have not survived intact. Cuthbert of Jarrow, who wrote a letter describing Bede's death, spoke of his "skill in our songs," and quoted five vernacular verses, presumably by Bede. At his death Bede was translating St. John's Gospel into English, but it cannot now be identified.

Letters. In cataloguing his works, Bede listed "a book of letters," specifying five. An unlisted sixth, written to Archbishop Egbert of York in 734, is normally published among his historical works; it describes elements of Northumbrian life and advocates reform. The listed letters deal with computistical and exegetical questions.

INFLUENCE

Often linked with the acknowledged doctors of the patristic period, Bede has without hyperbole been called the Father of English Scholarship, History, and Literature. He richly contributed to biblical tradition, latinity, literary criticism, chronology, and history, and he stimulated interest in natural phenomena and geography. Missionaries like Boniface and scholars like Alcuin rapidly disseminated his works about the Continent. Laistner's *Hand-list* of manuscripts of his writings is a comprehensive index to his literary remains. His textbooks controlled Christian education until diocesan schools replaced monastic schools in the twelfth century; but the popularity of his scriptural exegesis and especially of his *Ecclesiastical History* continued to grow. The papacy pronounced him Doctor Ecclesiae in 1899, and Sanctus in 1935. His relics were taken from Jarrow early in the eleventh century and buried in St. Cuthbert's coffin at Durham, whence they were translated to the galilee porch late in the twelfth century. That tomb was pillaged in 1541 and the relics dispersed, but it remains an object of veneration.

BIBLIOGRAPHY

Among the more recent editions of Bede's collected works are those of John Allen Giles, 12 vols. (1843–1844), which includes translations of Bede's historical works; and *Patrologia latina,* XC–XCV (1861–1862). The Corpus Christianorum Series Latina (1960–) has to date (1982) published critical editions of six exegetic and didascalic works.

The Alfredian translation of *Historia ecclesiastica* was first published in 1643, edited by Abraham Whelock. A critical edition, with modern English translation, is *The Old English Version of Bede's Ecclesiastical History of the English People,* Thomas Miller, ed. and trans., 2 vols. (1890–1898, repr. 1959). See also Putnam F. Jones, ed., *A Concordance to the Historia ecclesiastica of Bede* (1929).

Secondary literature includes Peter Hunter Blair, *The World of Bede* (1970); Whitney F. Bolton, *A History of Anglo-Latin Literature, 597–1066,* I (1967), 264–287; Gerald Bonner, "The Christian Life in the Thought of the Venerable Bede," in *Durham University Journal,* **63** (1970–1971); and *Famulus Christi: Essays in Commemoration of the Thirteenth Centenary of the Birth of the Venerable Bede* (1976); Patrick Echliñ, "Bede and the Church," in *Irish Theological Quarterly,* **40** (1973); T. J. M. van Els, *The Kassel Manuscripts of Bede's "Historia ecclesiastica gentis Anglorum" and Its Old English Material* (1972); Kenneth Harrison, "The *Annus Domini* in Some Early Charters," in *Journal of the Society of Archivists,* **4** (1973); Charles W. Jones, "Some Introductory Remarks on Bede's Commentary on Genesis," in *Sacris erudiri,* **19** (1969–1970); D. P. Kirby, "Bede's Native Sources for the *Historia ecclesiastica,*" in *Bulletin of the John Rylands Library,* **48** (1965–1966); Richard W. Southern, *Medieval Humanism and Other Studies* (1970); and Leslie Whitbread, "After Bede: The Influence and Dissemination of His Doomsday Verses," in *Archiv für das Studium der neueren Sprachen und Literaturen,* **204** (1967).

CHARLES W. JONES

[See also **Anglo-Latin Poetry; Anglo-Saxon Literature; Benedict Biscop, St.; Historiography, Western European.**]

BEDESTAN (also *bedesten, bezzeztan, besestan, bazzazistan, dar al-bazzaziyah).* The term, most widely used in the Ottoman Empire, means a place of textile *(baz)* dealers, and must have originated in the early Islamic period, when textiles, a state monopoly, were considered a luxury item and were protected. Special, well-guarded areas were developed for their storage and exchange. In time the items stored and exchanged came to include precious metals and minerals as well as imported goods such as Chinese porcelain. A *bedestan* or *bazzaztan* (the two most common forms of the word) was the central, enclosed structure of a market or commercial district. *Bedestan*s were built only in large, important trading towns.

Unlike a *han* or caravansaray, a *bedestan* did not offer lodging to the traveling or resident merchant; rather, it was locked up well before sunset. In addition to serving as a secure place for the storage and sale of luxury items, the *bedestan* had special coffers or pits for rent where merchants could deposit their money and documents for safekeeping. It also offered merchants a safe place to conduct their financial transactions and to organize overland caravans and sea voyages. In short, a *bedestan* was a secure commercial building that also served as a bank.

Commonly a *bedestan* was built by the sultan or his representative, the governor of a province, and therefore had state protection. The presence of a *bedestan* in a city or town promoted trade and drew merchants from beyond the borders of the state. As a rule the *bedestan* was built as *waqf,* an endowment for the support and maintenance of a charitable or pious foundation and its staff. The income came from the lease of space within the *bedestan.* The individual areas, devoted to storage and display, were highly coveted by the merchants, who concluded contracts for long- or short-term leases directly with the government officers.

Architecturally a *bedestan* was a compact, square or rectangular structure with high and thick walls and windows below the roof line. A single gate on each side of the building gave access to the interior. From each gate a street or hall stretched to intersect the others at the center. The streets were vaulted, and domed at the crossing. Individual shops lined both sides of each street at a level slightly above it. Each shop was domed separately. The shop had a shelf or counter on which goods were displayed.

A *bedestan* often became the center of a large commercial area. Stalls, shops, and streets lined with shops were built abutting its walls on all four sides, and soon a mazelike bazaar appeared.

BIBLIOGRAPHY

Halil Inalcik, "The Hub of the City: The Bedestan of Istanbul," in *International Journal of Turkish Studies,* 1 (1979–1980).

ÜLKÜ Ü. BATES

[See also **Han; Islamic Architecture; Markets, Islamic.**]

BEDLAM, with its modern connotation of insane confusion, is a shortened name for the Bethlehem Royal Hospital. A well-known sight of seventeenth- and eighteenth-century London, the hospital was England's most famous insane asylum. Yet its beginnings as a pious and obscure benefaction did nothing to signal this later role.

The Priory of St. Mary of Bethlehem was founded in 1247 on land deeded by Simon Fitz Mary, twice sheriff of London. Located just outside Bishop's Gate, the priory's original purpose was to accommodate the bishop of St. Mary of Bethlehem. Little is known of the early days. In 1330, Edward III, first mentioning its role as a hospital, granted it the right to collect alms. Throughout its history Bedlam was short of funds. In 1346 the priory petitioned the London city council for aid; although accepted as a ward by the council, the hospital remained the property of the bishop.

Such ownership eventually led to Bedlam's seizure in 1375 by Edward III. The bishopric of St. Mary of Bethlehem was in France, and this rendered the hospital forfeit to the crown during a desultory phase of the Hundred Years War. Bedlam remained under royal patronage. When Henry VIII around 1536 closed the monasteries, which had assumed much responsibility for the insane, considerable pressure was put on public authority to provide for these people. In 1547 the city of London bought Bedlam from the king, and from that time the hospital played a greater role in the treatment of the insane.

In 1598 the hospital housed twenty patients, of whom six were charity cases. Financial problems continued, and occasional scandals beset Bedlam. A new hospital, capable of housing 150 patients, was erected in Moorfields in 1674. This hospital charged a penny to view the patients. Records from the early nineteenth century indicate 90,000 visits per year.

The history of Bedlam in the medieval period was typical of establishments of its type. Most religious institutions treated the sick. In the early Middle Ages, monasteries had a near monopoly on medical knowledge and facilities. Even in the later Middle Ages, religious orders still provided much full-time care. When Henry VIII swept away the monasteries, secular authority was obliged to fill the gap. The purchase and public support of Bedlam was one such effort.

There is little information about the care of Bedlam's inmates during the Middle Ages. The presence of the insane is first mentioned in 1403, when Henry IV brought the hospital's porter, Peter Taverner, to trial for abusing his office. He was charged with stealing two stocks, various chains with locks, manacles, and some metal chairs. Apparently, these items were used routinely to restrain the patients. While this presents an unappealing picture, one should realize that no advances in the treatment of mental illness were made before the middle of the twentieth century. Previously, little could be offered beyond custodial care.

Sir Thomas More wrote of his early-sixteenth-century visit to Bedlam: "Think not that everything is pleasant that men . . . laugh at. For thou shalt in Bedlam see one laugh at the knocking of his head against a post, and yet there is little pleasure therein."

BIBLIOGRAPHY

Thomas Bowen, *An Historical Account of Bethlehem Hospital* (1783); Courtney Dainton, *The Story of England's Hospitals* (1961), 140–144; Michel Foucault, *Madness and Civilization: A History of Insanity in the Age of Reason* (1965), esp. chs. 2 and 3; Sir Thomas More, *English Works of Sir Thomas More,* W. E. Campbell, ed., I (1931), 461; Edward G. O'Donoghue, *The Story of Bethlehem Hospital from its Foundation in 1247* (1914); Robert Rentoul Reed, Jr., *Bedlam on the Jacobean Stage* (1952), 12–20.

STEPHEN R. ELL

[See also **Hospitals and Poor Relief; Insanity, Treatment of.**]

BEER. See **Brewing.**

BEGUINES AND BEGHARDS were urban women and men of continental northern Europe who led lives of chastity, poverty, and religious devotion without joining an approved order. Beguines first appeared in the Low Countries at the end of the twelfth

 BEGUINES AND BEGHARDS

century. Beghards, their male counterparts, appeared soon afterward, but there were always many more beguines than beghards. In fact, the beguinal movement was predominantly a female phenomenon, and was noteworthy for having been the only medieval female religious movement that did not owe its primary inspiration and guidance to men. From about 1220 to 1318, the period of its greatest vigor, the beguinal movement provided the opportunity for large numbers of women to satisfy both their spiritual desires and their material needs. Afterward beguines were forced to abandon most of their independence and the movement declined, but some beguinal communities continued to exist in the Rhineland and especially the Low Countries until modern times.

Medieval beguines and beghards followed one of four different patterns of life. In the first, individuals, almost always women, continued to live in their own homes and go about their own work, but they remained continent and otherwise lived as piously as they could. Sometimes they associated themselves with nearby friaries or other communities by offering services or donating property. In the second form, groups of from two or three to sixty or seventy women, or occasionally men, resided together in houses (female houses were called beguinages), leading lives of devotion, supporting themselves by their common labors, and remaining under the spiritual jurisdiction of the local parish priest. In the third, large agglomerations of two hundred to three hundred women (or, less often, men) formed their own walled-in "towns within towns" and constituted their own independent parishes. The fourth form of beguinal life, followed more often by men than by women, was wandering mendicancy.

The beguinal movement had its origins, around the turn of the twelfth century, in a widespread desire among upper-class women to lead "apostolic" lives of piety and simplicity. Until recently it was thought that women in the Low Countries started becoming beguines between 1170 and 1250 because they could no longer gain easy entry into the Premonstratensian and Cistercian orders—the two orders that until then had accepted the largest numbers of women. In fact, however, the Cistercians continued to found many new nunneries in the Low Countries and northern Germany throughout the thirteenth century. Some women may have become beguines because they could not gain entrance into nunneries, but many others must have chosen a beguinal form of life because it seemed more "apostolic"—because manual labor or mendicancy in the midst of the world must have seemed closer to the models provided by Christ and the apostles than did the lives of cloistered nuns. Thus, in the early period of the movement, the motivation for becoming a beguine was probably similar to that for becoming a Franciscan or Dominican friar.

The earliest communities of "holy women" *(mulieres sanctae)* who behaved like beguines without yet receiving that name were groups that arose spontaneously in and around Liège between about 1170 and 1210. The first well-known "holy woman" was Mary of Oignies, whose pious life became a model for others. The most influential early supporter of the beguinal movement was the canon (later bishop and cardinal) Jacques de Vitry: in 1213 he wrote a laudatory life of Mary of Oignies, and in 1216 he won verbal approval from Pope Honorius III for "pious women, not only in the diocese of Liège, but also in France and Germany, to live in communal houses and encourage each other to do good by mutual exhortation."

Honorius' verbal approval was followed in 1233 by Pope Gregory IX's bull *Gloriam virginalem,* which formally took "chaste virgins in Teutonia" (a term that probably encompassed Germanic-speaking areas of the Low Countries) under papal protection. With such official support the beguinal movement grew rapidly. The earliest evidence of beguines in Cologne dates from 1223; in Louvain, from 1232; in Mainz, from 1233; in Namur, Osnabrück, and Paderborn, from 1235; in Frankfurt, from 1242; and in Strassburg, from 1244. Scattered references to male counterparts of beguines first appear in sources from the Low Countries, northern France, and Germany dating from about 1220 to 1250. A community of semireligious males existed as far east as Wiener Neustadt by 1243.

The use of the words *beguina* and *beguinus* to designate the new semireligious women and men became widespread and standard by the 1230's. There is considerable uncertainty about the etymology of the word "beguine," especially because the original meaning had already been forgotten by the middle of the thirteenth century: Matthew Paris wrote in 1243 that "the meaning of the name is unknown."

The theory that the beguines were named after one of their earliest patrons, Lambert "le Bègue" ("the Stutterer"), is now universally rejected. This false etymology was first offered around 1250, in the mistaken belief that the beguines must have had a single founder: in fact Lambert, who died in 1177, was not even called "le Bègue" in any source earlier

BEGUINES AND BEGHARDS

than the one that offered the false etymology. It is possible that the term beguine really derived from the plain, beige-colored clothing (Old French: *bege*) that beguines wore, but it seems most likely that beguine came from a contraction for Albigensian heretic (Latin: *Al-bigen-sis*). At Cologne, Albigensian and Amaurian heretics were definitely called *beggini* between 1210 and 1220; most likely the term was first used loosely around the same time to apply to the new groups of semireligious women. In that case it would have originated as a term of abuse.

The name "beghard" first appears in sources from the Flemish-speaking Low Countries in the 1250's. Thereafter it became the standard form for the male beguine in Germanic-speaking areas (Romance areas retained the form *beguinus*). Most likely beghards gained their name from a combination of the prefix for beguine and the pejorative Germanic suffix *-hardus.*

The likelihood that both *beguinus* (with feminine *begina*) and *beghardus* were originally pejorative terms is strengthened by the certainty that beguines and beghards were regarded by many with suspicion and hostility throughout the thirteenth century. One reason for this was that religious traditionalists and members of the secular clergy were often hostile to the "apostolic" movement with which the early beguines and beghards were associated. Critics who thought that even the early Franciscans seemed like heretics because of their novel "apostolic" conduct found that spontaneous organizations of laywomen and laymen who dedicated themselves to chastity and poverty, and sometimes to mendicancy and Bible reading, were far too much of a novelty, and an implicit danger to traditional organs of authority.

After the semireligious groups gained papal support, the close association they maintained with the Dominicans and Franciscans continued to cause them difficulties. As laypeople the beguines and beghards formally remained under the spiritual jurisdiction of their parish priests, but very often they preferred to settle near Dominican and Franciscan friaries and develop close institutional and spiritual affiliations with the friars. Not surprisingly, the secular clergy resented this intimacy, and a strong sense of institutional rivalry ensued. Further reasons for hostility were that the beguines and beghards appeared too pious to some because of their seemingly "holier than thou" behavior, while others felt sure that beguines were really hypocrites who only pretended to be pious but really lived lives of scandalous self-indulgence.

For all these reasons, throughout the thirteenth century beguines and beghards were subject to abuse and often to restrictive legislation. The word *beguinus* was used as a term of derision for the overly pious, and poets such as Gautier de Coincy in the 1220's, Rutebeuf in the 1250's, and Jean de Meun in the 1270's excoriated beguines for religious hypocrisy. (In Jean's *Romance of the Rose* a beguine appears as the personification of Constrained Abstinence and the consort of a friar named False Seeming.) The leader of the secular theologians at the University of Paris, William of St.-Amour, attacked the beguines and beghards in the 1250's as a means of attacking the friars whom they resembled and who stood behind them. According to William, the beguines had no right to behave like religious people because they belonged to no approved order; worse, they were thoroughly evil because, though young and able, they lived on alms and refused to work.

In 1233 a synod of Mainz issued the earliest formal legislation against beguines. This stipulated that women who took vows of chastity and wore a habit without following any known rule should not wander about, but should live in their own houses, supporting themselves by their own income or labors, and recognize the authority of their parish priests. Other German synods of the thirteenth century similarly prohibited beguinal mendicancy and insubordination to parish priests; at least two (Trier, 1277, and Eichstätt, *ca.* 1284) went so far as to warn against the preaching of errors.

Despite hostility and restrictive legislation, the beguinal movement reached its apogee from about 1220 to 1318. Even though there were numerous critics, there were also numerous admirers and supporters of the movement. Robert Grosseteste, for example, stated around 1230 that beguines constituted the "most perfect and most holy form of religious life"—in his view even superior to that of the Franciscans—and an unidentified Parisian Dominican insisted around 1240 that beguines and beghards were the most devout Christians in the secular world. The vigorous early growth of the movement was treated by the chronicler Matthew Paris as one of the major religious events of the first half of the thirteenth century.

In the second half of the century, the pattern of beguines living together in houses became established as the dominant form of beguinal organization in Germany, while the pattern of beguines forming "towns within towns" was the dominant

BEGUINES AND BEGHARDS

form in the Low Countries. In Germany the largest center of beguinal life was Cologne, where more than one hundred houses had been established by 1320. The roughly one thousand beguines of Cologne in 1320 (a figure that excludes beguines living alone) accounted for about 3 percent of the total population of the city and about 15 percent of the adult females. (Even in the sixteenth century, when the number of beguines in Cologne had decreased, they were still said to have been "as numerous as drops in the sea.") In Mainz there were roughly one hundred beguines around 1300, but in Strassburg there were some six hundred, or about 2.5 percent of the total population, and in Basel the percentage was similar. Outside the Rhineland there were smaller numbers of beguines in most cities of the German Empire, including several as far east as Bohemia and Silesia. In the Low Countries large beguinages could be found in nearly every city. The largest, containing two hundred to three hundred women, were in such cities as Ghent and Bruges. There were many fewer beghard houses than beguinages, but one or two existed in German cities such as Cologne, Strassburg, and Frankfurt, and there were scattered beghard communities in the Low Countries in such cities as Brussels, Louvain, and Antwerp.

Beguines who lived in houses or large communities earned their livelihoods from one of three sources or a combination thereof: their own family incomes, gifts, and communal earnings. The most typical beguinal occupations were nursing, weaving, spinning, and embroidery, followed by funerary services, washing, and housework for others. Beguines were invariably committed to chastity, but were free to abandon their beguinal status and marry if the opportunity arose. Usually beguine houses and communities had their internal directresses (in Germany called Marthas), and extreme asceticism generally was not demanded (although there were great exceptions to this rule, as at Schweidnitz, where beguines engaged in severe corporal self-punishment). Most often beguines wore drab, homespun habits similar to those worn by members of female mendicant orders.

Although most of the early beguines seem to have come from the upper classes, as time went on, beguinages recruited more and more from the middling classes of the towns. The primary reason for this seems to have been that there was a surplus of unprotected women in medieval urban environments, owing to the number of men who died in war or became celibate priests or monks. In the countryside excess women could support themselves by agricultural labor and gain protection by belonging to extended family communities. But in cities the lives of unmarried women were far more precarious because there was less space for large families and there were fewer approved female occupations. By joining in beguinal communities, unattached urban women could pool their economic resources, find mutual protection, and gain a sense of identity.

Despite whatever material motivations there may have been for joining beguinal communities, the level of piety in most thirteenth- and early fourteenth-century beguinages appears to have been extremely high. Many beguines sought not just to imitate Christ but also to have ecstatic religious experiences; therefore many beguinages became quarters for the development of an intense mysticism that has an important place in both literary and religious history. Several beguines who described their ecstatic experiences in spontaneous outpourings produced the earliest mystical writings in the northern European vernaculars.

The first known mystical tract in a European vernacular was Beatrice of Nazareth's Flemish *Seven manieren van Minne* (Seven manners of love), written around 1233 by a nun who had been educated by beguines. This was followed around 1240 by the vernacular mystical letters, poems, and "visions" written by the Flemish beguine Hadewijch of Antwerp, and around 1265 by *Das fliessende Licht der Gottheit* (The flowing light of divinity), written in mixed poetry and prose by a north German beguine, Mechthild of Magdeburg. A final important early vernacular mystical text was the *Mirouer des simples ames* (Mirror of simple souls), written in Old French around 1300 by Marguerite Porete, a beguine from Hainaut. Most of these works have great literary worth because of their freshness and intensity.

The writings of the mystical beguines are particularly interesting to the historian of religion for two reasons. One is that some of them may have influenced the thought of major mystical theorists, such as Meister Eckhart and Ruysbroeck. The other is that they provide invaluable documentation for understanding actual mystical experiences: while there are numerous medieval tracts that teach about mysticism, and a few that describe the mystical experiences of others, the beguinal writings are among the very few that describe mystical experiences from the point of view of those who really had them.

After about a century of maligned but flourishing

BEGUINES AND BEGHARDS

existence, the beguinal movement received a sharp setback as a result of two decrees drawn up at the Council of Vienne in 1312 and formally promulgated late in 1317. In 1273 three reports written to advise the Second Council of Lyons expressed criticism of beguines in varying degree, but when the council met in 1274, no legislation directed specifically against the beguines resulted. It can only be surmised why the Council of Vienne acted so differently. Possibly real heresy had arisen in some beguinages and among some beghards. Unrestrained mysticism was always potentially dangerous because it opened the possibility for people to think that they could become fully one with God on earth by their own efforts and without the aid of sacramental intermediaries.

Certainly Marguerite Porete came close to espousing such views in her *Mirouer:* consequently she was burned for heresy at Paris in 1310, shortly before the gathering at Vienne. But whether Marguerite was really much more heretical than her predecessors Beatrice of Nazareth, Hadewijch of Antwerp, and Mechthild of Magdeburg is a moot point, and whether unrestrained mysticism in general was more prevalent among beghards and beguines around 1310 than in the previous half-century is almost impossible to determine. It is certain, however, that there were larger numbers of beguines and beghards around 1310 than ever before, that they were accordingly a greater irritant than ever to those who tended to be disturbed by them, and that the Dominican and Franciscan friars with whom they were associated were themselves being forced onto the defensive by their enemies. The beguines and beghards were bound to suffer from the last fact because the weakness of the friars made the beguines and beghards an easier target than ever, and also because the friars themselves were sometimes prone to turn against beguines and beghards to deflect attacks on themselves.

Of the two Vienne decrees that were directed against the beguinal movement, one, *Ad nostrum,* called for inquisitorial procedures against German beghards and beguines who were charged with spreading mystical and antinomian errors. (Taken together, these errors are now called "the heresy of the Free Spirit.") The other decree, *Cum de quibusdam mulieribus,* was a general prohibition of beguinal organizations. It declared that beguines could not be considered members of any regular order because they took no vows of obedience, did not renounce property, and did not profess any approved rule. Nonetheless, beguines wore habits, associated with members of religious orders (Franciscans and Dominicans were no doubt meant), and dared to dispute and preach about complicated theological matters, such as the Trinity and the divine Essence, thereby leading simple people into error.

Accordingly, *Cum de quibusdam* ordered that all beguinal communities be dissolved and that beguinal organizations be permanently forbidden. But it then concluded by saying that truly faithful women could continue to live lives of penance and humility in communal houses. The final clause reflects the uncertainty that the legislators felt on the entire subject: they were opposed to what they perceived to be the abuses of the beguines, but they also were forced to admit that there was no intrinsic harm in allowing pious women to lead communal lives of devotion without following an approved rule.

The publication of *Ad nostrum* and *Cum de quibusdam mulieribus* in 1317 initiated a century of confused or contradictory official policy and intermittent persecutions of the beguinal movement. Some bishops immediately took measures to dissolve beguinages in their dioceses, but some did not, especially because the final clause of *Cum de quibusdam* appeared to allow some escape. In 1318, in the bull *Racio recta,* Pope John XXII tried to clarify matters by making a distinction between "good" and "bad" beguines: the "good" ones should be supported, but the "bad" ones should not. This ruling, however, actually allowed much local discretion, because the distinction was extremely subjective. Thereafter papal policy on beguines was either similarly vague or oscillated between extremes of hostility and toleration until the popes of the fifteenth century finally established a consistent policy of toleration for the beguinal movement.

In the meantime, the Vienne legislation (which was never retracted) and *Racio recta* allowed local authorities to move against beguines and beghards more or less as they wished. The result was wide local variation in treatment: sometimes beguinages were left completely alone, sometimes they were dissolved, and sometimes beguines and beghards were subjected to heresy trials. The general tendency of the period, however, was for beguinages to continue to exist, but with more institutional and legal protection than before. In the Low Countries this meant that the pattern of walled-in communities with their own parish priests was consolidated, while in Germany it usually meant that beguines formally joined approved orders, most often the Third Order of St. Francis. Given those circumstances, after about 1420

BEGUINS

the beguinal movement was no longer very controversial, but it also had lost most of its earlier spontaneity and vigor.

BIBLIOGRAPHY

Brenda M. Bolton, "Mulieres Sanctae," in *Studies in Church History,* **10** (1973); John B. Freed, "Urban Development and the 'Cura Monialium' in Thirteenth-Century Germany," in *Viator,* 3 (1972); Herbert Grundmann, *Religiöse Bewegungen im Mittelalter,* 2nd ed. (1961), 170–198, 319–354; Robert E. Lerner, *The Heresy of the Free Spirit in the Later Middle Ages* (1972); Ernest W. McDonnell, *The Beguines and Beghards in Medieval Culture, with Special Emphasis on the Belgian Scene* (1954); A. Mens, "Beghine, Begardi, Beghinaggi," in *Dizionario degli Istituti di Perfezione,* I (1974); Eva Gertrud Neumann, *Rheinisches Beginen- und Begardenwesen* (1960); A. Patschovsky, "Strassburger Beginenverfolgungen im 14. Jahrhundert," in *Deutsches Archiv für Erforschung des Mittelalters,* **30** (1974); R. W. Southern, *Western Society and the Church in the Middle Ages* (1970), 318–331.

ROBERT E. LERNER

[See also **Beguins; Free Spirit, Heresy of; Hadewijch of Antwerp; Jacques de Vitry; Mechthild von Magdeburg; Mendicant Orders; Mysticism.**]

BEGUINS were male and female members of the Third Order of St. Francis (the semiregular Franciscan order for laypeople) who lived in Languedoc, Catalonia, and neighboring areas of southern France and northeastern Spain in the late thirteenth century and first quarter of the fourteenth century. Related to the Europewide movement of beguines and beghards (from whom they derived their name), the southern French and Spanish beguins were distinguished by their fervent dedication to the doctrine and practice of absolute poverty and by their belief in the imminent coming of Antichrist and a following wondrous new era of history. They were greatly influenced by the thought of the Provençal Franciscan Peter Olivi (*d.* 1298), and were offered guidance by the Catalonian physician and lay theologian Arnald of Villanova (*d.* 1311). The beguins' commitment to poverty and millennial eschatology resulted in conflicts with the hierarchical Church, which in turn led many beguins to become heretics. Inquisitorial persecution resulted in the rapid destruction of the movement.

Certainly the beguins were not heretics to begin with: they only wished to lead the most Christian lives they could while remaining laypeople. Their movement was exclusively urban: they lived either in cities such as Narbonne, Béziers, Carcassonne, Montpellier, Barcelona, and Valencia, or in smaller towns. Some lived communally in "houses of poverty"; others, in their own homes, coming together for conventicles in which they read religious works in the vernacular. Some gained their livelihood from begging, but many continued to follow their own professions or trades: the ranks of the southern French beguins included notaries, weavers, tailors, candlemakers, butchers, and smiths.

Whatever their occupations, many beguins wore coarse habits. Three works of instruction written for the beguins by Arnald of Villanova show that they sought to lead lives of the fullest "evangelical perfection," which they considered to be characterized most by the virtues of poverty, humility, charity, and chastity. Poverty, in their view, was paramount: truly evangelical poverty meant having only that which is absolutely necessary for sustaining the body's needs, and showing priority to the spiritual rather than the physical life by never laying away material goods. The beguins, furthermore, were opposed to any sort of "vain curiosity" and to indulging in any sort of litigation. Believing fervently that Christ and the apostles had owned no property and had lived in the world without being "worldly," they resolved to live as far as possible after the model of Christ's life and teachings.

How such people became radical heretics is a complex historical problem. Because some of the beguins' strongholds, especially those in Languedoc, had been strongholds of the Albigensian heresy a century or half a century earlier, some historians have been inclined to believe that the beguins were lineal descendants of the Albigensians. This, however, is certainly a distortion. Although both the Albigensians and the beguins were extreme ascetics, the beguins shared none of the Albigensians' dualist metaphysics, subscribing instead to an extreme evangelical Christianity that they inherited from the Franciscans. (Franciscans and Albigensians were always antagonists.) Conceivably the extraordinary intransigence of the southern French beguins stemmed in part from the sense of a need to preserve Provençal regional identity in the face of political centralization from the north, but this hypothesis is extremely difficult to prove.

Much more demonstrable causes of the beguins' turn toward heresy were the hostility that arose against them among the clergy; the role of the beguins' eschatological views; and the intervention of

Pope John XXII against Franciscan poverty after 1317. As often happened in the Middle Ages when groups of laypeople began to act "holier than the pope," the beguins quickly earned the suspicion and resentment of the clergy. Members of the clergy looked askance at the beguins because the latter were laypeople who wore habits in imitation of the regular orders and often behaved with greater piety than most clerics. Thus, as early as 1299 a Church council meeting at Béziers condemned beguins for violating a ban on new orders and for preaching without authorization. Similarly, in 1312 the Franciscans of Barcelona expressed their opposition to the presence of beguins in that city. Such protests neither stated that the beguins were doctrinal heretics nor served to make them such, but the antagonism of the clergy did have the effect of encouraging the beguins to feel more holy than ever.

Concurrently the beguins found confirmation of their sentiments that they were elected to suffer and to resist the attempts at discipline by the hierarchical Church in the eschatology they inherited from Peter Olivi and Arnald of Villanova. Both of these men had written that the world stood on the brink of cataclysmic change and that a chosen few who proclaimed and practiced the greatest poverty would be "witnesses" in an imminent struggle against Antichrist as well as heralds of a new age after Antichrist's death, when the world would be converted to a regime of evangelical perfection. The beguins considered themselves to be these "elect," and concluded that they were bound to be persecuted in the present but would certainly endure in the future because Providence was on their side.

Given the clergy's antagonism and the beguins' sense of mission, matters came quickly to a head in the years after 1317 when John XXII resolved to put an end to internal dissensions within the Franciscan order over the issue of poverty. The pope's intervention in Franciscan disputes at first had nothing directly to do with the beguins, but the beguins rallied to support the persecuted Franciscan upholders of rigorous poverty (known as "Spirituals"). When that happened, the beguins were persecuted in their turn, and were led by a dialectic of resistance and persecution into radical heresy.

The catalyst of these developments was the burning of four Franciscan Spirituals at Marseilles in 1318 for refusing to accept papal discipline. Outraged beguins believed that the four Spirituals were martyrs, and gathered relics from their remains. In the beguins' view John XXII had fallen into heresy by his actions, and all prelates installed after 1318 accordingly had no ecclesiastical power whatsoever. Some beguins went so far as to say that the pope was Antichrist and that the "carnal Church" was the Whore of Babylon, "drunk with the blood of martyrs." The response of John XXII and the Church hierarchy was to launch a series of inquisitions in southern France that reached their climax between 1319 and 1325. Many beguins chose death rather than submission, and the movement was wiped out by around 1330.

BIBLIOGRAPHY

Malcolm D. Lambert, *Medieval Heresy* (1977), 197–204; Gordon Leff, *Heresy in the Later Middle Ages,* 2 vols. (1967), I, 195–230; Raoul Manselli, *Spirituali e Beghuini in Provenza* (1959); William H. May, "The Confession of Prous Boneta, Heretic and Heresiarch," in *Essays in Medieval Life and Thought Presented in Honor of Austin P. Evans* (1955); Josep Perarnau, *L' "Alia informatio Beguinorum" d'Arnau de Vilanova* (1978); Walter L. Wakefield and Austin P. Evans, *Heresies of the High Middle Ages: Selected Sources, Translated and Annotated* (1969), 411–439.

ROBERT E. LERNER

[See also **Albigensians; Arnald of Villanova; Beguines and Beghards; Franciscans; Heresies, West European; John XXII; Peter Olivi.**]

BEIRUT (Arabic: *Bayrūt;* French: *Beyrouth*), city on the central Lebanese coast (now the capital of the Lebanese Republic). Though a town of great antiquity, it was during the Roman era that Beirut, then Berytus, rose to its greatest prominence in premodern times. Its port and central location on the eastern Mediterranean coast made it a natural focus for long-distance commerce and exchange, and by the first century it had become an important administrative center as well. Enormous sums were lavished on its public buildings and marketplaces, and the level of culture that accompanied this prosperity may be judged from the lofty reputation of the city's law school, founded in the third century.

Although it may have suffered somewhat from the general decline of urban life that beset the Hellenistic cities of the Near East in Byzantine times, Beirut in the sixth century was still resplendent enough for the historian Agathias to describe it as the "jewel of Phoenicia." All this was brought to an end, however, in July 551, when a violent earthquake (described in detail by Agathias, Malalas, the Pseudo-Dionysius, and the poet Joannes Barbucallus), accompanied by a great tsunami and a terrible fire, totally devastated the city. Efforts were made to restore Beirut to its earlier splendor, but with little success. When Nāṣir-i Khusraw visited the city in 1047, he found but a single arch surviving of the city's ancient edifices, the ruins of which littered the surrounding area.

It was thus a small urban center that the troops of Abū ᶜUbayda ibn al-Jarrāḥ occupied, apparently with little difficulty, in 635, during the Arab conquest of Syria. Nonetheless, Beirut never sank to insignificance, for its port gave it enduring strategic importance, as did its ease of access to iron from nearby mines and to timber from a pine forest to the south. Beirut flourished under the Umayyad caliphate because it served as the port for the imperial capital of Damascus, and the caliph al-Walīd ibn ᶜAbd al-Malik (Walīd I, 705–715) is said to have sung its praises in verse. A local silk industry was raised to prosperity, and new residents were moved in from Persia as part of the more general Umayyad practice of transferring populations *(nawāqil)*. The great Syrian religious scholar and jurist al-Awzāᶜī, whose reputation extended throughout the Islamic world, established himself in Beirut in late Umayyad times and remained the city's most famous son even after his death in 774.

With the fall of the Umayyad dynasty in 749, the urban centers of Syria all suffered, in varying degrees, the loss of imperial solicitude and maintenance. Beirut, for the strategic considerations mentioned above, probably fared better than most others. The Arab geographers of medieval times agree that it was fortified; European pilgrims speak favorably of it; and its history in this period attests to the continuing importance of its coastal position. The Byzantines attacked and captured it in 975, but shortly thereafter lost it to the Fatimids. The forces of the First Crusade bypassed Beirut on their way to Jerusalem in 1099, but returned in 1110, besieged the city, and captured it after a desperate defense (described in detail by William of Tyre). Beirut changed hands several times during the Crusades, and finally returned permanently to Muslim control in 1291.

Under the Mamluks and Ottomans, Beirut's history continued to be shaped by its role as a Mediterranean port. The long-established presence of an entrepreneurial Christian community, coupled with a European market for the region's products (particularly silk), attracted merchants from Italy and other European countries, and also made Beirut the object of European rivalries. Under the Lebanese emir Fakhr al-Dīn ibn Maᶜn (*ca.* 1591–1635), Beirut was particularly prosperous. The city remained small, however, because its dependence on its location and commercial connections made it inevitable that outbreaks of international or local strife should have a highly disruptive effect on its fortunes. In fact, only within the last century has Beirut been able to regain and surpass the levels of prosperity and culture it enjoyed in early medieval times.

BIBLIOGRAPHY

The history of medieval Beirut relies very heavily on a single source, Ṣāliḥ ibn Yaḥyā, *Taᵓrīkh Bayrūt,* Francis Hours and K. S. Salibi, eds. (1969). A good introduction is *Beirut: Crossroads of Cultures* (1970), with medievalist contributions in French; see also Guy Le Strange, *Palestine Under the Moslems* (1890), 408–410; Harvey Porter, *The History of Beirut* (1912), still useful but often mistaken; Louis Cheikho, *Bayrūt: Taᵓrīkhuhā wa-āthāruhā* (1925); René Dussaud, *Topographie historique de la Syrie* (1927), 58–60; Saïd Chehabe ed-Dine, *Géographie humaine de Beyrouth* (1960); Daᵓūd Kanᶜān, *Bayrūt fī l-taᵓrīkh* (1963); Nina Jidejian, *Beirut Through the Ages* (1973), with excellent bibliography.

LAWRENCE I. CONRAD

[See also **Crusades and Crusader States, 1095–1199; Lebanon; Umayyads.**]

BEKᶜA OPIZARI, the most renowned Georgian silversmith, active in the second half of the twelfth century in the monastery of Opiza. Three known works are the following: (1) The book cover of the Tskarostᶜavi Gospels (Institute of Manuscripts Tbilisi), commissioned by Ioane, bishop of Tbetᶜi. For this work, which was completed in 1195, Bekᶜa received 23 "drahma." The cover consists of two gilded silver plates executed in repoussé technique and embellished with precious stones. (2) The frame of the Anchiskᵓati Icon, commissioned by the bishop of Antsha. (3) A book cover of the Antsha Gospels (not preserved).

BIBLIOGRAPHY

Shalva Amiranashvili, *Beka Opizari* (1956), in Georgian; Giorgi Tshubinashvili, *Gruzinskoe Čekannoe Iskusstvo* (1959), 563–570.

WACHTANG DJOBADZE

[See also **Georgian Art and Architecture.**]

BELISARIOS (*ca.* 505–565), Byzantine general. After serving in the imperial guard, he was commander on the Persian front in 526 and was the victor at Dara in 530. He helped to crush the Nika riot at Constantinople in 532; then, as commander of a seaborne expedition against Vandals in 533, won decisive victories at Decimum and Tricamarum, and recovered Africa for Justinian. Belisarios commanded an expedition against the Ostrogoths in 535; took Rome in December 536; defended Rome against Gothic siege in 537–538; captured Ravenna in 540; and conquered the southeast corner of Spain in 554. He was commander of the eastern front in 541. Belisarios returned to Italy in 544, and remained there for four years. He defeated the Huns near Constantinople in 559. Despite his record, he was under suspicion of conspiracy against Justinian in 562–563. Belisarios was a brilliant commander, unshakably loyal to Justinian. His wife was Antonina, a close friend of Empress Theodora.

BIBLIOGRAPHY

L. M. Chaussin, *Belisaire* (1957); Berthold Rubin, *Das Zeitalter Justinians,* I (1960); J. L. Teall, "Barbarians in Justinian's Armies," in *Speculum,* **40** (1965).

ROBERT BROWNING

[See also **Byzantine Empire, 330–1025; Justinian I.**]

BELLINI, JACOPO (late 14th c.–1470), artist, was born at Venice. He was the father of Gentile and Giovanni Bellini and the father-in-law of Andrea Mantegna. His earliest certain recorded activity dates from 1430 at Padua. Jacopo's debt to his teacher Gentile da Fabriano was acknowledged in a Crucifixion fresco of 1436 formerly in the cathedral of Verona. It is possible that he became a pupil of Gentile's while the latter was working in Venice between 1408 and 1412, and probable that he accompanied Gentile to Florence in 1423. At Ferrara in 1441, Jacopo was acclaimed the winner of a competition for a portrait, now lost, of Lionello d'Este.

In the literature of his time Jacopo is praised as a teacher, portraitist, and painter of narrative cycles, and is recognized for his accomplishments in perspective. His known paintings consist of a few religious subjects, including the signed *Madonna and Child* now in the Accademia at Venice, and numerous attributions. Two albums of his drawings, one in the Louvre and the other in the British Museum, together form the most extensive collection of fifteenth-century drawings to survive intact. They provide evidence of Jacopo's roots in Paduan-Venetian tradition in the context of a rich variety of experimental essays reflecting his debt to Tuscan art as well as of his interests in secular subject matter and the secularization of religious iconography.

BIBLIOGRAPHY

Lionello Venturi, *Le origini della pittura veneziana 1300–1500* (1907), 99–137; Corrado Ricci, *Iacopo Bellini e i suoi libri di disegni,* 2 vols. (1908); Victor Goloubew, *Les dessins de Jacopo Bellini,* 2 vols. (1908–1912); Hans Tietze and Erica Tietze-Conrat, *The Drawings of the Venetian Painters in the 15th and 16th Centuries,* I (1944), 94–115; Marcel Röthlisberger, "Nuovi aspetti dei disegni di Jacopo Bellini," in *Critica d'arte,* **13–14** (1956); Christiane L. Joost-Gaugier, ed., *Jacopo Bellini: Selected Drawings* (1980).

CHRISTIANE L. JOOST-GAUGIER

[See also **Gentile da Fabriano.**]

BELLS. The ringing of bells in the Middle Ages provided the primary means for the organization of daily activity and the transmission of news and information to a largely illiterate population. Bells also served a variety of ceremonial purposes. The earliest descriptions of the use of bells in conjunction with Christian ritual date from the seventh century, although bell ringing is reported by Gregory of Tours (*ca.* 585), and was probably known in parts of Europe by the middle of the fifth century. Paulinus, bishop of Nola (in Campania, Italy), has traditionally been credited with the introduction of bells into European churches and cloisters (*ca.* 400). He does not, however, refer to their use in any of his writings. The practice more likely originated in Russia, and was exported across northern Europe to the British Isles in the second half of the sixth century.

The procedure of marking the canonical hours by the ringing of a bell is believed to have been officially instituted by Pope Sabinius (604–606), and is first described in an *ordo romanus* of the seventh century. The aural division of the liturgical day furnished the model for the use of bells in large town clocks of the later Middle Ages. In addition to sounding the prayer hours, bells were used to announce meals and other assemblies of the monastic community. Among the monastic orders the Benedictines displayed the greatest interest in the use of bells. One of the earliest references to the use of *signa* (large bells) occurs in the seventh-century rules of the order. Benedictine bell foundries are recorded as early as the eighth century. The most significant early work to discuss the technical aspects of bells and bell casting, the tenth-century *Schedula diversarum artium,* was written by Theophilus, a Benedictine monk. Extant bells from the period that conform to his descriptions are known as Theophilus bells.

Small bells *(tintinnabula)* were often used as ornaments on ecclesiastical vestments, a custom derived from the ancient belief that the sound of small bells hung on sacrificial animals offered protection against evil spirits. The tolling of the passing bell, customary in Christian ritual since the seventh century, was thought to afford similar protection to the souls of the recently deceased as they journeyed toward the afterlife. Beginning in the eighth century, the ringing of a bell was included as part of the solemn ritual of excommunication (performed with bell, book, and candle), and symbolized the public nature of the act.

By the end of the tenth century, bells had been introduced into the liturgy proper. A small bell was rung three times at the Sanctus, and another was rung for the elevation of the Host. The sounding of a public bell to prompt the faithful to recite the *Ave Maria* was officially instituted by Pope Urban II (1088–1099), and again by Gregory IX (1227–1241). The recitation of the threefold *Ave Maria,* signaled by the ringing of the so-called Angelus bell, was called for in papal and royal documents throughout the Middle Ages, and was finally codified (the prayer being recited thrice on three occasions daily) by King Louis XI of France in 1472. The association of bells with the *Ave Maria* frequently inspired bell founders to engrave the Virgin's name on their bells.

Bells were often consecrated and "baptized" with the name of a saint, usually the founder or patron of the religious institution for which the bell was made. Such a bell was treated with particular reverence, since it was believed to possess the mystical power of its saintly patron to punish or heal. The famous tenth-century bell named for St. Guthlac was said to cure headaches. Oaths sworn upon a saint's bell were considered more binding than those sworn upon the Gospels, owing to the miraculous ability of the bell to expose perjurers (by causing their faces to contort).

The tenth and eleventh centuries witnessed a tendency toward the use of multiple bells in Continental churches, with some cathedrals in France and the Low Countries boasting as many as twelve bells in a single tower. Multiple bells appeared with increasing frequency in England beginning in the twelfth century, probably as a result of French influence. The thirteenth century was marked by a general increase in the size of individual bells, a trend that reached its culmination in the great bells of the fifteenth century (for example, the Maria Gloriosa of Erfurt, cast in 1497). The introduction of cannon into fifteenth-century warfare signaled a period of improved social and financial status for bell founders, the only metalworkers experienced enough in the casting of large pieces to produce the new weapons.

In the secular realm bells represented order and temporal power. King Athelstan of England declared in 926 that possession of a bell tower (symbolizing the union of worldly power and divine right) should be a requirement for thanedom. In France and Germany the boundary of a lord's domain was often determined by the distance at which the manorial bell could be heard. The allocation of local bell-ringing rights was frequently a matter of legal contention.

In the towns, bells conveyed important information to citizens rapidly and simply. They marked the beginning and end of the workday, the opening and closing of the city gates, the opening of the market, the sale of particular items, the opening and closing of taverns, and they announced general assemblies and council meetings. The particular meaning was indicated by the number of rings or, in the case of multiple bells, a sequence of large and small bells. Larger bells were used as alarms to warn of storms, enemy attack, danger of fire, and approaching beasts of prey. Misuse of the alarm bell was severely punished by law. Contemporary documents usually referred to bells by their function: market bell, sleep bell, fish bell, enemy bell, death bell.

Bell ringers were usually drawn from the lower classes. The position entailed certain material benefits, such as exemption from military service and provision of free food and clothing. The bell ringer's duties were often extended to include occasional service as town crier or as a singer in the local lord's chapel on feast days.

BIBLIOGRAPHY

For complete bibliographies including secondary literature and historical sources, see J. Smits van Waesberghe, ed., *Cymbala: Bells in the Middle Ages* (1951), the most exhaustive study of the theoretical aspects of medieval campanology available. See also his "Cymbala," in *Die Musik in Geschichte und Gegenwart,* **2** (1952); Doris Stockmann, "Die Glocke im Profangebrauch des Spätmittelalters," in *Studia instrumentorum musicae popularis,* III (1974), provides many valuable references to French and German documentary material bearing on the legal and social implications of the use of bells in the Middle Ages. For more general historical accounts see John Camp, *Bell Ringing* (1974); John J. Raven, *The Bells of England* (1906).

MICHAEL P. LONG

[See also **Canonical Hours; Metalworking; Musical Instruments.**]

BEMA, Greek for speaker's platform. The term is applied to the chancel, usually raised, in early Christian and Byzantine churches. The bema often projected into the nave from the apsidal end of the church; it was reserved for the clergy and contained the altar. Usually the bema was curtained off, enclosed by parapets, or, in Byzantine churches, separated from the nave by an iconostasis. In synagogues the bema is the elevated pulpit.

LESLIE BRUBAKER

BENEDETTO ANTELAMI (*fl.* 1150–*ca.* 1233), sculptor and architect. The most important Italian sculptor before Nicola Pisano, Benedetto's oeuvre is reconstructed on the basis of his signed *Deposition* relief from a pulpit in Parma Cathedral (1178). His grave, monumental, and powerfully emotional style finds its greatest expression in the series of relief sculptures narrating Old and New Testament scenes and Labors of the Months on the portals of the Parma Baptistery, begun in 1196. The systematic union of sculpture and architecture has led scholars to conclude that Benedetto was responsible for the baptistery's overall design. The Cathedral of Borgo San Donnino (now Fidenza) is also attributed to Benedetto, although there is disagreement over his direct participation.

BIBLIOGRAPHY

Géza de Frankovitch, *Benedetto Antelami, architetto e scultore e l'arte del suo tempo,* 2 vols. (1952); Charles R. Morey, *Mediaeval Art* (1942), 220ff.; A. Kingsley Porter, "The Development of Sculpture in Lombardy in the Twelfth Century," in *American Journal of Archaeology,* **19** (1915).

ADELHEID M. GEALT

BENEDICAMUS DOMINO ("Let us bless the Lord"), the dismissal formula of each of the daily offices except matins, and of the Mass, in place of *Ite, missa est,* when the Gloria was not sung (during Advent, from Septuagesima until Easter), on the vigils of Easter and Pentecost, and when the Mass was followed by a procession (as on Maundy Thursday and the midnight Mass at Christmas). As in the *Ite, missa est,* the chorus makes the reply *Deo gratias* to the solo statement *Benedicamus Domino,* repeating the melody. Use of the formula is documented in the Gallican church about 800, and from about 1000 it had general currency in the Roman rite.

Some extant melodies for the *Benedicamus Domino* are original, while others are phrases borrowed from liturgical melodies, usually kyries or responsories. The source melody was often proper to the day for which the *Benedicamus Domino* was intended.

In the eleventh century, textual and musical tropes were added to the formula in Aquitaine for use on important feasts. By 1100 the tropes took the form of a rhymed metrical *versus* whose final line included a version of the formula and whose music was newly composed. From about 1100, polyphonic settings of the untroped formula, using melodies of the *Benedicamus Domino* and new melodies in their lower voices, and of the *Benedicamus Domino versus* appear. The double-texted *Benedicamus Domino versus,* wherein the formula is sung in the lower voice, and a *versus* in the upper, was also cultivated in Aquitaine. Pieces of these types occur in the repertories of Santiago de Compostela (*ca.* 1140), Notre Dame de Paris (*ca.* 1150–1250), and Las Huelgas at Burgos (*ca.* 1300). In the fourteenth century, polyphonic settings of the formula and its substitutes were common in Italy, Germany, and England, but had slipped from popularity in France.

BIBLIOGRAPHY

The best discussion of the liturgical use of *Benedicamus Domino* and its polyphonic settings is Barbara Marion Barclay, "The Medieval Repertory of Polyphonic Untroped Benedicamus Domino Settings" (Ph.D. diss., U.C.L.A., 1977). For tropes of and substitutes for the formula, see Léon Gautier, *Histoire de la poésie liturgique au moyen âge: Les tropes* (1886), 171–173; and Jacques Chailley, *L'école musicale de Saint Martial de Limoges* (1960), 275–285.

JAMES GRIER

[See also **Music, Liturgical; Tropes.**]

BENEDICT BISCOP, ST. (*b.* before 630). Biscop Baducing, who later assumed the cognomen Benedict, an Anglo-Saxon nobleman and thane of King Oswiu (or Oswy), was born in Northumbria. He determined to renounce the world about 652, and made the first of six pilgrimages to Rome. There and at Lérins he became acquainted with monastic observance and Roman liturgical practice, and acquired books, relics, and art objects. In 674 he founded the monastery of Wearmouth and, about 681, its sister abbey of Jarrow. Benedict was largely responsible for the Northumbrian cultural renaissance that culminated in the work of Bede, a monk of Jarrow.

BIBLIOGRAPHY

Source. Clinton Albertson, *Anglo-Saxon Saints and Heroes* (1967), 221–271.

Literature. Peter Hunter Blair, *The World of Bede* (1971); Gerald Bonner, ed., *Famulus Christi: Essays in Commemoration of the Thirteenth Centenary of the Birth of the Venerable Bede* (1976).

CLAUDE J. PEIFER, O.S.B.

[See also **Bede; England, Anglo-Saxon.**]

BENEDICT OF ANIANE (*ca.* 750–821). The Visigoth Witiza, called Benedict, abbot of the monastery of Aniane in southern France, is known primarily for the monastic reform that he accomplished along with Louis the Pious—a reform that gave official sanction to the Benedictine Rule, first in Aquitaine and later throughout the Carolingian Empire. He also played an important role in the development of the liturgy; he is undoubtedly the true author of the Supplement to the Gregorian sacramentary, often attributed to Alcuin.

BIBLIOGRAPHY

Philibert Schmitz, "Benoît d'Aniane," in *Dictionnaire d'histoire et de géographie ecclésiastiques,* VIII (1935), with bibliography; Jean Deshusses, "Le supplément au sacramentaire grégorien: Alcuin ou saint Benoît d'Aniane?" in *Archiv für Liturgiewissenschaft,* 9 (1965).

JEAN DESHUSSES, O.S.B.

[See also **Benedictines.**]

BENEDICT OF NURSIA, ST. (*fl.* first half sixth c.), monk and abbot, venerated since the eighth century as patriarch of Western monasticism. Benedict's influence depends entirely on the monastic rule attributed to him: he was not the founder of a religious order in the modern sense, but author of a document that became universally adopted, and hence shaped the form of monastic life throughout the Western church down to the present.

Benedict is not mentioned by any contemporary until the end of the sixth century, and left no written work in which he identifies himself. A generation after Benedict's death, Pope Gregory the Great wrote an account of his life and miracles that occupies the entire second book of his *Dialogues.* He identifies his sources as four abbots, all of whom had access to traditions about Benedict and at least two of whom must have known him personally. Gregory was not concerned with producing a biography, but with telling edifying stories to illustrate his moral teaching. Nevertheless, there is no serious reason to doubt the reliability of the basic outline of Benedict's career as described in the *Dialogues.*

Gregory tells of a visit to Benedict by the Gothic leader Totila (*d.* 552), which probably took place in 546. While Benedict's death is usually dated 547, he may have lived for up to another decade. The traditional dating of his birth in 480 is an approximation arrived at by counting backward from his death.

Benedict was from a prosperous family in the region of Nursia (now Norcia), near Spoleto in the mountains northeast of Rome. Nothing is known of his early life except that as a youth he was sent to Rome for study. Disillusioned by the licentiousness of the city, he felt a call to the monastic life and retired to the valley of the Anio, some seventy-five kilometers east of Rome. Assisted by a monk of a nearby monastery named Romanus, he spent three years in solitude in a cave at Subiaco. After an abortive attempt at governing a community of unruly monks at nearby Vicovaro, he returned to Subiaco, where he was joined by numerous companions, whom he grouped into twelve small colonies loosely organized under his overall direction.

After a stay of unknown length at Subiaco, Benedict migrated with some of his monks to Monte Cassino, a prominent hill more than 500 meters high, which towers above the ancient town of Cassinum, halfway between Rome and Naples. Here he established a single fully cenobitic monastery, preached the Gospel to the country people in order to purge them of vestigial paganism, and became a holy man of widespread renown in the region. People looked to him for guidance and assistance during the chaotic period of the Gothic War (535–553).

Benedict sent monks to found one other monastery, near Terracina. His sister, Scholastica, a consecrated virgin who visited him once a year, preceded him in death and was buried at Monte Cassino, in the same tomb in which he was subsequently laid. Before his death Benedict predicted the destruction of his monastery, though without loss of life; Gregory observes that this prophecy was fulfilled during the Lombard invasion.

Gregory testifies that Benedict wrote a rule "remarkable for its discernment and clarity of language." Through the centuries it has been assumed that the rule to which Gregory refers is the same document that has come down to us under the name *Regula sancti Benedicti* (RB), although Gregory does not identify the rule he has in mind or cite it anywhere in the *Dialogues.* He does cite it once elsewhere (*Commentary on 1 Kings,* 4:70, citing RB 58), though without naming the author. The RB is attributed to Benedict by most of the manuscript tradition, which goes back to the eighth century. Since it was never attributed to anyone else, Benedict's authorship was scarcely questioned until recent times.

In 1938, Dom Augustin Genestout advanced the thesis that the RB is dependent on the *Regula magistri* (RM), a long, anonymous rule of disputed provenance that contains almost all of the prologue and first seven chapters of the RB within its more ample introductory material and chapters 1–10. There followed a vigorous debate in which various conflicting views were presented, some even denying Benedict's authorship of the RB and relegating it to the seventh century. It is now widely agreed, however, that the RB is indeed a work of the mid sixth century, and that its traditional attribution to Benedict is highly plausible, even if incapable of apodictic proof. It is to be assigned to his mature years at Monte Cassino, completed probably in the 540's. He seems to have borrowed extensively from the RM, which appears to be only slightly earlier. Some have suggested that the RM may even be the work of Benedict, reflecting an earlier stage of his thought and experience.

The RB is a brief document of some thirteen thousand words, consisting of a prologue, seventy-two chapters, and an epilogue. It contains both theoretical teaching to expound the principles of monastic life and practical directives to regulate the life of the community. Stages in its growth can be discerned: chapters 67–72 are an appendix added after the original ending at 66.8, and sections such as the liturgical code (8–18) and penitential code (23–30) may have existed separately before being incorporated into the Rule.

While the religious wisdom of Benedict appears throughout the Rule, even in very prosaic contexts, his doctrine is elaborated principally in 1–7. This is the section that is most closely parallel to the RM (and dependent on it, in the view of most scholars), yet even here Benedict displays subtle but significant differences in what he adds or omits. The key to his cenobitism is the place he assigns to the abbot (2; 64): he is father and teacher of the monks with a personal relationship to each, a sacramental of Christ's presence among them; simultaneously he is the administrator of all the affairs of the community, both spiritual and temporal. While the RB confers awesome responsibility on the abbot, it is frankly conscious of his human weakness, as well as that of the monks. He is not an autocrat, but must constantly seek to discern the will of God, which may become known to him through the counsel of the monks (3).

The spiritual program of the monk is represented by the "tools for good works" (4), especially the three characteristic monastic virtues of obedience, silence, and humility (5–7). The remaining chapters of the RB regulate almost every aspect of the life of the monks: sleep (22), meals (39–41), clothing (55), work (48), material possessions (32–34), care for the sick and weak (36–37), travel (50–51; 67), guests (53), gifts (54), admission and training of members (58–61), priests (62).

Like most ancient monastic rules, the RB was written to govern the life of the particular monastery for which it was intended. However, a few references to such things as climatic differences show that its author considered the possibility of wider usage. The Rule's sole intent was to shape a life according to the Gospel; it did not envisage any apostolic or cultural purpose, but its insistence that guests be received as Christ led to extensive works of charity. Likewise, the fact that all monks had to learn to read and to spend much of their time in reading indirectly resulted in an emphasis on education and the growth of a literary culture that equipped the monasteries to become repositories of learning. Benedict could scarcely have foreseen this.

Although his work betrays little of the erudition one finds in Cassiodorus, Benedict had profoundly assimilated another kind of culture, simpler and more religious, from lifelong immersion in the Bible and the Church Fathers. He wished to be a faithful echo of monastic tradition. The index of sources to the RB is an impressive list, even if he did not know all these works at first hand. His chief debt was to the monastic tradition of Egypt, as mediated to the West chiefly by John Cassian. The influence of Augustine on Benedict was greater than the number of cases of strict literary dependence might suggest. The balance and sanity of the RB are largely due to the happy combination of these two diverse strains of tradition.

While the RB's eventual supremacy was due in part to political factors in Carolingian times, the decisive reason for its survival was its intrinsic value. Tradition has echoed Pope Gregory in singling out *discretio* as its outstanding quality. Benedict combined firmness of principle with a willingness to adapt to contingent possibilities. He shows remarkable compassion for weakness and failure, yet upholds the loftiest ideal. He respects human freedom and the complexity of reality. The RB is filled with trenchant, memorable phrases that enshrine important principles, but it leaves details to the improvisation of the abbot. For this reason it remains viable, whereas most other rules of its time now appear anachronistic.

The early diffusion of the RB is obscure; there are no sixth-century references to it aside from Gregory, though it may have been known to Columban (*d.* 615). In the seventh century it was propagated in Gaul chiefly by the Celtic monasteries; there it was combined with the *Rule of Columban* in the observance called *regula mixta.* In England it is first mentioned in Northumberland, where it may have been introduced by Wilfrid around 660. There is no evidence that Augustine brought it to Canterbury.

In the eighth century the Anglo-Saxon missionary monks carried the RB with them to the Continent. Boniface made it the basis of his reform of the Frankish monasteries, and Charlemagne saw it as a means of achieving uniformity of observance. It was imposed on all monasteries of the empire by Benedict of Aniane, on the authority of Louis the Pious, at the Synod of Aachen (816–817). While this regime was short-lived, the RB retained its role in the subsequent reform movements that began with the foundation of Cluny in 910. Almost all the orders that grew up in the High Middle Ages adopted the RB, so that the period from 800 to 1200 is known as "the Benedictine centuries." Since then it has been practically the only rule used in the West.

Because of its wide use in monasteries, the RB was copied more often than any other text except the Bible, and hundreds of manuscripts are still extant. Serious critical study of the text began only in the late nineteenth century; the work of Ludwig Traube was decisive for the distinction of text types into "pure" and "interpolated." The pure text is best represented by the ninth-century codex 914 of St. Gall, a lineal descendant of Charlemagne's copy of a Monte Cassino codex believed at the time to be the autograph. The Oxford codex Hatton 48, copied in England around 750, is the oldest manuscript extant, but it represents the interpolated text. The origin of this recension is obscure, but it apparently goes back to sixth-century Italy. More than 1,200 printed editions have appeared since the editio princeps (Venice, 1489).

The earliest evidence for a cult of St. Benedict is from the eighth century. He was venerated at Monte Cassino after its restoration in 720, and his tomb there was a place of pilgrimage, as we know from some verses by a certain Mark, and from the earliest Cassinese calendars and martyrologies, which place his feast on 21 March. Another tradition resting upon an eighth-century document claims that his relics were removed shortly before 700 and taken to the abbey of Fleury in France. The feast of this translation, 11 July, also dates from the eighth century. Despite extensive scientific studies in recent decades, it has proved impossible to verify the authenticity of either set of relics. In 1964, Pope Paul VI declared St. Benedict the patron of Europe.

The earliest extant representations of St. Benedict are frescoes in the Catacomb of Hermes at Rome (eighth or ninth century) and in the lower Church of St. Chrysogonus in Trastevere (ninth or tenth century); then miniatures in Cassinese manuscripts of the tenth and eleventh centuries. In these early portraits he is depicted as rather youthful, and either beardless or with a closely cropped beard. The now-familiar representation of him as an aged patriarch with a long beard dates from the late Middle Ages.

BIBLIOGRAPHY

Sources. Adalbert de Vogüé and P. Antin, *Grégoire le Grand: Dialogues,* 3 vols. (1978–1980), English trans. by Odo J. Zimmerman, *St. Gregory the Great: Dialogues* (1959); critical text of RB—Rudolphus Hanslik, *Benedicti regula* (1960, rev. ed., 1977), English trans. with much explanatory material and bibliography, Timothy Fry, ed., *RB 1980: The Rule of St. Benedict in Latin and English with Notes* (1981).

Studies. Lives—Justin McCann, *St. Benedict* (1937, repr. 1958); Ildefonso Schuster, *St. Benedict and His Times* (1951). Commentaries—the most exhaustive work on the RB is Adalbert de Vogüé and Jean Neufville, *La Règle de saint Benoît,* 6 vols. (1971–1972), including introduction, critical text by J. Neufville, manuscript readings, and historical and critical commentary, to be used with vol. VII, *Commentaire doctrinal et spirituel* (1977), and *La communauté et l'abbé dans la Règle de saint Benoît* (1961). See also Paul Delatte, *The Rule of St. Benedict: A Commentary* (1921); Ildefons Herwegen, *Sinn und Geist der Benediktinerregel* (1944); García Colombás and Iñaki Aranguren, *La Regla de San Benito* (1979).

Bibliographies. Bernd Jaspert, "Regula Magistri, Regula Benedicti: Bibliographie ihrer Erforschung 1938–1970," in *Studia monastica,* **13** (1971); Giuseppe Turbessi, *Ascetismo e monachesimo in S. Benedetto* (1965); periodically in *Regulae Benedicti studia* (Hildesheim).

CLAUDE J. PEIFER, O.S.B.

[See also **Benedict of Aniane; Benedictine Rule; Benedictines; Cassian, John; Gregory I, the Great, Pope; Monasticism, Origins; Monte Cassino.**]

BENEDICTINE RULE, a normative text written by St. Benedict of Nursia for use by cenobites. Its principal concerns are the government, the spiritual life, and the daily life of the monastery. It concludes by recalling the goal to be attained: union with God.

The Rule reflects Benedict's very humane conception of monasticism—in constrast with Eastern asceticism, for example. It does not impose austerity, and substitutes the authority of a code of permanent laws for the absolute will of the superior. The Benedictine Rule states the fundamental constitutive principles that can be adapted, in detail, to variable conditions of time and place.

The autograph copy disappeared in a fire in 896. All the manuscripts are one of three types: pure text (true copies, such as St. Gall MS 914), interpolated text (first appeared in the sixth century, such as Oxford, Bodleian Library, MS Hatton 48, *ca.* 700), and mixed text or *textus receptus* (first appeared in the eighth century, in Paul the Deacon).

BIBLIOGRAPHY

Anselmo Albareda, *Bibliografía de la Regla Benedictina* (1933). Current bibliographies and reports appear in *Revue Bénédictine, Revue Mabillon, Studien und Mitteilungen zur Geschichte des Benediktiner-Ordens und seiner Zweige,* and *Benedictina.*

An edition of the Rule is Adalbert de Vogüé and Jean Neufville, *La règle de St. Benoît,* 6 vols. (1971–1972), with a translation, a commentary, and critical apparatus. On the *Regula Benedicti-Regula Magistri* controversy, see Bernd Jaspert, *Die Regula Benedicti-Regula Magistri Kontroverse* (1975), with comprehensive bibliography.

ALAIN J. STOCLET

[See also **Benedict of Nursia, St.; Benedictines.**]

BENEDICTINES, the oldest and the premier form of organized monastic life in the Western church and the one from which all religious orders subsequently derived. The term "Benedictine" seems to have been coined by Giovanni Bona, abbot general of the Cistercian Order (*d.* 1674); it rarely appears before the seventeenth century. In the Middle Ages the Benedictines were called "black monks" because of the color of their habit, which distinguished them from other monks, such as the Cistercians, who wore white.

Benedictine life has always been based on two things: first and fundamentally, the Rule of St. Benedict (mid sixth century), which represents the accumulated wisdom of earlier centuries of monastic experience and which served as the constitution of Benedict's monastery at Monte Cassino; and second, the body of observances or customs, primarily interpretations of the Rule, that grew up at a particular monastery and gradually came to have the force of law for that house. Benedict legislated for a cenobitic community of laymen, governed benevolently by an abbot, a family whose purpose was the glorification of God and the salvation of the individual monk. Monastic profession, made after a year's novitiate or probation, included three vows—stability, the reformation of life, and obedience—that consecrated

BENEDICTINES

the monk to God. Benedictine life meant a routine dedicated to prayer and work, and characterized by moderation in all things; this moderation and a certain flexibility in the interpretation of the Rule distinguished the Benedictine from other forms of monastic life. Beyond the search for God, Benedictine life had no specific secondary goal.

Around 577 the Lombards sacked Monte Cassino and the monks fled to Rome, taking their Rule. From Rome in 596, Pope Gregory I sent the monk Augustine to convert Anglo-Saxon England, from which in the seventh and eighth centuries zealous monk missionaries such as Willibrord and Boniface evangelized the European continent. Among the many monasteries that later acquired fame, this period witnessed the foundation of Fleury (631), St. Ouen of Rouen (649), St. Denis of Paris (650), and Corbie (657) in France; of Canterbury (601), Peterborough (664), Wearmouth (674), and St. Albans (790) in England; of Echternach (708), Reichenau (724), Fulda (744), and St. Gall (750) in German lands; and of Bobbio (612), Farfa (restored 690), San Vincenzo at Volturno (703), San Salvatore (735), and St. Paul-Outside-the-Walls (restored 740) in Italy.

As to England and Germany, so to eastern Europe monasticism brought Christianity and classical culture: to Bohemia in the late tenth century; to Hungary through the support of King Stephen (*d.* 1038); and to Poland, where after 1050 numerous monasteries, including Tyniec near Kraków, were founded.

At the same time the broad river of Benedictinism gradually absorbed the three currents of monastic expression flowing through France and the British Isles: the stream in western Gaul associated with St. Martin of Tours (*d.* 397) and characterized by eremitical elements; the tide emanating from Lérins, widespread in the Rhone valley and manifested by the severe asceticism of Eastern monasticism; and the Celtic monasticism of Christian Ireland and Britain, which had a strongly anchoritic and penitential flavor. Because of its intrinsic common sense and broad humanity; through the support of popes, the emperors Charlemagne and Louis the Pious; and above all because of the work of the dynamic Boniface, by about 800, Benedict's Rule for Monks, as it was called, had replaced all other monastic codes in Italy, Britain, France, and the German Empire.

St. Benedict intended that the monk's day be oriented around the liturgy, the *opus Dei* (work of God), to which nothing ought to be preferred (ch. 43). The liturgical code was composed of the night office (vigils) and the seven day offices (lauds, prime, tierce, sext, none, vespers, and compline), as advised in Psalm 118 (119):147, 164. Although the offices changed slightly according to the season of the year, each office involved the recitation of psalms with refrains and versicles punctuated by silent prayer, a hymn, readings from the Old and New Testaments, and patristic commentaries on the Scriptures. The sixth-century practice was to recite the entire psalter (150 psalms) within a week's time. Gradually, between the seventh and eleventh centuries, the liturgy assumed new functions.

The spiritual goal of salvation for the individual monk yielded to the public and penitential needs of medieval society. People looked on the monks as spiritual soldiers who, through their prayers, fought important battles against the community's enemies; they believed that the temporal security of their societies and the eternal welfare of lay individuals depended on the prayers and penances of the monks. The *opus Dei* also fulfilled penitential obligations imposed on lay people. Penances were laid for all kinds of sins, and until satisfaction had been made, the sinner could not expect salvation. The monks, acting as substitutes, performed the penances due in their liturgical prayers.

Thus the number of prayers, offices, and chants multiplied. In the ninth century the practice of reciting the fifteen gradual psalms was introduced by Benedict of Aniane, and this observance spread throughout the Carolingian world. In the tenth century the English monastic movement associated with St. Dunstan and St. Ethelwold added to the liturgy the seven penitential psalms before the night office, as well as special prayers for the royal family in the morning. At Christ Church, Canterbury, in the time of Lanfranc (*d.* 1089), psalms for the royal family, a solemn community Mass, and vespers for the dead, all in addition to the regular liturgy, dominated the routine of the monastery.

At the end of the eleventh century, the abbey of Cluny, with its rich and elaborate ceremonial, represented the highest spiritual ideal of the Christian life. Describing his visit there in 1063, Peter Damian wrote, "For so great an amount of time was consumed in the continuous execution of the services of the house, and so great was the constant pressure of the Divine Office, that even in the great heat of summer, scarcely a half-hour through the entire day was free in which the brethren could speak together in the cloister." Virtually all of the monks' time was devoted to the work of God.

St. Benedict planned the monastery as a self-sufficient socioeconomic unit "so constructed that within it all the necessities, such as water, mill, and garden are contained, and the various crafts are practiced. Then there will be no need for the monks to roam outside, because this is not at all good for their souls" (ch. 66). Initially this conception suited the dangerous and localized conditions of the times. The gradual feudalization of Europe between the eighth and eleventh centuries, however, inextricably involved the Benedictines in all aspects of Western culture. The monasteries came to fulfill broad social functions.

As the Rule had anticipated (chs. 58–60), recruits to the Benedictine life came primarily from three groups: older, mature men; the clergy; and children given by their parents to the monasteries as oblates. Monasteries satisfied family and career needs in medieval society: they provided honorable, secure, and congenial life-styles for the children of noble families. From the seventh century the majority of monks were recruited from the military-aristocratic classes, frequently from the younger sons of the lesser nobility. While the Rule predicted the entrance of children of the poor (ch. 59), after about 1000 the dowries required for admittance, royal legislation, and aristocratic opposition tended to exclude members of the servile classes.

The size of monastic population varied with time and place. In the Carolingian period, while a few houses such as St. Riquier and Corbie had perhaps 300 monks, and Fulda 200, more typical numbers for the larger abbeys ranged between 70 and 150. About 1070–1130, when Benedictine expansion reached its peak, Cluny counted 300 monks and the greater houses, such as St. Wandrille, St. Albans, and Westminster, had between 80 and 120. In every age the hundreds of small priories across Europe had only six to fifteen monks. The number of lay brothers and domestic servants, who frequently equaled at least half the number of choir monks, swelled the total population of monastic establishments. After 1200 numbers tended to decline.

In return for the gifts of land and other properties for the support of established houses and the foundation of new ones, monasteries became the feudal vassals of kings and great lords. In frontier and disputed territories, monasteries served as politically stabilizing influences. At the same time, lay authorities came to participate in the selection of abbots. While Benedict had prescribed that except in cases of grave disorder, the community of monks should have complete jurisdiction in the election of their abbot (ch. 64), by the ninth century laymen exercised enormous influence. By direct appointment, by choosing from the monastery's nominees, or by their physical presence at the chapter (meeting) that chose the abbot, lay persons sought to protect and advance their military or financial or administrative interests. Blood relationships between monks and nobles, feudal contracts, and the pitiful conditions of society compelled the monks to perform a wide variety of functions for civil authorities, ecclesiastical officials, and lay people.

Thus, Benedictines served as royal advisers and as the regents of kingdoms—Lanfranc of Bec and Suger of St. Denis; as scribes, obviously, and as treasury or financial officials—Alcuin of York, abbot of St. Martin of Tours in the eighth–ninth centuries; as leaders of troops on military campaigns—Odo of Corbie in the eighth century, Gauzlin of Jumièges, whom Louis III commissioned in 880 to defend the entire West Frankish kingdom against the Norman invaders, Aethelwig of Evesham in the eleventh century; as royal judges in the civil courts—Einhard of St. Bavo in Ghent in the ninth century, Samson of Bury St. Edmund's in the late twelfth century, Simon of Reading in the thirteenth century; as physicians and teachers of medicine—Constantine "the African" of Monte Cassino, the nun Hildegard of Rupertsberg who treated the emperor Frederick Barbarossa, and Robert de Veneys, who advised Henry II of England; as architects or master masons—William of Volpiano, abbot of St. Bénigne-de-Dijon, and Desiderius of Monte Cassino, whose buildings greatly influenced Hugh of Cluny.

After the Norman Conquest the feudalization of the English church meant that monasteries had to provide military contingents for the "national" levy. In 1160, Peterborough, for example, owed the service of sixty knights; Glastonbury, forty; and Hyde, twenty. Monks, as feudal lords, sat and exercised political influence in royal councils and parliaments. The financial burdens connected with all these public duties fell upon the monasteries themselves. The successful performance of many of these activities rested upon some kind of formal education.

St. Benedict called his monastery "a school for the Lord's service" (prologue), and from his entirely spiritual conception there gradually evolved schools within monasteries whose practical purpose was the education both of the young monks and of children of the local nobility. Between about 600 and 1000, the period that John Henry Newman called "the Benedictine centuries," monastic schools provided much of the training available in western Europe. Books are a basic necessity for any school, and preparation of finely written books became the distinctly monastic craft. First for their own needs, then for those of friends and other monasteries, the Benedictines wrote in every literary genre. In addition to copies of, and commentaries on, the Scriptures, and psalters and liturgical books, monks produced meditations and ascetical writings, biographies and saints' lives, histories and chronicles, homilies and theological tracts, letters and instructional dialogues, and scientific and mathematical treatises.

From the thousands of monastic teacher-scholars who preserved the culture of classical antiquity and set down the world view of their own times, a few may be taken as representative: among chroniclers and historians, the Venerable Bede (*d.* 735), the paradigmatic example of the medieval monk who spent his life in the discipline of the cloister and in teaching and writing; Ordericus Vitalis (*d.* 1142) of St. Evroult in Normandy, whose *Ecclesiastical History* superbly illustrates the medieval practice of interpreting history from a religious vantage point; and Matthew Paris (*d.* 1259) of St. Albans, the artist and chronicler whose *Great Chronicle* provides unparalleled information about contemporary Europe and the Middle East, as well as an insight into the English national consciousness at the time of its birth. Among theologians and ascetical writers are John of Fruttaria (*d.* 1050), who wrote tracts on the moral foundations of the monastic life; Anselm of Bec (*d.* 1109), whose writings on the Incarnation, the Trinity, and the Virgin earned him a distinguished place in the development of Scholastic theology and of monastic piety; Rupert of Deutz (*d.* 1129), who wrote long commentaries on the Bible, including a Marian exposition on the Canticle of Canticles; and William of St. Thierry (*d.* 1148), whose treatises (often in the form of letters) on the love of God and on the contemplative life enjoyed wide popularity; and among scientists and mathematicians: Byrhthferth (tenth century), who wrote manuals on mathematics and on the nature of the physical atmosphere, and Notker Labeo of St. Gall (*d.* 1022), called "the German" because he translated into German works that show familiarity with music, astronomy, and mathematics.

The Benedictine economy rested overwhelmingly on agriculture. Although geographical conditions and local expertise determined the methods of exploiting the land and the specific crops grown, everywhere between the eighth and the thirteenth centuries monastic income derived primarily from manorial estates worked by servile tenants or lay brothers. Typically monastic lands, such as those of St. Emmeram at Regensburg, were subdivided into manorial units, each of which was required to provision the community for a specified length of time. The manors at first were entrusted to monks, and later to lay entrepreneurs, sometimes by a life contract, as at Cluny, and sometimes by an annual one, as at St. Denis.

In the late eleventh century, Benedictine houses represented the most advanced forms of medieval farming. The monks preserved careful records, both to extract as much revenue as possible from their estates and to defend them legally. Income also came from the incidents of feudal tenure, such as courts, mills, ovens, fairs, and serfs, and from ecclesiastical sources, such as tithes, the dowries of novices, private churches, and altar, burial, and preaching stipends.

Down to roughly the mid twelfth century, expansion continued with new foundations and a strong rate of recruitment; most houses enjoyed relative prosperity. After about 1150, however, smaller endowments, declining manorial revenues, and the attempt to maintain an extravagantly aristocratic lifestyle in the midst of increasingly complicated social conditions led to economic problems. Benedictines were not as enterprising as the Cistercians in exploiting commercial possibilities, such as mining. As revenues declined, the monasteries became socially exclusive. A conservative mentality prevented the reduction of expenses and the utilization of new methods of estate management and agricultural husbandry.

In addition to the expenses incurred in the service of public authorities, monastic revenues went to the predictable costs of clothing and feeding the monks—in the late eleventh century the ordinary diet included bread, meat, vegetables, eggs, fish, cheese, butter, and wine or beer (at Abingdon in England, each monk was allotted the heroic quantity of three gallons of beer a day); to hospitality to traveling nobility—the entertainment of a royal entourage (which was a basic feudal obligation in an age when government income was very limited and all governments traveled constantly) could severely deplete the year's receipts of even a wealthy monastery; to feeding the poor and giving medical attention to the neighborhood—Corbie in the eleventh century distributed two hundred loaves of bread a day; and to the costs related to the copying and illumination of books and manuscripts—gold leaf was very dear.

The basic duty of the monks remained prayer for the rest of society. Therefore a large part of their income was spent on the construction or redecoration of churches and on the liturgy. All houses sought to execute the work of God with the most dazzling sumptuousness, to accumulate around the altars and saints' relics vessels and vestments of the most glittering splendor. Thus the period from about 1070 to 1130 witnessed what the Cluniac monk Raoul Glaber described as "the white mantle of churches which the world put on." The monastic liturgy provided the impetus for the efflorescence of sacred and Romanesque art. Although monks did not monopolize any craft, Romanesque art was distinctly monastic.

What some scholars have called "the Benedictine plan" of Romanesque ecclesiastical architecture—semicircular apses at the east end of the choir and at the termini of both the side aisles and the arms of the transepts, with twin towers above the west front—swept across Europe. The apses contained altars, which in addition to allowing pilgrims to visit the church and its relics without disturbing the services in the choir, reflected the increased clericalization of the monastic order; as the practice developed of ordaining most monks, altars had to be provided for their Masses. The Romanesque style perhaps found its best expression in the monastic churches of St. Madeleine at Vézelay; Payerne, the Cluniac priory in Switzerland; St. Étienne and La Trinité at Caen in Normandy, Durham Cathedral Priory, and above all in the church that Kenneth J. Conant labeled Cluny II. The successful integration of the elements that made up the Gothic style by Abbot Suger at St. Denis (1144) quickly led to the development of Gothic architecture in the cathedral churches of Europe.

After 1200 the life of most Benedictine houses tended to blend into the social and economic world of their localities; monasteries adopted the interests and values of their environments. Building programs expanded and refurbished monastic churches, and made the monasteries more comfortable. Organs came into common use to accompany the chant. Intelligent young monks studied at the universities and returned to teach in their communities. Multiple lawsuits over property occupied the attention of monastic officials, and abbots, such as the practical and hard-driving Samson of Bury St. Edmund's, devoted most of their time to the administration of estates and the service of kings and popes.

In all these activities the purely spiritual ideal of the monastic life declined. The decree "In singulis regnis" of the Fourth Lateran Council (1215) prescribed that the superiors of all Benedictine monasteries in each ecclesiastical province should meet triennially in chapters for purposes of reform and common discipline. Although the chapters met fairly regularly until the fourteenth century and some minor reforms were effected, the black monks strongly resisted the centralizing tendencies of the papacy, preferring to continue the traditional local autonomy of each house. Strictly speaking, therefore, a Benedictine "order" never developed, but "national" congregations—most notably the English (1336)—did emerge.

Between 1200 and 1500 many factors contributed to the decline of Benedictine influence: the coming of the friars, who represented a more dynamic spiritual and intellectual force; the competition of professional copyists and then of the printing press, which, in meeting far larger markets for books, deprived many monks of their occupation; the system of commendatory abbots, which led to the spiritual impoverishment of some monasteries and the financial ruin of others; and the emergence of a class of administrative bureaucrats, able and eager to do the work of governments. But the root cause of Benedictine difficulties was reduced revenues. The attempt to live in the style and splendor of previous ages, in spite of weak management and rising inflation, proved impossible. The numbers of recruits fell everywhere—in Germany especially, but also in France, Italy, and England—not because they were not available or interested, but simply because monasteries could not afford to admit them.

The enduring legacy of the Benedictines to the modern world was a tradition of ordered and disciplined living, a deep appreciation for the ancient liturgy, the wisdom of a rich literary culture, and a compassionate understanding of the mysteries and difficulties of the human condition. In the seventeenth, the nineteenth, and again in the twentieth century, the Benedictines experienced a remarkable resurgence.

BIBLIOGRAPHY

Reference. Giles Constable, *Medieval Monasticism: A Select Bibliography* (1976); Oliver L. Kapsner, *A Benedic-*

tine Bibliography, 2 vols., 2nd ed. (1962), *First Supplement* (1982).

The Rule. Timothy Fry *et al., RB 1980: The Rule of St. Benedict in Latin and English with Notes* (1981); Adalbert de Vogüé, ed., *La Règle de saint Benoît,* 6 vols. (1971–1972); Leonard Doyle, trans., *St. Benedict's Rule for Monasteries* (1948).

Introductions and general surveys. Lowrie J. Daly, *Benedictine Monasticism: Its Formation and Development Through the Twelfth Century* (1965); David Knowles, *Christian Monasticism* (1969); Herbert Workman, *The Evolution of the Monastic Ideal,* 2nd ed. (1927); George Zarnecki, *The Monastic Achievement* (1972).

Advanced studies. Philibert Schmitz, *Histoire de l'Ordre de Saint Benoît,* I (1942); David Knowles, *The Monastic Order in England,* 2nd ed. (1963) and his *The Religious Orders in England,* 3 vols. (1948–1959); Friedrich Prinz, *Frühes Mönchtum in Frankenreich* (1965).

Recruitment and numbers of monks. Joseph H. Lynch, *Simoniacal Entry into the Religious Life from 1000 to 1260* (1976); Jacques Dubois, "Du nombre des moines dans les monastères," in *Lettre de Ligugé,* CXXXIV (1969); Bernard Guillemain, "Chiffres et statistiques pour l'histoire ecclésiastique du moyen âge," in *Le moyen âge,* 59 (1953).

Socioeconomic aspects. Richard W. Southern, *Western Society and the Church in the Middle Ages* (1970), 214–240; Georges Duby, *The Chivalrous Society,* Cynthia Postan, trans. (1977), *passim;* Jacques Dubois, "Les moines dans la société du moyen âge, 950–1350," in *Revue d'histoire de l'église de France,* 60 (1974); Penelope D. Johnson, *Prayer, Patronage, and Power: The Abbey of la Trinité, Vendôme, 1032–1187* (1981); J. Ambrose Raftis, *The Estates of Ramsey Abbey* (1957); Giles Constable, *Monastic Tithes: From Their Origins to the Twelfth Century* (1964); Lester K. Little, *Religious Poverty and the Profit Economy in Medieval Europe* (1978); and Georges Duby, *Rural Economy and Country Life in the Medieval West,* Cynthia Postan, trans. (1968), *passim.*

Learning and spirituality. Jean Leclercq, *The Love of Learning and the Desire for God* (1961); Pierre Riché, *Education and Culture in the Barbarian West,* trans. of 3rd French ed. by John J. Contreni (1976); Jean Leclercq, François Vandenbroucke, and Louis Bouyer, *The Spirituality of the Middle Ages* (1968), *passim* but esp. ch. 7, "The Benedictine Tradition"; and Beryl Smalley, *The Study of the Bible in the Middle Ages* (1964).

Art and architecture. Walter Horn and Ernest Born, *The Plan of St. Gall: A Study of the Architecture and Economy of, and Life in a Paradigmatic Carolingian Monastery,* 3 vols. (1979); Georges Duby, *The Age of the Cathedrals: Art and Society, 980–1420,* Eleanor Levieux and Barbara Thompson, trans. (1981); Erwin Panofsky, ed. and trans., *Abbot Suger on the Abbey Church of St.-Denis and Its Art Treasures* (1946); and Robert E. Swartwout, *The Monastic Craftsman: An Inquiry into the Services of Monks to Art in Britain and in Europe North of the Alps During the Middle Ages* (1932).

Individual portraits. John F. Benton, ed., *Self and Society in Medieval France: The Memoirs of Abbot Guibert of Nogent* (1970); and H. E. Butler, trans., *The Chronicle of Jocelin of Brakelond Concerning the Acts of Samson, Abbot of the Monastery of St. Edmund* (1951).

BENNETT D. HILL

[See also **Benedict of Nursia, St.; Benedictine Rule; Monte Cassino.**]

BENEDICTIONAL. In the Middle Ages the terms *liber benedictionalis* (mid tenth century) and *liber benedictionum* (late thirteenth century) were generally reserved for the special book containing episcopal benedictions of the Mass: this is what the liturgist N. K. Rasmussen calls the "simple benedictional." In England the pontifical (or expanded ben-

Benedictional of St. Aethelwold. The Nativity. BRITISH LIBRARY, MS Add. 49598, fol. 51v

BENEDICTIONS

edictional), or sometimes a part of it, was occasionally called *benedictionale.* In Germany at the end of the Middle Ages, *benedictionale* was synonymous with agenda, the ritual of priests. Benedictions were most often in the missal, the pontifical, or the ritual *(manuale).*

BIBLIOGRAPHY

Michel Andrieu, *Le pontifical romain au moyen-âge,* III (1940), 655; and *Les ordines romani du haut moyen âge,* II (1948), 361; William Dugdale, *The History of St. Paul's Cathedral in London* (1658), 221; John Wickham Legg and W. H. St. John Hope, *Inventories of Christchurch, Canterbury* (1902), 75.

PIERRE-MARIE GY, O.P.

[See also **Benedictions.**]

BENEDICTIONS, in medieval liturgy, are prayers of diverse length and nature, usually said by the bishop or priest to invoke the divine blessing on people and things that may be directly related to the sacraments or independent of them. Benedictions originated in biblical and Jewish prayers that blessed God and appealed for his blessing on mankind. In these prayers, however, the element of blessing God had already lost some of its importance in the patristic period. Later, especially in the Carolingian period, an apotropaic element—involving protection against the devil—was often added to the benediction. Since the twelfth century a clear theological distinction has been made between the essential prayers concerning the sacraments and other prayers, among which are benedictions. An attempt was made to distinguish "benediction" from "consecration" (the act of making people or things sacred), terms that until then had been inadequately differentiated.

Benedictions directly related to the sacraments are those of holy oils and of baptismal water. The texts of these benedictions appear in liturgical manuscripts of the eighth century.

The *Apostolic Tradition* of Hippolytus recognizes two types of oil: the oil of exorcism, destined to anoint the catechumens, and the oil of thanksgiving, over which the Holy Spirit had been invoked so that the Spirit might be spread by anointing the baptized. Later a further distinction was made between holy chrism, a mixture of oil and balm (primarily for postbaptismal unction and confirmation) and the oil for the sick. In the Middle Ages the holy oils were blessed by the bishop on Holy Thursday with solemn benedictions. In Rome the benediction of the oil for the catechumens *(Deus incrementorum)* resembled an exorcism, whereas the benediction of the oil for the sick and of the chrism were epicleses appealing for the presence of the Holy Spirit in the oil. The Romano-Frankish liturgical books also had prayers of exorcism preceding these benedictions. Other prayers were later added, making the rite more complex and solemn. In northern Italy the priests blessed the oil for the sick until the eleventh century, and the oil of the catechumens until the thirteenth century. In the High Middle Ages the oil for the sick was offered by the faithful; after it had been blessed, it could be used directly on them.

The benediction of baptismal water takes place during the Easter vigil with a very solemn prayer and many symbolic gestures, of which the most ancient is the plunging of two candles into the water, thus symbolizing the gift of the Holy Spirit. The prayer recalls the role of water in the history of salvation and asks that the baptismal water be liberated from the power of Satan, and that it receive the presence of the Holy Spirit. For the baptismal water, as for the holy oils, the fathers and the theologians of the High Middle Ages did not distinguish clearly between the benedictions and the essential rites of the sacraments. St. Thomas Aquinas still compared the presence of the Holy Spirit in the Eucharist to the presence of the Holy Spirit in baptismal water (*Summa theologica,* IIIa, Ques. 73, art. 1, 2m).

Other benedictions during the liturgical year are the blessing of the candles on the feast of the Presentation (2 February), the blessing of the ashes at the beginning of Lent, the blessing of the palms on the Sunday before Easter, the blessing of the Paschal candle on Holy Saturday, and the various blessings of food during the Easter celebration. Of these the blessing of the Paschal candle is the oldest ritual, originating with the *Lucernarium* of the ancient liturgy and in the Jewish blessing of the sabbath candle. Among its different forms the *Exsultet* of the Romano-Frankish liturgy (probably of Gallican origin, perhaps from the fifth century), while retaining traces of its primitive character as a benediction to God for the gift of light and the offering of this gift, appears especially as the great lyrical *praeconium* of Easter. Used everywhere except in Milan during the Middle Ages, the *Exsultet* was cut from the Praise of the Bee and, in the area of Romano-Germanic and Cluniac pontifical influence, from the passages on the happy fault *(felix culpa)* and the necessary sin of Adam *(necessarium Adae peccatum).*

The 2 February blessing of the candles, the blessing of the ashes, and the blessing of the palms are similar in terms of their history and liturgical form. Such rituals were used around the tenth century, about the time of the Romano-Germanic pontifical (earlier for the blessing of the palms), and were extensions of preexisting rites: processions with candles (2 February), processions with palms (for the entry of Christ into Jerusalem at Easter), and the penitential distribution of ashes. The blessing of the palms took on the appearance of a mass. Receiving the blessed ashes was at first reserved for public penitents; then, individual confession, along with the distribution of ashes, was recommended for all the faithful by the Romano-Germanic pontifical. The distribution of ashes to all was foreseen in the English monasteries by the *Regularis concordia* around 970 and was prescribed for all Christians by the Council of Benevento in 1091.

The benedictions celebrated at Easter form, in medieval practice, an important group including blessings of food *(benedictiones esculentorum praesertim in Pascha)* and the blessing of houses on Holy Saturday. The blessing of milk and honey during the Easter vigil, used until the thirteenth century, had its origin in the primitive Christian Paschal meal. The blessing of houses on Holy Saturday comes from the old Roman custom in which the faithful sprinkle their houses, vineyards, fields, and fruits with the baptismal water blessed that same day.

Episcopal benedictions generally occur before Communion during mass (after Communion, according to Gulielmus Durandus of Mende). These are inspired by the vetero-testamentary benediction of the Book of Numbers (6:22–26) and include three invocations, often rhythmic and rich with assonance, to which the people respond with "Amen." They were used in the ancient Gallican liturgy and in the Hispanic liturgy.

Episcopal benedictions had been part of the Romano-Frankish Mass since Carolingian times. They were adopted by the Benedictine abbots, probably by custom from the ninth century, and by papal concessions at the time of the Gregorian reform. After the Gallican and Hispanic episcopal benedictions, the main collections of these benedictions are the Gelasian Romano-Frankish collection of the eighth century, the supplement (by Benedict of Aniane) to *Sacramentaire grégorien,* and various later medieval collections, of which the most important is that of Gulielmus Durandus of Mende (end of the thirteenth century).

BIBLIOGRAPHY

The two essential works on medieval benedictions are Edmond Martène, O.S.B., *De antiquis ecclesiae ritibus,* 5 vols. (1690–1706), in conjunction with Aimé Georges Martimort, *La documentation liturgique de Dom Edmond Martène* (1978); and Adolf Franz, *Die kirchlichen Benediktionen im Mittelalter,* 2 vols. (1909, 2nd ed., 1960). Among the individual sources two especially important ones are *Pontifical romano-germanique du Xe siècle,* C. Vogel and R. Elze, eds., 3 vols. (1963–1972); and *Sacramentaire de Gellone,* A. Dumas, O.S.B., and J. Deshusses, O.S.B., eds., 2 vols. (1981). On chrism, see R. Béraudy, in Aimé Georges Martimort, ed., *L'église en prière,* 3rd ed. (1965), 557–558. Also see St. Bernard, *Ordo officiorum Ecclesiae Lateranensis,* L. Fischer, ed. (1916), 28; J. M. Pinell, "La benediccio del ciri pasqual i els seus textos," in *Liturgica,* **2** (1958); Hermann Gräf, *Palmenweihe und Palmenprozession in der lateinischen Liturgie* (1959); Pierre-Marie Gy, "Die Segnung von Milch und Honig in der Osternacht," in Balthazar Fischer and J. Wagner, eds., *Paschatis sollemnia* (1959); A. Olivar, "Vom Ursprung der römischen Taufwasserweihe," in *Archiv für Liturgiewissenschaft,* **6,** no. 1 (1959); P. Verbraken, "Une laus cerei africaine," in *Revue bénédictine,* **70** (1960).

Collections of benedictions are in *Le sacramentaire grégorien,* Jean Deshusses, ed. (1971), 576–598; and *Corpus benedictionum pontificalium,* Edmond Moeller, O.S.B., ed., 4 vols. (1971–1979).

PIERRE-MARIE GY, O.P.

[See also **Benedictional.**]

BENEDICTUS LEVITA (Benedict the Levite, or Deacon) is the assumed name of a forger who added three books and four appendixes to Abbot Ansegis of Fontenelle's authentic and widely used collection of Frankish capitularies. Scholars now place him in the circle of pseudo-Isidorean forgers active in West Frankland (probably the ecclesiastical province of Rheims) between 847 and 857. Of Benedictus' 1,721 chapters roughly one-fourth represent authentic capitularies; many of the rest derive from genuine ecclesiastical law, here presented as legislation issued by Pepin, Charlemagne, and Louis the Pious. The wholly forged chapters contain the same themes as the False Decretals: for instance, the right of accused bishops to their confiscated properties *(exceptio spo-*

lii) and the complicated procedural law designed to make bishops virtually untouchable. With numerous repetitions and rough transitions, Benedictus' capitularies show far less craft as forgeries than do the False Decretals, and, measured in terms either of extant manuscript copies or of influence on later legislation, they received comparatively little attention.

BIBLIOGRAPHY

Edition. F. H. Knust, in: *Monumenta Germaniae historica: Leges,* II (1837), 17–158. The greatest scholar of the false capitularies, charged with a new edition for the *MGH* which he never completed, was Emil Seckel, who summarized his views in Johann J. Herzog, ed., *Realencyklopädie für protestantische Theologie und Kirche,* 3rd. ed., XVI (1905), 296–304. See also G. May, "Die Infamie bei Benedictus Levita," in *Österreichisches Archiv für Kirchenrecht,* **11** (1960), and the good recent summary with additional bibliography in Horst Fuhrmann, *Einfluss und Verbreitung der pseudoisidorischen Fälschungen* (1972), 163–167.

JOHN VAN ENGEN

[See also **Capitulary; Decretals, False.**]

BENEFICE, ECCLESIASTICAL. Like the lay benefice, an ecclesiastical benefice was created by gifts of revenue-producing property to benefit the recipient. Such gifts could be made to support any continuing religious activity—to a bishop for administering his diocese or to an abbot for administering a monastery, to the canons of a cathedral or the monks of a monastery, to a parish church for the use of the parish priest, to charitable organizations such as hospitals. The person who received the income from such endorsements was said to hold a benefice, which hence came to mean any ecclesiastical office with a permanent source of income. The income usually came from land or rights associated with land, such as labor services, mills, markets, tolls, courts of justice, and even, for the great benefices, feudal service.

The grantor of the endowment that supported a benefice was almost always a layman, and he expected to retain some control over the use of the gift, notably over the choice of the person who was to hold the benefice. This caused endless friction with the church. Most dioceses had been endowed by kings or great lords, who naturally wanted to name the bishops—and very often did. Their powers were curtailed by the Investiture Struggle.

The same quarrels arose over lesser benefices, down to the parish level, where the lord of the village named the village priest. The papacy gradually gained control over appointments to all important benefices, and worked out a modus vivendi with kings and great lords. The pope named the bishops, but high royal officials were given a fair share of these appointments. Less important officials were named canons of cathedral or collegiate churches. In 1305, for example, Pope Clement V allowed the king of France to nominate one canon in each such church in France. At the lower level, village lords nominated parish priests to the bishop; their choices were accepted if the candidate could meet very limited educational standards.

Like many reforms, centralization of appointments to benefices in the papacy had unforeseen bad effects. Men with influence could be appointed to many benefices, and were not expected to perform the duties associated with each office. Pierre de Chalon, head of the French customs service in the early fourteenth century, had seven benefices. Obviously he did little in return for his income. Benefices could also be given to promising young scholars, but they were just as likely to go to favorites of a cardinal or a king. Pluralism—the possession of many benefices—was one of the grievances of late medieval and early modern reformers.

BIBLIOGRAPHY

The best overall summary is by G. Mollat in the *Dictionnaire de droit canonique,* II (1935), 406ff. Geoffrey Barraclough, *Papal Provisions* (1935), shows how the pope gained control of benefices. See also Glenn Olsen, "The Definition of the Ecclesiastical Benefice in the Twelfth Century," in *Studia gratiana,* **11** (1967); and Ulrich Stutz, "The Proprietary Church," in Geoffrey Barraclough, ed., *Mediaeval Germany,* II (1938).

JOSEPH R. STRAYER

[See also **Investiture and Investiture Controversy.**]

BENEFICE, LAY. In its broadest sense a benefice (Latin: *beneficium*) was a benefit—that is, anything (such as money, land, or office) that would be helpful to the recipient. It was, in this sense, an outright gift; the donor received only gratitude. In the Germanic kingdoms of the early Middle Ages, however, the benefice ceased to be a free gift. The donor retained some rights in the thing granted, and expected to receive some income or service from the recipient. The service was not necessarily military, and the holder

BENEVENTAN RITE

of a benefice could be a person fairly low on the social scale. As time went on, there was a tendency to use the expression primarily to describe grants made in return for military service and political support. "Benefice" came to be almost the equivalent of "fief."

The earlier, broader meaning, however, was never entirely forgotten, as is shown by a famous dispute between Pope Hadrian IV and Emperor Frederick I Barbarossa. When Frederick was holding a court at Besançon in 1157, the pope sent him a letter complaining about the mistreatment of an archbishop. In the letter Hadrian said that he had given Frederick the imperial crown and, if possible, would give him even greater "benefices." Frederick felt that this expression meant that he held the Empire as a fief from the pope, and became very angry. After some argument Hadrian finally explained that he had used the word "benefice" only in its old meaning of "favor." After 1200 "benefice" was almost never used to mean "fief."

BIBLIOGRAPHY

The fullest listing of the various meanings of the word *beneficium* is in Jan F. Niermayer, *Mediae latinitatis lexicon minus* (1976). See also François L. Ganshof, *Feudalism* (1961), 16–25; and Marc Bloch, *Feudal Society* (1961), 163–168. For the argument between Hadrian IV and Frederick Barbarossa, see Peter Munz, *Frederick Barbarossa* (1969), 142–145.

JOSEPH R. STRAYER

[See also **Fief; Frederick I Barbarossa.**]

BENEVENTAN RITE. The religious rite of the duchy of Benevento is accessible in relatively late works, the liturgical books of the tenth and eleventh centuries. Many parts of those books, such as *orationes, praefationes,* and readings, demonstrate that this rite originally corresponded essentially to the liturgy of Campania. From the eleventh century on, however, it was increasingly adapted to the liturgy of Rome.

Early liturgy of Campania and Benevento. In his *De viris illustribus* (*ca.* 467–480), Gennadius of Marseilles mentions the composition of a *(Liber) sacramentorum* by the Campanian bishop Paulinus of Nola (*d.* 431). This Mass book, like the other liturgical books of that period, has not been preserved, nor do we have a single complete copy of the Campanian sacramentary from more recent times. All we possess are a few remnants handed down in the Anglo-Saxon tradition.

That this kind of Mass book was used by the Anglo-Saxons came about through Hadrian of Canterbury, who, after having been abbot of the monastery of Niridan near Naples, became a companion to Theodore of Tarsus, who was appointed archbishop of Canterbury by Pope Vitalian in 668. The books needed for missionary work among the Anglo-Saxons were taken along by Hadrian from his Campanian monastery. Some of these books have been preserved, such as a diatessaron including the Epistles of St. Paul, with an attached list of the Epistle readings that were customary in Campania. The Latin Campanian Gospel list has been preserved only in copies made in Britain—for example, the Lindisfarne Gospels (*ca.* 700). The same is true for the sacramentary.

The influence of the sacramentary of Paulinus of Nola, from the fifth and sixth centuries on, throughout Italy (and presumably Gaul), has not been fully investigated. Today we can still recognize such an influence with special clarity in the *orationes* and *praefationes* of the Milanese Mass book *(Missale Ambrosianum),* which contains a large number of formulas otherwise found only in Campanian and Beneventan liturgical books. The great significance of Paulinus' sacramentary for the history of Western liturgy makes its loss, and the loss of the subsequent adaptations in the Anglo-Saxon Mass books, all the more deplorable.

Beneventan liturgical books. The most interesting Beneventan liturgical fragments are the extensive remains of a missal written around 1000 in the region of Bari and now in the libraries of Zurich, Payerne, and Lucerne. Most of the formularies still show three liturgical readings (one from the Old Testament, one from the "Apostle," and one from one of the Gospels). The gradual follows the first reading, and the "Alleluia" the second reading. There is also an "Oratio post evangelium," a remnant of an intercessory prayer following the Gospel, of which only an "Oremus" has survived in the Roman rite. Almost every formulary has its own *praefatio*—with the archaic title "Prex" (to be supplemented by the word "Oblationis," hence "sacrificial prayer"). Furthermore, there is a "Super populum" formula, which in the Gregorian sacramentary has become limited to the weekdays of Lent, representing the prayer of blessing for the departing community at the end of the Mass.

The incomplete Missal VI 33 in the archiepiscopal archive of Benevento, which also is from the period around 1000, must be considered less original than the fragments described above. In this missal the original order of the three pericopes and the "Oratio post evangelium" has been found only in Sunday Masses after Pentecost, but otherwise the content has been preserved. The same is true for an eleventh-century missal from Canossa (now in Baltimore, Walters Art Gallery, MS W 6) that is interesting largely because of its calendar, featuring numerous Byzantine saints. This liturgical book differs in its arrangement from the other known manuscripts. It begins with the votive Masses, followed by the canon, then by formularies for the most important holidays. There are no Sunday Masses. The original number of *praefationes* is intact.

Beneventan choral manuscripts. The text of these manuscripts largely corresponds to the Roman antiphonaries. Nonetheless, they have unique characteristics, especially of notation, and they include choral songs that are found nowhere else except in the Milanese liturgy books.

In 1058, Pope Stephen IX prohibited the "Ambrosian" choral song at Monte Cassino, but in the region of Benevento, as can be seen from the extant manuscripts, the traditional choral song continued to be in use for some time longer. The most important codices are in the archiepiscopal archives of Benevento and in the National Library at Naples.

Also noteworthy are the "Rotuli paschales," which contain the "Exultet" to be sung by the deacon on Holy Saturday. They are adorned with biblical illustrations that are upside down, so that while the deacon is singing, the congregation may look at the pictures on the *rotulus* hanging from the pulpit.

BIBLIOGRAPHY

Klaus Gamber, *Codices liturgici latini antiquiores,* 2nd ed. (1968), 226–258, with bibliography; and Das *Bonifatius-Sakramentar and Other Early Liturgy Books from Regensburg* (1975); Klaus Gamber and Sieghild Rehle, *Manuale Casinense (Cod. Ottob. lat. 145)* (1979); Sieghild Rehle, *Missale Beneventanum of Canosa* (1972); and "Missale Beneventanum (Codex VI 33 of the Archiepiscopal Archive of Benevento)," in *Sacris erudiri,* **31** (1972/1973).

KLAUS GAMBER

[See also **Ambrosian Chant; Manuscripts and Books; Paulinus of Nola; Theodore of Canterbury.**]

BENJAMIN OF TUDELA (*fl.* 12th c.), a famous Jewish traveler who lived in Tudela, in northern Spain. No biographical data are extant, not even the date of his birth or death. His journey to the Near East is thought to have taken place between 1165 and 1173, though it may have begun as early as 1159. It included Provence, Italy, the Balkans, Turkey, Rhodes, the Holy Land, Syria, Babylonia, and Persia. From Persia, Benjamin sailed through the Persian Gulf and around the Arabian Peninsula to Egypt, thence to Italy via Sicily, and from there returned to Spain through central Europe.

Benjamin's itinerary, the *Sefer Massao't* (Book of travels), contains important historical information and folkloristic traditions, both Jewish and non-Jewish. The descriptions include much imaginary material, especially concerning life in Yemen, India, Ceylon, and China, which he never actually visited. The purpose of the journey is not stated. Some suggest that Benjamin's goal was to investigate the status of the Jewish communities in the Mediterranean countries and the Near East. He reports on the social, economic, and spiritual life of the Jews in all the places he visited, and gives demographic data; in addition he frequently mentions prominent spiritual and communal leaders. Some of Benjamin's descriptions have been verified by other sources, including Petaḥia of Regensburg, who journeyed to the Near East ten years later. Frequently the two travelers received identical information.

Several Hebrew manuscripts of the itinerary are extant, and more than twenty editions have been published since the first (Constantinople, 1543). In addition, the book has been translated into most of the major Western languages. No contemporary report on the Mediterranean world or the Near East is of comparable importance.

BIBLIOGRAPHY

An English translation by A. Asher, based on the editio princeps and the edition of Ferrara (1556), is *The Itinerary of Rabbi Benjamin of Tudela,* 2 vols. (1840–1841, repr. 1927), with extensive notes and bibliographical information. A critical text, accompanied by a new translation, was edited by M. N. Adler, *The Itinerary of Benjamin of Tudela* (1907, repr. 1964). See also Salo W. Baron, *A Social and Religious History of the Jews,* VI (1958), 222–224.

ABRAHAM DAVID

[See also **Travel and Transport, Western Europe.**]

BENNO OF OSNABRÜCK (*ca.* 1028–1084), an Ottonian bishop in charge of the Office of Works under Emperors Henry III and Henry IV. Benno apparently was involved in the construction of Strasbourg Cathedral, and may have received further training at Reichenau; he also built castles for Henry IV in Saxony.

BIBLIOGRAPHY

Eberhard Hempel, *Geschichte der deutschen Baukunst* (1949), 73ff.

LESLIE BRUBAKER

[See also **Strasbourg, Cathedral.**]

BENOÎT DE SAINTE-MAURE (*fl.* 1160–1170) wrote the *Roman de Troie,* more than thirty thousand octosyllabic lines long, probably for Eleanor of Aquitaine; it is based on Dares' and Dictys' accounts of the Trojan War. Benoît prefers their version of the Trojan War to that of Homer because they were allegedly eyewitnesses, and because they do not make extensive use of mythological apparatus. Moreover, he amplifies considerably the sparse details of the sources by extensive descriptions, especially of battles, heroic figures, and architecture. There are also some additions, notably Jason's winning of the Golden Fleece, and there is greater emphasis on passionate love (Benoît invents the love of Troilus and Briseida). The *Troie* itself, and some thirteenth-century prose adaptations, were widely read: they influenced Guido delle Colonne's *Historia Troiana* as well as Boccaccio's and Chaucer's versions of the Troilus and Criseyde legend. Benoît's incomplete *Chronique des ducs de Normandie,* 44,544 octosyllabic lines long and written for Henry II, recounts Anglo-Norman history to Henry I.

BIBLIOGRAPHY

Le roman de Troie, Léopold Constans, ed., 6 vols. (1904–1912); *Chronique des ducs de Normandie,* Carin Fahlin, ed., 3 vols. (1951–1967).

DOUGLAS KELLY

[See also **French Literature; Troy Story.**]

BENZO OF ALBA (*d. ca.* 1090), named bishop of Alba before 1059, was one of the Italian prelates most devoted to the cause of the German monarchy in the Investiture Controversy. A propagandist for the imperial candidate, Honorius II, against the legitimate pope, Alexander II, Benzo later attacked Alexander on the Patarine question and defended Emperor Henry IV in his struggle with Pope Gregory VII.

BIBLIOGRAPHY

Hugo Lehmgrübner, *Benzo von Alba* (1887); *Monumenta Germaniae historica: Scriptores,* XI (1854), K. Pertz, ed. (for Benzo's panegyric in honor of Henry IV).

MARK D. MEYERSON

[See also **Alexander II, Pope; Henry IV of Germany; Investiture and Investiture Controversy.**]

BEOWULF is an anonymous Old English heroic poem whose 3,182 lines describe the hero's three fights against a background of migration-period Germanic legend and history. Although the date of its literary composition has never been fully established, *Beowulf* is nonetheless the earliest long heroic poem extant in any vernacular tradition, including even early Irish.

The story can be summarized with inevitably misleading brevity. The poem begins by establishing the genealogy and major exploits of the Danish king Hrothgar. Glorious evidence for his success in both arms and government is Heorot, a magnificent hall built by the king for the benefit of his people. Here all is peace and joy, until the sounds of happiness coming from the hall excite the envy of a fen-dwelling monster called Grendel, condemned by God and banished from the world of men with other descendants of Cain. For twelve years this monster nightly inhabits Heorot, killing and eating anyone foolhardy enough to remain, and driving most to dwell elsewhere.

News of Hrothgar's trouble reaches Beowulf, a young warrior belonging to the following of Hygelac, king of the Geats. Beowulf offers to fight the monster single-handed. Unferth, one of Hrothgar's counselors, expresses doubt because he has heard that Beowulf was beaten by Breca in a youthful ocean race. With some heat Beowulf replies that Unferth is misinformed, that Breca lost the contest, and that he, Beowulf, killed nine sea monsters during the race.

That night, when Grendel comes out of the misty

BEOWULF

moors and into Heorot, he and Beowulf fight, but only after the monster has consumed one of the sleeping Geats. Reaching out to grasp Beowulf's hand, Grendel is surprised to find a more powerful grip than he has ever encountered. The fight that follows does great damage to the fittings and ironwork of the hall, astounds the Danes who listen from outside, and ends only when Grendel's arm is torn off and he goes home to die, leaving a trail of blood across the moor.

In the morning Danish singers compose songs in honor of Beowulf, the hall is decorated, and a great banquet is held to celebrate the cleansing of Heorot. At the feast a poet sings of Hildeburh's grief at the slaying of her Danish brother, her Frisian husband, and their son in a double outbreak of violence and revenge (the so-called Finnsburg episode). Those in the hall celebrate, but the mood of the story anticipates doom to come.

In the night Grendel's mother returns to Heorot and slays one of Hrothgar's men in revenge for the killing of Grendel; and Beowulf must return to action. This fight is more difficult, for the hero must swim in full battle gear under the surface of a dreadful mere to reach the monsters' cave dwelling behind a waterfall. Here Beowulf is very near to losing his life as the troll-wife throws him to the ground and draws a bright knife, but the hero spies a huge magic sword that he uses to kill the she-monster and to cut the head from Grendel's corpse lying in the cave. On his return to Heorot, Hrothgar and his Danes praise, reward, and tearfully part from Beowulf, after giving him much salutary advice. At home Beowulf reports his Danish adventures with some interesting and significant additions.

Beowulf's third fight occurs fifty years later, when he is king and the Geats are being terrorized by a flying, fire-breathing dragon, who is stirred up when an intruder steals part of his treasure. The mood of the final part of the poem is somber and meditative, as Beowulf recollects the complex sequence of events that caused the deaths of Hygelac and his whole ruling family, and involved the Geats in bitter warfare with Swedes and Frisians. Cowardice and a sense of betrayal are evident as ten of Beowulf's followers abandon the doomed king to the power of the dragon. Only his young kinsman Wiglaf comes to Beowulf's aid, and between them they are able to slay the fifty-foot serpent, though not before Beowulf has been mortally wounded. Amid prophecies that war will follow when Frisians, Franks, and Swedes learn of the hero's death, the poem ends with twelve of Beowulf's followers riding about the burial mound and singing a funeral dirge in praise of his virtues.

Any summary of *Beowulf* is bound to involve more than ordinary distortion because of the poem's unusually complex narrative pattern. The earliest commentators noticed the uneven progression of the poem's story line, which was explained by the poet's lack of sophistication or by his only partially successful attempt to stitch together material of very disparate origin. More recent criticism has professed to see an intricate patterning beneath the episodes, digressions, and allusions—a pattern used by the poet to heighten dramatic irony, to suggest the ultimate consequences of an incident, or to reveal the essential similarity of events widely separated in time. Thus, the Finn episode, the digressions about Sigemund or Heremod or Ingeld and Freawaru, the many allusions to Hygelac's Frisian raid or the Swedish wars or Hrothulf, Hrethric, and Hrothmund, are not ornament but substance, and consequently are essential to the poem's meaning.

The oral-formulaic theory of poetic composition dominated much *Beowulf* criticism during the third quarter of the twentieth century. Originally modeled on a way of analyzing the Homeric epics, this theory holds that the presence of repeated poetic formulas in significant numbers is a reliable indicator of oral composition. To some this meant that *Beowulf*'s author could not have been literate and, further, that traditional methods of literary analysis had been, and would be, wholly inappropriate to the poem. Gradually, however, the idea has gained acceptance that *Beowulf* and some other poems could be transitional texts, whose authors may well have been literate, and yet have used traditional oral language and conventions. This has freed commentators to identify more sophisticated and conscious patterning of the kind noted above.

Roughly the same period also saw the first widespread application of Latin patristic thought to an understanding of *Beowulf*. Assuming the author's literacy as well as a certain amount of learning, commentators began to identify in the poem rhetorical commonplaces, theological themes, and Christian allegories drawn from the Church Fathers. The sharp differences in both methodology and assumptions between these scholars and those holding the oral-formulaic theory polarized the field of *Beowulf* criticism for many years, creating scholarly antagonisms that have not yet entirely disappeared.

Today the hero's moral stance at the end of the

poem is the most contentious interpretive issue in *Beowulf* studies. Although commentators of the nineteenth and early twentieth centuries always understood the poem to be a celebration of the hero's virtue, unblemished to the last, several important recent studies have professed to see in him elements of pride, greed, or rash folly, particularly in the decision to fight the dragon single-handed. Right or wrong, these analyses have done a valuable service to *Beowulf* scholarship through their careful assessment of the ironic futility and sense of doom pervading the final, climactic section of the poem.

Such problems of interpretation have been complicated by the somewhat parlous textual history of the poem. *Beowulf* survives, along with three prose pieces and the Old English poem *Judith,* in a single copy comprising the second part of the British Library manuscript Cotton Vitellius A.xv, copied by two scribes sometime in the late tenth or early eleventh century. The signature "Laurence Nouell 1563" at the top of the opening leaf indicates it had belonged to the dean of Lichfield at that time, but by the early seventeenth century it was part of the great antiquarian library of Sir Robert Cotton. There it was bound with a twelfth-century manuscript containing four more selections in Old English prose, including King Alfred the Great's version of St. Augustine's *Soliloquies* and the *Dialogue of Solomon and Saturn.*

In 1731 the Cotton collection suffered severe fire damage, and the edges of the *Beowulf* manuscript were scorched. The original damage must not have been extensive, for the Icelandic antiquarian Grímur Jónsson Thorkelin and an unknown assistant each made a full transcript during a visit to England in 1786–1787. These transcripts have become very important for later editors because the charred edges of the Cotton manuscript were allowed to crumble unhindered for more than a century and a quarter after the fire, so that today many words and letters have disappeared from the text and are available only in the Thorkelin transcripts. Sometime between 1860 and 1870 the whole manuscript was rebound, preventing further fragmentation.

Even more difficult to establish than the text of *Beowulf* has been the date of the poem's literary composition. Hygelac's raid on the Frisian coast is attested in Gregory of Tours's *History of the Franks,* and must have occurred between 520 and 530. The unique manuscript was copied within twenty-five years of A.D. 1000. Add the fact that we have no evidence for written Old English prior to the later seventh century, and the broad limits for the literary composition of *Beowulf* are 650 to 1025. Within these dates and in the absence of conclusive proof, scholarly opinion has generally but not universally preferred to consider the poem to be early. In the nineteenth and early twentieth centuries most considered *Beowulf* a work of the Northumbrian "Golden Age," roughly contemporary with Bede (*ca.* 673–735). In the third quarter of the twentieth century, many began to feel that the poem might well have been composed during the reign of Offa of Mercia (757–796), particularly since his Continental ancestor, Offa king of the Angles, is spoken of with high praise (lines 1955–1962).

More recently evidence has been brought forward to show that Scandinavian culture and traditions continued to be popular in England right through the Viking raids of the ninth century and, therefore, that period should not be discounted. Thus, in spite of numerous arguments based variously on language, meter, literary history, or historical analogy, the general tendency of twentieth-century scholarship has been to broaden the range of possible dates of composition for the poem. At the same time, the limit is unlikely ever to pass the mid tenth century, if only because *Beowulf* freely alliterates palatal and velar *g,* unlike poems of the late Old English period.

The discovery in the summer of 1939 of a magnificent Anglo-Saxon royal treasure in a burial mound at Sutton Hoo in Suffolk had a dramatic if not always salutary influence on *Beowulf* studies. The find did bring the poem's descriptions of royal splendor out of the world of apparent fancy and into contact with factual history. At the same time it inflamed the imaginations of scholars and encouraged some to posit connections between these treasures and the poem more precise than existing evidence will justify. However, the prudent and careful analysis of the material culture of Anglo-Saxon England at Sutton Hoo, as well as at many other less famous sites, remains among our best hopes for solving the many interesting and vexatious problems surrounding the poem.

Finally, a constant and valuable part of *Beowulf* studies has always been the identification and analysis of similar motifs found in other, particularly Germanic, literatures and legends. Best-known of these are the Old Icelandic *Grettis Saga,* Saxo Grammaticus' *Gesta Danorum,* the anonymous *Lives of the Two Offas,* and the folk theme known as the "Bear's Son Tale" found in various forms. Strictly speaking, none of these can be called a source for

Beowulf, since they were composed between one and three centuries after the poem's unique manuscript was copied, but in the absence of any medieval comment or even direct notice of *Beowulf,* this material can provide useful insights and helpful parallels for a powerful and intriguing poem.

BIBLIOGRAPHY

Bibliographical helps. Stanley B. Greenfield and Fred C. Robinson, *A Bibliography of Publications on Old English Literature to the End of 1972* (1980); and Douglas D. Short, *Beowulf Scholarship: An Annotated Bibliography* (1980). An annual bibliography has appeared in the *Old English Newsletter* since 1968, and in *Anglo-Saxon England* since 1972.

Manuscript and transcripts. Julius Zupitza, ed., *Beowulf* (facsimile), 2nd ed. (1959).

Editions. Friedrich Klaeber, ed., *Beowulf and the Fight at Finnsburh,* 3rd ed. (1950); C. L. Wrenn, ed., *Beowulf with the Finnesburg Fragment* (1953).

Prose translations. William Alfred, in *Medieval Epics* (1963), 3–83; Robert K. Gordon, in *Anglo-Saxon Poetry* (1927), 1–70. See also Garmonsway and Simpson (below).

Commentary. Larry D. Benson, "The Literary Character of Anglo-Saxon Formulaic Poetry," in *PMLA,* **81** (1966); Adrien Bonjour, *The Digressions in Beowulf* (1950); Arthur G. Brodeur, *The Art of Beowulf* (1959); Eamon Carrigan, "Structure and Thematic Development in *Beowulf,*" in *Proceedings of the Royal Irish Academy,* **66** (1967); Robert P. Creed, "On the Possibility of Criticizing Old English Poetry," in *Texas Studies in Language and Literature,* **3** (1961); Margaret Goldsmith, *The Mode and Meaning of Beowulf* (1963); Edward Irving, Jr., *A Reading of Beowulf* (1968); Alvin Lee, *The Guest Hall of Eden* (1972); John Leyerle, "The Interlace Structure of *Beowulf,*" in *University of Toronto Quarterly,* **37** (1967); Francis P. Magoun, Jr., "The Oral-Formulaic Character of Anglo-Saxon Narrative Poetry," in *Speculum,* **28** (1953); T. A. Shippey, *Beowulf* (1978); James Smith, *"Beowulf,"* in *English,* **25, 26** (1976–1977); J. R. R. Tolkien, "*Beowulf*: The Monsters and the Critics," in *Proceedings of the British Academy,* **22** (1936); Ann Chalmers Watts, *The Lyre and the Harp* (1969); Dorothy Whitelock, *The Audience of Beowulf* (1951).

Meter. Alan J. Bliss, *The Metre of Beowulf* (1958); Thomas Cable, *The Meter and Melody of Beowulf* (1974); John Collins Pope, *The Rhythm of Beowulf,* 2nd ed. (1966).

Analogs. R. W. Chambers, *Beowulf: An Introduction,* 3rd ed. with supp. (1959)—supplement contains material on Sutton Hoo, for which see also Rupert Bruce-Mitford, *The Sutton Hoo Ship-Burial,* 2 vols. (1975–1978); George N. Garmonsway and Jacqueline Simpson, eds. and trans., *Beowulf and Its Analogues* (1971).

COLIN CHASE

[See also **Anglo-Saxon Literature; Grettis Saga Ásmundarsonar; Saxo Grammaticus; Sutton Hoo.**]

BERBERS. The term "Berber" is most probably derived from the classical *barbar* (barbarians), employed in late antiquity for the peoples generally known to the classical authors as Libyans—that is, the native inhabitants of North Africa to the west of Egypt, as distinct from Carthaginians, Greeks, and Latins. For the Arabs, *Barbar* was the proper name of these peoples, considered as one of the races of mankind.

As descendants of Noah, the Barbar were by the ninth century regarded as a branch of the Canaanites, the offspring of Jālūt (Goliath), who had spread in North Africa under the various names encountered by the Arabs—Luwāta, Hawāra, Zanāta, and Maghīla, among others. Subsequently these peoples were structured by the genealogists into two main divisions, the Barānis and the Butr, descended from two eponymous ancestors, Barnis (or Burmus) and al-Abtar, the sons of a founding father, Barr, in the line of descent from Jālūt.

These two names date from the very earliest period of the Arab conquest in the seventh and eighth centuries, when they expressed a distinction perceived by the conquerors. The nature of this distinction is unknown; Gautier thought it was between nomads (Butr) and peasants (Barānis); Marçais that it might have been between people who wore a short garment (*abtar,* "cut off") and those who wore a hooded cloak (*burnus,* plural *barānis*).

As a family the Butr were represented principally by the Zanāta; among the Barānis the Sanhāja were prominent. In the fourteenth century Ibn Khaldūn gave this genealogical scheme a central place in the North African section of his *Kitāb al-ᶜIbar* (Universal history) when he arranged his information in accordance with its racial plan. By the eleventh century, however, there was already a strong tendency to consider the Barbar as Arabs who had emigrated from Yemen, for example, in the days before Islam. By the fifteenth century the topic was largely subordinated to concern not only for various kinds of Arab ancestry, but also for descent from the Prophet and for affiliation to some holy man.

Although "Barbary" has been a European name for North Africa since the Middle Ages, "Barbar" was not commonly employed by Europeans as a term for any of its inhabitants before the nineteenth century. Largely on the authority of Ibn Khaldūn, it was then applied generally, in the form of "Berber," to all the non-Arabic-speaking peoples of North Africa who spoke instead the dialects of a different language. This Berber language is one of the Hamitic group, and distantly related to ancient Egyptian. It is presumed, in the absence of firm linguistic evidence, to have been the native speech of North Africa to the west of Egypt in classical times, having spread from the east well before the desiccation of the northern Sahara at the beginning of the second millennium B.C. with the evolution and dispersion of the peoples who eventually appear in the descriptions of the region by Herodotus and Pliny. In this process, the language may well have spread to previously existing populations. The extension of Berber conceivably continued in the remote interior even while the language was in retreat in the areas dominated by the Greeks of Cyrenaica, the Carthaginians, and the Romans. Certainly the Berber languages of North Africa today show signs of having eventually taken over from Latin, no doubt in the late classical period before the Arab conquests, when the civilization of antiquity had itself been transformed.

At the time of the Arab conquests, the Berbers occupied the whole of the northern Sahara west of Egypt, plus the Atlas region, extending southward toward Senegal and Niger, but not Tibesti. They were predominantly rural, ranging from pastoral nomads to sedentary cultivators, and mainly tribal, with leaders rather than rulers. For the Arabs they were mostly not peoples of the Book, so that they were eligible for recruitment as *muslim* ("one who submits") clients and allies. In this way the Arabs obtained the numbers necessary for the progressive conquest of North Africa and Spain.

In the mid eighth century, however, these *muslim* Berbers jointed the Kharijite rebellion against the Umayyads, as a result of which all North Africa, except Ifrīḳiya, was lost to the Arab empire. Kharijite Islam continued to develop among the Berbers, forming communities that were instrumental in developing the trans-Saharan trade routes in the ninth and tenth centuries, but dwindled steadily after the Fatimids came to power in Ifrīḳiya.

The Fatimid revolution, based among the Kutāma Berbers of eastern Algeria, was followed by that of the Almoravids, based among the Ṣanhāja Berbers of the western Sahara, and that of the Almohads, based among the Maṣmūda of the High Atlas. Created by the appeal of militant prophets to tribal peoples between the ninth and the twelfth century, these revolutions represented an important stage in the Islamization of the Berbers, as well as in the political history of North Africa and Spain. As a result of their conquests, the Maghrib was ruled by dynasties of Berber tribal origin down to the sixteenth century, although the prophet gave way to the Sufi saint as the most influential Islamic figure in the countryside.

Nevertheless, the Berber language failed to establish its dominance. Despite the appearance of Libyan languages in inscriptions of the classical period; despite the existence of tifinagh, a Saharan Berber script; and despite occasional attempts to write in Berber with Arabic letters, Arabic quickly became the principal written language of the Muslim period, as well as the spoken language of the towns. Vernacular Arabic spread in the countryside in conjunction with the diffusion of Arab nomads from the eleventh century. By the end of the Middle Ages, Arabization was already far advanced, and the Berber-speaking population was being separated into discrete blocs in the mountainous regions of North Africa, such as the Rif, the High and Middle Atlas, Kabylia and the Aurès, and the Ahaggar region of the Sahara, each distinguished by its own dialect. In southern Tunisia and Tripolitania, and in the M'zab, Berber speech was becoming identified with the remnants of the Kharijite Ibadite sect.

BIBLIOGRAPHY

Gabriel Camps, *Berbères: Aux Marges de l'histoire* (1981); Émile-Félix Gautier, *Le passé de l'Afrique du Nord: Les siècles obscurs,* 2nd ed. (1952); Ibn Khaldūn, *Histoire des Berbères,* Baron de Slane, trans., 2nd ed., 4 vols. (1925–1956); William Marçais, "Les siècles obscurs du Maghreb," in *Revue critique d'histoire et de littérature,* n.s. **96** (1929), repr. in his *Articles et Conférences* (1961).

MICHAEL BRETT

[See also **Atlas Mountains; Heresies, Islamic; Islam, Conquests of; Khaldūn, Ibn.**]

BERCEO, GONZALO DE (1196?–1264?), the first Castilian poet identifiable by name, is the author of nine devotional works composed in *cuaderna vía.* His close association with the Benedictine monastery of San Millán de la Cogolla in La Rioja is made clear in the closing stanza of the *Vida de San Millán de la Cogolla:* "Gonzalvo was the name of the author of this treatise, / he was brought up as a child in Sant

Millán de Suso, / a native of Verceo, where sant Millán was born" (quatrain 489). Although it was once assumed that Berceo was a monk, it has now been established that he was a secular priest, and probably notary to the abbot at San Millán.

The view of Berceo as an ingenuous, facile versifier is now discredited, and it has even been suggested that he studied at the Estudio General founded at Palencia in about 1210–1214. It is believed that the University of Palencia, which was staffed by French and Italian teachers, may have been the center in which the *mester de clerecía* genre originated. The question of whether Berceo is the author of the *Libro de Alexandre* has yet to be resolved. Internal evidence in his writing suggests that he was acquainted with the Benedictine monastery of Santo Domingo de Silos, an establishment known to have had close links with the monastery at San Millán.

Leaving aside the three hymns translated from Latin, Berceo's writings may be divided into four hagiographic, two doctrinal, and three Marian works. His hagiographic writings are concerned with local Spanish saints; indeed, the earliest, the *Vida de San Millán de la Cogolla,* appears to have an economic motive, the intention behind its composition being to encourage the payment of tithes to the monastery of San Millán. While the first two sections of the poem are based on the seventh-century prose *Vita Beati Aemiliani* by Braulio, the final section appears to combine material from a variety of sources, including the forged *Privilegio de los Votos* and oral legends in circulation at San Millán. The *Vida de Santo Domingo de Silos* demonstrates Berceo's skill at transforming a Latin prose text designed for a learned audience into vernacular poetry intended for a more popular audience, and possibly even for oral delivery. It is based on the *Vita Beati Dominici* written by Grimaldus in the late eleventh century.

A didactic, popularizing intention is apparent in both the *Sacrificio de la Misa* and the *Signos del Juicio Final.* Sister Teresa Goode has shown that in composing the *Sacrificio,* Berceo employed material from a number of commentaries on the Mass. In the case of the *Signos,* Brian Dutton has identified a Latin poem in *cuaderna vía,* extant in several versions, as the source of the first twenty-two stanzas. None of these versions, however, provides a close counterpart for the remaining fifty-five stanzas of Berceo's poem.

Ostensibly a poem of praise to the Virgin Mary as the instrument of redemption, the *Loores de Nuestra Señora* includes a summary of events from the fall of man to the coming of the Holy Ghost at Pentecost, a meditation on the Crucifixion, and an excursus on the significance of the number seven. This profusion of didactic material has led Víctor García de la Concha to interpret the work as a "compendium historiae salutis." Berceo's desire to instruct his audience may be interpreted as an early Spanish response to the reforming movement initiated by the Fourth Lateran Council (1215).

The Virgin's redemptive role is explored from quite different angles in the *Duelo de la Virgen* and the *Milagros de Nuestra Señora.* The first of these takes the form of an account of the Crucifixion, as experienced by the Virgin, addressed to St. Bernard of Clairvaux. It appears to derive from an as yet unknown version of the *Liber de passione Christi et doloribus et planctibus matris eius,* attributed to St. Bernard. One section of the *Duelo* is not composed in *cuaderna vía.* This is the song of the soldiers who guard Christ's sepulcher, beginning "Eya velar." There have been several attempts to rearrange the sequence of the stanzas in order to produce better sense. Critical attention has focused on the popular origins of the song, evidence for which is detectable in its traces of parallel structure. The possibility of liturgical influence has also been raised.

Berceo's best-known work, the *Milagros de Nuestra Señora,* has as its theme the Virgin's capacity to save her loyal servants, no matter how serious their sins may have been. All but one of the twenty-five miracle stories are found in a Latin collection of twenty-eight prose miracles. The text published by Richard Becker in 1910 (Copenhagen, Royal Library, MS Thott 128) remains the closest source to date, despite the discovery by Richard Kinkade of a similar collection in Madrid's Biblioteca Nacional. Berceo's allegorical introduction is quite different from that found in the Latin source; critics have explored the possibility that Berceo created his own introduction under the influence of Bernardine texts. The miracle story that has no counterpart in the Latin text, "La iglesia robada," is set in Spain; it has been suggested that Berceo was working from oral material.

In his old age Berceo turned once more to hagiographic composition. The *Vida de Santa Oria* is an account of the life of a recluse living in the vicinity of San Millán in the eleventh century. Berceo cites as his source the biography of the saint written by her confessor, Muño; unfortunately this text is no longer extant. The otherwordly quality of the *Vida de Santa Oria* sets it apart from Berceo's earlier works; it is clear that his attention is fixed on the afterlife. The unfinished *Martirio de San Lorenzo* is generally believed to have been interrupted by Berceo's death. Set in Rome, the poem concerns a martyr who, according to pious tradition, was a native of Huesca. The exact source of this work has yet to be established.

BIBLIOGRAPHY

Gonzalo de Berceo, *Obras completas,* Brian Dutton, ed., 5 vols. (1967–1981); Joaquín Artiles, *Los recursos literarios de Berceo,* 2nd ed. (1964); Carmelo Gariano, *Análisis estilístico de los "Milagros de Nuestra Señora" de Berceo,* 2nd ed. (1971); Gaudioso Giménez Resano, *El mester poético de Gonzalo de Berceo* (1976); T. Anthony Perry, *Art and Meaning in Berceo's "Vida de Santa Oria"* (1968); Frida Weber de Kurlat, "Notes para la cronología y composición literaria de las vidas de santos de Berceo," in *Nueva revista de filología hispánica,* **15** (1961).

HELEN BORELAND

[See also **Cuaderna Vía; Spanish Literature.**]

BERENGAR OF TOURS (*ca.* 1000–1088), born at Tours in the late tenth or early eleventh century, was educated in the cathedral school of Chartres, and became *scholasticus* of the school at Tours and archdeacon at Angers. He was remembered by his contemporaries as a grammarian, but became notorious for aberrant teaching about the Eucharist. Building on the eucharistic treatise of Ratramnus of Corbie, which he believed to have been written by John Scotus Erigena, Berengar apparently taught that Christ's presence in the sacrament was figurative or spiritual, and not substantial. Details of his teaching are hazy because they must be gathered from the writings of his opponents, such as Lanfranc and Guitmund of Aversa, or from his own *De sacra coena* (Concerning the Holy Meal), a work that is very poorly structured and survives in only one manuscript.

Berengar's views were often condemned in councils between 1050 and 1079, and he himself was condemned in person at papal councils in Rome (1059 and 1079). Despite such adversity his views may have been more popular prior to the mid 1070's than is generally believed. Following the disgrace that he suffered at Rome in 1079, he was broken in spirit. Berengar died near Tours in 1088, seemingly unconvinced that he was a heretic.

BIBLIOGRAPHY

Jean de Montclos, *Lanfranc et Bérenger: La controverse eucharistique du XIe siècle* (1971), contains a full bibliography; see also R. W. Southern, "Lanfranc of Bec and Berengar of Tours," in *Studies in Medieval History Presented to Frederick Maurice Powicke* (1948); Robert Somerville, "The Case Against Berengar of Tours—A New Text," in *Studi gregoriani,* 9 (1972); Margaret Gibson, "The Dispute with Berengar of Tours," in her *Lanfranc of Bec* (1978).

ROBERT SOMERVILLE

[See also **Eucharist; Heresies, Western European; Lanfranc; Ratramnus of Corbie.**]

BERENGARII IMPERATORIS GESTA (Deeds of the emperor Berengarius) is an anonymous Latin epic in four books written in northern Italy between 915 and 924. The prologue laments the decline of poetry and expresses the hope that its prestige will be restored by the glorification of a Christian emperor in the way that classical authors praised pagan rulers. The poem relates the career of Berengarius up to his coronation as emperor in 915, but so many passages are taken directly from classical epics that the historical value of the work is diminished. The one extant manuscript (eleventh century) contains explanatory glosses that throw valuable light on contemporary knowledge of classical commentaries.

BIBLIOGRAPHY

Gesta Berengarii imperatoris, Ernst Dümmler, ed. (1871); Max Manitius, *Geschichte der lateinischen Literatur des Mittelalters,* I (1911), 632–635.

W. T. H. JACKSON

[See also **Epic, Latin; Latin Literature.**]

BERKELEY, WILLIAM, chief sculptor for the Royal Chapel at Windsor Castle between 1479 and 1483. Berkeley's work marks the reemergence of court patronage during the early Tudor period in England, and stands at the beginning of a development toward monumental and energetic sculptural forms that celebrate the monarchy.

LESLIE BRUBAKER

BERKRI (also Berkeri, Pergri; Byzantine: Perkri; Arabic: Bārghirī [now Muradiye]), a fortified Armenian town in the district of Aṛberani located on the lower course of the Arest or Berkri River (now the Bendimahi in modern Turkey). Berkri became important in the Arab period (mid eighth to early tenth centuries) when it was the seat of the ᶜUthmānids, a dynasty of Arab emirs. In the tenth century, under the Qaysite emirs, it became a station on the trade route from Marāgha to Mayyāfarīqīn via Xoy and Bitlis. Sacked by the Byzantines in 931, the town passed to local Qaysite heirs, who held it under the suzerainty of the Armenian Arcrunids of Vaspurakan. When Vaspurakan was ceded to the Byzantines in 1021, Berkri became part of the katepanate of Basprakania (Asprakania), but did not surrender to its new masters until 1034 or 1035. Berkri continued as a trade center under the Mongols, being now located on the route from Tabrīz to Trebizond via Xoy and Erzurum. After the Ottoman conquest of the region, however, Berkri declined in importance, though for a time it remained the capital of a sanjak of the vilayet of Van.

BIBLIOGRAPHY

Heinrich Hübschmann, *Die altarmenishchen Ortsnamen* (1904, repr. 1969), 341; Hakob Manandyan, *Trade and Cities of Armenia in Relation to Ancient World Trade,* Nina Garsoïan, trans. (1965), 105, 148, 156, 157; A. Ter-Ghewondyan, *The Arab Emirates in Bagratid Armenia,* Nina Garsoïan, trans. (1976).

ROBERT H. HEWSEN

[See also **Armenia; Vaspurakan.**]

BERLINGHIERI, BONAVENTURA (*fl.* 1228–1274), Lucchese painter, probably the second son of Berlinghiero Berlinghieri. Only one work is securely credited to him: the signed and dated (1235) retable depicting a full-length standing St. Francis surrounded by scenes from his life, in the church of San Francesco, Pescia. The earliest known example of a panel type that grew increasingly popular in the duecento and trecento, it stands as a key monument in the history of early Italian painting. Bonaventura's style, based on that of his father and on the Byzantine tradition, created monumental forms and highly expressive lines, paving the way for later developments in Florentine and Sienese painting with the works of Coppo di Marcovaldo and Guido da Siena.

BIBLIOGRAPHY

Edward B. Garrison, "A Berlinghieresque Fresco in S. Stefano, Bologna," in *Art Bulletin,* 28 (1946); "Toward a New History of Early Lucchese Painting," in *Art Bulletin,* 33 (1951); and "A New History of Bonaventura di Berlinghiero's St. Francis Dossal in Pescia," in *Studies in the History of Medieval Italian Painting,* I (1953).

ADELHEID M. GEALT

BERMEJO, BARTOLOMÉ (*fl.* 1470–1498), one of the greatest of the Hispano-Flemish painters, was active in Aragon and Barcelona. Perhaps he was trained by a Fleming, for his style displays a rugged realism, with somber figures, clad in heavy, angular drapery, placed in dark, dramatic landscapes. His most famous work, the Pietà in Barcelona Cathedral executed for Canon Luis Desplá in 1490, is a masterpiece of early Spanish expressionism. He also designed stained glass for the cathedral in 1494–1495.

BIBLIOGRAPHY

Chandler R. Post, *A History of Spanish Painting,* V (1934), 103–236; Jacques Lassaigne, *Spanish Painting,* Stuart Gilbert, trans., I (1952), 73–76.

JAMES SNYDER

BERNARD OF CHARTRES (*d. ca.* 1130), early Scholastic philosopher and grammarian born in Brittany, was the elder brother of Thierry of Chartres. (He should not be confused with Bernard Silvestris.) A master at the cathedral school of Chartres from 1114 until about 1119, he subsequently served as its chancellor until 1126. His works have not survived, but a later pupil at the school, John of Salisbury, has transmitted some of Bernard's views. His most famous and most controversial dictum concerns the relationship between the scholars of his own age and those of antiquity: "We are comparable to dwarfs perched on the shoulders of giants; as a result we can see more and farther than they, certainly not on account of our own vision or superior height, but because we are carried and lifted up by the great stature of giants." This statement should not be interpreted anachronistically as an expression of faith in the progress of history, but as unbounded admiration of the classics, combined with a sense of the extent to which moderns can benefit from them through careful study. It is not surprising, therefore, that John of Salisbury characterizes Bernard as the greatest classical scholar of his time.

As a teacher Bernard stressed the study of Latin language and literature through a comprehensive and strict program of studies. His teaching of the liberal arts was supported by a theory of the working of the intellect *(ingenium).* The imitation of the classics played a major role in language study, but students were punished for mere copying. In his lost commentary on Porphyry's *Isagoge,* Bernard reportedly attempted to reconcile the teachings of Plato and Aristotle. As the most eminent Platonist of his age, Bernard's solution to the problem of universals was to regard them as the Platonic Ideas, and therefore as real. Although the Ideas are divine and eternal, they are not coeternal with God, as the persons of the Trinity are. They exist in the mind of God as models of all things; but, like Boethius, Bernard holds that only copies *(formae nativae)* of them are found in matter. By subordinating the Ideas to God, Bernard attempted to fit Platonism into Christian doctrine: through the theory of native forms God is distanced from creation, and hence the charge of pantheism is avoided.

In the realm of speculative grammar, Bernard held that a word signifying a quality, such as "whiteness," is related to its derivatives as the Ideas are to the things modeled after them. Among Bernard's students were William of Conches and Richard the Bishop. His philosophical views were developed further by Gilbert de la Porrée.

BIBLIOGRAPHY

Primary sources. John of Salisbury, *Metalogicon,* C. C. J. Webb, ed. (1929), 1.5, 11, 24; 2.17; 3.2, 4; 4.35; also trans. D. D. McGarry (1955); and *Polycraticus,* C. C. J. Webb, ed. (1909), 7.13; Otto of Freising, *Gesta Friderici,* Georg Waitz and B. von Simson, ed., 3rd ed. (1912), 1.49; Édouard Jeauneau, "Deux rédactions des gloses de Guillaume de Conches sur Priscien," in *"Lectio philosophorum": Recherches sur l'École de Chartres* (1973), 199–200, 358.

Secondary sources. P. Calendini, "Bernard de Chartres," in *Dictionnaire d'histoire et de géographie ecclésiastique,* VIII (1935); Peter Dronke, "New Approaches to the School of Chartres," in *Anuario de estudios medievales,* 6 (1969); Étienne Gilson, "Le Platonisme de Bernard de Chartres," in *Revue néo-scolastique de philosophie,* 25 (1923); Édouard Jeauneau, *"Nani gigantum humeris insidentes:* Essai d'interprétation de Bernard de Chartres," in *"Lectio philosophorum"* (1973).

HAIJO JAN WESTRA

[See also **John of Salisbury; Philosophy-Theology, Western European, to Early Twelfth Century; Scholasticism.**]

BERNARD OF CLAIRVAUX, ST. (1090–1153), epitomizes the early-twelfth-century tension between tradition and innovation. He traveled the length and breadth of Europe, all the while insisting that monks had no place outside their monasteries. He sought the condemnation of two of the day's leading scholars; yet he shared with them a fascination with dialectic. He convinced two sovereigns and innumerable knights to set out on a disastrous crusade against the Muslims and wrote scathingly against heretics; but he preached that persuasion, not force, must be used against unbelievers. A polished writer and an all but irresistible speaker, he manipulated words brilliantly while maintaining their inadequacy to express truth. Born to Burgundian nobility, he possessed a quick temper and an engaging arrogance that made him a natural leader, yet he taught that the indispensable basis of the Christian life is unflinching humility.

LIFE

The third of six sons born at Fontaines-lès-Dijon to Tescelin le Saur and Aleth de Montbard, Bernard was imbued with the deep piety of his parents and was trained for a clerical career by the canons of Châtillon. A young man "of graceful body, pleasant face, very polished manners, shrewd wit, and persuasive eloquence," he enjoyed unlimited prospects (*Vita prima* 3.6). At the age of twenty, he abandoned them to enter a monastery—not a large, prosperous, well-established abbey, but the small, extraordinarily austere "new monastery" at Cîteaux, scarcely a decade old. With characteristic persistence he prevailed upon kinsmen and friends—even his eldest brother, a knight and a married man—to join him. Some thirty strong, they entered Cîteaux "shortly before Easter," probably in 1112.

After a requisite year as a novice and two more in profession, Bernard, then twenty-four or twenty-five years old, was named to make a new foundation in Champagne, at Clairvaux. Only three years later Clairvaux established its own daughter house, the first of sixty-eight founded during Bernard's thirty-eight years as abbot. Under his leadership Clairvaux became, by the Cistercian system of affiliation, the motherhouse of nearly half the Cistercian order.

Gradually Bernard learned from his monks and

his friends to temper his intensity, but not before his zeal for monastic austerities had caused him to become gaunt and pallid and to develop chronic gastric problems from which he never recovered. The young abbot inspired such awe in his monks that they seldom consulted him on any subject, and even less often understood his sermons in chapter. They felt—with good reason, Bernard admitted to his cousin—that he had little sympathy with ordinary human frailty. They had little doubt of his holiness. His first biographer, William of St. Thierry, reported that meeting Bernard was like approaching the altar to celebrate the Eucharist.

WORKS

Bernard wrote tirelessly, dictating to secretaries, revising, asking the opinions of friends, and rewriting. Sometime before 1124 or 1125 he published his first treatise, *The Steps of Humility and Pride,* an amplification of chapter 7 of the Rule of St. Benedict. At roughly the same time, while apart from the community recuperating from illness, he composed *Four Homilies in Praise of the Blessed Virgin,* to "satisfy my own devotion." When Cistercian "novelties" and Cistercian smugness came under criticism by affronted Benedictines, he responded, about 1125, with a public letter to his cousin Robert, who had fled Cîteaux for the more comfortable Cluny, and with a satirical *Apologia* to a Benedictine friend. At the request of the same friend, he composed a theological study, *On Grace and Free Choice,* between 1126 and 1135. For the newly founded Knights Templars he wrote *In Praise of the New Knighthood* (1128–1136).

For the papal chancellor Bernard composed the book *On Loving God.* Sometime before 1144, to answer a question from the monks of Saintes-Pères of Chartres, a mellower Bernard turned again to monastic subjects, writing *On Precept and Dispensation.* His vision of the reformed church found expression in his biography and eulogy of the monk-missionary bishop of Armagh, St. Malachy (1148–1152), and in the advice he proffered to his former monk, Pope Eugenius III, in *Five Books on Consideration* (1148–1153).

During these same years Bernard allowed the circulation of several series of sermons: on the liturgical year and on diverse subjects, and the incomparable eighty-six sermons on the *Song of Songs,* which he began in 1135. He died before having progressed further than chapter 2 of the *Song.*

Some five hundred letters written between 1116 and 1153 to emperors, kings, popes, archbishops, counts, dukes, abbots, monks, townsmen, canons, nuns, and countesses attest to the extent of Bernard's influence, and succinctly express his vision of the Christian life. Minor works include *Sentences, Parabolae*—perhaps outlines of unrealized works—and a prologue to the Cistercian antiphonary on how plainsong should be sung.

Five years before he died, Bernard set out to revise all his works. He was still dictating on his deathbed. He mastered every literary genre used by churchmen of the day, even the developing disputed question, which he slipped discreetly into book V of *On Consideration (De consideratione* V.6.14–V.7.17; compare *De gratia et libero arbitrio* VIII.21, Sermo in Cesto SS. Petri et Pauli 1). His works circulated widely throughout the Middle Ages. Many were translated into the vernacular and Bernard's name and authority were applied to non-Bernardine compositions. Several of the Protestant Reformers read and admired him.

ACTIVITIES

Bernard's literary works correspond to his activities. In the early 1120's, through acquaintances among the Black Monks, he was encouraging the simplification of Benedictine observances. He was active at the Council of Troyes, which in 1128 established the Templars. Two years later, at a council at Étampes, he spoke so eloquently on behalf of Innocent II, one of two contenders for the papal throne, that he won over King Louis VI. "Given the opportunity to express himself," remarked John of Salisbury in later years, "he succeeded in persuading nearly everyone to his point of view." A grateful and beleaguered pope quickly made Bernard his counselor and "troubleshooter," and launched him on a public career that kept him from his abbey for roughly one-third of his remaining lifetime.

After traveling extensively throughout France with, and on behalf of, Innocent in 1132, Bernard carried his campaign to the northern Italian cities of Genoa and Pisa the following year, and accompanied Innocent on his return to Rome. Within two years he had also been dispatched to Germany to persuade the emperor to accept Innocent's claim to the papacy, returned to Italy for the Council of Pisa, and made another visit to Rome. Wherever Bernard went, Cistercian monasteries sprang up. More than twenty-five new Claravallian foundations were made in France, Italy, and the Empire during the decade Bernard spent championing Innocent's cause.

 BERNARD OF CLAIRVAUX, ST.

Scarcely had the papal schism been settled when William of St. Thierry wrote to alert the now widely esteemed abbot to the dangers of the theology of Peter Abelard. At first hesitant to involve himself, Bernard soon took up the defense of traditional theology with the same zeal he had shown in advancing monastic and ecclesiastical reform. A spate of increasingly virulent letters warned pope, cardinals, and clergy of Abelard's heresy. At a synod at Sens, Bernard secured an episcopal verdict of condemnation before his adversary had even arrived to debate him.

In the same year, 1140, he preached at Paris a sermon, *On Conversion,* so persuasive that at least three students forthwith abandoned their studies for the cloister. Among them was Geoffrey of Auxerre, who was to become Bernard's secretary, his almost constant companion, and the chief advocate of his canonization. He accompanied his abbot in 1145 on a visit to Languedoc to preach against the errors of Pierre de Bruys and his disciple Henri.

When, in March 1146, Pope Eugenius III called for a crusade to relieve Levantine Christians after the fall of Edessa, it was Bernard he instructed to promote it. That summer, after meeting at Vézelay with King Louis VII, Bernard raised enthusiasm and troops throughout France and the Low Countries. In the autumn and winter of 1146–1147, he journeyed up the Rhine on the same mission. Encountering virulent anti-Semitism incited by a certain Rasul, Bernard issued a public letter against threatened Jewish massacres (*Epistles* 363). The utter failure of the Second Crusade brought Bernard reproach that, he wrote, he accepted gladly if it spared God's honor. Geoffrey, however, felt obliged to remind survivors that his abbot had undertaken the chore only under obedience and at the repeated urgings of the king, the bishops, and the pope himself.

At further cost to his reputation, Bernard attempted unsuccessfully in 1148 to secure the condemnation of the philosopher Gilbert de la Porrée, on a point of grammar. Gilbert had distinguished between *Deus* (God) and *divinitas* in the continuing discussion of universals. By setting the latter term in the ablative case, he implied, to Bernard's mind, that God's being was derivative from his divinity. "The abbot of Clairvaux," suggested the Cistercian bishop Otto of Freising loyally, "may in the frailty of humankind have been deceived in the matter."

Although his health was visibly deteriorating, Bernard traveled to Metz early in 1153 to arbitrate between the armies of bishop and duke. After his return home, he grew increasingly weaker and, on 20 August, he died.

A first request by the Cistercians for the canonization of their saint failed, and they busied themselves retouching his biography—begun to that purpose while he still lived—to make it more persuasive. A second attempt succeeded, and on 18 January 1174, Alexander III pronounced him Saint Bernard.

MESSAGE

Formed in the monastic tradition of scripture-reading, patristic exegesis, and liturgical celebration, Bernard added his personal experience and his great love of words. Unlike the emerging Schoolmen he moved not so much from logical premise to conclusion as from sound to sound, word to word, in a concatenation of verbal images that in their complementarity gradually disclose a hidden mystery. He spoke out sharply against the misuse of words, against carelessness or an overly rigid vocabulary, against a refusal to recognize the limitations of all verbal symbols of ineffable reality. But few have expressed more eloquently than Bernard the human need to employ words carefully and beautifully to communicate the thoughts of mind and heart. His sensitivity to words is revealed in his endless revising of his works, in his love of alliteration, of puns, of word games. Allusions to birds, beasts, and plants abound, suggesting an observant eye. Although his first biographer maintained that Bernard was so caught up in things heavenly as to be unaware of his physical surroundings, he also disclosed that Bernard enjoyed walking in the woods, a practice he recommended to at least one scholar who sought to discern God.

All creation spoke to Bernard of the glory of God, and all mankind should, in his opinion, praise and adore its loving and all-powerful Creator. Monastic observances, church polity, Christian marriage, an armed crusade—all should glorify God and bring the Christian closer to him. Whatever turned persons away from God he attacked, whether it was a sect that declared the body evil, an arrogance that put self before God or fellows, a method of theology whose goal was detached analysis rather than absorbed prayer, or an artful cloister arcade that dissipated the monk's attention.

Bernard wrote differently to monks than to kings or clerks. His essential message, however, never varied: God is love. In that love alone can the human person find the wholeness and the happiness that he craves and for which he was created. Made in the

BERNARD OF CLAIRVAUX, ST.

image and likeness of the loving Creator, man is capable of being "deified," of being united in some inexpressible way with God. This is difficult, for, having turned away from the source of love and life and become mired in self-seeking and superficiality, humankind has trapped itself in a "region of unlikeness," in disorder and disobedience. To those who have turned away from truth to embrace deception, God has manifested his love, his forgivness, and his truth in Christ. Bernard's confidence in God's love was absolute: "He will not turn me away seeking," Bernard was sure, "whom damned he sought out" (Sermon 84.5 on the *Song of Songs*).

Conversion is the response of the individual to God's call. The person who turns back to seek God must first work at knowing himself without dissimulation, for "nothing is more intimate to us than He, and nothing more incomprehensible" (Sermon 4.4 on the *Song of Songs*). In himself man discovers both an incomparable natural dignity and an abyss of godless misery. As a composite being made up of body, mind, and soul, fallen man is pulled in two directions: to God, his natural happiness, and to ultimately wretched self-gratification. In this unnatural state man is fragmented; he has splintered what should be, and must be, integrated. The soul made in God's image needs the body and its senses to achieve the knowledge by which alone one can recognize the truth essential to happiness. It needs the mind to be able to discern extrasensory reality and to judge right from wrong, truth from falsehood. When they are disordered, the body unrestrained seeks gratification in physical indulgence; the mind, undisciplined, flits in pointless curiosity; the soul, unaided, flies beyond its capacity. Order must be reestablished by discipline—physical, mental, and spiritual—if the person is not to be preoccupied with and distracted by superficialities.

Recognition of one's own misery and grandeur allows one to admit one's utter dependence on God's mercy; this is humility, the indispensable foundation of growth. To be humble is to be intellectually honest, to recognize one's own truest being, to despise one's own excellence. Only the humble person can be compassionate, for, knowing himself, he can discern the same dignity and the same dependence in others.

Humility breeds freedom, which, like knowledge, is progressive. Possessing after the Fall only freedom of choice, the convert gradually can acquire freedom from sin—that is, he becomes increasingly able not to sin as he conforms his will to God's. In personal integration and union with God in heaven, he will also regain freedom from misery.

Love also grows and is purified by stages, four of which Bernard outlined. Love, an innate, natural faculty, can be turned to God to be fulfilled, or it can be dissipated on trivia and perverted. Everyone, at some rudimentary level, loves and indulges himself. As one learns humility, this "carnal love" becomes a social love as well, for one realizes that his pleasures must not impinge on those of others. It becomes, too, a love of God for the things God can do for one. When one has come to seek not his pleasure from God, but God's pleasure, there develops a "filial love" that enables one to love himself truly, for God's sake, and in that mutual love to lose himself in the joy of experiencing God (*On Loving God,* 23–27).

Likewise, a very ordinary love of parents and friends ("carnal love") can predispose one to love Christ the man as the Bible depicts him. Reason then perceives within Christ the eternal godhead ("rational love"), and one gradually learns a "spiritual love" of transcendent and formless God (Sermon 20 on the *Song of Songs*).

Bernard's experience of pure love comes but rarely and fleetingly. He called it contemplation, self-forgetfulness in wondering absorption in God. It is a transformation of the human person in conformity with God. It is *excessus,* a stepping out of the narrow self into God, and like man himself it occurs at multiple levels, involving cognitive recognition and affective self-giving. It is a pure gift from God that comes to those who prepare themselves by choosing to reorder their being and by acting on that choice in response to God's love. God wants to share himself; he waits only for the development of the receptivity that enables the seeker to accept this experience.

To Bernard and the tradition that formed him, the contemplative experience was not an achievement that proved one's spiritual success; the effort, not the attainment, was what counted. Bernardine contemplation lacks late-medieval overtones of extraordinary "mystical vision." To be often in the presence of God, not to claim supernatural intimacy, was the goal of the Christian, especially of the monk, whose whole life was ordered toward that end and toward the full understanding, the perfect love, the complete vision of heaven.

Unaccompanied by visions or by voices, contemplative experience was a gentle *excessus* modestly described:

Only by the movement of my heart did I perceive His presence. . . . The coming of the Word was not perceptible to my eyes, for he has no color; nor to my ears, for there was no sound; nor yet to my nostrils, for he mingles with the mind, not with the air. . . . His coming was not tasted by the mouth, for there was no eating or drinking, nor could he be known by the sense of touch, for he is not tangible. How then did he enter? Perhaps he did not enter because he does not come from outside. He is not one of the things that exist outside us. Yet he does not come from within me, for he is good and I know that there is no good in me. . . . If I looked outside myself, I saw him stretching beyond the farthest I could see, and if I looked within, he was yet further within. Then I knew the truth of what I had read, "In him we love and move and have our being." (Sermon 74.5 on the *Song of Songs*)

BIBLIOGRAPHY

The bibliography of studies on Bernard is vast. Three bibliographic guides have been compiled to date and should be consulted by those interested in pursuing bernardine studies seriously: Leopold Janauschek, *Bibliographia Bernardina* (1891); Jean de la Croix Bouton, *Bibliographie Bernardine 1891–1957* (1958); Eugène Manning, *Bibliographie Bernardine (1957–1970)* (1972).

General studies. Bruno Scott James, *Saint Bernard of Clairvaux: An Essay in Biography* (1957); *Bernard of Clairvaux and the Cistercian Spirit,* Clare Lavoie, trans., Cistercian Studies Series, XVI (1976); Jean Leclercq, *Saint Bernard mystique* (1948); Ailbe J. Luddy, *The Life and Teaching of St. Bernard,* 2nd ed. (1937); Elphegius Vacandard, *Vie de saint Bernard,* 2 vols. (1895); Watkin Wynn Williams, *Saint Bernard of Clairvaux* (1935, 1953), and *Studies in St. Bernard of Clairvaux* (1927).

Collections. Mélanges Saint Bernard: XXIVe Congrès de l'Association bourguignonne des sociétés savantes (1953); *Saint Bernard Théologien: Actes du Congrès de Dijon* (1953).

Monographs. Étienne Gilson, *The Mystical Theology of Saint Bernard,* A. H. C. Downes, trans. (1940, 1955); Jean Leclercq, *Études sur saint Bernard et le texte de ses écrits* (1953), and *Recueil d'études sur saint Bernard et ses écrits,* 3 vols. (1962–1969); Henri M. Rochais, *Enquête sur les sermons divers et les sentences de saint Bernard* (1962); Emero Steigman, *The Language of Asceticism: A Study of Bernard of Clairvaux's Sermons on the Canticle* (1973).

Texts. Jean Leclercq, Henri M. Rochais, and Charles H. Talbot, eds., *Sancti Bernardi opera,* 8 vols. in 9 (1957–1979); Jean Mabillon, *Sancti Bernardi abbatis clarae-vallensis . . . opera omnia,* 4th ed., 2 vols. in 4 (1839); Jean Mabillon and P. F. Chifflet, eds., in *Patrologia latina,* CLXXXII–CLXXXV (1879, repr. 1978).

Translations. The complete works of Bernard of Clairvaux are being published serially in English in *The Works of Bernard of Clairvaux, The Cistercian Fathers Series* (1969–).

E. ROZANNE ELDER

[See also **Abelard, Peter; Biblical Interpretation; Cistercian Order; Councils, Western, 869–1179; Crusades and Crusader States; Gilbert de la Porrée; Mysticism; Philosophy-Theology, Western European, to Early Twelfth Century; Philosophy-Theology, Western European, Twelfth Century to Aquinas; Preaching, Sermon Literature, Western European; William of St. Thierry.**]

BERNARD OF SANTIAGO, a master mason, probably French, brought by Bishop Diego Peláez to supervise the construction of the pilgrimage church of Santiago de Compostela in 1075. Focus of the great Romanesque pilgrimage routes, Santiago de Compostela preserves one of the finest interiors of its period.

LESLIE BRUBAKER

[See also **Santiago de Compostela.**]

BERNARD OF SOISSONS, architect of Rheims Cathedral, possibly from about 1255 to about 1290. He is known to have been in the city in 1282 and 1287. A cathedral inscription (destroyed in 1779) recorded that Bernard was master for thirty-five years, and "opened the big 'O' and built five vaults," probably references to the western rose and the five western high vaults of the nave. Nothing else is known of his career.

BIBLIOGRAPHY

Francis Salet, "Chronologie de la cathédrale [de Reims]," in *Bulletin monumental,* **125** (1967), with complete bibliography.

CARL F. BARNES, JR.

[See also **Rheims Cathedral.**]

BERNARD SILVESTER (or Silvestris). Little is known with certainty about Bernard Silvester, formerly identified with Bernard of Chartres. A connection with the milieu of Chartres is attested by the dedication of his major work, the *Cosmographia,* to

Thierry, who became chancellor of Chartres in 1141. This work also contains a reference to Pope Eugenius III, who traveled in France in 1147–1148. Bernard probably was a teacher of letter-writing and poetic composition at St. Martin, Tours, where he taught Matthew of Vendôme, from roughly 1130 to 1140. In 1178 a nephew of Bernard disposed of a house in Tours willed to him by his uncle, suggesting that Bernard died before that date, possibly about 1160.

The *Cosmographia* (On cosmogony) and the *Mathematicus* (On destiny) can be attributed to Bernard with certainty. The same cannot be said of the allegorizing commentaries on Vergil's *Aeneid* and on Martianus Capella's *De nuptiis.* (The latter also refers to a yet undiscovered commentary on Plato's *Timaeus.*) Differences between these commentaries and the authentic works may be due to the demands of genre. Of the *Experimentarius* (on geomancy and astrology) only a brief preface can be attributed to Bernard. Attempts to identify an *ars poetica* and an *ars dictaminis* ascribed to Bernard by medieval sources have yet to produce conclusive results. A treatise on classical meters is contained in the commentary on Martianus. Two shorter poetic works, *De gemellis* and *De paupere ingrato,* based on juridical *enigmata,* have been attributed to Bernard as well.

Bernard's overall concern is the universe and man's place in it. In the *Cosmographia* he presents a mythico-scientific account of creation and the interrelationship of man (microcosm) and universe (macrocosm). He combines the manner of Plato's *Timaeus* with that of Calcidius' commentary by alternating philosophical myth *(narratio fabulosa)* with prosaic exposition, adding *encyclopaedia* and panegyric, and varying prose with poetry through the flexible genre of the *prosimetrum.* Creation is presented as a divinely instituted ordering process of primeval matter pregnant with creativity and longing for form.

Bernard's interest in astrology derives from his preoccupation with the problem of destiny and free will. Earlier views characterizing him as a determinist do not allow for the subtlety and complexity of his ideas about this matter. Bernard's desire for ultimate knowledge finds expression in the numerous quests—astral, terrestrial, and subterranean—that are of great importance structurally and imaginatively to his works. His use of philosophical myth, and his acceptance—indeed, celebration—of matter and procreation were particularly influential.

BIBLIOGRAPHY

Editions. Peter Dronke, ed., *Bernardus Silvestris: Cosmographia* (1978); Mirella Brini Savorelli, ed., "Un manuale di geomanzia presentato da Bernardo Silvestre da Tours (XII secolo): L'*Experimentarius,*" in *Rivista critica di storia della filosofia,* **14** (1959); Bernard Hauréau, ed., *Le Mathematicus de Bernard Silvestris et la Passio S. Agnetis de Pierre de Riga* (1895); Julian W. Jones and Elizabeth F. Jones, eds., *Commentum quod dicitur Bernardi Silvestris super sex libros Eneidos Virgilii* (1977); Jakob Werner, ed., *De gamellis,* in *Beiträge zur Kunde der lateinischen Literatur des Mittelalters,* 2nd ed. (1905); André Vernet, ed., *De paupere ingrato,* in "Poésies latines des XIIe et XIIIe siècles (Auxerre 243)," in *Mélanges dediés à la mémoire de Félix Grat,* II (1949), 256–257; Mirella Brini Savorelli, ed., "Il 'Dictamen' di Bernardo Silvestre," in *Rivista critica di storia della filosofia,* **20** (1965).

Studies and translations. Winthrop Wetherbee, trans., *The Cosmographia of Bernardus Silvestris* (1973); for a survey of the secondary literature see the bibliography of Brian Stock, *Myth and Science in the Twelfth Century: A Study of Bernard Silvester* (1972) and the bibliographies to the works of Dronke, Wetherbee, and Jones and Jones cited above; note also the following unpublished dissertation: André Vernet, "Bernardus Silvestris: Recherches sur l'auteur et l'oeuvre, suivies d'une édition critique de la *Cosmographia*" (École des Chartes, 1938).

HAIJO JAN WESTRA

[See also **Philosophy-Theology, Western European, Twelfth Century to Aquinas; Plato in the Middle Ages.**]

BERNARDINO OF SIENA, ST. (1380–1444), a member of the Observant branch of the Franciscan order and perhaps the outstanding popular preacher of the fourteenth century. He was canonized on 24 May 1450.

Born at Massa Marittima, the son of the Sienese noble Tollo di Dino di Bando Albizzeschi and the Massan noble Nera di Bindo Avveduti, Bernardino was orphaned by the age of six. He lived in Massa with a maternal aunt until, at eleven, he moved into the home of his paternal uncle and aunt, Cristoforo and Pia Albizzeschi, in Siena. There two pious widows, a cousin and another aunt, became central figures in his life. These influences help explain his later religious calling and his interest in the spiritual and ethical well-being of women. In Siena, Bernardino studied canon law for three years, although he did not obtain the doctorate.

At eighteen Bernardino joined the aristocratic flagellant confraternity of the Disciplinants of Santa Maria della Scala, named after the great hospital in

Benardino with his plaque. Palazzo della Signoria, Siena. ALINARI/ EDITORIAL PHOTOCOL

which they met. There he cared for the ill for four months during the plague epidemic of 1400. After experimenting with the eremetic life, Bernardino entered the Franciscan order in 1402. A short time later he joined the Observant branch of the Minorites, and moved into their monastery called the Colombaia (dovecote) on Mt. Amiata, south of Siena.

Bernardino preached his first sermon in 1405. Henceforth he lived as a wandering preacher, speaking most often in the towns of central and northern Italy, from Siena to Milan. Particularly well known are his Lenten sermons of 1424 and 1425, given in Florence, and that preached in the Campo, or main plaza, of Siena on Assumption Day, 15 August 1427.

Bernardino was preoccupied with Jesus. He adopted the Holy Monogram, the letters *IHS* from the name of Jesus (written in the Greek form), surrounded by the radiant sun and set in a field of blue, the color that signified faith. Bernardino would have had men substitute this emblem for their many contesting emblems, whether of noble families, guilds, or political parties.

Bernardino's attempt to spread the adoption of the Holy Monogram allowed religious enemies to charge him with heresy and idolatry several times before the papal curia. On each occasion he was absolved. He was authorized to use his emblem and continue preaching. Bernardino's fame brought him offers of several bishoprics, including those of Siena and Ferrara, but he declined. He received major positions within the Franciscan order in Italy. Bernardino strove to heal the divisions that separated the Observants from the more lax Conventuals, while trying to prevent the former from straying in their zeal into the errors of the condemned Spiritual Franciscans and of the persecuted Fraticelli. Though remaining within the fold of orthodoxy, Bernardino was strongly affected by some of the more suspect Franciscan authors, especially Peter John Olivi and Ubertino of Casale.

Bernardino's sermons eschewed great theological and theoretical issues. They dealt with the specific moral and religious concerns of his hearers, among them crime, strife, almsgiving, usury, the obligations of merchants, conjugal and family ethics, and sodomy—then seen as an especially serious problem in Siena. Bernardino filled his sermons with colorful illustrations drawn from everyday life, and often preached in the form of a running dialogue with his audiences.

BIBLIOGRAPHY

Iris Origo, *The World of San Bernardino* (1962).

WILLIAM M. BOWSKY

[See also **Franciscans; Minorites; Peter John Olivi.**]

BERNARDO CIUFFAGNI. See **Ciuffagni, Bernardo.**

BERNARDO DA VENEZIA, Italian master builder and woodcarver, active mainly in Pavia during the third quarter of the trecento. In 1391 he was called to Milan by Gian Galeazzo Visconti to direct work on the cathedral, and in 1392 he was part of a panel that reviewed its building plans. In 1392 he also received a commission to carve a wood Madonna and Child for the cathedral altar which is now in the Museo del Duomo. In 1396, Visconti commissioned the Certosa of Pavia, appointing Bernardo as its chief designer. Four years later he was active on Santa Maria del Carmine, Milan. His activities on the Certosa must have ceased sometime around 1428, when Solari is recorded as chief architect.

BIBLIOGRAPHY

Giacomo Bascapè, *Il Duomo di Milano* (1965); Angiola M. Romanini, *L'architettura gotica in Lombardia* (1964); John White, *Art and Architecture in Italy, 1200–1400* (1966), 347, 350.

ADELHEID M. GEALT

BERNART DE VENTADORN was one of the best-known and most frequently imitated troubadours in the twelfth century. According to the romanticized account of his life in the Old Provençal *vida,* he rose from his humble status as the son of a servant at the castle of Ventadorn to become the lover of his lord's wife and, later, of Eleanor of Aquitaine. The *vida* further states that he spent his final days in the monastery at Dalon. In fact, however, little can be firmly established concerning Bernart's life. He evidently had a long association with the castle of Ventadorn (whence his name), and he probably went at least once to England. He must also have spent some time in Toulouse at the court of Raymond V, whom he names in several of his poems. He may have begun his career as an apprentice to his patron, Eble of Ventadorn, himself a poet of some note though surviving manuscripts bear none of his pieces. Unfortunately it is impossible even to determine whether Bernart served Eble II or Eble III.

Bernart's songs, of which forty-four survive, probably date from between 1150 and 1180. Except for three *tensos,* all are *cansos.* His songs, which deal exclusively with *fin' amors,* are remarkable for the clarity of their language, the beauty of their images, and the wide range of emotions that they express.

BIBLIOGRAPHY

Carl Appel, ed., *Bernart von Ventadorn: Seine Lieder, mit Einleitung und Glossar* (1915); Moshé Lazar, ed. and trans., *Bernard de Ventadour, troubadour du XIIe siècle: Chansons d'amour* (1966); Stephen G. Nichols, Jr., ed., *The Songs of Bernart de Ventadorn* (1962). For references to a variety of articles on specific poems, themes, and techniques, see Robert A. Taylor, *La littérature occitane du Moyen Âge* (1977), 56–69.

ELIZABETH WILSON POE

[See also **Courtly Love; Provençal Literature; Troubadour, Trouvère, Trovadores.**]

BERNOLD OF CONSTANCE (or of St. Blasien, *ca.* 1050–1100) was canon of Constance; monk of St. Blasien and then of Schaffhausen; chronicler, canonist, liturgist, polemicist; and earliest and most influential disseminator of the ideas of Pope Gregory VII in Germany. His chronicle (autograph in Munich, MS lat. 432, the Codex latinus monacensis) is the most extensive source for the history of the Investiture Controversy.

BIBLIOGRAPHY

Johanne Autenrieth, *Die Domschule von Konstanz zur Zeit des Investiturstreits* (1956); I. S. Robinson, "Zur Arbeitsweise Bernolds von Konstanz und seines Kreises," in *Deutsches Archiv,* **34** (1978); J. G. Ernst Strelau, *Leben und Werke des Mönches Bernold von St. Blasien* (1889).

I. S. ROBINSON

[See also **Gregory VII, Pope; Investiture and Investiture Controversy.**]

BERNORINUS (*d.* 899), archbishop of Vienne, is known for his Latin poetry, among which is his epitaph. The poetry is primarily of a religious nature, and focuses on the life of Christ. It is conjectured that Bernorinus may have played a role in the building of a church at Clermont in honor of St. Allire.

BIBLIOGRAPHY

Monumenta Germaniae historica: Poetae Latini aevi Carolini, I, E. Duemmler, ed. (1881), 393–425; O. Schumman, "Bernowini episcopi carmina," in *Historische Vierteljahrschrift,* **26** (1931).

MARK D. MEYERSON

[See also **Latin Literature; Latin Meter.**]

BERNWARD (993–1022), bishop of Hildesheim, was born of a noble Saxon family. After education at the cathedral school of Hildesheim, in 987 he was installed in the Imperial Chapel and Chancellery by Willigis of Mainz. Subsequently he became tutor to Otto III. In January 1001, Bernward was in Rome to present his case for the rights of the bishop of Hildesheim over the convent of Gandersheim, and in 1006–1007 he took part in Henry II's war against Baldwin IV of Flanders.

Bernward is best known as the builder of the monastery of St. Michael, for which he commissioned the monumental bronze doors cast in 1015. Under his close supervision the Hildesheim workshops reintroduced bronze casting after a lapse in Germany of some two hundred years. These doors constitute an important first step toward the late-eleventh-century revival of monumental sculpture. Bernward was canonized in 1192.

BIBLIOGRAPHY

Thangmar, *Vita S. Bernwardi episcopi Hildesheimensis,* in *Monumenta Germaniae historica: Scriptores,* IV, G. H. Pertz, ed. (1841), 754–782; Francis Joseph Tschan, *Saint Bernward of Hildesheim,* 3 vols. (1942–1952); Rudolf Wesenberg, *Bernwardinische Plastik* (1955).

PETER HUENINK

BÉROUL. See **Tristan, Roman de.**

BERRUGUETE, PEDRO (*fl.* 1477–1504), Hispano-Flemish painter active in Castile and Italy. He is probably the "Pietro Spagnuolo" listed in the archives of Urbino who collaborated with Joos van Ghent in decorating the Ducal Chamber in the palace of Federigo da Montefeltro. Back in Toledo in 1483, Berruguete headed a large workshop that produced numerous sizable retables that display strong Flemish and Italian influences.

BIBLIOGRAPHY

Chandler Post, *A History of Spanish Painting,* IX (1947), 17–161; Jacques Lassaigne, *Spanish Painting,* Stuart Gilbert, trans., I (1952), 84–87.

JAMES SNYDER

BERSERKS. In Old Norse two compound nouns, *berserkr* and *úlfheðinn,* described certain warriors who entered battle screaming and biting the rims of their shields, fought without byrnies in a frenzied state, vanquished all foes without being injured, and fell immobile into a deep sleep afterward. They were as strong as bears or bulls, as crazed as wolves or dogs, and they had the power to render their enemies blind, deaf, or witless from fear. The words themselves mean "bear shirt" and "wolf coat," respectively, and presumably arose as part of ancient initiation rites involving the totemistic clothing in animal skins of young men during their advancement to adulthood and warrior status. The presence of such warriors in battle and the reputation of the *furor teutonicus* is well attested as a trait common to North, East, and West Germanic groups. Further confirmation of their existence is the pictorial representation on the Torslunda helmet plate, from the time of the Germanic migrations, showing a man with a sword and dressed in a pelt with head. An early medieval chess figure in the form of a warrior biting the edge of his shield was found in the Hebrides.

Expressions such as *skipta hǫmum* ("change shape") or *hamask* ("to rage, be taken in a fit of fury") both contain the word *hamr* ("skin, shape"; compare Latin *camisa*), and indicate that the donning of pelts fitted into a larger tradition of totemistic identification, whereby the warrior would merge with his animal alter ego. The *hamr* could take the spirit from the human body and transport it away. Those who let their spirits travel in the form of their *hamhleypa* ("*hamr*-runner") on *hamfarir* ("*hamr*-journeys") rendered their human forms comatose, as the *berserkr* was at the end of battle. The most famous example is perhaps that of Úlfr (Wolf) in *Egils saga Skallagrímssonar,* who after life as a warrior retired to his farm. When evening came, he would often become short of temper (*styggr,* which also means "wary" when applied to animals) and fall into a doze. Men said that he was then *hamrammr* ("able to change shape").

BIBLIOGRAPHY

Georges Dumézil, *The Destiny of the Warrior* (1970), 141–147; Nils Lid, "Berserk," in *Kulturhistorisk leksikon for nordisk middelalder,* I (1956); Jan de Vries, *Altgermanische Religionsgeschichte,* I (1956), 222–224, 431–432, and pl. 11.

JAMES E. CATHEY

[See also **Egils Saga Skallagrímssonar; Scandinavian Mythology.**]

BERTHARIUS (*d.* 884), made abbot of Monte Cassino in 848. As defense against Muslim attacks, he fortified his monastery and built a walled town, St. Benedict, at the base of the mountain. He obtained exemption for his abbey from episcopal jurisdiction and cultivated the study of Scripture there, himself writing grammatical and medical treatises, sermons, and poetry. Bertharius was martyred by Muslim raiders.

BIBLIOGRAPHY

Luigi Fabiani, *La terra di S. Bendetto: Studio storico-giuridico sull'Abbazia di Montecassino dall'VIII al XIII secolo* (1950), 30–35; Maximilianus Manitius, *Geschichte der lateinischen Literatur des Mittelalters,* I (1911), 608–609.

MARK D. MEYERSON

[See also **Monte Cassino.**]

BERTHOLD VON HOLLE, author of the three courtly romances *Demantin, Crane,* and *Darifant,* presumably belonged to a family of nobility from the region of Hildesheim (Lower Saxony). He may be identical with Bishop Conrad of Hildesheim's lord high steward, whose name appears as Bertoldus de Holle on legal documents dated between 1219 and 1245, or with the steward's son, who is mentioned in documents between 1235 and 1247, or with the steward's nephew Berthold, mentioned between 1251 and 1270.

In *Crane* the author states that he owes the source of his story to "the young duke John of Brunswick." This is without doubt the Guelph duke John I, great-grandson of Henry the Lion. John I was, with his brother Albrecht I, duke of Brunswick from 1252 to 1277. *Crane* must have been composed during the earlier part of John's reign. *Demantin* was written before *Crane,* since it is mentioned in the latter work. Of *Darifant* only fragments have survived, and its relative chronology is uncertain. The reference to Duke John suggests that Berthold was associated with, and composed all three works for, the Guelph court at Brunswick, which in times past had been an important cultural center and still held some significance in the second half of the thirteenth century. It is doubtful, however, whether the language of Berthold's works, a mixture of Middle Low and Middle High German, reflects the prevailing form of communication at the Brunswick court.

In *Demantin,* a work of approximately 12,000 lines, Berthold tells a long-winded story about the adventures of the young knight Demantin of Antriun; his wooing of Sirgamot, the daughter of the king of Greece; and his friendship with Firganant, the king of England. In one series of adventures, which includes tournaments, battles, single combats, and encounters with monsters and fairies, Demantin is the hero; a second series is centered on Firganant. The bipartite structure is reminiscent of the Parzival/Gawan partition in Wolfram von Eschenbach's *Parzival.* At the end Demantin marries Sirgamot and rules as the king of Greece.

Crane, shorter (approximatley 5,000 lines) and better constructed than *Demantin,* is a story about three friends, Gayol, Agorlin, and Agorlot, who are squires and pages at the emperor's court and are given the nicknames Crane, Valke ("falcon"), and Stare ("starling") by the emperor's daughter Acheloyde. One might suspect a certain symbolism behind the bird names, but nothing of the kind emerges clearly in the action of the poem. Gayol-Crane, the son of the king of Hungary, loves Acheloyde, and as the victor in a tournament arranged by the emperor, wins her hand. After an additional series of adventures Crane returns to Hungary and rules as a just and liberal king.

The 265 extant lines of *Darifant* tell of the wedding of Balifeit and his beautiful bride Locedia. Balifeit's friend Darifant leaves the festivities accompanied by a fairy. Later he fights a single combat with Offart.

The literary merits of Berthold's works are rather limited. Whether the three epics, or at least *Crane,* served a certain function within the court culture of the Guelph dukes is difficult, if not impossible, to determine.

BIBLIOGRAPHY

Berthold von Holle, [no title], Karl Bartsch, ed. (1858, repr. 1967), contains portions of *Demantin, Crane,* the *Darifant* fragments; *Demantin,* by Karl Bartsch, ed. (1875); Gabriele von Malsen-Tilborch, *Repräsentation und Reduktion: Strukturen spähöfischen Erzählens bei Berthold von Holle* (1973), with bibliography.

BERND KRATZ

[See also **German Romance.**]

BERTHOLD VON REGENSBURG (*ca.* 1210–1272), the most gifted and influential preacher of the

BERTHOLD VON REGENSBURG

German Middle Ages. We know nothing certain about the date and place of his birth, or about his family except for a sister, Elisabeth. Possibly he studied at Magdeburg, where a school of theology was founded in 1228, and certainly he became a member of the Minorite order in Regensburg. Various chronicles report that Berthold preached in Augsburg in 1240, before 1253 in nearby Bohemia, in 1253 in Landshut, in 1254 and 1255 in Speyer. In 1255 he was also in Colmar, then moved south and east to Konstanz, Winterthur, Zug, Thun, Zurich, and on to Austria. Everywhere Berthold drew huge crowds. Although the congregations of forty thousand and two hundred thousand mentioned by chroniclers are scarcely realistic, he often had a pulpit constructed in front of a church or even in an open field, and asked his listeners to sit downwind, the better to hear.

Berthold's reputation grew. In 1263, Pope Urban IV called him to help Albertus Magnus preach for the Crusades, and he traveled through Germany, France, and Switzerland again for two years. His influence was great both in the church and in the political life of the times, and he was often called on to settle quarrels in both church and state. Berthold was buried in Regensburg, and in 1692 his relics were moved to a shrine, where they are still preserved, in the Regensburg Cathedral.

Older church historians mention various writings by Berthold, but only his Latin and German sermons are preserved. The Latin sermons consist of five collections: *Rusticanus de Dominicis, Rusticanus de sanctis, Rusticanus de communi sanctorum, Sermones ad religiosos et quosdam alios,* and *Sermones speciales et extravagantes.* The first three collections were compiled 1250–1255, and are authentic. Cross-references make it clear that they are a unit, and some of the manuscripts of *Rusticanus de Dominicis* contain a preface by Berthold in which he explains that he was forced to record the sermons "because, when I preached them before the people, certain simple monks . . . wanted to note down for themselves what they were able to understand and thus made many mistakes."

The authenticity of the sermons in the last two collections is often questionable, and the number varies from manuscript to manuscript. In addition we have scattered sermons in other collections, some ascribed to Berthold but probably not his, some anonymous or ascribed to others but recognizable for internal reasons as Bertholdian. Most of the Latin sermons have never been printed. Casutt counts 55, 124, 75, 87, and 48, respectively, in the five collections. Many contain German glosses. Their popularity is evinced by the large number of manuscripts. Casutt lists 259 codices with Latin sermons by Berthold, and a few months before his death in 1967 he had discovered forty-three more.

Approximately 125 German texts stem from Berthold, some in the form of well-structured sermons, some tracts or mere fragments. Their authenticity has long been questioned. The problem is not whether they originated with Berthold but whether he himself wrote or approved them in the form in which they are preserved. Most likely to be authentic in this sense are PS (Pfeiffer and Strobl) I–XXXV plus perhaps XXXVII and XXXVIII. They are marked as a unit through cross-references (for example, PS VI, pp. 83, 84, 86, 87, 92); through the repeated use of self-apostrophe for dramatic effect (PS III, pp. 34, 36 twice, 42, 43, 46); and through their appearing in unbroken sequence in the Heidelberg and Berne manuscripts, with one break in the Schloss Harburg manuscript, and (with a break at the same place) from PS XXII on in the Brussels manuscripts, possibly the second part of a two-volume codex.

If the reference to an eclipse in PS XXV, p. 401, as having occurred *vernent an Sant Oswaldes tage* ("last year on August 5" [1263]) is correct, and if we ignore as a later addition a following reference to another eclipse *an der mittewochen in den cruce tagen vor den pfingesten* ("on Wednesday on the day before Ascension" [1267]), this sermon was written down in 1264, when Berthold was still alive and could have approved it.

More certain than the date is that they were edited in Augsburg, as is established by references to local conditions and the repeated phrase *hie zu Augespurg.* Schönbach and (with convincing detail) Hübner have argued that the German texts were edited in Augsburg by the same Minorites who produced the *Deutschenspiegel* and the *Schwabenspiegel.* No German sermon corresponds to any Latin sermon in toto. Rather, it seems that various Latin sermons were used in part as source material for German texts. Several German texts are longer and shorter expositions of the same material: PS XIX and LI, XXIII and LVII, XXVII and LIX. Richter has shown that *Sermo ad religiosos* 11 was the source for at least four different German texts. It is very unlikely that Berthold, whose attitude toward his work we know from the Latin preface quoted above, saw and approved all of them.

The style of the German texts is lively and popular, the structure of the sermons, easy for an audience to follow. Most often they are organized around some number of objects or concepts, as the titles indicate: "On the Seven Planets," "On Eight Kinds of Food in Heaven," "On the Four Servants of God." They are filled with stories and illustrations, with direct address and dialogue, with humor and fulmination and the call to repent. Berthold was aware of his language, and made a conscious effort to speak so that the simplest listener could understand him and to avoid local dialect peculiarities. His texts constitute one of the most extensive and significant prose monuments in Middle High German. They also give us a rich picture of daily life and are the best witness we possess for the spoken language of the thirteenth century.

BIBLIOGRAPHY

Laurentius Casutt, *Die Handschriften mit lateinischen Predigten Bertholds von Regensburg O. Min. ca. 1210–1272* (1961), contains designation and location of 263 Latin MSS with Berthold sermons; Alfred Hübner, *Vorstudien zur Ausgabe des Buches der Könige* (1932); Franz Pfeiffer and Joseph Strobl, *Berthold von Regensburg: Vollständige Ausgabe seiner deutschen Predigten*, 2 vols. (1862–1880, repr. 1965): the reprint has an updated bibliography and list of manuscripts by Kurt Ruh; Dieter Richter, *Die deutsche Überlieferung der Predigten Bertholds von Regensburg* (1969); Karl Rieder, *Das Leben Bertholds von Regensburg* (1901), has the best bibliography; Anton Schönbach, "Die Überlieferung der Werke Bertholds von Regensburg," in *Sitzungsberichte der Kaiserlichen Akademie der Wissenschaften, Philosophisch-historische Klasse*, **151–153** (1905–1906).

FRANK G. BANTA

[See also **Preaching, Sermon Literature, Western European.**]

BERTRAM, MEISTER (*fl. ca.* 1365–1415), leading painter of late Gothic style in Germany. Born in Westphalia, he settled in the prosperous Hanseatic port of Hamburg (1367), where he headed a large workshop. His panels for the Grabow Altarpiece (*ca.* 1379; now in Kunsthalle, Hamburg), consist of twenty-four paintings of Old and New Testament scenes. His art is typical of the German international style: stocky figures clad in delicate Gothic draperies executed in bright colors and simple, direct outlines.

BIBLIOGRAPHY

Alfred Stange, *Deutsche Malerei der Gotik,* II (1936), 132–154.

JAMES SNYDER

BERTRAND DE BAR-SUR-AUBE, born in the late twelfth or early thirteenth century in the region of Champagne, is the author of the early-thirteenth-century epic *Girart de Vienne,* in which he gives himself the title "gentil clerc" and proposes a method of classifying the chansons de geste into three cycles: those of Charlemagne, Garin de Monglane, and Doon de Mayence. Although he has been named as the possible author of *Aymeri de Narbonne, Les Narbonnais, Bueve d'Hantone,* and *Doon de Mayence,* his authorship of the last three poems has been strongly contested.

BIBLIOGRAPHY

A. H. Krappe, "Bertrand de Bar-sur-Aube, and Aymeri de Narbonne," in *Modern Philology,* **16** (1918–1919); Prosper Tarbé, ed., *Le roman de Girard de Viane* (1850, repr. 1974), 5, 29; Wolfgang Van Emden, ed., *Girart de Vienne* (1977), 35–37.

MINNETTE GRUNMANN-GAUDET

[See also **Chansons de Geste; French Literature.**]

BERTRAN DE BORN (*ca.* 1140–*ca.* 1215), a troubadour known best as an unscrupulous warmonger and prolific writer of political *sirventes.* Born a petty nobleman, perhaps at Born in Salagnac, he originally held a castle, Hautefort, in joint ownership with his brother Constantine. Bertran's first major dispute seems to have been with this brother, over the control of their common inheritance. When Bertran managed to have Constantine expelled from the estate, the latter turned for help and protection to the viscount of Limoges and Richard, duke of Aquitaine, the future Richard the Lionhearted. As a result of this allegiance, and possibly for other reasons as well, Bertran conceived a fierce hatred for Richard and his father, Henry II, king of England. At the same time he allied himself to King Henry's eldest son, also Henry, known to all as the "Young King."

Testimony to the depth of friendship between the poet and this prince survives in the beautiful *planh* composed by Bertran on the occasion of the young

Henry's death in June 1183. Less than a month later, Henry II confiscated Hautefort and turned it over to Constantine. But Bertran's disfavor with the king did not last very long. According to the tradition of the Old Provençal *razos,* it was Bertran's manifest grief over his companion's death that moved both the father and the brother of the slain man to take pity on the poet. His castle restored to him, Bertran began to use his poetic skill to attack enemies of the king of England.

Although the troubadour evidently shifted his loyalties, there is a certain consistency in the positions he took. He never claimed to be a great patriot or political ideologist; rather, he advocated war for war's sake. He loved war because it brought wealth to minor noblemen like himself, and made great lords more generous and conciliatory than they were in times of peace. Bertran's image as a fomenter of discord has been immortalized by Dante, who depicts him in the twenty-eighth canto of the *Inferno* with his head detached from his body, a fitting punishment for the man who, in Dante's judgment, pulled apart the members of the royal family.

Bertran spent the latter years of his life as a monk in the abbey of Dalon, where he died. Thirty-nine of his poems have been preserved. Bertran de Born seems to have cut a figure intriguing even to his contemporaries, for there are more and older *razos* surviving about him and his poetry than for any other troubadour.

BIBLIOGRAPHY

Carl Appel, ed., *Die Lieder Bertrans von Born* (1932); Albert Stimming, ed., *Bertran von Born* (1892, 2nd ed. 1913). For references to recent studies on Bertran de Born, see Robert A. Taylor, *La littérature occitane du Moyen Âge* (1977), 60–62.

ELIZABETH WILSON POE

[See also **Provençal Literature; Troubadour, Trouvère, Trovadores.**]

BERTUCCIO (or Bertucius), Venetian sculptor, goldsmith, and bronze caster who signed and dated (1300) the bronze doors of the left-central porch of San Marco: "MCCC Magister Bertucius aurifex Venetus me fecit." Composed of openwork scale patterns, decorated with rosettes and busts of saints, the left doors bear a compelling likeness to the doors of the central porch, indicating that Bertuccio may have cast them as well. The central porch doors include several busts and figures that are clearly taken from classical originals, indicating a new phase in Venetian taste for classical antiquity. Bertuccio's doors signal the long history of Venetian sculpture, among the oldest on the Italian Peninsula.

BIBLIOGRAPHY

A. Prosdoscimi, "Le porte antiche dell'atrio di San Marco a Venezia," in *Accademia Nazionale dei Lincei: Rendiconti della classe di scienze morale,* 8th ser., 2 (1947); Otto Demus, *The Church of San Marco in Venice* (1960), 139, 181.

ADELHEID M. GEALT

BERWICK, TREATY OF, was an agreement ending the eleven-year sojourn of David II of Scotland as Edward III's prisoner in England. Captured in 1346 at the battle of Neville's Cross, David was finally set free on 3 October 1357. According to the treaty's conditions, Scotland agreed to pay a ransom of 100,000 marks sterling due in ten equal instalments made annually on 24 June, the feast of the Nativity of St. John the Baptist. During these years a truce would also be in effect. In addition to the ransom, Edward demanded twenty-three hostages, three of whom would serve as hostages on a rotating basis from a list of nine top-ranking nobles. Their maintenance costs would be solely Scottish responsibility. In case of default, David was supposed to return to captivity until arrears were paid (a clause never enforced despite frequent defaults). The treaty, ratified by a general council at Scone on 6 November 1357, emphasized the determination of the Scots to ransom their king rather than include Edward and his heirs in the Scottish succession.

BIBLIOGRAPHY

For a text of the treaty in English see Alec R. Myers, *English Historical Documents,* IV, *1327–1485* (1969), 101–103. Ranald Nicholson, *Scotland: The Later Middle Ages,* vol. II of *The Edinburgh History of Scotland* (1974), 146–183, provides an excellent assessment of the treaty. See also William Croft Dickinson, *Scotland from the Earliest Times to 1603,* 2nd rev. ed. (1961), 177–185.

MARILYN KAY KENNEY

[See also **Edward III of England; Scotland.**]

BESANT (Latin: *byzantius*), used in the Latin West to denote gold coins (*nomismata*) struck at mints in the Byzantine Empire. Latin authors associate the word with Byzantium, the alternative designation for the city of Constantinople. For example, Baldric of Dol, a historian of the First Crusade, upon noting the name Byzantium, writes: "from whence, to this time, coined money [denarii] of that city [Byzantium], we call *Byzanteos.*" With adjectives, the word signifies a variety of issues, other than Byzantine, used in Mediterranean trade. Of importance are: "white besants" *(byzantii albi),* coinage of the Kingdom of Cyprus; and "Saracen besants" *(byzantii saraceni),* Muslim coinage.

BIBLIOGRAPHY

Mittellateinisches Wörterbuch, O. Prinz and J. Schneider, eds., I (1959), 1637–1638; Gustave Schlumberger, *Numismatique de l'Orient latin* (1954), 130–131, 174–183.

JOHN W. NESBITT

[See also **Mints and Money, Byzantine.**]

BESESTAN. See **Bedestan.**

BESSARION (*ca.* 1403–1472), Byzantine prelate and exponent of Palaiologan-Renaissance learning, was the chief Byzantine unionist at the Council of Ferrara-Florence. Greek rejection of ecclesiastical union brought him to Rome, where as Roman cardinal he headed (under Nicholas V) an academy to produce new and more accurate translations of Greek philosophical and scientific works and of Greek Church Fathers. The patron of Byzantine humanists in Italy, he bequeathed his vast library of Greek manuscripts to Venice. From these Aldus Manutius printed many first editions, and other scholars made new or improved translations of such works as the pseudo-Aristotelian *Mechanica,* Theon's commentary on Ptolemy's *Almagest,* and Plato.

BIBLIOGRAPHY

Henri Vast, *Le Cardinal Bessarion* (1878); Ludwig Mohler, *Kardinal Bessarion als Theologe, Humanist, und Staatsmann,* 3 vols. (1923–1942); L. Labowsky, "Il Cardinale Bessarione e gli inizi de la Bibliotheca Marciana," in *Venezia e l'Oriente,* Agostino Pertusi, ed. (1966).

DENO J. GEANAKOPLOS

[See also **Councils, Western (1315–1445); Translations and Translators, Western European.**]

BESTIAIRE D'AMOUR. Richard de Fournival (*d.* 1260?) in his *Bestiaire d'amour* takes the animal symbolism inherited from the *Physiologus,* which had been used primarily in moral and religious didactic contexts, and adapts it to the purpose of courtly casuistry. Under the guise of an autobiography the poet, an unrequited lover, illustrates the circumstances and stages of an amorous quest and the causes of its failure. The animals serve to illustrate the variety of strategies of the lover and his lady while presenting many traditional themes of courtly lyric poetry. To appreciate fully the medieval author's text, readers must see the illustrations of the original manuscript, for they and the text are closely related.

BIBLIOGRAPHY

Gabriel Bianciotto, ed., *Bestiaires du moyen âge* (1980), 125–168; *The Bestiary: A Book of Beasts,* T. H. White, ed. and trans. (1960).

THOMAS E. KELLY

[See also **Bestiary.**]

BESTIARY, a medieval compilation of stories in which the supposed characteristics of real and imaginary animals, plants, and stones serve as Christian allegories for the purpose of moral and religious instruction. It derives from a Greek work probably written at Alexandria early in the Christian era by a scholar known only as Physiologus. The Greek word φυσιολόγος, from φύσις (nature) and λόγος (word or reason), was used by Aristotle, Diodorus Siculus, and others in different ways; but under the influence of Neoplatonic philosophy in the first two centuries of the Christian era, patristic writers such as Clement of Alexandria and Origen gave the word a mystical dimension: it meant one who interpreted the natural world morally and metaphysically, and provided an initiation into a knowledge of the heavenly mysteries. In particular, the author of the book now known as *Physiologus* sought to show the nature of God himself by unveiling the correspondences between the phenomenal world of nature and its heavenly ar-

BESTIARY

Vulture. BRITISH LIBRARY, MS 3244, fol. 51

chetype. He took material for his book from fables in classical mythology, the sacred books, the accounts of Aristotle, Pliny, and other natural historians, and from oral tradition, then reshaped it to conform with preconceived allegories.

Neither the identity nor the date of the author of this early work has been firmly established. A Greek recension assigns the interpretations to St. Basil, and a Syriac version makes a similar ascription. The author has also been identified with Peter of Alexandria, Epiphanius, John Chrysostom, Athanasius, Ambrose, and Jerome. Francesco Sbordone, from a study of seventy-seven Greek manuscripts and their genealogies, concluded on purely textual grounds that the original Greek text was composed around A.D. 200. Friedrich Lauchert considered that the work was in circulation around A.D. 140 because similar material appeared in some of the homilies of the Greek church fathers of the time. However, the specific reference to *Physiologus* in Origen's seventeenth homily on Genesis 4:9 appears to have been an interpolation by Rufinus toward the end of the fourth century, and the echoes that Lauchert found in the works of Clement of Alexandria and others are probably no more than a reflection of common traditions of folklore. The work certainly appears to have circulated before the end of the fourth century. As Max Wellmann demonstrated, the work was quoted verbatim both by the author of the *Hexaemeron* commentary of Eustathios and by St. Ambrose. The *Physiologus* ascribed to Ambrose also appeared on the first list of books endorsed and prohibited by the church in the famous *Decretum Gelasianum* of 494, but, as Nikolaus Henkel points out, the prohibition could have referred to a different work of the same name.

The first Latin translation of the Greek text probably appeared between the fourth and sixth centuries, and translations into other languages of the Near East—Ethiopian, Syriac, and Armenian—were made in the fifth century. Subsequently translations appeared in almost every European vernacular. The earliest of these was an Old English metrical fragment preserved in the Exeter Book. Written in the latter part of the eighth century, it described the panther, the whale, and a bird (possibly a partridge). From the ninth century on manuscripts became very numerous, and scholars such as Charles Cahier, F. J. Carmody, M. R. James, Florence McCullogh, and Nikolaus Henkel have established various families of them.

By the end of the twelfth century the early text had expanded and developed into a collection of popular moralized nature stories under the name "bestiary." The bestiary could contain as many as 150 chapters, more than three times the number in the early work. Beasts, birds, reptiles, and fish were put into separate classes, and passages from the church fathers on trees, the creation, the ages of man, and the nature of man were sometimes added.

The most substantial additions derived from *Etymologiae sive originum* attributed to Isidore, archbishop of Seville, early in the seventh century. The bestiary reproduced Isidore's incorrect etymologies, often using them as a starting point for a disquisition on the fabulous or natural traits of the subject. The lamb was called *agnus* because the word meant "chaste" in Greek; the viper *(vipera)* was so named because it gave birth with violence *(vi);* the cat *(cattus)* got its name from *captare* (to seize). Although Isidore himself omitted the moralizations, his derivations not only strengthened ancient legends but also provided material that reinforced the didactic approach.

For example, the bestiaries used Isidore's derivation of the beaver *(castor)* from *castrando* (castrating), in confirmation of the beaver's well-known peculiarities. According to Pliny: "The beavers of the Black Sea region practice self-amputation of the same organ [their genitals] when beset by danger, as they know that they are hunted for the sake of its secretion, the medical name of which is beaver-oil." Because of this alleged trait, Juvenal regarded the beaver as a symbol of prudence. He told of how the

Siren. BRITISH LIBRARY, MS Add. 24686, fol. 13

wealthy Catullus, faced with imminent shipwreck, threw his possessions into the sea to save his life, just as the beaver casts off its genitals to preserve its life.

Isidore treated the subject at length, describing how the animal bit off its testicles and threw them at the hunter, who thereupon picked them up and ceased the chase. If the beaver was pursued by another hunter, it showed its incompleteness and was left unharmed. Many of the bestiaries repeated Isidore's statement before pointing out the allegory: "If you have had wicked inclination toward sin, greed, adultery, theft, cut them off from you and give them to the devil. The Apostle said, 'pay all of them their dues, taxes to whom taxes are due, honor to whom honor is due' [Rom. 13:7]." As Michael Curley has remarked, "With a deft application of hermeneutics an ancient legend is transformed into a Christian fable."

Isidore's animal lore and the pseudozoology that was incorporated into the encyclopedic writings of Thomas of Cantimpré, Vincent of Beauvais, Albertus Magnus, Hugh of Folieto, Alexander Neckam, and others came largely from the sources used by *Physiologus.* As a result, the same animal tales were constantly repeated. Alexander Neckam in *De naturis rerum* did, indeed, dismiss the story that the weasel conceived by the ear and gave birth by the mouth, but he affirmed that the lion slept with its eyes open. Albertus Magnus regarded the self-castrating beaver and the life-restoring pelican as fiction, but in 1230 Bartholomew the Englishman, in his popular *De proprietatibus rebum* (translated into Middle English in the fourteenth century), was less skeptical, juxtaposing accurate descriptions of domestic animals with those of fire-extinguishing salamanders and panthers with sweet breath. Although there is abundant evidence of a different, more scientific approach in the period, the bestiary, tending to absorb all animal fables indiscriminately, was in keeping with the didactic encyclopedic taste of the time.

The augmentation of material from *Physiologus* with encyclopedic lore in later writings gave rise in the bestiaries to some variety of treatment. An eleventh-century metrical version, the so-called *Theobaldus-Physiologus,* described thirteen animals and included an original chapter on the spider. A Middle English metrical translation of some eight hundred short lines dealt with the lion, eagle, serpent, ant, hart, fox, spider, whale, mermaid, elephant, turtledove, and panther but omitted the centaur and took material on the dove from another source. It also replaced the Latin meters with English alliterative patterns and rhyming lines. In some manuscripts moralizations were omitted; for instance, one of the most popular French bestiaries was the *Bestiaire d'amour* of Richard de Fournival (mid thirteenth century), which replaced the labored Christian moralizations with a lover's witty plea for his lady's favor.

A very different treatment occurred in the *Bestiaire divin,* a bestiary of 3,426 lines written in the same century. The author, Guillaume le Clerc, embellished traditional material and occasionally added a personal plea on the importance of faith and good works. The fourteenth-century Waldensian bestiary derived less than half its material from *Physiologus.* Apparently composed for students, it drew on a

Elephant. Latin Bestiary. BRITISH LIBRARY, MS Harl. 4751, fol. 8

number of sources outside *Physiologus,* and tended to replace the mystical interpretations of the original with moral lessons.

When *Physiologus* doubled in size, deluxe editions appeared with brilliant, meticulously painted miniatures, framed and decorated with gold. Compared with the Greek manuscript, the Smyrna Codex of about 1100, some manuscripts contain twice the number of miniatures. Bodleian MS 764, for example, has some 135 illustrations. Many Latin bestiary manuscripts were illustrated and, according to Florence McCulloch, a French manuscript without illustrations is rare. A large number of the most attractively illustrated manuscripts were made in England, and consequently, as M. R. James states, the Latin bestiary ranked with the psalter and the Apocalypse as one of the leading picture books of twelfth- and thirteenth-century England. Some bestiaries that include passages on fabulous nations or prodigies have lively illustrations of monsters such as giants, pygmies, cynocephali, cyclopes, sciapods, and a huge dragon called Geryon that is composed of three men together. Two twelfth-century Icelandic fragments, comprising the only bestiary to appear in a Scandinavian language, contain illustrations that correspond to at least six English manuscripts of Latin bestiaries, indicating that the fables they represent were known in Iceland at the time.

There may have been numerous model books available, such as the Hofer Bestiary, and some of the miniatures show similarities in style. Characteristic of the finest illustrated manuscripts is a use of brilliant color, symmetrical pattern, and exquisite line drawing. Except in the case of very familiar animals, such as the horse and the dog, the artists appear to have been little concerned with reproducing details based on actual observation. Most of the subjects lent themselves to graphic visual representation. The man-eating griffin, with its lion's body and wings and head of an eagle, holds the head of its prostrate, suffocating victim in its mouth. The manticore, with its lion's body and man's face, has evidently eaten most of its victim, and only a man's legs protrude from its treble row of teeth. Unwary sailors are shown trying to picnic on the back of an aspidochelone or whale that they have mistaken for an island.

Because of the allegorical values assigned to the animals and their frequent depiction in the miniatures, the illustrations had a profound influence on medieval art and architecture. Ecclesiastical sculptures, carvings, frescoes, and paintings, as well as illustrations in other medieval manuscripts, often used the same subjects. It is largely through such treatment that the Christian iconography popularized by the bestiary has survived. Even today the symbolism of the pelican, the eagle, the lion, and other beasts is well known.

The lore of the bestiary lasted for many centuries in literature and daily life. Early in the Renaissance the illustrated emblem books, secularizing the moral, gave further currency to this lore, which was also a very fruitful source of imagery for Elizabethan and Jacobean dramatists. Today no one believes that the lion's cubs are born dead and that the lion resuscitates them after three days, and the medieval concept that this lion symbolized God raising Christ from the dead on the third day is alien to modern thought.

But even if the phoenix, the sacrificial torch from whose ashes a new bird emerges, is no longer regarded as a symbol of the risen Christ or of eternity, it still gives its name to building societies and other commercial ventures, as well as to certain kinds of heroic endeavor. The swan that, despite the harshness of its voice, was fabled to sing so gloriously at death may no longer serve as a type of martyrdom, the repentant sinner, or of Christ himself speaking from the cross, yet the meaning of "swan song" is still current, and the significance of Coleridge's amusing couplet "swans sing before they die; 'twere no bad thing / Did certain persons die before they sing" remains. As for the hedgehog, the traditional symbol of the Devil, that bowled along with the fruits from orchard or vineyard stuck to its quills, at least one modern naturalist claims to have seen the animal flat on its back, deliberately impaling falling apples. Because of the bestiary, abstruse animal stories, perpetuating misconceptions of the early natural historians, are still part of our culture, although their origins are forgotten.

BIBLIOGRAPHY

Charles Cahier and Arthur Martin, *Mélanges d'archéologie, d'histoire et de littérature,* 4 vols. (1847–1856); and *Nouveaux mélanges,* 4 vols. (1874–1877); Francis Carmody, ed., *Physiologus latinus: Éditions préliminaires, versio B.* (1939); and *Physiologus latinus, versio y* (1941), 95–134; Michael J. Curley, trans., *Physiologus* (in English) (1979); Nikolaus Henkel, *Studien zum Physiologus im Mittelalter* (1976); Montague R. James, ed., *The Bestiary, Being a Reproduction in Full of the Manuscript Ii.4.26 in the University Library, Cambridge* (1928); Jan P. N. Land, ed., *Anecdota Syriaca,* 4 vols. (1862–1875), contains the Syriac translation of *Physiologus;* Friedrich Lauchert, *Ge-*

schichte des Physiologus (1889); Florence McCulloch, *Mediaeval Latin and French Bestiaries,* rev. ed. (1962); Francesco Sbordone, ed., *Physiologus* (1936); and *Ricerche sulle fonti e sulla composizione del Physiologus greco* (1936); Max Wellmann, "Der *Physiologus,* Eine Religionsgeschichtlich-Naturwissenschaftliche Untersuchung," in *Philologus,* suppl. **22.1** (1930).

BERYL ROWLAND

[See also **Allegory; Beast Epic; Isidore of Seville.**]

BETANIA, a cruciform domed church near Tbilisi, the capital of Georgia, built between the end of the twelfth and the early thirteenth centuries. The exterior walls, particularly the porch, the dome, and window frames, are richly decorated with carvings of geometric and vegetal motifs. The church is renowned for its extensive wall paintings, a large portion of which are still well preserved, particularly the concha of the eastern apse, where the deesis theme is depicted. Below the apse are full-length portraits of the prophets en face, holding scrolls, and underneath them are the apostles. As customary, historical personalities and donors are depicted on the northern walls. Among them are the king of kings of Georgia, Giorgi III (*d.* 1184), Queen Tamar (*d.* 1213), and her husband, David Soslani (*d.* 1207).

BIBLIOGRAPHY

R. Schmerling, V. Dolidze, and T. Barnaveli, *Okrestnosti Tbilisi* (1960), 83–86.

WACHTANG DJOBADZE

[See also **Armenian Art.**]

BETH DIN. See **Jewish Communal Self-Government.**

BETH HA-. See **Schools, Jewish.**

BETHENCOURT, JEAN DE. See **Canary Islands.**

BETROTHAL in the Middle Ages was a mixture of Roman and Germanic customs. The Romans did not regard betrothal as legally binding. Either party to the agreement could withdraw without providing grounds for legal action. Nevertheless, betrothal was a social and moral commitment. The agreement was solemnized at a festive social ceremony at the girl's home. Her parents specified the amount of her *dos,* or dowry, in the agreement. In an exchange of formulas, her father promised to give her to her suitor as the man's wife. Then the suitor gave her gifts and a ring, the ancestor of the modern engagement ring.

The Germanic tribes regarded betrothal, called *beweddung* in Old English, as a legally binding contract, the first step in marriage. In its earliest stages marriage among the Germanic people was a sale of the bride by her father or legal guardian to the groom. The phrase "buying a maid" appears in the Anglo-Saxon laws. In German the expression "to buy a wife" was used for marriage throughout the Middle Ages. Wife purchase was practiced in Denmark as late as the fifteenth century. The procedure consisted of two parts: the first was *beweddung,* the pledge to give the bride to her suitor; the second was *gifta,* the actual giving of the bride.

The earliest description of a betrothal among the Germanic people appears in chapter 18 of Tacitus' *Germania.* He contrasts the practical, austere Germanic customs with the opulent, festive Roman ones. He states that the dowry is brought by the husband to the wife. By this he meant the bride price, which he interpreted as a reverse dowry. The gifts given by the husband were not rich objects to adorn or please a woman, but practical things, such as oxen, horses, a shield, a spear, or a sword. The woman in turn brought some present of arms to her husband. The gifts signified that the woman was coming to share a man's toils and dangers, that she was to be his partner in all his sufferings and adventures, in peace and war.

Among the Salian Franks, and later among other tribes, the suitor paid the bride's guardian *arrha,* or earnest money, at the betrothal rather than the full bride price. This sum was often used to entertain guests at the wedding. The *arrha* came to be paid to the bride. Under Roman influence this took the form of a ring.

Between the sixth and ninth centuries the entire bride price came to be paid to the bride. It was under the husband's control during their marriage, as was all the wife's property; but at his death it became hers. At this stage betrothal was no longer a contract of sale. It gave the bride some financial security instead of making her into an object of sale. The most important part of the agreement was the promise to pay the bride price to the bride. This obligation was symbolized by a ceremony involving the exchange of an object, such as a straw, a piece of cloth, an arrow, or a glove. The couple took an oath, which they sealed with a clasp of hands.

It was customary to give the bride a morning gift after the first night of marriage. This also came to be specified in the betrothal agreement. The bride price and the morning gift were merged to form a legal provision for the widow, the predecessor of the English dower. This form of betrothal prevailed after the beginning of the tenth century.

During the later Middle Ages the old Roman practice of bestowing a dowry on the bride was revived. One of the reasons for this was that the increasing life expectancy of women made them less scarce and less valuable. Families had to provide dowries for daughters and sustain the principal costs of marriage in order to attract prospective husbands. The dowry was specified in the betrothal agreement. Like the dower, it was in the husband's control while he was alive but became the property of the wife at his death. Between the dower and the dowry, a betrothal agreement could give a woman a considerable amount of future financial security.

The betrothal agreement was always phrased in the future tense. Nevertheless, it was a legal contract that was as binding as marriage. If a betrothed woman had sexual relations with a man other than her betrothed, it was considered adultery. The arrangement and enforcement of the agreement was in the hands of the family. Young people, particularly in wealthy families, rarely chose their own mates in the Middle Ages. The Church recognized self-betrothal, but if a couple betrothed themselves against the wishes of their parents, they risked ostracism and disinheritance. Thus, young people usually followed the wishes of their parents unless they had a strong antipathy to the person who was selected. This situation made betrothal a business agreement rather than a romantic commitment.

BIBLIOGRAPHY

Georges Duby, *Medieval Marriage* (1978); Willystine Goodsell, *A History of Marriage and the Family* (1935); David Herlihy, "Life Expectancies for Women in Medieval Society," in *The Role of Woman in the Middle Ages,* Rosmarie T. Morewedge, ed. (1975); George E. Howard, *A History of Matrimonial Institutions* (1904); John Leyerle, ed., "Marriage in the Middle Ages," in *Viator,* 4 (1973).

DIANE BORNSTEIN

[See also **Family, Western European; Law, Early German.**]

BEVERAGES, ISLAMIC. Drink, for the Arab of Muḥammad's time, usually meant one of three things: water, when it was available; milk; or juices or infusions of various fruits and grains. Potable water, at least for the bedouin, was difficult to obtain, and as often as not they were forced to refresh themselves from a muddy or brackish source. Milk, especially that of camels, sheep, and goats, formed a common part of the nomadic diet. While viticulture was practiced to some extent by the sedentary inhabitants of the Hejaz, grape wine *(khamr)* was chiefly imported from Syria, and as such was an expensive luxury. Those with a taste for intoxicants turned more frequently to *nabīdh,* a fermented beverage made from the infusion *(naqīᶜ)* of dates, raisins, or grains. Honey was used to produce a sort of mead *(bītᶜ),* which enjoyed particular popularity in the Yemen. There is evidence also that the bedouin drank an intoxicant made from fermented milk.

The well-known Islamic prohibition of wine, as it is presented in the Koran, apparently took some time to evolve. An early verse (47:15) describes "rivers of wine, delicious for the drinker" as among the delights of paradise. Soon after Muḥammad's flight to Medina (622), the attitude and tone of the revelation changes. At first believers are admonished, "Do not go unto prayer when you are drunk" (4:43), and in a verse of later origin (2:219) Muḥammad is instructed to tell his people, "in wine and games of chance [*maysir*] there is both injury and benefit for mankind, but the injury is greater." In a subsequent revelation wine, along with gambling, worship of stone idols, and use of divining arrows is called "an abomination, the work of Satan," by which Satan wishes to sow enmity among men (5:90–91).

These verses, and the motive force behind them, have caused some puzzlement among scholars. W. M. Watt suggests that since wine in all these verses is grape wine *(khamr),* instead of the more common *nabīdh,* Muḥammad was in part trying to prohibit trade in this commodity with hostile lands: Byzantine Syria and Sasanid Iraq. He also sees the connection of wine with manifestations of pagan practice as significant. Ignazio Guidi has pointed out that *khamr,* being expensive, may have contributed to the social ill of prodigality on the part of those fond of treating themselves, and others, to this luxury. Another social ill linked to wine, of perhaps more pressing importance, is the civil violence alluded to in 5:90–91.

While 5:90–91 was interpreted as a strict prohibition by all but a few, later jurists found considerable latitude for disagreement concerning what was included under the rubric "wine." Almost every major collection of legal codes contains a chapter on the legal status of various beverages. Some, citing a saying attributed to Muḥammad, maintain flatly that even a small amount of any intoxicant is prohibited to believers. Others, stressing that *khamr* has a precise, limited definition, allow other drinks, even alcoholic, as long as neither the intent nor the result of consumption is drunkenness. They reject the notion that *khamr* is any substance that takes possession of and overwhelms one's mind *(khāmara* ᶜ*alā al-*ᶜ*akl).* The canonically prescribed penalty for drunkenness is forty to eighty lashes, to be administered after the offender has regained sobriety.

The extent to which these rules were observed varied considerably according to time and place. There is little to suggest that in Syria and Mesopotamia, where wine had long been produced and a large part of the population remained Christian until the Mongol invasion, either the production or the consumption of wine ceased with the Muslim conquest. While some rulers are reputed to have been zealous in suppressing wine production and consumption, reports concerning the alcoholic excesses of others abound. Even when a sovereign did take measures against drinking, the records of these attempts, detailing the multitudes of the great and small who are prosecuted, speak more of the universality of drinking than of the ruler's own piety, while the frequency of these reform campaigns attests to their lack of effectiveness. We even have indications that some of the military elite were rewarded with tax revenues on wine and, in Egypt, beer *(mizr),* a beverage known there since pharaonic times.

Other beverages that, because of their legal neutrality, were not mentioned in canonical texts continued to be drunk. In Syria, Mesopotamia, and the Nile Valley, the supply of water was generally good. Sherbets—cool, sweet drinks made of water and syrups—seem to have appeared fairly early. Tradition has it that in the time of the first caliphs, people were already preparing a syrup *(tilā*ᵓ*)* by boiling down grape juice to one-third its original volume, and then diluting it as desired. Rosewater, which became a popular flavoring agent for these concoctions, was introduced by way of Persia (Arabic: *jullāb,* from the Persian *gul āb).* Numerous sources attest to the popularity of these drinks in Abbasid times. To cool them and other drinks, ice and snow were brought to the cities from the mountains; the Mamluks even employed their postal routes to transport ice from the Syrian mountains to Cairo.

Other beverages were introduced during the late Middle Ages. The Turks and Mongols who entered the Islamic world brought with them *koumiss* (Arabic *qūmīz),* a powerful drink made of mare's milk known to be a favorite of certain Mamluk sultans, though few outside their circle seem to have acquired a taste for it. Coffee, which has become a Near Eastern staple, was introduced relatively late. Only in the fifteenth century do we first find coffee being used, and then only by mystics in the Yemen, to which the plant had come from Ethiopia some time earlier. It took another century to gain general acceptance in Egypt, Syria, and Turkish Anatolia and even then this stimulant met with a certain amount of pious and official opposition.

BIBLIOGRAPHY

W. M. Watt, *Muhammad at Medina* (1956), 299; Ignazio Guidi, *L'Arabie anté-islamique* (1921), 56; Maxime Rodinson, "Recherches sur les documents arabes relatifs à la cuisine," in *Revue des études islamiques,* 17 (1949). M. M. Ahsan, *Social Life Under the Abbasids* (1979), devotes a section to food and drink. Ibn Qutayba's *Kitāb al-ashriba,* an informative ninth-century work on beverage laws, has yet to be translated, though a French introduction to it appears in Gérald Lecomte's *Ibn Qutayba: L'homme, son oeuvre, ses idées* (1965), 111–115. A sixteenth-century account of the origins and growth of coffee drinking is found in Sylvestre de Sacy's French translation of ᶜAbd al-Qādir al-Jazīrī's ᶜ*Umdat al-ṣafwa fī ḥill al-qahwa,* in his *Chrestomathie arabe,* 2nd ed. (1826).

RALPH S. HATTOX

[See also **Brewing; Dietary Laws, Islamic; Mead; Wine, Winemaking.**]

BEVERS SAGA is a Norse translation of the early-thirteenth-century Anglo-Norman *Boeve de Haumtone,* and is therefore to be compared with two other translations of the Anglo-Norman work, the Middle English *Sir Beues of Hamtoun* and the Middle

Welsh *Ystorya Bown de Hamtwn.* Statements in some handbooks and survey articles to the effect that *Bevers saga* is a translation of a Middle English text are based on a tentative and incorrect suggestion in the first edition of the saga (1884).

Bevers saga survives only in Icelandic manuscripts: two fragments (*ca.* 1350 and *ca.* 1400), two almost complete texts (*ca.* 1400 and *ca.* 1470), and a copy (1690) of a medieval manuscript that is now lost (Sanders, 1979). Other copies in paper manuscripts all derive from the surviving medieval texts.

Because *Bevers saga* belongs to the genre of translated romances *(riddarasǫgur)* that is mainly associated with Norway, it has been assumed to be a Norwegian translation. In the absence of a Norwegian text or any internal proof to support this assumption, the possibility that *Bevers saga* was translated in Iceland cannot, however, be excluded.

Various suggestions have been made concerning when *Bevers saga* was translated, but none of them is satisfactory. Cederschiöld's adduction of linguistic features is of limited help, since these may reflect the norms of later copyists rather than the usage of the translator. Kölbing suggested that part 2 of *Karlamagnús saga, Af fru Olif ok Landres* (translated, according to its prologue, in the winter of 1286–1287), borrowed a number of features from *Bevers saga,* which must therefore be the elder of the two works. Later work on *Olif ok Landres* (by Smyser) suggests, however, that it follows its lost original closely; thus the common features in *Bevers saga* and *Olif ok Landres* must also have been common to their respective originals, and the one Norse work cannot be proved to be dependent on the other.

The Anglo-Norman *Boeve de Haumtone* survives in two manuscripts from the thirteenth and fourteenth centuries; and at the points at which they overlap, they are sufficiently similar for them to be described as belonging to one and the same version. Earlier scholarship (by Kölbing) has suggested that *Bevers saga* was translated from a version of *Boeve de Haumtone* different from the one that survives, but an examination of the material suggests that the text used for the Norse translation need have been only slightly different from the existing Anglo-Norman work.

The principal surviving texts of *Bevers saga,* while consistently abbreviating the Anglo-Norman poem, reproduce its narrative content quite faithfully, with only a few significant deviations; there are a greater number of changes in the second half of the saga, where the narrative structure in the original is in any case repetitive. The style of the surviving texts of *Bevers saga,* with the exception of the text from 1690, is comparatively free of rhetorical ornament.

BIBLIOGRAPHY

Editions. Gustaf Cederschiöld, *Fornsögur Suðrlanda* (1884), ccxvi–ccxli (including a German summary of *Bevers saga*), ccxlvi, ccxlvii, text pp. 209–267; Bjarni Vilhjálmsson, *Riddarasögur,* I (1954, repr. 1961), 283–398; new edition (Sanders) forthcoming in the publications of Stofnun Árna Magnússonar á Íslandi.

Literature. Eugen Kölbing, "Studien zur Bevis Saga," in *Beiträge zur Geschichte der deutschen Sprache und Literatur,* **19** (1894); Christopher Sanders, "The Order of Knights in *Ormsbók,*" in *Opuscula,* **7,** *Bibliotheca Arnamagnæana,* **34** (1979); H. M. Smyser, "The Middle English and Old Norse Story of Olive," in *PMLA,* **56** (1941).

CHRISTOPHER SANDERS

[See also **Boeve de Haumtone.**]

BIBLE

THE HERITAGE OF THE BIBLE AT THE BEGINNING OF THE MIDDLE AGES

The Masoretic text of the Hebrew OT. The canon of the Hebrew OT was established in the second century A.D. and is attributed to Rabbi Akiba ben Joseph. The twenty-four books included in the text were divided into three main groups: Pentateuch, Prophets, and Hagiographa. The most ancient extant Hebrew text is the Ben Asher manuscript, originally of Aleppo, dating from the ninth century and based on earlier traditions. The Masoretic (traditional) text was widely diffused among Jewish communities, serving liturgical and scholarly purposes. Its holy character imposed uniformity on the text, making possible the development of a common Jewish exegetical tradition.

Jewish translations. From the second century B.C., Bible texts were translated into Aramaic and Greek, in response to the needs of those communities where Hebrew ceased to be spoken. Gradually complete translations emerged, such as the Aramaic translation of the Masoretic text by Aquila (Onkelos) and the Greek Septuagint, produced in Egypt. The Septuagint was a translation of a pre-Masoretic version, with differences both in the text and in the order of the forty books included. Adopted by Christian communities from the second century, its most ancient extant manuscripts are the Sinaitic texts of the fourth century.

CHRISTIAN TEXTS AND TRANSLATIONS

Greek. The Septuagint included by the third century the NT, whose canon had been established in Greek in the second century. Its text was emended by Origen, who compared variants and other Greek translations. His Hexapla, completed by 235, rendered a critical Septuagint version, becoming the authoritative version of the Greek Orthodox church, and served as the basis for translations into Latin and Oriental languages.

Old Latin translations. Liturgical needs of Christian communities in the western provinces of the Roman empire required translations into Latin of fragments or full books from the Septuagint, especially of the NT and Psalms. Limited to liturgical uses, these translations never obtained official status or uniformity. The Old Latin versions, however, became part of the heritage of many communities and continued to be used in the early Middle Ages, even though the authoritative text of the Vulgate was of superior quality.

The Vulgate. At the request of Pope Damasus, St. Jerome translated the NT into Latin by 384. After his establishment at Bethlehem (386), he translated the OT from the Septuagint, as emended by Origen and interpreted by Eusebius of Caesarea, also using his knowledge of Hebrew where problems of understanding made him resort to the *Hebraica veritas.* The result is the Vulgate, which became during the fifth century the authoritative Latin text of the Bible and gradually replaced the Old Latin versions.

Oriental translations. During the same period, Eastern Christians who did not speak Greek made translations from the Septuagint into their own languages. Some were dependent on versions not emended by Origen. The most important among them is the fifth-century Syriac Peshitta, based on the Septuagint and the Jewish-Aramaic text. The Armenian translation was made from an independent version of the Septuagint. The Georgian, Coptic, and Ethiopian versions served the needs of autonomous Eastern churches and their independent theologies.

The evolution of the Latin text (fifth–ninth centuries). The Vulgate was adopted at Rome and during the fifth century, in Italy. The growth of papal authority was an important factor for its diffusion, which was also furthered by the spread of Benedictine monasticism. At the end of the fifth century Pope Gelasius I recognized it as the official Bible of the Roman Catholic church. Misreadings by copyists led to the multiplication of variants, which have been classed under the general headings of Roman, Gallican, and Monte Cassino versions. Their diffusion was in turn facilitated by the Arab conquest of North Africa (657–690), where the best versions of the Old Latin Bible ceased to be used. In Visigothic Spain, the Old Latin version served as the basis for the early-seventh-century text of Isidore of Seville. This text spread along with Vulgate versions to other countries. It was introduced in Anglo-Saxon England and studied in the Northumbrian schools. Bede used an Isidorean version for his works and corrected it.

While full texts of the Bible represented a mass of material (the *Bibliotheca*) accessible only to scholars, the rest of the clergy and learned lay persons used florilegia, manuals of selected texts, which were composed from the seventh to the ninth century.

The Vulgate was finally adopted at the end of the eighth century under Charlemagne. His capitulary on "the letters," imposing uniformity on Bible texts, especially the Psalms, had an important influence. His adviser Alcuin worked on a revision of the Vulgate until 800. It was completed by Theodulf, bishop of Orléans, who used Spanish versions for reference. This revised Vulgate was spread under imperial authority. Under the influence of Anglo-Saxon and Irish scholars, it was improved in the ninth century, producing the Gallican Vulgate. The Carolingian scriptoria supplied the churches, monasteries, and lay palaces with copies of the corrected text, often richly illuminated, as with the Bible of Charles the Bald, a famous achievement of Carolingian art (Bibliothèque Nationale, Paris, fonds Latin 1). These Bibles were widely used for scholarly purposes, for historical writing, and in liturgy and preaching. The book of precepts by Dhuoda, of the mid ninth century, demonstrates fair knowledge of the Bible by a woman of the nobility trying to educate her son in the light of biblical morals.

The Gothic translation. Accomplished from the Septuagint (*ca.* 350) by Ulfilas, who was ordained Arian bishop of the Goths, the Gothic translation did not include the books of Kings. It was widely disseminated, helping to convert Germanic tribes to Arian Christianity. Only a few verses from Ezra and Nehemiah are extant, in addition to the NT fragments whose versions were emended between the fifth and the seventh century in Italy and Spain, under the influence of Old Latin versions.

BIBLICAL EXEGESIS IN THE MIDDLE AGES

Jewish. The Talmud is essentially a compilation of OT exegesis, composed between the second century B.C. and the sixth century A.D. The sages codified Jewish law according to the letter and spirit of the OT. They commented on the Scriptures in four levels of interpretation: *peshat* (literal), *remez* (sense), *derash* (homiletic interpretation), and *sod* (hidden or allegorical meaning).

Their activity was continued in the early Middle Ages by the geonim, the heads of Mesopotamian academies, whose interpretations of the OT and Talmud were adapted to changing conditions and used for that purpose merely the homiletic level. The rise of the Karaite sect in the eighth century and the Karaite-Rabbanite polemics contributed to the development of literal and allegorical senses. Karaite exegetes such as Anan ben David and Benjamin Nahawāndi commented on the OT to assess their opposition to the Talmud, while Rabbanites tried to prove its sanctity. The most important geonic exegete was Saadiah Gaon, whose anti-Karaite treatises resulted in a broad interpretation of the OT, especially the Pentateuch. His Arabic translation of the Bible is also a literal commentary. Combining literal meaning with linguistic and philosophic research, he innovated in the field of exegesis.

The Judeo-Spanish (Sephardic) exegetical school emerged in the tenth century. Its philological orientation, under the impact of such grammarians as Menahem ben Saruq and Dunash ben Labrat, became the dominant factor of its work. In the eleventh century this orientation merged with a philosophical approach, leading such exegetes as Isaac Alfasi to analytical methods of interpretation. From the twelfth century the Sephardic school was producing synthetic commentaries, embodying philological and philosophical methods of the four levels of interpretation. Scholars such as Abraham ibn Ezra (*d.* 1164) and Maimonides brought this work to its peak. David Kimḥi of Narbonne (*d.* 1235) enhanced the Sephardic legacy with the literal and homiletic achievements of the northern French schools. During the second half of the thirteenth century, Nahmanides added allegorical elements, already used by Cabalists.

The Franco-German school emphasized from the eleventh century literal and homiletic exegesis. The work of Rashi, the greatest medieval exegete, who commented on the OT and the Talmud and expounded the text in the light of this literal-homiletic method of interpretation, was continued in the twelfth century by his pupils, among them Samuel ben Meir, Joseph Kara, Eliezer of Beaugency, and Joseph Bekhor Shor. Their explications were universally accepted and had a certain influence on Christian exegetes, especially the Victorines.

The allegorical interpretation of the OT began as a pious explication of texts. Under the influence of Islamic mystical methods, the *kalām* (a method of speculative thought, conditioned by revealed knowledge and limited by faith) and *taʾwīl* (metaphoric interpretation of sacred texts), Jewish exegetes worked, from the tenth century, on allegorical explanations of biblical visions. The Kairouan school of North Africa, led by Jacob ben Nissim, developed this method, adapting the Scripture's meaning to the mentality of their own times. The emergence, in the twelfth century, of mystical groups, and finally the *Cabala* movement, led to radical changes of allegorical interpretation. Cabalist exegetes attempted to explain hidden meanings of the Scriptures, thus developing a cosmological image of the Messianic era that manifested the salvation of the Jewish people. Combining a philosophical approach and allegorical interpretation, they produced a Neoplatonic mysticism that influenced the works of exegetes such as Levi ben Gerson (Gersonides) and Joseph Albo.

Christian: Roman-Catholic. Roman Catholic exegesis was also based on four levels of interpretation, the literal, historical, moral, and allegorical. The church fathers used them to develop a concordance between the OT and NT, emphasizing the accomplishment of Messianic promises in the Revelation of Christ. Another topic was the spiritual interpretation of religious observance, distinguishing between Christianity and Judaism.

The spread of the Vulgate led early medieval exegetes to discuss the differences between the Old Latin versions and the Vulgate. For that purpose, they emphasized literal and historical senses, attempting to establish the correct text. Textual scholarship, used mainly in Spain by Isidore of Seville and his associates and in the Northumbrian schools by Bede and his pupils, became the legacy of the text correctors of the Carolingian epoch.

The exegetical work of Gregory the Great was based on the allegorical interpretation, tending to explore the inner meaning of the Scripture. His goal was to emphasize that there is only one way of salvation, that revealed by Christ. In the *Moralia in Job,* where he developed his didactic approach, he traced the spiritual and moral values of Christianity. Gregory's prestige and authority assured the wide diffusion of his works in the West, where they served as a model for subsequent Roman Catholic exegesis. In the Irish monasteries, allegorical interpretation was used to develop piety.

In the Carolingian epoch, exegesis was mainly effected in the *quaestiones,* treatises written in the form of answers to questions, designed to enlighten clergy and laity about problems raised by obscure texts or contradictory passages. Initiated by Alcuin in his *Interrogationes in Genesis,* this technique was developed by the ninth-century exegetes, among them Hrabanus Maurus, Walafrid Strabo, Paschasius Radbert, John Scotus Erigena, and Remigius of Auxerre. Some of them, like Agobard of Lyons, used it for anti-Jewish polemics.

In the tenth and eleventh centuries some commentaries ceased to be scholarly works. Their goal was the use of Scripture as a basis for the monastic and Gregorian reforms. This practical purpose required a mystical approach, such as the interpretation by Bernard of Clairvaux of the Song of Songs as the expression of the spiritual union of God and the believer's soul.

Other exegetes emphasized the literal sense in order to correct textual variants caused by the increased production of biblical exempla. Some of them sought the assistance of Jews, seeking the true version in the Hebrew text. Their combined efforts resulted in the twelfth-century "Paris versions," which became the standard text of the Vulgate.

Scholarly exegesis was pursued in the eleventh century by Fulbert of Chartres and his pupils, among them Berengar of Tours and Lanfranc of Bec. Their commentaries were based on literal, moral, and historical meanings. At the beginning of the twelfth century these notes became, at the school of Anselm of Laon, a complete gloss of the Bible. With additional notes, it became the *Glossa ordinaria,* the standard commentary, whose arrangement is attributed to Gilbert Crispin, bishop of London.

The twelfth century was a crucial epoch in the history of medieval Bible studies. Based on the Paris version of the Vulgate and the *Glossa ordinaria,* new works were undertaken. The rise of the new urban schools, the core of the future universities, created new structures of study. The development of Scholasticism was closely linked with the rise of the new generations of exegetes.

The Cistercian order had a special place in that evolution. Even before the establishment of the Paris version, Abbot Stephen Harding, worried by numerous variants of the text, produced his Cîteaux Bible, corrected with the help of a Jewish scholar, who translated Hebrew and Aramaic versions into French for him. In the middle of the century at Rome Nicholas Manjacoria established the text of the Psalms, with help by Jews in understanding the text.

Exegesis was influenced by spiritual and political evolution. Monasteries were centers of allegorical and mystical interpretation; St. Bernard of Clairvaux was the leading figure of this trend, expressing his belief that "Clairvaux is Jerusalem," a symbol of the unity of biblical legacy and monastic life. Visionaries such as Hildegard of Bingen used these methods to express the allegorical image of their visionary world.

The most spectacular progress was achieved in the schools, where systematic study of the Bible embodied the four exegetical levels of interpretation. The school of St. Victor at Paris became the most important European center of exegesis, gathering scholars from the entire Catholic world. The Victorines, led by Hugh, Richard, and Andrew of St. Victor, concentrated their work on the literal and historical interpretations, attempting to produce logical commentaries on the Scripture. Through contacts with Jewish exegetes, they became aware of Rashi and his pupils' commentaries; assimilating the homiletic and historical senses, they introduced some of the Hebrew exegesis into their works.

Besides the Victorines, other scholars included Peter Abelard, whose philosophical approach, especially dialectics, brought him into conflict with the church establishment. The *Sentences* by Peter Lombard had an important impact on Scholasticism because of its methodology and use of biblical quotation. Peter Comestor's *Scholastic History* was an attempt to write an intellectual history based on the Bible. Herbert of Bosham commented on the Psalms; through his contacts with Jewish exegetes at Paris, he became aware of the Sephardic philological approach. The scholarly achievements of the century were furthered by Stephen Langton, who also produced a Hebrew-Latin vocabulary of biblical terms.

Political events, such as struggles between church and state, the establishment of centralized monarchies, and the Crusades, influenced exegesis, especially of the books of Kings, which were used to produce suitable arguments for the parties involved. Such were the attempts to explain the term "liberty," in defining the rights of the church in the state as well as the divine character of kingship, and the topography of the Holy Land.

The study of theology at the universities was connected with biblical exegesis. To the main trends of the twelfth century, philological and philosophical approaches were added. The example of scientific and philosophical translations incited exegetes to study Greek and Hebrew texts in order to interpret their Latin versions. Robert Grosseteste, bishop of Lincoln, used Greek and Roger Bacon used Hebrew sources. New chairs of Greek and Oriental languages provided linguistic training for exegetes. The work of Christian Hebraists, many of them converted Jews, enabled scholars such as Nicholas of Lyra to study the achievements of Jewish exegesis and use them in their works.

The mendicant friars supplied the best Bible scholars. The Dominicans, influenced by Thomas Aquinas, tended to philosophical interpretation, while the Franciscans, including Nicholas of Lyra, based their works mainly on literal commentaries or on spiritual interpretation of the NT doctrine of poverty.

In the second half of the fourteenth century scholarly exegesis declined in the West. The rise of the mystical movements in the fourteenth and fifteenth centuries brought a revival of allegorical interpretations designed to improve the lives of the faithful through the "imitation of Christ," as in the famous work of Thomas à Kempis.

Christian: Greek Orthodox. Greek exegesis developed under the impact of the theological disputes from the fourth to the seventh century. The Arian, Nestorian, Monophysite, and Monothelite controversies led exegetes to concentrate on the interpretation of the NT, either to find textual support for their theories or to refute those of their opponents. The philosophical approach, especially that of the Neoplatonic schools of Alexandria and Antioch, imposed methods of exegesis, always under the shadow of the four great heresy disputes. A final Septuagint text was established in the ninth century, when the "Alexandria" and "Antioch" versions were abandoned. The "Vatican manuscript" became the standard version.

After the Arab conquest of the seventh century, the early Greek Bible-study centers of Alexandria, Antioch, and Palestine declined. The Constantinopolitan monastic schools of Asia Minor and Greece became the centers of Byzantine Bible studies. Included in the curricula of both lay and ecclesiastical schools, texts were taught in their literal and moral meanings. At the end of the ninth century, Patriarch Photios, who based his doctrine of *filioque* on interpretation of the NT in opposition to the Roman church, produced at his school thousands of pamphlets, summarizing Byzantine exegesis. In monastic schools, especially at Studion in Constantinople and in the ascetic centers of Mount Athos, the mystical sense of exegesis was developed. It reached its climax in the work of the eleventh-century poet Simeon the Young, seeking the ecstasy of the Divine Light as a goal of pietism.

The tenth and eleventh centuries, the golden age of Byzantine civilization, were a flourishing period of biblical studies. Scholarly commentaries, both philological and philosophical, were pursued. Moral and mystical exegeses were expressed in prose and poetry, seeking the deification of perfect faithful. Missionaries, chiefly among the Slavs, beginning with Cyril and Methodius, brought about the translation of the Septuagint into Slavic, which was accompanied by exegetical activity designed to expose the sense of the Scriptures for the newly converted peoples.

After the separation of the churches in 1054, the last four centuries of Byzantium were a period of continuous polemics with Rome. Byzantine theologians used exegesis of the NT to support the *filioque* doctrine.

Christian: Oriental. Syriac, Armenian, Georgian, Nestorian, and Coptic exegeses are rooted in their polemics with Greek Orthodox theologians. With the development of their own ecclesiastical organizations, from the seventh century Oriental exegetes concentrated their work on literal interpretation of the Scriptures, both in order to defend their own translations against the Septuagint versions and to provide textual understanding for the faithful. Moral and allegorical interpretations were used to reinforce religious practices in an effort to prevent mass conversions to Islam. Armenian exegesis sought to establish rules of moral behavior, in accord with the political structure of a national-religious kingdom. To this end, Armenian exegetes turned to the OT emphasizing the unity of the chosen people, the sacred monarchy, and the holy faith.

Muslim. From the time of Muḥammad, Muslims became aware of the Bible first in the form of tales included in the Koran. The *ḥadīth* interpreters of the Koran turned also to biblical exegesis. Their work was mainly based on literal and historical interpretation, tending to explain the inner meaning of the Koran suras, especially through the study of the Pentateuch. The material was gathered in the ninth-century anthology of commentaries by al-Tabarī. Converted Jews, the *Isrāʾīliyyāt,* introduced homiletic interpretations of religious practice. NT texts were also commented on, owing to the recognition by Islam of Jesus Christ as a prophet and to the place given to his family in the Koran. The rise of the mystical schools in Islam (the *Kalām*) is also linked with metaphoric interpretation of the Bible as an aid to Muslim piety.

VERNACULAR VERSIONS

English. In Old English there are frequent biblical paraphrases in the poetry; and the eighth-century Northumbrian masters translated whole books for the education of the laity. Ælfric translated the Pentateuch and other OT books near the end of the tenth century. John Wycliffe's nonconformist movement of the fourteenth century was based on biblical evidence, although the complete Bible translation attributed to him was actually a group effort, completed after his death in 1384. Condemned by the authorities, it nevertheless became popular and was frequently revised and commented on in the fifteenth century.

French. Early translated Bible verses appeared in the passion dramas of the eleventh century, and the Bible was paraphrased in other popular poems. By 1100 there was an Anglo-Norman Psalter, and by 1200 large excerpts of the OT had been translated from the Hebrew for Jewish use. Herman of Valenciennes completed a metrical version of the Bible in 1190. At the same time, Waldensian and Albigensian versions in Provençal led to a prohibition of suspect translations by Pope Innocent III in 1199. Nevertheless, translated glosses continued to popularize the use of the vernacular. The "Arsenal Bible," translated and illuminated at Acre in 1250, and presented to St. Louis, is the masterpiece of Crusader civilization. It was followed by a full French version commissioned by Louis IX.

German and Netherlandish. A Frisian Psalter of the late eighth century is extant, and in the same period there was a Bavarian version of the Gospel of Matthew. Notker Labeo (*ca.* 950–1022) of St. Gall translated the Psalms, Song of Songs, and Job. Systematic translations were continued in the eleventh and twelfth centuries. Before 1200 a Waldensian translation into Flemish was completed, which served as the basis for translations by heretical sects into German in the thirteenth century, as well as for the Dutch *Statenbijbel.* In 1350 a complete NT, the Augsburg Bible, was translated, followed in about 1390 by the Wenzel Bible, a German OT translated by Martin Rother. The fifteenth-century revision of these works, the Mentel Bible, was the first complete German Bible, printed in 1466 at Strassburg.

Italian. The earliest Bible texts in Italian are from the thirteenth century. They consist of a Waldensian version in the north Italian dialect, translations of Psalms and Gospels, and a Jewish version, translated from the Hebrew in the central Italian dialect, which produced the *giudeo-italiano* idiom. Full translations were current in the fourteenth century, related to the growth of urban civilization. Influenced by French and Provençal versions, they were mainly produced at Florence. In the fifteenth century, Venetian versions appeared.

Spanish and Catalan. From the twelfth century Hebrew texts were translated for the use of Jewish communities. Under the impact of philosophical and scientific translations from the Arabic into Latin, Spain became the sole country where Bible translations were produced through Jewish-Christian collaboration in the thirteenth century: OT books were translated directly from the Hebrew and NT from the Vulgate. The opposition of church hierarchy led King James I of Aragon to prohibit the practice in 1233. In Castile, however, it was continued under the royal patronage of Alfonso X the Wise, who regarded the Bible as a record of history. The translation he commissioned was included in a compilation of world history of 1270. In the fourteenth century, Latin exegesis was translated into Spanish and added to new translations, including the Vulgate, Hebrew, and Spanish versions combined as Polyglot Bible. The fifteenth-century Alba Bible (1422–1433), translated by Moses Arragel of Guadalajara, included both Jewish and Christian exegesis.

Translations into Catalan were influenced by French and Provencal versions. Commissioned by Alfonso III of Aragon, the Catalan Bible was translated in 1287 from a French prototype. Revised in the fourteenth century, it was replaced by the Valencian full translation by Boniface Ferrer accomplished in 1417.

Other vernacular versions. The Slavic translation from the Septuagint by Cyril and Methodios and its subsequent versions became the official text of the Orthodox churches of Russia, Bulgaria, and Serbia, losing thus the character of a vernacular version. The oldest vernacular translation used in the Slav Catholic countries is a Polish selection of Psalms and Gospels of the late thirteenth century, the Queen

Margaret Psalter. It was followed by other Psalters in the fourteenth and fifteenth centuries. In 1346 a Welsh version of excerpts was achieved and became a prototype for Celtic translations. Under the influence of the Wycliffite movement, John Hus translated the Bible into Czech, completed by his followers. This translation became the basis of further Hussite vernacular versions, among them the fifteenth-century Hungarian Bible.

BIBLICAL IMPACT ON DAILY LIFE

Liturgy. From late antiquity, Jewish and Christian services and prayer books incorporated Bible readings. Sung psalms and canticles became the core of the medieval hymnal. Scripture readings demonstrated OT prefiguration of the NT, and homilies and sermons in turn expounded the moral message of the Bible as a mirror of Christian life.

Popular culture. Medieval folklore, perhaps modeled on Jewish Haggada (OT episodes told in legendary form), was important in the popularization of the Bible. Free, vernacular versions in the manner of popular legends tended to arouse popular imagination and involvement in the Bible stories. From the twelfth century, exegetical works were used to enrich popular tales, as demonstrated in condensed form in the fourteenth-century *Biblia pauperorum* (Bible of the Poor).

Decoration of churches, altars, and liturgical instruments was another means of popularization. The image thus became a visual exposition, a "Bible in stone," for the masses unable to read its text. In the West, murals, sculpture, and stained-glass windows represented whole Bible stories.

Pilgrimages and Crusades. The goals of all the major pilgrimages—Rome, Santiago de Compostela, Jerusalem—all had biblical associations; the Crusades were intended to deliver the Holy Land of the Bible from infidel subjection. Accordingly, the Bible became the source of preaching to promote the Crusades, as can be seen in the sermons of Pope Urban II and St. Bernard of Clairvaux. The Latin Kingdom of Jerusalem was considered a "new spiritual Israel," restoring David's realm, and clerical criticism of the Crusaders' profane behavior took on the style of the OT prophets.

Political thought. Biblical concepts of the "chosen people," "sacred kingship," and "promised land" were adopted by Western political thinkers from the beginning of the Middle Ages to replace the Roman imperial legacy. Developed by St. Augustine, these ideas became incarnated in the kingdom of the Franks, in Charlemagne's empire, and thus in the actual political structures of the later Middle Ages. The Covenant served as the model for the mutual alliance of God, the chosen people, and the sacred, anointed king, for government by divine grace. Accordingly, tyranny was considered a sin, causing a break in the alliance and imposing on the church the duty of correcting the vice by excommunication. After the Gregorian reform of the twelfth and thirteenth centuries, papal claims came increasingly to be based on this sense of prophetic mission. The political philosophy of Thomas Aquinas finally synthesized the earlier doctrines into a coherent theory of the Christian state and monarchy.

Theology and scholarship. More than any other field, theology was linked to the biblical message and its exegesis. Theologians were supposed to interpret the meaning of the "divine page," the entire truth, in order to solve the problems of the faith. Canonists of the eleventh and twelfth centuries oriented their study to biblical precepts, and the decretalists of the twelfth through fourteenth centuries used the Bible as the source of their legislation. The historical books of the OT also served as the model for medieval chroniclers and historians, who drew from the Bible their notions of the didactic character of history. Bible history itself joined the classical heritage—"Rome, Athens, and Jerusalem"—as one of the key roots of civilization. Indeed, from the *Etymologies* of Isidore of Seville to the thirteenth-century *specula* (mirrors) of Vincent of Beauvais, the Bible was considered an essential root of all kinds of knowledge and science. In the fourteenth century, Raymond Lull even insisted on the biblical legacy in the training of a knight.

Popular literature. Not only were saints' lives modeled on the Gospel accounts of the life of Christ, but even heroic poetry followed the biblical model. Aside from the specifically biblical narratives of certain Germanic and Old English poems, there developed in *Beowulf,* the Spanish *cantilenas,* and the French *chansons de geste* an ethos of the Christian warrior, implying (as in the Charlemagne cycle) piety, fidelity to the church, and readiness to fight the opponents of the faith. This influence is felt even in poems of more pagan character, such as the *Nibelungenlied.* Lyric, romance, and especially drama were all deeply influenced by the Bible. Dramatic cycles explicitly retold the OT and NT history, and even the lay theater included Bible verses and episodes. In sum, no aspect of medieval European culture escaped the pervasive influence of the Bible.

BIBLE, ARMENIAN

BIBLIOGRAPHY

A full bibliography of the Bible in the Middle Ages would be enormous. Among more recent works the following will give adequate guidance to additional sources: Beryl Smalley, *The Study of the Bible in the Middle Ages* (1952); Geoffrey W. H. Lampe, ed., *The Cambridge History of the Bible,* II (1962); *La Bibbia nell'alto Medioevo,* Centro Italiano di Studi sull'alto Medioevo, Settimane di studio, X (1963), consisting of contributions to a conference held at Spoleto in 1962; Beryl Smalley, *The Becket Conflict and the Schools* (1973); Jean Leclercq, *The Love of Learning and the Desire for God* (1974); Aryeh Grabois, "L'idée de la royauté biblique dans la pensée de Thomas Becket," in Raymonde Foreville, ed., *Thomas Becket* (1975); and "The *Hebraica Veritas* and Jewish-Christian Intellectual Relations in the Twelfth Century," in *Speculum,* 50 (1975).

ARYEH GRABOIS

[See also **Alcuin; Allegory; Exegesis; Gloss; Jerome, St.; Jews and the Catholic Church; Rashi; Talmud; Translations and Translators; Vulgate;** and articles on individual figures and national literatures.]

BIBLE, ARMENIAN. The Armenian translation of the Bible, known as *Astuacašunč^{c} Girk^{c}* (Scriptures inspired by God; compare 2 Tim. 3:16), is one of the "ancient versions" and is of great importance because of its variant readings and early date (fifth century). According to the direct testimony of Koriwn, the pupil, collaborator, and biographer of the vardapet Mesrop Maštoc^{c}, the latter with the help of his pupils, Yovhan of Ekełik^{c} and Yovsēp^{c} of Pałnatun, began to translate the Proverbs of Solomon during his short stay in Samosata about 405 or 406. The work was subsequently continued on Armenian soil and was presumably brought to completion soon afterward. Thus, the translation of the Bible was the first document written in Armenian. Details about the language of the original are unfortunately not given by Koriwn, who states only that the translation was made in haste. After the Council of Ephesus in 431, four of Maštoc^{c}'s pupils, Yovsēp^{c}, Eznik, Łewond, and Koriwn himself, who had been sent to Constantinople at an earlier date—returned with an "authentic" copy of the Scriptures that served as the basis of subsequent revisions supervised by Bishop Sahak of Armenia and Eznik of Kołb. Koriwn is again silent about the nature of the revisions and the characteristics of the "authentic" copy, which was probably in Greek.

The origin of the Armenian version has preoccupied scholars for three centuries. All agree that the present text of the Old Testament is a version of the Septuagint and that the New Testament was translated from Greek. Yet, they have difficulty explaining the numerous Syriacisms not only in the Old and the New Testaments but also in the ancient Georgian version, which was translated from an archaic Armenian copy. Earlier scholars had suggested that the Armenian translation was originally made from Syriac and that the revision was based on a Greek text, presumably the Caesarean version.

The problem, however, seems to be more complex, since the variations of the Armenian from the Septuagint and the Greek text of the New Testament do not always correspond to those in the Syriac Peshitta. Modern scholars are more inclined to consider the Greek as the original and explain the Syriac influences as a result of the acquaintance of the Armenian translators with the pre-Peshitta versions, the Diatessaron of Tatian, and several works of the Syriac church fathers. The complexity of the problem is compounded by the evidence of alternate ancient translations from Syriac of Chronicles I and II and of the apocryphal third Epistle of Paul to the Corinthians, and from Greek of Ecclesiasticus, Song of Songs, Sirach, and the Psalms. We also learn from a colophon of 1299 that the Armenian text was "corrected" on the basis of the Alexandrian, Caesarean, and tetraplaric versions.

The collective text of the Scriptures in Armenian was first edited by Nersēs, bishop of Lambron, in 1180. The earliest complete manuscripts do not predate the thirteenth century. However, there are codices of the gospels from earlier centuries. A comparison with the Septuagint reveals that the Armenian lacks Maccabees IV, which was probably never translated into Armenian, and that the Epistle of Jeremiah is not part of the present canon, even though it exists in certain manuscripts. The present text of the Apocalypse is a recension by Nersēs of Lambron; the original was not translated in the fifth century. The manuscripts of the Armenian Bible also include short introductions and tables of contents of the individual books, the Ammonian sections, the Euthaliana, the canonical tables of Eusebius of Caesarea, and the pseudepigrapha, but none of these is included in the present canon.

BIBLIOGRAPHY

The only critical edition of the Armenian Bible was published by Yovhannēs Zawhrabean (John Zohrabian) in

1805. A revised edition without the critical apparatus was published by Arsēn Bagratuni (1860); and a concordance was compiled by T^cadēos Astuacaturean (1895). Hakob Anasyan, *Haykakan matenagitut^cyun V–XVIII dd.*, II (1976), 309–668, provides an exhaustive bibliography. See also Koriwn, *Vark^c Maštoc^ci* (1941).

KRIKOR H. MAKSOUDIAN

[See also **Armenian Church; Armenian Language; Koriwn; Mesrob, St.; Nersēs of Lambron; Sahak, St.**]

BIBLE, CISTERCIAN. The program of spiritual renewal initiated by the founders of the Burgundian Cîteaux (1098) included a liturgical reform. It emphasized authenticity by going back to the earliest and most reliable sources. For the same reason one of the founders, the Englishman (St.) Stephen Harding, undertook the task of producing a Bible free, as much as possible, from the errors of copyists of past centuries. He not only collected the best Latin manuscripts of the Vulgate but also consulted the Hebrew text of the Old Testament with the help of Jewish scholars, and turned occasionally to the Greek original of the New Testament. Phrases or sentences that he could not verify from such sources were eliminated or corrected. The result was a critical edition of both Testaments that ranked among the best produced in the early twelfth century.

The work was completed in 1109, the year Stephen Harding became abbot of Cîteaux (1109–1133). In this capacity he made the use of the revised Bible compulsory at Cîteaux and subsequent Cistercian foundations, and strictly prohibited any further changes in the text. His purpose was, obviously, to ensure liturgical uniformity, since biblical texts featured both in the missal and in the books of the Divine Office. This goal, however, was never achieved. After the joining of St. Bernard of Clairvaux to the initial community (1113), new foundations multiplied at such a rate that the copying of Abbot Stephen's Bible could not keep up with the demand.

The original Bible consisted of three parchment volumes in folio, although the first volume, because of its bulk, was soon cut and arranged into two separate volumes. Thus the Bible, still preserved in the Municipal Library of Dijon, is in four volumes (as MSS 12–15).

The enduring fame of and interest in the Cistercian Bible, however, rests on its extraordinary beauty; it is decorated with elaborate initials and even full-page illustrations of great technical perfection and originality. This is particularly true of the last two volumes. Although the identity of the artists remains unknown, their work certainly belongs among the finest monuments of French Romanesque illuminations.

BIBLIOGRAPHY

Augustinus Lang, "Die Bibel Stephan Hardings," in *Cistercienser-Chronik*, **51–52** (1939–1940); Charles Oursel, "La bible de Saint Etienne Harding et le scriptorium de Cîteaux, 1109– vers 1134," in *Cîteaux*, **10** (1959); and *Miniatures cisterciennes, 1109–1134* (1960).

L. J. LEKAI

[See also **Cisterian Order; Harding, Stephen.**]

BIBLE, FRENCH. In France, as in most European countries, vernacular translations of Scripture began not with the whole Bible but with certain of its books. It is difficult to ascertain the exact dates of the earliest translations, but Walter Map in his *De nugis curialium* admits having seen at the Third Lateran Council of 1179 French translations of the psalter and other books of the Bible. Investigations undertaken on the order of Innocent III in 1199 revealed nothing in these works contrary to orthodoxy, although the translations were associated with the Waldenses, condemned as heretical at the Synod of Verona in 1184. The earliest book translated, as well as the most popular, was undoubtedly the psalter. Two early major traditions of French versions are represented in the Montebourg Psalter (Oxford, Bodleian Library, MS Douce 320, *ca.* 1200), a translation of the Gallican rendering, and in the Eadwine Psalter (Cambridge, Trinity College, MS R.17.1, *ca.* 1160), a translation of Jerome's *Hebraica.*

By the beginning of the fourteenth century these literal versions had been replaced by more idiomatic renderings. The revision of Raoul de Presles (*ca.* 1380), close to the Metz Psalter (*ca.* 1300), became so widespread that it reappeared in modernized form in the early printed editions of the Bible in the late fifteenth century. Beautifully illuminated French psalters exist, as well as a number of verse translations. Also popular were translations of major commentaries on the Psalms, for example Peter Lombard's *Magna glosatura* (Paris, Bibliothèque Nationale,

BIBLE, FRENCH

MSS fr. 963 and 22,892) and Augustine's *Ennarationes* (contained in essence in Durham Cathedral, MS A ii, 11–13, *ca.* 1195).

Numerous too are the translations of the Apocalypse, which had a wide appeal. The earliest, with commentary, may have appeared in the third quarter of the twelfth century in Normandy, and by around 1200, illuminated copies were in wide circulation. The texts, however, are frequently garbled and at times ill suited to the cycle of miniatures accompanying them (for example, Paris, Bibliothèque Nationale, MS fr. 403).

The outstanding work of translation in this period is the twelfth-century version of the four books of Kings (Paris, Mazarine, MS 70). It is both a masterpiece of French prose and a monument of erudition containing much of the exegetical materials found in the *Glossa ordinaria.* It is only fitting that this version should have been widely copied and should have found its way into a number of mid-twelfth-century compilations of Old Testament translations, including the most important, the Acre Bible (Paris, Arsenal, MS 3211), probably commissioned by St. Louis during the Sixth Crusade.

The late twelfth century, perhaps the period of most intense activity in biblical translation, produced the two major forms of later standard complete Bibles. The Bible of the Thirteenth Century (incomplete in Paris, Bibliothèque Nationale, MS fr. 899 [*ca.* 1280], and MS fr. 24,728) is for the most part an exact but pedestrian translation, although Acts and the Catholic Epistles are markedly inferior and the Apocalypse is often unintelligible. It contains some learned commentary (sections of the *Glossa ordinaria* for some of the books of the Octateuch, for example), but the glosses on the psalter and Gospels are often trivial and at times silly. It is a two-volume work wherein the Octateuch, Kings, Chronicles to Esther, Job, and the psalter appear in volume I and volume II contains the sapiential books, Maccabees, Prophets, and all of the New Testament. This collection of translations by diverse hands appears to have been compiled by a group of stationers in Paris or Picardy.

The second major translation had as its core Guyart des Moulins's *Bible historiale,* from which it took its name (Paris, Mazarine, MS 532 and Bibliothèque Nationale, MS fr. 155). Guyart had originally planned to present a faithful translation of Peter Comestor's *Historia scholastica,* adding to it a translation of those sections of the Vulgate that Peter's commentary elucidated. Although this plan limited Guyart to the historical books of the Old and New Testaments only, he decided to include a translation of Proverbs and parts of other sapiential books as well. Guyart's original work continued to be copied in the fourteenth and fifteenth centuries (London, British Library, MSS Royal 19 D. iii [1411], and Royal 15 D. i and 18 D. ix–x [purchased by Edward IV, 1479]), but Guyart no sooner released his edition than he lost control over its contents.

Other compilers retaining sections of Guyart's work added translations of other nonhistorical books, such as the psalter and Job, and frequently replaced Guyart's New Testament version with translations and glosses from the Bible of the Thirteenth Century until a complete Bible was formed. The most drastic but most common form (surviving in some forty manuscripts) appeared as early as 1317 (Paris, Arsenal, MS 5059), when most of the first volume of the *Bible historiale* (with added psalter) was retained but Guyart's second volume, containing his translation of Maccabees and Acts with selected glosses from the *Historia* and his gospel harmony according to Comestor, were replaced by volume II of the Bible of the Thirteenth Century.

Although the royal house of France encouraged revisions and new translations during the fourteenth and fifteenth centuries, as witnessed by the original but incomplete work of Jean de Sy (Bibliothèque Nationale, MS fr. 15,397 [1355]) and by the revisions of the Bible of the Thirteenth Century by Raoul de Presles (MSS fr. 20,065–20,066), it was the *Bible historiale,* as completed by volume II of the Bible of the Thirteenth Century, that found the greatest favor during the fourteenth and fifteenth centuries and became the basis for the early printed Bibles in France, appearing in some dozen editions between 1487 and 1545.

BIBLIOGRAPHY

Samuel Berger, *La Bible française au moyen âge* (1884, repr. 1967); Guy de Poerck and Rika Van Deyck, "La Bible et l'activité traductrice dans les pays romans avant 1300," in *Grundriss der romanischen Literaturen des Mittelalters,* VI, pt. 1 (1968), 21–39; VI, pt. 2 (1970), 54–69; C. A. Robson, "Vernacular Scriptures in France," in *The Cambridge History of the Bible,* Geoffrey W. H. Lampe, ed., II (1969), 436–452.

RAYMOND C. ST-JACQUES

[See also **French Literature; Waldensians.**]

BIBLE, GLOSSES AND COMMENTARIES (IRISH). The Bible was introduced to Ireland with the advent of Christianity in the fourth or fifth century. No copy has survived from this period, but the text used was probably an Old Latin type similar to that found in Codex Usserianus I (Dublin, Trinity College, MS 55), a manuscript of the four Gospels from around 600. During the late sixth or early seventh century Jerome's Vulgate reached Ireland. Its adoption as the standard text of the Bible was a gradual process—as regards both the various books of the Bible and the different churches of Ireland—accelerated by closer contacts with Rome in the seventh century but protracted, nevertheless, into the eighth century.

Because of the simultaneous use of both Old Latin and Vulgate texts during this period, the majority of Irish biblical texts have a "mixed" character: although based on an early and pure type of Vulgate (probably from Italy), they also carry extensive Old Latin readings, often irregularly distributed and varying for a given text from one manuscript to another. Another feature of Irish biblical texts is their frequent minor textual variations (insertions, omissions, changes in word order), probably provided to help persons not fully familiar with Latin. No full text of the Bible has survived from the early Irish church; the purest Vulgate texts are the Cathach Psalter (early seventh century) and the Book of Durrow Gospels (*ca.* 650); the Book of Armagh (*ca.* 807) contains the complete New Testament.

Commentaries. From the mid seventh to the early ninth century the Irish monastic schools produced a large volume of exegetical literature in Latin, most of it anonymous. Recent scholarship has identified over forty Hiberno-Latin commentaries. Although these works rely primarily on patristic exegesis, especially Hilary, Jerome, Augustine, Gregory, and Isidore, they also share features peculiar to the Irish monastic milieu from which they derive. Notable among such features are: (1) the use of unusual and uncanonical sources, for example, Pelagius (for the Pauline Epistles), Theodore of Mopsuestia (for the Psalms), and the grammarian Vergilius Maro Grammaticus (for etymologies); (2) the application of the rhetorical questions of time, place, and author to the individual books of the Bible; (3) the presentation of material in formulaic questions and answers, in imitation of native Irish oral pedagogy; (4) a predilection for triadic and tetradic schemes and structures; and (5) the rendering of key biblical words in the "three sacred languages" (Hebrew, Greek, and Latin). The biblical books most frequently commented on are the Gospels (especially Matthew), the Pauline Epistles, and the Psalter.

Biblical exegesis from the ninth century on was composed mainly in the Irish language—a reflection of the trend in the monastic schools in favor of the vernacular—but compares unfavorably with the earlier, Hiberno-Latin exegesis both in quantity and in quality.

Glosses. As evidenced by the interlinear glosses in Codex Usserianus I, Irish exegetes were glossing the Bible as early as the seventh century, in both Latin and Old Irish. By 700 the art of glossing had progressed from calques and single words to sentences providing different levels of interpretation and explanatory comments. The bulk of Irish biblical glosses (of which approximately 12,000 are in Old Irish) are found in two codices, an eighth-century Würzburg manuscript of the Pauline Epistles (MS M.p.th.f.12) and a late-eighth- or early-ninth-century commentary on the Psalms (Milan, Biblioteca Ambrosiana, C. 301 *inf.*).

BIBLIOGRAPHY

Bible. James F. Kenney, *Sources for the Early History of Ireland,* I (1929), repr. with addenda by Ludwig Bieler (1966), 624f., contains full bibliography (to 1929) and the best discussion of the Irish Bible. See also A. Cordoliani, "Le texte de la Bible en Irlande du Ve au IXe siècle," in *Revue biblique,* 57 (1950); Peter Doyle, "The Latin Bible in Ireland: Its Origins and Growth," in Martin McNamara, ed., *Biblical Studies: The Medieval Irish Contribution* (1976), 30–45.

Commentaries. The fundamental study is "Wendepunkte in der Geschichte der lateinischen Exegese im Frühmittelalter," in Bernhard Bischoff, *Mittelalterliche Studien,* I (1966), 205–273, translated in McNamara, *op. cit.,* 73–160.

Glosses. The Old Irish glosses have been edited by Whitley Stokes and John Strachan, *Thesaurus palaeohibernicus,* 2 vols. (1901–1903), and *Supplement* (1910). See also Maartje Draak, "Construe Marks in Hiberno-Latin Manuscripts," in *Mededelingen der Koninklijke Nederlandse Akademie van Wetenschappen, Afd. Letterkunde,* n.s. **20**, no. 10 (1957), 261–281.

PÁDRAIG P. Ó NÉILL

[See also **Gloss; Ireland, Early History; Celtic Church.**]

BIBLE, OLD AND MIDDLE ENGLISH. Medieval biblical materials in English divide readily into two periods: Old English, or Anglo-Saxon (600–1100),

BIBLE, OLD AND MIDDLE ENGLISH

and Middle English (1100–1500). The Old English biblical tradition comprises three kinds of texts: glosses, prose translations, and poetic paraphrases.

Glossing refers to the practice of inserting between the lines of the Latin, word by word, a vernacular translation of the text. This is the earliest form of Bible translation, though it is more precise to speak of glosses, since the word order strictly follows the Latin, and would sound awkward to native ears. The glosses are largely confined to manuscripts of the Gospels and the psalter, since these two parts of the Bible were used more extensively in the liturgy than any other. The most famous examples are the Lindisfarne Gospels of the late seventh century and the Rushworth Gospels (*ca.* 800). Glossed psalters are even more numerous (fourteen in all), the most important being the Vespasian Psalter. One other manuscript, the Paris Psalter, is unique in having the Latin text of the Psalms in one column, and an Old English translation in the other. Moreover, the first fifty psalms are in prose (attributed to King Alfred) and the remainder in alliterative verse.

The nearest thing to a translation in the modern sense is the tenth-century rendering of the Gospels into West Saxon prose. The word order of these, compared with the glosses, is much more natural. The West Saxon Gospel translations are anonymous. The only name that we can associate certainly with conventional Bible translation in the Old English period is that of Ælfric, a reformer, teacher, and scholar who did much to advance the cause of education in the years following the monastic reform of St. Dunstan. He produced sets of sermons, saints' lives, and translations of parts of the Old Testament that have been assembled under the title *Heptateuch* (Genesis through Judges). From the preface to his translation of Genesis, the *Questions on Genesis,* and his *Treatise on the Old and New Testaments,* all in Old English, we may infer a plan to present the entire Bible in the English language. His translation of the first half of Genesis is complete and literal; whether other books were to have been literal translations or homilies is not clear. In any case Ælfric should not be overlooked in any history of English versions of the Bible.

The final category of Old English biblical materials is the group of poetic paraphrases traditionally associated with the name of Caedmon. Nothing that survives is certainly his, except the hymn to the Creator (nine alliterative lines) quoted by Bede. Nevertheless, there are important and artistically impressive poetic paraphrases of Genesis, Exodus, and Daniel written in the same long line as *Beowulf.* There are also free adaptations of New Testament materials in the same poetic form under the modern titles *Christ and Satan* (which includes apocryphal materials) and *Christ* (parts I, II, III), the latter drawing on homiletic materials tied to the *temporale* (the church's calendar of biblical feasts), such as Gregory the Great's sermon on the Ascension (*Christ* II). We may conclude the canon of Old English translations with mention of the poetic paraphrase of Judith, one of the books of the Old Testament apocrypha most admired by the Anglo-Saxons. *Judith* is preserved, along with *Beowulf,* in a manuscript of about 1000.

The Middle English period presents a much greater diversity of materials, and there is not room here even to mention the categories, which range from biblical compendia like the *Cursor mundi* through such visionary poems as *Piers Plowman.* Sermons, legendaries, romances, and especially the drama (itself comprising whole cycles of Bible history) were all suffused with the influence and language of the Bible.

The most ambitious work of sustained direct paraphrase is a late-fourteenth-century metrical version of parts of the Old Testament, covering the Pentateuch (except Leviticus), Joshua, Judges, Ruth, the four books of Kings, Job, Tobias, Esther, Judith, and parts of Maccabees. This is followed in the manuscript by a brief prose *sanctorale,* or collection of saints' lives. The quality of this huge work leaves much to be desired, and is clearly inferior to an earlier poem (*ca.* 1250) having the modern title *Genesis and Exodus,* which actually contains sections from Genesis, Exodus, Numbers, and Deuteronomy, and is worth reading for its interesting blend of biblical and apocryphal materials. Its treatment of the narrative, however, is conservative when compared with *Jacob and Joseph* (*ca.* 1250) and *Susannah* (*The Pistel of Swete Susan, ca.* 1400), two very different poems that are both products of medieval minstrelsy.

Psalters and Gospels continued to be turned out, the most notable development being the psalter produced by the fourteenth-century mystic Richard Rolle, whose spiritual development was inextricably associated with the book of Psalms. His psalter presents the Psalms verse by verse: first the Latin, followed by a fairly literal translation of that verse into English, which in turn is followed by an English-language commentary on the verse, translated from the *Magna glosatura* on the Psalms by Peter Lombard but with changes and additions by Rolle himself that show considerable originality.

For the New Testament we have first the *Glossed Gospels,* consisting of the Gospel text in English, accompanied by commentaries derived mainly from the *Catena aurea* of Thomas Aquinas. The impulse behind this important text is still a matter of dispute, but it is most likely a part of the larger Wycliffite translation project undertaken by the Lollards. Very different in character and scope is the earlier *Stanzaic Life of Christ* (*ca.* 1350), a West Midland poem of more than ten thousand lines, structured to fit the commemorations of the *temporale* and derived in large part from extrabiblical sources such as the *Legenda aurea* and the *Polychronicon,* a fourteenth-century universal history, itself organized after the biblical pattern. There were also sporadic efforts to translate the book of Acts, the Pauline and Catholic Epistles, and the book of Revelation, this last based on an earlier French version of the Apocalypse.

The Wycliffe Bible itself was produced over a period of time during the latter half of the fourteenth century, in at least two distinct versions usually referred to as early (EV) and late (LV). Essentially, EV is a preliminary text in which the translators deliberately kept to the word order of the Latin; LV is a revision of this with corrections, in which the word order is that of English, hence a much smoother translation. The text is, as already mentioned, a complete English Bible, including apocrypha, and takes up four large volumes in the 1850 edition. Although this translation was banned by ecclesiastical authorities in 1407 on account of its Lollard associations, its continuing popularity is attested by the survival of some 230 manuscript copies.

The circumstances surrounding the composition of the Wycliffe Bible, and the date of its completion, are matters of conjecture. According to a note in one manuscript at Baruch 3:20, "Here endeth the translation of *N,* and now beginneth the translation of *J* and other men." From another manuscript with a note in exactly the same place we learn that "*N*" probably stands for Nicholay de Herford, but no other names are given, probably because the "other men" had not been publicly identified and were not anxious to be subjected to ecclesiastical examination. Nevertheless, records show that in the 1370's John Wycliffe, Nicholas Hereford, and John Trevisa were paying rent for quarters in Queen's College, Oxford, and it may be that here the EV of the Wycliffe Bible was taking shape up to the time these men left the college (*ca.* 1380). The LV is more of a mystery, and may have been undertaken elsewhere, following the retirement of Wycliffe from Oxford. It may not have been completed until well after his death in 1384. A prologue to the Wycliffe Bible, found in some manuscripts of LV, is well worth the attention of anyone seeking to understand the motivation behind the composition of the first complete Bible in English.

BIBLIOGRAPHY

Geoffrey W. H. Lampe, ed., *The Cambridge History of the Bible,* II (1969); Beryl Smalley, *The Study of the Bible in the Middle Ages* (1952); Minnie C. Morrell, *A Manual of Old English Biblical Materials* (1965); Jonathan B. Severs, ed., *A Manual of the Writings in Middle English, 1050–1500,* II (1970), esp. pts. II, III, and IV, 339–409, and corresponding bibliography, 503–552; Anna C. Paues, ed., *A Fourteenth Century English Biblical Version* (1904); Josiah Forshall and Frederic Madden, eds., *The Holy Bible Containing the Old and New Testaments with the Apocryphal Books, in the Earliest English Versions Made from the Latin Vulgate by John Wycliffe and His Followers,* 4 vols. (1850); Margaret Deanesley, *The Lollard Bible* (1920); Sven L. Fristedt, *The Wycliffite Bible,* pt. I (1953), pt. II (1969), pt. III (1973); Conrad Lindberg, "The Manuscripts and Versions of the Wycliffite Bible," in *Studia neophilologica,* **42** (1970).

DAVID C. FOWLER

[See also **Ælfric; Anglo-Saxon Literature; Gloss; Lollards; Middle English Literature; Mystical Writings, Middle English; Translations and Translators; Wycliffe, John.**]

BIBLE MORALISÉE, a commentary on the Bible derived from the *Postillae in Bibliam* of Hugues of St. Cher, in which excerpted passages are presented with moralized or allegorical interpretations. Three profusely illustrated copies of about 1250 survive, the earliest in four volumes in Oxford, London, and Paris, a fragment in French in Vienna (Österreichisches Nationalbibliothek, MS 2254), and a royal copy in Toledo and New York (Morgan Library, MS M. 240). Containing four sets of paired scenes in roundels, each page resembles the format of stained glass windows.

BIBLIOGRAPHY

Alexandre de Laborde, *La Bible moralisée illustrée,* 5 vols. (1911–1927); Reiner Haussherr, ed., *Bible moralisée: Faksimile-Ausgabe im Originalformat des Codex Vindobonensis 2254 der Österreichisches Nationalbibliothek* (1973); David M. Robb, *The Art of the Illuminated Manuscript* (1973), 214–215, 219.

ROBERT G. CALKINS

[See also **Biblia Pauperum; Manuscript Illumination.**]

Page from Bible Moralisée. ÖSTERREICHISCHES NATIONALBIBLIOTHEK, VIENNA, MS 2254

Page from Biblia Pauperum. BRITISH LIBRARY

BIBLIA PAUPERUM, a popular illustrated biblical commentary containing typological juxtapositions of two Old Testament scenes with one of the life of Christ. It appeared first in manuscript form in the thirteenth century, became a popular picture book with miniatures in the fourteenth, and then appeared as a printed book with woodcuts in the fifteenth. It served as an aid for preachers to demonstrate the unity of the Bible.

BIBLIOGRAPHY

Gerhard Schmidt, *Die Armenbibeln des XIV Jahrhunderts* (1959); Heinrich Theodor Musper, *Die Urausgaben der holländischen Apokalypse und Biblia pauperum* (1961); Erzsébet Soltész, *Biblia pauperum* (1967).

ROBERT G. CALKINS

[See also **Bible Moralisée; Manuscript Illumination.**]

BIBLICAL INTERPRETATION. Medieval interpretation of the Bible derived from methods and attitudes developed in the patristic school of Alexandria, most notably by Origen (*d. ca.* 254). Influenced by the Pauline reinterpretation of Old Testament events in relation to Christ (for instance, Galatians 4:24–31), and possibly by the Neoplatonic exegesis of Philo Judaeus (*d. ca.* 50), he taught that the Bible contained a multiplicity of meanings and senses. By an analogy with the division of human nature into body, soul, and spirit, he specified three senses of Scripture: the somatic, psychic, and pneumatic, or the literal, moral, and spiritual (*De principiis* 4.2.4).

Origen's hermeneutic reached the Latin West indirectly through the Latin patristic authors, including Ambrose, Hilary, Jerome, and Augustine, who used and systematized his method, and directly through Rufinus' translation of his works.

St. Gregory the Great (*d.* 604) is generally regarded as the initiator of the medieval fourfold interpretation of the Bible, in that he adapted and extended Origen's spiritual sense to include the anagogical and allegorical senses. In practice, medieval exegetes recognized and employed both the threefold and the fourfold senses of the Bible, with numerous variations. The Carolingians Paschasius and John Scotus Erigena seem to have employed a twofold division, the literal-historical sense intended by the biblical author and the spiritual sense, discovered by the commentator and transmitted through the exegetical tradition.

Guibert de Nogent (*d.* 1124) stated in his *Quo ordine sermo fieri debet (Patrologia latina,* CLVI, 25D) that the four senses constituted "rules by which every page of Scripture turns as if on so many wheels: history speaks of things done; allegory understands one thing by another; tropology is a moral way of speaking . . . and anagoge is the spiritual understanding by which we are led to things above." In his *Didascalicon de studio legendi,* Hugh of St. Victor (*d.* 1141) describes a threefold division of senses: the literal-historical, the allegorical or doctrinal, and the tropological or mystical. It was only in the thirteenth century that the fourfold division of senses was epitomized by the Dominican Augustine of Dacia, in this distich:

> Littera gesta docet, quid credis allegoria,
> Moralis quid agas, quo tendis anagogia.

> The literal tells of deeds; the allegory, what to believe;
> The moral, what to do; the anagogical, whither all is leading.

St. Thomas Aquinas defined the literal, or historical, sense as that by which words signify things or deeds. Hence, anything that may correctly be understood from the meaning of the words pertains to the literal sense. Not all scriptural texts, therefore, are open to interpretation according to the four senses; indeed, texts that contain a moral teaching, present an allegory, or are concerned with the future status of the church are susceptible of interpretation according to their literal sense only. The spiritual senses, including allegorical, moral, and anagogical, come into play where things or actions signified by the words of a text may be understood to signify other things. Thus, the allegorical sense is understood as the sense by which things in the Old Testament signify things in the New Testament—as, for example, the sacrifice of the Passover lamb represents the sacrifice of Christ.

The fourfold division prevailed, at least in theory, until well into the sixteenth century, although the importance of the spiritual senses was gradually undermined by increased appreciation for the literal and historical. Around 1330, Nicholas of Lyra cited Augustine of Dacia's distich in his *Postilla* on Galatians, but in fact concentrated on setting forth the literal sense of Scripture, which he considered the most important and decisive one, and the foundation of all spiritual interpretations. His mastery of Hebrew, familiarity with the rabbinical interpretations of Old Testament texts, and judicious originality of thought made his *Postillae* on the Bible a favorite exegetical manual with his contemporaries, and a model for later humanist and Reformation exegetes, including Martin Luther.

BIBLIOGRAPHY

Geoffrey W. H. Lampe, ed., *The Cambridge History of the Bible,* II (1969), 155–279; Henri de Lubac, *Exégèse médiévale: Les quatre sens de l'écriture,* 4 vols. (1959–1964); Beryl Smalley, *The Study of the Bible in the Middle Ages* (1952); Ceslaus Spicq, *Esquisse d'une histoire de l'exégèse latine au moyen âge* (1944).

WANDA CIŻEWSKI

[See also **Allegory; Exegesis; Gregory I, the Great, Pope; Guibert de Nogent; Hugh of St. Victor; Nicholas of Lyra.**]

BIBLICAL POETRY, GERMAN. The earliest German biblical poetry employs alliterative verse. A short text entered about 800 in a manuscript from Wessobrunn, Bavaria *(Das Wessobrunner Gebet),* consists of nine lines of verse describing the void before the Creation followed by a prayer to God the Creator, usually thought to be in prose, though it may be in free alliterative verse. The first sentence bears a striking resemblance to two strophes of the Old Icelandic mythological poem *Vǫluspá,* and may well be an adaptation of a piece of pre-Christian poetry. The prayer asks for strength to resist devils, possibly an allusion to pagan cults. It has been conjectured that the text may have been composed (or

BIBLICAL POETRY, GERMAN

compiled) for the purpose of converting the heathen or instructing new converts in the Christian faith.

Also from Bavaria (St. Emmeram, Regensburg) come about 100 lines forming part of an eschatological poem known as *Muspilli.* This treats the fate of the soul after death, the Signs, and the Last Judgment. It does not follow any biblical text closely. Before the description of the Signs preceding the Last Judgment is a section of eleven lines (37–47) describing the fight between Elias and Antichrist. In Malachi 4:5 the sending of Elias is promised, and in Revelation 11:3–7 God's two witnesses (identified in church tradition wth Enoch and Elias) are killed by the beast (identified with Antichrist). The fight between Elias and Antichrist is described as a trial by combat. In line 57 the word *muspille* occurs; the supposed nominative form of this word, *muspilli,* was used by Schmeller, the first modern editor of the text, as a title for the whole. Whatever its precise meaning, this word seems to be pre-Christian in origin and to evoke pagan conceptions of the end of the world by fire, for which, however, there is no lack of biblical support. It has also been held that the fight between Elias and Antichrist derives in part from pagan accounts of contests between giants (in the Old Norse account of the end of the world there is a fire-giant called Muspellr). The description of the Last Judgment is entirely clerical in inspiration. This text has been thought by some scholars to be a composite work, while others have argued for its essential unity. The verse technique is weak, and there are a few nonalliterating lines with terminal rhyme, which seems to suggest that *Muspilli* is a transitional work composed at a time when native forms were being replaced by others borrowed from the new Latin culture of the church.

From the second quarter of the ninth century we have the remains of two biblical epics in the Old Saxon language of northern Germany: three fragments (336 lines in all) of the *Altsächsische Genesis* and the greater part (5,983 lines) of the *Heliand,* a life of Christ based on the canonical Gospels (with a few unessential apocryphal elements added). Both works have connections with England: much of the *Genesis* (617 lines) exists in an Old English translation (known as *Genesis B* or *The Younger Genesis*), and the fullest manuscript of the *Heliand,* from the tenth century, was almost certainly made in England. The biblical epic in alliterative verse is often thought to be a form borrowed from Anglo-Saxon literature in the wake of English participation in the conversion of the Saxons under Charlemagne and Louis the Pious, and to have been employed as a means of religious instruction among the new converts; there is indirect evidence that Louis may have instigated the composition of these biblical epics.

The biblical narrative is accommodated to native ways of thought, especially where Christ is depicted as the leader of a band of loyal warriors and where vocabulary appropriate to Germanic notions of fate is applied to what has been preordained by God and is therefore bound to happen. Many exotic details are omitted and many elements of Saxon local color are added. The marriage feast at Cana is expanded into a grand carousal, and Herod feasts like a Germanic chieftain with his "ring-friends." The heroic spirit of native poetry is probably reflected in Peter's defense of his lord in the Garden of Gethsemane, by his declaration of loyalty at the Last Supper, and by Thomas' words exhorting the disciples to accompany Christ to Jerusalem, not to question his decision, and to die with their lord as a band of warriors. Such passages illustrate how the poet eagerly seizes upon any passage in his source that can fire the imagination of his audience. However, he does not falsify the teaching of the church, and the story of the Passion is told with no concessions to the martial spirit invoked elsewhere.

Even more imaginative are some passages of the *Genesis* (which might have been composed by the same poet, though this seems unlikely), such as the one in which Adam rails at Eve after they have been cast out of the Garden, or another in which Eve grieves for Abel as she washes his bloodstained clothes. Although the biblical sources are undoubtedly germanized in the Saxon versions, the degree of germanization has often been exaggerated, and much of what appears Germanic is merely a consequence of the poetic form in which the story is couched.

Henceforth all German biblical poetry was composed in rhyming verse, commonly thought to have been modeled on that of the Ambrosian hymn and introduced into Germany by Otfrid von Weissenburg, a monk of no mean erudition who, in the third quarter of the ninth century, completed his *Liber evangeliorum* (or *Evangelienbuch*), a life of Christ based on the canonical Gospels and incorporating much theological learning. In a letter to Liutbert, archbishop of Mainz, Otfrid acknowledges his debt to the works of Christian Latin poets, and in an early chapter of his work he states his literary ambition: to provide his people, the Franks, with a worthy German medium for the celebration of God's works.

BIBLICAL POETRY, GERMAN

His poem, divided into five books, traces the events of the Gospels from the story of Zacharias and the birth of the Baptist to the Ascension. The Last Judgment (largely according to Matthew 25) and a description of the joys of heaven are added. The first book deals with Christ's early life and ends with the teaching of John; the second begins with the doctrine of the Logos and ends with the Sermon on the Mount; the third recounts some of the miracles and Christ's teaching to the Jews; the fourth is devoted to the Passion and ends with the sealing of the sepulcher; the fifth treats the Resurrection and subsequent events. In general Otfrid follows the Gospel of John from the beginning of book II. For book I he had to resort to Matthew and Luke, and he often inserts matter from them into the framework provided by John. Mark is hardly used, since his Gospel was at the time held to be an abridgment of Matthew's. Precisely how Otfrid selected his material is not known.

Apart from adding exegetical comments to his narrative, Otfrid interpolates chapters headed *spiritaliter, mystice,* and *moraliter* to provide explications of the events just narrated according to different modes of interpretation. Otfrid was profoundly learned in the divinity of his age and a precise biblical scholar with a supreme respect for the sacred texts. He was a pupil of the great Hrabanus Maurus of Fulda, from whom he learned how to use the standard commentaries. He added not a single idea of his own, and his originality consists almost entirely in his having chosen German rhyming verse as the medium for his work—and perhaps in his having adapted rhyming verse to German. His work had a short-lived popularity, but after the beginning of the tenth century it was quickly forgotten.

From this early period only two other biblical pieces are preserved. A fragment of thirty-one lines of Otfridian verse known as *Christus und die Samariterin* (*ca.* 900) contains the beginning of a skillful rendering of the conversation between Christ and the woman of Samaria (John 4). The style has been thought to derive to some extent from that of contemporary oral poetry. *Psalm 138* is a free metrical paraphrase of a psalm—so free that scholars dispute the correct sequence of the lines.

This early efflorescence was succeeded by a century and a half from which no German poetry is preserved. When the tradition resumed about 1060, it yielded works of a very different kind: metrically primitive, naive in expression, and informed by a new religiosity. Typical of the new spirit is a song commissioned by Bishop Gunther of Bamberg and composed by one Ezzo *(Ezzos Gesang).* It tells of the Creation, the Fall, and the Redemption, partly in narrative addressed to "you lords" in the poet's audience, partly in the form of a hymn addressed to God. Two versions are preserved: of one, from Strasbourg, we have seven strophes; of the other, probably a sermonizing expansion of the original, we have thirty-three. The longer version is contained in an important manuscript from Vorau, to which we owe the preservation of most of the German biblical poetry that has survived from the eleventh and twelfth centuries. The manuscript also contains a poetic synopsis of the main articles of the faith, known as *Summa theologiae,* beginning with the creation of the angels and ending with the feast of the blessed. Moral teaching is linked with the dogma throughout.

Whereas Otfrid and the poet of the *Heliand* had given accounts of the life of Christ based almost exclusively on the canonical Gospels and added dogmatic interpretations where it seemed appropriate, later poets tended to start from the dogma and to employ the biblical texts as evidence—evidence that was necessarily incomplete and had to be supplemented from other sources. The scheme of divine history was laid down in the creeds, none of which mentions the earthly life of Christ between the Incarnation and the Passion. Thus the teaching of Jesus became dispensable. The Apostles' Creed, moreover, adds the Descent into hell; and for an account of this, one had to resort to the gospel of Nicodemus. The reign of Antichrist and the Fifteen Signs were included among those events that still lay in the future, and for details of these one could turn to such authoritative works as the tenth-century *Libellus de Antichristo* of Adso and the twelfth-century *Elucidarium* of Honorius Augustodunensis. The legends of the saints, many of which were rendered into German during the Middle Ages, contained further evidence of the wonderful work of God; incorporated into works based on the biblical texts, these might further contaminate the canonical material. Furthermore, in order to account for the Redemption, one had to add the fall of man from the Book of Genesis; and in order to account for the fall of man, one had to add the fall of Lucifer.

The first book of the Bible was important for the reason just mentioned, and the earliest biblical epic of this period is the *Altdeutsche Genesis* (or, since the manuscript is in Vienna, the *Wiener Genesis*), a work of more than 3,000 primitive rhyming couplets

BIBLICAL POETRY, GERMAN

that was probably composed by a Carinthian cleric about 1060. It recounts the creation of the angels, the fall of Lucifer, and then most of the story of Genesis, culminating in Jacob's blessing of his sons. There are some omissions, such as the destruction of the cities of the plain. The narrative has a naive charm and lacks the ascetic spirit of some slightly later works. God the Creator is "the lordly artisan" (*der hêre werchman*—he is called a *meister undi wercman* in *Summa theologiae*), fashioning man out of clay like one making a figure out of wax, starting with the head and then adding the other parts in turn. The dogmatic purpose is evident throughout; the sin of Adam and Eve is followed by forty-five couplets on the doctrine of sin and repentance, and the poet seeks to mitigate God's apparent severity by making him wait for Adam and Eve to repent, wishing to forgive them; only when they remain intransigent and insist on blaming each other are they cast out of the Garden.

A revised version of the epic was made roughly half a century later and was entered in a manuscript from Millstatt (Carinthia) together with the *Altdeutsche Exodus* (or *Millstätter Exodus*). This later epic takes the biblical events as far as Exodus 15, which contains Moses' hymn of thanksgiving for the crossing of the Red Sea. This book of the Bible was important for its prefigurative significance, of which the German poet was well aware but which he did not underline: the Egypian bondage represented man's bondage to sin; the Passover prefigured the Last Supper; the crossing of the Red Sea and the destruction of the Egyptian host, man's deliverance and the washing away of sins in baptism. The poet had considerable narrative skill. Echoes of German heroic poetry have been discerned in some of his imagery, as when he says that raven and wolf were denied their prey because the midwives spared the Israelites' children, or when the locusts with which God plagued the Egyptians are called "swift warriors" (comparisons between locusts and warriors are, however, found in clerical Latin writings). The poet commits a curious anachronism, though with clear dogmatic intent, when he makes Pharaoh observe that the Jews practice circumcision in place of baptism.

Another, largely independent, treatment of the books of Moses, taking the events as far as the fall of Jericho, is found in the Vorau manuscript already mentioned. It is known as *Die Vorauer Bücher Mosis* and dates from the second quarter of the twelfth century; opinion is divided as to whether the Vorau version of Genesis and that of the life of Moses are the work of one poet or two. The story of Joseph told in the *Genesis* is taken over from the earlier epic, but the rest is a new work, composed with a different intention. The biblical narrative as such is of little interest and is treated freely. What does concern the poet (or poets) is the theological meaning that can be read from it. The Trinity is seen at work in the creation of the choirs of angels, of the world, and of man. The interpretive culmination of the work is the extensive allegorization of the Tabernacle. Toward the end the narrative becomes perfunctory, and the death of Moses is not even recounted in German; moreover, it is given in the words not of the Vulgate, but of an apocryphal work.

The same manuscript contains German versions of other Old Testament stories. One is that of Balaam and his ass, told with some comic verve; here the interpretive commentary is kept separate from the narrative. Another short text, *Das Lob Salomonis,* comprises three parts: first, an account of how God tried Solomon and gave him wisdom, power, and riches; second, a description of the building of the Temple; and third, an account of the visit of the queen of Sheba. This text, which embodies much allegorical interpretation and some nonbiblical material, may have been compiled from three separate poems. The text known as *Nabuchodonosor* is, no doubt, similarly a conflation of two originally separate works. It relates the story of Shadrach, Meshach, and Abednego in the fiery furnace, followed by that of Judith. The link that probably occasioned the combination of the two stories is the name Nabuchodonosor (Nebuchadnezzar), which is shared by the kings in both. The three men in the former have become Christian martyrs, declaring their faith in Christ, "who created all things and called heaven and earth into being."

The story of Judith, which breaks off before the slaying of Holofernes, is told with élan and has features of the popular poetry known as *Spielmannsdichtung*. It differs conspicuously from another version of the same story, the so-called *Jüngere Judith,* which is also preserved in the Vorau manuscript and dates from about 1140. This unremarkable short epic of more than 1,800 lines is a straightforward rendering of the biblical book, which shows us, says the poet in his introduction, how God protected his people so long as they obeyed him, in this case through a simple woman *(mit einem blôden wîbelîn).*

The Vorau manuscript also preserves the work of

BIBLICAL POETRY, GERMAN

the first German poetess, Frau Ava, who has been identified with a recluse of that name who died in 1127, probably at Melk (lower Austria). This is a life of Jesus *(Leben Jesu)* in very primitive verse. Ava tells us that she was instructed by her sons, who presumably were clerics. Her work follows the scheme already outlined, omitting most of Christ's teaching and drawing on apocryphal sources in its account of the Nativity (Pseudo-Matthew) and the Descent into hell (Nicodemus). Pieces on the Seven Gifts of the Holy Spirit, the reign of Antichrist, and the Last Things are added. In a thirteenth-century manuscript from Görlitz the whole is preceded by a life of John the Baptist; in this Ava follows the apocryphal tradition according to which he marries Mary Magdalene at Cana, where Jesus performs his first miracle. Such fiction is far removed from Otfrid's erudite interpretations and respect for the canonical text. It is possible that Ava's work affords us a glimpse of the contemporary religious drama, for where her narrative diverges from the biblical account, it is sometimes in agreement with the Latin Easter plays of a slightly later date.

Other works from the early twelfth century combine biblical and legendary material. One such is the *Mittelfränkische Reimbibel,* known only in fragments and formerly, when only legendary portions were known, called *Das mittelfränkische Legendar.* It includes the story of Susanna from the Old Testament as well as the legends of Veronica, Simon Magus, Helena, and others.

A few fragmentary remains of other renderings of Old Testament material survive from the eleventh century: parts of a version of Genesis with allegorical interpretation, of a rendering of the Books of the Maccabees, and of the Book of Tobit. The last is the work of a cleric called Pfaffe Lamprecht, who is better known for his *Alexanderlied;* it dates from about 1160.

At about the same time an Austrian poet well versed in contemporary theology composed a lengthy work called *Daz Anegenge* (The beginning), which sets forth the Creation as the work of the Trinity and the plan of redemption as the outcome of a celestial council in which the four daughters of God—Peace, Mercy, Truth, and Justice—dispute before his throne. This motif derives, it seems, from a sermon of Bernard of Clairvaux, but ultimately goes back to Psalm 84(85):10–11. (We shall encounter it later more than once.) A treatment of the Last Things, *Der Linzer Antichrist,* dates from this period and may be mentioned here because it draws on the Book of Revelation. It contains a good deal of theological speculation.

We may assume that before the late twelfth century all religious poetry was composed by clerics or, as in the case of Frau Ava, under clerical guidance. Hardly any secular works survive from the period before 1170. However, the introduction of the courtly romance from France and the cultivation of the courtly love lyric ended the church's monopoly of the written word. The great poets of the classical and postclassical ages (roughly 1170–1300) were mostly members of the knightly class. Knowing their station, they did not compete with the clergy in the composition of religious works, except in the field of the legend. Admittedly, Hartmann von Aue treated religious themes in his crusading lyrics and his courtly legends, and Wolfram von Eschenbach sought an accommodation between knighthood and the service of God in his *Parzival* and *Willehalm.* Walther von der Vogelweide, too, composed lyrics on religious themes and one lengthy poem, *Der Leich,* summarizing the principal tenets of the faith; and in the gnomic poetry *(Spruchdichtung)* that began to proliferate during this period, religious themes are frequently found. None of this, however, is biblical poetry. True, in an elegant strophe composed in 1212, Walther tells the story of Christ and the tribute money, but only to make a political point.

An apparent exception to what has just been said is a work known as *Die Kindheit Jesu,* composed about 1200 by an Austrian knight, Konrad von Fussesbrunnen. It is a work of great charm that owes much of its narrative skill to the poet's imitation of his contemporary, Hartmann von Aue. However, since it is based on an apocryphal source (Pseudo-Matthew), it need not concern us here. The style of the courtly writers could influence that of clerical writers, as is shown in *Diu Urstende* (The Resurrection), a work composed in the second quarter of the thirteenth century by a Swabian priest, Konrad von Heimesfurt. This pedestrian work relies as far as it can on the canonical Gospels, but for much of the narrative it resorts to apocryphal sources that tell, for instance, of the imprisonment of Joseph of Arimathea and his miraculous release by Christ, the death and Assumption of the Virgin, and the Descent into hell; this last, in agreement with the Gospel of Nicodemus, is recounted after the events of Pentecost.

The Bible was not just the chief source of man's knowledge of divine history; it also contained all there was to know about the early history of the

BIBLICAL POETRY, GERMAN

world. Its historical information was exploited by Rudolf von Ems, a knight who died shortly after 1250, in his last and unfinished work, the *Weltchronik.* This poem, a vast torso of more than 36,000 lines, was to have traced the history of the world up to Rudolf's own day, but he got only as far as the reign of Solomon. Not being concerned with theology, he confined himself to the biblical text, though at appropriate points he inserted geographical information (no doubt culled from the *Lucidarius*) as well as excursions on the Greek gods (from the *Pantheon* of Godfrey of Viterbo) and on the kings of Troy and the settlement of Italy (for which he probably used the *Historia scholastica* of Peter Comestor).

In the second half of the century, an anonymous Thuringian poet began his own world chronicle with the words *Christ herre,* whence it is known as the *Christherre-Chronik;* he, however, got no farther than the Book of Judges. About 1280 Jans Enikel, a Viennese burgher, composed another world chronicle. Lacking any sense of history, he recounted what he had heard or read in the spirit of contemporary profane writings. Old Testament figures are put into modern dress: the story of Joseph and Potiphar's wife (now Pharaoh's wife) is told as if it were a contemporary novella, and David fights Goliath, described like a giant from one of the Dietrich stories, for the hand of the king's daughter. In the first half of the fourteenth century, one Heinrich von München set about completing the *Christherre-Chronik;* in order to do this, he not only appropriated parts of the works of Rudolf von Ems and Jans Enikel but also plagiarized a number of earlier romances on historical subjects.

Jans was not the only one to modernize biblical material. One of the most learned German writers of the later thirteenth century was the Magdeburg constable Brun von Schönebeck, who produced, among other things, an extensive commentary on the Song of Solomon in somewhat clumsy verse. This book of the Bible called for extensive exegesis if it was to be used as evidence of the work of salvation. Brun gives a conventional interpretation: Solomon represents God, and the bride represents both the Virgin and the soul. Solomon's other brides are allegorized, and the mandragora, briefly mentioned in the biblical text, is said to represent Antichrist. This leads to a discussion of the Last Things. The work is exceedingly discursive and incorporates the most varied and curious learning. Latin quotations from the Bible and elsewhere are introduced and subjected to lengthy commentaries.

For us perhaps the most interesting part of the work is the introduction. In it Brun constructs a kind of courtly novella around the figures of Solomon and the queen of Sheba. Solomon sends his envoy Fortitudo to her with a letter declaring his love in words taken from the biblical source. There follows a dialogue between the queen and the messenger in which she declares her love for Solomon. The queen then sets out to visit Solomon. On her arrival there is a love scene between them and finally a marriage feast.

Shortly after 1300 an anonymous cleric from Hessen composed a poem of more than 7,000 lines that is now known as *Die Erlösung.* This account of Paradise lost and regained is undoubtedly the most masterly piece of biblical poetry in German since the *Heliand.* Like the Old Saxon epic it employs the idiom of its time, the language of courtly poetry. The poet is familiar with the works of the courtly writers, but he declares that he will avoid all flowery language *(allez florieren),* because his theme is serious *(ernestlich gevar)* and must be treated in plain words *(mit blôzen worten unde bar).* However, while eschewing courtly preciosity, he does not despise linguistic and metrical elegance. At the same time he often adopts the style of the preacher, frequently quoting from the Bible in Latin and then providing an elegant rendering in German verse.

The poem opens with a hymn in praise of the Trinity composed, like the prologue to Gottfried's *Tristan,* in four-line strophes with a single repeated rhyme. This is followed by a description of the wonders wrought by the triune God, from the stars in their courses to the opening of a flower and the hatching of an egg. There is no account of the Creation. The first event in the work is the fall of man, after which the fall of Lucifer is related. The scene then moves to heaven, where God calls a great council to deliberate on what is to be done with fallen man. God, *diu klâre majestat,* sits on a splendid throne set with precious stones, surrounded by the angels like a king in the circle of his retainers, and requires the company to pronounce judgment on man. His four daughters offer arguments; Peace and Mercy speak, as it were, for the defense, and Truth and Justice for the prosecution. After they have been heard, the Son, the "mirror of God," begs leave to speak. The Father courteously *(gezogenlîche)* accedes to the Son's request, promising him dominion over all kingdoms if he can find a solution. The Son unfolds his plan of redemption, which satisfies Truth and Justice as well as Peace and Mercy. The

BIBLICAL POETRY, GERMAN

company of heaven embraces it with great rejoicing, and the council is concluded.

Messengers are sent into the lands to proclaim the redeeming work that is to come. These are the patriarchs, kings, and prophets of the Jews and also, representing the gentiles, Sybilla, Nebuchadnezzar, and Vergil. There follow the events of the New Testament in the familiar narrative scheme. Apocryphal material is introduced in places—for example, the signs at Christ's birth and Herod's two-year imprisonment in Rome, as well as the Descent into hell (placed before the Resurrection). The death and Assumption of the Virgin are treated in hymns, and a hymn in praise of her precedes the Annunication. The earthly ministry of Christ is not ignored: the marriage feast at Cana is there to represent the miracles, and the Sermon on the Mount to represent his teaching.

As has already been said, the work has many courtly features. A monologue in which opposite emotions contend is spoken by the Virgin at the Annunciation, when she is torn between her unworthiness and her desire to be the chosen vessel of grace. This scene is probably in imitation of Gottfried. Herod greets the three kings with the courtly formula *Dê vô benîe,* and their conversation is conducted with courtly decorum. Indeed, the poet has a talent for dialogue and the construction of scenes. Not long after the work was composed, passages from it were worked into an Easter play, and it is not unlikely that there was a two-way traffic between the drama and narrative works based on the Bible. The poet's account of Mary Magdalene's meeting with the risen Christ would support the view that he had the Easter plays in mind when he wrote it: as in the drama, Mary does not go to the sepulcher alone, but with the other women; she stays behind to lament; when she sees the Lord and takes him to be the gardener, he has a spade in his hand. Hesse, the poet's home, was an important area for the development of the religious drama in the fourteenth century.

A comparable treatment of the same material is found in a Thuringian poem of less than 500 lines that opens with the words *Sich hûb vor gotes trône.* Here too there is a scene in heaven in which God's daughters appear, but the rest of the material is treated perfunctorily.

The Styrian poet Gundacker von Judenburg used the same material in a work known as *Christi Hort* (Christ's treasure). In three separate sections he treats the Creation, the fallen angels, the fall of man, and God's decision to redeem man; then the life of Christ from the Annunciation to Gethsemane; and last, the events from the Passion to Pentecost. After this the author recounts the legends of Joseph of Arimathea and Pilate. A number of events from the earthly life of Christ are included in the narrative. At times the author employs a kind of litany, addressing Christ rather than simply narrating events. A similar mixture of Gospel material and legend is found in a poem known as *Der Sælden Hort* (The treasure of blessedness), a phrase taken from the text. It was composed shortly before 1300 by an anonymous Swiss poet, whose chief interest was in the legendary material, especially that concerning Mary Magdalene. He was eager to emphasize the efficacy of penance as a means of grace and the need to shun carnal desire. He composed some memorable scenes, like that in which Salome dances for Herod and demands the head of John the Baptist; the horror of the scene is well captured.

From the first half of the fourteenth century comes a poem known as *Gottes Zukunft* (The coming of God), written by Heinrich von Neustadt (Wiener-Neustadt), a physician who also produced secular works. This poem begins with a grandiose allegory of the creation of man, based on the *Anticlaudianus* of Alan of Lille, then proceeds to treat the Redemption according to the familiar scheme. The poet is less concerned with the biblical events themselves than with arousing religious emotion, and he dwells on the scenes in which the Virgin Mary appears. His religiosity is in the tradition of Bernard of Clairvaux, to whom he often refers, and in his portrayal of Christ he borrows much from the ideas of chivalry.

In 1331, Tilo von Kulm, a nobleman who was also a canon of the see of Samland, completed his poem *Von siben Ingesigeln,* an abridged version in German of a Latin tractate, *Libellus septem sigillorum,* and dedicated it to Luder von Braunschweig, the grand master of the Teutonic Order. The seven seals of the title are the Incarnation, Baptism, Passion, Resurrection, Ascension, Pentecost, and the Judgment. In order to open the seals, the poet applies the customary exegesis to the Scriptures, prefacing his account of the Redemption with the creation of the angels and the events leading to the fall of man. He too has the daughters of God disputing before the throne. Being especially devoted to the cult of the Virgin, Tilo gives his fullest treatment to the Incarnation and the Passion, since he allows himself no legendary additions to the Scriptures and it is only here that the Virgin is assigned a significant role in

BIBLICAL POETRY, GERMAN

the canonical sources. For Tilo too the earthly life of Christ has little interest. He presumes no theological learning in his public, which no doubt consisted of Knights of the Teutonic Order.

Also from the east comes *Der Kreuziger* (The bearer of the cross), a work of more than 10,000 lines by the Silesian Johannes von Frankenstein. It is an account of the Passion with copious Scholastic commentary culled from the church fathers.

Yet another work on the Redemption of man, preserved only in fragments and also known as *Die Erlösung,* was composed by Heinrich Hesler in the first half of the fourteenth century. What survives treats the fall of Lucifer and the fall of man. Heinrich, who was probably a member of the Teutonic Order, also rendered the gospel of Nicodemus into German with a modicum of exegesis. By contrast a third work, a translation of Revelation, comments extensively on each verse in turn.

It was mentioned earlier that the knightly class had little to do with the composition of biblical poetry. This is true of the period up to 1300 and of the cultivated knights of western and southern Europe, who set the literary tone with their celebrations of courtly love and the chivalric ideal embodied in the court of King Arthur. However, the fighting knights of eastern Europe, the members of the Teutonic Order, did play a part in promoting and contributing to the last phase of medieval biblical poetry.

This order, founded at Jerusalem in the twelfth century, was engaged during the thirteenth and fourteenth centuries in the military subjugation and religious conversion of the heathen Prussians. Its members lived in communities under a strict monastic regime, one of the features of which was the reading of edifying books at mealtimes. Since few of the knights were learned in theology, the works chosen or commissioned for such readings were often straightforward renderings of the narrative books of the Old Testament. Particularly favored, it seems, were the later books, which told of the embattled Jewish people defending their faith, both in exile and in their own land, against the heathen hosts. In the heroic narratives of these books, the Teutonic knights no doubt found a life and a spirit comparable with their own. The order had its headquarters in the castle of Mergentheim, from whose library comes a splendid manuscript, now in Stuttgart, to which we owe much of our knowledge of the works composed by members of the order.

The first and no doubt earliest work in this codex is the third medieval German version of the Book of Judith, whose heroine, according to Pope Honorius III, was "worthy to be praised by every mouth until today." The narrator tells us that the work was composed 1,221 years after Christ's death—that is, in 1254. Since the literary activity of the order began later than this, it has been proposed either to emend the text at this point or to regard the work as having been composed by one who was not a member of the order. If the latter proposal is adopted, we may conclude that the work found a place in the manuscript because it was considered suitable reading matter.

The author addresses his work to a young man, his "friend and brother," in response to the latter's request for guidance from the Scriptures. The story is then rendered into adequate German verse, with a break and a resumption after a few hundred lines suggesting that the author dispatched his work in two installments. The poet was no great scholar: he now and then misconstrues the Latin of his source, and his exegesis does not go beyond the explication of a few proper names. Curiously, he bases his moral teaching not on the story of Judith but on that of Joseph and Potiphar's wife. His young friend should shun the temptations of the world and leave the garment of worldliness behind him, as Joseph left his garment in the hand of Potiphar's wife.

Next in the codex comes a rendering of the Book of Esther into unpretentious verse. It has been supposed that these two books owe their place in the collection to the fact that their heroines, both godly matrons, offer an antidote to the poisonous image of the courtly lady, the object and encourager of illicit desires. Then comes a rendering of the books of Ezra and Nehemiah. These were likely to find a sympathetic echo among the knights, who were not only fighting men but also builders of cities. A German rendering of the Books of the Maccabees is also found in the manuscript. These, the most warlike books of the Bible, could not fail to appeal strongly to these warrior knights, whom Pope Honorius III called "new Maccabees." The author tells us that he was a layman, and he also maintains that, while the Old Testament is within the grasp of a layman, only a priest can interpret the New Testament. It has been conjectured that the author was Luder von Braunschweig, later the grand master of the order, who is known to have composed a version of the legend of St. Barbara. The history of the Jews is pursued, beyond the point reached in the biblical books, up to the death of Herod, so that the German version ends in the age of the New Tesament. The poet's interest was not confined to the Bible, and he inserts the

BIBLICAL POETRY, GERMAN

history of Alexander and his successors into the text.

All the works in the codex that we have mentioned so far are narratives with little or no exegetical commentary. This is not true of two others, versions of the books of Daniel and Job. The former was composed, the author tells us, at the behest of Luder von Braunschweig. It gives an extensive interpretive gloss after the translation of each chapter. Sometimes a specifically Christian interpretation is added to a more immediate one contained in the scriptural text. Thus, while Daniel himself interprets Nebuchadnezzar's dream in chapter 4 as a prediction of the king's own future, the gloss at the end of the chapter relates it to the redeeming work of Christ. Sometimes the allegorization is based on very little in the text. For example, the plain of Dura, mentioned in chapter 3 as the site of the image of gold set up by Nebuchadnezzar, is credited in the gloss with fifteen kinds of vegetation. These are described and allegorically equated with all sorts and conditions of men. This equation then leads to a critique of contemporary morality. The whole work ends with a discourse on contrition and repentance. The translation of the Book of Job was completed in 1338 and dedicated to the grand master Dietrich von Altenburg. Here the exegesis, which is designed for a public not deeply versed in theology, is incorporated into the translation.

The last work in this series of versions of Old Testament matter, *Historien der alden ê,* was written about 1340 and was based not on the biblical texts themselves, but on the *Historia scholastica* of Peter Comestor. It is a dreary digest of miscellaneous stories and assorted information put together in an arbitrary manner, no doubt representing the bare minimum of knowledge required for understanding sermons that alluded to the Old Testament.

An interesting feature of some of these late works is their metrical form. Whereas in the early works of the eleventh and twelfth centuries, the number of syllables in the line was variable within wide limits, and the meter had to accommodate itself to the syntax, Heinrich von Hesler allowed himself an average of seven syllables to the line (falling occasionally to six and rising to nine). Within these limits he was still able to compose smooth and elegant verses. The translator of the Maccabees allowed himself much less latitude, strictly adhering to lines of eight syllables. The result was an unnatural contortion of the syntax, which now had to be accommodated as best it might to the meter.

Few of the authors we have discussed had any real poetic talent, and even the gifted author of *Die Erlösung* seems to have set no very high value on the poetic qualities of his work. Verse was not chosen for its aesthetic advantage over prose, but for its memorability. This was an important factor in an age when most men could not read, when all the important books were in Latin, and when even the literate few could hardly expect to have books constantly to hand for ready reference. By the middle of the fourteenth century, however, prose translations were taking over from verse renderings as a means of access to the sacred texts. The age of biblical poetry—although not, of course, of religious poetry in a broader sense—was over.

BIBLIOGRAPHY

Editions. (The following abbreviations are used for frequently cited series: ATB, Altdeutsche Textbibliothek; DTM, Deutsche Texte des Mittelalters; and LitVer, Bibliothek des Literarischen Vereins in Stuttgart.) Emil von Steinmeyer, ed., *Die kleineren althochdeutschen Sprachdenkmäler* (1916, repr. 1963); Theodor Wilhelm Braune, ed., *Althochdeutsches Lesebuch,* 15th ed., rev. by E. A. Ebbinghaus (1969)—both of these collections contain all the shorter Old High German texts discussed above, and the latter contains in addition *Ezzos Gesang* and excerpts from Otfrid's *Evangelienbuch,* the *Heliand,* and the *Genesis*—O. Behagel, ed., *Heliand und Genesis,* 7th ed., rev. by W. Mitzka, ATB IV (1958); Otfrid von Weissenburg, *Evangelienbuch,* O. Erdmann, ed., rev. by L. Wolff, ATB XLIX (1965).

V. Dollmayr, ed., *Die altdeutsche Genesis,* ATB XXXI (1932); E. Papp, ed., *Die altdeutsche Exodus* (1969); Joseph Diemer, ed., *Deutsche Gedichte des XI. und XII. Jahrhunderts aufgefunden im regulierten Chorherrenstifte zu Vorau* (1849); Karl Polheim, ed., *Die altdeutschen Gedichte der Vorauer Handschrift Kodex 276/II,* facsimile ed. (1958); Erich Henschel and Ulrich Pretzel, eds., *Die kleinen Denkmäler der Vorauer Handscrift* (1963); Friedrich Maurer, ed., *Die religiösen Dichtungen des 11. und 12. Jahrhunderts,* 3 vols. (1964–1970); W. Schroder, ed., *Kleinere deutsche Gedichte des 11. und 12. Jahrhunderts,* ATB LXXI–LXXII (1972); *Die jüngere Judith,* H. Monecke, ed., ATB LXI (1964).

Konrad von Fussesbrunnen, *Die Kindheit Jesu,* K. Kochendörffer, ed. (1881); Konrad von Heimesfurt, *Diu Urstende,* Karl A. Hahn, ed., in *Gedichte des XII. und XIII. Jahrhunderts* (1840); Rudolf von Ems, *Weltchronik,* G. Ehrismann, ed., DTM XX (1915); Jans Enikel, *Die Weltchronik,* P. Strauch, ed. (1891); Brun von Schönebeck, *Das Hohelied,* A. Fischer, ed., LitVer CXCVIII (1893).

Die Erlösung, Friedrich Maurer, ed. (1934)—the old ed. by Karl Bartsch (1858) contains the text *Sich hûb vor gotes trône*—Gundacker von Judenburg, *Christi Hort,* J.

Jaschke, ed., DTM XVIII (1910); *Der Sælden Hort,* H. Adrian, ed., DTM XXVI (1927); Heinrich von Neustadt, *Gottes Zukunft,* S. Singer, ed., DTM VII (1906); Tilo von Kulm, *Von siben Ingesigeln,* K. Kochendörffer, ed., DTM IX (1907); Johannes von Frankenstein, *Der Kreuziger,* F. Khull, ed., LitVer CLX (1882); Heinrich Hesler, *Die Erlösung,* O. von Heinemann and E. von Steinmeyer, eds., in *Zeitschrift für deutsches Altertum,* **32** (1888); *idem, Nicodemus-Evangelium,* K. Helm, ed., LitVer CCXXIV (1902); and *Apokalypse,* K. Helm, ed., DTM VIII (1907).

Judith, R. Palgen, ed., ATB XVIII (1924); *Esther,* C. Schröder, ed., in *Germanistische Studien,* **1** (1872); *Esras und Neemyas,* S. D. Stirk, ed. (1938); *Makkabäer,* K. Helm, ed., LitVer CCXXXIII (1904); *Daniel,* A. Hübner, ed., DTM XIX (1911); *Hiob,* T. E. Karsten, ed., DTM XXI (1910); *Historien der alden ê,* W. Gerhard, ed., LitVer CCLXXI (1927).

Studies. See *Die deutsche Literatur des Mittelalters. Verfasserlexikon* (1978–) for individual authors. Anonymous works are listed under titles. For the Old High German period see J. Knight Bostock, *A Handbook on Old High German Literature,* 2nd ed. (1976), 126–154, 190–211, 214–222; Helmut de Boor, *Die deutsche Literatur von Karl dem Grossen bis zum Beginn der höfischen Dichtung,* vol. 1 of Helmut de Boor and Richard Newald, *Geschichte der deutschen Literatur von den Anfängen bis zur Gegenwart* (1960), 52–65, 74–94. For the early Middle High German period see *ibid.,* 33–176; also Ursula Hennig, "Zur Gattungsbestimmung frühmittelhochdeutscher alttestamentarischer Dichtungen," Adrian Stevens, "Die 'Wiener Genesis' in ihrem Verhältnis zur Tradition der christlichen Rhetorik," and David A. Wells, "Die Erläuterung frühmittelhochdeutscher geistlicher Texte: Probleme und Methoden," all in L. P. Johnson, H.-H. Steinhoff, and R. A. Wisbey, eds., *Studien zur frühmittelhochdeutschen Literatur* (1974); David A. Wells, *The Vorau "Moses" and "Balaam": A Study of Their Relationship to Exegetical Tradition* (1970); Dennis Green, *The Millstätter Exodus: A Crusading Epic* (1966).

For the period 1170–1250 see Helmut de Boor, *Die höfische Literatur: Vorbereitung, Blüte, Ausklang,* vol. 2 of Helmut de Boor and Richard Newald, *op. cit.* (1962), 377–389. For the period after 1250 see *idem, Die deutsche Literatur im späten Mittelalter: Zerfall und Neubeginn,* vol. 3 of Helmut de Boor and Richard Newald, *op. cit.* (1962), 482–520; Karl Helm and Walther Ziesemer, *Die Literatur des Deutschen Ritterordens* (1951).

D. R. McLintock

[See also **Frau Ava; Heliand; Hrabanus Maurus; Middle High German Literature; Military Orders; Otfrid von Weissenburg; Rudolf von Ems.**]

BIBLIOTHECA. See **Photios.**

BIDUINO, a sculptor active around 1180–1200 in Tuscany. Biduino was among the earliest Tuscan Romanesque carvers influenced by antiquity. Though he retained vestiges of the earlier Byzantinizing damp-fold style (drapery that clings to parts of the body as if it had been dampened), Biduino introduced Roman decorative motifs such as strigilated panels (signed sarcophagus at the Camposanto, Pisa) and seems also to have studied late antique sarcophagi. Among his signed works are the lateral doors of San Cassiano a Settimo (*ca.* 1180) and the south portal at San Salvatore in Lucca (*ca.* 1200).

BIBLIOGRAPHY

Mario Salmi, *Romanesque Sculpture in Tuscany* (1928), 90–94.

Leslie Brubaker

BIEL, GABRIEL (*ca.* 1412–1495), sometimes called the last Scholastic of the Middle Ages, was born at Speyer, Germany. Ordained at an early age and provided with a house and a living at St. Peter's in Speyer, he received his arts education at Heidelberg, where he remained as regent master for several years after becoming master of arts in 1438. In 1451, Biel matriculated in theology at Erfurt, but soon transferred to Cologne. It was there, at a university noted for its Thomism and Albertism, that he acquired copies of Ockham's works and became committed to his thought. He returned to Erfurt in 1457 to complete his theological education. As licentiate in theology, Biel was cathedral preacher and vicar at Mainz from 1457 to 1465. He quickly established himself as a popular preacher in the middle Rhine valley.

Toward the end of the 1460's, Biel joined the Brethren of the Common Life. He was sent first to Butzbach (1468) as provost, participated in establishing a general chapter for the houses of the Upper Rhine region (1471), and was sent to Urach in 1477 to establish the first Brethren house in Württemberg, where he became provost in 1479.

The most productive period of Biel's life began with his appointment in 1484 as regent master of theology at Tübingen. In order to provide the necessary instruction in theology at the newly founded unversity (1477), Biel lectured on the *Sentences* of Peter Lombard and delivered in revised form the lectures on the canon of the Mass that his friend Eggeling Becker of Braunschweig had given at Mainz in the 1450's. He was rector of the university in 1485

BIEL, GABRIEL

and 1489. Through his students at Tübingen and his writings he exercised a profound influence on theologians of the next generation, as varied as Johann Eck, Johann Staupitz, Philipp Melanchthon, and Martin Luther.

Biel retired from teaching around 1490 and served as provost for the recently founded Brethren house at Einsiedel, near Tübingen, where he died.

Biel was probably the most significant and influential theologian in Germany in the generation before the Reformation. His collected sermons went through numerous editions, and his treatise on money and usury was widely read. But his major impact was through his *Collectorium* (his commentary on the *Sentences*) and his *Expositio* on the canon of the Mass. Among earlier doctors Biel generally favored William of Ockham and the *via moderna,* or *via Nominalium.* He was also conversant with, and at times dependent on, the thought of Alexander of Hales, Bonaventure, Aquinas, and John Duns Scotus.

Biel's works in logic (written at Heidelberg) and the philosophical positions expressed later in his *Collectorium* are nominalistic and dependent on Ockham, Marsilius von Inghen, and Pierre d'Ailly. This is particularly true of his treatment of universals, his epistemology, and his understanding of the categories of motion, place, quantity, and relation. But, far more than Ockham, Marsilius, or d'Ailly, Biel focused his attention on theology, in which he was heavily indebted to Ockham. At the heart of Biel's theology was the affirmation, developed especially within the Franciscan theology of Duns Scotus and Ockham, of an omnipotent God, ultimately free and unbound by any categories of time and space, the physical laws of the universe, or even human views of good and evil, who had nevertheless, through a covenant, bound himself to act according to the systems of nature and salvation he created. The themes of a contingent universe and church, of willed covenants between God and man, and causal relations based on ascribed rather than inherent value run throughout Biel's theology.

Biel argued that God's freedom, considered without regard for what he has chosen to do, is unlimited. God can, considering his power absolutely *(de potentia absoluta),* accept to salvation a sinner without grace, just as he can reject someone who stands in a state of grace. The meritorious quality of a human act is not based on its conformity to the commandments of God or the presence of the created habit of grace, but primarily on divine acceptation. Practically, however, according to God's ordained system *(de potentia ordinata),* God has committed himself to reward with grace the persons who do their best *(facere quod in se est)* on the basis of their natural powers *(ex puris naturalibus),* and to reward with eternal life those who persevere in grace and good works. The semi-Pelagian implication of this teaching, which had been under attack throughout the fourteenth and fifteenth centuries, found its crisis moment in the life and writings of Martin Luther.

Biel's sacramental theology combined a view of sacramental causality based on ascribed value with a strong defense of the sacrifice of the Mass. As a major exposition of the theology of the Mass, Biel's work was formative for the eucharistic piety of the late fifteenth and early sixteenth centuries.

The wide influence of Biel's theology for his and succeeding generations up to the Council of Trent resulted in part from the clarity and simplicity of his philosophical and theological system. But equally important was the fact that Biel's commentaries drew together many strands of late medieval Scholasticism, and his work was deeply grounded in the pastoral concerns of the average clergyman.

BIBLIOGRAPHY

Sources. Hanns Rückert *et al.*, eds., *Collectorium circa quattuor libros Sententiarum* (1501 and later); crit. ed. by Hanns Rückert *et al.* (1973–); Heiko A. Oberman and William J. Courtenay, eds., *Canonis misse expositio,* 4 vols. (1963–1967); *De potestate et utilitate monetarum* (1516); English trans. by R. B. Burke (1930); Heiko A. Oberman, Daniel E. Zerfoss, and William J. Courtenay, eds. and trans., *Defensorium obedientiae apostolicae* (1968); *De communi vita clericorum,* W. M. Landeen, ed., in *Research Studies of Washington State University,* 28 (1960).

Studies. Martin Elze, "Handschriften von Werken Gabriel Biels aus seinem Nachlass in der Giessener Universitätsbibliothek," in *Zeitschrift für Kirchengeschichte,* **81** (1970); W. M. Landeen, "Gabriel Biel and the Brethren of the Common Life in Germany," in *Church History,* **20** (1951), and "Gabriel Biel and the *Devotio moderna* in Germany," in *Research Studies of Washington State University,* 27 (1959), 28 (1960); Heiko A. Oberman, *The Harvest of Medieval Theology: Gabriel Biel and Late Medieval Nominalism* (1963), which includes a full bibliography.

William J. Courtenay

[See also **Brethren of the Common Life; Nominalism; Ockham, William of; Philosophy-Theology, Western European, Late Medieval.**]

BILLUNGS, a German dynastic family that created in the late tenth and eleventh centuries a lordship in Lower Saxony which filled the vacuum left by the atrophy of the Liudolfingian tribal duchy. The first Billungs, a name that does not appear in the chronicles until the thirteenth century, were Wichmann I (*d.* 944), who was married to the sister of Henry I's queen, and his younger brother Hermann (*d.* 973), whom King Otto I enfeoffed with the Nordalbingian mark in 936. When Otto's son Liudolf rebelled in 953 and Hermann's nephews joined the revolt, the king appointed Hermann his vicar in the Elbian borderlands. As a reward for his loyalty, Hermann obtained most of the alods and comital rights in Saxony previously held by the senior branch of the family. Otto renewed Hermann's vicariate in 961 and placed the rest of Saxony under his procuratorship in 966.

Hermann's son Bernhard I (973–1011) was called a duke, but his actual authority was confined to the Billungs' own domains. These were located in an arc stretching from the middle Weser to the Bardengau, the area around Lüneburg. The Billungs also possessed the advocacies of the dioceses of Minden and Verden, in which most of their lands were situated. As the kings' personal ties to their Saxon duchy became more tenuous, the Billungs were transformed from the kings' representatives into tribal spokesmen. At Henry II's accession in 1002, for example, Bernhard made Henry's confirmation of the Saxons' rights a precondition for their recognition of his election.

Bernhard's sons, Duke Bernhard II (1011–1059) and Count Thietmar, opposed Henry's alliance with the Liutizen, from whom they could no longer demand tribute, and rebelled against the king in 1019–1020. This incident was symptomatic of the estrangement between the dukes and the monarchy. The rival territorial ambitions of the Billungs and the archbishops of Bremen were at the heart of the conflict. The Billungs especially resented the Salians' support of Archbishop Adalbert, who was trying to obtain all the counties in his diocese. Thietmar was caught plotting against Henry III in 1047, and Bernhard's son, Ordulf (1059–1072), seized various properties and rights of the church of Bremen after Adalbert's dismissal from court in 1066. Henry IV imprisoned Ordulf's son Magnus, the last Billung duke (1072–1106), for joining Otto of Nordheim's revolt in 1070. After his release, Magnus, who was not directly affected by Henry's attempt to develop a royal domain in the Harz, played only a minor role in the fighting in Saxony during the Investiture Conflict.

After Magnus' death, Henry V granted the duchy of Saxony (that is, the Billungs' counties, advocacies, and fiefs) to Lothar of Supplinburg. Magnus' daughters, the wives of the Guelph duke of Bavaria, Henry the Black, and the Ascanian Count Otto of Ballenstedt inherited the alods. Lothar and his Guelph grandson, Henry the Lion, tried unsuccessfully to turn the Billung duchy into a territorial state, but the Billung alods formed the nucleus of the later kingdom of Hanover.

BIBLIOGRAPHY

Hans Joachim Freytag, *Die Herrschaft der Billunger in Sachsen* (1951).

JOHN B. FREED

[See also **Germany to 1125; Henry III of Germany; Henry IV of Germany; Saxony, Duchy of.**]

BIMARISTAN. See **Hospitals, Islamic.**

BIOGRAPHY, FRENCH. Although the term "biography" is apparently of medieval Greek origin (first used by the Syrian Damascius *ca.* 500, according to Charles Du Cange, in his *Glossarium mediae et infimae Latinitatis*), this word was not much used in the Middle Ages. In any case, many "lives," of various kinds but almost all exemplary, were written in France, as elsewhere in Europe, during the medieval period.

Lives of the saints were extremely numerous. Latin hagiography was practiced in Gaul as early as about 400 and continued in a wide stream for a millennium, drawing inspiration from the *vitae patrum* and other religious works, as well as from folklore.

The lives of the saints vary in form, in length, and in literary interest. Resemblances are, however, generally striking: the basic saintly models are few, and hagiography has clear rhetorical commonplaces. The majority of the vernacular lives are based on Latin models (whose authenticity the adapters do not question), and many are devoted to ancient and exotic saints: early Christian (with apocryphal "biographies"), Near Eastern, and Celtic, among others.

The line between life of the saint and edifying tale is therefore often hard to draw.

When the narrator is a contemporary of the saint, the text can have far greater biographical value, though the primary function of panegyric and the rhetorical conventions remain. Examples are the *Life of St. Martin* by Sulpicius Severus and the very important *Life of St. Thomas Becket* by Guernes de Pont-Sainte-Maxence, completed only about four years after the saint's martyrdom in 1170. Guernes did not know Becket, but did research, and his work is a genuine biography. Early in the fourteenth century, Jean de Joinville wrote his *Histoire de Saint Louis,* a work hard to classify because it is a mixture of autobiographical memoir, crusade chronicle, and biography of a saint. In any case, his text is full of personal reminiscences about the saintly ruler, and is generally unmarked by the conventions of hagiography.

The greatest proportion of vernacular hagiographical compositions dates from the twelfth and thirteenth centuries. During the fourteenth and fifteenth centuries hagiographers continued to compose, and especially to rewrite, put into prose, and compile into *légendiers* (often modeled on Jacobus da Voragine's *Legenda aurea*) earlier verse lives. The biographical character of these works is generally negligible: the very techniques of abbreviation and compilation into hagiographical cycles worked against any real concern with the biography of a given saint. In this period hagiographical inspiration moved largely first into the miracle plays (with their strong interest in the Virgin), then into the mystery plays, which often focus on the life of Christ (as well as on the saints).

Secular biography flowed primarily from classical sources, though it, too, often shows a marked influence of hagiography and of patristic writing (such as Jerome's *De viris illustribus*). It is frequently difficult to distinguish secular biography from other historical writing in the Middle Ages; the blending of Latin biographers (such as Suetonius) with Latin historians (such as Sallust and Lucan) as sources points up this lack of distinction between genres. There is in France a strong tradition of royal biography, first Frankish, then clearly French; first in Latin, later (by the thirteenth century) also in the vernacular. (The first important model is Einhard's *Vita Karoli,* unclaimable as "French"; Einhard had primarily followed Suetonius in his presentation of material.) About 827, Ermoldus Nigellus wrote his *Life of Louis the Pious,* in Latin elegiac verse. Ermoldus refers to Louis as "Caesar Augustus," and his work is full of classical (especially Vergilian) reminiscences and of epic features—but his basic model is hagiographical. Helgaud's *Life of Robert the Pious* (written soon after Robert's death in 1031) is still more fundamentally hagiographical, and he omits all less-than-saintly details, such as Robert's excommunication.

Suger, abbot of St. Denis, wrote a Latin *Life of Louis VI* (commended for his pious zeal, but not "canonized"). Soon thereafter, between 1185 and 1204, the royal abbey produced the official *Historia regum Francorum.* (The parallel to and rivalry with the *Historia regum Britanniae,* composed *ca.* 1135 by Geoffrey of Monmouth, is clear.) Rigord, monk of St. Denis, and Guillaume Le Breton wrote encomiastic histories of Philip Augustus (Rigord first called the monarch "Augustus"). Nicolas de Bray composed a massive but uncompleted *Gesta Ludovici VIII.*

Around 1250, at the initiative of the abbot of St. Denis, Matthew of Vendôme, a vast compilation of Latin chronicles and *gesta* was made (including the *Historia regum Francorum* and the works by Suger and Rigord). This set of chronicles, an official history of the French monarchy through 1223, was in 1274, again under Matthew, translated into French by a monk named Primat, and presented to Philip III. This work constituted the kernel of the *Grandes chroniques de France,* which were later continued, at various times, through the reign of Charles VIII. They were printed as early as 1476–1477.

There is also a tradition of panegyric biography and genealogy of feudal dynasties, Wace and Benoît de Sainte-Maure providing the prototypes.

Yet another strain of medieval biography is represented by the strong interest in the life of Julius Caesar. Perhaps the most significant of such works is *Li fet des Romains, compilé ensemble de Saluste et de Suetoine et de Lucan,* composed in 1213–1214 by a cleric of Lille.

Around 1226 the son of William Marshal (earl of Pembroke and Striguil, regent of England in 1216–1219) had a talented minstrel write his father's life in French verse, *L'histoire de Guillaume le maréchal.* This is the first in a series of chivalric biographies, in which the narrator stresses the conformity between his model and chivalric ideals, bending historical reality or suppressing details that depart from this ideal image—an image derived from romance and from manuals of chivalry, rather than from hagiography (though piety is a "chivalric" virtue).

It is worth noting that both romance and epic had pseudohistoriographic roots, and often produced an illusion of biography—for instance, the story of Tristan and Iseult is also the "Life of Tristan"; Arthur's life is elaborated in romance as it had been in chronicle; epic cycles focus on the lives and fill out the family trees of the members of the great (largely fictitious) dynasties. This tradition of chivalric biography extended through the end of the Middle Ages, and influenced other genres: in his *Chronicles* Froissart focuses on chivalric personalities and deeds.

By contrast, in his *Memoires* Philippe de Comines (fifteenth century) by no means idealizes Louis XI, or other French and Burgundian leaders; his is a more realistic and cool (if not impartial) assessment of historical figures. He has clearly broken with the chivalric tradition of biographical-historical writing.

Approximately one hundred Provençal poets had their *vidas* written in the thirteenth century. These short prose vernacular lives were based largely on what the poets said about themselves in their poetry. Although the *vidas* present considerable literary interest, their biographical value is limited.

There was a modest amount of autobiographical writing in France in the Middle Ages, mostly in Latin. Abelard wrote his *Historia calamitatum* (the authenticity of which has been questioned) to set the record straight; it bears a disconcerting resemblance to hagiography. Suger wrote an account of his career at St. Denis, and Guibert de Nogent wrote his memoirs.

An autobiographical or confessional strain also runs through medieval lyric poetry and genres influenced by it: Guillaume de Lorris' *Roman de la rose* is a first-person account of love; Rutebeuf and Villon both reflect, movingly, on their lives, supplying pieces of information about themselves that are often historically inaccurate if poetically or psychologically "true."

BIBLIOGRAPHY

Hippolyte Delehaye, *The Legends of the Saints,* Mrs. V. M. Crawford, trans. (1907, repr. 1961); Paul Zumthor, *Histoire littéraire de la France médiévale* (1954); J. D. M. Ford, "The Saints' Lives in the Vernacular Literature of the Middle Ages," in *Catholic Historical Review,* **17** (1931); Beryl Smalley, *Historians in the Middle Ages* (1974); James W. Thompson with Bernard J. Holm, *A History of Historical Writing,* I (1942); Jan M. Romein, *Die Biographie: Einführung in ihre Geschichte und ihre Problematik* (1948); Charles Homer Haskins, *The Renaissance of the Twelfth Century* (1927); Larry D. Benson and John Leyerle, eds., *Chivalric Literature: Essays on Relations Between Literature and Life in the Later Middle Ages* (1980); Georg Misch, *Geschichte der Autobiographie,* 3rd ed., II–IV (1955–1969).

EVELYN BIRGE VITZ

[See also **Abelard, Peter; Anglo-Norman Literature; Chronicles; Comines, Philippe de; Einhard; Ermoldus Nigellus; Froissart; Guibert of Nogent; Guillaume Le Breton; Hagiography, French; Helgaud; Matthew of Vendôme; Rigord; Rutebeuf; Suger, Abbot of St. Denis; Wace; William Marshal.**]

BIOGRAPHY, ISLAMIC. Islamic biographical dictionaries represent an indigenously Arabo-Islamic literature that appears to have no significant pre-Islamic antecedents and no parallel in the medieval West. The genesis of the biographical dictionary has often been linked to the science of *ḥadīth* criticism. Some scholars, however, prefer to relate this genre to Arab genealogical storytelling and poetic traditions. It would appear that the biographical dictionary, with its characteristic principles of arrangement, reflected basic Arab mental structures, since examples devoted to varied types of individuals appeared almost simultaneously.

The arrangement of these compendia is linked to the concept of *ṭabaqāt*, or classes. In *ṭabaqāt* works the biographies were divided into groups that could be based on generations (as with *ḥadīth* transmitters) or on levels of merit or skill (as with poets). In a possibly later development this term was also applied to compendia limited to a given type of individual but not divided into classes (for example, the *Ṭabaqāt al-shuʿarāʾ* of Ibn al-Muʿtazz, *d.* 908). Finally, in certain cases *ṭabaqāt* simply seems to be synonymous with biographical dictionary. Although biographical literature may have originated in *ṭabaqāt* format, it developed into a diverse and sophisticated historical and literary genre that saw its golden age under the Mamluk sultanate (*ca.* 1250–1500).

Compendia included general works stretching from the advent of Islam to the author's time (for example, the fourteenth-century *al-Wāfī bi'l-wafayāt* of al-Ṣafadī) and more specialized collections that could be devoted to cities (the eleventh-century *Taʾrīkh Baghdād* of al-Khaṭīb al-Baghdādī) or occupations ranging from scholar and Koran reciter to singer and dream interpreter. Specializations were not limited to occupations, but could be based on the interests of the biographer: al-Ṣafadī compiled collections both of the blind and of the one-eyed.

BIOGRAPHY, ISLAMIC

The number of individual notices, and hence the length of the compendium, could vary from relatively short works describing one hundred personages to multivolume texts comprising thousands of notices. Besides *ṭabaqāt* arrangements, notices were also organized chronologically by death date or alphabetically by *ism* (first or given name, as distinguished from patronymics, nicknames, and the like) or by combination thereof.

The biographical notices themselves could vary sharply in length from a few lines to extended biographical or critical essays covering many pages. Most typically, however, notices ranged between about half a page and four or five pages. Most commonly the data presented include the date of birth (when available), the date of death, the genealogy of the subject, his education, his teachers, the books he wrote, and some anecdotal material (provided at the discretion of the biographer).

Almost invariably the notices began with an onomastic chain, a list of names, appellations, and titles that provides genealogical and onomastic information, setting the subject in his social and professional context. Following this varied information the biographer could proceed to what he considered most significant in the subject's life. This might include character traits, important events, or more "academic" concerns, such as the biographee's education, his teachers, and his travels in search of knowledge. The materials relating to the death of the person, be they the circumstances of death, the cause of death, or his appearance in dreams after his death, can most often be found at the end of the notice. Clearly, this order is not accidental.

In those parts of the notice that follow the onomastic chain, the biographer could choose among several discourse styles. One was the simple declaratory presentation of biographically significant information. Another was the anecdote, a sophisticated literary form. Anecdotes could be included because they illustrated an important characteristic of the biographee, because they transmitted a noteworthy biographical datum, because they were entertaining, or because they met a combination of all three criteria. The third major discourse style was poetry, and since most educated Muslims were at least occasional poets, the verses could be those of the biographee, those composed about him, or even those of the biographer. The literary skill of the biographer, therefore, involved the balancing and arrangement of these different discourse types in the notice.

Obviously the relative weight given to different discourse styles reflected the preferences and tastes of the authors. Poetry, of course, was an especially important element in the biographies of poets, and some collections, like the tenth-century *Kitāb al-aghānī* of Abū'l-Faraj al-Iṣfahānī and the eleventh-century *Yatīmat al-dahr* of al-Thaᶜālibī, hovered between biographical dictionaries and what were essentially literary anthologies in biographical form. At the other extreme, some biographers limited themselves almost exclusively to the onomastic chain and a few items of dry data (for instance, the seventeenth-century *Shadharāt al-dhahab* of Ibn al-ᶜImād).

Biographical compendia contain a great wealth of historical data, both about the subjects of the notices, and about the society in which they lived. The "reference" quality of these texts, however, should not lead us to forget that, at their best, they were finely crafted literary and biographical masterpieces. Muslim biographers copied freely from their predecessors, generally following a system of scholarly reference and citation. Each writer, however, took artistic and historical responsibility for the precise form and wording, as well as for the selection and arrangement of borrowed materials. One onomastic or honorific element added or deleted, one anecdote lengthened, shortened, or commented upon, could alter the image of the subject. Indeed, such biographical variations could lead to controversy and polemics. For this reason the proper understanding of the biographer's intent is often dependent on the deciphering of sets of codes ranging from the onomastic to the oneirocritical.

Different biographers, naturally, had their own styles, reflected in the tone and organization of their notices. In his *Wafayāt al-aᶜyān,* for example, Ibn Khallikān not only follows a relatively consistent pattern of organization but also tends to paint his subjects as the "ideal type" of the appropriate social or personal category. He reinforces this quality by avoiding either a polemical tone or controversial incidents. The fifteenth-century Abu'l-Maḥāsin Ibn Taghrībirdī, by contrast, in his *al-Nujūm al-zāhira,* opts for the pithy phrase or description, seemingly avoiding intricate details but in fact providing the reader with a forceful portrait of the personages he treats (be the portrait negative, as in the case of the historian and *ḥadīth* authority al-Khaṭīb al-Baghdādī, or more positive, as in the case of the Andalusian poet Ibn Zaydūn). Biographical peculiarities such as these are important not only directly, for the picture they provide of the biographee, but also indirectly, for what they tell us of the historical and literary preferences of the biographer.

BIBLIOGRAPHY

Hartmut E. Fahndrich, "The *Wafayāt al-A*ᶜ*yān* of Ibn Khallikān: A New Approach," in *Journal of the American Oriental Society,* **93** (1973); Ulrich Haarmann, "Auflösung und Bewahrung der klassischen Formen arabischer Geschichtsschreibung in der Zeit der Mamluken," in *Zeitschrift der Deutschen Morgenländischen Gesellschaft,* **121** (1971); Ibrahim Hafsi, "Recherches sur le genre *'Ṭabaqāt'* dans la littérature arabe," in *Arabica,* **23** (1976) and **24** (1977); Donald Presgrave Little, *An Introduction to Mamlūk Historiography* (1970); Fedwa Malti-Douglas, "Dreams, the Blind, and the Semiotics of the Biographical Notice," in *Studia Islamica,* **51** (1980); Franz Rosenthal, *A History of Muslim Historiography,* 2nd ed. (1968).

FEDWA MALTI-DOUGLAS

[See also **Arabic Literature; Ḥadith; Khallikan, Ibn.**]

BIOGRAPHY, RELIGIOUS. See **Hagiography.**

BIOGRAPHY, SECULAR. Compared with the rich biographical literature of antiquity and its luxuriant growth from the Renaissance on, medieval descriptions of individual lives were meager both in quantity and, above all, in quality. Furthermore, it is difficult at times to distinguish between the strictly biographical and the more general doctrinal, historical, didactic, and moral elements in medieval secular biography.

The ancient biographical tradition was continued in the medieval collections of lives by famous Christian writers, much concerned with the history of doctrine. St. Jerome should be considered the inventor of this subgenre. His *De viris illustribus* (the title, echoing the ancients, was to be used often in the Middle Ages) is a series of lives of Christian thinkers beginning with Sts. Peter and Paul and ending with Jerome himself. Written around 395, this collection was imitated and brought up to date by, among others, Gennadius of Marseilles; Isidore of Seville in his *De viris illustribus liber;* and, in the seventh century, by St. Ildefonsus, archbishop of Toledo, in his *De virorum illustrium scriptis* (known also as *De viris illustribus*). This biographical and theological genre was revived in the eleventh century by Sigebert of Gembloux. His *De viris illustribus* was continued by a contemporary clerk referred to as Anonymus Mellicensis, who gave the more exact title of *De scriptoribus ecclesiasticis* to his compilation, and, in the twelfth century, by Honoré of Autun (Honorius Augustodunensis) in *De luminaribus ecclesiae.*

The traditional title *De viris illustribus* was used again by Petrarch, whose conscious imitation of the ancients was to include the abridged lives of the most important "men and heroes" of all epochs and countries. The project, begun in 1337, was never finished. Petrarch did complete a collection of biographical sketches of famous Romans from Romulus to Julius Caesar. His venture into the biography of secular heroes doubtless encouraged Boccaccio, who, between 1356 and 1374, wrote *De casibus virorum illustrium,* a collection of lives of men and women spanning all of history from Adam to Boccaccio's own contemporaries, such as Charles I of Anjou, Jacques de Molay, and Philippa of Catania. As the title indicates, *On the Downfall of Famous Men* is also a commentary on the fickleness of fortune. Boccaccio's *De claris mulieribus,* the final version of which was completed after 1362, contains the biographies of 104 famous—and notorious—women, from Eve to Giovanna of Naples. This compilation enjoyed widespread influence: among other things, it bestowed an air of authenticity on the legend of the mythical Pope Joan.

Probably more important than the above collections of lives were accounts written by historians. They offered either full-fledged biographies or biographical sketches incorporated into their presentations of deeds *(res gesta).* Such biographical accounts, which are quite numerous, are not always easily distinguishable either from history or from panegyric. Only a few typical examples can be mentioned here. In the sixth century Gregory of Tours incorporated vivid presentations of many contemporary figures in his *Historia Francorum.* More properly biographical is the *Vita Karoli magni imperatoris* by Eginhard or Einhard (*ca.* 770–840), probably the greatest monument of secular biography of the Latin Middle Ages. A conscious imitation of Suetonius, the work presents the splendid Charlemagne at the end of his reign and offers many important details about the emperor's private and public life.

The *Annales rerum gestarum Alfredi magni* by Asser is the first biography of the English king. Suger treated Louis VI the Fat in his *Vita Ludovici Grossi,* written before 1145, and Otto von Freising wrote a history of Frederick II Barbarossa *(Gesta Friderici imperatoris).* In 1196 Rigord, who described himself as "chronicler of the French Kings," completed the *Gesta Philippi Augusti,* abridged and continued by Guillaume le Breton as the *Gesta Philippi II regis Francorum.* Giraldus Cambrensis (or Gerald de Barri) left many striking individual portraits scattered throughout his numerous writings, especially in his *Typographia Hiberniae.* Historicobiographical accounts continued to be written throughout the Middle Ages. Thus in 1382, the Italian vernacular chronicler Filippo Villani included in his *Liber de civitatis Florentiae famosis civibus* biographies of some thirty-five prominent Florentines.

Perhaps the best way to grasp the character of medieval secular historicopolitical biography is to turn to the writings of the eleventh-century Byzantine politician and polygrapher Michael Psellos. His *Chronographia,* available in an excellent modern English translation, contains lifelike portraits of several Greek rulers between 976 and 1077. Paul Kirn considers Psellos and Giraldus Cambrensis the "masters of medieval biography."

In the vernacular, little secular biography was written. The only outstanding example (and a true masterpiece in its own right) is the early fourteenth-century mixture of hagiography, history, biography, and autobiography presented by Jean de Joinville in his *Histoire de saint Louis.*

Provençal literature left us a curious biographical genre. The *vidas* are brief prose notes on the troubadours included in collections of their songs. About a hundred such biographies are known; all date from the thirteenth century, and all but two are anonymous. They give the name and the geographic and social origins of the troubadour. Many elaborate on the amorous life of the poet, usually by paraphrasing information culled from the poetry.

Secular biographies in the vernacular tended to be panegyrical. Boccaccio's *Trattatello in laude de Dante* (completed before 1362) is a panegyric of the poet, an idealization of his love for Beatrice, and above all an encomium of the *Divine Comedy* and of poetry in general. Idealized biographies, such as the anonymous *Livre des faicts du bon messire Jean le Maingre, dit mareschal Boucicaut* (completed around 1409), the *Livre des fais et bonnes meurs du sage roy Charles V* by Christine de Pisan, and other works, continued to be written throughout the fifteenth century. The century ended with the *Mémoires* of Philippe de Comines. His highly realistic portraits of Louis XI and other nobles confirm the success of Renaissance life accounts in Italy and elsewhere and foreshadow the imminent universal triumph of secular biography.

BIBLIOGRAPHY

There is no single exhaustive study of secular biography in the Middle Ages. See Robert Bossard, *Über die Entwicklung der Personendarstellung in der mittelalterlichen Geschichtsschreibung* (1944); Wilbur L. Cross, *An Outline of Biography from Plutarch to Strachey* (1924); Paul Kirn, *Das Bild des Menschen in der Geschichtsschreibung von Polybios bis Ranke* (1955); Nancy Partner, *Serious Entertainments: The Writing of History in Twelfth-Century England* (1977); Michael Psellus, *Chronographia,* Edgar Sewter, trans. (1953, repr. 1979); Jan Romein, *Die Biographie* (1948); Donald A. Stauffer, *English Biography Before 1700* (1930), 22–32.

PETER F. DEMBOWSKI

[See also **Asser; Boccaccio, Giovanni; Einhard; Giraldus Cambrensis; Gregory of Tours; Honorius Augustodunensis; Ildefonsus, St.; Isidore of Seville; Jerome, St.; Petrarch; Psellos, Michael; Sigebert of Gembloux.**]

BIOLOGY. The term "biology" dates from the nineteenth century. During the Middle Ages, there was no discipline corresponding to modern biology. If we very roughly take biology to be the study of plants and animals, we can consider how it was studied in the Middle Ages, what taxonomies and methods were applied to it, and what information was available from it. It cannot be stressed too strongly, however, that the Middle Ages possessed no discipline readily comparable to biology as we know it today.

The lack of correlation between modern and medieval disciplines will be more apparent when we consider the medieval classifications of the intellectual disciplines. Medieval writers placed biological science very close to, if not in, the realm of philosophy. When one examines the literature regarding plants and animals, one is struck by the profound difference in method that separates the medieval and modern disciplines. The difference in method underlines a difference in intent as well. Medieval studies of plants and animals did not serve the same functions as modern ones. Thus what is often interpreted as fantasy or sheer misinformation usually served a specific end.

The medieval study of animals, with the exception of a few descriptive tracts written for a practical purpose, existed on two levels. At the more popular and simpler level, works listed animals, gave descriptions that are often ludicrous to modern eyes, and noted the symbolic or spiritual significance of the species. At a loftier level, intellectuals tried to deduce the matter of physiology from general principles, or to see in animals the imperfect reflections of ideal forms.

Medieval plant studies had, in general, a more practical bent, for plants made up the raw material of medications. It was this aspect of plant life that received most attention. When botany was treated more theoretically, the approaches were the same as those applied to animal studies.

For all the difficulty inherent in trying to examine in a past society a discipline not recognized by it, such an exercise is nonetheless rewarding. Viewed within the medieval conceptions of their place within intellectual life and the functions they were to perform, the studies of plants and animals stand as a consonant and satisfying reflection of a particular world view. To the extent that we can abandon the prejudices of modern science and adopt those of the Middle Ages, we can see the strengths and limitations of science in both periods.

CLASSIFICATION OF INTELLECTUAL DISCIPLINES

Despite an overlay of Christianity, the subjects of medieval education derived from classical times. The classical liberal arts, conventionally divided into the trivium (grammar, logic, and rhetoric) and the quadrivium (geometry, arithmetic, astronomy, and music) formed the bedrock of medieval education. Indeed, before the twelfth century, it was often difficult to find instruction beyond the trivium. The mastery of the liberal arts equipped one to study philosophy, though the two overlapped. Philosophy in both the classical and the medieval sense was a much broader subject than it is today.

The first widely held medieval subdivision of philosophy was that of Boethius, a sixth-century thinker who stands as a link between antiquity and the Middle Ages. Boethius divided philosophy into practical and speculative branches. Practical philosophy comprised ethics as applied to different human groupings. Speculative philosophy was divided further into theology, mathematics, and physics. Theology dealt with timeless and immaterial things. Mathematics treated of the material but only in its timeless and unchanging aspects (those that can be measured or counted). Mathematics, in Boethius' scheme, comprised the quadrivium, in effect further removing it from basic education. Physics dealt with material and changeable bodies. It is to physics that those studies related to biology belong. It should be noted that physics was the lowest part of philosophy. Cassiodorus in the middle of the sixth century and Isidore of Seville in the seventh repeated this subdivision of philosophy.

These schemata of knowledge had little influence before the recovery of the Aristotelian corpus in the twelfth century. The early medieval period was relatively barren in terms of philosophy. Further, the Neoplatonism that permeated early medieval thought taught that physical objects and observed phenomena were imperfect reflections of Ideas. It was better to study pure ideas than their imperfect copies. Although theoretical physics was neglected, descriptions of plants and animals were compiled.

As the horizons of knowledge expanded, so did the classification of intellectual disciplines. The scope and ends of the disciplines were elaborated. The medieval theoretical study of physics was dominated by Aristotle. Whether accepted, modified, or rejected, the Greek thinker's work could not be ignored, for it represented the most systematic and coherent body of thought available.

In the high and late medieval periods, physics received much more attention and its subject matter was delineated. According to a twelfth-century Salernitan writer, Marius, excerpts of whose work have been translated by Dales, "nothing can exist in the world except animals, vegetables, and minerals." These, then, are the fit subject of physics, which treats of material things in this world.

Hugh of St. Victor in the *Didascalicon* states that physics searches for causes as found in their effects, quoting Vergil on the question of why plants grow and what causes animals to act as they do. Physics, according to Hugh, is the only discipline to deal with things rather than concepts of things. Physics tries to separate the compounded actualities of things into their elements: fire, air, earth, and water.

The lesser-known twelfth-century author Domingo Gundisalvo, in his *De divisione philosophiae* (*ca.* 1140), sets out to define philosophy and its branches. He quotes Ibn Sīnā in stating that the purpose of philosophy is to learn the truth of everything as far as it is possible for man to do so. His division of the branches of philosophy is conventional. He divides the natural sciences into eight, of which two involve the properties of plants and animals.

Later periods saw further elaborations and var-

BIOLOGY

ious reclassifications of the branches of philosophy, but the subject matter of biology remained within it. The importance of this fact is that philosophy represents a discipline of deduction, reasoning, and discourse. Observation and experimentation, the methods of modern science, had relatively insignificant roles. In the early Middle Ages, Neoplatonism assigned a trivial importance to material things. Aristotelian science, as practiced in the later medieval period, was largely deductive, concerned to separate accident from essence. As Albertus Magnus, generally regarded as the greatest medieval biologist, wrote in *De vegetabilibus et plantis,* "we intend to consider in this book the things common to plants . . . since particulars are infinite and no discipline can be made from them." Those features common to plants (the essential) can be deduced from more general principles, and the particulars (the accidental) can be ignored. No observation is required, although it is not rejected. Albertus Magnus was himself a superb observer of plants, but his method did not require such a talent.

It should be apparent also that the study of plants and animals occupied a relatively low position in the hierarchy of intellectual pursuits. Thus, when studied by the best minds, biology tended to be either a minor interest of an encyclopedic mind or another field for the rigorous application of a philosophic method.

All of this explains, at least in part, why biology was not intensively studied in the Middle Ages and why the approach to it was so radically different from our own. That is not to condemn medieval biology, however. The study of plants and animals fitted into a hierarchy and could be viewed in its relation to all other branches of intellectual endeavor. Such an integration of intellectual life is no longer feasible. Further, the proper method of one discipline, usually rigorous deductive logic, was applicable to any other. Again the fragmentation of modern science stands as a counterpoint. In the Middle Ages, higher truths were used to deduce mundane ones. The world was described as it must be rather than as the illusions of experience might make it appear. To the extent that there was something like biology in the Middle Ages, it aimed at a truth different from that of its modern counterpart. The success of each must be judged on its own grounds.

THE STUDY OF ANIMALS

Two main approaches to the study of animals came together in the High Middle Ages. In a continuous tradition from the period before 1050 came the encyclopedic approach. The Roman forebears were Pliny and Seneca, the early medieval masters Isidore of Seville and Hrabanus Maurus. The encyclopedist tradition was that of cataloging. When the works of Aristotle were recovered via Islam, a more rigorous and systematic approach to the study of animals became possible. Although most works of the high and late medieval period owe something to both the encyclopedic and the systematic approaches, there was a distinctive type of literature arising from each. Albertus Magnus stands as the greatest representative of Aristotelian zoology. Representing the other tradition are the medieval bestiaries, catalogs of animals filled with a fascinating blend of practical information, symbolism, allegory, and sheer nonsense. A third type of work about animals is the hunting manual. Of these rather practical works, the falconry treatise of Fredrick II Hohenstaufen stands as probably the finest biological work of the medieval period, a unique masterpiece still consulted for the art it instructs.

The encyclopedists and the bestiaries. Early medieval thought was dominated by Neoplatonism, which taught that the significance of things lay outside the world. The creatures of this world were imperfect reflections of ideal forms. Practical information tended to be disregarded in favor of an examination of the symbolic, figural, and allegorical significance of worldly experience. This viewpoint, though often bizarre to modern eyes, was intellectually satisfying and retained a profound influence throughout the Middle Ages.

Isidore of Seville proved to be one of the most widely read authors of the early Middle Ages. His *Etymologiae* was the sort of work any respectable medieval library would contain. In the *Etymologiae,* Isidore wrote about nearly all aspects of human knowledge. For each entry, he gave an etymology of the term under discussion. These derivations, usually fanciful, became a common feature of medieval bestiaries. Isidore drew on a variety of sources, some of which he appears to have deliberately misrepresented, for his biological information. The quality of his information is precipitously uneven, and Isidore was not one to let observation hinder his descriptions.

Hrabanus Maurus, ninth-century abbot of Fulda and a thinker of somewhat higher stature, also wrote about almost everything. He emphasized the allegorical significance of the species he described. His pupil, Walafrid Strabo, also wrote about plants and animals. Their work never enjoyed the popularity of the *Etymologiae* but remained a standard source of zoological and botanical information.

The encyclopedists, according to Jerry Stannard's analysis, divided animals into *quadropedia,* mostly mammals; *aves,* birds and other flying animals; *pisces,* comprising most marine life, fish, dolphins, and other sea creatures; *serpentes,* reptiles and amphibians for the most part; and *vermes,* a catchall category including many insects, worms, spiders, larvae, and difficult-to-categorize creatures of various types.

It was the bestiary, however, that typified medieval writing on animals. Many followed Isidore's habit of offering an etymology of the species name and of discussing an animal's moral and allegorical significance. The archetypal bestiary was the work of an unknown author called "the Physiologus," whose tract on animals, written sometime between the second and fifth centuries, was widely translated, modified, and embellished.

A representative bestiary, copied in the twelfth century, was superbly translated by T. H. White and published in 1954. A few examples of its entries will give a hint of the flavor of this peculiar literary genre: The lion sleeps with his eyes open just as Christ, sleeping in the body, was buried after crucifixion. As God, however, he remained awake. Lions are compassionate; they eat men but not women or children. Sick lions eat monkeys as medicine. Lions fear a white cock.

The beaver is gentle and his testicles make a fine drug. When pursued, he bites them off and tosses them in front of his hunters. Thus everyone who would follow God's commandments should cut himself off from vices and cast them away.

The onager, or wild ass, is a large, untamable desert creature. After the twenty-fifth day of March, it brays twelve times in the day and twelve times at night. This symbolizes the devil, who makes a lot of noise seeking his victims.

The elephant and his mate symbolize Adam and Eve. Elephants fear mice. Stallions lose their virility if their manes are cut. As for the unicorn, its having only one horn reminds us of Christ's statement, "I and the Father are one."

The rambling, often bizarre nature of bestiary entries is difficult to explain. Stannard has said that they are like "scrapbooks: the beliefs and claims regarding the creatures of nature are like so many clippings . . . representing the random notices concerning a single species." There is much truth in this observation, and it is worth considering why this genre took its intriguing form.

In the first place, much of the survival of classical writing was fortuitous and unrelated to quality. Thus the Physiologus represented one of only a few sources on animals and perhaps the only one exclusively devoted to them. The peculiarities of the original were adopted and modified from the few other sources available. Second, the study of animals had no real claim to importance in the hierarchy of knowledge and, until the reintroduction of Aristotle, was not the primary concern of major intellectuals. To have any value from a Neoplatonic and Christian point of view, a bestiary had to consider the allegorical and moral. Thus the third factor in the peculiar nature of bestiaries is their need for legitimization through allegorization. If the study of animals led one to think of Adam and Eve and their fall, or the injunctions of Christ, it was valuable. To do so, the bestiary might be presented as entertainment, which indeed it remains to this day.

Aristotelianism and Albertus Magnus. Most of the Aristotelian corpus was lost to western Europe in the early Middle Ages. By 1200, however, essentially the whole of Aristotle had been translated into Latin along with the commentaries of great Arab scholars such as Ibn Rushd. Aristotle's works contained many basic propositions unacceptable to the Roman church—the eternity of the world, determinism—and were condemned in 1210 and 1231. Even in 1277 the University of Paris condemned a variety of Aristotelian "errors."

Still, the intellectual force of Aristotelianism could not be condemned out of existence, and the great thinkers of the thirteenth century assimilated Aristotle into Christian thought; by 1300, Aristotle was usually referred to simply as "the philosopher." Thomas Aquinas is justly most famous for the "Christianization" of Aristotle, but his teacher, Albertus Magnus, occupies the more important position in the history of biology.

Albertus was exceptionally versatile as a scholar, writing in the areas of biblical commentary, metaphysics, medicine, zoology, and botany, among others. His main studies of animals were *Quaestiones super de animalibus* and *De animalibus libri XXVI.* The first nineteen books of the latter work comprise a paraphrase of Aristotle and are followed by Albertus' more original thought. Both works demonstrate Albertus' critical spirit and powers of observation. Often he listed those animals that he had observed personally, and in such cases his information is of

BIOLOGY

high quality. For example, his description of the beaver is much more accurate than that in most bestiaries. Further, he dismissed as fanciful the story of the animal's self-castration.

Albertus also wrote much theoretical zoology. He examined general questions about all living things and deduced the answers from Aristotelian principles using Aristotelian categories and logic. He answered the question, "Does every animal breathe air?" for example, by deduction based on the supposed physiology of breathing. To the question, "Is there a mean [i.e., an intermediate state] between living and nonliving things?" he replied that fungi and sponges represent such a mean because they live near plants or animals on whose vapors they exist. Albertus' answers to such questions were closely reasoned and followed from his premises. Unfortunately, nearly all of the premises were incorrect.

Albertus' unquestioned talent as an observer did not lead him to experimentation, the only means by which he might have disproved Aristotle's physiology. While medieval science is often criticized for its nonobservational bias, it was, rather, its lack of experimental method and acceptance of physics as a deductive discipline that crippled its potential.

The thirteenth-century natural philosopher Roger Bacon believed that experimental science was the highest type and viewed knowledge as the product of experience. The role of such experimentally derived knowledge was to confirm revelation. Bacon, however, did not experiment in biology and is a solitary medieval advocate of an approach that was not adopted until several centuries later.

As an example of the method, potential, and limitations of medieval animal studies, let us consider a lesser scholar, Adelard of Bath, extensively studied by Richard Dales. Adelard criticized the scholars of his day on the grounds that they valued authority over reason and that they ignored the Arab masters. Asked how different parts of the brain were known to have different functions, he replied that presumably this was first learned from sensory experience by considering the results of certain head injuries. Adelard saw the importance of this type of observation in its demonstration of the existence of the incorporeal within the body.

Adelard's remark demonstrates again the effort to make the study of earthly things lead to spiritual truths. Spiritual truths were already known, and observation merely confirmed them; there was no need to expand the means of corroboration through experiment or any other new method.

Hunting. For the medieval nobleman, hunting was the most passionately pursued sport. Hunting provoked a literature of its own. Among the hunting tracts of the Middle Ages, Fredrick II Hohenstaufen's *De arte venandi cum avibus* stands out as a masterpiece. This work on falconry contains a wealth of material on birds in general and is still authoritative on falconry.

Fredrick, like Albertus Magnus, possessed tremendous intellectual versatility, and his range of interests and abilities surpassed those of the Dominican scholar. Fredrick was aware of his capabilities also. He felt free to criticize Aristotle's knowledge of birds as inadequate when not erroneous. He attributed this failing to the acceptance of hearsay, which was never, in his opinion, an adequate road to knowledge. Aristotle, said Fredrick, did not verify his authorities through experience.

Fredrick himself knew a great deal about birds. He classified them by preferential habitat (aquatic, terrestrial, or versatile) and described the mating habits of different species. He experimented with the incubation of eggs. Fredrick meticulously described the migration patterns of various species, including those birds that guide the others. He delineated the anatomy of birds and described their molting, and his knowledge of hunting with birds is consummate. In tone and substance, *De arte* is unlike any other medieval treatise on animals. To be sure, it, too, contains errors, but they are exceptional and not, even as in the case of a great writer like Albertus Magnus, the very basis of his work. *De arte venandi cum avibus* remains a unique masterpiece of medieval thought, but one quite outside the main currents of the study of animals.

THE STUDY OF PLANTS

Compared to zoology, medieval botany was in general a more practical and less fanciful discipline, since the study of plants centered on their medicinal properties. The characteristic medieval treatise on plants was the herbal, usually based on a classical model but often supplemented by the author's experience. Botany owed a huge debt to medicine, and the vast majority of herbalists were physicians. Despite its practical aims and relation to medicine, the study of plants was a peculiar blend of classical knowledge, superstition, and imagination.

Just as Aristotle towers over the highest works of medieval zoology, so does his pupil Theophrastus dominate botany. And just as Aristotle's work en-

BIOLOGY

joyed nothing of the popularity of the Physiologus, so Theophrastus was largely ignored in favor of Dioscorides.

Little is known of Dioscorides, who probably lived in the first century A.D. His work, usually known under the title *De materia medica,* includes about 500 plants and was the main source of medicinal botany until the seventeenth century. Other classical writers were important to medieval botany, but none to the extent of Dioscorides. Although Pliny the Elder described more plants than did Dioscorides, he based his descriptions on other books, rarely supplementing his work with personal observation. His encyclopedic approach, however, was much admired in the Middle Ages. Apuleius Barbarus, also called Pseudo-Apuleius, wrote his *Herbarium* around A.D. 400. This was another widely copied work. Apuleius saw plants as "simples," or elements in complex medications. His writing could reach real heights of fancy, as when he states that the mandrake shines in the dark and will flee the unclean man, but his descriptive powers are meager, at best.

The same figures who dominate the early medievial study of animals also loom large in the study of plants. Isidore of Seville listed hundreds of plants, giving each the usual fanciful derivation. Already in Isidore we see the character of monastic botany. To a great extent, the study of plants by religious writers was a literary venture. The symbolic, religious, and philosophic importance of plants always vied with their medicinal powers. Hrabanus Maurus, in particular, tried to discern the symbolic significance of plants. Of the lily, he wrote, "The lily signifies Christ, for in the Song of Songs, it says, 'I am a flower of the field, a lily of the valley.'"

In the twelfth century, Hildegard of Bingen wrote extensively on animals and plants, and her works *Physica* and *Causae et curae* contain much botanical lore. Most of her interest in plants was medical, and she is justly famous in the history of medicine. Where no Latin word existed for a local plant, Hildegard employed the German. Her list of the medicinal plants is vague as to the preparation of drugs. Nonetheless, many of her drugs sound intriguing, even if they were probably of little therapeutic value. For example, Hildegard describes the clinical presentation of peripheral edema and offers a remedy. One thinks at once of congestive heart failure and digitalis. Her medication is topical, however, and its exact plant source unclear. We will probably never know what the drug was or if it could be effective.

The medical school at Salerno was the most practically oriented of the medieval medical centers. The *Regimen sanitatis Salerni* (date uncertain) catalogs the medicinal properties of plants and, in a characteristically honest appraisal, states that, "Against the power of death, the garden contains no medicine."

Among other medieval writers who deserve some mention in regard to the study of plants are Vincent of Beauvais, Thomas of Cantimpré, and Bartolomeus Anglicus. All lived in the thirteenth century. Bartolomeus, like the others, wrote widely; his *De proprietatibus rerum* is encyclopedic, as its title implies. Bartolomeus wrote about the sky and about the creatures thereof (birds and insects), and did the same for earth and water. His work was widely imitated. Thomas of Cantimpré's *De naturis rerum* is another work of broad scope.

The anonymous herbal is, however, more typical of medieval plant studies. Almost all such works were elaborations of Dioscorides, Apuleius, or both. A typical herbal has entries for 400 to 500 plants, some of which might not be found in Europe but were carried over from classical authors. Herbals brimmed with superstitions: for example, it was sometimes said to be necessary to draw three circles around a mandrake with a sword and then cut it while facing west. These ideas had already been ridiculed by Theophrastus but apparently seemed less silly to the audience of the herbals.

Herbals contained remedies for nearly everything; there were medicines for melancholy, fear, and forgetfulness. Hair dyes and nail polishes could be prepared from the herbal's instructions. When we turn to specific medicines, the impression can be confusing. A single plant was said to treat anal prolapse, epilepsy, mania, exanthems, parasites, and migraine. The same plant could be prepared as an aphrodisiac. Cinnamon was recommended for angina pectoris. Licorice was used for coughs, probably because it is locally soothing. Cuttlefish bone would keep teeth white and is today used to keep birds' beaks clean and sharp. Besides the purely fanciful and possibly effective, there were some genuinely useful agents, notably opium and the belladonna alkaloids.

Before the sixteenth century, illustrations of plants were so conventional and so unlike the plants that it was probably impossible to identify a plant by using an herbal. There may have been an oral tradition of plant identification, with the herbal being used primarily to prepare the medications. Certainly illustrations of mandrake showing the root as a human body or of narcissus showing human faces in the flowers would be poor tools for identifying the actual plants.

It would be tempting to dismiss the herbals as so much rubbish. Unlike bestiaries, they are usually not even entertaining. The medicinal value of the listed remedies is almost impossible to determine but was probably nearly nonexistent. Still, placebo reactors are common enough in all ages, and carefully prepared and presented medications have a value beyond ingredients. Moreover, as in the case of bestiaries, herbals led men's minds to ponder what lay behind the material world, to consider the links between matter and spiritual forces. The herbal fitted medieval medicine as well as today's pharmacology text fits its modern counterpart.

As in the case of animal studies, Albertus Magnus stands also as the greatest medieval botanist. Where nearly everyone else, and especially the herbalists, were content to list plants alphabetically without any effort at classification, Albertus made the classification of plants a primary goal. His basic distinction was between leafy and leafless plants. He distinguished three basic types of flowers and divided trees into those with and without gum. The latter group was further divided on the basis of a variety of other characteristic features. Believing that the bodies of plants were to be understood through their parts, Albertus likened the bark of a tree to the skin of an animal and the roots to the mouth.

Albertus was also a great descriptive botanist. His descriptions of flowers are meticulous and accurate, even though he did not understand the functions of flower parts. The descriptions of the oak and the acorn are justly famous.

Using Aristotelian logic and categories, Albertus determined the requirements for plant growth. On the basis of their mixtures of elements, he explained why some plants bear fruits, others flowers, others only leaves. He saw trees as the most nearly perfect plants, just as he considered large animals more nearly perfect than small ones.

For all its impressive qualities of description and systematization, Albertus' botany had little future. His work was completely bound up with Aristotelianism. The future of botany lay in new systems of classification, more realistic illustration, and even more meticulous observation. The herbal, on the other hand, did not die with the Middle Ages, and seventeenth-century physicians still compiled alphabetic lists of medicinal plants. Even if, like William Turner, they denied that the mandrake had tiny hands and feet, they still revered Dioscorides.

CONCLUSION

Medieval thinkers assumed that certain general principles ruled creation and that creation was tied to spiritual forces. These were things of which man wished and needed to be reminded. It is in the effort to understand these attitudes that we come closest to understanding biology in the Middle Ages, rather than in the facile demonstration of factual errors.

BIBLIOGRAPHY

Albertus Magnus, *De vegetabilibus libri VII,* Ernst Meyer and Karl Jessen, eds. (1867); and *Quaestiones de animalibus,* Bernhard Geyer, ed., in *Opera omnia,* XII (1955); Agnes Arber, *Herbals, Their Origin and Evolution* (1938), 264; Heinrich Balss, *Albertus Magnus als Biologe* (1947); Richard C. Dales, *The Scientific Achievement of the Middle Ages* (1973), 2–37; Friedrich II Hohenstaufen, *The Art of Falconry,* Casey A. Wood and F. M. Fyfe, eds. and trans. (1943, repr. 1955); Edward Grant, *A Source Book in Medieval Science* (1974); and *Physical Science in the Middle Ages* (1977); Isidore of Seville, *Etymologiarum sive Originum libri XX,* Wallace M. Lindsay, ed. (1911); Florence McCulloch, *Medieval Latin and French Bestiaries* (1962); Pierre Riché, *Education and Culture in the Barbarian West,* John Contreni, trans. (1976); Jerry Stannard, "Natural History," in David C. Lindberg, ed., *Science in the Middle Ages* (1978), 429–460; James Weisheipl, "The Nature, Scope and Classification of the Sciences," *ibid.,* 461–482; Terence Hanbury White, trans., *The Bestiary, A Book of Beasts, Being a Translation from a Latin Bestiary of the Twelfth Century* (1954, repr. 1960).

STEPHEN R. ELL

[See also **Adelard of Bath; Albertus Magnus; Aristotle in the Middle Ages; Bestiary; Herbals; Hildegard of Bingen; Hrabanus Maurus; Hunting; Isidore of Seville; Medicine.**]

BIRGITTA, ST. (1303–1373), was the daughter of the lawgiver of Uppland, Sweden. In 1316 she was married to Ulf Gudmarsson, lawgiver of Östergötland, who died in 1344; the couple had eight children, seven of whom reached maturity. After being widowed, she moved first to the Alvastra Cistercian Abbey, then in 1349 to Rome, where she lived first in San Lorenzo in Damaso, and then (1353) in the present Piazza Farnese, where she died. During Birgitta's Cistercian years prophetic and mystic gifts and an enduring deep religious feeling (with emphasis on Christ's passion, asceticism, and frequent confession of sins) first took shape in the revelations she received concerning universal and particular issues of Christian life and faith, society and politics, the church, the papacy, bishops, priests, and monks. Through priestly assistance (Matthias, the two Petrus Olavis) her messages were formulated in Latin and were distributed to, among others, King Magnus II Eriksson of Sweden, Pope Clement VI, and the kings of England and France at the renewed outbreak of war in 1346.

Birgitta's criticism is rooted in the aristocratic and particularistic feelings that led Swedish landowners and officials to introduce a German princely dynasty on the Swedish throne in the person of Albrecht of Mecklenburg (1363–1389), while she herself worked in Rome to promote the religious causes to which she felt drawn: to urge the pope to return from Avignon to Rome and to approve a special type of monastic life, according to the *regula salvatoris* revealed to her by Christ. To provide for an abbey under this rule, King Magnus (1346) and his son King Erik (1362) secured the royal estate of Vadstena, Östergötland, where construction was begun in 1369 according to Birgitta's plans (papal permission was granted in 1370). To her numerous pilgrimages (Spain, Trondheim, Cologne, Italy) Birgitta added the journey to Jerusalem in 1372. The flow of revelations continued until her death. She committed the collected materials to the Spanish bishop-hermit Alfons Pecha in Genoa, and it was he who arranged them in seven books, political texts later being added as book 8.

Birgitta's daughter Catherine (born 1331 or 1332) lived with her in Rome, and in 1374 returned with her mother's body to Vadstena, where Birgitta's veneration as a saint started. From 1375 to 1380, Catherine, first superior of the convent, was again in Rome, where Birgitta's warning that the papacy must quit Avignon was most valuable to Urban VI after the outbreak of schism. In December 1378 he approved a revised version of the rule and issued privileges for the new abbey, which drew French criticism from John Gerson, among others. After Catherine's death in 1381, Vadstena developed under the supervision of Blessed Nicolaus Hermanni, bishop of Linköping. Birgitta's canonization in 1391 stimulated the spread of the *Revelations* to secular and ecclesiastical centers (Oxford, Prague, Kraków) and of the order itself. In 1500 there were twenty-six abbeys: dynastic (England, Denmark, Poland), princely (German territories), and urban foundations (Florence, Genoa, Hanseatic towns on the Baltic and in the Netherlands). At the Council of Basel, Cardinal Juan de Torquemada defended Birgitta's *Revelations* against the charge of heresy.

BIBLIOGRAPHY

Bibliographies. Igino Cecchetti and Maria Vittoria Brandi, "Brigida di Svezia," in *Bibliotheca sanctorum,* III (1963), 527–530, 532–533; Tore S. Nyberg and J. Berdonces, "Brigida di Svezia" and "Brigidini/brigidine," in *Dizionario degli istituti di perfezione,* I (1974), 1577–1578, 1591–1593; Birgit Kockers, Merete Geert Andersen, and Curt Wallin, "Birgitta," in *Kulturhistorisk leksikon för nordisk middelalder,* XXI (1977), 113–114, 120–121; Tore S. Nyberg, "Birgitta/Birgittenorden," in *Theologische Realenzyklopädie,* 2nd ed., VI (1980), 651–652.

Latin editions. Many works of St. Birgitta have been edited in the series Samlingar utgivna av Svenska Fornskriftsällskapet, Latinska skrifter, vols. V, VII.1, VII.5, VII.7, VIII.1, and VIII.2. Other editions are Jan Öberg, ed., *Kring, Birgitta* (1969); and Tryggve Lundén, ed., *Den helige Birgitta och den helige Petrus af Skänninge, Officium parvum beate Marie Virginis,* 2 vols. (1976).

For studies of the life and work of St. Birgitta, see the bibliographies listed above.

TORE S. NYBERG

[See also **Mysticism, Western European.**]

BIRKA, a town that flourished in the ninth and tenth centuries in the Uppland district of east-central Sweden. It was located on Birch Island (Björkö) in Lake Mälaren. Extensive archaeological evidence of its significance as a trade emporium was uncovered in excavations made there in the late nineteenth and early twentieth centuries. Written evidence of the town's importance is preserved in the contemporary (*ca.* 865) *Life of St. Ansgar (Vita Anscharii)* of St. Rimbert.

A black-earth zone and adjoining cemeteries containing about two thousand graves (approximately eleven hundred excavated) have provided a remarkable quantity of remains that, along with the slaves and biodegradable commodities that also were traded at Birka, give an idea of the town's commercial activity. The finds include weapons, tools, pottery, glassware, remnants of clothing and other textiles, personal ornaments, coins, and lump or chopped silver.

Most of the objects uncovered at Birka appear to have been made locally, but some raw materials, such as silk, must have been imported. Our best indicator of the town's far-reaching trade is numismatic evidence. The greater part of the coins found in the Birka graves are Islamic in origin. They outnumber issues deriving from western European mints by eight to one, and locally produced issues by four to one. Coinage of Byzantine origin is limited to very few examples.

Another indicator of Birka's fame is the effort mounted by the missionary St. Ansgar to establish a church there and convert the town's inhabitants to Christianity. Ansgar arrived in 830, under the sponsorship of the Carolingian emperor Louis the Pious, and was given protection either by a certain Björn, whom the saint's biographer calls "king," or by his "prefect" *(prefectus regi).* Ansgar's mission was partially successful because a substantial Christian population was already there. The *Life* specifically mentions Greek (Byzantine) *negociatores,* who were to be distinguished from the local inhabitants *(populi).* Ansgar's church may have survived for about thirty years, but the saint was not successful in converting the region.

Excavations conducted at Birka in the nineteenth century did not uncover a ground plan, but it is clear that the town was originally unwalled. The finds are rich enough to suggest that Birka was in existence for about 175 years (*ca.* 800–*ca.* 975), and that political turmoil in the Mälaren region along with changes in the level of the lake bottom brought about the town's demise.

BIBLIOGRAPHY

Holger Arbman, *Schweden und das karolingische Reich* (1937); *Birka: Sveriges äldsta handelsstad* (1939); *Svear i Österviking* (1955); and "Birkahandel," in *Kulturhistorisk leksikon för nordisk middelalder,* I (1956), 582–586.

SIDNEY L. COHEN

[See also **Missions and Missionaries; Trade.**]

BĪRŪNĪ, MUḤAMMAD IBN AḤMAD ABŪ'L-RAYḤĀN AL- (973–*ca.* 1050), an encyclopedist who distinguished himself in astronomy, mathematics, mathematical geography, and history.

The exact location of Bīrūnī's native town is unknown. But from the adjective Khwārizmī that is usually appended to his name in the medieval biographical dictionaries, we conclude that he must have been born in the district of Khwarizm (or Khwārazm) of northwest Iran (modern Kara-Kalpak A.S.S.R.). The medieval biographers attempt to read into the adjective *Bīrūnī* the ordinary meaning of the Persian word *bīrūn* (outside), and deduce that he must have been born, or lived, outside the confines of the city (of Kāth) or, in this case, the whole district of Khwarizm. While such an identification is possible, it nevertheless sounds like a popular etymology that remains as the only instance of its kind in the history of Islamic annals.

Very little is known of Bīrūnī's early life. While a child he seems to have studied with the distinguished mathematician of the district, Abū Naṣr Manṣūr ibn ᶜIrāq (*d. ca.* 1036), who later wrote to Bīrūnī or in collaboration with him several treatises, most of which are extant. In his twenties Bīrūnī seems to have been in the service of the rulers of his native Khwarizm, presumably as an astrologer, and in his late twenties to have briefly entered the service of various competing rulers of Jurjān on the Caspian Sea. Although it was to the ruler of Jurjān, Qābūs ibn Washmgīr, that Bīrūnī dedicated his most famous book, *al-Āthār al-Bāqiyah ᶜan al-Qurūn al-Khāliyah* (Vestiges of bygone eras), he quickly returned to the service of the Maʾmūnid house of Khwarizm.

This association did not last very long, for sometime between 1000 and 1007 the whole area fell within the sphere of influence of the Ghaznavid ruler Maḥmūd, whose dynasty took its name from the Afghan city of Ghazna (now Ghazni), and was actually conquered in 1016/1017. It was during this conquest that Bīrūnī and other scientists of the Khwarizm court were taken prisoners by Maḥmūd. It was Bīrūnī's knowledge of astrology that saved him from death and allowed him to be promoted at the court of Maḥmūd's son Masᶜūd, even though Bīrūnī himself did not give the subject much credence. As a typical medieval astrologer, Bīrūnī accompanied Maḥmūd on his campaigns into India, which lasted for about thirteen years 1017–1030). It was during these campaigns that Bīrūnī learned Sanskrit and took extensive notes, which he later published in what is now considered the most authoritative account of medieval India. After Maḥmūd's death in 1030, the services of his astrologer were inherited by his son Masᶜūd, to whom Bīrūnī dedicated his most extensive astronomical work, *al-Qānūn al-Masᶜūdī* (Masudic canon). How long Bīrūnī served after that is not known, but he seems to have survived the death of Masᶜūd in 1040 and lived to a ripe old age. In the introduction of his book on pharmacology, which he did not dedicate to a specific patron, he complains that old age (he was more than eighty) had brought him weakness of sight and hearing.

WORKS

Bīrūnī's total intellectual production exceeds 146 titles in more than twenty different disciplines, ranging from astronomy to mathematics, mathematical geography, chronology, mechanics, pharmacology, mineralogy, history, literature, religion, and philosophy. But the bulk of his work lies in mathematics and related disciplines (ninety-six titles). Only twenty-two works, fairly evenly spread over the various disciplines, have survived the ravages of time; and only thirteen of these have been published. The following is a synoptic assessment of each of the most famous works of Bīrūnī.

Chronology (al-Āthār . . .). This text is unique in the Muslim Middle Ages because it combines the purely literary and historical sources of medieval sects and nations with the astronomical lore about their calendars, feasts, and astronomical parameters used in their rituals. All other Arabic medieval works on chronology fall short of this encyclopedic work, in that they were restricted either to one sect or nation, or to one literary tradition. Bīrūnī's discussion of the Jewish calendar, for example, is the most extensive medieval technical and dogmatic exposition on the subject. It was never matched, even by the Hebrew sources.

India (Mā li'l-Hind min Maqūla . . .). In Bīrūnī's own words, "The book is nothing but *a simple historic record of facts*" about Indian society in all its facets. Being an encyclopedist scientist, he in effect managed to bring together a comprehensive survey of Indian intellectual achievements and social practices as they existed around 1030. Being also conscious of his readers, who were not necessarily Indians, he adopted what we would now call a comparative analytical approach in order to highlight some of the details of Indian science and philosophy that Islamic society of the time had already encountered in other contexts. Otherwise he let the Indians speak for themselves.

Like others of his writings, this one is a mine of historical information on Bīrūnī's society as well. Between the lines he allows the reader to identify his views of events in Islamic history as far as these are relevant to India. Moreover, we are explicitly told that he did not satisfy himself with a general survey, and went as far as to translate representative religious and philosophical books from Sanskrit into Arabic.

Mathematical Geography (*Taḥdīd* . . . , The determination of the coordinates of cities). The underlying reason for writing this book was the determination of the *qibla* of the city of Ghazna, Bīrūnī's home in exile. The *qibla* is the direction on the local horizon that a Muslim faces during the five daily prayers. To face in the proper direction, one has to know with some precision the longitude and latitude of both Mecca, the city toward which one must face, and Ghazna. Once that is determined, the values are applied to a spherical triangle, and the angle from the local meridian to the required direction of Mecca can be determined. The problem admits of more than one method of solution, and Bīrūnī did his share in supplying the various methods in this book.

Bīrūnī occupied himself as well with the empirical question of determining the local meridian and the coordinates of any locality. Once that was done, he applied this information to problems of distances between cities, a use that was of great political and economic value.

It is in the introduction of this book that Bīrūnī gives his general overview of the sciences of his time and attempts to justify his work as a religiously condoned one. One can not help but feel that the tense situation between the religious and rational sciences that came to be of paramount importance half a century later was beginning to take shape during Bīrūnī's lifetime.

Masudic Canon (al-Qānūn al-Mas^{c}ūdī). This is Bīrūnī's most extensive astronomical encyclopedia. The published edition falls slightly short of 1,500 pages. It has the general outline of a usual Islamic *zīj* (astronomical handbook), but is much more detailed and analytical in its approach to observations and numerical tables. It is in this book, for example, that Bīrūnī determines the motion of the solar apogee, in contradistinction to Ptolemy's findings, and is able to state for the first time that the motion is not identical to that of precession, but comes very close to it. In this book, too, Bīrūnī employs mathematical techniques unknown to his predecessors that involve analysis of instantaneous motion and acceleration, described in terminology that can best be understood if we assume that he had "mathematical functions" in mind.

It is unfortunate that this text has not yet been translated and studied by modern scholars, for it not only promises to be of great importance to historians of Islamic astronomy but also may change our accepted ideas about the general history of mathematics.

Shadows (Ifrād al-maqāl). This treatise, written sometime after 1015, begins with a general defense of science, echoing the sentiments that were expressed in the *Taḥdīd,* in which Bīrūnī tries to distinguish science from philosophy, as if anticipating the attack on the latter that was to come a generation later. After discussing the linguistic application of the word *ẓill* (shadow) and the astronomical phenomena associated with it, he goes on to give a definition of shadow functions (tangent and cotangent), and to explain in great detail the ensuing identities, theorems, and special applications. He then applies himself to the problem of determining the time of day from shadows, and quickly exploits that to connect his discipline with the time of the Muslim daily prayers that are astronomically defined.

Astrolabe. Although the astrolabe was the most famous instrument of medieval astronomer-astrologers, there is not a single known Arabic treatise in which one could find as thorough a discussion of its history and various types as that in the introductory part of this treatise of Bīrūnī. As in his other works, one can also find here many references to the status of science during his lifetime. For example, Bīrūnī lists all the contemporary astrolabes that he knows of, and the theories underlying their construction. While discussing the astrolabe of Abu Saᶜīd al-Sizjī (*d. ca.* 1024), he states that Sizjī had constructed his astrolabe "employing the principle believed by some people that the apparent rising motion is due to the movement of the earth and not that of the heavens [as is traditionally believed]. I earnestly believe that this problem of whether the earth or the heaven is the one that moves is very difficult to determine and either motion is equally valid for geometricians and astronomers who employ mathematical lines exclusively. The final solution, however, concerns only the natural philosophers, for it is within their own domain of study."

Elements of Astrology (Tafhīm . . .). By Bīrūnī's own admission this book is the most comprehensive of his works on astrology. It was written at the request of Rayḥāna, the daughter of al-Ḥasan of Khwarizm, in a question-and-answer style, and includes a long introduction on preliminary principles of geometry, arithmetic, astronomy, astronomical problems in relation to the earth, chronology, and the astrolabe. This introduction takes up some 346 paragraphs of the total 530, well over half the book.

Because of this book S. H. Nasr, historian of science, has gone to great length in apologizing for Bīrūnī's belief in astrology, not recognizing that expounding the theory of a discipline and believing in its basic tenets are two different things. Although we do not have the exact statement of Bīrūnī's beliefs either way, there is enough evidence to suggest that his heart was not in astrological doctrines. At several points in this text on astrology, he warns his reader against excessive belief in astrology. Moreover, the astrological sections of the *Masudic Canon* are also prefaced by warnings against belief in astrology. At one point he goes so far as to say that he discussed astrology in detail in order to warn the intelligent man away from it. Bīrūnī's only book that would have elaborated his attack against astrology is unfortunately known to us only by name, and seems to have been lost during his lifetime. But the title, *Warning Against the Craft of Deceit,* meaning astrology, leaves very little doubt as to Bīrūnī's position and belief.

Gems (al-Jamāhir . . .). Bīrūnī's work on jewels and minerals is similar to that on pharmacology, in that they are both compilations of what he had gathered from earlier sources. After discussing the value of the study of precious stones and metals, and their economic and social values, thereby producing a theory of government and ethics, he offers a list of individual precious stones, in most cases giving their names in several languages (including Persian, Syriac, and Sanskrit) and their medical uses. He also gives the physical characteristics of each stone, its known varieties and their relative values, and the semiprecious stones that are similar to it. He adds stories and anecdotes involving each stone (when they exist). Of course, the more precious the stone, the larger the section devoted to it.

The second of the two treatises on minerals is devoted to metals, with large sections on gold and silver. Gold is then used as a base weight, and the specific weights of other metals are recorded with respect to it. A comparison of these weights with the modern values confirms Bīrūnī's highly scientific methods.

Pharmacology (Ṣaidanah). This compilation is devoted to drugs as they were known in medieval times and from the tradition of Dioscorides. But, unlike Dioscorides, who arranged his book by subject matter, Bīrūnī lists his drugs in strictly alphabetic order, be they derived from plants, minerals, metals, or animals. He tries whenever possible to list the following properties with each drug: name (in Arabic, Syriac, Greek, Sanskrit, Hebrew, Persian, Sogdian, and other languages), physical description, literary sources, provenance, medical uses, and varieties.

Because of the several languages quoted by Bīrūnī, it has been contended that he knew these languages. But from his own statement in the introduction concerning the dictionaries that he used, and other instances in the *Masudic Canon* and *Chronology,* one can say only that Bīrūnī may have been able to read the alphabets of several languages, and knew enough of them to use a dictionary.

Moreover, this book has given rise to a controversy concerning Bīrūnī's national origin and allegiance. The controversy is a result of modern politics, and he has been claimed by several nations: the Soviet Union because he was born in what is now Soviet Central Asia; Iran because he spoke Khwarazmian, a kin dialect of Persian; Pakistan and Afghanistan because he lived a good part of his life in Sind and near modern Kabul; the Arab nations because he wrote most of his works in Arabic. As a result his millennary celebrations in 1973 were held in more than one country, and he was honored as the national scientist of each. It is in the introduction of the *Pharmacology* that Bīrūnī speaks of himself as being first and foremost a Muslim who thinks that of all the languages he spoke or learned, Arabic is the most suitable for scientific discourse, and that Persian is good only for evening entertainments.

BĪRŪNĪ AND PHILOSOPHY

Although Bīrūnī's education and intellectual production is all philosophical, in the sense of medieval natural philosophy, he was not especially keen to dwell on philosophical issues. Only once did he correspond with his contemporary Ibn Sīnā; and from a close reading of the contents of the questions that he asked Avicenna and the responses that he supplied, one feels that Bīrūnī's heart and talent were somewhere else. This disdain of philosophical questions was also apparent in his quick dismissal of the motion of the earth as mathematically insignificant, and it explains why Bīrūnī never produced an astronomical text of the type written by his contemporary Ibn al-Haytham or the later astronomers of Marāgheh. The Ptolemaic philosophical problems that gave rise to objections and disputations by almost every Islamic astronomer of any repute, and later by Copernicus and others, never attracted the attention of Bīrūnī as far as we can tell. A mathematical description of astronomical phenomena of the highest possible precision seems to have satisfied him.

BIBLIOGRAPHY

The most recent biographical essay on al-Bīrūnī is that of Edward S. Kennedy in *Dictionary of Scientific Biography,* II (1973), 147–158, where most of the standard biographical and bibliographical sources are cited. In addition to that consult the following selected works: *The Chronology of Ancient Nations,* Edward C. Sachau, ed. and trans. (1879); *Al-Bīrūnī's Book on Pharmacy and Materia Medica,* Hakim M. Said and Sami K. Hamarneh, eds., Hakim M. Said, trans., 2 vols. (1973); *Alberuni's India,* Edward C. Sachau, trans. (1888), abridged in Ainslie T. Embree, ed., *Alberuni's India* (1971); *Taḥdīd Nihāyāt al-Amākin,* Pavel G. Bulgakov, ed. (1962), trans. by Jamil ᶜAlī as *The Determination of the Coordinates of Positions for the Correction of Distances Between Cities* (1967), commentary by Edward S. Kennedy, *A Commentary upon Bīrūnī's Kitāb Taḥdīd al-Amākin* (1973); *Al-Qānūn al-Masᶜudī,* complete Arabic edition, 3 vols. (1954–1956), abstract in English in Edward S. Kennedy, *A Survey of Islamic Astronomical Tables* (1956), 157–159, English table of contents by Kennedy, "Al-Bīrūnī's Masudic Canon," in *Al-Abḥāth,* **24** (1971); W. Hartner and M. Schramm, "Al-Bīrūnī and the Theory of the Solar Apogee: An Example of Originality in Arabic Science," in Alistair C. Crombie, ed., *Scientific Change: Symposium on the History of Science, Oxford, 1961* (1963); Edward S. Kennedy, *The Exhaustive Treatise on Shadows* (1976); *The Book of Instruction in the Elements of the Art of Astrology,* Robert Ramsay Wright, trans. (1934); *Kitāb al-Jamāhir fi Maᶜrifat al-Jawāhir,* F. Krenkow, ed. (1936); *Abu Raiḥān Bīrūnī wa Ibn Sīnā al-As'ilah wa-l-Ajwibah,* ed. with English and Persian introductions by Sayyid H. Nasr and Mahdi Muhaqqiq (1973). Several articles dealing with Bīrūnī's works can be found in the following commemoration volumes: *Al-Bīrūnī Commemoration Volume,* Iran Society, Calcutta (1951); *The Commemoration Volume of Bīrūnī International Congress in Teheran* (1976); *Al-Bīrūnī Commemoration Volume,* Hakim M. Said, ed. (1979).

GEORGE SALIBA

[See also **Arabic Numerals; Astrology/Astronomy, Islamic; Historiography, Islamic; Mathematics; Sīnā, Ibn.**]

BISAT. See **Rugs and Carpets, Islamic.**

BISHAPUR (medieval Bishavur, Sabur, or Shapur), in southern Iran, was founded in 266 by the Sasanian king Shapur I (240/241–272), according to inscriptions excavated at the site. The archaeological remains include a palace complex with classically influenced mosaics, a Zoroastrian temple with curious subterranean water channels, and a city laid out on a rectangular plan with two main intersecting avenues. Nearby cliffs bear six reliefs, three of Shapur and three of his successors. In the rough hills above the town is the Grotto of Shapur, a cave with a colossal statue of the monarch, who is believed to have been buried there. The city may have had a population of fifty thousand to eighty thousand before some of the inhabitants were removed to nearby Kāzerūn in the fifth century. In 637 the city was captured by the Arabs, and began to fade as a regional center. By the twelfth century it was in ruins.

BIBLIOGRAPHY

Roman Ghirshman, *Bischapour,* 2 vols. (1956–1971); Hubertus von Gall, "Die Mosaiken von Bishapur," in *Archäologische Mitteilungen aus Iran,* **4** (1971); Klaus Schippmann, *Die iranischen Feuerheiligtümer* (1971), 142–153; Richard Ettinghausen, *From Byzantium to Sasanian Iran and the Islamic World: Three Modes of Artistic Influence* (1972).

TRUDY S. KAWAMI

[See also **Sasanian Art; Shapur I.**]

BISHOP. See **Clergy.**

BISHOPS' SAGAS (Icelandic, *biskupa sögur*), a class of Old Norse saga literature describing the lives of some of the bishops of the two Icelandic sees, Skalholt (from 1056) and Hólar (from 1106). Taken together, they give a vivid and fairly full picture of Icelandic church history from the time of the conversion to Christianity, about 1000, down to the beginning of the fourteenth century.

The Skalholt sagas are *Hungrvaka,* the sagas of St. Þorlákr, *Páls saga biskups, Árna saga biskups,* and a brief sketch of Bishop Jón Halldórsson (*d.* 1339); those of Hólar are *Jóns saga helga, Guðmundar saga biskups,* and *Laurentius saga.*

The missionary period, until the first bishop of the Icelanders, Ísleifr Gizurarson (*d.* 1080), took office, is briefly described in *Hungrvaka* and in greater detail in *Kristni saga,* which is sometimes classified with the bishops' sagas.

The earliest biographies of Icelandic bishops were the Latin lives of the two national saints, St. Þorlákr of Skalholt (*d.* 1193) and St. Jón of Hólar (*d.* 1121), composed at the time of their elevation to sainthood (1198 and 1200, respectively). Apart from fragments of a vita of Þorlákr, they are now lost, but the earliest sagas of the saints in the vernacular are based on these lives. The sagas of Þorlákr and Jón exist in several versions, and are best classified as hagiographic narrative in the tradition of the early Old Norse–Icelandic saints' lives of the twelfth century, adapted from foreign sources. Whereas *Jóns saga* is considered of slight value as a historical source, *Þorláks saga* is assumed to contain a good deal of authentic information. The so-called *Oddaverja þáttr* (Story of the people of Oddi) in one of the versions of *Þorláks saga* describes the saintly bishop's disputes on behalf of the church with the mighty secular chieftains.

Slightly later than *Þorláks saga,* and possibly written by the same author, are *Hungrvaka* and *Páls saga biskups.* They are a happy blend of ecclesiastical and secular history, and, in the case of *Hungrvaka,* have a touch of hagiographic diction.

The bishops' sagas are sometimes divided into two categories, hagiographic and nonhagiographic, but this is probably not a very useful distinction within a body of texts united by a common interest in hagiography, edification, and history.

The oldest bishops' sagas are among the earliest attempts at writing biographies of Icelanders. They had foreign models but at the same time were very much part of a native historical tradition, and it is more than likely that they in some measure served as an inspiration for the authors of *Íslendinga sögur* and the so-called contemporary sagas.

BIBLIOGRAPHY

Editions. Biskupa sögur, Jón Sigurðsson and Guðbrandr Vigfússon, eds., 2 vols. (1858–1878); *Byskupa sögur,* Guðni Jónsson, ed., 3 vols. (1948).

Literature. Hans Bekker-Nielsen, *Old Norse–Icelandic Studies: A Select Bibliography* (1967), 34–35; and "Hungrvaka and the Medieval Icelandic Audience," in *Studi germanici,* n.s. **10** (1972); Régis Boyer, *La vie religieuse en Islande (1116–1264) d'apres la Sturlunga saga et les sagas des évêques* (1972); Peter Foote, "Aachen, Lund, Hólar," in *Les relations littéraires franco-scandinaves au moyen âge* (1975), 53–76; Jørgen Højgaard Jørgensen, *Bispesagaer-Laurentius saga* (1978), with many references; E. O. G. Turville-Petre, *Origins of Icelandic Literature* (1953), 196–212.

HANS BEKKER-NIELSEN

[See also **Árna Saga Biskups; Guðmundar Saga Biskups; Hungrvaka; Jón Qgmundarson; Jóns Saga Helga; Kristni Saga; Laurentius Saga; Páls Saga Biskups.**]

BITEROLF UND DIETLEIB. The epic *Biterolf*, 13,510 verses long, is transmitted in only one manuscript, the Ambraser Heldenbuch (Cod. Vindob. seria nova 2663, Österreichische Nationalbibliothek, Vienna). The language of the manuscript, which was written by Hans Ried at the behest of Emperor Maximilian I between 1504 and 1516, is Early New High German. The poem itself, written in couplets, dates from the 1250's, and was originally in Middle High German. It combines two themes of German heroic poetry: the north German narrative of Dietleib, the inexperienced young hero who seeks adventure (which also plays a role in the *Thidreks saga*), and the battle between the two paramount heroes of German heroic epic, Dietrich von Bern and Siegfried, which is transmitted in *Laurin* and the various versions of the *Rosengarten.* It is the latter that takes pride of place in the epic, and gradually crowds Dietleib and his adventures into the background. Both themes, being part of the German epic tradition, inevitably function not only as an example of the union of a Low German and a High German narrative but also as a commentary on the tradition.

Although these themes are part of the oral heroic epic tradition, the treatment in *Biterolf* is courtly, and to a great extent determined by the conventions of Arthurian narrative. The fight between the two principal figures, for instance, has the character of a tournament rather than of a battle like that at Etzel's court in the *Nibelungenlied* or that on the "Wülpensand" in the *Kudrun.* The possibilities of epic tragedy are therefore skirted. This transformation is in keeping with the function of *Biterolf* as commentary, as an epic on epic, a function achieved in part by a conversion of heroic material into a courtly work, both thematically and metrically. The most obvious evidence for such a function is the text's combination of a Low German and a High German theme of heroic poetry—itself an exercise in epic theory, aided by the close narrative relationship of Dietleib to Dietrich, to which the *Thidreks saga* testifies.

Of particular significance for the narrative are the themes and figures of *Waltharius* and the *Nibelungenlied,* but it is the courtly convention that governs the action, not heroic necessity. The characters of the heroic epic are transformed into the figures of chivalric romance, without, however, a conversion of the narrative into a romance: there is no knight-errant encountering monsters and marvels, and courtly love plays no role at all. The knight acts conventionally in realistic space and time, and the narrator's position in regard to those actions is reminiscent of that of a chronicler. In this respect the narrative of *Biterolf* exemplifies a phase in the development of illusionistic fiction in the vernacular.

BIBLIOGRAPHY

Biterolf and Dietleib, Oskar Jänicke, ed., in *Deutsches Heldenbuch,* I (1866, repr. 1963); Michael Curschmann, "Biterolf and Dietleib: A Play upon Heroic Themes," in S. J. Kaplowitt, ed., *Germanic Studies in Honor of Otto Springer* (1978). For bibliographies of secondary material, see Helmut de Boor, *Geschichte der deutschen Literatur* (1962), III, pt. 1, 186; Ruth R. Hartzell Firestone, *Elements of Traditional Structure in the Couplet Epics of the Late MHG Dietrich Cycle* (1975).

FRANZ H. BÄUML

[See also **German Romance; Kudrun; Middle High German Literature; Nibelungenlied; Rosengarten; Sigurd; Theodoric the Ostrogoth; Thidreks Saga; Waltharius.**]

BITSHVINTA (Pitsunda), one of the most significant centers of Christian activity in the late antique and early Christian period in northwestern Georgia. Its excavation began in 1952, and still continues. Within the late Roman-Byzantine walls surrounding the city, archaeologists have found a fourth-century basilican church with three naves, a spacious narthex, and a baptistery. The mosaic pavements preserved in the apse, the narthex, and the baptistery of the church are from the fourth and fifth centuries. They reveal close stylistic and formal affinities with Syro-Palestinian floor mosaics. This church has been identified as the cathedral of Bishop Stratophilos, who in 325 participated in the Council of Nicaea.

BIBLIOGRAPHY

A. Apakidze, ed., *The Great Pituint,* 3 vols. (1975–1978), in Russian with English summary.

WACHTANG DJOBADZE

[See also **Georgian Art and Architecture.**]

BJARKAMÁL. The Old Norse heroic lay known as *Bjarkamál in fornu* (The old lay of Böðvar Bjarki) has its background in the cycle of Danish legends about the Skjoldung dynasty. *Bjarkamál* describes the fall of Hrólf Kraki, the greatest ruler of that family, in the course of a treacherous attack on his hall at Lejre by his sister, Skuld, and her husband, Hjartvar. The last struggles of the king and his men in the flaming hall are recounted by means of a dialogue between two of Hrólf's most famous champions, Böðvar Bjarki and his comrade Hjalti. Hjalti is the first to notice the attack. He wakes the sleeping Bjarki and exhorts him to fight and die for his lord, reminding him of Hrólf's own deeds of courage and of his generosity. Bjarki replies in the same tone. Both heroes fight and die, falling at either end of the king's body.

The text of the lay has come down to us in a fragmentary and indirect manner. We have five sources.

First, four historical accounts of the Battle of Stiklestad (1030), in which King Olaf (St. Olaf) of Norway fell before heathen forces. All four mention that the court poet Þormóðr Kolbrúnarskáld recited the lay to fire the courage of Olaf's men on the morning before the battle. The accounts are found in Snorri Sturluson's saga of Olaf the Saint in *Heimskringla,* the Legendary Saga of Olaf, the "Greater Saga" of Olaf the Saint, and *Fóstbroðra saga* (The saga of the foster brothers). Snorri quotes two stanzas from the lay, the first describing dawn and the waking of the thralls to their tasks, and calling for "Aðils' men" to rise, the second declaring that the call is not to awaken to the pleasures of wine and women, but to the hard game of war. Diction and meter are Eddic; most half-lines consist of five syllables *(málaháttr),* a few only of four *(fornyrðislag).* The stanzas are of four long lines each.

Second, in his discussion of poetic diction ("Skaldskaparmál") in the *Prose Edda,* Snorri Sturluson quotes three more stanzas, which contain several kennings, or poetic circumlocutions, for "gold." The stanzas probably belong in Hjalti's panegyric of Hrólf's generosity. Meter and language are those of the historical accounts. Kennings are more abundant than we would otherwise expect in an Eddic poem, but that is the reason these fragments are preserved and quoted here.

Third, the Laufáss Edda preserves two fragmentary *málaháttr* stanzas that show little agreement with or similarity to the other fragments, but echo certain phrases in *Hrólfs saga kraka.*

Fourth, in his account of Hrólf Kraki in Book II of the *Gesta Danorum,* Saxo Grammaticus gives a spirited free version of the entire lay in 298 Latin hexameters.

Fifth, the fourteenth-century legendary saga of Hrólf Kraki *(Hrólfs saga kraka)* contains a prose version of the lay, to which certain novelistic motifs have been added: Hrólf speaks; a mysterious bear replaces the sleeping Bjarki in the struggle.

From Saxo's version of the lay, which he analyzed for echoes of the original, Axel Olrik constructed a hypothetical model of *Bjarkamál* in modern Danish. More recently Åke Ohlmarks has made a similar attempt, basing his Swedish reconstruction on the *Hrólfs saga kraka* and the preserved stanzas in the historical accounts and the *Prose Edda.*

It is likely that our various sources for *Bjarkamál,* including the Norse stanzas, go back to a lost Old Danish lay. This, however, is not a necessary assumption: the legendary material is certainly Danish, but it could have found its first poetic expression in western Scandinavia (Norway and Iceland). On the strength of the preserved stanzas and Saxo's hexameters, Olrik dated the original lay around 900, in the "classical" period of Nordic heroic poetry. More recent scholarship has pointed out that the rather theatrical heroics of the poem may reflect the romanticism of a later period.

With the Anglo-Saxon *Battle of Maldon, Bjarkamál* stands as a surpreme poetic statement of the ethics of the Germanic comitatus and of the mutual obligations of lord and vassal. It also gives clear expression to the standard heroic theme of self-immolation for a lost cause. It therefore seems particularly appropriate that it should have been recited at Stiklestad by one of King Olaf's most loyal retainers. Klaus von See, however, has attempted to dismiss the traditions as historically unlikely and as an adaptation by Norwegian historians of William of Malmesbury's account of the singing of the *Song of Roland* before the Battle of Hastings.

BIBLIOGRAPHY

Sources. Snorri Sturluson, *Heimskringla,* II, Bjarni Aðalbjarnarson, ed., Íslenzk Fornrit no. 27 (1945), 361–363; with English translation, *Heimskringla: History of the Kings of Norway,* Lee M. Hollander, trans. (1964), 498–500; for prose versions, see *Hrólfs saga kraka,* Desmond Slay, ed. (1960), 113–122; with English translation, "King Hrolf and His Champions," in *Eirik and Red and Other Icelandic Sagas,* Gwyn Jones, trans. (1961), 311–317; and *Saxonis Gesta Danorum,* I, Carl Knabe and Paul Herrmann, eds., revised by Jørgen Olrik and Hans Raeder

(1931), 53–61, with English translation in *The First Nine Books of the Danish History of Saxo Grammaticus,* Oliver Elton, trans. (1894), 71–80.

Reconstructions. Swedish: *Den glömda Eddan (Eddica minora),* Åke Ohlmarks, trans. (1955), 125–130, 232–235; Danish: *Danske oldkvad i Sakses historie,* 2nd ed. (1918), 5–15, with English translation, "The Old Lay of Bjarki," in *Old Norse Poems: The Most Important Non-Skaldic Verse Not Included in the Poetic Edda,* Lee M. Hollander, trans. (1936), 3–11.

Literature. Klaus von See, "Hastings, Stiklastaðir und Langemarck. Zur Überlieferung vom Vortrag heroischer Lieder auf dem Schlachtfeld," in *Germanisch-romanische Monatsschrift,* n.s. **26** (1976).

JOAQUÍN MARTÍNEZ-PIZZARRO

[See also **Eddic Poetry; Fóstbroðra Saga; Hrólfs Saga Kraka; Olafs Saga Helga; Saxo Grammaticus; Snorri Sturluson.**]

BJARNAR SAGA HÍTDŒLAKAPPA. *Bjarnar saga* is one of the less well-known Icelandic family sagas, and no English translation has appeared. It tells the story of a feud between the Icelanders Bjǫrn Arngeirsson (nicknamed "Champion of the Dwellers of Hot River Dale") and Þórðr Kilbeinsson. Bjǫrn is betrothed to Oddný, but before marrying her he undertakes a voyage abroad for three years. Circumstances prevent a timely return, and Þórðr rumors Bjǫrn's death, then marries Oddný himself. When Bjǫrn learns of her marriage, he is loath to return to Iceland, and continues his life of Viking adventure. He encounters Þórðr, who has spent the winter with King Olaf Haraldsson (ruled 1015–1028), off the Norwegian coast. He spares his life for the sake of King Olaf, but seizes his property. The king subsequently mediates the quarrel.

Once back in Iceland, Þórðr seeks to maintain the reconciliation by inviting Bjǫrn to stay the winter, but the old irritations persist and give rise to an exchange of provocative stanzas. They part on hostile terms, and the main body of the saga is devoted to a crescendo of animosities, a continued exchange of biting stanzas, sexual slander, a series of unsuccessful ambushes laid by Þórðr, and the institution of legal proceedings. Eventually the way is cleared for a settlement when Bjǫrn offers one of Þórðr's partisans, Þorsteinn Kuggason, shelter during a blizzard. Þorsteinn undertakes to mediate the dispute, but his mission fails when Þórðr insists on tallying up the offensive stanzas and evening the score. Subsequently he organizes yet another ambush, and this time Bjǫrn falls after a heroic defense. Þorsteinn Kuggason leads the prosecution, outlaws Bjǫrn's killers, and imposes a heavy settlement on Þórðr.

Bjarnar saga belongs to the category of so-called skald sagas, characterized by a large admixture of skaldic verse and a lovers' triangle in which the hero loses the woman to a rival (this is also the underlying plot of *Hallfreðar saga, Kormaks saga,* and *Gunnlaugs saga*). In the other examples of the genre the skald-hero emerges as a sharply profiled personality with a troublesome temperament. The interset in these sagas lies in the realm of artistic or romantic biography. In *Bjarnar saga* the emphasis is on the feud; the relationship of the protagonists to their poetry and to Oddný is less important. Bjǫrn is clearly marked as the hero. He is frank and fearless, while Þórðr is depicted as deceitful and cowardly. *Bjarnar saga* thus belongs to a rather large group of pessimistic sagas in which the superior man succumbs to ignoble enemies.

There are no clear criteria for dating *Bjarnar saga,* and it has few points of contact with other family sagas. The most recent editor, Sigurður Nordal, placed it in the period 1215–1230 on the basis of style and an apparent unfamiliarity with *Egils saga* (1220–1240?), but a later date is also possible. The transmission of the saga is imperfect, and the beginning is extant only in an adapted form included in a redaction of *Óláfs saga helga* (The saga of Saint Olaf).

BIBLIOGRAPHY

The most recent edition is Sigurður Nordal and Guðni Jónsson, eds., *Borgfirðinga sǫgur* (1938), 111–211. A German translation is Felix Niedner, trans., and Helmut Voigt, ed., *Vier Skaldengeschichten* (1964), 67–141. Critical works are Walther Heinrich Vogt, "Die Bjarnar saga hítdœlakappa: Lausavísur, frásagnir, saga," in *Arkiv för nordisk filologi,* **37** (1921); and Bjarni Einarsson, *Skáldasögur: Um uppruna og eðli ástaskáldasagnanna fornu* (1961), 234–256.

THEODORE M. ANDERSSON

[See also **Family Sagas; Gunnlaugs Saga Ormstungu; Hallfreðar Saga; Kormaks Saga; Skaldic Verse.**]

BJARNI KOLBEINSSON (*ca.* 1150–1223), Norse poet, was consecrated bishop of the Orkneys in 1188. Little is known about his life, except that his Icelandic connections were excellent: the physician-skald Hrafn Sveinbjarnarson and Loptr, the son of Bishop Páll, were among his important visitors.

The last folio of the Codex Regius of *Snorra Edda* contains two poems: *Jómsvíkingadrápa* and *Málsháttakvæði*. Bjarni Kolbeinsson is named as the author of the first; the second has no attribution, and may or may not be by him. The end of *Jómsvíkingadrápa* is missing. Three additional stanzas and two half-stanzas from *Óláfs saga Tryggvasonar en mesta* are appended to the forty-stanza Codex Regius poem in the standard editions.

Jómsvíkingadrápa tells of the famous expedition of the Jómsvíkings to Norway and their defeat at the Battle of Hjǫrungavág. The story is related in sagas of Óláfr Tryggvason and in *Jómsvíkinga saga;* the most probable date for the battle is between 974 and 985. The chief actor is Vagn Akason, the Jómsvíking who had vowed not to return from Norway until he had slain Þorkell Leira and gone to bed with his daughter Ingibjǫrg. Despite Vagn's defeat, he is given the girl as a reward for his bravery.

The poem is in a meter called *munnvǫrp* (literally "mouth-throw" or improvisation), a *dróttkvætt* variant in which odd lines have no rhyme and even lines have half rhyme. (The first known stanzas in this measure are attributed to Torf-Einarr, a tenth-century earl who, like Bjarni, was from the Orkneys.) The skald's kennings are simple and used sparingly; his vocabulary is somewhat repetitive; his syntax, straightforward.

The *drápa* has three parts: an introductory section of fourteen stanzas; a central section of twenty-one stanzas, opening and closing with a refrain and including four identical refrains inserted at four-stanza intervals (stanzas 15, 19, 23, 27, 31, 35); and a final section, now ten stanzas in length. The refrain is: "One nobleman's wife destroys all my joy; the offspring of a great family makes me suffer terribly." This refrain occupies lines 1, 4, 5, and 8 of each of the six refrain stanzas; lines 2, 3, 6, and 7 describe the battle. The poet's juxtaposition of troubadour love-longing and Viking carnage strikes an odd and perhaps not totally humorless note, as in stanza 31:

> One nobleman's wife—
> the she-wolf went upon the swollen corpse,
> there stood the wolf in the feed—
> destroys all my joy;
> the offspring of a great family—
> the wolf gaped over the bones,
> the hunger of the wolf's cubs diminished—
> makes me suffer terribly.

Bjarni's poem breaks with tradition in several ways. The skald's initial plea for silence, the bid for a hearing that for more than three centuries had opened the formal *drápa,* becomes in *Jómsvíkingadrápa:* "I'll say my poem even if no one is listening." Bjarni's second stanza carries parody a step further by rejecting Odin's mead, the liquid metaphor for poetry invoked by scores of skalds before him; Bjarni insists that he never took Odin's booty, yet he is still composing poetry. Other light touches are the poet's critical comments on his own poem (stanza 11: "that is particularly composition-worthy material"; stanza 34: "no need to tell any more in this section"), intrusions that seem to satirize the professional skald's tendency to put himself squarely into his verse. In *Jómsvíkingadrápa* the poet portrays himself as a naive, ignorant, unlucky-in-love narrator who seeks relief from his misery by telling what he knows of a hero whose wooing was successful. Bjarni Kolbeinsson's sophisticated, almost Chaucerian irony has a double target: the conventions of contemporary European love poetry (young men's passion for married noblewomen), and those of the skaldic *drápa* with its fondness for battles, carrion beasts, and beefy breakers-of-rings in their cups.

BIBLIOGRAPHY

Lee M. Hollander, *A Bibliography of Skaldic Studies* (1958), 66; Finnur Jónsson, *Den norsk-islandske skjaldedigtning* (1912–1915), IIA, 1–10, IIB, 1–10; Ernst A. Kock, *Den norsk-isländska skaldediktningen* (1946–1950), II, 1–6; Jan de Vries, *Altnordische Literaturgeschichte,* 2nd rev. ed. (1964–1967), II, 33–37.

ROBERTA FRANK

[See also **Jómsvíkinga Saga; Málsháttakvæði; Skaldic Verse; Snorra Edda.**]

BLACHERNAE, COUNCIL OF. See **Councils, Byzantine.**

BLACHERNITISSA, a Byzantine iconographic type of the Virgin, showing Mary standing, orant, with the Christ child suspended in front of her. Several variants of the Blachernitissa exist, the most common of which presents Christ enclosed within a mandorla (Virgin *Platytera*). The type takes its name from the location of the prototypical representation, the sixth-century church of Blachernae in Constantinople.

LESLIE BRUBAKER

[See also **Byzantine Art; Iconography.**]

Virgin Platytera, marble. Constantinople, mid 11th century. COURTESY OF SANTA MARIA MATERDOMINI, VENICE

BLACK DEATH, the first epidemic of the second plague pandemic. A combination of plague strains, it devastated Europe from 1347 to 1351, killed between 25 and 45 percent of Europe's population, and caused or accelerated dramatic political, economic, social, and cultural changes. In all, it was the single most important natural phenomenon in European history, one whose impact is perhaps best described by Petrarch: "O happy posterity who will not experience such abysmal woe, and will look on our testimony as fable."

NATURAL HISTORY

The Black Death was caused by the plague bacillus *Yersinia pestis.* Because of its peculiar etiology, plague has traditionally been the most deadly infectious disease. *Y. pestis* can present itself in three, perhaps four, guises: bubonic, pneumonic, septicemic, and enteric plague. The bacillus is indigenous to certain regions of the world, including southern and central Asia, the Arabian peninsula, and east Africa, existing there in localized, balanced circumstances with its hosts. *Y. pestis* thrives in the stomach of a particular flea, *Xenopsylla cheopis,* which in turn lives in the fur of small mammals, especially rodents, and particularly the black rat, *Rattus rattus.* Hence, in its natural circumstance plague is primarily an affliction of rodents, and has minimal effect on human populations.

Occasionally the ordered existence of *Y. pestis,* flea, and rodent is disrupted. The causes are not fully understood, but climate and changes in insect or rodent ecology are most likely. In these aberrant circumstances *Y. pestis* multiplies in enormous numbers in the flea s stomach, eventually blocking the digestive tract and preventing it from swallowing. While attempting to feed, the "blocked flea" will retch and regurgitate very large numbers of the bacillus into the bloodstream of its rodent host. This marks the first step of a plague epidemic, the transfer of disease vectors from flea to rat. When sufficiently virulent, an epizootic will break out among the rodents; and should they die, the flea will look for a new host. If the new host is man and *Y. pestis* is injected into the human bloodstream in sufficient numbers, a plague epidemic will erupt.

Plague is comparatively slow to spread in its epizootic form, but when it reaches a particular area, it tends to become embedded in the local rodent population. In human terms it becomes pandemic, a series of outbreaks linked in cyclic intervals that last for hundreds of years and come more frequently than any other major disease save influenza. Plague combines high degrees of visitation with high levels of virulence. Indeed, it is among the most lethal of all infections; in its most "benign" bubonic form it kills about 50 percent of those infected, while the pneumonic and septicemic strains are almost 100 percent fatal.

Like all infectious diseases, plague operates

BLACK DEATH

within particular constraining factors. Bubonic plague, named for the subcutaneous hemorrhages, or buboes, that appear on its victims, is the most common as well as the least lethal variant. Since it is strictly insect-borne, and can never be passed directly from human to human, its spread is dictated by the habits of the flea *X. cheopis. X. cheopis* is active only between 20°C. and 25°C., thus limiting plague's potential presence to select portions of spring, late summer, and early autumn, depending on local climatic variations.

Pneumonic plague, which develops when the bacillus moves into the pulmonary system, is communicable, like all respiratory diseases, and is highly virulent. But it needs bubonic plague to trigger a respiratory reaction; it usually occurs only when there is a sharp temperature drop during a bubonic epidemic, followed by continuing colder weather. It is so lethal that it tends to self-destruct by killing off all its available hosts, a problem also common to septicemic and enteric plague. Septicemic and enteric plague are the deadliest strains, killing all their victims. The former attacks the blood system, while the latter infects the digestive tract. Both are rare, however, and some scholars question their presence in the Black Death. Irrespective of which strains were present, it takes a combination of events to set off any type of plague epidemic, and an even more unusual combination to set off an epidemic with several plague varieties. Unfortunately, such a combination took place in the middle of the fourteenth century.

ORIGINS AND SPREAD TO EUROPE

There are dozens of explanations for the sudden appearance of the Black Death. The most convincing attributes it to a combination of Mongol domination of Asian trade routes in the thirteenth and fourteenth centuries, and drier climatic conditions. One of the indigenous plague regions is Yunnan, in south China. Late in the thirteenth century it was penetrated by Mongol horsemen. Paleoclimatological evidence suggests that plague fleas and perhaps rodents were taken back to central Asia, where they either established plague or added to an existing reservoir of *Y. pestis* among the local animal population. Some authorities claim that the disease was native to wild rodents of the Gobi area, but virtually all agree that by 1300 at the latest, plague was enzootic throughout central Asia.

In the 1320's and 1330's there was a series of prolonged droughts throughout Asia, with 1333 proving especially dry. Steppe nomads, their flocks, rodents, and other animals were forced to migrate east and west, to greener pastures. Ironically, 1334 was quite wet, compounding the environmental dislocation, followed by drought in 1335 and 1336, and an attack of locusts in 1337. Although the specific mechanism is uncertain, it is clear that in some way these events shattered the ecological balance of bacillus, insect, and rodent. At some point early in the 1340's—a more precise date cannot be isolated—the plague epizootic ensued, and then a human plague pandemic, the first epidemic of which became known as the *swarta döden,* the Black Death, by the sixteenth century.

By 1346 word of a pestilence of unprecedented fury filtered back to the commercial and maritime corners of Christendom. Traders and sailors told of massive depopulation in Cathay, south Asia, and the Tartary, but for Europe proper the plague remained a distant disaster, one that the Piacenzese chronicler Gabriel de Mussis thought would never reach the Christian West. All of this changed early in September. The Black Death had worked its way west to the Crimea, around the Italian trading entrepôts along the Black Sea. The springboard of the plague into Europe is traditionally considered to be the Genoese settlements at Tana and Caffa (Feodosiya). A dispute between the merchants and the local Tatar khan caused the Italians to take refuge in Caffa. The Tatars besieged them, but during the siege, plague broke out in their army. Decimated by disease, the khan decided to share his woe, loading victims' bodies on catapults and tossing them into Caffa. As the rotting bodies proliferated and the Black Death spread throughout the compound, the Genoese took to their ships and sailed back to Italy. With them went the Black Death.

There are several implausible aspects to this traditional account. Given plague's complex etiology and the necessity of the insect/rodent vectors or live human victims with pneumonic plague to facilitate its spread, the catapulting of dead bodies, however numerous, could not have started an epidemic. More likely, the urban Caffa rodent population was infected by its rural counterparts. But however accurate the particulars of the Caffa account, the story tells a great deal about the mechanism of plague's spread. It moved overland until it reached the terminus of European sea travel. Once there, like an invading army it followed major routes of trade and communication, traveling across the open seas, up rivers, and along major highways, then branching

BLACK DEATH

back and "mopping up" areas it had initially bypassed. The Black Death finally struck Russia proper four years after the siege of Caffa, via Western trading routes rather than moving north across the steppes from its starting point in the Crimea.

A few Genoese ships from the Black Sea were not the only carriers. The Black Death came from dozens, perhaps hundreds, of small ports throughout the eastern Mediterranean. By autumn 1346, Syria, Mesopotamia, and Palestine had all been infected. By the mid fourteenth century a complex system of transport and communication connected the Middle East with virtually all of Europe. This system ensured that the Black Death would touch all corners of Christendom.

ITALY

The first definitive record of the Black Death in Europe proper is in October 1347 at the Sicilian port of Messina, when a Genoese fleet of a dozen ships, probably from the Black Sea, put in for provisions. Plague had already erupted on shipboard, and the Genoese were not permitted to spend much time ashore. But the stay was long enough; within a few days the rodent and human populations of Messina had been infected and, through contact and flight, plague spread through the island. The nearby city of Catania was stricken by late October, and by early November most of Sicily had been visited. From Sicily the Black Death moved to the Italian mainland. Italy was the most urbanized, economically sophisticated part of Europe, with many ports and fishing villages. Genoa and Pisa were the first towns on the west coast to be infected; Bari and Venice, the first on the east coast. From these ports the Black Death moved up and down both coasts, and then inland, through market towns, smaller villages, and finally more remote rural environs. Within six months all of Italy save a few Alpine villages had been stricken.

The best information on the effects of the Black Death in Italy comes from Tuscany, particularly Florence and Siena. Florence was one of late medieval Europe's most illustrious and prosperous cities, but in the few decades preceding the Black Death it had undergone a series of political and economic traumas, exacerbated by the failure of two of the city's most important banks. The Black Death reached Florence by the winter of 1348, an indication that the bubonic plague of autumn had become pneumonic. A graphic description was written by Boccaccio, in the preface to his *Decameron.*

> In the year of our Lord 1348 the deadly plague broke out in the great city of Florence, the most beautiful of Italian cities. Whether through the operation of the heavenly bodies or because of our own iniquities, which the just wrath of God sought to correct, the plague had arisen in the East some years before, causing the death of countless human beings. It spread without stop from one place to another until, unfortunately, it swept over the West. Neither knowledge nor human foresight availed against it, although the city was cleansed of much filth by chosen officers in charge and sick persons were forbidden to enter it, while advice was broadcast for the preservation of health. Nor did humble supplication serve. Not once but many times these were ordained in the form of processions and other ways for the propitiation of God by the faithful, but, in spite of everything, toward the spring of the year the plague began to show its ravages in a way just short of miraculous. It did not manifest itself as in the East, where, if a man bled at the nose he had certain warning of inevitable death. At the onset of the disease both men and women were affected by a sort of swelling in the groin or under the armpits, which sometimes attained the size of a common apple or egg. Some of these swellings were larger and some were smaller, and all were commonly called boils. From these two starting points the boils began in a little while to spread and appear generally all over the body. Afterwards, the manifestations of the disease changed into black or lurid spots on the arms, the thighs, and the whole person. In many ways, these blotches had the same meaning for everyone on whom they appeared. . . .
>
> Such was the cruelty of heaven and to a great degree of man, that between March and the following July it is estimated that more than 100,000 human beings lost their lives within the walls of Florence, what with the ravages attendant on the plague and the barbarity of the survivors toward the sick. Who would have thought before the plague that the city held so many inhabitants?

While Boccaccio's figures of morbidity are too high—Florence's 1348 population probably did not exceed 100,000—scholarly estimates of the death toll range from 45 to 75 percent of total population. Shops and factories were closed immediately afterward, and prices for commodities and foodstuffs soared as the market system that brought goods in from the surrounding countryside collapsed. The wealthy fled the city, doctors and apothecaries charged exorbitant fees for their services, and the nearly empty streets resonated with the sound of carts and wagons assigned to pick up the dead. Boccaccio continues,

> It was common practice of most of the neighbors, moved no less by fear of contamination by the putrify-

> ing bodies than by charity toward the deceased, to drag the corpses out of the houses with their own hands . . . and to lay them in front of the doors, where anyone who made the rounds might see them, especially in the morning, more of them than he could count; afterwards, they would have biers brought up. . . . Nor was it once or twice only that one and the same bier carried two or three corpses at once, but quite a considerable number of such cases occurred, father and son, and so forth. And times without number it happened that, as two priests bearing the cross were on their way to perform the last office for someone, three or four biers were brought up by the porters in the rear of them so that, whereas the priests supposed that they had but one corpse to bury, they discovered that there were six to eight, or sometimes more. Nor for all their number were their obsequies honored by either tears or lights or crowds of mourners; rather, it was come to this, that a dead man was then of no more account than a dead goat would be today.

Many Florentines adopted an Epicurean attitude, drinking, reveling, and spending. Parents abandoned children, husbands left wives, and sick relatives were forsaken. The political, social, and economic tensions of the 1340's worsened.

All of Tuscany was devastated. Siena, thought by some historians to have suffered less than its surrounding *contado,* still lost between 40 and 50 percent of its population. One of its municipal chroniclers wrote:

> Father abandoned child, wife husband, one brother another, for the plague seemed to strike through breath and sight. And so they died. And no one could be forced to bury the dead for money or friendship. . . . And I, Agnolo di Tura, called the Fat, buried my five children with my own hands and so did many others likewise. And there were many also dead throughout the city who were so sparsely buried with earth that the dogs dragged them forth and devoured their bodies.

Siena was left with a telling memento of the Black Death. Its new cathedral, with transept, choir, and nave completed, and towers in progress, was interrupted. When the plague subsided, a combination of a shortage of labor, high wages, and civic funds directed elsewhere caused temporary, and then permanent, cessation of construction.

At Orvieto news of the Black Death reached the town council by March 1348. On 12 March the council met, agreed that little could be done to halt the progress of the plague, and decided to keep the news to itself. Orvieto's medical community, representative of the more sophisticated Italian towns, shows how poorly equipped even the most advanced fourteenth-century communities were to deal with the Black Death. There was a single municipal physician, a single municipal surgeon, and fifteen to twenty private doctors, all serving a community of 12,000 to 15,000. There were one public and two private hospitals, and sanitation laws designed to curb industrial pollution. It was a relatively advanced system, but against a novel, complex, and highly lethal contagious disease like the Black Death it proved useless.

The Black Death came to Orvieto in April, probably with the entourage of the ambassador of Perugia. It raged through the balance of spring and into summer, during which the weather may have been too warm to sustain bubonic plague. Continual references to victims dying within twenty-four hours of infection suggest the presence of the deadly septicemic strain, as does the disease's abatement in September and October, normally the peak season for bubonic plague. At its peak contemporary observers claimed 500 people died each day. While this figure may be too high, Orvieto probably did lose 50 percent of its population.

Italy was struck as hard by the Black Death as any part of Europe. In Venice attempts at quarantine failed, and by 1351 its population had fallen by more than 50 percent. Quarantine efforts in Milan seem to have been more successful. Municipal authorities walled up those houses in which plague victims were discovered, isolating the healthy as well as the sick. In a technical sense such measures should not have made much difference, yet Milan's death rate was only about 10 to 15 percent of total population. Milan, however, proved exceptional; estimates of overall Italian mortality range from 30 to 60 percent.

FRANCE AND NORTHERN EUROPE

From western Italy the Black Death spread to France, Europe's most populous kingdom, which, in contrast to highly urbanized Italy, was overwhelmingly rural. But different patterns of settlement were of no account; like Italy, France was devastated by the Black Death. It entered Marseilles in January 1348, and Provence a month later. In the urban centers of the south—Marseilles, Narbonne, Toulouse, Bordeaux, Perpignan—mortality exceeded 40 percent. In Avignon, the residence of the pope, 400 persons were said to have perished each day between February and May 1348. In six weeks, 11,000 folk were buried in a single graveyard, one out of three cardinals died, and total mortality probably ex-

BLACK DEATH

ceeded 50 percent. At Montpellier only 7 of the town's 140 Dominican friars survived. In the villages of the rural Midi, mortality was about 40 percent; in Languedoc it was 45 percent.

In northern France mortality patterns in the great cities approximated those of the south. In Caen and Rouen, the two largest towns in Normandy, mortality ranged between 40 and 50 percent. Some of the rural areas of the north suffered less severely, with overall mortality running between 20 and 25 percent, but even there some localities were devastated. The village of Givry in Burgundy had a population in 1340 of between 1,200 and 1,500. Its parish records from 1348 show 615 deaths in a single fourteen-week period, as against a 1338–1348 annual average of only 30.

In Paris, the largest city of northern Europe, with a population of 80,000 to 100,000, the Black Death came late in the spring of 1348, probably along the trade routes from Lyons. Mortality rose through the hot summer months, suggesting the presence of a septicemic strain, then reached an apex in late autumn and early winter, suggesting pneumonic plague. In the peak months of November and December, 800 people a day were said to have died. Interesting evidence comes from the account of the parish of St. Germain l'Auxerrois. From 1340 through May 1348, a total of 78 people bequeathed legacies to the parish church "fabrice." From June 1348 through January 1349, the total rose to 419. Among the casualties were several members of the French peerage; in Paris as elsewhere, the Black Death recognized no class barriers.

From northern France the plague continued to spread in steady, relentless fashion. It went from Picardy into the Low Countries, where it continued to defy categorization and stereotype. Boccaccio and many other contemporary observers, including the medical faculty at the Sorbonne, felt the Black Death was most severe in towns, and urged flight to the countryside. In the Netherlands this pattern was reversed. Mortality in heavily industrialized Flanders was "only" about 15 to 20 percent, while that in rural Holland exceeded 30 percent.

In Scandinavia, rural and sparsely populated, mortality was even higher, running to almost 50 percent of total population, perhaps as the result of the cold northern climate's facilitating pneumonic plague. The Black Death entered the far north through the Norwegian port of Bergen in the spring of 1349. In May a London wool ship was seen drifting in Bergen harbor. Plague had broken out and killed all the crew members before they reached port. It finally ran aground, and was boarded by municipal authorities; before they could impose a quarantine, the Black Death spread inland. Although it may be apocryphal, this traditional story captures the image of terror and havoc that the plague caused. By the end of 1350, it had ravaged all Scandinavia, its effects reflected in the statement of the Swedish king Magnus II: "God for the sins of men has struck the world with this great punishment of sudden death. By it, most of our countrymen are dead."

Even more grisly and macabre was the course of the Black Death in Greenland. Small groups of Norwegians and Icelanders had steadily migrated west, and established settlements on the island's east and west coasts. Heavily reliant on provisions from Scandinavia, the Greenlanders probably got the plague from a supply ship in the winter of 1350. There are no population records for Greenland from before or after the Black Death, and only a few scattered records of the plague's devastation. But when Norwegian ships put into the western settlements in the early fifteenth century, they saw only cattle roaming through deserted villages. In Scandinavia proper the Black Death probably killed more than 45 percent of the population. In Iceland it seems to have taken in excess of 50 percent, and in Greenland it combined with deteriorating climatic conditions to bring settlement to an end altogether.

BRITISH ISLES

For the rest of Europe, the best information survives for the British Isles and Germany. The Black Death first came to England in September 1348, probably via a Gascon ship trading in the small Dorset port of Melcombe Regis. This initial contact was followed by many others, including penetrations at Bristol, Southampton, Great Yarmouth, King's Lynn, and the Thames estuary. Bristol and Southampton probably were the points of entry for plague strains from Italy, the Thames estuary for plague from France, and East Anglia for plague from the Netherlands. Because of this, England was subjected to different plague varieties, and suffered one of the highest death rates in all of Europe—more than 35 percent.

By November 1348, barely two months after its introduction, the Black Death had begun to cause massive social disorder. Church officials were hard pressed to keep parish clergy working at their daily routines. Ralph of Shrewsbury, bishop of Bath and Wells, responded to the desertion of many of his priests by issuing an edict in January 1349 that commanded them to stay at their posts, administer last rites, and supervise burials on penalty of being defrocked. Data on clerical mortality suggest why such an edict was imperative; it reached 45 percent in Bath and Wells, and 50 percent in Devon and Somerset. In Bristol, probably the second largest city in England, fifteen of the fifty-two members of the town council were dead within three months of the plague's arrival; throughout the town mortality was probably between 40 and 45 percent.

In Oxford, 45 percent of the town's nonacademic clergy died; in Woodstock, 42 percent; and in Bicester, 40 percent. At Cuxham Manor, on the upper Thames, two reeves administered the estates continuously from 1288 to 1349. The old reeve died in March 1349, his successor in April, a third in June, a fourth in July, and a fifth within a year. In Wycombe, Buckinghamshire, 60 percent of the beneficed clergy died; in Winchester, the ancient seat of the Exchequer, the figure was 49 percent. Like Siena, Winchester was left with a physical reminder of the Black Death. Its cathedral never received two towers that were part of the original design, and a temporary west facade was shored up and made permanent when high costs after the plague curtailed a more ambitious plan.

The Black Death reached London by late September 1348. It came from the west and the south, and probably directly up the Thames. With about 45,000 people, London was England's largest town, and by fourteenth-century standards it had a fairly elaborate system of sewers and public sanitation. Its walls were beginning to crumble, but with the Thames running along its south side and the Tower covering much of the east, it could still be isolated from most of the surrounding countryside. This was what municipal authorities tried to do, but to no avail. As in Orvieto, the public health laws were designed primarily to reduce industrial pollution and dispose of human waste; a quarantine system designed to restrict people rather than rats and fleas was doomed to failure.

By winter the plague had become pneumonic, and the death rate began to rise. From 2 February until 2 April, more than 2,000 people were buried in a single cemetery, and the worst was yet to come. From June through September civic reports listed an average of 290 deaths per day. Three of the seven major benefices of the Abbey of Westminster fell vacant in June and July. John de Stratford, archbishop of Canterbury, died in August 1348; his successor, John Offord, died in May 1349, before he had been enthroned; and Offord's successor, the Oxford don Thomas Bradwardine, died in August. Scheduled to convene at Westminster in 1349, Parliament never assembled. The Black Death lingered until the late spring of 1350, and killed 35 to 40 percent of London's population. A magnet for immigrants, the city was fairly quick to recover, but its population did not reach preplague levels for 175 years.

Of all England's regions the most severely afflicted was East Anglia. In many other ways a microcosm of the larger kingdom, it was cut off from much of the rest of England by fen and marshlands, and thus developed close ties with the Netherlands. It was probably through ships plying the Netherlandish trade that the Black Death was introduced in the spring of 1349. In all likelihood separate strains came overland from London, and from Essex and Kent in the south. From May to September, contemporaries claimed, a third of the population died. In Cambridgeshire three villages suffered losses of 53 percent, 57 percent, and 70 pecent; at Cambridge University, 16 of 40 resident scholars died between April and August. Sudbury, an important market town along the River Stour, had 107 market stalls in 1340; by 1361 it had 62. Bishop Bateman of Norwich spent much of 1349 moving about his diocese, a step ahead of the plague. In June he fled Great Yarmouth for Norwich; from there he went south to Ipswich, west to Bury St. Edmunds, southwest to Sudbury, and finally north to safety at his rural estate in Hoxne.

The Black Death took nearly as great a toll in northern England. In Newark, Nottinghamshire, 48 percent of the beneficed clergy died; in Stow, Lincolnshire, it was 57 percent; in Lincoln town it was 56 percent; and in Doncaster, 58 percent. North of the border, the Scots delighted in the woes of the "auld" enemy. An army was raised in the summer of 1349, to take advantage of English weakness, but it never marched. In July the Black Death reached Scotland, and did there what it had done in the rest of Europe. Throughout the British Isles the Black Death probably killed a third of the population.

GERMANY: FLAGELLISM AND ANTI-SEMITISM

Germany was less severely afflicted than Italy, Scandinavia, or England. Although some regions in the Rhineland lost more than 40 percent of their population, overall mortality in central Europe probably averaged about 25 percent and some regions, including Alsace and Lorraine and Bohemia, and some towns, including Nürnberg, seem to have lost barely

BLACK DEATH

10 percent of their people. But from Germany came two distinct phenomena that are closely identified with the Black Death: the flagellant movements and pogroms against the Jews.

Flagellism was not unique to Germany or to the mid fourteenth century. It appeared late in the tenth century at the approach of the millennium, and in the course of the later Middle Ages cropped up in Iberia, France, and the Low Countries. But its most intensive manifestation began in the Rhineland in 1349. The best description comes from the French chronicler Froissart:

> The penitents went about, coming first out of Germany. They were men who did public penance and scourged themselves with whips of hand-knotted leather with little iron spikes. Some made themselves bleed very badly between the shoulder blades and some foolish women had cloths ready to catch the blood and smear it on their eyes, saying it was miraculous blood. While they were doing penance, they sang very mournful songs about the Nativity and Passion of our Lord. The object of this penance was to put a stop to the mortality, for in that time . . . at least a third of all the people in the world died.

The flagellants moved in long, snakelike processions, two by two, in groups of a few hundred. A master led, followed by men and then by women. Dressed in cowled hoods and carrying crosses, they chanted hymns. When they reached a town or a village, they proceeded to the main square or church. There they flagellated themselves three times a day, twice in public, all the time crying, "God spare us." Throughout the process the flagellants tried to recruit new members, to form cohorts for thirty-three and a third days, each day representing a year of Christ's life on earth.

The flagellants drew their members from all ranks of society, and perhaps because of the presence of landed and bourgeois elements, they were initially tolerated by both ecclesiastical and civil authorities. The movement therefore spread from the Rhineland to southern and central Germany, the Low Countries, and Eastern Europe. But as the Black Death worsened, the fringe aspects began to dominate, and flagellism became increasingly violent. Early in 1349, Pope Clement VI asked the faculty of the Sorbonne for its opinion on the flagellants. The faculty advised condemnation, which Clement enacted late in October. Lay leaders, including the kings of England and France, soon joined in, and by 1350 the movement had all but disappeared.

Among the doctrines the flagellants preached was anti-Semitism. From at least the time of the First Crusade, organized, large-scale anti-Semitism had been commonplace in many parts of central Europe. Between 1290 and 1310, Jews were expelled from England, France, and parts of the Low Countries, and by the mid fourteenth century there were large Jewish communities in the Rhineland. As the Black Death continued through 1348 and 1349, one of the more popular explanations attributed the plague to the Jews' ritual poisoning of wells. This in turn was supposedly part of a larger plot hatched by the rabbis of Toledo to provide victims for Passover services.

Such claims were hotly denied by responsible church authorities, including Clement VI, and by the medical faculties of the universities of Paris and Montpellier; they ignored the facts that Jews partook from the same wells as their Christian neighbors, and suffered similar losses. Clement even issued a bull ordering his parish clergy to protect their local Jewish communities, but in Germany all these things were ignored. In Strasbourg the town council protected the Jews; the local merchant guild opposed and then deposed it, replacing the old members with a new, anti-Semitic council. In February 1349 the new council burned all 2,000 Strasbourg Jews. In Basel the Jews were gathered on an island in the Rhine and immolated. As an afterthought the Basel town council passed a law prohibiting new Jewish settlement for 200 years.

The overall effect on European Jewry was calamitous. In some towns the massacres took place as the Black Death raged; in others the mere news of its approach was sufficient to set them off. In the summer of 1349, the large Jewish community at Frankfurt am Main was destroyed: later in the year those at Mainz and Cologne were annihilated. By the end of the year, the pogroms began to wane in the Rhineland, not coincidentally as the Black Death wound down, but they picked up anew in the Hansa towns of the east Baltic, and in all of eastern Europe save Poland. By 1351, 60 major and 150 smaller Jewish communities had been exterminated, and more than 350 separate massacres had taken place. The overall effect, an important legacy of the Black Death, was to encourage the eastward movement of what was left of north European Jewry to Poland and Russia, where it remained until the twentieth century.

Other parts of Europe suffered the Black Death as severely as Italy and England. Regions of Iberia, especially Catalonia, were devastated, and in the entire peninsula only Portugal lost less than 30 percent of

BLACK DEATH

its population. Eastern Europe, except for parts of Poland and Lithuania, probably lost in excess of one-third of its people; as the Black Death began to wane in the West, it started to hit its stride in the East, perhaps as a result of Western plague varieties joining those from the steppes. By 1351, when it had finally run its course, virtually all of Europe had been affected. Pope Clement VI calculated the number of dead at 23,840,000. If European preplague population is reckoned at about 75 million, this accounts for about 31 percent of the total, roughly equidistant from the high estimation of close to 50 percent for East Anglia, Tuscany, and parts of Scandinavia, and from the low estimates of less than 15 percent for Bohemia and Galicia. It is unerringly close to Froissart's claim that "a third of the world died," itself drawn from St. John's figure of mortality from plague in Revelation, a favorite medieval source.

MEDICAL RESPONSE

Europe's medical community was not able to deal successfully with the Black Death. Medicine had become highly complex by the fourteenth century, with a tripartite division of apothecaries, surgeons, and university-trained physicians, who at least in theory supervised much of the practice of the other two. Further, hospitals were beginning to devote time to curing rather than just isolating the sick. But, for all these signs of nascent professionalism, late medieval medicine was still largely rooted in Greek method, which stressed observation and debate rather than clinical and experimental science. This method was often adequate in coping with "well-established" diseases and more mundane problems, but had no mechanism to deal with a new, essentially unknown epidemic.

Galen's *Book of Fevers,* the most heavily used epidemiological reference, said practically nothing about plague, thereby forcing many physicians to treat the disease with remedies for smallpox or malaria. Other physicians deserted their patients and fled. According to Guy de Chauliac, doctor to the pope, "The plague was shameful for the physicians, who could give no help at all, especially as, out of fear of infection, they hesitated to visit the sick." Such actions brought considerable condemnation on many physicians and surgeons, but demand for their services remained high. Many doctors realized profits unimaginable before the Black Death. In Orvieto, for example, the town physician received a stipend of £25 per year in 1345. In 1349 this was raised to £200, plus exemption from municipal tithing. For Europe's medical community the Black Death proved to be a crisis, but a profitable one that hastened its professionalization.

The crucial role of fleas and rodents in causing plague was never correctly identified. The medical faculty of the University of Paris stressed astral causation. There had been a triple conjunction of Saturn, Jupiter, and Mars in the fortieth degree of Aquarius on 20 March 1345; the Parisians did not know exactly why it caused the Black Death—"this is hidden from even the most highly trained intellects"—but felt it clearly responsible. This was to become the most popular theory.

Another explanation was the miasma-contagion theory, a general exposition taken from Galen. This stressed that plague came from the south, carried by warm, wet, infected winds. Accordingly, marshes, coastal areas, and lowlands were hazardous; mountains and their valleys were safe; and all houses should be built so that the doors and windows faced north. It was circumspect to burn incense, since pleasant smells, such as those from juniper, rosemary, thyme, or rosewater, drove away foul smells. One physician, Dionysius Colle, further developed this odor variation of the miasma-contagion theory. He stressed the disruptive role of malodorous places such as latrines and charnel houses, and urged their isolation or elimination. Virtually all authorities stressed the importance of moving slowly, especially when infection was suspected, and warned against exercise and baths, which opened the pores and facilitated penetration by plague winds.

Other medical men, particularly surgeons, stressed phlebotomy and cautery as plague treatment. John of Burgundy presented a detailed plan for bloodletting of particular veins, designed to restore the balance of humors disrupted by the disease. This need for restoration was stressed in other plague treatises. The Italian professor of medicine Simon de Covino felt that pregnant women had to take special precautions, a view supported by the Arab Ibn Khātima, who argued that they and people of hot temper were in the most peril.

Apothecaries, the third component of the medical profession, stressed the curative powers of various ointments and potions. Figs, filberts, aloe, myrrh, saffron, and a variety of treacles were recommended, but all were as ineffectual as phlebotomy.

Deperation produced new theories, some of which stressed environmental factors and included elements of truth, but all neglected the crucial roles

BLACK DEATH

of insects and rodents. A series of earthquakes in 1345 was linked to the miasma-contagion theory; the earthquakes were thought to allow noxious gases to seep up to the earth's surface. Another theory blamed a change in ocean tides, which killed millions of fish and sent forth foul odors that in turn caused the Black Death. And many, professors and peasants as well as clerics, simply attributed it to the wrath of God. The Florentine chronicler Giovanni Villani claimed that God brought vengeance on his native town because of its people's sins of avarice, usury, worldliness, adultery, and blasphemy. Clement VI organized huge processions, usually dedicated to the Virgin Mary, in hope that she might allay God's fury. And a new plague saint, St. Roch, was added to the litany of those to whom one might pray for relief when the old saint, Sebastian, proved insufficient.

SOCIAL AND ECONOMIC EFFECTS

In the short span of five to ten years, the Black Death had an immediate and dramatic effect on all aspects of political, social, economic, cultural, and intellectual life. Demographically, it meant the end of Europe's Malthusian crisis, a chronic condition of overpopulation that had retarded growth and diminished standards of living for several decades. As successive waves of plagues from the second pandemic became cyclic, population loss became chronic. European population would not reach preplague levels until early in the sixteenth century. Accompanying this depopulation was a fundamental change in patterns of settlement, the *Wüstungen,* the abandonment of villages and arable land settled during the halcyon days of of high medieval expansion.

During the course of the Black Death, both wages and prices rose, often several hundred percent. But within months of its end, a new wage-price pattern appeared. Food prices stabilized while commodity and luxury goods continued to become dearer. But these increases were dwarfed by an enormous jump in wages, one so great that it effected a drop in real prices. The English chronicler Henry Knighton observed this new relationship:

> There were small prices for vitually everything. A man could have a horse, which before was worth forty shillings, for six shillings, eight pence; a fat ox for four shillings, a cow for twelve pence. . . . Sheep and cattle went wandering over fields and through crops, and there was no one to go and drive or gather them together.

At Cuxham Manor in England, a plowman paid two shillings a week in 1347 received seven shillings by 1349, and ten shillings, six pence by 1350. The net result was a marked rise in standards of living for most segments of society, especially in the lower strata. William Langland noted in *Piers Plowman* that hunger was no longer the peasants' master, that many beggars now refused an old standby, bread made from beans, and insisted on alms in white bread and milk. Day laborers not only received higher wages but also asked for, and got, lunches of meat pies and golden ale. The new era of plenty did not go on unabated; it was most marked in the late 1350's, and by the 1380's and 1390's there were occasional spot famines. But for more than a century the secular trend of standards of living was upward.

Rising living standards produced serious strains in Europe's social structure, as traditional roles of landlord and peasant were knocked askew. Exacerbating this was the acceleration of the decline of customhold tenure and manorialism. The manorial system, affecting upward of 75 percent of Europe's population, depended on cheap, immobile labor and relatively high food prices, all of which the Black Death irrevocably altered. Any peasant unhappy with his lot on one manor could sneak off to another, and probably would be welcomed. Any lord hoping to keep his peasants had to offer them better terms of land tenure, the eventual result being lower rents and the commutation of traditional obligations. In western and central Europe most peasants held land by copy rather than by custom within a few generations of the Black Death.

Many lords were forced to lease their entire estates, collecting cash as rentiers rather than exploiting them directly. Those lords who did continue direct farming often turned from labor-intensive crops, such as grains, to land-intensive production, such as herding. In southern Germany woad, a blue dyestuff, was planted; in England many fields were enclosed and turned into sheep runs; in France and Italy viticulture spread. Only in eastern Europe, one of the Continent's finest corn-producing areas, did the traditional manorial economy persist.

The Black Death engendered or exacerbated sociopolitical crises. As financial distinctions became blurred, the governing classes became more conscious of their social positions. Fashions were more extravagant and colorful than they had been in generations, with men affecting tight, tailored pantaloons and long, pointed shoes, and women wearing hairpieces and dresses with plunging necklines, some almost to the point of baring their breasts. Matteo Villani noted that instead of making people more contemplative and virtuous, the Black Death left them with more material possessions than they had ever had, and an unquenchable desire to accumulate even more. Within a few months of the plague's termination, authorities all over Europe began to enact sumptuary laws. In France a 1349 statute of labor tried unsuccessfully to limit wages to pre-1347 levels; two years later a new law was passed that allowed for a 33 percent rise. In 1351 the English Parliament issued its own statute of laborers that not only pegged prices and wages but also insisted that all able-bodied men work. As in France, it was generally ignored.

Occasionally attempts to prevent the changes resulting from the Black Death brought violent responses from the newly prosperous, or from those whose expectations were not fully realized. In 1358 the peasantry of northern France rose against their seigneurs in the Jacquerie; in 1378 the disenfranchised guild members of the city of Florence rose in the Ciompi; in 1381–1382 the poor in Paris and several towns in Flanders, and the peasants throughout eastern England, took up arms against their rulers. The Black Death was an important, if not the sole, factor in all of these rebellions.

The Black Death and subsequent depopulation contributed to a decline in industrial productivity, a great spurt in technological innovation, a decline in Europe-wide patterns of trade, and a general urban crisis. It helped in the economic rise of some places, such as southern England, southern Germany, and Holland, and in the decline of others, such as Flanders, northern Germany, and parts of France and Italy. It produced tremendous educational and cultural changes. Europe's university population was depleted, and many of its greatest scholars, including William of Ockham and Thomas Bradwardine, were dead. Of about thirty-nine pre-Black Death universities, fourteen had withered away by 1400.

RELIGIOUS AND CULTURAL EFFECTS

The effect of the Black Death on the church was highly complex. English and Italian wills show dramatic increases in gifts to virtually all church institutions. Financially, while some ecclesiastical landholders suffered, papal and other major church officers probably emerged unscathed. Demographically, however, things were less positive. The number of churchmen shrank, especially in select monastic orders. In England, for example, monastic mortality has been estimated at about 51 percent, at least 10 to 15 percent higher than that of lay society. Religious attitudes in the plague's aftermath seem to have been ambivalent. While some chroniclers point to a decline in moral standards, others stress a great flowering of personal piety and individual spiritual fervor. A few generations ago many historians linked the disruptions caused by the Black Death with the Protestant Reformation. This is unlikely, but the church, like most other institutions of authority, was shaken and markedly changed in the century after 1347.

The graphic changes brought on by the Black Death can be seen in art and literature. There were differences in the way death was depicted. Its new image, as found on the walls of the Camposanto in Pisa, was not an airy skeleton but an old woman, black-cloaked, with wild, snakelike hair, bulging eyes, clawed feet and talons, and a scythe to collect her victims. In England funereal brass monuments, which before the Black Death most commonly had representations of knights and their ladies bedecked in finery, often took new images of death—shrouded, macabre corpses, with snakes and serpents surrounding their bones, and grisly smiles on their faces. In Tuscany portraiture reflects a loss of optimism. Trinity scenes painted in the thirteenth and fourteenth centuries show individualistic touches and lavish backgrounds. After the Black Death distinctions between artists disappeared almost entirely. The new trinities show impersonal, uniform figures, the divine counterparts of the downtrodden Ciompi workers.

Art historians have also noted changes in artists' conceptions of the Resurrection. After the Black Death, Christ was endowed, in the words of Millard Meiss, "with more decisive hierarchal superiority," and his miraculous character and supernatural nature were stressed more than ever. Post-Black Death art also shows a great deal of moralizing. In his *St. John the Evangelist,* Giovanni del Biondo has the great evangelist trampling Avarice, Pride, and Vainglory. Another of his works has the Madonna as a decaying corpse, consumed by toads and snakes, a motif unprecedented in Tuscan art. Plague and death had become a new, popular theme for bourgeois and aristocratic patrons alike.

Like art, literature reflected the new social realities and contradictions. The *Decameron* may have been guilt-free, but Boccaccio's later works show the more somber side of the postplague era. The *Corbaccio,* written in 1354–1355, his next work after the *Decameron,* is far different from its predeccesor. It is gloomy, pessimistic, truculent, and ascetic, attitudes that hardened as Boccaccio aged. In a 1373 letter he condemned the *Decameron,* and urged a friend to discourage young women from reading it.

More difficult to assess are the psychological changes wrought by the Black Death. Although there was some social and economic continuity during the worst periods of the plague, the loss of one-third of Europe's population must have had profound effects on even the most stable people. From some it seems to have elicited an Epicurean attitude; from others, despair and depression; and from still others, an increased sense of religiosity and commitment, or contempt for authority and social hierarchy. Perhaps most significant were the surprisingly low levels of fertility suggested by data from the 1350's, despite optimum conditions and opportunity for parenthood. In the aftermath of the great crisis, many people seemed reluctant to bring children into the world.

The impact of the Black Death has been compared with those of the world wars of the twentieth century. Existing social and political systems stagnated, changed, or simply collapsed. Deep-rooted moral, philosophical, and religious convictions were tested, and often found wanting. Expectations, once slowly or never realized, and perhaps never even held by some members of society, were achieved more quickly than ever before; in general, earlier standards seemed no longer to apply. For many people there must have been a new sense of the power of nature, perhaps a power somewhat divergent from traditional images of divinity. In the long term the Black Death changed Europe profoundly. It provided the major theme of depopulation for the later Middle Ages, and accelerated the transition from medieval to modern. In this context alone the Black Death, the greatest biological-environmental event in history, was one of the major turning points in the development of Europe.

BIBLIOGRAPHY

Good presentations of the fundamental issues and fairly complete bibliographies are in Robert S. Gottfried, *The Black Death* (1983); Philip Ziegler, *The Black Death* (1969); and William Bowsky, ed., *The Black Death* (1971), the latter containing portions of many of the works cited below. Other basic surveys include G. G. Coulton, *The Black Death* (1908); and Johannes Nohl, *Der schwarze Tod* (1924). The seminal book on plague, superseding all others is Jean-Noël Biraben, *Les hommes et la peste,* 2 vols. (1975).

Among the best contemporary descriptions of the Black Death are Boccaccio, *Decameron; Cronica de Giovanni Villani; Cronica senese di Agnolo di Tura del Grosso;* and *Chronicon Henrici Knighton.* A good contemporary medical tract is Guy de Chauliac, *La grande chirurgie;* a good modern one is Leonard F. Hirst, *The Conquest of the Plague* (1953).

There are many fine regional and national studies. For Britain see Charles Creighton, *A History of Epidemics in the British Isles* (1894); John F. D. Shrewsbury, *A History of the Bubonic Plague in the British Isles* (1971); and A. R. Bridbury, "The Black Death," in *Economic History Review,* 2nd ser. **25** (1973). For Italy see Elisabeth Carpentier, *Une ville devant la peste: Orvieto et la peste noire de 1348* (1962); William Bowsky, "The Impact of the Black Death upon Sienese Government and Society," in *Speculum,* **39** (1964); and David Herlihy, "Population, Plague, and Social Change in Rural Pistoia," in *Economic History Review,* 2nd ser. **18** (1965). For France see Elisabeth Carpentier, "Autour de la peste noire," in *Annales: Économies, Sociétés, Civilisations,* **17** (1962); R. Emery, "The Black Death in Perpignan," in *Speculum,* **42** (1967); and Guy Bois, *Crise du feodalisme* (1976). Carpentier also discusses the Black Death in Germany and eastern Europe; for a further breakdown on the national and regional literature, see the bibliography in the Biraben book.

Other excellent, more specialized studies include Raymond Crawfurd, *Plague and Pestilence in Literature and Art* (1914); Ada E. Levett, *The Black Death on the Estates of the See of Winchester* (1916); Stephan D'Irsay, "The Black Death and Medieval Universities," in *Annals of Medical History,* **7** (1927); Anna Campbell, *The Black Death and Men of Learning* (1931); Séraphine Guerchberg, "La controverse sur les prétendus semeurs de la peste noire," in *Revue des études juives,* **8** (1948); Millard Meiss, *Painting in Florence and Siena After the Black Death* (1951); J. C. Russell, "The Effects of Plague and Pestilence," in *Comparative Studies in Society and History,* **8** (1966); William J. Courtenay, "The Effect of the Black Death on English Higher Education," in *Speculum,* **55** (1980); and Robert E. Lerner, "The Black Death and Western European Eschatological Mentalities," in *American Historical Review,* **86** (1981). Outside the scope of this essay but worthwhile is Michael W. Dols, *The Black Death in the Middle East* (1977).

ROBERT S. GOTTFRIED

[See also **Anti-Semitism; Boccaccio, Giovanni; Trade; Death and Burial; Feudalism; Flagellants; Medicine; Plagues, Islamic World.**]

BLACKS. In the Middle Ages blacks were known to Europeans mostly as imported slaves, whereas the Muslim world was in direct contact with black Africa. Thus the Muslims drew far more black slaves from Africa than did the Europeans, who until the fifteenth century could acquire them only through Muslim merchants.

Muslim Egypt received black slaves, partly as part of the annual tribute *(baḳṭ)* of Nubia and partly from caravans of merchants. This trade extended to all of North Africa, from Tripoli to Morocco. From Morocco, black slaves were sent to Spain, both in the Umayyad period and in that of the petty kingdoms *(taifas)* that succeeded the Umayyads. ᶜAbd-al-Raḥman I, who founded the Umayyad dynasty of Córdoba in the eighth century, had a black slave in charge of his harem, but it was only much later that blacks became really numerous in Muslim Spain. From the end of the eleventh century, Islam expanded rapidly in the area from the Sudan to Guinea; this led to a large number of enslavements. By the beginning of the twelfth century a notarial formulary shows that there were Sudanese slaves at Córdoba, and a later collection mentions natives of Guinea who were employed on harbor works at Algeciras.

As the Christians of northern Spain gradually reconquered Muslim Spain, they encountered black slaves, most of whom had been converted to Islam. There is abundant evidence about the enslavement that followed the conquest of the island of Minorca by Alfonso III of Aragon in 1287. Many Muslims were auctioned off at Ciudadela; among them were blacks who were already slaves. Some of the buyers were foreign merchants who subsequently distributed these slaves throughout Christian Spain and Italy. The same result was produced by donating slaves to pay off debts.

In the Muslim world and in the Christian countries of the Mediterranean, blacks, like other slaves, were most often used as domestics in private homes. In Muslim countries, however, there were armies of black slaves, especially in Egypt and in North Africa. Black eunuchs were numerous in the palaces of Muslim rulers and great men. Some Islamic governments employed black slaves on public works—harbors and monumental buildings—but the use of slaves on plantations was rare. In the ninth century, however, the Abbasid caliphs of Baghdad used slave labor to drain and cultivate the marshes of lower Mesopotamia. They imported a large number of black slaves from central Africa. These slaves, known as the Zanj, launched a long and bloody revolt during the second half of the century (869–883).

The number of black slaves increased in the kingdoms of Aragon and of Majorca during the fourteenth and fifteenth centuries. Many were bought by rural landlords, but some served in the royal court. In 1438 the queen of Aragon wrote to the Muslim king of Tunis, asking him to permit one of her merchants to bring her six female blacks without paying an export tax. These slaves doubtless had been brought to Tunis by a trans-Saharan caravan. Caravans also went to the peninsula of Barca in Cyrenaica. Blacks imported from "the mountains of Barca" could be found even in rural regions of Catalonia—for example, at Santa Coloma de Queralt in 1447. In 1489 a twenty-five-year-old black slave from Guinea was sold with his two-year-old daughter by a Portuguese merchant at Barcelona. The merchant had imported them directly from the African regions in which the Portuguese were beginning to practice the slave trade on a large scale. There were so many black slaves in Barcelona that by the middle of the fifteenth century there was a fraternity of black Christians, composed of freed slaves, in the town. There was another such group at Valencia.

From Spain slaves were exported to southern France (Roussillon, Languedoc, Provence) and to the kingdom of Naples. As the export of slaves from the west coast of Africa grew with the establishment of Portuguese trading posts, first at Arguim (1448) and then at São Jorge da Mina (1482), eastern Spain was often a transmittal point from which they could be sent to Italy.

In the kingdom of Castile, black slaves were especially numerous in Seville. There, in 1475, a royal order established a special judge for blacks and mulattoes, whether slave or free. The magistrate was a black who had served in the royal court. The black converts of Seville also had their own fraternity.

Black slaves in Portugal were acquired primarily through naval warfare and the voyages of discovery down the Atlantic coast of Africa. From 1425 on, the Portuguese seized the slaveships of the Muslims off the Moroccan coast and took the slaves. In 1444 a slave-trade company was founded at Lagos in the Algarve. The entire coast from Rio de Oro to Guinea was a hunting ground. Missionary zeal played a singular role in enslaving Africans. A bull of Pope Nicholas V, sent in 1454 to King Alfonso of Portugal, mentions the happy fact that enslavement led to the conversion of pagans and other enemies of Christ.

BLACKS

In Senegal the Portuguese continued the system established by Muslim slave traders. The black ruler of Senegal at times sold his own subjects. He also captured slaves in neighboring regions, either to cultivate his own lands or to sell them to the Arab merchants who supplied him with horses and other goods. A good horse was worth ten to fourteen blacks. The Portuguese at first got ten to twelve slaves for any kind of horse, but as the market became saturated, they received only six.

The most distant regions were most profitable for the European slave traders. In 1479, Eustace de la Fosse of Tournai, sailing on a Spanish ship, dropped anchor on the coast of Malaguette (Maniguette). Native canoes brought out women and children to sell. A mother and child could be bought for a barber's basin and three or four copper rings. The ship then sailed to São Jorge da Mina, where Eustace sold his slaves for gold washed out from the alluvial banks of the lower Niger. In this case black slaves were being sold to other blacks, but when the Portuguese had established their fort at Mina (1482), they began to monopolize the trade. The merchants used as interpreters slaves who had been captured earlier and who had lived in Portugal. At least at first, these interpreters could be freed if they brought back four slaves for their master.

The Portuguese trading stations of Arguim and Mina gradually supplanted the older center of Barca in Cyrenaica. Tripoli had at first directly provided Sicily with slaves (numerous there in the fifteenth century), but soon the Portuguese had a monopoly of the trade in the Mediterranean lands of Europe. Slave traders had to check in at Lisbon, where they received a license to export. By 1462 they were permitted to export slaves from Cape Verde and further south directly to Castile. In 1456 the slave trade from Arguim was controlled by the king of Portugal, who farmed out his rights.

African rulers realized that the trade was coming more and more under government control. The Guinean prince Bemoin therefore sent one hundred slaves directly to the Portuguese ruler. From this time on, we can follow the activities of the Casa dos Escravos at Lisbon. Between 15 June 1486 and 31 December 1493, 3,589 slaves were brought to Lisbon. The Florentine merchant Bartolomeo Marchionni at that time had a royal license to trade at the Rio dos Escravos. Besides Lisbon, Lagos in the Algarve continued to be a center of the trade and kept its own accounts.

We are particularly well informed about black slavery in Sicily and Naples at the end of the Middle Ages. In Sicily during the first half of the fifteenth century, 70 percent of the black slaves were men and 30 percent were women. Of the men, 66 percent were under the age of twenty. In the second half of the century, black women became more numerous. In the castles of Francoforte and Cadera in the southeast part of the island, there were, in 1491, ten black males (all baptized) and eight black women, four of whom had one young child each. Slave breeding had become more common than before. In 1497 the baroness of Cadera had eight female and twelve male slaves, all black except for two of the women. Most of the men performed agricultural labor, while the women did domestic or farmwork. The number of black slaves grew rapidly throughout Sicily during the second half of the fifteenth century, and the number of women became equal to that of the men. This encouraged slave breeding and the development of agricultural slavery, since at least some of the workers were born on the master's estate.

At Naples during the late fifteenth century blacks formed 83 percent of slave labor, but slave breeding was less common there than in Sicily. In spite of this difference, slavery in southern Italy for several decades became more and more like colonial slavery, both because it was based on imported black Africans and because it was used for agriculture. In Sicily slaves were used to cultivate sugarcane, vineyards, and other crops, as well as to herd cattle. Work in vineyards is also mentioned in Naples.

The number of black slaves also increased during the fifteenth century in southern France, Catalonia, and even great urban centers such as Genoa and Venice, as well as in the eastern Mediterranean colonies of those two cities. While most of these slaves were brought from Barca and other Barbary coast ports on Italian ships until about 1460, they arrived directly from West Africa by way of Portugal after that date. The Portuguese slave trade had begun earlier, but it was only after 1460 that its influence was felt in Mediterranean Europe and especially in the lands of the Crown of Aragon, both in Italy and in Spain.

Even central Italy was affected by the Portuguese slave trade. In 1473 the accounts of the Florentine firm of Cambini show the arrival, at one time, of twenty-six black slaves in Pisa, which was then the distribution center. Bartolomeo Marchionni, who had bought the monopoly of the slave trade of the Rio dos Escravos from the king of Portugal, sent black slaves from Lisbon to Porto Pisano.

In the Aragonese kingdom of Valencia, slaves were used in agriculture. This was not a matter of hundreds of slaves, as in the ancient world or in the American colonies, but of groups of twenty slaves at the most, largely black, who had the same master. The slaves imported at the end of the century via Valencia were especially numerous. After 1457 blacks from Guinea came in by way of Portugal. After 1489 there were shiploads of savage Jolofs from West Africa, who knew only their own language and could be employed only in agricultural gangs. They came in by the hundreds or more from Rio dos Escravos, where Marchionni had the monopoly. His agent at Valencia, Cesare de Barchi, brought in 2,004 of these blacks. It is clear that such a large number of black slaves, brought in by a single trader, could not have been absorbed by the town of Valencia alone. Many of them must have been sent to the country, or reexported. When one considers that on the island of Majorca (also under the Crown of Aragon), slaves were 18 percent of the population in 1428, one can see that black agricultural slavery was an important element in the economies of some regions of southern Europe.

The black African slave trade was, in fact, directed toward this area during the last four decades of the fifteenth century and the first three or four decades of the sixteenth. In 1542, when Hernando Cortés agreed to buy 500 blacks (two-thirds male, one-third female, fifteen to twenty-five years old) to work his New World plantations, it was stipulated that if the seller, Leonardo Lomellini of Genoa, could not find them in the trading posts of Cape Verde, Cortés could buy them in Spain at Lomellini's expense. This proves that up to that time, the normal destination of black slaves was southern Europe.

The Byzantine Empire, and the countries of northern, central, and eastern Europe, had no direct contacts with black Africa during the Middle Ages. Although slavery existed in all these regions, blacks were not members of the slave class.

BIBLIOGRAPHY

Charles Verlinden, *L'esclavage dans l'Europe médiévale,* I (1955), 358–362, 615–629, 762–765, and II (1977), 208–220, 320–332, 353–358, 474, 489, 657; "Esclavage noir en France méridionale et courants de traite en Afrique," in *Annales du Midi,* 78 (1966); and "Les débuts de la traite portugaise en Afrique (1433–1438)," in *Miscellanea in memoriam J. F. Niermeyer* (1967), 366–377; V. Cortes Alonso, "Procedencia de los esclavos negros en Valencia (1482–1526)," in *Revista española de antropología americana,* 7 (1972); R. Brunschvig, "Abd," in *Encyclopédie de l'Islam,* 2nd ed., I (1953).

CHARLES VERLINDEN

[See also **Exploration by Western Europeans; Slavery, Islamic World; Zanj.**]

BLANCHE OF CASTILE (1188–1252), the daughter of Alfonso VIII of Castile, brought order to France during the minority of Louis IX. It was this achievement rather than her marriage to the future Louis VIII of France in 1200 or her brief reign as queen with him (1223–1226) that merits a biography. Her extraordinary administrative ability was demonstrated between 1226 and 1252. For most of that period she was regent for her young son, Louis IX (St. Louis), a task entrusted to her by her husband's testament. Indeed, until 1244 she was the guide and chief adviser of her son.

Several accomplishments that scholars assign to this period of Louis's reign ought rightly to be credited to Blanche: (1) she several times frustrated in battle or thwarted the plans of rebellious nobles; (2) by remaining a widow despite the importunities of Count Thibaut of Champagne, she did not furnish aristocratic factions, which would have opposed her alliance with a particular baronial family, with any additional cause for discontent; (3) she defeated Henry III of England in his efforts to foment uprisings in France that might have led to his reconquest of Normandy; and (4) she steered a steady course in the mounting crisis between the empire and the papacy.

Blanche's morality was strict and uncompromising—and her duty as a mother, as she saw it, was to transmit her religious values to her children. (In this she shared the concerns of her sister Berenguela, the queen of Leon and mother of St. Ferdinand, king of Castile and Leon.) Louis IX and his sister Isabelle (ultimately Saint Louis and Blessed Isabelle) received her impress willingly. Three younger sons—Robert of Artois, Alphonse of Poitiers, and Charles of Anjou—seem to have been more conventional in the degree of their piety.

But Blanche's strength of character had irritating aspects even for the two children who most successfully lived up to her moral standards. The late 1230's and mid 1240's, when both these children became adults, saw a series of conflicts develop (over

Blanche's plans for the marriage of Isabelle to a Hohenstaufen prince; over her coolness toward Louis IX's bride, Margaret of Provence; over her son's vow in 1244 to go on crusade) that increasingly reduced her prominence in political life. She was never eclipsed, for the king recognized his need for her good advice on many issues and did not respect his wife's political sense. But Blanche's opposition to the Crusade necessitated her retreat from the center stage of public life.

Curiously, it was the Crusade (1248–1254) that also reversed the process. Louis chose his mother as regent during his absence, and it was she who finished a great many of the tasks he had started in preparation for the Crusade (notably, the reforms of the royal administration and the completion of the construction of the port of Aigues-Mortes). But during his absence Blanche did more. She negotiated additional levies from the church to finance her son's Crusade; she supervised the transmission of the county of Toulouse to her son Alphonse, then on Crusade, following the death of his father-in-law, Count Raymond VII; and she dealt with the menace of the Pastoureaux (1251)—though her originally lenient handling of this movement of peasants who intended, so they said, to help her son in the East has been vigorously criticized. By the time she died in November 1252, Blanche had done as much as or more than most French kings in laying the foundation of the authoritarian French monarchy. One chronicler gave her what he considered the supreme compliment: she ruled as well as a man.

BIBLIOGRAPHY

The standard scholarly biography is Élie Berger, *Histoire de Blanche de Castile* (1895). See also William C. Jordan, *Louis IX and the Challenge of the Crusade* (1979), chs. 1, 5. A readable popular study is Régine Pernoud, *Blanche of Castile,* Henry Noel, trans. (1975).

WILLIAM CHESTER JORDAN

[See also **France, 987–1223; France, 1223–1328; Louis IX of France (St. Louis); Pastoureaux.**]

BLANCHEFLOUR ET FLORENCE, an Anglo-Norman version in verse of the *Jugement d'amour* (see also *Melior et Ydoine*), a debate brought by two sisters, Blancheflour and Florence, to the God of Love on the relative merits of knights and clerks as lovers. The dispute is decided by a combat between a sparrow hawk representing the knight and a lark taking the side of the clerk, the latter being defeated. The defeat causes the death of Blancheflour. The text is the work of one Brykhulle, who claims to be adapting an English source by an unidentified Banastre.

BIBLIOGRAPHY

An edition is Paul Meyer, "Notice du MS. 25970 de la Bibliothèque Phillips," in *Romania,* 37 (1908).

BRIAN MERRILEES

[See also **Anglo-Norman Literature; Courtly Love; Melior et Ydoine.**]

BLASPHEMY is a malediction against God. To blaspheme, according to the standard medieval definition, is to "put forward any abuse or disparagement tending to the injury of the Creator." Strictly speaking, it is distinguishable from heresy. Whereas heresy amounts to mistaken religious belief, blasphemy is not necessarily inconsistent with orthodoxy. The latter requires only the expression of ill will or rancor toward God and religion. A slightly different, but no less important, distinction is that the offense of blasphemy does not presuppose that the speaker share the basic beliefs of the dominant group. Heresy does. Thus (in Christian doctrine), a Jew who openly reviled the Christian religion might be guilty of blasphemy. A Jew could not be a heretic, however, because he had never accepted the teachings of Christianity.

Blasphemy was defined broadly in medieval thought, and was always considered to include the expression of a wide range of opinion contrary to the Christian religion. For example, it was clearly blasphemous to say that God was a great deceiver, because this ascribed to God a property that was not his. It was likewise blasphemous to say that fate ruled men's lives, because this ascribed to something or someone else a property that belonged preeminently to God. It was, in addition, considered blasphemous to malign a specific saint, this being classed as "blasphemy by implication." It was not even necessary, according to some formulations, that words be spoken aloud, for Scholastics held that there was "blasphemy of the heart" as well as "blasphemy of the mouth."

The practical consequence of this broad definition was that considerable overlap existed between blasphemy and heresy. Almost all heretical opinions in medieval Europe were also considered blasphemy, and legal commentators treated a blasphemous utterance as raising a legitimate suspicion of the speaker's heresy. The theoretical difference was always maintained, of course, but certainly one of the principal reasons for not making them equivalent was that blasphemy might be uttered in a fleeting rage or without serious intent. Heresy required persistence.

Even without the element of heresy, blasphemy was a theoretically criminal act almost everywhere in medieval Europe. By an edict of 538, the emperor Justinian decreed the death penalty for persistent blasphemers, citing as justification the calamities that he believed blasphemers had visited upon the empire by arousing the wrath of God. Visigothic law specifically punished blasphemy by whipping and imprisonment, and the Diet of Aachen of 818 treated blasphemy as a capital offense. However, these severe sanctions seem rarely, if ever, to have been imposed.

In practice during the High Middle Ages, punishment of blasphemy was largely left to the church, which maintained a system of public courts throughout Europe with canonical jurisdiction over all Christians. There was specific canonical legislation against blasphemy, an enactment of Pope Gregory IX (*ca.* 1230), and the ecclesiastical courts could punish persons convicted of blasphemy by means of public penance or money fines. Even in these courts, however, it is difficult to find evidence that such prosecutions were frequent, except when the blasphemy was accompanied by actual heresy. Medieval moralists ascribed this infrequency of prosecution to a contemporary decline in moral standards, but it seems more likely that the relative frequency of casual blasphemy and the much greater perceived danger of heresy accounts for the small place that blasphemy had in medieval law.

The real development of blasphemy as a crime separate from heresy is therefore postmedieval. The spread of religious toleration made a diversity of beliefs acceptable, or at least not punishable crimes. But a line was drawn at blasphemy. Public reviling of God and religion continued to be punished, resulting in the growth of a body of law relating to blasphemy that retains some theoretical vitality even today.

BIBLIOGRAPHY

Leonard W. Levy, *Treason Against God: A History of the Offense of Blasphemy* (1981); Gerald D. Nokes, *A History of the Crime of Blasphemy* (1928); Werner Schilling, *Gotteslästerung strafbar?* (1966).

R. H. HELMHOLZ

[See also **Heresies.**]

BLAZON, in the Islamic world an emblem of status first adopted for public display just prior to the beginning of the Mamluk period (1250–1517) and particularly characteristic of it. The best-known examples refer to their owners' early careers as *mamlūks,* male slaves—usually Turks from outside the Islamic world—purchased in childhood, converted to Islam, and brought up to serve as the military elite in Mamluk domains (encompassing Egypt, Palestine, Syria, and parts of the Arabian Peninsula, Anatolia, and North Africa). Of these boys a privileged few were chosen for the *khāṣṣakiyyah,* a special group raised at the sultan's court; members of the *khāṣṣakiyyah* were appointed to ceremonial posts: cupbearer, sword-bearer, and polo master, for example. When granted their freedom in early adulthood, these Turks frequently adopted the badges of their former court posts as emblems of their special status and closeness to the sultan. The emblems—goblets, swords, polo mallets, and so on, most often framed in roundels—were then used as identification marks on personal property of every description, ranging from buildings to saddles to household objects.

This custom appears to have been inaugurated under the last powerful Ayyubid sultan in Cairo, al-Malik al-Ṣāliḥ Najm al-Dīn Ayyūb (1240–1249). The chronicler Abū˒l-Maḥāsin ibn Taghrībirdī reports that, when Aybak received his freedom from al-Ṣāliḥ and was made an *amīr,* or commander, he was given the table *(khānjā)* as his emblem, in reference to his former service as taster for the Sultan. He subsequently married al-Ṣālih's widow and became the first Mamluk sultan.

The earliest surviving such emblem, two bows addorsed in a roundel, occurs twice on the facade of the mausoleum of Aydakīn in Cairo and five times on an enameled glass lamp from the same building (now in The Metropolitan Museum of Art, New York). Aydakīn (*d.* 1285) had served al-Ṣāliḥ as *bunduqdār,* or bowman, some forty years earlier.

Blazon of two bows in a roundel on Syrian mosque lamp of enameled glass, late 13th century. THE METROPOLITAN MUSEUM OF ART, GIFT OF J. PIERPONT MORGAN, 1917

As time passed, men who had begun in the *khaṣṣakiyyahs* of the successive Mamluk sultans continued to adopt such emblems, which became more varied and eventually more elaborate. After the fourteenth century it was common to combine emblems of different posts in a single frame, and by the end of the fifteenth century combinations of four or five such emblems had become the rule.

As early as the late thirteenth century, military men who had not begun their careers as *mamlūks,* and thus were not entitled to display badges of courtly service, began to follow the fashion of displaying emblems, usually in the form of abstract designs, the individual significance of which has yet to be explained.

When an *amīr* succeeded in becoming sultan, he almost always abandoned the use of his personal emblem in favor of the exclusive panoply of attributes that were attached to the sultanate. Furthermore, the emblems were not hereditary; they announced the status of individuals, rather than of families. Indeed, for the former *mamlūks,* aliens taken from their parents at an early age, these emblems served as substitutes for the secure position conferred by family in Islamic society, "placing" their owners as preferred servants of the sultan, rather than as sons of identifiable fathers.

For these reasons and despite superficial similarities to "coats of arms," the Mamluk system of "blazons" bears little fundamental resemblance, either in its origins or in its social functioning, to European heraldry.

BIBLIOGRAPHY

David Ayalon, *L'esclavage du mamelouk* (1951) and "Studies on the Structure of the Mamluk Army—I," in *Bulletin of the School of Oriental and African Studies,* **15** (1953); Leo A. Mayer, *Saracenic Heraldry* (1933); M. Meinecke, "Zur mamlukischen Heraldik," in *Mitteilungen der Deutschen Institut in Kairo,* **28** (1972); Estelle Whelan, "Representations of the *Khaṣṣakiyyah* and the Origins of Mamlūk Emblems," in *Memorial Volume for Richard Ettinghausen* (forthcoming).

ESTELLE WHELAN

[See also **Heraldry; Mamluk Dynasty; Mamlūks.**]

BLESSED VIRGIN MARY, LITTLE OFFICE OF. It is often said that the Little Office of the Blessed Virgin Mary is an abridged version of the Common Office of the Blessed Virgin Mary. But the earliest evidence in medieval manuscripts seems to indicate that the first offices of devotion to the mother of Christ were indeed "little" and eventually developed into the extensive full office, which was then shortened for convenient use, especially by the laity.

Votive offices of the Blessed Virgin Mary seem to go back at least to the eighth or ninth century, for in a sermon inserted into Bede's *Homilies* a certain Roman cleric is said to sing daily all the hours of St. Mary. Also, it is surmised by some scholars that the votive masses to the Blessed Virgin Mary introduced into Carolingian liturgical practice must have been complemented by a votive office. In any event, by the tenth century there is substantial evidence for the recitation of an office of the Blessed Virgin Mary throughout northern Europe. At Verdun during the time of Bishop Berenger (940–962) a matins of the Blessed Virgin Mary was sung; in the Life of St. Ethelwold of Winchester (963–984) there appears to be another report of such an office; and Bishop Ulrich of Augsburg (*d.* 973) used a "cursus in honor of St. Mary."

During the late eleventh and early twelfth centuries and the beginnings of high medieval Mariological devotions, a rapid growth of the votive office of the Blessed Virgin Mary seems to have taken place both in the north and south of Europe. Udo of Toul (1052–1059), Gerard of Gsanad (*d.* 1047), William of Hirsau (*d.* 1089), Gandulf of Rochester (*d.* 1110), Peter de Honestis (*d.* 1119), Stephen of Grandmont (*d.* 1124), Honorius Augustodunensis, and Peter the Venerable (*d.* 1156) are all associated with Marian offices, and it is even reported by Geoffroy de Vigeois that at the Council of Clermont (1095) Urban II prescribed that clerics recite the Office of the Blessed Virgin Mary to win success in the First Crusade. In Italy the growth of the office is associated with the names of Gregory VII and the Countess Matilda, but it was Peter Damian (*d.* 1072) who was seen as the great promoter and whose name was often attached in manuscripts to the text of the elements in the office. During the twelfth century many of the new orders such as the Premonstratensians and Knights of Santiago adopted the rite, although the Cistercians seem to have adopted it officially later.

The earliest texts of the Marian Office studied by Dom Leclercq display great diversity beginning with three lessons, often borrowed from the works of the ninth-century Mariologue, Ambrosius Autpertus, and then develop into a full cursus for all the hours with lessons and responses, psalms and hymns.

By the later Middle Ages the Little Office of the Blessed Virgin Mary had become one of the most popular forms of devotion used by clergy and laity alike, and as such it became the essential component of the Books of Hours, whose many sumptuously illuminated representatives grace public and private collections of manuscripts throughout the world.

BIBLIOGRAPHY

Dictionnaire d'archéologie chrétienne et de liturgie 21.2012–2015; Edmund Bishop, "On the Origins of the Prymer," in *Liturgica Historica* (1962), 211–237; Jean Leclercq, "Fragmenta Mariana" and "Formes anciennes de l'office marial," in *Ephemerides liturgicae,* 72 (1958), 74 (1960); *The Hours of Catherine of Cleves,* intro. by John Plummer (1966); *The Visconti Hours,* intro. by Millard Meiss and Edith W. Kirsch (1972).

ROGER E. REYNOLDS

BLIGGER VON STEINACH (*ca.* 1152–*ca.* 1210), Middle High German poet, wrote a now lost epic lauded by Gottfried von Strassburg in *Tristan,* lines 4691–4722, and by Rudolf von Ems (*Willehalm,* lines 2192–2197 and *Alexander,* lines 3205–3218). Gottfried's praise gives us some assurance that Bligger's poem was of rare quality and of unusual form and content (which may account for its loss). He praises the luster of Bligger's words and the inspiration of his ideas—the former as woven from gold and silk threads, the latter as cut of cloth spun by fairies or goddesses.

The images of weaving and dyeing may give some indication of the poem's form and content. Gottfried refers to it as "the tapestry" *(der umbehanc),* which may merely continue the weaving images or possibly indicate the form, or even the title, of the work. A well-known form of narrative in medieval Latin and vernacular poetry was the description of stories and scenes woven onto tapestries, and it may well be that this form became an independent vehicle of narration in Bligger's *umbehanc.* A possible model for Bligger was Ovid's tale of the sisters Procne and Philomela (*Metamorphoses* 6.423–674), in which Philomela weaves the story of her rape and mutilation into a tapestry.

Two of the late-thirteenth- to early-fourteenth-century collections of German courtly lyrics—the Weingartner Liederhandschrift and the Grosse Heidelberger Liederhandschrift—contain three lyric poems ascribed to a Bligger von Steinach, who may or may not have been the same poet. The name Bligger was traditional in the von Steinach family, traceable since 1100 to the present Neckarsteinach on the lower Neckar River near Heidelberg. The first two of these poems (*Minnesangs Frühling,* 118, 1, and 119, 12) are conventional love lyrics. The third (119, 13–27) is a short didactic poem *(Spruch)* in prasie of generosity.

BIBLIOGRAPHY

Herbert Kolb, "Über den Epiker Bligger von Steinach: Zu Gottfrieds Tristan vv. 4691–4722," in *Deutsche Vierteljahrsschrift,* 36 (1962); and "Bligger von Steinach," in *Die deutsche Literatur des Mittelalters: Verfasserlexikon,* 2nd ed., Kurt Ruh *et al.,* eds., I (1978), 895–897; Joachim Bumke, *Ministerialität und Ritterdichtung: Umrisse der Forschung* (1976), 41, 95–96; Helmut de Boor, *Die höfische Literatur: Vorbereitung, Blüte, Ausklang 1170–1250,* 10th rev. ed. (1979), 81.

C. STEPHEN JAEGER

[See also **Gottfried von Strassburg; Middle High German Literature; Rudolf von Ems.**]

BLOCK BOOK

BLOCK BOOK, a type of book belonging to the first century of printmaking. Whereas Gutenberg's press produced books that were printed from assembled groups of cast letters, the block book was printed from page-size blocks of wood into which texts were entirely hand-cut. And, whereas the printed book emphasized text, the block book was invariably illustrated. Thus, the block book was inevitably a simpler production, often of a devotional nature, and intended for a less educated audience. One essential economic difference between the two types of book production must be borne in mind: the block book could be printed on demand, by hand or on a small press, but the printed book required its publisher to produce all copies at once (because so much type could not be tied up for an extended period). Printed texts often included secular, formal treatises for wealthy patrons, while the block books were more likely to be instructive tracts of a moral or religious nature. Many of the block books contained manuscript text passages that provided more elaborate commentary; these are sometimes referred to as chiroxylographic block books.

Although there are still those who favor dating the first, Netherlandish block books to 1420–1440 (Hind, 1935; Musper, 1961), it is generally agreed that in Europe they developed contemporaneously with the first type-printed books of 1450–1460. In other words, the block book is no longer regarded as a precursor of the printed book, but as a product of the same impulse to reproduce texts and imagery by mechanical means. Among the thirty or so surviving block-book titles, there are three important groups. The first includes the *Exercitium super pater noster,* the *Apocalypse,* and the *Ars moriendi,* all of which bear unmistakable relationships to Flemish painting of 1430–1460. There is no reason to date these block books earlier than 1450; one has to assume that older manuscript sources provided prototypes for these admittedly conservative books. The technique of these block books agrees with that of single woodcuts that may be dated between 1450 and 1460, such as the *Mass of St. Gregory* (Schreiber 1462 in Nuremberg).

The second group of block books is probably north Netherlandish in origin and encompasses the *Biblia pauperum,* the *Canticum canticorum,* and the *Speculum humanae salvationis.* Their technique and style have recently been related to a group of manuscripts associated with the *Hours of Anne of Cleves,* all dated 1440 or later. The third group, consisting of seven block books, is contained in one bound volume in the University Library, Heidelberg (CPG 438): a German-Latin *Biblia pauperum, Decalogus, Septimania poenalis, Symbolum apostolicum,* the *Fable of the Sick Lion,* a *Dance of Death,* and a *Book of the Planets.* All have been associated with a group of Upper Rhenish woodcuts (Schreiber 84, 98, 28a, 1349, and 1218) by numerous authorities. Style, technique, coloring, watermarks, and many iconographic features and even aspects of the contents confirm that these block books must be the earliest produced in Germany.

Virtually all of the above block books were copied during the years of greatest popularity, 1450–1480. This is especially the case in Germany, where the quality of style and technique was considerably lower than the sophisticated accomplishments of the earlier productions. Numerous other titles are scrupulously indexed by Schreiber in his *Manuel,* volume IV (Leipzig, 1902), and very little has been uncovered to enlarge his listings. It is likely that no block books were produced on French soil (although we possess a fragment of an *Ars moriendi* in French), while the lone Italian fifteenth-century *Passion* appears to be an isolated phenomenon. Recent research has concentrated on production methods (Geldner), textual analyses (Werner), the uncovering of illustrated manuscript models (Bing, Saxl, von Wilckens), and a consideration of the block books as cultural objects (Field, Hindman and Farquhar).

BIBLIOGRAPHY

Richard S. Field, *The Fable of the Sick Lion* (1974); Sandra Hindman and James Douglas Farquhar, *Pen to Press* (1977); Paul Kristeller, *Biblia pauperum* (1906); Heinrich Theodor Musper, "Die Urausgabe des einzigen italienischen Blockbuchs," in *Die graphischen Künste,* n.s. 6 (1941); and *Die Urausgaben der holländischen Apokalypse und Biblia pauperum,* 3 vols. (1961); Wilhelm Schreiber, *Manuel de l'amateur de la gravure sur bois et sur métal au XVe siècle,* 8 vols. (1891–1911), esp. vol. IV; and "Darf der Holzschnitt als Vorläufer der Buchdruckerkunst betrachtet werden?" in *Centralblatt für Bibliothekswesen,* **12** (1895); Allan Stevenson, "The Quincentennial of Netherlandish Blockbooks," in *British Museum Quarterly,* **31** (1966–1967); Leonie von Wilckens, "Hinweise zu einigen frühen Einblattholzschnitten und zur Blockbuchapokalypse," in *Anzeiger des germanischen Nationalmuseums* (1978).

RICHARD S. FIELD

[See also **Codicology, Western European; Manuscripts and Books; Printing, Origins; Prints and Printmaking; Woodcut Printing.**]

BLONDEL DE NESLE. Some twenty songs (composed *ca.* 1175–1200) survive from the repertory of this French trouvère, who should not be identified with Jean II de Nesle (*d. ca.* 1241). Legend glorified Blondel as a delicate lover, probably because he regularly adopted troubadour motifs such as separation of heart from body, dying by loving, and mistreatment by the god of love. The Ménestrel de Rheims fictionalized an account (*Récits, ca.* 1260) in which Blondel allegedly freed Richard the Lionhearted from his Austrian prison.

BIBLIOGRAPHY

Roberto Crespo, "Briciole di un antico canzoniere francese," in *Medioeva romanzo,* 2 (1975); G. Muraille, "Blondel de Nesle," in *Dictionnaire des lettres françaises: Le Moyen Age* (1964); Leo Wiese, ed., *Die Lieder des Blondel de Nesle* (1904).

JOHN L. GRIGSBY

[See also **Troubadour, Trouvère.**]

BLOOD LIBEL. The presence of Jews constantly reminded Christians of their Lord's Passion and still-incomplete mission. Several therapeutic fantasies resulted, constructed from ancient blood superstitions and atrocity accusations once leveled against early Christians. Supposedly a Christian child was sacrificed annually, to insult Jesus or (in a form dating from 1235) to provide blood for ritual or medicinal use. The origins certainly precede the first full description (Norwich, 1144), but the idea then spread rapidly and helped to create lucrative shrines to supposed martyrs. Thousands of Jews suffered (many died) through false allegations frequently accepted even by the learned, who judged them compatible with imputed Jewish characteristics. In fact, they contradict basic Jewish tenets and seldom, if ever, had factual basis. Nevertheless, this phenomenon of northern popular religion penetrated Mediterranean Europe in the late thirteenth century behind the Inquisition, and survived with horrifying effect into modern times.

BIBLIOGRAPHY

Augustus Jessop and Montague Rhodes James, *The Life and Miracles of St. William of Norwich* (1896); G. I. Langmuir, "The Knight's Tale of Young Hugh of Lincoln," in *Speculum,* 47 (1972); Joshua Trachtenberg, *The Devil and the Jews* (1943); and Marie H. Vicaire and B. Blumenkranz, eds., *Juifs et judaïsme de Languedoc, XIIIe siècle–début XIVe siècle* (1977).

PAUL R. HYAMS

[See also **Anti-Semitism; Host Desecration Libel; Jews in Europe (900 to 1500).**]

BLOOD MONEY, ISLAMIC LAW. The great majority of offenses against the person, ranging from physical assault and woundings to homicide, are treated by Islamic jurisprudence as civil, rather than criminal, offenses in the technical Western sense of these terms.

As a result of this classification of offenses, the victim, or the victim's immediate family relatives in the case of homicide, have the right to demand compensation for the loss occasioned, even though, in cases where the intention to wound or to kill was deliberate, the alternative sanction of retaliation or *qiṣāṣ*—the imposition of an exactly equivalent loss upon the offender or one of the offender's family—may be invoked. In Islamic law the compensation payable for such physical assault, wounding, or death is known as *diya* (blood money).

It follows from this notion of physical injury as a civil or private wrong that cases of assault or homicide that are nonactionable at the instance of the victim or the victim's family are extremely limited. They are confined, in fact, to lawful physical punishment or execution effected as the result of a court judgment, physical injury to or the killing of an outlaw (one who, by rebellion or apostasy, has put himself outside the protection of the law), and injury or death resulting from the lawful use of self-defense.

Traditional Islamic law observes a strict and meticulous tariff of blood money. At the top of the scale is the *diya* payable in cases of homicide. This is fixed, following explicit rulings in the text of the Koran and the Sunna, or precedents, of the Prophet, at 100 camels or 1,000 gold dinars. The camels due in cases of deliberate or intentional homicide should be of a higher quality and value than those due in cases of accidental homicide. These sums apply when the homicide victim is a male Muslim. Where the victim is a female Muslim, half of these sums is due.

Three examples may be taken from the tariff of blood money for nonfatal injuries: First, for the loss of an eye, half of the maximum *diya,* or fifty camels, is due. Second, a wound that bares the flesh to the bone *(mūḍiḥa)* is assessed at 5 percent of the maximum *diya,* or five camels. Third, the loss of a tooth rates 5 percent of the maximum *diya,* or five camels. As with the *diya* for homicide, such injuries caused to a female bring only half of this compensation.

A particular case of the application of the rules of blood money occurs when a child is stillborn as a result of a physical injury, intentional or accidental, caused to the mother. For such destruction of a fetus (which Islamic law holds has a legal existence from the time of conception), the blood money payable is five camels or fifty gold dinars, and is known by the specific Arabic term of *ghurra.*

The offender is personally liable for any injury caused to the victim that is assessed at one-third or less of the maximum *diya.* Where the injury caused is assessed as greater than one-third of the maximum *diya,* or where the act of the offender has resulted in a death, then a collective responsibility for the payment of *diya* falls upon the group known as the *ᶜāqila.*

The *ᶜāqila,* a group of persons in some way closely tied to the offender, has been variously defined: for example, the army unit whose members were all on the same payroll as the offender, or the merchants who plied the same trade in the same market. But the definition of the *ᶜāqila* most commonly applied in Islamic legal practice has been that of the male agnate blood relatives *(ᶜaṣaba)* of the offender.

Following normal principles of reciprocity of legal rights and obligations, because the *ᶜāqila* shoulders the burden of paying the *diya* for an offense committed by one of its members, it also has the right to share in any blood money received for injury to, or the death of, one of their group.

From the point of view of those who receive it, the *diya* is undoubtedly compensation for a loss, through injury or death, that has been inflicted upon the *ᶜāqila.* But in cases of shouldering the burden of payment of the *diya,* the *ᶜāqila* forms a type of mutual assurance society. Each member of this society is "covered" for tortious acts that accidentally cause injury or death and that entail a liability of more than one-third of the maximum *diya.* Each member is similarly covered for intentional injury or homicide, in the sense that he or she is secured from retaliation by the injured party where the injured party—the victim or the victim's relatives—is prepared to accept compensation in place of retaliation. This insurance cover extends to the maximum value of 100 camels or 1,000 gold dinars.

NOEL COULSON

[See also **Homicide, Islamic Law** (with full bibliography); **Wergild.**]

BOCCACCIO, GIOVANNI (1313–1375), Latin encyclopedist and founder of Italian prose literature, was born in Tuscany (probably Florence) during the summer of 1313, the illegitimate son of an unknown mother and of Boccaccino di Chellino, a merchant banker closely allied with the Bardi banking company.

Perhaps because the writer was sensitive about his lower bourgeois origins and his illegitimacy, he provided the protagonists of his fictional works with varied, exotic backgrounds. The amount of apparently autobiographical material contained in his works once led romantic and positivistic scholars to ascribe all the protagonists' circumstances and adventures uncritically to the author himself. Thus the error of the second version (1826) of Filippo Villani's life of the writer, giving Boccaccio's birthplace as Paris, was revived and embroidered. Boccaccio became the abandoned natural child of an anonymous French girl of high lineage, perhaps (if the confession, in the *Filocolo,* were to be believed), even of royal blood. The record of a "Boccasin lombard et son frère," discovered in the Parisian *Livre de la taille* of 1313, added illusory credence to the invention.

By the beginning of the fourteenth century the Boccaccio family had emigrated from Certaldo to establish itself in Florence, twenty miles to the northeast. During his early childhood in Florence, Boccaccio was first set to study with Giovanni Mazzuoli da Strada, the father of Boccaccio's friend and later social rival, the poet Zanobi da Strada. At fourteen, Boccaccio was taken, or sent, to Naples (extant records show that his father was there in 1327 and 1329 executing business on behalf of the Bardi firm). Despite the boy's early penchant for letters (he was, he later said, "ad poeticas meditationes dispositum ex utero matris"), Boccaccino hoped that his son would follow him into the banking profession and apprenticed him to a Florentine counting house in Naples, where he was forced to study arithmetic for six years—"without profit," as Boccaccio later complained in the *Genealogia.* For another six years his father constrained him to study canon law, just as fruitlessly.

Angevin Naples, heir to the prestige of the extinct

BOCCACCIO, GIOVANNI

Hohenstaufen court, and closely associated with Byzantium and Avignon, was at the time the major cultural, intellectual, and artistic center of the Latin West. Here Boccaccio may have met Giotto, who from 1329 to about 1333 was painting allegorical frescoes in the Castel Nuovo. The young Boccaccio also frequented the vast royal library directed by Paolo da Perugia and knew many of the city's scholars, such as Andalò del Negro, the Genoese astronomer (whose treatises Boccaccio transcribed into his notebook, the *Zibaldone laurenziano*); Barlaam, the Calabrian Greek scholar; the jurists Barbato da Sulmona, Pietro Piccolo da Monteforte, and Giovanni Barrili; and the Augustinian theologian, Dionigi da Borgo San Sepolcro. All were humanists and lovers of poetry. In particular, from 1330 to 1332, Cina da Pistoia, poet and friend of Dante and Petrarch, taught civil law at the University of Naples. Boccaccio was thus able to assimilate much from this cosmopolitan milieu: the classics, French courtly and popular traditions, Byzantine narrative, and north Italian traditions of the *dolce stil nuovo* were all formative in the creation of his early compositions.

EARLY WORKS

Boccaccio's literary career began in Naples with *La caccia di Diana* (Diana's Chase) of perhaps 1333–1335. Taking his cue from a lost sirvente of Dante that listed the sixty most beautiful women of Florence, Boccaccio gallantly named and celebrated sixty chosen beauties of the Angevin court. Comprising eighteen short cantos of terza rima, the poem often echoes Dante and is heavily influenced by the courtly tradition of France and Provence. Two other major sources have been suggested: the amorous hunt sequence of the maiden Rhodopis and Euthynicus in book VIII of the second-century Greek novel, *Leucippe and Kleitophon* by Achilles Tatius of Alexandria; and the beginning of Xenophon of Ephesus' *Ephesiaca (Abrokome and Antheia)*. Boccaccio later used Achilles Tatius' episode as the major plot of the *Ninfale fiesolano.*

The plot of the *Caccia* is somewhat thin. While musing about love, the poet-narrator hears a spirit calling the fair ladies of Naples to Diana's hunt. Led by the poet's unnamed beloved, they all gather in a pleasant valley and bathe in a river. After Diana has divided them into four separate squads and, as we later learn, turned the poet into a stag, the hunt begins with the prolix and repetitive description of the action lasting several cantos. When the chase is over, the goddess invites the band to sacrifice their animals to herself and Jove and to devote themselves to perpetual chastity; but the poet's unnamed lady at last rebels. The annoyed Diana disappears. The beloved lady prays to Venus, and that deity appears as a naked damsel who changes the animals into handsome young men and restores the poet to human form. She then disappears into heaven, and the poem ends with an encomium of the poet's beloved in the *dolce stil nuovo* style.

The work is a bagatelle of little intrinsic value beyond its picture of the refined Neapolitan court, its gallant tribute to the ladies, and its witty, parodic reversal of the Circe myth, altered to show the ennobling power of earthly love.

To his second work (*ca.* 1335) Boccaccio gave the title *Filostrato,* based on a Greek etymology suggesting "one vanquished by love." Here the writer used the ottava rima of the medieval *cantari* to tell the tale of the "ill-conceived love" of Troiolo for Creseida. Creseida's father, Calcas, the Trojan soothsayer who has foreseen the destruction of the city, secretly escapes and takes refuge with the Greek enemy. Meanwhile, Troiolo, son of the Trojan King Priamo, is helplessly smitten by Calcas' widowed daughter and has ended his proud scorn of love. He is abetted throughout his tragic affair by Creseida's cousin, his beloved friend, Pandaro, who acts as go-between. The lovers enjoy a period of unalloyed pleasure. In an exchange of prisoners, however, Creseida is requested by her father; the lovers are deeply grieved but Creseida promises to return to Troiolo in ten days. On Pandaro's suggestion Troiolo thinks of fleeing with her but fails to act. Diomede, after escorting her to the Greek camp, falls in love with her and wins her. The unknowing and sorrowful Troiolo seeks consolation for her absence with Sarpidone, but to no avail. When Creseida fails to return, his life becomes unending grief. Later Troiolo recognizes Creseida's golden brooch, which Deifobo has snatched from the wounded Diomede in battle. Now aware that she has betrayed him, Troiolo sets out to avenge himself on Diomede, but Achille slays him before he can achieve his purpose. The author ends his lovers' tale with a warning to young men to bridle their amorous desires for fickle young women.

The fictionalized author himself assumes the name "Filostrato" in the proem's dedication to his lady, here designated with the name Filomena, and he sets out to relate his own sufferings "in the person of another." The statement led late-nineteenth- and early-twentiety-century followers of the critic, Vincenzo Crescini, to interpret much of the plot as pure

BOCCACCIO, GIOVANNI

autobiography, even those parts calqued on traditional commonplaces.

The subject matter of the story is taken from a subplot in Benoît de Sainte-Maure's *Roman de Troie* (*ca.* 1160), probably via its translation by Binduccio dello Scelto or, less likely, through its Latin adaptation in the *Historia troiana* (1287) by Guido delle Colonne. Boccaccio's poem provided the plot for Chaucer's *Troilus and Criseyde* and Shakespeare's *Troilus and Cressida,* among others.

The work, despite its Greek title and classical setting, is actually popular in tone, and aimed at Boccaccio's refined middle-class audience. Centering on the sufferings of the lovesick hero, it renews the theme of love-passion celebrated by Guido Cavalcanti and the young Dante.

Filocolo, the third work of Boccaccio's Neapolitan period (*ca.* 1336–1338) has been justly accused of being learned to the point of pedantry. It is a complex display of the young writer's newly acquired knowledge, much of it undigested. Boccaccio larded the work with Latinisms and archaisms and followed an elevated and difficult style, clearly intending it to be a tour de force. He dressed the plot, taken from two short French poems recounting the story of Blancheflour and Florence, with lengthy digressions.

Like the other early works, the *Filostrato,* the *Teseida,* and the *Ameto,* the *Filocolo* is a composite of various sources and influences from Ovid, Vergil, Dante, French romances and fabliaux, Italian *novellini,* and Byzantine narrative—all combined curiously, and not always successfully, with raw technical learning and exotic and romantic adventure. The introduction begins at Easter as the narrator sees Fiammetta amidst the "priestesses of Diana beneath white veils and black vestments"—a contemporary convent of nuns. She urges him to set down the "ancient" tale of Florio and Biancifiore in a little book in the vernacular. The traditional identification of "Fiammetta," the *senhal* of Boccaccio's beloved, with a supposed illegitimate daughter of King Robert, "Maria d'Aquino," has proved groundless; no record of such a person is found in the genealogical records of the families involved.

The five books of the *Filocolo* open with the contemporaneous birth of the two protagonist lovers. The Christian Quinto Lelio Africano, a noble descendant of the Roman Scipio, and his wife, Giulia Topazio of the line of Julius Caesar, make a pilgrimage to the Santiago de Compostela to give thanks for her pregnancy. Through the intervention of the devil the couple is waylaid, Lelio killed, and his wife taken to the court of the pagan king of Spain. Here both she and the queen give birth on the same day: Giulia to a daughter, Biancifiore, and the queen to a son, Florio.

Giulia dies in childbirth but the children grow up together and love each other. Felice, the king, now assuming Biancifiore to be of plebeian blood, separates the lovers, sending Florio away with his friend and mentor, Ascalion, to be educated at the court of his uncle, Ferramonte, duke of Montoro. The lovers faithfully resist the strongest attempts to arouse discord between them. In collusion with his steward, the king accuses Biancifiore falsely of lèse majesté but she is saved by a disguised Florio. The latter's friends and hosts at Montoro tempt him with two fair ladies as consolation, but his devotion remains steadfast. Finally the king and queen sell Biancifiore to Eastern merchants; his father first tells Florio that his beloved has died but the queen relents and confesses the truth when her son threatens suicide. Florio then adopts the name "Filocolo" (which according to Boccaccio's faulty Greek etymology means "love's labors") and, receiving a magic ring to protect him against the fire and water, he sets out on an odyssey to find his beloved.

These wanderings, whose narrative fills most of the fourth book and part of the fifth, cover most of Italy and the Mediterranean basin. Leaving Alfea (Pisa) by boat, he is surprised by a storm and seeks shelter in Partenope (Naples). At this point comes the most famous episode of the book, the so-called "Thirteen Questions of Love." During his long sojourn in the city, Filocolo accepts Fiammetta's invitation and takes part in an afternoon festival during which thirteen love problems are recounted to the presiding "queen," Fiammetta, for solution. Later Filocolo continues his journey, following Biancifiore to Sicily, Rhodes, and finally to Alexandria, where she is held in the Arab stronghold to be one of thirty girls doomed to form part of a ten-year tribute from the amiraglio of Alexandria to the "correggitore" of Babylonia. Over a game of chess, the castellan befriends Filocolo and decides to help him; Biancifiore's nurse arranges a night tryst. Filocolo succeeds in penetrating the tower in a basket of roses, and surprises his beloved in her chamber. The two are wedded in a pagan rite of their own devising. Two days after the consummation of their love, the amiraglio, who has also conceived a lustful passion for Biancifiore, discovers the pair asleep. When he tries to kill them Venus' power makes them invulnerable. Condemned to be burned at the stake, they are saved by Filocolo's magic ring. Through the aid of Ascalion and other friends summoned by Mars, they are freed; Filocolo then reveals that he is the amiraglio's nephew. A public wedding celebration follows.

The last book deals with the couple's return from Alexandria to Marmorina, but even this is not recounted without major digressions. After several tangential visits, they stop at Naples and go to view the ancient ruins of Pozzuoli; here Filocolo tries to shoot a deer, but his arrow hits a pine tree which, like Vergil's Polydorus in the *Aeneid* and Dante's Pier della Vigna in the *Inferno* XIII, begins to bleed and speak. In this arboreal guise the noble shepherd, Idalogo, recounts his unfortunate love story and metamorphosis, including in his account a tedious lesson on astronomy. Together with Caleon, the Neapolitan lover forsaken by Fiammetta, the pair change course again to found Certaldo, leaving Caleon as its ruler. In Rome the priest Ilario converts Filocolo and his retinue to Christianity.

After their final arrival in Marmorina, King Felice is converted to the True Faith by a dream. Filocolo and the whole company set out to complete the pilgrimage to Compostela that had been started by Biancifiore's parents. Felice is left at Cordoba, and the couple return to Rome to give long-neglected funeral rites to the bones of Lelio and Giulia, who are reunited in their tomb. In Rome they learn that Felice is dying, and Filocolo returns to Cordoba for his father's blessing. Filocolo and Biancifiore are then crowned king and queen. The priest Ilario, who attends the coronation, describes the whole adventure in the "Greek tongue" before his return to Rome.

With the *Teseida delle nozze d'Emilia* (The Theseid of the Marriage of Emilia), begun in 1339 and preserved in an autograph manuscript in the Laurentian Library in Florence, Boccaccio planned to answer Dante's challenge, pronounced in the *De vulgari eloquentia,* of restoring the classical epic and introducing it into the Italian vernacular. In imitation of the *Aeneid* and the *Thebaid,* Boccaccio planned the work in twelve books. For the rhyme scheme, however, he again took the traditional octaves of the *cantari.* In fact, the poet only barely maintained the epic tone and adventure in the first two books. Here Theseus, duke of Athens, battles the Amazons in Scythia and, on his victory, marries their queen Ippolita. Obeying a dream, he returns home with his wife and her beautiful sister, Emilia. After another war with Creonte, king of Thebes, Theseus reenters his city in triumph with many prisoners, among whom are Arcita and Palemone.

Books III to X are not epic in nature, but deal with the major plot, that of the rivalry of the two captured warriors for possession of Emilia. Seeing her in a garden from their cell window, both conceive a consuming passion for the young girl. Eventually Arcita is released from prison by Theseus on condition that he leave the kingdom; however, changing his name he returns to Athens and, unrecognized, enters Theseus' service in order to be close to his beloved. One day as he bemoans his love in a forest grove, he is overheard and recognized by a servant of Palemone. The latter escapes from prison himself, follows Arcita to the woods and challenges him to a duel. They are discovered first by Emilia, who calls for Theseus. The duke, on learning their identities, separates the warriors, who agree to settle their suit by a tournament. Arcita wins, but on Venus' intervention on behalf of Palemone, the victor is mortally wounded as he falls from his horse and eventually dies, giving Emilia to Palemone. Book XI deals with Arcita's funeral and the funeral games; book XII concerns Emilia's wavering between dedicating herself to Diana or giving herself in wedlock, and recounts her ultimate marriage to Palemone at the urging of Theseus.

The disjointed plot, especially in the last two books, shows that the writer had to stretch his material to fill the traditionally required twelve. The epic was clearly a genre alien to Boccaccio's gifts. The tone and style of the *Teseida* wavers from the pompous to the melodramatic. The most poetic sections are the amorous and elegaic interludes and the least successful are those that strive to be "epic." Boccaccio later added to the work his dedication to "Fiammetta," an introductory sonnet to each of the books, and the heavily erudite glosses in imitation of Lactantius' commentary on the *Thebaid.* Chaucer used the plot of the *Teseida* in The Knight's Tale and also imitated the vision of Arcita's soul as it mounts to heaven in *Troilus and Criseyde.*

COMPOSITIONS OF 1340–1350

Boccaccio returned to Florence probably during the winter of 1340–1341, where, at first disconsolate, he settled in to begin his Latin eclogues, the *Buccolicum carmen.* This work, which took a decade to complete (until 1350), is dedicated to Donato Albanzani and is preserved in the *Zibaldone laurenziano.* Except for the first two eclogues, and despite the allegorical form, they contain valuable historical and autobiographical information. In particular the third, "Faunus," was inspired by Louis I of Hungary's descent into Italy in 1347 to avenge the assassination of his brother Andrea, the first husband of Queen Giovanna of Naples.

The writer also completed two Italian works in swift succession. The first of these, the *Comedìa delle ninfe fiorentine* (Comedy of the Florentine Nymphs, or the *Ameto*, 1341–1342) has been traditionally termed a "little *Decameron*," and superficially it resembles the masterwork by having seven *novelle*, or short stories, recounted within a frame tale employing both prose and verse. But the comparison actually ends there, since the tales make up only a relatively small part of the total book. The cornice plot takes place during one spring afternoon: wandering in the woods between the Arno ("Sarno") and Mugnone rivers the boorish hunter Ameto comes upon a group of Venus' nymphs bathing in a stream. In a pleasant reversal of the traditional Actaeon story, the nymphs call off their dogs, which have attacked the watcher in his hiding place; Ameto then joins Lia and her six companions as they sing in the forest glade. Each nymph in turn recounts her life and love affair, ending her *novella* with a song. Through the course of their narrations, Ameto is sensually stimulated but is gradually ennobled through the power of love; finally the goddess Venus appears preceded by seven storks and seven swans; the swans, representing the seven virtues, vanquish the storks, the seven vices. On orders from the goddess the seven nymphs clear Ameto's vision. They then bathe him and adorn him in rich clothing. At last he understands the true nature of love, and, suddenly able to avoid lasciviousness, he sees the nymphs now as more attractive to his intellect than to his senses.

Boccaccio ends the work with a dedication not to a lady but to his friend, Niccolò di Bartolo del Buono, lamenting "the spines of adversity" he suffers in Florence. Boccaccio's belated attempt to inject allegory into the work is artificial and unconvincing. Although there is some suggestion that the seven nymphs themselves are to be interpreted as the seven virtues, the sensuousness and sexuality in the rest of the work overwhelm the ascetic, moralizing intention of the ending.

The *Amorosa visione* (The Amorous Vision, 1342), extant in two versions, is a vast acrostic: the poem is prefaced by three sonnets made up of the initial letters of all the *terzine* in the poem. This obviously greatly impeded the free artistic flow of poetry. From the initial sonnets we learn that the "donna gentile" to whom the poem is dedicated is, as before, "madama Maria," the "beloved flame" ("Fiammetta").

The plot again is intricate and confused. Told in the first person, it recounts a dream-vision sent to the protagonist by Amore, god of Love. Having fallen into an unusually deep sleep, he dreams that he is running by the sea and meets "a shining lady," who urges him to follow her on the path of virtue. She remains unidentified; but because of her iconographic attributes of a golden apple and purple vestments, critics have suspected that she represents the celestial Venus. The two arrive at a "nobile castello" where there are two doors, one straight and narrow, leading upward to virtue, and the other, wide and luminous, from which issue the sounds of festivities. Urged by two youths (similarly unidentified) who appear from within, the dreamer rebels and insists on entering the wide door on the left and is, surprisingly, followed by his guide.

Within they find a great hall decorated with allegorical frescoes equal, we are told, only to the genius of Giotto. The ecphrasis of these depictions of earthly delights and pursuits occupies most of the work from canto IV to canto XXX; one after another are described the triumphs of Learning, Glory, Wealth and, especially, of Love. Boccaccio gives little adornment to the monotonous lists of the famous who figure in the processions, a concatenation of names from the Bible, literature, myth, and history. Cantos XXXI–XXXVI contrast with the first in showing the caducity and wretchedness of human joys in the triumph of destructive Fortune.

Once more, in canto XXXVII, the guide urges the dreamer to enter the narrow gate, but again he turns left into a garden of delight dominated by a beautiful red marble fountain of love (the fountain-theme repeated in *Decameron,* III). Here the dreamer meets among other ladies his beloved, who, he explains, is of the family of St. Thomas Aquinas and whose first name is that of the Blessed Virgin. Eventually he finds himself alone with her in a secret part of the garden and, forgetting her saintly associations, is about to possess her sleeping person when he suddenly awakens and the lady disappears. In a waggish reversal of dream-vision logic, however, the guide bewilderingly reappears, defying her oneiric origin; she again urges the narrator to follow her (this time, back to his beloved!) and to sing of what he has seen in his dream.

The controversy surrounding identification of the characters and the plot's inconsistencies have given rise to varying interpretations. Some scholars see the work as subversively hedonistic, a playful allegory of a soul refusing redemption, while others view it as a semiserious depiction of the foolishness of earthly indulgence. The work, at all events, is also an erudite *ludus* in which the author inverts the outcomes of almost every tradition of which he makes use.

Written between 1343 and 1345, the *Elegia di Madonna Fiammetta* reverses to a certain extent the plot of the early *Filostrato.* This time Boccaccio does not set his tale in exotic lands or in mythical times but instead chooses contemporary Naples: "You will not find adorned lies, Trojan battles gory with blood," his narrator-heroine tells us. She dedicates the confession of her adultery to the "noble ladies" and seeks their compassion. Fiammetta, a medieval rival to Dido, is abandoned by her paramour Panfilo after a brief period of love. Returning to Florence on the pretext of caring for his aged father, Panfilo promises to rejoin her within a few months but is never seen again.

When he does not return, she self-indulgently pines and languishes; no doctor, not even the gay resort of Baia (where her abused and tender husband sends her) can cure her overwhelming sadness. When she hears from a servant that Panfilo has fallen passionately in love with another lady, her laments echo Ariadne, Medea, and Oenone in Ovid's *Heroides* and the rhetoric of Seneca's *Hercules furens.* She calls down the revenge of the gods and hell's demons upon her unknown rival. She attempts suicide by jumping from her house but is saved by her confidante, a wise old nurse, and several maidservants; in response she shreds their clothing, scratches their faces, and rips their hair out by the roots. Finally, after a report of Panfilo's return proves to be a case of mistaken identity, she returns, inconsolable, to her weeping. Her literary cousin, the Florentine widow of Boccaccio's later *Corbaccio,* will repeat her sins, often almost verbatim.

Without doubt, the *Elegia* is the most successful work before the *Decameron,* and it has justifiably been considered to be a precursor of the modern psychological novel. Although the work indeed succeeds as a prototype for this genre, the technique and intent of the writer were clearly quite different. Again Boccaccio gives surprising twists to the traditional elements he employs: in particular Fiammetta herself repeats the various shopworn antifeminist charges of women's lies, fraud, and vanity—tiresomely repeated by theological moralists—as if they were her normal attributes, praiseworthy habits, or extraordinary achievements. Clearly the moral significance of the work is to show the foolishness of the self-inflicted wounds of love, although that message is precariously balanced by the sympathy that the heroine elicits. Boccaccio stresses the absurd sinfulness of her passion in her frequent worship of and idolatrous sacrifice to the ancient pagan gods and in her prayer to Christ, where she begs Him to act as go-between to restore her lover. Such analysis and depiction of sado-masochistic love falls directly within the tradition encountered in many poems of Guido Cavalcanti and in Dante's *Rime petrose.*

During roughly 1344–1346, Boccaccio wrote the etiological fable in octaves entitled the *Ninfale fiesolano* (The Nymphs of Fiesole). The work, again based on Achilles Tatius' *Leucippe and Kleitophon,* XIII.12, is set in the mythical Golden Age and recounts the fictional histories of two Florentine rivulets, the Africo and the Mensola, in a tale of the adolescent love of a shepherd (Africo) for a nymph (Mensola). After he meets her one day among other nymphs of Diana, sworn to perpetual chastity, Africo suffers a deep passion for her and, ignoring his father's warnings, searches for his beloved night and day. When he finds her, she rejects him; and he sadly seeks solace in his mother's tender caresses. Eventually Venus gives aid, counseling him to disguise himself in female attire. Stealing his mother's dress, he goes hunting with the nymphs, gains Mensola's admiration, and finally deflowers her. From their union, recounted in comical sexual metaphors later to be the hallmark of such episodes in the *Decameron,* is born a son, Pruneo.

When Mensola, regretting her seduction and grieving in her shame, refuses ever to see him again, the young and impetuous Africo commits suicide beside the Florentine stream to which he leaves his name. Mensola, in dread of Diana's wrath, confides her son to the care of the aged nymph Sinidecchia, but does not escape the goddess' revenge. When she tries to cross a brook she is metamorphosed into its waters.

The founding of Fiesole takes place in an artificial coda. Attalante passes through the region and, forcing Diana's nymphs to become wives for his men, builds the city. Meanwhile Pruneo, who, brought up by his grandparents, has grown into a valorous youth, progresses from cupbearer, to counselor, to the position of Attalante's seneschal. On the various deaths of these characters, the Romans arrive to found Florence.

Despite the absurd, disjointed quality of the plot as it hobbles to its end, the work is significant in Boccaccio's development in several ways. First, the charming description of the love affair shows great growth in his poetical power; he captures realistically and economically the psychology of his protagonists: the devotion of Africo's parents moves the reader as does the delicacy of Sinidecchia's understanding for Mensola's plight. Last, by avoiding the pomposity of language and the exaggerated number of literary allusions that weigh down even the accomplished *Elegia,* Boccaccio arrives at a simpler, more direct vernacular prose style, which later reached its fulfillment in the Hundred Tales.

THE GENEALOGY OF THE PAGAN GODS

Sometime between 1340 and 1350 Boccaccio started collecting information for his Latin encyclopedia *De genealogia deorum gentilium* (The Genealogy of the Pagan Gods), which he completed in a first draft probably about 1360; throughout his life, as new manuscripts and material came into his possession, he corrected and added to it. Especially important was the knowledge he obtained about the *Odyssey* and the *Iliad* from Leonzio Pilato in 1360–1362, knowledge that enabled him to include some fifty quotations in Greek. The *Genealogia* is an immense encyclopedia, gathering into one place the scattered references to the gods in the classics and in the moralizing mythologies of the Middle Ages. Partially because of its vast scope, comprising fifteen long books, and because of its convenience, it was translated into every major European language and remained a classic reference work for about four centuries. Today it is still useful as a reflection of fourteenth-century knowledge and interpretation of classical mythology, and it is indispensable for an understanding of not only the writer's own works but also those of his near contemporaries.

Boccaccio's interpretation allows that the gods were often merely personified astrological influences and that some were the unrecognized agents of God, such as demons administering justice or angels dispensing mercy. In general, though, he continues the long tradition of Christian euhemerism, which explained away the gentile gods as falsely deified heroes and rulers. Boccaccio insists, however, that mythology can prefigure or reflect tenets of the Christian religion. The concluding two books, XIV and XV, constitute the most frequently read selections today: they defend the liberal arts and especially poetry in an amalgam of arguments taken from different poetic treatises written throughout the centuries; Boccaccio includes ideas from such writers as Horace, Suetonius, Varro, St. Gregory of Tours, Isidore of Seville, Macrobius, Lactantius, St. Jerome, St. Augustine, and Petrarch. He champions the pursuit of (specifically pagan) literature by claiming that myth and poetry, which for him are one, teach great eternal truths: as the reader penetrates the superficial veil of fiction, the author's true meaning is revealed. Although unoriginal and conventional, it amply illustrates Boccaccio's rhetorical eloquence and shows how responsible and lofty he considered his calling as *poeta.*

Boccaccio dedicated the work to Hugo IV of Lusignan, king of Cyprus and Jerusalem, and indeed (if we can believe his preface), he may have begun the work at Hugo's suggestion. Most probably Boccaccio was trying to curry favor with the king in order to gain a position at court and escape the penury that he and his brother Jacopo then suffered; but his hopes were dashed in 1359 when the king died. Perplexingly, the writer makes no reference to this event in the work and, in the book's conclusion, he continues to address Hugo as if he were still alive.

THE DECAMERON

Boccaccio probably began the *Decameron* about 1350, with perhaps his most intense effort coming between 1351 and 1353. The title itself is another of Boccaccio's attempts at Greek etymology: it is formed of two words meaning "ten" and "day." In the proem the author dedicated the work to the ladies of the time who did not have the diversions open to men—those of falconry, hunting, fishing, riding, and business—and who were forced to conceal the flame of amorous passion as they stayed idly enclosed in their rooms. The book is subtitled *Prencipe Galeotto,* that is, Galehaut, the go-between of Lancelot and Guinevere, a waggish nod, in particular, to Dante's allusion to "Galeotto" in *Inferno* V, blamed for the arousal of carnal lust in the episode of Paolo and Francesca.

Boccaccio's hundred tales are set in a most elaborate frame story. During the height of the Black Death that ravaged Florence in 1348, seven young ladies meet in the church of Santa Maria Novella and decide to remove themselves from the infection of Florence in the company of three young men. Boccaccio documents the structural breakdown of all so-

BOCCACCIO, GIOVANNI

cial, civil, and religious institutions and laws in the city as a background to the ideal, earthly society that his protagonists create during their two-week sojourn in two successive villas and gardens in the countryside of Florence. Their storytelling takes place in three locations, each more remote and more ideal than the last: first and second the gardens of the two villas and, in day VII, "the Valley of the Ladies," a circular garden of perfect delight.

Despite the ribaldry of some of the tales, the ten characters conduct themselves with impeccable decorum: Fridays and Saturdays are reserved for fasting and bathing, while the other ten days are given over to the various amusements of walking, singing, dancing, eating, and especially storytelling. Each evening the *brigata* or company selects one member as "king" or "queen" of the next day's festivities; the ruler chooses the topic of the tales to be told. Each member in turn recounts one story; and, when the ten recitations are completed, the day concludes with dancing and the performance of a ballata. The structure of the framework brings to fruition the form that Boccaccio had earlier essayed in the "Thirteen Questions of Love" episode of the *Filocolo* and again in the *Ameto.*

The strategy of the cornice, or framework, for the stories serves to give a sense of the exceptional, a sense of moral and physical "time out" or simply of a vacation from the regular course of events; the fictional sojourn—and, thus, the book that describes it—is a legitimate festival (akin to the ecclesiastical period, perhaps, of carnival time, after the rigors of winter and before the solemnity of Lent). As the *brigata* arrives in the countryside, the members lose their sense of social and spiritual urgency and begin to enjoy their sojourn as an escape from destruction and responsibility. Their stories are thus an escapist distraction and consolation both for themselves and for the reader. As the temporary world of the *brigata* is separated from the destructive, vulgar society of the pestilence, so the retold tales also form a world apart from their own, an enclosed, nearly perfect, yet, ultimately, finite creation. By decree the "queen," Pampinea, banishes from the festivities any base, bad report or tragedy that might detract from their pleasure. Yet in the introduction to day VI, vulgarity does impinge as the servants engage in a comic spat over the virginity of new Florentine brides; the theme of day IV, "those whose love has an unhappy ending," upsets the company forced to deal with the tragedy of love.

Indeed in the hundred narratives the theme of love preponderates, appearing in all its metamorphoses, from the brutally erotic (as in the second half of the Cimone story, V.1, which inverts the "ennobling-power-of-love" theme, and in the sado-masochistic tale of the scholar and the widow, VIII.7) to the morbidly tragic (the story of the eaten heart, IV.9); from the stoic and noble (the Ghismonda-Guiscardo-Tancredi tale, IV.1) to the frankly erotic (Masetto, the gardener of III.1, the tale of the tub, VII.2, and, especially, Alibech III.10). But love is not the only theme. Other topics—wit and witticism, practical jokes, worldly initiation (Andreuccio da Perugia, II.5)—also form part of Boccaccio's varied mosaic.

Throughout, as Branca noted, the mercantile ethic prevails, with the commercial values of quick wit, astuteness, and *savoir-vivre* being treasured while the vices of stupidity or inarticulate dullness are cured or punished. The *Decameron* concerns only the immanent. Theological doctrines are not contradicted; they are merely left aside since their seriousness would necessarily banish the freedom from care in which the *brigata* temporarily tries to rest. Thus, Boccaccio does not present the canonization of Ser Ciappelletto (I.1) as morally shocking but as a neat and natural outcome of his dilemma and lying confession. His outrageous, yet comic, performance saves his money-lending hosts by permitting them to dispose of his corpse in a way which will not incite the Burgundians' hatred to a pogrom of usurious "Lombards." God's ways are unfathomable, we are assured; perhaps Ciappelletto did repent in his dying breath, but his astuteness has avoided a real secular danger.

Boccaccio seldom, if ever, invents the stories he retells; in fact, the members of the *brigata* themselves indicate that they have already heard some of the tales. The sources include writings from Spain, France, Provence, Byzantium, the Near East, as well as native Italian chronicles and histories. Most, though not all the tales, are set in the period immediately preceding the author's own generation; tales V.1 and X.8, occurring in classical settings, are major exceptions. Many of the characters in the work really existed, and they include not only such well-known contemporaries as Giotto and Guido Cavalcanti, but also some who might seem most unlikely, such as the criminals from the Andreuccio tale and the tricksters in Frate Cipolla's dilemma (VI.10).

Despite the many calques and borrowings (Branca has shown that even the description of the plague, which Boccaccio witnessed personally, is based on the *Historia gentis Langobardorum* of Paul the Deacon), the *Decameron* displays a perfection of unity and unfailing appropriateness of style; it is perhaps no accident that Madonna Oretta's censure of a knight's inarticulate narration (VI.1) holds a near-central position in the structure. In this, his masterwork, the writer at last avoided the awkwardness and exaggerated rhetoric that mar many of his earlier pieces. Here he achieves a new Italian prose based on the Latin cursus forms. Measured to the canons of *ars dictaminis,* his sentences, which often include internal rhyme, form poetic units in prose as firm as the metrical units of poetry. The *Decameron* was to be used, and often abused, as the model of Italian narrative until the nineteenth century.

Perhaps the unity of the *Decameron* consists not only in the frame story and in the style, but also in the philosophical outlook the work implies. Although in the *Genealogia* XIV Boccaccio described the tradition of medieval poetics, which held that poetry was a veil of exquisite fiction, concealing from the dull-witted, but revealing to the wise, an inner kernel of truth, the writer was to subvert the process. Boccaccio had been nourished by the technique of Dante, who used the various levels of meaning in his *Commedia* to involve his reader's mind, engaging him in a process of intellection and free will so that he might grasp the congruence between the sense of the literal veil and the teaching of the hidden allegory. In the *Decameron,* however, Boccaccio was to demonstrate that, for him, Dante's way of allegory was artistically incompatible.

Boccaccio's stories, in fact, often take up a Dantean model only to satirize or reverse the didactic process. Alibech enters the Egyptian desert, not to be slowly tested and purified like Christ, St. Anthony, Mary Magdalen, and Dante in the *Commedia,* but to succumb forthwith to bawdy sensuality (Cassell). Ser Ciappelletto is, like Dante's Ser Brunetto Latini, a sodomitic notary employed in France. But where Latini is damned in hell, Ciappelletto (also slyly teaching "how man becomes eternal"; compare *Inferno* XV.85) receives the highest reward heaven and earth can bestow—sainthood (Hollander). Cimone's indulgence in piracy, rape, pillage, and murder after his enamorment parodies the whole tradition of Dante and the *dolce stil nuovo* school, which celebrates the cathartic and edifying power of earthly love (Marcus). Gualtieri's savage trial of his patient, but rather inane, Griselda reflects God's testing of Job and Abraham and echoes the grief of the Blessed Virgin suffering her Child to be killed. Yet Griselda is cowlike in her meekness, and the narrator of the *brigata* stigmatizes Gualtieri's whimsical arrogance as mere "mad, brute foolishness." In Boccaccio's art allegory becomes, incongruously, a major source of comedy.

The healthy and subversive intellectual games of the *Decameron* seem to have been too advanced for some contemporary men of letters. Boccaccio's friend Petrarch translated and adapted "Griselda" into Latin, entitling it *De obedientia* where, with an oddly literal mind, he exalted the marquis Gualtieri, and made his abused spouse the very ideal of the obedient Christian wife. Chaucer used Petrarch's reactionary version in The Clerk's Tale, and scribes substituted it for Boccaccio's original version in many copies of Laurent de Premierfait's French version of the *Decameron;* moralists also used Petrarch's version in dozens of didactic works on the "mirror of marriage" theme. Notably it was not, in the main, the intellectuals, scriptoria, and learned libraries that disseminated Boccaccio's work, but the Italian merchants who made for themselves the early copies and carried them to the world's main trading centers.

LATER WORKS

The Italian prose *Corbaccio* (The Evil Crow) of 1355 (the work is internally dated and its diatribes against feminine finery correspond in tone with the strict Florentine antifeminist sumptuary laws of 1355 and 1356) is the last work of fiction that Boccaccio wrote in Italian. In form it is another parody on the conventional dream-vision. An aging man of letters, who has been rejected and mocked by a certain widow, first seeks solace from his friends, then retires to the solitude of his room, where he falls asleep. In a dream he finds himself walking along a pleasant path adorned with trees and flowers; but as he progresses, rocks, nettles, and thorn bushes block his way and the howls of wild animals threaten him. Suddenly a spirit appears, garbed in flames: it is the shade of the widow's husband sent from Purgatory to instruct the dreamer about love and women and, in particular, to inform him about the wickedness of the woman who has victimized them both. In rollicking detail the spirit tells of the corrupt and conceited habits of his widow and revels in the outrageous description of her aging body. He orders the dreamer to hate what he has loved and to take revenge on the woman by exposing her in writing. The dreamer awakes bathed in sweat and swears to carry out this literary revenge "if the Giver of all Grace grants it."

The ribaldry of the story (like that of the tale of Alibech, *Decameron* III.10) offended the modesty of earlier generations, but the spirit of dark comedy makes the work more acceptable to modern tastes. It is heavily calqued on Dante's *Commedia,* although the imitations and quotations are used mostly for parody. In intention it is a negative answer to Dante's *Vita nuova,* for where Dante had promised to say of Beatrice "that which had never been said of any woman," the dreamer promises to slander the widow with the detractions with which men have always vilified every woman. Indeed, the work is a collection of every known antifeminist denigration. (Boccaccio had started such a collection in his *Zibaldone laurenziano* in 1350.)

Despite all the instruction the dreamer has received, he awakes still enmeshed in his self-inflicted distress, and the reader is left in some doubt about the work's moral intent: although even Ovid and Christian sources agreed that lovers should separate in peace and not hatred, Boccaccio's lover is counseled, supposedly by divine intercession, to pursue hate and revenge as his remedy. Such an outcome reverses the cleansing effect of vision literature and the salubrious lessons of classical *remedia amoris.* Boccaccio once more indulges his penchant, displayed constantly in his Italian works, for giving surprise antiallegorical reversals to traditional forms.

Boccaccio began the nine books of the Latin *De casibus virorum illustrium* (On the Fates of Illustrious Men) probably in 1355 and completed it in its original form in 1360; in 1373 he expanded it, revised it stylistically, and dedicated it, at last, to his friend Mainardo Cavalcanti. Boccaccio's stated purpose is to put his efforts and studies to didactic use by retelling the unfortunate ends of famous people. He tries to show the vanity and caducity of earthly things by showing the unhappy fate of those men and women foolish enough to rise up in pride only to fall into the abjectness that God's justice provides for them, through the agency of Fortune. Boccaccio selects his myriad exempla from the entire gamut of history. Many of the tales Boccaccio chose judiciously from the *Gesta* of Fra Paolino da Venezia (*d.* 1344), which he had copied into his notebook, the *Zibaldone magliabechiano.*

In the *De casibus* Boccaccio successfully reworks the vision-procession form, which he had attempted earlier in the *Amorosa visione.* Here, as he muses in his study, the shades of ancient heroes, rulers, and leaders parade before him and engage in a dialogue as they insist on being included in his work. As promised in the proem, he varies the long list of tales of misfortune with various admonitions against vice and useful persuasions to virtue (these chapters are on such topics as the "Encomium of Paternal Love" and the "Praise of Patience"). The ending demonstrates the moralizing tone of the whole: Boccaccio warns his readers that whenever Fortune seems to promise stability she merely plots to deceive those who would put their hopes in her; he exhorts mankind to hold God in reverence, to follow wisdom, and to keep to virtue, honor, and benevolence. Man should seek honor, praise, glory, and fame with humanity and justice, so that he may seem worthy of such gifts and so that, should he fall, others will know that it was not through his personal fault but through the fault of Fortune, who turns all according to her will. The work had vast influence: Chaucer used it extensively, especially in The Monk's Tale (itself subtitled "De casibus virorum illustrium"), and John Lydgate made an English paraphrase of Laurent de Premierfait's French translation.

Boccaccio first put his hand to composing the vast *De montibus, silvis, fontibus, lacubus, fluminibus, stagnis seu paludibus et de nominibus maris* (On Mountains, Forests, Springs, Lakes, Rivers, Marshes, or Swamps and on the Names of Seas) at about the time he was writing the vernacular *Corbaccio,* the Latin *De casibus,* and the *Genealogia;* with the latter work in particular the *De montibus* shares much material. The work is again aimed at teaching and utility, an encyclopedia of geography intended to help scholars understand references in classical and contemporary literature. Boccaccio divided the various geographical features into separate categories, giving an alphabetical listing for each. Much credit for the work's genesis goes to Petrarch, who lent his friend the manuscripts of Pliny and other classical geographers for intensive study. Although the work was heavily used and enjoyed much esteem, it seems never to have been translated into English, and has been neglected by modern publishers.

Another example of the productive tie between Petrarch and Boccaccio are the 104 chapters of *De mulieribus claris* (On Famous Women); Boccaccio's volume complements Petrarch's *De viris illustribus* (On Famous Men) by celebrating the virtues and censuring the vices of women. Roughly chronological in order, it covers all history from Eve to contemporaries such as Queen Giovanna of Naples. This last chapter and the initial dedication to Niccolò Acciaiuoli's sister, Andrea, were added in 1362, when Boccaccio, then recently invited to Naples, still cherished the hope of gaining patronage. Boccaccio most likely composed the first version in the summer of 1361, after having the opportunity of reading some of Leonzio Pilato's Latin translation of Homer. This is especially clear in such chapters as those on Clytemnestra, Helen, and Penelope. Boccaccio revised the work several times and continued to rework and amplify it until about a year before his death.

The *De mulieribus* is not precisely historical since it contains, for example, some thirty-eight chapters on women from myth and fiction and includes such fabulous biographies as that of Pope Joan. In tone it is more moralizing even than the *De casibus*, and is much closer in purpose to medieval collections of moral exempla; it surpasses most of these, however, in possessing the organic unity of a treatise rather than being simply a listing of items. Going beyond the usual Christian tradition of celebrating only martyrdom, virginity, and sanctity, the work also celebrates examples of feminine heroism and magnificence. Chaucer translated the whole chapter on Zenobia into the *Canterbury Tales* (The Monk's Tale), and Henry Parker dedicated a complete English version to Henry VIII. Translations and adaptations were also made into German, Spanish, and French.

LATER LIFE

When in 1340–1341 Boccaccio returned to his father's house in Florence after a thirteen-year absence, the city seemed bleak compared with the glamour of the Neapolitan capital. To shake off his gloom Boccaccio devoted himself more than ever to humanistic studies and to writing. Besides composing original works, he indulged his insatiable appetite for reading and copied many important texts both for himself and for his friends (especially, later, for Petrarch); many are preserved in his two notebooks, now called the *Zibaldone laurenziano* and the *Zibaldone magliabechiano.*

The decade after 1341 was one of misfortune. When after 1339 King Edward III of England repudiated his vast debts to the Florentine banking firms of the Bardi and Peruzzi, they collapsed within six years. Boccaccino suffered bankruptcy with them in 1345, leaving his son to live the rest of his life in straitened circumstances. Boccaccio's second stepmother, Bice de' Bosticchi, died during the plague year of 1348 and his father in 1349, burdening the writer with the upbringing of his half-brother Jacopo.

Meanwhile the writer sought unsuccessfully for patronage. In 1346 he went to Ravenna as guest of Ostasio da Polenta, for whom he translated the *Decades* of Titus Livy. In 1347 he accepted an invitation to visit Forlì from its ruler Francesco Ordelaffi, whom Boccaccio was to allegorize as "Faunus," the title character in the third eclogue of the *Buccolicum carmen.* A decade later, Florentine factionalism also troubled the writer. During early 1358, strife arose in the sole ruling Guelph party over the issue of admonishment, an act which proscribed suspected Ghibellines and excluded them from public office by declaring them magnates. In fact, the Guelph hierarchy used the law to bar their rivals and enemies from public life; various powerful magnate families and some nouveaux-riches, victimized by the law, formed a conspiracy, which the republic severely crushed in late 1360.

Boccaccio's letter, the *Epistola consolatoria a messer Pino de' Rossi* (*ca.* 1361–1362), sent from his Certaldo retreat, shows both his bitterness against the ruling newcomers in Florence and his anxiety for Rossi and his friend's fellow exiles. Among others known to Boccaccio, two conspirators, Niccolò di Bartolo Del Buono (to whom Boccaccio dedicated his *Comedìa*) and Domenico Bandini lost their heads on 30 December 1360. During Boccaccio's retirement to Valdelsa, he received many important visitors, such as Coluccio Salutati and the Villanis, in the surroundings of his ancestral home. Frequent trips to Florence punctuated his sojourn, enabling him to supervise the work of his protégé, Leonzio Pilato, whom Petrarch had commissioned in 1359 to translate the first five books of the *Iliad.* Boccaccio obtained for Leonzio an appointment to the first Western chair of Greek at the Studium (University) of Florence; their collaboration marks the first serious intellectual interest in Greek in the Renaissance.

Significant for the study of Boccaccio's works and for the history of nascent civic humanism is the poet's involvement in Florentine affairs. Through his literary success, he enjoyed great respect and esteem in the governing circles of Florence, and except for the troubled period between 1360 and 1365, he filled many civic offices. These ranged from delicate missions of negotiation to the papacy and other foreign powers, to relatively minor administrative duties. Perhaps the most touching of these minor tasks took place during his embassy to the lords of Romagna in 1350: the captains of Orsanmichele entrusted him

BOCCACCIO, GIOVANNI

with ten gold florins to be given to Dante's daughter, "Suora Beatrice," who had become a nun in a convent near Ravenna.

Most important for the artistic development of Boccaccio and Petrarch had been their meeting in the autumn of 1350, when Petrarch was fêted by his admirers as he passed through Florence on his way to the Jubilee in Rome. Their friendship and reciprocal influence lasted until Petrarch's death in 1374. In the year following their first encounter, the priors of the commune and the gonfaloniere di giustizia chose Boccaccio to go to Padua to offer Petrarch the restitution of his family property, which had been confiscated from his father, Ser Petracco, in October 1302. The city's offer was contingent on Petrarch's acceptance of a chair in the Florentine studium, but Petrarch refused. The episode, however, had no effect on the friendship between the two humanists. Boccaccio's admiration for the man he called his *preceptor inclitus* (glorious teacher) approached adulation; on reading some of the elder poet's *rime,* he burned his own early poetic compositions. Petrarch's coronation as poet laureate on the Capitoline in 1341 prompted Boccaccio's tribute in the *De vita et moribus domini Francisci Petracchi.* Wherever Boccaccio lived or stayed, whether in Naples, Florence, or Ravenna, he frequented scholars with similar interests and shared their reading of the "master's" works. Boccaccio did not, however, hesitate to reprove his friend indignantly for accepting a position in June 1353 at the court of the Milanese archbishop, Giovanni Visconti, then Florence's bitterest enemy.

In 1362, Ciani, a messenger from a certain Carthusian monk, Pietro Petroni, brought the latter's deathbed warning that both Petrarch and Boccaccio would be damned in hell if they did not renounce their profane literary pursuits. The warning had little effect on Petrarch, but it touched Boccaccio to the quick. Always a man of great sensitivity and sudden emotions, Boccaccio apparently decided to give up all worldly pursuits, including his studies, and offered to sell Petrarch his library. Boccaccio's initial letter has not survived, but the soothing reply from Petrarch has been preserved (*Seniles* I.5); Petrarch's consolation of his friend demonstrates their familiarity. Gently he entices Boccaccio to continue his writing and studies, and ends his letter, as he was to many times, by inviting his friend to share his home.

In his later years, Boccaccio combined the *studium alma poesis* with a stricter religious and moral ethic; his later works, such as the Italian *Trattatello in laude di Dante* and his Latin works, particularly the revisions of the *De casibus,* the *De mulieribus,* and the *Genealogia* demonstrate his efforts at didacticism and moralizing. A papal dispensation of 2 November 1360, *super defectu natalium,* which legitimized the writer and described him as *clerico florentino,* suggests that he took minor orders in later life; and his will, which leaves a breviary, maniple stole, chasuble, and various relics, has aroused speculation that Boccaccio might even have become a priest. Despite his susceptibility to great fears and intermittent religious asceticism, his overpowering literary interest in the legitimate, immanent concerns of human love, marriage, and parenting, and his devotion to humanistic studies persisted throughout his life.

In the same inauspicious year of 1362, Boccaccio made an unhappy return to Naples with his half-brother and ward, Jacopo, then nineteen years old. Although Boccaccio had many reasons to dislike his now vain and pompous childhood friend, Niccolò Acciaiuoli—perhaps because of some jealousy of Niccolò's amazing success; or because the grand seneschal to Queen Giovanna of Naples had passed over Boccaccio and appointed another old friend, Zanobi da Strada, as court poet; or simply because Niccolò's habit of abusive epithet had offended him (Acciaiuoli will forever be remembered for having labeled Boccaccio *Johannes tranquillitatum*)—the writer nevertheless accepted Acciaiuoli's invitation to come to the court as a way out of his straitened circumstances.

Niccolò, however, offered his hospitality at a price: apparently, he wanted Boccaccio to write a eulogy of his social career. The consequences of the author's refusal are eloquently described in Boccaccio's letter to Francesco Nelli (1362): the writer was treated shamefully, forced to dwell with the servants; conditions became so bad that Boccaccio took refuge in the house of another Florentine, Mainardo Cavalcanti. However, when Acciaiuoli invited Boccaccio to rejoin his household at his villa in Tripergoli near the resort of Baia (so often celebrated in Boccaccio's early works), the writer accepted—only to be again consigned to a "sink" to live in, with a bed "neither wide enough nor long enough for a dog." The grand seneschal then returned abruptly to Naples, leaving Boccaccio and his servant without food or aid and encumbered by the large library that Boccaccio had brought with him in the belief that his transfer to the south was to be permanent. The poet fled this unmerited neglect, and after visiting Petrarch in Venice, he retired to Certaldo, where he

BOCCACCIO, GIOVANNI

remained in fairly continuous residence except for brief excursions, such as that to Avignon in 1365.

Adding insult to injury, Niccolò's secretary, Francesco Nelli, wrote to Boccaccio censuring his sudden departure and stigmatizing him as "thin-skinned" *(un uomo di vetro)* and "rash" *(sùbito)*. Unfortunately, the writer's vitriolic Latin reply has come down to us only in an Italian translation, but we can immediately recognize in it the author of the *Decameron* and the *Corbaccio.* Boccaccio revels in bawdy narrative: the mighty grand seneschal evacuates his bowels while holding court, selecting officials, writing to emperors and popes, all the while surrounded by a retinue of adulating women, "truly not whores, since that would seem indecent—yet not sisters, nor cousins, nor nieces."

Elsewhere in his correspondence Boccaccio's gentler, more tender side can be glimpsed. In a touching letter to Petrarch, we learn that in 1367 he went to Venice seeking Petrarch only to find that his friend had left for Pavia. Boccaccio was placed in the embarrassing situation of being entertained by Petrarch's daughter Francesca without the presence of her husband or father to protect her reputation. He confesses that on seeing Petrarch's grandchild, Eletta, he felt he was beholding one of his own (five illegitimate) children, his little Violante, who had died when she was a mere five years old.

Humiliations occurred again for Boccaccio when he made another return to Naples in the autumn of 1370. (Niccolò Acciaiuoli was now dead and buried in his sumptuous tomb in the Certosa near Florence.) From Boccaccio's calm letter of 20 January 1371 sent from Naples to an old friend, Niccolò da Montefalcone, abbot of Santo Stefano in Calabria, we learn that Boccaccio had arrived on the worthy abbot's invitation only to find that the latter had left for some southern destination, taking with him a copy of Tacitus which Boccaccio had lent him. This time Boccaccio consoled himself most pleasantly in Naples with other friends until the spring of 1371.

Boccaccio returned to the Arno city knowing that he was considered the leading scholar of Florentine humanism. He now lived surrounded by gifted disciples, such as Coluccio Salutati and Benvenuto da Imola, and found religious solace in the circle of the Augustinians from the church of Santo Spirito, to whom he willed his library. Offers of patronage and protection abounded for the writer as he approached the end of his life; yet now experienced, settled, and perhaps mistrusting, he declined them all. He returned to Certaldo early in 1371, refusing invitations not only from Petrarch, but from Ugo da San Severino (who made offers both on his own behalf, and on that of Giovanna of Naples), from Giacomo di Maiorca, the queen's third consort, and from the powerful Niccolò Orsini, count Palatine and count of Nola. Boccaccio devoted himself peacefully to poetry and, in 1370, to the revision of his masterpiece, the *Decameron,* extant only in this autograph, now the Hamiltonian MS 90, in West Berlin. A later letter of 1373, in which he jokingly cautions the ladies of Mainardo Cavalcanti's household against reading the hundred tales, shows the confident modesty of one aware that his masterpiece is the reading choice of a vast middle-class public.

On 25 August 1373, the Signoria of Florence commissioned Boccaccio to comment publicly on "el Dante" for a fee of one hundred florins. He began his lectures from the steps of the Church of Santo Stefano di Badia on 23 October (according to Monaldi's *Diario,* two weeks after the contractual October 8) and continued every day, except for feast days. After some sixty brave lectures (published as the *Esposizioni sopra la Comedìa di Dante,* and including commentaries from *Inferno* I to *Inferno* XXVII), ill health forced Boccaccio to abandon his task and return to Certaldo in January of 1374. His letters refer to his various ailments, gout and scabies, both exacerbated by obesity. Early the next year, news of Petrarch's death (19 October 1374) reached him after a three-month delay. His friend had willed him a costly fur coat to warm him as he studied during winter evenings. Boccaccio's letter of condolence to Francescuolo da Brossano, Petrarch's son-in-law, expresses deep regret at his own infirmity and a touching desire to visit Arquà, where his friend had died.

On 21 December 1375 Giovanni Boccaccio himself died in Certaldo, leaving behind a literary legacy that won him a place among the "three crowns of Florence," equal to the poets he had loved and admired the most, Dante and Petrarch.

BIBLIOGRAPHY

Modern editions. Il Decameron, Charles S. Singleton, ed., 2 vols. (1955); *Decameron: Edizione critica secondo l'autografo hamiltoniano,* Vittore Branca, ed. (1976); *Decameron: Edizione diplomatico-interpretiva dell'autografo Hamilton 90,* Charles S. Singleton, ed. (1974); *Tutte le opere di Giovanni Boccaccio,* Vittore Branca *et al.,* eds., 12 vols. to date (1964–), with a valuable biographical profile in vol. I.

English translations. [*De casibus virorum illustrium*]: *The Fates of Illustrious Men,* Louis Brewer Hall, trans. (1965). [*Il Corbaccio*]: *The Corbaccio,* Anthony K. Cassell, ed. and trans. (1975). [*Il Decameron*]: *The Decameron,* George Henry McWilliam, trans. (1972); *The Decameron,* James M. Rigg, trans., 2 vols. (1930, repr. 1955). [*Eclogue XIV*]: *Boccaccio's Olympia,* Israel Gollancz, ed. and trans. (1913); repr. in *Pearl: An English Poem of the XIVth Century* (1921). [*L'Elegia di Madonna Fiammetta*]: *Amorous Fiammetta,* Edward Hutton, ed. (1931, repr. 1970), a republishing of Bartholomew Young's 1587 translation. [*Il Filocolo*]: *The Most Pleasant and Delectable Questions of Love,* Henry Grantham, trans., Thomas Bell, ed., illustr. by Alexander King (1931, repr. 1950); *Thirteene most pleasaunt and delectable questions, entituled, A disport of diverse noble personages . . . in his booke named "Philocopo"* (1927), a reprint of Henry Grantham's translation (1567) of the "Questions of Love" from *Filocolo.* [*Il Filostrato*]: *The Filostrato of Giovanni Boccaccio,* trans. with parallel text by Nathaniel Edward Griffin and Arthur Beckwith Myrick (1929, repr. 1967); *The Story of Troilus,* Robert Kay Gordon, trans. (1964). [*Genealogie deorum gentilium libri*]: *Boccaccio on Poetry, Being the Preface and the Fourteenth and Fifteenth Books of Boccaccio's Genealogia Deorum Gentilium,* Charles G. Osgood, ed. and trans. (1930, repr. 1956). [*De mulieribus claris*]: *Concerning Famous Women,* Guido A. Guarino, trans. (1963). [*Il Ninfale fiesolano*]: *The Nymph of Fiesole,* Daniel J. Donno, trans. (1960); *Nymphs of Fiesole,* Joseph Tusiani, trans. (1971). [*Teseida*]: *The Book of Theseus,* Bernadette Marie McCoy, trans. (1974), is faulty and must be used with great care. [*Trattatello in laude di Dante*]: *The Earliest Lives of Dante,* James Robinson Smith, trans. (1901, repr. 1968); Nicholas R. Havely, ed., *Chaucer's Boccaccio* (1980), a translation of the sources that Chaucer used in *Troilus and Criseyde* and in the Knight's and Franklin's Tales.

Studies. Book-length studies in English include Guido Almansi, *The Writer as Liar: Narrative Technique in the Decameron* (1975); Erich Auerbach, *Mimesis: The Representation of Reality in Western Literature,* Willard R. Trask, trans. (1953, repr. 1968); Thomas Goddard Bergin, *Boccaccio* (1981); Vittore Branca, *Boccaccio: The Man and His Works,* Richard Monges and Dennis J. McAuliffe, trans. (1976); Thomas Caldecot Chubb, *The Life of Giovanni Boccaccio* (1930, repr. 1969), useful if used with care; Marga Cottino-Jones, *An Anatomy of Boccaccio's Style* (1968), comprises essays on the *Decameron,* with some chapters in Italian; Hubertis Maurice Cummings, *The Indebtedness of Chaucer's Works to the Italian Works of Boccaccio: A Review and Summary* (1916, repr. 1967); Stavros Deligiorgis, *Narrative Intellection in the Decameron* (1975); Robert S. Dombroski, ed., *Critical Perspectives on the Decameron* (1976); Robert Hastings, *Nature and Reason in the Decameron* (1975); Robert Hollander, *Boccaccio's Two Venuses* (1977), interprets Boccaccio's works as a moral satire on the cult of sensual love; Alfred Collingwood Lee, *The Decameron: Its Sources and Analogues* (1909, repr. 1966); Millicent Joy Marcus, *An Allegory of Form: Literary Self-Consciousness in the Decameron* (1979), includes a judicious bibliography; Aldo D. Scaglione, *Nature and Love in the Late Middle Ages* (1963), a good general and philosophical background to the text; Bernard N. Schilling, *The Comic Spirit: Boccaccio to Thomas Mann* (1965); T. K. Seung, *Cultural Thematics: The Formation of the Faustian Ethos* (1976); John Addingon Symonds, *Giovanni Boccaccio as Man and Author* (1895, repr. 1968), a delightful example of Victorian criticism; Herbert Gladstone Wright, *Boccaccio in England from Chaucer to Tennyson* (1957).

ANTHONY K. CASSELL

[See also **Dante Alighieri; Florence; Italian Literature; Petrarch.**]

BOCHKA (plural, *bochki,* literally "barrel" in Russian), the peculiarly shaped vault preserved on secular and religious Russian wooden buildings of the seventeenth and eighteenth centuries, but in use much earlier. This particular kind of vault is pointed and extends outward from its springing, giving the silhouette of an "onion dome."

GEORGE P. MAJESKA

[See also **Kokoshnik; Russian Architecture.**]

BODEL, JEAN. Jean (or Jehan) Bodel of Arras (1165/1170–1210), a Picard trouvère and polygraph, is best known for the *Jeu de saint Nicolas,* the earliest extant miracle play in the *langue d'oïl.* From his literary production, which spanned little more than a decade (*ca.* 1190–1202), we also possess nine fabliaux, five pastorelles, the epic *Chanson des Saxons,* and a lyric poem, the *Congés.*

Bodel, who was also a city clerk and member of the Confrérie des Jongleurs et des Bourgeois d'Arras, was the first major figure in what became, during the thirteenth century, an important center of literary activity—the prosperous cities of northern France. The *Congés* (1202), in which the poet bids farewell to his friends before entering a leper colony, inaugurated an Artesian poetic genre, anticipating by approximately seventy-five years the *congés* of Baude Fastoul and Adam de la Halle. The local tavern in the *Jeu* became an important locus in thirteenth-century Artesian dramatic literature (see *Courtois d'Arras* and Adam de la Halle's *Jeu de la feuillée*). Word play in the *Jeu*'s tavern scenes also prefigured the nonsense poetry *(resverie, fatrasie, fatras, coq-à-*

l'âne) that flourished in northern France during the thirteenth and fourteenth centuries.

The *Chanson des Saxons* (*ca.* 1198) and the *Jeu* (1200) show Bodel to be both highly conscious of the Old French literary tradition and daring in generic experimentation. The former work, an account of the war between Charlemagne and the Saxons, constitutes an attempt to revive the old Carolingian epic by incorporating elements from chivalric romance. The *Jeu,* generally considered to be a masterpiece of Old French theater, is a work of complex versification and literary composition. Although it has received considerable scholarly attention, the *Jeu* resists easy classification and interpretation. Building on, and transforming into theater, a traditional Nicholas narrative about the theft and restoration of a treasure, Bodel drew from epic literature, as well as from the crusading spirit that prevailed in northern France around 1200, to construct a pagan-Christian battle. Local Artesian lowlife supplied the material for a tavern in which approximately half the action of this surprising miracle play—drinking, dicing, and verbal games—takes place.

BIBLIOGRAPHY

Editions and translations. Jean Bodel, *Le Jeu de saint Nicolas,* rev. ed. by Albert Henry (1881); *Jean Bodels Saxenlied,* Friedrich Menzel and Edmund Stengel, eds., 2 vols. (1906–1909); Pierre Ruelle, *Les congés d'Arras* (1965).

Secondary works. Charles Foulon, *L'oeuvre de Jehan Bodel* (1958); Henri Rey-Flaud, *Pour une dramaturgie du Moyen-Âge* (1980).

T. S. FAUNCE

[See also **Adam de la Halle; Drama, Western European; Fabliau; French Literature; Pastourelle; Troubadour.**]

BOETHIUS, ANICIUS MANLIUS SEVERINUS (*ca.* 480–524/526), was born into one of the foremost patriarchal families of Rome. His father died while he was still very young, at which time he was taken in by the powerful family of Quintus Aurelius Memmius Symmachus. Under Symmachus' tutelage Boethius was introduced to two pivotal elements in his formation, Greek philosophy and orthodox Christianity. Courcelle's hypothesis that Boethius studied in Alexandria under Ammonius is difficult to prove or to set aside entirely. Boethius is clearly influenced by Neoplatonic thought of the period as found in Alexandria and Athens, and his program of studies and early writings clearly follows the pattern of the Greek tradition rather than the Latin. Boethius subsequently, during a period of difficult doctrinal and political struggle within the church, applied the language, concepts, and logical method learned in the Greek philosophical tradition to present a strong apology for orthodox Christian positions.

Although his political career was to some degree predetermined by his birthright, his career seems unusually precocious and distinguished. In 510 he was honored with the consulship and began an accomplished career in the senate. In 522 he was named *magister officiorum* by King Theodoric and saw his sons installed as consuls in Rome (he had married Rusticiana, Symmachus' daughter).

In 523, Cyprian, Theodoric's referendary, brought charges of treason against the senator Albinus, accusing him of having corresponded with intimates of the Byzantine emperor Justin and thereby of having conspired against Theodoric's kingdom. Boethius, who was quick to come to Albinus' defense, was soon implicated in the conspiracy and was further accused of having used his obscure studies as a kind of occult power to further his ambition. Moreover, Boethius' strong defense of orthodox Christianity at the court of an Arian king cannot be discounted as an incriminating factor. Arrested in 523, he was imprisoned at Pavia and after an unusually long imprisonment, was executed sometime between 524 and 526.

Boethius' works can be divided into four categories, in approximate chronological order: didactic works, logical works, theological treatises, and the *Consolation of Philosophy.*

Written at the request of Symmachus and dedicated to him, Boethius' didactic works expound the four mathematical disciplines forming the basis of the Neoplatonic educational program: arithmetic, music, geometry, and astronomy. Boethius called these disciplines the *quadruvium* (which became *quadrivium* in the Middle Ages), the fourfold path to knowledge of "essences." Of these four works, only the *De institutione arithmetica* and the greater part of *De institutione musica* survive. Boethius' contemporary Cassiodorus seems to imply that Boethius finished all four works, although some scholars question this possibility. The work on arithmetic is a translation of Nicomachus' *De arithmetica,* while the musical treatise presents a translation of Nicomachus' lost *De musica* and Ptolemy's *Harmonica.* The work on geometry would have presented Euclid's *Elements* in Latin, and the astronomical treatise would have been based on Ptolemy's *Almagest.*

BOETHIUS, ANICIUS MANLIUS

The logical treatises constitute the largest category of Boethius' works. Their composition covers a major span from around 505 to about 523, according to de Rijk. Boethius began with translation of and commentary on Porphyry, the late Platonist who had become the principal pedagogue of logic in the Greek schools of the fourth and fifth centuries. Translations of Aristotle's *Prior Analytics* and *Posterior Analytics* form the major division within the logical works and became the principal source of Aristotelian logic for the Latin Middle Ages. Boethius also wrote commentaries on Aristotle's and Cicero's *Topics,* major commentaries on Aristotle's *Categories* and *Interpretation,* and a series of short monographs on logic. A work of particular importance and even originality is the *De hypotheticis syllogismis,* which criticizes and clarifies linguistic imprecisions of his Greek schoolmasters.

Boethius never clearly sided with either the Stoics or the Peripatetics on whether logic was a proper division of philosophy itself or merely a discipline treating propositions, syllogisms, and terms; yet at times he presents both positions without overwhelming criticism. His own position, following his Neoplatonic masters, seems to be that logic, like the mathematical disciplines, is propaedeutic to philosophy, the queen of disciplines. The scope and seriousness of the logical works testify to their centrality in Boethius' thought. Their language and methodology become crucial factors in the composition and understanding of the theological treatises and of the *Consolation of Philosophy.*

After more than a century of scrutiny and doubt concerning their authenticity, the five short theological treatises known as *Opuscula sacra* are now generally accepted as authentic. Only the genuineness of the fourth treatise, "De fide catholica," remains in doubt, principally because of its catechetical rather than philosophical nature. (Recent studies by Henry Chadwick argue convincingly for its authenticity.) The second, third, and fifth works are dedicated to John the Deacon, who seems to have been responsible for much of Boethius' formation in Christian doctrine. The first and second treatises are the result of Boethius' reflections on the Trinity. The third addresses the problem of the goodness of substances by virtue of their existence.

Boethius applied his logical and linguistic skills to christological problems in the fifth treatise; his bold analysis of the use of such terms as *natura, persona,* and *substantia* make this his most original theological work. While Augustine is cited only in "De trinitate," the first treatise, the resonances with his thought that recur throughout the works bear witness to Boethius' knowledge of him. Considerable study remains to be given to these important documents, which have led scholars to call Boethius "the first of the Scholastics."

Consolation of Philosophy, Boethius' final work, represents his reflections during imprisonment on the suffering of the innocent and the reconciliation of divine providence with human freedom. The work mixes dense prose sections with verse; the latter, added to lighten a difficult subject, reveals a poetic gift considerably above the commonplace. Philosophical and literary resonances range from Plato and Aristotle to the Neoplatonists, from Cicero and Ovid to Augustine. The absence of any reference to Christian faith or dogma makes the work all the more unusual. The work is that of a philosopher trying—as far as possible within the limits of reason alone—to understand the problem of evil, the distinction between providence and fate, and the apparent contradiction between divine foreknowledge and free will. The *Consolation* was considered essential for almost every library from the Carolingian period through the fourteenth century, and the manuscript tradition is one of the richest of any medieval work. The *Consolation* was one of the first works to be translated into modern vernacular languages, and its influence in Western literature remains an active area of research.

The integrity and influence of Boethius' life and works have led Edward K. Rand to group him with Ambrose, Augustine, and Jerome as one of the "founders of the Middle Ages."

BIBLIOGRAPHY

Editions. Boethius' *Opera omnia* were published in *Patrologia latina,* LXIII–LXIV (1847); *De institutione arithmetica* and *De institutione musica* were edited by Gottfried Friedlein (1867). Logical works include *In Ciceronis topica commentarium,* Johann Kaspar Orelli and Johann Georg Baiter, eds. (1833), published in Cicero's *Opera; Commentarii in librum Aristotelis Perihermineias,* Karl Meiser, ed., 2 vols. (1877–1880); *In Isagogen Porphyrii commenta,* Georg Schepss and Samuel Brandt, eds. (1906); Boethius' translation of Aristotle's *Organon,* edited by Lorenzo Minio-Paluello, published in *Aristoteles Latinus* (1953–); and *De hypotheticis syllogismis,* Luca Orbetello, ed. (1969). The *Opuscula sacra* were published in Rudolf Peiper's edition of the *Consolation of Philosophy* (1871);

the latter work was also edited by Wilhelm Weinberger (1934) and Ludwig Bieler (1957).

Translations. Lorenzo Pozzi, ed. and trans., *Trattato sulla divisione* (1969); H. R. Stewart and E. K. Rand, eds. and trans., *The Theological Tractates; The Consolation of Philosophy* (1918), rev. ed. by S. J. Tester (1973); Eleonore Stump, ed. and trans., *Boethius's De topicis differentiis* (1978).

Studies. B. Bischoff, "Das griechische Element in der abendländischen Bildung des Mittelalters," in *Byzantinische Zeitschrift,* **44** (1951); Calvin M. Bower, "Boethius and Nicomachus: An Essay Concerning the Sources of *De institutione musica,*" in *Vivarium,* **16** (1978); Samuel Brandt, "Entstehungszeit und zeitliche Folge der Werke von Boethius," in *Philologus,* n.s. **62** (1903); Henry Chadwick, "The Authenticity of Boethius' Fourth Tractate *De fide catholica,*" in *Journal of Theological Studies,* n.s. **31** (1980); Pierre Courcelle, "Boèce et l'école d'Alexandrie," in *Mélanges de l'école française de Rome,* **52** (1935), *La Consolation de philosophie dans la tradition littéraire: Antécédents et postérité de Boèce* (1967); and *Late Latin Writers and Their Greek sources,* Harry E. Wedeck, trans. (1969); M. T. Gibson, ed., *Boethius, His Life, Thought, and Influence* (1981); Joachim Gruber, *Kommentar zu Boethius De consolatione philosophiae* (1978); Alfred Kappelmacher, "Der schriftstellerische Plan des Boethius," in *Wiener Studien,* **46** (1928); Arthur P. McKinlay, "Stylistic Tests and the Chronology of the Works of Boethius," in *Harvard Studies in Classical Philology,* **18** (1907); and "The De syllogismis categoricis and Introductio ad syllogismos categoricos of Boethius," in Leslie W. Jones, ed., *Classical and Mediaeval Studies in Honor of Edward Kennard Rand* (1938); Howard R. Patch, *The Tradition of Boethius* (1935); Ubaldo Pizzani, "Studi sulle fonti del 'De institutione musica' di Boezio," in *Sacris Erudiri,* **16** (1965); Edward K. Rand, *Founders of the Middle Ages* (1928); Lambertus M. de Rijk, *Logica modernorum,* 2 vols. (1962–1967); and "On the Chronology of Boethius' Works on Logic," in *Vivarium,* **2** (1964); G. Schrimpf, *Die Axiomenschrift des Boethius (De hebdomadibus) als philosophisches Lehrbuch des Mittelalters* (1966); James Shiel, "Boethius' Commentaries on Aristotle," in *Mediaeval and Renaissance Studies,* **4** (1958); and "Boethius and Eudemus," in *Vivarium,* **12** (1974); Edmund T. Silk, "Boethius's Consolatio philosophiae as a Sequel to Augustine's Dialogues and Soliloquia," in *Harvard Theological Review,* **32** (1939); Eleonore Stump, "Boethius' Works on the Topics," in *Vivarium,* **12** (1974); Hermann K. Usener, *Anecdoton Holderi, ein Beitrag zur Geschichte Roms in ostgothischer Zeit* (1877, repr. 1969); C. J. de Vogel, "Amor quo caelum regitur," in *Vivarium,* **1** (1963); and "The Problem of Philosophy and Christian Faith in Boethius' Consolatio," in *Romanitas et Christianitas: Studia Iano Henrico Waszink* (1973).

CALVIN M. BOWER

BOEVE (BEUVES) DE HAUMTONE, an early thirteenth-century Anglo-Norman adventure romance written in 3,850 alexandrines and decasyllables grouped in laisses, which recounts at a rapid pace the many bizarre adventures of Bevis, son of Guy of Hampton, and of Bevis' bride, Josiane, an Oriental princess. The Anglo-Norman text, which is probably based on an earlier insular version in French, gave rise to versions in Middle English, Welsh, and Old Norse. On the Continent there were three distinguishable French forms, all much longer than the Anglo-Norman. The story is also found in Italian (two versions), Romanian, Russian, Dutch, and Yiddish.

BIBLIOGRAPHY

An edition is Albert Stimming, *Der anglonormannische Boeve de Haumtone* (1899). Also see M. Dominica Legge, *Anglo-Norman Literature and Its Background* (1963), 156–161.

BRIAN MERRILEES

[See also **Anglo-Norman Literature.**]

BOGOLIUBSKII, ANDREI (1109?–1174), son of a Cuman princess and Iuri Dolgorukii. Succeeding Iuri as prince of (Rostov-)Suzdal in 1157, Andrei built up Vladimir as his capital and established the policy of attempting to dominate Russia from there. He expanded his influence over the Volga Bulgars (1164) and Novgorod (1170), and is most renowned for his armies' sack of Kiev (1169) and his building activities: the Vladimir Uspensky Cathedral and Golden Gate, the Church of the Intercession on the Nerl River, and the palace in Bogoliubovo. His ambitions to be "autocrat" in Russia, influenced by Byzantine political theory, prompted the successful resistance of other Russian princes (1173), and his domestic tyranny led to his assassination by his top officials (1174).

BIBLIOGRAPHY

David Goldfrank, "Andrei Bogoliubskii," in *Modern Encyclopedia of Russian and Soviet History,* I (1976); Ellen Hurwitz, "Andrej Bogoljubskij: Policies and Ideology" (Ph.D. diss., Columbia Univ., 1972).

DAVID GOLDFRANK

[See also **Russian Architecture; Vladimir-Suzdal.**]

BOGOMILISM, a heretical religious sect, arose in Bulgaria during the reign of the Bulgar czar Peter (927–969). It was said to have been first preached by a certain Pop Bogomil (whose title suggests he originally was an Orthodox priest). Dualist in theology, its adherents believed in two principles: a good principle identified with spirit and an evil principle identified with matter. The evil principle was believed to have created the world and every material thing in it, including human bodies. However, it was incapable of creating life, which had to come from the good principle. Since the God of the Old Testament was the creator of the earth, the Bogomils identified him with the evil principle. They accepted only the New Testament and believed its god was the good principle, and thus a different god from that of the Old Testament. Jesus Christ was sent to earth by the good principle with a message of salvation, explaining how human souls could escape from matter and return to the spiritual heaven. Because matter was evil, Jesus Christ could not really have taken on a human body or undergone any true human experiences; it only appeared that he did this. As a consequence the Bogomils rejected the cult of Mary.

The Bogomils also rejected much of earthly life (such as sexual activity, marriage, eating meat, drinking wine), advocated an ascetic ideal, and banned anything material from their religious services (church buildings, icons, relics, the cross, water for baptism, bread and wine for the Eucharist). In fact, they rejected all sacraments as practiced in the Orthodox church and the Mass. They said only the Lord's Prayer, which was recited a set number of times a day, and it did not matter where one said it. They confessed their sins to one another. They rejected the cults of saints and all miracles, saying that the evil principle worked miracles to seduce men. By all accounts they seem to have led ascetic and moral lives, and their faith allowed them to hide their beliefs (even to participate in Orthodox services) in order to escape persecution.

The best and most detailed source describing Bulgarian Bogomils is a tract written by the Bulgarian priest Cosmas around 970. His information is confirmed in two other, less detailed sources: a letter from Theophylact, patriarch of Constantinople, to Czar Peter, written around 940, the earliest description of heresy in Bulgaria—Theophylact does not call the heretics Bogomils but simply "a newly appeared heresy"; and the edicts of a church synod held in 1211 by the Bulgarian czar Boril, which condemned the Bogomils.

Bogomilism is often considered one link in a chain of heresies reaching back to the Gnostics and Manichaeans. Scholars believed that dualist beliefs survived in the East in the tenets of the Paulicians in Armenia and the eastern regions of Byzantium. Since many Paulicians had been transferred by the Byzantines to defend their border with Bulgaria in the ninth century, they were seen as the source of Bogomil beliefs. Recently, however, doubt has been raised as to whether the Paulicians were really dualists. If they were not, then probably an indigenous origin should be sought for Bogomilism. Recent missionaries have observed that certain newly converted people, by exaggerating the role of the devil, have spontaneously arrived at a dualist Christian cosmology. Such could have occurred among certain newly-converted Bulgarians—whose official conversion was in 864—who did not grasp or like the subtleties of Orthodox theology.

The Bogomils probably were not very numerous. After Theophylact's letter (*ca.* 940) and Cosmas' tract (*ca.* 970), for roughly a century no source mentions them in Bulgaria or Macedonia (a region that was Bulgarian until conquered, along with Bulgaria, by Byzantium in 1018). Then a patriarch of Constantinople named Cosmas (probably Cosmas I, 1075–1081) wrote to the metropolitan of Larissa (in Thessaly) referring to the progress of "Manichees" in all regions of Bulgaria and in the western Byzantine provinces. Shortly thereafter, William of Tyre, a chronicler of the First Crusade, referred to Crusaders passing through western Macedonia and conquering (1096) a fortress in Pelagonia inhabited by "heretics." Scholars usually think he meant Bogomils, but the heretics could well have been Paulicians. Next, during the reign of Manuel I Komnenos (1143–1180), Bishop Hilarion of Moglen (in southeastern Macedonia) is described, in a late-fourteenth-century saint's life, as fighting various heretics including Bogomils. Around 1190 an Italian Cathar bishop named Nazarius visited Bulgaria for his spiritual baptism and brought home a copy of a sacred Bogomil text, the *Interrogatio Johannis.*

In the period 1186–1393 (from the time Bulgaria regained its independence from Byzantium until the Ottoman conquest) references to Bogomils remain equally infrequent. In 1211 Czar Boril's synod condemned the Bogomils, claiming the devil "has sowed all the Bulgarian land with heresy"; the synod's edicts briefly described Bogomil beliefs and practices, and condemned certain Bogomils by name. In 1238, Pope Gregory IX, angry at the Bulgarian ruler

John Asen II complained of "heretics" in Bulgaria in a letter to Bela IV of Hungary. In 1250 an Italian inquisitor, Rayner Sacconi, mentions in an inquisitorial manual the Bulgarian dualist church as one of six churches in the East. Together, he says, the six had a total of 500 "perfecti" (roughly equivalent to priests). It is doubtful that more than 150 or 200 of these 500 would have been Bulgarian. And, if there were only 150–200 perfecti for all Bulgaria, it suggests that Bogomilism was not a large movement there. The sources are then silent for almost a century until 1350, when a church council held in Trnovo, the capital of the Second Bulgarian Empire, condemned a particular Bogomil (who had come from the Byzantine Empire). Finally, in 1360, Bogomils were condemned in passing at a second Trnovo church council that devoted most of its attention to other problems. After this, Bogomils are not heard of again in Bulgaria. The scarcity of references to them during the 400 years they existed in Bulgaria suggests they were not numerous there.

Certain scholars have tried to depict the Bogomils as a national movement of Bulgarians against Byzantium. Yet in no Bulgarian war against Byzantium (when Bulgaria was independent) and in no Bulgarian revolt against Byzantium (when Bulgaria was subjected) are Bogomils ever mentioned. Such notice would be expected in Byzantine sources if Bogomils had been active, for the presence of heretics would have served to discredit the Bulgarians.

Other scholars have tried to claim that Bogomilism was a movement of social protest. However, Bogomils are not mentioned as participating in any such movement in Bulgaria. The only suggestion that they were social rebels is found in Cosmas, who says that certain Bogomils taught their adherents not to submit to authority, and goes on to say, "they slander the rich; they hate the emperors; they mock their superiors and insult their lords. They claim that God has horror of those who work for the emperors and recommend that servants not work for their masters." No evidence, however, shows any Bogomil ever acting on this teaching.

Since no Bogomil is ever found active in any social or political event in Bulgarian history, and since no prominent Bulgarian is known to have been a Bogomil, Bogomilism probably had little impact on Bulgarian state affairs.

However, these Bulgarian dualists did have a major role in sowing the seeds of the dualist movement that spread throughout the Mediterranean (with a strong assist from the Byzantine Bogomils, who seem to have been the chief middlemen) and had great prestige among foreign dualists, as is indicated by the Italian Nazarius coming to Bulgaria for his ordination.

Bogomilism spread from Bulgaria to the Byzantine Empire. The earliest information on this expansion is found in a letter of the monk Euthymius of Peribleptos (a monastery in Constantinople), written between 1034 and 1050. He refers back to the reign of Basil II (976–1025) when he had been in Acmonia, in the Opsikion theme (a province in northwestern Anatolia). There he had met many heretics and witnessed the trial of a heresiarch named John Tzurillas. Euthymius describes John as the first teacher of a newly appeared heresy that he had preached in Thrace and Smyrna, where he had won many disciples. In the Opsikion theme the heretics were called Phundagiagitae ("bag-men," presumably reflecting their wandering life), while in the Cibyrrhaeot theme (in the southwest corner of Anatolia) they were called Bogomils. Presumably John acquired his doctrine in Bulgaria and then, taking advantage of the elimination of that frontier by the Byzantine conquest of Bulgaria, moved into Thrace, where he began preaching; later he crossed over into western Anatolia. He is the earliest known Bogomil teacher in the empire.

By the end of the eleventh century, Bogomil ideas had spread to Constantinople. In about 1110, during the reign of Alexios I Komnenos (1081–1118), an arrested Bogomil revealed the name of the leader of the congregation in the capital: a monk named Basil, who had taught Bogomilism for more than forty years. Basil had twelve disciples and had won numerous adherents among the aristocratic families of Constantinople. He was arrested along with his leading followers. Some of them were brought back to Orthodoxy; those who refused to recant were imprisoned for life, and Basil himself was burned at the stake. A dramatic account of his arrest, interrogation, and death is given in Anna Komnena's *Alexiad.*

Alexios also took active measures to convert heretics in Philippopolis in Thrace. Most of these were Paulicians, but Anna mentions Bogomils being there as well. To meet this threat of heresy, the emperor asked the monk Euthymius Zigabenus to write a tract refuting all heresies. His tract, the *Panoplia dogmatica* (written between 1111 and 1118), did just that and includes a detailed section on Bogomilism as taught by Basil. Euthymius presents detailed legends showing the two principles (two sons of God) in action, the Creation, the significance of biblical

BOGOMILISM

events, and the means to salvation; all are marked by allegorical interpretations of biblical passages. These beliefs are far more sophisticated than the simple dualism described by Cosmas in tenth-century Bulgaria. This development of Bogomil ideas almost certainly occurred in the Byzantine capital among its philosophically minded intellectuals. Thus, Bogomilism in Constantinople became a complex theological system whose tenets could appeal to intellectuals. In this form it was carried from Constantinople along the Mediterranean to Dalmatia, Italy, and France.

Both the Bulgarian and the Byzantine Bogomils—as described by Cosmas and Zigabenus—were mitigated dualists. They believed in a single major God who had two sons: an elder son (Satanail), who fell and created the material world, and was the evil principle, and a good young son (Christ). In this scheme good would triumph in the end. A second, less popular current, found in the Thracian Dragovica church and later also represented by Niketas of Constantinople, was absolute dualism. This doctrine visualized two equally powerful and coeternal principles (good-spirit against evil-matter) that would battle eternally with no final triumph for either.

The action of Emperor Alexios seems to have been effective in the capital and little is heard about Bogomils in Constantinople thereafter. However, Bogomils were still active in Anatolia, where their faith was popular among some monks and penetrated certain monasteries. In August 1143 a synod in Constantinople deposed two Cappadocian bishops (Clement of Sosandra and Leontius of Balbissa) as Bogomils. Their beliefs, if accurately recorded, were not pure Bogomilism; however, certain of their views reflected the influence of Bogomil ideas. In October 1143 a Cappadocian monk named Niphon was charged with preaching Bogomilism; he was found guilty by the synod and shut up in a Constantinopolitan monastery. He seems to have been a popular figure, and by 1146 Patriarch Cosmas II had befriended him and procured his release. Other church leaders did not believe Niphon had reformed, and used their association to depose Cosmas II on charges of Bogomilism. Possibly Cosmas was innocent and his enemies simply used this friendship to depose him.

At roughly the same time, as noted above, in Moglen (Macedonia), Bishop Hilarion battled Paulicians, Monophysites, and Bogomils. Testimony at a heresy trial early in the fourteenth century mentions the town of Pokovik in Thrace as having many Bogomil adherents. In the late fourteenth century Bogomil ideas are mentioned as disturbing certain Thracian and Macedonian monasteries. Finally Archbishop Symeon of Thessaloniki (1410–1429) wrote a tract against heretics. Part of this work was directed against the Bogomils (whom he also calls Kudugers). Symeon considered them the most dangerous heretics in his city.

From Bulgaria and Macedonia, Bogomilism may have spread to Serbia. In the 1180's the Serbian ruler Stefan Nemanja held a synod against some unnamed heretics who did not believe that Jesus Christ was the Son of God. Nothing more is said about their doctrines. Most scholars think they were Bogomils, and they may well have been. However, after Nemanja took strict action against them, nothing more is heard of heretics in Serbia until the fourteenth century. At that time articles against the Bogomils (referred to as Babuni) were included in both church synodial edicts (as one of several heresies to be cursed on the Day of Orthodoxy) and in the law code of Czar Stefan Dušan (1349). Since Dušan had by then conquered Macedonia and much of northern Greece, possibly the heretics against whom he felt it necessary to legislate lived in the newly conquered lands rather than in Serbia proper.

From Constantinople dualism spread west along the Mediterranean to Dalmatia, Italy, and southern France. In Dalmatia the heretics formed the Ecclesia Sclavoniae and were particularly active in the late twelfth and the thirteenth centuries. Persecuted by Catholic bishops on the coast, some of them fled to Bosnia, where they seem to have acquired a small following. Many scholars have tried to identify this Bosnian following with the Bosnian church. However, the Bosnian dualists seem to have been a movement separate from the Bosnian church, which most probably was not dualist.

Dualist ideas possibly reached France and Italy in the eleventh century. Under different names (such as Cathars, Albigensians, Patarins) dualism became a flourishing movement there in the second half of the twelfth century. The dualists were wiped out in France in the early thirteenth century but survived in Italy through the fourteenth. Many sources have survived that describe the organization and beliefs of these Western heretics. Since their doctrines arose in Bulgaria, many of these Western beliefs were also Bulgarian. However, since new doctrinal ideas also developed in the West, it is dangerous to assume that any particular Western belief not documented for Bulgaria was actually held there. Thus, no Western beliefs or practices—not specifically corroborated for Bulgaria—have been included in this account. Western sources also describe the organization of the sect; we have no sources about organizational matters for Bulgaria. Some scholars have assumed that Bulgarian Bogomils followed (possibly even originated) the Western system. But however likely this view may be, it should be stressed that it cannot be proved that Bulgarian Bogomils organized their society as their Western counterparts did.

However, it is evident that the ascetic ideals held by both the Bogomils and Western dualists were impossible to realize. Therefore, Western dualist society was divided into two orders: the perfecti (priesthood), who underwent a spiritual baptism and became possessed of the Holy Spirit, and the common believers. That the Bulgarians probably had such a spiritual baptism is suggested by the fact that the Italian Cathar Nazarius went to Bulgaria to receive his baptism. The believers led normal lives and then late in life (when widowed or on their deathbeds) received the spiritual baptism and became perfecti. A person who failed to receive this baptism would, after death, be reborn as a man again. The perfecti led wandering ascetic lives, doing no manual labor and fed by the believers. One who sinned after baptism had to be baptized again.

The Western dualists were divided into several different currents (each tracing its baptism back to a particular heresiarch), each with its own bishop under whom were two subordinates—an Elder Son and a Younger Son. Each current was known as a church. The French bishoprics tended to be territorial. In Italy a church tended to be the following of particular leaders with territories overlapping. In 1250, according to Rayner Sacconi, there were not over 4,000 perfecti overall.

In the East, with which we are concerned here, there were six churches: Bulgaria, Dragovica (in Thrace), Sclavonia (Dalmatia), Philadelphia (in Anatolia), and Latin and Greek churches of Constantinople. (Rayner wrote when the Crusaders held Constantinople.) The six Eastern churches contained a total, Rayner claimed, of 500 perfecti. No evidence exists to show that the Eastern churches had Elder Sons and Younger Sons. It also cannot be proved that the Eastern churches even had a dominant bishop, though certain sources suggest this: Boril's synod condemned a Ded'ec of Sardica (modern Sofia), and in 1167 a Byzantine dualist named Niketas came to the Cathar council of St. Felix-de-Caraman in southern France, where he played a dominant role. The Westerners referred to him as a "bishop" from Constantinople. However, since most of our information about dualist church organization comes from Inquisition sources and since the Inquisition was not active in the East, we are very ill-informed about organizational aspects of Bulgarian and Byzantine Bogomilism.

On the cultural side, very little has survived from the Bogomils. Since they rejected church buildings and religious art, a major category of long-lasting cultural artifacts was never created. About all that can be pointed to are certain manuscripts containing apocryphal tales about biblical figures. Recently scholars have shown that the legends themselves are far older than the Bogomils, dating back to the first centuries of Christianity. Thus, the tales are not original Bogomil works. However, they reappeared in large numbers when the Bogomils were active in Bulgaria, and evidently there is a connection between the revival of these tales and the heresy. It should be noted, however, that in both eastern and western medieval Europe these tales were popular with all Christian groups and also among the Jews. Thus, it is difficult to connect particular manuscripts with the Bogomils. However, the themes of certain tales fit well with a dualist world view. An important text of this sort is the documented Bogomil text, the *Interrogatio Johannis,* which the Italian Cathar Nazarius brought back to Italy from Bulgaria and which has survived in two manuscripts.

BIBLIOGRAPHY

Dimitŭr Angelov, *Bogomilstvoto v Bŭlgariia* (1969); John V. A. Fine, "The Bulgarian Bogomil Movement," in *East European Quarterly,* **11** (1978); Dmitri Obolensky, *The Bogomils* (1948); Henri Puech and A. Vaillant, *Le traité contre les Bogomiles de Cosmas le prêtre* (1945); A. Solovjev, "Fundajajiti, Patarini i Kudugeri u vizantiskim izvorima," in *Zbornik radova Vizantološkog Instituta* (Serbian Academy of Sciences), **1** (1952).

JOHN V. A. FINE, JR.

[See also **Albigensians; Bosnia; Bosnian Church; Bulgaria; Dualism; Heresies, Byzantine; Heresies, Western European; Paulicians; Stefan Dušan; Stefan Nemanja.**]

BOHEMIA-MORAVIA. Bohemia is named for a Celtic tribe, the Boii, who lived near the headwaters of the Labe (Elbe) River as early as the fourth century B.C. Moravia (Morava in Czech) takes its name from the Morava River or from the Marvani, a people first

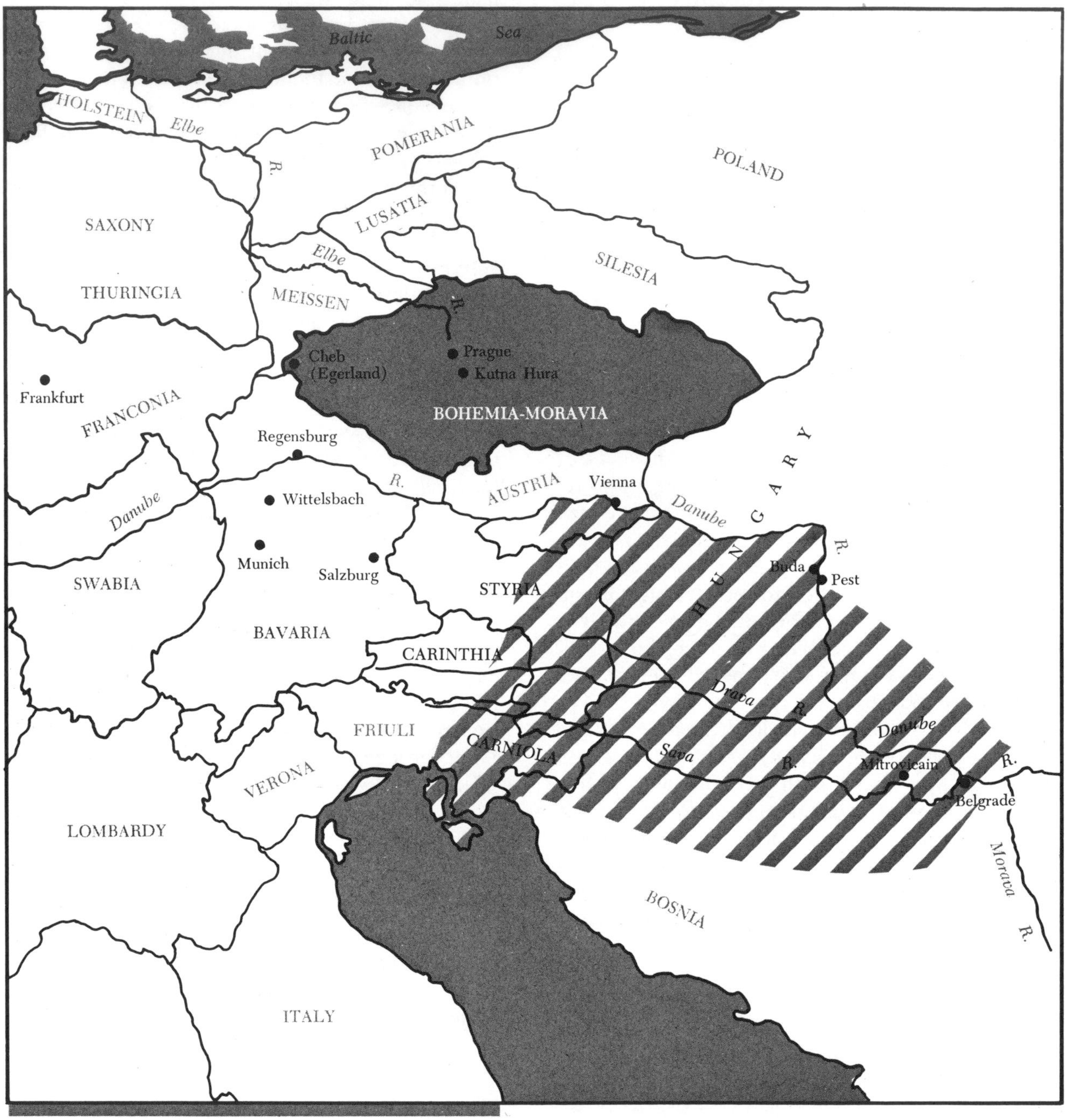

BOHEMIA-MORAVIA during the MIDDLE AGES

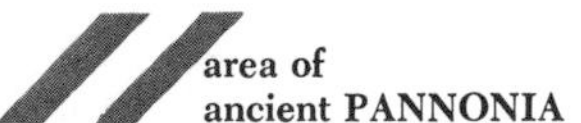

BOHEMIA-MORAVIA

mentioned in 882 in a reference to a group of Slavs, possibly in Pannonia, paying homage to the Frankish king at Frankfurt. Both names are of foreign origin. The Slavs living in the region of modern Bohemia-Moravia referred to themselves as Czechs (Češi) and to their land as Čechy.

By the fifth or sixth century the population of this region had become predominantly Slavic. It was conquered in the sixth century by the Avars; in 623 some of the Slavs revolted under the leadership of a Frankish merchant, Samo, who established a short-lived empire that died with him in 659. Thereafter the Slavs felt the presence of the Franks and other Germanic tribes. They accepted the rather loose suzerainty of Frankish rulers, under whom Christian missionaries entered Bohemia. In 845 fourteen Czech nobles traveled to Regensburg to accept baptism into the Christian faith of their Frankish-Bavarian neighbors.

GREAT MORAVIA

In the tenth century the land called Great Moravia by the Byzantine emperor Constantine VII Porphyrogenitos was a major center of political, cultural, and religious development and rivalry. The principality of Moravia was founded by Mojmír in the 830's, when he drove out the pro-Frankish Pribina, under whom the Franks had increasingly taken possession of the land. Mojmír's successor, Rastislav (846–870), successfully outflanked a combined Frankish-Bulgar alliance against him by establishing one with the Bulgars' southern neighbor, the emperor of Byzantium.

One of the results of the Moravia-Byzantium compact was a cultural and diplomatic mission sent by the emperor to the Moravians. The delegates were the brothers Constantine-Cyril and Methodios, both highly educated. Methodios was the protégé of the patriarch scholar Photios. Both brothers had gone to the Khazars on a mission in 860. Constantine knew well the Slav dialect of the Macedonians and had developed a special alphabet to express the significant features of the Slavic language. He brought this alphabet to Moravia, and he and his brother and disciples began to translate the Scriptures and liturgical works into Old Church Slavonic. The brothers, finding themselves opposed by Frankish missionaries and in a jurisdictional dispute between the bishop of Rome and the patriarch of Constantinople, decided they would be more effective cooperating with Rome. In 867 they traveled to Rome, seeking the pope's approval. Their efforts were rewarded and Methodios was named archbishop of the ancient and now-restored metropolitan see of Sirmium, capital of Pannonia (modern Mitrovica, Yugoslavia) by Pope Adrian II in 869. The realm of Moravia and the archbishopric were destroyed by the Bavarians and nomadic Magyars shortly after the death of Svatopluk in 894.

Traditionally the personalities and issues surrounding Great Moravia have been placed by historians in the region north of the Danube. Recently, Imre Boba has argued convincingly that people such as Methodios and Mojmír acted not in what is today called Moravia but, rather, in the area along the Sava and Drava rivers, south of the Danube. If that is so, a major revision of the ninth-century history of central Europe will be needed.

POLITICAL DEVELOPMENTS

In Bohemia the nobility, perhaps wishing for an alliance against the threatening Magyars, in the late ninth century turned to the East Frankish king Arnulf and declared their allegiance at Regensburg. The nobles were led by Spytihněv, the founder of the Přemyslid dynasty that ruled Bohemia for the next four centuries. Almost from the very beginning the Czechs deferred to their more powerful western neighbors. In the late ninth and early tenth centuries Czech nobles and rulers traveled to nearby cities and castles, declaring their allegiance to Frankish kings. Up to the end of the twelfth century, disputes within the Czech ruling family and between it and the nobility gave the Frankish kings opportunities to intervene in, and often to dominate, Bohemian affairs. At the same time the Czech princes were able to extract benefits from the Frankish monarchs, not only for themselves personally but for their lands as well. In exchange for their support the Czech princes successively recognized the sovereignty of the German kings.

Perhaps the most significant such step came in 1035, when Břetislav I (1035–1055) accepted Bohemia as a fief from Emperor Conrad II. In 1085 the German king, Henry IV, rewarded Duke Vratislav II for the contribution his troops had made when the king fought against his Saxon nobles and then the Roman pope. By refusing to participate in Pope Gregory VII's attempt to encircle the German king, Vratislav very likely saved Henry IV. In return Henry personally crowned Vratislav king, raising Bohemia from the status of a duchy to that of a kingdom. In 1114 King Henry V supported Vladislav I (1109–1125) against his rivals. Eventually Vladislav

BOHEMIA-MORAVIA

was appointed imperial cupbearer, a position that later secured the office of imperial elector for the Bohemian kings. Similarly, for his aid to Frederick Barbarossa against the Lombard towns, Vladislav II (1140–1172) extracted recognition for his claim to be hereditary king of Bohemia in 1158. The next year he was one of the electors at the imperial diet at Bamberg.

Under Přemysl Ottokar I (1197–1230) the position of the ruling dynasty was established on a secure enough footing that the independent status of the kingdom of Bohemia, although still within the empire, could be consolidated. Taking advantage of a struggle for the imperial throne, Přemysl had his family's hereditary rights to the Bohemian throne confirmed by the emperor. Pope Innocent III also recognized his royal title. The relations between the king of Bohemia and the emperor were given official recognition in the Golden Bull of Sicily, issued by Frederick II in 1212. It established Bohemia's internal independence from imperial intervention and declared its boundaries inviolable. The Czech king's obligation to provide 300 knights escort for the emperor's coronation in Rome was transformed into the nominal payment of 300 marks. Furthermore, he was required to come to the imperial diet only if it met in a city near the Czech border.

The Přemyslids reached the summit of their power under Přemysl Ottokar II (1253–1278). Přemysl built up his power base on the growing towns and the money economy. His income from granting charters of self-government to cities, and especially from the silver mines at Kutná Hora, led him to believe that he could act independently from his nobility. When the Babenberg dynasty died out in Austria in 1246, the estates there elected Přemysl their duke. In 1260 he took Styria by force; in 1269 he inherited Carinthia and part of Carniola, and in 1270 he obtained the greater part of Istria on the Adriatic. By 1270 he was the strongest ruler in central Europe, but his conquests in Austria were safe only as long as the emperor did not intervene. Přemysl decided therefore to seek the imperial crown for himself. The imperial electors had no desire for a strong king, so they elected Rudolf of Habsburg in 1273. The result was war. Přemysl, deserted by his ally, the duke of Bavaria, and betrayed by his Czech nobility, fell in the battle of Moravské Pole (modern Dürnkrut) in 1278. He was succeeded by several weak kings, during whose reigns Bohemian society and polity suffered the violence resulting from the nobles' fighting for power. After the death of the last male Přemyslid in 1306, the nobility reasserted its leading role in the realm by electing the king.

By 1310, growing tired of the disorder that marked public life, part of the nobility, cooperating with the church hierarchy and with leading elements in the cities, made overtures to Emperor Henry VII to have his son, John, come as king. Henry was agreeable, and had John marry Elizabeth, the last of the Přemysl family. After John of Luxemburg granted the nobility's demands (among others, that the officials of the land be native-born), it recognized him as king and a new dynasty was established. Under the two following monarchs, Charles IV and Wenceslaus IV, also kings of the Germans—and, in Charles's case, emperor—Bohemia reached its most notable status on the European stage. By this time the lands of the Crown of St. Wenceslaus included Bohemia, Moravia, Cheb (the Egerland), and parts of Lusatia and Silesia. By the fourteenth century Moravia was a margravate, the holding of the cadet members of the royal family. Charles especially built up the realm and its major city, Prague. He made it the imperial residence, had the bishopric raised to the status of an archbishopric, founded at Prague the first university in central Europe, including Germany, and in general attracted scholars, artists, and religious leaders to the city.

Wenceslaus started strongly but lost prestige after his imprisonment by the Czech nobility, intent on putting a stop to the growth of royal government. As he retreated into Bohemian affairs and into bouts of drinking, the German princes lost patience and deposed him from kingship in Germany, giving it eventually to his half brother, Sigismund, king of Hungary and heir apparent of Bohemia. Because of the Hussite revolution Sigismund was able to hold the Bohemian throne for only two trouble-filled years (1436–1437).

Like most medieval polities, Bohemia was riven by competition between monarch and nobles. All lay landowners participated in the political structure, with the wealthiest dominating it. This so-called land-community *(Landgemeinschaft)* had a unified system of laws and customs defined by the land court. The king or prince, as the single most powerful landowner, had the strongest voice, but he could not interpret the law alone. If the land-community felt he had violated its rights, it was justified in resisting the ruler with arms.

In the early Middle Ages the rulers of Bohemia paid their retainers with land given as fiefs. Since most were given to the retainer and his heirs in per-

BOHEMIA-MORAVIA

petuity, these holdings came to be regarded as their own by the nobles, who thus shook off feudal restrictions. By the eleventh century nobles regarded their lands as alods. Their extensive estates gave them a great deal of political power, which they used to interfere in the ruling dynasty's attempt to make its throne hereditary. In general the nobility expected to dominate the king's governing council and the provincial posts of administrator of justice *(popravci).*

Until the thirteenth century one governmental apparatus had been sufficient to provide the administrative and juridical needs of all the landowners, including the king. But as the interests and needs of the Crown diverged from those of the other landowners, the kings developed a separate administration. By the fourteenth century there were two spheres of government: the royal and the land.

The royal government had jurisdiction over church lands, royal towns, and royal estates, including lands that during the fourteenth century the monarchs gave in fief to the nobility. In this sphere the king was sovereign and did not need the approval of a diet when he levied a tax.

In the land government the king was only the first among equals. The highest powers were the land court, to which even the king could be cited, and an executive committee made up of four barons responsible for the smooth running of the court and the carrying out of its decisions. They also exercised great power between the court's sessions. All free landholders, knights, and nobles were under the jurisdiction of the land court and of the justices of the rural districts. The upper nobility was responsible only to this court, except in cases involving those lands held in fief from the king. The cases of the gentry, unless they exceeded a value of 600 groschen, were heard in a lower court.

In the fourteenth century both Charles IV and Wenceslaus IV tried to weaken the position of the nobility. They used the tried and true methods of appointing their friends who were nonnobles, and—in Wenceslaus' case—foreigners to high office. Charles's most ambitious action was his attempt to draft a statement of Bohemia's land law, the *Majestas carolina,* in the spirit of the Roman law, an action that would have undermined the nobility's position as the law-interpreting body. A written constitution would have given rise to a class of lawyers and specialists competent to define its meaning by virtue of their education. As expected, the nobility refused to ratify the *Majestas,* persuading Charles to keep the "old and customary law," the interpretation of which would remain the task of the land court.

In addition to appointing loyal friends to high office, King Wenceslaus IV attacked the nobility's economic base. Having filled strategic government offices with his own men, he obtained favorable decisions in land disputes. The king carried through claims that lands the owners thought were alodial were held in fief from the crown. In response the nobility revolted in the 1390's and reversed the trend toward greater royal power. In 1405 they regained control over appointments to important government offices. Although the Hussite revolution interrupted their drive to power, by the second half of the fifteenth century the nobility fully dominated the realm. At the bottom they extended their powers over the peasantry, and at the top they dominated both the land court and the king's council.

SOCIETY AND ECONOMY

Just as Bohemia's political forms resembled those of the rest of medieval Europe, so in general did its social patterns. There, as elsewhere in Europe, almost all people made their living off the land. The major food items for all were grains ranging from wheat to millet; vegetables such as peas, beans, and lentils; and livestock, including cattle, swine, and sheep. Hunting, fishing, and beekeeping represented only minor sources of food because by the tenth century they were monopolized by the nobility. Draft horses were found only on the estates of the nobility and of the wealthy peasants.

From the tenth century both the scratch (or hook) plow, used on lighter soils, and the moldboard, used on the heavier and more fertile soils, were employed. Also from the tenth century on, a fairly advanced harrow with iron spikes set in squares was used, as were hoes, spades, and rakes. The scythe was used in harvesting hay, but because the scythe would scatter the kernels if used in cutting grain, the sickle was used instead for this purpose. The grains were threshed with flails, never by being trodden upon by cattle. Although grain was ground mostly in the mills of the lords, many peasants kept primitive hand mills in order to avoid the lord's fees.

Bohemian and Moravian society resembled that of the rest of Europe. Only briefly in the tenth and eleventh centuries were slaves found. They were taken in war and were either sold in lands to the south or moved into the general servile class, having

BOHEMIA-MORAVIA

been granted a piece of land from which they paid the lord a rent. The status of the servile population varied, depending on the obligations imposed by the lord. The peasants' range of obligations included the older *daň,* paid to the prince in the form of corvee *(robota)* or in kind; the rent paid to the lord in kind, in corvee, or increasingly, in the thirteenth century and after, in money; the tithe to the church, which mostly ended up in the hands of the nobility; and fees to avoid having their property revert to the lord. The fines that the lord's court levied for various infractions also represented a considerable drain on the peasants' income.

Within the village society there were divisions. There are references to free peasants in the tenth century, after which this group apparently greatly diminished, entering either the servile class or the lesser nobility. As the economy became increasingly moneyed, village society grew more stratified. The wealthiest were those whose abilities and initiative had caught the eye of the lord, who took them into his administrative and judicial service, where they had ample opportunity to enrich themselves. The next group was the village artisans, including smiths, millers, and innkeepers, who had the chance to overcharge or dilute their products and so acquire the means to rise above the standard of living of the ordinary peasant. The extent of social stratification in a rural village by the end of the fourteenth century can be seen from a survey of villages belonging to the Strahov monastery. It shows that out of a total of 550 tenants, 163 had less than a quarter of a field and some had only the ground on which their home stood. At the other extreme were 136 wealthy tenants, with a full field or more. A little less than half (251) were peasants with moderate-size holdings.

Toward the end of the Middle Ages several developments contributed to improving the peasant's lot. Beginning in the thirteenth century, the transformation of the obligation to the lord from tribute in kind or work to a money rent gave the peasant greater incentive to increase the productivity of his land, since to a greater extent he was farming for himself. Many responded to the challenge and improved their material circumstances. Furthermore, the colonization of new lands with both German and Czech peasants helped bring about conditions more favorable to the peasants. Most colonists worked their land under the so-called emphyteutic law, according to which peasants and their families enjoyed the perpetual use of the land in exchange for an annual payment of a rent, most of which was in money. Most contracts set it at sixty groschen, where it remained up to the revolution in 1419.

We do not know to what extent prices increased in the thirteenth and for most of the fourteenth centuries. We do have figures for the years 1379 to 1401 that show prices for wheat and barley in the country remaining relatively static while those in Prague, over a similar period, rose slightly. By the end of the fourteenth century the Bohemian peasant paid, on the average, 10 percent of his income as rent. The emphyteutic law did, however, give the peasant security of tenure and the freedom to pass his holding on to his son without having to pay a humiliating and costly fee. Last, in certain regions peasants were able to purchase what was called "the rights of towns." According to these charters, peasants received a degree of self-government and could bequeath their property to whomever they wished. Thus, if a peasant had no natural heir, he could will his holding to a friend or a neighbor in exchange for cash. If he died without a will, his land went to the nearest relative, male or female. Obviously these developments did not mean improved conditions for all. Only those who understood and took advantage of the changes, especially the commercialization of agriculture, benefited. Those unable to avoid the pitfalls of the money economy remained where they were or became impoverished.

Bohemian and Moravian town society resembled that of Europe in general. By the tenth century Prague was a true medieval city: it had a monopoly on a market and stone walls for protection, and artisans lived off the production of goods, exchanging them for the surplus produce of the rural population. The more general growth of towns, though, had to await the commercialization of agriculture in the thirteenth century. By that time two types of town emerged: the royal, of which there were more than twenty, including Prague and Brno, and the dependent, those belonging to a baron or prelate. Most of the towns belonging to the archbishop acquired the same rights and privileges as the king's.

Residents of royal towns, although the nobility regarded them with scorn, were freemen. Their freedom was secured by a charter and based on the medieval understanding of Roman principles. It diverged from the feudal laws of the nobility in that it recognized private or emphyteutic property. The town courts, in adjudicating disputes, appealed to their own written law or, when this failed, to the precedents set in other cities, both at home and abroad. But free status did not mean communal au-

BOHEMIA-MORAVIA

tonomy. In the thirteenth century even royal towns were governed by the king's official, working with an advisory body made up of townspeople. This town council gained more extensive jurisdiction in the fourteenth century, so that the royal official became little more than a policeman carrying out the will of the council. However, even Prague never became totally independent in terms of electing its own council. In fact, it was the people's insistence that King Wenceslaus IV remove his anti-Hussite council that initiated the revolution in 1419.

Residents of dependent towns were not freemen. In some cases they were liable to perform labor services for their lord, and they generally could not dispose of their property without his consent.

Prague was by far the major city in Bohemia. By the fourteenth century its territory extended over five and one-half hectares, and with its population of between 30,000 and 40,000, it was the biggest city east of the Rhine. Most of its growth had occurred in the second half of the fourteenth century as rural people moved there. As a result a new section of the city, called New Town, was established with its own government. Most of the residents were Czech, whereas Old Town and Lesser Side, across the Vltava River, were predominantly German-speaking.

The source of the city's livelihood came mostly from within the kingdom. Bohemia exported only a few products, mostly leather and metal goods in the form of arms, which paid for the citizens' imports, such as Italian and French wines, Oriental textiles, and precious stones. The city of Zgorzelec (Görlitz) in Silesia was one of the main purchasers of Prague armaments. The fact that Prague was the administrative center for empire, kingdom, and Bohemian church also brought money to the city. Surrounding princes and towns frequently sent delegations whose members purchased goods and services in the city. The dukes of Saxony owned a house in Prague for their frequent visits. The Czech nobility also spent much time in the city, the seat of the land assembly, the land court, and the royal court. Furthermore, up to 1409 some 1,500 university students from all over central Europe brought in money. However, most of Prague's wealth came from the surrounding peasants, especially from the tenants paying rent on the extensive landholdings of the chapters and monasteries of Prague. The estimated 1,200 clergy living in the city spent some of their earnings on the craft products of the Prague artisans.

At the top Prague society had a small, wealthy group of merchants, nobles, prelates, and some of the more successful butchers and bakers. Next came a moderately wealthy group of artisan masters who were independently employed. Toward the end of the Middle Ages it was increasingly difficult for newly trained artisans to become self-employed masters, for the guilds closed ranks in order to protect their status. These frustrated skilled workers then had to seek work with the established masters. Prague also had groups of unskilled workers seeking employment on a daily basis. Bohemia was one of the few areas in Europe relatively untouched by the plague. As a result, by the late fourteenth century there were more workers than there was work, which meant both high levels of unemployment and depressed wages. At the edge of Prague society and of its laws lived the beggars, gamblers, and prostitutes. The prostitutes, who numbered in the hundreds, were organized by and worked for their "madams" in their own section of the city. Judging from the tax lists, Bohemian and Moravian towns had large populations of poor people. Anywhere from 25 to 50 percent of the people on the tax lists were exempted for reasons of poverty.

The Bohemian economy entered a recession at the end of the fourteenth century. Wages apparently remained static, or perhaps even fell, because the currency in which workers were paid had been debased. At the same time the costs of food, fuel, and housing increased. That this was a critical time for many ordinary city dwellers is reflected in the fact that more and more defaulted on what was the equivalent of a house payment, losing their homes to their creditors. Furthermore, as collateral for small loans, pawnshop keepers were taking objects essential to the owner for making his or her living. Of the more than 3,100 items pawned and recorded between 1388 and 1416 in the New Town, Prague, more than 80 percent were essential articles such as wagons, knives, shoes, caps, and half-completed artifacts. Evidently the demands of staying alive were forcing people to desperate actions. Both the church and preachers of reform chastised the wealthy and powerful for gaining their status at the expense of human suffering.

THE CHURCH

Christianity was brought into Bohemia in the ninth century by Frankish missionaries trained at St. Emmeram's monastery in Regensburg. By 845 their success was marked by the baptism of fourteen Czech nobles in Regensburg. Bohemia initially was ecclesiastically subordinate to the bishop of Regens-

BOHEMIA-MORAVIA

burg. However, Otto I, in order to thwart the growing power of the duke of Bavaria, in 973 successfully negotiated to have a new bishopric of Prague created and made subject to the archbishopric of Mainz. Not until 1344 did Prague become ecclesiastically independent, when the pope, at Charles IV's intercession, raised it to the status of archbishopric. The bishopric of Olomouc in Moravia was established in 1063 and that of Litomyšl in 1344.

Missionary work by the Franks meant not only converting people from one faith to another but also a particular method of church planting. It was customary to have the landowner undertake the building of a church on his land. He, in turn, considered the church to belong to himself, hence the "proprietary church." Even the tithe, the payment of the faithful that was supposed to go to the clergy, went mostly to the lord of the estate, who considered the parish church just another source of income on his estate. The demands and expectations that lay lords had of the church was a source of conflict between church and secular power in Bohemia, just as it was in the rest of Europe. The priests themselves were considered merely servants of the lay lord, and the bishop of Prague, until the end of the twelfth century, was considered a princely or royal chaplain.

It was the church's growing wealth that helped it to free itself partially from the laity. Landowners donated property to church institutions to relieve their consciences, but also for the satisfaction they derived from having what they liked to think of as their own monastery. From the twelfth century on, the church acquired large tracts of land, so that by the beginning of the fifteenth century it owned about 30 percent of the land in Bohemia. Its land gave it a strong base from which to resist the secular power.

One of the first church leaders in the struggle with the kings was Bishop Andrew (1215–1224), who was aided by the papacy. Andrew's goal was to free the clergy from lay control and make it responsible to the bishop. Among other things, he demanded of the laity that it not interfere with the clergy's right to the tithe, that the investiture of priests be reserved to the bishop, and that the clergy be tried only by ecclesiastical courts. By 1222 King Přemysl I had granted a charter conceding Andrew's demands. Until the fourteenth century the charter remained mostly unenforced. Bishop John of Dražice (1301–1343) vigorously supervised the installation of priests by insisting that they have his approval before taking office. In several church synods the first archbishop of Prague, Ernest of Pardubice (1344–1364), threatened lay patrons with revocation of their rights if they protected improperly installed priests, collected part of a priest's endowment, or abused priests. In order to increase his own control and to uphold clerical morality, he instigated a system of clerical supervision and visitations modeled on that of the archbishopric of Mainz.

The charter of 1222 left to the laity the right of patronage, which meant that patrons presented their candidates for parishes to the episcopal office for confirmation. The church soon launched a campaign to persuade the laity also to donate its patronage rights to ecclesiastical institutions. The effort was only moderately successful, because by the end of the Middle Ages the church owned patronage to only 28 percent of the parishes, the nobility to about 60 percent, the king to about 7 percent, and townspeople to about 3 percent.

Despite the church's efforts, the laity continued to exercise control over its parishes and priests. Patronage remained a part of the total rights of dominion a lord had on his lands that could be sold or traded just like any other property. Complaints that nobles treated their priests violently, that they removed and installed clergy at will, that they compelled candidates to give up part of a benefice's income, and that they ignored the ecclesiastical judiciary continued until the end of the Middle Ages. Whereas Archbishop Ernest had the support of his monarch, Charles IV, Archbishop John of Jenšteýn did not, and his term of office (1378–1400) was marked by continuous violent struggle with Wenceslaus IV, resulting in his early retirement. In the fifteenth century the church faced a threat from a popular reform movement, the Hussites, which eventually totally withdrew its obedience from Rome. It was not until the seventeenth century that the armies of the Habsburgs, in service to the Catholic reformation, compelled their return.

Throughout much of their history the Czechs have had their fate determined by the superior force of their neighbors. Briefly, near the end of the Middle Ages, it was otherwise. From 1420 to 1434 during the Hussite revolution, Bohemian and Moravian armies made up of peasants, gentry, and barons, of men and women, struck terror in the hearts of Europeans. Four times they repulsed Crusaders, who came from as far away as England and Spain. Almost at will they raided nearby lands including Hungary, Silesia, Saxony, Franconia, Bavaria, and Austria. At one point they went as far north as the Baltic Sea. It was the effect of these armies that compelled the medieval church to do something it had done for no other party charged with heresy. The military victories convinced the church to invite the Hussite theologians to present their program freely, without the hindrances and limitations usually placed on persons charged with heresy, before the Council of Basel (1433). It was from this council that the Czech Hussites wrung the concession to use the chalice in Communion and to confirm and ordain their own priests. Although not accepted by the papacy, this agreement from Europe's most powerful and influential prelates was an accomplishment unprecedented in the Middle Ages.

BIBLIOGRAPHY

One of the most helpful sources for beginning a study of Bohemia and Moravia in the Middle Ages is *Přehled dějin, československa* I/1 (1980), 1–480, published by the Czechoslovak Academy of Sciences (Historical Section); it contains an extensive bibliography of study aids, published sources, serials, and monographs. Jarold K. Zeman, *The Hussite Movement: A Bibliographical Study Guide* (1977), refers to many works on late medieval history, mostly in Western languages.

The most extensive survey is *České dějiny*, 16 vols. (1912–1966), edited by Václav Novotný and Kamil Krofta, which includes František M. Bartoš' classic *Čechy v době Husově, 1378–1415* (1947); see also Berthold Bretholz, *Geschichte Böhmens und Mährens*, I (1921). Other general treatments are Karl Bosl, *Handbuch der Geschichte der böhmischen Länder*, I (1967); and Francis Dvornik, *The Slavs: Their Early History and Civilization* (1956); *The Slavs in European History and Civilization* (1960); and *The Making of Central and Eastern Europe*, 2nd ed. (1974). Books dealing specifically with Great Moravia include Imre Boba, *Moravia's History Reconsidered* (1971); and L. Havlík, *Moravia in the 9th–10th Centuries* (1978).

Works concerned primarily with political developments include František Graus and Herbert Ludat, eds., *Siedlung und Verfassung Böhmens in der Frühzeit* (1967); Jan Kapras, *Přehled právních dějin zemí České koruny*, 2nd ed., I (1921); Bohuš Rieger, *Regional Government in Bohemia*, I (1894); Ferdinand Seibt, "Land und Herrschaft in Böhmen," in *Historische Zeitschrift*, **200** (1965); and Václav Vaněček, *Dějiny státu a práva v Československu do roku 1945*, 2nd ed. (1970). John Klassen, *The Nobility and the Making of the Hussite Revolution* (1978), offers a brief treatment of political developments and of parish-patron relations, as well as a summary of social and economic history.

The best works on social and economic history are in Czech: František Graus, *Chudina městská v době předhusitské* (1949); and *Dějiny venkovského lidu v Čechách v době předhusitské*, 2 vols. (1953–1957), are basic. See also Bedřich Mendl, "Hospodářské a sociální poměry v městech Pražských v letech 1378 až 1434," *in Český časopis historický*, **22** (1916) and **23** (1917); Jaroslav Mezník, "Der ökonomische Charakter Prags im 14. Jahrhundert," in *Historica*, **17** (1969); and Václav Tomek, *Dějepsis města Prahy*, I–IV (1855–1879), which is still useful.

The history of the church is treated in the general summaries mentioned above. In addition, H. F. Schmid, "Die rechtliche Grundlagen der Pfarrorganization auf westslavischen Boden," in *Zeitschrift der Savigny Stiftung für Rechtsgeschichte*, Kanonistische Abteilung, **14** (1926), provides a useful discussion of clergy-laity relations on the parish level. Ferdinand Seibt, ed., *Bohemia sacra* (1974), contains a wide range of articles by Czech and German scholars on the church and on culture; Ruben E. Weltsch, *Archbishop John of Jenstein, 1348–1400* (1968), is an informative study on church-monarch relations and also contains useful material on cultural developments. For a description of some aspects of late medieval piety in Bohemia, with bibliographical references for further study, see Howard Kaminsky, *A History of the Hussite Revolution* (1968), 5–55. On cultural developments, see Albert Kutal, *Gothic Art in Bohemia and Moravia* (1972); S. H. Thompson, "Learning at the Court of Charles IV," in *Speculum*, **25** (1950); and Eduard Winter, *Frühhumanismus: Seine Entwicklung in Böhmen und deren europäische Bedeutung für die Kirchenreformbestrebungen im 14. Jahrhundert* (1964).

JOHN KLASSEN

[See also **Cyril and Methodios, Sts.; Feudalism; Hussites; Land Tenure, Slavic; Přemyslid Dynasty; Slavic Languages and Literatures.**]

BOHEMIAN BRETHREN. The names Bohemian Brethren, Czech Brethren, and Moravian Brethren are used interchangeably by modern writers to describe a religious group that evolved from the radical wing of the Hussites in Bohemia during the 1450's. Under continuing threat of persecution, groups of the Brethren sought exile in other countries: temporary refuge in Moldavia in 1481, and permanent exile in Poland and east Prussia after 1547. In the sixteenth century their congregations flourished mainly in the margravate of Moravia, which had a high degree of religious toleration, until the suppression of all Protestants in the Habsburg lands after 1620. Thereafter the Brethren were scattered to many lands. In 1722 a few descendants settled at Herrnhut in Saxony and played a part in the restoration of some traditions of the old Brethren in the "renewed" Unitas Fratrum under Nikolaus von Zinzendorf. The modern Moravian church claims continuity of

BOHEMIAN BRETHREN

episcopal order with the original Bohemian Brethren.

In the fifteenth and sixteenth centuries, the group was known under several names: Brethren *(Fratres)*, Brothers of the Law of Christ *(Fratres Legis Christi)*, Unity of Brethren *(Unitas Fratrum)*, the Waldensian Brethren *(Fratres Waldenses)*, and Picards *(Picardi, Pighardi, Beghardi)*. The term Bohemians *(Bohemi)* was usually applied to members of the large national Hussite church (the Utraquists or Calixtines); Moravians *(Moravi)* sometimes referred to Brethren residing in Moravia. The designation *Unitas Fratrum (Jednota bratrská)* was derived from the distinctions made by the Brethren in their concept of the church. The term "church" *(ecclesia, církev, Kirche)* was reserved for the church universal, which on earth was divided into several "unities" (*unitas, jednota, Unität;* a synonym for denomination), such as the Roman or Lutheran unity. The local church was described consistently as "congregation" *(congregatio, sbor, Gemeinde)*.

THE OLD BRETHREN

The first generation of original Brethren (1457–1490) can be seen as a climax to the spiritual evolution of the Hussite movement, which served as a bridge between the late-medieval reform movements within and outside the church (Devotio moderna, the Waldensians, and the Lollards) and the Protestant Reformation. Disillusioned with the religious and political stalemate that characterized the situation in "heretical" Bohemia after the Hussite wars (1420–1434), small groups of religious seekers appeared in many places. Some gathered around "good priests," whose moral character was perceived as a safeguard of efficacious ministration of sacraments (the Donatist tradition). Others sought instruction in the Bible from ordained church teachers or from lay theologians.

The most original among the latter was Peter Chelčický (*ca.* 1380–*ca.* 1460), a country squire with limited formal education, but a creative thinker and author of fifty-six preserved Czech writings. In his best-known work, *The Net of Faith* (*Sít'víry,* written *ca.* 1440 and first published in 1521), he adopted the Waldensian view of history. The fall of the church occurred when "two monstrous whales," Emperor Constantine and Pope Sylvester, tore the net of faith (Luke 5:6) to pieces. Chelčický rejected the close ties between medieval church and state. He also renounced the system of parish churches to which every citizen belonged by virtue of birth and infant baptism. He envisaged small local congregations formed by voluntary commitment of adult disciples. To Chelčický the cross of Christ represented not only the atoning sacrifice for the sins of humanity but also a call to radical obedience: to take up the cross and follow Christ on a path of self-denial and suffering. The church was to be restored to its pre-Constantinian poverty and powerlessness in society.

An eyewitness to the bloodshed of the Hussite wars, Chelčický became a consistent pacifist (*On Spiritual Warfare, O boji duchovním, ca.* 1421). He also rejected the feudal division of society into three classes (nobility, clergy, and commons) as incompatible with the love of God. His vision of a classless society included a call for the abolition of serfdom and the demand that all men, even the priests, support themselves by physical work (*On the Triple Division of Society, O trojím lidu, ca.* 1425). His egalitarian vision was likely not intended as a blueprint for society as a whole, but as a life-style for a minority of true Christians. Nonetheless, he has been considered the first genuine revolutionary ideologist, the only one to separate the secular from the sacred.

Chelčický's vision of radical Christian primitivism and social separatism became a reality when, in the winter of 1457–1458, a small group of earnest seekers, led by Gregory (Řehoř) of Prague (*d.* 1474), established a religious community at Kunvald in the mountains of eastern Bohemia. Gregory's plan had been approved by his uncle, Jan Rokycana (*ca.* 1395–1471), archbishop of the Hussite (Utraquist) church. He was initially sympathetic to such renewal strivings, but when the network of the Brethren assemblies grew, and when in 1467 they cast lots (Acts 1:26) to choose their own priests, independent of the apostolic succession in the Roman and Hussite churches, Rokycana agreed to persecution of the Brethren by the "Hussite king," George of Poděbrady (reigned 1458–1471).

In 1480 several hundred German-speaking Waldensian refugees from the Mark of Brandenburg settled around Lanškroun and Fulnek in eastern Bohemia and Moravia. They were received into the Unity, and formed its small German-speaking branch. The vast majority of the Brethren were Czech-speaking.

During the first generation the Brethren practiced consistent separation from society. They lived mostly in isolated rural settlements and supported themselves by physical work as peasants and artisans. They did not admit into membership persons with higher education or members of nobility,

BOHEMIAN BRETHREN

wealthy burghers, and members of specified occupations. They disallowed the taking of oaths (Matthew 5:33–37), service in government, and bearing of arms. They stopped short of communal sharing of property. Their ascetic life-style resembled monastic rules, and was governed by the Sermon on the Mount, which they regarded as the key to the understanding of Scripture.

Up to 1530 the Brethren retained all seven sacraments but reinterpreted their meaning, particularly the presence of Christ in the Eucharist. Baptism was administered to adults (rebaptism) by threefold pouring of water in the hands of the candidate, who then washed his or her face. Infant baptism was retained for children born to members of the Unity. The practice of rebaptism was discontinued in 1534. There were strict rules for church discipline and for admission to membership, which was understood as a lifelong process of spiritual formation in three stages: beginners (*incipientes,* inquirers and young people under catechetical instruction); progressing members (*progredientes, proficientes,* after baptism); and mature members *(perfecti),* from whom lay leaders and church officers were recruited.

CHANGES IN THE SECOND GENERATION

In the 1480's the social character of membership began to change. Increasingly, townspeople and persons with higher education sought to join the Unity. The leading congregations were now located in manorial towns such as Litomyšl and Mladá Boleslav, where they enjoyed protection by sympathetic nobility. The changes in the socioeconomic profile of membership led to ideological conflict. The younger generation sought to modify the rigid social and ethical separatism of the Old Brethren. There were important theological issues as well. The emphasis on obedience to the law of Christ was increasingly condemned as legalism (salvation by good works) and was replaced by focus on salvation provided by God's free grace, which believers receive through the voluntary response of faith, as a gift (similar to Luther's *sola fide,* "by faith alone").

The main spokesman for the changing outlook was Luke (Lukáš) of Prague (*ca.* 1460–11 December 1528). Reared in a Hussite home in Prague, he received the bachelor's degree at the university in October 1481. After a spiritual crisis he moved to Litomyšl, and joined the Brethren there in 1482. Luke was ordained priest, elected to the Central Council of the Unity (1494), and consecrated a bishop (1500). In 1491–1492 he and others visited southeastern Europe and the Near East in a vain search for remnants of the uncorrupted apostolic church. In 1498, Luke sought contacts with the Waldensians in northern Italy, was appalled by conditions in papal Rome, and likely witnessed the burning of Savonarola in Florence.

In the mid 1490's the Unity divided into Major and Minor parties. The latter, led by Amos (*d.* 1522), sought to retain the original rigoristic stance of the Old Brethren. The Amosites survived in a few rural settlements until the mid sixteenth century. The Major Party gained control of the Unity under the leadership of Luke, author of 150 Czech works. Influenced by humanism, he took full advantage of the printing press. Several editions of a new Czech translation of the New Testament, Czech and German hymnbooks, as well as Czech, German, and Latin confessions and polemical works were published from 1501 on. Messengers of the Unity visited Erasmus at Antwerp in 1520, and Luther at Wittenberg several times in the 1520's. Luke wrote polemical works against specific doctrines of Luther, Zwingli, and the Anabaptists. He defended the unique character of the Unity as a church built on the principles of regenerate church membership, church discipline, and separation of church and state.

Luke provided a theological basis on which the Brethren in his and later generations could become champions of religious toleration as well as pioneers of wide ecumenical contacts with all branches of the Christian church.

After Luke's death in 1528, the Unity underwent further changes in its theological orientation. A period marked by strong Lutheran influence (1528–1546) was followed by a period of transition (1546–1575). Ultimately the Brethren sought closer ideological and political alignment with the Calvinistic Reformation. However, despite such shifting international ecumenical contacts and increasing cooperation with the national Utraquist church at home (*Confessio bohemica,* 1575), the Brethren never fully surrendered their identity as the oldest "believers' church" and "free church."

BIBLIOGRAPHY

Jarold K. Zeman, *The Hussite Movement and the Reformation in Bohemia, Moravia, and Slovakia (1350–1650)* (1977), exhaustively lists materials in English, other Western languages, and selective Slavic and other languages.

The Moravian Archives in Bethlehem, PA, contain a large collection of printed sources on the Czech Reformation, as well as microfilm of the chief manuscript source, *Acta Unitatis Fratrum,* 14 vols.

Edmund A. De Schweinitz, *The History of the Church Known as the Unitas Fratrum* (1901), is outdated. Standard general works are Joseph T. Müller, *Geschichte der Böhmischen Brüder,* 3 vols. (1922–1931); and Rudolf Říčan, *Die Böhmischen Brüder,* Bohumír Popelař, trans. (1961).

Studies on the first and second generations of the Unity are Peter Brock, *The Political and Social Doctrines of the Unity of Czech Brethren in the Fifteenth and Early Sixteenth Centuries* (1957); Jaroslav Goll, *Quellen und Untersuchungen zur Geschichte der Böhmischen Brüder,* 2 vols. (1878–1882); and *Chelčický a Jednota v XV. století* [Chelčický and the Unity in the fifteenth century] (1916); Amedeo Molnár, *Boleslavští bratří* [The Brethren of Boleslav] (1952); Victor-Lucien Tapié, *Une église tchèque au XVe siècle: L'Unité des Frères* (1934); Rudolf Urbánek, *České dějiny* [History of Bohemia], III, pts. 3 and 4 (1930–1962); Jarold Knox Zeman, *The Anabaptists and the Czech Brethren in Moravia* (1969).

Chelčický's "Treatises on Christianity and Social Order," Howard Kaminsky, ed. and trans., in *Studies in Medieval and Renaissance History,* **1** (1964). On Chelčický, see Matthew Spinka, "Peter Chelčický: The Spiritual Father of the Unitas Fratrum," in *Church History,* **12** (1943); Murray Wagner, *Peter Chelčický* (1982). See also the works by Brock, Goll, and Urbánek listed above. An English translation of *The Net of Faith* and a volume of selected sources on the Unitas will appear in the series Classics of the Radical Reformation. See also Donald F. Durnbaugh, *The Believers' Church* (1968).

On Rokycana, see Frederick G. Heymann, "John Rokycana: Church Reformer Between Hus and Luther," in *Church History,* **28** (1959); and *George of Bohemia: King of Heretics* (1965).

On Lukáš, see Amedeo Molnár, *Bratr Lukáš, bohoslovec Jednoty* [Brother Luke, theologian of the Unity] (1948) and "Luc de Prague," in *Communio viatorum,* **3–6** (1960–1963).

JAROLD K. ZEMAN

[See also **Devotio Moderna; Hussites; Lollards; Reform, Idea of; Waldensians.**]

BOHEMOND I, PRINCE OF ANTIOCH (*ca.* 1050/1058–1111). Fact and fiction are interwoven in the history of the Normans, and no Norman offers a better example than Bohemond, perhaps the most glamorous of the leaders of the First Crusade. His incredible feats of arms, his cunning diplomacy, and his struggle with the Byzantine and Islamic worlds have caught the interest of many generations of historians.

He was christened Marc, son of Robert Guiscard and Alberada, but his nickname, Bohemond, was taken from a legendary giant. Vague contemporary descriptions lead us to believe that he was a magnificent physical specimen, and his later feats of endurance corroborate such a description. The exact date of his birth is unknown. In any event, while in his teens he became a leader in his father's mercenary army. The birth of his half brother, Roger Borsa, posed a problem for Bohemond, who realized that his stepmother, Sigelgaita, would deny him his patrimony. This turn of events forced him to turn to Byzantine lands, and in 1081, Bohemond captured Avlona. In the same year Alexios I Komnenos became emperor of Byzantium, a state beset by the Normans, the Seljuks, and the impending wave of Latin Crusaders. During the next three decades Bohemond and Alexios clashed. Robert Guiscard and Bohemond won in the initial phases of the struggle, and posed a threat to Byzantium. However, Bohemond lost Larissa to Alexios in 1083, and his father's death in 1085 ended the first phase of his struggle with the Greeks.

Despite initial failures Bohemond attempted to wrest lands from Roger Borsa, and succeeded in gaining Bari. Conveniently for Bohemond, Pope Urban II initiated the First Crusade in November of 1095 with a call for Christians to take up arms against the Muslims and recover the Holy Sepulcher. Bohemond had not only papal sanction for the acquisition of new lands but also promises of spiritual rewards. He took the cross, assembled a small band of Normans, and left Bari in October 1096. In the following months Bohemond crossed Greek lands with a minimum of incidents. He left his troops in Roussa (now Keshan) and journeyed to Constantinople, where he received an honorable welcome from Alexios. In secret negotiations Alexios and Bohemond made a compromise, the terms of which are poorly recorded. Certainly, Bohemond took an oath of allegiance and promised to return Greek lands captured by the Crusaders. What Alexios promised in return is left unclear by the Latin chroniclers, who were intent on justifying Bohemond's later seizure of Antioch.

The main contingents of the crusading forces crossed the Bosporus, and besieged Nicaea on 16 May 1097. Nicaea surrendered to the Greeks on 19 June in order to avert a sack of the city at the hands of the Latins. The ensuing Latin resentment of the Greeks opened the way for the renewal of Bohemond's quarrel with Alexios. The Crusaders soon renewed their march, with Bohemond in the vanguard. Kīlīj Arslan, who had lost Nicaea, awaited the arrival of the Crusaders at Dorylaeum on 1 July. Bohemond's forces bore the brunt of the Turkish ambush, but repulsed the enemy attack until the main contingents arrived and routed the Turkish troops.

The Christian armies, after great suffering, arrived before the walls of Antioch in October, and besieged the city until 3 June 1098. During the long siege Bohemond engaged in numerous skirmishes. News of a relief force headed by Kerbogha, the Turkish governor of Mosul, caused many of the city's leaders to consent to Bohemond's ownership of Antioch unless Alexios came to claim the city.

After the opening of the gates of Antioch, the Crusaders sacked the city and slaughtered the inhabitants. The relief army of Kerbogha arrived before Antioch on 5 June, and made the situation of the Christians difficult. Bohemond restored order in the ranks, and the crusading forces marched out of Antioch and routed the forces of Kerbogha on 28 June. In the ensuing months the Crusaders remained in the city, and Bohemond claimed Antioch on the basis of Alexios' failure to aid the Westerners. Finally, Bohemond used force to oust the followers of Raymond de St. Gilles, who supported Alexios, and to establish his hold on Antioch. The main contingents of the Christians resumed the march to Jerusalem, leaving Bohemond in possession of Antioch.

After the fall of Jerusalem, Bohemond, in the company of Baldwin, count of Edessa, and Daimbert, an archbishop who hoped to become patriarch of Jerusalem, visited the Holy City and completed his earlier vows to recover the Holy Sepulcher. Before his return to Antioch, he aided Daimbert in his quest for the patriarchate. Returning to Antioch soon thereafter, Bohemond found that his hold on the city was threatened by Alexios, who claimed his right to it, and by his Muslim neighbors, who viewed him as an intruder. He led a campaign against the Turks, but was captured by Malik-Ghāzi Gûmûshtigin, the Danishmendid emir of Sivas. In 1101, Crusaders trying to release him fell into a Turkish ambush. Following this disaster the main force was decimated by a superior Turkish force.

During Bohemond's captivity his nephew Tancred served as regent of Antioch. The Turks offered to release Bohemond upon payment of a heavy ransom, but Tancred was reluctant to raise it. However, Bohemond managed to have his friends pay the money, and immediately returned to Antioch (1103).

Two years later Bohemond renewed his struggle with Alexios. In order to gain sympathy for his cause, he had an interview with the pope; journeyed through France, telling of the perfidious acts of Alexios; and strengthened his cause by marrying Constance, daughter of Philip I of France. In September 1105, Bohemond launched an offensive against Alexios, but encountered strong resistance. In the ensuing stalemate Alexios accepted Bohemond's claim to Antioch with a provision requiring vassalage. The landless Bohemond had in a few decades extended his holdings from Apulia to Antioch, using the Crusades as a vehicle for his personal ambitions. Bohemond's death on 7 March 1111 prevented inroads into Byzantium, but his heirs acquired the principality of Antioch and played an important role in the Levant for several decades.

BIBLIOGRAPHY

Ralph B. Yewdale, *Bohemond I: Prince of Antioch,* 2nd ed. (1924); Robert L. Nicholson, *Tancred: A Study of His Career and Work* (1940).

JOHN H. HILL

[See also **Alexios I Komnenos; Antioch; Byzantine Empire; Crusades and Crusader States; Normans and Normandy; Tancred (Crusader).**]

BOIS PROTAT. Although the *Bois Protat* is probably the oldest European block intended for printing, its uniqueness limits its significance. Because similar objects have not survived, we may never be certain that it is in fact a Burgundian artifact of the last quarter of the fourteenth century, as is widely believed. Nevertheless, it is the only block that could lay claim to such an early date; and it is, in any case, the only extant French block cut before 1500.

Discovered in 1898 in the vicinity of the abbey of La Ferté-sur-Grosne, near Dijon, the block has ever since been the property of the Protat family in Mâcon. It is probably of walnut and measures 600 by 230 by 25 millimeters. The lines are crudely and rather shallowly executed. One side of the block is a fragment of an Annunciation, while the verso carries a larger fragment of a Crucifixion. Whereas the former would transpose the normal right-left arrangement of the Annunciation if printed, the reversed inscription of the Crucifixion ("Vere filius Dei erat iste") was clearly meant to be printed. It is not certain, however, whether the total image, whose original dimensions might have reached 700 by 600 millimeters, was intended to be printed on cloth or on paper.

Because the *Bois Protat* does not really resemble any of the surviving fifteenth-century blocks in technique, the historian must rely on stylistic rather than technical evidence when assessing its place and date of origin. Although crudely executed, the drawing of the Crucifixion is endowed with considerable character and grace. Its style argues for a date between 1370 and 1390 and an assignment to Burgundy. Not only do details of costume and armor support the dating, but the treatment of faces, of the long drapery folds, and of the space itself seems thoroughly consonant with works in many media produced around 1370–1390 under Charles V and his brothers. In other words, this block may quite reasonably be regarded as a reflection of a courtly style just prior to the full flowering of the International Style. The obvious point of comparison is the sublime *Parement de Narbonne.*

There remain two peculiarities not generally noted. The design of the Annunciation is far less accomplished than that of the Crucifixion; perhaps this explains why the floor pattern was left unfinished, implying also a date later than that of the Crucifixion. Second, the block itself conforms precisely to the standard thickness of all other known printing blocks (with one or two exceptions) of the fifteenth and sixteenth centuries. This might be considered surprising in an object thought to be the first of its kind. It could, however, indicate that the practice of printing on textiles had achieved a standardization far earlier than one may suppose from the surviving evidence.

BIBLIOGRAPHY

Henri F. X. M. Bouchot, *Un ancêtre de la gravure sur bois* (1902), and *Les deux cents incunables xylographiques du Département des Estampes,* 2 vols. (1903); Max Lehrs, review of Bouchot's *Un ancêtre de la gravure sur bois,* in *Repertorium für Kunstwissenschaft,* **25** (1902); Wilhelm L. Schreiber, "M. Bouchots Ansichten über die Erstlinge der Holzschneidekunst," in *Zeitschrift für christliche Kunst,* **21** (1908).

RICHARD S. FIELD

[See also **Printing, Origins; Prints and Printmaking.**]

BOISSEAU (Middle French, *boissel;* probably from Old French *boisse,* a measure of grain; perhaps from Vulgar Latin *bostia, boistia,* "what one can hold in the hands"), the principal measure of capacity for dry products throughout France. The Parisian standard was defined in an ordinance of 1670 as any vessel being 8 pouces, 2.5 lignes, in height and 10 pouces in diameter, making a total of 655.78 cubic pouces (13.008 liters). The boisseau for wheat traditionally contained 4 quartes or 16 litrons, and was equal to 1/3 minot, 1/6 mine, 1/12 setier, and 1/144 muid; for oats, 4 picotins, equal to 1/24 setier and 1/288 muid; for charcoal, 2 demi-boisseaux, equal to 1/8 minot, 1/16 mine, and 1/328 muid; for salt, 2 demi-boisseaux or 16 litrons, equal to 1/4 minot, 1/16 setier, and 1/192 muid; for plaster, 1/12 sac and 1/432 muid; and for lime, 1/2 minot and 1/144 muid. Variations of the boisseau were numerous, however, with some cities and locales having more than one acceptable, customary standard. In the departments of Aisne, Bouches-du-Rhône, Marne, and Oise it was used as a measure of area for land.

RONALD EDWARD ZUPKO

[See also **Bushel; Weights and Measures, Western European.**]

BOLL (from Old English *bolla,* a bowl, beaker, or measure), a measure of capacity for dry products used principally in Scotland, where it was first standardized under David I at 12 gallons, or the capacity of a vessel 9 inches deep and 72 inches in circumference. Throughout the Middle Ages it was commonly regarded as any vessel capable of holding 164 pounds of the clear water of the Tay River. By 1600 it was fixed at 4 firlots or 8,789.34 cubic inches (1.441 hectoliters) for wheat, peas, beans, rye, and white salt, and at 12,822.096 cubic inches (2.101 hectoliters) for oats, barley, and malt. Both bolls were equal to 16 pecks or 64 lippies. Regionally, however, there were hundreds of variations for these and other products.

In medieval England the boll was 1/20 of the Newcastle coal chalder or 2.1 hundredweights (106.684 kilograms). Several adjustments were subsequently made in its size until it was finally standardized in 1695 at 1/24 Newcastle chalder of 53 hundredweights or 247.3 pounds (112.187 kilograms). As in Scotland, there were numerous local variations.

RONALD EDWARD ZUPKO

[See also **Weights and Measures, Western European.**]

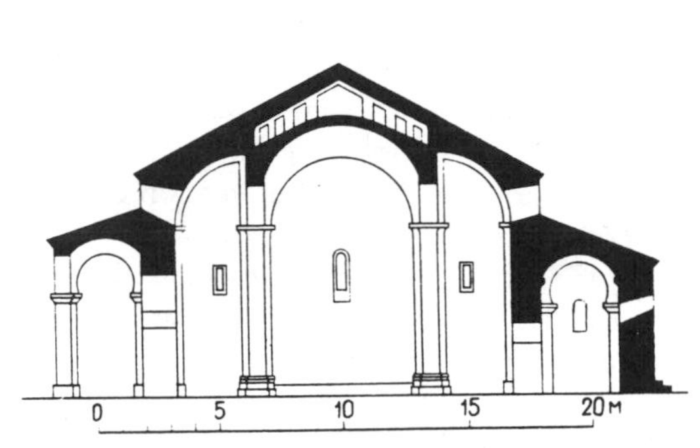

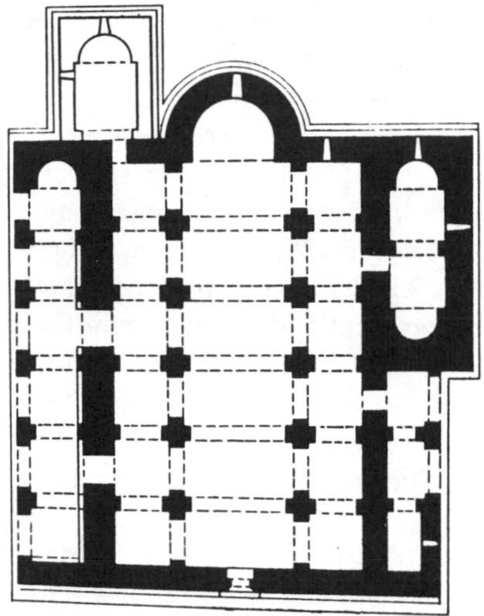

Bolnisi Seon, 478–493 A.D. Transverse section and ground plan. DRAWINGS FROM G. YSHUBINASHVILI, BOLNISSKIJ SION (1940)

BOLNISI SEON. The Basilica of Zion, located in the southern part of the Georgian province of Kartli, is the earliest and largest (exterior, 27.8 meters by 24.5 meters) three-naved vaulted basilica in Georgia. It is built of greenish tufa, and an inscription dates its construction from 478 to 493. On the north side is a longitudinal gallery to accommodate the catechumens. On the south are a smaller gallery and a compartment used as baptistery. Originally the basilica was accessible from the north and south; the western doorway derives from the seventeenth century. The small chapel on the northeastern side was added in the eighth century.

Typical of Bolnisi Seon are the cruciform piers of the nave. The arms of the crosses support the arches of the barrel vaults and the arcuation of the piers. Such piers are regarded as a prototype for the medieval complex bundle columns. The pastophories are absent. The pier and pilaster capitals, as well as some bases, are decorated with reliefs of animal, geometric, and plant motifs.

BIBLIOGRAPHY

G. Tshubinashvili, *Bolnisskij Sion* (1940), 62–78; F. W. Deichmann, "Zur Entwicklung der Pfeilerbasilika: Die Basilika Sion von Bolnisi," in *Second International Symposium of Georgian Art* (1977), 1–10.

WACHTANG DJOBADZE

[See also **Georgian Art and Architecture.**]

BOLOGNA, UNIVERSITY OF. Bologna vies with Paris for the title of oldest and most distinguished university of medieval Europe, but whereas Paris was essentially a guild of masters, Bologna was in origin an association of students. The *universitas scholarium* emerged around 1190 as an organization of the non-Bolognese law students resident in the city, and rapidly developed a complex constitution rather like that of contemporary communes. By 1204 there were apparently four *universitates,* later reduced to two, one for Italian and one for non-Italian students, each with an elected rector and *consiliarii* responsible to a general congregation; each body was divided into a number of constituent "nations" that provided the rectors in rotation.

Originally intended only to safeguard the civil rights of the students who lacked the protection of Bolognese citizenship and, being laymen, also of the church courts, the student organization soon began to take over the supervision of the teaching in the schools, despite the objections of the doctors, who claimed that mere apprentices should not wield such powers. The university statutes, which were confirmed by the commune and the papacy in 1252–1253, have survived only in a revised version begun in 1317, but these still show the extent of student power in its thirteenth-century heyday when the student body hired the doctors on stringent conditions, paid their salaries, and fined them for the slightest dereliction of their duties. The attempt to define all duties and obligations in legalistic terms was typically Italian, but the exclusion of the doctors and all Bolognese citizens from any voice in the ruling body was a flaw that was never overcome.

By 1300 student power was retreating in the face of the commune, which began to pay the salaries of some doctors in 1280 and was appointing all of them by about 1350. Between the powers of the students on the one hand and of the commune on the other, the teaching doctors controlled little except the all-important examinations; the role of the church, which through the archdeacon granted the *licentia docendi* (license to teach), was little more than nominal.

The university developed in Bologna because the city had long been the home of a widely renowned law school that seems to have arisen through private initiative to meet the needs of the developing European society of the late eleventh century. The seminal influence was that of Irnerius (*d. ca.* 1130) who is said to have been a teacher of liberal arts before he began to study Justinian's *Corpus iuris civilis*, especially the hitherto neglected *Digest*. The impetus he gave to the study of these sixth-century texts was maintained by a succession of distinguished doctors throughout the twelfth century, and culminated in the compilation of the definitive *glossa ordinaria,* completed about 1228 by the Florentine Accursius. There followed the post-Glossators, who devoted themselves to the application of Roman law to contemporary problems, such as feudal customs and the drafting of communal statutes.

Meanwhile, Bologna had also achieved fame as a center for the study of canon law, grounded on the *Concordance of Discordant Canons* or *Decretum* compiled by the monk Gratian around 1140. From the pontificate of Alexander III (1159–1181), a former doctor of canon law, the university was increasingly recognized by the papacy, while the earlier imperialist tradition stemming from Irnerius declined. Canon and civil law were taught side by side, and a surprising number of Italian canonists were laymen. In the fourteenth century, the study of the laws of war by Giovanni da Legnano was a new departure.

Compared with the school of law, which was second to none in Europe, the other faculties at Bologna were of more limited significance. The faculty of arts and medicine, which emerged in the second half of the thirteenth century, had to struggle at first to secure its independence from the jurist universities; the faculty of theology was not founded until 1364. A school of rhetoric was initiated by Adalberto Samaritani, a contemporary of Irnerius and now regarded as the originator of the medieval *dictamen:* with Boncompagno of Signa (teaching from about 1195, *d.* after 1240) and his successor Guido Fava, rhetorical studies moved from letter writing to other practical concerns, including politics, and the first steps were taken toward the application of rhetoric to the vernacular.

At around the same time, notarial studies were established as a separate discipline by Ranieri da Perugia; the *Summa artis notariae* of Rolandino Passeggieri (*ca.* 1255) was established as the definitive textbook until the sixteenth century. By contrast, the Bolognese contribution to natural science was small, and humanism was slow to take root, although Theodore of Candia was teaching Greek there in 1426. In 1450, Pope Nicholas V created the first university chair of music in Europe at Bologna.

The work of the studium was often interrupted by war, plague, imperial bans, and papal interdicts. Some early divisions within the academic body led to migrations and the establishment of daughter universities, but these were generally short lived; Padua, founded in 1222, was unique in its inheritance of Bologna's vitality as well as most of its constitutional characteristics. Bolognese influence on other Italian and a few non-Italian universities (such as Prague) was modified by their being under the control of princely or municipal authority from the start.

The colleges at Bologna remained small and provided little teaching. The strength of Bologna lay in its power to attract students and outstanding teachers from the whole of Italy and beyond. The position of the city at the crossroads of Lombardy and Tuscany was paramount in this respect; only in the late Middle Ages did the growth of local universities begin to undermine Bologna's supremacy as a center for legal and medical studies. The university reflected the strengths of the communal tradition: lay despite the teaching of much canon law, and strongly directed toward the skills of everyday life, free from the domination of any prince or even of the papacy, protected by a wealthy commune that valued it above all as a unique financial asset.

BIBLIOGRAPHY

Chartularium studii Bononiensis, 13 vols. (1909–1939); J. K. Hyde, "Commune, University, and Society in Early Medieval Bologna," in John W. Baldwin and R. A. Goldthwaite, eds., *Universities in Politics* (1972); Carlo Mala-

BONAVENTURE, ST.

gola, ed., *Statuti delle università e dei collegi dello studio bolognese* (1888); Berthe M. Marti, *The Spanish College at Bologna in the Fourteenth Century* (1966); Albano Sorbelli, *Storia della università di Bologna,* I (1944); Sven Stelling-Michaud, *L'université de Bologne et la pénétration des droits romain et canonique en Suisse aux xiii*[e] *et xiv*[e] *siècles* (1955). Detailed studies are in *Studi e memorie per la storia dell' università di Bologna,* 1st ser., 18 vols. (1907–1950); n.s. 2 vols. (1956–1961), published by the Istituto per la Storia dell' Università di Bologna.

J. K. HYDE

[See also **Boncompagno of Signa; Glossators; Gratian; Irnerius; Law, Schools of; Medicine, Schools of; Schools; Universities.**]

BONAVENTURE, ST. (*ca.* 1217–15 July 1274), christened Giovanni, was born at Bagnoregio (near Viterbo), the son of Giovanni di Fidanza, a physician, and Maria Ritella. At the age of about ten, he fell ill and was saved miraculously from death by the intercession of St. Francis. Giovanni got his early schooling from the Franciscans at Bagnoregio. In 1235 he entered the University of Paris, where he studied grammar, rhetoric, logic, and philosophy. He became bachelor of arts in 1241 and, after teaching the liberal arts, became master of arts in 1243. He joined the Franciscan order in Paris, and made his religious profession, with the name Bonaventure, in 1244.

Bonaventure received his theological education in the Franciscan school at the University of Paris, under Alexander of Hales and John of La Rochelle (1243–1245) and Eudes Rigaud (1245–1248). He studied Scripture, the church fathers, and medieval Doctors, consolidated his knowledge of Aristotle, and read Ibn Sīnā and Ibn Rushd. After becoming bachelor of Scripture under William of Meliton (1248), Bonaventure lectured on the Bible, notably the Gospel of St. Luke. As bachelor of the Sentences (1250), he taught Peter Lombard's *Sentences.* Having become a formed bachelor around November 1252, he helped William of Meliton with his lectures and was trained, until December 1253, in the art of preaching, or Christian eloquence. It was probably at this time that he was ordained a priest.

Bonaventure's teachers recognized his fine memory and rare intelligence. Alexander of Hales said that Adam seemed not to have sinned in Bonaventure. Uniting a life of prayer with the study of theology, he adapted his scholastic formation as a theologian to his religious development as a friar of the Order of St. Francis. The depth of his theological reflection as a student and the wealth of his personal experience as a Franciscan came together to form an original thinker.

By Easter 1254, Bonaventure was master of theology in the chair of the Franciscan school at the University of Paris. On his inception he defended a series of disputed questions *De scientia Christi.* He showed that Christ, as Divine Word, knows an infinite number of things by their divine ideas. These ideas are identical with God's essence. Under the influence of his eternal light, ideas cause the natural certitude of science and wisdom. As man, Christ did not comprehend the divine wisdom nor all things known to it. The prescribed sermon or *principium* affirmed Christ as the source of illumination for every science and wisdom. For the theologian, Christ is our way by faith, our truth by understanding, and our life by cleanness of heart. The theologian must honor Christ by word and deed, listen to him with humble faith, and question him with a studious, not a curious, mind. Christ will teach him all truth by sending the Holy Spirit.

Shortly afterward, as master of theology, Bonaventure debated another series, *De mysterio Trinitatis*, on the being and attributes of God. Bonaventure indicated how the divine essence is knowable by reason and faith, then how it is knowable with reference to the Trinity. The two series and the sermon testify that he had an unusual ability to reconcile diverse doctrines, while unifying them by his fervent love of God, in an original synthesis of reason and faith.

From 1254 to 1257, Bonaventure taught and preached at the University of Paris. His scriptural commentaries present his sacred science, founded on faith, and the basis of his science of theology, developed in his commentary on the *Sentences* of Peter Lombard. United, the two sciences formed one sacred doctrine. In his commentary on Ecclesiastes, taking the theme of God as our eternal and beatific good, Bonaventure compares our love for the Creator and for the creature, which is good and directed to God, but empty because of a natural tendency toward its original nonbeing; he also examines the emptiness of sin in the fool and the true way of life in the wise man. Seeing futility in mundane wisdom, he nevertheless recognizes that "every creature, because it speaks God, is a divine word." Ecclesiastes opened hidden doors to Bonaventure's heart and mind: he found much wisdom, reflecting his Franciscan view of life, on our use of temporal goods as means to our eternal good.

In his commentary on St. Luke's Gospel, Bonaventure directs his attention to the mission of preachers: anointed with the grace of the Holy Spirit, they are sent with due authority to teach the word of God with fraternal love for their hearers. This Gospel portrays Christ the mediator preaching salvation to men, and Christ the redeemer triumphing over sin and death in his passion, resurrection, and ascension. It manifests the mystery of the incarnation, the healing power of Christ's preaching, the truth of our redemption, and our reward of eternal life. Bonaventure used this work to share with his Franciscan brothers, in their preaching of the Gospel, the treasures of science and wisdom he had found in pondering the life and mission of Christ.

In his commentary on St. John's Gospel, Bonaventure employed reasons founded on faith to support a theological understanding of the divinity and humanity of Christ. Coming from the Father, the Son is the Divine Word through whom the Father speaks and creates all things. Assuming a human nature, the Son is the incarnate Word attesting the Father and speaking the words of truth for eternal life. This work reveals the depths of Bonaventure's contemplation and love of Christ, Son and Word of God.

Bonaventure's theological commentary on Peter Lombard's *Sentences* (1254–1256) is without doubt one of the finest treatments of this work. He visualizes theology as a spiritual river: perennial in the unbeginning and unending emanation of the Divine Persons, spacious in the extensive work and wise order of God's creation, circular in the Incarnation uniting beginning to end or man to God in Christ, and abundant in the sacraments of living water washing away sins and giving life through grace. The subject of theology is the object of faith made understandable by uniting it to reason.

Bonaventure thus set out from God as one and triune, proceeded through Christ the integral exemplar of truth, natural and revealed, and achieved a theological understanding of the Trinity from its universal effects in nature and grace. Subordinated to Scripture through divine authority, theology has certitude from reason perfected by a loving faith and the gifts of knowledge and understanding. It seeks the good of the Christian in the contemplation, and mainly the love, of the gift of wisdom. Theology is distinct from the science of Scripture, which seeks the good of eternal life and to which theology is ultimately directed. This commentary shows Bonaventure's originality as a theologian and philosopher. Relying chiefly on his own reasons and arguments, he forged a masterful and mature synthesis rooted firmly in Scripture and formed within Christian faith.

The one sacred doctrine derived from Bonaventure's two sciences of Scripture and theology was sketched in *De reductione artium ad theologiam* (1256), and developed in *Breviloquium* (1256–1257). Identifying theology and Scripture, he saw them coming from the Trinity through revelation, advancing according to human reason illumined by faith, describing the contents of the whole universe, and leading to the fullness of eternal life. This doctrine has a fourfold vision of man and the universe. Enfolding the Scriptures, the *width* of the doctrine has a single knowledge of what to believe and to do (unlike philosophy, which separates the speculative from the practical), and so reaches the supreme power, wisdom, and beneficence of God. Going from beginning to end, or creation to last judgment, the *length* includes the three times (laws) and seven ages of the world. Moving from man to God, the *height* of the doctrine grounds philosophy within theology by subjecting human knowledge and the things of nature to faith and grace, thus erecting a ladder touching heaven and earth, but built around Jesus Christ, God and man. Containing all the senses of Scripture, the *depth* holds its many mystical meanings, which signify what we must believe, do, and desire for eternal beatitude. Bonaventure manifests here an astounding ability to transport his personal (Franciscan) experiences to the universal level of a sacred doctrine based firmly on the truth of Scripture.

In all these writings Bonaventure supported Scripture and confirmed his own reasons with many Greek and Latin sources. Although Aristotle was much used in philosophy, the most favored source was St. Augustine, whom Bonaventure preferred to all non-Christian philosophers because he excelled them in describing the created world. Bonaventure transcended his sources, reconciled and united them by his own principles, giving to each source a due share in the Bonaventurean synthesis.

As master of the Franciscan School, Bonaventure preached nearly eighty sermons. Most were University sermons, some were given before the royal family, and a few were presented to other Parisian audiences. All of his sermons were based on the Gospel of the day, normally Sunday, but also major feasts of Mary, angels, and saints. Exhibiting the pastoral aspects of his doctrine and exposing his great versatility as a preacher, they showed his thoughts constantly on Christ our redeemer and exemplar, revealed his horror of sin and love of virtue, and displayed his fraternal compassion and Christ's saving mercy.

Early in 1256, William of St. Amor called the Dominican and Franciscan friars false apostles and, by their mendicant poverty, defamers of the Gospel. He also questioned their place, upheld by the papacy, as teachers at the University of Paris. In reply, *De perfectione evangelica,* Bonaventure defended the Franciscan ideal of the Christian life. He based his defense on humility as the summit of evangelical perfection and the sum of the precepts of the Christian religion. On this ground, from love of Christ, he built a powerful doctrine of poverty, chastity, and obedience in the religious life conforming to the Gospel counsels. William's views, condemed in October 1256 by Pope Alexander IV, were in part a reaction to erroneous teachings (condemned by Alexander in October 1255) of the Franciscan Gerard of Borgo San Donnino, who followed Joachim of Fiore but held that a new age of the Spirit would begin in 1260.

The Franciscan order was already threatened internally by the Spirituals, who wanted to live unchanged the austere life exemplified by Francis. They accepted the Joachimite teachings, to add a new dimension to the dissension within the order. John of Parma, the minister general, was a Joachimite. When Pope Alexander persuaded him secretly to resign, he convoked a general chapter in Rome. At the chapter he said that he knew no one better to follow him than Bonaventure. His personal integrity and recent defense of the order brought Bonaventure election as minister general on 2 February 1257.

Informed of his election, Bonaventure on 23 April sent the order a letter stating the policy that he would pursue. He planned to share his office in order to stamp out evil, to stir up good, to fortify the weak, and to refresh the strong. He promised to consult prudent men in the course of rectifying the discord in the order without new regulations. Listing the abuses to be uprooted, he asked the brothers to renew their zeal and loyalty, to keep the rule exactly, and to live their profession of perfection personified by Francis. Bonaventure wanted to reunify the order, so he sought to restore fidelity to its principles. He ruled so vigilantly and with such wise authority, backed by personal holiness, that he rid the order of abuses and reconciled its different factions, thus unifying it during his many years as minister general. Because of his untiring visits, despite poor health, to every part of the order and his own realization of the Franciscan ideal, the order was reformed in the true spirit of Francis.

Leaving Paris, Bonaventure went to Italy and presented himself, in May or June, to Alexander IV, who reaffirmed the order's pastoral privileges. Upon returning to France, he took up residence at Mantes-sur-Seine, near Paris. In the summer of 1258 (probably), he had Gerard of Borgo San Donnino brought to Paris to retract his Joachimite views; Gerard refused to retract, and was imprisoned. Bonaventure visited England, in November and December, but spent Christmas at Rouen with Eudes Rigaud. He was at the provincial chapter of St. Omer in July 1259, and preached at Arras on 27 July. When visiting the provinces of the order, he took along his secretary, Bernard of Bessa, and a dear friend, Mark of Montefeltro. Mark spoke of Bonaventure as a kind and patient man walking in the footsteps of Francis. Bonaventure rejoiced in Mark, who gave him an opening for humility and better foresight. Mark recorded the numerous sermons of Bonaventure on his many journeys, and helped him to retain his high standard of preaching.

Bonaventure preached to popes, his friars, other religious, and the laity. The majority of his sermons have survived, but some are only schemata. They show why he was revered as a very eloquent preacher, all others keeping silent when he spoke. Based solidly on Scripture, his sermons were suited to their occasions and hearers. He preached fervid fidelity to Christ and his way of life; he spoke often, in his later years, as a man experienced in contemplation and a Franciscan whose mystical thought was fired by a most ardent charity.

Bonaventure made a pilgrimage, in October 1259, to La Verna (Alverna), where Francis received the stigmata. While there, Bonaventure wrote his best-known and most popular mystical work, *Itinerarium mentis in Deum* (The mind's road to God), organized as a seven-stage journey. Stage one takes him from the perfections of irrational creatures to their Creator; stage two takes him back to the reflections of the Trinity in the same creatures. Stage three goes up from the image of God in man to the principle of image in the Creator; stage four, reforming the image by grace and its virtues, returns to consider the Trinity reflected in the Christian soul and the

Church. Stage five rises from the contingent and multiple being of creatures to the necessity and unity of the Creator, whose essential name is Being; stage six moves on to Good, the name of God in the personal processions of the Trinity. Stage seven, going above the intellect, rests in the love and peace of a mystical contemplation of the Trinity and the incarnation of Christ, the door and the path for everyone entering paradise. The whole journey, pervaded by the spirit of Francis, depends on a Christian esteem of God's work in creation and a heartfelt response in the Spirit to the redeeming action of the crucified Christ in his church.

Retiring to Lyons from November 1259 until Easter 1260, Bonaventure wrote additional mystical works. *De triplici via* deals with reflection, prayer, and contemplation as necessary dispositions for mystical union with God. *Soliloquium* has the soul speaking, as the inner voice of God, to man about the state of his nature, the vanity of the world, the certitude and outcome of death, and the joy of paradise. *Lignum vitae* sees Christ's cross as a tree rooted in his origin, supporting him in his passion, and raising him to glory. Each of these mysteries has four flowers bearing forty-eight fruits, providing abundant contemplation from the Gospel on the mysteries of the crucified Christ. *De perfectione vitae ad sorores* was a response to Isabella, abbess of Longchamp and sister of Louis IX. More spiritual than mystical, it shows Bonaventure's doctrinal respect for the true way of religion according to the Gospels.

These five works, voicing Bonaventure's personal experience, indicate the mystical and spiritual unity of his doctrine, his harmony as master of theology and minister general, the stress on the church in his thought and the life of the Christian, and his awareness of the evangelical mission of the Franciscan order.

At Lyons, Bonaventure prepared to pacify the dissident elements in the order by restoring it according to the true Franciscan ideal of following Christ. To achieve this, he made ready for the general chapter at Narbonne, 23 May 1260, by reorganizing and codifying the existing constitutions. Having no new regulations, yet showing his ability as a wise legislator, his code was adopted by the chapter, which had all the older forms of ordinances destroyed. The adoption of the code brought peace to the order by reconciling diverse groups and correcting delinquent friars. Thus, ruling the order, he proved to be a kind and moderate disciplinarian.

It was probably at this chapter that Bonaventure won approval for his codified rules for novices. Ratifying his work and respecting his judgment, the chapter commissioned him to write a new life of Francis that would be more authentic than the current variant lives, in order to stabilize the peace and unity of the order in the spirit of Francis. Bonaventure, loving original sources, decided to visit the scenes hallowed by Francis and to talk with his surviving companions, especially Leo and the simple but saintly Giles. He was at La Verna on 23 August, he then went to the Valley of Rieti, the hermitages in Umbria, and other places frequented by Francis. On 3 October he was in Assisi at the transfer of St. Clare's body to a church erected in her honor.

Back in France, Bonaventure settled down at Mantes, late in November, to compose his life of Francis. Bonaventure organized his topics especially from Thomas of Celano, around the original data gathered in his talks with the surviving companions of Francis and other reliable witnesses. In May 1261, finishing the first draft, he returned to Italy for the summer to revisit the companions and resorts of Francis. He also presented himself to Pope Urban IV, elected 29 August. Bonaventure retired in October to southern France, where he remained until about March 1262, when he was again at Mantes. During the next several months he made the final draft of his life of Francis. He took the completed draft to Italy, where he stayed from November 1262 to November 1263.

It was probably early in 1263 that Bonaventure, with Cardinal Gaetano Orsini (protector of the order), visited John of Parma in his hermitage at Greccio. They wanted him to forsake his rigid Joachimite views. John relented by a profession of faith and a recitation of the Creed. Bonaventure was in Padua on 8 April, at the transfer of St. Anthony's remains to the basilica built in his honor. He was in Pisa for the general chapter, 20 May 1263, which approved the two forms of his life of Francis. One, *Legenda maior,* treated at length the life, death, and canonization of Francis, and his miracles after death. The other, *Legenda minor,* was a shorter form in nine liturgical readings for the feast and octave of Francis.

Bonaventure noted that he had composed his work chiefly with gratitude and dedication to Francis. Moved also by love for the brothers, he had carried out their commission to recount more accurately the truth of Francis, especially as his own companions remembered him. Bonaventure chose not always to follow a chronological order, but to arrange his materials so that the reader could behold the spirit of Francis. Using history rather than simply recording it, he produced a spiritual portrait more than a mere historical picture of Francis. The chapter also reorganized the order into new provinces and completed several decades of liturgical renewal by enacting about forty decrees on the liturgy, with many new feasts, such as the Visitation of Mary and her Immaculate Conception.

Bonaventure was at the papal court in Perugia from June to October, and made a few visits to Assisi. He was busy mainly with matters concerning the Poor Ladies of St. Clare. To handle their affairs, a committee directed by Bonaventure and guided by Cardinal Orsini was set up by the Pisa chapter. The two men, working together, recodified and unified the legislation on the sisters (Poor Ladies). Urban IV approved their new rule on 18 October 1263. Bonaventure then set about regulating the relations between the sisters and the friars, a task that took more than a year to complete. He left the papal court to winter in southern France, mostly at Montpellier. He was in Rome on 30 March 1264, and at a papal consistory in Orvieto on 31 August. After a short stay at Assisi, he left Italy in October and resided at Lyons until the end of January 1265.

Bonaventure presented himself to Pope Clement IV at Perugia in March 1265, and remained at his court until the autumn, then returned to Mantes. He received word there, on 24 November, of his nomination as archbishop of York. Clement IV thought that Bonaventure was the best choice because of his virtuous life, eminent knowledge, remarkable foresight, illustrious works, and excellent government of his order. Alarmed by his nomination, Bonaventure immediately set out for Perugia, arriving there before 20 December. He begged the pope to withdraw his nominations, and Clement yielded. Bonaventure spent Christmastime in Assisi, was in Mantes by March 1266, and attended the provincial chapter at Lens on 18 April.

Bonaventure presided over the general chapter at Paris on 16 May 1266. Because the new *Legenda* on Francis had been accepted officially, the chapter ordered all the older liturgical readings on him to be destroyed. It also passed decrees on poverty, prayer, preaching the Gospel, rules for novices and students, correcting incorrigible offenders, and preserving peace with the secular clergy. Bonaventure added a brief commentary on the Narbonne Constitutions. After the chapter he visited the order in northern and central France, and resumed residence at Mantes in December.

It was probably between June 1266 and May 1268 that Bonaventure wrote *De regimine animae* in response to a request from Queen Blanche of Castile, daughter of Louis IX and wife of Alfonso X. The tract presents concisely Bonaventure's doctrinal conception of the spiritual life and its practical exercises. He conceives the spiritual life as based on a knowledge of God, in whom man must believe most highly, most devoutly, and with the greatest holiness. The exercises are continual moderation in the use of material things, unswerving justice toward all persons, true piety in divine worship, and aiding our neighbor.

New threats to the order surfaced in 1266 at the University of Paris. Siger of Brabant, using Ibn Rushd, was teaching philosophy as though natural reason had to accept as true things known to be false by divine revelation. Bonaventure could not ignore the evident peril to the Christian faith of students in the Franciscan school. Moving to Paris in February 1267, he gave talks on seven successive Lenten Sundays (6 March to 17 April), *Collationes de decem praeceptis* (Sermons on the Ten Commandments), in which he opposed the unorthodox teaching. His primary aim was to show the commandments coming from the mercy of God: by the blood of Christ, all men were freed from the death of sin; by his resurrection, they were offered the life of grace and promised eternal life in glory. To have such life, the Christian must keep the commandments and be conformed to Christ with the aid of the Father and the Holy Spirit. Bonaventure spoke particularly of errors among philosophers, who went too far in their investigations, as the fashioning of idols. He cited two errors: an eternal world, which destroyed the whole truth of Scripture and the Incarnation, and one intellect for all men, which denied the truth of faith on salvation, obeying the commandments, and our resurrection.

Resuming his attack in September, Bonaventure preached vehemently against the unorthodox teaching at least seven times up to February 1268. He stepped up his attack in another Lenten series of talks (26 February to 7 April), *Collationes de septem donis Spiritus sancti* (Sermons on the seven gifts of the Holy Spirit). In them he first examines the origin, use, and fruit of grace, then presents a very practical doctrine on each gift of the Holy Spirit. He scolds impious Christians who doubt God's omnipotence and wisdom, insists on the superiority of theology over philosophy—the occasion, not the cause, of error in philosophers—and names the two errors cited in 1267, to which he adds a third that destroys divine providence: fatal necessity negating freedom, merit, and eternal reward.

Replying to Gerard of Abbeville, who reopened the assault on the mendicants, Bonaventure contrasted with Christ, the good counselor, three sorts of bad counselors. One despises great things by spurning the mendicant life as false and of small spiritual significance. A second makes good things bad by reputing as evil the advice to become a friar, thus perilously and wickedly perverting the counsel of Christ. A third casts doubt on certitude by turning away from religious life, though ignorant of it, those wanting to enter it. Bonaventure urged his audience to seek counsel from Scripture, Christ, and his saints.

Bonaventure left Paris about 17 May, was at the papal court in Rome on 8 July, spent most of December at Assisi, and was there again for the general chapter on 12 May 1269. This chapter settled problems on the rule and constitutions. It passed more liturgical decrees, some of which were to become universal in the church (for instance, on the Angelus and the Saturday Mass of Mary). After the chapter he returned to Mantes, but again had to defend the order in September, at Paris, against the assaults of Gerard of Abbeville.

This defense came mainly in the *Apologia pauperum,* in which Bonaventure rebutted Gerard by citing against him numerous texts from several Latin and Greek sources. He thus exposed Gerard as going contrary to Scripture, the teaching of the church, canon law, papal and conciliar decrees, the example of the saints, and the unbroken tradition of the Fathers, Doctors, and theologians. He opposed Gerard in particular on evangelical perfection, penance and self-renunciation, voluntary poverty, and the mendicant way of religion. He based his opposition on the counsels of the Gospel, and so defended the Christian life in its Franciscan form, a mendicant style of life ratified by papal authority.

In February 1270 Bonaventure left Paris for a six-month visit to Spain. He was back in Paris on 1 November, in Cologne on 7 December, and at Saarburg on 6 January 1271. He was in Italy in late February, at Viterbo in August, at Naples in November, at Assisi for Christmas, and at Rome on 27 March 1272 for the coronation of Pope Gregory X. On 13 April the pope called an ecumenical council and utilized Bonaventure in preparing its agenda on church reform, reunion of the Greeks with Rome, and the safety of the Holy Land.

Bonaventure was again in Paris on 16 May, then in Lyons for the general chapter on 12 June 1272. Besides the newly assigned papal tasks, it handled more constitutional and liturgical matters, and further questions on the relations of the friars and Poor Ladies of St. Clare. Bonaventure was in Toulouse on 12 August, on a second visit to Spain in September and October, and in Lyons for Advent and Christmas. By 11 March 1273 he was once more in Paris, where the unorthodox masters of arts were again teaching erroneous opinions (though condemned on 10 December 1270) taken from Islamic philosophers, while some masters of theology belittled the life of Christ, to the scandal of students.

Provoked by the audacity and disbelief of such masters, Bonaventure fought them in a third series of talks (9 April to 28 May), *Collationes in Hexaëmeron* (Sermons on the six days of Creation). Their general theme is a sixfold vision (or illumination) of the church, prefigured by the six days of creation. Bonaventure sets out to draw his hearers away from the false wisdom of mundane masters, whose errors he recites, to the true wisdom of Christ. He shows how natural reason can know its proper objects with the infallible certitude of science and wisdom. From the truth in philosophers, conceited in their science, he isolates errors concerning irrational creatures, our moral life, and the divine exemplarity. He traced the latter error to the Islamic errors cited in 1267–1268.

The unorthodox masters, however, lap up the words of philosophers in so idolatrous a fashion that, perverting the wine of Scripture, they turn it into the water of philosophy. But through Scripture philosophy should be brought back to God, the first origin of philosophy. He warns the theologian not to become too involved in the human sciences, for if he strays far from Scripture, he may not return, becoming vain and supercilious by seeking to know and not to love. A right study of Scripture requires holiness of mind in the charity of wisdom, the gifts of the Holy Spirit, and keeping to the limits of the student's own intelligence.

Bonaventure never finished these talks. On 28 May he learned of his nomination as cardinal bishop of Albano, with a clear indication from the pope not to refuse. He left Paris to join Gregory at Mugello (north of Florence). Bonaventure was made a cardinal there, about 16 July. Remaining at the papal

BONAVENTURE, ST.

court, he went with it to Lyons, where Gregory consecrated him bishop on 11 or 12 November, along with the new archbishop of Lyons, the Dominican Peter of Tarantaise (future Pope Innocent V). Bonaventure was then appointed (with Peter) to synthesize the reports of the commissions preparing for the second Council of Lyons (7 May–17 July 1274).

Bonaventure continued as minister general of the Franciscan order until a general chapter at Lyons on 20 May 1274, when he resigned and was replaced by Jerome of Ascoli (future Pope Nicholas IV), who had brought Greek delegates to the council. The Greeks arrived on 24 June; a reunion was celebrated with them on 29 June, Bonaventure preaching the sermon. Shortly afterward he fell critically ill, and died before dawn on 15 July. He was buried at Lyons on the same day, with the pope and the council fathers assisting, and Peter of Tarantaise giving the sermon. His death, seen as the loss of a wise and holy man full of compassion and virtue, evoked much sorrow and tears, for God gave him this grace, that all who knew him were captivated by a boundless love for him.

The exemplary life of Bonaventure as a Franciscan and the abiding influence of his thought and love on the life and devotion of the Latin church brought his canonization by Pope Sixtus IV on 14 April 1482, and the further honor as a doctor of the church by Sixtus V, on 14 March 1587. St. Bonaventure has always been seen as a truly great theologian, a Franciscan of ardent devotion, and an eminent leader in his own day. Known as the Devout Doctor in the fourteenth century, he has been called the Seraphic Doctor since the fifteenth. His many and masterful writings (and sermons) on the religious and the spiritual life, especially their Franciscan form, his restoring of the order to its original ideal of evangelical perfection, his renewal of the order in the true spirit of St. Francis, and the success in unifying the order and preserving its unity earned St. Bonaventure the later title of Second Founder of the Order. He is considered today as one of the prominent men of his era, a fearless defender of truth, and a striking symbol of a mystical and Christian wisdom.

BIBLIOGRAPHY

Works. S. Bonaventurae opera omnia, 10 vols. (1882–1902); *Collationes in Hexaëmeron et Bonaventuriana quaedam selecta* (1934); *S. Bonaventurae opera theologica selecta,* 5 vols. (1934–1965); *Obras de San Buenaventura,* 6 vols. (1945–1949).

English Translations. Works of Saint Bonaventure, Emma T. Healy and Philotheus Boehner, trans., 2 vols. (1955–1956); *The Works of Bonaventure,* José de Vinck, trans., 5 vols. (1960–1970); *Bonaventure: The Soul's Journey into God, The Tree of Life, The Life of St. Francis,* E. Cousins, trans. (1978).

Authenticity, Biography, Chronology. G. Abate, "Per la storia e la cronologia di S. Bonaventura," in *Miscellanea francescana,* **49** (1949), and **50** (1950); Jacques G. Bougerol, *Saint Bonaventure: Un maître de sagesse* (1966); Ignatius C. Brady, "The Writings of Saint Bonaventure Regarding the Franciscan Order," in *Miscellanea francescana,* **75** (1975); "St. Bonaventure's Sermons on St. Francis," in *Franziskanische Studien,* **58** (1976); and "The Edition of the *opera omnia* of Saint Bonaventure," in *Archivum franciscanum historicum,* **70** (1977); André Callebaut, "Le chapitre Général de 1272 célébré à Lyon," in *Archivum franciscanum historicum,* **13** (1920); and "La date du cardinalat de S. Bonaventure (28 Mai 1272)," *ibid.,* **14** (1921); Theodore Crowley, "St. Bonaventure Chronology Reappraisal," in *Franziskanische Studien,* **56** (1974); P. Glorieux, "Essai sur la chronologie de saint Bonaventure 1257–74," in *Archivum franciscanum historicum,* **19** (1926); and "La date des *Collationes* de saint Bonaventure," *ibid.,* **22** (1929); Ephrem Longpré, "Bonaventure (saint)," in *Dictionnaire d'histoire et de géographie ecclésiastiques,* IX (1937); John F. Quinn, "Chronology of St. Bonaventure (1217–1257)," in *Franciscan Studies,* **32** (1972); and "Chronology of St. Bonaventure's Sermons," in *Archivum franciscanum historicum,* **67** (1974).

General Studies. Jacques G. Bougerol, *Introduction à l'étude de saint Bonaventure* (1961), trans. by José de Vinck as *Introduction to the Works of Bonaventure* (1963); Lorenzo di Fonzo, "Bonaventura da Bagnoregio," in *Bibliotheca Sanctorum,* III (1963), 239–283; *S. Bonaventura 1274–1974,* Jacques G. Bougerol, gen. ed., 5 vols. (1972–1974) (vol. V is a bibliography with 4,842 entries); *San Bonaventura maestro di vita francescana e di sapienza cristiana,* A. Pompei, ed., 3 vols. (1976).

Doctrinal Studies. Jules d'Albi, *Saint Bonaventure et les luttes doctrinales de 1267–1277* (1922); Ewert H. Cousins, *Bonaventure and the Coincidence of Opposites* (1977); Étienne Gilson, *La philosophie de saint Bonaventure,* 3rd ed. (1953), trans. by Illtyd Trethowan and Frank J. Sheed as *The Philosophy of Saint Bonaventure,* (1938, repr. 1965); John F. Quinn, *The Historical Constitution of St. Bonaventure's Philosophy* (1973), with bibliography; and "The Rôle of the Holy Spirit in St. Bonaventure's Theology," in *Franciscan Studies,* **33** (1973); Joseph Ratzinger, *Die Geschichtstheologie des heiligen Bonaventura* (1959); and *The Theology of History in St. Bonaventure,* Zachary Hayes, trans. (1971).

J. F. QUINN

[See also **Alexander of Hales; Franciscans; Joachim of Fiore; Mysticism; Paris, University of; Peter Lombard; Philosophy-Theology; Sentences.**]

BONCOMPAGNO (BUONCOMPAGNO) OF SIGNA (*ca.* 1170–after 1240) was a leading master of rhetoric and major contributor to the study of the *ars dictaminis* at the University of Bologna. Born at Signa (near Florence), he was trained in the liberal arts at Florence and Bologna, where he probably also studied law. He flourished as a teacher and author from about 1194 to about 1235, mainly at Bologna but with intervals at Rome, Vicenza, Venice, Padua, and Reggio, as well as outside Italy. Boncompagno served as a legate to the papal curia between 1229 and 1234, but in 1240 his application for a position in the curia was rejected. He died, impoverished, in a hospital at Florence.

Few sources refer to Boncompagno. His imaginative, witty, and dynamic personality was recorded by the thirteenth-century Franciscan chronicler Salimbene, who described his antics and called him *maximus trufator* ("greatest wiseacre"). Two of Boncompagno's former students, Rolandinus de Padua, a chronicler, and Boto da Vigevano, a *dictator,* acknowledged their teacher's legendary success. Only two thirteenth-century *dictatores,* Gaufridus Anglicus and Conradus de Mure, cited him in scholarly references.

Boncompagno was a severe critic of the Orléans school, which relied heavily on classical style and models. By contrast, he established doctrines for writing letters and legal documents that followed simple Latin style and observed the practical needs of law and the notarial arts.

His most ambitious work was the *Rhetorica antiqua sive Boncompagnus,* a collection of more than a thousand model letters. The use of his name as the title testified to Boncompagno's pride of authorship. The book was crowned with laurel before an assembly of faculty and students at Bologna in 1215, and again at Padua in 1226 or 1227.

Boncompagno's first work was *V tabulae salutationum,* a model collection of salutations for letters that he compiled about 1194–1195. He subsequently revised the collection to include privileges and wills, under the title *X tabulae salutationum.* About 1196–1197, Boncompagno produced *Tractatus virtutum,* in which he discussed writing and the virtues and vices of words. As an appendix to the *Tractatus* he then wrote *Notule aureе,* on the ways to open model letters. *Palma,* an *ars dictaminis,* followed in 1198, and *Oliva,* a treatise on the writing of privileges and confirmations, both ecclesiastical and secular, probably in 1199.

The *Liber de obsidione Ancone,* composed between 1198 and 1200, concerns the siege of Ancona in 1172, and was Boncompagno's only historical work. *Cedrus,* a treatise on writing statutes, was written about 1201. It was followed by *Mirra,* which dealt with the writing of wills. *Breviloquium,* a study of introductions to letters, was his next work. In 1204, Boncompagno wrote *Isagoge,* a well-organized work on introductions and salutations to persons of both genders. Also in that year he turned to morality, writing *Liber de amicitia* and thus continuing a tradition established by Cicero. *Rota Veneris,* written before 1215, is a manual on the art of writing love letters, with attention to rhetorical doctrines and erotic literature.

In 1235 the second of Boncompagno's longest works appeared. The *Rhetorica novissima,* a textbook on judicial oratory, was his contribution to a genre related to the *ars dictaminis* and known as the *ars arengandi,* the art of composing speeches. About 1240 he wrote his last work, *Libellus de malo senectutis et senii,* another moral treatise, which shares the sentiments expressed by Cicero on old age.

Boncompagno's life, writings, and their influence remain to be carefully studied.

BIBLIOGRAPHY

Robert L. Benson, "Protohumanism and Narrative Technique in Early Thirteenth-Century Italian 'Ars Dictaminis,'" in *Boccaccio: Secoli di vita: Atti del Congresso Internazionale Boccaccio 1975, Università di California, Los Angeles, 17–19 ottobre 1975,* Marga Cottino-Jones and Edward F. Tuttle, eds. (1977); Louis J. Paetow, "The Arts Course at Medieval Universities with Special Reference to Grammar and Rhetoric," in *The University Studies* (Illinois University), **3** no. 7 (1910, repr. 1966), 1–112; Josef Purkart, ed. and trans., *Rota Veneris* (1975); Carl Sutter, *Aus Leben und Schriften des Magisters Boncompagno: Ein Beitrag zur italienischen Kulturgeschichte im Dreizehnten Jahrhundert* (1894); Helene Wieruszowski, "Rhetoric and the Classics in Italian Education of the Thirteenth Century," in her *Politics and Culture in Medieval Spain and Italy* (1971), repr. from *Studia Gratiana,* **11** (1967).

E. J. POLAK

[See also **Bologna, University of; Dictamen; Rhetoric, Western European.**]

BONDOL, JEAN (*fl.* 1368–1381), court painter of Charles V of France, was also known as Jehan de Brugis or Hennequin de Bruges. He signed a frontispiece in the Bible of Charles V (now in The Hague,

Meermanno-Westreenianum Museum, MS 10 B 23), and may also have painted some miniatures in the Bible of Jean de Sy (Paris, Bibliothèque Nationale, MS fr. 15397).

BIBLIOGRAPHY

Erwin Panofsky, *Early Netherlandish Painting* (1953), 36ff.; Jean Porcher, *Medieval French Miniatures* (1959), 56ff.; Millard Meiss, *French Painting in the Time of Jean de Berry: The Late Fourteenth Century and the Patronage of the Duke* (1967), 20–23.

ROBERT G. CALKINS

[See also **Manuscript Illumination.**]

BONIFACE, ST. (*ca.* 675–754). Boniface (baptized Winfrid) was born to a landed family near Exeter, in Devon. The conventional stories of his early piety told by his biographer, Willibald, ring somewhat true in depicting the opposition of his father to his monastic vocation. However, after his father's death Winfrid entered the Benedictine monastery at Exeter. Apparently this house did not fulfill the intellectual needs of the young man, and he soon transferred to the abbey of Nursling (Nhutscelle), whose abbot, Wynbercht, had an excellent reputation for learning. Winfrid himself gained some repute as a scholar. He taught in the monastery school and wrote a grammar in this period. Around 705 he was ordained a priest, and soon began to attract notice beyond the monastery's walls. A synod of Wessex clergy presided over by King Ine was troubled by some difficult problems that it decided to refer to the archbishop of Canterbury. On the recommendation of several abbots, including Wynbercht, the king entrusted the mission to Winfrid, who carried it off successfully. It seemed that an ecclesiastical career beckoned, but Winfrid, like so many of his Irish and Anglo-Saxon contemporaries, was drawn to missionary work.

In 716, with the permission of his abbot, Winfrid set out for Frisia, landing at Durstede. But conditions there were most unfavorable for the novice missionaries. The Frankish mayor of the palace, Pepin of Héristal, who had conquered part of Frisia, had died in 714, and a pagan reaction had set in under the Frisian leader Radbod. Archbishop Willibrord (Clement) of Utrecht had been forced to withdraw. Although Winfrid approached Radbod, he and his companions found no support for their work and decided to return to England.

Undeterred by this early failure and unwilling to accept the abbacy of Nursling after the death of Wynbercht, Winfrid, armed with a letter from his bishop, Daniel of Worcester, set out once more. This time, however, his destination was Rome, where Pope Gregory II received him kindly, gave him the name Boniface, after the Roman martyr, and charged him to preach to the heathens. From Rome, Boniface returned to Frisia, where the death of Radbod and the accession of Charles Martel created more favorable conditions than before. Under the leadership of Willibrord, Boniface labored for about three years—a kind of missionary apprenticeship, one must assume. However, his success was such that Willibrord attempted to persuade him to become his auxiliary bishop. Boniface refused, ultimately on the ground that his mission as a papal representative would not allow him to confine his activity to Frisia without the concurrence of the pope. Boniface, therefore, moved the center of his mission to Hesse. He instructed the lapsed rulers of Amöneburg, Dettic and Deorulf, and won over a large number of pagans. Frankish rule had caused great hardship among the poor; Boniface concentrated on charitable works that soon led to numerous converts.

In the meantime, he had sent a messenger to Rome to report on his work and seek further advice. The pope called him to Rome, administered a profession of faith similar to that taken by bishops of the Roman province, and consecrated him a bishop on 30 November 722. Gregory gave Boniface a broad commission to carry out missionary work among the Germans, and provided him with a letter asking Charles Martel to take him under his protection. Boniface returned to Hesse, where he made a frontal attack on paganism by cutting down one of the famed sacred oaks at Geismar (near Fritzlar). This action made so strong an impression on pagan witnesses that news spread throughout the region and brought success to this second mission.

Boniface next moved to Thuringia, which had been partially conquered and Christianized by the Franks, and where other missioners, including St. Kilian, had also worked. But the Frankish effort had met with little success, and there apparently were serious problems among the local clergy, some of whom were teaching heresy. Boniface was ardent in seeking advice on the best way of dealing with these issues. While he showed great tact and even tolerance in dealing with new converts, he was firm in upholding Roman liturgical practice and orthodox doctrine in the face of these clerics. It was perhaps as a result of this experience, as well as of his learning of the accession of Pope Gregory III (731), that he wrote a report on his work. Gregory's response was to name him archbishop and to send him the pallium, thus increasing the power and prestige of the papal representative in Germany.

During the next several years Boniface labored in Bavaria, where he enjoyed the protection of Duke Hubert I. But he had made little provision for the organization of the German church, despite his own position as archbishop. In the fall of 737 he made his third trip to Rome. Although one papal letter from this period mentions the expansion of missionary work into the land of the Old Saxons, the chief topic was the organization of the church in Germany. The sources are not clear, but it is probable that serious opposition to plans for the establishment of bishoprics in Germany came in part from the clergy and in part from the lay aristocracy. Now armed with the support of the pope, Boniface returned to Germany, where, in addition to the diocese of Passau already established by the pope with his consecration of Bishop Vivolo, Boniface organized dioceses at Salzburg, Regensburg, Freising, Buraburg, Würzburg, Erfurt, Eichstätt, and Neuberg. During this period he also founded the monastery of Fulda (744), which he placed directly under the protection of the pope. Although papal support no doubt played a significant role in these decisions, Boniface worked with a consciousness of the need for lay protection. He founded the first three bishoprics in Bavaria, where he enjoyed the favor of Duke Hubert. Moreover, he made no important efforts to reform the Frankish church until after the death of Charles Martel, an evident sign that opposition from that quarter had impeded his work.

With the death of Charles in 741, Boniface was able to draw greater support from Charles's sons and successors in Austrasia and Neustria. At about the same time that he was confirmed as legate by Pope Zacharias in 743, he cooperated with Carloman of Austrasia in the Concilium Germanicum which enacted a series of reform decrees under Carloman's name. At Liftina (now Estinnes), in 744, another council was held. There may also have been a council of all bishops in the kingdom in 745, but this has recently been denied.

There has been some controversy among historians regarding the degree to which Boniface's efforts were constrained by secular powers and the extent to which he subordinated them to these controls. On the one hand, it seems clear that he worked closely with the papacy and regarded himself as the representative of the pope. On the other hand, his reform program was promulgated in councils where the influence of the mayors of the palace was paramount. Boniface, in his letters, provides little definite reaction on this problem; he was more concerned about the manner in which insidious clerical influences at court impeded his work. Both he and the pope accepted the necessity of lay protection in order to carry out his mission, but Boniface maintained a careful distance between himself and secular powers. To him this was the proper role for a cleric.

Clerical politics, which relied heavily on secular support, seriously affected Boniface's plan for the organization of the German church. It was his intention to establish his archdiocese at Cologne, but he was forced to make his headquarters in the diocese of Mainz. Fear of this powerful papal legate no doubt dictated the opposition of the Frankish bishops to the selection of Cologne, which might too easily become a thorn in their side because of its position in the Frankish heartland.

In the last year of his life, Boniface returned to the mission field. He made provision for the succession of his disciple Lull to the diocese of Mainz, and sought to ensure that there would be no reaction against his fellow Anglo-Saxon missionaries. Then he returned to Frisia, to work among the pagans beyond the Zuider Zee. On 5 June 754, near Dokkum, a group of pagans attacked at dawn, and massacred Boniface and his companions. Within a short time the feast of the martyr was being celebrated both on the Continent and in England.

BIBLIOGRAPHY

Ephraim Emerton, ed. and trans., *The Letters of Saint Boniface* (1940); George W. Greenaway, *Saint Boniface* (1955); Jörg Jarnut, "Bonifatius und die fränkische Reformkonzilien (743–748)," in *Zeitschrift der Savigny-Stiftung für Rechtsgeschichte: Kanonistische Abteilung,* **96** (1979); Wilhelm Levison, *England and the Continent in the Eighth Century* (1946); Heinz Löwe, "Vom Bild des Bonifatius in der neueren deutschen Geschichtsschreibung," in *Geschichte in Wissenschaft und Unterricht,* **6** (1955); Theodor Schieffer, *Winfrid-Bonifatius und die christliche Grundlegung Europas* (1954).

JAMES M. POWELL

[See also **Fulda; Germany, 843–1137; Missions and Missionaries, Christian; Willibald of Mainz.**]

BONIFACE OF MONTFERRAT (*ca.* 1155–1207), successor to Count Thibaut of Champagne as one of the leaders of the Fourth Crusade. He was a cousin of the French king Philip II Augustus, had two brothers married into the family of the Byzantine emperor Manuel I, and was related to the rulers of the Latin Kingdom of Jerusalem. He took the cross in 1201, despite the reservations of Pope Innocent III, who thought him insufficiently pious. Boniface got along well with the Greeks, and was a party to the treaty of 1204 dividing the Byzantine Empire. He married Margaret of Hungary, the widow of Emperor Isaac II Angelos, in order to strengthen his claims to the imperial throne, but he lost the election for that office to Baldwin of Flanders. He received instead the Kingdom of Thessalonica, where he had previously held lands. Boniface was killed in an ambush by the Bulgars.

BIBLIOGRAPHY

George Ostrogorsky, *History of the Byzantine State* (1957).

LINDA ROSE

[See also **Baldwin I of the Latin Empire; Crusades and Crusader States: Fourth; Latin Empire of Constantinople.**]

BONIFACE VIII, POPE (*ca.* 1235–11 October 1303) was born Benedict Gaetani in the Ernican hill town of Anagni; he became pope on 24 December 1294, taking the name of Boniface VIII. Because his stormy pontificate led almost immediately into what Petrarch dubbed the "Babylonian Captivity of the Church," it is generally seen as marking the effective end of the medieval papacy.

Trained as a canon lawyer, Gaetani entered papal service at an early age and rose rapidly through the ranks. By the 1260's he was frequently employed on diplomatic missions—for example, to England and France—and in 1281 Pope Martin IV recognized his talents by making him a cardinal deacon. Ten years later Nicholas IV promoted him to cardinal priest.

When Nicholas died (4 April 1292), selecting a successor proved difficult: the cardinals were badly split but subject to rules that called for unanimity. An interregnum of twenty-seven months therefore ensued, ending only on 5 July 1294, when the desperate College of Cardinals finally agreed upon Peter of Morrone, a hermit of eighty, who took the name of Celestine V. Since Celestine's talents ran more to the spiritual than to the administrative, his rule threatened quickly to become a pious disaster. Finally recognizing the problem, the pope first consulted the leading cardinals; next issued a bull affirming his right to resign; and then actually did so on 13 December 1294. Eleven days later Cardinal Gaetani succeeded him.

The unusual circumstances surrounding Boniface's elevation ensured that his would be a difficult reign, but a further complication lay in the fact that Celestine had enjoyed the fervent support of such millenary groups as the Franciscan Spirituals, people unwilling to accept either that he had resigned voluntarily or that he had the right to abdicate. Boniface made matters infinitely worse, first by confining his predecessor to Castello di Monte Fumone (to guard against schism) and then, on 1 August 1296, by declaring the Spirituals to be heretics. In this case, as in others, Boniface's personality tended to multiply his problems, for he was never a man to suffer fools gladly. Always haughty and proud, in his papal years he displayed an increasingly imperious irascibility, a propensity doubtless caused partly by painful attacks of "the stone" and partly by his determined attempts to live up to a high conception of office which never seemed able to distinguish between those matters which pertained only to Benedict Gaetani, the private man, and those which belonged solely to Boniface VIII, the pope.

Boniface's greatest struggle, that with France, began early in 1296, when the French Cistercians protested against royal taxation and appealed to Rome. The pope replied on 24 February with *Clericis laicos,* a bull prohibiting all secular taxation of the clergy without prior papal approval. The French countered on 17 August by prohibiting the export of gold and silver, thereby hoping to cut papal revenue significantly.

Simultaneously, however, Boniface found himself embroiled in a dispute with the Colonna family, two of whose members were cardinals. The pope had been using his powers to increase Gaetani land holdings near Anagni, but since the Colonnas coveted these properties, hard feelings arose. Matters came to a head on 2 May 1297, when Stephen Colonna ambushed a papal treasure train to prevent yet another acquisition. In his anger Boniface excommunicated the Colonnas and, on 27 November, proclaimed what amounted to a crusade against them. He was not to be satisfied until the Colonna cardinals had been seized and imprisoned, and their principal residence, Palestrina, both razed and sown with salt. Nevertheless, faced with opposition so close to home, Boniface decided to make peace with the French, capitulating completely in the summer of 1297, when he gave way on clerical taxation and announced the canonization of Louis IX, grandfather of the reigning French king, Philip the Fair.

With the possible exception of the publication in 1298 of the *Liber sextus,* Boniface's compilation of canon law, the high point in his pontificate came in 1300, his year of Jubilee. With indulgences promised to all, hundreds of thousands made the pilgrimage to Rome, thereby convincing the pope of his popular support. Thus, on 12 July 1301, when Philip the Fair ordered Bernard Saisset, bishop of Pamiers, arrested for treason, Boniface was in no mood to accept the French impertinence. In *Salvator mundi* and *Ausculta fili* (4–5 December 1301), he suspended all privileges of clerical taxation, reproved Philip for his conduct, and summoned all the French bishops to Rome for a review of the king's government and of the state of religion in France.

In April 1302, Philip convoked an assembly of clergy, nobles, and towns in support of his policies, but after a French army was disastrously beaten by the Flemings at Courtrai in July, Boniface felt confident enough on 18 November to issue *Unam sanctam,* a ringing declaration that it was "altogether necessary to salvation for every human creature to be subject to the Roman pontiff." In February, March, and June of 1303, Philip responded with more assemblies, which, following the lead of the Colonna cardinals, proclaimed Boniface a usurping heretic and called on the king to aid in summoning a general council of the church to depose him. A French lawyer, Guillaume de Nogaret, was dispatched to Italy to arrest him, and on 7 September troops under Nogaret and Sciarra Colonna stormed the papal palace at Anagni, taking Boniface prisoner. Although he was freed two days later, he returned to Rome a broken man, and soon died.

In 1311 the first Avignonese pope, Clement V, was to issue a bull, *Rex gloriae,* in which he ordered many of Boniface's later bulls quashed and then praised his enemies for having attacked him with "an estimable, just, and sincere zeal and from the fervor of their Catholic faith."

BIBLIOGRAPHY

Thomas S. R. Boase, *Boniface VIII* (1933); Georges Digard, *Philippe le Bel et le Saint-siège de 1285 à 1304,* 2 vols. (1936); Georges Digard *et al., Les registres de Boniface VIII,* 4 vols. (1904–1939); Pierre Dupuy, *Histoire du différend d'entre le pape Boniface VIII et Philippe le Bel, roy de France* (1655, repr. 1963); Charles T. Wood, ed. and trans., *Philip the Fair and Boniface VIII,* 2nd ed. (1971, repr. 1976).

CHARLES T. WOOD

[See also **Bull, Papal; Celestine V, Pope; Clement V, Pope; Nogaret, Guillaume de; Papacy, Origins and Development of; Philip IV the Fair.**]

BONINO DA CAMPIONE (*fl.* after 1349; *d.* 1397), Lombard sculptor who was the best-known member of the Campionesi, a group that also included Ugo and Giovanni da Campione. A sculptor of considerable talent, his works include the tomb of Lambertino Balduino in the Duomo Vecchio, Brescia (after 1349), and the monuments of Stefano and Valentina Visconti, and of Prostaso Caimi, in S. Eustorgio, Milan. He also executed the sarcophagus of Folchino de' Schizzi (*d.* 1357) in the Duomo at Cremona.

Records date Bonino's equestrian monument of Bernabò Visconti (now at Castello Sforzesco, Milan) before 1363, although the sarcophagus dates after Bernabò's death in 1385. During the lifetime of Can Signorio della Scala (*d.* 1375), Bonino carved the enormous and complex tomb in the Sagrato di Santa Maria Antica, Verona. The Visconti and della Scala monuments rank Bonino as one of the outstanding sculptors of trecento northern Italy.

BIBLIOGRAPHY

John Pope-Hennessy, *Italian Gothic Sculpture* (1972), 200.

ADELHEID M. GEALT

BONNANO (BONNANUS) DA PISA (*fl. ca.* 1174–1186), sculptor and architect, is documented as architect of the campanile of Pisa Cathedral (the Leaning Tower), begun, according to inscriptions, in 1174. His exact involvement is unclear. Inscribed bronze doors with reliefs of Old and New Testament scenes done for Pisa Cathedral (1180) and Monreale Cathedral (1186) are his chief works. They established the great school of Pisan sculpture, which blossomed in the following century with Nicola and Giovanni Pisano.

BIBLIOGRAPHY

Tanfani Centofani, *Notizie di artisti* (1897), 156; Pietro Toesca, *Storia dell'arte italiana, II medioevo* (1927), 564, 754, 840, 900, 902, 1140; Adolfo Venturi, *Storia d'arte italiana,* II (1902), 606; and III (1904), 152, 622, 839, 958.

ADELHEID M. GEALT

BOOK. See **Manuscripts and Books.**

BOOK OF HOURS, a compendium of prayers and devotions that became the most popular devotional book of the later Middle Ages. The name comes from their central and essential text, the Hours of the Virgin—more properly, the *parvum officium beatae Virginis Mariae* (little office of the Blessed Virgin Mary)—which consists of certain psalms, lessons, hymns, responses, prayers, and antiphons. It is called an "Hours" *(Horae)* because it provides texts to be recited and sung at each of the eight periods, or "hours," of the liturgical day: matins, lauds, prime, terce, sext, none, vespers, and compline.

The Office of the Virgin was apparently developed by Benedict of Aniane (*ca.* 750–821) as a supplement to the canonical Office. It spread quickly from French monasteries to England, where it was firmly established by 1050 and was adopted by the secular clergy for cathedral use during the twelfth and thirteenth centuries. It also became popular with the laity, who used it for both public and private devotions. The "Little" Office of the Virgin had only one nocturn and three lessons in place of the breviary's three nocturns and nine lessons. In the late twelfth century it was grafted onto the Psalter; later this composite book, the Psalter-hours, became the pure book of hours by losing the full Psalter. Many supplemental texts, mostly prayers and various short offices modeled after the Little Office, were added.

Whereas the recitation of the canonical Office was primarily a public, obligatory function for monks, nuns, and clergy, the recitation of the Little Office by the laity was an act of private devotion. The use of books of hours can be documented to

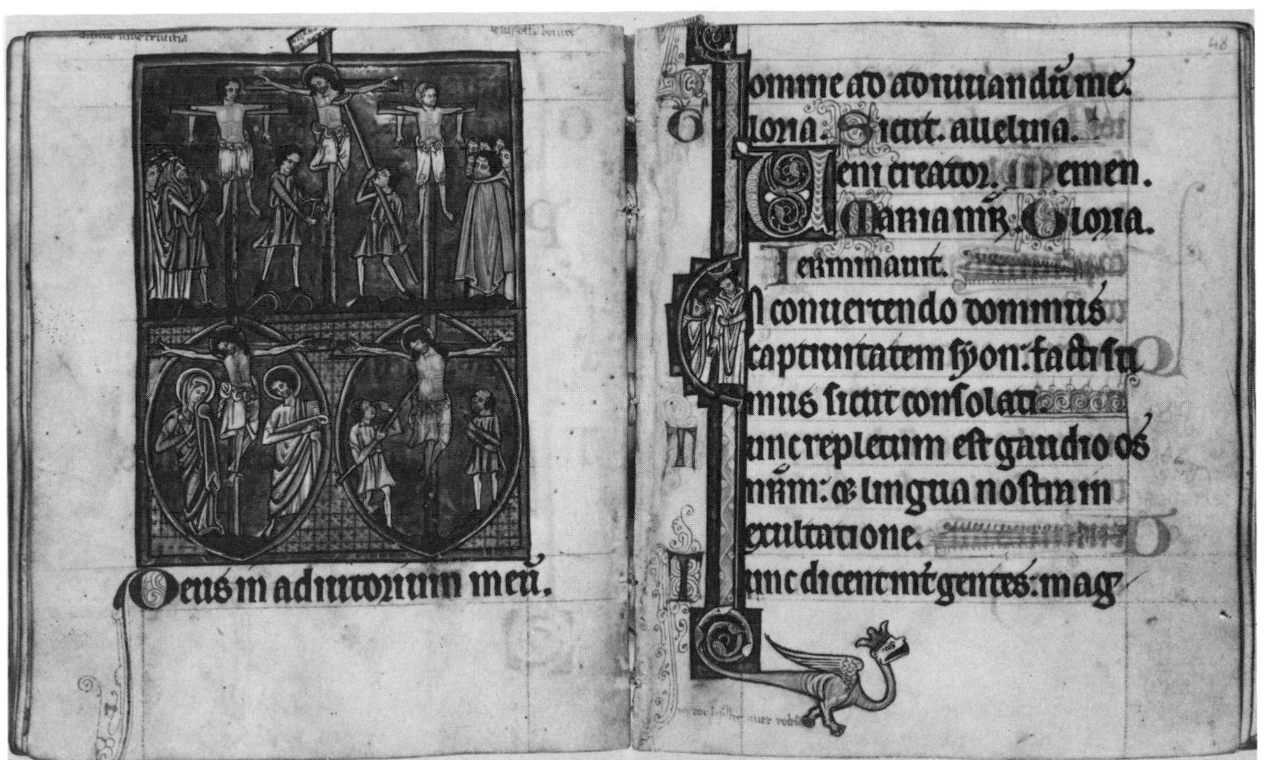

Page from a book of hours depicting the crucifixion of Christ with text on the life of Thomas Becket. MS Add. 49999, fol. 47–48v. THE BRITISH LIBRARY

England in the middle of the thirteenth century, yet it was on the other side of the Channel that it rapidly became a standard form of private prayer book for wealthy persons. On the Continent books of hours had their greatest popularity in the fifteenth century and at the beginning of the sixteenth. Artists depicting the Annunciation customarily showed the Virgin occupied in reading her hours, much as any noble or royal lady would do; they portrayed the child Mary learning to read the hours of her mother Ann. The book of hours was the sole book possessed by many households; it was the book that many a mother in the Middle Ages used to teach her children to read.

The breviary and the missal, the official books of priestly and liturgical prayers, were carefully controlled by ecclesiastical authority; the Divine Office, contained in the breviary, was very complicated in structure, and its observance required considerable time, effort, and concentration by the clergy. As pious laymen and women tried to model their life as much as possible on that of clerics, religious, and monks, they found a substitute for the breviary in the simpler observances composing the book of hours. Thus, Abbé Leroquais has fittingly called the book of hours "the breviary of the laity." As such, the books of hours were free productions of individual piety. Surviving manuscripts differ greatly in their selection of supplementary texts, the interests of patrons, and the practices of different scriptoria. There is great variety in the format and in the arrangement of the prayers; in the texts included in addition to the Little Office; in the saints singled out for special honor; and in the special devotions and personal prayers requested by the owner.

The Little Office of the Virgin forms only a small part of most books of hours; a number of other services and series of prayers soon came to be considered essential. During their greatest vogue (in the fifteenth century) and in the city of Paris, where most of them were copied and illuminated (and later printed), books of hours were composed of nearly identical elements that appeared in the following order:

A calendar of Church feasts and commemorations of the saints. Generally a page is devoted to each month, for which the various liturgical feast days are indicated in different colors.

A series of Gospel excerpts, which the faithful knew well from having heard them on four great feasts: John 1:1–14 (Christmas); Luke 1:26–38 (Annunciation); Matthew 2:1–12 (Epiphany); and Mark 16:14–20 (Separation of the Apostles, July 15). There is often a fifth: John 18–19 (the Passion).

Two long prayers to the Virgin, designated by their incipits: *Obsecro te* (usually illustrated with a portrait of the person who had commissioned the book kneeling before the Virgin) and *O intemerata.*

The Little Office of the Virgin, of which the prayers to the Virgin form the introduction. This office is the central part of the book of hours, but it, like the breviary, varied from diocese to diocese in western Europe; the Office of the Virgin is designated as "according to the use of the Roman curia," or the use of Paris, or the use of Sarum (which dominated in England).

The seven penitential psalms (Vulgate 6, 31, 37, 50, 101, 129, 142). Sometimes the fifteen gradual psalms (119–133) were also included.

The litanies of the saints.

The suffrages, which are memorials and prayers addressed to certain saints in order to obtain a particular intercession.

The Office of the Dead.

The standard body of the fifteenth-century book of hours concludes with various offices or hours, especially the Hours of the Cross and the Hours of the Holy Spirit.

Finally, to these standard elements were added, from time to time and from diocese to diocese, a vast body of additional prayers and sundry devotions for particular occasions. The Mass of the Virgin is a frequent item. The prayers, some of them in the vernacular, were probably written by the patrons themselves for specific occasions. These prayers sometimes appear to reflect local problems: a large number of prayers to saints asking for preservation from plague seems to attest its present danger.

Books of hours are one of the most common of all types of surviving manuscripts of the late Middle Ages. The number, design, and quality of the illuminations in a book of hours varied greatly according to the needs, whims, wealth, and taste of the person who commissioned it. The felicitous accord between patron and artist could result in books of sumptuous beauty, as in the various hours of Jean, duke of Berry, King René, and Étienne Chevalier. It is unclear to what extent patrons decided on the themes to be illustrated in their books, how far the patrons were guided by their spiritual directors, and how far the illuminators were free to choose and interpret their subjects.

Late medieval spiritual writers constantly advised the laity to put themselves in the place of Christ and his mother, and to identify themselves with the events of Christ's ministry and passion. Artists who worked on books of hours came to have a similar purpose: biblical personages appear in contemporary clothing and local settings; the great sacred figures thus occupy a much more familiar world and acquire more comprehensible personalities. The miniatures evoke a lilliputian world alive with throngs of people and vast, luminous landscapes. The *Très riches heures,* a fifteenth-century manuscript executed under the direction of Jean, duke of Berry, and reputed to have been illuminated by the Limbourg brothers, contains a calendar embodying a concrete, naturalistic conception of the seasons, perhaps the first attempt at modern landscape art.

Standard sets of illustrations evolved in the fourteenth and fifteenth centuries, serving to mark the divisions of the text and to aid devotion. Scripture texts illustrated with miniatures, along with legends of the saints, served as a kind of brief sermon with accompanying visual aids. Not all illustrations had so lofty a purpose: fourteenth-century marginal decoration in the form of droll and grotesque figures is often humorous, eccentric, or plainly irreligious. Through the whimsy of the imaginative artist, the value that medieval men and women placed on play and fun was reflected in their private prayer books.

Around 1480, the engraved illustrations of the printed book, which were much cheaper than illumination, began to satisfy the average bourgeois bibliophile; as a result, painters were left with mainly royalty and high nobility for clients. Around 1475–1480 a number of women of high station (perhaps the French queens) became infatuated with very small but exquisitely crafted books of hours, perhaps regarding them as enchanting but pious toys. Some of the very large and pretentiously illuminated books of hours were not regarded as everyday prayer books, whose pages were turned endlessly and replaced when worn out; the edifying value of such large books was probably more artistic than spiritual.

BIBLIOGRAPHY

Editions. The Grandes heures of Jean, Duke of Berry, intro. and legends by Marcel Thomas (1971); *The Hours of Étienne Chevalier,* pref. by Charles Sterling, intro. and legends by Claude Schaefer (1971); *The Rohan Master: A Book of Hours,* intro. by Millard Meiss, intro. and commentaries by Marcel Thomas (1973); *The Très riches heures of Jean, Duke of Berry,* intro. and legends by Jean Longnon and Raymond Cazelles, pref. by Millard Meiss (1969).

Studies. Edmund Bishop, *Liturgica historica* (1918), 211–237; John Harthan, *The Book of Hours* (1977); Paul Lacombe, *Livres d'heures imprimés au XV*[e] *et au XVI*[e] *siècle, conservés dans les bibliothèques publiques de Paris* (1907, repr. 1963); Victor Leroquais, *Les livres d'heures manuscrits de la Bibliothèque Nationale,* 3 vols. (1927), with valuable introduction; and *Les bréviaires manuscrits des bibliothèques publiques de France,* 5 vols. (1934).

MICHAEL KWATERA, O.S.B.

[See also **Bible Moralisée; Blessed Virgin Mary, Little Office of; Breviary; Canonical Hours; Divine Office; Limbourg Brothers; Manuscript Illumination.**]

BORDEAUX (Burdigala, Bordeus) is situated in southwestern France on the west bank of the Garonne River, 24 kilometers (15 miles) above its junction with the Dordogne to form the Gironde and 96 kilometers (60 miles) from the mouth of the Gironde. Burdigala was founded by the Celts in the third century B.C. as a shipping point for the tin trade with Brittany and the British Isles. The city (*castrum*) that replaced it was founded by the Romans in the first century A.D. and from the beginning was closely linked to the wine trade. In 408, en route to Spain and Africa, the Vandals appeared before it and pillaged the Girondin countryside.

Domination by Visigothic princes began ten years later, followed by the Merovingian Frankish kings (Clovis himself was at Burdigala in 507), who minted the first local coinage and maintained antique culture and traditions, including schools. In 732 it was sacked by the Muslim ᶜAbd-al-Raḥmān Ghāfiqī. In 768 it fell to the Carolingians, whose kings and counts ruled it until 887. In 844 a Viking fleet first appeared in the mouth of the Gironde, and four years later the Normans captured and burned the city. The advent of the Normans marks the end of antique civilization, and, under the territorial counts who succeeded the Carolingians, society became feudalized. The history of medieval Bordeaux begins with the last quarter of the ninth century.

Under Guillaume-Sanche (*d. ca.* 996) the county of Bordeaux became merged with the duchy of Gascony. The last count of Bordeaux was his son, Sanche-Guillaume (1009–1032), who restored the abbeys of Ste. Croix, La Réole, and St. Sever, nominated bishops, and resumed minting. After his death Bordeaux became part of the duchy of Aquitaine, whose dukes ruled the city by appointing *viguiers* and *prévôts.* In time these offices became hereditary. Their holders took Bordeaux as a patronymic and became the first noble family. In the last half of the eleventh century two dozen lordships can be counted in the Bordelais. Many of these lords participated in the *Reconquista.* A large number were alodialists owing neither homage nor feudal services and whose peasants owed no rents or land service, so that at the beginning of the twelfth century in Bordeaux and the Bordelais the dukes found themselves without sufficient territorial base and proper resources to have real power. From about 1058 onward Bordeaux was the great city and religious metropolis, if not the capital, of Aquitaine. Construction of the castle of L'Ombrière had begun, along with the church of St. Seurin, to be followed by the cathedral of St. André. After 1154 the dukes of Aquitaine were also kings of England, and the history of English rule of Bordeaux begins.

During the seige of the city in 1205–1206 by Alfonso VIII of Castile, the Bordelais had to fend for themselves and of necessity created the first municipal institutions. In 1206 King John recognized the de facto situation: his letters mention a mayor, jurats, a seneschal, a commune, and royal baillis. The name of the first mayor (1208) was Pierre Lambert. In 1224 Henry III granted the right to have a mayor and commune and confirmed it by charter in 1235. The *Établissements de Bordeaux,* which detail the organization of the city, belong to the years 1253–1254 and were confirmed by Henry III in 1257.

The *Établissements* provide for a mayor elected by the jurats for a one-year term (and not eligible for reelection for three years) who was paid a salary of 1,000 *sous bordelais,* with all other compensation prohibited. The fifty jurats were also elected for one year. Their first act was to swear fealty to the king-duke and then to take an oath before the entire commune to govern well and faithfully, to do equal justice to all, and to elect a mayor who would be faithful to the king. The mayor and jurats together constituted the *jurade,* the governing body, whose deliberations were secret. The *jurade* elected annually from among the burghers thirty councillors who commanded the 300 burghers charged with maintaining the peace, who aided in governing, advised in difficult cases, and who were held to obedience and secrecy.

Bordeaux was really a tight-knit corporation controlled by noble families, such as the Bordeaux, and by nouveaux riches, such as the Caillau and the Colomb, who were rivals of the Delsoler. It became the economic capital of Aquitaine. As early as 1214, John exempted the burghers from all customs on wines from their vineyards, and this exemption was one basis of their commercial prosperity, which was to last for more than two centuries. After 1225 Bordeaux replaced La Rochelle as the principal Atlantic port of the English domain and became the sole supplier of wine to England, where Gascon merchants enjoyed special privileges. The customs on wine (the great custom of 5*s.* 4*d. petits tournois* per tun; the small one called *issac* of 2*s.* 8*d. petits tournois* per tun) were so lucrative that they were pledged in 1267–1268, 1280, and 1289 to the merchants of Cahors and in 1284–1296 to the Ricciardi of Lucca in return for enormous loans to the king-duke.

After the Gascon War of 1294–1303, when the French seized the city and were driven out by an insurrection led by Arnaud Caillau, Bordeaux entered on its first great century. Its prestige in Christian Europe was enhanced by the election of its archbishop, Bertrand de Got, to be Pope Clement V. The prosperity of its 30,000 inhabitants and their loyalty to their English dukes were built solidly on the wine trade with England. For the five years between 1305 and 1337 where accounts are complete, 384, 654 tuns (307,723,200 liters) were exported from Gascony. Of these, 337,424 tuns were laded at Bordeaux, and of these, 53,509 tuns were wines grown by burghers, nobles, and ecclesiastics of the city. In 1344–1346 the gold ecu and florin were minted. From 1355 to 1372 Bordeaux became the capital of the principality of Aquitaine, and the future Richard II was born there in the sumptuous court of his father, the Black Prince.

The period 1372–1429 was one of stagnation. By 1400 wine exports had dropped to 11,000 tuns annually. The ravages of the Hundred Years War and the Black Death reduced the population to 20,000. In 1429 the French began their reconquest of Gascony. But even in the midst of war, in 1441, the archbishop, Pierre III, was successful in obtaining a papal bull establishing a university. Bordeaux was invested in 1442 and capitulated in 1451. The English returned the next year to a joyous welcome but on 17 July 1453 lost the battle of Castillon, and on 19 October the armies of Charles VII entered the city. He promptly revoked the liberties and privileges of Bordeaux, but they were partially restored by Louis XI.

BIBLIOGRAPHY

Charles Higounet, ed., *Histoire de Bordeaux,* 8 vols. (1962–1974), supersedes all previous publications. The first three volumes are: Robert Étienne, ed., *Bordeaux antique* (1962); Charles Higounet, ed., *Bordeaux pendant le haut moyen âge* (1963); and Yves Renouard, ed., *Bordeaux sous les rois d'Angleterre* (1965).

G. P. CUTTINO

[See also **Aquitaine; France; Hundred Years War; Wine.**]

BORIS (*ca.* 830–907), khan/prince/archon of Bulgaria from 852 to 889. Boris succeeded Presiam, who was either his father or his uncle. He fought a series of wars early in his reign against the Franks, Byzantines, Serbs, and Moravians. Except possibly the Byzantine war, all were unsuccessful. Through outstanding diplomacy Boris emerged from the wars without territorial losses. The results of the Byzantine war (*ca.* 853) are unknown. Possibly he occupied Macedonia (if it had not been taken by Presiam in 846). But, though held throughout Boris' reign, Macedonia was not recognized as Bulgarian by Byzantium until 904.

Attracted to Christianity, Boris planned to receive it from the Franks, with whom he was allied against Moravia. However, Byzantium attacked Bulgaria in 863, forcing Boris to break that alliance and accept Christianity from Byzantium. Boris was baptized in 864, taking the name Michael from Emperor Michael III, who stood as his godfather. Byzantine clerics then began entering Bulgaria. In 866 some Bulgarian boyars revolted against Christianity and the new legal order. Boris suppressed their revolt, and fifty-two leading boyars (and their families) were executed. Boris sought an independent church but failed to acquire it from Byzantium, so in 866 he turned to Rome for a mission. After the papacy refused his requests for an archbishop, he turned to the Council of Constantinople (869–870), which, being overwhelmingly Eastern in composition, decided Bulgaria belonged under Byzantium. The Byzantines sent an archbishop with considerable autonomy. Thus Bulgaria became part of the Orthodox world.

Boris built many churches throughout Bulgaria, including seven cathedrals, one of which, the Great Basilica at his capital of Pliska, at a length of ninety-nine meters, was then the largest church in Europe. In 886 he welcomed the Slavic mission expelled from Moravia and encouraged its work that led to Bulgaria's acquiring a Slavonic liturgy and literature. Boris stimulated translations from Greek to Slavonic, and supported the beginning of Bulgarian monasticism. Under him Preslav and Ochrid developed as religious, educational, and translation centers, at which a native clergy was trained.

The Bulgarian people had consisted of Slavs and Turkic Bulgars. By Boris' reign the Bulgars were on the way to being assimilated by the more numerous Slavs. Under Boris this process was greatly accelerated through Christianity and the use of Slavonic as the literary language. After his reign sources no longer make distinctions between Bulgars and Slavs. Boris greatly weakened the hereditary Bulgar boyar aristocracy with its right to participate in governing through family ties; he crushed many old families (by the 866 executions, for example) and replaced some of them with his own men (including some Slavs in leadership positions). He declared himself ruler by Grace of God. He had some success in establishing rule from the center, but did not really create a permanent centralized administration.

Boris was an outstanding diplomat whose last twenty-five years (864–889) had Bulgaria involved in no wars. A devout Christian, after an illness he abdicated to a monastery in 889. When his son and successor Vladimir tried to alter Boris' policies (restoring the Frankish alliance and reverting to paganism), Boris came out of his monastery in 893 to overthrow Vladimir. He then directed the Council of Preslav (893), which officially deposed and blinded Vladimir, placed Boris' younger son Symeon on the throne, made Preslav the capital, and established Christianity in Slavonic form as the official religion of Bulgaria. Boris then returned to his monastery, where he died in 907. He was canonized locally before 923.

BIBLIOGRAPHY

John V. A. Fine, Jr., *The Early Medieval Balkans: A Critical Survey from the Sixth to the Late Twelfth Century* (1983), 112–131; Vasil Gjuzelev, *Knjaz Boris Prvi* (1969).

JOHN V. A. FINE, JR.

[See also **Bulgaria; Byzantine Empire; Michael III; Slavic Languages and Literatures; Symeon of Bulgaria.**]

BOROUGH (ENGLAND–WALES). Medieval England and Wales were noteworthy for the effectiveness of their local governments. Of the many varieties of government, one of the richest, most dynamic, and hence most important was the borough. William Stubbs, a pioneer in the field of constitu-

BOROUGH (ENGLAND–WALES)

tional history, believed that boroughs evolved from fortified Anglo-Saxon camps called *burhs,* and that by the eleventh century they could be distinguished from villages by the growth within them of semiautonomous governments. F. W. Maitland, probably the most influential of all constitutional historians, developed a variation on Stubbs's interpretation that he called the "garrison theory." He, too, claimed that English urban communities started as fortresses, but emphasized the growth of royal government after the Norman Conquest. Boroughs then became administrative centers, which spurred more general development.

Carl Stephenson built further on the foundations of Stubbs and Maitland, stressing the importance of a continental connection in English urban growth and redoubling Maitland's emphasis on administrative functions. This view was challenged by James Tait, who emphasized the crucial role of commerical activity in the development of boroughs, claiming that the general increase in trade during the twelfth and thirteenth centuries led to a growth in urban markets, incomes, and tax bases. Kings, eager to tap new sources of money, offered municipal liberties in exchange for steady incomes. Tait also downplayed the constitutional distinctions between boroughs or *burhs* and other urban settlements, *ports* and *vills,* claiming that they were all, by and large, towns. His views, although modified, remain the most widely accepted interpretation.

Little detailed evidence survives about the administration of Anglo-Saxon towns. England was overwhelmingly rural, and towns played a comparatively small role in society. Most boroughs were royal foundations and, like other royal estates, were administered by a reeve, who was responsible for rents, tolls, and the profits of justice. Major changes in borough government began in the late eleventh century, stemming in part from the Norman Conquest and the sophisticated administrative techniques that the Normans introduced. But more important was the economic development of western Europe, based to a large degree on the establishment of a market economy rooted in towns. Other types of local government—seigneurial, ecclesiastical, franchisal—drew income mainly from landed sources, while borough income was primarily from profits in trade and industry. Townsmen usually had more capital, which made them immediately valuable to the Crown.

The new importance of boroughs is evident in the Domesday Book, a survey taken in 1086 by William I to measure the wealth of his realm. The results distinguish separate rights and privileges for boroughs and burgesses, indicate a limited sense of the boroughs' incorporation, and reveal borough courts, which defended something called burgage tenure. This was a heritable form of tenure held by a fixed money rent, normally in lieu of all services. Burgage tenure was a key to urban autonomy, for it effectively provided the right to sell, alienate, or otherwise transfer ownership and possession of property without license.

In the twelfth and thirteenth centuries, town liberties were extended through the purchase of charters from the king. The process was begun in the reign of Henry I (1100–1135), and usually granted the right of incorporation to merchant and craft guilds, the full or at least partial recognition of free borough status, the right to farm the Crown's revenues directly, the right to local tolls (and sometimes exemptions from tolls and customs in other parts of the kingdom), additional powers for local borough courts, the return of writs, and the right to choose local authorities. The spirit of the liberties appears in a charter granted to Newcastle:

> Pleas which arise in the borough shall there be held and concluded except those which belong to the king's crown.... If a burgess has a son in his house and at his table, his son shall have the same liberty as his father. If a villein comes to reside in the borough for a year and a day, he shall always remain there. A burgess can give or sell his land as he wishes and go where he will, freely and greatly, unless his claim to the land is challenged.

Henry II (1154–1189) resisted burghal encroachments on royal prerogatives. He was not hostile to urban or commercial activity, but opposed any weakening of his authority, and was wary of the spread of the revolutionary communal activity that had beset towns in his French domains. Hence, although he issued more than fifty town charters, he never allowed the use of the expression "commune," and issued nothing in perpetuity. One result was the emergence, late in the twelfth century, of town guild merchants, corporations made up of local elites that took certain civic powers to themselves without official royal sanctions. Ironically, it was the guild merchants that, in the fourteenth and fifteenth centuries, helped guide town governments to virtual autonomy.

Conditions changed during the reigns of Henry's sons, Richard I and John. Each needed money—Richard for his crusade and ransom, and John for his efforts to recapture Normandy—each was willing to grant borough liberties, even in perpetuity, for cash. Both shied away from granting full communal authority, but each sold exemptions from taxes, county court attendance, and other obligations. By the end of John's reign, the structure of borough government had acquired most of the characteristics it would have until the nineteenth century.

Burghal courts were unchallenged in their jurisdictions, which usually included police activities, public health, defense, the setting of assizes, and regulations for local markets. Councils were formed from the *probi homines* (great men), the leading gentlemen, merchants, and craftsmen. The councils concerned themselves primarily with local projects such as building and sanitation, and farms of murage, pavage, and pickage. Permanent staffs of municipal officials were hired, some of whom were lawyers and notaries. Reeves, bailiffs, and sometimes even sheriffs, once exclusively the king's men, now reported to the councils. Coroners, clerks, escheators, customs collectors, gaolers, and even librarians were hired, and permanent records were kept. This was an expensive but essential process, for records helped to safeguard borough privileges and to engender civic spirit. Henry III (1216–1272) and Edward I (1272–1307) resisted some of these liberties, but townsfolk, richer than ever, were in a position to buy or confirm most of the privileges the Crown questioned.

Another aspect of burghal autonomy was representation in Parliament, in which burgesses participated from the first. The 1295 parliamentary returns show their role. Summonses were sent to county sheriffs, who asked for two representatives from each town. The elections were held locally, usually by the *probi homines,* with 114 towns making returns. In all, burgesses made up about one-sixth of Parliament, a proportion that rose to one-fifth by 1500. Attendance was expensive, and in 1300 many burgesses avoided it; by 1500, however, buoyed by mercantile wealth, most townsmen regarded it as a privilege, and the urban parliamentarians were drawn from the town elites—gentlemen, merchants, and lawyers. The burgesses played a small role in the national aspects of Parliament, concerning themselves mostly with local fiscal and commercial issues. But their continued participation in representative government was another aspect of burghal independence.

Burghal autonomy continued to grow apace in the later Middle Ages. Fourteenth- and fifteenth-century kings, like their predecessors, needed cash, and several towns were able to purchase another privilege, the right to complete incorporation. This allowed them to sue (and be sued) and to acquire a town seal. Town corporations could hold lands and divide them as they saw fit, and issue bylaws. No town, not even London, was able to affect the title "commune," and none was entirely free of the power and authority of the king. But beyond these limitations there were few constraints, and by the late fourteenth century, beginning with Bristol in 1373, several important towns were made counties.

Taxation increased, but municipal government was offering more services, especially in public health and education, as is illustrated in the 1440 charter of Kingston upon Hull, which served as the model for all future incorporations. The charter confirmed burgage tenure, free transfer of land, a distinct borough court, independence from the sheriff and other royal officials, and freedom from tolls. It recognized that income from tolls was not sufficient for expanding town governments, and guaranteed burgesses' right to hold property. Holdership of land was a crucial issue in the struggle for autonomy because income from property taxes and rents was the principal source of the funds that paid for the expanding borough governments.

In sum, economic prosperity was the major force behind the emergence of autonomous borough governments. Towns offered kings a source of ready cash. From the late eleventh century, as a European market economy developed and townsmen grew richer, burgesses were able to buy liberties—first piecemeal, then by charter, and finally as independent corporate bodies. This freed boroughs from all layers of local government and made them answerable only to the king.

BIBLIOGRAPHY

Frederick Pollack and F. W. Maitland, *The History of English Law,* 2 vols., S. F. C. Milson, ed. (1968), is basic to constitutional history. Helen M. Jewell, *English Local Administration in the Middle Ages* (1972), is an excellent survey; and Norman F. Cantor, ed., *William Stubbs on the English Constitution* (1966), is a fine introduction to Stubbs.

Sources on borough government can be found in Mary Bateson, ed., *Borough Customs,* 2 vols. (1904–1906); Adolphus Ballard, ed., *British Borough Charters, 1042–1216* (1913); Adolphus Ballard and James Tait, eds., *British Borough Charters, 1216–1307* (1923); Martin Weinbaum, ed., *British Borough Charters, 1307–1660* (1943).

General issues are covered in Carl Stephenson, *Borough and Town* (1933); James Tait, *The Medieval English Bor-*

ough (1936); Colin Platt, *The English Medieval Town* (1976); and Susan Reynolds, *An Introduction to the History of English Towns* (1977).

Particular issues are covered in May McKissack, *The Parliamentary Representation of English Boroughs During the Middle Ages* (1932); Gwyn Williams, *Medieval London: From Commune to Capital* (1963); Charles Phythian-Adams, *Desolation of a City: Coventry and the Urban Crisis of the Late Middle Ages* (1979); and Robert S. Gottfried, *Bury St. Edmunds and the Urban Crisis, 1290–1539* (1982).

ROBERT S. GOTTFRIED

[See also **Burgage Tenure; England, Norman–Angevin; England, 1272–1485; Law, English Common; Trade.**]

BOROUGH-ENGLISH is the English form of ultimogeniture, the rule that all of a deceased person's lands and tenements pass by inheritance to his youngest son. It was a widespread local custom but never especially characteristic of boroughs, and the name is a whimsical latecomer, used generally for the institution only from the 1450's and merely recalling that the English borough within Nottingham was one of the localities that knew this law. Borough-English governed a little free land in the countryside and was the custom of some boroughs, but was principally important as a manorial law for unfree holdings. Manors that observed it were common in the south, especially the southeast; in Sussex it was something like the normal rule. Details varied. In Nottingham the youngest son received the whole heritage; if there was no son, it was divided among daughters; and if there were no children, the youngest brother, or uncle, was the heir. Elsewhere the youngest daughter sometimes inherited alone if there were no sons; the eldest brother, if there were no children. Some manorial customs were very intricate.

Borough-English was first noticed in the tract called Glanvill, about 1188. Further evidence of it accumulates by bits and pieces from the following centuries. But its history has not been written, and we understand it badly. No one knows just how common it was. It may be very ancient, or it may have arisen as late as the 1100's, imposed, like primogeniture, by lords who wished to keep tenements undivided. Concentrated in the southeast in areas close to those where partible inheritance persisted, it may represent a less complete concession than primogeniture to pressures for impartibility. It could hold an orphaned family together until the youngest brother came of age to take control of the heritage, and it might help equalize the fortunes of brothers by favoring the youngest, whom the parents, while they lived, would have least time to assist.

BIBLIOGRAPHY

Mary Bateson, ed., *Borough Customs,* II (1906), xcv, 130–131; Charles I. Elton, *Origins of English History,* 2nd ed. (1890), 178–216; Rosamond Jane Faith, "Peasant Families and Inheritance Customs in Medieval England," in *Agricultural History Review,* **14** (1966); George C. Homans, *English Villagers of the Thirteenth Century* (1941), 121–132; Frederick Pollock and F. W. Maitland, *The History of English Law,* 2nd ed. (1898), I, 647, and II, 268–283.

DONALD W. SUTHERLAND

[See also **Inheritance, Western Europe; Land Tenure, Western European.**]

BORRASSÁ, LUIS (*fl. ca.* 1380–1424), leader of the Spanish international style of painting in Barcelona. Borrassá established a large atelier that produced numerous retables featuring colorful narratives executed in rich, bright colors with a decorative treatment of draperies and figure types revealing Italian influence. A characteristic work is the elaborate *Retable of St. Peter* in Santa María in Tarrasa (*ca.* 1411–1413).

BIBLIOGRAPHY

Chandler R. Post, *A History of Spanish Painting,* II (1930), 315–361; Jacques Lassaigne, *Spanish Painting,* I (1952), 47ff.

JAMES SNYDER

[See also **International Style, Gothic.**]

BORRE STYLE, a style of Viking art named after a Norwegian ship burial containing decorated bridle mounts. It employs three main motifs: the "ring-chain" pattern of two-strand interlace bound by rings; a single "gripping beast"; and a backward-looking animal. The style developed about the mid ninth century, and continued in use until the late tenth.

BIBLIOGRAPHY

James A. Graham-Campbell, *Viking Artefacts: A Select Catalogue* (1980), ch. 9; D. M. Wilson,"The Borre Style in

Gripping beast pendant, Sweden. COPYRIGHT: DAVID WILSON, THE BRITISH MUSEUM

Cross-slab with ring chain motif from Kirk Michael, Isle of Man. COPYRIGHT: EVA WILSON THE BRITISH MUSEUM

the British Isles," in Bjarni Vilhjálmsson *et al.*, eds., *Minjar og Menntir* (1976); and D. M. Wilson and Ole Klindt-Jensen, *Viking Art*, 2nd ed. (1980), ch. 3.

JAMES A. GRAHAM-CAMPBELL

[See also **Viking Art.**]

BÓSA SAGA OK HERRAUÐS is an Icelandic prose narrative of the *fornaldarsaga* genre. The older and better of the two versions probably dates from the fourteenth century; its four principal manuscripts have been dated between the late fourteenth and early sixteenth centuries. The story is also told in a later, relatively independent redaction from the seventeenth century, and in a number of *Rímur*.

The older *Bósa saga* relates the adventures of the impetuous Bósi and his loyal friend Herrauðr, son of King Hringr of East Gautland (the Swedish province of Östergötland). Sentenced to death by King Hringr, the two sworn brothers are rescued by the sorcery of Bósi's foster mother Busla and sent on a mission to Permia (Bjarmaland) to obtain the egg of the fabulous *gammr*, apparently a kind of monstrous vulture. At the temple of the god Jómali they find the egg and rescue the maiden Hleiðr, sister of King Goðmundr of Glæsir Plains (Glæsisvellir). They return home and are reconciled with King Hringr, but before Herrauðr can marry Hleiðr, the comrades are called upon to fight in the famous battle of Brávellir. In their absence King Goðmund's retainers Hrærekr and Siggeir attack and kill the defenseless King Hringr, and carry Hleiðr back to Glæsir Plains, where she is to be married to Siggeir.

Bósi and Herrauðr set off again, joined by Bósi's brother Smiðr, and succeed in disrupting the wedding and recapturing Hleiðr. On the way back to Gautland, they stop off at Permia, where Bósi abducts the princess Edda. Forces from both Permia and Glæsir Plains pursue them, but are defeated in a huge battle fought with the aid of magic spells. The heroes marry their princesses; Herrauðr rules over East Gautland, and Bósi over Permia.

The saga, which draws on a number of conventional themes and motifs (quest for fabulous treasure, rescue of maiden, bride-stealing, heroic battles), is one of the more entertaining and well-composed examples of the genre. Far from being a monotonous concatenation of heroic adventures, the story is shaped by a structure of symmetrical narrative patterns (for example, journey-abduction-battle) and imaginative variation. Unusual and interesting material is found in Busla's rune-magical curses (the so-called *Buslubæn*) and Bósi's coarsely humorous sexual encounters with a series of farmers' daughters. (Both curses and encounters were omitted from some of the manuscripts and from the first printed edition.)

Despite the Swedish names and setting, the story does not appear to be based on historical tradition; nor have attempts to derive it, in whole or in part, from either Swedish legend or the Russian Bylina been convincing. Some literary borrowing or influence from other (written) sagas is evident, but the author's main inspiration no doubt came from the world of folktale and ballad. However, it is not impossible that a coherent story of Bósi and Herrauðr existed in some oral form prior to the extant fourteenth-century composition.

BIBLIOGRAPHY

Editions. Otto L. Jiriczek, ed., *Die Bósa-Saga in zwei Fassungen, nebst Proben aus den Bósa-Rímur* (1893); Guðni Jónsson and Bjarni Vilhjálmsson, eds., *Fornaldarsögur Norðurlanda,* II (1944), 463–497. An English translation is in *Gautrek's Saga and Other Medieval Tales,* trans. with an introduction by Hermann Pálsson and Paul Edwards (1968), 57–88.

Studies. Hermann Pálsson and Paul Edwards, *Legendary Fiction in Medieval Iceland* (1971); Claiborne W. Thompson, "The Runes in *Bósa saga ok Herrauðs,*" in *Scandinavian Studies,* **50** (1978).

CLAIBORNE W. THOMPSON

[See also **Sagas, Legendary.**]

BOSNIA. Today the Republic of Bosnia is in Yugoslavia, lying south of the Sava, east of the Dalmatian coast, and west of the Drina, which forms the border with Serbia. The name Bosnia has designated different areas at different times, and is derived from the River Bosna, which flows from its source near modern Sarajevo (medieval Vrhbosna) north into the Sava. The term then came to refer to the *župa* (county) of Bosnia, which included the area of Vrhbosna-Kreševo-Fojnica-Visoko-Zenica and was the direct holding of the ban (ruler) of Bosnia. However, at various times in the medieval period, the ban of Bosnia was also suzerain over various territories to the north of his banate as far as the Sava River. These lands (Soli, Usora, Glaž, Vrbanja, Zemljanik, and the Donji Kraji) were frequently referred to as Bosnian lands. The diocese of the Catholic bishop of Bosnia included the central core of the state and all the territory in the north as far as the Sava. The Franciscan Bosnian vicariate, founded in the 1340's, included all the territory in southeastern Europe where Franciscans were operating.

HISTORY

The Slavs settled in greater Bosnia in the late sixth and early seventh centuries. The previous population (which included many Illyrians) emigrated, was killed, or was gradually assimilated. Most of the incoming Slavs were under Avar rule. In the second quarter of the seventh century, the Croatians (who were probably Iranians) invaded, defeated the Avars, and asserted their overlordship over the Slavs in Croatia and parts of Bosnia. In regions south and east of Bosnia, the Serbs came to predominate over the Slavs. In time, these seventh-century invaders were assimilated by the more numerous Slavs. However, they provided the names for the resulting population, among whom Slavic culture and language triumphed. At first the Croatians and Serbs did not form single states; different leaders controlled smaller county units called *župas.* Constantine Porphyrogenitos, writing in the tenth century, mentions eleven Croatian *župas,* four of which were in the north and west of greater Bosnia. He also mentions three towns in the territory of Bosnia.

In the tenth century, Bosnia was briefly part of the Serbian state of Prince Časlav. After he died in battle (*ca.* 960), much of it was incorporated into the Croatian state of Kresimir II; Czar Samuil of Bulgaria marched through Bosnia in about 997, and may well have asserted his overlordship over part of it. After Emperor Basil II defeated Samuil's state in 1018, Byzantium asserted its suzerainty over Bosnia; this lasted until later in the eleventh century, when some of Bosnia was incorporated into Croatia and some into Duklja. With the decline of Duklja after Constantine Bodin's death (*ca.* 1101), that part of Bosnia seems to have been briefly independent prior to its annexation (before 1137) by the Hungarian king (ruler also of Croatia and its part of Bosnia since 1102). Hungarian suzerainty over Bosnia was to last, except for a brief period of Byzantine overlordship (1167–1180), throughout the Middle Ages. However, for much of this time this suzerainty was only nominal.

Bosnia's location put it between East and West. But, because of its mountainous terrain and poor communications, it was more a no-man's-land than

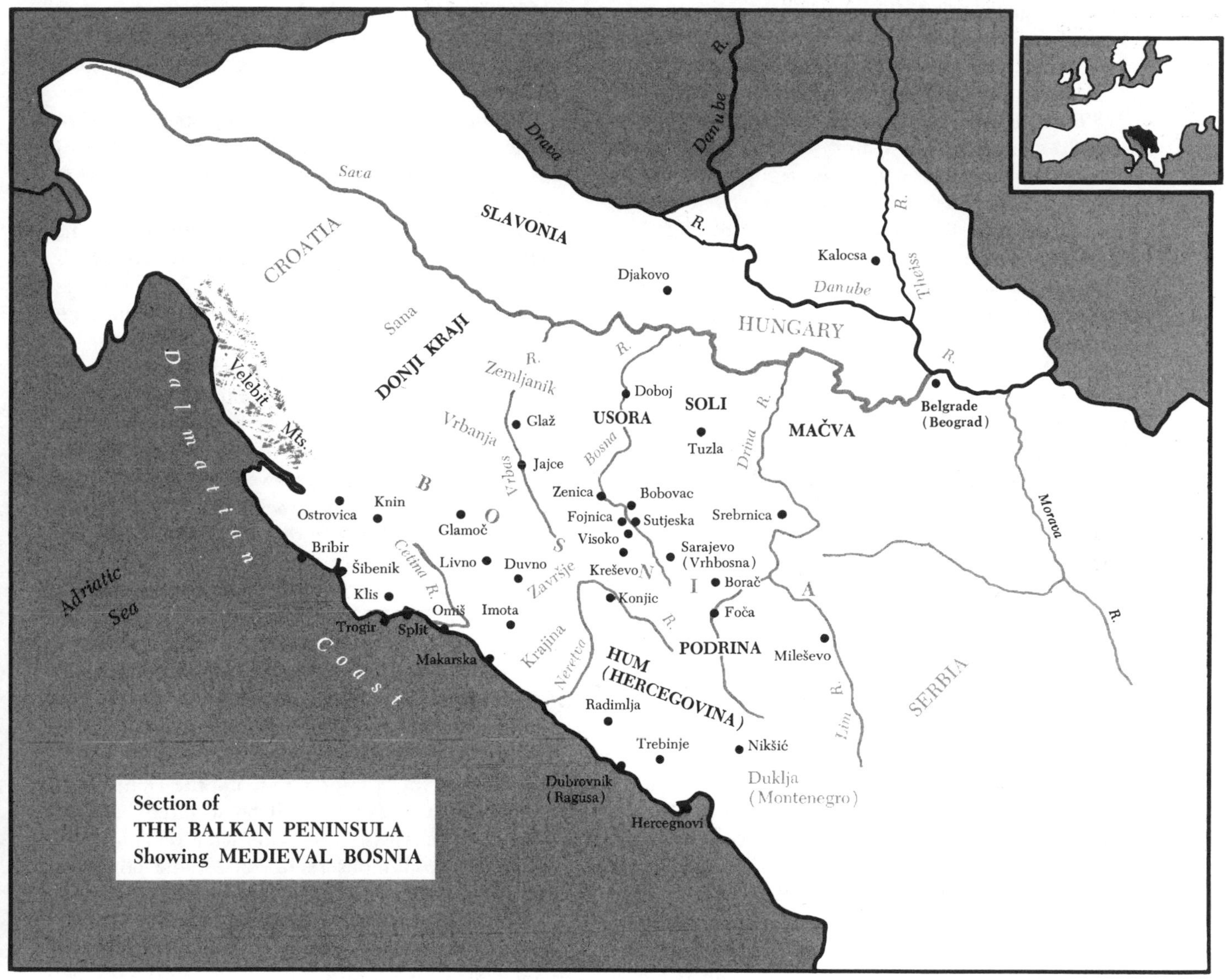

Section of
THE BALKAN PENINSULA
Showing MEDIEVAL BOSNIA

a meeting ground between the two worlds until the fifteenth century, when increased trade opened it up to Western cultural influences. By the tenth century most Bosnians probably were nominally Catholic, converted by missionaries from the Dalmatian coast. By the twelfth century, Bosnia was under the archbishop of Dubrovnik. The mountainous terrain encouraged localism; Bosnia was divided into various regions (e.g. the Podrina, Bosnia [the central part], Hum [more or less corresponding to modern Hercegovina], Soli [Tuzla], Usora, the Donji Kraji); each region had local traditions and its own hereditary nobility. A region was divided into *župas* ruled by the more important nobles, often bearing the title *župans.* These local traditions lasted throughout the Middle Ages, and made the ban's task of centralizing Bosnia difficult. Thus periods of expansion were frequently followed by separatism. Regionalism was seen in cultural phenomena (gravestone motifs, folk songs, folk costumes), and later was intensified by differing and uneven economic development and varying foreign influences. Different religious faiths dominated in different areas.

In the twelfth century central Bosnia was governed, under Hungarian suzerainty, by its ban; northern Bosnia seems also to have been ruled by one or more bans of the same family, also under Hungarian suzerainty. From 1168 to 1326, Hum (formerly Zahumlje) was separate from Bosnia under members of the Serbian dynasty. Except for the

BOSNIA

coastal regions and Trebinje, where there were also Catholics, Hum belonged to the Serbian Orthodox church and had its own Orthodox bishopric.

Sources increase from the time of Ban Kulin (*ca.* 1180–*ca.* 1204). He granted Ragusan merchants duty-free trade in his realm. Under him heretics fleeing Dalmatia (particularly Split) sought refuge in Bosnia; sources also show the Bosnian Catholic church to have been in need of reform. Various Catholic missions failed to solve these problems. The Hungarians, wanting to assert their suzerainty over Bosnia, used heresy as an excuse and obtained papal permission to crusade against the Bosnians. The war began in 1235. Meeting stout resistance from Bosnians of all faiths who rallied around their ruler, Ban Ninoslav, the Hungarians conquered only about half of Bosnia by 1241, when they had to withdraw their forces to meet a Tatar invasion of Hungary. Thus the Bosnian state survived.

In about 1252 the pope removed the Bosnian Catholic church from the jurisdiction of Dubrovnik and assigned it to the Hungarian archbishopric of Kalocsa. The Bosnians refused to accept the change, and the Bosnian Catholic bishopric had to migrate to Djakovo in Slavonia, where it remained, having no role in Bosnia, throughout the Middle Ages. The Bosnians created their own autonomous Bosnian church, which is first documented from the early fourteenth century but probably dates to the mid thirteenth century.

Ninoslav is last mentioned in sources from the 1240's and no more information exists about the Bosnian banate in that century, although the banate most probably maintained its independence under Ninoslav's heirs. The Hungarians retained their suzerainty over the territory north of the banate (Soli, Usora, Vrbanja, Sana), as various surviving Hungarian charters reveal. In the 1280's this northern territory was divided between Ban Prijezda and the former Serbian ruler, Stefan Dragutin, who was granted Mačva and Usora by his brother-in-law, the Hungarian king. Prijezda's son, Stjepan Kotroman, married Dragutin's daughter and emerged as the major figure in the north, but he was soon eclipsed by the Šubići, who began expanding into Bosnia from Bribir. In 1299, Pavao Šubić was called ban of Bosnia (which probably still referred to the northern territory). In 1305 he was called "Ban of All Bosnia"—which, if taken literally, would suggest he governed the banate too. We do not know whether Kotroman was expelled, or if he remained in his former lands as a Šubić vassal. Kotroman died between 1305 and 1315. Then disorders in his lands (wherever they then were), if we can believe a seventeenth-century source, caused his widow and son to flee to Dubrovnik.

Around 1318, Kotroman's son, Stjepan Kotromanić (*ca.* 1318–1353), established himself as ban of Bosnia holding the central Bosnian banate. Whether Kotroman had ever held this territory and how Kotromanić obtained power there are unknown. The Šubići, by then in decline, recognized Kotromanić's rule in the banate. The Hungarian king, Charles Robert, also had domestic troubles. Kotromanić supported him, and received Hungarian blessing for his activities in Bosnia. Thus Kotromanić could consolidate his state without foreign interference. He involved himself in a Croatian civil war to take from Nelipić territory to the west of his banate—Makarska, the Krajina (the land between the Neretva and Cetina rivers), and Završje (including Imota, Duvno, Livno, Glamoč). This territory was Catholic and had two Catholic bishoprics.

After the death of Serbia's King Milutin in 1321, disorders followed among the Serbs. As a result, Kotromanić was able to annex Hum in 1326. Here most of the population was Orthodox. The dominant family were the Draživojevići, who from the 1330's were vassals—not always loyal—of the Bosnian ban. Two charters from about 1324 confirm the rights of certain local nobles in Usora, Soli, and the Donji Kraji to lands they already possessed, but asserted the ban's suzerainty over them. The Donji Kraji remained basically an autonomous region under the powerful Hrvatinić family.

The ban supported a Franciscan mission initiated in the 1340's against "heresy" in Bosnia. By 1342 the Franciscan vicariate of Bosnia was established; eventually its territory came to include all those parts of southeastern Europe where Franciscans worked. By 1385 the Franciscans had four convents in Bosnia proper; another dozen were built before the Turkish conquest (1463). Throughout the Middle Ages the Franciscans were the only Catholic clergy (excluding a handful of court chaplains) in Bosnia proper. By 1347, Stjepan Kotromanić had accepted Catholicism. From then on, all Bosnian rulers, except possibly Ostoja, were Catholics. Under Kotromanić Bosnian mines, particularly silver and lead, were opened, which paved the way for Bosnia's economic development and greatly increased its commercial contacts with the coast. Now many merchants from Dubrovnik came; some settled, forming colonies. These Ragusans played major roles in the ban's financial administration and also supported the Franciscans. The commercial towns that developed were Catholic in character.

Stjepan Kotromanić died in 1353; his nephew Tvrtko (1353–1391) succeeded. Kotromanić had established little state apparatus, and generally left his vassals in outlying regions to administer their own lands. Tvrtko was only fifteen, and few of these nobles felt obliged to serve him. He held only the central banate and had the task of acquiring the loyalty of other regions that were seceding from his state. The Hungarian king was actively wooing the northern nobles. The Hrvatinić family split; some for Tvrtko, some for Hungary. The Hungarian king (Louis the Great), who had just married Kotromanić's daughter, compelled Tvrtko to come to Hungary in 1357, and to surrender as her dowry Završje and the lands between the Cetina and Neretva rivers. Tvrtko then was confirmed, as a Hungarian vassal, as ruler over Bosnia and Usora. Having strengthened his position by winning the support of many nobles, he successfully stopped a major Hungarian invasion in 1363. In 1366 various Bosnian nobles revolted, putting Tvrtko's brother Vuk on the throne. Tvrtko received Hungarian aid, and by 1367 had recovered all his territory. The nobles shifted sides throughout this conflict, as suited their own interests.

Reestablished in power and with the northern lands secure and loyal again, Tvrtko began meddling in the feuds of the Serbian nobility to his southeast. Through these activities he was able, in 1374, to annex the Upper Drina and Lim regions (giving him all Hum) and, in 1376, Trebinje. As a result of the acquisition of this Serbian territory, plus the extinction of the Nemanjić dynasty in Serbia (in 1371), to which he belonged through Dragutin's daughter's marriage to Kotroman, Tvrtko claimed the Serbian kingship. He was crowned king of Serbia and Bosnia in 1377 at Mileševo on the recently conquered Lim. From then on, the rulers of Bosnia, instead of being bans, would be kings, and would bear this double title even though they held very little Serbian territory.

Next, Tvrtko sided with Charles III (and subsequently his son Ladislas) of Naples in his struggle against Sigismund of Luxembourg for the Hungarian throne. As a result, Tvrtko made himself overlord of much of Croatia (south of Velebit, including Knin, Ostrovica, Klis) and Dalmatia (including Omiš, Split, Trogir, Šibenik), and in 1390 even called himself king of Croatia and Dalmatia. In this he was actively supported by the Hrvatinići, whose leader in the 1380's was Hrvoje Vukčić. After Tvrtko's death in 1391, Hrvoje became the most powerful man in Bosnia and continued Tvrtko's Dalmatian activities on behalf of Ladislas.

Tvrtko was succeeded by an elderly cousin, Dabiša (1391–1395); a council *(sabor)* of nobles now becomes prominent in the sources. The council's role at this time resulted from Dabiša's weakness; the king had no choice but to summon the leading nobles to gain their agreement on important questions, lest they revolt. The general cooperation of the nobles basically held the state together; but separatism remained strong, and the great nobles took advantage of Dabiša's impotence to gain more autonomy in their own regions. Although much of their territory had been under the ban/king since the 1320's, local traditions remained strong.

The lesser nobles were often more loyal to their regional lord than to the king. There were three leading families. First, the Hrvatinići, the most powerful; but after Hrvoje's death in 1416, they were to decline in state affairs though continuing to dominate the Donji Kraji. Second, the Kosača family: Vlatko Vuković (*d.* 1392), Sandalj Hranić (1392–1435), and Stefan Vukčić (1435–1466), who controlled part of Hum; they acquired control of most of the rest after Sandalj eliminated the Sankovići (descendants of the Draživojevići) by blinding Radič Sanković and letting him die in prison in 1404. Third, Raden Jablanić (succeeded by Pavle Radenović and his heirs the Pavlovići) in eastern Bosnia (Borač, Vrhbosna). After 1391 the Hrvatinići and Kosače held more territory than the king.

Dabiša was forced to make peace with Sigismund at Dobor in 1394. He made Sigismund his heir, renounced the Croatian-Dalmatian kingship, and returned to Hungary the Dalmatian and Croatian territory that Tvrtko had gained. After Dabiša's death in 1395, the Bosnian nobles rallied to prevent Sigismund from becoming their king, and put on the throne Dabiša's widow Jelena, who ruled as a puppet of the nobles until 1398, when she was deposed for another family member, Ostoja (first reign 1398–1404). Sigismund could not intervene, owing to the disasters that befell him while fighting against the Turks at Nicopolis (1396). This disaster aided Ladislas' cause and allowed Hrvoje to gain control over parts of Croatia and Dalmatia. In 1403, Ladislas came to Zadar, but, fearing to move against Buda, made Hrvoje his deputy and gave him the title *herceg* of Split.

In 1404 the Bosnian nobility, angry at Ostoja for

a war against Dubrovnik and his attempt to confiscate the estates of a middling nobleman (Pavle Klešić), ousted him for Tvrtko II (a son, probably illegitimate, of Tvrtko I); Ostoja fled to Sigismund in Hungary, received military support, and occupied part of Bosnia, including the major royal residence of Bobovac. There Ostoja ruled as a puppet king for Sigismund while most of the nobility supported Tvrtko. Skirmishes, chiefly fought in the north between the nobility and the Hungarians, continued until 1409, when Hrvoje submitted to Sigismund. Hrvoje now held Dalmatia from Sigismund. Ostoja, never partial to Hrvoje and jealous of Sigismund's favor to him, which threatened Ostoja's position in Bosnia, moved closer to the Bosnian nobility, which agreed to accept him as king (1409–1418).

Because Ostoja was supported by Ladislas' partisans, Sandalj and Pavle Radenović, Sigismund and Hrvoje went to war against Ostoja. In the end, by 1411, Sandalj, Pavle, and Ostoja submitted to Sigismund. Ostoja was recognized as king by Sigismund, while Ostoja recognized Sigismund as his suzerain and yielded Soli and Usora to him. That same year Sigismund assigned the richest silver-mining town in Bosnia, Srebrnica on the Drina, to Stefan Lazarević of Serbia. For most of the rest of the fifteenth century—until the Turkish conquest—Srebrnica was Serbian, and Bosnian attempts to regain it caused several wars with Serbia.

In 1412, Hrvoje was declared a rebel by Sigismund, who accused him of dealing with the Turks because he had attacked Sandalj's lands when Sandalj was fighting the Turks in Serbia. As a result, Sigismund dropped Hrvoje as his deputy for Dalmatia. By then Venice, as a result of purchase from Ladislas and war with Sigismund, had acquired several Dalmatian cities. Split immediately ousted Hrvoje's officials, showing his unpopularity there. With this loss of support, Hrvoje turned to the Turks and received mercenaries from Isak-Beg, the Ottoman governor in Skopje. They won a major victory over the Hungarians at Doboj in 1415. As a result, Sigismund lost his influence in Bosnia. Sandalj and Ostoja made peace with Hrvoje, and the Ottomans and Hrvoje confirmed Ostoja as king. For the next twenty years Ottoman soldiers were to be active in Bosnia as mercenaries in various civil wars.

In August 1415, Sandalj and Ostoja held a conference at Sutjeska; Pavle Radenović was invited and murdered. The cause was probably Pavle's current association with ex-King Tvrtko II. His son Radoslav Pavlović immediately went to war in revenge and acquired Ottoman mercenaries. Hrvoje, who had no role in this struggle, died in 1416; his nephew Djuraj Vojsalić obtained a dominant role in the Donji Kraji, but had much less influence in general Bosnian affairs. This was partly owing to loss of territory. Omiš and the Krajina were taken by the Croatian nobleman Ivaniš Nelipić. Furthermore, Ostoja, after Hrvoje's death, divorced his own wife to marry Hrvoje's widow, who brought with her considerable territory (including Jajce, to be the last Bosnian capital).

By 1417, Ostoja had joined the Pavlovići against Sandalj. The following year Ostoja died. His son Stefan Ostojić (1418–1420) succeeded. That same year Sandalj obtained Ottoman mercenaries. A peace conference was held at which Isak-Beg, the Ottoman commander, killed Radoslav's brother Peter. Thus war continued, and Sandalj, with his Turkish mercenaries, won back much of the territory he had lost early in the war; he then deposed Stefan Ostojić. Tvrtko II was restored to the throne (second reign 1420–1443). By October 1420, Radoslav had made peace with Sandalj and recognized Tvrtko II. However, Sandalj and Radoslav would continue to feud; warfare broke out between them in 1423 and 1429.

In 1426 Tvrtko patched up relations with the Hungarians, a situation that led to a damaging Ottoman raid causing Tvrtko to accept Ottoman suzerainty. In 1433, Radivoj, another son of Ostoja, was recognized by the Ottomans as king, and Sandalj supported him too. This threat caused Tvrtko to improve relations with the Hungarians. In 1435 he again accepted Hungarian suzerainty; in 1437 the Ottomans forced him to renounce this suzerainty and to accept Ottoman overlordship again.

In the 1430's the Franciscans became more active, building several new monasteries. In this and the following decade, considerable building of Catholic churches took place, and many nobles accepted Catholicism. The towns in which the Franciscans were active, a high percentage of whose populations were Catholic merchants from the coast, were essentially Catholic. Despite Catholic gains, the Bosnian church—whose monasteries were chiefly rural—continued to be tolerated; the Orthodox church maintained its dominance in Hum (though Sandalj and his successor, Stefan Vukčić, supported the Bosnian church as well), and had some following in Bosnia near the Drina and the upper Neretva where ran the border between Bosnia and Hum.

BOSNIA

Sandalj died in 1435 and was succeeded by his nephew, Stefan Vukčić, who inherited a vast territory, from Konjic on the upper Neretva to Nikšić in "Montenegro," and from the upper Drina and Lim to the "Montenegrin" coast. In the late 1430's destructive Ottoman raids against Bosnia increased. Radoslav and Stefan Vukčić fought a brief war, followed by a peace in 1439. Radoslav died in 1441, and was succeeded by his son Ivaniš. Tvrtko II died in 1443 and was succeeded by another son of Ostoja, Stefan Tomaš (1443–1461), the brother of Radivoj.

Stefan Vukčić disapproved of the succession, and supported Radivoj against Stefan Tomaš. Warfare broke out, and Stefan Vukčić found himself losing territory as most of the Bosnian nobility rallied around the new king. As a result Stefan Vukčić turned to the Ottomans and, with their support, began regaining his lands. His success led to peace between him and the king, who now married Katarina, Stefan Vukčić's daughter. The Ottomans, unhappy at this peace, stepped up their raids against both their lands. In 1448 Stefan Vukčić, to assert his independence, dropped his title *vojvoda* of Bosnia, which reflected subordination to the Bosnian king, and took the title *herceg* of Hum and the Coast. The following year he changed it to *herceg* of St. Sava (a Serbian saint, whose relics were at the monastery of Mileševo on the *herceg*'s lands). Soon his lands became known as Hercegovina, a name that lasted to the present.

By this time the Ottomans were annexing parts of eastern Bosnia, and their chief gains were at the expense of the Pavlovići. Ivaniš Pavlović died in 1450; the following year the Ottomans took Vrhbosna, which (under its new name of Sarajevo) rose to become the major city in Bosnia during the Turkish period. Greatly weakened by territorial losses, Ivaniš' brother and successor, Peter, became vassal to *Herceg* Stefan.

As Turkish vassals both the king and *Herceg* Stefan owed Ottoman tribute. The king had prosperous mines in his lands and was in a much better position to raise this money; the *herceg* had just a few poorer mines, and was chiefly dependent on customs revenues for his income. To improve his economy, he tried to develop his port of Novi (Hercegnovi); he attempted to break Dubrovnik's salt monopoly by establishing his own salt works and salt trade, as well as a textile industry at Novi. Dubrovnik also accused him of interfering with the activities of its merchants in Hercegovina. This quarrel led Stefan Vukčić to invade Dubrovnik's territory in 1451; the next year, stirred up by Dubrovnik, the *herceg*'s son, Vladislav, revolted against his father and took much of western Hum and the lower Neretva. Venice intervened on behalf of the *herceg* in the lower Neretva, and the Bosnian king was briefly involved against him. The warfare ended with peace treaties in 1453 (between the *herceg* and Vladislav) and 1454 (between the *herceg* and Dubrovnik). The treaties restored the prewar status quo.

With the Ottoman threat increasing, Stefan Thomaš sought papal aid; the pope would give it only if action was taken against the Bosnian church. So, for the first time, a Bosnian ruler turned to persecution; in 1459 he gave Bosnian churchmen the choice of conversion to Catholicism or exile. We are told that some 2,000 chose conversion, whereas only forty chose exile. The exiles emigrated to Hercegovina, where no persecutions occurred. In fact, the *herceg*'s leading diplomat, *Gost* Radin, was a leader of the Bosnian church. No papal aid followed. In 1461, Stefan Tomaš died and his son Stefan Tomašević (1461–1463) received a crown from the pope. In 1462 the *herceg*'s son, Vladislav, revolted again and sought Turkish aid.

In 1463 the Ottomans sent a major army bent on conquest. Through clever ruses the invasion was a surprise attack. Unprepared, most of Bosnia's and Hercegovina's fortresses were in Turkish hands within a few months. Stefan Tomašević was captured and beheaded. The *herceg* retreated with his armies to the coast. At the end of the invasion, the main Ottoman forces withdrew, leaving behind garrisons in certain major fortresses. Then the *herceg* brought his army back and recovered much of his former territory, while the Hungarian king, Mathias Corvinus, attacked from the north and conquered part of northern Bosnia, including its last capital, Jajce. The *herceg* and his now reconciled son, Vladislav, aided the Hungarians in this recovery, and were rewarded with the regained Krajina and Završje. The Hungarians established a banate centered in Jajce.

The unpopularity of the Hungarians is seen in the action of a group of Bosnian nobles who, following the conquest, went to Venice, seeking aid and Venetian overlordship. They stated that if Venice refused, they would stay under the Turks, for under no circumstances would they accept the Hungarians. The Turks attacked again over the following years, and quickly recovered most of Hercegovina and much of

BOSNIA

the territory the Hungarians had regained. However, the last Hungarian fortress in Bosnia, Jajce, held out until 1527. The last fortresses in Hercegovina held out until 1481. *Herceg* Stefan had died in 1466; his son Vladislav then succeeded him.

ECONOMY

Until the fourteenth century Bosnia and Hum were economically backward, less developed than many of the other regions comprising modern Yugoslavia. The majority of the population was engaged in agriculture, farming or stock raising (particularly sheep). The shepherds were called Vlachs, a term originally signifying an ethnic group (a pre-Slavic people linguistically related to the Romanians) which, because many Vlachs had retreated to the mountains and there herded sheep, had acquired the occupational meaning of "shepherd."

Bosnia's counties were dominated by hereditary county lords *(župans),* under whom were the lesser gentry. It appears that by the thirteenth and fourteenth centuries, most of the peasants *(kmets)* were dependent, either working the nobles' lands through work-dues or else farming lands assigned to them for natural rents. By the end of the fourteenth century, the title *župan* was dying out (though it was retained by the Draživojević-Sanković family until Sandalj eliminated them in 1404). But though the middling nobles were subjected, the great nobles, as noted above, kept their control over vast territories (often encompassing several *župas*). In the fourteenth and fifteenth centuries the rulers (bans/kings and also leading nobles, such as the Kosače, Hrvatinići, and Pavlovići) tried to replace the hereditary local rulers of fortresses and counties with their own appointees. They seem to have been fairly successful (though the king succeeded only in his direct holdings, and not in the lands of the great nobles who were his vassals), and these appointees, bearing the title of *knez,* commanded various castles.

In the fourteenth century, under Stjepan Kotromanić, Bosnian mining began, with further mines opening up under his successor, Tvrtko. The leading metals were silver and lead. Technical expertise was provided by Sasi (Saxons, chiefly from Hungary), while Ragusans took over their administration and financial operation. The laborers were local Bosnians. Dubrovnik soon acquired a monopoly on silver; the most important silver center was Srebrnica. In these mining towns Ragusans established colonies of merchants and mining administrators. They established a consulship to govern each Ragusan colony according to Ragusan law. The Sasi were governed by their own law code. In time, craftsmen settled at these commercial centers growing up around mines. Many of the more skilled ones came from the coast, but soon many locals joined their ranks. The ruler of the town (whether the ban/king or the great nobleman on whose lands the town lay) appointed a *knez* to keep order and be the chief legal figure. The town *knez* tended to be a literate and astute financier; he was frequently a Ragusan merchant. If the town was fortified, a garrison commander was also appointed.

The Bosnians were gradually, by the end of the fourteenth century, entering the crafts and also becoming merchants. By the fifteenth century some Bosnians were trading widely in Bosnia and even on the coast and in Italy. However, the major merchants continued to be Ragusans. The Ragusans kept their monopoly on silver, though certain Bosnians became successful in the lead trade. Bosnia's prosperity grew rapidly, because by the mid fourteenth century, most of Europe's mines were in decline. Such was not true of the new mines of Bosnia and Serbia. By 1422, Serbia and Bosnia together were exporting more than one-fifth of Europe's silver. This led to great urban prosperity; certain merchants made great fortunes, and through customs revenues certain nobles became very wealthy. All sorts of luxury textiles and metal products were imported into Bosnia. At the same time certain Bosnian craftsmen achieved great skill in metal crafts; Bosnian silverwork (cups and belt buckles) was in demand on the coast.

The rulers in the twelfth and thirteenth centuries (Kulin, Ninoslav), wanting to encourage the circulation of more goods in Bosnia, had allowed Dubrovnik to trade duty-free. But when the mines opened, possibilities arose for earning much revenue. Kotromanić therefore began imposing customs duties. By the end of the century, the great nobles were doing the same. Customs were of three types: export duties collected at the point of purchase (for example at the mine where the silver was bought for export), which seem to have been 10 percent of the purchase in kind; import duties, collected at the market where the goods were sold, which also seem to have been 10 percent in kind; and duties on passage, collected generally in cash at toll stations.

The nobles frequently tried to establish more toll stations on routes crossing their lands, which Dubrovnik regularly, and sometimes successfully, protested. The major customs collections were farmed out to particular rich merchants (regularly Ragusans), who paid the ruler the sum expected for the year and then collected the actual customs revenues for themselves, hoping for a profit. On one occasion in 1376 one wealthy Ragusan, Žore Bokšić, and two partners purchased all the customs stations in Bosnia.

Besides the towns growing up around commercial enterprises, like mines, others grew up at major crossroads. Important commercial routes to Serbia, Bulgaria, Constantinople, and Hungary ran through Bosnia. Some places on routes became centers for selling local goods—for instance, Foča was important for selling wax, sheepskins, and other pastoral products. The Vlachs, who wandered with their flocks, had horses. By the fifteenth century certain Vlachs, particularly those of Hercegovina, acquired great wealth by running caravans. Other Vlachs (as well as some nobles and their retainers) enriched themselves by plundering caravans.

Certain towns grew up, not for commercial reasons but as suburbs of major castles; often chosen as a local market, the area below a castle in time might acquire shops in which craftsmen sold goods daily, rather than only at a weekly market. The noble in control of the castle collected the market duties. But, with the prosperity from the mines and trade, we find (for example, in lists of goods pawned in Dubrovnik) that in the fifteenth century some Bosnians had considerable wealth; some nobles maintained luxurious courts stocked with rich textiles and metalwork from Italy and western Europe. Actors and musicians performed at their courts. These performers were not limited to the courts of the nobility; documents show them performing in commercial towns as well.

ART

Bosnia and Hercegovina are famous for their enormous medieval gravestones (particularly from the fourteenth through sixteenth centuries) known as *stećci*. Sometimes erroneously called "Bogomil tombstones," they were, in fact, erected by wealthy people of all faiths. They were carved in various shapes: great sarcophagi, standing slabs, great crosses. Although the majority are unmarked, some have carved motifs, from simple geometrical designs (spirals, rosettes, crosses) to elaborate scenes (tournaments, hunting scenes, round dances). Some of their creators were excellent artists. The most elaborate and interesting motifs are found on stones erected by Vlachs. Particularly famous are the stones at the Orthodox Vlach cemetery at Radimlja.

Bosnia was studded with imposing stone fortresses; certain of the palaces (such as the king's at Bobovac) not only were impressive architectural structures but also were decorated with excellent stone reliefs and frescoes. Medieval Bosnia also had many churches, but in general they were small and do not compare favorably with the handsome Catholic churches along the coast or the Orthodox monastery churches in nearby Serbia. That Bosnian patrons invested less in their churches probably reflects the indifference of the Bosnian nobles to formal religion.

In addition to stonecarvers and stonemasons, Bosnia also had fine metalworkers. Although most of the known goldsmiths came from Dubrovnik, Bosnians were silversmiths. As noted above, certain Bosnian-style silver products were in demand on the coast. Bosnia was also the first inland Balkan country to produce firearms and cannons; it seems the original masters of this trade were Germans working in Bosnia. Bosnian textile products were never comparable to those produced by the coastal cities; however, we suspect that, quite early, different regions of Bosnia already had the elaborately embroidered, homemade folk costumes for which they later became famous. Bosnians also produced several surviving Gospel manuscripts, some of which have exquisite miniatures.

BIBLIOGRAPHY

Alojz Benac *et al.*, *Kulturna istorija Bosne i Hercegovine od najstarijih vremena do početka turske vladavine* (1966); Sima Ćirković, *Istorija srednjovekovne bosanske države* (1964); John V. A. Fine, Jr., *The Bosnian Church: A New Interpretation* (1975); Desanka Kovačević-Kojić, *Gradska naselja srednjovjekovne bosanske države* (1978).

JOHN V. A. FINE, JR.

[See also **Bosnian Church; Hungary; Kulin; Ottomans; Samuil of Bulgaria; Sandalj Hranić; Serbs and Serbia; Stefan Dušan; Stefan Tomaš; Stefan Tomašević; Stjepan Kotromanić; Tvrtko I; Tvrtko II.**]

BOSNIAN CHURCH, a schismatic institution in medieval Bosnia, is documented from the early fourteenth century—though probably it dates back to the mid thirteenth—until a little beyond the Turkish conquest of Bosnia in 1463.

At the beginning of the thirteenth century, Bosnia was part of the Catholic world; its church, under the archbishop of Dubrovnik, was dominated by a local

BOSNIAN CHURCH

monastic order whose head was often bishop of Bosnia. Bosnia had a peasant society and no centers of education. Latin was hardly known, and its bishops had to be consecrated in Slavic. Through ignorance, errors crept into the practice of local Catholics, including the leaders. Missions from Rome early in the century failed to reform Bosnia; as a result, Hungary, seeking a pretext to reassert political control over Bosnia, led a "crusade" against Bosnia (1235–1241) that had limited success. Finally, about 1252, the Bosnian Catholic church was subjected by Pope Innocent IV to the Hungarian archbishop of Kalocsa. Because of these actions the Bosnians severed connections with international Catholicism. The Catholic bishop of Bosnia had to leave Bosnia, settling in Slavonia, where the bishopric's seat remained throughout the Middle Ages.

What happened inside Bosnia remains cloudy, owing to the lack of sources. When we have information again, early in the fourteenth century, we find a Bosnian church established under its own bishop, called the *djed.* Later documents show the Bosnian church to have been a monastic institution; thus, it probably was simply a continuation of the early-thirteenth-century local Catholic monastic order which, around the middle of that century, severed its international ties and became an independent local organization, keeping its former institutional structure. No sources suggest that any change of theology occurred at the time, and almost all later local and Ragusan sources on the Bosnian church suggest it was mainstream Christian in its theology throughout its existence. Thus the Bosnian church most probably retained the beliefs and practices it held up to its schism with Rome. But, though it retained its "Catholic" theology, it surely had various "errors" in practice owing to its peasant composition.

Throughout its history the Bosnian church retained both its more-or-less Catholic theology and its monastic character. Its clergy (except for a few living at royal or aristocratic courts) resided in monasteries. The clergymen bore the title of Christians *(krstjani)*—usually rendered as *Patarini* in Ragusan Latin-language sources. The head of a monastery *(hiža)* was often called a *gost.* The *djed* and his council (of twelve *strojnici*), chiefly composed of *gosts,* provided what overall supervision there was. Their monasteries were not found throughout Bosnia, but were clustered in the center of the state and extended east toward the Drina and south toward and beyond the Neretva, with a few on the lands of the Kosača family in Hercegovina. Some monasteries served as hostels for travelers and were used by Ragusan merchants. The Bosnian church never established a secular clergy or any sort of territorial organization. Thus, calling it a "church" may be somewhat misleading. It seems to have consisted only of a series of scattered monastic houses with a relatively small number of monks. Probably peasants could go to these monasteries for services. Gravestone inscriptions show that *krstjani* participated in burials of laymen.

The Bosnian church was tolerated by the state even after the 1340's, when a Franciscan mission was established and the rulers became Catholic. The Bosnian church did not play a major role in the state and was not a state church. For most of its existence, it had no political role—other than occasionally allowing its hierarchs to witness charters. Such a role can be shown only early in the fifteenth century—particularly 1403–1405—when the *djed* was an influential adviser at court. His influence then was probably owing to the particular sympathy of King Ostoja to his church.

Since other rulers after the 1340's were Catholics, it is not surprising that the Bosnian church was not a major state institution. Though some scholars have argued that an alliance existed between the Bosnian church and the nobility, this too is greatly exaggerated. Connections between the church and specific noblemen can be shown for only about ten families; all these ties appear in the last seventy years of the state. For most of these few noblemen, the services noted were religious. For only a very small number did the Bosnian church provide political or secular services (usually as diplomats or mediators of quarrels) and for only two families—the Kosače and Radenović-Pavlovići—did these ties last longer than one generation.

Few Bosnian church texts survive. Of these, most important are the surviving pages of Gospel manuscripts, some of which are beautifully illustrated: the Radosav Ritual, the Hval Gospel, Tepčija Batalo's Gospel. Certain other surviving Bosnian Gospels may also have been from Bosnian church circles, but proof is lacking. The will of *Gost* Radin (1466)—a church leader and important diplomat for *Herceg* Stefan—survives; it testifies not only to his great wealth but also to his orthodox religious beliefs. A letter from the *djed* (1404), concerning a dispute between the king and a nobleman, also provides in passing some information on the church.

The Bosnian church continued to exist—as a

small organization—until finally in 1459, under papal pressure (papal aid against the Turks was conditional on persecuting the Bosnian church), King Stefan Tomaš gave Bosnian churchmen the choice of conversion or exile. Most accepted Catholicism (showing morale was poor), while a minority (about forty) sought refuge in Hercegovina with *Herceg* Stefan. Thus the church, weak throughout its existence, was weakened further on the eve of the Ottoman conquest. It disappeared entirely soon after as its members were absorbed by Islam, Orthodoxy, and Catholicism.

Many scholars have depicted the Bosnian church as dualist (Bogomil), but domestic sources about the church (Bosnian and Ragusan) do not suggest this. They show that the Bosnian church, unlike the Bogomils, accepted an omnipotent God, the Trinity, church buildings, the cross, the cult of saints, religious art, and at least part of the Old Testament. Furthermore, the cordial relations these sources depict between Bosnian churchmen and both Orthodox clerics and Catholic officials (from both Dubrovnik and Hungary) could not have occurred had these Bosnians been Manichees. The only contemporary sources speaking of dualism in Bosnia are foreign (chiefly Italian), from the Inquisition and, only from the late 1440's, the papacy. Most of these sources do not specifically refer to the Bosnian church, but just to "Bosnian heretics" and, to the degree that they are accurate, probably refer to a separate and small dualist current also existing in Bosnia that was derived from a Dalmatian dualist church (Ecclesia Sclavonia).

BIBLIOGRAPHY

Sima Ćirković, "Die Bosnische Kirche," in *Accademia nazionale dei Lincei, Problemi attuali di scienza e di cultura* (1964), 547–575; John V. A. Fine, Jr., *The Bosnian Church: A New Interpretation* (1975); Fra L. P. (Petrović), *Kršćani bosanske crkve* (1953); Jaroslav Šidak, *Studije o "Crkvi bosanskoj" i bogumilstvu* (1975).

JOHN V. A. FINE, JR.

[See also **Bosnia; Stefan Tomaš.**]

BOSPORUS. Lying between the continents of Europe and Asia, the Bosporus is the strait connecting

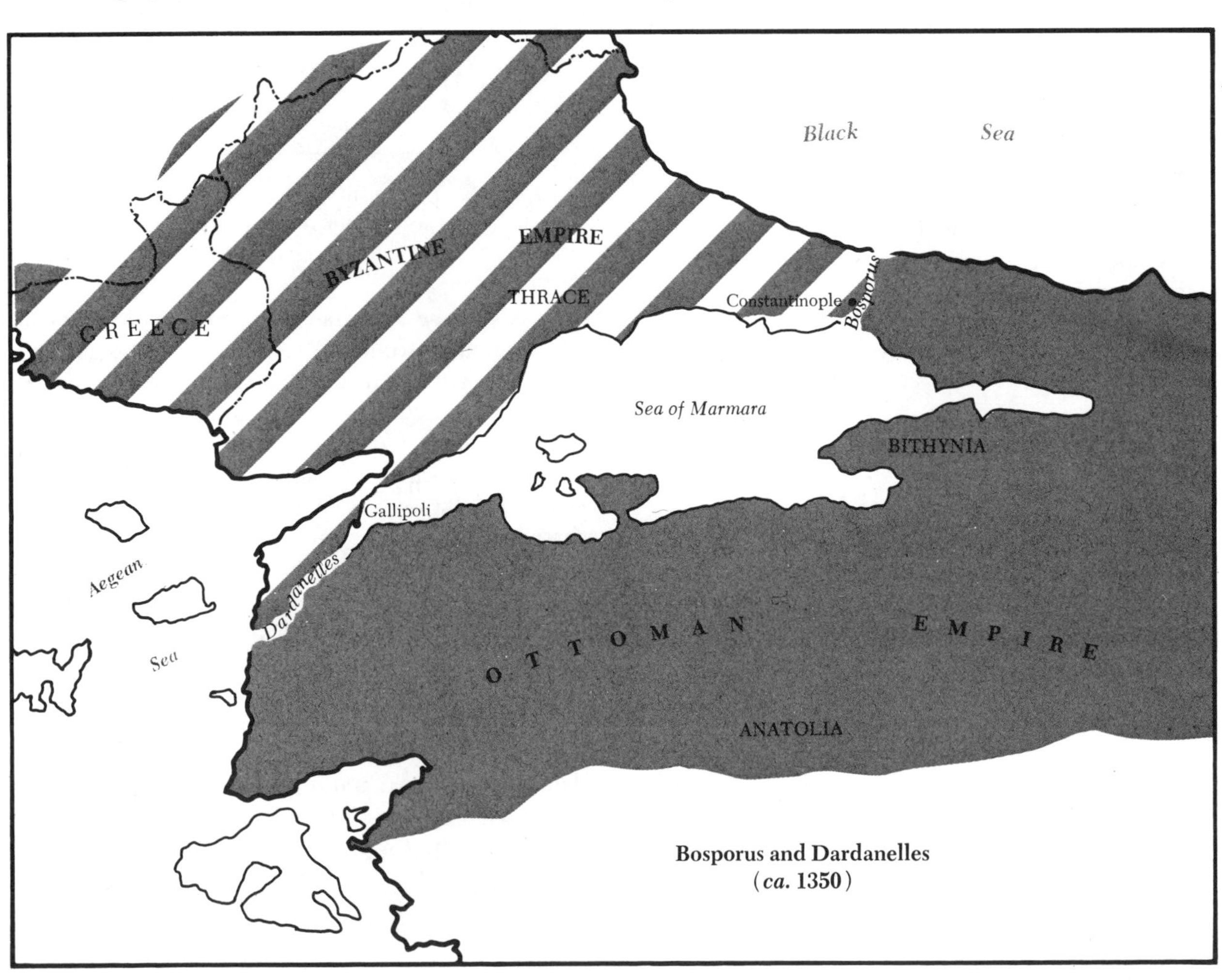

Bosporus and Dardanelles
(*ca.* 1350)

the Black Sea with the Sea of Marmara. Because of its strategically important location, it played a significant role in Byzantine history. It was the site of the ancient Greek colony of Byzantium, and in 324 Emperor Constantine began construction of Constantinople on the western (European) shore. In 330, Constantinople became the capital of the Eastern Roman Empire, and it remained the capital of the Byzantine Empire until its fall to the Ottoman Turks in 1453.

As the gateway to Constantinople, the Bosporus was the site of many invasion attempts. In 615 and again in 625, a Persian army got as far as the Bosporus before being repelled, as did Arab armies in 717 and again in 782. In 941, Russian invaders landed on the Bithynian coast and pillaged the Asiatic shore, but they were defeated in a naval battle in which the Byzantines employed their so-called Greek fire.

The Bosporus was extremely vital to Byzantine and international commerce, and as the empire weakened, its control was contested by several groups. In 1080 the Seljuk Turks established themselves on the Asiatic shore and set up customhouses in order to control shipping. Two centuries later the Venetians and the Genoese each sought to control the Bosporus, and in 1348 the Genoese built a naval station there. In 1352 a large naval battle took place in the Bosporus between these traditional rivals.

In 1452 the Ottoman Sultan Mehmed II began to construct a fortress on the European side of the Bosporus about five miles above Constantinople, in preparation for a siege of the city that began in the spring of 1453 and ended with the Ottoman capture of the city on 29 May 1453, marking the end of the Byzantine Empire.

BIBLIOGRAPHY

George Ostrogorsky, *History of the Byzantine State* (1957).

LINDA ROSE

[See also **Constantinople; Dardanelles; Greek Fire; Mehmed II; Seljuks.**]

BOSS, an ornamental knob or projection that covers the intersection of ribs on a vault or ceiling; a decorative form that projects from the center of a panel or coffer is also called a boss. Elaborately carved ceiling bosses were particularly popular in English Gothic architecture.

LESLIE BRUBAKER

Ceiling bosses. Château of Blois, *ca.* 1500. FROM SIR BANISTER FLETCHER'S A HISTORY OF ARCHITECTURE

BOTANY, the scientific study of plants and plant life, originated around 1830; consequently botany, as such, was unknown in the Middle Ages. That does not mean, however, that nothing was known of plants or that references to herbs and trees were restricted to poetical effusions and allegorical representations. In point of fact, a large amount of information (and misinformation) about the appearance, uses, and properties of plants was generally available throughout the Middle Ages. That body of data, serving practical needs and illustrating philosophic principles, was assembled over a period of many centuries, in different cultures, by different individuals; and although much was committed to writing, not all of it was published until modern times. Those data were obtained and organized in ways quite different from modern botanical research. In order to understand the form and content of medieval bot-

BOTANY

any, we must place it within the appropriate context, however unfamiliar that may appear today, and organize it in accordance with medieval modes of experience and expression, whether or not they accord with modern botany.

Before we examine the various kinds of botanical data recorded during the Middle Ages, it will be useful to consider briefly the historical background and to review the sources available to the historian of medieval botany.

HISTORICAL BACKGROUND

As in many other branches of medieval science and medicine, beliefs about the nature of plants and their properties had a twofold base. On the one hand there is a literary tradition that, though discontinuous, goes back to Greco-Roman writings. Not all of the classical writers whose names appear in medieval botanical texts were known at first hand; nevertheless, the written tradition of medieval botany, in a real sense, begins with Theophrastus' *Historia plantarum,* which was transmitted principally through Pliny's *Historia naturalis,* probably the single most influential text for medieval botany. The medicinal use of plants goes back to Dioscorides' *De materia medica,* which was known in the West chiefly through Galen.

Over against the literary tradition there was a folk tradition in which plants were both valued and used for various practical and domestic purposes. This was essentially an oral tradition in which hard-won empirical data were preserved, though not always susceptible to philosophic explanation.

These two traditions—a school or academic tradition and an oral folk tradition—rarely came together until the end of the Middle Ages, when medical and craft handbooks and Books of Secrets began to recognize the value of each. In the early Middle Ages, what botanical learning had survived the dissolution of the Roman Empire was chiefly confined to glossators who strove to identify the plants known to the ancients—for example, Isidore of Seville—and to the anonymous compilers of recipes. With the rise of Scholasticism, botanical knowledge was not appreciably bettered, though access to Latin translations of Greek and Arabic medical texts greatly increased the amount of book learning about plants.

Throughout the Middle Ages, therefore, there was a fund of information concerning plants: at the folk level it satisfied the requirements of daily life in which plant products played an essential role; at the academic level theories about the nature of plant life were disputed with the tools and by the methods of Scholasticism.

SOURCES FOR MEDIEVAL BOTANY

The foregoing summary of the historical development of medieval botany, though brief, is sufficient to indicate the variety of potential sources covering a wide field and widely distributed over space and time. For purposes of convenience, those sources will be divided into literary and nonliterary.

Our primary literary source for medieval botany is the herbal, which brings together more pertinent data than any other single literary genre. A herbal may be defined as a series of descriptions of plants believed to be of therapeutic value, accompanied by medical, pharmacological, and botanical data regarded as useful.

Closely related to the herbal, and nearly as valuable a source, is the leechbook, a general medical handbook designed to include all that was thought necessary to the practicing physician. The leechbook and a third source, the recipe collection, may be considered together. Though they differ in format, they are both medical texts and, like the herbal, they demonstrate the dependence on medicaments of plant origin. Frequently the leechbook included a connected series of sections, each of which dealt with the uses and properties of one plant species. A recipe collection contained similar material but was arranged in terms of the complaints for which the recipes were designed. Moreover, the less formal nature of a recipe collection permitted its compiler to take full advantage of local plants and folk uses, with the result that oftentimes valuable data are preserved concerning names and uses of plants and their preparation and administration.

A fourth source, the encyclopedias, though often conveniently accessible, seldom contain original material. Nevertheless, as compilations, they faithfully reflect what was known and believed about many hundreds of plant species.

The fifth class, glossaries and lexica, is intrinsically much more important. They must, however, be used with caution, because their compilers were always more concerned with names than with their denotata. By their uncritical acceptance of names, synonyms, and the data associated therewith, errors were perpetuated and many fanciful beliefs were transmitted.

The above naturally do not exhaust our literary sources, for such genres as dietaries, cookbooks, cartularies, and commentaries on the Hexaemeron may profitably be examined, especially in connection with the nonliterary sources.

Iconographic data concerning plants are primarily confirmatory. That is, few new data regarding plants will be found by examining medieval sculpture or even the naturalistic illustrations found in devotional texts. The pictorial record does, however, enable one to correlate the uses of plants, especially for nonmedicinal purposes, with the widely scattered textual references. A second class of nonliterary data must also be mentioned: the European flora. Only by means of a thorough familiarity with European herbs and trees, growing in their natural habitat, can one appreciate the subtle references to plants in medieval literature. Failure to know European plants has resulted in many ludicrous errors by well-intentioned but botanically naive translators.

Although the European landscape clearly has undergone major changes in the past millennium, a knowledge of the medieval flora will enable one to take full advantage of the toponymic and paleobotanical data that have accumulated since the mid 1940's. Owing to the accidental preservation of plant material, usually in carbonized or fossilized form, abundant material awaits the student interested in correlating medieval material culture with the better-known literary material.

On the basis of the foregoing sketch of the historical development of the knowledge of plants, plus our own sources, literary and nonliterary alike, the following is a brief summary of the different classes of data pertaining to plants, arranged within a framework that was known to and accepted by the major writers of the Middle Ages.

DESCRIPTION OF PLANTS

Because of the practical purpose of herbals, plants were described in such a way that most of them can be identified today. The descriptive data were primarily morphological: habit; size, shape, color, and texture of leaves; presence of thorns; and so on. Anthological data are also frequent: color, shape, and odor of flower, fruit, and seed capsule. But equally important was specification of habitat; not infrequently some detail concerning its domestic uses was an additional aid in locating and collecting the desired species. Closely related species were often lumped together, though they may have been distinguishable by the herbalist in their fresh state. Often the formulaic phrase "known to all" occurs; in such cases the descriptive data are meager because the species was both common and widespread, and served many different uses. Approximately fifteen hundred species can be identified today as having been known in the Middle Ages; naturally the number and reliability of the data vary considerably from one species to another.

NOMENCLATURE

After descriptive data, plant names, especially when correlated with their synonyms, are the most important means to the identification of medieval plants. The great majority of plant names are Latin, though many hundreds of vernacular names occur in late medieval texts. Most of the common species had several synonyms, sometimes ranging up to fifteen. Latin transcriptions of Greek names are common—for instance, *mentha (μίνθη),* our mint—and in late medical texts a few Arabic names also occur. In addition, some of the more commonly used medicinal plants had distinctive apothecary names. The plurality of species names created much confusion and, to solve this problem, many Latin-vernacular glossaries were compiled. Modern binomial scientific nomenclature, codified by Linnaeus in 1753, in many cases can be traced back to medieval polynomials.

TAXONOMY

Although taxonomy was not an end in itself, a loosely formulated classification was implicitly accepted. Following the common class words of Latin, one distinguished trees *(arbores),* shrubs *(frutices),* herbs *(herbae),* and grasses *(gramina).* From an agricultural standpoint it was useful also to distinguish the cereal grains *(cerealia).* Outside of this generally accepted schema, which indirectly goes back to Theophrastus' *Historia plantarum,* were the cryptogams (mosses, ferns, fungi). Because their life cycles were unknown and because they lacked the floral parts associated with the flowering plants or angiosperms, a special category was sometimes created for them. For purposes of finer discrimination, especially among common herbs and garden plants, closely related species were distinguished by the use of pairs of adjectival modifiers—for example, *major/minor* or *albus/niger*—some of which were perpetuated in later botanical systems.

PHILOSOPHIC BOTANY

This division takes the place of such modern subdisciplines as physiology, anatomy, pathology, and genetics, each of which depends upon controlled experiments conducted under laboratory conditions with specialized, precise equipment. In the absence of the latter, the medieval writer could only speculate about the causes of normal and abnormal plant processes. The method most commonly adopted to explain what we regard as physiological and chemical processes was the so-called doctrine of the four elements (earth, air, fire, water) and its corollary, the four qualities (cold, hot, dry, wet). By supposing that all plants and plant substances were composed of varying amounts of each of the elements (or qualities), and by interpreting natural processes as changes in the relative proportions thereof, reasonable, naturalistic explanations were formulated, in terms of which both properties and behavior appeared plausible. This philosophic method of explanation was as widely used in medicine, pharmacy, and dietetics to explain drug action and nutrition as it was applied to botany to explain such processes as germination, growth, and ripening of fruit.

MEDICINAL USES

Approximately five hundred different species of plants are recorded in medieval medical literature. They were used either singly, both externally and internally, or as ingredients in compound medicines, again having both internal and external applications. While many of them appear today not to possess any specific therapeutic value, others may have been useful for the amelioration of symptoms (such as colchicum for gout, squill for dropsy). Because the ingestion of some plant substances led to predictable, often dramatic, physiologial responses (such as emesis, purge, diuresis, poisoning), those species were well known, and were prepared and administered accordingly. Many (such as rhubarb, aconite, wormwood) remained in medical practice until the early nineteenth century; many still are used in folk medicine for the same purposes as in the Middle Ages (for instance, dill as a carminative).

ALIMENTARY USES

With the exception of several dozen poisonous species, probably every plant species was employed somewhere, sometime, for alimentary purposes, particularly in times of famine. For the common people, plant products constituted the normal diet: legumes (beans, peas); roots (carrots, parsnips); fruits and nuts (apples, hazelnuts), and some leafy vegetables, especially cabbage. For rich and poor alike the basic diet was, if available, composed of cereals, especially wheat and barley, the olive (for oil), and the grape (for wine). For the more fortunate the diet of flesh, fish, and fowl was flavored by exotic spices (pepper, ginger, cloves, cinnamon), all of which also served medicinal purposes. But even among the wealthy, whose diets are known from medieval cookbooks, local herbs were used as seasonings—for instance, parsley, fennel, sage, thyme. It must be borne in mind that, with very few exceptions (such as the medlar), our modern fruits and vegetables are the result of many years of deliberate breeding and selection; their medieval ancestors were, by our standards, small, woody, and misshapen, but eaten nonetheless.

DOMESTIC AND ECONOMIC USES

Daily life was inseparable from plant products, especially for the lower classes. From house construction to furniture and heating, to utensils, tools, and toys, a wide variety of wood was used. Moreover, for clothing, basketry, and cordage the preparation of flax, hemp, nettles, and the bast fiber of the linden tree was one of the principal domestic operations. Large timbers, principally oak, were necessary for major building projects, ships, and wagons; oak was, with the beech, preferred for charcoal making. Other, more specialized uses of plants included dyes (indigo, woad), perfumes, cosmetics, and liqueurs. There was also an ongoing need for supple willow twigs for wattle. The use of wood for ecclesiastical art required an enormous amount of linden and box; weaponry required yew (for bows) and ash (for spears); and cutting peat was a full-time task for many. As a commercial enterprise, import of spices from the Levant ranked first, though timber from the Norse lands, especially fir, was a close second.

AGRICULTURE AND HORTICULTURE

Although agriculture and horticulture have progressively diverged since the Middle Ages, they were originally concerned with maximum yields of varieties of the same species (as with olives and grapes), or of related species (wheat and barley), the surplus of which was bartered or sold for other commodities. There is a continuum between the kitchen garden, small, freehold plots, and the large manorial or ecclesiastical holdings, the latter tending toward monoculture. A wide variety of species grew in gardens and orchards, though they were always supplemented by the use of wild, native species. The kitchen garden, even on the larger monastic estates, typically might contain plants for alimentary pur-

BOTANY

poses (peas, lentils), herbs for seasoning foods and/or medicinal purposes (thyme, crocus), plus a few ornamentals (rose, lily); the orchards included cherry, plum, and, if the climate was favorable, apricot and pomegranate trees. Bee plants and fodder plants also constituted an important part of medieval crops, as did the raising of hops.

FOLK BELIEFS

Folk botany, as a separate discipline, is relatively new, yet an enormous amount of data regarding medieval folk beliefs and practices has been published. Beliefs about the poisonous, aphrodisiacal, or sacred nature of particular species are among the most common. The medieval attitude toward the pagan veneration of certain species—for example, Yggdrasil of the Norse—took two forms: pagan beliefs were Christianized (for example, the yule tree) or prohibited, with varying degrees of success (as was the case with the oak and mistletoe). Numerous indications survive of the attribution of miraculous properties to ordinary plants, such as verbena or rue; these are termed magiferous plants, as opposed to the wholly fabulous or magical plants (for example, the Peridexion tree, vegetable (or Scythian) lamb, and barnacle goose tree).

RITUAL USES AND SYMBOLISM

It is convenient to group together ritual uses and the symbolic associations of various plants because they were often two aspects of a single, multistage ceremony. The locus classicus is, of course, the use of incense, oil, and greenery (olive leaves and "palms") for liturgical purposes. On a lower plane there were numerous rituals for the blessing of plants for specific purposes, especially agrarian rites. On a still different level were the cultic practices involved in the collection of plants. Sometimes a specific time was stipulated (before sunrise), or the collection was to be performed by ritually purified persons on special days, St. John's Eve being the most famous. After the collection other rituals might be involved in the preparation, administration, or use of such plants—for example, for purposes of prognostication.

PLANTS IN LITERATURE

Because of the many diverse roles played by plants in medieval life, it is not surprising that trees and flowers, often not further specified, are commonly mentioned in all literary genres. Often they serve to reinforce a naturalistic setting; at other times a symbolic value may be hinted at or openly allegorized, as in the *Roman de la Rose.* Plant fables and biblical stories involving plants (the Holy Rood, Crown of Thorns) were popular and were transmitted, by way of sermons, to the folk level, where vestiges often remain in the form of proverbs. Reference to Near Eastern species growing in a literary garden was a common technique to indicate an exotic provenance.

ICONOGRAPHY

Medieval floral iconography is so vast and diverse that one can only note three major developments: (1) the delicate, naturalistic flowers, drawn from life, that appear as marginal illustrations in books of hours; (2) the stiff stereotypes appearing in various literary genres—the plants so depicted would not be identifiable in the absence of the associated, written account; and (3) the use of floral or arboreal motifs in sculpture, carving, coins, and tapestries—for example, the Tree of Jesse or the millefleurs tapestries. In paintings all three of the above types appear, though usually not in one single painting.

BIBLIOGRAPHY

On the historical background, see Dioscorides, *De materia medica,* Max Wellmann, ed., 3 vols. (1906–1914); Isidore of Seville, *Etymologiarum sive originum libri XX,* Wallace M. Lindsay, ed., 2 vols. (1911); Pliny the Elder, *Natural History,* Harris Rackham *et al.*, eds., 10 vols. (1938–1962); and Theophrastus, *Enquiry into Plants,* Arthur Hort, trans., 2 vols. (1916).

Sources for medieval botany. On herbals in general, see Jerry Stannard, "Medieval Herbals and Their Development," in *Clio medica,* 9 (1974); on leechbooks, see Jerry Stannard, "Medieval Italian Medical Botany," in *Atti del XXI Congresso internazionale di storia della medicina* (1970), 1554–1565; on recipe collections, see Jerry Stannard, "Botanical Data and Late Medieval *Rezeptliteratur,*" in Gundolf Keil, ed., *Fachprosa-Studien* (1981), 119–130; and on glossaries, see Hermann Fischer, *Mittelalterliche Pflanzenkunde* (1929), 290–318. For paleobotanical data with reference to medieval times, see Lanfredo Castelletti, "Materiali botanici dalla fornace da campane (sec. XII) e resti di un sarcofago ligneo (sec. XIV) da Sarzana," in *Archeologia medievale,* 2 (1975); and Heinrich Werneck, "Ur- und frühgeschichtliche sowie mittelalterliche Kulturpflanzen und Hölzer," in *Archaeologia austriaca,* 30 (1961).

Aspects of medieval botany. On plant description, see Jerry Stannard, "The Botany of St. Albert the Great," in Gerbert Meyer and Albert Zimmerman, eds., *Albertus Magnus, Doctor universalis* (1980), 345–372; on nomenclature, see T. A. Sprague, "Botanical Terms in Isidorus," in *Kew Bulletin,* **8** (1933); and Jerry Stannard, "Identification of the Plants Described by Albertus Magnus, *De vegetabilibus,* lib. VI," in *Res publica litterarum,* **2** (1979); on taxonomy—on which subject no major modern monograph exists—see Hermann Fischer, "Vitus Auslasser, der erste deutsche Florist, und sein Kräuterbuch vom Jahre 1479," in *Berichte der deutschen botanischen Gesellschaft,* **42** (1924); on philosophical botany, see Karen Reeds, "Albert on the Natural Philosophy of Plant Life," in James A. Weisheipl, ed., *Albertus Magnus and the Sciences* (1980), 341–354; on medicinal uses of plants, see Jerry Stannard, "Albertus Magnus and Medieval Herbalism," *ibid.,* 355–377; on alimentary uses, see Francesco Zambrini, ed., *Il libro della cucina del secolor XIV* (1863).

There is no single study in which the practical economic and domestic uses of plant substances have been assembled, specifically for the Middle Ages, but see *Mappae clavicula: A Little Key to the World of Medieval Techniques,* Cyril S. Smith and John G. Hawthorne, trans. (1974). On agriculture and horticulture, see Rudolph von Fischer-Benzon, *Altdeutsche Gartenflora* (1894); on folk beliefs, see Wilfrid Bonser, *The Medical Background of Anglo-Saxon England* (1963); Max Höfler, *Volksmedizinische Botanik der Germanen* (1908); and Paul Sébillot, *Le folk-lore de France,* III (1906); on plants in literature, see Charles Joret, *La rose dans l'antiquité et au moyen âge* (1892, repr. 1970); and Philipp Strauch, "Palma contemplationis," in *Beiträge zur Geschichte der deutschen Sprache und Literatur,* **48** (1924); and on iconography, see Felix Andreas Baumann, *Das Erbario Carrarese und die Bildtradition des Tractatus de herbis* (1974); and Lottlisa Behling, *Die Pflanzenwelt der mittelalterlichen Kathedralen* (1964); and *Die Pflanze in der mittelalterlichen Tafelmalerei,* 2nd ed. (1967).

JERRY STANNARD

[See also **Beauty Aids, Cosmetics; Dyes and Dyeing; Folklore and Magic, Western European; Herbals; Tapestry, Millefleurs; Tree of Jesse.**]

BOTTEGA, Italian for shop, warehouse, or office (from Latin *apotheca,* "storeroom"), refers to the studio or shop of an artist or sculptor. Medieval artists often worked anonymously in teams; at best the name of the master craftsman in charge of a team may be known. A group project is thus sometimes identified as the product of a known *bottega* or, if the master craftsman has been identified, as the product of a given master and his *bottega,* or shop assistants. Works that show characteristic traits of a known artist but are of less than top quality are sometimes attributed to his *bottega.*

LESLIE BRUBAKER

BOUCHER, GUILLAUME, a Parisian goldsmith imprisoned in Hungary by the Tatars, was taken to the Mongolian capital. In 1254, as the only Frenchman in Karakorum, he received Louis IX's envoy to the great khan. For the khan he built a silver tree intertwined with pipes belching fermented mare's milk, wine, honey, and rice mead through gargoyles. An angel blowing the trumpet at the top of the machine signaled the pouring of the liquor.

BIBLIOGRAPHY

Alfred Chapuis and Édouard Gélis, *Le monde des automates* (1928), I, 63; Willem van Ruysbroek, *The Journey of William of Rubruck to the Eastern Parts of the World,* William W. Rockhill, ed. and trans. (1900).

PHILIPPE VERDIER

BOUCICAULT, JEAN. See **Jean Boucicaut.**

BOUCICAUT MASTER (*fl. ca.* 1400–1420), an anonymous manuscript illuminator active at Paris. He is named after his most famous work, a book of hours made for Maréchal de Boucicaut, Jean Le Meingre II, marshal of France (Paris, Musée Jacquemart-André, MS 2). He is sometimes identified as Jacques Coene from Bruges. His characteristic style appears in many early-fifteenth-century manuscripts, and he is therefore believed to have headed a large and prolific atelier. Innovative in his use of architectural perspective and landscape settings, he was a major contributor to the development of the International Style in France.

BIBLIOGRAPHY

Paul Durrieu, "Le maître des heures du maréchal de Boucicaut," in *Revue de l'art ancien et moderne,* **19** (1906); Millard Meiss, *French Painting in the Time of Jean de Berry: The Boucicaut Master* (1968).

ROBERT G. CALKINS

[See also **Books of Hours; International Style, Gothic; Manuscript Illumination.**]

BOURDICHON, JEAN (*fl. ca.* 1475–1521), French painter active at Tours. He served as court painter for Louis XI, Charles VIII, and Louis XII. His most famous surviving works are the Hours of Anne of Brittany and the Hours of Frederick of Aragon (Paris, Bibliothèque Nationale, MSS lat. 9474 and 10532).

BIBLIOGRAPHY

Raymond Limousin, *Jean Bourdichon* (1954); Bibliothèque Nationale, *Manuscrits à peintures du XIIe au XVIe siècle* (1955), 151–152, 163–166; Janet Backhouse, "Bourdichon's Hours of Henry VII," in *British Museum Quarterly,* **36** (1973); R. Flot, "L'art en Touraine au temps du Vinci: Jean Bourdichon," in *Bulletin de l'Association Leonardo da Vinci,* **13** (1974).

ROBERT G. CALKINS

BOURGEOISIE, RIGHTS OF. See **Rights of the Bourgeoisie.**

BOUTS, DIRK (*ca.* 1420–1475). One of the foremost Netherlandish painters of the mid fifteenth century, Bouts was born and probably trained at Haarlem. By 1457 he had settled permanently in Louvain, where he was named city painter in 1468. His early works, such as the Infancy Altarpiece (*ca.* 1445), now in the Prado, Madrid, display his Haarlem background through stocky, peasantlike figures placed in ample spatial settings with colorful landscape backgrounds. After establishing his workshop in Louvain, Bouts came increasingly under the influence of Rogier van der Weyden, the leading painter in nearby Brussels, and his mature style features a charming blend of his Haarlem manner with the more sophisticated styles of the South Netherlandish masters. The Altarpiece of the Holy Sacrament (in St. Peter's, Louvain, 1464–1467), his best-known work, has four Old Testament panels forming the wings for a central panel, the Last Supper, executed in rich colors. Bouts's style was widely imitated in the Netherlands, and his workshop (including his sons) produced numerous altarpieces.

BIBLIOGRAPHY

Max J. Friedländer, *Early Netherlandish Painting,* III (1968); Wolfgang Schöne, *Dieric Bouts und seine Schule* (1938).

JAMES SNYDER

[See also **Altarpiece; Weyden, Rogier van der.**]

BOVO II OF CORVEY, abbot of Corvey from 900 to 916, wrote a commentary on the ninth poem of the third book of Boethius' *Consolation of Philosophy,* emphasizing the contrast between the Platonic and the Christian interpretations of Creation. Bovo is said to have known Greek and to have translated a letter from that language for King Conrad I.

BIBLIOGRAPHY

Maximilianus Manitius, *Geschichte der lateinischen Literatur des Mittelalters,* I (1911), 526–529.

MARK D. MEYERSON

BOW AND ARROW/CROSSBOW. The bow is the oldest mechanical device designed by man for the use of stored energy, its invention surely having occurred during the Mesolithic Age.

Material and Construction. There are two basic types of bow: the *self bow,* a straight wooden stave of round or *D*-shaped cross-section, held by the string in a shallow curve; and the *composite bow,* built up in three to five sections of alternately stiff and flexible elements, with strongly double-curved outline.

The self bow (its best known representative is the English longbow) was preferably of yew wood; in northern continental Europe, where the yew does not grow, it was elm. The composite bow in its most sophisticated form, used by the Mongols of Genghis Khan and the Turks, had a central handgrip of hardwood, to which were spliced two highly flexible arms of laminated horn having a sinew backing bonded with glue. These flexible arms were joined to stiff wood or bone tips containing the string notches. The arms were constructed to bend forward, against the way they would be curved, when strung; this reflex curve added enormous power to the draw, and made it possible to keep the composite bow much shorter (less than four feet) than the self bow (an English longbow averaged more than six feet). Self-bow strings were of hemp; reflex bows often had silk strings.

Asiatic bowmakers were highly specialized craftsmen; a composite bow would take at least two years to finish, with time to let the wood dry, to let the glue set, and so on, interspersed between the actual working stages. The manufacture of a self bow, provided properly seasoned wood was at hand, would take only days. Another advantage of the self bow

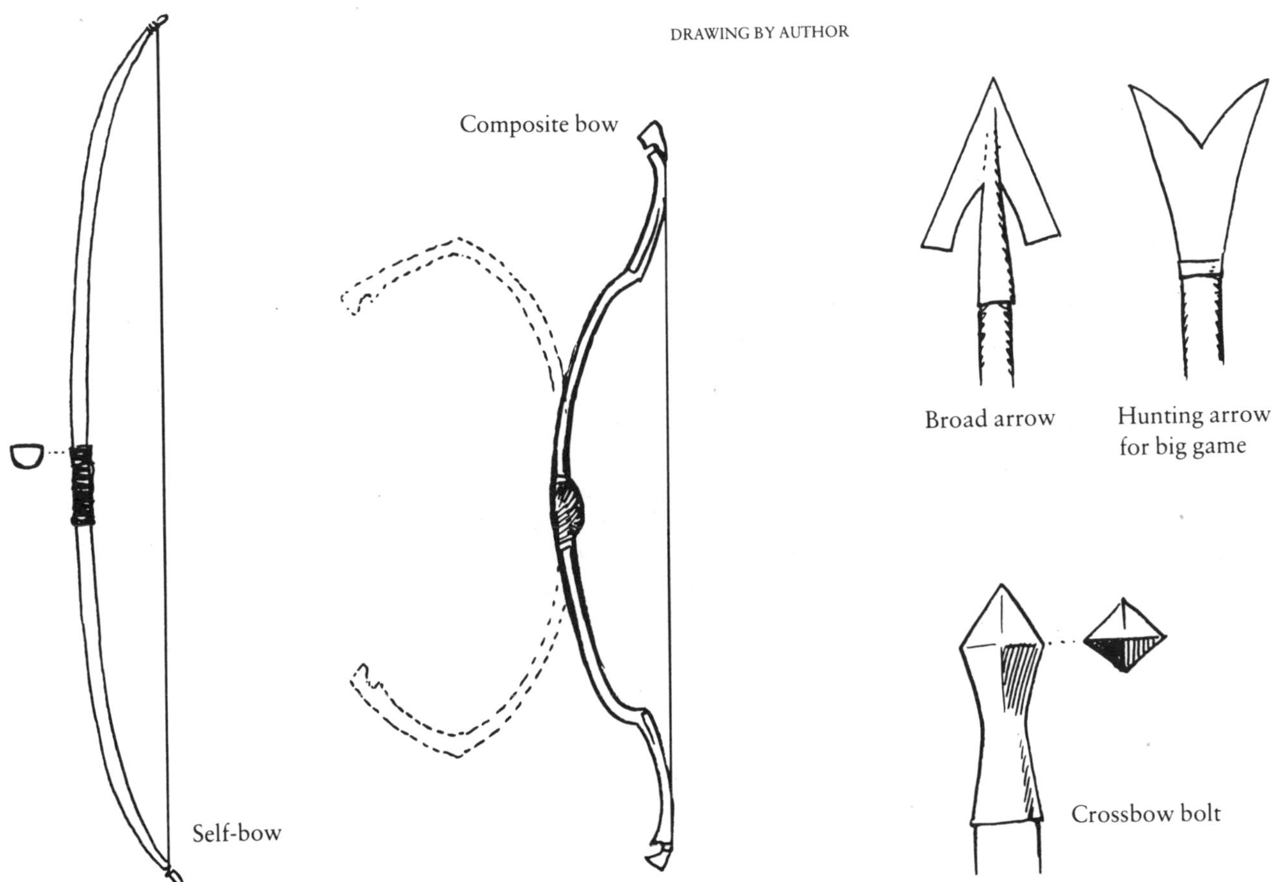

DRAWING BY AUTHOR

was its relative immunity from adverse weather conditions; an occasional greasing with tallow or rubbing with beeswax sufficed as weatherproofing. The composite bow, by contrast, had to be carefully protected from wetness, in order not to damage the glue bonding. For this reason composite bows had to be given a coating of water-repellent birchbark (in northern zones) or of waterproof lacquer. In order to preserve their elasticity, both types of bows had to be unstrung when not in use.

Arrows could be made of any straight-grained wood, reed, or bamboo cane; in Europe the preferred wood was ash. To stabilize the arrow's flight, radial fletchings were attached to its rear end, just short of the nock, the notch with which the arrow was fitted to the string. These fletchings were halved feathers of geese, swans, hawks, or—for show—peacocks. They were glued and tied on in sets of three, with the two so-called "hen feathers" pointing up and down, when the arrow was fitted to the bow, and the "cock feather" pointing away from the bow. As a help in speedy nocking of the arrow, the cock feather was usually of a different color than the hen feathers. Arrowheads in medieval Europe were triangular, with two cutting edges, and fitted to the shaft with a socket. Asiatic arrowheads, by contrast, had tangs set into the hollowed shafts. On impact the tang would split the shaft, making the arrow useless for an enemy, who otherwise could recover spent arrows and shoot them back.

The length of the arrow depends on the size of the bow; when the latter is fully drawn, the arrowhead should just protrude in front of the bow-holding hand. The arrows for the English longbows were called "cloth-yard shafts" because of their standardized length of thirty-seven inches. Arrows for Mongol bows were twenty-six inches long.

No operable medieval longbows survive, but it has been estimated that the English longbow must have had an average pull of about seventy-five pounds. Its extreme range was roughly 300 yards, with an effective range up to 200 yards. Asiatic bows had an extreme range exceeding 800 yards and an effective range of more than 300 yards.

BOW AND ARROW/CROSSBOW

In Europe the bow was drawn with the arrow held between forefinger and middle finger of the right hand, while the string was pulled back by the first three fingers. Asiatic composite bows were drawn by hooking the right thumb behind the string, with the forefinger locked over the tip of the thumb. As protection for the thumb against the cut of the string, a special archer's ring with slide was worn.

Quivers. The cloth-yard shafts of the English longbowmen were carried in sheaves, bundles of twenty-four arrows. Archers of other nations, including the Normans in 1066, using shorter bows (and therefore shorter arrows), carried their arrows in cylindrical quivers on their belts, at the right hip. The quiver slung diagonally across the back—so familiar from Robin Hood movies—is postmedieval, borrowed from the American Indian. In the thirteenth century the Seljuk Turks carried their arrows in boxlike quivers on their belts at the right side; the arrows were stored with their points up. This way the fletchings did not get ruffled when the arrow was pulled out of the quiver. Later Turkish and Mongol warriors carried bowcase and arrow quiver hung from the belt, bowcase on the left, quiver on the right. This quiver was a flat pouch of several layers of felt and leather, with separately sewn pockets for the individual arrows. With additional quivers on the saddle, the Mongol horseman-archer carried a minimum of sixty arrows.

History of the Bow. Though originally designed as a hunting weapon, the bow must have been used in warfare at a very early stage in history. Late Stone Age cave paintings in Spain and North Africa show battles between archers, and one of the earliest surviving relief carvings from predynastic Egypt (before 3000 B.C.) depicts archers marching in formation behind a military standard. "Egyptian" and "Cretan" were synonyms for "archer" in antiquity; they seem to have carried self bows, while in the steppes north of the Black Sea, the famed horsemen-archers known as Scythians (whose name seems to be derived from the same root as "to shoot") used composite bows. Greeks and Romans made scant use of archers; their armies relied on heavy infantry formations armed with spear and sword. Archers were used only as light auxiliary infantry without tactical importance. In the Dark Ages following the fall of Rome, the Huns swept into Europe, for a short time spreading terror as horsemen-archers by means of their composite bows.

During the Middle Ages the use of the composite bow in Europe remained limited to Hungarians, Poles, and Russians. In Scandinavia the self bow became a favorite weapon of the Vikings, and at the Battle of Hastings (1066) it was one of the decisive factors of the Norman victory.

In western Europe the outstanding archers of the Middle Ages were the English longbowmen, who won the celebrated victories of Crécy (1346), Poitiers (1356), and Agincourt (1415). However, though the longbow was a sturdy, all-weather weapon of highest efficiency, it had the severe drawback of being so long that it could be handled only on foot, and foot archers were not mobile enough to be used except in defensive positions. All English victories in the Hundred Years War were won by longbowmen behind field fortifications, such as ditches or stakes, shooting down the horses of charging French knights. When the French learned to outflank the English battle line, to separate the archers from their supporting men-at-arms, or to catch them before they could set up defensive positions, the archers were lost, particularly when their arrows were spent. Because of the high speed with which a skilled archer could shoot arrow after arrow, the problem of an adequate ammunition supply was a grave one.

Another contributing factor to the gradual phasing out of the longbow was the introduction of massed pikemen's squares on the continental battlefields. In the Battle of Grandson (2 March 1476), the disciplined Swiss vanguard stoically weathered the arrow storm of 6,000 English archers in Burgundian service. The upright pikes of the close-packed square served as a screen rendering the arrows harmless. When their main force arrived, the Swiss charged, and swept the Burgundians off the field, archers and all. The same sort of confrontation was repeated at Murten (22 June 1476) and Nancy (7 January 1477) with the same results, thus ending the longbowmen's reign over the battlefield.

The Bow in Sport. After the bow had ceased to be a military weapon in western Europe, it remained popular as a sporting weapon. Target shooting at the butts once was a demanding military practice (one-eighth of a mile was standard distance in Henry VIII's time); today archery is an Olympic discipline. On the Continent the archers' guilds of the Flemish cities once almost rivaled the fame of the English longbowmen. These guilds still exist, and their annual shooting contests at a wooden popinjay (in earlier days a live rooster was tied and hoisted on the

BOW AND ARROW/CROSSBOW

wing of a windmill) are colorful folk festivals in many Belgian towns. The Flemish archers used a special cuff (brassard) with a bone or ivory plaque to protect the left wrist against the snap of the bowstring. Antique brassards, engraved with city and guild arms and folk-art motifs, are desirable collectibles.

Bow hunting, a revival of medieval and American Indian traditions, is becoming an increasingly popular sport. A special sporting variant is the pellet bow, used in hunting birds and small mammals, whose plumage or fur would be spoiled by blood from arrow-inflicted wounds. The pellet-bowstring is doubled and has a small pouch in its center for the clay or lead pellet. Medieval European pellet bows had a metal handgrip with a window through which the pellet passed. Persian pellet bows had an arrow-length rod with a cup at its fore-end tied to the bowstring. The pellet was placed in the cup, and the rod gave it its direction.

Crossbow. The medieval crossbow (or arbalest) was a powerful bow fitted to a stock containing an arresting and a releasing device, the nut and the trigger. The nut was a pivoting bone cylinder with a semicircular cutout to receive the bowstring. On its underside was a notch in which the fore-end of the trigger locked. When the trigger was pressed, it slipped out of the notch, thus freeing the nut to pivot and letting the string go. The bows of crossbows were laminated from horn and whalebone, bonded with glue, and coated with birchbark for weather protection. In northern Europe special slipcovers were placed over the bows on the march. During the fifteenth century steel bows were introduced, but were of only limited use because they tended to snap in extreme cold.

Crossbows were standardized in three sizes: full, half, and quarter, with a pull of 150 to 500 pounds. Even a quarter bow could not be spanned by strength of the arms alone; therefore mechanical devices had to be employed. The simplest device was a belt hook. The crossbow was set on the ground upside down, the crossbowman squatted, hooked the belthook into the string, and stood up (the thigh muscles are the strongest muscles in the human body) until the string locked into the nut. Another device was the goat-foot lever, consisting of a long arm with a short fork hinged to it. The long arm was hooked into a ring at the fore-end of the stock, and the hinged fork was set against the string. As the long arm was pulled back, the fork moved the string into the lock-

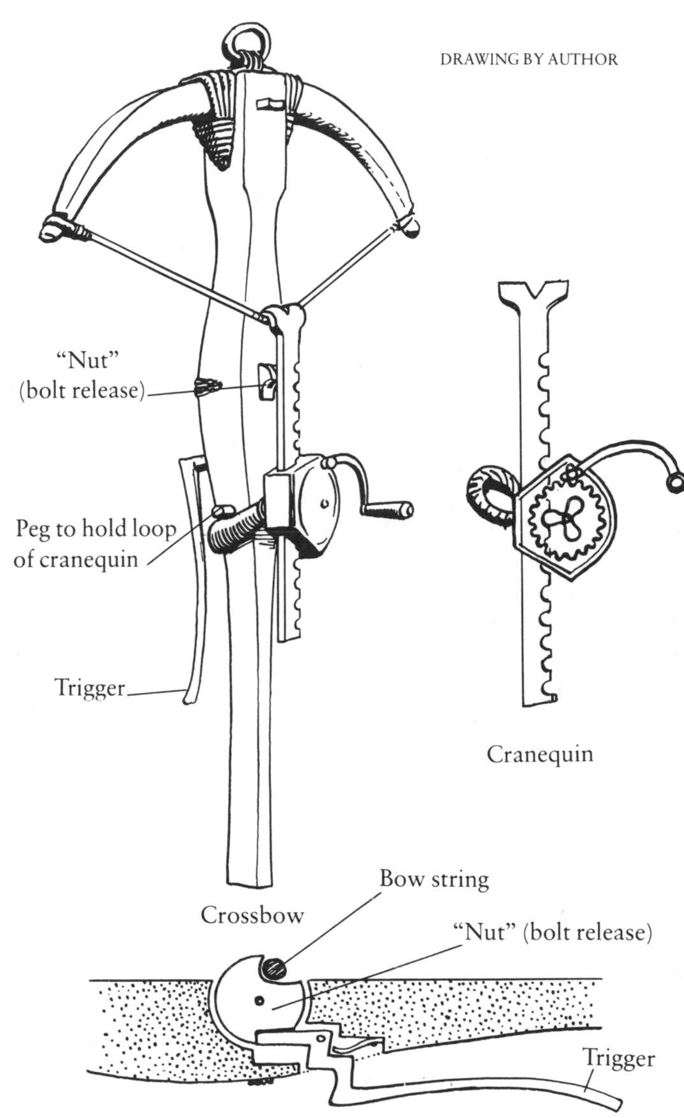

ing position. The most efficient device was the cranequin, a rack-and-pinion mechanism operating like an automobile jack. For oversize rampart crossbows a windlass with claws and pulleys was used, but this device was not practical in the open field.

Missiles. Because of its greater power the crossbow did not shoot slender arrows, but sturdy bolts, or quarrels, about fifteen inches long and three-quarters of an inch thick. Their socketed steel heads were almost square in cross-section ("quarrel" is derived from French *carreau:* square); hunting bolts for big game had chisel-shaped heads for inflicting hamstringing wounds. The fletchings of bolts were two strips of leather or thin slats of wood, set at a slight

DRAWING BY AUTHOR

Spanning with belthook Goat's foot lever

Cranequin

angle to give the bolt a flight-stabilizing spin (the forerunner of the spinning rifle bullet). The maximum range of a crossbow was about 300 yards; its effective range, about 150 yards.

Quivers. Crossbowmen carried fourteen bolts, points up, in a lidded, boxlike quiver on their belts, at the right side. These quivers were usually covered with badger fur against wetness; they also held a compartment for a spare string.

History of the Crossbow. The crossbow was invented by the Chinese about 1200 B.C.; there was even a repeating crossbow with integral magazine holding twenty-five or more bolts, activated by a pumping lever. In Europe crossbowlike weapons appeared in Roman times *(gastaphretes, catapulta),* but the fully developed crossbow was used from the tenth century on. As a "too murderous" weapon, it was banned in 1139 by papal edict for use against Christians (though against infidels and heathens it was highly recommended), but without success. Although Emperor Maximilian I of Germany abolished it in 1517 as obsolete for his armies, the Spanish conquistadors used it in the conquests of Mexico and Peru.

BIBLIOGRAPHY

James Duff, *Bows and Arrows* (1932); Egon Harmuth, *Die Armbrust* (1975); Ernest Heath, *The Grey Goose Wing* (1971); Daniel Higson, *The Bullet Crossbow* (1923); Paul E. Klopsteg, *Turkish Archery and the Composite Bow* (1934); Gervase Markham, *The Art of Archerie,* facsimile ed. by Stephen V. Grancsay (1968); Edward S. Morse, *Additional Notes on Arrow-Release* (1922); Sir Ralph Payne-Gallwey, *The Crossbow* (1903).

HELMUT NICKEL

[See also **Agincourt, Battle of; Arms and Armor; Hundred Years War; Hunting, Western European.**]

BOYAR *(boyarin),* probably a Bulgar (Turkic) term *(bolyarin)* introduced into Old Bulgarian by the Danubian Bulgars and later found in Old Russian and Ukrainian. It was originally employed to identify the rich and wellborn, landholders, as well as the senior servitor-councillors of princes.

These untitled aristocrats were found in every principality as well as in republican Novgorod and Pskov. In the princely territories they were the military chieftains, often bringing their own retainers in support of their lords' enterprises. Their rewards came in the form of social prestige, war booty, income from temporary governorships, and presents from their princes. Since they served voluntarily they were not contractually obligated to follow their prince if they disagreed with his policies. A boyar, like any other freeman in service, could resign without endangering his possessions; and he might transfer service to another prince, even though his lands were located in the principality of his former lord. His rewards came from past and present service.

Prior to the mid fifteenth century only two restrictions were imposed upon the departure of freemen in service. First, transfer of allegiance to an enemy could not take place during time of war; second, a servitor who had left could not encourage his new lord to wage war upon his former employer. In such instances the penalty could be death, blinding, or imprisonment, along with confiscation of worldly goods. Such, at least, was the case in Muscovy, for which we have evidence.

In fourteenth- and early-fifteenth-century Muscovy the boyars were drawn from the thirty-five to forty leading aristocratic serving families. By this time the title was employed only for councillors of the prince. Their number at any given time was small. In the later fifteenth century, for which reasonably good evidence exists, the boyars numbered between six and twelve at any given time. Presumably their number had not been greater before then.

The social composition of the boyar class began to change in the course of the fifteenth century. As princes entered the Muscovite service rolls, a handful eventually reached the top of the service ladder and were named boyars. They obtained their positions as a result of advantageous marriages with members of the ruling house, for meritorious service in time of crisis, or because of unusually distinguished lineage; but none could be appointed if he retained unusual military power or governmental rights in his hereditary lands. As Muscovy continued to absorb the surrounding principalities the aristocrats were assimilated into the Muscovite service system, and a larger percentage of princes rose to boyar rank in the sixteenth century. At the same time the boyars (along with all freemen in service) lost their traditional right of departure, and that deprived them of their leverage against the rapidly growing power of the crown.

BIBLIOGRAPHY

Gustave Alef, "Das Erlöschen des Abzugsrechts der Moskauer Bojaren," in *Forschungen zur osteuropäischen Geschichte,* **10** (1965); and "The Crisis of the Muscovite Aristocracy," *ibid.,* **15** (1970); Jerome Blum, "The Beginning of Large-Scale Private Landownership in Russia," in *Speculum,* **28** (1953); Alexandre Eck, *Le moyen âge russe* (1933), 114–118, 188–193; Alexander E. Presniakov, *The Testaments of the Grand Princes of Moscow,* Robert C. Howes, trans. and ed. (1967), 69–72; and *The Formation of the Great Russian State,* A. E. Moorhouse, trans. (1970), 396–397; George Vernadsky, *Kievan Russia* (1948), 139–140, 169, 184, 220; and *The Mongols and Russia* (1953), 346–349, 367–370.

GUSTAVE ALEF

[See also **Duma.**]

BRACKET CAPITAL. See **Capital, Types of.**

BRACTEATES. The name is derived from Latin *bractea,* meaning thin metal plates or disks, usually of gold or silver, which were originally ornamental in character but later were employed as a coinage. The term generally signifies coins stamped on one side only, where the thinness of the metal makes the underside (reverse) of the coins hollow, whereas the topside (obverse) is convex. In medieval studies, "bracteate" designates three separate numismatic categories. The first category comprises gold medallions stamped on one side only with crude designs, inspired by fourth-century Byzantine gold prototypes. They were minted in the period 450–650. The original homeland of these medallions is unknown, but it is likely to have been somewhere in Scandinavia, where the majority have been found. The "half-bracteates" are a second category, dated to the ninth and tenth centuries, and found principally at Hedeby (German: Haithabu) in Schleswig and at Birka in east-central Sweden. A third kind of bracteate includes one-sided coins minted in Scandinavia and especially Germany in the twelfth through fourteenth centuries.

The migration-period bracteates vary in size from two to twelve centimeters. There are four principal types, designated *A, B, C,* and *D* by Swedish archaeologists and numismatists in the nineteenth century. All the bracteates have eyelets by which they were attached to necklaces or sewn to clothing. When the last complete census was made in 1952, there were 760 known bracteates, of which 623 were found in Scandinavia.

Bracteates of the *A* group most closely resemble Byzantine prototypes. Their outstanding feature is the centrally placed bust or head of a man wearing

Albrecht, Sweden, 1364–1389 (*left*). Sverre, Norway, 1177–1202 (*center*). Knut, Sweden, 1167–1196 (*right*). COURTESY OF THE AMERICAN NUMISMATIC SOCIETY

elaborate regalia, surrounded by hands of geometric, zig-zag, or ribbon ornament. *B* bracteates are less distinctive. One or more male figures, placed among various symbols and sometimes with runes, crowd the surface of the disk, and the banding associated with type *A* is absent. *C* bracteates are the largest in size, and always depict a mounted warrior. The *D* bracteates are decorated exclusively with animal ornament, without representations of the human figure. A backward-glancing, bird-beaked fantastic animal is a characteristic design in the *D* group.

The "half-bracteates" of the Carolingian era were attributed by nineteenth-century Danish and Swedish numismatists to their respective countries, but it is not possible to describe this coinage as anything more specific than "Scandinavian" in origin. Most of the "half-bracteates" are stamped on both sides, but the coins are often so thin that the obverse and reverse designs are confused. Three types can be distinguished: *pictorial,* with motifs drawn from Scandinavian art or mythology (a man, a house, roosters facing one another, a ship, or a deer); *Carolingian,* imitations (often poorly made) of Carolingian coins, particularly those minted at Dorstad; and *crosses.* The pictorial and Carolingian types belong to the ninth century, while the coins with crosses, whose motif is never combined with the motifs of the other two groups, are probably of the tenth century.

The Scandinavian bracteates of the later Middle Ages appeared briefly in Denmark in the period 1150–1160, and were minted, with a very low weight in proportion to other twelfth-century Danish coinage, only in Jutland. In Sweden the later bracteates originated at about the same time (*ca.* 1160) in all parts of the country, with differing but related weights, and continued to be issued (with a fifty-year hiatus in the first half of the fourteenth century) until the end of the Middle Ages. In Norway the minting of bracteates began in the first half of the twelfth century and continued until the sixteenth century. All the later Scandinavian bracteates were used in exchanges of the most modest character.

BIBLIOGRAPHY

For literature on Scandinavian bracteates see especially Mogens B. Mackeprang, *De nordiske Guldbrakteater* (1952); and Johannes Brøndsted, *Danmarks Oldtid,* III: *Jernalderen* (1960), 316f., for discussions of the migration-period material. Brita Malmer, "Nordiska Mynt före År 1000," in *Acta archaeologica lundensia,* ser. 8° no. 4 (1966), is the standard work on the half-bracteate series. N. L. Rasmusson (with Hans Holst), "Brakteat," in *Kulturhistorisk leksikon for nordisk middelalder,* II (1957), is basic to the study of the bracteates of the later Middle Ages. See also Herje Öberg, *Guldbrakteaterna från nordens folkvandringstid* (1942); and M. Stenberger, "Vikingatida smyckebrakteater," in *Fornavännen,* **46** (1951).

SIDNEY L. COHEN

[See also **Mints and Money.**]

BRACTON, HENRY DE (*d.* 1268), English justice and author of the legal treatise *De legibus et consuetudinibus Angliae* (On the laws and customs of England). The surname likely comes from one of several Devonshire villages named Bratton, the most common form of the name during the Middle Ages. Bracton, the modern version, comes from the earliest printed text of *De legibus.* He was an ecclesiastic and held several church preferments, ending his life as chancellor of Exeter Cathedral.

One of Bracton's patrons was William Raleigh, bishop of Winchester and a former royal justice. Bracton may well have been one of Raleigh's clerks when the latter was senior justice of the court *coram rege* (before the king) in the 1230's. However, nothing certain is known of Bracton's judicial career prior to 1240, when he received the sum of forty marks a year for maintenance in the king's service. From 1247 to 1251 and from 1253 to 1257 he was justice *coram rege.* After 1259 Bracton served several times as justice of assize for Devonshire. In 1267 he was appointed to the commission hearing claims from those who had forfeited lands by siding with Simon de Montfort during the Barons' War. On the whole, Bracton's was an interesting, although not especially distinguished, judicial career. His posthumous fame results entirely from his association with *De legibus.*

De legibus is the most important literary source

in English legal history. It is distinguished from both its predecessors and its successors by its comprehensive scope and analytic approach to law. The treatise is so detailed and accurate a picture of native English law that it is without a peer, not only in England but in the whole legal literature of the Middle Ages. One of the most significant problems associated with *De legibus* is the nature of its relationship to Roman and canon law texts of the period. From the scholarly edition of the text it is clear that its overall organization cannot have been taken from either Justinian's *Code* or *Digest,* although the early printed text made this seem likely.

Nevertheless, the influence of Roman jurisprudence permeates the whole work. The author, according to S. E. Thorne, the latest editor and translator of *De legibus,* "was a trained jurist with the principles and distinctions of Roman jurisprudence firmly in mind, using them throughout his work, wherever they could be used, to rationalize and reduce to order the results reached in the English courts." Subsequent writers on English law did not share this background or approach. Within fifty years of Bracton's death the law fell into the hands of those without experience or learning in Roman or canon law. The approach of the author of *De legibus* was not repeated in England until Blackstone's *Commentaries,* some five centuries later.

Apart from its Roman elements, *De legibus* is of great significance in quite another way. The treatise follows earlier tradition by its extensive comment upon writs—that is, those authorities that entitle litigants to a hearing before the courts. Here, too, *De legibus* broke new ground by introducing specific cases from the plea rolls to illustrate what the author believed the law should be. Moreover, when in 1884 Paul Vinogradoff discovered a mid-thirteenth-century manuscript in the British Library containing a collection of plea roll cases, including some of the cases cited in *De legibus,* he took this collection to be the source used by Bracton. Three years later the manuscript was edited by F. W. Maitland under the title *Bracton's Note-Book.* The notion that specific cases were useful and important in any discussion of the law is first found in *De legibus.* It was an idea with a distinguished future, one that before the end of the thirteenth century had given birth to the Year Books.

The text of *De legibus* presents especially difficult problems. No edition based upon the examination of a substantial number of the manuscripts was available until that done by G. E. Woodbine, who between 1915 and 1942 produced a text based on the collation of more than forty late-thirteenth- and early-fourteenth-century manuscripts. This edition revealed a text plagued with lapses, omissions, and errors of the most grievous sort, which led most scholars to suppose that the work had suffered at the hands of some incompetent editor/redactor after Bracton's death.

Woodbine's text has since been translated with revisions and notes by S. E. Thorne in four volumes. In his introduction to the last two volumes (1977) Thorne put forth views that radically alter the accepted relationship between Bracton and the treatise. Thorne argues that *De legibus* was conceived and largely written in the 1220's under the inspiration of William Raleigh. This work was revised and enlarged by Bracton and others between 1230 and 1260. Traces of this chronology can be seen clearly in the treatise. However, the work was never thoroughly revised. Many of the difficulties in the text result from the fact that copies were made at various times for a variety of reasons during that thirty-year period. In addition Thorne argues that the collection of plea-roll extracts known as *Bracton's Note-Book* has no connection with *De legibus.*

It is probably too soon to say whether these views will meet with general approval. They do offer the most convincing explanation yet put forth for the many problems associated with Bracton and *De legibus.*

BIBLIOGRAPHY

Henry of Bracton, *De legibus et consuetudinibus Angliae,* George E. Woodbine, ed., 4 vols. (1915–1942), also trans. with revisions and notes by Samuel E. Thorne, 4 vols. (1968–1977); *Bracton's Note Book,* F. W. Maitland, ed., 3 vols (1887); C. A. F. Meekings, *Studies in Thirteenth-Century Justice and Administration* (1981), chs. 1, 7, 11; T. F. T. Plucknett, *Early English Legal Literature* (1958), 42–79; H. G. Richardson, *Bracton: The Problem of His Text* (1965); Samuel E. Thorne, *Henry de Bracton, 1268–1968* (1970).

T. A. SANDQUIST

[See also **Law, Canon; Law, English Common; Law, Civil.**]

BRADWARDINE, THOMAS (*ca.* 1300–1349), English Scholastic and archbishop of Canterbury was probably born at Hartfield, Sussex. He studied at Oxford, where he was a fellow of Balliol College in 1321 and, by 1323, a fellow of Merton. During his regency in arts, he composed *De insolubilibus,* an influential treatise in logic later developed by Richard Swineshead. In 1328, while a student of theology, he wrote his most important treatise in natural science, *De proportione velocitatum in motibus,* in which variation of velocity (effect) was seen to be a function of the whole ratio of mover over moved (cause) in geometric, rather than arithmetical, proportionality. The influence of this short treatise in four chapters was enormous throughout the century; it was twice abbreviated and popularized for beginners in arts, and was the basis for the later work of Nicole Oresme at Paris. It provided the distinction between dynamics, the analysis of causes producing motion, and kinematics, the analysis of distance moved in time (effect).

Later, in *De continuo,* Bradwardine assembled an arsenal of arguments against a contemporary view (held by Robert Grosseteste, Walter Chatton, and Henry of Harclay) of the continuum as composed of indivisible points. The main contention in both treatises is that mathematics can provide the key to understanding nature (*De continuo,* MS Erfurt, Amplon. 4° 385, 31v; *De prop. vel. in motibus,* preface), thereby enlarging the scope of "middle sciences" between pure mathematics and natural philosophy. The last chapter of *De proportione* even tried to unify celestial and terrestrial motion, an idea that was not pursued by his successors at Merton—William Heytesbury, John Dumbleton, Richard Swineshead, and others—who were more interested in "calculations" *de motu.*

While a fellow of Merton, Bradwardine was twice elected proctor of the university (1325–1326 and 1326–1327). By 1333 he had become a bachelor of theology and canon of Lincoln. Although the earliest reference to him as master in theology is dated 7 December 1340, Bradwardine must have become master within one year of 19 September 1337, when he became chancellor of St. Paul's Cathedral, London. In the summer of 1335, Bradwardine relinquished his fellowship at Merton and joined the household of Richard of Bury, bishop of Durham.

Bradwardine's most important theological work was *De causa Dei contra Pelagium et de virtute causarum,* completed at London in 1344, while he was chancellor of St. Paul's. It is a massive and systematic proof of the primacy of God's free and efficacious grace and will over all secondary causes, both necessary and free. It is a work of theological reason against unnamed "modern" Pelagians who would exempt man's free will from God's prior causality in both nature and grace. These Pelagians claimed that Pelagius could never have been disproved by reason and Scripture alone, but was silenced simply by ecclesiastical authority (*De causa Dei,* preface). For this reason the whole of *De causa Dei* is a systematic demonstration of the primacy of God's universal causality (Book I), the reality of man's free will under grace (Book II), and the solution of difficulties involving God's foreknowledge and the reality of future contingent events (Book III).

Bradwardine's main sources, besides Scripture, were Augustine, Anselm, and Thomas Aquinas. Although he in no way exceeded the bounds of orthodoxy, many modern historians consider him a "theological determinist" or "predestinarian" because he held the Pauline and Augustinian doctrine of predestination and efficacious grace. Many attempts have been made to identify the *Pelagiani moderni,* without unanimous success; among the more likely candidates are William of Ockham, Adam Woodham, Robert of Holcot, John Rodynton, and Thomas Buckingham. That the problem was not merely academic can be seen in Chaucer's Nun's Priest's Tale.

Bradwardine's first election to the see of Canterbury (31 August 1348) was cassated by Edward III because *congé d'élire* (formal permission to elect) had not been obtained by the prior and convent. This in no way reflected on the esteem Edward had for Bradwardine, who had long served as chaplain and confessor to the king. He accompanied Edward on the first French campaign in 1346, and he preached a remarkable victory sermon *(Sermo epinicius)* to the king and his troops in France after the battle of Crécy and shortly after news reached the king of the English victory over the Scots at Neville's Cross near Durham (17 October 1346). This sermon, though preached in English, exists only in a Latin translation lacking the last folios.

On the death of John of Ufford, archbishop of Canterbury, a *congé d'élire* was obtained, and Bradwardine was elected to succeed on 4 June 1349. He was appointed on 19 June by Pope Clement VI, and was consecrated at Avignon on 19 July 1349. Despite prevalence of the plague, he immediately returned to England, and received the temporalities of the see from the king at Eltham on 22 August. He died of the plague at the residence of the bishop of Rochester in Lambeth on 26 August 1349.

Bradwardine is sometimes referred to under the Scholastic title of Doctor Profundus.

BRAGI BODDASON THE OLD

BIBLIOGRAPHY

Works. De causa Dei contra Pelagium, Henry Savile, ed. (1618, repr. 1964); H. Lamar Crosby, ed. and trans., *Thomas of Bradwardine: His Tractatus de Proportionibus . . .* (1955); *De continuo,* J. E. Murdoch, ed., in *Geometry and the Continuum in the Fourteenth Century* (diss., Univ. of Wisconsin, 1957); H. A. Oberman and James A. Weisheipl, "The *Sermo epinicius* Ascribed to Thomas Bradwardine (1346)," in *Archives d'histoire doctrinale et littéraire du moyen âge,* **25** (1958).

Literature. Alfred B. Emden, *Biographical Register of the University of Oxford to A.D. 1500,* I (1957), 244–246, and III (1959), xv–xvi; Brian Fleming, *Thomas de Bradwardine: Oxford Scholar, Royal Servant and Archbishop of Canterbury* (1964); Gordon Leff, *Bradwardine and the Pelagians* (1957); Anneliese Maier, *Die Vorläufer Galileis in 14. Jahrhundert* (1949), esp. 81–110; Konstanty Michalski, "Le problème de la volonté à Oxford et à Paris au xive siècle," in *Commentariorum Societatis philosophicae polonorum. Studia philosophica,* II (1937); Heiko A. Oberman, *Archbishop Thomas Bradwardine: A Fourteenth Century Augustinian* (diss., Univ. of Utrecht, 1957).

JAMES A. WEISHEIPL

[See also **Edward III of England; Oresme, Nicole; Scholasticism, Scholastic Method; Swineshead.**]

BRAGI BODDASON THE OLD, the earliest skald whose work is believed to have survived, shares his first name with the Norse god of poetry and eloquence. Rather little is known about the historical Bragi. He is named several times in *Skáldatal,* which states that he composed for Eysteinn Beli and Bjǫrn á Haugi, kings of the Swedes. In the opinion of Jón Jóhannesson, Bjǫrn was in western Norway at the time of Haraldr Hárfagri (Harald Fairhair, 860–931). Bragi's fragmentary *Ragnarsdrápa* narrates the scenes painted or possibly carved on each quarter of a ceremonial shield given to him by a prince, Ragnarr Sigurðarson, identified by Snorri Sturluson with the legendary Ragnarr Loðbrók.

Twenty-nine half-stanzas apparently belonging to *Ragnarsdrápa* have been preserved in manuscripts of *Snorra Edda:* eight and a half narrate the death of Hamðir and Sǫrli in Jǫrmunrekkr's hall; eight and a half, the everlasting battle of Heðinn and Hǫgni; two describe Gefjon plowing the island of Zealand out of Sweden; seven, Thor's contest with the world serpent. Two introductory half-stanzas address a certain Hrafnketill (perhaps the presenter of the shield), asking him to listen to the *drápa,* which the poet hopes will be "a good reward" for the beautiful shield that "Sigurðr's son" gave him. In the two-line refrain, which occurs twice in the extant fragments, the giver is further identified: "Ragnarr gave me the moon of the sea-king's chariot [that is, the shield, visualized as hanging over the gunwale of a Viking ship] and a multitude of tales."

The original structure of the poem cannot now be determined. The poet appears to relate the four episodes through the repeated image of a circle or shield rim, each reflecting the shape of the gift itself, "the ringing round of Hildr's wheel." There are other Old Norse shield poems, the best preserved of which is *Haustlǫng* by Þjóðólfr ór Hvíni. Hellmut Rosenfeld has suggested that the genre is related to the shield descriptions in Homer and Hesiod, and should be seen against a background of cult, the use of votive shields in pagan religious practice.

The complex diction of *Ragnarsdrápa* and the lateness of the tradition that Bragi composed it cast some doubt on its authenticity. The most important arguments for the relative antiquity of the poem have to do with its metrical structure, which is less regular than that of *dróttkvætt* composed from the tenth century on. In *Ragnarsdrápa,* for example, the rhyme does not always fall on the penultimate syllable of the line (six times), and a syllable can precede the alliterating sound in the even line (four times). Despite this metrical freedom, all the chief characteristics of *drótkvætt* style are present and even heightened: alliteration, internal rhyme, a regular syllabic meter, and an obscured, periphrastic language. Perhaps the very originality and brilliance of the poem ensured its survival when a duller *drápa* might have perished.

Bragi's 120 lines do more than comment on the nature and disposition of what he sees before him on the shield; his stanzas are intense, poetic reshapings of the content of their graphic art original. The poet's anatural, compressed syntax and diction seem to be competing with the lines, colors, and symbolic details of the artist.

BIBLIOGRAPHY

Jón Jóhannesson, "Bjǫrn at Haugi," Gabriel Turville-Petre, trans., in *Saga-Book of the Viking Society,* **17** (1966–1969); Vilhelm Kiil, "Gevjonmyten og *Ragnarsdrápa,*" in *Maal og minne* (1965); Hallvard Lie, "Skaldestil-studier," in *Maal og minne* (1952), 5–53; and *"Natur" og "unatur" i skaldekunsten* (1957), 19–42, 65–66; Hellmut Rosenfeld,

"Nordische Schilddichtung und mittelalterliche Wappendichtung," in *Zeitschrift für deutsche Philologie,* **61** (1936).

ROBERTA FRANK

[See also **Scandinavian Mythology; Skaldic Verse; Snorra Edda.**]

BRAILES, WILLIAM DE (*fl. ca.* 1230–1260), an English Gothic illuminator who worked probably at Oxford. He signed his name and portrayed himself as a cleric in a psalter (Cambridge, Fitzwilliam Museum, MS 330, leaf of Last Judgment) and a book of hours (London, British Library, MS Add. 49999, fols. 43, 47). Two more psalters, thirty-five picture leaves of Old and New Testament subjects, and nine Bibles are attributed to him.

BIBLIOGRAPHY

Sydney C. Cockerell, *The Work of W. de Brailes* (1930); Hanns Swarzenski, "Unknown Bible Pictures by W. de Brailes and Some Notes on Early English Bible Illustration," in *Journal of the Walters Art Gallery,* **1** (1938); Eric Millar, "Additional Miniatures by W. de Brailes," in *Journal of the Walters Art Gallery,* **2** (1939); Graham Pollard, "William de Brailles," in *The Bodleian Library Record,* **5** (1955); and Nigel Morgan, *Early Gothic Manuscripts,* vol. 1: *1190–1250* (1982), 30, 114–123 (nos. 69–74), ills. 226–248, figs. 14, 15.

ADELAIDE BENNETT

BRANDENBURG. The mark of Brandenburg, the heart of the later kingdom of Prussia, was created by the Ascanians in colonial Slavic territory that was Germanized in the twelfth and thirteenth centuries. Charlemagne had forced the Slavs east of the Elbe to accept his overlordship, but they had freed themselves by the end of the Carolingian period and had allied with the Magyars. Henry I, the first Saxon king, crossed the Elbe in the winter of 928–929 and captured the chief fortress of the Havelli, Brennaburg, the first reference to Brandenburg.

Otto the Great appointed Gero as the margrave along the middle Elbe and Saale in 937, and established the bishoprics of Brandenburg and Havelberg as mission centers in 948. After Gero's death in 965, his mark was divided. The territory inhabited by the Ljutizi between the Elde and Peene rivers in the north and Lusatia in the south formed what was later called the Nordmark (North Mark). The Slavs rebelled in 983 against the harsh German exactions and their enforced Christianization, and for nearly two centuries the bishops of Brandenburg and Havelberg, and the margraves of the Nordmark, were titular dignitaries.

Emperor Lothar III appointed an Ascanian, Albrecht the Bear (*d.* 1170), a grandson of the last Billung duke of Saxony, as margarve of the Nordmark in 1134. Albrecht captured Havelberg during the Wendish Crusade in 1147. To protect his lands, the last Slavic prince of Brandenburg, Pribislav, named Albrecht as his heir. Pribislav died in 1150, but Albrecht gained firm possession of his new domains only in 1157, after suppressing a revolt. He then assumed the title of margrave of Brandenburg.

The new mark was not identical with the Nordmark, but was a new territorial lordship. Its main components were the Havelland, which Albrecht had inherited from Pribislav; the Ascanians' other alods and fiefs east of the Elbe, such as the Zauche and the city of Brandenburg; and their holdings west of the Elbe, in the area that came to be known in the fourteenth century as the Altmark (Old Mark). Albrecht encouraged German colonists, many of whom came from the Low Countries, to settle in the mark; and the native population was gradually Germanized. Albrecht's eldest son, Otto I, inherited Brandenburg, and his youngest son, Bernhard, acquired the duchy of Saxony after the fall of Henry the Lion in 1180.

Otto's grandsons, John I (1220–1266) and Otto III (1220–1267), transformed Brandenburg into a major German principality. They established Brandenburg's feudal suzerainty over Pomerania, acquired the Uckermark (the area around Prenzlau), obtained Upper Lusatia in fief from Bohemia, acquired half of the province of Lebus (the region around Frankfurt an der Oder), and expanded east of the Oder in what was later called the Neumark (New Mark).

John and Otto founded or promoted the development of approximately thirty cities, including Berlin-Cölln and Frankfurt, and provided for their subjects' spiritual well-being by patronizing the friars. Although they had ruled together in complete harmony for decades, in 1258 they divided their income and vassals, in order to prevent disputes among their numerous sons. This division proved to be unimportant because the Brandenburg line of the Ascanians died out with Margrave Woldemar, John's grandson, in 1319.

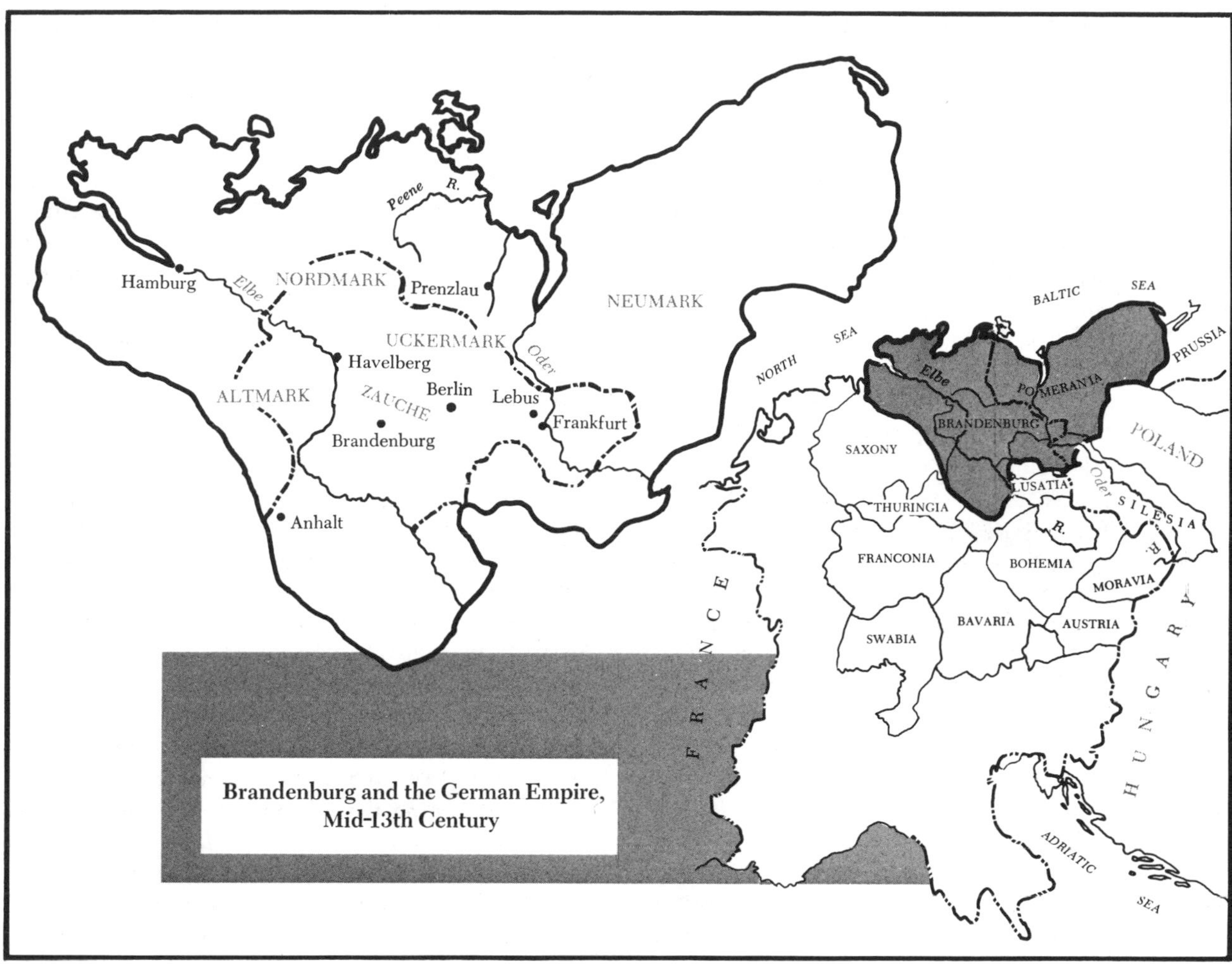

Brandenburg and the German Empire, Mid-13th Century

The fourteenth century was the low point in the history of Brandenburg. The mark became a pawn in imperial politics, neglected by its absentee, foreign rulers and valued chiefly as a source of revenue. Following the example of the Habsburgs and Luxemburgs, Louis the Bavarian used his position as king to enfeoff his eldest son, Louis, with the vacant fief in 1323. In 1348 a pilgrim appeared, claiming to be the long-dead Woldemar. King Charles IV and the Ascanian dukes of Saxony and counts of Anhalt, who may have arranged for the impostor's appearance in order to embarrass the Wittelsbachs, recognized Woldemar as the true margrave.

Louis' reconciliation with Charles ended the game, but in 1351 Louis granted Brandenburg to his half brothers, Louis the Roman and Otto, receiving Upper Bavaria in exchange. The Wittelsbachs had incurred vast debts in fighting Woldemar, and were forced to pledge many properties and rights to raise funds. The Brandenburgers distrusted the Wittelsbachs as foreigners, and the estates assumed control of the bankrupt principality. Angry with their Bavarian relatives, Louis the Roman and Otto recognized the sons of Charles IV as their heirs in 1363. When Otto tried to abrogate the agreement, Charles invaded the mark in 1373 and forced Otto to surrender Brandenburg to the Luxemburgs.

The Golden Bull of 1356 had recognized the margrave of Brandenburg as one of the seven electors. Since Charles' eldest son, Wenceslaus, could not simultaneously be an elector and king, he granted the mark to his half brother Sigismund in 1378. Ten years later Sigismund pledged the mark to his cousin Jobst of Moravia, to raise the large sums he needed to obtain the Hungarian crown. Sigismund, who had sold the Neumark to the Teutonic Knights in 1402, regained Brandenburg after Jobst's death in 1411. A century of ineffective princely authority had left the mark in a state of anarchy. The knights practiced highway robbery as a profession, the cities were virtually independent republics, and the population had been decimated by warfare and plague.

Recognizing the need to restore order, Sigismund appointed his loyal supporter, Frederick Hohenzollern, the burgrave of Nürnberg, as governor of the mark in 1411, and formally enfeoffed him with the electorate in 1417. Although Frederick (*d.* 1440) and his sons John the Alchemist (*d.* 1464), Frederick II (*d.* 1471), and Albrecht Achilles (*d.* 1486) were chiefly interested in their Franconian lands, they forced the knights, church, and cities to submit to princely authority, and redeemed pledged property. Frederick II purchased the Neumark from the Teutonic Knights in 1455.

After Albrecht's death Brandenburg was permanently separated from the Hohenzollerns' Franconian lands, and the dynasty became firmly rooted in the mark. Albrecht's grandson, Joachim I (1499–1535), a devout Catholic, has been called the last medieval ruler of Brandenburg.

BIBLIOGRAPHY

Francis Ludwig Carsten, *The Origins of Prussia* (1954, repr. 1958); *Codex diplomaticus Brandenburgensis,* Adolph Friedrich Riedel, ed., 41 vols. (1838–1869); *Regesten der Markgrafen von Brandenburg aus dem askanischen Hause,* Hermann Krabbo and Georg Winter, eds. (1910–1955); Johannes Schultze, *Die Mark Brandenburg,* I–III (1961–1963).

JOHN B. FREED

[See also **Germany: 843–1137; Germany: 1138–1254; Germany: 1254–1493; Otto I the Great.**]

BRANDEUM is a loanword from the Greek πράνδιον, referring to a piece or type of linen or silk cloth. The recorded uses of this material suggest that it was costly and luxurious, for it is mentioned primarily as a wrapping for relics and as an altar cloth or corporal. In these functions *brandeum* shows a significant degree of synonymity with the words *palla* and *pallium.* In accordance with the conception that spiritual force flowed from one object to another through physical contact, a *brandeum* enveloping a relic was thought to absorb holiness from the object it enclosed and, thus, to become a relic itself. In this case the spiritual change in the cloth was incidental to its use as a wrapping, but *brandea* might also be intentionally sanctified for use as relics.

In 594, Empress Constantina asked Pope Gregory I to send her the head of St. Paul. Gregory (*Registrum epistolarum,* IV, 30) refused the request on the ground that the Romans, unlike the Greeks, considered it a sacrilege to disturb the bodies of the saints. He explained that the Roman practice was to enclose a *brandeum* in a box and place it next to the saint's body, where it could absorb holiness. In this way the cloth acquired all the miraculous potency of the body, and became in fact a relic (*reliquiae,* physical remains). To emphasize the equivalence of these cloths to corporeal relics, Gregory related that Pope Leo I had demonstrated the authenticity of a sanctified *brandeum* to doubting Greeks by cutting the cloth, whereupon blood flowed from the incision. Later, the Lives of Gregory I attributed this miraculous proof to Gregory himself.

Gregory of Tours described the sanctification of a small cloth *(palliolum)* at St. Peter's shrine in Rome (*Liber in gloria martyrum,* 27) and of a piece of silken cloth *(partem pallii sirici)* at St. Martin's tomb (*De virtutibus s. Martini,* I, 11). In 519 the papal legates at Constantinople wrote to Pope Hormisdas, requesting that he send *sanctuaria* from the apostles' tombs to Justinian (*Avellana collectio,* ep. 218). All these texts speak of similar procedures for the creation of relics through contact with tombs, but Pope Gregory's word *brandeum*—like Gregory of Tours's *palliolum*—appears to refer to the cloth itself, while *sanctuaria* specifies the result of the sanctification.

The veneration as relics of cloths from saints' tombs probably originated in the early Christian practice of soaking up the blood of martyrs with pieces of material, which were sometimes interred with the body as part of the physical remains. The belief that other cloths—whether deposited with the corpse at the time of burial or placed temporarily in the tomb at a later date—might acquire sanctity through contact with the remains reflects a pattern of thought that has parallels in non-Christian magic. The use of these objects as relics became popular in early medieval Europe, and in Rome in particular, because it made possible the distribution of relics without dismembering the bodies of the saints, an act that was contrary to both Roman law and papal tradition.

Despite papal efforts to emphasize their value, these contact relics gradually became less attractive, even in the West, as the force of Roman sepulchral

BRANT, SEBASTIAN

customs and regulations diminished; and their importance declined even more when the popes of the eighth and ninth centuries began to practice translation and dismemberment, thus making corporeal relics more readily available. Nevertheless, inventories of collections from the High Middle Ages reveal that cloths from tombs were still granted and treasured as relics.

The occasional designation of these cloths as *brandea,* particularly in Pope Gregory's letter, has led many modern scholars to employ the word as a generic term for sanctified cloths and even for so-called secondary or representative relics of all kinds (such as dust, oil, water, flowers) that derive their holiness from contact with a tomb or another relic. Ample evidence exists that, like *brandea,* such objects were thought to possess miraculous powers, and some authors referred to them as *reliquiae,* implying their conceptual equivalence to physical remains.

Nevertheless, this broad modern application of the term *brandeum* departs from medieval usage. In the Middle Ages *brandea* were always cloths but not necessarily holy. A *brandeum* might also be a relic but, at least in its original sense, the word described the object's physical form rather than its spiritual qualities.

BIBLIOGRAPHY

See articles on *brandeum* in *Dictionnaire d'archéologie chrétienne et de liturgie; Lexikon für Theologie und Kirche,* 2nd ed.; and *Reallexikon für Antike und Christentum.* See also Martin Heinzelmann, *Translationsberichte und andere Quellen des Reliquienkults* (1979), 22–23; John M. McCulloh, "The Cult of Relics in the Letters and 'Dialogues' of Pope Gregory the Great: A Lexicographical Study," in *Traditio,* **32** (1976); and "From Antiquity to the Midde Ages: Continuity and Change in Papal Relic Policy from the 6th to the 8th Century," in Ernst Dassmann and K. S. Frank, eds., *Pietas: Festschrift für Bernhard Kötting* (1980); H. Wagenvoort, "Contactus," in *Reallexikon für Antike und Christentum,* III (1957).

JOHN M. MCCULLOH

[See also **Gregory I the Great, Pope; Gregory of Tours; Relics, Western European; Translation of Saints.**]

BRANT, SEBASTIAN (1457–1521), was born at Strassburg and studied at the University of Basel from 1475 until 1484. In 1489 he joined the law faculty there, and also became active as an editor of scholarly texts, such as the works of Petrarch. In 1499 or 1500 he returned to Strassburg, where he served as city clerk until his death.

Brant wrote many pamphlets in German and Latin, as well as occasional, religious, didactic, and political poems. In them he emerges as a patriot, an ardent supporter of emperor and empire. Among his more important translations are works of Cato, Facetus, Moretus, and the German didactic poet Freidank.

Brant's fame stems from *Das Narrenschiff* (The ship of fools), published in 1494. The book became so popular that within the first year it went through three editions. In all, six editions were published during Brant's lifetime. The book's success was due in no small measure to the excellent woodcuts, many of them by Albrecht Dürer, that accompanied it. A Low German translation by Hans van Ghetelen appeared at Lübeck in 1497; one in French in the same year; one in Dutch in 1500; and one in English in 1509. The Latin translation by Jacob Locher *(Stultifera navis)* of 1497 is particularly to be credited with the acclaim the book received outside Brant's homeland, as well as with the respectability it enjoyed in humanistic circles.

In concept and style *Das Narrenschiff* belongs to the satiric genre of the Middle Ages, and stands in an old tradition, to a degree biblical in origin. With focus on moral-didactic-religious values, on what is wisdom in the eyes of God, and on the welfare of the soul, Brant seeks to teach; didacticism is the purpose of his work. But this didacticism is not predicated on an ascetic outlook or on world denial. Instead, it is paired with the view that man must seek to be effective in this life.

Brant sees follies as sins. This concept makes up the framework of his book: a ship—an entire fleet at first—sets off from Basel to the paradise of fools. Thus a touch of humor is added to the often scathing criticism Brant delivers. The motif of the ship, however, remains superficial; it is not developed into a coherent concept binding the disparate materials together.

The book contains 112 chapters arranged in what seems to be random order, without any transitions between them. Each chapter chastizes a type of fool who is depicted graphically in the accompanying woodcut. There is thus a pamphletlike quality about each chapter.

According to its preface, Brant's book means to be useful, to teach, to lead to disdain of all follies. All imaginable sins and weaknesses are scrutinized, but the order in which they appear defies any attempt at fathoming hierarchies of values. The Seven Deadly Sins are there, but so are fornication, adultery, ingratitude, blasphemy, dancing, shooting, gambling.

Brant writes in a vivid, clear style (although there is hobbling syntax), with a regular rhythm and constant rhyme scheme. A three-line motto closes most of the chapters.

Brant must be understood within his milieu, the urban bourgeoisie. In 1498 his friend Johann Geiler von Kaysersberg wrote a series of 146 sermons based on his book. Although a writer for the people, Brant belongs to the current of humanism through his studies and knowledge of classical literature, which provided him with much of his material for his collection of fools.

BIBLIOGRAPHY

Aurelius C. G. Pompen, *The English Versions of The Ship of Fools: A Contribution to the History of the Early French Renaissance in England* (1925, repr. 1967); Mary A. Rajewski, *Sebastian Brant: Studies in Religious Aspects of His Life and Works with Special Reference to the Varia Carmina* (1944); Manfred Lemmer, "Sebastian Brant," in *Die deutsche Literatur des Mittelalters: Verfasserlexikon*, Kurt Ruh, ed., I (1978), 992–1005.

HUGO BEKKER

BRASS. See **Bronze and Brass.**

BRATTISHING, a carved decorative parapet or cresting on top of a screen, cornice, or shrine. Brattishing is a feature of Gothic ornament, the most popular motifs being leaves, flowers, and crenellations.

LESLIE BRUBAKER

Detail of Brattishing. Shrine of St. Anno, 1175–1183. PHOTOGRAPH, RHEINISCHES BILDARCHIV, COLOGNE

BRAULIO OF SARAGOSSA, ST. (585/590–651), born at Ozma or Saragossa, came from a notable Spanish family: his father, Gregory, was a bishop; his brother John preceded him as bishop of Saragossa. His other brother, Fronimian, was abbot of the monastery of St. Emilian of Cogolla in the Rioja. Braulio was educated by his father and brother John, and later by Isidore of Seville. He is believed to have returned to Saragossa in 619 or 620 to serve as archdeacon, and he became bishop in 631. He was present at the fourth, fifth, and sixth councils of Toledo (633, 636, 638). He died at Saragossa.

Braulio's major literary contribution was a life of St. Emilian, a saint from the Rioja, to whom he and his brothers were devoted. He also left a collection of forty-three letters, most of which were written by him but some were written to him. Many concern matters of religious practice and doctrine, but some are personal, including several letters to Isidore of Seville.

BIBLIOGRAPHY

Braulio's *Epistolario de San Braulio* (1975) and *Sancti Braulionis vita sancti Emiliani* (1943) are translated in Claude W. Barlow, comp. and trans.,*The Fathers of the Church: Iberian Fathers,* II (1969). See also Charles Henry Lynch, *Saint Braulio, Bishop of Saragossa (631–651): His Life and Writings* (1938).

LEAH SHOPKOW

[See also **Isidore of Seville.**]

BREAD. A bread of sorts can be made from the flour of any cereal, but the quality varies enormously, depending on the source of the flour and the method of preparation. It is probable that, throughout the Middle Ages, the majority consumed more cereal as porridge than as bread. Einkorn and the Italian (foxtail) and panic millets were usually eaten in this form. The most common type of bread was a flat, unleavened "cake" cooked on an iron griddle and most frequently made from barley and oats. Emmer and durum wheat could make raised breads of sorts, but were distinctly inferior to bread wheat and spelt for that purpose. Rye, unadulterated with wheat, yielded a very dark, heavy bread. Raised breads were baked in oval ovens like those used by the Romans. Brewer's yeast was the usual leaven.

Fine, white flour was produced, but was expensive and only for special occasions or for the rich and privileged. A carefully adjusted mill could grind off the bran, which could be screened from the groats. The mill could then be reset, and the groats ground to white flour. Fine flour was "bolted," passed through a cloth sieve. Another method of debranning was to grind the grain rather coarsely, then pass it through a searce, or hair sieve. The bran was sometimes fed to livestock, but could also be mixed with flour and eaten by the poor. Most country mills could not be adjusted very finely, and usually ground the grains whole. Many households had hand mills that ground whole grains. Whole wheat flour was brownish, and since it was not degermed the oils in it tended to become rancid. Bleached flour was unknown. Stone grinding added significant quantities of grit to the flour, and teeth were often worn to the gum line by middle age.

Raised white bread was the standard in imperial Rome, and spread through Gaul and Britain; in the north brown and black bread were the rule. Brown breads were usually prepared from maslin flour (from field mixtures of wheat and rye). Drage flour (from field mixtures of barley and oats) was used for flat bread. The black breads were primarily of rye flour.

The transition from porridge to griddle cakes to baked raised bread was slow in the north. According to Gille, the Old German word for bread did "not become differentiated from other culinary terms until the tenth century." Nevertheless, white flour was a prestige item, and as the economy prospered, more white bread was consumed and the black breads were lightened by addition of wheat flour. In periods of economic decline and depopulation, the people reverted to heavier, coarser breads and porridge.

Contamination of flour by organic poisons was a chronic problem, and occasionally resulted in severe outbreaks of neurological disorders. Rye is especially susceptible to ergot *(Claviceps)* infection, and ergotism was often serious in wet years. Tares *(Lolium temulentum)*, a common weed of wheat, was often infested by a fungus also causing nervous disorders. Contamination by weed seeds, chaff, weevils, and flour beetles was also common.

BIBLIOGRAPHY

Bertrand Gille, "The Medieval Age of the West," in Maurice Daumas, ed., *A History of Technology and Invention,* I, E. G. Hennessy, trans. (1969).

JACK R. HARLAN

[See also **Agriculture; Cookery; Food Trades; Grain Crops; Mills; Ovens.**]

BREHON LAW. See **Law, Irish.**

BRETA SQGUR, a translation of Geoffrey of Monmouth's *Historia regum Britanniae* (late 1130's) into Old Norse, is preserved in two vellum manuscripts: *Hauksbók* (AM 544 4°) and AM 573 4°. Only the *Hauksbók* redaction has been published in its entirety, but a critical edition of the saga is being prepared (Editiones Arnamagnaeanae, ser. A, X).

In both manuscripts *Breta sǫgur* is a continuation of *Trójumanna saga,* the story of the Trojan War. Vergil's *Aeneid* provides most of the transitional material, and the translation of Geoffrey's history begins in chapter 6 with the legendary tale of Brutus, the great grandson of Aeneas and eponymous ancestor of the British. Major sections deal with King Lear, the Roman invasions (Julius Caesar), the coming of the Angles and Saxons (Hengist and Horsa), King Vortigern and Merlin the Magician, and King Arthur. Geoffrey's history ends in A.D. 689 (*Hauksbók,* 679), but an epilogue in *Breta sǫgur* contains, in addition to material from Geoffrey's prologue, a list deriving from the Icelandic annals of later English kings.

The text in *Hauksbók* (early fourteenth century) is complete but abridged. The scribe, Haukr Erlendsson (*d.* 1334), shortened, in particular, longer conversations and lists of names, and revised and polished the language. AM 573 4° (fourteenth century) is defective and has many lacunae but the fragments contain a more complete translation than *Hauksbók.* Some materials are interpolated, including *Valvens Þáttr* (a translation of Chrétien de Troyes's *Perceval*), in the midst of which this manuscript breaks off. Each manuscript preserves some original material not found in the other.

Merlínusspá, a poetic translation of Geoffrey's "*Prophetiae Merlini,*" is interpolated into the *Hauksbók* version of *Breta sǫgur* at the appropriate place (chs. 28–29; *Historia* 7. 3–4, or chs. 111–117 in Faral's edition). AM 573 4° mentions the work but does not include it because "many people know it by heart." Both manuscripts attribute the verse translation to Gunnlaugr Leifsson, a monk at the Benedictine monastery at Þingeyrar in northern Iceland (*d.* 1218–1219) known primarily as the author of Latin hagiographic works. The two sections of the "Prophetiae Merlini" are rendered in *Merlínusspá* as two independent long poems (the two poems are inexplicably reversed in the manuscript). The composition

BRETHREN OF THE COMMON LIFE

mixes Eddic and skaldic meter and is technically proficient but poetically mediocre.

The translation of *Breta sǫgur* is generally good. Some passages are translated verbatim, but most sections are only roughly rendered into Old Norse. The date of the original translation is uncertain. It may have been made in Iceland soon after 1200, or it may be a Norwegian courtly translation from the mid thirteenth century. The translation of *Merlínusspá* is usually assigned to about 1200. Gunnlaugr must have known more of the *Historia regum Britanniae* than only Merlin's prophecies, and his rendering of the prophecies may have been the impetus for the translation of the entire history of the kings of Britain into Old Norse.

BIBLIOGRAPHY

"Trójumanna saga ok Breta sögur, efter Hauksbók," Jón Sigurðsson, ed. and trans., in *Annaler for nordisk Oldkyndighed og Historie* (1848), 102–215, (1849), 3–145; Geoffrey of Monmouth, *Historia regum Britanniae,* in *La légende arthurienne: Études et documents,* III pt. 1, Edmond Faral, ed. (1929); A. G. van Hamel, "The Old-Norse Version of the *Historia regum Britanniae* and the Text of Geoffrey of Monmouth," in *Études celtiques,* **1** (1936); J. S. Eysteinsson, "The Relationship of *Merlínússpá* and Geoffrey of Monmouth's *Historia,*" in *Saga-Book of the Viking Society for Northern Research,* **14** (1953–1957).

James E. Knirk

[See also **Geoffrey of Monmouth; Trójumanna Saga; Troy Story.**]

BRETHREN OF THE COMMON LIFE. The Brethren of the Common Life were part of a late medieval religious movement that emphasized communal living and meditation. The broader movement, called the Devotio Moderna, included the Brethren, the Sisters of the Common Life, and the Congregation of Windesheim. These communities sprang up in the Low Countries between 1380 and 1400, and expanded into Germany before most of them lost vitality and disappeared after 1600.

The Devotio Moderna was influenced by the monastic atmosphere of the period, but its adherents were by no means all monks. The Sisters were laywomen who lived together in houses and gave their property to the community. This common ownership distinguished them from groups of women like Beguines, who were frequently suspected of heresy. The Brethren also practiced common ownership of property, but they included priests in their number. In fact, the Brethren were a heavily clerical community: during the first thirty years, sixteen of twenty-five members were priests. The Congregation of Windesheim consisted of cloisters that contained regular canons bound to the communities by monastic vows. Both the Congregation, which owed its founding to the Brethren, and the Sisters surpassed the Brethren in numbers of houses during the fifteenth century. Around 1460 the historian of the Devotio Moderna, John Busch, counted eighty monasteries belonging to the Congregation, thirty-two houses of Sisters, and only eighteen houses belonging to the Brethren of the Common Life.

A major purpose of the Brethren was to prepare young men for the priesthood and the monastery. They provided lodging and board for schoolboys, and served as spiritual counselors and tutors for them. The Brethren seldom had schools of their own, although they would occasionally teach in a city or parish school. In their own houses, however, they held colloquies *(collationes)* for schoolboys after church on Sundays. Brief addresses were followed by conversation in small groups or by an interview with a priest. As part of their spiritual task, the Brethren served as chaplains in houses of the Sisters. They spent the rest of their time copying books, worshiping, preaching, meditating, and attending to the upkeep of their houses.

These tasks corresponded to the ideals of Geert de Groote, who laid the foundation for the Brethren before he died in 1384. Born into a wealthy family at Deventer in 1340, Groote studied law in Paris before he was converted to the ascetic life in 1374. He returned to his hometown and turned over most of his house to a few women for their use. Groote then retired to the Carthusian monastery of Monnikhuizen near Arnhem. Encouraged by the monks to go out into the world and preach, he left the monastery and was ordained a deacon in the diocese of Utrecht in 1380. The last four years of his life were filled with activity. Groote traveled throughout the Low Countries, preaching reform and discipline. A strong denunciation of the clergy of Utrecht who were living as married men resulted in the suspension of his right to preach. He also counseled young persons seeking to enter monasteries, gave legal advice, corresponded with school rectors, studied a variety of books, and arranged to have good books copied by young assistants. By the time Groote died, small groups of disciples had begun to gather in Zwolle, Deventer, and Kampen.

BRETHREN OF THE COMMON LIFE

One of these disciples, Florens Radewijns, a priest in Deventer, gathered in his vicarage "young men of good will," and became the leader of the Brethren. He moved rapidly to expand the group. The brothers soon moved out of the vicarage, making room for schoolboys under their guidance, and by 1402 a new house was constructed for the young scholars in Deventer. They did not study with the Brethren, however, since few of the brothers had formal theological training. Rather, they lived with the Brethren while studying at the well-known school in Deventer, then joined the Brethren as clerics (candidates for the priesthood), entered the monastery, or left the tutelage of the Brethren and pursued other careers.

When an epidemic struck Deventer in 1398, Florens and several colleagues left to reinforce a new community that had just been founded in Amersfoort. The house at Deventer was also responsible for foundations in Delft, Louvain, and Emmerich. After spending a year in Deventer, Henry of Ahaus established a community in Münster (1401), which became the center of the movement in Westphalia; he also founded the houses in Cologne (1417) and Wesel (1435). Further east, the Brethren settled in Hildesheim, Marburg, and Rostock. Brothers from a short-lived community in Osnabrück founded the house in Herford around 1430. Another early group of the Brethren flourished in Zwolle, especially under the leadership of Dirk of Herxen, the energetic rector of the house from 1410 to 1457. By 1482 the Zwolle house had increased its membership to thirty-five brothers. During these same years five new houses were founded from Zwolle: 's-Hertogenbosch (1424), Doesburg (1426), Groningen (1435), Harderwijk (1441), and Culm (Chelmno).

From the statutes *(consuetudines)* that Dirk of Herxen wrote for the Zwolle fraternity in 1415 we receive a clear picture of the life of the Brethren. The priests and clerics rose at half past three and prepared themselves for reading the canonical hours. Every morning an hour was set aside for the study of Scripture, and the brothers went to the parish church to hear Mass. They labored at their copying for seven to eight hours per day. There was reading aloud during meals, with checks to see if the brothers were listening; on Sundays and feast days the brothers came together for discussion of a Scripture passage. Only one hour per day remained at the personal disposal of the brothers. They elected a rector to preside over each house and a procurator to assist him.

The life of the Brethren resembled the life of monks or of chapter clergy. This similarity was reinforced by two developments. First, some houses sought the status of a chapter; second, houses formed themselves into associations around important foundations like Zwolle and Münster. In addition, the Brethren were closely related to the Windesheim Congregation and to houses along the Rhine and in southern Germany that strongly resembled clergy chapters. A loose union of these canon-brotherhouses included the establishments at Marienthal, Königstein, and Butzbach.

The Brethren helped to found the first monastery at Windesheim in 1386, and several brothers from Deventer were among the first inhabitants. The earliest monasteries joined together in the Windesheim Congregation in 1394–1395; three years later the monastery at Mount St. Agnes, near Zwolle, was placed under the direction of Windesheim. The cloisters in the congregation supported each other in matters of personnel and discipline, and cooperated in carrying out the annual inspection of the houses. The first prior of the house at Mount St. Agnes was John Hemerken of Kempen, the older brother of Thomas Hemerken of Kempen (à Kempis), who followed his brother into the monastery. The Windesheim cloisters were well equipped for the task of preparing uniform liturgical texts and a new edition of the Vulgate, their most impressive accomplishment. The Council of Basel entrusted the Congregation with the reform of monasteries in the dioceses of Verden, Halberstadt, and Hildesheim.

These chapters or monasteries differed from the brotherhouses in important ways. The property of a chapter belonged to the church, and burial rights were granted on the property. The authority of a superior was established by church law, and the singing of canonical hours and of festival Masses was required. None of these stipulations, including monastic vows, applied to the Brethren. They promised only to live together purely and harmoniously, and with all property held in common. Still, in their daily routine they followed so many monastic practices that they were accused of starting a new monastic order without ecclesiastical sanction. More and more brotherhouses applied for chapter status in the fifteenth century, and almost all of the sisterhouses ended up adopting the rule of a third order.

A special similarity to monasticism was the cultivation of the spiritual life through meditation. The Brethren did not exalt meditation above the singing of canonical hours and other external forms of worship, nor did they set aside long periods of medita-

BRETHREN OF THE COMMON LIFE

tion on a daily basis. Instead, they encouraged the practice of meditation throughout the day as rumination upon a designated text or religious topic. The Brethren did, however, possess several masters of meditation who wrote about the art and provided material for others. Gerard Zerbolt of Zutphen, according to R. R. Post, "was the most fertile and the most successful writer the Brothers ever produced." Before he died in 1398, Gerard wrote two widely circulated devotional treatises: *The Reform of the Soul's Powers* and *Spiritual Ascents.* Both works describe the way in which the soul can overcome the damage it suffered in the Fall, and attain to pure love of God. These works may have influenced Ignatius of Loyola, and anticipated the form of his *Spiritual Exercises.*

The rector of Zwolle, Dirk of Herxen, composed material for meditation on seven topics, including the Passion of Christ, the Lord's Prayer, the Ave Maria, and death and heaven. He also suggested writing key words on the hand in order to assist concentration. This technique was later advocated by the Windesheim canon, John Mombaer, in his popular devotional work, *The Rose Garden of Spiritual Exercises* (1494). Mombaer intended to help the Brethren cultivate the three beds in the rose garden of their spiritual life: the canonical hours, Holy Communion, and meditation. In order to prevent distraction, he suggested the *chiropsalterium.* It reminded the person praying the hours to reflect on a devotional theme by stroking the fingers of one hand with the thumb. Mombaer also provided schematic devices for meditating on Communion. The *Rose Garden* illustrates two characteristics of the devotional life of the Brethren. First, it demonstrates that external forms of worship were as important as private meditation. Second, it provides a method whereby a brother could focus on meditation while engaged in other tasks throughout the day. Like the monasteries, the houses of the Brethren combined communal worship with private devotion, and refused to separate even manual labor from the devotional life.

The most famous spiritual writer associated with the Brethren was Thomas à Kempis, a canon at Mount St. Agnes and therefore not, strictly speaking, a member of the Brethren. As a Windesheim canon, however, he had close contact with the Brethren and compiled his treatises as guides for the spiritual life of the monks and of the brothers. The *Imitation of Christ* is his best-known work, and one of the most popular devotional works of all time. It consists of four treatises, each written separately and circulated before they were combined in a manuscript dating from the 1440's. Serious doubts have been raised about Thomas' authorship, and there is good reason to believe that he may have served as editor rather than as author of the material. A strong tradition nevertheless attaches his name to the work as a whole.

The first three books deal with the spiritual life in general, whereas the last is a treatise on preparation for Holy Communion. Although the counsels are directed specifically at the ordered religious life, their simplicity and directness have endeared the work to generations of religious people. "He rides very pleasantly who is carried by the grace of God" (2.9) is a typical statement from the *Imitation* that could appeal to many outside the cloister. The injunctions against vain and worldly learning are also typical of the attitude of the Brethren toward academic pursuits. Like Thomas, they believed that one should study only to refresh the soul.

Despite this attitude, several important figures in late medieval theology, in the humanist movement, and in the Reformation have been linked to the Brethren. Wessel Gansfort (*d.* 1489), born in Groningen, lived in one of the brothers' hostels and attended their colloquies while he was a pupil in Zwolle. After years in university circles in Cologne, Heidelberg, and Paris, Wessel returned to his hometown as a scholar of renown. He then made contact with the canons at Mount St. Agnes and dedicated to them a book that may have influenced Mombaer's writings on meditation. Although Wessel wrote a number of ascetic works, his theology was shaped by the nominalism he encountered in Paris rather than by the Brethren.

Unlike Wessel, the principal late medieval representative of nominalism, Gabriel Biel (*d.* 1495), did belong to the Brothers of the Common Life. For nine years (1468–1477) he served as prior of the chapter in Butzbach, and in 1471 he founded a general chapter of Brethren houses on the Upper Rhine. In 1477 Biel was invited to establish the first chapter of the Brethren in Württemberg, at Urach. After retiring from his teaching post at the University of Tübingen, he served as rector of the house of St. Peter at Einsiedel near Tübingen in Schönbuch. It was a unique community of Brethren consisting of three separate classes (canons, nobles, burghers) and adapting the principles of the common life to each class.

BRETHREN OF THE COMMON LIFE

Although Biel did not owe his nominalist theology as such to the Brethren, his life as a brother enriched his theology and influenced the religious atmosphere at Tübingen. In a treatise on the common life, Biel contrasted the freedom of life among the Brethren with the obligation of the monks to obey additional precepts. His contribution to the Brethren as a leader and organizer was substantial, but his position as a university-trained prior was not typical.

The prince of the humanists, Erasmus of Rotterdam, had contact with the Brethren, but he did not think very highly of them. In 's-Hertogenbosch he lived in the Brethren hostel (1484–1487) and received instruction from one of the brothers because he was too advanced for the city school. Erasmus scorned his teacher, however, and felt that these years of his life were wasted. The simple piety that Erasmus advocated in his writings was not unlike that of the Brethren, but influence is difficult to prove. The suspicion of learning that prevailed among the Brethren was shared by Erasmus only in regard to Scholastic theology. It did not extend to the humanist interest in the ancient sources and in education that permeated northern Europe in the late fifteenth century.

More Brethren houses established schools in the late fifteenth and early sixteenth centuries, but they were joining a movement that had preceded them. Their copying activity was gradually rendered obsolete with the advent of printing, although some houses established presses. The well-known humanist teacher Alexander Hegius (*d.* 1498) was a friend of the Brethren in Deventer, but the Brethren as a whole are better described as occasional participants in the humanist movement than as pioneers of that movement in northern Europe.

The Brethren contributed little to the Reformation, and no Protestant leaders of note belonged to the brotherhood. Martin Luther may have lived in their hostel in Magdeburg in 1497, but they had no school in Magdeburg for him to attend. Some houses of the Brethren had direct encounters with Protestantism. Both Luther and his colleague Philipp Melanchthon advised the Brethren at Herford how to survive by adopting Protestantism, and Luther defended their house against the city council and the Protestant preachers. The brothers observed the communal life as Protestants by substituting the study of Scripture for daily Mass and by celebrating Holy Communion on Sundays in Protestant fashion. The house in Rostock printed a Low German New Testament based on Jerome Emser's version of Luther's translation. Luther protested, and the city council of Rostock eventually shut down the brothers' press. In 1559 the house ceded all its property to the city at the order of the Protestant city council.

Most houses were likewise stifled by the Reformation, and soon disappeared. Either they were unable to gain new recruits or they were dissolved, like the monasteries, when Protestantism was established in a territory. The founding houses of Deventer and Zwolle suffered the latter fate around 1580, after holding out for half a century. Most of the houses had disappeared by 1600, except for Herford and the house at Münster, which remained Catholic and continued to function until 1803.

The Brethren of the Common Life represented a resurgence of monastic spirituality on the eve of the Reformation. They anticipated the Protestant movement only superficially in their focus on Scripture as the basis of meditation and as a text to be preserved. They were partly swept up in the new wave of learning called humanism, but they did not effectively promote it. Their success in living a common life of regular devotion outside the walls of the cloister and without monastic rules was a significant departure from monastic forms. But their disdain for higher learning and their strict religious observance marked them as genuinely expressing a piety that was still vibrant at the end of the Middle Ages.

BIBLIOGRAPHY

Bibliographical Works. Erwin Iserloh, "The Devotio Moderna," in Hans-Georg Beck *et al.*, eds., *From the High Middle Ages to the Eve of the Reformation* (1970), 723–727; Ernest Persoons, *Recente publicaties over de moderne devotie 1959–1972* (1972).

Sources. Johann Busch, *Des Augustinerpropstes Johannes Busch Chronicon Windeshemense, und Liber de reformatione monasteriorum,* Karl L. Grube, ed. (1886); Albert Hyma, *The Christian Renaissance* (1925), 440–476; Thomas Hemerken à Kempis, *Opera omnia,* M. J. Pohl, ed., 7 vols. (1902–1922).

General Studies. Stephaan Axters, *Geschiedenis van de vroomheid in de Nederlanden,* III (1956); Ernst Barnikol, *Studien zur Geschichte der Brüder vom Gemeinsamen Leben* (1917); Albert Hyma, *The Brethren of the Common Life* (1950); Regnerus R. Post, *The Modern Devotion* (1968).

Specific Studies. Georgette Epiney-Burgard, *Gérard Grote (1340–1384) et les débuts de la dévotion moderne* (1970); Paul Mestwerdt, *Die Anfänge des Erasmus: Humanismus und "Devotio moderna,"* Hans von Schubert, ed. (1917); Heiko A. Oberman, *Werden und Wertung der Reformation: Vom Wegestreit zum Glaubenskampf*

(1977), 56–71; Robert Stupperich, *Das Herforder Fraterhaus und die devotio moderna* (1975); T. P. van Zijl, *Gerard Groote: Ascetic and Reformer, 1340–1384* (1963).

SCOTT H. HENDRIX

[See also **Biel, Gabriel; Chapter; Devotio Moderna; Groote, Geert de; Thomas à Kempis.**]

BRETON LAYS. See **Lai.**

BRETON LITERATURE. The Old Breton period extended from the fifth to the eleventh century and was followed by the Middle Breton period, ending in the seventeenth century. The only Old Breton words still extant are glosses in Latin manuscripts of the ninth and tenth centuries, now scattered all over Europe because of the exodus from Brittany caused by Norman invasions, and personal and local names in eleventh- or twelfth-century charters, such as those of Redon, Landévennec, and Bégard.

It is likely that there was a very highly developed oral tradition in Brittany in the Middle Ages. The Quimperlé Cartulary mentions several authors' names: Dunguallun (*cantor*), Cadiou (*citharista*), and Riuallon (*filius an Bard*). The twelfth-century lais of Marie de France—narrative poems sung with musical accompaniment—follow such a Breton oral tradition; and on the evidence of names, it would appear that the Old Breton literature inspired much in the Arthurian cycle, the story of Tristan and Iseult, and the romances of Chrétien de Troyes.

The earliest piece of connected Breton known to us is found in a fourteenth-century manuscript. It is a short love poem of four lines by a scribe weary of his toil, beginning

> An guen heguen am louenas
> An hegarat an lacat glas.
> [The fair one, her cheek gladdened me,
> The lovable one of the blue eye.]

This poem might have been common knowledge at the time and therefore typical of Middle Breton poetry. The versification of Breton poetry is very complex. Its main principle is that the penultimate syllable in a line should rhyme with one or more other syllables in the same line.

Several texts date from the fifteenth century: fragments of the *Destruction of Jerusalem* and the *Life of Saint Gwenole;* a 247-line poem, the *Dialogue Between Arthur and Guynglaff,* which has been transmitted in very damaged form through successive copies; the *Life of Saint Nonn and Her Son Devy;* and the Middle Breton Hours, a religious book drawn up for the use of the nobility. What is left to us of medieval Breton literature is of less interest than the indirect evidence.

BIBLIOGRAPHY

Claude Evans, "Les noms bretons dans les chartes de l'Abbaye de Bégard 1156–1450: Étude philologique et pièces justificatives" (Ph.D. diss., Univ. of Toronto, 1975); Léon Fleuriot, "La littérature bretonne dans ses rapports avec l'histoire," in Jean Delumeau, ed., *Documents de l'histoire de Bretagne* (1971), 97–98, 155–169; Roparz Hemon and Gwennole Le Menn, eds., *Les fragments de la Destruction de Jérusalem et des Amours du vieillard* (1969); Roger S. Loomis, *Arthurian Literature in the Middle Ages* (1959); Joseph Marie Loth, "Le plus ancien texte suivi en Breton," in *Revue celtique,* **34** (1913, repr. 1923).

CLAUDE EVANS

[See also **Arthurian Literature; French Literature (after 1200); Marie de France; Tristan.**]

BREVIARUM. See **Nikephoros, Patriarch.**

BREVIARY, the liturgical book of the Roman Catholic church that, before the reform ordered by the Second Vatican Council, contained the formularies of daily prayer. The Latin *breviarium* means "an abridgment"—in this case a combination and reduction into a more convenient form and size of various books (psalter, antiphonary, lectionary, homiliary, passional, hymnal, collectarium) that were used as an ensemble in the recitation or chanting of the Divine Office.

In the eleventh century small groups of clerics (later known as canons regular) sought by their common life to improve the status of the clergy. These communities of canons, inspired by monastic practices, accepted the obligation to maintain the Divine Office, but their small size made it impossible for them to do so in any elaborate way. Whereas large monastic communities had the personnel to arrange the various books needed for the offices of the different hours, seasons, and feasts, the small communities of canons lacked such resources. A guide that would

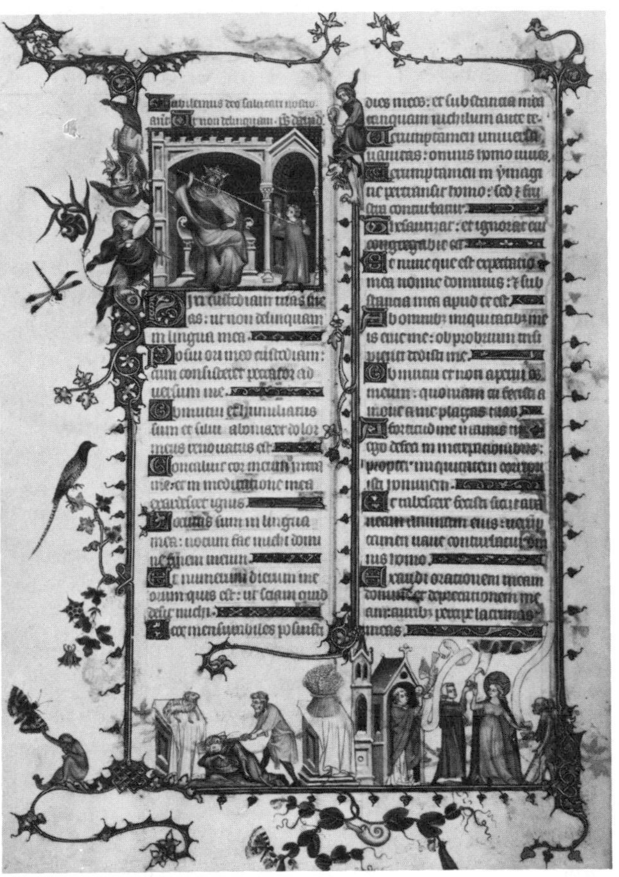

Page from the Belleville Breviary by Jean Pucelle (*ca.* 1325). BIBLIOTHÈQUE NATIONALE

help them to assemble the necessary texts and provide a clear "order of service" would be very welcome. Out of this need came the ordo, a kind of outline, which later served as the nucleus of the *breviarium.*

The desire for order in the offices is seen in the process by which the collectariums—the books of collects to be read by the celebrant, especially at the end of each canonical hour of prayer—attracted other texts to themselves. Some of these composite books contain whole offices (apart from lessons) that seem to have served as samples to indicate the order of texts for other occasions; some contain the psalter with the necessary antiphons; some contain only texts for feasts; and some have only the commons of the saints. To one such book, obtained by the monastery of Monte Cassino about 1100, was attached an ordo specifying for each day and for each canonical hour the texts to be sung, with their incipits. Its title is significant: *Breviarium sive ordo officiorum per totam anni decursionem* (A short conspectus or order for the services of the whole year). Dom Pierre Salmon thinks that this is doubtless the origin of the word "breviary" for the book containing the Divine Office. All that remained to be done to produce the breviary properly so called was to reunite the full texts with their incipits.

Thus the origin of the breviary is not to be found in the desire to provide a short, handy version of the Office for increasingly mobile clergy, although it became such in the thirteenth century and later. By far the greatest number of the oldest breviaries are monastic, choral and noted for singing (though some monastic breviaries are not noted); also, since these breviaries are books of 200 to 300 folios, they can scarcely be considered portable or handy. If larger than twenty centimeters, they were used only in the choir; if smaller, they could be carried around and used for private recitation. Breviaries rarely were richly illustrated except by individual commission—for instance, by Jean Pucelle for Jeanne de Belleville about 1325, and by the Bedford Master for the duke of Bedford, 1424–1425.

The Monte Cassino manuscript is the most ancient one known to contain within one volume the whole of the canonical Office: psalter, canticles, litanies, hymnary, collects, blessings for the lessons, short Scripture readings, antiphons, responsories, and lessons for certain offices. Another manuscript, contemporary with the preceding one and also from Monte Cassino, contains propers of each season and of the saints, thus serving to complete the first-mentioned one. Other examples of the breviary date from the twelfth century and are all Benedictine; they testify that even monks needed and welcomed such assistance as they arranged the many texts for the offices.

The reforms of the Office under Innocent III (1198–1216) further promoted the process of consolidation. Innocent supervised the reorganization of the Office of the *capella papalis,* the papal chapel in which the pope and his chaplains celebrated the Office whenever the pope was not celebrating the liturgy in one of the Roman stational churches. In the eleventh century, under Gregory VII, the Office of the Papal Chapel was still the old Roman Office (marked, for example, by the exclusion of three-lesson feasts in Lent and a sparing use of antiphons). As the papal chaplains became curial officials, they lacked the time and inclination to sing the full offices with their sometimes difficult and ever-changing antiphons. Thus, the public Office was celebrated as

BREVIARY

usual in the Lateran basilica, while the "papal" Office was recited less solemnly and quasi-privately in the papal chapel (later known as the *curia romana,* and finally as the *ecclesia romana*).

To alleviate further the burden on his chaplains, Innocent ordered a codification of the books of the Lateran that resulted in the simpler ordo that bears his name. All the elements of the Office were then gathered together for convenience, though it is not clear whether the result was one book or two. The new Office was more convenient, better adapted, and less cumbersome; its contents were generally a monastic Office in the old Roman basilican tradition (a mixture of Roman, Germano-Gallican, and monastic customs). There was the age-old distribution of psalms throughout the week, as well as some hymns and responsories, antiphons, and lesser elements. Scripture reading had a generous place in this Office (whole epistles sometimes being read in a week); the patristic texts were drawn from wider sources than those found in the earlier Roman Office. Such was the office known as the Office of the *ecclesia romana* (the title by which the papal curia was known), although its use was still a privilege reserved to the curia.

In the early thirteenth century the privilege of using this relatively brief and simple Office was extended to the newly formed Order of Friars Minor, or Franciscans. Unlike the monks or canons, the Franciscans were not a sedentary order vowed to stability, but a mobile, preaching order. As their order developed, the friars came to be inscribed in a "province" according to a decision of their provincial, or even to work across different provinces; thus, they needed to adopt liturgical practices that were uniform and not subject to frequent change. They sought an abridged Office, convenient to handle and contained in a single volume small enough to be carried on their missionary journeys and by which they could remain united in prayer. Their brotherhood could thus be liturgically expressed by common forms of the Office in whatever location or occupation they found themselves.

The Franciscans adopted the *breviarium romanae curiae* with papal permission in 1223, but adapted it to their own needs in 1240; further abbreviation of the curial Office was found necessary to produce a truly portable book. Under their general, Haymo of Faversham, and with the approval of Gregory IX, the Franciscans shortened the scriptural and patristic lessons into simple excerpts. The Gallican version of the psalter was substituted for the Roman.

Such changes reflected the increased concern for those who could not pray the Office corporately in choir. Although the Middle Ages saw an increasing tendency to insist on the private recitation of a canonical hour by an individual monk or cleric who for some reason had to be absent from choir, the obligation to pray the Office had long been regarded as one invested in a local church or religious community. Now the obligation became increasingly seen as one invested in an individual by reason of religious or clerical status—an obligation thus divorced from place. As the obligation of daily recitation developed from the community to the indivdual, it became increasingly necessary for each person so obligated to have a portable breviary containing all the necessary texts; previously memory had supplied choir parts of the Office, and there had been at least eight special books for different liturgical roles.

The handiness of the book that became known as the "Roman breviary" appealed to clerics who could not assist at the Office in choir but still had to recite it in private. This obligation had been gaining pace from the eleventh century, and later there was a tendency to insist on the value of the Office in itself, abstracted from its celebration. Eventually those who could not say the Office in choir were expected to do so alone. At the same time there was an increasing desire to obtain dispensations from the choral Office because of the demands of pastoral, academic, and political life. As time passed and dispensations multiplied, clerics began to forget that solitary recitation of the Office was supposed to occur only when one was unavoidably absent from choral celebration. Thus the breviary became not only the name of a book but really a whole attitude toward prayer.

The Franciscan order assured that the breviary approved by Gregory IX had a wide diffusion and a considerable success. As its convenience became appreciated throughout western Europe, this single book gradually came to replace the host of books formerly needed for the celebration of the Office. Nicholas III (1277–1280), a Franciscan tertiary, adopted this Romano/Franciscan breviary not merely for the curia but also for the Roman basilicas—thus replacing their ancient Roman Office. Benedict XII made it obligatory at Avignon in 1337; when Gregory XI and the papal court returned to Rome in 1376, the curial Office as modified by the Franciscans was retained, and Gregory made it obligatory at the Lateran. The printing press later made this breviary available and popular on a large scale, and the printing on a smaller scale of more cumbersome, local (non-Roman) Offices became prohibitive.

Thus the Roman breviary came to predominate in the Western church, although each diocese retained its particular features (principally local feasts). Yet widespread feeling that the Office was filled with complexities and inaccuracies led to increasing agitation for a reform of the breviary under papal supervision. This was accomplished by Cardinal Francisco de Quiñones, general of the Franciscan order, under Paul III in 1535, and more definitively by a commission under Pius V in 1568. The breviary of Pius V, the first universal breviary, remained substantially unchanged as the official book of the Divine Office until the *Liturgia horarum* was approved by Paul VI in 1970.

BIBLIOGRAPHY

Primary sources. The Hours of the Divine Office in English and Latin, 3 vols. (1963); *The Roman Breviary,* John, marquess of Bute, trans. (1908).

Secondary sources. Pierre Batiffol, *History of the Roman Breviary,* Atwell M. Y. Baylay, trans. (1898); Dom Suitbert Bäumer, *Geschichte des Breviers: Versuch einer quellenmässingen Darstellung der Entwicklung des altkirchlichen und des römischen Officiums bis auf unsere Tage* (1895); James D. Crichton, *Christian Celebration: The Prayer of the Church* (1976); S. J. P. van Dijk, ed., *Sources of the Modern Roman Liturgy,* 2 vols. (1963); S. J. P. van Dijk and J. H. Walker, *The Origins of the Modern Roman Liturgy* (1960); Dom Pierre Salmon, "Aux origines du bréviaire romain," in *La maison-Dieu,* 27 (1951); *L'office divin: Histoire de la formation du bréviaire* (1959), trans. as *The Breviary Through the Centuries* by Sister David Mary, S.N.J.M. (1962); and "L'office divin au moyen âge: Histoire de la formation du bréviaire du IXe au XVIe siècle," in *Lex orandi,* 43 (1967).

MICHAEL KWATERA, O.S.B.

[See also **Antiphon; Antiphonal; Books of Hours; Curia, Papal; Divine Office; Franciscans; Lectionary (Liturgy); Psalter, Liturgical.**]

BREVIARY OF ALARIC, a collection of laws copied between 804 and 814 by the scribe Audgarius; now in Paris (Bibliothèque Nationale, cod. lat. 4404). Although the character of the script is adequate, the inferior quality of the illustrations suggests that the

Page from the Breviary of Alaric showing emperors and jurisconsults, *ca.* 804–814, cod. lat. 4404. BIBLIOTHÈQUE NATIONALE

manuscript was produced in a provincial area, possibly Narbonne. The opening pictures of emperors and jurisconsults show interlace frames that Porcher believes indicative of Hiberno-Saxon influence on the Continent.

BIBLIOGRAPHY

Jean Porcher, "La peinture provenciale," in Wolfgang Braunfels, ed., *Karl der Grosse. Lebenswerk und Nachleben,* vol. III: *Karolingische Kunst* (1965), 63.

LESLIE BRUBAKER

BREWING. Most preliterate peoples have known beer and wine. One or the other was an ingredient of 15 percent of the recipes in an Egyptian medical tract (papyrus Ebers) of about 1500 B.C. But they were also consumed by the healthy; it has been estimated that as much as 40 percent of the cereal production of ancient Mesopotamia (4000–3000 B.C.) was used in brewing. Small wonder that the regulation of drinking hours appears as early as Hammurabi (*ca.* 1770 B.C.). It must be added, however, that the hazardous quality of "drinking" water gave ample incentive for the substitution of wine and beer, both relatively "germfree" because of the care exercised (to prevent souring) in their production. Intoxication was very probably the lesser evil.

As primordial beverages, wine and beer had many names, and were not always clearly distinguished. Mead (Latin, *hydromel*), a drink made with fermented honey, was probably as early, and it was often mixed with wine. Both were flavored by adding spices of various kinds. In the Middle Ages the beverage made by fermenting grain, most commonly known in Latin as *cervesia,* would have been what we call ale, unless hops were added, a practice known in ancient Mesopotamia but apparently not in western Europe before the eighth century.

The basic discovery was "malting," a process in which grain, particularly barley, is wetted and allowed to swell. When the resulting "malt" is treated with hot water ("mashing"), the product is a brown liquid known as wort, which, when drained off the spent grain and allowed to ferment, yields ale. The fermentation was facilitated by the addition of yeast as early as the second millennium B.C., although yeast was not clearly defined before the nineteenth century of the Christian era. Today the name "yeast" applies to various unicellular organisms found throughout nature. These organisms make fermentation possible, and make it efficient when added in sufficient quantity. They are concentrated in the froth and sediment from brewing, and it is likely that the purposeful addition of these residues to subsequent batches was an empirical discovery that led to their deliberate use by the brewer and to their identification as a discrete material. "Yeast" appears in the English language as early as A.D. 1000 as "yest," "zest," or "berme."

We are informed by Pliny the Elder that the Celts were brewing in his time (first century), and the ancient miracle of converting water into wine was repeated, in a manner appropriate to northern Europe, by St. Brigid (fifth century) and St. Columban (*d.* 615), who turned water into beer, or "multiplied" it. Charlemagne's capitulary *De villis* (812) obligated the manors to provide the court with beer, mead, cider, vinegar (sweetened vinegar was a beverage), and other drinks. (The early-eleventh-century glossary of Aelfric lists more than forty "beverages and fluids.")

Breweries are mentioned in the Domesday Book (1086), which says that the monks of St. Paul's Cathedral were brewing ale at the rate of nearly 68,000 gallons per year—no more than enough for 185 monks, at the consumption rate of a gallon a day that prevailed a century later; in the fourteenth century nuns were said to be consuming nearly twice this much. And an account of outfitting a fleet for the Hanseatic town of Lübeck in that century states that 40 percent of the cost went for beer.

Beer "proper" is distinguished from ale through the addition of hops to the wort. Although "hopping" was known in ancient Mesopotamia, early "beers" in medieval Europe were flavored with other aromatic herbs and spices, notably bog myrtle, rosemary, and yarrow, in mixtures known as gruit. This was the only secret involved in brewing, and the composition of gruits was a trade secret, susceptible to control by makers and governments. The hop plant was widespread, and the hopped beverage thus was not susceptible to this control. But, despite vigorous opposition from vested interests, the hopped beverage, beer, was to prevail. It tasted better.

The use of hops appears in documents as early as the reign of Charlemagne's father, Pepin the Short, and is thought to have been introduced to western Europe by the Finns. Hildegard of Bingen wrote in her *Physica sacra* (*ca.* 1150–1160) that the hop plant is of "a heating and drying nature," conducive to melancholy, but making beverages resistant to putrefaction.

France belonged to southern Europe in its preference for wine; as early as the time of Charlemagne the French were said to be "obsessed" with wine, and considered beer-drinking a penance. Still, Paris had a brewery and the drink was popular, at least among the lower classes. There was a corporation of brewers in Paris in the thirteenth century.

North central Europe was the land of beer. The ninth-century plan of the monastery of St. Gall in Switzerland shows in some detail two breweries, presumably for two grades of beer, and soon four or five hundred monasteries in Germany were engaged in brewing. The art moved from the monastery to the castle and then to the commercial brewery. About 1370 nearly half of the "master artisans" registered in Hamburg were brewers.

In England, where ale remained popular, the typical castle had a brewery operated by an "alewife," whose product, according to Peter of Blois (*d. ca.* 1205), was "horrid to the taste and abominable to the sight." But it cheered the common folk. Henry II of England appears to have been the first to levy a tax on beer, in 1188 (to finance a crusade); but on the whole beer and ale were lightly taxed, for with bread they constituted the essential diet of the common people.

Innovation was modest. Much attention was given to the quality of water used in brewing, which needed to be "soft" (relatively free of minerals). Burton-on-Trent was a brewing center from 1295 because of the quality of its water. An inventory of a London brewery in 1335 indicates that the apparatus cost less than £1 (equivalent, according to Corran, to £240 today). A similar brewery, founded in the fourteenth century, existed at Queens College, Oxford, until after 1945. It had a mash tub with two outlet pipes protected by metal screens and a (sixteenth-century) pump for transferring the wort through lead pipes to the "copper" (a boiling pan of that material), to cooling tubs, and to fermenting casks. A batch was 216 gallons.

Germany, especially Bavaria, and Bohemia were pioneers in large-scale production and innovation in brewing. Cold, or "bottom," fermenting, in which the yeast is made to settle to the bottom, was first mentioned in Munich in 1420. The product was, and is, called lager.

BIBLIOGRAPHY

John P. Arnold, *Origin and History of Beer and Brewing* (1911); Johann Beckmann, *Beiträge zur Geschichte der Erfindungen* (1780–1805), available in many editions and translations, has an article on hops (in the 1846 English translation, II, 376–387); H. S. Corran, *A History of Brewing* (1975). Gesellschaft für die Geschichte und Bibliographie des Brauwesens, *Jahrbuch* (1928–), contains annual bibliographies and articles on all aspects of the subject, mostly in relation to Germany—see esp. Wolfgang Röllig, "Das Bier im alten Mesopotamien" (1971), 1–104; Wolfgang Helek, "Das Bier im alten Ägypten" (1972), 9–120; and Fritz Eyer, "Brauer und Brauen im alten Frankreich" (1973), 9–28.

ROBERT MULTHAUF

[See also **Aelfric; Agriculture; Hildegard of Bingen, St.**]

BRICK, either sun-dried or baked, has been used in almost every part of the Old World. It was a common building material in Europe in the Middle Ages, especially in regions that had little or no stone available, such as the Low Countries, eastern England, southern France, and northern Italy. Since there was considerable rainfall in all these regions, only baked bricks could be used. Churches, public buildings, towers and other fortifications, and private dwelling places could all be built in brick. Brick could be adapted to any style of architecture—late Roman at Ravenna, Romanesque as in a cluster of churches at Bologna, Gothic, as in the cathedral at Albi.

There was no standard size for bricks in the Roman Empire or medieval Europe. Each builder had his own moulds and these could be altered to suit the needs of the job. Variations in length were especially great; some bricks could be 18 inches long. There was, however, a clear difference in thickness between Roman and medieval bricks. Roman bricks were thin, often no more than 1 inch, seldom more than 1.5 inches. The Romans used a great deal of mortar to support these rather fragile bricks, which were often scarcely more than tiles. Medieval bricks were thicker, averaging around 2 inches in this dimension and sometimes going up to 3 inches. Medieval bricklayers also used much less mortar than their predecessors. Thicker bricks and less mortar saved time and labor.

In England something very like our standard brick developed in the fourteenth century (9″ × 4.5″ × 2″) and the fifteenth (9″ × 4.4″ × 2.06″). By the end of the Middle Ages 8.5″ × 3.75″ × 2″ was standard. This was probably due to Flemish influence; Flemish bricklayers dominated early English brickwork.

The new type of brick was so different from the Roman that the Latin word for brick *(later)* was almost forgotten, even in the Romance languages. The French dropped it entirely and used the Flemish word *brique.* The Italians kept *laterizio* as an elegant word for brickwork, but the working words were *mattone* (brick), *mattonaio* (brickmaker), and *mattonaia* (brickyard). The Spaniards kept *ladrillo* but also used *briqueta* for a brick-shaped object.

BIBLIOGRAPHY

American Face Brick Association, *Brickwork in Italy* (1925); Guglielmo De Angelis d'Ossat, "Tecniche edilizie in pietra e laterizio," in *Settimane di studio del Centro italiano di studi sull'alto medioevo,* **18** (1971); Nathaniel Lloyd, *A History of English Brickwork* (1925).

JOSEPH R. STRAYER

[See also **Construction and Building.**]

BRIGIT (BRIGID), ST.

BRIGIT (BRIGID), ST., the most celebrated female saint of Ireland, second only to St. Patrick in importance and popularity. Although a large body of hagiology on Brigit has survived, some of it from as early as the mid seventh century, it contains scarcely any concrete or reliable information about her. She belonged to the Fotharta Airbrech, in her time a subject people settled in northwest Leinster. She probably lived in the second half of the fifth and the early sixth century—the entries on her death in the *Annals of Ulster* (for 524, 526, and 528) are unreliable—the period after the mission of St. Patrick, which witnessed the consolidation of Christianity and the beginning of Irish monasticism. Assisted by the hermit (later bishop) Conláed, Brigit founded a monastery at Cell-dara (present-day Kildare), perhaps on the site of what had been a pagan sanctuary. This foundation enjoyed the notable distinction of having a double monastery—one part for women, the other for men—for which Bishop Conláed (and his successors) performed episcopal and sacerdotal functions. Overall control, however, rested with the abbess. By the mid seventh century Cell-dara had become the principal ecclesiastical foundation of the Lagin, the ruling people of southeastern Ireland, and Brigit their tutelary saint.

The early Irish biographers of Brigit extravagantly compensated for the lack of historical information with a wealth of mythological and folkloristic matter. They related that Brigit was born at sunrise, neither within nor without a house; that the house in which she was staying seemed to onlookers to be on fire; and that sunrays supported her wet cloak. That she and nineteen other nuns tended a perpetual sacred fire is mentioned by Giraldus Cambrensis, who testified to the continuation of the tradition in Kildare as late as the 1180's.

Besides associating her with the cult of fire and sun, biographers emphasized her supernatural powers of fertility and healing. Thus many of her miracles demonstrate her power over animals (especially livestock), food production (especially dairy products), and brewing. Her feast day, February 1, corresponds to *Imbolc,* the pagan Celtic festival of spring and one of the four major dates of the Celtic year. These aspects and functions of her person suggest that the historical St. Brigit usurped the mythological roles and rituals of her namesake, the Celtic goddess *Brigit* (literally, "the exalted one"), who, among the insular Celts, was revered as the patroness of learning, of healing, and of craftsmanship, and whose name commanded such respect as to be synonymous with "goddess."

The hagiology on Brigit is remarkably early in date and innovative in character. An Old Irish genealogical poem on the Fotharta, dated about 600 (though probably a little later), describes her as "another Mary," implying that like the Blessed Virgin she was patroness of Ireland—an indication of Cell-dara's early aspirations for its patron.

From the second half of the seventh century comes the first attempt at writing formal hagiography in Ireland, the Latin life of Brigit by the monk Cogitosus. His detailed description of the church and congregation at Cell-dara (in his own time) and the extravagant claims to ecclesiastical supremacy in Leinster and even all Ireland which he makes on behalf of its abbess indicate that he wrote as a devoted member of the community.

In his prologue Cogitosus admits his indebtedness to earlier accounts of Brigit's miracles handed down by the elders and scholars of Cell-dara. From this and other references (notably two ninth-century Latin poems on Brigit by Irish exiles on the Continent, which name previous biographers of Brigit) Mario Esposito postulates that prior to Cogitosus two other hagiographers—Ultán, bishop of Ardbreccan (*d.* 657 or 663), and Aileran the Wise (*d.* 665)—each wrote a Latin Life of Brigit. One of these putative Lives Esposito identifies with the anonymous *Vita prima Brigidae* (also known as the *Vita tertia*), attributing it (tentatively) to Aileran the Wise; the other putative Life, the work of Ultán, provided the main source for the *Vita prima.* According to Esposito, both of these Lives, though mainly the *Vita prima,* were used by Cogitosus.

Most scholars agree with Esposito that an early collection of miracles about Brigit, a primitive Life, preceded Cogitosus. They do not accept, however, Esposito's hypothesis that the *Vita prima* was used by Cogitosus, arguing instead for either *Vita prima*'s dependence on Cogitosus or their common dependence on a primitive Life. Further evidence for the existence of this primitive Life comes from the Old Irish Life of Brigit, *Bethu Brigte* (first half of the ninth century), containing extensive passages in Latin, which is based on a Latin original more archaic in character than the *Vita prima* or Cogitosus. Only a reconstruction of the primitive Life (partial at best), combined with a closer textual study of the *Vita prima* and Cogitosus, will make it possible to determine the precise relationship between the three extant Lives and their indebtedness to the primitive Life.

Another Life of Brigit, in Latin hexameters, was composed on the Continent by the Irishman Donatus, bishop of Fiesole (*ca.* 829–876), who probably drew on the *Vita prima, Bethu Brigte,* Cogitosus, and an additional source, perhaps the primitive Life. From the twelfth century come two Lives, the so-called *Vita quarta* attributed to a certain Animosus, and a Life by Laurence of Durham (*d.* 1154), both lengthy narratives of Brigit's miracles but neither offering any insights on the relationship of the early Lives.

In Britain and continental Europe the cult of Brigit was propagated by Irish missionaries and pilgrims from the seventh to the twelfth century. Among the most notable manifestations of this cult were the inclusion of Brigit's name in ecclesiastical calendars, martyrologies, and other related liturgical documents; the dedication to her of churches and holy places; and numerous folk beliefs and practices associated with her name. These influences are well attested throughout the Middle Ages, especially in Scotland, Brittany, northeastern France and Belgium, Alsace, Switzerland and southern Germany, Sweden, and northern Italy; vestiges survive to the present day.

BIBLIOGRAPHY

For a complete bibliography up to 1931, see Charles Plummer, "A Tentative Catalogue of Irish Hagiography," in *Miscellanea hagiographica hibernica* (1925), 171–285, nos. 11, 86, 87, 88, 219; and James F. Kenney, *The Sources for the Early History of Ireland: Ecclesiastical* (1929, repr. with addenda by Ludwig Bieler, 1966).

Since 1931 the following new editions of Lives of Brigit have appeared: D. N. Kissane, ed., "*Uita metrica sanctae Brigidae:* A Critical Edition with Introduction, Commentary and Indexes," in *Proceedings of the Royal Irish Academy,* **77C** (1977); and Donncha Ó hAodha, ed. and trans., *Bethu Brigte* (1978). The following articles (after 1931) on the Lives are valuable: Mario Esposito, "On the Early Latin Lives of St. Brigid of Kildare," in *Hermathena,* **24** (1935); Ludwig Bieler, "The Celtic Hagiographer," in *Studia patristica,* **5**, pt. 3 (1962); Felim Ó Briain, "Brigitana," in *Zeitschrift für celtische Philologie,* **36** (1977). On the cult of St. Brigit outside Ireland, see Louis Gougaud, *Les saints irlandais hors d'Irlande* (1936), 16–45.

PÁDRAIG P. Ó NÉILL

[See also **Hagiography; Ireland, Early History; Irish Literature, Religious; Monasticism, Origins.**]

BRITTANIE DE ENGLETER. See **Livre de Reis.**

BRITTANY, DUCHY. The fundamental characteristics of the medieval duchy of Brittany were chiefly shaped by two geohistorical factors. First, an important inheritance was handed down from the Celtic and Gallo-Roman society created after the conquest of Armorica in 56 B.C. Second, from the fourth century A.D. the migration in waves of Celtic peoples from Roman Britain, who settled principally in the west and north, imparted to Armorica not only a new name, Britannia minor, but also a distinctive ethnic, linguistic, and cultural pattern that still persists. The medieval duchy was permanently divided in language and, to a lesser extent, by private customs, art, and law. For its political and cultural life this division between Celtic and Latin traditions was crucial, being both creative and destructive.

Recent archaeological finds show that Armorica, containing five main tribes, was extensively romanized. The capitals of three of these tribes (Rennes, Nantes, and Vannes) survived to form nuclei of later counties. Corseul, capital of the Coriosolites, was replaced by Alet (now St. Malo, a later bishopric) in the late third century. Brest and Quimper took over, respectively, the military and ecclesiastical roles of Vorgium (Carhaix) at this time. Similarly, lesser urban centers, rural villas, and coastal industrial complexes decayed unevenly. The role of migrant Britons in this decline is uncertain. Some probably arrived to shore up the Roman province; later they occupied deserted sites or conquered larger regions like that around Vannes in the late sixth century. Civilized Gallo-Roman society gave way to a fragmented, rural, Celtic one. It is still a matter of lively debate whether incoming Britons imposed their own language or adapted local Gaulish, a closely related tongue.

Accounts of the migrations have until recently been based on saints' lives. The earliest Breton example is that of St. Samson, founder of the abbey-bishopric of Dol about 550. A first recension dates from the seventh century. Other lives—of St. Paul Aurelian, eponymous founder of the bishopric of St. Pol de Léon, or of St. Guénolé, founder of Landévennec abbey—date from the ninth century, while most are later still. They describe movements led or inspired by Christian priests, monks, and hermits,

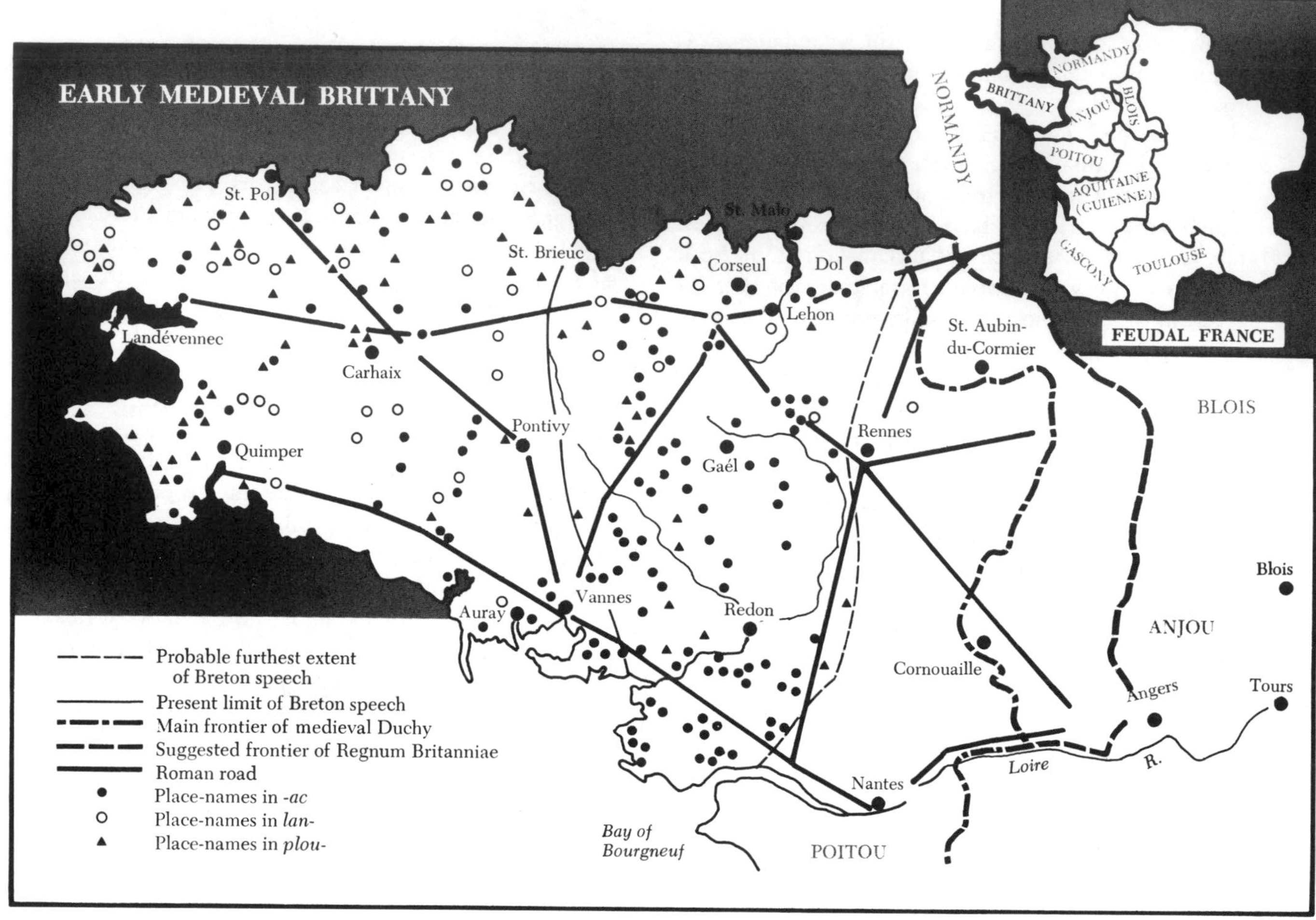

drawn mostly from the aristocracy of Devon, Cornwall, and Wales.

Place-names, especially those incorporating personal names together with prefixes like *plou-* (Latin, *plebs,* "people," normally representing an ancient parish; compare Welsh, *plwyf*), *lan-* (a church or monastic enclosure; compare Welsh, *llan*), *tre-* (a parish division), and *loc-* (Latin, *locus,* [a holy] "place," an element normally indicative of later settlement), testify to this tradition in which small groups of settlers from the same family, kinship, or tribal groupings established themselves. Another group of place-names with the suffix *-ac,* widespread in eastern Brittany, are former Gallo-Roman names ending *-acum* (normally transformed in later French-speaking regions to *-é* but fossilized before that change could be completed). They probably represent the broad measure of interpenetration of indigenous and incoming people during the migration period.

In the sixth and seventh centuries, the regions under migrant control and those still held by descendants of the Gallo-Romans stabilized. Breton bishops attended Frankish church councils. Small Breton principalities were set up. Judicael, ruler of Domnonia (in modern Côtes-du-Nord) recognized the suzerainty of the Merovingian king Dagobert in 635. A march district, dominated by Frankish dukes *(duces),* formed around Rennes and Nantes. After 753 it was governed by a marquis—Roland, immortalized in the later *Song,* being the most notable of the line.

The Carolingian dynasty sought to extend its authority over the Breton princes. In 818, Emperor Louis the Pious defeated the chieftain Morvan. Monastic reforms were instigated. Nomenoë, a local aristocrat from Vannes, was appointed imperial *missus* in Brittany in 831. By this time Celtic familial and public institutions were certainly in retreat be-

BRITTANY, DUCHY

fore Carolingian ones around Redon, as the unique cartulary of the abbey founded there in 832 indicates. The incorporation of Brittany into a wider world is evident in later ninth-century cultural contacts with Italy and eastern Francia, and a modest revival of learning centered at Landévennec, Redon, and other monasteries. This was typified by a highly ornate Latin style, similar to contemporary Irish and Anglo-Saxon Hisperic Latin, and by distinctive illuminated manuscripts, the origins of which are revealed by Breton glosses.

Divisions among the Carolingians following the death of Louis the Pious (840) and the beginning of Viking raids (Nantes was sacked in 843) allowed Nomenoë to create a more independent principality. He defeated Emperor Charles the Bald at Ballon in 845, annexed the marcher counties of Rennes and Nantes, and negotiated for the elevation of Dol to archiepiscopal rank, seeking to free Brittany from the metropolitan jurisdiction of Tours; the dispute was finally settled in favor of Tours by Innocent III. After Nomenoë's premature death in 851, his son Erispoë negotiated with Charles the Bald, who recognized him as ruler of the *regnum Britanniae*. He was succeeded by Salomon (857–874). All three rulers pursued an expansionist policy, and the *regnum* reached its greatest extent in 867.

Internal dissensions and Norse pressure brought expansion to a halt. Alan the Great (*d.* 907) was the last Breton king. Viking raids intensified about 913. Many monastic communities and chapters dispersed or sought refuge in other parts of France. There was a similar flight by some comital families. Refugees from Cornouaille were welcomed by Athelstan of England. The Carolingians abandoned Brittany as they had Normandy. Norsemen who had settled on the Loire threatened to create a second Viking state. Their advance was halted by Bérenger, count of Rennes (probably descended from a Carolingian family), who had not fled, and by Alan Barbetorte, grandson of Alan the Great, who returned from England. Barbetorte took up residence in Nantes while retaining links with Cornouaille. In the next century the counts of Rennes and Nantes vied for control of the duchy. Initially the counts of Nantes (supported by the counts of Anjou) were dominant, but the victory of Conan I of Rennes at Conquereuil in 992 enabled his family to assert its ascendancy, though in turn it fell under Norman influence. The death of Conan II in 1066 brought his son-in-law, Hoël, count of Cornouaille and Nantes, to the ducal title.

In the meantime important changes had been occurring in Breton society. Overshadowed by powerful neighbors, the duke ceased to do homage to the king of France after 983. After 1000 in Brittany, as elsewhere in France, Carolingian institutions crumbled and were replaced by more strictly feudal ones. Great families, basing their power on fortified residences, began to usurp public authority, even in traditional Celtic regions. Adopting the chivalric culture of their eastern neighbors, this aristocracy looked to the reformed Benedictine monasteries of Normandy and the Loire valley for aid in establishing new priories and restoring older houses.

A revival of urban life also occurred: Nantes, Rennes, and Vannes began to expand beyond their late Roman fortifications and many new, albeit small, towns grew up in the shadow of seigneurial castles or important ecclesiastical centers. From about 1140 internal colonization of forest, marsh, and waste was advanced particularly by the Cistercians and military orders of the Hospital and Temple. Commerce began to revive. There was renewed naval activity. From the late thirteenth century Breton shipmasters began to carry salt from the Bay of Bourgneuf and Gascon wine along European trade routes. In the later Middle Ages export of canvas and linen became important, though commercial institutions and the scale of Breton economic activity remained backward.

The one natural resource that the duchy always possessed was a fecund population. Because of limited natural wealth this surplus sought outlets in more favored regions. An important Breton contingent accompanied William of Normandy to England in 1066. Long-lasting territorial links were established, not least for the ducal family that held the honor (or future earldom) of Richmond at the time of Domesday (1086) and enjoyed possession intermittently until 1399. Other Bretons took part in the conquest of southern Italy and the Crusades, joined the great religious orders, or made their way, like Peter Abelard, to the incipient universities—that at Nantes was not founded until 1460.

In the twelfth century the dukes, under Anglo-Norman suzerainty and harassed by a turbulent nobility, lost political authority. Eventually Henry II of England brought Brittany into the Angevin sphere by marrying his son, Geoffrey, to Constance, heiress of Conan IV (1156–1171). Administrative and legal reforms followed, including the Assize of Count Geoffrey (1185), a measure designed to preserve noble primogeniture and safeguard military services.

BRITTANY, DUCHY

But the murder of Arthur, Geoffrey's heir, by his uncle, King John of England (1203), and John's subsequent defeat by France reopened Brittany to French royal influence.

Philip Augustus married the Breton heiress to a distant Capetian cousin, Peter of Dreux, surnamed Mauclerc because of subsequent battles with ecclesiastical authorities. Their descendants ruled the duchy until its final incorporation into the kingdom by the successive marriages of Duchess Anne to Charles VIII (1491) and to Louis XII (1499). Mauclerc and his son, John I (1237–1286), were particularly successful in containing noble pretensions, expanding ducal demesnes, and implementing other sources of wealth. Breton court culture, law, and institutions were increasingly shaped by French example.

But about 1300 a reaction against enmeshing royal doctrines of sovereignty began. In 1297, Philip IV promoted John II (1286–1305) to the peerage of France, expecting him in return to do liege homage, to perform certain military services, and to acknowledge the judicial superiority of the Parlement of Paris. But the duke began to challenge royal claims to exact taxation in Brittany, restricted appeals to Parlement, objected to royal nominations to Breton benefices, and asserted his own right to issue coinage (including gold from about 1345) and to control private warfare in the duchy. There developed claims to ducal "regalities," which in practice nullified royal rights.

These developments, characteristic of relations between France and Brittany in the late Middle Ages, were further promoted by the almost simultaneous outbreak of general war between England and France (1337) and civil war in Brittany. In the *Arrêt de Conflans* (7 September 1341) Philip VI accepted claims by his nephew, Charles of Blois, on behalf of his wife, Jeanne de Penthièvre, niece of the late John III (1312–1341), to perform homage for Brittany. Edward III of England had already offered aid to John de Montfort, half brother of John III, and fighting broke out. Despite Montfort's death in September 1345, Anglo-Breton forces won many notable victories, most significantly when his son defeated and killed Charles of Blois at Auray (29 September 1364). John IV (1364–1399) was now recognized as rightful duke by Charles V of France, and Jeanne de Penthièvre renounced her claims (first Treaty of Guérande, 12 April 1365).

Though exiled from 1373 to 1379, John IV modernized his administration, endowing it with a more efficient *chambre des comptes* and regular taxation *(fouages);* checked noble powers; revived trade by commercial treaties; and protected merchants. Despite both financial and moral debts to the English, who needed his alliance in order to protect lines of communication with Guienne during the Anglo-French war, John IV pursued policies that avoided deep commitment to either great power. His successors followed his example until expulsion of the English from Normandy and Guienne (1449–1453) left Brittany exposed.

King Louis XI (1461–1483) used every means to undermine ducal independence. Enormous efforts were made to counter this threat—frontiers were fortified, artillery was stocked, foreign alliances were arranged—but in comparison with the Crown, ducal resources were limited. The weak rule of Francis II (1458–1488), serious factional quarrels, lack of a direct male heir, and failure by Brittany's allies to provide sufficient reinforcements led to military defeat (notably at St. Aubin-du-Cormier, 28 July 1488) in the war, which had begun in 1487. Duchess Anne, born on 25 January 1477, recognized by the Breton *états* as heiress and married by proxy to Maximilian, king of the Romans (19 December 1490), was finally besieged at Rennes in the autumn of 1491. Terms were arranged with Charles VIII that guaranteed Breton privileges and institutions. Charles and Anne were married on 6 December 1491. With minor modifications Brittany retained its administrative independence until the end of the ancien régime.

Throughout the later Middle Ages dukes and their advisers appealed continually to history, legal precedent, ceremonial, and legend to sustain arguments for independence. In the end, despite creating an advanced territorial state, their efforts were rendered nugatory by the Crown's ability to attract into its service not only the greater nobles but also all those who had been accustomed by opportunities in the Anglo-French war and by economic exigencies to seek their livelihood outside Brittany. The duchy produced three outstanding constables of France (Bertrand du Guesclin, Olivier de Clisson, and Arthur de Richemont), several marshals and admirals, and thousands of ordinary soldiers. In the late fifteenth century the soldiers and others who sought employment in France were forced to choose between the duchy and the kingdom; they chose the latter in expectation of future rewards. But assimilation of a duchy that had endured so long, enjoyed such practical autonomy, and possessed such cultural individuality (notably displayed in its ecclesiastical

BRITTANY, CELTIC

architecture), the result of a unique combination of Celtic and Latin strains, was a long process after 1491. Some would argue it is not yet complete.

BIBLIOGRAPHY

Jean Delumeau, ed., *Histoire de la Bretagne* (1973), has a full bibliography. On Roman Armorica see Louis Pape, *La civitas des Osismes à l'époque gallo-romaine* (1978); and Patric Galliou, "La défense de l'Armorique au Bas-Empire," in *Mémoires de la Société d'histoire et d'archéologie de Bretagne (MSHAB),* 57 (1980). On Carolingian and early feudal Brittany see Hubert Guillotel, "Les vicomtes de Léon aux XIe et XIIe siècles," in *MSHAB,* 51 (1971); "L'action de Charles le Chauve vis à vis de la Bretagne de 843 à 851," *ibid.,* 53 (1975–1976); and "Le premier siècle du pouvoir ducal breton (936–1040)," in *Actes du 103e Congrès national des sociétés savantes, Nancy-Metz 1977* (1979). John Le Patourel, *The Norman Empire* (1976), is the most recent account of Anglo-Norman suzerainty. Michael Jones, "The Defence of Medieval Brittany," in *Archaeological Journal,* 138 (1981), reviews recent work, much of it by Jean-Pierre Leguay, whose *Un réseau urbain au moyen-âge: Les villes du duché de Bretagne aux XIVème et XVème siècles* (1981) is comprehensive. Hervé Martin, *Les ordres mendiants en Bretagne, vers 1530* (1975), is the most important recent contribution to ecclesiastical history. Franco-Breton relations after 1297 have been the concern of Michael Jones. In addition to *Ducal Brittany 1364–1399* (1970), see his "The Breton Civil War," in J. J. N. Palmer, ed., *Froissart, Historian* (1981); and "The Breton Nobility and Their Masters from the Civil War to the Late Fifteenth Century," in J. R. L. Highfield and Robin Jeffs, eds., *The Crown and Local Communities in England and France in the Fifteenth Century* (1981). André Mussat, *Arts et cultures de Bretagne: Un millénaire* (1979), is an impressive survey by the leading Breton art historian; other recent literature is cited in Michael Jones, "Bulletin historique: L'histoire du bas Moyen Âge breton (1200–1500)," in *MSHAB,* 56 (1979).

MICHAEL JONES

[See also **Carolingians and the Carolingian Empire; France to 987; France, 987–1223; France, 1223–1328; France, 1314–1494; Hundred Years War; Normans and Normandy.**]

BRITTANY, CELTIC. It is believed that as early as the Iron Age Brittany had absorbed the Celtic culture that had developed in eastern Europe. Sometime between 800 B.C. and 500 B.C. Gaulish began to be spoken in the peninsula. It is not known whether it disappeared completely after the Roman conquest, which took place between 59 B.C. and 49 B.C., and before the second Celtic penetration. The new wave of settlers, fleeing Anglo-Saxon invaders, came from Wales, Devon, and Cornwall between the fifth and the seventh centuries.

The colonization of Brittany was carefully planned. Settlements were made by "saints"—that is, by the educated members of the community—and were frequently named after them: hence the numerous place-names formed with the characteristic Breton prefixes *plou-* ("plebs," "parish," or rather "those belonging to the parish"), *tre-* ("subdivision of the plebs," French: *trève*), and *lan-* ("monastery") followed by the saint's name.

The language spoken by the settlers, Brittonic (or Brythonic), belonged to the *p* branch of the Celtic family. Early in the fifth century Brittonic was still a relatively uniform speech, but within 150 years (450–600) it had split into three forms: Welsh, Cornish, and Breton. We know of only two continuous texts in Breton dating from before 1500. The oral character of Celtic tradition and the countless wars and invasions of Brittany might account for this scarcity of written evidence.

The religious rites and traditions that the settlers brought had developed in the British Isles. Christianity had been established in the peninsula before their arrival; by the fifth century the existence of the three episcopal churches of Rennes, Nantes, and Vannes is attested. Their organization was that of the bishoprics of Gaul; Armorica, being situated in Lyonnaise (one of the three provinces of Roman Gaul), depended on Tours as its ecclesiastical metropolis.

Because of the isolation and structure of Celtic society, the predominant element of Christianity was monastic. Each monastery was connected with a single tribe and acknowledged no ecclesiastical superior entitled to control its abbot. The "abbey-bishopric" is characteristic of these areas. The pope tolerated this custom, and in the ninth century Dol even became the seat of an archbishopric. Tours disputed this and in 1199 Pope Innocent III finally disallowed the claim of Dol to the metropolitan see.

There were several differences between the Celtic and Roman rites. Easter was celebrated at a different date in each tradition. Other points of divergence were the form of tonsure, baptism, consecration of bishops, and the liturgy. While the Roman style of tonsure was a shaven circle on the crown of the head, the tonsure of Celtic monks was frontal, but the exact form is not known. There is also some doubt about the exact nature of the baptismal rite. The Celts apparently performed a single immersion—still the custom in Brittany in the early seventeenth century—instead of the three immersions recommended by the apostolic canon. They did not observe the canonical rule requiring the participation of three bishops at another bishop's consecration. In the sixth century two Breton priests, Lovocat and Catihern, were accused of allowing women to help celebrate the Mass. This seems to have been an Eastern practice, and the Eastern influence on the Celtic church is well documented.

After the Synod of Whitby (663 or 664) decided in favor of Roman usage, changes were slowly effected throughout Celtic Christianity. As late as 818, after questioning Matmonoc, abbot of Landévennec, Louis the Pious addressed an order to the Breton bishops and to the clergy enjoining the adoption of the Roman tonsure and of the Rule of St. Benedict. Even after its submission, however, the Breton church remained deeply influenced by its Celtic origins, retaining its monastic character and devotion to its founding saints.

In civil government, the principles expressed in the *Très ancienne coutume de Bretagne,* an early-fourteenth-century codification of common law and Christian ethics, are not different from contemporary laws in the neighboring provinces. At the time of the Celtic colonization, Breton law must have been somewhat elementary, and distinctively Celtic characteristics appear mostly in matters of custom.

In Celtic lands inheritance was usually shared equally among all brothers. These equal rights were not enforced by law, but as the father's or elder brother's will ruled supreme in actual fact, shares were often on a par. At the beginning of the eleventh century, Duke Alan III of Brittany gave his brother Eudo the appanage of Penthièvre, which covered one third of Brittany. Rohan, a larger territory than the one granted to his elder son, was given to a younger son of the house of Porhoët. Similar situations occurred in the houses of Gaël, Montfort, Dinan, and Donges. The practice continued until 1185, when *L'assise au Comte Geoffroy* forbade the dismemberment of the fiefs as disruptive to the feudal system. The right of the younger son also partly defines the *quévaise,* a kind of landholding to be found in Lower Brittany in the lands belonging to the Cistercians of Bégard and Le Relec and to the Hospitallers.

In the arts, some of the most interesting mementos of early Celtic times are the Christianized menhirs, such as Men ar Manac'h on the island of Locoal off the coast of Morbihan. Breton medieval religious iconography has preserved some of the druidic traditions: St. Tugdual, St. Efflam, and St. Brieuc are represented fighting the dragon, the Nwywre. This could be interpreted as Christianity fighting Celtic tradition, but in fact the Breton Middle Ages are pervaded with Celtic influence.

BIBLIOGRAPHY

E. G. Bowen, *Saints, Seaways and Settlements in the Celtic Lands* (1969); Nora Chadwick, *Early Brittany* (1969); Edmond Durtelle de Saint Sauveur, *Histoire de Bretagne,* 2 vols., 4th ed. (1957, repr. 1975); François Falc'hun, *Histoire de la langue bretonne d'après la géographie linguistique,* 2 vols. in 1 (1963); François Gourvil, *Noms de famille bretons d'origine toponymique* (1970); Kenneth H. Jackson, *A Historical Phonology of Breton* (1967); Arthur Le Moyne de La Borderie, *Histoire de Bretagne,* 6 vols. (1896–1914); Jeanne Laurent, *Un monde rural en Bretagne au XVe siècle, la Quévaise* (1972); Joseph Loth, *L'émigration bretonne en Armorique* (1883); Olivier Loyer, *Les chrêtientés celtiques* (1965); Marcel Planiol, *Histoire des institutions de la Bretagne,* 3 vols. (1953–1955).

CLAUDE EVANS

[See also **Celtic Art; Celtic Church; Celtic Languages; France.**]

BRITTON was an English lawyer, and perhaps a judge, during the reign of Edward I. He composed a treatise on English law, written in Old French (the language of the royal courts), in the 1290's. It is a summary of Bracton brought up to date, a well-arranged and useful book for a practicing lawyer. It is especially strong on the writs and procedures used to prove title or gain possession of land. The book was very popular in its day, judging by the number of manuscripts that survive, and it was one of the first of the older books on English law to be printed (1540).

BIBLIOGRAPHY

F. W. Nichols published the text of Britton with a translation, biography, and useful notes (1865). The English translation alone was published in 1901. There is a good account of Britton and his work in William S. Holdsworth, *A History of English Law,* 3rd ed., II (1923), 319–321.

JOSEPH R. STRAYER

[See also **Bracton, Henry de; Law, English Common.**]

BROEDERLAM, MELCHIOR, Flemish painter active at Ypres between 1381 and 1395. He was appointed court painter to Philip the Bold, duke of Burgundy in 1385, and was active at Paris between 1390 and 1395. His only surviving documented work is the pair of painted panels for an altarpiece sculpted by Jacques de Baerze for the Chartreuse de Champmol (Dijon, Musée des Beaux Arts). Broederlam's work reveals a familiarity with Italian art, perhaps as a result of a trip to Italy, and he introduced a new sense of architectural and landscape space, volumetric figural style, and brilliant palette into French art—perhaps the earliest manifestation of the developing international Gothic style.

BIBLIOGRAPHY

Louis Dimier, "Les primitifs français," in *Gazette des beaux arts,* **16** (1936); Erwin Panofsky, *Early Netherlandish Painting* (1953), 86–89, 111–115; Georg Troescher, *Die burgundische Malerei* (1966), I, 96ff.; Charles D. Cuttler, *Northern Painting from Pucelle to Bruegel* (1968), 21–25.

ROBERT G. CALKINS

[See also **Flemish Painting.**]

BRONZE AND BRASS. Excluding the use of gold and silver for the manufacture of luxury items and coinage, the Middle Ages opened in Europe with a civilization thoroughly dependent on two very different metals—iron (and its alloy steel) for the making of tools, weapons, and armor; and copper (and its alloys bronze and brass), for the manufacture of decorative metalwork.

Copper was fairly readily available from a number of mining areas in Europe, but it is of very little practical use alone because it is too soft to be made into useful tools and utensils, and has too high a melting point for easy casting into decorative objects. Hence it was almost always alloyed with tin, lead, and/or zinc.

Since the early Bronze Age tin had been the usual additive, and the resulting copper-tin alloy is known as bronze. The melting point of this alloy falls to about 960°C. when it contains 15 percent tin, but for casting purposes the alloy is improved by the addition of lead. In fact, Roman bronze statuary contains an average of about 10 percent tin, 20 percent lead, and 70 percent copper, although these amounts all vary within wide limits.

The addition of tin to copper serves two purposes: the lowering of the melting point and the hardening of the resulting bronze. In fact, by the time 20 percent tin has been added, the alloy has become both extremely hard and very brittle, so it will not easily deform without cracking. Hence, bronze that is to be raised into cooking vessels or made into sheet usually contains less than 10 percent tin, so that it can be fabricated by working (hammering) without cracking.

Bronze was made by adding tin to copper and melting the two together in a crucible. However, one great mystery surrounds the production of bronze in antiquity: where the tin came from, and in what form it was traded. Although the Greeks knew Britain as the "Tin Islands," very few other tin deposits were known in Europe, and the Middle East seems to be singularly lacking in supplies of this essential metal. Hence the discovery of brass in the first millennium B.C. and its large-scale production from the first century B.C. on must have relieved a supply problem that was, no doubt, gradually worsening.

Brass differs from bronze in that zinc has such low melting and boiling points (420°C. and 907°C., respectively) that it cannot be extracted from the ore by the usual methods without losing the metal as a vapor. Hence zinc metal was not widely known in Europe until the eighteenth century, when apparatus had been invented for condensing the vapor (although the metal had probably been isolated in India by the seventh century). Thus, from the Roman period and throughout the Middle Ages, brass was made by heating small pieces of sheet copper with zinc ore (calamine) and charcoal in a sealed crucible. Temperature control is essential, since it is necessary to have a high enough temperature for reduction of the zinc ore to take place (about 930°C.), but to keep it below the melting point of the copper. The zinc vapor is then absorbed into the surfaces of the sheet copper to produce brass. This method of production is known as the cementation process, and is capable of producing brass with up to about 30 percent zinc, but no more. Brasses with a higher level of zinc were unknown in Europe until supplies of zinc metal became available either by import from China, probably sometime in the seventeenth century, or by indigenous manufacture from the eighteenth century on.

Besides differing from bronze in method of manufacture, brass is not hard enough to be made into tools; but it is a pleasing yellow (almost golden)

BRONZE AND BRASS

color, and the ease with which it can be cast and worked makes it a natural choice for decorative metalwork.

For the early medieval period very little evidence is available about the copper alloys that were in use, and it is often assumed that the main source of metal was Roman scrap. Recently collected analyses, however, show that much of the early medieval "bronze" contains zinc and lead, as well as tin, and suggest that, in addition to the certain reuse of Roman scrap, supplies of brass were either imported from the East or made within Europe itself.

If early medieval European bronze was very heterogeneous in composition, the meager evidence available for the Celtic fringe on the western seaboard and in Ireland indicates the continuation of a tradition of tin bronze, containing a small percentage of lead but almost no zinc, while the opposite is true for the Byzantine Empire. Here the analyses of Coptic bronzes show that brass or leaded brass (containing an average of only 2 to 3 percent tin) had become the main alloy. Coptic bronzes were widely imported into Europe during the Dark Ages, and their tradition was inherited by the medieval Islamic world, where brass or leaded brass was the rule.

It is uncertain how far the industrial-scale fabrication of metalwork survived the Roman Empire, but certainly by the Carolingian period large-size cast metalwork was possible, and numerous examples of bronze doors for churches and cathedrals are known. This is the period when the Meuse valley of Belgium, particularly the town of Dinant, began to establish a reputation for the production of copper-based wares, using imported supplies of copper but locally mined calamine (zinc ore). Mosan wares became famous throughout Europe, so much so that brass and bronze articles became known as *dinanderie* after the most celebrated center of production. Brass was the main alloy, and was known in English as "latten" (probably from the Old French *laton*). However, tin rarely is completely absent and lead is invariably present in cast objects, such as candlesticks and crucifixes.

The techniques of manufacturing objects (either working or casting) were unchanged from the Roman period and are well described in a surviving metalworker's handbook of the period, published under the pseudonym "Theophilus." Apart from the method to be used for manufacturing an object, one other factor was relevant to the composition of the brass or bronze: the proposed method of decoration. Copper-based articles for gilding by the fire-gilding (mercury-gilding) technique had to be free from lead, and preferably free from zinc. In fact, gilded Romanesque bronzes were often made of almost pure copper, or at least low-alloy bronze and brass. The same is true for enameling; the Mosan enamels of the twelfth century were invariably on almost pure copper sheet.

Apart from the usual domestic, architectural, and ecclesiastical metalwork, there were three other important uses for copper alloys in the medieval world: coinage, church bells, and memorial brasses. With the demise of the Roman Empire in the West, copper-alloy coinage essentially disappeared from Christian Europe until after 1500, apart from a few isolated places. It continued, however, to be standard in the Byzantine Empire and the Islamic world. Little is known about the composition of these coins, but some evidence shows that copper was widely used for the Byzantine coins, although bronze was issued from certain mints or for some of the lowest denominations.

With the widespread introduction of the use of stone for church buildings came an increased demand for bells to hang in the towers. Bells were cast in high-tin bronze, known as bell metal, and Theophilus prescribes the presence of 20 percent tin in this alloy. Two techniques were used for making the mold: lost-wax casting, described by Theophilus in the early twelfth century, and more permanent molds, described by Biringuccio in the *Pirotechnia* (1540).

Engraved memorial brasses were an important art form from the mid thirteenth century on, and now provide valuable sources for the history of costume and of arms and armor. The "brasses" were made from sheet metal containing tin, lead, and sometimes iron, in addition to zinc in the copper. Zinc content was usually on the order of 20 percent, with a small percentage of tin and a variable amount of lead.

For the first half of the Middle Ages surviving metalwork is rare, because after the introduction of Christianity, burial of objects in tombs was forbidden and the ravages of time have left relatively little. It is not until the upsurge of building with stone in the eleventh century, which created "permanent" structures, especially churches, that we have a supply of metalwork that has survived above ground. At about the same time bronze or brass casting on a large scale became more common, and if, in contrast to the Roman period, the human statuary commemorated the dead rather than the living, those cast medieval tomb effigies now found in the cathedrals of western Europe provide a foretaste of what was to follow in the Renaissance flowering of the art of monumental bronze sculpture.

BIBLIOGRAPHY

Maurice Lombard, *Les métaux dans l'ancien monde du Ve au XIe siècle* (1974); W. A. Oddy, "Bronze Alloys in Dark-Age Europe," in R. Bruce-Mitford, *The Sutton Hoo Ship Burial,* III (1983); P. T. Braddock, "The Copper Alloys of the Medieval Islamic World: Inheritors of the Classical Tradition," in *World Archaeology,* **11** (1979); Otto Werner, "Analysen mittelalterlicher Bronzen und Messinge," in *Archäologie und Naturwissenschaften,* **1** (1977); Malcolm Norris, *Monumental Brasses: The Craft* (1978).

See also Leslie Aitchison, *A History of Metals,* 2 vols. (1960); Charles Singer *et al., A History of Technology,* II (1956), III (1957); R. F. Tylecote, *A History of Metallurgy* (1976).

W. A. ODDY

[See also **Bells; Dinanderie; Metals and Metallurgy; Mints and Money; Mosan Art; Theophilus.**]

BROT AF SIGURÐARKVIÐU. See **Sigurðarkviða in Forna.**

BROUN, ROBERT (*fl.* 1415–1425), a sculptor from London habitually employed by the English monarchy. Broun carved both wood and alabaster, and was probably responsible for the realistic alabaster tomb effigies of Henry IV and his wife at Canterbury (*ca.* 1420).

BIBLIOGRAPHY

Lawrence Stone, *Sculpture in Britain: The Middle Ages* (1955), 197–198.

LESLIE BRUBAKER

BRUCE, ROBERT. See **Robert I of Scotland.**

BRUDER HANS. Around 1400 a poet who called himself "broeter Hanze" wrote in a mixture of Low and High German a cycle of seven *Marienlieder,* poems in praise of the Virgin Mary. He was probably from the lower Rhineland, the region between Cologne and Cleves. Presumably he had become a lay brother in a religious order, for he indicates in his work that he had left his beloved wife in order to devote himself entirely to Mary's service.

The form of the *Marienlieder* is highly elaborate. Poems II–VI have the same structure: each consists of one hundred stanzas that follow the intricate seven-line pattern of the *Titurelstrophe.* Poem VII also consists of one hundred stanzas, but each stanza has sixteen lines with only two different rhymes. The introductory poem I is a tour de force: its fifteen twelve-line stanzas are written in four different languages: German (lines 1, 5, 10), French (lines 2, 6, 12), English (lines 3, 7, 11), and Latin (lines 4, 8, 9):

> Ave alpha du stercher god!
> Je diroy volentiers un mot
> Of that swete ladi deer,
> Cuius venter te portavit.
> Ich meyn miin vrou dye alrebest,
> Qui dam de toutes dammes est . . .
> (I, 1–6)

Each poem has the same acrostic: the initial words of the stanzas in poem I and the initial letters of the stanzas in poems II–VII form the Latin Angelic Salutation (Hail Mary) in its shorter version, common until the sixteenth century.

The main themes are as follows: poem I, commentaries on the words of the Angelic Salutation; poem II, the succession of generations from Adam and Eve to Joseph and Mary; poem III, meditations on the meaning and power of the word *ave;* poem IV, the strife of the four daughters of God (Mercy, Truth, Justice, and Peace; cf. Psalm 84[85]:11) over man's sin and redemption, Gabriel's annunciation and Mary's visit with Elizabeth, and Marian interpretations of passages from the Song of Songs and Ecclesiasticus; poem V, recapitulation of the biblical accounts of Christ's birth, the coming of the Magi, the flight to Egypt, and the presentation in the temple, as well as rejection of the concept of *felix culpa,* the idea that Mary would not have given birth to Christ if Adam had not sinned; poem VI, Mary amid the joys of paradise and the heavenly Jerusalem; poem VII, a concluding hymn in Mary's praise.

Bruder Hans's work is an interesting representative of a literary tradition that reflects the popularity, especially widespread in the late Middle Ages, of devotion to the Virgin Mary.

BIBLIOGRAPHY

Bruder Hansens Marienlieder aus dem 14. Jahrhundert, Rudolf Minzloff, ed. (1863, 1967); *Bruder Hansens Mar-*

ienlieder, Michael S. Batts, ed. (1963); Michael S. Batts, *Studien zu Bruder Hansens Marienliedern* (1964).

BERND KRATZ

[See also **German Lyric.**]

BRUGES. The administrative center of the Belgian province of West Flanders, Bruges, known in Dutch as Brugge (bridge or site of bridges), is located in the northeast of the province on extremely low and marshy land about ten miles from the North Sea coast. During the sixth and seventh centuries the territory of Flanders was part of the Merovingian state; from the eighth century to the second half of the ninth it was Carolingian until, as the county of Flanders, it became virtually independent under such feudal adventurers as Count Baldwin Iron Arm (864?–879) and his son Baldwin II (879–918). As a defense against the Vikings, one of these counts built a castle at Bruges, situated then at the head of the Gulf of Zwyn on the Rei River. The area around Bruges had been Christianized by missionaries at least as early as the seventh century. Beside this new castle the town was to develop.

Around the castle, guarded by a castellan of the count, there arose in the tenth and early eleventh centuries an urban agglomeration of merchants and artisans engaged in commerce and industry. This area, known as a *portus* or *suburbium,* embraced the marketplace and the halls and houses of the new bourgeois inhabitants, who by the eleventh century had acquired from the counts the elementary social, economic, and legal privileges that distinguished them from the feudal and peasant classes and made them free. Strategically located next to the North Sea and near the great rivers of western Europe, Bruges early became a trade center for the Scandinavian and north German regions, as well as for England. From Bruges was exported the fine Flemish wool cloth, and to Bruges came products in Scandinavian ships from as far afield as Russia and Byzantium. By 1089 a wall had been constructed around an urban area of about 175 acres.

Though preeminently a commercial center, Bruges was also a favorite residence of the counts in the eleventh and twelfth centuries, and therefore housed the principal departments of the comital government, such as the chancery and treasury. In 1089 the provost of the collegiate church of St. Donatian was appointed chancellor, with control of the seals and of the treasury that received and stored the revenues from the various castellanies of Flanders. Besides St. Donatian there were in Bruges such churches as Notre-Dame and St. Sauveur, all subject to the dioceses of Tournai and Utrecht. In a letter of 1067 the archbishop of Rheims described in glowing terms the prosperity of Bruges and its environs.

A detailed description of Bruges is included in an eyewitness account by a Brugeois notary, Galbert de Bruges, of the assassination of Count Charles the Good on 2 March 1127, while he was praying in St. Donatian. This graphic report gives a fine picture of the churches, castle, fortifications, streets, marketplace, and houses, and of some of the leading personages. Galbert writes that the murder and civil war following it were immediately known in London through merchants from Bruges who lived there, and in Laon through Flemish students studying at the cathedral school. During the civil war among the contenders for the countship, Bruges and other prominent Flemish towns bargained for and received charters of self-government that freed them from the supervision of comital administrators. Henceforth, although a part of the county of Flanders, Bruges was responsible for all such local urban matters as justice, finance, fortifications, public works, police, and regulation of the guilds and commerce.

As leaders in the struggle for self-government, the principal members of the merchant guild naturally assumed direction of these urban functions and formed a council to administer them. The members of the council known as an *échevinage* were called *échevins.* For the rest of the Middle Ages membership in the *échevinage* became progressively exclusive, being limited to a few great families, who even schemed to make membership hereditary. Known as patricians, the members of these families were rarely challenged seriously for political power by the lower classes. By the late thirteenth century the patricians governed Bruges primarily for their economic and social interests, blatantly exploiting those whom they employed in their commercial enterprises. Particularistic politically, they envisaged winning total independence from the counts and becoming a city-state like those in northern Italy.

By the end of the twelfth century, Bruges was the greatest commercial center not only of Flanders but also of northern Eruope, a position it would hold until late in the fourteenth century. As a trade and financial center for merchants and bankers from all over Europe and the Middle East, Bruges was comparable to Venice in southern Europe and to Antwerp in the sixteenth century and Amsterdam in the seventeenth century. During the thirteenth century, when receding waters, silting, and land reclamation had deprived Bruges of direct access to the sea, a canal was built linking Bruges to Damme, which served as its port until the end of the medieval period. Unlike the great Italian trading centers with their fleets, Bruges was an emporium without its own ships. The Brugeois merchants, relying on other merchants to come to them, served principally as middlemen for buying and selling of goods on a wholesale level. Bruges attained its economic apogee early in the fourteenth century, when Italian ships began to sail directly to the North Sea from such ports as Genoa and Pisa.

Records from this time list scores of products from Russia, Sweden, Spain, Africa, the Middle East, and all over western Europe. Merchants from some thirty Christian and Muslim states traded at Bruges and established facilities for their business. Streets were even named after the foreign states represented. The need for increased credit and money changing led bankers from Italy and southern France to open branches at Bruges, a development that anticipated the organization of the Medici in the fifteenth century. In the thirteenth and fourteenth centuries such impressive buildings as the cloth hall, the town hall, and various guild and market halls were erected. By the early fourteenth century Bruges, with a population of about 50,000, was not much smaller than Ghent, the primary industrial town of Flanders.

In the struggle between King Philip IV the Fair of France and Count Guy of Dampierre in the late thirteenth century, Bruges was a leader in supporting Guy's fight to retain territorial independence. This alliance came only after the patricians, who supported Philip the Fair (called Leliaerts after the French symbolic fleur-de-lis), had been driven from power by the lower classes (called Clauwaerts because of their loyalty to the clawed lion of Flanders). At first the struggle went well for Philip, whose forces occupied Flanders and by 1300 had it under French rule. The harsh administration and financial exactions by hated French officials, however, fomented a bloody revolt led by the Clauwaerts of Bruges, headed by a simple weaver, Peter de Coninck. Slipping into Bruges in the early morning of 8 May 1302, Coninck and his followers slaughtered all but a few of the French soldiers and officials, as well as French sympathizers, in what has since been called the Matins of Bruges.

This event led most of Flanders to revolt. To punish Bruges and to reduce Flanders to obedience, Philip the Fair sent an imposing army. It was met by a Flemish force composed mostly of foot soldiers from the towns, those from Bruges being the most prominent. On 11 July 1302 the French were put to rout at Courtrai, in the famous Battle of the Golden Spurs, an event that enabled Flanders to remain independent and that became celebrated in Belgian history.

Bruges was never again to play such a role of leadership. In the 1330's and 1340's Ghent was dominant in allying Flanders with England against France in the early phases of the Hundred Years' War. In the region around Bruges a smoldering hatred for the Flemish count Louis of Nevers—who had concluded a humiliating peace with Philip the Fair that surrendered Flemish land, forced heavy indemnities, and guaranteed the return of those Leliaerts who had fled to France—led to a fierce uprising in Bruges and Maritime Flanders against the pro-French count Louis. For five years (1323–1328) revolt persisted under the leadership of Nicolas Zannekin, who skillfully united the lower classes of Bruges with the peasants in the countryside in a kind of jacquerie that promised social and economic reform in a society based on primitive Christian ideals. Only the intervention of a French army and the defeat of the insurgents in the Battle of Cassal (23 August 1328) ended the uprising and restored Louis of Nevers to power.

When Flanders came under the rule of the dukes of Burgundy in 1384, Bruges, though already in decline, was still an important economic center. Serious decline came at the beginning of the sixteenth century, when Antwerp, with its superior location on the Scheldt River, supplanted Bruges as the commerical and financial center of northern Europe. Meanwhile the strong Burgundian dukes sharply reduced the local political power of Bruges by integrating it into the ducal territorial administration of the county. By the end of the fifteenth century, Bruges was well on the way to becoming "Bruges la Morte," an economic backwater with a declining population. But is was to play another role. With its soaring belfries and network of canals lined with beautiful stepped buildings, it became the "Venice of the North," an artistic center for the Flemish masters who in their paintings immortalized the urban panorama of Bruges and the faces of some of its leading burghers.

BIBLIOGRAPHY

Two good popular accounts are M. H. Letts, *Bruges and Its Past,* 2nd ed. (1926); and Patricia Carson, *The Fair Face of Flanders* (1969). Bruges has a prominent place in the following scholarly works: Henri Pirenne, *Early Democracies in the Low Countries* (1971); and *Histoire de Belgique,* 3rd rev. ed. (1922), II, and 5th rev. ed. (1929), I; F. L. Ganshof, "Iets over Brugge gedurende de preconstitutioneele Periode van haar Geschiedenis," in *Nederlandsche Historiebladen,* **1** (1938); Henri Nowé, *La bataille des éperons d'or* (1945); J. A. van Houtte *et al.,* eds., *Algemene Geschiedenis der Nederlanden* (1950–1951), II and III; and Jean Lestocquoy, *Les villes de Flandre et d'Italie sous le gouvernement des patriciens (XIe–XVe siècles)* (1952). For the account of Galbert de Bruges, see *The Murder of Charles the Good Count of Flanders,* J. B. Ross, trans. (1960).

BRYCE LYON

[See also **Baldwin I of Flanders; Banking, European; Burgundy, Duchy; Commune; Échevin; Flanders and the Low Countries; Flemish Painting; Patrician; Philip IV the Fair; Trade, European; Wool.**]

BRUNELLESCHI, FILIPPO (1377–1446), Florentine sculptor and architect. The greatest architect of early Renaissance Italy, Brunelleschi began his career as a metalsmith, matriculating as a goldsmith in 1404. His sculptural activity continued sporadically throughout his career and included silver reliefs and statuettes that he provided for the altar of San Jacopo in the Pistoia cathedral (documented 1399) with Lunardo di Matteo Ducci. Sometime between 1401 and 1403 he submitted a bronze relief, the *Sacrifice of Isaac* (now in the Museo Nazionale, Florence), for the second door of the Baptistery, a competition won by Ghiberti. Brunelleschi is credited with a wooden crucifix in the Gondi Chapel of Santa Maria Novella, Florençe (*ca.* 1410–1415), as well as with the design of other sculptural decoration, including four terra-cotta reliefs of seated evangelists in the spandrels of the Pazzi Chapel, Santa Croce; the lavabo for the north sacristy of the Duomo; and the tomb and altar for the Old Sacristy of San Lorenzo.

Brunelleschi's style is characterized by bold, simply arranged forms that retain their integrity while harmoniously relating to the other forms of the composition. This style helped make Brunelleschi an architect of exceptional genius whose numerous commissions changed the direction of Italian architecture.

According to early sources, Brunelleschi's architectural career began sometime after 1402, on a trip with Donatello to Rome, where he was drawn to the remnants of ancient monuments. Exposure to classical examples and his own sense of purity and elegance produced a number of revolutionary buildings.

Brunelleschi's first great achievement was the successful capping of the Duomo, begun in 1296 by Arnolfo di Cambio. For it he designed and built the largest dome since the Pantheon, and the highest built until then. Brunelleschi is first mentioned in documents relating to the Duomo in 1404; he submitted designs in 1417, was appointed and began construction in 1420, and submitted a new model of the entire cathedral (assisted by Ghiberti) in 1429. In 1436 the double-shelled dome was closed over and blessed; the lantern was designed in 1437 and put in place after his death. An aesthetic as well as an engineering feat, the dome still dominates the Florentine skyline.

In 1419, Brunelleschi began work on the Ospedale degli Innocenti (completed mid fifteenth century), designing an elegant loggia having smooth columns with Corinthian capitals and arches spar-

Sacrifice of Isaac, bronze relief, 1401–1403, Museo Nazionale, Florence. ALINARI/EDITORIAL PHOTOCOLOR ARCHIVES

Florence Cathedral with dome designed by Brunelleschi, 1420–1436. ALINARI/EDITORIAL PHOTOCOLOR ARCHIVES

Interior, S. Spirito, designed by Brunelleschi, 1434, Florence. ALINARI/EDITORIAL PHOTOCOLOR ARCHIVES

Pazzi Chapel of the Church of S. Croce, Florence, 1429–1430. ALINARI/EDITORIAL PHOTOCOLOR ARCHIVES

ingly decorated with glazed terra-cotta reliefs by Andrea della Robbia. The completed building deviates from his original design, but the loggia and square are true to Brunelleschi's revolutionary concepts of architectural design and city planning. The parts are integrated through carefully estimated proportional relationships that provide a new sense of totality and logic to the whole.

In 1421 Brunelleschi began work on the Church of San Lorenzo, which remained unfinished at his death. It still lacks a facade, but in 1428 the Old Sacristy was completed, and by 1438 the transept was finished.

Among his most successful works is the Pazzi Chapel of Santa Croce, begun in 1429 and completed in 1443. The dome was finished in 1459, and the cupola inside the portico in 1461.

In 1434 Brunelleschi began work on the design for Santa Maria degli Angeli, of which only the foundation was completed in his lifetime (the rest is a twentieth-century construction). In the same year designs for Santo Spirito were undertaken; construction commenced in 1444 and two columns were in place at his death in 1446. The remaining structure was faithful to his design, although it was not completed until 1487.

Hampered by heavy demands on his time, and the slow pace of construction, Brunelleschi failed to see much of his work completed in his lifetime, nor did work always follow his designs. What remains, however, testifies to his extraordinary vision. Using simple geometrical forms—the square, the circle, the hemisphere, the arch—combined as regular, modular components, he created environments that were spatially and structurally finite and comprehensible to those understanding mathematics and proportion. Architecture no longer soared heavenward physically, but employed one's sense of logic to find principles that, in Brunelleschi's mind, applied equally to mankind, architecture, and the universe. In Brunelleschi's architecture, the proportions are decidedly human and express his belief that man embodies the proportional relationships that also structure the cosmos. In this respect, Brunelleschi contributed to the new view of humanity that helped distinguish the Renaissance from the Middle Ages. His buildings, colored with a restrained palette of whites and grays, provided a new sense of order, serenity, and purity.

According to Manetti, who is credited with Brunelleschi's earliest biography, Brunelleschi also codified a mathematical system of perspective for painters; some scholars suggest this took place around the years 1415–1420. He reportedly painted some examples, which are now lost, to illustrate his system. Whether or not this is true, Brunelleschi's interest in mathematics probably does anticipate a similar interest in mathematical perspective found in the works of Masaccio and Uccello. Brunelleschi's architecture undoubtedly inspired many generations of architects including Alberti and Michelangelo.

BIBLIOGRAPHY

Giulio C. Argan, *Brunelleschi* (1955); Piero Sanpaolesi, *Brunelleschi* (1962); E. Luporini, *Brunelleschi, forma e ragione* (1964); Heinrich Klotz, *Die Frühwerke Brunelleschis und die mittelälterliche Tradition* (1970); F. D. Prager and G. Scaglia, *Brunelleschi: Studies of His Technology and Inventions* (1970).

Adelheid M. Gealt

[See also **Donatello; Florence; Ghiberti, Lorenzo.**]

BRUNETTO LATINI. See **Latini, Brunetto.**

BRUNHILD. See **Brynhild.**

BRUNI, LEONARDO (*ca.* 1370–1444), was born at Arezzo, in Tuscany, according to Hans Baron. Little is known about his early life. He went to Florence around 1384, and as a promising student of Latin he came to the attention of the Florentine chancellor Coluccio Salutati. The humanist circle around Salutati decisively influenced Bruni's education, and he studied rhetoric, law, and Greek. Profound classical scholarship and participation in Florentine politics distinguish Bruni's humanism.

Bruni made his reputation as a writer by contributing to Florentine propaganda in the city's struggle against Giangaleazzo Visconti of Milan. *Laudatio florentinae urbis,* written in 1401 or shortly thereafter, displayed humanist values and a keen ear for what the Florentine patriciate wanted to hear about their city and its tradition of independence. In 1405 Bruni went to Rome to further his career, and Innocent VII placed him in the papal chancellery. Bruni spent the next ten years serving the "Pisan" curia, and he was disappointed in 1406 when he was not selected to succeed his mentor Salutati. Bruni prospered under the antipope John XXIII and fled the Council of Constance with him in 1414.

In 1415 Bruni returned to Florence and shortly thereafter began his great project, the *Historia florentini populi.* This archetype of humanist historiography remained influential for over a century and set the tone for the writing of history in Italy. Bruni borrowed from the medieval chronicle tradition the idea of writing about a single city, and he took from classical models an eloquent Latin style, speeches, and a sharp political focus. Bruni lent his considerable talents as a writer to a single theme—the greatness of Florence and its people. While this work was mainly political in content, Bruni believed that history ought to be useful, so he emphasized accuracy and readability (an Italian translation that appeared in 1473 added to Bruni's enduring fame). In 1416 Cosimo de' Medici helped Bruni to become a citizen of Florence.

Bruni's other works include a discussion of the military and important Latin translations of Aristotle. In the 1420's, Florence, again facing a threat from Milan, benefited from his services as a polemicist. In 1427 Bruni was the city's foremost man of letters and the obvious choice to fill the post of chancellor. The great tax survey of that year also revealed that his net assets placed him in the top 1 percent of Florentine taxpayers. This fortune originated in the papal service, was augmented by a highly advantageous marriage in 1411 or 1412, and flourished in a city that patronized his talents. Bruni survived the fall of the Albizzi oligarchy in 1434 and continued to serve his old friend and new master Cosimo. In the same year he wrote his famous lives of Dante and Petrarch in Italian. Numerous orations and diplomatic letters testify to his contribution to civic affairs. Florence honored him with a magnificent tomb in S. Croce.

BIBLIOGRAPHY

There is no standard edition of Bruni's many works. See the bibliography in Hans Baron, *Leonardo Bruni aretino, humanistisch-philosophische Schriften* (1928); and Baron's *The Crisis of the Early Italian Renaissance* (1955). The *Historia* is in *Rerum italicarum scriptores,* Emilio Santini, ed., 2nd ed. XIX (1914). Bruni figures prominently in Eric Cochrane, *Historians and Historiography in the Italian Renaissance* (1981); Eugenio Garin, *L'umanesimo italiano* (1952); and Lauro Martines, *The Social World of the Florentine Humanists* (1963). There is an interesting fifteenth-century biography by Vespasiano da Bisticci, published in numerous editions.

S. Epstein

[See also **Florence; Historiography.**]

BRUNO OF MAGDEBURG (*fl.* 1084), chronicler and cleric at the court of Archbishop Werner of Magdeburg (leader of Saxon uprising and opponent of Henry IV). In 1082 he wrote *De bello saxonico liber,* covering the period 1073–1081. His work is inexact but valuable for its vivid portrayal of contemporary events.

BIBLIOGRAPHY

Maximilianus Manitius, *Geschichte der lateinischen literatur des mittelalters,* III (1931), 398; Hans Eberhard Lohmann, ed., *De bello saxonico liber* (1937).

Edward Frueh

[See also **Henry IV of Germany.**]

BRUNO OF QUERFURT, ST. (*ca.* 974–1009), an "archbishop of the barbarians" martyred by East Prussians. Nobly born and well educated, he accompanied Emperor Otto III to Rome where, impressed by Adalbert of Prague and Romuald of Ravenna, he began to expound and live an ascetic progress from monasticism to hermitism to missionary martyrdom.

BIBLIOGRAPHY

To the editions of Bruno's writings listed in the *Repertorium fontium historiae medii aevi,* II (1967), 592–594, can be added those by Jadwiga Karwasińska in *Monumenta Poloniae historica,* n.s. IV (2, 3) (1969, 1973). On Bruno see Bernard Hamilton, "The Monastery of S. Alessio and the Religious and Intellectual Renaissance of Tenth-century Rome," in *Studies in Medieval and Renaissance History,* 2 (1965), repr. in his *Monasticism, Catharism and the Crusades (900–1300)* (1979); Jean Leclercq, "Saint Romuald et le monachisme missionnaire," in *Revue bénédictine,* 72 (1962); and Hanns Leo Mikoletzky, "Zur Charakteristik Bruns von Querfurt," in *Festschrift zur Feier des zweihundert-jährigen Bestandes des Haus-, Hof- und Staatsarchivs,* Leo Santifaller, ed., I (1949).

John Howe

BRUNO OF SEGNI, ST. (*ca.* 1040–1123), theologian and exegete, was appointed bishop of Segni in 1079 and served as counselor to three popes: Victor III, Urban II, and Paschal II. He entered Monte Cassino in 1103 and was elected abbot in 1107. After criticizing the Concordat of Sutri (1111), Bruno was forced to return to Segni, where he died. He was canonized in 1183. His works include commentaries on the Old and New Testaments, a life of St. Leo, a life of St. Peter, sermons, letters, and *sententiae*.

BIBLIOGRAPHY

R. Grégoire, *Bruno de Segni, exégète médiéval et théologien monastique* (1965); Max Manitius, *Geschichte der lateinischen Literatur des Mittelalters,* III (1931), 398; *Monumenta Germaniae historica: Libelli de lite,* II (1892), 546–562; *Patrologia latina,* MDCCCLXIV–MDCCCLXV (1854), 1–1142.

NATHALIE HANLET

BRUNO OF WÜRZBURG, ST. (*ca.* 1005–1045), born at Linz, was bishop of Würzburg from 1034 and author of a commentary on the Psalms and of catechetical works. A nobleman, he held influential offices under King Henry III and Emperor Conrad II. Bruno died in an accident at Persenbeug. Although never canonized, he was venerated in Germany as a saint; his feast day is 17 May.

BIBLIOGRAPHY

Bruno's writings are in *Patrologia latina,* CXLII (1853), 39–568. A biography is in *Acta sanctorum* for May, IV (1866), 38–41.

EDWARD A. SYNAN

BRUNO THE CARTHUSIAN, ST. (*ca.* 1030–1101), founder of the Carthusian order of hermit-monks, studied and taught at Cologne and Rheims, and was summoned by his former student, Pope Urban II, to participate in the "Gregorian Reform." In 1083 he undertook the eremetical life at Sèche-Fontaine and founded the Carthusian order at Grande Chartreuse the following year. After being summoned to Rome in 1090, Bruno retired, with the pope's permission, to the Calabrian wilderness, where he died. He was buried at a hermitage that he had founded, Santa Maria de la Torre.

BIBLIOGRAPHY

Bruno's writings are in *Patrologia latina,* CLII (1854), 637–1420, and CLIII (1854), 11–566. A biography is André Ravier, *Saint Bruno: Le premier des ermites de Chartreuse* (1967).

EDWARD A. SYNAN

[See also **Carthusians; Gregory VII, Pope.**]

BRUNSBERG, H(E)INRICH VON (*d.* 1430), architect of northeastern Germany. He was influenced by the work of the Parlers in the use of irregular wall planes and, especially, in decorative details. H(e)inrich treated similarly both his religious buildings (Marienkirche at Stargard, upper part of the choir, begun *ca.* 1390; Katharinenkirche at Brandenburg an der Havel, choir, begun 1390/1395) and his civil buildings (town halls at Stargard, *ca.* 1390; Königsburg im Neumark, *ca.* 1400; and Tangermünde, *ca.* 1430).

BIBLIOGRAPHY

Paul Frankl, *Gothic Architecture* (1962), 181–183; Louis Grodecki, *Gothic Architecture* (1977) 307, 313, 318; M. Säume, "H(e)inrich von Brunsberg," in *Baltische Studien,* **28** (1926).

CARL F. BARNES, JR.

[See also **Parler, Johannes; Parler, Peter.**]

BRUSA (Greek: Prusa; Turkish: Bursa), an important fortified Byzantine town in Bithynia in Asia Minor (40° 10′N., 29° 3′E.), about seventy-five miles opposite Constantinople across the Sea of Marmara and a bit inland. Because of its location it was of great strategic importance to the Byzantines. Theodore I Laskaris established himself there after the Latin occupation of Constantinople during the Fourth Crusade in 1204. The Byzantines managed to hold the city against the Ottomans until 1326, when the Turks took it and made it their capital. Brusa became the burial place of the early Ottoman sultans, who did a great deal of building there: mosques, religious schools, baths, and public kitchens. In 1402 the city was captured and pillaged by the Mongol leader Tamerlane.

BIBLIOGRAPHY
George Ostrogorsky, *History of the Byzantine State* (1957).

LINDA ROSE

[See also **Ottomans; Tamerlane; Theodore I Laskaris.**]

BRUT, THE. Layamon's *Brut* is a Middle English narrative poem of 16,095 long lines (as it appears in the Early English Text Society edition). We are aware of no other work by the author, details of whose life are known only from the opening lines of the poem, in which he tells us that his name is Layamon, and that he is a priest at Erneleye (the modern parish of Areley Kings in Worcestershire).

The *Brut* recounts the mostly legendary history of the British, who are said to be descended from the Trojans in bondage in Greece after the fall of Troy. Under their leader, Brutus, from whom they take their name, they rebelled, escaped, and eventually settled in Britain. There follows a lengthy account of succeeding ancient kings, including Cymbeline, Lear, and Vortigern (and his dealings with Hengist and Horsa), down to Arthur, whose story first appears in English here. His life is the climax of the poem, and Layamon devotes the middle third of it to him. The story continues to the death of Caedwalla (Cadwallon) and the dominance of the Anglo-Saxon invaders.

Layamon acknowledges three sources: the French verse *Brut* of Wace (a translation of Geoffrey of Monmouth's Latin prose *Historia regum Britanniae*), the Old English translation of Bede's *Ecclesiastical History of the English People,* and a "Latin book by St. Albin and St. Augustine, who brought baptism here," which may be the Latin version of Bede's *History.* Wace, the broad outline of whose story is followed throughout, was undoubtedly the main source.

Many other sources have been postulated, but although Layamon may well have been familiar with and influenced by them, it is difficult to establish direct, conscious derivation from the text. Layamon cites Merlin's prophecies about the fate of Rome and Winchester as recollections at the time of their fulfillment. Since these two prophecies appear among the "Prophecies of Merlin" in Geoffrey's *Historia regum Britanniae*—but nowhere in Wace—it is possible that Layamon derived them from it; but little else in the *Brut* suggests that Layamon knew Geoffrey's work. Welsh sources have also been cited and may account for some of Layamon's departures from Wace—for example, the elves who conduct Arthur to Avalon and, more particularly, the name of their queen: Argante.

The poem is extant in two manuscripts, both in the British Library Cotton collection. The basic text appears on folios 3–194 of Cotton Caligula A. IX. The dialect suggests that it emanated from Worcestershire. The second, and possibly slightly later, text appears on folios 1–146 of Otho C. XIII. This text has much greater significance than most variant versions of medieval works. It is probably from the Somerset area. Otho has been shortened with considerable skill by an unknown editor or scribe, and is of particular significance to students of the English language because it has a much more modern orthography and vocabulary than Caligula.

The earliest likely date of composition is 1189, when Henry II died, for Layamon refers to Eleanor, who was Henry's queen. Recent paleographic reassessments of the date of the Caligula manuscript suggest that it was written in the third, rather than the first, quarter of the thirteenth century. A later date of composition for the poem is consequently possible, but since the language seems to favor an earlier date of composition, those who support a late date suggest that the poet may have used archaic forms for effect.

Layamon expands and completely alters the emphasis and tone of his French exemplar. Wace quotes important speeches only, and merely reports others; Layamon not only supplies appropriate speeches—persuasive or belligerent—whenever the occasion demands but also invents realistic dialogue to dramatize the story. In Wace messages are usually written and not reported verbatim. Layamon frequently provides named messengers who deliver their messages verbally. He even adds whole new scenes to illuminate Wace's terse reportage. His most notable amplifications are the feast he invents to illustrate the need for the Round Table and the mysterious carpenter who is able to so construct it that it can seat 1,600 and yet be transported at will.

Wace looks to the contemporary Norman court for a model for his kings and their followers, particularly Arthur's, whereas Layamon looks back to the heroic tradition for his. Layamon's characters are fierce and passionate; in war, more interested in glory earned through individual bravery than in strategy, and in peace more concerned with the security of their domains than with the brilliance of their courts.

Because of this heroic slant in Layamon's poem, and because it is the only other extant epic in early English literature, the *Brut* inevitably invites comparison with *Beowulf.* The differences are greater than the similarities. Unlike classical Old English verse, which adheres to strict rules, Layamon's verse is unconstrained in its use of alliteration, is variable in stress, and occasionally employs rhyme and assonance, both eschewed by most Anglo-Saxon poets. The traditional assumption that Layamon's verse medium originated in Old English "popular" poetry is being reexamined in the light of comparative studies of alliterative homilies and the loose verse of late chronicle poems. Moreover, a detailed analysis of Layamon's vocabulary shows closer kinship with early Middle English works than with Old English epic.

Like other medieval storytellers, Layamon uses stock phrases, often as mechanically, but rarely as inappropriately, as they do; occasionally he uses them with great skill, as when he points out an irony of fate by changing the key word in an oft-repeated phrase to its opposite. He occasionally uses similes, all short, mostly simple, one- or two-line comparisons, except for a group of six hunting images that are multifaceted and sustained for several lines. All of these occur in the account of Arthur's pursuit of the Saxons. Because of the sudden appearance and disappearance of these similes, it has been suggested that Layamon took them over, ready-made, from a source that he used for this part of the story. Two factors must be borne in mind when assessing this theory: first, these similes are peculiarly apt for this part of the story alone; second, there is not the slightest change in Layamon's idiom within them. Indeed, in the longest of them he incorporates five of his stock phrases.

We have, then, a poet who stands between two cultures, echoing the values of the old, aware of the new but rejecting its values, and using the language of his time with intelligence and a dramatic flair unequaled by his contemporaries in either culture.

BIBLIOGRAPHY

Editions. G. L. Brook and R. F. Leslie, eds., *Laȝamon: Brut,* I (1963), II (1978), III in process—this is the only modern edition of the full text; Sir Frederic Madden, ed. and trans., *Laȝamon's Brut, or Chronicle of Britain,* 3 vols. (1847, repr. 1970), contains a literal translation of the poem, and textual apparatus.

Concordance. R. F. Leslie and Alan Tweedale, A Keyword-in-context (KWIC) concordance to the Caligula and Otho texts of Layamon's *Brut,* available on magnetic tape from the University of Victoria—full details in *Computers and Medieval Data Processing,* **10.1** (June 1980), item 247.

Studies. Roger Sherman Loomis, "Layamon's *Brut,*" in *Arthurian Literature in the Middle Ages: A Collaborative History* (1959), provides a succinct survey of the poem. Herbert Pilch, *Layamons "Brut": Eine literarische Studie* (1960), is a learned analysis of the sources, structure, and style of the *Brut,* particularly useful for the study of possible Welsh sources. Håkan Ringbom, *Studies in the Narrative Technique of Beowulf and Lawman's Brut* (1968), is a useful analysis, although too much is made of the continuity of Old and Middle English; it is valuable for its detailed appendixes comparing Wace's *Brut* with Layamon's. E. G. Stanley, "The Date of Laȝamon's *Brut,*" in *Notes and Queries,* **213** (1968), is a critique of hitherto accepted criteria for dating the poem, suggesting that many are vague or doubtful. J. S. P. Tatlock, *The Legendary History of Britain: Geoffrey of Monmouth's Historia regum Britanniae and Its Early Vernacular Versions* (1950), 483–531, is a monumental study of the background of the *Brut,* still the most comprehensive survey yet made (though a number of its suppositions have been questioned).

ROY F. LESLIE

[See also **Arthurian Literature; Geoffrey of Monmouth; Middle English Literature; Wace.**]

BRYNHILD is the most impressive female figure in Germanic heroic poetry. She is the focus of three Eddic poems *(Sigurðarkviða in forna, Sigurðarkviða in skamma, Sigurðarkviða in meiri)* and the sections of *Vǫlsunga saga* that combine these poems. She has a somewhat less central role in *Þiðreks saga* and the *Nibelungenlied.* In the earliest form of the Norse legend *(Forna),* she is wooed by Sigurd on Gunnarr's behalf after Gunnarr is stymied by a magic flame wall designed to admit only the most distinguished suitor, whom Brynhild has vowed to marry. Sigurd crosses the flame wall disguised as Gunnarr, obliges Brynhild to comply with her vow, and shares her bed for three nights, separated from her by his drawn sword. He then departs, and she is wed to the real Gunnarr. One day Brynhild and Sigurd's wife, Gudrun, quarrel as they bathe in the Rhine, and Gudrun humiliates her rival by revealing that she was won by Sigurd, not Gunnarr. Bent on revenge, Brynhild claims that Sigurd abused Gunnarr's trust by sleeping with her, and she incites Gunnarr to take Sigurd's life. Gunnarr agrees, and Sigurd is killed in the forest.

In a later, more elaborate version *(Sigurðarkviða in meiri)* we learn that Sigurd was betrothed to Brynhild before wooing her for Gunnarr. In this version Gunnarr's mother, Grimhild, administers a potion of forgetfulness that blots out Sigurd's memory of his prior commitment and allows him to marry Grimhild's daughter, Gudrun. The deception of Brynhild and the subsequent revelation are analogous to the older poem. Sigurd and Brynhild then confront one another over the issue of broken faith. He confesses his love and offers to abandon Gudrun, but Brynhild rejects any accommodation and plots Sigurd's death. In this version he is slain by Gunnarr's younger brother, Gotþormr, as he lies in bed next to Gudrun. Originally Brynhild probably survived, but in the later story she commits suicide after leaving directions that she and Sigurd are to lie side by side on the same funeral pyre.

The older story concentrated on the forceful heroine determined to fulfill her desires. The later story is more romantic, and emphasizes the erotic and psychological factors by adding the prior betrothal, a strong tinge of jealousy, a series of probing dialogues, and Brynhild's pathetic suicide. This was the form of the legend in *Sigurðarkviða in meiri,* a poem that is missing from the only full manuscript of the *Poetic Edda.* The story therefore survives only in the prose reworking in *Vǫlsunga saga.* A late Eddic poem entitled *Helreið Brynhildar* tells how Brynhild encountered a witch on her journey to the underworld and recounted the story of her life.

In the German version of the legend represented by *Þiðreks saga* and the *Nibelungenlied,* Brynhild's dominant role is diminished. Her prior betrothal to Siegfried is implicit but largely suppressed. Instead of being wooed behind a magic flame wall, she is subdued in a series of athletic contests *(Nibelungenlied).* In addition, she is deflowered by Siegfried *(Þiðreks saga)* or wrestled into submission in Gunther's bed *(Nibelungenlied).* The slaying of Siegfried is explained less by her initiative than by Hagen's, and she subsequently recedes from view quietly instead of dying in a grand finale.

BIBLIOGRAPHY

For editions and translations, see the entries under the individual texts. The critical literature is surveyed by Theodore M. Andersson, *The Legend of Brynhild* (1980).

THEODORE M. ANDERSSON

[See also **Nibelungenlied; Sigurd; Sigurðarkviða in Forna; Sigurðarkviða in Meiri; Sigurðarkviða in Skamma; Þiðreks Saga; Vǫlsunga Saga.**]

BUCENTAUR (Latinized form of *bucintoro,* probably from *buzo,* Venetian dialect for *burchio,* "big barge," and *d'oro,* "of gold"). To symbolize its maritime supremacy, the Republic of Venice in 1177 inaugurated under the auspices of Pope Alexander III the annual ceremony of the "wedding of the sea" *(sposalizio del mare)* on the feast of the Ascension. In a richly decorated, sailless barge called *bucentaur,* some thirty-five meters long and some eight meters wide, the doge and the governing council, followed by a cortege in another barge or a gondola, went to the entrance of the port of the Lido. When at sea the doge dropped a consecrated ring in the water and announced: "We wed thee, sea" *(desponsamus te, mare).* In early times the barge was towed. Later, as seen in pictures from the sixteenth century, it was furnished with oars. The last *bucentaur* was destroyed by the French in 1798; in the Arsenale of Venice there is a reconstruction executed in 1829. The *bucentaur* is depicted in the *Veduta prospèttica di Venezia* of Jacopo de' Barbari (1500) and in eighteenth-century paintings by Canaletto, Guardi, and Marieschi.

BIBLIOGRAPHY

Antonio M. Luchini, *La nuova regia su' l'acque nel Bucintoro* (1729); Giovanni Casoni, *Il bucintoro di Venezia* (1837); Pompeo Molmenti, *Storia di Venezia nella vita privata* (1922–1926), index. Illustrations are in *Encyclopedia Treccani,* VIII (1930), 15–16.

ANGELO PAREDI

[See also **Venice.**]

BUCH VON BERN, DAS. Also known as *Dietrichs Flucht,* this poem is, with *Alpharts Tod* and *Die Rabenschlacht,* one of the medieval German historical Dietrich epics. It is found together with *Die Rabenschlacht,* to which it is related in plot, in four of the five manuscripts that survived to modern times. These manuscripts, anthologies collected for the nobility from the late thirteenth to the early sixteenth century, show chronological and editorial differences but no great variation in plot or composition.

Dietrichs Flucht was written in Bavarian-Austrian territory, in the rhymed couplets of the courtly narrative. Heinrich der Vogler names himself (line 8,000) during an excursus decrying irresponsible treatment of the lower nobility by the princes. He may have written only this and similar excursuses, or he may be the author in the sense that he reshaped a traditional tale for the edification of the thirteenth-century nobility. The early date of the Riedegg manuscript suggests that *Dietrichs Flucht* was composed sometime toward the end of the first half of the thirteenth century, though the political situation criticized by Heinrich closely resembles that of the last quarter of the century, after the Hohenstaufens had lost control of the Holy Roman Empire.

The basic theme of *Dietrichs Flucht* is reciprocal loyalty between those higher and lower in the feudal hierarchy. There is a fairy-talelike prologue recounting the succession of six kings of Italy (including Otnit and Wolfdietrich). Prior to Dietrich's birth Italy has been divided among his father, Dietmar, and his two uncles, Diether and Ermrich. Ermrich, ruler of Rome, attacks young Dietrich in order to take over northern Italy. Advisers help Dietrich win a battle at Milan. The hero's plans to reward his men are foiled when Ermrich's forces take a number of Dietrich's men hostage. Dietrich goes into exile so that the hostages can be released. He obtains the support of Etzel (Attila) in order to go back to Bern (Verona) and face Ermrich again. He wins a partial victory. Returning to Etzel, he must marry Herrat, Queen Helche's niece, in order to obtain further support. A third battle occurs when the treacherous Witege gives Raben (Ravenna) back to Ermrich. Although Dietrich again wins a partial victory, he suffers heavy losses. He laments for the men, then returns to Etzel.

The narrative's combination of historical, realistic, and fictional elements is not unlike that of the *Nibelungenlied.* The names of leading characters reflect those of historical figures of the Germanic migrations, but the events, reshaped in oral tradition, do not resemble those of the migration period. Battle tactics and geography are realistic. The author seems to rely for irony on the audience's perception of the discrepancy between Dietrich's realistic, thirteenth-century plight and the fairy-tale epics popular at the time, in which he is invincible.

BIBLIOGRAPHY

The critical edition is in Ernst Martin, ed., *Deutsches Heldenbuch,* II (1866, repr. 1967), 57–215. See also Helmut de Boor, *Die deutsche Literatur im späten Mittelalter: Zerfall und Neubeginn,* vol. III, pt. 1 of Helmut de Boor and Richard Newald, *Geschichte der deutschen Literatur von den Anfängen bis zur Gegenwart* (1973), 147–152. Hugo Kuhn, "Dietrichs Flucht und Rabenschlacht," in *Verfasserlexikon,* 2nd ed., rev., II (1978–1979), lists all texts and gives a brief outline of the present state of research.

RUTH H. FIRESTONE

[See also **Alpharts Tod; Eckenlied; Middle High German Literature.**]

BUDA (German: Ofen). Superseding the early princely residence of Óbuda (Buda Vetus; Alt-Ofen) near the Roman site of Aquincum and the older market town of Pest (across the Danube), Buda, built on a defensible hill and fortified after the Mongol invasion of 1241, became the capital of Hungary in 1361. Its early-fifteenth-century castle was a famous proto-Renaissance monument, and its privileges (of 1244) became the model of many town charters. Under Ottoman occupation from 1541 to 1686 and destroyed during the Turkish wars, Buda regained its leading position only in the nineteenth century.

BIBLIOGRAPHY

László Gerevich, *The Art of Buda and Pest in the Middle Ages* (1971); László Gerevich *et al.,* eds., *Budapest története* [History of Budapest], 2 vols. (1973), with extensive bibliography; András Kubinyi, "Topographic Growth of Buda up to 1541," in Commission Nationale des Historiens Hongrois, *Nouvelles études historiques,* I (1965); and *Die Anfänge Ofens* (1972); Károly Mollay, ed., *Das Ofner Stadtrecht: Eine deutschsprachige Rechtssammlung aus dem 15. Jahrhunderts aus Ungarn* (1959).

J. M. BAK

[See also **Hungary.**]

BUILDING. See **Construction and Building.**

BUKHARA, a city in Transoxiana (today the western Uzbek S.S.R.), in the lower course of the Zeravshan River, one of the main centers of urban culture in central Asia. A settlement on the site of modern Bukhara apparently existed already in the middle of the first millennium B.C. The first dated source mentioning Bukhara is the book of travels of the Chinese

Buddhist pilgrim Hsüan Tsang from about A.D. 630. The name probably comes from the Sanskrit *vihāra* (Buddhist monastery), which may imply a connection to the spread of Buddhism in central Asia under the Kushan, but this etymology is not certain. By the time of the Arab conquest, Bukhara was the principal town of the oasis bearing this name; the original name of the town itself was apparently Numidjkath. The pre-Islamic rulers of Bukhara had the title Bukhār Khudāh.

The city was conquered by Qutayba ibn Muslim in 709 and since then has remained in the hands of Muslims. The local dynasty, having converted to Islam and been subjected to the Arabs, retained some authority until 782, when the last Bukhār Khudāh was executed by order of the caliph. From 875 Bukhara became the capital of the Samanids; the tenth century was the most brilliant period in the history of the city. After its conquest by the Karakhanid Turks in 999, Bukhara became second in importance only to Samarkand, its rival in Transoxiana. The city was completely destroyed and its inhabitants slaughtered by the Mongols in 1220. It had recovered already by the second half of the same century, although it was again ravaged by the Mongols in 1273 and 1316. ᶜAbd Allāh ibn Iskandar, of the Shaybanid dynasty, made Bukhara his residence in 1557, and the city remained the capital of the Uzbek khanate in Transoxiana until its abolition in 1920.

Even more than a seat of government, Bukhara was important as a major commercial city of central Asia (surpassed only in the nineteenth century by Tashkent) and as the center of religious learning. Since the Samanid time, Bukhara has been one of the world centers of the Sunnite orthodoxy and it has a greater number of madrasas than any other city in central Asia.

At the time of the Arab conquest, Bukhara was a comparatively small city, occupying an area of about eighty-five acres with an estimated population of about 10,000. It had an almost square configuration, with seven gates and two main streets crossing in the center; the citadel was outside the city wall, at a distance of about 400 feet. As distinct from most other ancient cities of central Asia, in Bukhara the pre-Islamic city (Persian: *shahristān*) was not abandoned with the growth of the city beyond the original walls, but was incorporated, together with the citadel, in the larger city limits. In 849–850 (and probably earlier) the expanding suburbs *(rabad),* which encircled the old *shahristān,* were also surrounded by walls. The area of the city at the time of its greatest expansion during the pre-Mongol period is not clear; estimates vary between 420 and 1,180 acres. The number of inhabitants is even less certain, probably not much greater than the 75,000 of about 1900.

Although famous for its many outstanding buildings (the so-called Mausoleum of the Samanids was built in the tenth century), Bukhara was also notorious for the scarcity and bad quality of water, density of buildings, and lack of vegetation; an Arab geographer of the tenth century, Muqaddasī, called it "a latrine of that region and the most cramped of the cities of the East." The fact that the densely built city has always remained on the same site has prevented any large-scale archaeological excavations. Extensive ethnographic study between the 1940's and the 1960's has helped to reconstruct important details of city life in the nineteenth and the early twentieth centuries, and to some extent in earlier periods as well.

BIBLIOGRAPHY

Vasilii Barthold, *Turkestan down to the Mongol Invasion,* Mrs. T. Minorsky, trans., 3rd ed. (1968), 100–113; Richard N. Frye, *Bukhara: The Medieval Achievement* (1965); Narshakhī, *The History of Bukhara,* R. N. Frye, trans. (1954); *Architectural Monuments of Middle Asia: Bukhara, Samarkand* (1969).

YURI BREGEL

[See also **Karakhanids; Samanids.**]

BUKHĀRĪ, AL-, Muḥammad ibn Ismāᶜīl al-Bukhārī (810–870), was born in Bukhara. His scholarly activity earned him considerable renown during his lifetime, and in the centuries that followed his death he became known as the foremost "traditionist" of Sunni Islam. A Muslim traditionist concerns himself with the traditions of Islam (Arabic singular and plural, *ḥadīth*), which are the oral and written transmission of the sayings and actions of the prophet Muḥammad, his family, and his close associates, as well as of the practices that evolved in the early Muslim community. Each tradition consists of a text *(matn)* and a chain of transmission *(isnād).* The first transmitter of the text was usually someone who had personally known the prophet Muḥammad or had known one or more of his contemporaries. The second transmitter was someone who knew the first transmitter and heard the text from him, and so on through successive generations.

BUKHĀRĪ, AL-

Initially, early Muslims collected and recorded traditions for their own religious purposes. But, during the first two and one-half centuries of Islam, as the prophet Muḥammad's explicit legislative and legal legacy proved inadequate for the religious and political needs of the peoples of the expanding Muslim world, traditions became an important source for guidance in both private and public affairs. At the same time there is evidence that they were used tendentiously for a variety of sectarian and political purposes, and that a great many traditions were fabricated and put into circulation to support a particular position. By the third century of Islam the sheer number of traditions in circulation throughout the Muslim world, along with their continued importance as a source of guidance for Muslim belief and practice, led to the development of tradition criticism as an important scholarly discipline. Tradition criticism was concerned with determining which among the many thousands of traditions available for scrutiny were reliable. Bukhārī, from a very early age, gained prominence for working out criteria for the reliability of traditions and for collecting and transmitting them in accordance with these criteria.

To determine the reliability of a given tradition, the chain of transmission and the text were examined separately, although more attention was given to the individual transmitters than to the text, and a seemingly reliable text might be rejected by a traditionist because of a faulty chain of transmitters. By Bukhārī's era many traditions had chains of transmission with one or more persons missing or with improbable juxtapositions of transmitters, such as *x* having heard a tradition from *y*, who had died before *x* was born. A perfect chain of transmission went back in uninterrupted succession to the Prophet; each person, or link, in the chain actually heard the text from the person before him. Multiple transmitters in each generation were desirable.

Interest in transmitters at first was chronological. Then, as the Muslim world expanded, their relative geographical locations were considered, and finally attention was given to the personality of a particular transmitter, his reputation for integrity and piety, and his capacity for transmitting accurately. This multifaceted interest in transmitters led to the compilation of biobibliographical dictionaries of prominent transmitters that could be consulted by traditionists eager to decide on the relevant merits of different chains of transmission.

Even before Bukhārī's time, custom dictated the preferability of oral to written transmission of traditions. Thus, a student wishing to collect traditions traveled wherever necessary to acquire them directly from particular transmitters before adding his own name to the end of the chain of transmission. Although oral transmission was the rule, scholars often taught by using written manuscripts of their own works. Students or fellow scholars would copy a particular manuscript under supervision and then be granted permission to transmit it to others. Under Bukhārī's influence strict rules were developed for accurate copying of manuscripts of tradition collections. He insisted that all texts be reproduced exactly as heard and that doubts about accuracy, textual criticism, and particularly critical comments on content be relegated to glosses and ascribed to the individual collector.

Bukhārī traveled extensively throughout the Middle East to study and collect traditions. He visited the main centers of Muslim learning, and he is said to have heard traditions from more than 1,000 scholars. In later life he settled in Neyshābūr, where his reputation for learning and the popularity of his teaching aroused the jealousy of other scholars. Because of a doctrinal position he held on the recitation of the Koran, he was accused of heterodoxy and forced to leave Neyshābūr. He then taught for a while in Bukhara, but was expelled from that city for refusing to give the local governor or his children private instruction in tradition. He spent the remainder of his life among relatives in a village near Samarkand.

Bukhārī is the author of a biographical dictionary on tradition transmitters, but he is best known for his collection of traditions, the *Ṣaḥīḥ,* which contains, not counting repetitions, 2,762 traditions. They are arranged in chapters with headings that correspond to the ritual, legal, and dogmatic concerns of the Muslim community. There are also chapters that deal with other material, such as revelation, the acquisition of knowledge, the creation of the world, the Koran, and historical and pseudohistorical information on various prophets, including Muḥammad. Some chapters consist only of their headings, which indicates that Bukhārī drafted the outline of his collection before critically sifting his tradition material, and that his standards were such that he was unable to find any reliable traditions for those particular chapters.

After Bukhārī's death his *Ṣaḥīḥ* was widely disseminated and studied, as were numerous other tradition collections. In the course of the seventh century of Islam (the thirteenth century of the Christian

era), along with five other collections, it came to be considered one of the most important sources for religious learning in Sunni Islam. Although these "Six Books" all acquired virtually canonical standing, Bukhārī's *Ṣaḥīḥ* and the collection of a contemporary, Muslim ibn al-Ḥajjāj (*d.* 875), are considered especially authoritative.

BIBLIOGRAPHY

Ignaz Goldziher, *Muslim Studies,* S. M. Stern and C. R. Barber, trans., II (1971); *Selections from the Ṣaḥīḥ of al-Bukhārī,* Charles C. Torrey, ed. (1906, repr. 1969).

SUSAN SPECTORSKY

[See also **Hadīth; Islam.**]

BULBOUS DOME. See **Dome, Types of.**

BULGARIA. The territory in the southeastern corner of the Balkan peninsula which came to be known as Bulgaria had been part of the Byzantine Empire. By the fifth century Slavic tribes (in two large groups, though not unified political units, the Antes and Slaveni) had settled across the Danube in what is now Wallachia. In the middle of the sixth century Procopius listed various Slavic place-names along the Timok River and in northern Bulgaria. In the late sixth century, partly as a result of Avar pressure, larger numbers of Slavs in small tribal groupings began crossing the Danube and settling. The Byzantines were too weak to prevent their settlement. The Slavs who migrated to Bulgaria and Macedonia were chiefly of one linguistic group, probably already distinguishable from those who settled in Serbia and Croatia. The indigenous population (Thracians and Dacians) emigrated, were killed, or were gradually assimilated. Some of the Dacians took to the mountains and as shepherds retained their identity, reappearing in eleventh-century sources as Vlachs.

Meanwhile, in the seventh century a Turkic tribe of Onogur Bulgars, under its ruler Kovrat, was living north of the Sea of Azov. These Bulgars, an ethnically mixed group under a Bulgar chief, were seminomadic. In about 635 Kovrat threw off Avar suzerainty and united most of the Bulgars in that general region under his rule. After his death (*ca.* 642) his tribe split among his several sons. One son, Isperikh (Asperukh), migrated with his followers into what is now Romania, and then in the 670's crossed the Danube and subjected the Slavs settled there.

The Slavs seem already to have been moving toward state formation, for we are told that Isperikh subjected "the Seven Tribes," a term suggesting that they had formed a federation. Unhappy with this development, the Byzantine emperor Constantine IV led a major campaign to expel the Bulgars. Isperikh defeated the Byzantine army and in 681 forced the empire to sign a treaty recognizing the Bulgar state. This state extended north from the Balkan Mountains and included territory a little beyond the Danube. (At least early Bulgar sites are found on both banks of the river.) Probably much of the territory north of the Danube, however, was still Avar; this land would become Bulgar after the collapse of the Avar Khaganate in the 790's. The Bulgars themselves do not seem to have been particularly numerous—a twelfth-century source gives their numbers as 10,000—and were concentrated along the Danube, particularly from its right bank east to the Black Sea including the Dobrudja.

The Bulgars established their capital at Pliska, which was a huge walled camp on a plain. It encompassed some twenty-three square kilometers and contained the khan's palace, the yurts of his fellow tribesmen, warehouses, shops, and space for flocks and horses. Nearby Madara was their religious center; it exhibits a fine carved horseman on the face of a steep cliff rising above a temple at its base. Archaeology shows that for a while many Bulgars kept settlements distinct from those of the Slavs. They had a mixed pastoral and agricultural economy. Trade was important; the ruins of Pliska show caravanserais, warehouses, and many shops, and an early treaty with Byzantium (716) had commercial clauses.

The Slavs were settled agriculturists, living chiefly in villages, and provided foot soldiers and tribute to the Bulgars. In time (and it seems in some cases quite early) mixed settlements of Slavs and Bulgars appeared in some places, as archaeology has shown. Archaeologists have also noted that the Bulgar towns were new ones rather than continuations of earlier cities. In most cases there is a gap from the sixth to the ninth century at the sites of classical towns. Pure Bulgar sites show variations in burial practices, suggesting the Bulgars were drawn from more than one ethnic group, and the cultural syntheses between Slavic and Bulgar practices (and Byzantine influences) varied from region to region.

The Bulgars rose to international prominence

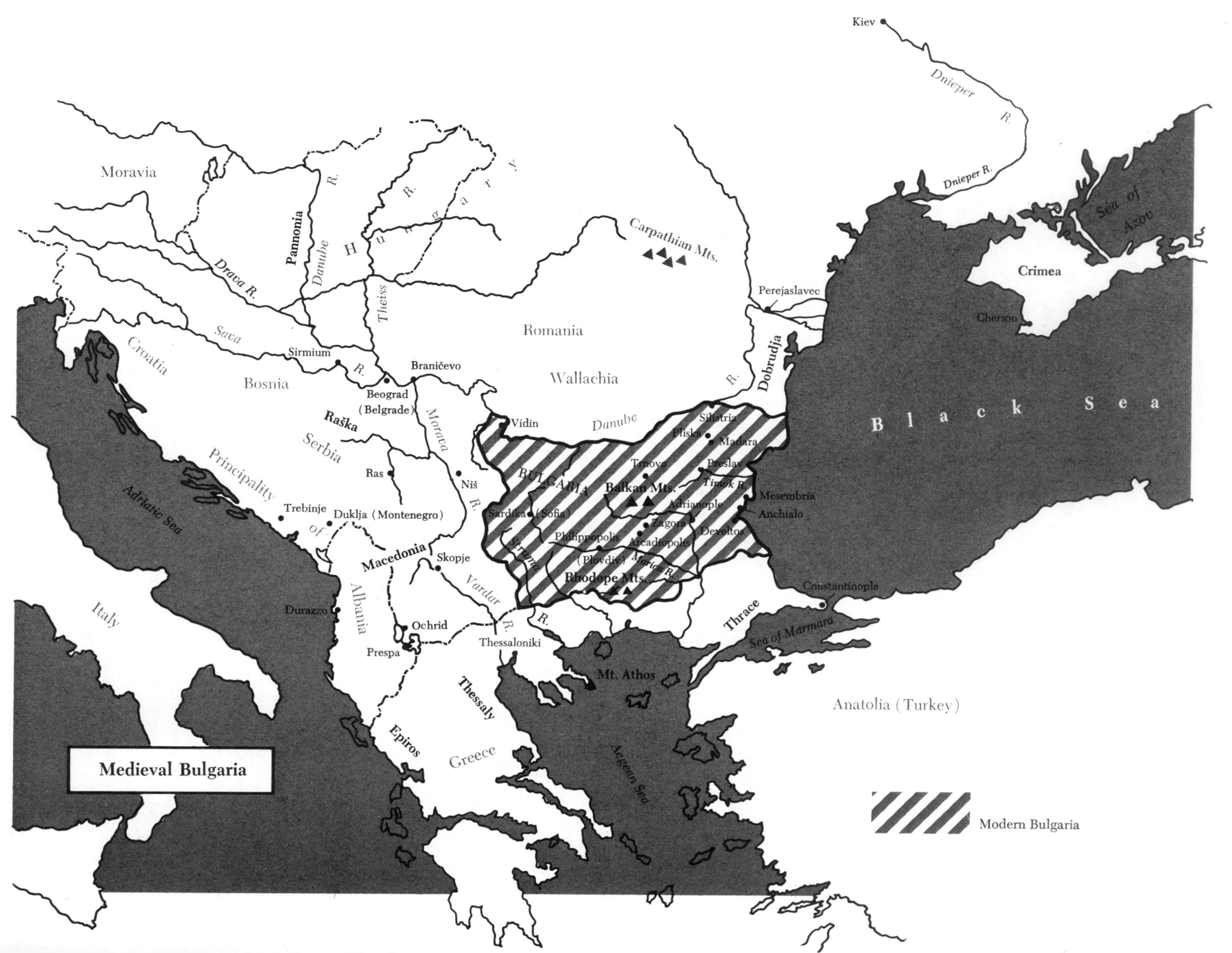
Medieval Bulgaria
Modern Bulgaria
Kiev
Dnieper R.
Moravia
Pannonia
Danube R.
Hungary
Theiss
Drava R.
Sava
Croatia
Sirmium
Bosnia
Beograd (Belgrade)
Braničevo
Carpathian Mts.
Romania
Wallachia
Perejaslavec
Dobrudja
Crimea
Cherson
Sea of Azov
Black Sea
Raška
Serbia
Ras
Morava
Niš
Vidin
Danube
Silistria
Pliska
Madara
Preslav
Trnovo
BULGARIA
Balkan Mts.
Timok R.
Mesembria
Anchialo
Adrianople
Zagora
Develtos
Sardika (Sofia)
Philippopolis
Arcadiopolis
(Plovdiv)
Marica R.
Rhodope Mts.
Struma
Principality of Trebinje
Duklja (Montenegro)
Adriatic Sea
Macedonia
Skopje
Vardar R.
Albania
Durazzo
Ochrid
Prespa
Thessaloniki
Italy
Thrace
Constantinople
Sea of Marmara
Mt. Athos
Anatolia (Turkey)
Thessaly
Epiros
Greece
Aegean Sea

early in the eighth century when Khan Tervel (701–718) helped the exiled Justinian II regain the Byzantine throne in 705. Tervel was honored with the title caesar. Shortly thereafter in 717–718, the Arabs launched a major attack against Constantinople, which, if successful, would have led to an Arab offensive against eastern Europe. The Bulgars sent aid to the beleaguered Byzantines and played a significant role in breaking the Arab siege.

In 739 the Bulgar royal house of Dulo—according to its traditions descended from Attila—died out, setting off a series of civil wars because the jealous boyars (military aristocrats) did not want to be ruled by other boyars. From then until the 770's frequent skirmishes, coups, and changes on the throne occurred. The Byzantines intervened frequently, both by intrigue from within and by military campaign from without. The great military emperor Constantine V (741–775) led nine campaigns against the feuding Bulgars, but though successful in battles he was unable to destroy the Bulgar state. After his death the Bulgar state remained, probably stronger than before, with the Slavs increasingly identifying their cause with the Bulgars and both peoples becoming more hostile to the Byzantines. In border skirmishes after Constantine's death the Bulgars were more successful.

In the 790's Charlemagne conquered the main Avar center on the Theiss (Tisza) River. In about 803 Krum, a Bulgar chief from Pannonia, somehow gained the Bulgar throne at Pliska. He renovated the palace there, built with massive blocks of stone. In 805 he attacked the declining Avars and wrested away their eastern European territory, adding what is now eastern Hungary and southern Romania (east to the Dnieper and north to the Carpathians) to the Bulgar state. (In the 820's either Krum or his successor Omurtag extended Bulgaria's northwestern border to the Theiss River, where a frontier with the Franks existed.)

In 807 Byzantium launched a raid against Krum, an action that led him to attack and conquer Sardika (modern Sofia) in 809. In retaliation Emperor Nikephoros I directed a major attack in 811 against Pliska, much of which he destroyed. However, the Byzantine army dawdled on its way home as the emperor suffered a nervous breakdown. Krum successfully attacked the Byzantine camp, killing the emperor (whose skull was fashioned into a goblet) and mortally wounding his son and heir, Staurakios. Krum seized the Byzantine Black Sea port of Develtos in 812 and sent an ultimatum for a truce; the Byzantines rejected it over a clause about returning deserters. Krum won a major victory over the Byzantines in 813 and plundered the suburbs of Constantinople, which led to the overthrow of the incompetent Michael I. In 814, en route to Constantinople with a massive army, Krum died of a stroke.

Besides expanding Bulgaria's borders to the north, east, and west, and strengthening its armies, Krum issued a law code (the text of which, except for two articles, is lost). It seems to have been the first Bulgarian attempt to have a state law rather than to allow each tribe to follow its own customs under its own tribute-paying chief. In this period Greek was the official written language. Many inscriptions from the pre-Christian Bulgars survive; except for a small number of runic ones, all are in Greek.

After brief disorders—and possibly one or two extremely short reigns or regencies—Krum's son Omurtag (814–831) succeeded. A thirty-year peace was concluded with Byzantium that reestablished the Balkan Mountains as the Byzantine-Bulgarian border, restoring to the empire the Thracian cities conquered by Krum. With the exception of a brief war in 836, peace with Byzantium lasted until 846. Omurtag aided Emperor Michael II in 822–823 against the rebel Thomas the Slav, an action that contributed to breaking Thomas' siege of Constantinople. Peace with Byzantium enabled Omurtag to concentrate on his western border, where the Slavs of the Timok River had seceded and accepted Frankish suzerainty. The Franks ignored Omurtag's protests, so he attacked them in 827, expelled the local Slavic chiefs, installed Bulgar governors, and acquired Beograd (Belgrade), Braničevo, and Sirmium. By the end of the campaign he had brought or restored Bulgaria's border to the Theiss River.

Omurtag disliked Christianity (probably chiefly because Christians were seen as Byzantine agents) and actively persecuted the growing numbers of Christians both in the interests of Bulgar religion and as imperial spies. Various Christians were martyred, but despite persecutions the religion continued to spread.

Omurtag was a great builder. He rebuilt Pliska, destroyed by Nikephoros, making it more grandiose than it had been before; he founded the future capital city of Preslav, building a splendid palace and bridge there as well as another impressive palace on the Danube. He also erected shrines, particularly a great temple at the religious center of Madara. To assert his authority over the boyars, he claimed divine origin for his rule. A Preslav inscription states that Omurtag "from God rules in the land where he was born."

Omurtag died in 831. His eldest son, Enravota, had become a Christian and was excluded from succession. (He was executed soon thereafter when he refused to give up his faith.) A younger son, Malimir, succeeded. He is mentioned until 836; then a military commander named Presiam (or Persian) seems to be the ruler. Two theories exist: either Presiam was a second name for Malimir (and double names did exist), who would continue to reign until 852, or else Malimir was succeeded by Presiam in the middle of the Byzantine war of 836. With the expiration of their treaty in 846, Bulgaria attacked Byzantium. The results are unknown. Presiam also made an unsuccessful attack on Serbia at some time before 850. In 852 Presiam died and was succeeded by his son or nephew (depending on the source) Boris (852–889). Boris immediately went to war against Byzantium. In either this campaign or Presiam's 846 campaign the Bulgarians occupied most of Macedonia. This doubled the size of their state and brought into it an area almost exclusively Slavic, which would increase the influence of the Slavs. Byzantium, unhappy with this expansion, did not recognize Bulgaria's control of Macedonia until 904.

BORIS

At the start of Boris' reign Bulgaria also fought unsuccessful wars with the Franks, Serbs, and Moravians, but through skillful diplomacy Boris suffered no territorial losses. Despite persecutions under Boris' predecessors, Christianity was increasingly penetrating Bulgaria. Bulgarian territory had been, on paper, under the Byzantine patriarch since 731, when Emperor Leo III, angry at a papal condemnation of his iconoclastic policy, had transferred most of the Balkans to the jurisdiction of the patriarch of Constantinople. The papacy did not accept this change and was then trying to make papal recognition of a new patriarch, Photios, conditional on Byzantium's admission that these lands were papal.

Until the 860's the matter had been academic (because the population was pagan), but now it was taking on significance because Boris was attracted to Christianity. He was allied with the Franks against his northwestern neighbor, Moravia, and believed that he would have more flexibility if he received a mission from the distant Franks rather than from neighboring Byzantium. Byzantium objected to this, and in September 863, when Bulgaria's armies were on their western border, preparing to fight Moravia, the Byzantines attacked by land and sea. Boris, without troops to meet them, at once capitulated. He agreed to accept a Byzantine mission and was himself baptized in 864, taking the name Michael after Emperor Michael III, who stood as his godfather. The Byzantines recognized Bulgarian possession of Zagora, a small strip of territory on their common border.

In 866 a group of boyars revolted against the new religion and the new legal order. The latter may have been equally galling to them, because Boris wanted to create a new legal basis for his state modeled more on Byzantium than on the old Bulgar customs, based on their paganism, which supported privileges to the old Bulgar families. Boris had obtained Byzantine legal texts, and their influence is already seen in 866 in some of the questions on legal practice that he directed to Pope Nicholas I. Thus, the boyars' position, long guaranteed through belief in divinely established clans, was threatened.

Furthermore, Boris no longer claimed to be first among equal clan leaders, but prince by Grace of God. Finally, many of the boyars had long resented Byzantium; they surely considered the entering Byzantine mission a threat to Bulgarian independence. The boyars marched on Pliska, and Boris suppressed the revolt. Our only source about this event, a Western one, attributes his victory to miracles. Boris executed fifty-two leading boyars and their families but pardoned the lesser rebels. This weakened the old aristocracy and probably enabled him to advance some of his own people into positions of power. Thus, possibly, he laid the basis for a service nobility and, to some degree, strengthened the central administration.

Bulgaria was then divided into ten regions, each under a great nobleman. In the First Bulgarian State (681–1018)—except for the governors sent to the Timok region by Omurtag—it is not known whether regional governors were local magnates or appointees of the prince. Under Boris many of the important old boyar families were liquidated, and some scholars have assumed that they were replaced by a service nobility dependent not on birth but on the prince. Though plausible, this view cannot be proved because of the meager details supplied by the sources.

Some boyars evidently remained influential under Boris, for popes wrote to individual boyars, urging them to exert influence on Boris. In Boris' period we hear of "greater" and "lesser" boyars. In the tenth century Constantine VII Porphyrogenitos refers to "inner" and "outer" boyars. Most probably the outer boyars were those living in the provinces and having their own local power bases, and the inner ones were those based at court and presumably dependent on the prince. It would be interesting to know to what extent the prince succeeded in appointing inner boyars to positions of provincial authority. But references to outer boyars in the tenth century suggest that Boris, despite eliminating certain powerful families, did not break the power of provincial boyars as a class. Furthermore, little evidence exists to show much state apparatus. Under Peter (927–969) various Byzantine titles appeared at court, but we cannot assume that their holders were part of a bureaucracy similar to that of their Byzantine namesakes.

Throughout his reign Boris concerned himself with legal matters. His letter to the pope in 866 sought legal texts, secular as well as religious. And subsequently under him the text of *Zakon sudnyi ljud'm* (Court law for the people), based heavily on the Byzantine *Ecloga* but adapted for Bulgarian conditions, appeared in Bulgaria. Whether it was compiled in Bulgaria or brought there from Moravia is heatedly debated among scholars. Byzantine canon law texts were also brought to Bulgaria.

Like the boyars, Boris worried about Byzantine influence in his state and sought an autonomous church with its own patriarch. The Byzantines did not respond, so in 866 he approached Pope Nicholas I. The pope sent a mission, detailed responses to 106 questions on religious practice that Boris had sent him, and, though refusing Boris' request for a patriarch, promised him an archbishop in the future. Boris accepted this and expelled the Byzantine mission. Within a year he asked that the pope make Formosus, leader of the papal mission, his archbishop. Nicholas refused and recalled Formosus. The following year Boris asked Nicholas' successor, Adrian II, for the appointment of an archbishop. Rebuffed again, Boris sent a delegation to a council of the whole church, meeting in Constantinople (869–870), asking to whom Bulgaria belonged. The majority there were easterners and declared for Constantinople. The Byzantines, having learned their lesson, at once sent Boris an archbishop with considerable autonomy who controlled at least five dioceses. Greek clerics returned and the Latin mission was expelled. Thus, Bulgaria became permanently part of the Orthodox world.

The Greek mission preached in Greek; but in 886 a Slavic mission, founded by Constantine-Cyril and Methodios and by then led by Clement and Naum, was expelled from Moravia. Boris welcomed them to Bulgaria, and soon two major Slavonic centers were established: at Ochrid in Macedonia under Clement and at Preslav in northeastern Bulgaria. Clement set up a school at Ochrid that, according to his *Life,* trained 3,500 native Bulgarians in reading, writing, and Christianity. Its graduates created a native clergy. Boris encouraged translations from Greek to Slavonic (of both religious and legal texts), which were carried out at Preslav and Ochrid. Thus, the work of the Slavonic mission was saved, and Bulgaria acquired church services and a literature in the vernacular (for Old Church Slavonic, the language of the mission, was based on Bulgaro-Macedonian Slavic).

By this time, after some 200 years of living together, the more numerous Slavs seem to have been well on their way to assimilating the Bulgars. The process had been gradual, but the final stage seems to have occurred under Boris. It may be partially attributed to his liquidating many leading Bulgar families after their revolt. But Boris also made it national policy to mix the two nationalities into a single culture by using a new doctrine, neither Slavic nor Bulgar in origin, as a cement to unify them; yet by making Slavic—the language of the majority—the official language of church and state, he increased the prestige of the Slavs. It has been said that prior to Boris there was a Bulgarian state but no Bulgarian people and no nationwide cultural consciousness. These Boris' policies created. After his reign sources no longer distinguish between Bulgars and Slavs; and the term "Bulgarian," despite its origins, came to signify the population of Bulgaria among whom Slavic triumphed. Presumably Boris' Slavic policy rallied the Slavs behind him, too. The Bulgar tongue died out, and modern Bulgarian retains less than a dozen words from it.

Boris erected many churches, including seven cathedrals in different dioceses of Bulgaria. The most spectacular was the great basilica built at his capital of Pliska, seat of the archbishop, which at ninety-nine meters in length was the longest church in Europe of its day. Boris also encouraged the development of monasticism; various monasteries were built, some becoming intellectual centers, and tracts of land began to be donated to them. Thus, Boris Christianized his state, laid the foundation for a Slavic literary culture (which, based on translations from Byzantine texts, meant bringing to Bulgaria elements of the rich Byzantine culture), and reduced considerably the position of the old boyars.

After an illness Boris, who seems to have been genuinely religious, abdicated, retiring to a monastery. His son and successor, Vladimir (889–893), sided with the remnants of the old aristocracy and set about reversing Boris' policies. He tried to restore the Frankish alliance and paganism. Various churches were destroyed, including the Pliska basilica. This state of affairs brought Boris out of his monastery in 893. He overthrew Vladimir and convened the Council of Preslav. This major council deposed and blinded Vladimir; declared as ruler Boris' younger son, Symeon (he was a monk at Preslav; having been well educated in Constantinople, he was carrying out translations from Greek to Slavonic); made Preslav the capital; and, according to a later Russian source, declared Christianity in Slavonic the official religion of state. With this achieved, Boris returned to a Preslav monastery, where he died in 907.

SYMEON AND PETER

Symeon (893–927) took over. The Greek mission was expelled. No major Byzantine protests are known to have occurred, but that there must have been some grumbling is suggested by a defense of Slavic letters written by a monk under the pseudonym Hrabr' (the Brave One). In this period Slavic written in Cyrillic triumphed over that in the Glagolitic alphabet. Symeon also appointed the first Slavic-rite bishops, Clement (894–916) for Macedonia and Constantine for Preslav. But despite the expulsion of the Greek mission and considerable autonomy for the archbishop of Preslav, Bulgaria did not break with Byzantium. The Slavonic clergy was partly of Byzantine origin (some of its members were trained at the Patriarchal School in Constantinople), and the Bulgarian archbishop remained subject to the Patriarch of Constantinople. Symeon encouraged culture. Further legal and religious texts (as well as certain Byzantine historical works) were translated. Symeon was associated with a major collection *(sbornik)* named after a Kievan prince, Svjatoslav (1073–1076), because the text survived in his copy. Fine miniatures illustrated many texts. Under Symeon the first original Bulgarian works appeared: the treatise of Hrabr', the first saints' lives, and the prolific writings of John the Exarch, which, in addition to their religious content, shed light on social and religious conditions in Bulgaria.

Symeon encouraged monasticism; at least eight monasteries existed around his new capital of Preslav. Preslav grew. Its palace was renovated, new churches were built, and its commercial quarter had active shops in which artisans specialized in ceramics, stone, glass, wood, and metals (in particular gold and silver). Exquisite examples of these craftsmen's skill have survived. Bulgarian tile work (in the "Preslav style") was particularly famous. Beautiful examples have survived, and because Bulgarian tiles achieved a higher quality than Byzantine, they were imported to Byzantium and Russia.

Almost immediately after Symeon's accession, some cronies of Emperor Leo VI, scheming for profits, convinced the emperor to move the Bulgarian market from Constantinople to Thessaloniki. This transfer meant less state control on customs and a smaller assortment of goods (and these goods were no longer purchased directly in Constantinople but at higher prices from those who carried them to Thessaloniki). When his protests were ignored, Symeon went to war. He was successful until the Byzantines convinced the Magyars (Hungarians) to attack Bulgaria from the north. They did considerable damage. Symeon summoned the Pechenegs to attack the Hungarians. They did it so effectively that the Hungarians were driven out of the Steppes and settled in modern Hungary. This caused the loss of some of Bulgaria's northern territory.

In 897, after a stunning victory over the Byzantine army (now fighting alone without Magyar allies), Symeon obtained a treaty restoring the market to Constantinople; the Byzantines also agreed to pay the Bulgarians tribute. In 904, after an Arab raid destroyed part of the walls of Thessaloniki, Symeon advanced his armies toward that city, which lay open before him. The Byzantines quickly negotiated with him, recognized Bulgaria's possession of Macedonia, and allowed the Bulgarians to occupy part of western Thrace to within twenty-two kilometers of Thessaloniki.

In 912 Emperor Leo VI died and was succeeded by his brother Alexander, who refused to pay the Bulgarian tribute. As a result Symeon went to war against Byzantium, raiding Thrace in the spring of 913. By this time he was probably seeking a pretext for war. Emperor Alexander died after a year, and his successor, Constantine VII Porphyrogenitos, a little boy, was under the control of a feuding regency council. Symeon brought his armies before the walls of Constantinople. Nicholas Mystikos (head regent and patriarch) agreed that Constantine should be betrothed to Symeon's daughter and crowned Symeon, most probably, with the title Emperor of the Bulgarians. Constantine's mother, resenting this, engineered a coup, established a new regency, and repudiated Nicholas' treaty. Symeon resumed the war; fighting continued from 913 to 927.

Symeon inflicted massive destruction on Thrace and Greece and delivered to the Byzantine army at Anchialo in 917 one of its greatest defeats, but he could not take the capital. He also, at some time between 914 and 925, on his own raised his archbishop to the rank of patriarch and then had the new patriarch crown him czar. Since he probably had already been crowned emperor of the Bulgarians by the patriarch of Constantinople, he would not have needed a new coronation for that title. Presumably his patriarch crowned him "Emperor of the Romans" (the title of the one authentic emperor, the Byzantine emperor). A seal of Symeon survives with that title on it.

During the long war the Byzantines tried to strengthen the Serbian state to the west of Bulgaria. After much meddling by both Bulgarians and Byzantines (each trying to establish its own puppets in Serbia) Symeon annexed Serbia in 924. During that campaign Zaharija, the last pro-Byzantine ruler of Serbia, fled to Croatia, with which, after the annexation of Serbia, Bulgaria had a common border. Croatia was allied to Byzantium. Its ruler, Tomislav, had received the Byzantine honorary title of proconsul and could pose a danger to Symeon whenever he concentrated his forces toward the east. Therefore, in 926 Symeon invaded Croatia. Tomislav's Croatians routed his army. But although Symeon certainly lost many soldiers, his military strength remained powerful enough for him to plan a major attack against Constantinople the following year. Symeon died of a stroke at the start of that campaign.

He was succeeded by his son Peter (927–969), who at first was guided by his maternal uncle, George Sursuvul. They at once attacked Thrace in order to negotiate a treaty with Byzantium from a position of strength. This plan succeeded, and the treaty agreed to in late 927 recognized Peter's title Emperor of the Bulgarians, and the title "Patriarch" for the head of the Bulgarian church. Tribute was restored, and Peter married the granddaughter of Emperor Romanos Lekapenos. At roughly the same time (927 or 928) Serbia reasserted its independence. Peter's reign has usually been depicted by scholars as a disaster and he as a weak ruler. But almost nothing is really known about his reign. He maintained peace with Byzantium from 927 to 965. In his first years (928–930) he successfully put down two uprisings by brothers. After that, there were no further domestic disturbances. The only known destructive events were four Magyar raids that passed through Bulgaria en route to ravage Byzantine Thrace. Thus, for nearly forty years Bulgaria enjoyed peace, a situation that encouraged increased trade (particularly with Byzantium, with which commercial ties had certainly ceased during Symeon's long war).

The *Russian Primary Chronicle* depicts Bulgaria as richer commercially than Kiev. It states that at Perejaslavec on the Danube were concentrated "gold, silks, wine and various fruits from Greece, silver and horses from Hungary and Bohemia and from Rus furs, honey, wax, and slaves." No evidence exists to show that Peter was a poor ruler. His reputation in later popular tradition was high. He was canonized, and when the Second Bulgarian Empire was established in 1186 Asen's brother and coruler took the name Peter. Thus, we should probably regard him as a reasonably successful and popular ruler until the disastrous warfare at the end, which he did not seek and which was against two powerful opponents, including a Byzantium far stronger than the one Symeon had faced.

Under Peter monasticism developed further, accompanied by the increasing growth of monastery estates. John of Rila established the greatest monastic center in medieval Bulgaria. He gained a great reputation as a hermit; disciples flocked to him, and a little community grew up. John abandoned this for a mountain retreat, leaving behind a spiritual testament that contained a rigorous monastic rule combining individual asceticism with community life. He stressed the value of manual labor and urged the monks to live in harmony, following the Christian faith taught by the church fathers and never aspiring to riches or power. The monks were urged to have nothing to do with the princes of this world, and the story has it that John refused to receive Czar Peter when Peter came to his retreat. Under Peter, the Bogomil heresy also arose. The heresy was to last until the fourteenth century and from time to time bothered Orthodox churchmen. However, it seems to have had a small following and played little or no role in national events.

Like the rest of eastern Europe, Bulgaria was overwhelmingly peasant. It is usually stated that by the tenth century the great majority of peasants were serfs on great estates, and the size and number of these estates was on the increase. We know that monastic estates were expanding, but we know almost nothing about secular landholding. Boyars of great wealth, and surely great estates, existed then, but it is not known whether great boyars of the tenth century held more land than figures like Kavkhan Isbul of the early ninth century, who had sufficient wealth to present Malimir with an aqueduct. In fact, we do not know enough to speak of trends in landholding or in the enserfment of peasants. There may well have been many free peasants in the tenth century whose existence is noted in no surviving sources. Many scholars have based their depiction of Bulgarian trends on what was occurring in the Byzantine empire at the same time. However, considering the great differences between the two societies, it does not seem warranted to assume parallel developments without documentation.

BYZANTINE DOMINATION

In 965 Bulgarian envoys went to Constantinople for tribute to find Nikephoros Phokas, one of Byzantium's greatest generals, on the throne. He refused to pay, whipped the envoys, and attacked some border fortresses. Then he summoned Svjatoslav's Russians from Kiev to attack Bulgaria, which they did in 967. The reason for involving the powerful Russians seems to have been to divert them from Cherson in the Crimea by offering them plunder in Bulgaria. The Russians' attack was successful and, contrary to the initial agreement, Svjatoslav decided to remain in Bulgaria. Peter suffered a stroke and retired to a monastery, where he died in 969. He was succeeded in Preslav by his son Boris II.

How much of Bulgaria was held by Svjatoslav and how much by Boris is not known. Svjatoslav wanted to control the Danube and planned to settle in the commercial town of Perejaslavec. Seeing what was happening, Nikephoros tried to improve relations with the Bulgarians and summoned the Pechenegs to attack Kiev in 968. This attack briefly drew the Russians away; but after driving the Pechenegs back into the Steppes, Svjatoslav returned in 969 to Bulgaria, defeated the Bulgarian army at Perejaslavec, and soon subdued Bulgaria. Boris was allowed to hold Preslav as a vassal ruler. The Russians and Bulgarians thereafter fought as allies and jointly raided Thrace.

In 971 the new emperor, John I Tzimiskes, conquered Bulgaria and forced Svjatoslav's withdrawal. At the end of this campaign Tzimiskes annexed Bulgaria, making it into a military province, and took Boris back to Constantinople as an honorary captive. Various leading boyars were also taken to the empire, where they were given estates, an action depriving the Bulgarians of their natural leaders. Tzimiskes reduced the rank of the patriarch to archbishop. Thus, Byzantine rule was restored to the Danube for the first time in centuries.

However, Tzimiskes conquered only the eastern regions. Macedonia remained unoccupied. When the emperor died in 976, this unsubdued region revolted under the four sons of a Count Nicholas. The sources do not state what this uprising consisted of; presumably the four expanded their control over a larger part of Macedonia. To oppose this threat, the Byzantines released Boris II and his younger brother, Romanos. Boris was killed by mistake by a Bulgarian border guard, but Romanos reached Bulgaria, where he joined the rebels. Within ten years three of the sons of Nicholas were dead (including Aaron, who was killed by Samuil, the surviving brother, in 986 for dealing with the Byzantines). Samuil acquired the holdings of his brothers and maintained cordial relations with Romanos. Some sources claim he recognized Romanos as czar, others deny that he did. In any case Samuil held de facto power. His state was centered in the region of Ochrid and Prespa in western Macedonia. Both he and the Byzantines called his state Bulgarian.

The deposed patriarch of Preslav, Damian, joined Samuil, who made him patriarch of a new patriarchate of Ochrid, which he established. The Byzantines could do little to prevent him at the time because they were involved in a serious civil war. When a break came in that war in 986, Basil II attacked Samuil but was badly defeated. Then Byzantium was embroiled in another long civil war, which enabled Samuil to begin a decade of expansion. By 997 he held all Macedonia, Bulgaria, Thessaly, Epiros, the important port of Durazzo (Dyrrhachium), and most if not all of Albania. He was also overlord of princes in Duklja (present-day Montenegro), Raška (Serbia), Trebinje, Zahumlje (roughly present-day Hercegovina), and some of Bosnia. In 997 he had himself crowned czar.

In 1001, with peace finally established in Byzantium, Basil II launched his counteroffensive. Brutally bloody warfare followed, with Byzantium making slow, steady gains against great resistance until 1014, when Basil surrounded the main Bulgarian army near the Struma River. We are told he captured 14,000 men and had them all blinded, sparing one eye of every hundredth man so that the one-eyes could lead the blind back to Samuil. At the sight of his blinded troops, Samuil died of a stroke.

Resistance continued until 1018 under Samuil's

son Gabriel Radomir, and then under Aaron's son, John Vladislav, who murdered Gabriel Radomir in 1015. In 1018 Basil II conquered Ochrid and the war ended. He annexed all Bulgaria, dividing it into three themes (military provinces) centered in Skopje, Silistria, and Sirmium. He appointed Byzantine generals as commanders and left garrisons in major fortresses. He transferred to Byzantium many of the leading Bulgarian nobles, granting them lands in Asia, and thus deprived the Bulgarians of their former leaders. The lesser nobility was left in possession of its lands and local positions, under the supervision of the Byzantine military administration. Basil reduced the title of the patriarch of Ochrid to archbishop, but left Ivan, Samuil's bishop, in office and the Bulgarian church in the hands of Bulgarians. He gave the see of Ochrid considerable autonomy and allowed it to retain all its suffragan bishoprics in Bulgaria and Macedonia. He also decreed that since the Bulgarians were accustomed to paying taxes in kind—no Bulgarian coinage existed—they could, unlike the rest of his empire, continue to do so. Bulgaria was to remain under Byzantine rule until 1186.

The Bulgarian national consciousness, established over the preceding centuries, was severely tested during this period, for the sensible postconquest policies of Basil II were not continued after his death. In 1036 or 1037 the archbishop of Ochrid, Ivan, died and Emperor Michael IV appointed a Constantinopolitan cleric, a Greek named Leo, to replace him. From then on, Greeks were appointed to Ochrid and to other bishoprics in Bulgaria and Macedonia. Efforts were made to hellenize the Bulgarian church; they became particularly intense under Archbishop Theophylact (*ca.* 1090–1109), whose surviving letters are a major source for this period. Theophylact closed Slavic schools, introduced Greek-language services in many places, and encouraged the translation from Slavonic into Greek of local texts; Theophylact himself translated into Greek the Life of St. Clement. There also seems to have been a systematic destruction of Slavic manuscripts. Not one Slavic manuscript survived inside Bulgaria from the period before the establishment of the Second Bulgarian Empire in the 1180's. In this atmosphere Bulgarian culture seriously declined. No major Bulgarian writers were active during the Byzantine period.

To make matters worse, in the 1030's Macedonia and Bulgaria suffered a series of droughts leading to bad harvests. In the midst of these Emperor Michael IV abolished Basil's policy of allowing taxes in kind and demanded cash payments while increasing the tax rate. A serious revolt broke out in 1040 under Peter Odeljan (Deljan), possibly the son of Gabriel Radomir. After being crowned in Beograd he moved south, acquiring much support and taking Niš and Skopje. Meanwhile, a second revolt broke out in Durazzo under a certain Tihomir; a meeting was held between the two rebel groups to coordinate their efforts. At it Tihomir was murdered, an act that presumably disillusioned many of his followers. The revolt spread into northern Greece; then a son of John Vladislav, called Alusianos in Byzantine sources, appeared and joined the rebels. He received a major command and attacked Thessaloniki. His attack was a fiasco, and he lost many men. Shortly thereafter his men seized and blinded Odeljan, and Alusianos became the sole leader. After he suffered another defeat at the hands of the Byzantines, the revolt fizzled out in 1041. Alusianos surrendered and was richly rewarded. One strongly suspects that he was a Byzantine agent from the start, sent out to destroy the rebellion from within.

In the 1030's—and in the decades that followed through the 1070's—Bulgaria suffered severely from Pecheneg raids from across the Danube. In 1072 a landowner, George Vojteh of Skopje, revolted; he dispatched a delegation to Michael, the ruler of Duklja, who sent the rebels military support under Michael's son, Constantine Bodin. The rebels accepted Bodin as their leader and crowned him czar. After various rebel successes the Byzantine armies proved stronger, and in two separate victories they took Vojteh and Bodin prisoner and crushed the revolt.

THE SECOND BULGARIAN EMPIRE

The Bulgarians did not raise another major rebellion for more than a century. But by the late eleventh century the Byzantine empire was in decline; its thematic armies were deteriorating, and the land that had supported them was increasingly falling into the hands of provincial magnates who had amassed enormous estates. On the periphery of the empire, some of these aristocrats were becoming more or less independent princes. In 1185 two brothers from Trnovo, Peter and Asen, sought a *pronoia* (fief) from Emperor Isaac II Angelos. Rudely rebuffed, they returned to Trnovo, where the population (including many Vlachs) was angry at high taxes in general and at an extraordinary imperial wedding tax in particular; the brothers mobilized resistance and soon captured Preslav.

In this revolt both Vlachs and Bulgarians participated; the two leaders may well have been Vlachs.

However, the state they established was called Bulgarian, and like other medieval Balkan states it was multiethnic, with little or no favoritism along ethnic lines. The imperial army under Isaac attacked in 1187 with success, causing Peter and Asen to flee beyond the Danube. Thinking the revolt was crushed, Isaac returned to Constantinople without bothering to subdue all Bulgarian fortresses; the brothers recruited many Cumans (Turkic nomads) beyond the Danube and returned to regain Bulgaria. A second imperial attack in 1187 failed to engage the rebel army, and Cuman raids followed into Thrace. In 1188 the Byzantines recognized Bulgarian independence between the Danube and the Balkan Mountains. Kalojan (Joanica), the youngest brother of Peter and Asen, went to Constantinople as a hostage; within two or three years he escaped and returned home. Trnovo became the capital of Bulgaria, and an archbishopric was established there. Soon the archbishop crowned Asen as ruler. Asen ruled in Trnovo, while his brother Peter moved to Preslav, which he governed. Warfare and raids continued over the following years; the Bulgarians' victory over the Byzantines at Arcadiopolis in 1193 gained them much of central Thrace.

After nearly two centuries of Byzantine rule, many old Bulgarian institutions had been replaced by the Byzantine administrative and landholding system. Inheriting this system, the rulers of the Second Bulgarian Empire retained it and modeled their state institutions and court ceremony on the Byzantine. But despite the model the Bulgarians never achieved a truly nationwide bureaucracy. The boyars were no longer from ancient families, but rose from their roles in the liberation struggle or from royal appointment. Thus, most families began as service nobility. In time, though, some acquired vast estates and local authority, becoming autonomous rulers in their provinces during times of central instability. In this period many important boyars were of Cuman origin. The overwhelming majority of the population still were peasants. Our limited sources suggest that most of them were serfs on royal, boyar, or monastic estates.

In 1196 a boyar named Ivanko murdered Asen in a personal quarrel; he tried to take power in Trnovo while seeking Byzantine aid. When this aid failed to materialize, with Peter besieging Trnovo, Ivanko fled to Byzantium and Peter took over in Trnovo. He died the following year. Upon his death the youngest brother, Kalojan, who had been prominent in the preceding military activities, became the ruler. He stepped up raiding for plunder, causing much devastation, until the Byzantines convinced the Kievan Russians to attack the Cumans. Many Cumans left Bulgaria to defend their homeland, considerably weakening Kalojan, who consented to a treaty with Byzantium (1201) which restored Thrace to the empire. Kalojan meanwhile expanded his state to the north and west, taking Niš (where he installed a Bulgarian bishop) and Braničevo at the junction of the Danube and Morava Rivers. He began negotiating with the pope for a crown. A papal legate arrived shortly after the Fourth Crusade took Constantinople (1204); he crowned Kalojan king and recognized his Trnovo archbishop as a primate. These were lesser titles than Kalojan sought, so he simply called himself czar and his church leader patriarch, anyway.

These papal ties had few internal effects and were short lasting. After the Crusaders took Constantinople, Kalojan began expanding into Thrace. He regularly removed Greek bishops and replaced them with Slavs. Being hostile to the Greeks, he offered the Crusaders an alliance. But the Crusaders, ambitious for Thrace themselves, refused. In 1205 the Greeks of eastern Thrace revolted against the Crusaders; they sought and received military aid from Kalojan. The Latin Emperor Baldwin I marched against them. The armies met at Adrianople, where the Bulgarians won a massive victory; Baldwin was captured and died in captivity. The Bulgarians then ravaged to the walls of Constantinople, occupied more of Thrace, and took most of Macedonia. Kalojan died in 1207 during a siege of Thessaloniki. His death ended the siege.

The heir to the throne, John (Ivan) Asen II, was around eleven years old, so Kalojan's nephew Boril (1207–1218) took over. Whether it was a usurpation or an act to keep the family in power by having an adult more or less as regent is unknown. Whatever the initial motivation, Boril, once in power, decided to retain it. He married Kalojan's widow, a Cuman princess, to increase his legitimacy and also to keep Cuman military support. The little heir was smuggled away by his supporters, first to the Cumans and then to exile in the Russian principality of Galich. Under Boril different boyar factions emerged, and some peripheral territories seceded. It is evident that Kalojan's state lacked strong central institutions; it was a federation of local units (each under a local chief) who supported Kalojan either for booty from

BULGARIA

raids or from fear of punitive attack. After his death little existed to hold the state together.

A certain Alexios Slav seceded in the Rhodope Mountains, with a principality, centered from 1211 in Melnik, which lasted until 1230. Strez, who had held Prosakon (Prosek) and a strip of territory between the Struma and Vardar Rivers, which he had wrested from the Byzantines, allied himself with the Serbs and took much of Macedonia. Immediately, in 1207, the Hungarians also attacked, conquering the towns along the Morava, including the major commercial center of Braničevo. Shortly thereafter, in a treaty with the Hungarians, Boril recognized these losses. In 1208 Boril was defeated by the Latins near Philippopolis (modern Plovdiv). Alexios Slav, seeing an opportunity, accepted Latin suzerainty, married the daughter of Emperor Henry I, and was promised support to obtain the Bulgarian crown.

Nothing was to come of this promise, but it threatened Boril. As a result of the activities of the Latins and of Strez, all Bulgarian territory south of the Balkan Mountains was lost. A revolt next broke out (between 1211 and 1213) at Vidin on the Danube, which Boril suppressed with Hungarian aid. In 1213 Boril made peace with the Latins—the resulting alliance remained in effect until Boril's death—and they jointly planned an attack on Serbia. Strez, who had submitted to Boril about 1209, joined the anti-Serb coalition. The Serbs in 1214 stopped the invading armies, and Strez was killed. In 1216 Boril's ally, Emperor Henry, died, and the following year his other ally, the Hungarian king, went east to crusade. Since Boril now lacked outside support, John Asen's supporters summoned him back from Russia; they marched on Trnovo, whose citizens opened the gates to him. Boril was blinded, and John Asen II (1218–1241) became czar.

He inherited a weak state; the dominant power in the region was Epiros, under Theodore Angelos Komnenos Doukas. Through conquest and easy annexation after Strez's death, Theodore had in 1216–1217 acquired most of Macedonia. In Ochrid he had established a Greek, Demetrios Chomatianos, as archbishop. Asen set about rebuilding his state and its armies. By 1225 Bulgaria had become strong enough that Theodore, bent on taking Constantinople, made an alliance with Asen. Faced with this threat, the Latins turned to Asen for aid, offering a marriage between the young Baldwin II and Asen's daughter, with Asen becoming regent in Constantinople. In the midst of these discussions Theodore marched toward Constantinople, but suddenly turned against Bulgaria. Possibly he had learned of Asen's negotiations with the Latins and feared being attacked from the rear during a siege of Constantinople. The armies met at Klokotnica (1230), and Asen won a massive victory. Theodore was captured and blinded; he remained Asen's prisoner until his release in 1237. As a result of this victory and its aftermath, John Asen II was able to take from Epiros all Macedonia and most of Albania. He also held much of Thrace and had regained many of his northern lands from the Hungarians, and now held Beograd, Braničevo, Vidin, and most of the Dobrudja.

With Theodore eliminated, the Latins no longer needed Asen and saw no reason to allow him into Constantinople as regent. So they broke off discussions and made an aged knight, John of Brienne, regent. Angered, John Asen negotiated a military alliance against the Latins with the Greek state of Nicaea. He recognized the primacy of the Nicene church (that its patriarch was the ecumenical patriarch), and Nicaea recognized the prelate in Trnovo as a patriarch. The status of the Bulgarian church was officially recognized in 1235 at the wedding of Asen's daughter and the heir to the Nicene throne. The allies then besieged Constantinople. Asen soon realized that if their attack succeeded, Nicaea would obtain Constantinople, and it would be worse for Bulgaria to have a strong Greek emperor in Constantinople than the weak Latins. He withdrew his troops and attacked a Nicene fortress in eastern Thrace. An epidemic of the plague followed, killing Asen's wife, his son and heir, and the new patriarch. Asen saw this as a sign of God's anger for breaking his alliance and made peace with Nicaea in 1237. In that year he fell in love with his captive's (Theodore's) daughter, married her, and allowed her blinded father to return to Thessaloniki.

DECLINE OF THE SECOND BULGARIAN EMPIRE

John Asen II died in 1241. His heir was his seven-year-old son, Koloman; as usual no apparatus existed to hold the state together. The boyars broke into squabbling factions, peripheral territories seceded, and neighbors wrested away territory. Bulgaria rapidly declined, never to regain its former position. Koloman had no choice but to submit to Nicaea. The Tatars swept through Bulgaria in 1242, causing much devastation and imposing tribute. Other Tatar raids followed. In 1246 Koloman died and was succeeded by his younger half brother, Michael Asen, son of Theodore's daughter, who became regent. Nicaea immediately attacked, taking Thrace to the upper Marica and Macedonia to the Vardar. The Hungarians attacked and retook Beograd and Braničevo. Macedonia west of the Vardar and Albania were taken by Epiros, but in 1251 were acquired by Nicaea. When John Vatatzes, the able Nicene emperor, died in 1254, the Bulgarians overran Macedonia from the Vardar to Albania. Nicaea regained this territory by 1256 and forced Bulgaria into an alliance.

In 1256 Michael Asen was assassinated. He was succeeded by his cousin and murderer, Koloman II. Before his demise Michael had married the daughter of Rostislav Mihajlović, son-in-law of the king of Hungary and ban of Mačva (in northwestern Serbia). Rostislav, using his daughter's safety as an excuse, attacked Bulgaria, rescued the girl, deposed Koloman (who was soon killed), and may have ruled Bulgaria briefly. But he could not solidly establish his authority and retreated to Vidin, which he retained as a Hungarian vassal. A peace concluded eventually between Bulgaria and Hungary in 1261 recognized Hungarian suzerainty over Vidin. In Bulgaria (in 1257) a boyar named Mico proclaimed himself ruler, but he may never have established himself in Trnovo and was soon eclipsed and deposed by another boyar, Constantine Tih (1257–1277)—a grandson of Stefan Nemanja, former ruler of Serbia—who held large estates near Sofia. To give himself legitimacy, Constantine in 1258 married a granddaughter of John Asen II who was the daughter of Theodore Laskaris of Nicaea.

In 1261 the Nicenes recovered Constantinople and restored the Byzantine Empire. By then a general, Michael VIII Palaiologos (1258–1282), had usurped the throne from the Laskaris family. Constantine's Laskarid wife incited him to attack Byzantine Thrace. The Byzantines counterattacked and in 1262 wrested from Bulgaria the two important Black Sea towns of Mesembria (Nesebŭr) and Anchialo, as well as the district around Philippopolis. The Bulgarians appealed to their Nogaj Tatar overlords, and together the Tatars and Bulgarians raided Thrace. Previously, a Russian, Jakov Svetoslav, had fled the Tatars to Bulgaria. John Asen II, who had spent his exile in Russia, had given him lands in southwestern Bulgaria. Jakov Svetoslav by 1261 bore the title despot. In 1263 the Byzantines invaded his territory; having procured Hungarian aid, he repulsed their attack. With the encouragement of the Hungarians he then seceded from Bulgaria and was granted Hungarian-held Vidin, which was added to his territories. He now styled himself czar of Bulgaria.

Thus, Bulgaria was divided into two states, Trnovo and Vidin, the ruler of each styling himself czar. The 1264 alliance between Constantine Tih and the Nogajs was directed not only against Byzantine Thrace but also against Jakov Svetoslav, who quickly improved his relations with Constantine; together they attacked Hungarian territory. A Hungarian invasion in 1266 brought Jakov Svetoslav back into the Hungarian fold. In 1271 the Hungarians were again referring to him as czar of the Bulgarians. He ruled Vidin until murdered in 1275 by agents from Trnovo; this act allowed Trnovo to regain Vidin briefly.

After a serious Nogaj raid against Byzantium in 1271, the Byzantines negotiated an alliance with the Nogajs. As a result Emperor Michael VIII pressured Constantine Tih, now a widower, to marry Maria, Michael's niece. They agreed that she would bring as her dowry the disputed Black Sea cities of Mesembria and Anchialo. However, the Byzantines failed to relinquish them. The angry Bulgarians raided Thrace, and the Byzantines persuaded the Nogajs to attack Bulgaria. Angry at this attack and the failure to regain the cities, the Bulgarians joined the coalition of Charles of Anjou, bent on restoring a Latin empire in Constantinople. To face this threat and to convince the pope to restrain Charles, Michael VIII agreed to the Union of the Churches at Lyons (1274). This act horrified much of the Byzantine population, including Michael's sister, Irene (the mother of Constantine Tih's wife, Maria). Irene emigrated to Trnovo, as did various other Greeks; it became a center for anti-Union intrigue.

Boyar squabbles, separatism, Tatar raids, and popular discontent increased. In 1277 a swineherd named Ivajlo emerged as leader of a popular movement; having won great acclaim by repelling Tatar raids, he then marched on Trnovo. Constantine Tih was killed opposing him. Trnovo held out under Maria, but most of eastern Bulgaria recognized Ivajlo. The Byzantines, seeing an excellent chance to intervene, dispatched an army with a pretender, Mico's son, who called himself John Asen III. Maria, hostile to her imperial uncle for his "heresy," in the face of the approaching Byzantine army, yielded Trnovo to Ivajlo and married him. Once in power, surrounded by his Byzantine wife and the Trnovo aristocrats, Ivajlo gave up whatever social program

BULGARIA

he had had and joined the establishment. His following drifted away. The aristocrats, scorning his origins, had little use for him; and as Ivajlo lost his popular following, the nobility had less reason to fear (and therefore accept) him. Late in 1279, when Ivajlo was away opposing a Tatar attack, Byzantine troops appeared at the gates of Trnovo. The boyars now agreed to accept their demands and John Asen III was installed as a Byzantine puppet; Maria was taken back to the empire. Ivajlo returned to defeat the Byzantine troops left to prop up John Asen III; John fled to Constantinople. But the boyars disliked Ivajlo also and selected one of their number, George Terter, of Cuman origin, as czar (1280–1292). Ivajlo fled to the Nogajs, who murdered him.

George Terter was czar of a very weak state and lacked the power either to prevent Tatar raids or to retain his outlying provinces. Soon he held only the eastern part of Bulgaria as various boyars broke away to establish their own petty principalities. Some of these were supported by the Nogajs. The two most important secessionist principalities were centered in Braničevo and Vidin. The Braničevo state was soon conquered by the principality of Mačva, under Dragutin. Vidin was ruled by a boyar of Cuman origin named Šišman, who bore the title despot. Šišman also had difficulty in maintaining his independence; he survived a Nogaj attack, only to see Vidin fall to the Serbs under King Milutin. He fled to the Nogajs, who, claiming overlordship over all Bulgaria, used his misfortune as an excuse to attack Serbia. Milutin made peace with the Nogajs by agreeing to let Šišman return to Vidin. To seal this arrangement both Šišman and his son, Michael, acquired Serbian brides. Vidin thus found itself a client of Serbia, and this subordination increased with the fall of the Nogajs in 1299.

In 1292, under Nogaj pressure, George Terter fled to Byzantium, and the Tatars installed as their puppet czar in Trnovo Smilec, a boyar, who had already established a secessionist principality in the southern province of Srednogora. After Smilec's installation Srednogora remained separate under his brothers Voisil and Radoslav. Smilec maintained good relations with the Nogajs and Byzantium, and did nothing to aid Braničevo and Vidin in their difficulties. He died in 1298, and after brief attempts at reigns by his widow and then by Čaka, a Nogaj son-in-law of George Terter, George Terter's son, Theodore Svetoslav, took power in 1300. He was able to succeed in this take-over because in 1299 the Nogajs had been wiped out by the Golden Horde. The horde did not interfere in Bulgaria, which now found itself free of Tatar domination.

In fact, Theodore Svetoslav soon asserted his overlordship in what is now southern Bessarabia up to the Dniester, and from this territory he recruited many Tatars for his armies. He immediately started rebuilding his shattered state, reincorporating seceded territories—including Srednogora, the rulers of which fled to Byzantium—and terrorizing the independent-minded boyars. From Byzantium he conquered part of Thrace, Anchialo, and Mesembria; through these ports he increased foreign trade (particularly on Venetian and Genoese ships). The Byzantines, weakened by the Catalans, made peace with him and recognized these conquests in 1307. As a result of the treaty, probably in 1308, Theodore Svetoslav married Theodora, granddaughter of Andronikos II.

SERBIAN ASCENDANCY

When Theodore Svetoslav died in 1322 and his son, George Terter II, died later, probably in the same year, the line died out. Skirmishes had taken place all that year between Bulgaria and Byzantium, and during the interregnum Byzantium obtained the voluntary submission of a long strip of southern Bulgaria from Sliven to Mesembria. The fact that much of this region's population was Greek probably contributed to this willingness. Philippopolis was besieged by Byzantine troops. Faced with this major threat from Byzantium, the boyars, some of whom had lands in the lost or threatened territory, turned to the strongest local figure they could find. Between the end of 1322 and June 1323, they elected as czar Michael Šišman, son of Šišman of Vidin. Michael had succeeded to Vidin before 1313 on Šišman's death. Both father and son had been vassals of the Serbian king, and Michael's wife, Anna, was the daughter of the late King Milutin (*d.* 1321) and the sister of the present ruler of Serbia, Stefan Dečanski.

Michael's election united the two parts of Bulgaria into one state again. The Šišman dynasty was to rule Bulgaria until the Ottoman conquest. Michael immediately went to war against Byzantium, broke the siege of Philippopolis, and won back the lost southern territory, much of which had been ceded to Smilec's disgruntled brother Vojsil, who was allied to Byzantium. A subsequent Byzantine attack regained Philippopolis. Negotiations followed, and Michael agreed to divorce his Serbian wife, who, along with their son John (Ivan) Stefan (who had been coruler and heir, but was now deprived of his rights), was imprisoned, and to marry Theodora, widow of Theodore Svetoslav and sister of Andronikos III of Byzantium. For most of the Byzantine civil war between Andronikos II and Andronikos III, Michael supported Andronikos III, who eventually obtained Constantinople and became sole emperor in 1328.

Michael's relations with Serbia had begun deteriorating on the death of Milutin in 1321. He had supported a rival, Vladislav, against Stefan Dečanski, the heir who succeeded in obtaining the throne. His divorcing and incarcerating Dečanski's sister did little to improve matters. The Serbs, meanwhile, were expanding into Macedonia, which threatened both Bulgaria and Byzantium. Michael and Andronikos III formed an alliance to attack Serbia. Dečanski sought peace, but Michael refused. The venture was badly coordinated and the Byzantine army did not appear, leaving the Bulgarians to face the Serbs alone at Velbužd (modern Kjustendil) on 28 July 1330. The Serbs won an overwhelming victory, and Michael was killed. The battle resulted in the Serbs' gaining what was to be a permanent edge (at times even hegemony) over Bulgaria and meant that the Serbs would gain Macedonia. A delegation of Bulgarian nobles immediately sought out Dečanski for negotiations. He demanded the return to power of his sister Anna and his nephew, John Stefan, who was then about thirty years old. The boyars, led by Michael's brother Belaur, agreed, and Serbian troops installed the pair in Trnovo in August or September 1330. Theodora and her children fled to Constantinople.

The Serbs' new influence within Bulgaria was not popular with Byzantium, and the exile of Theodora gave the empire an excuse to intervene. The boyars who held lands in the south, like Michael's brother-in-law, Stracimir, were threatened by the possibility of a Byzantine attack, and the boyars who in 1324 had supported the policy change that ousted Anna for Theodora and the Byzantine alliance were in danger of revenge from Anna. Thus, tensions immediately developed in Bulgaria; these were increased when the Byzantines launched their expected invasion and again annexed Mesembria, Anchialo, and whatever territory Michael had recovered south of the Balkan Mountains.

Anna's inability to defend this territory and the threat of further Byzantine gains led a group of Trnovo boyars, headed by the protovestijar Raksin and the logothete Filip, early in 1331 to overthrow John Stefan for John (Ivan) Alexander (1331–1371). John Alexander, who was Michael's nephew and Stracimir's son, had been governing the province of Loveč and probably was party to the plot. Anna and John Stefan emigrated to Serbia. The overthrow of Dečanski in August or September 1331 created instability in Serbia, thereby preventing Serbian intervention on behalf of John Stefan. John Alexander, aware of future danger from Serbia, made peace with the Serbs in the spring of 1332; it was sealed by the marriage of the new Serbian ruler, Stefan Dušan, to John Alexander's sister Helena.

Good relations with the Serbs continued over the next half century; John Alexander was thus able to attack the Byzantines and to regain Mesembria and Anchialo. Byzantium recognized his possession of them in a treaty of 1332. In 1343, in return for supporting the Constantinopolitan regency against John Kantakuzenos in another Byzantine civil war, John Alexander received the upper Marica with Philippopolis. He had abandoned his first wife and married Theodora, a converted Jewess; under her influence he disinherited the son of his first marriage, John Stracimir, and declared his son by her, John Šišman, as heir. As compensation for Stracimir, he granted him Vidin before 1360, thereby dividing the realm again.

In 1365 the Hungarians took Vidin, establishing a Hungarian banate there. They called in the Franciscans to catholicize the population. In 1370 John Stracimir recovered Vidin. To maintain his rule there without further wars, he recognized Hungarian suzerainty. Dissatisfied with his father's policy, Stracimir assumed the title of czar, removed his church from Trnovo's jurisdiction and subjected it to the patriarch of Constantinople, and began coining his own money. On John Alexander's death in 1371 his eldest son by Theodora, John Šišman, received the bulk of his dominions with Trnovo. Stracimir immediately attempted to conquer all Bulgaria; he seized Sofia but retained it for only a year or two. In northeastern Bulgaria a boyar named Balik had already—possibly in the mid 1340's—defected. He was succeeded by his brother Dobrotica, for whom part of his holdings, the Dobrudja, received its name. Dobrotica too separated the church in his lands from Trnovo, recognizing the jurisdiction of the patriarch of Constantinople. He also acquired much of the Black Sea coast and carried on considerable trade in the Black Sea. Thus, the czar in Trnovo suffered losses of trade and income. The income loss and territorial fragmentation were disastrous because the Turkish offensive against the Balkans was under way.

OTTOMAN DOMINATION

Different groups of Turks had been involved in the Balkans—as raiders and mercenaries—from the middle of the fourteenth century. Their activities increased at the end of the 1360's, and a group of Turks (probably not Ottoman) conquered Adrianople in 1361. From then on, raids were stepped up against the Balkans. Bulgaria's internal disturbances greatly reduced the effectiveness of Bulgarian resistance. In the mid 1370's the Ottomans, under Sultan Murad I, became seriously involved in the Balkans and began seizing the gains made by other Turkish military groups. In 1377 the Ottomans acquired Adrianople. Although many scholars have stated that Bulgaria became vassal to the Ottomans in 1372 or 1373, as a result of the Battle of Marica (1371), most Ottomanists would date Ottoman suzerainty over Bulgaria to 1376. This later date corresponds to the time that the Ottomans became active in the Balkans. Vassalage to the Ottomans meant that Bulgaria was obliged to pay tribute and to supply troops for Ottoman campaigns. In addition, John Šišman's sister, Tamara, had to enter Murad's harem.

Vassalage did not stop the Turkish raids for plunder that swept through parts of Bulgaria from time to time, nor did it prevent the Ottomans from conquering towns near the border, such as Sofia, which was taken, probably in 1385. In 1388 it seems the Bulgarians tried to shed their vassal ties, but a major Ottoman attack brought them back into vassalage with a considerable loss of territory. Because certain early Ottoman sources do not mention the 1388 campaign and because later accounts of it bear similarities to the 1393 campaign, certain scholars have wondered whether the events of 1388 really took place. In 1393 the Ottomans, having learned of secret Bulgarian negotiations with Hungary, invaded and conquered Bulgaria; Trnovo put up a heroic three-month defense before it fell. The last part of independent Bulgaria, Stracimir's Vidin principality, remained an Ottoman vassal state. But Stracimir supported the crusade that was defeated at Nicopolis in 1396; then his state, too, was annexed. The Turks sent in administrators and settled their cavalry on military fiefs *(timars)*. They quickly and effectively established such firm control that Bulgaria remained Ottoman even after the Turkish defeat at Ankara (1402) and throughout the Ottoman civil war (1403–1413). It was to remain under the Ottomans until 1878.

BULGARIAN CULTURE IN THE FOURTEENTH CENTURY

The fourteenth century, despite its tragic political history, was a period of cultural flowering. Bulgaria was part and parcel of the Byzantine "Palaiologan renaissance," for in these years Orthodoxy was truly an international movement with an international culture and with the different churches cross-fertilizing one another. In the thirteenth and fourteenth centuries fine Byzantine-style churches with Byzantine-style frescoes were built in Trnovo and other towns. Particularly splendid are the frescoes of the church at Bojana, outside Sofia, painted under Constantine Tih.

The mystical movement of hesychasm had an impact on certain Bulgarian monasteries. The leading propagandist for hesychast ideas, Gregory of Sinai (1290–1346), settled in the Bulgarian monastery of Paroria and enjoyed the patronage of John Alexander. Gregory acquired a number of Bulgarian disciples, the most prominent being Theodosios of Trnovo. Theodosios knew Greek well and translated various of Gregory's hesychast works into Bulgarian, making them accessible to the Slavs. Hesychasm was extremely popular on Mount Athos, where the Bulgarians had a foundation (Zografou Monastery), which was a second source for hesychast ideas in Bulgaria, since Bulgarian monks passed to and fro between Athos and Bulgarian monasteries. Theodosios spent some time on Athos and died in 1363 in Constantinople. Then, illustrating the international character of hesychasm, the hesychast Byzantine patriarch Kallistos wrote a Life of Theodosios. This Life was soon translated into Bulgarian.

The most prominent disciple of Theodosios, Euthymios, the last patriarch of Trnovo (1375–1393), was a famous religious writer who turned out a series of important saints' lives, eulogies, and letters. He worked on an orthographic reform and also corrected and revised various liturgical texts that had been inaccurately translated from Greek. He and his disciples were responsible both for translations from the Greek and for original works. In this period many Bulgarian church intellectuals knew Greek well. And the traveling of educated monks from monastery to monastery, including to monasteries across international borders (to Byzantium, Bulgaria, and Serbia), facilitated the circulation of ideas.

Turkish raids and the eventual conquest of Bulgaria caused the emigration of many Bulgarian intellectuals to Serbia and Russia, whither they brought their talents and many texts. So many texts were then brought to Russia that scholars speak of a second South Slavic influence on Russia. These intellectuals had a major impact on both Serbian and Russian letters. Particularly prominent in this regard were the two Tsamblaks: Gregory, who first went to Serbia, where he became abbot of Visoki Dečani and wrote a major Life of Stefan Dečanski before moving to Russia; and Cyprian, who became metropolitan of all Russia (1390–1406) and made major efforts to correct Russian liturgical texts and to revise canon law.

BIBLIOGRAPHY

John V. A. Fine, Jr., *The Early Medieval Balkans* (1983); Peter Mutafčiev, *Istorija na bŭlgarskija narod,* pt. 2 (1944), a good survey for the period after 1280, where Zlatarski ends. Mutafčiev died before completing the work, and I. Dujčev wrote the concluding section, covering the period 1323–1393. Steven Runciman, *A History of the First Bulgarian Empire* (1930); Stančo Vaklinov, *Formirane na starobŭlgarskata kultura* (1977); Vasil N. Zlatarski, *Istorija na bŭlgarskata dŭržava prez srednite vekove,* 3 vols. in 4 (1918–1940), covering the period up to 1280.

Many major contributions on Bulgarian history have appeared as articles by scholars whose collected works are in the process of being issued. Under the title *Izbrani proizvedenija* [Collected works] multivolume collections of articles (chiefly in Bulgarian) by A. Burmov, Peter Mutafčiev, and Vasil N. Zlatarski are being republished in a project begun in the late 1960's in Sofia. Collected studies by I. Dujčev have also been published; some of his Bulgarian articles are collected under the title *Bŭlgarsko srednovekovie* (1972), and his Western-language articles are being republished in Rome in a multivolume collection begun in 1965, *Medioevo Bizantino-Slavo.*

JOHN V. A. FINE, JR.

[See also **Avars; Basil II; Bogomils; Boris; Boyar; Bulgarian Art and Architecture; Bulgarus; Byzantine Empire; Constantinople; Croatia; Epiros, Despotate of; Hesychasm; John Asen I; John Asen II; Kalojan; Krum; Land Tenure, Slavic; Magyars; Messembria; Nicaea, Empire of; Ochrid; Peter of Bulgaria; Philippopolis; Russian Nomads, Invasions of; Samuil of Bulgaria; Serbs and Serbia; Sirmium; Slavic Languages and Literatures; Slavs; Stefan Dušan; Symeon of Bulgaria; Thessaloniki; Vlachs.**]

BULGARIAN ART AND ARCHITECTURE. In their need to create a national art and architecture for the First Bulgarian Empire (681–1018), Bulgarian patrons and artists drew on varied sources. The Roman basilica provided the most typical church form. Sveta Sofia, a brick cruciform basilica with a barrel vault and dome, possibly fortified, is typical of fifth- and sixth-century churches. Other structures, such as the sixth-century Red Church near Perushtica, an aisled tetraconch, copy Roman and Byzantine centralized plans.

The palace at Pliska, which served as the capital from 681 to 893, was laid out as a double fortress. A huge rectangular earthwork topped by a wooden palisade and surrounded by a moat formed the outer defense. Inside was space for dwellings, workshops, and trade, and the inner palace of the khan, protected by stout stone walls, towers, and gatehouses. The palace at Preslav, seat of government from 893 to 972, had a similar layout. The outer fortress here had thick limestone walls with towers and fortified gates. The inner palace was also built of stone. These palaces have been linked to Sasanian prototypes, but they have even closer parallels in late Roman structures such as Diocletian's palace in Split.

One example of Sasanian influence is the Madara horseman, the only rock-cut relief in Europe. The rider, with a dog running behind and a dead lion below, is surrounded by several inscriptions in Greek. Recent studies date these to the eighth and early ninth centuries. The relief itself, originally carved to represent Khan Tervel (701–718), was reused as a symbol of divinely invested royal power under Omurtag (814–831). The Madara relief is based on Sasanian prototypes mixed with the Thracian rider image and its reflection in Roman and Byzantine art. A similar eclecticism is found in the Bulgarian metalwork treasure of Nagy-Szent-Miklós from the second half of the ninth century.

Preslav preserves the most important remains of the arts of the First Empire. Foremost is the Round Church attributed to Symeon by an inscription from 907, a rotunda enlivened by eight niches. The atrium, added later, repeats the pattern. Both the church and the narthex were double-storied; the ensemble was decorated with opus sectile floors, carved marble, mosaics, and decorative tilework. The Round Church and other buildings in Preslav contained stone carvings, many in the flat-relief style of the Madara horseman. Some decorative carvings from the tenth century reflect contemporary work in

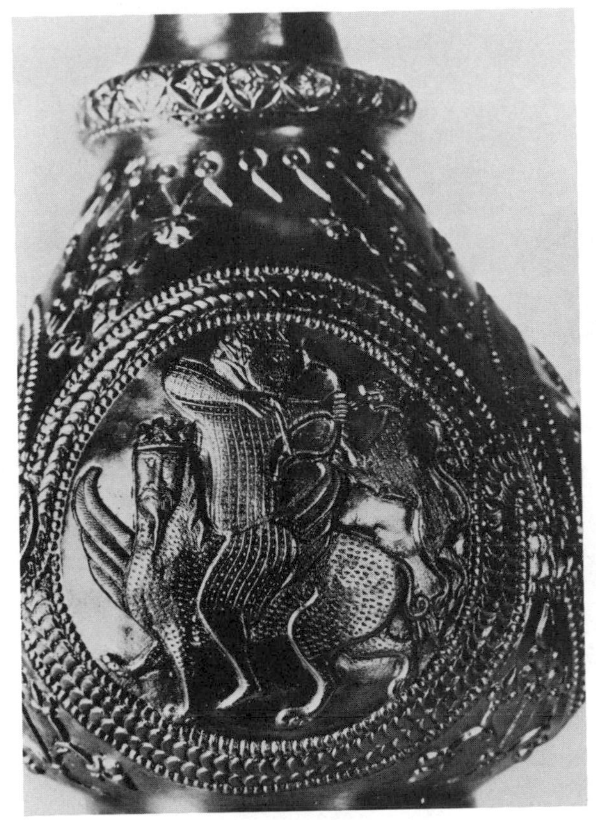

Gold vessel (*left*), Nagy-Szent-Miklós treasure. Second half of 9th century. PHOTOGRAPH, KUNSTHISTORISCHES MUSEUM, VIENNA. Exonarthex and western façade of narthex (*above*), Round Church, Preslav. Late 9th or early 10th century. PHOTOGRAPH, STFAN BIODZHIEV. St. Theodore icon (*below*). Patlejna, 9th–10th century. PHOTOGRAPH, ELLEN C. SCHWARTZ

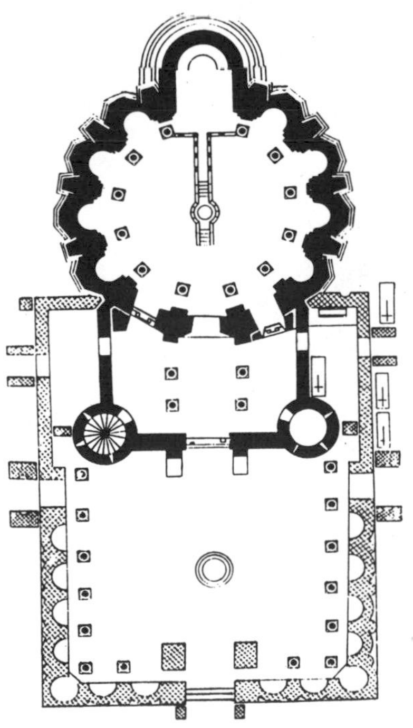

Ground Plan, Round Church, Preslav. FROM KRŬSTJU MIJATEV, DIE MITTELALTERLICHE BAUKUNST IN BULGARIEN

Portraits of donor Kalojan and his wife, Desislava. Bojana, 1259. PHOTOGRAPHS, TSENTRAL FOTO

St. George icon, Plovdiv. Late 13th century. PHOTOGRAPH, NATIONAL ARCHAEOLOGICAL MUSEUM, SOFIA

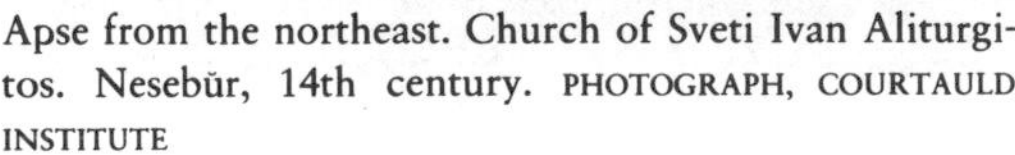

Apse from the northeast. Church of Sveti Ivan Aliturgitos. Nesebŭr, 14th century. PHOTOGRAPH, COURTAULD INSTITUTE

Constantinople; others, such as the column capital with rabbits or the sculptures from nearby Avradaka, are unique and represent some of the earliest animal decoration of pre-Romanesque times.

Another usual feature is the use of glazed ceramics for decoration. Icons, including the twenty-tile representation of St. Theodore from Patlejna and the single-tile figures from Tuzlalŭk, have been found, along with flat tiles and pieces of ceramic cornices. These tiles adorned walls and floors in imitation of more costly media. Designs on the tiles were inspired by classical, Byzantine, and Sasanian decorative motifs; the contemporary development of this art form in Bulgaria and Byzantium must have been due to contact with the Arab civilizations of the Near East or North Africa.

The Byzantine occupation of Bulgaria (1018–1185) saw the introduction of artistic styles that served as models for later Bulgarian art. An important monument from this time is the charnel house *(kostnica)* of the Bachkovo monastery, built by the Bakuriani brothers in 1083. It comprises two stories; the lower was used for burial, and the upper served as a chapel. The paintings inside belong to the Byzantine style of the late eleventh century.

The rich remains of the Second Bulgarian Empire (1185–1396) show Bulgarian art to be a dialect of the Byzantine artistic language at that time. New developments in church architecture include the two-story church. These structures, often single-aisled and capped by a dome supported on pilasters, are exemplified by Kalojan's church at Bojana (1259) and the Church of the Virgin Stanimaka (*ca.* 1230). The latter shows another new element, a bell tower placed over the narthex. Of growing importance was elaborate architectural decoration that did not express the structure or the internal layout of the building. This decoration reached its climax in the local school of Nesebŭr (Mesembria). The fourteenth-century Church of Sveti Ivan Aliturgitos there is covered with a pseudo-structural arcade framing blind niches filled with varied geometric patterns of stone, bricks, and glazed ceramic inserts.

Bulgarian medieval painting shows both a reliance on older models and an awareness of current Constantinopolitan trends. The Bojana paintings of 1259 by artists from Trnovo show archaic elements of style such as the tall, slim figures found in Komnenian art. This ensemble is pervaded by a mood of gentleness as well as an awakening interest in realism seen in the donor portraits and the scene of the Christ child in the temple. The later ensemble at Zemen (*ca.* 1354) shows archaic elements mixed with a local, folk style. A knowledge of up-to-date metropolitan painting is visible in the frescoes of the "Tsŭrkvata" of Ivanovo, a rock-cut chapel commissioned by Ivan Alexander about 1350. Its small, lively figures in exotic headgear are rendered in an energized version of the style found at the Kariye Camii in Constantinople.

Manuscript and icon painting show similar trends. The luxurious Gospels of Ivan Alexander in the British Museum contain royal portraits in contemporary dress along with miniatures that closely copy an eleventh-century model. An icon of St. George crowned and enthroned (*ca.* 1300) from Plovdiv is done in pure Palaiologan style. Other arts and styles appear to have a more local origin, such as the bronze icon plaque of the Virgin and Child in Plovdiv (first half of the thirteenth century) and the icon of the Bulgarian saint Ivan Rilski at Rila with its rich complementary colors and glittering highlights (fourteenth century). Late monuments such as the frescoes at Dragalevci (1476) and Kremikovci (1491) near Sofia show a continuation of these Palaiologan and local trends into the early years of the Ottoman occupation.

BIBLIOGRAPHY

Bŭlgarska Akademija na Naukite, Institut za Izkustvoznanie, *Istorija na bŭlgarskoto izobrazitelno izkustvo* (1976); André Grabar, *La peinture religieuse en Bulgarie,* I–II (1928); Nikola Mavrodinov, *Starobŭlgarskoto izkustvo* (1959); Nikola Mavrodinov, *Starobŭlgarskoto izkustvo XI–XIII vek* (1966); Krŭstju Mijateve, *Die mittelalterliche Baukunst in Bulgarien* (1974); Stancho Vaklinov, *Formirane na starobŭlgarskata kultura VI–XI vek* (1977).

ELLEN C. SCHWARTZ

[See also **Byzantine Art; Early Christian and Byzantine Architecture.**]

BULGARS. See **Bulgaria.**

BULGARUS (*d.* 1166), one of the "Four Doctors" (students of Irnerius), continued his teaching of Roman law at Bologna in the twelfth century and thus firmly established Bologna's reputation as the leading center for legal studies in western Europe. (The other three "doctors" were Martinus Gosia, Hugo de Porta Ravennate, and Jacobus da Voragine). Like his colleagues, Bulgarus was an adviser of Emperor Frederick Barbarossa and with them was consulted at the Diet of Roncaglia (1158), at which Frederick asserted his rights over Lombardy. These rights were based on ancient customs rather than on Roman law, and Bulgarus himself had upheld the right of a city to abrogate general rules of law. Bulgarus had distinguished students who in turn taught Azo, one of the most influential medieval writers on Roman law.

BIBLIOGRAPHY

R. W. Carlyle and A. J. Carlyle, *A History of Mediaeval Political Theory in the West,* II (1909, repr. 1979), 15–16, 32–36, 57, 65–66, 69, quotes passages from Bulgarus; Peter Munz, *Frederick Barbarossa* (1969), 165–169, discusses the Diet of Roncaglia. On Bulgarus' role in the revival of the study of Roman law, see Charles H. Haskins, *The Renaissance of the Twelfth Century* (1927), 200–208.

JOSEPH R. STRAYER

[See also **Bologna, University of; Irnerius; Law, Schools of; Martinus Gosia.**]

BULL, PAPAL, a special kind of document or charter issued by a pope and named from the seal *(bulla)* that was appended to authenticate it. The coin-shaped seal was almost invariably leaden, but a golden one was occasionally used. The kind of document to which the term was first applied by the papal chancery itself, if only in an unofficial fashion, appeared toward the middle of the thirteenth century. In the fifteenth century one of the offices of the chancery was called the register of bulls *(registrum bullarum).*

In terms of content, what the chancery called a bull was originally used for decrees or other dispositions of general validity and in particular for politically important excommunications. Eventually it was also used for constitutions, canonizations, convocations or confirmations of ecumenical councils, and many other less significant purposes, though it was not used for any of these purposes consistently. In fact, almost the only unexceptionable generalization about the contents of bulls may be that they seem never to have dealt with purely private matters.

The bull's format began with a one-line protocol in tall, elongated letters containing the pope's name, his title *(episcopus servus servorum Dei),* and a phrase indicative of a perpetual purpose as a record (e.g., *ad perpetuam rei memoriam).* The body or text of the bull could be relatively simple in form, not even needing to have a sanction clause at the end. The final protocol consisted of a short *datum* formula, mentioning only the place of issuance along with the day of the month and the year of the pope's pontificate, and of course the seal, attached with silk strings. Pope Boniface VIII's famous declaration of 1302, *Unam sanctam,* known as other bulls were from the opening words of its text, was in this form.

Retroactively the name bull also came to be applied by scholars to more elaborate papal documents issued in the form of privileges (solemn or simple) and to some less elaborate ones issued in the form of letters, to which the leaden seal was attached with silk strings; and sometimes the name has been popularly applied to any papal document with a leaden seal. The issuing of solemn privileges became much less frequent after the emergence of the new type of bull in the mid thirteenth century, and eventually the new type of bull in turn lost some of its functions to the more simple *breve* (brief), starting from the first half of the fifteenth century. Original papal privileges survive in appreciable numbers only from the eleventh century onward, when more durable parchment was used for copying them instead of fragile papyrus; and none survives in its entirety from before 819. Original leaden seals, however, survive from the sixth or seventh century. The earliest ones have the pope's name in the genitive case on one side and the title *PAPAE* on the other. Those from the later Middle Ages bear the effigies of Sts. Paul and Peter, identified by the letters *S(anctus) PA(ulus)* and *S(anctus) PE(trus),* on one side; on the other side they bear the pope's name with his title *P(a)P(a)* and number.

BIBLIOGRAPHY

Giulio Battelli, *Acta pontificum,* 2nd ed. (1965); Harry Bresslau, *Handbuch der Urkundenlehre für Deutschland und Italien,* 2nd ed., I (1912, repr. 1958), 72–85; Arthur Giry, *Manuel de diplomatique* (1894, repr. 1925), 661–699; Peter Herde, *Beiträge zum päpstlichen Kanzlei- und Urkundenwesen im dreizehnten Jahrhundert,* 2nd ed. (1967), 57–71; Reginald L. Poole, *Lectures on the History of the Papal Chancery down to the Time of Innocent III* (1915), 20–25, 37–50, 98–122; Michael Tangi, ed., *Die päpstlichen Kanzleiordnungen von 1200–1500* (1894, repr. 1959).

JAMES J. JOHN

[See also **Charter; Papacy, Origins and Development of.**]

BUNDAHISHN. The *Bundahishn* (Creation) is one of the most important pieces of Zoroastrian Middle Persian literature. Composed after the Arab conquest of Persia (641), it nevertheless makes use of much ancient material from diverse sources. It was transmitted in two versions, the Greater, or Iranian, *Bundahishn* and the Indian *Bundahishn.* Although the former conveys a greater wealth of material, the latter deserves study in its own right because it contains some material not found in the larger version as well as important variant readings.

The *Bundahishn,* which is also called *Zand Āgāhīh* (Knowledge of the *zand* [interpretation of the Avesta]), has three major themes: the creation of the world and the future course of world history, descriptions of the natural world, and Iranian legendary history.

Of particular interest is the creation account, which conforms to the "great year" pattern. This great year is divided into the four "seasons" of *mēnōg,* or "spiritual" creation, *gētīg,* or "material" creation, mixture with evil, and separation and renewal of the material world. Central to this concept is the distinction between finite and infinite time. The god Ohrmazd (Ahura Mazda), who is not omnipotent in an absolute sense, creates finite time and space as a strategem to entrap and destroy his adversary Ahriman (Angra Mainyu). By creating a finite context, Ohrmazd is able to limit and defeat the previously limitless power of evil. The great year, then, is finite time, created once and for all for the express purpose of eradicating evil.

Man is the major actor in this drama, since he is the warrior against evil in this finite world. The turning point, the beginning of the separation of good from evil leading to the final cleansing and renewal of the world, is the birth of the prophet Zarathustra (Zoroaster).

BIBLIOGRAPHY

Mary Boyce, "Middle Persian Literature," in *Handbuch der Orientalistik,* IV, 2 (1968), 40–41, and bibliography in note on 41.

DALE L. BISHOP

[See also **Avesta; Zoroastrianism.**]

BUON, GIOVANNI (*ca.* 1355–*ca.* 1443) and **BARTOLOMEO** (*ca.* 1374–*ca.* 1467), Venetian sculptors. In 1392 Giovanni, assisted by his son Bartolomeo, worked on the facade of S. Maria dell'Orto. The two collaborated in 1422 on the Ca' d'Oro, an activity documented until 1434 and involving a wellhead (a masterpiece of its kind), perhaps done in connection with Nanni di Bartolo, and a frieze on the facade. In 1438 they carved the Porta della Carta for the Doge's Palace. Between 1441 and 1445 Bartolomeo designed and executed the facade of the Scuolo della Misericordia (lunette now in the Victoria and Albert Museum, London), and in 1442–1450 he worked on S. Maria della Carità. He was at work again on the Doge's Palace in 1463. Giovanni and Bartolomeo incorporated a pragmatic and evocative realism inspired by German sculptors into an ornate profusion of sculpted figural and decorative elements wonderfully compatible with their architectural settings.

BIBLIOGRAPHY

John W. Pope-Hennessy, *Italian Gothic Sculpture,* 2nd ed. (1972), 221–222; Wolfgang Wolters, *La scultura veneziana gotica (1300–1460)* (1976), 90–93.

ADELHEID M. GEALT

BUONACORSO, NICOLO DI. See **Nicolo di Buonacorso.**

BURĀQ, the celestial animal that conveyed the prophet Muḥammad during his Night Journey from Mecca to Jerusalem *(isrāʾ)* and thence through the realms of paradise *(miʿrāj).* According to al-Ṭabarī's commentary on the Koran, earlier prophets had also ridden it. Burāq is described in the principal collections of Islamic canonical Tradition *(al-ḥadīth)* as being white, larger than a donkey but smaller than a mule, and able to reach the horizon with one stride. Iconographically, Burāq developed in Persian miniature painting into a highly elegant creature, generally depicted with wings and a human or angelic face, and colored either in vivid hues or white.

BIBLIOGRAPHY

Muḥammad ibn Ismāʿīl al-Bukhārī, *The Translation of the Meanings of Ṣaḥīḥ al-Bukhārī,* Muḥammad Muḥsin Khān, trans., English and Arabic, rev. ed., V (1976), 143;

Burāq carrying Muḥammad. Persian Manuscript, fifteenth century. THE METROPOLITAN MUSEUM OF ART, GIFT OF ALEXANDER SMITH COCHRAN, 1913

Muslim ibn al-Ḥajjāj al-Qushairī, *Ṣaḥīḥ Muslim . . . Under the Title al-Jamiᶜ-uṣ ṣaḥīḥ, by Imām Muslim,* ᶜAbdul Ḥamīd Ṣiddīqī, trans., I (1971), 101; Sir Thomas W. Arnold, *Painting in Islam* (1928), 117–122.

MUHAMMAD ISA WALEY

[See also **Ascension of the Prophet.**]

BURCHARD OF WORMS (*ca.* 965–1025) was deacon and treasurer of Mainz and later bishop of Worms, where he became the intimate of emperors Otto III, Henry II, and Conrad II. A Latin work of thirty-two chapters, written just before his death, illustrates his main interest, codification. He tried to clarify current practice in all types of law in the interest of those suffering abuse by authority. His best-known work, probably called *Decretorum libri XX* (Twenty books of decisions) but popularly simply *Burchardus,* drew on numerous sources to substitute a clear code of Christian penitential discipline for the prevailing confusion of practices. He was especially concerned with penitence and the sacerdotal duties of priests and bishops.

BIBLIOGRAPHY

Court Law of Worms, Ludwig Weiland, ed., in *Monumenta Germaniae historica: Constitutiones,* I (1893), 640–644; *Decretorum libri XX,* in *Patrologia latina,* CXL (1853), 537–1058; Max Manitius, *Geschichte der lateinischen Literatur des Mittelalters,* II (1923), 56–61.

W. T. H. JACKSON

[See also **Confession; Law, Civil; Law, German.**]

BURGAGE TENURE, in Normandy and the British Isles a form of land ownership characteristic of boroughs (*bourgs,* burghs). The typical burgage holding was a messuage: a house and garden in the town. Agricultural land in the outlying fields was also held by the tenure.

Burgage was free ownership, distinctively free and beyond the measure of other free tenures. To begin with, he who held in burgage ought to be a free man, and his property had a special power to make him so; commonly the tenant who held for a year was beyond further challenge of his status. Burgage was especially free, secondly, because the rights of the lord sat exceedingly lightly upon it. It was held in perpetuity, with only the possibility of escheat reserved. The lord usually received a fixed annual rent, but this was of small value, often merely nominal, and there was generally no other service. The onerous "incidents" of many other tenures were absent. In some small boroughs the lord took a military heriot or a relief when the owner died, but that was all. Finally, burgage tenure was free because the owner had wide powers to dispose of it as he liked. He could grant it out at a rent, subdivide, mortgage, give, or sell it. In most English boroughs (though not in the Norman or Scottish) he could "devise" it by his will. There were sometimes light restraints on his powers of disposition in favor of the lord, often more substantial restraints in favor of kindred. The

English law of other tenures came in time to invest owners with equally great powers, but only by about the end of the Middle Ages.

Burgages never lay scattered about. Where the tenure was found, it was the tenure of a whole town in nearly all its messuages and lands. Nothing more might be needed to give a community the name of borough. But most boroughs possessed the privilege of having lawsuits that arose there settled in courts held within their bounds. Thus even in lands of English rule, where a common law for free tenures was built up from the twelfth century, this freest of all tenures paradoxically escaped the centralization and remained subject to local custom.

As a name for a tenure the term "burgage" emerged only in the twelfth century, and it was almost always confined to Normandy and the British Isles. But the form of property that it designated originated earlier, in the eleventh century if not before, and became familiar throughout Roman Catholic Christendom. It arose where a king or lord wished to promote the growth of a community whose value to him would lie in something other than its agriculture. In the commonest case what was desired was a commercial center, whether a local market town or an international emporium. The lord's dues had to be kept light in order to allow the indispensable accumulation of wealth and, in the case of new foundations, to attract settlers. The dues that arose from the land itself could be made negligible, for the hope was to create commercial wealth, in which the lord would share not through ground rents but through market tolls and tallages.

BIBLIOGRAPHY

Robert Génestal, *La tenure en bourgage* (1900); Morley de Wolf Hemmeon, *Burgage Tenure in Mediaeval England* (1914); James Tait, "Liber burgus," in A. G. Little and F. M. Powicke, eds., *Essays in Medieval History Presented to Thomas Frederick Tout* (1925).

DONALD W. SUTHERLAND

[See also **Borough; Land Tenure, Western European.**]

BURGH. See **Borough.**

BURGH, DE. The family of de Burgh belonged to the local gentry of Norfolk and achieved prominence in England with Hubert, who acted as a justiciar for King John. The family involvement with Ireland began with William, who accompanied Lord John (later king) on his expedition of 1185 and was later granted lands in what is now County Tipperary. When he married a daughter of Donal O'Brien, king of Thomond, forging an alliance that was to last for generations, he committed himself to Ireland. The future of the family, though, lay not in Munster but to the north, first in Connacht and then, more importantly, in Ulster. William procured a speculative grant of Connacht in the 1190's and began the process of colonization before he died in 1205. His son Richard, with the help of his uncle Hubert de Burgh, chief justiciar of England, procured a new charter for Connacht and led the "conquest of Connacht" in 1235. By 1236 he had begun building his castle at Loughrea, which was to be the center of his new lordship, and in the following years the settlement of his new lands was completed. His heir, Walter, thus inherited a vast estate in Tipperary and Connacht when he obtained seisin in 1250. There was a spectacular addition when he was granted the earldom of Ulster by Henry III in 1263.

As earl of Ulster and lord of Connacht, Walter was the most important magnate in Ireland. Almost immediately he was involved in a fierce struggle with Maurice fitz Maurice and other Geraldines, which erupted into civil war. At base this was a struggle for power in Connacht, which Walter regarded as his sphere and where he resented Geraldine intrusion. The bitter rivalry between the two families, complicated by involvement on different sides in Gaelic dynastic struggles in Thomond, reached its climax under Richard de Burgh, the "red" earl, who obtained seisin of his lordship in 1280. His feud with John fitz Thomas, later first earl of Kildare, was finally healed in a settlement in 1298 that saw the Geraldines withdraw from Connacht.

Earl Richard proved himself the greatest of the de Burghs by consolidating his hold on Connacht and greatly expanding his Ulster earldom. He was a great builder of castles, influenced by what he saw when in Wales with King Edward I; a great soldier (he twice led expeditions from Ireland to fight in the Scottish wars); and a diplomat of skill, demonstrated not only in his dealings with Gaelic dynasts in Ulster and Connacht, but also in his work in Scotland on behalf of the English king. His sister was married to James the Stewart of Scotland and, more notably, his daughter was married to King Robert Bruce. Because of this connection Richard played a dubious role in the resistance to the Scottish invasion of Ireland in

1315, was arrested and imprisoned by the citizens of Dublin, and saw much of his earldom fall into Scottish hands. But after the defeat of the Scots he rapidly recovered his position. When he died in 1326, the de Burgh inheritance was intact.

But already there were signs of fatal factional fights among minor de Burghs, especially in Connacht, which were to destroy the estate. The murder of William, the "brown" earl, in 1333 was a catastrophe. His inheritance passed to his daughter Elizabeth, wife of Lionel of Clarence, and through that marriage to the Mortimers and finally to the house of York and the English Crown. The minor de Burghs in Connacht gradually became Gaelicized as Burkes and emerged in the later Middle Ages as the two great lines of Clanricarde and Clanwilliam Burkes.

BIBLIOGRAPHY

M. J. Blake, "William de Burgh: Progenitor of the Burkes in Ireland," in *Journal of the Galway Archaeological and Historical Society,* 7 (1911–1912); Edmund Curtis, *A History of Medieval Ireland* (1938); H. T. Knox, "The de Burgo Clans of Galway," in *Journal of the Galway Archaeological and Historical Society,* **1** (1900–1901), and **4** (1905–1906); T. E. McNeill, *Anglo-Norman Ulster* (1980); G. H. Orpen, *Ireland Under the Normans,* 4 vols. (1911–1920); A. J. Otway-Ruthven, *A History of Medieval Ireland* (1968).

JAMES F. LYDON

[See also **Connacht; Ireland Under English Rule; Ulster.**]

BURGHAUSEN, HANNS VON (*d.* 1432), late German Gothic architect until recently misidentified as Hanns Stethaimer, a contemporary. Burghausen was creator of the Landshut School of Bavarian-Austrian *Hallenkirchen* and a master of unified spatial volumes. His principal works are the churches of Sankt Jakob at Straubing, begun about 1395; Sankt Martin at Landshut (nave), begun between 1400 and 1410; Heilig Geist at Landshut, begun in 1407; and the Franciscan church at Salzburg, begun shortly after 1408.

BIBLIOGRAPHY

John W. Cook, "A New Chronology of Hanns von Burghausen's Late Gothic Architecture," in *Gesta,* **15** (1976), with extensive documentation and bibliography.

CARL F. BARNES, JR.

[See also **Gothic Architecture.**]

BURGUNDIANS. Scholars agree, on the basis of linguistic evidence and various written traditions from the early Middle Ages that can justly be characterized as folkloric, that the Burgundians originated in Scandinavia and then migrated eastward toward the Vistula during the first century of the Christian era. The reasons for the migration of this particular Germanic tribe are the subject of substantial speculation, but there is no scholarly consensus—and very probably never will be. From their new settlements the Burgundians moved westward during the middle of the third century and took advantage of the civil wars that bedeviled the Roman Empire following the murder of Maximinus in 238 to raid imperial territory. For the next century and a half the Burgundians were in close contact with the Romans. Burgundian settlements reached the east bank of the Rhine no later than 359.

On the last day of 406, the freezing of the Rhine provided the opportunity for a large mass of barbarians to cross the river. The Burgundians were an important part of this group that penetrated the Roman frontier. They and a band of Alani were separated from the rest through the diplomacy of imperial agents, and these barbarian defectors were settled along the west bank of the Rhine in the region of Coblenz (rather than Worms, as maintained in later medieval legend). Burgundian efforts to extend their settlements were discouraged by the Roman authorities, and finally in 436, after the Burgundians had been engaged in several plots, the Roman military commander in the West, Aëtius, used his Hunnic auxiliaries to punish these Germans for their attempts to expand the area under their control. The Burgundians were so severely mauled by Aëtius' men that "the war between the Huns and the Burgundians" captured the popular imagination and became the basis for the *Nibelungenlied.* The practical results of this encounter were the deaths of several thousand Burgundians, the death of King Gundahar, and the resettlement of the remnant of the tribe to the south, in the region of Geneva, in 443.

After being resettled, the Burgundians cooperated with the Romans and fought against the Huns at Châlons in 451. Indeed, following the death of Emperor Majorian in 461, Burgundian rulers accepted imperial military titles and were styled *patricius* (patrician, noble). On two occasions the Burgundians were responsible for establishing emperors: Olybrius in 472 and Glycerius in 473. In 490 they supported Odoacer against Theodoric. These involvements in imperial affairs did not hinder Burgundian expansionist efforts in Gaul. By about 470 Lyons was in Burgundian hands, and Langres was under their control by 485. Before the end of the century the Burgundians dominated most of eastern Gaul from the southern limits of Champagne to the Alps.

Although the Burgundian rulers were Arian Christians, they enjoyed good relations with the Gallo-Roman inhabitants of the lands that they now occupied. The Burgundian laws were written down in Latin, and it is clear that the Roman population was well treated. Mixed marriages between Burgundians and Romans were not prohibited, and the Romans were not disarmed. The Burgundian king, who made his capital at Lyons (the royal heir was probably established at Geneva), bore the Germanic title king and the Roman title *patricius.*

It should be emphasized that the Romans were permitted to live according to their own laws, and it would appear that a regime of personal law existed. Some scholars reject this interpretation, insisting that the Burgundian law was territorial and that the surviving *Lex romana Burgundionum* (Roman law of the Burgundians) was simply a "private collection." Whatever the final determination on this issue may be—that it was personal or territorial—the fact of cooperation between the Burgundians and the Gallo-Romans will not be undermined. Perhaps the best illustration of this cooperation is the *hospitalitas* agreements arranged by Roman officials: the Burgundians received the tax revenues from two-thirds of the land, one-third of the slaves, half of the forests, and half of the farm buildings. These divisions of the revenues were carried out smoothly and were in marked contrast to the practices of the Arian Vandals, who dispossessed the Roman landholders, and the pagan Franks, who did not utilize *hospitalitas* agreements.

The flourishing Burgundian kingdom of the later fifth century was severely endangered by conflict among the members of the ruling family by aggressive neighbors. Godegisel married an orthodox Christian while his brother Gundobad remained Arian. Gundobad murdered Godegisel, giving the Frankish ruler Clovis the opportunity to exploit the subsequent Burgundian unrest. He married the Burgundian princess Clotilda, who was an orthodox Christian, and in 500–501 the Franks campaigned, unsuccessfully, against Gundobad. Thereafter, Gundobad's son Sigismund converted to orthodox Christianity, an action that appears to have discouraged further Frankish efforts for a time.

The Arian Goths took Sigismund's conversion as a casus belli, and although the conflict was inconclusive, the Burgundians suffered considerable losses. Clovis' son, Chlodomer, took advantage of this situation to invade in 524. He captured and murdered King Sigismund, whose brother defeated and killed Chlodomer. A decade later Chlodomer's brothers destroyed the remnants of the Burgundian ruling family and integrated their kingdom into the Frankish kingdom. Thereafter, Burgundian history follows the road of Frankish history, although the Burgundians and their Gallo-Roman neighbors were permitted to maintain their separate legal identities.

BIBLIOGRAPHY

Maurice Chaume, *Les origines du duché de Bourgogne,* 4 vols. (1925); Alfred Coville, *Recherches sur l'histoire de Lyon du Ve au IXe siècle* (1928); Albert Jahn, *Geschichte der Burgundionen und Burgundiens bis zum Ende der I. Dynastie,* 2 vols. (1874); Lucien Musset, *The Germanic Invasions,* Edward and Columba James, trans. (1975).

BERNARD S. BACHRACH

[See also **Alani; Barbarians, Invasions of; Clovis; Nibelungenlied; Roman Empire, Late.**]

BURGUNDIO OF PISA (*d.* 1193), canonist and translator, had a long and distinguished career. He must have been born early in the twelfth century, since he was one of the learned scholars who conferred with the archbishop of Nicomedia at Constantinople in 1136. He was trained as a jurist and became a judge in Pisa, but he had also studied medicine and acquired a thorough knowledge of Greek. He served Frederick Barbarossa as envoy to Ragusa (1169) and Constantinople (1172), and dedicated his translation of Nemesius' *De natura hominis* to the emperor.

Burgundio's most important work was the translation of *De fide orthodoxa* of St. John of Damascus. This book, "the theological code of the Greek church," written by a scholar who has been called "the Thomas Aquinas of the East," had a great influence on Western theologians such as Peter Lombard. Burgundio also translated works by St. John Chrysostom, ten medical treatises of Galen, and the Greek quotations in Justinian's *Digest.* He was one of the most active and most accurate of the many Western scholars who translated Greek texts in the twelfth century. His work was still being used in the fifteenth century.

BIBLIOGRAPHY

Maurice De Wolf, *History of Mediaeval Philsophy,* E. C. Messenger, trans. (1926), 204–205, 217–218; Charles Homer Haskins, *Studies in the History of Mediaeval Science,* 2nd ed. (1927), 206–209; Joseph de Ghellinck, *Le mouvement théologique du XIIe siècle* (1948), 375–386.

JOSEPH R. STRAYER

[See also **Translations and Translators.**]

BURGUNDY, COUNTY OF. This region, also known as the Franche-Comté, occupied the eastern frontier of medieval France in the watershed of the Saône, with Helvetia on the east, Lorraine and Alsace on the north, and Bresse on the south. It originally made up the southern half of what the Romans called Gallia Belgica and was inhabited by a Celtic people known as the Sequani. In A.D. 411 the region was overrun by the Burgundians, and in 534 the Merovingian Franks conquered Burgundy. Under Charlemagne the northern half was divided into five *pagi,* or districts: Ajoie (Granges, Rougemont), Portois (Luxeuil, Faverney, Traves), Varais (Baume-les-Dames, Salins), Amaous (Gray, Dôle, Neublans), and Ecuens (Lons-le-Saunier to the Juras). The counts established in the new *pagi* were aided by archbishops at Besançon, who had jurisdiction over the churches of the region.

In the treaty of Verdun (843) Langres, Chalon, Mâcon, Autun, and other areas west of the Saône went to Charles the Bald, while the counties between the Saône and the Juras went to Lothair. Between 888 and 1032 the latter region formed part of a kingdom of Transjurane Burgundy, which was created by princes of the German house of Welf on the breakup of the Carolingian kingdom of Lotharingia. Rudolf II of Burgundy (912–937) even tried to acquire the crown of Italy. On the death of Rudolf III without heirs in 1032, Emperor Conrad II sought to incorporate Transjurane Burgundy into the empire, but real power in the region continued to be exercised by great barons like the lords of Salins, who also held Ornans and Vuillafans, and the counts of Montbéliard, who dominated the northeastern frontier. The weakness of the Burgundian kings had forced the population to look to such as these for protection against invaders, notably the Magyars, who sacked Luxeuil, Mandeure, and Besançon in 927, while the clergy tried to protect the population from the warlords themselves.

Otto-Guillaume (*d.* 1027) attempted to establish his power over both Burgundies but was thwarted by the Capetians; and his son Renaud, lord of Salins and "count of Burgundy," formed an alliance with the Salian emperors. Archbishop Hugues de Salins (*d.* 1066/1067), the rebuilder of Besançon, became archchancellor of the kingdom of Arles (of which Burgundy formed a part), with imperial confirmation of his authority over Besançon in 1043.

Count Guillaume le Grand aided Henry IV during the Investiture Struggle, but his son Renaud II went on the First Crusade and another son, archbishop of Vienne, became Pope Calixtus II in 1119. Renaud III refused to recognize the election of Lothair of Supplinburg as emperor in 1125, however, and he remained unsubdued after ten years of war against Lothair's rector in the kingdom of Arles, Conrad of Zähringen. It was this fierce and successful resistance that earned him the appellation "the free count"; and when in 1156 the new emperor, Frederick Barbarossa, married Renaud's only child, Béatrice, the "free" character of the county as directly dependent on the empire was preserved.

Hohenstaufen efforts to attach the Franche-Comté permanently to the empire encountered stubborn resistance among the French-speaking nobility. When Frederick's youngest son, Count Otto I, was succeeded by his son-in-law, Otto of Meran, in 1201, Étienne II, count of Auxonne and Chalon, laid claim to the succession and formed an alliance with Duke Hugues IV of Burgundy. This coalition was too strong for Otto II, who in effect was forced to share comital authority in Burgundy with Étienne II, a situation that lasted throughout the thirteenth century.

In 1237 Jean "l'Antique" (or "le Sage") ceded his counties of Auxonne and Chalon to Hugues IV in return for his possessions in Franche-Comté: Salins, Ornans, Vuillafans, Val de Miège, and Les Clées across the Juras. For the next thirty years this remarkable personage exploited the large revenues from the saltworks at Salins, made himself master of the export routes, granted municipal charters and founded new towns at strategic points, and populated the county with some sixteen children by three successive wives (founding the dynasties of the Chalon-Vienne, the Chalon-Auxerre, and the Chalon-Arlay, who became princes of Orange in 1386). While the last Meran count, Otto IV, allied himself with the Capetians (his daughter Jeanne married the future Philip V in 1295), Jean I de Chalon-Arlay turned to the Habsburgs, who in 1288 gave him the lucrative *péage* (toll rights) on the Jougne-

Verdun
Paris
CHAMPAGNE
LORRAINE
KINGDOM OF GERMANY
Seine R.
Troyes
Clairvaux
Sens
ANJOU
Langres
Luxeuil
Auxerre
Châtillon
UPPER BURGUNDY
Blois
Gray
Baume-les-Dames
Dijon
Tours
Besançon
Citeaux
FRANCHE-COMTÉ
Dôle
Beaune
Nevers
Autun
Salins
TRANSJURANE BURGUNDY
Chalon
CISJURANE BURGUNDY
Cluny
Mâcon
BRESSE
Geneva
Saône R.
Rhône R.
Forez
SAVOY
Lyons
Eleventh-century Burgundy
Vienne
KINGDOM OF ITALY
KINGDOM OF BURGUNDY
DUCHY OF BURGUNDY
DAUPHINÉ
COUNTY OF BURGUNDY
(Franche-Comté)
Valence
Ste. Columbe
Viviers
LOWER BURGUNDY
(KINGDOM OF PROVENCE)
KINGDOM OF FRANCE
Nice
Arles
Toulouse
Aix
Marseilles
Mediterranean
Sea

BURGUNDY, COUNTY OF

Pontarlier route and helped him subdue rivals in the county.

The Chalon, who had begun by resisting imperial domination in favor of the French, now became champions of the county's independence against the French. In 1294 Jean de Chalon-Arlay and twenty-eight barons took an oath never to become vassals of the king of France, but the power of Philip IV and Duke Robert II of Burgundy was too great. Jean de Chalon became "guardian" of the county in 1301, and a *parlement* like that of Paris was established at Dôle in 1306. Under Eudes IV and his grandson, Philip de Rouvre, ducal government met considerable resistance in the county. A measure of independence followed the latter's death in 1361 when Franche-Comté passed to Margaret of Flanders, the younger daughter of King Philip V. She supported the aspirations for independence but was finally induced to allow her granddaughter, widow of Philip de Rouvre, to marry the new duke of Burgundy, Philip the Bold (1363–1404). The latter eventually inherited the counties of Artois and Burgundy, except for Montbéliard, which had earlier passed to the landgraves of Württemberg.

Under the Valois dukes, Franche-Comté was divided into three bailliages with a superior council, a *parlement,* and estates (all resident at Dôle) that were often able to moderate ducal fiscal demands. After the death of Charles the Rash in 1477 and the marriage of his only child, Marie, to Maximilian of Habsburg, Louis XI tried to arrange for the annexation of Franche-Comté through the betrothal of his son Charles (VIII) to Marguérite, daughter of Maximilian and Marie. In 1493 Charles chose to marry instead the heiress of Brittany, and Franche-Comté thus remained with the house of Habsburg for the next 185 years.

Franche-Comté benefited economically from its position on two major commercial routes: that from Italy to the north, and that from Lyons to the Rhine. The expansion of trade and the fairs of Champagne after the eleventh century fostered the growth of fairs at Besançon, Seurre, Gray, and Ronchamp. Besançon received a charter of liberties in 1184 and became an independent commune after 1290. Between 1246 and 1260 Pontarlier, Salins, Neublans, Ornans, and Chaussin were enfranchised; and between 1272 and 1293 St. Amour, Dôle, Faucogney, Arlay, Arbois, Bletterans, Poligny, and Lons. The eastern part of the county was heavily forested and mountainous, but great progress was made in clearing, founding new settlements, and marketing forest products. There were iron mines at Gouhenans and Grandvelle, but the chief industry of the region was salt, notably the works at Lons and Salins.

As early as the fifth century, monasticism had come to the county. Condat and St. Romain in the Juras were soon followed by houses at Grandvaux, Ilay, Cusance, and Fontenelle. In the sixth century, St. Columban founded Luxeuil on the Lorraine frontier and Baume, near Lons, from which the founders of Cluny came. The most important indigenous foundation was the abbey of St. Claude, to which the miracles of the holy Oyend (Eugendus, sixth century) and Claude (seventh century) attracted crowds of pilgrims; by the twelfth century some 1,500 religious populated its holdings scattered throughout the Jura region. The monastic impulse was renewed under the influence of the Cluniac and Cistercian movements with new or reformed houses both in the lowlands of the northwest (Bellevaux, Acey) and in the mountains to the south and east (Lieucroissant, Mouthier, Montbenoît). Important churches, Romanesque and Gothic, were built at Besançon, Salins, Goailles, and St. Claude, which also has remarkable choir stalls by Jean de Vitry (fifteenth century). There was a university at Dôle (1423) and institutions of higher learning at Besancon and Poligny by 1500. The most notable secular building of the period was the chateau of the Chalon-Arlay at Nozeroy, which was completely reconstructed in the fifteenth century and sumptuously decorated by artists from the court of ducal Burgundy.

BIBLIOGRAPHY

Bibliographie franc-comtoise, 1940–1960, Claude Fohlen, ed. (1961); *Bibliographie franc-comtoise, 1960–1970* (1974); *Cartulaire des comtes de Bourgogne,* in *Mémoires et documents inédits pour servir à l'histoire de la Franche-Comté,* VIII (1908); Vital Chomel and Jean Ebersolt, *Cinq siècles de circulation internationale vue de Jougne* (1951); Edouard Clerc, *Essai sur l'histoire de la Franche-Comté,* 2 vols. (1870); Aristide Déy, *Étude sur la condition des personnes, des biens, et des communes au comté de Bourgogne pendant le moyen âge* (1870–1872); Lucien Febvre, *La Franche-Comté* (1912); Jean-Yves Mariotte, *Le comté de Bourgogne sous les Hohenstaufen, 1156–1208* (1963); Edmond Préclin, *Histoire de la Franche-Comté* (1947); Louis Stouff, *Les comtes de Bourgogne et leurs villes domaniales: Étude sur le régime communal, XIIIe et XIVe siècles* (1899).

EUGENE L. COX

[See also **France; Germany; Trade.**]

BURGUNDY, DUCHY OF. That part of the fifth-century Burgundian kingdom which later became the duchy of Burgundy had no natural frontiers. It was a land of hills, plateaus, and river valleys that made it primarily a zone of transit between north and south, east and west. It was first separated politically from the eastern half of the kingdom by the treaty of Verdun in 843, when the regions between the Saône and the Juras were awarded to Lotharingia while the territory west of the Saône went to Charles the Bald. That territory consisted of fourteen *pagi,* or districts: Autunois, Beaunois, Avalois, Lassois (Bar-sur-Seine, Châtillon), Dijonnais, Mémontois (Mâlain), Attuyer, Oscheret, Auxois, Duesmois, Auxerrois, Nivernais, Chaunois (Chalon-sur-Saône), and Mâconnais. These *pagi* were more or less under the domination of Richard le Justicier (*d.* 921), whose brother Boso married the sister of Charles the Bald and received the region of Provence.

Richard, styled "duke of the Burgundians," actively supported Charles and his successors, led a successful defense against Norman invaders, and established law and order in his dominions. His son and successor, Hugues le Noir, tried to annex territories east of the Saône; struggles later ensued with Hugues le Grand, count of Paris, who seized some of the *pagi* in western Burgundy and whose son Othon succeeded to the ducal title on the death of Hugues le Noir in 952. In 1002 King Robert the Pious acquired the duchy for his son Henri (II). When the latter succeeded to the Frankish throne in 1031/1032, he conferred the duchy on his younger brother Robert, who thus founded a line of Capetian dukes that continued unbroken until the death of Philip de Rouvre in 1361. By that time the duchy was bounded on the north by the county of Champagne, on the west by the counties of Auxerre and Nevers, on the south by the Forez and Mâconnais, and on the east by the Franche-Comté (that is, the county of Burgundy), which the dukes were in the process of acquiring.

The Valois dukes who succeeded the Capetians ruled an extensive collection of territories stretching from the Burgundies to the Low Countries: Philip the Bold (1363–1404), John the Fearless (1404–1419), Philip the Good (1419–1467), Charles the Rash (1467–1477). The duchy proper was enlarged by the acquisition of the counties of Nevers and Charolais, the latter serving as appanage for the ducal heir. By the end of the thirteenth century there were six bailliages in Burgundy. The baillis were primarily judicial officers, while castellans and *prévôts* conducted ducal administration on the local level. Above them all were the ducal *grand conseil* and an appeals court, *les jours généraux,* which sat about six times a year at Beaune, where a *parlement* also convened almost annually. Philip the Bold introduced receivers for ducal revenues into each bailliage in 1366 and in 1386 reorganized the *chambre des comptes.* The estates of Burgundy usually met at Dijon after 1386, mainly to vote on the dukes' requests for *aides* (special taxes). The highest ducal officer was the chancellor, the most famous of whom was Nicolas Rolin (*d.* 1461), a bourgeois from Autun who was Philip the Good's "prime minister" for almost forty years, founder of the great Hospices de Beaune (1443), and patron of Jan van Eyck and Rogier van der Weyden.

The medieval duchy of Burgundy was rich in agricultural resources, and easy access to major routes and waterways generally made for prosperity. Auxerre, Langres, Autun, and Dijon were already major settlements in Roman times, and impressive Roman monuments still remain at Autun. The Capetian dukes were mostly docile allies of their royal cousins, and the duchy's interior location protected it from the ravages of many outside invaders. Thus, Burgundy was one of the earliest regions to benefit from the economic revival of the eleventh century, and by the thirteenth century there was scarcely a barony in the duchy that did not have a town with markets and fairs. Dijon received the earliest charter of liberties in 1183, and dozens of other towns were enfranchised during the next century, though the Burgundian lords were somewhat backward in granting franchises to rural communities. Mortmain persisted longer in Burgundy than elsewhere, and the much-hated *brennerie* (obligation to feed the lord's dogs) was not wholly suppressed until 1360. The power of the Valois dukes usually protected Burgundy from the ravages of the Hundred Years War, however, and taxation for Valois military and political policies was borne chiefly by their northern provinces.

Ecclesiastically, the duchy lay mainly in the dioceses of Chalon, Autun, and Langres. The bishops of Langres ranked as peers of France; since Carolingian times they had held comital powers and extensive dominions (including Dijon) that once rivaled those of the dukes. It was the king of France, however, not the duke, who confirmed episcopal elections. Burgundy was also the birthplace of many important monastic reform movements, notably those of Cluny (not in ducal dominions, but considered part of Burgundy) and Cîteaux, near Dijon. St. Bernard, born to a Burgundian noble family, studied at St. Vorles in Châtillon and founded Clairvaux just over the frontier in Champagne. A century earlier the Cluniac reform affected Burgundy before spreading elsewhere and stimulated other related reform movements, such as that of Guillaume da Volpiano at St. Bénigne-de-Dijon, Bèze, Réome, St. Michel-de-Tonnerre, Molosme, and Vergy. Other monastic centers were the abbeys of Flavigny and Vézelay, the latter a major pilgrimage center, where St. Bernard preached the Second Crusade in 1146 and where Richard the Lionhearted and Philip Augustus took the cross in 1190. In the thirteenth century, Cluniacs, Cistercians, Carthusians, Grandmontains, canons regular, and members of crusading orders were joined by orders of friars, all of whom contributed to the duchy's religious and economic life. The Cistercians in particular, with their emphasis on manual labor and exploitation of unused or waste lands, played a great role in agricultural development, including viticulture. The building done at Cluny during the formative period of Romanesque style was influential all over western Europe; the abbey's third church (twelfth century) was an outstanding example of "high" Romanesque and the largest church in Christendom until the building of St. Peter's. La Charité-sur-Loire, also Romanesque, was the second largest church in France. Under the influence of St. Bernard, the Cistercians developed a simpler version of Burgundian Romanesque (as at Fontenay), which also expanded widely with the spread of the Cistercian order.

Although the Valois dukes were celebrated patrons of the arts, they were not great builders and much of their cultural legacy remained in their northern dominions. Burgundy was, however, the scene of two celebrated feats of chivalry: Jacques de Lalaing's yearlong challenge to all comers in 1449–1450 at the Fontaine aux pleurs near Chalon, and the *pas d'armes* held by Pierre de Bauffremont at the "Tree of Charlemagne" near Dijon for two months in 1443. The greatest artistic contribution of the Valois was doubtless Philip the Bold's removal in 1385 of the Flemish sculptor Claus Sluter and his atelier to Dijon. Among the results were the ducal tombs and the work of Sluter and his nephew Claus de Werve for the Carthusian monastery of Champmol, which Philip founded as his final resting place. The portal and some of the surviving full-sized figures sculpted for a monumental Calvary (the so-called *Puits de Moïse*) are regarded as masterpieces of late medieval art.

BIBLIOGRAPHY

Bernard Bligny, *L'église et les ordres religieux dans le royaume de Bourgogne aux XIe et XIIe siècles* (1960); Otto Cartellieri, *The Court of Burgundy* (1929); Maurice Chaume, *Les origines du duché de Bourgogne,* 4 vols. (1925–1931); Charles Oursel, *L'art de Bourgogne* (1953); Ernest Petit, *Histoire des ducs de Bourgogne de la race capétienne,* 9 vols. (1885–1905); Jean Richard, *Les ducs de Bourgogne et la formation du duché du XIe au XIVe siècle* (1954); Richard Vaughan, *Philip the Bold: The Formation of the Burgundian State* (1962); *John the Fearless: The Growth of Burgundian Power* (1966); *Philip the Good: The Apogee of Burgundy* (1970); *Charles the Bold: The Last Valois Duke of Burgundy* (1973); and *Valois Burgundy* (1975).

EUGENE L. COX

[See also **France; Valois Dynasty.**]

BURGUNDY, KINGDOM OF. Two Carolingian successor states, Provence and Upper or Jurane Burgundy, formed the kingdom of Burgundy, which was also known after the twelfth century as the kingdom of Arles and Vienne. It was an artificial political creation and possessed no inherent linguistic, geographic, or economic unity. The Rhône-Saône Valley and the Alpine passes linking Germany, France, and Italy made the region strategically important. French efforts to obtain the kingdom, which was part of the Holy Roman Empire, placed Burgundy at the center of international politics for centuries.

Emperor Lothair I assigned Provence itself and the duchy of Lyons, that is, the Lyonnais and the Viennois, in 855 to his youngest son, Charles. After Charles's death, his brothers, Emperor Louis II and Lothair II, divided the kingdom. Charles the Bald obtained the duchy after Lothair's death in 869 and named his brother-in-law, Boso, count of Vienne. Charles also placed Boso in charge of Provence after Louis's death in 875. Goaded on by his wife, a daughter of Louis II, Boso arranged for his own coronation as king of Provence in 879, after the death of Louis the Stammerer, the son of Charles the Bald. Charles the Fat acquired Provence after Boso's death in 887, but Charles's successor, Arnulf, permitted Boso's young son, Louis the Blind, to be proclaimed king of Provence in 890. Louis tried to obtain the

BURGUNDY, KINGDOM OF

Italian crown in 905 but was captured and blinded by his rival, Berengar. Real power passed into the hands of Louis's cousin, Hugh of Arles. Hugh and King Rudolf II of Upper Burgundy fought for the Italian crown in the 920's, but in 933 Hugh relinquished his sovereign rights in Provence to Rudolf, who in return recognized Hugh as king of Italy.

Rudolf's father, Rudolf I (888–912), a member of the Welf family, had inherited the Transjurane duchy, roughly equivalent to French Switzerland. In the chaos that followed the deposition of Charles the Fat in 887, Rudolf tried to make himself king of Lorraine but had to content himself with a smaller kingdom composed of his own duchy and four counties in the diocese of Besançon, the later Franche-Comté. Rudolf II's enlarged kingdom stretched from Basel to the Mediterranean and from the modern Italian-French border to the Saône-Rhône. It included Lyons and Viviers, which were located on the west bank of these rivers.

Hugh tried to take Burgundy from Rudolf's son Conrad, but Otto the Great intervened and took Conrad into protective custody. Assured of his fidelity, Otto permitted Conrad to return to Burgundy in 942. Conrad's father and grandfather had already acknowledged the overlordship of the German king, and the ties between the two rulers became even closer when Otto married Conrad's sister Adelaide in 951.

Conrad and his son Rudolf III (993–1032) were weak monarchs, whose power was largely confined to their hereditary domains in Transjurane Burgundy. The great feudal magnates, such as the count of Provence or the archbishop of Lyons, were virtually independent of royal authority. It is noteworthy that the Burgundian kings were able to nominate bishops in only four or five of the approximately thirty bishoprics in their kingdom.

The childless Rudolf designated his nephew, Emperor Henry II, as his heir in 1006. Conrad II then claimed the Burgundian throne as Henry's successor. The Burgundian nobility, fearful of being ruled by the strong German king, supported the claims of Rudolf's nephew, Count Odo of Blois. After Rudolf's death in 1032, Conrad defeated Odo and Burgundy was joined to the empire. Henry III tried to strengthen his position in the kingdom by supporting the peace movement and the bishops, but imperial authority collapsed in Burgundy during the Investiture conflict.

By marrying the heiress to the county of Burgundy in 1156, Frederick Barbarossa tried to establish a new territorial base for the monarchy, but his conflict with Pope Alexander III undermined his efforts. Frederick II shifted the focus of imperial attention from the Franche-Comté to Provence, where he intervened in the protracted quarrels between the counts of Provence and Toulouse. The Capetians were, however, the real victors. St. Louis's brother, Charles of Anjou, obtained Provence by marrying the heiress to that county in 1245; and Toulouse passed in 1249 to the king's other brother, Alphonse of Poitou.

After the Interregnum, the German kings offered the Burgundian crown to various princes in hopes of obtaining diplomatic support for turning Germany into a hereditary monarchy. These schemes failed on account of the Capetian-Angevin rivalry, the opposition of the Burgundian princes, and papal fears of the growing power of the French monarchy.

In the meantime, France was gradually absorbing the various Burgundian territories. Count Otto IV of Burgundy first agreed to marry his daughter and heir to a French prince and then in effect sold the Franche-Comté to Philip the Fair in 1295. The bishop of Viviers accepted French suzerainty a decade later, and in 1312 Lyons was added to France. Philip VI exerted pressure on the archbishop of Vienne by fortifying St. Columbe on the right bank of the Rhône, opposite Vienne. He purchased the Dauphiné in 1349, and henceforth the French king's oldest son held it.

These annexations aroused considerable resentment in Germany, and Emperor Charles IV responded by asserting his nominal rights as feudal suzerain. He even had himself crowned in Arles in 1365, the first monarch since Frederick Barbarossa to do so. It was also the last time that this ceremony was performed. To obtain French support, Charles finally appointed the dauphin, the future Charles VI of France, as his vicar in most of the kingdom of Burgundy. The establishment of this vicariate in 1378 transferred de facto suzerainty to France, even though Burgundy remained nominally part of the empire until its dissolution. Louis XI obtained Provence in 1481, but France did not acquire the last fragments of the kingdom, Savoy and Nice, until 1860.

BIBLIOGRAPHY

Paul Fournier, *Le royaume d'Arles et de Vienne (1138–1378)* (1891); and "The Kingdom of Burgundy or Arles from the Eleventh to the Fifteenth Century," in *The Cambridge Medieval History,* VIII (1936), 306–331; Louis Halphen, "The Kingdom of Burgundy," *ibid.*, III (1922), 134–147; Louis Jacob, *Le royaume de Bourgogne sous les empereurs Franconiens (1038–1125)* (1906); René Poupardin, *Le royaume de Provence sous les Carolingiens (855–933?)* (1901); and *Le royaume de Bourgogne (888–1038)* (1907); Theodor Schieffer and Hans Eberhard Mayer, eds., *Die Urkunden der burgundischen Rudolfinger*, in *Monumenta Germaniae historica: Regum Burgundiae e stirpe Rudolfina diplomata et acta* (1977).

JOHN B. FREED

[See also **Carolingians; France; Germany.**]

BURIAL. See **Death and Burial.**

BURIDAN, JEAN (*ca.* 1295–*ca.* 1358). The little we know of Jean Buridan, the most distinguished natural philosopher among the masters of arts at the University of Paris in the fourteenth century, derives from the records of the latter institution or from his own writings. Born in the diocese of Arras, Buridan studied at the College of Cardinal Lemoine and then joined the College of Navarre as a teacher. He is mentioned as rector of the University of Paris in 1328 and 1340 and is recorded as the recipient of revenues from benefices in at least four separate years (1329, 1330, 1342, 1348). Prior to 1334 he appears to have made a trip to Avignon. Following mention in a statute of 12 July 1358, Buridan disappears from the records, perhaps having succumbed to the plague in that year.

During the whole of his academic career, Buridan was a secular cleric and master of arts who apparently never sought a theological degree and was therefore forbidden to write on theology. As a master of arts, though, he had a professional commitment to Aristotelian thought. Most of his works are commentaries or questions on the works of Aristotle, including the *Topics, Prior Analytics,* and *Posterior Analytics* in logic; the *Metaphysics, Physics, De anima, Parva naturalia, De caelo et mundo, Meteorology,* and *On Generation and Corruption* in natural philosophy; and the *Ethics, Economics, Politics,* and *Rhetoric.* To these works must be added at least three additional logical treatises: *Summulae de dialectica, Consequentiae,* and *Sophismata.* The first is an updated textbook, whereas the latter two are concerned with advanced problems in logic derived from the work of William of Ockham. Only in the twentieth century, when developments of a similar nature have been made, has the high level of Buridan's logic been appreciated.

In the realm of natural philosophy, his ideas and contributions appear exclusively in the commentaries and questions on the works of Aristotle mentioned above. Although the hundreds of distinct problems with which Buridan was concerned in all these treatises were typical of the period, his treatment was not. Guided by a significant methodology, Buridan's interpretations were often brilliant and won numerous followers. In the aftermath of the condemnation of Aristotelian thought of 1277, Buridan and his fellow masters of arts were confronted with serious difficulties. Theologians had become preoccupied with God's absolute power to effect any action that did not involve a logical contradiction. It was thus customary to formulate hypothetical situations that were often naturally impossible within Aristotelian science and from which consequences were drawn that conflicted with it. In this intellectual atmosphere the validity of scientific truth, and even the possibility of attaining it, had been called into question.

Buridan's tactic was to concede God's power to effect anything short of a logical contradiction but to question, and often to doubt, whether God had performed, or would perform, the numerous hypothetical actions commonly imagined for him. Rather than focus on supernatural actions, Buridan sought to investigate the physical world in the "common course of nature" *(communis cursus nature).* It was not essential that the principles of natural science be known with absolute certainty—for that was an unrealizable goal—but only that they be derived from inductive generalization, in which any particular principle is observed to be true in many instances and false in none. This was all the certitude one could expect, and it ought to suffice. Generally, Buridan's methodology involved the skillful combination of empiricism, reason, and Ockham's Razor, whereby the simplest of two or more explanations is to be preferred.

Because Buridan's natural philosophy has not yet been systematically studied, his opinions on most of the issues he discussed are unknown. On at least two major problems though—impetus theory and the possible axial rotation of the earth—his views are quite well known and form the basis of his reputation.

The Latin term *impetus* was used to describe an immaterial, impressed force transmitted from a mover to a projectile and assumed to cause the continuing motion of the latter when it lost contact with its initial mover. Impetus theory was a replacement for Aristotle's discredited explanation that the violent upward motion of a stone, for example, required an external motive power—air in this case—in continuous contact with it. Although impressed-force theories had first been formulated by the Greeks and elaborated by the Arabs, Buridan's account probably represents the most thorough and systematic application of it during the Middle Ages. In the terrestrial region below the moon, he invoked it to explain the violent motion of a stone hurled upward, during which movement the impressed impetus was gradually destroyed by external air resistance. The downward accelerated fall of that same stone was also explained by impetus, newly generated. Ignoring external air resistance, Buridan now assumed that successive and cumulative increments of impetus were produced by the heaviness of the stone, which thus received successive proportional increments of velocity resulting in a continuous acceleration until it reached the ground.

Turning to the heavens, Buridan boldly suggested that impetus might also be the cause of the incessant, uniform, circular motions of the celestial spheres. Rather than intelligences or angels as the source of celestial motion, Buridan conjectured that, in creating the celestial orbs, God might have impressed a certain quantity of impetus on each sphere. Since the heavens were assumed to be free of external resistances, a given quantity of impetus would remain forever constant and thus cause its sphere to rotate indefinitely with a uniform circular motion. The extent to which Buridan's impetus theory may have influenced the new dynamics of Galileo and Newton in the scientific revolution of the seventeenth century has been much debated, without conclusive results.

Impetus theory also bears on Buridan's resolution of the possibility that the earth might rotate daily from west to east on its axis (while the sphere of the fixed stars remained stationary). Employing arguments based on the relativity of motion, Buridan held that the earth's axial rotation was astronomically as plausible as the universally received opinion of Aristotle that the earth was motionless at the center of the universe while the planets and fixed stars rotated around it.

An empirical consequence drawn from the application of his impetus theory led Buridan to reject the earth's physical rotation. An arrow shot straight up by the impetus imparted to it should lag behind a rotating earth and fall noticeably to the west of its launching site. Since this is contrary to experience, Buridan denied the earth's daily axial rotation. Embodied in this illustration are the typical ingredients of Buridan's methodology: reason and experience are combined to arrive at the kind of scientific knowledge that could constitute the basis of our understanding of the physical world. In both logic and natural philosophy Buridan exerted a considerable influence during the fifteenth and sixteenth centuries, especially in eastern Europe. Not only were his works widely read in scholastic circles, but commentaries were written on them as well.

BIBLIOGRAPHY

For a thorough bibliography of primary and secondary sources that extends to the year 1966, see Ernest A. Moody's article in *Dictionary of Scientific Biography,* II (1970), 608. Additional primary sources have subsequently been published in logic (see *Iohannis Buridani Tractatus de consequentiis,* Hubert Hubien, ed. [1976] and Buridan's *Sophismata,* Theodore K. Scott, ed. [1977]) and politics (*Questiones super octo libros Politicorum Aristotelis* [1513, repr. 1968]). Selections in translation from Buridan's *De caelo* and *Physics* appear in Edward Grant, ed., *A Source Book in Medieval Science* (1974), 50–51, 203–205, 275–284, 326–327, 360–367, 500–503, 524–529, and 621–624. Various aspects of Buridan's logic are described and evaluated by Hans Freudenthal, "Les faits et gestes de l'âne de Buridan," in *Revue de synthèse,* **89** (1968); Alan R. Perreiah, "Buridan and the Definite Description," in *Journal of the History of Philosophy,* **10** (1972); and *The Logic of John Buridan, Proceedings of the IIIrd European Symposium on Medieval Logic and Semantics, Copenhagen 16–21 November 1975* (1976). Analyses of Buridan's opinions on a wide variety of philosophical topics, especially ethics and metaphysics, may be found in the following articles: Alessandro Ghisalberti, "Necessita e liberta nelle *Quaestiones in Metaphysicam* di Giovanni Buridano," in *Medioeva* (Padua), **1** (1975); James J. Walsh, "Some Relationships Between Gerald Odo's and John Buridan's Commentaries on Aristotle's *Ethics,*" in *Franciscan Studies,* **35** (1975); and two articles by Jerzy B. Korolec: "La philosophie de la liberté de Jean Buridan," in *Studia Mediewistyczne,* **15** (1974); and "Les principes de la philosophie morale de Jean Buridan," in *Mediaevalia philosophica polonorum,* **21** (1975). On Buridan's theology, see Alessandro Ghisalberti, "La teologia razionale di Giovanni Buridano," in *Rivista di filosofia neo-scholastica,* **65** (1973). His methodology and physical thought, especially impetus theory, are treated in the following: Ernest A. Moody, "Galileo and His Precursors," in Carlo L. Golino, ed., *Galileo Reappraised* (1966); *La teoria dell'impeto: Testi latini di filosofia medievale [Francesco de Marchia, Giovanni Buri-*

dano, Alberto de Sassonia, Marsilio d'Inghen] (1969); Alessandro Ghisalberti, *Giovanni Buridano dalla metafisica alla fisica* (1975); Stillman Drake, "Impetus Theory Reappraised," in *Journal of the History of Ideas,* 36 (1975), and "A Further Reappraisal of Impetus Theory: Buridan, Benedetti, and Galileo," in *Studies in History and Philosophy of Science,* 7 (1976); Allan Franklin, *The Principle of Inertia in the Middle Ages* (1976), 42–54, and "Stillman Drake's 'Impetus Theory Reappraised,'" in *Journal of the History of Ideas,* 38 (1977); Edward Grant, "Scientific Thought in Fourteenth-century Paris: Jean Buridan and Nicole Oresme," in Madeleine Pelner Cosman and Bruce Chandler, eds., *Machaut's World: Science and Art in the Fourteenth Century* (1978); and Bert S. Hall, "The Scholastic Pendulum," in *Annals of Science,* 35 (1978).

EDWARD GRANT

[See also **Aristotle in the Middle Ages; Astrology/Astronomy; Ockham, William of; Physics.**]

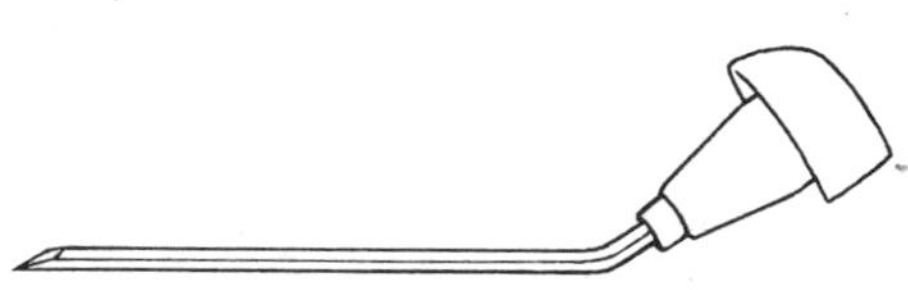

BURIN, an engraver's tool consisting of a four-sided steel rod the blunt end of which forms a lozenge-shaped section. The engraver rests the butt end in the palm of one hand and pushes the point of the lozenge-shaped cutting edge through the copper to engrave the design. The engraved plate is then inked, wiped so that ink remains in the incised lines, and used to make a printed impression.

BIBLIOGRAPHY

Felix Brunner, *A Handbook of Graphic Reproduction Processes* (1972), 73–84, 101–103.

MARTHA WOLFF

[See also **Engraving; Prints and Printmaking.**]

BURLEY (BURLEIGH), WALTER (*ca.* 1275–sometime after June 1344), English scholar-diplomat, exemplifies the diversity in fourteenth-century intellectual life. A diocesan priest from Yorkshire, he was educated at Oxford (master of arts by 1301) and Paris (doctor of theology by 1324), and subsequently taught in both universities. In 1327 Burley became an attaché to the Avignon papacy for Edward III and remained in royal service for at least a decade, including appointment as tutor to the king's heir, Edward of Woodstock (later the Black Prince). He was also associated with the noted bibliophile Richard de Bury, under whose patronage he composed several of his commentaries on Aristotle. The last known official record of Walter Burley involves his acquisition on 19 June of a rectory in Kent, though there is no evidence that he ever took up this holding. His last years appear to have been spent in southern France and northern Italy, where he may have written his popular history *De vita et moribus philosophorum.* These dates and associations place Burley at the center of the political and intellectual turmoil characteristic of his era.

Although Burley was involved in public life, his true career was as a scholar and philosopher. Among his surviving writings are as many as eighty-three distinct works on no fewer than fifty distinct topics, ranging from the full corpus of Aristotle to a popular text on astrology and the famed history of the philosophers. Missing are any theological writings, though Burley must have completed at least those required for the Paris doctorate. The wide circulation of his writings is evident from the vast number of manuscript copies that survive. As modern editions of Burley's writings appear, the importance especially of his commentaries on the texts of Aristotle and of his own treatments of philosophical issues becomes more and more evident, for they reveal with clarity the intellectual growth and transition that took place in Europe after the condemnations of 1270 and 1277. Three areas of Burley's philosophical activity are especially significant: logic, science, and the problem of Averroism.

Burley has been famed as a logician since his own day, and it is this aspect of his career that has received the most attention from modern scholars. In addition to commentaries on all of Aristotle's logic, he composed two versions of his own *De puritate artis logicae,* thought by some to be the earliest attempt at a complete Scholastic system of logic. On the pivotal issue of the universals, Burley held a realist position against Ockham's radical nominalism, though it is disputed whether his realism is a moderate one deriving from Thomas Aquinas or a radical one deriving from John Duns Scotus. In spite of the indisputable opposition between them, recent study of Burley's treatise *De suppositionibus* reveals that he had a positive influence on Ockham, who even incorporated some of Burley's positions into the *Summa logicae* as verbatim borrowings.

That Burley is significant in the history of science is not surprising, given his association with Merton College, Oxford. Noteworthy are his study of the *Physics* and his treatise *De intensione et remissione formarum.* His consideration of motion in a void uses techniques of logical analysis to attempt a reconciliation of Ibn Rushd's and Ibn Bajja's (Avempace's) interpretations of Aristotle, and he notes the theological implications of the concept of "separated quantity" with respect to the Eucharist. The treatise on forms examines an issue in physics the solution of which was eventually mathematized by Nicole Oresme.

Burley's writings on the nature of man and the human intellect indicate a striking change in the attitude toward Ibn Rushd that produced the great condemnations. Charges that Burley was a culpable Averroist who argued for the unicity of the human intellect are not borne out by textual study: *De potentiis animae* and the *Questiones circa tercium de anima* both specifically reject the Averroistic psychology, and Burley's major *Expositio super libros de anima,* far from being an Averroistic interpretation of Aristotle, is an orthodox study of Ibn Rushd's own commentary on Aristotle. That such a pedagogical exercise was possible within fifty years of the condemnations suggests a remarkable intellectual vitality in the fourteenth-century schools and attests to the value of further study of Burley and his peers.

BIBLIOGRAPHY

Sources. De puritate artis logicae, Tractatus longior, with a Revised Edition of the Tractatus brevior, Philotheus Boehner, ed. (1955); *De vita et moribus philosophorum,* Herman Knüst, ed. (1886); M. Jean Kitchel, ed., "The *De potentiis animae* of Walter Burley," in *Mediaeval Studies,* 33 (1971); Stephen F. Brown, ed., "Walter Burleigh's Treatise *De suppositionibus* and Its Influence on William of Ockham," in *Franciscan Studies,* 32 (1972).

Studies. M. Jean Kitchel, "Walter Burley's Doctrine of the Soul: Another View," in *Mediaeval Studies,* 39 (1977); Anneliese Maier, "Ein unbeachteter 'Averroist' des XIV. Jahrhunderts: Walter Burley," in *Medioevo e rinascimento: Studi in onore di Bruno Nardi,* II (1955); Conor Martin, "Walter Burley," in *Oxford Studies Presented to Daniel Callus* (1964).

M. JEAN KITCHEL

[See also **Aristotle in the Middle Ages; Nominalism; Ockham, William of; Realism; Rushd, Ibn; Universals.**]

BUSANT, DER. See **Bussard, Der.**

BUSCHETO OF PISA (*d. ca.* 1100), Italian architect credited, according to an inscription on his grave, with the design of the Pisa cathedral (begun 1063), one of the most important Italian Romanesque churches. Documents accord him the unusual position of both artisan and member of the Duomo Opera, which regularly passed judgment on artistic works. This indicates the high position Buscheto must have attained in his lifetime.

BIBLIOGRAPHY

H. Swarzenski, "Busketus," in Ulrich Thieme and Felix Becker, eds., *Allgemeines Lexikon der bildenden Künstler,* II (1911), 289.

ADELHEID M. GEALT

BUSHEL, the principal measure of capacity for grain in England, where the standard, or Winchester, bushel (35.238 liters) contained 4 pecks, or 8 gallons, equal to 1/8 quarter or 1/80 grain last. During the Middle Ages the bushel of wheat was supposed to weigh 64 tower pounds, but after the tower system was abolished in the sixteenth century it was described in statutes as weighing 56 avoirdupois pounds. The bushel was used regionally for many other products, with variations from 35 to more than 100 liters. It was rarely employed in Ireland, Scotland, or Wales.

RONALD EDWARD ZUPKO

BUSSARD, DER *(Der Busant),* an early-fourteenth-century Middle High German verse tale *(Märe)* of 1,074 lines preserved in four manuscripts. The son of the king of England, studying in Paris, is introduced at court and meets the daughter of the French king. They fall in love and, since she is already affianced to the king of Morocco, decide to elope. During a brief rest in the forest a hawk *(busant)* steals her ring. The prince pursues the bird, loses his way, lapses into madness, tears off his garments, and lives like an animal in the woods. The princess, meanwhile, has found shelter with a miller's family, where she supports herself by selling fine needlework until she is found the following spring by the duke and duchess of Engelstein and taken to their castle. Another year passes before hunters bring in a wild man, who is slowly nursed back to health. At the sight of a hawk he suffers a severe relapse and tears the bird to pieces with his teeth. This strange incident arouses the curiosity of the duke and leads to the happy reunion of the faithful lovers. Messengers are dispatched to both England and France and arrangments made for an elaborate wedding.

The courtly sentimental theme of true love triumphant is told by an anonymous Alsatian poet who is indebted to Konrad von Würzburg, most notably in his style but also in his handling of the wild man episode in the woods. Other influences can be traced to Hartmann von Aue's *Iwein* and to Rudolf von Ems's *Willehalm von Orlens.* The poet's immediate source may have been a French tale, now lost, descended from the Old French epic *L'escoufle* (*ca.* 1200). The motif of a bird's theft of a precious item as the cause of the lovers' separation occurs also in the *Thousand and One Nights* (Tale of Qamar al-Zamān and Princess Budūr).

BIBLIOGRAPHY

Die deutsche Literatur des Mittelalters: Verfasserlexikon, 2nd ed., Kurt Ruh, ed., I (1978), 1145–1148; Hanns Fischer, *Studien zur deutschen Märendichtung* (1968), 303.

KLAUS WOLLENWEBER

[See also **Hartmann von Aue; Konrad von Würzburg; Mären; Middle High German Literature; Rudolf von Ems.**]

BUTLER. The term "butler" was used in the Middle Ages for a person doing work not unlike that done by a modern butler. But "butler" also denominated a great official in the household of a prince. Though usually less high in status than the constable or seneschal, he possessed wide powers and influence. As the word *butticularius* implies, the origin of the butler must be sought in the need for procuring butts of wine for the prince's hall. The learned Latin word *pincerna* (cupbearer) was used as a synonym, and in England this was the epithet applied to the royal butler as early as the reign of Edward the Confessor. In the Holy Roman Empire there was even a *summus pincerna* (archbutler).

Whatever the original task of the butler (that is, with regard to providing the princely household with wine and, in France, supervising the vintage and the income therefrom), his duties were soon enlarged. In the households of the Anglo-Saxon and Norman kings the process went less far than on the Continent, though ceremonially the butler played an important role in the English coronation—bearing the king's cup and receiving it back as his own—and in the customs service he formally collected the duties on wine (butlerage). In France butlers were important members of the royal council, a fact attested by their witnessing royal charters and their supervision, to some extent, of princely finances, especially in the Chambre des Comptes.

The office of butler in England was hereditary in the family of the earls of Arundel. In Ireland the hereditary butlers actually took their title as a surname; the family became one of the most influential on the island. In the Holy Roman Empire the office of archbutler was held from the twelfth century by the dukes of Bohemia. In France several important families, including the La Tour, Brienne, and Saint-Pol, supplied the royal butlers, but the office was suppressed during the reign of Charles VII.

BIBLIOGRAPHY

J. H. Round, *The King's Serjeants and Officers of State* (1911), 140–172; Ferdinand Lot and Robert Fawtier, *Histoire des institutions françaises au moyen âge,* II (1958), 54–57; Heinrich Mitteis, *Der Staat des hohen Mittelalters* (1968), 393–394, trans. by H. F. Orton as *The State in the Middle Ages* (1975), 365; Bryce Lyon, *A Constitutional and Legal History of Medieval England,* 2nd ed. (1980), 53, 155, 522.

WILLIAM CHESTER JORDAN

[See also **Household, Chamber, and Wardrobe.**]

BUTTRESS, a massive pier that projects from or is built against a wall to give additional strength and,

Flying buttress. Rheims Cathedral, 13th century. FROM SIR BANISTER FLETCHER'S A HISTORY OF ARCHITECTURE

often, to counteract the lateral thrust of an arch or vault behind the wall. Exterior buttresses are placed at right angles to a wall, encase a corner (clasping buttress), or extend on the diagonal from a corner of the wall (diagonal buttress). A flying buttress consists of a quadrant arch or a masonry strut that channels the lateral thrust of a building's vaulting across an open space, usually above the side aisles or ambulatory, to an outer buttress. The flying buttress was used during the Romanesque period (Cluny III) but did not become common until after 1180. In Gothic architecture the flying buttress allowed a greater verticality and a decreased wall surface; and since the buttress was placed to counter the lateral thrust on each main pier of the building's interior, it united the interior and the exterior of the church into an organic whole by expressing the bay system of the inside of the church on the outside of the building.

LESLIE BRUBAKER

[See also **Gothic Architecture.**]

BUYIDS (Arabic, Buwayhids; contemporary Persian, Āl-i Būyih), a dynasty founded in the 930's by soldiers from the province of Daylam, a mountainous region overlooking the coastal plain through which a major river, the Safīd-Rūd, flows from the Iranian plateau into the Caspian Sea. The Buyids were the most important of several dynasties established in the ninth, tenth, and eleventh centuries in the Middle East by foot soldiers from the Caspian provinces of Persia. Consequently, in this period such soldiers were called Daylamīs (men from Daylam), and the sources frequently refer to the Buyids as "the Daylamī dynasty."

The mountains separating the Iranian plateau from the coasts of the southern half of the Caspian have been refuge areas throughout Persian history and remained largely independent of the control of the caliphs of Damascus and Baghdad for more than a century after the Iranian plateau had been conquered by Muslim armies. Even after the Muslims had finally subdued the coastal plain in the early ninth century, they allowed some local families to continue to rule in the hills and mountains in exchange for their nominal allegiance to the Abbasid caliph in Baghdad. These local families traced their origin to the Sasanian, Parthian, and even pre-Parthian nobility of Persia, and they were repositories of real or imagined tradition, which the Buyids reintroduced in other parts of Persia.

As the peoples of the mountainous areas converted to Islam, many chose Shiism, a form of Islam that restricted the right to rule to the Alids, the descendants of Muḥammad through Ali, the cousin and son-in-law of the Prophet. This choice gave them a new ideological basis for their opposition to the Abbasid caliphs, and Shiite Daylamīs at first supported the Alids who appeared in their region, then formed states of their own when ambition overcame their religious convictions.

The Buyids were not of noble lineage and served first the Alids and then the Daylamī aristocrats. They were the descendants of a common soldier, Būyih, who gave his name to the dynasty. But in the early tenth century, when the Abbasids were no longer able to field armies in western and central Persia, the Buyids found that as capable and generous officers they could count on an adequate following of Daylamīs with which to establish a state of their own. In 924 ^{c}Imād al-Dawla subdued the southwestern Persian province of Fārs and established his capital of Shiraz. From Fārs he sponsored the conquest of central Persia by his younger brother, Rukn al-Dawla, and the conquest of Iraq by his youngest brother, Mu^{c}izz al-Dawla. Rukn al-Dawla's control of central Persia was disputed by the powerful Samanids, who ruled much of eastern Persia and, being Sunnis, were displeased at the rise of a Shiite dynasty in the central lands of the Sunni Abbasid caliphate.

Mu^{c}izz al-Dawla established Buyid rule in Iraq much more easily and occupied Baghdad in December 945. This event had far greater significance than the conquest of southwest or central Persia because it made a Shiite dynasty guardians of the Sunni Abbasid caliphs. In 946 Mu^{c}izz al-Dawla deposed the reigning caliph and replaced him with another member of the Abbasid family, al-Mutī^{c}. It then became clear that Buyid mayors of the palace were going to

BUYIDS

use the Abbasid caliphs as instruments of their policy.

For generations before the coming of the Buyids, the Abbasid caliphs had given diplomas of investiture to local rulers who were virtually independent of Abbasid control and who properly petitioned for the caliph's recognition. These diplomas had considerable symbolic value, because the majority of Muslims were Sunnis and accepted the consensus of the religiously learned Sunnis who saw in the caliphate a symbol of the continuing unity of the Islamic world as a legal community.

Control of the Abbasid caliph therefore gave the Buyids influence with their Sunni subjects and control over the titles and diplomas of investiture that the caliph granted to other Muslim rulers. In any case, had the Buyids wished to replace the Abbasid with an Alid caliph, as the theoretical principles of Shiism required, they would have created a potential focus of loyalty for their Shiite Daylamī troops, who might have become a troublesome rival.

The remarkable cooperation of the Buyid kings helped to establish them in an unstable period, but it did not last after the death in 977 of Rukn al-Dawla, the last of the three brothers. At this point ^{c}Aḍud al-Dawla, the son of Rukn al-Dawla, deposed his cousins and brothers and established direct rule over Fārs and Iraq, while leaving central Persia in the control of his obedient brother, Mu$^{\supset}$ayyid al-Dawla. ^{c}Aḍud al-Dawla also extended Buyid rule by sending successful expeditions to northern Iraq, Oman, and southeastern Persia, while his brother took control of the northeastern province of G̣orgān. ^{c}Aḍud al-Dawla was undoubtedly the most powerful and widely admired ruler of the Buyid dynasty, but at his death in 983 he left a heritage of internecine warfare that would trouble the Buyids until their disappearance.

In 1029 the increasing weakness of the Buyids tempted Maḥmūd the Ghaznavid, the successor of the Samanids as the great Sunni power of eastern Persia, to conquer the Buyid kingdom centered at Rayy (near modern Tehran); probably only the death of Maḥmūd and the struggles between his successors, and then between the Ghaznavids and the Seljuk Turks of central Asia, saved the other Buyid kingdoms from intermediate conquest. After the Seljuks had established themselves in eastern Persia, they advanced on the Buyids and extinguished Buyid rule completely in the 1050's.

As heirs to Iraq, the central province of the last universal Islamic caliphate, the Buyids acquired an important legal, cultural, and administrative role that was to influence the Islamic Middle East for centuries. The constitutional problems created by the presence of the Shiites as mayors of the palace favored a reinterpretation of both Shiism and Sunnism. The Buyids found the Abbasid caliphs increasingly valuable to their foreign policy, particularly after 969, when the Fatimid countercaliphs conquered Africa and, in accord with their more activistic version of Shiism, called Ismailism, worked openly to create a new universal caliphate and to remove or subordinate the many local dynasties then present in the Middle East.

The Shiism of the Buyids had at first been doctrinally vague, but they soon became important patrons of Twelver Shiism, the form that had the largest constituency in succeeding centuries. This form of Shiism was less politically aggressive than Ismailism, since it held that the descendants of Muḥammad through Ali, who was the rightful ruler of all Muslims, had disappeared a century before the rise of the Buyids, and an Alid would return as a messiah. In the meantime, temporary practical arrangements for government were permissible, and the Buyid use of the Sunni Abbasid caliphs was one such arrangement.

Sunni constitutional theory also adapted to the new situation of the caliphate, and near the end of the Buyid period this theory found its classical expression in a book by the jurist al-Māwardī, who held that the caliph could delegate virtually full executive authority to a mayor of the palace, such as the Buyid king, just as in earlier times the caliph had delegated extensive administrative authority to his first minister, the vizier. The appearance of an aggressively pro-Abbasid sentiment in the Baghdad mob and of the aggressively Sunni Ghaznavid dynasty in eastern Persia made the later Buyids far more deferential to the Abbasid caliphs. The new respect shown the caliph continued under the successor dynasty, the Seljuk sultans, and sultanate and caliphate became the twin focuses for most subsequent Sunni political theory.

The Buyid sphere of rule corresponded to the western half of the Sasanian empire, which had ruled for four centuries before the Islamic conquests. It is therefore not surprising that the Buyids, who came from an area that preserved many Sasanian traditions, forged genealogies connecting themselves with pre-Islamic Persian royalty and used ancient

Persian regalia in their courts and pre-Islamic Persian symbolism in their public art. Their interest in the pre-Islamic culture of Persia formed an important link between the Sasanian past and subsequent Persian "revivals," although—unlike their eastern Persian neighbors—they were not important patrons of Persian literature.

The varied cultural orientation of the Buyids, as patrons of both the Arabic humanities and the Persian royal tradition, together with the tolerance that, as Shiite rulers of a population primarily Sunni, they found it wise to display, helped to make the tenth and eleventh centuries a period of great cultural efflorescence in which figures such as the poet al-Mutannabi received the patronage of Buyid courts. The competition between Buyid courts not only encouraged tolerance and offered a great choice of patronage, but also helped the diffusion of court culture from Baghdad to provincial centers. The Buyids were guided in their patronage by highly cultivated viziers whose number included the philospher Ibn Sīnā.

This cultural efflorescence took place against a background of economic decline and political instability. In the tenth century the Middle East fell under the control of its indigenous tribesmen, such as the Daylamī tribesmen who formed the original core of the Buyid armies. The Buyids, like other such governments, did not prove to be effective guardians of agriculture. Agriculture was probably also damaged by an institution that first became prevalent under the Buyids: the *iqṭā*ᶜ, or assignment of government tax rights to bureaucrats and army officers in lieu of salary. The economic decline of the Buyid domain was aggravated by the gradual shift of the route for trade between the Indian Ocean and the Mediterranean from the Persian Gulf to the Red Sea.

The weakness of central government under the Buyids threw society back on its own resources, and in the Buyid period there was a growth of self-regulation in local life. Some local offices, such as judgeships, became hereditary. Local paramilitary groups called ᶜ*ayyārūn* became more important, and the organized Sufi brotherhoods began to appear. Succeeding dynasties, even when they were more powerful than the Buyids, used the *iqṭā*ᶜ and other Buyid administrative practices that were conducive to a more decentralized form of rule. Later dynasties also were obliged to accept the presence of the arrangements for local self-regulation that had evolved in the Buyid period, and these arrangements helped to make Middle Eastern life remarkably resilient even in periods of severe political turmoil.

BIBLIOGRAPHY

Heribert Busse, *Chalif und Grosskönig: Die Buyiden im Iraq (945–1055)* (1969); "Iran Under the Būyids," in *The Cambridge History of Iran,* IV, R. N. Frye, ed. (1975), 250–304; R. P. Mottahedeh, *Loyalty and Leadership in an Early Islamic Society* (1980).

ROY PARVIZ MOTTAHEDEH

[See also **Abbasids; Alids; Baghdad; Fars; Ghaznavids; ᶜImād al-Dawla; Iran, History (After 650); Iraq; Muᶜizz al-Dawla; Shiᶜa; Shirāz; Sunni.**]

BVM, LITTLE OFFICE OF. See **Blessed Virgin Mary, Little Office of.**

BYZANTINE ARCHITECTURE. See **Early Christian and Byzantine Architecture.**

BYZANTINE ART. This subject is treated in two articles: **Byzantine Art (843–1453)** and **Byzantine Minor Arts (843–1453).** For discussions of the earlier period, the reader should consult **Early Christian Art** and **Early Christian and Byzantine Architecture.**

BYZANTINE ART, 843–1453. There have been great advances in the study of Byzantine art since the early 1950's. These have been due to new discoveries from excavation and from restoration of churches, to the fresh examination of long-known material (sometimes from old drawings and photographs because of modern destruction), and to systematic publication of materials such as manuscript illuminations. Not all of this activity has been accompanied by interpretative discussions of the new materials or by wide-ranging reviews of the present state of knowledge. As a consequence of these circumstances this article will be empirical in approach to the period, and will identify the main materials for the study of Byzantine art and the current interests of scholarship. It should be remembered throughout that the losses of works of art from the period are enormous, and only a small fraction of the art produced has survived to the present day. It follows that any new discoveries in the future will radically change our perspective.

Anyone wishing to understand the Byzantine period in the history of art must take into account a number of factors that inhibit the formulation of any considered statement. The fragmentation of the material is the chief problem and is reflected on many levels. Although the extent of the eastern Mediterranean controlled by the Byzantine emperor, based in Constantinople, progressively diminished throughout the period, at its greatest extent, in the eleventh century, the Byzantine provinces included southern Italy, Greece and much of the Balkan Peninsula, Asia Minor, and Cyprus. The surviving art from this area is of random dates and uneven in quality. We never have a fair cross section of the artistic production of any community at a clear moment in time.

As for the monumental art of the capital of this centralized empire, most of the production of the tenth through thirteenth centuries in Constantinople has now disappeared, even though Ottoman tolerance after 1453 allowed the survival of a number of the major churches for use as mosques. Only from the first half of the fourteenth century does a significant proportion of monumental decoration survive in the capital and in Greece and the Balkans.

Apart from this geographical and chronological fragmentation of the material, a further obstacle is that virtually no church that has preserved its decoration is architecturally intact—either its dome or its vaults will have fallen as a result of earthquake, subsidence, or simply age, or it may have been altered in other ways. Its decoration is unlikely to be from one homogeneous period, and may reveal several phases of restoration; it will certainly have deteriorated through time and will have been defaced as a result of Muslim iconoclasm or Christian graffiti. It is generally accepted today that the great achievement of the Byzantine civilization was the use of monumental mosaic or fresco for visual expression of Christian belief in unified schemes over the interior surfaces of domed churches. Yet it is no longer possible to experience the full conception of this art.

There is another kind of obstacle to the study of Byzantine art that results from the Christian function to which most work was dedicated. Works normally were didactic in intention or had some part in worship. As in Byzantine literature, this function led to a conscious attempt to produce works that would not reflect the temporary fashions of any age but would translate topical concerns into timeless forms of expression. This situation creates a problem for the historian, who has the greatest difficulty in trying to reconstruct the precise circumstances and the intended purpose of each work of art. The art historian must penetrate this screen and "decode" the work of art if each age is to be understood. The same point may be made conversely: this art was not the product of a faceless community, and the anonymity of both patrons and artists should not be seen as the key feature of Byzantine art.

In order to emphasize the influence of personalities on the development of Byzantine art, this article will divide the period according to the imperial dynasties and will note the importance of individual patrons. In the present state of scholarship, it is difficult to assess the contribution of individual artists, especially since most studies avoid their identification and instead speak in terms of "workshops." Probably future research will attribute some changes in Byzantine art to the impact of dominant artists on their generation. One named artist of this caliber was Pantoleon, the early-eleventh-century painter of icons and manuscripts. He not only imposed his style on his seven collaborators in the production of the illustrations for the *Menologion* of Basil II (Vatican Library, MS gr. 1613) but also influenced other surviving manuscripts of this period; there was even a revival of this style in the early Komnenian period. Another famous artist, the twelfth-century Eulalios, is known only from textual sources (he was, for example, the mosaicist of a new decoration in the Church of the Holy Apostles in Constantinople), but it seems reasonable to suppose that he was one of the artists who caused the changes in Byzantine art in the course of the twelfth century.

The complex artistic achievements of the "Orthodox Christian" Byzantine civilization are sketched out in this article by the identification of the main monuments that have survived. Works of high quality show a considerable range and variety of means of expression that was achieved despite the theoretical church control over art imposed by the Second Council of Nicaea in 787. The idea that there is a "Byzantine style" to be identified as a monotonous sequence of identical schematic saints and unchanging iconography has no justification in fact, even if the modern observer's attention is confined to third-rate works from the provinces. Byzantine art was the "superior" art of the Middle Ages, and Constantinople may for much of the period be regarded as a "high-pressure" center that overshadowed and intimidated the rest of Europe and the Near East in cultural matters.

THE MACEDONIAN DYNASTY (867–1056)

In 843, after the death of the Iconoclastic emperor Theophilos I (829–842), the ban that had been imposed on the use of figurative paintings in Byzantine churches was finally lifted. Iconoclasm had forced theologians to define the allowable uses of art by Orthodox Christians, and from this time on, church art remained distinct from that of the mosque and the synagogue. But the period after Iconoclasm was not revolutionary in its forms of art. Instead of innovating, artists continued to use the forms of art developed before Iconoclasm. The destruction of images was far from complete under the Iconoclasts (in Thessaloniki, for example, considerable amounts of mosaic decoration remain from the pre-Iconoclastic centuries), and it would seem that ninth-century artists had access to works, including manuscripts, preserved from the age of Justinian (527–565).

Whether the revival of art after Iconoclasm led to the adoption of a more iconic and hieratic style is difficult to decide on the basis of the few surviving mosaics and manuscripts. What is clear is that there was a rapid expansion of monasteries after 843, and that the monks encouraged the use of art. The mosaics of the Monastery of the Dormition at Nicaea (destroyed in the 1920's but known from photographs) may have been among the first new works after Iconoclasm, if the patron of the restored sanctuary scheme (the Virgin and Child with archangels) is to be identified with a known Naukratios who died in 847.

Otherwise, the ninth- and tenth-century wall paintings in the numerous rock-cut churches of Cappadocia in central Anatolia or the vast number of icons in the Monastery of St. Catherine on Mt. Sinai provide ample evidence that the monastic environment was filled with icons. Over the whole period the wealth and artistic patronage of the monks grew at the expense of the secular clergy. The Byzantine city and countryside were dominated by clusters of monastic buildings; cathedrals and parish churches were sparse and progressively impoverished.

The initial commissions after 843 were decorations of the Great Palace of the emperors; the first mosaics of Hagia Sophia were not begun until 29 March 867. Most likely the money for the restoration and decoration of this sixth-century cathedral

Virgin and Child mosaic, before 869. The apse, Hagia Sophia, Istanbul. COURTESY OF DUMBARTON OAKS, CENTER FOR BYZANTINE STUDIES, WASHINGTON, D.C.

was supplied by the emperors, but the scheme was planned and carried out by the scholar-patriarch Photios (*d. ca.* 893). The program of iconography executed under the direction of Photios no doubt had precedents in churches before Iconoclasm (though not in Hagia Sophia, which was given a nonfigurative decoration by Justinian), and also had parallels in the earlier ninth-century palace church of the Virgin of the Pharos (864), but as the decoration of the main church of the empire it must have influenced all future schemes (directly or indirectly).

Photios planned the layout of figures in hierarchical order, with the most holy personages relatively higher in the vaults. He allocated particular figures to special architectural spaces: Christ to the dome and the Virgin to the apse. Photios' final choice of figures and scenes must have been determined by the extent and shape of areas available for adornment and by the specific theological points he wished to illustrate. All later Byzantine planners must have worked within the same parameters; hence the subsequent scope for variety within the same general principles.

Although the general theme of the mosaics of Hagia Sophia could be characterized as the representation of the heavenly cosmos, Photios made some choices of iconography on the basis of current topical reasoning. In the apse he chose to show the Virgin with the Child, and the conch was bordered with an anti-Iconoclastic epigram ("The images that the impostors had cast down here pious emperors have set up again"). The inclusion of the Christ Child makes a good theological point against Iconoclasts: that it was entirely legitimate to represent God in human form on icons because Christ took on human form at the time of the Incarnation. Similarly in the great tympana below the dome, the particular choice of church fathers represented was made to give prominence to saints who were the subject of special annual commemorations in the liturgy of Hagia Sophia.

The meaning or meanings of the panel in the narthex of the church, above the main entrance into the nave, is more difficult to substantiate. In this mosaic an emperor is shown prostrate before Christ enthroned; the Virgin and an angel are set in medallions on each side of Christ. The emperor, who is not named in an inscription, can be interpreted as one of the early Macedonians praying for the help of the Holy Wisdom of Christ or, alternatively, as the penitent Leo VI (886–912) after he disobeyed church law by marrying for a fourth time. An explanation along the lines of the former alternative seems more in line with Byzantine thinking.

The figure style of these ninth-century mosaics is bold, linear, and flat, but it clearly continues the methods of artists of the ancient world. Similar work is found in manuscripts from Constantinople (for example, *Homilies* of Gregory of Nazianzus, Paris, Bibliothèque Nationale, MS gr. 510; *Christian Topography* of Cosmas Indicopleustes, Vatican Library, MS gr. 699), and the style spread to the provinces, either taken by artists sent from Constantinople (as in the Ascension in the dome of Hagia Sophia at Thessaloniki, *ca.* 885) or as an imitative response by local artists (as in the rock-cut churches of Cappadocia).

The artistic endeavors of the ninth century are a self-conscious and intellectual response to the freedom of visual expression initiated in 843. The subtlety and erudition of manuscript illustration has only recently been recognized by modern scholarship; the best-studied are the Chludov Psalter (Moscow, State Historical Musuem, MS no. 129D) and the *Homilies* of Gregory of Nazianzus, both of which may have been painted under the direction of Photios, and a Bible (Vatican Library, MS Reginensis gr. 1) that was illustrated in the second quarter of the tenth century for a certain Leo Patrikios.

The importance of the Macedonian emperors for the development of Byzantine and western European art is well recognized, as is clear from the following statements of two modern scholars: "Modern Art may be considered to have begun with the Byzantine renaissance of the tenth century" (Kingsley Porter); and Emperor Constantine VII Porphyrogenitos (913–959) was "a patron of the arts whose like the world hardly saw in the thirteen centuries which divided Hadrian from Lorenzo the Magnificent" (R. J. H. Jenkins). Both statements are exaggerations, but it is true that the contemporaries of Constantine were enthusiastic about his interest in art, and indeed went so far as to say that he was himself an expert painter. Sufficient tenth-century art survives, at least in the so-called minor arts, to establish that it was a time of great production and refinement. Certain media were developed under the patronage of court circles, particularly enamels, glassware, and techniques employing precious metals. Several tenth-century works of this kind are in the Treasury of San Marco in Venice, and a major enamel work is the reliquary of the true cross at Limburg-an-der-Lahn (dating from the 950's or 960's).

A feature of many of these works produced for the Constantinopolitan aristocracy is their combination of traditional Byzantine figure styles with the characteristic ornamental forms of Islamic art. The palace of Constantine Porphyrogenitos must have had many similarities with that of the Abbasid court of Baghdad. His throne in the audience hall of the Magnavra was popularly known as the throne of Solomon, but its model was Islamic; it was of gilded bronze, and had lions that roared and birds that twittered.

The term "Macedonian Renaissance" has frequently been applied to the art of the tenth century. Both the legitimacy and the meaning of the term are in dispute. For some art historians the term means no more than that there was a revival of the arts after Iconoclasm, but for others the term has all the connotations of a full-scale return to the aesthetic ideals of pagan classical antiquity. Furthermore, this view is argued on the ground that in literature too there was a rediscovery of ancient authors and a consequent reediting and reissue of their texts.

Two aspects of this controversy need mention. In the first use of the term "Macedonian Renaissance," it could not be denied that under the Macedonians the Byzantine world was at the peak of its cultural activities. This forms a striking contrast with the preceding centuries after Justinian, when the empire was fighting for survival in the face of aggressions from Persian, Arab, and Slavic invaders. But "Renaissance," at least as an art history term having an association with Italian art, is too strong a term for mere "artistic expansion."

In the second use of the term—to denote a return to the classical ideal—in which the Italian analogy is obviously felt to be appropriate, art historians have, it must be pointed out, very little evidence on which to reach a decision. The whole concept depends on a small number of famous manuscripts with miniatures of superb quality, notably a Gospels in a monastery on Mt. Athos (MS Stauroniketa, codex 43), a Book of Joshua in roll format (Vatican Library, MS Palatina gr. 431), and a psalter (Paris, Bibliothèque Nationale, MS gr. 139). A number of ivory carvings add some further substance to the argument, but it must be emphasized that the small amount of material is not conducive to proving the historical fact of a movement of widespread significance.

The Paris Psalter is one of the great achievements of Byzantine miniature painting. Fourteen full-page miniatures are preserved in a tenth-century psalter, though it is apparently not the original book for which they were painted. It is generally proposed that the pictures are copies of an even better model that was produced for Constantine Porphyrogenitos himself, possibly intended as a gift from him to his son Romanos in 952. On this interpretation the copy was made around 975. It does not seem obligatory to accept that we do not have the original set of paintings. The cycle represents the life of David, the author of the Psalms, and each of the authors of the Old Testament odes that were included in the Greek Psalter. Each scene is portrayed in a style highly reminiscent of the illusionistic narrative art of classical antiquity. Despite inadvertences that show the artist was a copyist of pictorial models rather than an observer of living models, the figures are solid in appearance and placed in atmospheric settings. It has been argued that the artist knew classical paintings and composed his new schemes out of such models; against this it has been countered that the invention of the schemes out of classical prototypes must have occurred in the early Christian period, and that the tenth-century artist's expertise lies in his ability to copy and rearrange these early models.

There are flaws in both arguments. The discovery (in 1944) of wall paintings in the small church at Castelseprio in northern Italy (perhaps from the first half of the eighth century), which are in a related style and must be the work of a Byzantine artist, makes it unlikely that the Paris Psalter is a total invention of the tenth century. However, the artist might have had full models for only some of the miniatures and might have been more inventive in others. The fundamental problem of method in such approaches is that since both depend on the theoretical reconstruction of lost models, the hypotheses put forward cannot be tested. Further studies are needed before a full characterization of the tenth century can be made. One area that is still insufficiently exploited is Cappadocia, where much painting from the tenth century is preserved—some of

Representation of David, author of the Psalms. The Paris Psalter, 10th century. PHOTOGRAPH, BIBLIOTHÈQUE NATIONALE, PARIS

high quality and reflecting the art of the capital, some of lesser sophistication but equally important as evidence of regional activity and interests.

Two other imperial patrons dominate the Macedonian period: Basil II (976–1025) and Constantine IX Monomachos (1042–1055). In character, scarcely a greater contrast of types can be imagined than Basil II and Constantine VII Porphyrogenitos. Basil was a successful general who spent years on campaign and lived in austerity while amassing plundered treasure "in vaults dug beneath the Palace" (to quote the Byzantine writer Michael Psellos). Constantine was a recluse in the Great Palace who relished pompous ceremonial and surrounded himself with beautiful objects. His learning and scholarship were famous. Art historians have sensed the reign of Basil II as the termination of a period rather than the beginning of positive new trends. On this view the reign is convenient as marking the end of the "Macedonian Renaissance" and was a fallow period before new, more "spiritual" currents in art emerged in the eleventh century. Basil is seen as "a philistine who resented spending money on the arts" (Runciman).

Probably a reassessment of this period is due, for while he was not a great builder and did not maintain or expand the Great Palace in Constantinople as his predecessors had done, Basil was lavish enough in supporting the restoration of Hagia Sophia after the earthquake of 989, and his partronage may be suggested in a small number of important commissions. These attributions and the evidence of other artistic enterprises at this time document a growing support for monastic values that influenced the nature and appearance of art. Imperial sponsorship can be argued for four luxurious manuscripts produced during the reign of Basil II: the (so-called) *Menologion* of Basil II (Vatican Library, MS gr. 1613), the Psalter of Basil II (Venice, Biblioteca Marciana, MS gr. 17), and two lectionaries (Mt. Sinai, Monastery of St. Catherine, codex 204; Mt. Athos, Great Laura, MS Skevophylakion). The two lectionaries were donated to monasteries, but the other two, apparently intended as a pair, are of unknown destination. Considered as a group, these books bear witness to the intense piety of the donor.

One major enterprise is in all likelihood to be associated in part with the patronage of Basil II. This is the mosaic decoration of the main church of the Monastery of Hosios Lukas in central Greece. The dating of this church is a highly controversial issue, but it must, on grounds of style, lie within the first half of the eleventh century. A time as late as the reign of Constantine Monomachos can be argued. This monastery, a center of pilgrimage from the middle of the tenth century, grew up around the death site of a popular local saint, the hermit Luke of Stiris. Because of its growing popularity, the buildings of the monastery were expanded, at first probably with the cooperation of the rich landed gentry of the nearby city of Thebes. An arrangement to employ mosaicists who must have come from Constantinople was perhaps the outcome of a visit by Basil II to central Greece in 1018, after his final triumphant campaign against the Bulgarian Empire.

Hosios Lukas is the best place to appreciate the expressiveness of Macedonian-period art. The architecture is of the cross-in-square type, and the nave is surmounted by a wide dome. The sanctuary is divided from the nave by an ornately carved templon screen. The vertical walls are faced with veined marble slabs, and carved cornices articulate these surfaces. The church was built with interior galleries and thus is tall and spacious. The upper curving vaults and the narthex are decorated with mosaics, while the corner bays of the church and the crypt below it have a contemporary decoration of wall paintings. The tesserae used by the mosaicists consist of cubes of cut colored glass, stone, or marble. The gold and silver cubes were made by sandwiching gold or silver leaf between wafers of glass.

The patron saint of the monastery, St. Luke, is prominently represented in the cycle (his relics were placed in a shrine in the northwest bay of the church). A conspicuous feature of the program is the inclusion of portraits of dozens of sainted monks and hermits. This interest in the visual portrayal of monks is matched in a series of manuscripts from Constantinople, where for the first time in the eleventh century, a text written at the close of the sixth century was illustrated. This book, the *Heavenly Ladder* by John Climacus of Sinai, received illustrations showing each step a zealous monk could take as a sure means of ascent to heaven. The emphasis on portraits of the saints of the Orthodox church calendar at Hosios Lukas marks a new stage in the development of "monastic" art.

The program includes a small number of narrative scenes. All derive from the New Testament except for one, the Anastasis, or Descent into Hell, which derives ultimately in art from the Apocrypha. Their purpose is to illustrate the main events in the life of Christ that are celebrated in the annual church festivals. The decoration of the church therefore encapsulates in visual form the annual cycle of the liturgy.

The style of these mosaics is bold and linear, and the figures and scenes are set against glittering gold grounds. The effect is one of unity, reinforced by the apparent absence of distracting topical references. But under analysis the inclusion of references to the function of the memorial church and current monastic thought can be detected. Hosios Lukas documents again how Byzantine art translates the particular into the general.

The first half of the eleventh century, after the death of Basil II in 1025, was a time of political and military decline in the Byzantine Empire. Economically this resulted in a series of debasements of the gold coinage. For his part in this devaluation, Constantine IX Monomachos has been widely condemned by modern historians, though a new assessment of the period is being made by numismatists. So far as the art historian is concerned, the reign of Constantine marks a major injection of funds into the patronage of the arts.

Constantine is described in the contemporary sources as a man of great piety, and he was personally involved in a great number of projects. He gave an enormous donation to Hagia Sophia at Constantinople and recorded this in a mosaic panel in the south gallery. The oddity of this panel is that while the faces of Constantine, Christ, and Empress Zoe belong to this reign, the background and the bodies are earlier and were set by Zoe's first husband, Romanos III Argyros (1028–1034), on the occasion of his donation to the cathedral. Other works of Constantine were the Church of St. George of the Mangana at Constantinople (today known only partially from an excavation), the restoration of the Church of the Holy Sepulcher at Jerusalem, and the Nea Moni (New Monastery) on the island of Chios, for which an architect and mosaicists were sent from Constantinople. Constantine must also have been associated with the mosaic decoration of the Church of Hagia Sophia at Kiev (founded in 1037).

A feature of the mosaics of Nea Moni and of some mid-eleventh-century manuscripts, such as the Psalter of Theodore of 1066 (British Library, MS add. 19352) and the Gospels (Paris, Bibliothèque Nationale, MS gr. 74), is the use of bright, highly saturated colors in the rendering of figures. But there was no single line of development in Byzantine art of this period in either the minor arts or painting; different in treatment from the works mentioned above are the wall paintings of Hagia Sophia at Ochrid and the "churches with columns" in Cappadocia.

THE ART OF THE KOMNENOI AND ANGELOI (1081–1204)

The reign of Alexios I Komnenos (1081–1118) reestablished the stability of the empire, though in a somewhat changed and less centralized form. In terms of art the twelfth century was a period of enormous activity by emperors and the rich in the provinces. New fashions in stylistic expression spread rapidly from one end of the empire to the other, documenting the movements from one job to another by professional artists. A new self-consciousness was shown in the growing tendency of artists to sign their works. It would seem to follow from the amount of work available to hired artists in the provinces that these men spent much time outside the capital, even if their apprenticeship had been there. Komnenian art is therefore very much the art of the Byzantine Empire rather than that of Constantinople. Nevertheless, at present art historians tend to attribute any work of high quality to an artist from Constantinople.

Art in the twelfth century was more open than ever before to influences from foreign culture. For example, in the middle of the century Seljuk Turk artists were employed inside the Great Palace to erect a large building in Islamic style, the Mouchroutas. Contacts with western Europeans were even more frequent because of the presence of Crusaders and the predilection of the Komnenian dynasty for choosing Western princesses as wives.

Little Komnenian art is left in Constantinople, but one desolate group of buildings there still conveys something of the nature of the pretensions of the imperial family. The present Zeyrek Camii was originally the Monastery of Christ Pantokrator. This complex was founded to serve as the family mausoleum by John II Komnenos (1118–1143) and his wife Irene (*d.* 1134). Its foundation charter (the Pantokrator *Typikon*) of 1136 is an extant document of great historical value. The main south church of the complex would have been decorated not only with marble fittings and mosaics but possibly also with some of the enamels that now form the Pala d'Oro of the Church of San Marco in Venice. It was discovered during restoration of the church that its windows were filled with a figurative stained glass decoration.

There is no good reason to doubt that this glass belonged to the original foundation. The corpses of the emperors were laid in sarcophagi in a central church called the Heroon, while empresses were placed in the narthex. The continued prosperity of the empire under the early Komnenoi can be appreciated from this evidence of multimedia adornment.

The main artistic developments of the Komnenian period can be recognized through the selection of a number of key monuments from the considerable number of churches that have survived. The state of mosaic production at the beginning of the period is well displayed by the Church of Dafni, near Athens, though the exact date of this work is unknown and estimates still range from the mid eleventh to the mid twelfth century. Dafni was a monastery, and the church must have been built and decorated by workers familiar with Hosios Lukas. The church is of the same architectural type as Hosios Lukas but is smaller and lacks the galleries. The mosaics give the impression of artists who were striving to react against the aesthetic means employed in the earlier church. The number of portraits of saints is greatly reduced, and more space is allotted to narrative scenes; a cycle of the life of the Virgin is introduced into the program.

What is more, quite different attitudes to the portrayal of figures are seen at Dafni. The artist who set the bust of Christ Pantokrator in the apex of the dome set a face that is aesthetically pleasing yet conveys the fear of the Christian who will confront God at the Last Judgment. Lower in the church the narrative panels, which must be the work of a different artist or artists, are more mundane. The events are shown as true narratives with well-modeled and lifelike actors.

The comparison of the mosaics of Hosios Lukas and of Dafni is ideal for demonstrating the great potential open to the Byzantine artist. At first sight both decorations might be characterized as linear. Observation soon shows that line is used in quite a different way in each church; in Hosios Lukas the lines of tesserae run in decorative patterns over the figures, while at Dafni the lines model the figures and their drapery. The artists of Dafni work with economy of touch, producing static compositions and calm figures. This feature has encouraged some art historians to see Dafni as a "classic" moment in the history of Byzantine art.

Other paintings that have some of the calm narrative qualities of Dafni have survived. For example, three contemporary churches on Cyprus show the use of art by imperial agents in this province around 1100: the Church of St. Chrysostomos at Koutsovendis, the Church of the Virgin at Trikomo, and the Church of the Virgin Phorviotissa at Asinou (dated 1105–1106). These churches were decorated by a group of painters influenced by the same principles as the Dafni mosaicists.

Crucifixion mosaic, *ca.* 1100. Church of Dafni. ALINARI/EDITORIAL PHOTOCOLOR ARCHIVES

One of the greatest Byzantine painters of the twelfth century is documented by the survival of one decoration in the Balkans: the wall painting of the Church of St. Panteleimon at Nerezi, near Skopje in Yugoslavia. This was the main church of a small, remote monastery founded by a member of the Komnenos family in 1164 (the foundation date is recorded in an inscription). Despite the small size of this cross-in-square church, the main artist achieved compositions that convey spaciousness and grandeur. The lowest zone of painting is filled with standing saints; the upper surfaces contain a cycle of the lives of Christ and the Virgin. The patron saint of the monastery has a section of the narthex devoted to a cycle of his life and miracles.

The astonishing feature of these frescoes is their emphatic portrayal of emotion. These are not abstract artistic statements of the Christian truths of the New Testament; rather, the spectator is made to see the dramatic moments of the passion of Christ and to appreciate the sorrow of the Virgin at the death of her son. The artist not only is able to show emotion through facial expressions, but reiterates feelings by the postures of the figures and the composition of the background elements.

It is generally assumed that the Master of Nerezi received his training in Constantinople, but at present it is not possible to unravel the influences on his development. One manuscript from Constantinople shares some of the elements of his style. This is an illustrated edition of the *Homilies* of Monk James Kokkinobaphos, which is now in the Vatican Library (gr. 1162). It is not known where else the Master of Nerezi worked, and so the nature of his personal influence on other artists cannot be assessed. However, even in Macedonia it is clear that the presence of Nerezi had a great impact on local artists, as, for instance, in more than one church in the town of Kastoria and in the church at Kurbinovo, near Lake Prespa. Certain features of the Nerezi paintings were taken up and exaggerated by later twelfth-century artists throughout the Byzantine world, and even beyond it in Sicily and Russia.

The dominant mode of expression in the late twelfth century was a style marked by facial contortion and excessive agitation of drapery. The whole posture of figures was affected by this new kind of treatment. Artists also gave greater attention to the portrayal of background elements, and a new interest in perspectival effects is sometimes found. In iconography there was a growth in the proliferation of details in narrative scenes, an interest that continued to develop in late Byzantine art. Art historians have been concerned to recognize this late-twelfth-century art and to give it an identifying label, such as "manneristic," "baroque," "rococo," "dynamic," "agitated," or "storm style." It must be remembered, though, that at the time this mode must have been found especially expressive and attractive, even though it must finally have cloyed, for in the last decade of the century there is evidence of a reaction and the use of simple, calm figures (as in the Last Judgment wall painting in the Church of St. Demetrios at Vladimir around 1194).

Although the late Komnenian artists who worked in this style shared similar aims of expression, a comparison of only a few works of quality can show the possibility of individual techniques and interpretations. A good mosaic example of the style is the decoration of the cathedral of Monreale in Sicily. The vast ensemble was executed by mosaicists sent from Constantinople and dates from the 1180's. This was not the first time that the Norman kings of Sicily had used Byzantine mosaicists (twelfth-century decorations survive also at Cefalù, and at Palermo in the Palatine Chapel and the Martorana), but the surface area covered is the greatest in Italy. For the iconographical program the mosaicists clearly were instructed to repeat some of the cycles found on the walls of the earlier Palatine Chapel (dating from the 1140's and 1150's), but the later artists transformed their models into the new style of exaggeration.

Painters had greater opportunities than the mosaicists of Monreale to intensify this style. An extreme development is found in the Church of St. George at Kurbinovo (dated by an inscription to 1191). The artist of Kurbinovo (who also worked in the Church of the Anargyroi at Kastoria) never missed a chance to introduce a distorted posture or an extra cluster of fluttering draperies. The painting is carried out with a speed and sureness of touch that show the confidence with which the artist worked.

Another wall painting in this style is found on Cyprus, high up in the Troodos Mountains, in the Church of the Panagia tou Arakou at Lagoudera (dated by an inscription to 1192). This small cupola church retains a large proportion of its original painting, and the work of the main master is seen at its best in the dome and the pendentives below it. (Although the name of the artist is not found among the surviving paintings, there is the possibility that this is a later work of the artist Theodore Apseudes, who signed his work of 1183 in the Enkleistra of St. Neophytos near Paphos.) The Lagoudera Master is more restrained in his mannerisms than the painter (or painters) of Kurbinovo. He can also be distinguished by his greater interest in the portrayal of space. This interest is seen both in the design of complicated background architecture in several scenes and in his ability to portray the human body twisting in space. A good example of this breaking up of the picture plane is the representation of the Annunciation angel in the northeast pendentive.

Another version of this style is known from a small icon of the Annunciation in the collection of the Monastery of St. Catherine on Mt. Sinai. Like the Lagoudera Annunciation angel, the figure of Gabriel in the icon is shown turning in space. The event takes place in a landscape setting peopled with many

The Annunciation, 12th century. Monastery of St. Catherine, Mt. Sinai. PUBLISHED THROUGH THE COURTESY OF THE MICHIGAN-PRINCETON-ALEXANDRIA EXPEDITION TO MT. SINAI

kinds of birds—the idea for this motif came into art from sermons that connected the feast of the Annunciation (25 March) with the coming of spring.

These four examples of late Komnenian art show, in addition to the diffusion and popularity of one style of painting, the adaptability of Byzantine artists to work on extremely different scales, yet produce images that may fairly be described as "monumental."

THE LATIN OCCUPATION OF CONSTANTINOPLE (1204–1261)

The sack of Constantinople in 1204, during the Fourth Crusade, meant, in the first place, that many preciously mounted relics and portable works of art were removed to western Europe. But other factors affected the continuation of Byzantine art. There was a hiatus in the production of art for an Orthodox imperial court in the capital, and there is no known instance of the execution of a mosaic decoration in the eastern Mediterranean during this period (mosaicists in the Byzantine tradition still operated in Italy, in the Veneto and in Rome). Of the various Greek courts in exile, the Laskarid emperors of Nicaea, who controlled the westernmost parts of Asia Minor, were probably the most energetic patrons of art, but much work was done in the Empire of Trebizond and in the despotate of Epiros.

Artists did have the option to stay in Constantinople and work for the Frankish Crusaders, and there is documentary evidence that some did stay. (There is also a controversial attribution of some bilingual manuscripts to such natives—for instance, Athens, National Library, codex 118, an illustrated Gospels in which the Evangelists hold Latin-text scrolls of their individual gospels.) Nevertheless, most artists probably worked outside the capital. They must have found the most promising region for large-scale enterprises to be the expanding Serbian Empire in the Balkans, where the building of a series of royal mausoleums in monasteries must have provided almost continuous employment through the thirteenth century. The Nemanjid dynasty of Serbia managed to obtain the services of great Byzantine masters throughout the century, in particular at the following monasteries: Studenica, for the Church of the Virgin in 1208–1209; Žiča, for the Church of the Ascension in about 1220; Mileševo, for its Church of the Ascension in the 1230's; Peć, for the Church of the Holy Apostles in the 1240's or 1250's; and Sopočani, for the Church of the Trinity in (probably) the 1260's.

While there is no continuous evolution in style from church to church in Serbia and it is not known where else these artists worked, the wall paintings in the churches mentioned above are the best source of information about the formation of a new phase in Byzantine art. The common feature of these works is the portrayal of idealized figures in a naturalistic manner. By the time of Sopočani, the figures had become so bulky and their drapery so expansive that art historians have used the term "volume style" to characterize the trend. The figures at Studenica and Mileševo are rather more slender and delicate, and form a great contrast with the popular style of the last Komnenian period. While the faces at Studenica are still quite linear in their modeling, those in the main church of Mileševo (distinct from those in the narthex) display great softness in touch.

There can be little doubt that the interests and

achievements of these various artistic personalities who worked in Serbia were known to and influenced Italian artists of the Dugento. Another wall painting in the Balkans that has been cited as evidence of Byzantine influence on the West is in the church of St. Panteleimon at Boiana in the suburbs of Sofia, Bulgaria (the phase of 1259). This work participates in the same artistic development but is of lesser quality than the Serbian examples.

Further evidence of the vitality of this trend and its development outside the Balkans has been supplied by the restoration of the Church of Hagia Sophia at Trebizond. It was also a mausoleum church in a monastery, and was the pretentious foundation of one of the Grand Komnenoi, Manuel I (1238–1263), who ruled the Empire of Trebizond. The wall painting is probably to be attributed to the 1250's; in some respects (such as the treatment of the faces) the work is similar to Sopočani, but in others (the forms of the drapery) it exhibits an interest in decorative effects unparalleled there.

The presence of the Crusaders in the eastern Mediterranean in the twelfth and thirteenth centuries theoretically brought Orthodox and Catholic Christians into closer contact with each other, and the question of how this influenced artists needs to be considered. The best evidence is in the form of manuscript illumination and icon painting. (Other evidence, such as the mosaics in the Church of the Nativity at Bethlehem, is at present insufficiently studied.) The conclusions of research so far undertaken suggest that the works of major importance—for example, among the manuscripts, the Psalter of Queen Melisende (London, British Library, Egerton 1139), dating between 1131 and 1143, and produced at the Holy Sepulcher, Jerusalem, and the Arsenal Bible (Paris, Bibliothèque de l'Arsenal, MS 5211), dating around 1230 and produced at Acre—were painted by artists who traveled from the West and fell under the spell of Byzantine art. On this view the presence of the Crusaders brought no apparent changes to artists in the Greek East. This whole question of Western influence on the East needs further investigation, as does the problem of whether Crusader artists or their products had any impact in western Europe.

An example of Crusader style in a monumental painting, representing St. Francis of Assisi and scenes from his life, was discovered during the restoration of the Kalenderhane Camii. This Constantinopolitan building must in the course of the thirteenth century have been converted from Orthodox use to a Franciscan house (after 1261 it was reconverted). The painting is related in style to the Arsenal Bible, and on these grounds has been attributed to a Western artist.

THE PALAIOLOGAN DYNASTY (1261–1453)

In August 1261 the Nicaean emperor, Michael VIII Palaiologos (1259–1282), regained control of Constantinople and had the Orthodox liturgy celebrated in Hagia Sophia. The returning Byzantines found a city severely depopulated and full of open spaces and ruined buildings. The main patrons of art in the capital during this period were the imperial family and a small number of rich families who were closely interrelated by marriage. Outside the city there continued to be extensive works undertaken by the Slavic rulers of the Balkans. In Greece, particularly in towns such as Thessaloniki, Veroia, and Mistra, an impressive quantity of painting was executed. (Indeed, the full extent of late Byzantine painting that has survived in Greece remains to be surveyed.) It can be said that the art of the Palaiologan period is of more significance than its politics.

The painters of Sopočani in Serbia worked in the style that had the greatest influence on subsequent generations, and much work of the early fourteenth century reflects that influence. The first monumental mosaic in Constantinople after the restoration of the empire was the Deesis mosaic of the south gallery of Hagia Sophia, and in it the fully modeled faces of the figures are reminiscent of the wall paintings of Trebizond and Sopočani. There is good reason to date this mosaic of the Virgin and John the Baptist in prayer on each side of the enthroned Christ to the redecoration of Hagia Sophia in the fall of 1261, when the liturgical fittings of an Orthodox cathedral replaced those of a Catholic one. This panel, which has no parallel in style in any other mosaics in Hagia Sophia, seems at first sight more like a painting than a mosaic. The flesh is rendered as if by brushstrokes, and with subtle gradations of shading. The expressions are sad, almost sentimental. The artist of this panel is successful in presenting figures with which the viewer can make intimate contact in moments of prayer, but which are at the same time composed on a monumental scale.

The artist of the Deesis mosaic has not so far been recognized as the author of other works, though there are some panel paintings that can be associated with the facial style of the Deesis mosaic—for example, an icon of Christ Pantokrator in the collec-

The Virgin Mary and John the Baptist on either side of Christ, 1261. The Deesis mosaic, Hagia Sophia.
COURTESY OF DUMBARTON OAKS, CENTER FOR BYZANTINE STUDIES, WASHINGTON, D.C.

tion of the Monastery of Chilandari on Mt. Athos, and two panels of the Virgin and Child now in the National Gallery of Art, Washington D.C. (the Kahn and Mellon Madonnas). The dating and attribution of the two panels have been the subject of considerable and continuing controversy. This group of works is highly relevant to the question of how much the Sienese painter Duccio owed to Byzantine models.

Study of thirteenth-century manuscripts and icons will add to the knowledge of the nature of art in Constantinople after 1261, for in many cases the same artists must have worked in both media. In late-thirteenth-century monumental art a series of church decorations in Macedonia are signed by two remarkable artists, Michael and Eutychios. Their earliest dated work was the Church of the Virgin Peribleptos (now St. Clement) in Ochrid (1294/1295).The figure style seems purposely inelegant, and the iconography is notable for its complexity and the unusual choice of scenes. The place of training of these artists who were in the service of the court of Milutin (1282–1321) is unknown, but Thessaloniki has been proposed on various grounds. One of these is that their work is similar to the wall painting of the Church of the Protaton on Mt. Athos; this work is traditionally attributed to a Manuel Panselinos of Thessaloniki.

The rich families of early-fourteenth-century Constantinople took care to provide a place of rest for their bodies after death. They restored and endowed monasteries so that their tombs would be appropriate in the grandeur of their setting, and also to ensure the regularity of commemorative services after their death. As a result of such arrangements there was a flowering of tomb sculpture in the city. Some pieces are still in their original places (as in the Kariye Camii, or Kariye Djami), while others are found in the Archaeological Museum of Istanbul. Two of these mortuary chapels have survived in good condition: the parekklesion of the Monastery of the Virgin Pammakaristos (now the Fethiye Camii) and the parekklesion of the Monastery of Christ in Chora (now the Kariye Camii).

The parekklesion of the Fethiye Camii is a miniature cross-in-square church with a full cycle of mosaics. It was built and decorated for Michael Glabas and his family in the first decade of the fourteenth century. The mosaics are best preserved in the apse and the cupola. The face of Christ Hyperagathos in the apse Deesis owes some of its stylistic character to the earlier Deesis in the south gallery of Hagia

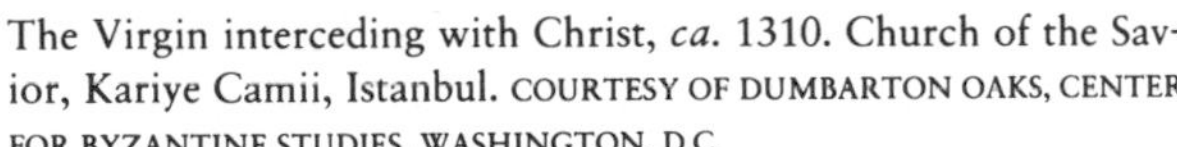
The Virgin interceding with Christ, *ca.* 1310. Church of the Savior, Kariye Camii, Istanbul. COURTESY OF DUMBARTON OAKS, CENTER FOR BYZANTINE STUDIES, WASHINGTON, D.C.

The parekklesion, Kariye Camii, Istanbul. COURTESY OF DUMBARTON OAKS, CENTER FOR BYZANTINE STUDIES, WASHINGTON, D.C.

Sophia, but has a new miniature quality of its own. This may be connected with another development of the early Palaiologan period, the manufacture of miniature mosaic icons in which tiny tesserae are set in a wax base.

The Kariye Camii is perhaps the most informative monument for the study of Byzantine art, because the personality of the patron, Theodore Metochites, is ascertainable from his writings, which are virtually all extant, and because the mosaics and paintings have been carefully studied and published. Theodore Metochites (1270–1332) was at the height of his career as the grand logothete, the highest state officer, when he restored the dilapidated Komnenian Monastery of the Chora, roughly between 1316 and 1321. He was a man of great erudition—flatterers called him "Philosophy personified," his enemies called him verbose, pompous, and a bore. His modern biographer, Ševčenko, gives this judgment of his character: "To have given us the Chora he had to be a man of wealth, taste, and intelligence. He did not have to be a perfect gentleman."

The main church and its two narthexes received mosaic decorations, and the parekklesion on the south side received a fresco decoration that included an extended cycle of the Last Judgment, an appropriate choice for its funerary function. The same artists worked in both media, and the parekklesion seems to be relatively later than the church. The mosaics of the narthexes illustrated the life of the Virgin and the early life and miracles of Christ. The main festival scenes would have been shown inside the main church, but of this set only the Dormition of the Virgin has been preserved. A panel above the main door from the inner narthex into the church showed Metochites himself offering a model of the church to Christ. To the right of this doorway was a large panel of the Deesis, and Metochites was moved to refer specifically to this composition in his writings.

Theodore Metochites intended the Chora to be more than a haven for his old age, and he repeatedly wrote that it would, as an artistic achievement, ensure the perpetuation of his memory on earth. His attitudes toward his literary scholarship help to account for the nature of the cycles of the Kariye Camii. He believed his generation had come too late in history to be able to have original ideas—all possible ideas had already been formulated. In any case in theology it was wiser to avoid originality or to raise problems; instead, one should worship in silence. The only possible kind of originality of which he could conceive was in expression or in style. The iconographic program of the church is in keeping with his character, being on the whole conservative but with a wealth of intellectual references.

Metochites had used his political offices to increase his wealth, and was in a position to hire the best artists who would work for him. Some seem to have come to him after being employed by the (corrupt) patriarch Niphon I (1310–1314), for workmanship similar to that in the Chora also appears in the mosaic decoration of the Church of the Holy Apostles at Thessaloniki. Their work in that city had a definite impact on the flourishing local artists. An example of this is seen in the Church of Christ (originally of the Anastasis of Christ) at Veroia, where in the wall paintings of 1315 the figure of St. John of Damascus composing his writings derives in type from the mosaic in the Holy Apostles of St. Kosmas the Poet. The foundation inscription of the Veroia church pretentiously describes the artist, who is named Kalliergis, as "the best painter of the whole of Thessaly." The same artist seems to have participated in the painting of the Church of St. Nicholas Orphanou at Thessaloniki, another tiny monastic church built and preciously adorned under family patronage.

The decoration of the Kariye Camii may be properly assessed as the best work produced at the time and the work of mature artists for one of the most ambitious men in the state. In its turn the church must have acted as a source of inspiration to other artists. Its direct influence was felt as far afield as the Church of St. Nicholas at Curtea-de-Arges in Romania and the monastery of Kalenić in Yugoslavia. The style of the Kariye Camii owes much to the treatment of figures and space developed at Sopoćani, but the introduction of elements of motion into the compositions and elegance into the drawing of drapery and background props may well be the self-conscious development of the artists engaged in this special project.

Soon after the completion of the Chora monastery, civil war broke out between Emperor Andronikos II (1282–1328) and his grandson. With the fall of Andronikos, Theodore Metochites was stripped of his possessions and sent into exile; in 1330 he was allowed to return to the Chora, where he died as a monk two years later. Further civil wars followed in the 1340's; the result of these wars and the decline of the Byzantine Empire in the face of the Turkish advance was that the decoration of the Chora can be seen as the last major project in Constantinople.

In the Balkans the Bulgarian and Serbian courts continued as important patrons of the arts of the Byzantine tradition, but for the most important new monastery of the time, Dečani in Yugoslavia (built between 1327 and 1335), with its vast frescoed wall surfaces, the artists, including one Sergios, seem to have come from the Dalmatian Coast. There can be no doubt, though, that a trickle of commissions in Constantinople kept a number of artists in business. The wall paintings of the Church of the Virgin Peribleptos at Mistra in southern Greece (third quarter of the fourteenth century) have usually been seen as the work of an artist trained in Constantinople. This view seems to be confirmed by the identification of a painter working in the same style in the production of a number of important manuscripts, notably in the theological works of Emperor John VI Kantakouzenos (1371–1375; Paris, Bibliothèque Nationale, MS gr. 1242). This artist, who received the main manuscript commissions of his time, continued the tradition of the Chora painting but exaggerated the bulkiness of drapery and the body beneath. It may have been in his workshop that Theophanes, the most remarkable late Palaiologan artist, was trained.

Theophanes (*d.* between 1405 and 1415) worked first in Constantinople but moved north, painting churches in the Crimea and Novgorod before settling in what is now Moscow. Known in Russia as Theofan Grek, he produced icons and book illuminations as well as monumental art. In his time the high iconostasis screen in the Orthodox church was being developed. His major surviving work is the wall painting in the Church of the Transfiguration at Novgorod (1378). These show a strikingly original style (later copied in Novgorod) of figures first blocked out in a flat red and then modeled with black outlines and slashing white highlights. Theophanes' lightning speed of painting and his visual memory were seen as exceptional by a Russian monk who observed him and wrote an appreciation.

The nature of Byzantine art in the declining years of the empire still needs to be defined. The painting of the Church of the Pantanassa at Mistra (1428) is entirely retrospective, and a fifteenth-century tomb painting in the outer narthex of the Kariye Camii (tomb G), showing the deceased standing in front of the enthroned Virgin and Child, appears to be the work of a Byzantine artist working in an up-to-date Italian quattrocento manner.

RETROSPECT

Byzantine art after Iconoclasm continued a tradition of figurative art that derived ultimately from the repertory of expression established in the Greco-Roman world. This legacy caused a perpetual tension as artists tried to use the formulas of classical temporal narrative to portray an unchanging, eternal Christian world. Over the whole period artists developed a number of different solutions for the treatment of their subject matter. Historical scholarship has tried to formulate explanations for the appearances of changes in style.

One influential theory to explain differences of style was that of the separate identity of "regional schools," a concept no doubt applied to the Byzantine world because such categories had proved useful in Italian art history. The main "schools" postulated were Cappadocian, Greek, Macedonian, Cretan, and of course Constantinopolitan (in the early Christian period the equivalents were the schools of Antioch and Alexandria). Analysis in terms of these schools has not proved useful—not because there were no local artists, but because travels of artists and works of art were frequent, and so the regions were not distinct units isolated from contact with each other. Kalliergis has already been cited as a painter in Macedonia who was quick to assimilate the latest ideas of artists from Constantinople through his observation of their work at Thessaloniki. The misleading aspect of this theory is that it underestimates the "internationalism" of Byzantine art. However, a much modified and refined version of this theory could in future be developed through the identification of regional artists and their pupils and influence. The differences observed between contemporary artists in, say, Macedonia and Attica do require an explanation.

The other influential interpretation of changes is in terms of "renaissance"; this also derives from an Italian theoretical model. Some art historians have identified "Macedonian," "Komnenian," and "Palaiologan" renaissances. The label is meant to give a cultural context to an intense interest in "narrative realism" by suggesting a renewed study of the art of classical antiquity. Such study is particularly hard to justify in the two later periods, and the Palaiologan period was more obviously retrospective to the manuscripts of the tenth century—the Paris Psalter was copied in the thirteenth century, and for the library of the Chora, Theodore Metochites had his own writings copied on parchment with the titles of the sections in lettering that imitated that of the time of Constantine Porphyrogenitos. The evidence for a "renaissance" in the tenth century is more difficult to assess, but the danger of overemphasizing the continuation of classical principles into this time needs to be avoided, and this theory seems to suggest that classical antiquity never ended. On the contrary, it is desirable to substantiate the new principles of the art of the Middle Ages and to recognize an essential discontinuity between the pagan and Christian worlds.

This article has sought to underline the individual contibution of patrons and artists to the development of Byzantine art. The recognition of the importance of personalities for the directions taken in medieval art is of course only a partial explanation of the period, but in the present state of Byzantine art history the identification of precise issues is still a priority.

It is common to estimate the importance of Byzantine art as lying in its influence on the West, and in particular in acting as a "catalyst" in the Italian rediscovery of classical antiquity. Rather than to treat Byzantine art as "relevant" to something else, it deserves study primarily for its own qualities and for its particular success in molding one form of Christian art.

BIBLIOGRAPHY

General. Jelisaveta S. Allen, ed., *Dumbarton Oaks Bibliographies, Literature on Byzantine Art 1892–1967,* 2 vols. (1973–1976), updated since 1967 by *Byzantinische Zeitschrift;* V. Glasberg, *Répertoire de la mosaïque médiévale pariétale et portative* (1974).

See also Otto Demus, *Byzantine Mosaic Decoration* (1948); Clive Foss and Paul Magdalino, *Rome and Byzantium* (1977); Irmgard Hutter, *Corpus der byzantinischen Miniaturenhandschriften,* vol. 1: *Oxford, Bodleian Library* (1977); Romilly Jenkins, *Byzantium: The Imperial Centuries A.D. 610–1071* (1966); Victor N. Lazarev, *Storia della pittura bizantina* (1967); Cyril Mango, *The Art of the Byzantine Empire 312–1453, Sources and Documents* (1972); Thomas F. Mathews, *The Byzantine Churches of*

Istanbul (1976); Gabriel Millet, *Recherches sur l'iconographie de l'Évangile* (1916); W. F. Volbach and Jacqueline Lafontaine-Dosogne, eds., *Byzanz und der christliche Osten* (1968); Kurt Weitzmann *et al., Icons from Southeastern Europe and Sinai* (1968).

The Macedonian dynasty. Anthony Bryer and Judith Herrin, eds., *Iconoclasm* (1977); Hugo Buchthal, "The Exaltation of David," in *Journal of the Warburg and Courthauld Institutes,* **37** (1974); Anthony Cutler, "The Mythological Bowl in the Treasury of San Marco at Venice," in *Near Eastern Numismatics, Iconography, Epigraphy, and History,* Dikran K. Kouymjian, ed. (1974); Sirarpie Der Nersessian, "The Illustrations of the Homilies of Gregory of Nazianzus: Paris Gr. 510, a Study of the Connections Between Text and Images," in *Dumbarton Oaks Papers,* **16** (1962); André Grabar, *L'iconoclasme byzantin* (1957), and *Sculptures byzantines du Moyen-Âge* (1976); Cyril Mango, *The Mosaics of St. Sophia at Istanbul* (1962); John R. Martin, *The Illustration of the Heavenly Ladder of John Climacus* (1954); Thomas F. Mathews, "The Epigrams of Leo Sacellarios and an Exegetical Approach to the Miniatures of Vat. Reg. Gr. 1," in *Orientalia christiana periodica,* **43** (1977); Arthur Kingsley Porter, *Romanesque Sculpture of the Pilgrimage Roads* (1923); Ihor Ševčenko, "The Illuminators of the Menologium of Basil II," in *Dumbarton Oaks Papers,* **16** (1962); Kurt Weitzmann, *Studies in Classical and Byzantine Manuscript Illumination,* H. L. Kessler, ed. (1971).

The Komnenoi and the Angeloi. Otto Demus, *The Mosaics of Norman Sicily* (1949); Vojislav J. Djurić, *Die byzantinische Fresken in Jugoslavien* (1975); Ernst Kitzinger, *The Art of Byzantium and the Medieval West,* W. E. Kleinbauer, ed. (1976).

The Latin occupation. Hugo Buchthal, *Miniature Painting in the Latin Kingdom of Jerusalem* (1957); Vojislav J. Djurić, *Sopoćani* (1963); David Talbot Rice, ed., *The Church of Haghia Sophia at Trebizond* (1968).

The Palaiologan dynasty. Hans Belting, *Das illuminierte Buch in der spätbyzantinischen Gesellschaft* (1970); Paul A. Underwood, *Kariye Djami,* I–III (1966); *idem,* ed., *Studies in the Art of the Kariye Djami* (1975).

Retrospect. Otto Demus, *Byzantine Art and the West* (1970); Steven Runciman, *Byzantine Style and Civilisation* (1975).

ROBIN CORMACK

[See also **Athos, Mount, Monuments of; Basil II; Byzantine Church; Constantine VII Porphyrogenitos; Constantine IX Monomachos; Constantinople; Deesis; Early Christian Art; Fresco Painting; Hagia Sophia (Constantinople); Hagia Sophia (Kiev); Hosios Lukas; Iconoclasm, Christian; Iconography; Kariye Djami (Camii); Macedonian Renaissance; Menologian Art; Menologion; Mosaic and Mosaic Making; Parekklesion; Photios; Psalter; Serbian Art; Theophanes the Greek; Thessaloniki.**]

BYZANTINE MINOR ARTS (843–1453). The term "minor arts" is misleading in the Byzantine context if understood to imply anything other than the small scale of the objects that art historians assemble under this head. There is no reason to believe that artifacts in precious metals, ivory, enamel, and silk were of less significance to their sponsors than major programs of church decoration. Indeed, it is the habit of Byzantine chroniclers to ascribe to emperors acts of patronage and even personal intervention in the creation of both sumptuous gifts sent overseas and elaborate fittings for the Great Palace in Constantinople.

Even if such reports generally have the character of a topos (a conventional figure of speech), it would be wrong to discount them all since some tell of an emperor's interest in the arts that can be independently verified. For example, Constantine VII Porphyrogenitos (913–959) is said to have been a painter in his own right and to have advised marble- and metalworkers. He is credited with a fountain in the vestibule of his apartment in the palace adorned with a silver eagle holding a snake in its claws. Such a motif had appeared four centuries earlier among the palace's floor mosaics; this sort of attention to the past is consistent with what we know of Constantine's interests from other sources. We know his fountain and hundreds of analogous works only from written documents.

As has been pointed out in the general article on Byzantine art, our picture of the industries of art is severely limited by the survival of only a small fraction of the objects produced. The magnitude of this loss can be understood, if not estimated, only in light of references in chronicles, wills, monastic typika, inventories, and other deeds to splendid Byzantine possessions in all mediums.

If the picture that results is restricted, it is still a useful corrective for the distortions created by unsupported hypotheses. For instance, it is commonly assumed of the middle and late Byzantine periods that sumptuous objects of art were made in the imperial palace. Save perhaps for silk weaving and the manufacture of ceremonial costumes and some forms of insignia, proof of an aulic origin (as opposed to aulic patronage) for most such objects is lacking. And given repeated textual references to the importation of both raw silk and silk clothing, it is doubtful that the imperial *gynaikion* could have supplied all Constantinople's needs.

Silk manufacture is known in Corinth and Thebes

in the eleventh century and the fabrication of gold cloth in Cyprus not much later. Constantinopolitan texts imply, and occasionally stipulate, the existence in the city of workshops making everything from sails to jewelry, to which presumably imperial and other courtly commissions were delivered. The tenth-century Book of the Eparch (prefect) regulates the division of labor among these trades and the location of their ateliers, controls that would hardly have been necessary if these shops had been located in the palace precinct. Nor should one take the various treasuries in the palace—the Idikon, the Vestiarion, the Koiton—for the sites where the precious objects that they contained were made. Aulic manufacture attested to in the early Byzantine period does not mean that craftsmen continued to work in the Great Palace and its successors down to the end of the empire.

Suppositions about the chronology of manufacture can be equally misleading. While it is possible to discern some broad technical, stylistic, and iconographic characteristics that serve to support the idea of temporal development, any notion of a simple linear evolution is to be avoided. Changes in form are to be explained not only in terms of time. Different regional traditions and skills, the diverse talents of individual craftsmen, the varying constraints of different mediums, the nature of the models employed, and the social status of a patron and the size of his purse are among the factors that, while complicating the art historian's task, invalidate the notion that we should seek to unravel a single strand of stylistic development. It is perhaps for this reason that most useful accounts of this region's minor arts have been "vertical"—studies of a single medium and its historical development. Yet, fraught with difficulty though the venture may be, if the achievements of any period are to be understood its productions must be considered "horizontally"—the "minor arts" of a period related to other crafts, and to the culture that commissioned, made, and paid for them. One way to approach this end is to pursue a path signposted with "landmark" objects that can plausibly be connected with particular patrons or artifacts that on other grounds are either dated or datable.

If the ascription to various emperors of a direct interest in the arts is a commonplace in the Byzantine sources, so too is the assertion that in times of economic stress, they melted down the imperial, ecclesiastical, and monastic patrimony of objects in precious metal. Again, some of these statements are likely to be true. The repeated destruction of expensive works of art may well have been as responsible as iconoclasm for the loss of many objects. Michael III (842–867) is said to have melted down the finest examples of goldsmiths' work from his father's reign as well as court costumes woven with gold thread. Yet this emperor, like others, may have given as much as he took. The monumental bronze door which survives in the southwest vestibule of St. Sophia is inlaid in silver with the monograms of Theophilos, his father, and Michael. This and the great gates that Justinian had installed in the narthex of the Great Church were only the most famous of several such doors in Constantinople.

Michael III is credited with many other gifts to St. Sophia and to Rome, including a Gospelbook illuminated by the famous icon painter Lazaros covered in gem-studded gold, a golden chalice, and a figured purple silk. He sent to Pope Nicholas I (858–867) a fabric woven with pictures of Christ and the Apostles. These and other lost objects show that the industries of art were alive and well in the aftermath of iconoclasm, even if monumental painting does not seem to have been revived until the very end of his reign.

Michael's successor, Basil I (867–886), the founder of the Macedonian dynasty, continued these traditions both as acts of foreign policy—notably a great rock-crystal vase adorned with gold and precious stones sent to Louis II the German—and as domestic demonstrations of piety. Basil gave to the Nea, his "New Church" in the palace, a silver chancel barrier decorated with precious stones and pearls, while the pavement of the chapel of the Savior in the same precinct was covered with leaves of hammered silver enriched with niello. That the craft of enamel, represented during iconoclasm by the lavish reliquary cross commissioned by Pope Paschal I (817–824), returned to flower in early Macedonian Constantinople is attested by the gold entablature of the *templon* in the same Savior chapel, on which "the image of our Lord, the God-man, is represented several times in enamel."

This is reported in the *Life* of Basil by his grandson Constantine VII. Born in the palace's "purple chamber"—a locus that denoted dynastic authority as much as luxury to the Byzantines—the third Macedonian emperor is rightly understood as turning the attention of craftsmen toward the past in a movement often hailed as a "renaissance." But the

Ivory triptych, 925–950. Palazzo Venezia, Rome. ALINARI/EDITORIAL PHOTOCOLOR ARCHIVES

justification for such a term should encompass both style and subject matter, conditions met by ivories such as the great triptych in the Palazzo Venezia in Rome and manuscripts such as the Joshua Roll in the Vatican Library (Pal. gr. 431). While the inscription on the triptych seems to allude to Constantine, the Joshua Roll and other manuscripts are more likely to be connected with other tenth-century patrons. There can be no doubt that this style does not revert to the beginning of the Macedonian dynasty. Ivories such as the casket with scenes from the life of David, probably made for the accession of Basil I as coemperor in 866, and this ruler's great copy of the *Homilies* of Gregory of Nazianzus (Paris, Bibliothèque Nationale, MS gr. 510) prepared between 880 and 883, show few signs of the figure style of the "renaissance."

Once established, however, this manner dominated the production of precious artifacts into the eleventh century. Indeed, only recently has a group of ivories made under Romanos IV (1068–1071) been categorically distinguished from similar pieces carved more than a century earlier. There were no fewer than four emperors of this period named Romanos, a fact that enormously complicates the dating of ivories and other luxurious objects (such as a magnificent sardonyx chalice in the treasury of S. Marco in Venice) inscribed with this name.

Problems other than dating beset the notion of a "Macedonian renaissance." First, one may ask whether the classical models supposedly tapped for the production of objects such as the Veroli Casket in London were known directly or through early Byzantine intermediaries. While an enameled bowl in Venice, bearing figures from antique life and myth, seems to have drawn indiscriminately on a group of Hellenistic and Roman gemstones, a book like the Bible of Niketas (now divided between libraries in Florence, Turin, and Copenhagen) has been shown to copy a prototype of Justinian's time. So, too, many motifs on middle Byzantine ivories are demonstrably dependent on forms carved in the same medium in the sixth century. Niketas was a *protospatharios,* an official at the court of Basil II (976–1025). The decoration of his Bible shows that the "renaissance" style was a court style, a claim confirmed by the chalcedony goblet in Venice of Sisinnios, patrician and logothete of the treasury under Romanos II.

The second question born of this matter of patronage is, then, the extent to which a particular style or medium is coextensive with a particular social stratum. The surviving evidence, where it can be connected with specific individuals, suggests that, rather than style, a sense of luxury was the objective of patrons and customers from high court officials to individuals much further down the social scale. Certainly the use of semiprecious stones was no aulic prerogative. The *Life* of St. Nikon Metanoietes (*d.* 998) tells of a curious scoop (or spoon?) made of sardonyx that was the only possession taken by the saint from his father's house. Similarly, not all objects in which much older forms are revived can be attributed to a taste for the past. A middle Byzantine lead pendant (Houston, Menil Collection) showing

Ring of Michael Attaleiates, gold and enamel, 2nd half of 11th century. COURTESY OF THE DUMBARTON OAKS COLLECTION, WASHINGTON D.C.

St. Symeon Stylites upon his column in a fashion very similar to sixth-century examples in clay is better explained by the Byzantine reconquest of the region of Antioch under John Tzimiskes (969–976), and the consequent reopening of the area for pilgrimage, than by any "renaissance" instinct.

The passion for lavishness in a man's own possessions and his donations to holy sites made not only for "norms" in Byzantine decoration but also for a socially acceptable means of expressing his vanity and ambition. The common factor binding works in many mediums, produced in very different parts of the empire, is an ostentatious display of richness and color. In their descriptions of books and liturgical vessels, two eleventh-century figures, Michael Attaleiates and Eustathios Boilas, stress the gold bindings and brilliance of the objects that they record as gifts to monasteries they had founded. This predilection is seen in the polychrome marquetry that decorated the monastery church of Constantine Lips, founded in Constantinople in 908 and today known as Fenari Isa Camii; the ring of Michael Attaleiates, preserved at Dumbarton Oaks, is the enameled embodiment of the same taste.

Among the preserved objects the fondness for color and luxe is found at its purest in enamels, which from the tenth century were generally set in a gold ground, in contrast to the earlier technique of all-over glass flux used on the cross of Paschal I and the votive crown of Leo VI in Venice. The new manner is supremely exemplified in the reliquary of the True Cross at Limburg an der Lahn, inscribed for Basil, illegitimate son of Romanos I and bearer of the title *proedros* created for him in 963. As many as four different shades of blue are used on the costumes of the archangels on the inside of this box. Yet, singular object that the reliquary is, it should still be recognized that most enamels were probably made in series. The features and nimbus of Christ on the reverse of the Limburg reliquary are identical in form and color to those on an enamel clasp at Dumbarton Oaks.

This method of production was necessitated by the prodigal use of enamel in secular decoration (ceremonial shields and the like) and imperial objects such as the sarcophagus of John Tzimiskes. In this respect, the production of enamels differs from the illumination of books which nonetheless, in the

Reliquary of the True Cross, gold and enamel 10th century. Cathedral Treasury, Limburg an der Lahn. BILDARCHIV FOTO MARBURG

eleventh and twelfth centuries, exhibit the same aesthetic of small polychrome figures glinting like gems against a golden ground. Clearly color was prized for its own sake. Ivory panels, often used as icons in the form of diptychs and triptychs, were painted, and the soft stone known to us as steatite was prized not so much as a substitute for ivory but for the range of hues—reddish brown, yellow, and jade green—that it offered. Even the great bronze doors sent from the capital to the West, like those made in 1070 for the Church of S. Paolo Fuori le Mura in Rome, were inlaid with silver and enamel and represent a stage of embellishment beyond that of early Byzantine doors. It is unlikely that such works were made only for export and probable that they were considered masterpieces in their time: defying the supposed anonymity of Byzantine art, the S. Paolo doors are signed by the caster Stavrakios.

Imperial and aristocratic costume is a genre of Byzantine art that is all but lost to us and knowable only through texts and its depiction in manuscript illumination. The *Cletorlogion* of Philotheos (899) suggests a strict hierarchical distribution of aulic garments and insignia, a rigidity presumably moderated beyond the throne room by fashion and social aspiration. That the early Byzantine taste for figured textiles did not disappear is indicated by descriptions of furnishings of the palace in the tenth-century Book of Ceremonies as well as by examples of silks exported to the West and used in the graves of kings and ecclesiastics. In the early-eleventh-century Menologion of Basil II, emperors and empresses of the past are shown in richly colored and pearl-bedecked regalia as spectators at the invention or translation of relics, while the saints themselves are frequently dressed as high officials of the middle Byzantine court. The motifs on their garments are generally either geometrical or stylized vegetal motifs, particularly rosettes and ivy leaves. Such ornament swiftly migrated to the decoration of Christian subject matter in wall painting and books.

The recurrence of figural and ornamental motifs in various mediums is due not to their manufacture by the same artists but to the taste of the patron and the concerns of his milieu. It is this taste that links objects normally, and inappropriately, separated by art historians into categories of "religious" and "secular" art, a distinction that would never have occurred to Byzantines, who were at once connoisseurs of Classical literature and Orthodox Christians. Basil the *proedros,* the donor of the Limburg reliquary, commissioned not only a manuscript of the works of St. John Chrysostom (Athos, Dionysiu cod. 70) with ornament similar to that on the reliquary but also a luxury edition of an ancient work on naval tactics.

Mobility can be recognized not only with regard to geography—as in the case of enamels from the mid-twelfth-century Pantokrator monastery that seem to have been reused on the Pala d'Oro in S. Marco, Venice—but across different mediums and transcending social classes in Byzantium. Thus already in the eleventh century we find the transformation of St. Dimitrios from a courtier in civil garb to an armed warrior on ivories, enamels, manuscripts, and metalwork. And within a short span of time (the second half of the twelfth century) the iconography of the Man of Sorrows occurs on a steatite (Leningrad, Hermitage) and in a Gospelbook of provincial origin (Leningrad, Public Library, cod. 105, fol. 65v).

Each of these examples demonstrates what are

Enameled glass bowl with mythological figures, 11th century. Treasury of St. Mark's, Venice. PHOTOGRAPH, OSWALDO BÖHM

only superficially paradoxes: that out of the increasingly military, clan-dominated society that was Komnenian Byzantium was born an interest in the pathetic, human aspects of Christ and his Mother; and that Western feudal and chivalric elements were known in Byzantine art and literature in the century immediately before the Crusaders seized Constantinople (1204). Ceramics, by contrast, produced for local consumption and a broader audience, often exhibit distinct regional techniques and sometimes forms influenced by Islamic rather than Western sources.

The occupation of the capital and the reduction of the empire's dimensions have overshadowed two social processes that found expression in the "minor arts" of the twelfth century. The fact that provincial aristocrats and ecclesiastics preferred to live in Constantinople meant that there they could commission works that they often removed to far-flung localities. Thus, objects bearing their names rehearse both metropolitan style and iconography. This tendency was reinforced at the regional level by imitations of Constantinopolitan manners and materials, such as the fragmentary, provincial imitations of middle Byzantine ivory triptychs preserved in Leningrad. Similarly, bronze and lead enkolpia (pendants) and crosses faithfully reproduce exemplars in silver. And beyond the empire, even before the Fourth Crusade, Venetian workshops were producing almost indistinguishable copies of Byzantine glass and gemstones.

Even though some Constantinopolitan craftsmen stayed in the capital and others went abroad to work for Latin patrons, during the residence of the emperors in Nicaea an edict of John III Vatatzes (1222–1254) forbade the import of "barbarian" products. This is obviously an imperial attempt to protect locally made products in an era when commerce was increasingly dominated by the West. Yet Orthodox patrons continued to patronize Greek artists: an icon of the Virgin, now in Freising Cathedral, is surrounded by archangels, apostles, and the *hetoimasia* (the "prepared throne") and bears a dedicatory inscription of Manuel Disypatos, metropolitan of Thessaloniki (1235–1261). This swiftly reached the West (Milan) and already exhibits traits associated with the art of the Palaiologan period (1261–1453). So, too, a sardonyx cameo in the Metropolitan Museum of Art, New York, bearing an image of the archangel Michael, has the tiny head and sinuous form of the military saints painted in the monastery

Sardonyx cameo of the archangel Michael, 1316–1321. THE METROPOLITAN MUSEUM OF ART, THE MILTON WEIL COLLECTION: GIFT OF MRS. EDITH WEIL WORGILT, 1940 (40.20.58)

Church of the Chora (Kariye Camii) between about 1316 and 1321.

The Chora is a reminder that Byzantine construction at many periods employed elements from past buildings. Some of its sculpture has been shown to revert to the sixth century. It is dangerous to identify this pragmatic use of *spolia* with the "renaissance" movement that has been suggested for the first half of the fourteenth century, as for many other periods. But it is certainly true that notable individual works depended on earlier achievements. A fourteenth-century sarcophagus in the Archaeological Museum, Istanbul, directly copies a fourth-century child's sarcophagus now in the same museum; and Palaiologan icons, like one of the Annunciation in the Pushkin Museum, Moscow, derive motifs from the Macedonian era. Rather than a programmatic renaissance, a self-conscious use of the Byzantine past of all periods seems evident in the creations of an empire limited to Constantinople and portions of the Greek mainland.

This inward-looking society, its artistic attentions focused on aristocratic families and the monasteries they had founded or restored, still sponsored elaborate objects. Imperial commissions are rare, but one undisputed example is a tiny ivory box, preserved at Dumbarton Oaks, depicting scions of the family of John V Palaiologos (1347–1391). Men of the rank of Theodore Metochites, patron of the Chora, ordered miniature mosaic icons, of which some forty specimens survive; the patrons of other panels are celebrated in epigrams by Manuel Philes and other paid poetasters. Beyond this small, precious body of work in the capital, manuscripts were still illuminated (just as churches were still decorated) in Thessaloniki and

Ivory pyxis showing scenes commemorating the installation of John VII Palaiologos as emperor. Thessaloniki, *ca.* 1403/1404. COURTESY OF THE DUMBARTON OAKS COLLECTION, WASHINGTON, D.C.

southern Greece. It was in the Peloponnese, in the fifteenth century, that the last monuments of Byzantium were created. At Mistra in particular, nuns produced embroidery in a tradition that continues to this day.

BIBLIOGRAPHY

General. Alisa Bank, *Byzantine Art in the Collections of the U.S.S.R.* (1966), in Russian and English; Anthony Cutler, "Art in Byzantine Society," in *Jahrbuch der österreichischen Byzantinistik,* **31** (1981); Jean Ebersolt, *Les arts somptuaires de Byzance* (1923); André Grabar, "Le succès des arts orientaux à la cour byzantine sous les Macédoniens," in *Münchner Jahrbuch der bildenden Kunst,* **3** (1951); Hans R. Hahnloser, ed., *Il tesoro di San Marco,* 2 vols. (1965–1971); Cyril Mango, *Art of the Byzantine Empire* (1972).

Specific mediums. Margaret English Frazer, "Church Doors and the Gates of Paradise: Byzantine Bronze Doors in Italy," in *Dumbarton Oaks Papers,* **27** (1973); Adolph Goldschmidt and Kurt Weitzmann, *Die byzantinischen Elfenbeinskulpturen des X.–XIII. Jahrhunderts,* 2 vols. (1930–1934); André Grabar, *Sculptures byzantines de Constantinople (IVe–Xe siècles)* (1963); "La verrerie d'art byzantin au moyen âge," in *Monumenta Piot,* **57** (1971); and *Sculptures byzantines du moyen âge (XIe–XVe siècles)* (1976); Ioli Kalevrezou-Maxeiner, "Eudokia Makrembolitissa and the Romanos Ivory," in *Dumbarton Oaks Papers,* **31** (1977); and *Byzantine Steatites* (in press); W. Eugene Kleinbauer, "A Byzantine Revival: The Inlaid Bronze Doors of Constantinople," in *Archaeology,* **29** (1976); Marvin C. Ross, *Catalogue of the Byzantine and Early Medieval Antiquities in the Dumbarton Oaks Collections,* 2 vols. (1962–1965); Marvin C. Ross and Glanville Downey, "An Emperor's Gift—and Notes on Byzantine Silver Jewelry of the Middle Period," in *Journal of the Walters Art Gallery,* **19–20** (1956–1957); Gary Vikan, *Byzantine Pilgrimage Art* (1982); Kurt Weitzmann, *Catalogue of the Byzantine and Early Mediaeval Antiquities in the Dumbarton Oaks Collection,* III (1972); Klaus Wessel, *Byzantine Enamels from the 5th to the 13th Century,* Irene R. Gibbons, trans. (1967).

ANTHONY CUTLER

[See also **Costume, Byzantine; Enamel, Enamel Making; Icons, Manufacture of; Ivory Carving; Manuscript Illumination.**]

BYZANTINE CHURCH. The transfer of the capital of the Roman Empire to Constantinople in 324 and the protection accorded to the church by Emperor Constantine and his successors created an entirely new condition in Christendom. In the West barbarian invasions soon greatly reduced the influence of the empire, but in the East it stood firm. Constantinople, the "New Rome," also called Byzantium—the name of the ancient city on the Bosporus, chosen by Constantine as the location of the new capital—survived in that role until 1453. For more than a millennium it was the recognized center of Orthodox Christianity for much of eastern Europe and the Middle East. The term "Byzantium" is used today to designate both the city of Constantinople and the Eastern Roman Empire, in order to distinguish them from the "Old Rome" and from the pagan empire. The role of the church of Constantinople in Christianizing the East is in almost every way similar to the achievements of the Roman church in the Latin West. One should note, however, that the word "Byzantine" was seldom used in the Middle Ages: the "Byzantines" spoke Greek and called themselves Romans. The Latin West also designated the empire as Romania; the Muslims, as Rum.

CHURCH AND STATE

The survival of the empire in the East assured an active role for the emperor in the affairs of the church. This does not mean, however, that the relations between church and state in Byzantium can be expressed in any simple formula or concept, such as "caesaropapism." Unquestionably the Christian empire inherited from pagan times the administrative and financial routine of overseeing religious affairs, and this routine was applied to the Christian church, almost automatically and without objections from anyone, by Constantine. But the Christian faith was incompatible with the Hellenistic and Roman idea of the emperor as a divine being: Christ was the only king, the only *kyrios.* So, following the pattern set by Eusebius of Caesarea, who delivered a funeral oration for Constantine (337), the Byzantines thought of the emperor as Christ's representative or messenger, "equal to the apostles" *(isapostolos),* responsible particularly for the propagation of Christianity among pagans and for the "externals" of the Christian religion, such as administration and finances (hence the title used by Eusebius, *episkopos tōn ektos*).

This imperial role in the affairs of the church never developed into a fixed, legally defined system. It was clearly conditioned by one decisive factor: the emperor's doctrinal orthodoxy. A heretical emperor was not to be obeyed. Numerous heroes of the faith—Athanasius of Alexandria (*d.* 373), John Chrysostom (*d.* 407), Maximus the Confessor (*d.* 662), John of Damascus (*d. ca.* 750), Theodore of Studios (759–826)—were venerated as saints after their deaths because of their resistance to imperial will, and the memory of many emperors, particularly Constantius I (337–361), Leo III (717–741), Constantine V (741–775), and Michael VIII (1259–1282), was formally cursed because of their support for heterodox doctrines.

The text that comes closest to a theoretical definition of church-state relations in Byzantium is *Novella* 6 of Justinian (527–565), which defines the priesthood and the imperial dignity as "the two greatest gifts of God" to mankind, and insists on their common divine origin. The ideal, as presented in the *Novella*, is a "harmony" between the two powers. The idea of a joint responsibility to God of the emperor and the patriarch of Constantinople is expressed in the *Epanagoge,* a legal compendium of the ninth century. These texts, however, sound more like pious exhortations than legal definitions. The Byzantines were well aware of the difficulty of expressing, in terms of the Christian faith, the dynamic and polarized relationship between the "earthly" and the "heavenly," the "old" and the "new," the "secular" and the "holy."

In court ceremonial and in official texts the emperor was often described in terms of Old Testament kingship; but as David and Solomon anticipated the kingdom of the Messiah, so the emperor of the Christians was necessarily seen as an image of Christ. He convened councils and could, if he wished, exercise a decisive influence on ecclesiastical appointments, including those of the patriarch of Constantinople and of those prelates who played an important diplomatic role in Byzantine foreign affairs (such as the archbishop of Ochrid, and the metropolitan of Russia). Out of 122 patriarchs of Constantinople elected between 379 and 1451, thirty-six were forced to resign under imperial pressure. But the relative dependence of the patriarchal office upon the emperor must be understood in the context of the instability of the imperial office itself: two-thirds of all Byzantine emperors were either killed or dethroned, and many were, at least partially, the victims of their own religious policies.

THE EASTERN PATRIARCHATES

As Christianity was becoming the official religion of the Roman state—a process that began under Constantine and was completed under Theodosius I (379–395)—the church had no administrative structure on a universal scale. The Council of Nicaea (325) acknowledged only the authority of provincial episcopal synods, presided over by their "metropolitans" and invested with the power of appointing new bishops (canons 4 and 5). It also recognized that some episcopal sees enjoyed traditional prestige that transcended the limits of a single province: the three sees mentioned specifically are Alexandria, Antioch, and Rome (canon 6). In the East both Alexandria and Antioch played a significant role in ecclesiastical affairs and theological controversies of the fourth century; they were unquestionably the intellectual and cultural centers of Eastern Christendom, and by the fifth century their incumbents were generally using the title "patriarch."

The archbishop of Alexandria—also designated "pope"—headed a church that not only had its roots in early Christianity (for instance, the prestige of the school of Origen in the third century), but also controlled the three civil "dioceses" (large administrative units) of Egypt, Libya, and Pentapolis, where the Christian faith had early been accepted by the masses. Missionaries from Alexandria converted Ethiopia to the Christian faith in the fourth century. Athanasius of Alexandria had been the hero of the anti-Arian struggle. His successor, Cyril, obtained the condemnation of Nestorius at the Council of Ephesus (431). However, Cyril's nephew and successor, Dioscorus, rejected the Definition of the Council of Chalcedon (451) that Christ had two distinct natures—one divine and one human—existing inseparably in one person. These theological developments all expressed the typical Alexandrian concern for the divinity of Christ, even at the price of minimizing the reality of his humanity. The anti-Chalcedonian schism of the Monophysites, followed by the majority of the Coptic population in Egypt, was instrumental not only in permanently breaking the religious unity of the Byzantine Empire, but also in facilitating the Muslim conquest of Egypt.

In Antioch the exegetical tradition was different from that of Alexandria, less philosophical and more oriented toward biblical history. There was a long resistance to the Nicaean (and Alexandrian) identification of Christ as "one substance" with the Father, and after the triumph of Nicaean orthodoxy, some Antiochenes defended a Christology that emphasized the genuine humanity of Jesus. Ecclesiastically the "patriarchate" of Antioch, which included the civil "diocese" of the East, was less monolithic than Egypt: it included a mixed (Greek and Syriac) population and sent successful missions to Persia, Armenia, and Georgia. After 431 some of its theologians who followed the condemned teaching of Nestorius emigrated to Persia. Divided, in the fifth and sixth centuries, between Chalcedonians and Monophysites, Antioch lost much of its prestige and influence before being taken over first by the Persians, then by the Arabs.

In the decades following the Council of Nicaea (325), a third major ecclesiastical center developed in the East. Constantinople had nothing of the antiquity and prestige of Alexandria or Antioch, but closeness to the imperial court gave its bishop a singular advantage in influencing ecclesiastical affairs. Thus in 381, as Theodosius I gathered the second ecumenical council to settle the Arian dispute, the bishop of the new imperial capital was formally recognized as having "priority of honor" after the bishop of Rome, because Constantinople was "the New Rome" (canon 3). The frankly political grounds for Constantinople's elevation were further emphasized in canon 28 of the Council of Chalcedon (451), which became the charter of the capital's ecclesiastical rights:

> The Fathers rightly granted privileges to the throne of old Rome, because it was the imperial city. And one hundred and fifty most religious bishops [at Constantinople in 381], actuated by the same considerations, gave equal privileges to the most holy throne of New Rome, justly judging that the city, which is honored with the presence of the emperor and the Senate and enjoys equal [civil] privileges with the old imperial Rome, should, in ecclesiastical matters also, be magnified as she is and rank next after her.

The text goes on to grant the bishop of Constantinople jurisdiction over the civil dioceses of Pontus, Asia, and Thrace—creating a "patriarchate" comparable with those of Rome, Alexandria, and Antioch—and bestows upon him the right to send missionary bishops to "barbarian lands" situated beyond these dioceses.

Historically, the creation of a Constantinopolitan primacy by the councils of Constantinople and Chalcedon was directed primarily against what the emperors considered an exaggerated power of Alexandria, which tended to impose its particular (and sometimes extremist) interpretation of the faith defined in Nicaea and in Ephesus. The councils of Constantinople and Chalcedon gave a more balanced definition of that faith that was more acceptable in Antioch and in Rome.

The formulation of canon 28 of Chalcedon had even wider implications: it affirmed that the privileges of the "Old Rome" were, like the new privileges of Constantinople, granted by "the Fathers," that consequently they were of human origin and had no connection with the logia of Christ addressed to the apostle Peter. In the fifth century the idea that the Roman bishop enjoyed primacy because he was the successor of Peter was firmly implanted in Rome, and served as the main argument for Pope Leo the Great (440–461) when he protested against the adoption of canon 28 at Chalcedon. Furthermore, the prevailing Roman interpretation of the Eastern primacies was that they also were created by Peter, who personally preached in Antioch (Galatians 2) and, according to tradition, sent his disciple Mark to Alexandria. In this scheme there was no place for any primacy of Constantinople.

To the Easterners the scheme seemed quite artificial. They did not consider that the apostolic foundation of a church involved jurisdictional rights, since so many Eastern cities—Jerusalem in the first place—could claim them, and they interpreted all primacies, including those of Alexandria, Antioch, and, indeed, Rome, in a pragmatic way, as a natural consequence of their being "major cities." Hence, the new role of Constantinople appeared quite natural to them.

The difference between the Eastern and the Western approach to the problem of primacies is best illustrated by the history of the church of Jerusalem.

Mentioned under its Roman name of Aelia by the Council of Nicaea (canon 7), it remained in the orbit of Antioch until after 451. Using its prestige as a pilgrimage center, it then acquired the status of a separate patriarchate, including the three provinces of Palestine, as a result of clever maneuvering by its bishop, Juvenal (422–458). However, in the order of the five main patriarchates its apostolic, or indeed divine, foundation was never used to justify anything but a last place.

Thus, as Justinian embarked on a major attempt to restore the empire's universality by reconquest of the West, the Byzantine vision of the universal church was that of a pentarchy of patriarchs—of Rome, Constantinople, Alexandria, Antioch, and Jerusalem—united in faith, equal in rights, but strictly bound by an order of precedence enshrined in imperial law. The Monophysite schism, the Islamic conquest, and, in the West, the rise of the papacy soon ended the pentarchy as a concrete historical reality, but it survived as an ideal of the Byzantine vision of the Christian universe.

THE "GREAT CHURCH" OF CONSTANTINOPLE

With the decline of ancient Rome and internal dissensions in the other Eastern patriarchates, the church of Constantinople became, between the sixth and the eleventh centuries, the richest and the most influential center of Christendom. As a symbol and expression of this universal prestige, Justinian built a church that remains the masterpiece of Byzantine architecture: the temple of the Holy Wisdom, Hagia Sophia. Completed in the amazingly short period of four and a half years (532–537), it became the heart of Christian Byzantium. The term "Great Church," first applied to the building itself, also designated the patriarchate, of which Hagia Sophia would remain the cathedral church for more than nine centuries. Its main and most visible structure consists of an immense square hall, covered by a wide dome. The light coming from all directions, the marble walls, and the golden mosaics have often been seen as representing the cosmos, upon which heaven itself had descended. The overwhelming impression produced by the building upon Greeks and foreigners alike is recorded in numerous contemporary texts.

Under John the Faster (582–595) the title "ecumenical patriarch" was adopted by the archbishop of Constantinople. This title was interpreted by Pope Gregory the Great as a challenge to papal primacy, but in fact it did not imply a claim to universal jurisdiction but, rather, to a permanent and essentially political position in the *oikoumene* (the *orbis christianorum*, the Christian world), which was ideally headed by the emperor. Together with the latter, the patriarch was responsible for the well-being of society, occasionally substituting for the emperor as regent. This was the case, for example, with Patriarch Sergios (610–638) under Emperor Heraklios (610–641) and with Patriarch Nicholas Mystikos (901–907, 912–925) during the infancy of Emperor Constantine VII. The respective rights and duties of the dyarchy of emperor and patriarch are described in the *Epanagoge,* a legal compendium of the ninth century.

Ecclesiastical canons and imperial laws regulated the election of patriarchs. Justinian (*Novella* 174, issued in 565) required that an electoral college of clergy and "important citizens"—not unlike the college of cardinals in Rome—participate in the election, but the laity, with the exception of the emperor, were soon eliminated from the process. According to Constantine Porphyrogenitos, the metropolitans of the synod chose three candidates so that the emperor could pick one, while reserving for himself the option of making another choice as well. This openly admitted role of the emperor—which formally contradicted canonical proscriptions against the choice of clerics by civil rulers—was perhaps understandable in view of the political functions of the "ecumenical" patriarch in the state.

Once enthroned in Hagia Sophia, the patriarch administered the church together with a "permanent synod" of metropolitans and a large staff. His jurisdiction covered the civil dioceses of Asia, Pontus, and Thrace, which in the seventh century included 424 episcopal sees. In the eighth century the dioceses of Illyricum and southern Italy were included in the patriarchate of Constantinople, at the expense of the church of Rome. In addition numerous missionary dioceses, subject to the patriarchate, existed in the Caucasus, the Crimea, and Slavic lands. A spectacular new expansion took place with the conversion of Russia (988–989).

Chosen mostly from the secular clergy of Constantinople in the earlier period, more frequently from the monastics after the thirteenth century, and sometimes promoted directly from the lay state, the patriarchs, with a few exceptions, were men of learning—and sometimes authentic saints. Their list includes Gregory of Nazianzus (379–381), John Chrysostom (398–404), Tarasius (784–806), Nikephoros (806–815), Photios (858–867, 877–886), Arsenios Autoreianos (1255–1259, 1261–1265), and Philotheos Kokkinos (1353–1354, 1364–1376). The often stormy politics of the court and the never-ending christological controversies necessarily involved the patriarchs. Some of them, such as Nestorius (428–431), entered history with the reputation of heresiarchs. Others, particularly during the reign of Heraklios and Constans II, followed the imperial policy of the moment and gave active support to Monotheletism (which stated that Christ had two natures but only one will). This was the case with Sergios (610–638), Pyrrhus (638–641), Paul (641–653), and Peter (654–666). They were condemned as heretics by the Third Council of Constantinople (680).

The Roman popes, although they never formally recognized the title "ecumenical patriarch" for the incumbents of the see of Constantinople and occasionally obtained from them the verbal acknowledgment of their "Petrine" succession as an important factor in the exercise of their primatial authority, could do nothing but admit the real influence of the imperial church, especially during their visits to Constantinople. One of them, Pope Martin I (649–655), was judged and deposed in Constantinople by an ecclesiastical tribunal presided over by the Monothelite patriarch Peter.

Thus, the see of Constantinople's "equal privileges" with "Old Rome" was an essential fact of history, but it certainly could not pretend to doctrinal infallibility.

THE ARAB CONQUEST AND ICONOCLASM

In the seventh century, when the Islamic wave swept over the ancient Christian and Byzantine provinces of Palestine, Syria, Egypt, and North Africa, stopping only at the gates of Constantinople, most Christians of those areas had already severed their ties with the imperial Orthodox church. Egypt had been almost entirely Monophysite since the middle of the fifth century; so were the Armenian regions in eastern Asia Minor and at least half of the population in Syria. The efforts of Justinian, and later the doctrinal compromises of Heraklios and his Monothelite successors, had failed to unify the empire religiously. Furthermore, the Monophysite schism that started with a dispute between Greek-speaking theologians over the true identity of Jesus Christ had developed into cultural, ethnic, and political antagonism. In the Middle East in the seventh century, the Chalcedonian Orthodox camp was composed almost entirely of Greeks loyal to the empire, whereas the indigenous communities of Copts, Syrians, and Armenians refused to accept the decree of the Council of Chalcedon and resented the brutal attempts of the imperial authorities to exile their leaders and impose religious conformity by force.

The Monophysite schism, followed by the Arab invasion, the success of which was partially due to dissension among Christians, left the patriarch of Constantinople alone as the foremost representative of Eastern Christianity within the borders of the empire. In Alexandria, Antioch, and particularly Jerusalem there remained "Melchite" (imperial) minorities, headed by their partiarchs, but they could have little influence in the universal church. For them, during the long centuries of Islamic occupation, the problem was one of survival, which they solved primarily by seeking and receiving cultural, psychological, and material help from Constantinople.

Reduced in size to the limits of western Asia Minor, the southern Balkan Peninsula, and southern Italy, the Byzantine Empire found enough strength for successful resistance to Islam. But during that struggle, between 726 and 843, Byzantine Christendom went through a major crisis that contributed much to its medieval shape: the crisis of iconoclasm and the eventual triumph of Orthodox *iconodulia* (reverence for images).

The doctrinal, philosophical, and theological background of Byzantine iconoclasm cannot be reduced to a simple scheme. The reluctance to use and venerate images in worship goes back to the prohibition of any representation of God in the Old Testament. Iconoclasm also was consistent with a certain Platonic spiritualism popular among Greek Christians, which explains why trends hostile to images existed in early Christianity. It is beyond doubt, however, that the iconoclastic movement of the eighth century was started by imperial initiative and had political implications in the framework of the struggle of the empire against Islam. Indeed, the Islamic belief in the absolute transcendence and invisibility of God and sharp polemics against Christian "idolatry" were essential arguments of the Muslim anti-Byzantine propaganda. Emperors Leo III (717–741) and Constantine V (741–775), sponsors of iconoclasm, decided to "clean" the Christian church of "idolatry," in order to fight Islamic ideology more successfully.

As images of Christ, the Virgin, and the saints began to be removed from public places and churches by order of Leo III (beginning in 726), the patriarch Germanos (715–730)—and also Pope Gregory II (715–731)—defended the veneration of icons, and John of Damascus, a theologian living in Muslim-dominated areas, wrote treatises against iconoclasm. The argument was that God, though invisible by nature, can and must be represented in his human nature, as Jesus Christ. According to the Orthodox, iconoclasm amounted to a denial of the Incarnation. An iconoclastic council, organized by Emperor Constantine V in 754, answered that a representation of Christ in his human nature implied either a denial of his divinity, which is inseparable from his humanity, or a Nestorian breaking up of his one person into two beings.

The debate continued—primarily on those christological grounds—for more than a century. Iconoclastic repressions were severe, and the Orthodox counted many martyrs in their midst. Besides John of Damascus, two major Byzantine theologians stood for the veneration of icons: Theodore of Studios (759–826) and Patriarch Nikephoros (806–815). Popular support of the veneration was led by the influential and numerous monastic communities, which then faced imperial wrath. Finally, the seventh ecumenical council (also known as the Second Council of Nicaea) was gathered by Empress Irene in 787. It rejected iconoclasm and endorsed the veneration *(proskynēsis)* of icons, carefully distinguishing it from worship *(latreia)*, which is due to God alone. After a second upsurge of iconoclasm there was a final "triumph of Orthodoxy" in 843.

The consequences of the crisis were both theological and cultural. In the Orthodox East images were accepted as a major means of communion with God, so that art, theology, and spirituality became inseparable. On another level the struggle on behalf of the icons enhanced the prestige of monasticism, which was acknowledged, more than in earlier centuries, as an effective counterweight to the arbitrary rule of the emperors. At the same time the iconoclastic crisis furthered the estrangement between the Eastern and the Western halves of Christendom. Fully involved in the struggle with Islam, the iconoclastic emperors neglected their power and influence in Italy. Furthermore, in retaliation against the pope's opposition to their religious policies, they transferred Illyricum, Sicily, and southern Italy from papal jurisdiction to that of the patriarchate of Constantinople. Humiliated and abandoned by his traditional protectors, and fearful of Lombard invasions, Pope Stephen II met with the Frankish king Pepin the Short at Ponthion (754), accepted the king's protection, and obtained his sponsorship in the creation of a papal state in Italy made up of former Byzantine territories.

MISSIONS: THE CONVERSION OF THE SLAVS

The loss of the Middle East to the Arabs and the gradual estrangement between East and West could have led the partiarchate of Constantinople to become the center of a Greek church, limited ethnically and culturally. However, immediately following the end of iconoclasm, the church of Byzantium began a spectacular missionary expansion that led to the Christianization of eastern Europe.

In 860–861 two brothers from Thessaloniki, Constantine and Methodios, successfully preached Christianity to the Khazars in the Crimea. In 863 they were sent to the Slavs of central Europe because Rastislav, prince of the Moravians, had requested missionaries from Byzantium. The Moravian mission of the brothers began with a complete and literal translation of Scripture and liturgy into the language of the Slavs. In the process the brothers created a new alphabet and vocabulary suitable for Christian usage. Furthermore, they justified the policy of translating essential Christian texts into the vernacular by references to the miracle of Pentecost (Acts 3).

This policy was fiercely opposed by competing Frankish missionaries, with whom the brothers had discussions in Moravia and later in Venice, and whom they accused of holding "the heresy of the three languages" (the belief that Christian worship is possible only in Hebrew, Greek, and Latin). In a prologue to the Gospel of John written in Slavic verse, Constantine (better known under his monastic name of Cyril) paraphrased St. Paul (1 Corinthians 14:19) in proclaiming the right of the Slavs to hear the Word in their own language: "I had rather speak five words that all the brethren will understand than ten thousand words which are incomprehensible."

Eventually the Byzantine missionaries were forced by the Germans to leave Moravia. Traveling to Rome, they received the formal support of popes Adrian II (867–872) and John VIII (872–882). After the death of Constantine-Cyril in Rome, Pope John consecrated Methodios as bishop of Sirmium and charged him with the mission to the Slavs. However, the authority of the pope was insufficient to secure the success of the mission; Methodios was tried and imprisoned by German bishops, so that Moravia joined Latin Christianity. Eventually the entire Western church adopted the principle of accepting only Latin in the liturgy, in sharp contrast with the

Byzantine missionary development, based upon translations and use of the vernacular. The Moravian disciples of Constantine-Cyril and Methodios found refuge in Bulgaria, particularly in the Macedonian center of Ochrid (St. Clement, St. Naum), where Slavic Christianity prospered in accordance with the Byzantine model.

The conversion of Bulgaria was practically contemporary with the Moravian mission. As in Moravia and many other areas of Europe, the political leadership of the country was instrumental in the conversion, which had been prepared by missionaries and diplomats from Byzantium. In 865 Khan Boris of Bulgaria became a Christian, with emperor Michael III acting as his godfather. After an attempt to join the jurisdiction of Rome (866–869), Boris placed his country in the Byzantine religious orbit. His son and successor, Symeon (893–927), and later the western Bulgarian czar Samuel (976–1014), made their respective capitals of Trnovo and Ochrid into important religious centers where Byzantine liturgy, theology, and religious culture were successfully appropriated by Slavs. And since Byzantine canon law in principle admitted a multiplicity of ecclesiastical centers, Bulgarian czars created independent patriarchates in their capitals. However, as they began to claim the imperial title for themselves, Byzantium, having regained its former military might, especially under Emperor Basil II (976–1025), put a temporary end to the independent existence of Bulgaria, but it did not entirely suppress the principle and the practice of worship in the Slavic tongue.

Also contemporary was the Byzantine mission to the Russians. In 866 Patriarch Photios, in an encyclical to Eastern patriarchs, announced that the Russians had been converted and had accepted a bishop from Constantinople. This initial conversion concerned only Byzantine cities in the Crimea. More significant were the conversion of Olga, the powerful princess of Kiev (957), who assumed the Christian name of Helen in honor of the reigning Byzantine empress, and the "conversion of Russia," which occurred in 988–989 under Prince Vladimir, who took the name of Basil and married Emperor Basil II's sister, Anna. Under Vladimir, Byzantine Orthodoxy became the official religion of the Russian state, with its major centers in Kiev and Novgorod.

Byzantine documents from the same period indicate missionary activities in the Caucasus, particularly among the Alani, under the initiative of patriarch Nicholas Mystikos (901–907, 912–925).

Thus, around the beginning of the second millennium, the Byzantine church exercised its ministry in a territory extending from northern Russia to the Arab-occupied Middle East, and from the Adriatic to the Caucasus. Its center, Constantinople, seemed to have no rival—not only in terms of power or wealth but also in terms of intellectual, artistic, and literary achievements.

SCHISM BETWEEN EAST AND WEST

A certain theological polarization between the Greek East and the Latin West goes back at least to the fourth century. For instance, Trinitarian theology was formulated differently by the Cappadocian fathers and by St. Augustine, with a greater insistence by the Greeks upon personal distinctiveness, and a greater emphasis by the Latins upon a philosophical definition of God as one simple essence. Also, Latins and Greeks often adopted divergent attitudes toward the Monophysites, with Rome remaining much more rigidly attached to the formula of the "two natures" adopted at Chalcedon, whereas Constantinople was more ready to remember that St. Cyril of Alexandria had spoken of "one incarnated nature." There was also increasing variety in disciplinary and liturgical practices.

More than any other difference, ecclesiological issues, in particular the increasingly divergent understanding of the primacy of Rome, began to strain relations between East and West. The leadership position of Rome—never denied in Byzantium—continued to be explained there (along with the eminence of the various Eastern sees) in a pragmatic way, without any decisive importance being attached to apostolicity. This explanation was enshrined in conciliar legislation, which the East considered as common tradition, even though the Romans in due time protested the publication of texts denying that Rome had received its primacy from Christ, through the apostle Peter. Fortunately both sides refrained for centuries from pushing these divergent positions to the point of final rupture. In the ninth, tenth, and eleventh centuries, however, conflicts arose in which cultural and political elements were intermingled with doctrinal and disciplinary issues.

The issue of the *Filioque* became, in the iconoclastic and posticonoclastic periods, a major source of conflict. The creed of Nicaea-Constantinople, which served as the principal expression of faith in the universal church, had been interpolated in the West with the Latin word *Filioque.* The interpolation, first made in Spain in the seventh century, affirmed that the Holy Spirit proceeded from the Father and the Son. The interpolated text soon became popular—partly because it suited the Augustinian explanation of the Trinity better than the original version—and in the eighth century it was used throughout Frankish Europe.

Charlemagne and his theologians, who were looking for an opportunity to accuse the competing Eastern Empire of heresy, refused to accept the Acts of the Second Council of Nicaea (787) because they contained the original form of the creed and traditional Greek formulations of the Trinitarian dogma. The *Libri Carolini* addressed to the pope by Charlemagne to justify his position were thus the first written monuments in a polemic that lasted for centuries. At first the popes defended the Greek position and opposed the interpolation. Only in 866 did Pope Nicholas I sponsor the activities of German missionaries in Bulgaria, implicitly condoning the use of the interpolated creed among newly converted Bulgarians.

Patriarch Photios, who considered Bulgaria part of his jurisdiction, became the first Greek theologian to give a complete refutation of the *Filioque*. The conflict between Pope Nicholas and Photios, which concerned issues of authority as well as the *Filioque* problem, was eventually solved. In 879–880 a solemn council, with legates of Pope John VIII present, condemned the interpolation and sanctioned a reconciliation between Rome and Constantinople. However, Frankish influence upon the weakened papacy of the tenth century led to an almost routine acceptance of the *Filioque* in Rome (probably in 1014), which made the schism practically inevitable.

Other issues of discipline and liturgy contributed to the division. These included the use of unleavened bread *(azymes)* in the Eucharist by the Latins, the enforced celibacy of priests in the West (while the East allowed the ordination of married men), and differences in the rules of fasting. These issues were particularly prominent during the famous incident that opposed the legates of Pope Leo IX to Patriarch Michael Keroullarios (1054).

When the Latins condemned certain Greek liturgical practices in southern Italy, Patriarch Keroullarios at first retaliated by ordering Latin churches in Constantinople to adopt the Greek rite. But he soon shifted to conciliation to comply with Emperor Constantine IX's policy of courting the support of Rome against the Normans. Subsequently, a papal legation was sent to Constantinople to negotiate. It pursued a strategy calculated to separate the emperor from the patriarch. But attacking Keroullarios only inflamed passions and increased support for him. What began as an effort to negotiate ended with mutual excommunications. The incident is frequently—and mistakenly—seen as the beginning of the schism. In reality it was an unsuccessful attempt to heal a division that already existed.

As polemics continued—and were greatly enhanced by national hatred after the sack of Constantinople by the Fourth Crusade in 1204—other issues were added to the list, such as the Latin doctrine of purgatory and the exact moment of consecration of the holy gifts in the Eucharist (the "words of institution" in the Latin tradition, to which the Greeks opposed the existence in all Eastern liturgies of an invocation of the Holy Spirit, or epiclesis, after the words of institution). Each of these issues, like that of the *Filioque,* could have been resolved if the two churches had been able to agree upon a criterion of authority. Especially after the Gregorian reform of the eleventh century, however, the papacy could not allow its unique authority to be questioned. On the Byzantine side the official position of the church was always that differences between churches were to be solved only by councils, and that the honorary primacy of Rome did not exempt the pope from being answerable to conciliar judgment.

Numerous attempts at reunion took place in the late Byzantine perod, initiated by the popes and by emperors of the Palaiologan dynasty (1261–1453). In 1274 representatives of Emperor Michael VIII were present at the Council of Lyons, where his personal acceptance of the Roman faith was read. Motivated primarily by political reasons, Michael imposed a pro-union patriarch, John Bekkos, on the church of Constantinople. But such a union, established basically by force, did not survive the death of Michael (1282). In 1285 a council in Constantinople formally rejected it, and approved a detailed—and in some ways open-minded—refutation of the *Filioque,* drafted by Patriarch Gregory II of Cyprus (1283–1289). More union negotiations took place throughout the fourteenth century, which saw the personal conversion to Roman Catholicism of Emperor John V (1369), a conversion that was not followed by the church and that was tacitly renounced by John himself.

It was the Western conciliar movement that provoked a radical change in the attitude of the papacy toward the idea of a real council of union. After long preliminary negotiations with Popes Martin V and Eugenius IV, Emperor John VIII, Patriarch Joseph

II, and numerous Greek prelates went to Ferrara, and then to Florence, where the council took place (1438–1439), as Byzantium stood under the immediate threat of Turkish conquest. After months of debate an exhausted Greek delegation signed the decree of union, which accepted the major doctrinal positions of the Roman church. Only one Greek bishop, Mark of Ephesus, refused to sign, but upon the delegation's return to Byzantium, Mark's position was endorsed by the vast majority of the population and the clergy. The fall of Constantinople in 1453 put an end to the union and to further negotiations.

Provoked by gradual estrangement, the schism cannot be formally associated with any particular date or event. Its ultimate root, however, was clearly a different understanding of doctrinal authority, which in the West had been concentrated in the person of the pope; the East never considered that truth could be formally secured by any particular person or institution, and saw no seat of authority above the conciliar process, which involved the bishops but also required a popular consensus.

THEOLOGY AND CANON LAW

Throughout its history Byzantium maintained an uninterrupted tradition of learning going back to antiquity and to the Greek fathers of the church. Although the imperial university of Constantinople and, particularly, the separate patriarchal school were training future officials of state and church, these institutions were neither the exclusive nor even the principal centers of theological development. Byzantium never witnessed the role of universities and formal Scholasticism, which appeared in the West in the twelfth century. Most Byzantine theologians wrote in an ecclesiastical or monastic context. But theology never became a monopoly of clerics: books on theology were published not only by bishops or monks but also by lay intellectuals.

The absence of a structured system of schools provides the probable explanation of why Byzantine theologians seldom undertook systematic presentation of their theology. St. John of Damascus (*d. ca.* 750) wrote *Exact Exposition of the Orthodox Faith,* a short textbook that faithfully adheres to formulations accepted in the past, not an original "system." In general, Byzantine theologians limited themselves to particular issues or denounced the heresies of their day. This lack of systematization does not imply that they did not believe in the effectiveness of theology. On the contrary, Byzantine spirituality, liturgy, and thought always affirmed the possibility of communion with God, accessible to every Christian in the life of the church.

But this accessibility did not include the essence of God, whose transcendence made intellectual or philosophical concepts—the basis for all structured theological "systems"—irrelevant, or at least unconvincing. This simultaneous perception of divine transcendence and accessibility was well expressed in the fourth century by St. Gregory of Nyssa, one of the most influential fathers of the Greek church: "In speaking of God," he writes, "when there is question of His essence, then there is the time to keep silence [see Ecclesiastes 3:7]. When, however, it is a question of His operation, a knowledge of which can come down even to us, that is the time to speak of His omnipotence by telling of His works and explaining His deeds, and to use words to this extent" *(On Ecclesiastes).*

In the East the definition of the canon of Scripture—that basic source of all Christian theology—did not receive its final form before the Council in Trullo, or Quinisext Synod (692), which endorsed the "longer" canon, including Old Testament books preserved in Aramaic and in Greek (also known as the Apocrypha). But several earlier Fathers stood for the "shorter" (Hebrew) canon, and even John of Damascus, in the eighth century, considered Wisdom and Ecclesiasticus "admirable," but did not include them in the canon proper. The book of Revelation was generally omitted from the canon in the fourth and fifth centuries, and never entered liturgical usage in Byzantium.

The magisterium of the church—which obviously was not limited by Scripture alone—found its most authoritative expression in the so-called ecumenical councils. (The word comes from *oikoumene*, meaning the entire inhabited world.) Seven "ecumenical" councils were formally accepted as such: Nicaea I (325), Constantinople I (381), Ephesus I (431), Chalcedon (451), Constantinople II (553), Constantinople III (680), and Nicaea II (787). Imperial convocation and approval gave the councils their authority in the empire, but for the church a lasting consensus, or "reception," was also necessary. Thus, several councils—Ephesus II (449), Hieria (754), Florence-Ferrara (1438–1439)—received imperial sanction, but were eventually rejected by the church. Other councils, though not formally "ecumenical," were recognized as highly authoritative—for instance, the Photian "great council of Hagia Sophia" (879–880) and the councils of 1341, 1347, and 1351, held in

Constantinople, which endorsed the distinction between essence and energy in God in connection with the hesychast controversies.

The Trinitarian theology of the Cappadocian fathers (fourth century) and Chalcedonian and post-Chalcedonian Christology, as defined by the recognized ecumenical councils, provided the fundamental framework of all theological thought. It is in the same framework that the so-called mystical theology of the Byzantines must be interpreted.

The term "mystical theology" comes from the title of one of the treatises of Pseudo-Dionysius (*ca.* 500). It reflects the notion that communion with God cannot be identified with any form of created knowledge, and that it is best expressed in negative, or "apophatic," terms: God is nothing of what the created human mind is able to conceive. At the same time the Greek patristic tradition affirms deification (*theōsis*) as the goal of human existence; it became accessible in the God-man, Jesus Christ.

Best formulated by perhaps the most creative of all Byzantine theologians, St. Maximus the Confessor (*ca.* 580–662), who was also the main spokesman against Monothelitism, the doctrine of deification inspired a number of spiritual and mystical writers. The Byzantines generally recognized that, inasmuch as deification "in Christ" was not a doctrine reducible to rational categories, it was best expressed by those who experienced it. In general, Byzantine Christianity gave greater credit to saints or prophets, as authorities in the field of theology, than did Christianity in the Latin West. Perhaps the greatest and the most striking of Byzantine prophets and mystics is Symeon the New Theologian (*d.* 1022). In some circles, particularly monastic, charismatic mysticism led to a denial of sacraments and of the institutional church. This sectarian form of charismaticism, repeatedly condemned, is known as Messalianism, or Bogomilism.

One of the areas of intellectual and spiritual tension for Byzantine theology was the definition of relationships between the Christian faith and the legacy of ancient Greek philosophy. As a Greek-speaking civilization, Byzantium preserved the writings of ancient authors, and in every generation there were scholars and intellectuals enthusiastically committed to the traditions of ancient philosophy. Some of them, following the example of Origen (*d. ca.* 254), attempted to synthesize Greek philosophy and Christian revelation.

Although Origen and Origenism were condemned (by the ecumenical council of 553), notions from Greek philosophy still remained necessary tools to express the basic dogmas of Christianity. But at the same time a great number of Byzantine theologians, particularly among the monks, were insisting upon the basic incompatibility between Athens and Jerusalem, the Academy and the Gospel. They were particularly opposed to Platonic idealism and spiritualism, which they considered incompatible with the Christian doctrine of the Incarnation. Sometimes they obtained from church authorities the formal condemnation of Platonism (see particularly the case of John Italos, 1076–1077). Until the end of Byzantium, scholarly humanists (for instance, Michael Psellos, Theodore Metochites, Nikephoros Gregoras, Bessarion, and George Gemisthos Plethon) staunchly defended the heritage of antiquity, but they always did so against some opposition. The tension was never resolved, and in this respect the Byzantine Christian tradition can be easily contrasted with the contemporary Latin West, where since the beginning of Scholasticism a new synthesis between Greek philosophy and Christian theology was in the making.

As Byzantine theology avoided rationally structured systematization, so the Byzantine church never bound itself with an exhaustive code of ecclesiastical laws. The councils issued canons related to the structure and administration of the church and to discipline, but all these texts reflected the requirements of concrete situations. The canonical requirements were seen as absolute, inasmuch as they reflected the permanent norms of Christian doctrine and ethics, but in many cases the Byzantine church also recognized the possibility that these same norms could be preserved not by applying the letter of the law, but by exercising mercy or condescension.

This latter attitude was identified as *oikonomia.* In the New Testament this term is used to designate God's plan for the salvation of mankind (Ephesians 1:9–10, 3:2–3) and also the stewardship entrusted to the bishops (1 Corinthians 4:1; Colossians 1:24–25; Titus 1:7). This biblical origin of the term helps to explain the Byzantine canonical notion of *oikonomia,* which was not simply an exception to established rules but "an imitation of God's love for man" (Nicholas Mystikos), and implied repentance by the pardoned sinner. Thus, Patriarch Nicholas was ready to exercise *oikonomia* by recognizing the legitimacy of an imperial child born to emperor Leo VI (886–912) from his uncanonical fourth marriage, but refused to legitimize the marriage itself.

The sources of Byzantine canon law, as they were

included in the most standard and comprehensive compendium—the so-called *Nomokanon in XIV Titles,* issued by Patriarch Photios in 883 and including imperial laws *(nomoi)* and church canons *(kanones)*—include the so-called Apostolic Canons (a collection of rules reflecting the practice of the church in Syria in the fourth century), the canons of ecumenical councils, a collection of canons of "local" councils (mainly of the fourth century), and another collection of "canons of the Fathers" (an anthology of opinions by prominent bishops of the early church). In many cases these materials were to be used as authoritative precedents rather than as formal rules. They were combined in the *Nomokanon* with imperial laws regulating disciplinary matters, setting guidelines for the election of bishops, and defining borders of ecclesiastical provinces and patriarchates. Later, Byzantine canonists used these texts together with commentaries composed in the twelfth century (a period of development in canon law) by Balsamon, Zonaras, and Aristenos.

LITURGY AND HYMNOGRAPHY

The centrality of the liturgy in the life of Byzantine Christian society was perceived by Byzantines and foreigners alike. Celebrated in the magnificent structure of Hagia Sophia—the "Great Church" built by Justinian—it was remembered by the envoys of Prince Vladimir of Russia who came to Constantinople in 987 as a "heavenly" reality. Its original forms were directly influenced by the traditions of the church of Antioch, which was closely connected with the new capital in the late fourth and early fifth centuries. As Constantinople became the center of the Christian world, its practices became more eclectic. In the late medieval period the typikon (Ordo) of Hagia Sophia was combined with the monastic traditions, particularly those of the monastery of Studios, and produced a synthetic system of liturgical celebrations, which in turn integrated (in the thirteenth and fourteenth centuries) the liturgical traditions of the Lavra of St. Sabas in Palestine.

By the ninth century the two eucharistic canons in standard use in Byzantium were those attributed to St. Basil the Great and St. John Chrysostom. Translated into many languages, they were adopted in the entire Orthodox world. The ancient liturgy attributed to St. James was also used locally. From the sixth century the eucharistic liturgy—now celebrated in the huge cathedral of Hagia Sophia before big crowds—was embellished with a number of symbolic actions, thereby losing some of its original communal character. Symbolic interpretations, inspired particularly by the book of Pseudo-Dionysius known as *Ecclesiastical Hierarchy,* presented the liturgy as an earthly representation of heavenly realities, standing between the individual Christian and God. Such ideas were primarily the result of an integration of Neoplatonic ideas into Christian thought. However, the original, mostly pre-Constantinian meaning of the liturgy was generally well preserved in the central parts of the rite, as distinct from its interpretations. Later commentators—for example, Nicholas Kabasilas in the fourteenth century—recovered the Christocentric, communal, and sacramental dimensions of the Eucharist.

Besides the central mystery of the Eucharist, the Byzantine tradition insisted upon the importance of baptism (always celebrated through triple immersion), of chrismation (the equivalent of the Western confirmation, but celebrated by a priest anointing the candidate with holy chrism), and of other sacraments, which sometimes included the rites of monastic tonsure and of burial.

After the merger of the "cathedral" and the "monastic" liturgical traditions, the liturgical year combined several cycles, each providing its own hymnographical material. The regular daily cycle, included in a book called Horologion (the Book of Hours), comprised the unchangeable structure of vespers, compline (apodeipnon), midnight prayer (mesonyktikon), matins (orthros), and the four canonical "hours." The feast of Easter is the changeable key for the yearly and weekly cycles. The Easter cycle covered the period of Lent, with proper hymns included in a book known as the Triodion, and the festal period itself, with hymns included in the Pentekostarion. A cycle of eight weeks repeated itself throughout the year, starting after Pentecost, with hymns contained in the Oktoekhos. The twelve parts of the Menaion (Book of Months) contained all the hymnographic material proper to the saints of each day. The detailed and highly complicated regulations about the various combinations, which occur with the changes of the date of Easter, were described in the typikon, the final form of which dates from the fourteenth century.

Of all Christian medieval traditions, the Byzantine one is the richest in terms of its hymnographic legacy. Poetically and theologically the Byzantine hymns constitute an immense literary corpus that has often served as an effective substitute for both school and pulpit. Unfortunately the Byzantine neumes, or musical signs, have not yet been deciphered, except for the liturgical manuscripts of the later period (thirteenth–fourteenth centuries). It has been demonstrated, however, that Byzantine music has its roots in the traditions of the Jewish synagogue of the early Christian period and that its medieval form was similar to—though probably richer than—Western Gregorian chant.

In composing their hymns Byzantine hymnographers had to combine theological, poetic, and musical skills. They include the great Romanos Melodos (sixth century) and many authors of the iconoclastic and posticonoclastic periods (Andrew of Crete, John of Damascus, Kosmas of Maiuma, Theodore of Studios). Romanos wrote kontakia, poetic homilies composed of metric stanzas sung by the precentor and accompanied by a refrain repeated by the congregation. The most famous Byzantine kontakion is probably the *Akathistos Hymn* to the Virgin Mary, the popularity of which never diminished throughout the centuries. In the seventh and eighth centuries, however, the kontakia were, in most cases, replaced with a more structured and sophisticated form of liturgical poetry, the *kanōnes*, which combined Old Testament odes, such as Exodus 15, Deuteronomy 32, and the Magnificat (Luke 1), with newly composed hymns. Hymnographic creativity, roughly following the models set in the eighth and ninth centuries, continued throughout the medieval period.

THE LEGACY OF CHRISTIAN BYZANTIUM

During the Palaiologan dynasty (1258–1453) the Byzantine Empire barely survived under the steady advance of Turkish power in Asia Minor and, later, in the Balkans. During the same period the patriarchate of Constantinople, adapting to the new political situation, succeeded not only in maintaining its jurisdiction over vast territories but also in acquiring greater prestige and authority. As the Latins occupied Constantinople (1204–1261), the patriarch went to exile in Nicaea, but continued to be recognized as the head of the mother church of the Orthodox Slavs. From his exile he was more flexible and more generous toward them than his predecessors, who had resided in the imperial city at the height of its power. In 1219 he appointed St. Sava as the first archbishop of an independent Serbian church. Sixteen years later he recognized the Bulgarian patriarchate of Trnovo.

In 1261 the patriarchate returned to Constantinople, recaptured from the Latins. Throughout the entire period of Latin domination Russia, destined to become the most powerful heir of Byzantine civilization, remained firmly under the patriarch's ecclesiastical control. As most of the Russian principalities were conquered by the Mongols (1237–1240), the "metropolitan of Kiev and all Russia," appointed from Byzantium (or from Nicaea) and frequently a Greek by birth, remained as the single most influential power in Russia. Politically his prestige was enhanced by the good diplomatic relations that existed between the Byzantine court and the Mongol khans residing in Sarai on the lower Volga.

Abandoning his traditional seat in Kiev, which had been destroyed by the Mongols, the metropolitan moved to northern Russia and established a residence in Vladimir (1300), then in Moscow (1326), which eventually became both the political and the ecclesiastical capital of Russia. This rise of Moscow, supported by Byzantium, provoked centrifugal movements in the western dioceses of the Russian metropolitanate. For short periods in the fourteenth century, and under the pressure of the grand prince of Lithuania and the king of Poland, the patriarch was forced to create separate metropolitanates in Novgorodok (Lithuania) and Halich (Polish-occupied Galicia). By 1390 Byzantine ecclesiastical diplomacy succeeded in reuniting the metropolitanate.

This extraordinary diplomatic activity of the patriarchate throughout eastern Europe was no longer based on the power of the emperor—now quite negligible—but on the prestige of Constantinople as a spiritual and intellectual center of a "commonwealth" of nations. A particular role in maintaining cultural ties was played by the monasteries. The "hesychast" revival, endorsed in Constantinople by a series of church councils (1341, 1347, 1351), had repercussions in all Orthodox countries. Mount Athos, the center of hesychast spirituality, was an international center where Greek, Slavic, Moldavian, and Georgian monks received their spiritual formation, copied manuscripts, translated Greek texts into their own languages, and frequently served as diplomatic emissaries of the patriarchate. They frequently occupied episcopal sees throughout eastern Europe.

However, Serbia (1389) and Bulgaria (1393) soon fell to the Ottoman Turks, and the harmonious relations between the mother church of Constantinople and the daughter church of Russia were broken by events connected with the Council of Ferrara-

Florence (1438–1439). The Greek Isidore, a Byzantine appointee to the metropolitanate of Russia, signed the decree of union in Florence, but was rejected by his flock upon his return to Moscow (1441). In 1448 Russian bishops elected a successor, Metropolitan Jonas, independently from Constantinople, and interpreted the fall of Byzantium to the Turks (1453) as a divine punishment for the betrayal of Orthodoxy perpetrated at Florence.

In spite of these tragic events, the intellectual and spiritual dynamism shown by the Byzantine church in the last year of its existence made possible the survival of what the French historian Charles Diehl has called "Byzance après Byzance." Within the borders of the Ottoman Empire a patriarchate of Constantinople continued to exist. The patriarch could not use his magnificent cathedral of Hagia Sophia, which was transformed into a mosque, but by decree of the sultan he became politically responsible for the entire Christian population of the empire, which gave him new powers not only over the Greeks but also over the Slavic and Romanian populations of the Balkans. Preserving the full splendor of the Byzantine liturgy and maintaining the traditions of monastic spirituality, particularly on Mt. Athos, the patriarchate was occasionally the victim of Muslim persecution and corruption of the Ottoman court, but it carried on its Byzantine legacy into modern times.

In Russia, meanwhile, Grand Prince Ivan III married Sophia, the niece of the last Byzantine emperor (1472) and the Russians began to see in their powerful capital of Moscow a "new Constantinople" or a "third Rome." Nevertheless, it was still from Turkish-held Constantinople that the Muscovite princes sought and obtained the recognition of their imperial title and, in 1589, the establishment of a patriarchate in Moscow. The Byzantine legacy remained valid even for them.

BIBLIOGRAPHY

The Byzantine church. I. D. Andreev, *Konstantinopolskie patriarkhi ot vremeni khalkidonskogo sobora do Fotiia* (1895, repr. 1981); Basile (Krivochéine), *St. Syméon le nouveau theologien* (1980); Anton Baumstark, *Liturgie comparée* (1953); Hans-Georg Beck, *Vorsehung und Vorbestimmung in der theologische Literatur der Byzantiner* (1937), and *Kirche und theologischen Literatur im Byzantinischen Reich* (1959); Hendrikus Berkhof, *Kirche und Kaiser: Eine Untersuchung der Entstehung der byzantinischen und theokratischen Staats-auffassung im vierten Jahrhundert* (1947); R. Bornaert, *Les commentaires byzantins de la divine liturgie du VIIe au XVe siècle* (1966); Louis Bréhier, *Le monde byzantin,* II (1949), 430–579; Demetrios J. Constantelos, *Byzantine Philanthropy and Social Welfare* (1968); Hippolyte Delehaye, "Byzantine Monasticism," in *Byzantium,* Norman H. Baynes and H. St. L. B. Moss, eds. (1948); Aleksei Dimitrievsky, *Opisanie Liturgicheskikh Rukopisei,* I–II (1895–1901); A. Dubroklonsky, *Prepodobny Theodor, igumen Studiisky,* 2 vols. (1913–1914); Francis Dvornik, *The Photian Schism* (1948), *The Idea of Apostolicity in Byzantium and the Legend of the Apostle Andrew* (1958), and *Byzantine Missions Among the Slavs* (1970).

A. Erhardt, *Überlieferung und Bestand der hagiographischen und homiletischen Literatur der griechischen Kirche von Anfängen bis zum Ende des 16. Jahrhunderts,* I, III, 1 (1943); George Every, *The Byzantine Patriarchate (451–1204),* 2nd ed. (1962); Augustin Fliche and V. Martin, *Histoire de l'église,* 21 vols. (particularly vols. 3–7) (1934); Enrica Follieri, *Initia hymnorum ecclesiae graecae,* 4 vols. (1960–1963); Joseph Gill, *The Council of Florence* (1959), and *Byzantium and the Papacy, 1198–1400* (1979); Venance Grumel, ed., *Les régestes des actes du patriarcat de Constantinople,* fascs. I–III (1932); Joseph Hajjar, *Le synod permanent σύνοδος ἐνδημοῦσα dans l'église byzantine dès origines au XIe siècle* (1962); Joseph Hergenröther, *Photius, Patriarch von Constantinople,* 3 vols. (1867, repr. 1966); J. M. Hussey, *Church and Learning in the Byzantine Empire, 867–1185* (1937).

Martin Jugie, *Le schisme byzantin* (1941); A. A. King, *The Rites of Eastern Christendom,* 2nd ed. (1947); Kilian Kirchhoff, *Die Ostkirche betet. Hymnen aus den Tagzeiten der byzantinischen Kirche,* 4 vols. (1934–); Vitalien Laurent, *Les "mémoires" du grand ecclésiarque de l'église de Constantinople, Sylvestre Syropoulos sur le Concile de Florence (1438–1439)* (1971); Joseph Lebon, *Le Monophysisme sevérien* (1909); Jean Meyendorff, *Orthodoxy and Catholicity* (1966); and *Byzantium and the Rise of Russia* (1980); Anton Michel, *Die Kaisermacht in der Ostkirche (843–1204)* (1959); Franz Miklosich and J. Müller, *Acta et diplomata graeca medii aevi sacra et profana,* I–II (1860–1862); L. Möhler, *Kardinal Bessarion als Theologe, Humanist, und Staatsman,* I–III (1923–1942); Dimitri Obolensky, *The Byzantine Commonwealth: Eastern Europe, 500–1453* (1971).

Jules Pargroire, *L'église byzantine de 527 à 847* (1905); Alphonse Raes, *Introductio in liturgiam orientalem* (1947); Steven Runciman, *The Eastern Schism* (1955); Alexander Schmemann, *Introduction to Liturgical Theology* (1966); K. M. Setton, *The Papacy and the Levant (1204–1571),* I–II (1976–1979); Nikolai Skabalanovich, *Vizantiiskoe gosudarstvo i tserkov v XI veke* (1884); Polikhronii Syrku, *Kistorii ispravlenia knig v Bolgarii v XIV v* (1898); A. E. Tachiaos, Ἐπιδράσεις τοῦ Ἡσυχασμοῦ εἰς τὴν Ἐκκλησιαστικὴν Πολιτικὴν ἐν Ῥωσίᾳ, *1328–1406* (1962); Otto Treitinger, *Die oströmische Kaiser- und Reichsidee nach ihrer Gestaltung im höfischen Zeremoniell* (1938, repr. 1956); Jan Louis Van Dieten, *Geschichte der Patriarchen von Sergios I. bis Johannes VI. (610–715)* (1972); Egon Wellesz, *History of Byzantine Music and Hymnography,* 2nd ed. (1961).

Theological trends. Jean Dauvillier and C. de Clercq, *Le marriage en droit canonique oriental* (1936); Franz Diekamp, *Die origenistischen Streitigkeiten im sechsten Jahrhundert und das fünfte allgemeine Concil* (1898); Hermann Dorries, *Symeon von Mesopotamien: Die Überlieferung der messalianische "Makarios"-Schriften* (1941); Werner Elert, *Der Ausgang der altkirchlichen Christologie* (1957); Juan M. Garrigues, *Maxime le Confesseur. La Charité. Avenir divin de l'homme* (1976); Stephen Gerö, *Byzantine Iconoclasm During the Reign of Leo III* (1973); J. Gouillard, "Le synodikon de l'orthodoxie: Édition et commentaire," in *Travaux et mémoires,* II (1967); André Grabar, *L'iconoclasme byzantin: Dossier archéologique* (1957); Antoine Guillaumont, *Les "Képhalaia gnostica" d'Évagre le Pontique et l'histoire de l'Origénisme chez les Grecs et chez les Syriens* (1962); Richard Haugh, *Photius and the Carolingians* (1975); Karl Holl, *Enthusiasmus und Bussgewalt beim griechischen Mönchtum* (1898); Martin Jugie, *Theologia dogmatica Christanorum orientalium ab ecclesia catholica dissidentium,* I–V (1926–1935); Kilian Kirchhoff, *Symeon: Licht vom Licht, Hymnen* (1930).

Joseph Ledit, *Marie dans la liturgie de Byzance* (1976); Vladimir Lossky, *Vision of God* (1963), *In the Image and Likeness of God* (1973), and *The Mystical Theology of the Eastern Church,* 2nd ed. (1975); Eric L. Mascall, ed., *The Mother of God* (1949); I. Medvedev, *Vizantiisky gumanizm XIV–XV vv* (1976); John Meyendorff, *Introduction à l'étude de Grégoire Palamas* (1959), and *Byzantine Theology* (1974), *Byzantine Hesychasm* (1974), *Marriage: An Orthodox Perspective,* 2nd ed. (1974), and *Christ in Eastern Christian Thought,* 2nd ed. (1975); and John Meyendorff *et al., The Primacy of Peter in the Orthodox Church* (1963).

Nikodim Milas, *Das Kirchenrecht der morgenländischen Kirche,* 2nd ed. (1905, repr. 1981); Georg Ostrogorsky, *Studien zur Geschichte des byzantinischen Bilderstreites* (1929, repr. 1964); Jaroslav Pelikan, *The Christian Tradition,* I–II (1971–1974); Theodore de Regnon, *Études de théologie positive sur la Sainte Trinité,* 3rd ser., II (1893, repr. 1981); René Rogues, *L'univers dionysien* (1954); Basile Tatakis, *La philosophie byzantine* (1949); Claude Tresmontant, *La métaphysique du christianisme et la naissance de la philosophie chrétienne* (1961); Harry Wolfson, *The Philosophy of the Church Fathers* (1956); Joseph Zhishman, *Das Eherecht der orientalischen Kirche* (1864).

JOHN MEYENDORFF

[See also **Azymes; Caesaropapism; Clergy, Byzantine; Councils, Byzantine; Councils, Ecumenical; Cyril and Methodios, Sts.; Filioque; Hesychasm; Hymns, Byzantine; Iconoclasm; John of Damascus, St.; Liturgy, Byzantine; Metropolitan; Monothelitism; Mysticism, Byzantine; Nestorius; Patriarch; Photios; Russian Orthodox Church; Schisms, Eastern-Western Church.**]

BYZANTINE EMPIRE. This topic is covered in a series of articles comprising the following: **Bureaucracy; Economic Life and Social Structure; History (330–1025); History (1025–1204); History (1204–1453).**

BYZANTINE EMPIRE: BUREAUCRACY. The Byzantine Empire was a bureaucratic state throughout its existence. Its bureaucracy owed some of its origins and traditional practices to Hellenistic Egypt and to the Roman Empire, particularly major administrative restructuring during the reigns of Diocletian and Constantine I; in any case its structure was the product of a long evolution and did not appear suddenly, as the creation of any one emperor. Constantinople was always the center of Byzantine administration. In addition to complex imperial and provincial bureaucracies, there was a large ecclesiastical bureaucracy that is outside the scope of this article. A prerequisite of the effective functioning of the bureaucracy was an adequate pool of literate men. Although education was not a state responsibility, candidates for higher bureaucratic posts were expected to have acquired a sound literary education.

Principal sources about the Byzantine bureaucracy include, in the absence of any surviving archives, protocol lists, the Book of Ceremonies of Emperor Constantine VII Porphyrogenitos (913–959), legal codes and commentaries, documentary lead seals, references in histories, correspondence, rhetoric, inscriptions, and some travelers' reports.

The bureaucracy possessed some constant characteristics throughout its history. Its posts were the coveted objects of intense competition and personal rivalries. Its nominal salaries were frequently inadequate, and often the candidate was expected to purchase his post. The result was graft and corruption that repeated efforts at reform never eliminated. Rank-consciousness permeated the bureaucracy as well as Byzantine society in general. Throughout its history the concept of taxis (order) is central for understanding the mentality and operations of the bureaucracy. Levels of efficiency varied, and the quality of an administration ultimately determined an emperor's ability to wield effective authority. There was no hereditary possession of bureaucratic offices, but emperors and their subordinates often filled posts for personal or factional reasons, rather than on the basis of strict merit. The term of office for the most prominent positions depended on the will of the emperor. The bureaucracy was never static; it was always subject to change. Some ranks and titles continued to be mentioned in the protocol lists after they had become obsolete and their functions forgotten.

The history of Byzantine bureaucracy may be divided into three periods: early Byzantine, from the fourth through the sixth centuries; middle Byzantine, from the seventh through the eleventh centuries; and late Byzantine, from the end of the eleventh century through the disappearance of the empire in the fifteenth century.

The early Byzantine bureaucracy derived from late Roman bureaucracy. The imperial comitatus, the group of ministries attached to the person of the emperor that formed the central government, included the *sacrum cubiculum* (household) with its *cubicularii* (chamberlains), *castrensiani* (domestic personnel), *silentiarii* (ushers), *scholae* (guards), and the *consistorium* (the most important officials and advisers of the emperor, the *notarii* [secretariat], and several other prominent officials). The quaestor was the emperor's chief legal adviser and drafter of legal documents; the *magister officiorum* (master of the offices) controlled the administration and distribution of palace offices and commanded the *scholae.*

The count of the sacred largesses directed the mines and mints; collected some taxes and paid *stipendia* or donatives; directed the imperial weaving factories and the issuance of clothing or clothing allowances to the court, the army, and the civil service; and controlled customs duties, certain special taxes on senators, and the military recruit substitute tax called the *aurum tironicum.* The *comes rei privatae* (count of the privy purse) administered and collected rents from state property, claimed and confiscated property (such as escheat property) for the state, and handled the sale of state property and payments in cash from its treasury. The vast praetorian prefecture of the east, directed by the praetorian prefect, was responsible for levying taxes; issuing rations to the army and the civil service, and fodder or fodder allowances to high officers and officials; managing the postal service; supervising arms factories, and maintaining such public works as roads, bridges, posthouses, and granaries. The praetorian prefecture contained an elaborate hierarchy of officials and secretaries.

There are no reliable statistics for the total number of bureaucrats in the Byzantine civil service at any time in its long history. Official pay varied strictly according to rank, but gifts often supplemented low nominal salaries.

Most provincial governors in the early Byzantine period were called *praesides* (singular, *praeses*), although occasionally they were *moderatores* or *correctores*, or even, in certain cases, *proconsules* or *consularii.* These governors held supreme civilian authority and only in rare cases of emergency exercised any military authority. They wielded legal authority subject to appeals to the courts of the praetorian prefecture. There are, however, several cases of combined civilian and military authority, in the reign of Justinian, because of security threats: the proconsul of Palestine, the count of Isauria, the proconsul of Armenia III, the proconsul of Cappadocia, the *quaestor Justiniani exercitus,* and the dux of Arabia had all normally enjoyed such dual authority. Therefore, the joining of civil and military authority was not a radical departure but an extension of existing practices for insecure regions. Nevertheless, these dual civil-military jurisdictions may justly be regarded as anticipations of what happened in the middle Byzantine period.

The bureaucracy and civil administration underwent substantial change in the seventh and eighth centuries, even though much of the nomenclature originated in earlier Latin terminology; the best sources date from the late ninth and tenth centuries. Two fundamental classes of offices *(axiai)* are those granted by insignia *(dia brabeiōn)*, which were honorific and might be held by someone who also held an office with a function, and offices granted verbally *(dia logou)*, which included the most important imperial administrators.

Offices granted through insignia were subdivided into those granted to bearded men and those granted to unbearded men (eunuchs). The honorific offices of bearded men included such elevated ones as caesar, *nobilissimus*, and *curopalates,* all of which were reserved to members of the imperial family until a very late period; *zoste patrikia, magistros, vestes, anthypatos* (proconsul), and *patrikios* (patrician); such senatorial ranks as *dishypatos* (twice consul), *hypatos* (consul), *vestitor, silentiarios, apo eparchon (praefecturius),* and *stratelates;* and distinguished imperial dignities that originally involved personal service to the emperor and required payment of money, but for which the rank holder received an annual salary: *protospatharios, spatharocandidatos, spatharios, strator, candidatos,* and *mandator.* Among the offices *dia brabeiōn* that eunuchs held were *vestes, patrikios, praipositos, protospatharios, primikerios, ostiarios* (doorkeeper), *spatharokoubikoularios, koubikoularios,* and *nipsistarios* (holder of the imperial washbasin).

Certain offices that were awarded *dia logou* were reserved for eunuchs: *parakoimomenos* (head of the imperial bedchamber), *protovestiarios* (head of imperial wardrobe and its treasury), *ho epi tēs trapezes* (head of the imperial table service), and *pinkernes* (head of the imperial wine service) were among the most important.

Major bureaucrats included the *protoasekretis,* who prepared the final revisions of imperial acts and could exercise some legal authority; the logothete of the drome, who controlled the roads and imperial post, and was in charge of foreign relations; the *sakellarios,* the general supervisor of imperial finances; the *logothete tou genikou* (general treasurer), whose treasury assessed and collected land and some commercial taxes, and kept the relevant tax registers; and the *logothete tou stratiotikou* (military treasurer), whose treasury kept the registers of soldiers, their obligations and lands, and paid soldiers' maintenance in wartime.

By the ninth century *chartularioi* had replaced some previous head officials. *Ho epi tou sakelliou* was imperial treasurer, and his subordinates were imperial notaries who kept central account books and the protonotaries responsible for the civilian affairs of individual themes; *ho epi tou vestiariou* (head of a public wardrobe that included a treasury and an arsenal for the fleet); *ho epi tou eidikou* (the head of the special treasury, which paid senatorial salaries, outfitted the fleet, and controlled precious objects of gold and silk made by imperial factories); *megas kourator* (administrator of the private estates of the emperor); *kourator tes manganes* (another administrator of particular imperial domains); and the *orphanotrophos* (director of the major orphanage at Constantinople). These new fiscal bureaus replaced the defunct *comitiva sacrarum largitionum,* the treasuries of the praetorian prefectures, the *res privata,* and special treasuries for certain imperial estates. Each major office had its own *officium* of subordinate officials.

Important legal officials included the eparch or prefect of Constantinople, who supervised the administration of the city, including its police, commerce, provisioning, prices, trades, morals, spectacles, and a special civil and criminal court as well as an appellate jurisdiction. Other important legal authorities were the *kuaistor,* who investigated falsification of documents and problems of familial law and supervised provincials who came to Constantinople, and *ho epi ton deeseon,* who studied petitions addressed to the emperor, as well as other judges *(kritai)* of tribunals. Among the major supplementary officials was the *mystikos,* or confidential officer of the emperor, who appeared in the ninth century.

The *stratarch* class included the *hetaireiarch,* who commanded several contingents of foreign mercenaries that guarded the palace in the eighth, ninth, and tenth centuries; the *drungarios tou ploimou,* who commanded the imperial fleet; the *logothete ton agelon* (logothete of the flocks and herds), who supervised imperial estates for the raising of horses for the army; the *comes tou stablou* (count of the stable); and the *protospatharios epi ton basilikon,* who headed an imperial guard of *spatharioi, candidatoi,* and *mandatores.*

Military administration changed dramatically in the middle Byzantine period, with the strategoi of themes replacing the *magistri militum* and, by the eighth century, thematic administrations replacing the old provincial structures. The *protonotarios* of each theme, who was ultimately subject to the *chartoularios tou sakelliou,* headed each civilian administration in his themes. By the tenth and eleventh centuries the judges *(kritai)* of themes were assuming control of finances and other aspects of civilian administration. The other principal class of military commanders was the *domestici,* who commanded the respective bodies of *tagmata*; the domestic of the theme of the Optimaton; and the count of the walls *(komes ton teicheon),* who supervised the walls of the palace at Constantinople.

The eleventh century witnessed the appearance of the *megas logiarist* as supreme minister of the budget and of financial administration, and of the *vestiarion* (wardrobe) as the sole central treasury. The logthete of the *sekreta* (administrative agencies) became the head of most of the civil service and ultimately was called the grand logothete *(megas logothetes),* who headed the civil service. The *mesazon* (intermediary) also appeared in the eleventh century. He was a chief imperial secretary who often acted as chief minister; he dispatched petitions and assisted the emperor with all aspects of administration, mediated between the emperor and his subjects, and made some judicial decisions. The keeper of the inkwell *(epi tou kanikleiou)* was responsible for the contents of imperial acts and for affixing authentication. The *vestiarion* became the sole treasury in the Komnenian period and continued to be so in subsequent centuries; its scope included all aspects of fiscal administration and maintenance of fiscal records that comprised both taxes and exemptions.

The Latin conquest of Constantinople in 1204 did not permanently destroy the Byzantine bureaucracy, for much of it was reconstituted at Nicaea. The Nicene civil service included imperial secretaries and some members of the imperial household: the *protovestiarios* (keeper of the imperial wardrobe), *epi tes trapezes* (steward), *pinkernes* (butler), and the *parakoimomenos* (chamberlain).

The most complete list of imperial ranks and bureaucratic officials from the late or Palaiologan period is provided by Pseudo-Kodinos in the middle of the fourteenth century, but his offices include many anachronisms. Meticulous rank-consciousness continued to permeate the bureaucracy and court. As in earlier periods there were honorific offices without any genuine function, such as despot, *sebastokrator, panhypersebastos, protosebastos, curopalates, megas papias,* and *megas archon.* Some of these titles reflected a trend to extreme excess in their pretensions. Each major office carried with it special forms of dress and insignia. Court ceremony continued to take elaborate form. The *protostrator* (chief groom) was responsible for the emperor's horse; the *megas primikerios* watched order of precedence and the imperial scepter; the *parakoimomenos* of the seal affixed the emperor's seal on wax and lead; the *protovestiarites* was in charge of ceremonies of reception; the *parakoimomenos* of the bedchamber headed the pages and servants of the imperial bedchamber, and his immediate subordinate was the *prokathemenos* of the bedchamber. Among other prominent court officials was the *megas diermeneutes* (grand interpreter).

There was no fixed *cursus honorum* for holders of office to follow in the late period. Most administrative training appears to have taken place at the imperial court. The imperial household officers had formerly been eunuchs, but from the twelfth century on, these posts tended to be occupied by members of the great aristocratic families.

Officials who assisted the functioning of the army included the grand stratopedarch, who was in charge of supplies and provisions, and the judge of the army, who adjudicated disputes between soldiers.

In the twelfth and thirteenth centuries the chief administrative division of a theme district was the *katepanikion* under a *praktor* (later an *energon,* who was appointed by the duke of a theme and exercised fiscal, and later also judicial, responsibilities). Fiscal surveys were made in the themes by *exisōtai* (who performed the far-reaching reassessment of *exisōsis,* equalization) and the *apographeis* (who performed the *apographē,* survey). The duke of a theme apointed his own *grammatikos* (secretary) and his *logiaristēs* (financial controller). The duke still wielded authority over soldiers within his theme, but such soldiers had lost most of their effectiveness. The best soldiers were salaried mercenaries, and the theme was primarily an administrative and judicial unit by this date; it retained only a vestige of its military origins.

It is incorrect to assume the existence of any monolithic bureaucratic party at any moment in the history of the Byzantine Empire. Bureaucrats and soldiers were not normally polarized rival factions. In fact, bureaucrats were related by marriage and by personal rivalries and interests to particular larger factional and familial groupings. Even in the late tenth and eleventh centuries there were bureaucrats who possessed marital ties with so-called great military families. One cannot hypothesize any simplistic rivalry of bureaucrats and military leaders; factional alignments were more complex and more fluid. Furthermore, bureaucrats who lived in and around Constantinople often possessed properties and enjoyed familial relations with those who resided in rural regions far from Constantinople, whether in Europe or in Anatolia. Therefore one should avoid assuming that bureaucrats developed an exclusively Constantinopolitan perspective in their policy-making and factional groupings.

Bureaucrats probably did identify with Constantinople and its suburbs, but they often maintained or developed wider ties with other, scattered areas of the empire. Even the eunuchs were often recruited from within the borders of the empire, and therefore were likely to favor their families and regions of origin. (The Byzantine practice of sometimes giving important posts to eunuchs of domestic origin contrasts with the practice in many other bureaucratic or slave empires, such as that of the Mamluks, of acquiring eunuchs only from distant regions, so that they could have no potential domestic loyalties or conflicts of interest.)

The Byzantine bureaucracy, despite its limitations, contributed to the lengthy endurance of the

Byzantine Empire. Its formalized procedures helped make the empire itself more important than any particular political or intellectual or military leader. The empire did not depend exclusively on finding exceptional leaders; it possessed methods of government and financing that could function in a more or less satisfactory fashion even during a period of mediocre leadership at the top. Because of the importance of this bureaucracy—many of the actions of which were performed silently, secretly, perhaps even without explicit verbal, let alone written, authorization—many aspects of Byzantine bureaucratic history may remain obscure or ambiguous—yet it cannot be ignored.

BIBLIOGRAPHY

Michael Angold, *A Byzantine Government in Exile: Government and Society Under the Laskarids of Nicaea, 1204–1261* (1975); John B. Bury, *The Imperial Administrative System in the Ninth Century* (1911, repr. 1958); Arnold H. M. Jones, *The Later Roman Empire 284–602,* 2 vols. (1964); Ljubomir Maksimović, *The Byzantine Provincial Administration Under the Palaiologi* (in Serbo-Croatian with English summary) (1972); Nicolas Oikonomidès, *Les listes de préséance byzantines des IXe et Xe siècles* (1972); Léon Pierre Raybaud, *Le gouvernement et l'administration centrale de l'empire byzantin sous les premiers Paléologues (1258–1354)* (1968); Ernst Stein, *Histoire du Bas-Empire,* 2 vols. in 3 (1949–1959), and *Studien zur Geschichte des byzantinischen Reiches vornehmlich unter den Kaisern Justinus II und Tiberius Constantinus* (1919); Jean Verpeaux, ed. and trans., *Pseudo-Kodinos: Traité des offices* (1966); G. Zacos and A. Veglery, *Byzantine Lead Seals,* I pts. 1–3 (1972).

WALTER EMIL KAEGI, JR.

[See also **Household, Chamber, and Wardrobe; Logothete; Postal and Intelligence Service, Byzantium; Praetorian Prefect; Protospatharios; Scholae; Themes.**]

BYZANTINE EMPIRE: ECONOMIC LIFE AND SOCIAL STRUCTURE. The Byzantine Empire, more appropriately referred to as the later Roman Empire, lasted for more than 1,000 years. The date of its end, 29 May 1453, is definitely known, but the date of its beginning is related to a series of military, economic, and administrative changes that extended over a number of years before they were consolidated to form what historians have come to call, in order to distinguish it from its earlier period, the later Roman Empire. This consolidation took place at the end of the third and the early part of the fourth century. The persons responsible for it were Diocletian (284–305) and Constantine (324–337).

General immobility of its social and economic structure was the principal feature of the later Roman, or Byzantine, Empire as it evolved following the reforms of Diocletian and Constantine. Those who actually worked the fields, whether they possessed them or not, became attached to the soil; and those in the cities who were engaged in any trade or profession of public interest became attached to their trade or profession. In neither case was there any freedom of choice; one was legally bound to follow the trade of his father. The tax known as the *jugatio-capitatio* was the principal factor in the evolution of this basically agrarian system.

The three elements that played the predominant role in the establishment of this system were the dangerous external situation of the empire, the decline in the population, and the ever increasing financial needs of the state. The reorganization of the empire by Diocletian and Constantine, designed to establish internal stability, greatly increased the complexity of the government, and thereby its financial needs, while the defense of the frontiers against the invasions of the barbarians and the Persians was making greater and greater demands upon the treasury. To meet these demands the empire had at its disposal land, a limited supply of agricultural labor, and certain organized services in the cities, notably those connected with the supply of food. And it was by a systematic exploitation of these resources that the empire could find the necessary funds with which to defend its frontiers and to maintain its governmental establishment.

Freedom of choice gave way to strict control and supervision. Land and its cultivator were bound together; one could not leave the land, nor could the land be taken away from one, for the empire obtained its revenues mainly from the land, and it was imperative that it be cultivated. But these revenues were chiefly in kind; they had to be transported, transformed, and distributed; and to achieve these processes the state turned to existing organizations of transport and industry, imposed its control upon them, held their members responsible for the performance of the services required of them, and rendered their trade hereditary. The shipowners *(navicularii),* the bakers *(pistores),* and the pork dealers *(suarii)* were those chiefly affected. Those working in the state factories, where arms and certain garments, destined for the use of the imperial court, were manufactured, or in the state mints, also were attached to their work and their trade was made hereditary. Attached to their social position, which was hereditary, were the urban aristocracy, the *curiales,* who performed public services, notably the collection of the taxes. The evolution of this social structure was complete by the end of the fourth century.

This was a hard system, but the times were hard. The empire was faced everywhere by formidable enemies; it was fighting for its very existence, and it had no recourse but to exploit fully the resources at its disposal. The fact is that it survived. Furthermore, the social immobility never became complete. There were free peasants who were at liberty to move, provided they did not stay on the same land for more than thirty years. And in the towns the majority of the artisans, particularly those whose trades were not connected with any public service, though organized into guilds and their activities regulated, enjoyed considerable freedom of action. Their trades were not forcibly hereditary, although the son usually followed the trade of his father, which was what the government wanted and encouraged. The artisans were even free to strike for higher wages, as is shown by an inscription at Sardis (459), and their intervention in politics often had important results; the title of the inscription serves well as illustration: "Declaration under oath of the builders and artisans of . . . Sardis." The ability of members of guilds engaged in public services to find substitutes for themselves proves further that there were people for whom the security afforded by membership in such guilds outweighed the curtailment of freedom and the heavy obligation that such membership carried with it.

But there were abuses and weaknesses, and these had serious consequences. The burden of taxation was heavy, and to this was added the maladministration of the lower officials, who usually exploited the poor beyond the requirement of the law while dealing much more leniently with the wealthy. Many peasants ran away or sought the protection of the large landowners, who were also great civil or military functionaries, turning over to them their land and becoming simple *coloni* (serfs).

The *patrocinium* (services of a patron) was perhaps the greatest evil, for it not only deprived the state of some of its revenue but also lessened the number of the small peasant proprietors. At the same time it increased the power of the wealthy, who, with their private armies, often defied the central government, thus adding to the maladministration of the empire. Nor did it help to ameliorate the condition of those peasants who resorted to it, for in place of the state they were now exploited by private masters—and much more ruthlessly.

The condition of most of the *coloni* was miserable. Some even chose to live among the barbarians rather than in the Greco-Roman world. And as the free peasants continued to disappear, while the great magnates were permitted to substitute money payments for the serf-recruits they were required to furnish to the state, the army of the empire became an army of mercenaries. The state required its citizens to work and pay taxes while it entrusted the defense of its frontiers to barbarians and other foreigners.

The emperors of the fifth and sixth centuries, especially Justinian, sought to eliminate some of these abuses, but the measures they adopted were palliatives, designed to work within the cadre of the existing organization. They did not succeed. At the close of the sixth century the only sizable social classes in the empire were the large magnates and *coloni,* although the free peasant proprietor had not completely disappeared.

The two centuries that followed form one of the darkest and most critical periods in the history of the empire. It was almost ripped to pieces by the Persians and then by the Arabs in the East, and by the Avars and the Slavs in the Balkan Peninsula. In the face of these external dangers, important measures were taken that transformed the social structure of the empire, gave new life to its society, and enabled it not only to stop the Saracens but also to regain the dominant position in the East.

Scholars generally agree, despite some unresolved questions, that the characteristic feature of the rural society which had come to obtain in the Byzantine Empire between the end of the sixth century and the beginning of the ninth was the free village community inhabited by peasants who owned their land and usually cultivated it themselves. Each free village community formed a fiscal unit for purposes of taxation. The peasants living in it were collectively responsible for the taxes, the assessment of which was now divorced from the head tax of the earlier period, allotted to their community. If a peasant, for instance, abandoned his land and there was no one to pay the taxes, the neighboring peasants were held responsible for these taxes and, in return, enjoyed the usufruct of the land. In practice, though, this responsibility was often lifted, and in such cases the abandoned land, after thirty years, became state property.

The *epibole* or *allelengyon,* as this collective responsibility for the tax was known, was doubtless designed to ensure the collection of the land tax from all the land, to keep the land under cultivation, and to encourage cooperation and mutual assistance among the peasants so that they might stay on the land. This free village community had existed before, but by the end of the sixth century it had virtually disappeared. Its restoration and extensive development, which no doubt had already begun in the seventh century, led to the remarkable revival of Byzantium, after the shattering blows it received in the seventh century at the hands of the Persians, Arabs, Avars, and Slavs. The general assumption is that the restoration of the free village community took place in Asia Minor, but there is some reason to believe that it may first have begun in the Balkan Peninsula, more specifically in Thrace, in connection with the settlement there of numerous Armenians. The theory that the Byzantine village community was of Slavic origin, first advanced in the nineteenth century by Russian scholars and since revived by Soviet scholars, has no basis in fact.

The free village community did not remain the dominant feature of the agrarian society of Byzantium. It began to lose its original character by the end of the ninth century. Everything being equal, the small farmer, with his strip of land, a pair of oxen, and a mule or donkey, managed to provide for his family and sometimes even to prosper. In general, though, he found it difficult, if not impossible, to accumulate a reserve with which to meet an emergency. Any misfortune, such as the loss of one of his animals, might endanger his social and economic position, for it would lessen his productivity and might prevent him from paying his taxes or meeting the demands of his creditors, had he been unfortunate enough to have resorted to borrowing. In either case he might abandon his land and run away. Protracted service in the army might have the same results. Or his existence might be endangered by incursions of the enemy, an earthquake, or crop failure. Wars were perennial and crop failure not infrequent. Under these circumstances the small farmer was tempted to sell his land and try to eke out a living by working for a large landed magnate. And there was no lack of purchasers.

The landed aristocracy had become weakened in the course of the seventh and eighth centuries, but it had never ceased to occupy a very important position in the society of the empire. Before the end of the ninth century it had become a powerful and wealthy group, controlling the high military functions of the empire and enjoying many economic privileges. The ninth century also saw the multiplication of monastic establishments endowed with land and ever ready to acquire more. This aristocracy, both lay and ecclesiastic, found its way into the village communities and began to absorb by various means, but principally at least in the tenth century, by purchase, the holdings of the small farmers, for land offered the most promising outlet for economic expansion, as the economy of the empire remained basically agricultural.

The imperial government, by a series of laws, tried to check this absorption. Said Romanos Lekapenos in one of these laws:

> It is not through hatred and envy of the rich that we take these measures, but for the protection of the small and the safety of the empire as a whole. . . . The extension of the power of the strong . . . will bring about the irreparable loss of the public good, if the present law does not bring a check to it. For it is the many, settled on the land, who provide for the general needs, who pay the taxes and furnish the army with its recruits. Everything falls when the many are wanting.

The substance of this law was repeated on various occasions, the last and most severe during the reign of Basil II. But in the end the aristocracy won. Its victory, anticipated by the death of Basil II (1025), was complete by the end of the eleventh century.

Urban society, too, went through some important changes during this period. The loss of Egypt and Syria and the consequent abolition by Heraklios of the gratuitous distribution of bread doubtless affected the corporation or guild of the shipowners, the *navicularii* of the earlier period. Under Justinian they had won some important concessions, and during the reign of Maurice (582–602) a decree was issued "enacting that the captain of a vessel should not be subjected to punishment and made to render compensation when his ship was wrecked, but that the loss should be put down to the imperial revenue." During and after the reign of Heraklios, the sources give the impression that the shipowners were comparatively free agents, plying the seas for their own personal gain. It would seem, on the basis of the general economic organization characteristic of the period, that one was free to enter or abandon this trade. There can be little doubt, though, that the activities of the *navicularii,* whether or not they were still organized into a corporation, were regulated, for the provisioning of Constantinople was one of the deepest concerns of the central government.

The abolition of the gratuitous distribution of bread probably affected the organization of the guild of the bakers. The *Book of the Prefect* has now been definitely confirmed as the work of Leo VI (886–912), but the various trade organizations that it regulates were not the creations of that emperor; they were the continuation, no doubt in a modified form, of the trade guilds of the early centuries of the later Roman Empire. The impression given by this document is that the bakers, for example, were not attached to their trade, nor was that trade hereditary. That was the status of every trade and profession referred to in that document.

When these changes took place is, of course, impossible to determine, but that they may be associated with the abolition of the gratuitous distribution of bread in the seventh century is not at all improbable. In any case, by the end of the ninth century, attachment to one's profession and its hereditary transmission no longer seem to have been features of at least the private corporations. This development must have taken place during the seventh or eighth century, the result of the force of circumstances rather than of the conscious efforts of the government. All corporations, though, whether public or private, were strictly regulated. These regulations had in view the interest not only of the state but also of the public at large, as well as of the trades. For example:

> The bakers shall make their profits according to the amount of grain purchased at the order of the prefect. They shall purchase the proper amount of grain by the nomisma from their assessor. When they have ground it and leavened it, they shall calculate their profit at a *keration* and two *miliaresia* on the nomismata. The *keration* will be pure profit, while the two *miliaresia* will go for the support of their workmen, the food of their mill animals, the fuel for the ovens, and the lighting. . . . Whenever there is an increase or decrease in the supply of grain, the bakers shall go to the prefect to have the weights of their loaves fixed by the assessor in accordance with the purchase price of the grain.

The organization of the trades in Byzantium during this period was more balanced and freer than during the early centuries of the empire. All was not always orderly, though, for some of the most violent scenes in the life of the empire, particularly in the eleventh century, were brought about by the activities of the trade organizations. In the period that followed, beginning about the end of the eleventh century and continuing to the end of the empire, these organizations declined. But they continued to exist and sometimes were the source of violence, although they had long lost all significance. Economic power was now in the hands of the Venetians, the Genoese, the Pisans, and other Westerners.

One of the most important features of the social and economic structure of the Byzantine Empire was monasticism. Associated in its origins with the ascetics of Egypt, it was soon introduced into the empire as a whole, thereby affecting its urban and rural life. By the end of the fourth century, monasteries were being founded virtually everywhere, the preference usually given to localities with difficult access. The monk was rapidly becoming one of the most vital elements of Byzantine society.

One may distinguish three chronological phases in the development of monasticism: (1) the period extending from its inception in the fourth century to about 741, when Constantine V became sole emperor; (2) the phase associated with iconoclasm, its first period in particular, covering the reigns of Constantine V (741–775) and Leo IV (775–780); and (3) the period that began with enthronement of Irene (797–802) and continued, with some interruptions in the course of the first half of the ninth century, until 1453 and beyond. It was in the course of the third phase that Byzantine monasticism experienced its greatest development, both in the number of its monastic establishments and in their regional distribution. The attempts made by Nikephoros II Phokas (963–969), then by Basil II (976–1025), and finally by Manuel II (1143–1180) to check the growth of its properties all ended in failure. By 1453, the church was virtually in control of what was left of the empire and the monk had become the dominant influence in its life.

The monks, who had always been an omnipresent part of Byzantine society, became very powerful, particularly in the later centuries of the empire. Nothing short of a thorough overhauling of the life of that society, a complete change in its constituents, could have altered their position. They furnished the church with its bishops and patriarchs. According to L. Bréhier, between 705, when Cyrus, a hermit of Amastreia who had predicted to Justinian II his restoration to the throne, became patriarch, and 1204, when Constantinople fell to the Latins, forty-five of the fifty-seven patriarchs were monks. The situation was not much different in the period that followed. In Byzantium the populace respected and admired the monks, and frequently turned to them in time of need. Emperors loved them, shared their table with them, sought their blessing, and, when on the point of launching some important undertaking, often consulted them. Monks were considered to be a spiritual force upon which the safety of the empire depended. There were emperors who placed greater faith in monasteries than in fortresses. The power and influence of the monks continued even after the fall of the empire.

In the course of the tenth century, the landed aristocracy came to dominate the society of the empire. The failure of the government to check this domination solidified the aristocracy's position and gave rise to the agrarian picture that obtained during the last centuries of the empire. The prevalent element of this domination was the landed magnate, who was also a powerful figure in the political and military life of the empire. His possessions, usually acquired through imperial grants, but also by purchase and even outright seizures, were vast, in some instances stretching over entire regions. This was true both in the Asiatic and the Balkan regions of the empire, but the former had been lost roughly by the beginning of the fourteenth century.

In Thessaly the region of Demetrias was dominated by the Maliasenoi family. Constantine Maliasenos, married to the niece of Theodore Komnenos Doukas, the despot of Epiros, was at the beginning of the thirteenth century a veritable dynast and the virtual owner of the entire region. His position, influence, and vast possessions were inherited by his son and successor, Nicholas, who lived during the reign of Michael Palaiologos. The Maliasenoi were relatives of the Palaiologoi. Their possessions included many villages over whose peasant inhabitants (and their property) they were absolute masters.

Besides the Maliasenoi there were other big magnates in Thessaly. Indeed, Thessaly was the country among the Greek lands where "feudalization" reached its greatest development. Powerful families such as the Strategopouloi and the Gabrielopouloi held vast possessions, and there were others whose influence and wealth, if somewhat lesser, was still considerable. For example, a certain Marmaras may be mentioned. He was a *protonobilissimus,* a title that appears for the last time in Byzantine documents, and held the village of Trnovo, which had been granted to him as a *pronoia* by the emperor, probably Michael Palaiologos. Like others of his class, Maramaras tried to increase his holdings by the seizing of neighboring properties that did not belong to him. He ultimately failed, but his attempt illustrates one of the ways the powerful sought to add to their properties.

What was true of Thessaly was also true of Macedonia and Thrace. There were located the vast estates of the powerful Byzantine families, whose members dominated the political life of the empire—the Angeloi, the Kantakouzenoi, the Tzamblakoi, the Synadenoi. Their great holdings, the existence of which is well attested by fourteenth-century sources, were doubtless already in their possession in the thirteenth century. The Tzamblakoi, who in the fourteenth century possessed vast domains in the region of Christopolis, Serrai, and Thessaloniki, were in the service of the Palaiologoi and, before them, of John III Vatatzes, and were amply rewarded. This is also true of the Angeloi. It is known from a document, dated 1306, that Manuel Angelos, described as a relative of the emperor, possessed a number of villages in the neighborhood of Serrai and Thessaloniki. These villages had belonged to his father, having been granted to him by an imperial chrysobull.

The possessions of the Kantakouzenoi in Thrace were fabulous, and those of the Synadenoi were considerable. The Synadenoi are known to have possessed important properties in the region of Serrai, granted to them by an imperial chrysobull, and the vast wealth of John Kantakouzenos was in the possession of the family by the end of the thirteenth century. The Kantakouzenoi also possessed lands in the Morea, where the agrarian situation was very much like that in Thessaly. In every region there were vast stretches of land owned by monasteries and the church.

In the meantime the village communities underwent important changes. No longer inhabited by free peasant proprietors but by dependent tenants, the *paroikoi* of the Byzantine texts, they had become the "property" of powerful magnates, both lay and ecclesiastical. Some peasant proprietors did continue to exist, but whether this was true of entire free village communities is a matter upon which no definite pronouncement can be made. What can be said definitely, though, is that in the later period, particularly that of the Palaiologoi, what characterized the agricultural landscape of the Byzantine empire was the dependent village. If villages inhabited entirely by small peasant proprietors did in fact survive, they must have been very few and far between, and hardly any better off economically—certainly in the fourteenth century—than the nonfree ones.

The peasants inhabiting the dependent villages were subject to various dues and obligations, known collectively as their burden (*βάρος*), payable to their lord. In the payment of these dues there are instances of "voluntary" collective responsibility, an indication perhaps of the previous free state of the village.

It is possible to look, at least to some extent, inside the village of the later centuries of the Byzantine Empire, especially in the first half of the fourteenth century. This possibility exists through the survival of the so-called *praktika,* inventories of dependent villages drawn up for purposes of taxation. These *praktika* list by name the peasants and their property, the latter consisting primarily of land, livestock, and trees. Besides the land devoted to the cultivation of cereals and other crops, vineyards and vegetable gardens are often mentioned. Among the livestock, oxen used for plowing, hogs, and sheep predominate, while among the trees those frequently mentioned are the fig, the olive, and the walnut. But what makes the *praktika* of the fourteenth century important as sources is that they deal with the same villages at different dates. This makes possible an examination of the social and economic situation of these villages as it changed from year to year.

The following analysis relates to two villages: Melintziani, located in the administrative district of Strymon (Struma), to the west of that river; and the village of Gomatou, located in the administrative district of Hierissos, immediately west of Mount Athos. Both villages belonged to the Athonian monastery of Iviron. The dates involved are 1301 and 1317 for Melintziani; 1301, 1317, and 1341 for Gomatou.

In both villages there was a decrease in the number of large households. This decrease was apparently general, if one may judge from the statistical information available for other villages. Underlying this decrease was a decline in the population of the villages, quite evident in Gomatou, less so in Melintziani. Those who owned the villages tried to offset this decline by settling newcomers, peasants who had come from other villages and other regions. Mentioned in the *praktika* which have been analyzed are an Anatolikos, a Boleros, and a Lemnaios, names derived no doubt from the geographical origins of those who bore them. The mobility of peasants that may be inferred from this should not be exaggerated. Most peasants died in the villages where they were born and registered. This, too, is shown in the *praktika.*

While some villages suffered a decline in population, others became deserted. About the latter, something is now known thanks to a preliminary survey published in 1966 by Hélène Antoniadis-Bibicou. The survey covers the regions that constitute modern Greece and extends from the eleventh through the nineteenth century.

Eighty-six villages, according to Antoniadis, were deserted during the eleventh century, 3 during the first half and 83 during the second. For the twelfth century she found only 30, and 20 of these were deserted in the second half of that century. The thirteenth century saw the desertion of 66 villages, of which 57 were deserted after 1250. About two-thirds of these villages were located in the islands, perhaps an indication that their desertion was the result of piracy, an activity that was widely prevalent during the second half of the thirteenth century and later. But by far the greatest number of villages became deserted in the fourteenth century. Antoniadis counted a total of 458 villages deserted, 136 of which were deserted during the first half, and 322 during the second half, of that century. They were in every region of the empire, but the majority were in Macedonia and Thrace. The villages deserted in the fifteenth century number 65 for the first half and 58 for the second half. The damage had obviously been done in the fourteenth century.

Thus the decadence of the Byzantine village, begun in the tenth century, reached its culmination in the fourteenth with the final disintegration of the Byzantine countryside. By then virtually every village was in a state of decline, deserted, or in the process of being so. Oppressed by magnates whose dependents they were, there was very little that the peasants could do. They might agitate, as they apparently did, or even break into open rebellion, as did the Thracian peasants inhabiting the villages in the neighborhood of Didymotichon in 1342, but all to no avail. So flagrant were the abuses to which they were subjected that the Turks saw in them one of the important reasons for their success. "God has decreed," said the Turks, "that we should take the land from the Christians because they do not conduct their affairs . . . with justice, because they look to wealth and favor, and the rich treat the poor with haughtiness, and do not help them either with gifts or with justice." The central government, its powers gone, with no money and manpower, was in no position to help.

In his struggle against his grandfather, Andronikos III (1328–1341) did indeed promise to reduce the burden on the peasantry in Thrace, but nothing concrete seems to have come out of this promise. In 1367 Emperor John V submitted meekly to the church when it rejected his plea to turn over to him some of its property in order that he might settle soldiers on it. Some years later Manuel II secularized half the monastic estates so that he might turn them into allotments for soldiers, but in so doing he met with the vigorous opposition of ecclesiastics. Much later he returned at least part of the confiscated property to their original owners. Meanwhile, the dynastic wars, which were also social wars, and the continuous incursions of foreigners wrought havoc everywhere. Peasants were killed or fled—perhaps to another village, where the same fate almost certainly awaited them—or sought refuge in a city, where they helped to swell the ranks of the poor and intensify the social tension. The countryside lay prostrate, ready to be seized by the willing foreigner.

BIBLIOGRAPHY

Hélène Antoniadis-Bibicou, "Villages désertés en Grèce: Un bilan provisoire," in *Rivista di storia dell'agricoltura,* 6 (1966); A. E. R. Boak, "The Book of the Prefect," in *Journal of Economic and Business History,* **4** (1929); J. B. Bury, *History of the Later Roman Empire,* 2 vols. (1923, repr. 1931), 55ff.; Peder Charanis, "On the Social Structure of the Later Roman Empire," in *Byzantion,* **17** (1947); and "Town and Country in the Byzantine Possessions of the Balkan Peninsula During the Later Period of the Empire," in Henrik Birnbaum and Speros Vryonis, Jr., eds., *Aspects of the Balkans* (1961); Franz Dölger, *Beiträge zur Geschichte der byzantinischen Finanzverwaltung* (1927); Angeliki Laiou-Thomadakis, *Peasant Society in the Late Byzantine Empire* (1977); Paul Lemerle, "Esquisse pour une histoire agraire de Byzance," in *Revue historique,* **219** and **220** (1958).

Georg Ostrogorsky, "Agrarian Conditions in the Byzantine Empire," in *The Cambridge Economic History of Europe,* 2nd ed., I (1966); M. M. Postan, *Pour l'histoire de la féodalité byzantine,* French trans. by H. Grégoire (1954); *Quelques problèmes d'histoire de la paysannerie byzantine* (1956); "The Byzantine Empire in the World of the Seventh Century," and "Byzantine Cities in the Early Middle Ages," in *Dumbarton Oaks Papers,* **13** (1959); Germaine Rouillard, *La vie rurale dans l'empire byzantin* (1953); N. G. Svoronos, *Études sur l'organisation intérieure de la société et l'économie de l'empire byzantin* (1973); Speros Vryonis, Jr., "Byzantium: The Social Basis of Decline in the Eleventh Century," in *Greek, Roman, and Byzantine Studies,* **2** (1959); and "Byzantine Demokratia and the Guilds in the Eleventh Century," in *Dumbarton Oaks Papers,* **17** (1963); Dionysios Zakythinos, *Byzance: État—société—économie* (1973).

PETER CHARANIS

[See also **Agriculture, Byzantine; Guilds, Byzantine; Monasticism, Byzantine; Taxation, Byzantine; Trade, Byzantine.**]

BYZANTINE EMPIRE: HISTORY (330–1025). The Byzantine Empire was the continuation of the Roman Empire in the eastern Mediterranean during the Middle Ages. Chronologically it spanned the period from about 330 to 1453, and at its height ruled the lands from the Euphrates in the east to the Strait of Gibraltar in the west. Ethnically the empire was diverse, its subjects including Greeks, Armenians, Slavs, Arabs, Egyptians, and Latins, although its culture, from the seventh century on, was predominantly Greek. Politically the empire was an autocracy in which the emperor was viewed as the vice-regent of God. The empire was seen as having been established by God to last until the end of the world. Among its primary characteristics were cultural and political continuity with ancient Greece and Rome, and a Christian ethic that permeated nearly every institution and aspect of life. The center of the empire, in both cultural and political terms, was Constantinople (previously Byzantium, today Istanbul), the site of the court of the emperor, with its many bureaus and complex ceremony, and the seat of the patriarch of Constantinople, the spiritual leader of Byzantine Christianity.

The Byzantine Empire thus stands as a bridge between the ancient world and the medieval and modern worlds. When much of western Europe was plunged in the depths of barbarism, the Byzantine Empire maintained a high level of civilization and political order. It preserved and then transmitted many of the ideas of ancient classical civilization, first to the Arabs and later to the Slavs and western Europeans. Much of medieval commerce, science, and learning would not have existed without the Byzantine contribution. Yet the Byzantine Empire was much more than a conduit, passively transmitting the fruits of classical experience to willing receivers. It had a life of its own and a set of ideas that borrowed heavily from the classical tradition but selected and combined those elements according to its own needs and interests. The Byzantines had a highly integrated view of life that saw clearly the re-

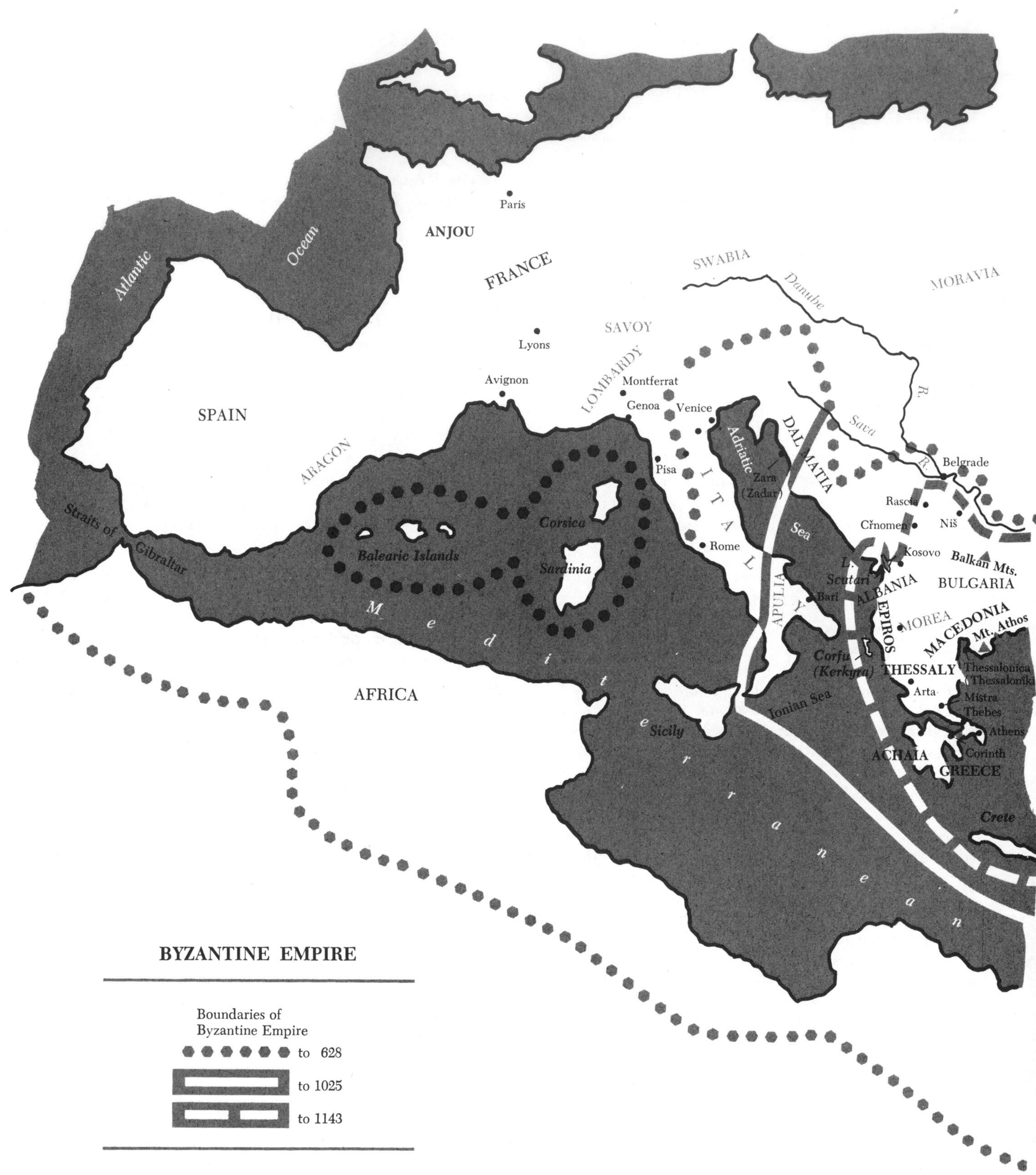

BYZANTINE EMPIRE

Boundaries of Byzantine Empire

to 628

to 1025

to 1143

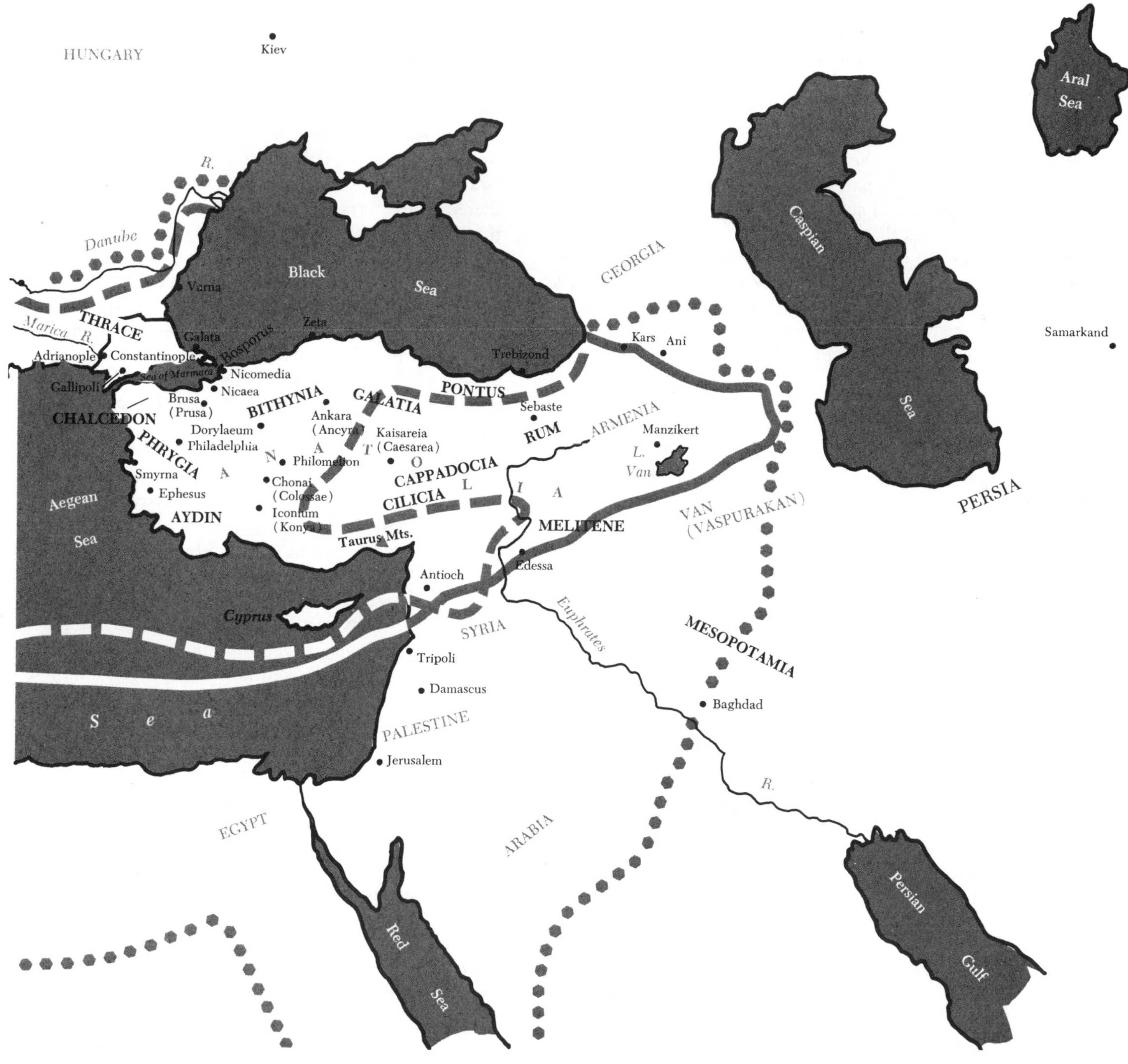
RUSSIA
HUNGARY
Kiev
Aral Sea
Caspian Sea
Black Sea
Danube R.
GEORGIA
Varna
THRACE
Marica R.
Galata
Zeta
Bosporus
Adrianople
Constantinople
Trebizond
Kars
Ani
Samarkand
Gallipoli
Sea of Marmara
Nicomedia
Nicaea
PONTUS
Brusa (Prusa)
BITHYNIA
GALATIA
Sebaste
CHALCEDON
Ankara (Ancyra)
ARMENIA
Dorylaeum
Kaisareia (Caesarea)
RUM
Manzikert
PHRYGIA
Philadelphia
A N A T O L I A
L. Van
Philomelion
CAPPADOCIA
Smyrna
Ephesus
Chonai (Colossae)
CILICIA
Aegean Sea
AYDIN
Iconium (Konya)
MELITENE
VAN (VASPURAKAN)
PERSIA
Taurus Mts.
Edessa
Antioch
Cyprus
SYRIA
Euphrates
MESOPOTAMIA
Tripoli
Damascus
Baghdad
S e a
PALESTINE
Jerusalem
R.
EGYPT
ARABIA
Red Sea
Persian Gulf

lationships among God, the emperor, and his people, and that witnessed deep penetration of the human sphere by the supernatural. The value system of the Byzantines was not the same as that of the largely warrior societies with which the empire came into contact in the later Middle Ages. Thus, Western misunderstandings of Byzantine society were largely responsible for the reputation for perfidy and intrigue that Byzantium has held since medieval times and that has caused the Byzantine Empire to be little understood even in modern times.

It should also be noted that the term "Byzantine Empire" is a creation of modern historians and that the "Byzantines" called themselves *Romaioi* ("Romans") and their empire the *Basileia tōn Romaiōn* ("Empire of the Romans"). They therefore saw themselves as part of a long historical continuum that stretched back to the kingdoms of the Old Testament and that found its fulfillment in the creation of the Roman Empire and its conversion to Christianity. The Byzantines saw no fundamental break with the past, continuing to refer to Constantinople as "New Rome" and to themselves as "Romans" until the conquest of the empire by the Turks and even long afterward.

THE EARLY BYZANTINE EMPIRE: 330–602

The Byzantine Empire grew gradually and organically from the old Roman Empire, and it is not possible to assign any precise date for its "founding." It is best to see the creation of the Byzantine Empire as a process rather than a single event and to view the early Byzantine period as one of gradual transformation, wherein the ideas and institutions of the ancient world were being replaced by those of the medieval East.

Naturally there were many fundamental changes during this period, and the fully developed Byzantine world was very different from the ancient world that preceded it. Two of these important changes were the foundation of Constantinople and the conversion of the empire to Christianity, both of which are closely connected with Constantine I the Great (306–337), generally recognized as the first Byzantine emperor. Constantine was not primarily an innovator, and he built firmly on the foundations of his predecessors. He did, however, build a great eastern capital at Constantinople (dedicated 11 May 330); he also became a Christian and encouraged his subjects to do likewise. Constantine's Christianity is perhaps best understood in terms of earlier Roman thought: the Christian God was understood to be directly involved in human affairs, and earthly success was largely determined by maintaining a correct relationship with him. These principles became a mainstay of Byzantine political thought from Constantine's time on. As a result, the Byzantine state became involved in the disputes concerning the definition of Christian doctrine, especially the controversies over the nature of the church and the Trinity (and later the person of Christ). Thus, at the time of Constantine the emperor was called upon to take a position on the Donatist and Arian controversies, and Constantine called and presided over the First Council of Nicaea in 325.

The age of Constantine also witnessed the culmination of a process of political reorganization that had begun in the third century and had been furthered by the tetrarchs. The loose administration of the Roman Empire was replaced by a tightly organized structure that was, at least theoretically, personally coordinated by the all-powerful emperor. In contrast with the Roman system, civil and military functions were carefully distinguished, and a separate administrative structure was created for each branch of the government. Cities remained the fundamental subdivision of the empire and some of the large cities retained their civic pride and a good deal of individualism, but on the whole they had lost their political independence and had become tax-collecting bodies for the central administration. The empire was divided into provinces, all of which were grouped into one of four great prefectures. The prefectures were governed by praetorian prefects, great officials of state who were responsible to the emperor for the day-to-day functioning of the state. Both the provincial governors and the praetorian prefects had lost their military function and they were purely civilian officials. On the military side a distinction was made among three kinds of troops: the frontier militia *(limitanei)*, the mobile field armies *(comitatenses)*, and the palace guard. The dux, or local military commander, generally reported to the comes, who was in turn responsible to the *magister militum.* The *magistri militum* and the praetorian prefects, along with a number of other officials chosen by the emperor, formed the imperial court, which made the basic decisions of state.

The emperor was in general secluded from ordinary individuals and his person elevated far beyond that of mere mortals. His sacred character as the vice-regent of God was emphasized by distinctive clothing and confirmed with an elaborate ritual that was borrowed extensively by the emerging liturgy of the church.

Constantine was succeeded by his three sons, with the eldest, Constantius II (337–361), reigning at Constantinople and ultimately seizing sole power in his own name. Constantius was an ardent Arian, having been raised in the Christian faith, and for a time it appeared that the decisions of the First Council of Nicaea might be reversed. He also furthered and completed many of the projects begun by his father, including construction of buildings in Constantinople and the city's elevation to a position equal to that of old Rome. A temporary reaction to the policies of the house of Constantine took place during the brief reign of Julian (361–363), frequently known as the Apostate. Julian was a nephew of Constantius II, and most of his immediate family had been murdered at the time of the latter's accession. His brief reign was characterized by his efforts to establish organized paganism as a rival to Christianity and by his attempt to revive the old civic structure of the empire. Julian died suddenly while on campaign against Persia and his policies came quickly to an end.

Under Valentinian I (364–375) and Valens (364–378) the empire was ruled by two emperors. Valens, who ruled from Constantinople, was an Arian, and the church continued to be plagued by dissension. Even more serious was the growing barbarian menace, as Hunnic peoples from east and central Asia appeared among the Germanic tribes and sent many of them plunging headlong across the Danube frontier. Many of these Germans were enrolled as Roman allies, and some were given land and settled within the empire. Such groups were an unstable and potentially disruptive element, and in 378, some Gothic allies revolted and ravished Thrace. Valens met the Goths on the battlefield at Adrianople, where he was decisively defeated and lost his life.

The situation after Adrianople was salvaged by Theodosius I (379–395), the last of the early Byzantine warrior-emperors and also the last to rule an undivided empire. Theodosius was an autocrat and a strong personality; he made concessions to the Goths but generally kept the barbarians at bay through a vigilant military policy. Also an ardent orthodox Christian, he summoned the First Council of Constantinople (381) which again condemned Arianism and elevated the church of Constantinople to a position second only to that of old Rome. Arianism remained a potent force, especially since it had been spread widely among the Germans, but it was no longer supported by imperial policy and slowly disappeared within the empire.

Theodosius left the empire to his two sons, Honorius, who ruled the West, and Arcadius, who held the throne in Constantinople. Theoretically the empire remained united, but from this point on, no emperor was able to hold effective power over both parts. The barbarians took advantage of the death of Theodosius to rise in revolt, this time under the leadership of Alaric, king of the Visigoths. Alaric ravaged Thrace, descended into Greece, and finally made his way to the West, where he sacked Rome in 410, shocking the world by this demonstration of imperial weakness. The rest of the fifth century was characterized by continued barbarian pressure, much of it directed against the Danube frontier. The Huns continued their westward movement, and one Germanic group after another crossed into Roman territory. The government at Constantinople was able to deal with this threat by means of a combination of military preparedness and a diplomacy supported by liberal payments to cooperative barbarian leaders. In addition, Constantinople was defended by a powerful system of fortifications completed under Emperor Theodosius II (408–450).

The rulers of the West had neither the manpower nor the financial reserves to meet the barbarian challenge, and Germanic groups began to settle in growing numbers throughout the western provinces. The emperors in Constantinople offered what assistance they could, but by the end of the fifth century all of the West had fallen to the barbarians, many of whom continued to recognize, if only formally, the emperor in the East as their ultimate sovereign.

In the East theological controversy continued. At the Council of Ephesus (431) Nestorius, patriarch of Constantinople, was condemned for allegedly stressing Christ's humanity at the expense of his divinity (Nestorianism). In reaction to this, Monophysitism emphasized a single divine nature in the person of Christ, a teaching that gained considerable support, especially in Egypt and Syria. After much turmoil, however, Monophysitism was condemned at the Council of Chalcedon (451) and a doctrine of two natures (divine and human) was declared orthodox. The decision of the Council of Chalcedon seriously split the church in the East, and many Christians were never reconciled to its teaching. The council also asserted the virtual equality of the bishops of Constantinople and Rome, and from this point on, the Byzantine church generally recognized the spiritual preeminence of the pope but denied him any administrative jurisdiction over the East.

The emperors of the second half of the fifth century sought to defend the empire against the barbarian threat and to find some solution to the schism caused by the decisions at Chalcedon. Zeno (474–491), for example, issued a decree, the *Henotikon* (Edict of Union, 482), which called upon both sides to abandon the struggle. Needless to say, the issue was more important to the contending parties and the injunction fell on deaf ears. Anastasius (491–518) even adopted Monophysite ideas in an effort to put an end to the controversy, but this also was unsuccessful. He was, however, able to bring considerable stability and prosperity to the state, and as a result he was able to carry out important economic and administrative reforms.

The reign of Justinian (527–565) represents the culmination of the early Byzantine period. The empire was prosperous, strong, and full of intellectual vitality; and with the assimilation of much classical thought by Christian theology, a new synthesis was beginning to emerge. Justinian was openly autocratic in temperament and policy; he believed firmly in his own abilities and his special relationship to God, and with his wife, Theodora, he ruled the empire with an iron hand.

This policy sparked resistance among both the aristocracy and the common people, resulting in the Nika Revolt of 532, which began as a riot of the circus factions ("clubs" or claques organized to applaud at the chariot races), but quickly expanded into a full-scale rebellion, destroying one-third of Constantinople and nearly costing Justinian his throne. Justinian survived this threat and used the destruction as a reason to rebuild Constantinople as a monument to himself. Among the buildings constructed at this time was Hagia Sophia ("Holy Wisdom"), the "Great Church" of Constantinople and probably the most spectacular example of Byzantine art and architecture.

Justinian also set himself the task of revising and codifying Byzantine law and legal education. The result was the *Corpus juris civilis,* which has served as the model of legal principle for much of European law. Justinian turned his attention also to the religious controversies, but his efforts there were no more successful than those of his predecessors.

In foreign affairs Justinian reconquered much of the West from the barbarians. Under the command of generals such as Belisarios and Narses, Byzantine troops defeated the Vandals in North Africa and the Ostrogoths in Italy. Byzantium was once again mistress of the whole Mediterranean basin.

Justinian's accomplishments were indeed spectacular, but they were also expensive, and his methods of taxation were harsh in the extreme. Thus, his reign can be viewed in two ways: it was a brilliant climax to the early Byzantine age, but it was also a prelude, and perhaps a contributor, to the age of disaster and disintegration that was to follow.

LOSS AND REORGANIZATION: 602–843

The centuries after Justinian were characterized by devastating military defeats and the loss of much of the empire's heartland. These losses threatened the empire's very existence, and required not only administrative changes but also a reconsideration of many of the bases of Byzantine civilization. It is a measure of the strength of Byzantine society and culture that the empire was able to survive these difficulties and to emerge from them, changed but full of vitality and energy.

The nature and the effects of the disasters that befell the empire in the years after Justinian are relatively well understood, but their causes are not. Thus, it is common to refer to the overextension of the empire under Justinian and the financial problems caused by the conquests, and to point to a long series of conflicts with Persia, but these do not seem sufficient fully to explain the collapse, particularly when the collapse is compared with the splendor and apparent prosperity of the earlier period. Instead, fundamental changes must have been taking place within Byzantine society, perhaps including the destruction of much of the empire's productivity and cohesiveness, and possibly serious demographic changes.

In any case, Justinian's conquests did not long survive him. Within a few years of his death (565) the Lombards began their invasion of Italy and, more seriously, the Sasanid Persians became an ever increasing threat on the empire's eastern frontier while barbarian pressure built along the Danube. The barbarians in the north were now the Avars and the Slavs, and they pushed deep into the Balkan peninsula in the latter years of the sixth century, destroying settlements that had survived the earlier invasions and altering the ethnic character of the area. The successors of Justinian resisted these pressures as best they could, but after 602 the frontiers, both north and east, collapsed completely.

Some measure of stability was brought by Emperor Heraklios (610–641), who probably saved the empire from complete destruction. In the early years of his reign he naturally could not rectify the situation, and by 626 the Persians and the Avars combined their forces to attack Constantinople. The Byzantines still had control of the sea, however, and the city was saved. Heraklios introduced new military tactics, including a greater reliance on heavy cavalry, and the tide of battle began to turn. The emperor spent years in the field, especially in the East, and by 628 he had decisively defeated the Persians and made their king his vassal.

Both sides were exhausted by the long struggle, and neither was a match for the Arabs, who had been united by the teachings of Islam and who quickly overran both the Persian Empire and the eastern Byzantine provinces: Syria in 636, Egypt in 642. Thus, the richest and most populous areas of the empire fell to the Arabs, and Justinian's dream of a united world was only a distant memory.

The Arabs pushed into Asia Minor and raided many key cities, further disrupting trade and settled life within the empire, but their lines of communication were strained and they could not conquer territory beyond the Taurus frontier in southern Asia Minor. A new threat was added, however, when they built a fleet that allowed them to attack the islands and coastal cities and to strike directly at Constantinople. The Byzantine capital endured two terrifying sieges, from 674 to 678 and again from 717 to 718. On both occasions Byzantine resolve remained high, while continued Byzantine naval supremacy and the use of Greek fire ensured the safety of Constantinople.

During the seventh-century invasions the old administrative system had broken down almost completely: the Balkans were now largely in the hands of the Slavs, while the East had been devastated first by the Persians and then by the Arabs. Byzantine resistance focused on fortified cities and other fortresses that could be held against the enemy, and the complex provincial system of Constantine was essentially abandoned. The historical sources for this period are unusually poor, and the details of the reorganization that followed the invasions are not entirely clear. Thus, some scholars wish to date the reorganization of the empire as early as the reign of Heraklios and to see it as a result of imperial policy, while others view the changes as taking place over a longer period, as necessity and circumstances demanded.

In any case, a fundamental aspect of the new system was the creation of the theme (Greek: *thema*) as the basic unit of imperial administration. The theme was essentially a military district governed by a *strategos* (general) who had both civil and military authority. With the breakdown of the distinction between civil and military power, the praetorian prefects lost their positions and the *strategoi* were made directly responsible to the emperor. This gave the *strategoi* considerable power and independence of action, both of which were necessary in the chaotic situation of the age.

At the central level, administration was coordinated by the logothetes in charge of the various accounts of state. These officials had originally been little more than accountants, but they gradually became more important until some were virtual ministers of state or department heads. For example, the logothete of the drome was originally in charge of the imperial post, including the messengers sent on diplomatic missions, and from this function he attained a position very much like that of a foreign minister.

The military disruptions of the seventh century had obvious social and economic effects, as revenue was lost to the state and trade and population were seriously displaced. There were considerable ethnic changes within the empire, but the overall result was to emphasize its cultural unity. Areas that had been different in either speech or religion had been lost to the western barbarians or the Arabs, and the remaining central part of the empire was overwhelmingly Hellenic in language and culture, and orthodox in religious sentiment. During the reign of Heraklios, for example, Greek finally replaced Latin as the language of administration.

The invasions had also broken up the large landed estates of the empire, and it was probably from this source that the state made distributions to individuals on condition that they provide their own military equipment and devote some of their time to military service. These "soldiers' lands" *(stratiotika ktimata)* saved the state the considerable expense of hiring mercenary troops and provided a loyal native soldiery that was the basis of the Byzantine army during the centuries to come.

The difficulties of this period may also have contributed to an increase in religious devotion and to the growth of the cult of icons. Not everyone was pleased with the veneration of icons, some regarding it as idolatry and ultimately responsible for the military disasters of the age. Such opposition remained in the background throughout much of this period, but it came to the fore in the early eighth century when a sympathetic emperor came to the throne.

Leo III (717–741) rose to prominence at a time when the empire was suffering from a series of weak emperors. The Arabs were poised for their second siege of Constantinople, and Leo's first task was to defend the empire from this mortal danger. As emperor he was a shrewd administrator and a talented military strategist. Particularly toward the end of his reign Leo enjoyed considerable success against the Arabs. He also sought to render more effective imperial control over the *strategoi* by founding new themes in frontier areas and by dividing the existing themes into more manageable units. In addition, Leo issued a codification and simplification of Byzantine law, the *Ekloga* (726), that demonstrated a concern for the realities of provincial life and sought to apply Christian principles to the legal structure of the state.

Leo III is, however, best known as the first of the iconoclast emperors. He probably was personally opposed to the veneration of icons, and he seems to have felt that the disasters of the age were the result of God's displeasure with the practice. As a result, Leo began to speak openly against the veneration of icons, and in 730 he issued an edict ordering the destruction of all icons. Opinion naturally was divided on this issue, among both clergy and laymen, and feelings were deeply held. The iconoclastic controversy therefore affected nearly every aspect of Byzantine society and went far beyond the religious issues. First, iconoclasm naturally had a tremendous impact on religious art, since all figural representations were forbidden. Second, the monasteries were severely affected, not so much under Leo III as under his son and successor, Constantine V (741–775), since the monks were the foremost supporters of the veneration of icons. Iconoclasm also raised the question of the ability of the emperor to intervene in religious disputes and even to define Christian truth. Finally, iconoclasm can be seen as the last great struggle between "Eastern" and "Western" ideas in the formation of Byzantine culture.

The successes of Leo III and Constantine V against the Arabs, and the removal of the caliphate from Umayyad Damascus to Abbasid Baghdad in 751–752, allowed the empire to turn its attention to the Balkans, where the foundation of the Bulgarian state in the seventh century had raised a new danger. Constantine V overwhelmingly defeated the Bulgars and put a stop to their advance into Thrace. Meanwhile, he devoted practically no attention to the West, where the pope was already alienated by iconoclasm and was seeking alliance with the Frankish kings, signaling an end to Byzantine political influence in central Italy.

Unlike her predecessors, Empress Irene (780–802) was a supporter of the icons and arranged for their restoration at the Second Council of Nicaea (787). The monks and their supporters, however, did not favor her willingness to allow the reconciliation of former iconoclasts and opposed the empress and her patriarch, Tarasius. This disagreement between the "Zealots" (monks and their supporters) and the "politicians" (those willing to bend strict church regulations for the greater good) was to trouble the empire for several centuries.

At the same time, Byzantium had to face the threat posed by the growing power of the Frankish monarchs and, more particularly, the military power of Charlemagne and his coronation as emperor in 800. To the Byzantines this latter action was a direct affront and a challenge since, in their view, there could be only one empire and one imperial power. Charlemagne, for his part, realized that no claim of imperial power was worthwhile without some reference to Byzantium, so he used his military success in Dalmatia to put pressure on the empire. He proposed some form of marital alliance, first through marriage of his daughter Rotrud to Irene's son Constantine VI and later through his own marriage to the empress herself. Opinion at the Byzantine court, however, was unanimous against any such arrangement, and this contributed to Irene's fall from power in 802.

Emperor Nikephoros I (802–811) was a moderate iconophile and an administrator of considerable ability. He made important changes in the imperial fiscal system and established Byzantine control on a firmer basis, especially in the Balkans, where he prepared the way for a large-scale campaign against the Bulgars. After notable successes, however, Nikephoros fell into a trap set by the Bulgarian khan Krum, and he and his army were destroyed.

The foreign failures of Irene and Nikephoros gave rise to an iconoclast reaction led by Emperor Leo V (813–820), who modeled himself on the great iconoclast emperors of the past. Under the intellectual leadership of John Grammaticus, iconoclasm again became a potent force, but it was opposed by the no less resolute leadership of the monks, especially the learned Theodore of Studios. Theophilos (829–842) provided the last impetus for that revived movement. He had an eclectic mind and was genuinely interested in the art and learning of Baghdad, even constructing his palace on an Arab model. The period of revived iconoclasm, however, was not one of military success. The revolt of Thomas the Slav (821–823), the beginning of the Arab invasion of Sicily (827), and successful raids in Asia Minor all weakened the credibility of the emperors and made the collapse of the iconoclastic movement all but inevitable.

THE BYZANTINE GOLDEN AGE: 843–1025

The invasions and the iconoclast crisis had put a strain on Byzantine civilization and had altered many of the fundamental institutions of the Byzantine state. Nevertheless, the Byzantine Empire survived these difficulties and emerged with a renewed sense of direction and imperial destiny. With these it entered a phase of expansion and growth that was to be a new golden age.

The restoration of the icons was largely the work of Empress Theodora, widow of Theophilos and regent for her son Michael III (842–867). John Grammaticus was deposed as patriarch and replaced by the layman Methodios, and a synod in 843 solemnly proclaimed the restoration of the icons. Naturally, the Zealots were not pleased and controversy continued, but the monks had been the overall victors in the struggle over iconoclasm and they came generally to dominate the ecclesiastical structure after 843.

Young Emperor Michael III was surrounded by individuals of brilliance and greatness of vision, and together they laid the foundations for the age that followed. Among these individuals were Michael's uncle Caesar Bardas, the scholar Leo the Mathematician, and Photios—perhaps the leading figure of the age, an intellectual who was later patriarch of Constantinople. Photios and Caesar Bardas were largely responsible for one of Byzantium's greatest achievements, the Christianization of the Slavs and their exposure to the richness of Byzantine civilization. Photios organized a mission to the Russians (860) that was the prototype for the great mission of Constantine (Cyril) and Methodios to Moravia. In order to further this mission, Constantine developed the so-called glagolithic alphabet with which to write Slavonic translations of the Bible, the liturgy, and other Christian writings. This development marked the real beginning of Slavonic civilization.

The mission to Moravia naturally had political as well as religious ramifications, for Byzantium hoped to neutralize Frankish and Bulgarian activity in this area. Ultimately Latin Christianity prevailed in Moravia, and Byzantine missionary activity was transferred to Bulgaria, where the Bulgarian prince Boris was baptized in 864, Emperor Michael being his godfather. With this policy of cultural expansion Byzantium was able to influence an area far larger than its army could ever control, and the various south and east Slavic peoples were brought slowly into the Byzantine cultural sphere.

The revived power of the Byzantine church and its missionary ambitions brought it into direct conflict with the papacy, which was experiencing a period of growth. The result was a schism between the two churches in which the issue of the *Filioque* played an important role but cultural differences and the question of papal supremacy and the independence of the Byzantine church remained crucial.

Ultimately Michael III fell victim to the political ambitions of Basil I (867–886), the founder of the Macedonian dynasty that was to dominate the empire over the next century and a half. Despite his questionable rise to power, Basil was a capable and farsighted ruler, continuing and carrying to completion many of the policies of Michael III and his advisers—for instance, he supported the missionary activity in Bulgaria and pursued an active military policy in Italy and in the East. Despite his lowly origins, Basil was an ardent supporter of the best in Byzantine civilization, and he encouraged the cultural developments begun under his predecessor. He also undertook a full compilation and revision of Byzantine law, which was completed by his son and successor, Leo VI (886–913).

Leo was intelligent, well educated, and pious; his sermons and theological works earned him the title of Leo the Wise. In foreign affairs Leo had to face a new threat from the Bulgarian czar Symeon (893–927). Symeon had been educated at Constantinople, and he was the empire's first adversary who thoroughly understood its policies and methods. When Symeon threatened the Byzantine northern frontier, Leo called upon the Magyars to attack Bulgaria. Not to be outdone, Symeon made an alliance with the Pechenegs, who attacked the Magyars, driving them into their present home in the Danube plain and relieving the pressure on Bulgaria. Under Leo the Byzantine advance in the East stalled, and Sicily fell to the Arabs in 902. In 904, an Arab force under the renegade Leo of Tripoli sacked Thessaloniki, the second city of the empire.

In addition, Leo had serious problems stemming from his failure to produce an heir despite three marriages. Ultimately his mistress produced a son, the future emperor Constantine VII Porphyrogenitos (913–959), and Leo forced his recognition over the vociferous objections of the Zealots. Leo's death in 913, while Constantine was still a minor, led to a succession of regencies formed against the background of Symeon's depradations in the Balkans and his open ambition for the imperial throne. Ultimately, power was seized by the talented and ambitious Romanos I Lekapenos (920–944), who managed to stalemate Symeon's aspirations until the latter's death in 927.

Peace on the Bulgarian frontier gave Romanos the opportunity to turn his attention to the East, where the power of the caliphate was rapidly waning and where a major Byzantine offensive was now begun. Under generals such as John Kurkuas, the Byzantine army defeated the Arabs on several fronts and prepared the way for the victorious advance over the next half century. In internal matters Romanos turned his attention to the growing power of the landholding aristocracy, which threatened to overturn the social and economic system that had brought the empire military and economic stability. Ironically, the military successes of the recent past had enriched the local military commanders and allowed them to increase their landholdings considerably, at the expense of the small peasant farmers, who were the backbone of both the Byzantine army and its fiscal structure. Romanos saw this danger and initiated a policy designed to protect the small farmer and to make it difficult for the powerful to acquire additional lands. This was the beginning of a long struggle that pitted the emperor against the hereditary aristocracy. It lasted well into the next century, bringing with it many fundamental changes in the Byzantine state.

Romanos had planned to pass the imperial power on to his sons, but after a brief period of confusion the legitimate emperor, Constantine VII, came to the throne in his own name in 945. Constantine Porphyrogenitos is best known as an author, painter, and patron of a notable intellectual circle, but he was also an emperor of ability and foresight who generally continued the policies established by his predecessor.

Constantine's son, Romanos II (959–963), died at an early age, leaving two young sons, Basil and Constantine, as the legitimate emperors. The political void was filled by two talented generals, Nikephoros II Phokas (963–969) and John Tzimiskes (969–976). Nikephoros Phokas was a member of the hereditary aristocracy of Cappadocia who under Romanos II had distinguished himself as a general in the East and in Crete. As emperor the "Pale Death of the Saracens" broke through the Taurus frontier and took the war to the Arabs' homeland. He naturally did not pursue the same social and economic policies as his predecessors, and the great landowners were given a respite from imperial pressure. Nikephoros, an ascetic by temperament, ardently supported the development of Mt. Athos as a spiritual center and encouraged movements for monastic reform.

Like his predecessor, John Tzimiskes was a great general; he led the Byzantine army to its deepest penetration of the East since the days of Heraklios. He marched through Syria and Palestine, carrying all before him, and stood within striking distance of Jerusalem.

Upon the death of Tzimiskes the legitimate emperor, Basil II (976–1025), asserted his claim to the throne. Dynastic sentiment still existed, but there were rival claimants to the throne and Basil had to fight a long series of civil wars to maintain his birthright. In addition, he had to contend with the might of Bulgaria under the leadership of Czar Samuil. The struggle was long and protracted, but Basil was finally victorious and Bulgaria was annexed to the empire. Throughout the Balkan peninsula the force of Byzantine arms was triumphant.

Basil II was also active in the East, and just before his death he contemplated a campaign against the Arabs in Sicily. A man of single-minded purpose, Basil had little time for culture or the refinements of life. He was a staunch opponent of the hereditary aristocracy, especially after the years of civil war against the aristocrats, and he followed and strengthened the regulations of his predecessors against the growth of large landholding.

At the death of Basil II in 1025, the Byzantine Empire stood at a pinnacle of power and influence. Its borders were expanding, and its culture and wealth were the envy of most contemporary states. Basil had recently (989) presided over the baptism of Prince Vladimir of Kiev and the Christianization of Russia. There were weaknesses, it is true, and Byzantium's enemies were gathering strength for a new assault, but for the moment the empire stood as the dominant power in the Mediterranean world.

BIBLIOGRAPHY

General works. The most useful single-volume introduction to the history of the Byzantine Empire is George Ostrogorsky, *History of the Byzantine State,* rev. ed. (1969). See also Cyril Mango, *Byzantium: The Empire of*

New Rome (1981); and Alexander Kazhdan and Giles Constable, *People and Power in Byzantium* (1982). Older but still useful are N. H. Baynes and H. St. L. B. Moss., eds., *Byzantium: An Introduction to East Roman Civilization* (1948); Charles Diehl, *Byzantium: Greatness and Decline* (1957); J. M. Hussey, *The Byzantine World* (1957); and Steven Runciman, *Byzantine Civilisation* (1933).

Early Byzantine Empire. Robert Browning, *Justinian and Theodora* (1971); J. B. Bury, *History of the Later Roman Empire,* 2 vols., 2nd ed. (1923); Arnold H. M. Jones, *Constantine and the Conversion of Europe* (1948, repr. 1979); *The Later Roman Empire,* 2 vols. (1949); Ernst Stein, *Histoire du bas-empire,* 2 vols. (1949–1959).

Loss and reorganization. P. J. Alexander, *The Patriarch Nicephorus of Constantinople* (1958); Anthony Bryer and Judith Herrin, eds., *Iconoclasm* (1977); Stephen Gero, *Byzantine Iconoclasm During the Reign of Leo III* (1973); Constance Head, *The Emperor Justinian II of Byzantium* (1972); R.-J. Lilie, *Die byzantinische Reaktion auf die Ausbreitung der Araber* (1976); Andreas N. Stratos, *Byzantium in the Seventh Century,* 5 vols. (1968–).

The Golden Age. J. B. Bury, *The Imperial Administrative System in the Ninth Century* (1911); Francis Dvornik, *Byzantine Missions Among the Slavs* (1970); Romilly J. H. Jenkins, *Studies on Byzantine History of the Ninth and Tenth Centuries* (1970); Dimitri Obolensky, *The Byzantine Commonwealth: Eastern Europe, 500–1453* (1971); Steven Runciman, *The Emperor Romanus Lecapenus and His Reign* (1929); Arnold Toynbee, *Constantine Porphyrogenitus and His World* (1973).

Sources. Byzantine sources for the period that are available in English include the following: Ernst Barker, ed., *Social and Political Thought in Byzantium from Justinian I to the Last Palaeologus* (1957); Constantine Porphyrogenitos, *De administrando imperio,* G. Moravcsik, ed., R. Jenkins, trans. (1949); Elizabeth Dawes and N. H. Baynes, trans., *Three Byzantine Saints* (1948); Eusebius of Caesarea, *Ecclesiastical History,* K. Lake and H. J. Lawlor, trans., 2 vols. (1926–1932); Nikolaos I, patriarch of Constantinople, *Letters,* R. J. H. Jenkins and L. G. Westerink, trans. (1973); Photios, *The Homilies of Photius,* Cyril Mango, trans. (1958); Procopius, *Works,* Henry B. Dewing, trans., 7 vols. (1914–1940).

T. E. GREGORY

[See also **Alaric; Basil I; Basil II; Bulgaria; Constantine I; Constantine V; Constantine VII Porphyrogenitos; Constantinople; Corpus Juris Civilis; Councils, Byzantine; Councils, Ecumenical; Cyril and Methodios, Sts.; Dux; Henotikon; Heraklios; Huns; Iconoclasm, Christian; Irene, Empress; Julian the Apostate; Justinian I; Leo III the Isaurian; Leo V the Armenian; Leo VI the Wise; Limitanei; Logothete; Magister Militum; Michael III; Monophysitism; Nestorianism; Nicaea, Councils of; Nikephoros I; Nikephoros II Phokas; Photios; Praetorian Prefect; Roman Empire, Late; Romanos I Lekapenos; Romanos II; Russian Nomads, Invasions of; Schisms, Eastern-Western Church; Slavs; Strategos; Themes; Theodosios II; Zealots; Zeno.**]

BYZANTINE EMPIRE: HISTORY (1025–1204). At the end of Basil II's reign, the Byzantine Empire stretched from the Danube and the Sava to the heart of Armenia and northern Syria; the southernmost part of Italy was Byzantine.

At Basil's death (15 December 1025) the throne passed to his brother, Constantine VIII (1025–1028). The latter's daughters, Eudokia (a nun), Zoe, and Theodora (who became a nun), were the last members of the Macedonian house. Zoe (born *ca.* 978–980) married successively Romanos III Argyros (1028–1034) and Michael IV the Paphlagonian (1034–1041), then adopted the latter's nephew, Michael V Kalaphates ("the Calker" 1041–1042). When the last-named attempted to force Zoe into a convent, the mob overthrew him and brought forth Theodora from her nunnery; Zoe and Theodora briefly held joint sovereignty (April–June 1042). Zoe then married Constantine IX Monomachos (1042–1055), during whose reign she died (*ca.* 1050). At his death, Theodora again ruled briefly (1055–1056) and nominated as her successor a civil servant, Michael VI Stratiotikos (1056–1057). Thus ended the Macedonian dynasty.

A military rebellion raised Isaac I Komnenos (1057–1059) to the throne, but he abdicated in favor of a bureaucrat, Constantine X Doukas (1059–1067). To secure the succession for the latter's young children, his widow Eudokia married a leading general, Romanos IV Diogenes (1068–1071). Once the latter was captured by the Turks at Manzikert, the courtiers installed Constantine X's son, Michael VII Doukas (1071–1078), as their puppet. Another military revolt brought to power Nikephoros III Botaneiates (1078–1081); he was displaced by the younger, more competent Alexios I Komnenos.

Few of these numerous rulers acted vigorously to confront the empire's difficulties. Michael IV proved abler than his low-born background suggested; Isaac I and Romanos IV tried to cope with the military situation, but Romanos' generalship was not suited to Turkish tactics. Constantine IX fostered art and learning; little else can be said in favor of these rulers.

Internally, one of the marks of the period was uprisings of subject national groups. The inhabitants of

Samuil's former "West Bulgarian" realm rebelled vainly in 1040–1041, and again in 1072. The Serbs of Zeta (north of Lake Scutari), who joined the first revolt, succeeded in holding a precarious independence until late in the eleventh century. In Anatolia those Armenians subject to Byzantine rule were restless under oppressive tax collectors and intolerant Orthodox clerics. Fearing Turkish invasions, many migrated from the Armenian homeland into Cappadocia, Cilicia, and northern Syria.

Rebellions by generals also characterized the period; only a few can be mentioned. George Maniakes, suddenly deprived of his command in Sicily, took his troops across the Adriatic but fell in battle (1043). Leo Tornikios failed in an attack on Constantinople in 1047; Isaac Komnenos, as indicated, was more successful. After Manzikert revolts proliferated. In 1073–1074 the commander of Norman mercenaries, Roussel de Bailleul, moved against Constantinople, then tried to establish a principality in northern Anatolia. In 1077 there were simultaneous uprisings in the Balkans by Nikephoros Bryennios and in Anatolia by Nikephoros Botaneiates; with Turkish assistance the latter triumphed. But Botaneiates in turn faced revolts by Nikephoros Basilakios (in the Balkans), Nikephoros Melissenos (in Anatolia), and Alexios Komnenos.

While rebels threatened Constantinople, conspiracies against the throne and intrigues to obtain a position of influence proliferated within the city and the palace. The post of chief minister or adviser was particularly important during the many weak reigns. The powerful eunuch John the Orphanotrophos influenced Zoe against her first husband and in favor of his own brother Michael: Romanos III perished under suspicious circumstances, and Michael wed the empress. As Michael IV suffered increasingly from epilepsy, John induced Zoe to adopt Michael Kalaphates but, once emperor, Michael V exiled the powerful eunuch. Around Zoe, Theodora, and Constantine IX there gathered an imposing group of intellectuals, including Michael Psellos, Constantine Leichoudes, and John Xiphilinos, who vied with other factions for power. While Psellos and his friends remained influential during many of the following reigns, the eunuch Nikephoritzes became all-powerful under Michael VII; his greed helped render that ruler unpopular. The Slavs Boril and Germanos dominated Nikephoros III's administration.

Underlying the conflicts of courtiers and the military revolts was a struggle between the great landowners and the civil bureaucracy. The death of Basil II ended efforts to protect the tax-paying villages of smallholders; some of Basil's regulations were annulled, others ignored. Great landowners expanded their properties; through their control of the provinces and the army, they aimed at domination of the government. They desired further relaxation of imperial control and, thus, greater opportunities to enrich themselves. The bureaucrats of the capital (such educated middle-class men as Psellos and his friends) wished to maintain their own power, and thus stood for centralized authority. To weaken the generals, the administrators reduced the military budget and the size of the army. Emperors from the military party—Isaac I, Romanos IV, and Nikephoros III—found their efforts hampered by officials of the capital.

In these struggles the populace of Constantinople and leading churchmen participated. Michael V's attempt to exile Zoe was thwarted by a spontaneous uprising; an armed mob besieged and captured the palace. Patriarch Alexios encouraged the rebellion. In 1057 Patriarch Michael Keroullarios used his influence with the people to turn them in favor of Isaac Komnenos and assure his peaceful entry into the city. Nikephoros III, too, succeeded in his usurpation because he won over a portion of the people, who opened the gates to him. Guilds of craftsmen and merchants often provided organization and leadership to these outbreaks.

While the empire was distracted by internal conflicts and ruled usually by weak emperors, some provinces were lost to invaders and others suffered devastation. Early in the eleventh century Norman mercenaries appeared in southern Italy, serving anyone for hire. After Maniakes' revolt, Norman leaders began to carve out principalities for themselves. Members of the Hauteville family, notably Robert Guiscard and his brother Roger, assumed leadership; in 1059 Robert obtained the title "duke of Apulia" from the pope. Guiscard's conquests culminated in the capture of Bari (1071), Byzantium's last possession in Italy.

The Danube-Sava frontier, attained by Basil II, proved insecure. The Pechenegs (Patzinaks), a Turkic people from the north shore of the Black Sea, raided the empire's Balkan territories in 1033, 1036, and from 1048 to 1053. In 1043 a Russian fleet attacked Constantinople, but was beaten off with the aid of Greek fire. In 1059 a joint Pecheneg-Hungarian expedition was checked by Issac I, but in 1064 an immense force of Ouzes (Oghuz Turks) ravaged the Balkans. Only an outbreak of disease halted them.

Hungarians, who had previously supported the rebel Serbs, made a serious attack in 1071, when they occupied Belgrade and Niš.

On the eastern frontier the situation was perilous. In the early eleventh century Turkoman bands had begun to move westward from the region of the Aral Sea. Their ravages helped induce Sennacherib, the Armenian ruler of the kingdom of Van (Vaspurakan) to surrender his territory to Basil II (1021–1022). For a time the Byzantines continued to press forward on the eastern frontier: George Maniakes occupied Edessa in 1032, and the Armenian Gagik II surrendered the kingdom of Ani to Constantine IX in 1045.

Meanwhile, Oghuz Turks of central Asia, led by the descendants of Seljuk—Tughril-Beg (*fl.* 1035–1063), Alp Arslan (1063–1072), and Malikshah (1072–1092)—occupied Iran and Mesopotamia; diverting their undisciplined Turkoman followers against Armenia, Georgia, and the Byzantine Empire was sound policy. An initial Seljuk onslaught (1048–1049) was defeated, but the Armenian kingdom of Kars was devastated, and Turkish raids became more frequent. Byzantium's absorption of the Armenian buffer states, the demilitarization and disaffection of the Armenians, the unreliable nature of the army's mercenary forces (Franks, Russians, Turks of all kinds, and others), and the heavy losses incurred in civil conflicts left Asia Minor open to Seljuk attack. In the early 1050's the Armenian borderlands suffered most, but in 1057 Melitene was pillaged, and in 1059, Sebaste. Ani and Kars were sacked in 1064. While Edessa and Antioch were repeatedly attacked, the Turkish raiders pushed westward: in 1067 Caesarea (Kayseri) was plundered; in 1069, Iconium (Konya); and in 1070 the Turks were at Chonai (Colossae) in west-central Asia Minor.

Romanos IV made a determined effort to repel the Turks. But his heavily armored troops moved slowly; while he campaigned in Cappadocia and Syria (1068–1069), Turks ravaged Pontus and Phrygia. When, in 1071, Romanos marched to recover the important fortress of Manzikert (north of Lake Van), Alp Arslan himself confronted him; because of treachery of members of the Doukas house within his army, Romanos was crushingly defeated and taken captive (19 August 1071). Once released, he was cruelly blinded by Michael VII's representatives and, as a result, died.

The Battle of Manzikert marked a turning point in Byzantine history: the end of the expansion begun under Michael III, and the loss of the bulk of Anatolia, the empire's chief recruiting ground. During the decade 1071–1081, Turkish bands ravaged every part of Asia Minor. With the consent of the usurpers Botaneiates and Melissenos, Turkish troops occupied Nicaea, where a branch of the Seljuk family established itself. The Norman Roussel and the Armenian Philaretos (former commanders in Romanos IV's army) took advantage of the confusion to attempt, unsuccessfully, to establish independent principalities in Pontus and Cilicia, respectively.

During this period of incompetent rulers, civil strife, and military disaster, important changes took place. As the army was reduced by Constantinopolitan officials, mercenaries became more prominent than in the past. The civil bureaucracy grew; Constantine IX and his successors enlarged the Senate with members of the Constantinopolitan middle class. Expenditures mounted and revenues declined; from the time of Michael IV, the nomisma (gold piece) began to be debased. From a theoretical twenty-four carat purity, maintained since Constantine the Great, the nomisma reached eighteen to twenty-one carats under Constantine IX, twelve to fourteen under Michael VII, and eight carats under Nikephoros III.

THE KOMNENIAN CENTURY, 1081–1180

With the accession of Alexios I Komnenos (1081–1118), the empire passed into capable hands. Alexios was accustomed to leading small, mixed bodies of inadequately trained soldiers; he gained victories as much by intrigue and diplomacy as by tactical skill. He was intensely pious, well educated, but narrowly orthodox. His son, John II (1118–1143), was a dedicated and capable soldier, puritanical, without interest in culture. Manuel I (1143–1180) came to the throne under unusual circumstances: he was the youngest of four sons and had a surviving elder brother. But when John died, under suspicious circumstances, Manuel, the only son present, was acclaimed by the troops. He favored Westerners, and in battle often engaged in daring single combat. His court was splendid but licentious; Manuel had an illegitimate son by a niece.

At Alexios I's seizure of power, a merciless sack of Constantinople left the populace cowed. Enemies threatened the empire from every side: the Seljuk Turks, from their base at Nicaea, raided as far as the capital's Asian suburbs; Pechenegs from beyond the Danube penetrated Thrace unopposed; Guiscard prepared for an attack on the western Balkans. Alexios dealt with these problems one by one; he mastered them more by diplomacy than by military force.

The Balkan frontier proved less difficult than the others for Alexios and his successors. In 1091 Alexios won the support of the Cumans (another Turkish tribe in south Russia) and used them to defeat the Pechenegs; the final Pecheneg incursion was crushed by John II in 1122. Cuman raids into the empire were repelled without great difficulty. In the western Balkans, Zeta was subdued by Byzantium, but the Serbs of Rascia (the valleys of the Ibar, Lim, and Tara) joined the rising power of Hungary to oppose the empire. John and Manuel repeatedly campaigned on this front. After a victory in 1150 at the Tara River over a combined Serbian-Hungarian force, Manuel brought Rascia to heel. Bitter conflicts with Hungary continued through the 1160's, and only in 1172 was Manuel's protégé Béla III placed on the Hungarian throne.

The Norman peril to the Byzantine Empire was real. The Byzantines never abandoned their desire to regain southern Italy; the Komnenoi hoped to enlist the pope or the German emperor on their behalf. Thus, when Robert Guiscard landed in 1081 on what is now the Albanian coast, defeated a series of Byzantine armies, and advanced into Macedonia and Thessaly, Alexios stirred up Henry IV of Germany to march on Rome. The beleaguered pope, Gregory VII, summoned home Guiscard, his principal secular ally. In Robert's absence Alexios skillfully sowed dissension among the Norman troops and drove them back.

In 1085, as he was about to renew his invasion, Guiscard died. The Normans did not abandon their ambitions; in 1107–1108 Guiscard's son Bohemond sought to avenge his own frustrations as prince of Antioch by securing papal support for a crusade against the Byzantines. Alexios shrewdly bottled up Bohemond's forces in the Albanian coastal plain, and forced a humiliating treaty upon him. Later, Roger II of Sicily launched repeated naval attacks on Byzantine territory; in 1147 he took advantage of the Second Crusade's passage through the empire to seize Kerkyra (Corfu) and plunder Corinth and Thebes. Only in 1149 did Manuel regain Kerkyra.

John and Manuel renewed Alexios' policy of alliance with the German empire against the Normans; they experienced some success with Lothair II and Conrad III. But Frederick I Barbarossa (1152–1190) was hostile to the Byzantines. Manuel took advantage of William I's accession in Sicily (1154) to appeal for Frederick's participation in a joint attack. Frederick declined, but Manuel sent several small expeditionary forces to southern Italy to support rebel Norman barons (1155–1157). Only after their defeat did he come around to the idea of a Norman-papal-Byzantine alliance against Frederick's expanding power in northern Italy. Manuel even hoped that the pope would depose Frederick and accept the Byzantine as the sole ruler of a unified Roman Empire. The Eastern emperor furnished encouragement and money to the Lombard League for its resistance to Frederick.

Relations with the West were complicated by the empire's dependence on Italian maritime cities for naval assistance. Finding the state bereft of a fleet and threatened by Normans, Alexios I in 1082 granted tax exemption, a quarter in Constantinople, and trading rights in most towns of the empire to the Venetians in return for naval aid. Benefiting from their tax-exempt status, Venetian merchants undercut and partially replaced Byzantines in their own territory. To check Venetian domination of the Byzantine economy, Alexios granted inferior, but still extensive, privileges to the Pisans (1111), while Manuel introduced the Genoese (1155) on similar terms. Aroused by Venetian arrogance, John in 1122 drove them from the empire, but their attacks on the Aegean islands forced him to reinstate them in 1126. Manuel, aggrieved by Venice's lack of cooperation in his Western policies, abruptly arrested and imprisoned all the Venetians in the empire (12 March 1171); this time the Venetian counterstroke was frustrated, and at Manuel's death peace had not been restored.

In the early years of his reign, Alexios I labored to repel the Turks from the immediate vicinity of Constantinople; he made a truce with the Seljuk ruler of Nicaea, and the latter furnished him with troops against the Normans. The two cooperated (*ca.* 1093) to dispose of a powerful Turkish emir, Tzachas, who from his base at Smyrna had ravaged nearby islands and threatened to create a permanent realm. This Byzantine-Seljuk equilibrium was upset by the advent of the First Crusade.

The pope's proclamation of the crusade was partially a response to Alexios' request for Western mercenaries, but the Crusaders had other goals than to rescue Byzantium from the Turks. The first to enter the empire, through Hungary and Thrace, were bands of peasants and poor knights (1096), enthusiastic but undisciplined. When they sought to plunder the countryside along the way, they suffered from the Pecheneg archers whom Alexios sent to control them. Despite the emperor's advice, the ill-armed troops insisted on crossing into Turkish territory, where they were destroyed. In the following year the nobles began to reach Constantinople, after experiencing their own conflicts with Byzantine police forces. Alexios insisted on an oath to restore any former Byzantine territory that they might regain; in return he promised his help. Only a few obdurate leaders refused the oath. With this powerful force Alexios dared to attack Nicaea (whose Seljuk ruler was absent); after a siege the city surrendered to the emperor. Later the Crusaders, supported by a small Byzantine army, defeated the Turks at Dorylaeum, and Alexios used the opportunity to regain the western part of Asia Minor.

During the Crusaders' siege of Antioch, Bohemond tricked the Byzantine forces into departing. Once the city fell, Bohemond claimed it for himself, alleging that Alexios had failed to keep his promise. Recovery of Antioch, or at least imposition of Byzantine sovereignty, became a goal of successive Komnenoi emperors. Alexios put so much pressure on Bohemond that, in 1104, he returned to Italy to enlist papal support and Western Crusaders for the attack he made on the Byzantine Empire in 1107.

During the early twelfth century the Armenians in Cilicia, led by the Roupenid family, sought independence. Frequently they had the help of the princes of Antioch. Imperial expeditions tried to impose Byzantine authority on both states. In 1137 John II reduced both to momentary obedience and enjoyed a triumphant reception in Antioch. Beginning about 1145, Ṭoros or Thoros II, the Roupenid, took advantage of Manuel's preoccupations to revolt, and Cilician Armenia was never again fully subdued. As a result of a great expedition (1158–1159), Manuel obtained acceptance of his sovereignty over Cilician Armenia and Antioch, but this proved a transitory success.

Alexios I and his successors did not abandon Byzantium's claims to the Holy Land. John II in 1138 joined with the Antiochenes to capture several small Syrian fortresses, but was defeated at Shaizar. The Second Crusade (1147–1148), which was intended to recover lost land in Palestine, clashed repeatedly with Byzantine forces during its passage through the empire. In 1169 a Byzantine fleet and expeditionary force attempted to cooperate with the Crusaders in Egypt. King Amalric I of Jerusalem came to Constantinople in 1171 and offered what a Byzantine author deemed to be homage, without substantial result.

The Komnenian emperors were too preoccupied with the Turkish problem to take action in Palestine. Following his recovery of Nicaea and western Asia Minor, Alexios waged a series of campaigns (1112–1116) to repel Turkish raiders; he advanced as far as Philomelion. John II reestablished Byzantine predominance along the north and south coasts of Asia Minor. When, in 1146, Manuel attempted an attack on Iconium, the capital of the Seljuks, he found he had overextended himself, and suffered severely in his withdrawal. In 1159, on his return from Antioch to Constantinople, Manuel dared to cross through Turkish territory; he again lost many troops. Peace was made in 1161, and the following year Kilij Arslan II, sultan of Iconium, was splendidly received in Constantinople. A decade later, however, Manuel became alarmed at the sultan's expansion in eastern Asia Minor. After some initial forays the imperial army advanced again on Iconium. En route, on 17 September 1176, the Turks intercepted the emperor near Myriokephalon and inflicted a crushing defeat. The greatest part of the Byzantine army was lost; Manuel and his immediate followers escaped only by courtesy of Kilij Arslan. Thereafter, Manuel could scarcely defend his frontiers from Turkoman raids.

Internally the Komnenoi emperors experienced less opposition than their predecessors; initially, consciousness of peril, and later, the rising prestige of the dynasty, contributed to the unusual calm. At John II's accession his mother, Irene, and sister, Anna, tried to place the latter's husband, Nikephoros Bryennios, on the throne, but at the last moment he refused to act. Manuel's unexpected succession brought special perils, but the ill-organized, hasty conspiracies that resulted were easily overcome. John II's brother Isaac had previously given trouble; Isaac's son Andronikos sustained a fixed opposition to Manuel. Charmed by Andronikos' brilliant personality, Manuel repeatedly gave him provincial governorships. On each occasion Andronikos conspired with the enemy beyond the frontier. Imprisonment, flight, and exile did not quell his spirit. Near the end of Manuel's reign, the two were reconciled; Andronikos was appointed governor of Pontus.

Conciliation of all factions, indeed, was a consistent Komnenian policy. Alexios I came to power as the candidate of the military aristocracy of Asia Minor and of the Doukas family, leaders of the bureaucratic party: Alexios' wife was Irene Doukas. The Komnenoi strove to create a solid bulwark around the throne by judicious marriages with members of the landholding class. Their adherents were rewarded with ceremonial titles, generalships, and political offices. Followers great and small might receive *pronoiai,* grants of land with peasants working on it, who rendered their taxes and other dues to the *pronoia* holder. Such grants were, at most, for life, and conditional upon continued loyal service.

While the peasants (or *paroikoi*) who fell under the sway of a monastery or great landlord suffered from oppression, the Komnenoi made an effort to revive the older militia of small property holders who owed military service instead of taxation. The perils of the empire, however, placed extraordinary demands on the taxpayers, and often tax farmers were allowed to exploit the populace. Immunities for monasteries and great landholders created gross inequalities of taxation. Favoritism and corruption were frequent. On the positive side, the Komnenoi improved and stabilized the coinage.

THE ERA OF COLLAPSE, 1180–1204

The death of Manuel left his only son, Alexios II (1180–1183), a youth of eleven, under the regency of his mother, Marie of Antioch. In 1182 a rebellion brought to power Manuel's cousin, Andronikos, as regent, then as coemperor, and from 1183 (when he secretly murdered Alexios II) as sole emperor (Andronikos I, 1183–1185). A popular uprising in the capital made Isaac II Angelos (1185–1195), a great-grandson of Alexios I, emperor. He was deposed and blinded by his brother Alexios III (1195–1203). The Fourth Crusade brought Isaac II back to the throne, with his son Alexios IV (1203–1204) as the real ruler. A popular reaction raised Alexios V Doukas to the crown (February–April 1204).

During Manuel's lifetime the power of the Latins (western Europeans) had increased in Constantinople. After the Venetians' expulsion in 1171, Pisan and Genoese merchants controlled trade. Manuel's widow was a Latin, as were spouses of other members of the imperial family. As regent, Alexios II's mother supported the pro-Latin faction among the aristocracy. In reaction the populace of the capital favored Andronikos, who opposed Latins. Once Andronikos' army, marching from Pontus, reached the Asian coast opposite Constantinople, a rioting mob massacred the Latins (April 1182). But Andronikos and his successors found that they needed Western merchants; Venetians and subsequently Pisans and Genoese regained their commercial dominance.

Andronikos, as well as being anti-Latin, was hostile to most members of the aristocracy; he practiced systematic terrorism against them. The Angeloi emperors revived the Komnenian policy of linking themselves by marriage to the principal families. Discontented aristocrats, however, repeatedly conspired against the government. In Constantinople popular uprisings showed antiaristocratic as well as anti-Latin prejudices.

In the provinces Andronikos attempted to restore good government. His governors were chosen on merit, and adequately paid; only lawful taxes were collected. His successors found themselves so hard pressed that tax farming and venality of office returned. Oppression by tax collectors became particularly harsh. Resistance to revenue collection rose: the people of Thebes turned back the collectors from their gates. Regions long part of the empire sought independence: a certain Isaac Komnenos on Cyprus (1184–1191), Theodore Mankaphas at Philadelphia (1188–1193 and again in 1204–1205), and Leo Sgouros in central Greece (1201–1205) created short-lived principalities.

The empire in this age encountered difficulties in the Balkans. Following Manuel's death the Serbs broke from Byzantine tutelage; Hungarian expeditions again appeared south of the Danube. In 1186 a revolt by Vlachs and Bulgarians (aided by Cumans) in the Balkan Mountains led to the establishment of the Second Bulgarian Empire. The Angeloi emperors waged exhausting, usually unsuccessful campaigns against the Vlach-Bulgarians.

In Asia Minor internal troubles in the Seljuk sultanate gave the Byzantines some respite, but Turkomans continued to raid. They pushed the frontier of Turkish control into Bithynia and the Lykos valley.

The Latin massacre of 1182 embittered relations with the Italian cities. Genoa and Pisa allowed their citizens to recoup their losses by ravaging the islands and coasts of the Aegean. By 1187 the Venetians were again allied with the empire, and in 1192 Genoa and Pisa regained their privileges. But individual acts of piracy continued, and Alexios III covertly hindered the Ventian merchants.

Western invasions threatened the empire. William II of Sicily in 1185 attacked by land and sea. His forces met at Thessaloniki, and the empire's second city fell; the Normans sacked it cruelly. Fear of them helped bring about Andronikos I's overthrow. Isaac II was able to repel the invaders, save that the Ionian islands remained in Norman hands. In 1189–1190 Frederick Barbarossa's portion of the Third Crusade passed through the empire; Isaac, by agreement with Saladin, committed himself to destroy it. Barbarossa withstood Byzantine attacks and planned an assault on Constantinople, until Isaac gave way. Frederick's son, Henry VI, once he had acquired the Norman realm of Sicily, threatened an attack on Byzantium; Alexios III was ready to pay tribute, until Henry's death (1197) ended the danger.

In the meantime, in 1191, Richard the Lionhearted's naval wing of the Third Crusade expelled the "tyrant" Isaac Komnenos from Cyprus. The island was permanently removed from Byzantine control and linked with the Crusader States of Syria.

The Fourth Crusade set out with the support of several enemies of Alexios III: Philip of Swabia, king of Germany, was married to the deposed Isaac II's daughter; Conrad of Montferrat had varied family claims at Constantinople; Pope Innocent III had little reason to trust the Byzantines; and the Venetians had old and new scores to settle. The appearance of Alexios, son of the deposed Isaac II, in the West at a crucial moment in the crusade's preparation (late 1201) provided a pretext for an attack on Constantinople. Deeply in debt to Venice, the French, German, and Italian Crusaders had to fall in with Venetian plans to attack rebellious Zara (1202). They then accepted their leaders' proposals to restore the young Alexios to his throne; he promised to make the empire obedient to the pope, pay what the Crusaders owed to Venice, and assist their expedition to the Holy Land. The Byzantine army in 1203 was small and the fleet in disrepair. When Alexios III fled, the courtiers restored Isaac II; at the Crusaders' insistence Alexios IV was to rule with him.

By oppressive taxation and acceptance of papal supremacy, the new emperors rendered themselves unpopular. An anti-Latin party among the nobles, led by Alexios Doukas, stirred popular opposition. The elderly Isaac died, and his son fell victim to a palace coup (January 1204). Angered by Byzantine duplicity, the Crusaders prepared a fresh attack on Constantinople. Alexios V defended the city valiantly, but on 12 April 1204 it fell. For Byzantium an era had ended.

BIBLIOGRAPHY

Recent editions of sources. Niketas Choniates, *Nicetae Choniatae Historia,* J. A. van Dieten, ed., 2 vols. (1975); Ioannes Skylitzes, *Ioannis Scylitzae Synopsis historiarum,* Hans Thurn, ed. (1973); Ioannes Skylitzes Continuatus, *He Synecheia tes Chronographias tou Ioannou Skylitse,* E. Th. Tsolakes, ed. (1968); Paul Lemerle *et al.*, eds., *Actes de Lavra,* pt. 1, 2 vols. (1970); Theodore Prodromos, *Historische Gedichte,* Wolfram Hörandner, ed. (1974).

Recent translations of sources. Nikephoros Chrysoberges, "Oration to Alexius IV Angelus," in Charles M. Brand, "A Byzantine Plan for the Fourth Crusade," in *Speculum,* **43** (1968); Anna Komnena, *The Alexiad of Anna Comnena,* E. R. A. Sewter, trans. (1969, repr. 1979); Ioannes (John) Kinnamos, *Deeds of John and Manuel Comnenus,* Charles M. Brand, trans. (1976).

Internal history. Centre de Recherche d'Histoire et Civilisation de Byzance, *Travaux et mémoires,* **6** (1976): an entire volume devoted to "Recherches sur le XIe siècle"; Charles M. Brand, *Byzantium Confronts the West 1180–1204* (1968); M. F. Hendy, "Byzantium, 1081–1204: An Economic Reappraisal," in *Transactions of the Royal Historical Society,* ser. 5, **20** (1970); Paul Lemerle, *Cinq études sur le XIe siècle byzantin* (1977); Demetrios I. Polemis, *The Doukai: A Contribution to Byzantine Prospography* (1968); Gustave Schlumberger, "Deux chefs normands des armées byzantines au XIe siècle: Sceaux de Hervé et de Roussel de Bailleul," in *Revue historique,* **16** (1881); Speros Vryonis, Jr., "Byzantine Δημοκρατία and the Guilds in the Eleventh Century," in *Dumbarton Oaks Papers,* **17** (1963).

The eastern frontier. T. S. R. Boase, ed., *The Cilician Kingdom of Armenia* (1978); Claude Cahen, *Pre-Ottoman Turkey: A General Survey of the Material and Spiritual Culture, c. 1071–1330,* J. Jones-Williams, trans. (1968); David Marshall Lang, *Armenia: Cradle of Civilization,* 2nd ed. (1978); Joseph Laurent, *Byzance et les Turcs Seldjoucides dans l'Asie Occidentale jusqu'en 1081* (1913); Speros Vryonis, Jr., *The Decline of Medieval Hellenism in Asia Minor and the Process of Islamization from the Eleventh Through the Fifteenth Century* (1971).

The Balkan frontier. Gyula Moravcsik, *Byzantium and the Magyars,* Samuel R. Rosenbaum *et al.*, trans. (1970); Andrew B. Urbansky, *Byzantium and the Danube Frontier: A Study of the Relations Between Byzantium, Hungary, and the Balkans During the Period of the Comneni* (1968); Robert Lee Wolff, "The 'Second Bulgarian Empire': Its Origin and History to 1204," in *Speculum,* **24** (1949), repr. in his *Studies in the Latin Empire of Constantinople* (1976).

Byzantium and the West: the Crusades. Frederic C. Lane, *Venice: A Maritime Republic* (1973); Donald E. Queller, *The Fourth Crusade: The Conquest of Constantinople, 1201–1204* (1977); Donald E. Queller, ed., *The Latin Conquest of Constantinople* (1971); Donald E. Queller, Thomas K. Compton, and Donald A. Campbell, "The Fourth Crusade: The Neglected Majority," in *Speculum,* **49** (1974); Donald E. Queller and Gerald W. Day, "Some Arguments in Defense of the Venetians on the Fourth Crusade," in *American Historical Review,* **81** (1976); Kenneth M. Setton, gen. ed., *A History of the Crusades,* new ed., I–II (1969).

CHARLES M. BRAND

[See also **Alexios I Komnenos; Andronikos I Komnenos; Bohemond I, Prince of Antioch; Bulgaria; Constantinople; Crusade, Fourth; Crusades and Crusader States to 1199; Doukas; Isaac II Angelos; Komnenoi; Latin Empire of**

Constantinople; Manzikert; Manuel I Komnenos; Normans and Normandy; Robert Guiscard; Romanos IV Diogenes; Roussel de Bailleul; Russian Nomads, Invasions of; Seljuks; Venice.]

BYZANTINE EMPIRE: HISTORY (1204–1453). After their capture of Constantinople (April 1204), the Crusaders began formal partition of Greek territories to build a new Latin Empire on the rubble of the Byzantine, unaware that, having seized an empire's head, securing its body was a separate and arduous task by itself.

While Byzantine government and society had been weakened by dissension and decadence when the Fourth Crusade shattered them, Byzantine civilization was far from moribund and soon demonstrated its basic vitality and resilience. Incredulous at the loss of their sacred capital, stunned Byzantine refugees, with no immediate aims or designated leadership, sought rallying places. In the provinces, already wracked by local separatism, chaos reigned. While Kalojan of Bulgaria gobbled up Balkan territory, local Greek magnates in Greece and Asia Minor created their own regional enclaves, mostly short-lived. Amid the turmoil three splinter states emerged as serious competitors for the anticipated role of restoring united Byzantine sovereignty in the old capital.

Already engaged, with help from the Georgian Kingdom, in carving out a separatist enclave around Trebizond, members of the once imperial Komnenos family exploited the confusion of 1204 to extend control along Asia Minor's northern shores, proclaiming their rights to the imperial heritage. Meanwhile, one of the few active leaders of resistance to the Latin siege, Theodore Laskaris, established himself and a following in the Bithynian city of Nicaea. And in Epiros in northwestern Greece, a relative of the recent imperial house, Michael Angelos, created a thriving independent regime around Arta.

Trebizond was quickly eliminated from the competition by Laskarid pressure. Within a decade Alexios Komnenos of Trebizond was restricted to the southeastern corner of the Black Sea coast, where he and his successors, still styled emperors, ruled in total detachment from the mainstream of Byzantine history. Meanwhile, Theodore Laskaris consolidated his position and image, securing a patriarchate and coronation as emperor (1208). Surviving Latin attacks, he defeated his menacing neighbor, the Seljuk sultan of Rum, in 1211, while his elimination or neutralization of localist regimes sped his achievement of coherent rule over the northwestern sector of Asia Minor. By his death (1222) Theodore had created a viable state that revived Byzantine hopes and seriously threatened the deteriorating Latin regime in Constantinople.

Nicaea's triumph was delayed by its remaining competition with the Epirote splinter state. Michael Angelos had been content to create a local principality, but after his death (*ca.* 1215) his successor, Theodore Angelos, set Epiros on a collision course with Nicaea. Grander in his pretensions and more aggressive in military exertions, Theodore moved first against the Latins in Europe. His stunning capture of Thessaloniki in 1224 gave him a capital of new status, and he proclaimed his new stature by having himself crowned emperor there. Theodore Laskaris' vigorous successor in Nicaea, John III Vatatzes (1222–1254), might well have been eclipsed had not a twist of fortune blocked an Angelan victory in the race for Constantinople.

Caught in a war with his former ally, John Asen II of Bulgaria, Theodore was unexpectedly defeated at Klokotnitsa (1230). Captured and then blinded, he was thus removed from the race for empire as quickly as he had entered it. Under his relatives Angelan power fragmented. A western branch lost Thessaloniki to the methodical Vatatzes in 1246, retaining only a minor Thessalian principality. Epiros itself fell to Michael II Angelos, who remained Nicaea's implacable foe.

Briefly left the real arbiter of Balkan affairs, John Asen wavered in his aims, and after his death (1241) the balance shifted steadily to favor Vatatzes. By 1254, when he died, he had consolidated Nicaea's Asian holding and added vast European territories, making his realm the only and inevitable Byzantine threat to the moribund Latin regime in Constantinople.

After the short reign of Theodore II (1254–1258), the usurpation of Michael VIII Palaiologos (1259–1282) gave Nicaea new assertiveness, soon tested. Determined to revive Angelan fortunes, Michael II of Epiros allied himself with Manfred, the ambitious Hohenstaufen king of Sicily, and Guillaume de Villehardouin, Latin prince of Achaia. Their joint forces were decisively defeated by a Nicaean army at Pelagonia (1259), leaving Nicaea a clear path to Constantinople. As part of his preparations, Michael

VIII won the Genoese as allies, to offset Venetian support for the Latin regime. But it was by chance that a small Nicaean force won entry into the poorly defended city and seized it on 25 July 1261, thus driving out Baldwin II. Michael's triumph was celebrated in fervent patriotic unity, but he quietly sealed his and his family's hold on the throne by having the rightful successor, John IV Laskaris, blinded and imprisoned.

For all its meaning to Byzantines, Constantinople's recovery was a burdensome victory. The great city had been devastated under the Latins and required great expenditures for restoration and maintenance. Its recovery also stirred the wrath or ambitions of Western powers, while generating costly Byzantine illusions about their status on the international scene. But the restored empire's territories (northwestern Asia Minor, Thrace, Macedonia) and resources were limited, while its commerce was largely taken over by the entrenched Genoese and the intrusive Venetians. Michael's usurpation made him bitter domestic enemies. From Villehardouin, his captive since Pelagonia, Michael wrung the cession of some fortresses in the Morea as a beginning of Byzantine recovery there, but ensuing military efforts to that end were not always successful, while machinations by Michael II of Epiros further engaged Byzantine energies.

The greatest menace was a new Western coalition against Michael VIII by the ambitious new ruler of southern Italy, Charles of Anjou, victor over Manfred (1266), in concert with Guillaume de Villehardouin of Achaia and Baldwin II, the expelled Latin emperor, with papal support. The real peril of this alliance against him drove Michael to prodigies of diplomacy meant to distract or neutralize this Angevin alliance. The papacy was the key to restraining Charles, and Michael wooed successive pontiffs with promises of ending pressure on Latin Greece and of the Greek church's reunion with Rome, on the latter's terms. Not content with promises, the papacy forced Michael to commit the Byzantine church to just such a submission, as agreed by his agents at the second Council of Lyons (1274). For this capitulation Michael paid dearly at home. His conflict with Patriarch Arsenios, loyal to the Laskarids, had already rent religious life. Now, outraged and adamant in their opposition to the union and fierce in their hatred for the Latins, the populace and most church leaders, joined by dissident Orthodox neighbors, refused to acquiesce.

Soured by Michael's failures or evasions, the papacy succumbed to Charles's pressures and renewed its support for Angevin aggressions. As almost certain disaster approached, Michael's diplomacy and money helped bring about the sudden rising in 1282 known as the Sicilian Vespers, which drove Charles's forces from Sicily and delivered the island to the rival Aragonese. With Angevin power broken, Michael and his restored empire were saved, but at devastating costs. Vast sums had been squandered, and religious controversy raged at home. Meanwhile, Balkan territories barely resisted cruel attacks from Mongols of the Golden Horde; and, most gravely, the Asian territories had been neglected and weakened, partly in hostility to pro-Laskarid military leaders there, partly in Michael's obsession with recovering European lands from the Latins and Angelans. Before he could vindicate his religious stance or redress the Asian situation, Michael died prematurely (11 December 1282), denied church obsequies and scorned by most of his subjects.

Michael's elder son, Andronikos, had been formally associated in power in 1272; his assumption of sole power confirmed Palaiologan dynastic succession. Mild and indecisive, often compared unfavorably with his forceful father, Andronikos II (1282–1321) had the unenviable task of adjusting Byzantium, its resources overextended by Michael, to the realities of seriously diminished circumstances. His long reign represented, if it did not actually accelerate, the restored empire's reduction from anachronistic grandeur to the pathetic status of a minor Balkan state.

Andronikos quickly abandoned Michael's odious religious policies, abrogating the union with Rome and striving to placate ecclesiastical factions. But religious peace and unity were elusive, and Andronikos quarreled chronically with one of his patriarchs, the austere but contentious Athanasios I (1289–1293; 1304–1310). The emperor bred domestic strife when he made a son by his first marriage, Michael (IX), his coruler (1295). His second wife, Irene of Montferrat, nagged him to partition the empire into principalities for their sons. Andronikos refused, to the ruin of his marriage, but he was later to begin the practice of appointing members of the reigning house to rule in local territories as a way of keeping the empire united under the central government. The old machinery of administration was disappearing, while an increasingly powerful landed aristocracy wielded the real power over the peasantry and provincial life.

Attempts to curb aristocrats' power and tax their inordinate wealth were futile. Coinage debasement and inflation were past control, while the Italians' commercial stranglehold completed the economic erosion.

Well aware of his handicaps, Andronikos compensated by reducing his army almost to nothing and all but abolishing the navy. To be sure, his diplomacy did neutralize or liquidate dangerous Latin claims and helped extend control in Thessaly and Epiros, while also placating the growing power of Serbia. But Byzantium was humiliated at sea by piracy and caught between the warring Venetians and Genoese. Most ominous was the erosion of the Asian lands that had once been the heart of the Nicene state. Disaffected, neglected, they began falling away to the small but growing emirate of the Ottoman Turks, who had established themselves in Bithynia, at Byzantine expense, in the late thirteenth century.

The belated efforts of the coruler, Michael IX, to stem this tide were unsuccessful, prompting Andronikos to engage the services of a formidable mercenary force known as the Catalan Company, under the opportunistic commander Roger de Flor. Hired at great expense, they were set to work late in 1303 and immediately showed their military effectiveness. But their irresponsible behavior forced the Byzantines to make new exertions and concessions in hopes of controlling them. As tensions mounted over the next winter, Roger de Flor was assassinated (April 1305). Released from all restraints, the Catalans broke out of their quarters at Gallipoli and ran wild over Byzantine Thrace. After spending three years of devastation there, they plundered their way across Macedonia and into southern Greece (1308–1310), where they eventually established themselves as rulers of Athens after defeating its Latin prince. From this bizarre episode Byzantium had gained only humiliation and new scars.

Woes deepened for the aging and dispirited emperor—a gentle, earnest man whose respect for learning and beauty made his era a bright one in Byzantine cultural history, but a sovereign unequal to his political problems. As difficulties mounted in both Asian and European territories, and disputes festered with his second wife, a tragic new chapter of domestic strife was added. Michael IX's elder son, Andronikos (*b.* 1297), was crowned in 1316 as coemperor. Spoiled, made reckless by bad company, the younger Andronikos fell into wild living, and a climactic escapade caused the accidental murder of his younger brother, Manuel. Their stunned father died of shock (October 1320), and the furious Andronikos II disinherited his grandson. Urged on by daring comrades, aware that the miseries of the old emperor's reign had generated wide disaffection, the young prince made a direct bid for the throne. Young aristocrats, especially his closest friend, John Kantakouzenos, were his key supporters, and the interests of the landed magnates merged with the ambitions of the prince and his circle. Byzantium thus slid into the first of a series of civil wars over succession that would deepen the empire's ruin.

Open civil war alternated with unstable truce over the next eight years, during which the young prince at times held independent enclaves of his own, while Byzantium's neighbors had new opportunities for intervention. In May 1328 the younger Andronikos finally compelled his grandfather to abdicate. After remaining in the palace for a while, old Andronikos II eventually retired to a monastery, where he died (13 February 1332), meanwhile leaving the ravaged, debilitated, and shrinking empire to the undisputed rule of Andronikos III (1328–1341).

Bored by administration, the restless new emperor left much of the governing to Kantakouzenos and other advisers while he indulged his taste for soldiering. He had some success in European regions, especially against the Bulgarians, but less luck against the Turks. During the civil war the Ottomans had captured Brusa (1326), making it their new capital, and thereafter their new emir, Orkhan (1326–1362), pressed his chances further. To stem this tide, Andronikos and Kantakouzenos led a counterattack, but they were badly defeated (June 1329) and the emperor was wounded. Subsequent Byzantine resistance in Bithynia virtually collapsed, and in March 1331 Nicaea capitulated. Six years later, Nicomedia surrendered, leaving to Byzantium only tiny fragments of Asian territory, for which the emperor agreed to pay tribute by a treaty personally settled between Andronikos and Orkhan in 1333.

Despite these reverses, Andronikos III did arrest some of Byzantium's deterioration. At home, with mixed success, he attempted to restore morale and curtail endemic corruption and institutional decay. Abroad, contacts with the West were limited, and involvement with a short-lived Latin Christian league in the Aegean was strained. But Andronikos recovered some territory from the Genoese, and he cultivated the emirate of Aydin as a valuable ally. His regime also restrained the restless new Serbian ruler,

Stefan Dušan (1331–1355), and, most impressively, completed Byzantine annexation of Thessaly and Epiros.

The relative recovery granted the empire by Andronikos III's energies was rudely cut short by his unexpected death, barely forty-five, in June 1341. As his closest friend and adviser, John Kantakouzenos attempted to maintain stability and continuity as unofficial regent for the young heir presumptive, John Palaiologos (*b.* June 1332). But his former protégé, the upstart Alexios Apokavkos, organized a plot against him, supported by the suspicious dowager empress Anna (of Savoy). Driven by his enemies to the step whose temptations he had previously avoided, Kantakouzenos proclaimed himself emperor (26 October 1341), while scrupulously guaranteeing the rights of the legitimate successor, young John Palaiologos.

A new civil war, more ruinous than the last one, ravaged Byzantium for the next six years. Both sides courted Serbia and the Turks, who won new advantages at Byzantine expense. Each side made humiliating concessions: Kantakouzenos had to give a daughter as bride to the Ottoman sultan to secure his alliance, while Anna of Savoy pawned the imperial crown jewels and regalia, never to be recovered, to Venice in order to raise money. Worst of all, the struggle released an unprecedented wave of social strife. For the lower classes, less protected than ever by agencies of a shriveled central government against the magnates' greed, usurpation by the great landowner Kantakouzenos was the last straw. Popular antiaristocratic sentiments in the capital were manipulated by Apokavkos as a base for his power, while he encouraged reactions against Kantakouzenos in provincial cities, notably Adrianople. The most dramatic outbreak came in Thessaloniki, largest city after the capital. An anti-Kantakouzenian rising there was led by a militant group called "Zealots," whose leaders bore the Palaiologos family name and who identified themselves with dynastic legitimism, whatever the radical social goals ascribed to them.

The murder of Apokavkos in June 1345 suddenly left the anti-Kantakouzenian party in disarray and turned the tide. His son John, ruling Thessaloniki with the Zealots, attempted to change sides and yield that city to the usurper. The Zealot-led populace responded by brutally massacring the conspirators and the city's magnates, and by establishing a renewed populist regime that ran Thessaloniki in relative independence for the next four years. Elsewhere, however, Kantakouzenos progressed: by February 1347 he entered Constantinople, arranging to rule jointly with young John V, who became his son-in-law.

Had not the price been so high, the reign of the able John VI Kantakouzenos (1347–1354) might have brought benefits. But the end of the civil war was followed by cruel ravages of the Black Death. Stefan Dušan's Serbians were overrunning European territories while the Turks were tempted to raid there, and Byzantium had become a pawn in Genoese-Venetian rivalries. Hoping particularly to curb the Genoese, entrenched in their colony of Galata across from Constantinople, John VI tried to rebuild Byzantine naval strength, but in the "Galata War" of 1348 the Genoese easily suppressed it. Religious strife raged over hesychasm, a doctrine of extreme monastic contemplativeness. Its main proponent, St. Gregory Palamas, had been harassed by the enemies of his friend Kantakouzenos. The latter's victory brought a vindication of the Palamite position and an effort to heal religious wounds. If social grievances could not be resolved, at least rebellions could be curbed: in 1350 Kantakouzenos suppressed the Zealot regime and recovered control of Thessaloniki.

Chafing in his subservient role, the maturing John V Palaiologos sought more power while John VI's elder son, Matthew Kantakouzenos, agitated for his own advancement. Dynastic strife was renewed in 1353, and Matthew was proclaimed coemperor. Kantakouzenos' weakened position was further undercut when the Ottoman Turks took advantage of earthquake damage to seize strategic Gallipoli on the Dardanelles, and make it their first foothold in Europe. Gaining momentum, John V entered Constantinople in November 1354; by negotiated agreement, Kantakouzenos abdicated. Matthew continued his own struggle until December 1357, when a new pact ended all Kantakouzenian claims to the throne although allowing the family to control the Morea. Within a decade of his abdication, however, John Kantakouzenos, become the monk Ioasaph, returned to the palace as adviser to his weak son-in-law.

John V's long sole reign (1354–1391) began the empire's final decline. Dušan's death (December 1355) at first removed Byzantium's most urgent menace as Serbia disintegrated under his successors. But this only left the field to the Ottoman Turks, who, first in disorganized raiding, then in more systematic conquest, began to absorb European cities and lands, especially under their astute new sultan, Murad I (1362–1389). Convinced that Western powers would join to expel the Turks from Europe while opportunity remained, John V committed himself to seeking their help. Initial communications (1355–1357) with the Avignonese papacy had no results. Suspicious of the West, meanwhile, some Byzantine leaders advocated cooperation instead with other Balkan Christians against the common foe. The patriarch Kallistos died during a fruitless mission to Serbia in 1363. And, despite dynastic marital ties with the Bulgarians, hostilities between them and Byzantium were more frequent than cooperation.

Clinging to his hopes, John personally visited the nearest Latin Catholic ruler, Louis the Great of Hungary, in 1366. But John was bluntly told that Western aid was conditional upon the Greek church's reunion with Rome on Latin terms. Blockaded by the Bulgarians on his return trip, John was rescued by a small but timely crusading expedition led by his kinsman Count Amadeo VI of Savoy, who had recaptured Gallipoli for Byzantium. Colloquies and religious debates that followed, also involving old Kantakouzenos, resulted only in John V's decision to travel to the West himself. Setting forth in 1369, essentially as an individual suppliant rather than as representative of the Orthodox church, John met the Avignonese pope Urban V in Rome and personally accepted the Roman faith, promising to work toward the similar submission of his Orthodox subjects. But no aid materialized, and when he subsequently visited Venice (1370), John was obliged to remain there until he could repay some of his debts to the Venetian government, with help from his younger son, Manuel.

Before John returned home, the south Serbian successors of Dušan were utterly defeated at the critical battle at Črnomen on the Marica River (26 September 1371). The destruction of medieval Serbia had begun, and all Macedonia lay open to Turkish conquest. From his base in Thessaloniki, young Manuel benefited briefly by seizing nearby lands, but his father concluded that Turkish power was as irresistible as Western aid was unattainable. By 1373 John despairingly reversed his policies and accepted subservience and military vassalage to Sultan Murad, much to Western shock and outrage. Meanwhile, domestic strife revived as John's eldest son and his coemperor, Andronikos, his loyalty already compromised, was caught in a conspiracy against his father, in concert with a son of Murad plotting against the sultan. John was compelled to partially blind his son, and the latter's own young son. The discredited Andronikos imprisoned, John crowned Manuel as the new successor.

The restless Andronikos escaped in 1376; wooing the Genoese and Turks for support, he forced his way back into Constantinople. Imprisoning his father and brothers, he attempted to rule on his own. But Andronikos IV (1376–1379) found himself friendless at home and exploited abroad. To his Turkish allies he had to return Gallipoli. Unable to fulfill promises to Genoa, he became disastrously embroiled, as its ally, in its latest conflict with Venice, the so-called Chioggia War.

In their turn John V and his sons escaped, made counteroffers to the Turks, and recovered Constantinople for themselves in 1379. Andronikos continued the struggle from Galata until a compromise settlement in 1381 restored Andronikos as successor and gave him his own territorial enclave. Unsatisfied, he resumed hostilities with his father until his unexpected death in 1385, which left his son John to maintain the elder line's claims. Excluded from his rights, Manuel set himself up independently in Thessaloniki, defying his father's policies of appeasement to rally Byzantine resistance against the Turks. Brief successes brought the full weight of Turkish arms down on Thessaloniki, besieged until Manuel was driven out in 1387. A discredited outcast, the prince found reconciliation easier with Murad than with his father, who treated him coldly and sent him into temporary exile.

The great Ottoman victory over the Serbians and their allies at Kosovo (15 June 1389) extended the Turkish grip on the Balkans, and the remaining Serbian princes joined the Bulgarians and the Byzantines in vassalage. Murad had been killed during the battle but his son and successor, Bayazid "the Thunderbolt" (1389–1403), pressed Turkish consolidation more aggressively and arrogantly than ever. With his encouragement John (VII), the late Andronikos IV's son, renewed Byzantine dynastic strife. First soliciting support in Genoa, John returned to force his way into Constantinople in April 1390 with Turkish backing. But John V held out in a fortress there and Manuel, now reconciled, brought aid that effected John VII's expulsion after barely six months of power. John V and Manuel paid for their victory with yet deeper servitude to Bayazid. Worn down by humiliation and futility, John V died on 16 February 1391, and Manuel just barely secured his succession.

Sensitive and refined, Manuel II (1391–1425) was also a man of energy, willpower, and talents worthy of a better age. For the moment he continued his father's policies: during 1391 he had to spend months serving in Bayazid's army on campaign in Asia Minor. On his return he married a Serbian princess, perhaps with hopes of Serbian military cooperation. But the Christian princes of the Balkans were powerless to cooperate or resist, as they found during the winter of 1393–1394. Bayazid whimsically brought them all together then as his vassals, alternately threatening to kill them all and then showering them with favors. Manuel left this bizarre gathering determined that resistance was not only more honorable than appeasement but perhaps more safe. Defied at last, Bayazid began besieging Constantinople in spring 1394, while Manuel relied jointly on the city's great defensive walls and on appeals for Western aid. On a scale more systematic than his father's before him, Manuel directed his pleas to every Western ruler who would listen.

Initial responses were few and indirect. The main Western effort, the crusade organized by Sigismund of Hungary, ended in utter disaster at Nicopolis (25 September 1396), leaving Bayazid more secure than ever and free to resume attacks on Constantinople, which he knew he must capture to complete the reality of his Turkish empire. Redoubling his appeals, Manuel won mostly promises and gestures, most tangibly a small expeditionary force sent by Charles VI of France under Marshal Boucicaut in 1399. Results were trivial, and Boucicaut persuaded Manuel to go in person to the West to plead for the larger military effort that was needed. Boucicaut even reconciled Manuel with the pretender John VII, so that the latter would serve as loyal regent in Constantinople during his uncle's absence. Leaving his family with his brother Theodore—ruler in the Morea since 1382—Manuel set sail in early 1400 to undertake the most elaborate of the late Byzantine imperial visits to western Europe.

After stops in Italy, Manuel was welcomed to Paris by Charles VI, and hopes soared for an international army to be organized. But Charles's episodes of insanity disrupted plans, and Manuel's brief visit to Henry IV of England yielded only promises. The remainder of Manuel's sojourn in Paris became a dreary wait, while the fate of Constantinople and Byzantium was decided in the East. The desperate John VII was actually planning to submit to Bayazid when the latter was struck down by the onslaughts of Tamerlane of Samarkand. Unexpectedly defeated at Ancyra (28 July 1402) and taken prisoner, Bayazid died in captivity the following year, leaving the nascent Ottoman state in complete disarray. As John coped with these altered conditions, Manuel began his return journey, renewing pleas for Western aid in this new time of opportunity.

When he returned home in the spring of 1403, Manuel had a falling-out with his nephew, but eventually he kept his promises to John VII and gave him a separate government of his own in Thessaloniki; there he settled until his death (1408) ended this latest dynastic tension. Meanwhile, Manuel continued his call for Western action against the Turks. As hopes for that paled again, Manuel allowed himself to meddle in the struggles among Bayazid's four sons, profitably playing the arbiter as they fought for the Turkish succession. With the triumph of Manuel's last candidate, Mehmed I (1413–1421), Byzantium won some small territorial gains and a superficial peace. Manuel used this interlude to tour and strengthen parts of his tattered empire, notably in the Morea and Thessaloniki, where sons of his represented the dynasty's name. In his contacts with the West, Manuel gave new stress to the idea of church reunion, but his carefully balanced policies were upset as his eldest son, John VIII, emerged to share power. Made coemperor in 1421, John urged greater initiative. When Mehmed I died, John's attempt, over Manuel's objections, to support a Turkish pretender brought the wrathful hostilities of the new sultan, Murad II (1421–1451). Amid this turmoil Manuel suffered a paralytic stroke that incapacitated him until his death (July 1425). Assuming power in earnest, John made a fruitless journey to Italy and Hungary (1423–1424) to seek aid, but peace was restored in his absence, and John VIII's sole reign (1425–1448) commenced in a respite totally of the sultan's making.

Unable to maintain Thessaloniki against Turkish pressures, Byzantium had ceded it in 1423 to the Venetians, from whom Murad captured it in 1430. But Murad left John himself in relative peace. In contrast with the stagnation of Constantinople and its pathetic environs, the empire had its bright spot in the Morea, where John VIII and his brothers, especially Constantine, completed the recovery of the remaining Peloponnesus from the Latins. Mindful of the ultimate Turkish danger, John renewed his father's quest for Western help, but with more intense emphasis upon church union, which Westerners insisted was the necessary prerequisite for any military aid. Only with full discussion of differences in a formal church council could John meet the minimal expectations of Orthodox believers, so he courted the

Western church with offers of serious negotiation. Despite skepticism or outright opposition from most Greek churchmen, John pressed forward and himself headed a distinguished delegation, including the patriarch and leading intellectuals, to a council in Italy. First convened at Ferrara in the spring of 1438 and reconvened the following year at Florence, this council produced, after long debates, a reunion formula that for many Greeks would mean a compromise of their faith more terrible than conquest by the Turks.

John returned home to his subjects' scorn, powerless to implement the union, which itself became a new issue in quarrels among his brothers. As for the benefit that might have come, another Western military expedition in the Balkans was disastrously defeated by Murad at Varna (10 November 1444); a subsequent unsuccessful effort by the Hungarians against the Turks was also defeated (October 1448), ending Latin ventures to save the Balkans. Spent and discredited, John died soon after (31 October 1448). Childless, he was succeeded, after family bickering, by his eldest surviving brother, Constantine, then despot of the Morea; he was crowned at Mistra, to avoid union-tainted ceremonies in Constantinople, and then sailed there to begin his doomed reign (1448–1453).

Constantine XI tried to reconcile union opponents while under papal pressure to implement union as the price for aid. Lulled by old Murad II's leniency, meanwhile, Constantine misjudged the new sultan. Energetic, autocratic, vastly ambitious, young Mehmed II (1451–1481) was determined to take Constantinople. Constantine might plead diplomatically for aid and allies, but Mehmed Fatih ("The Conqueror") was to be the true arbiter of Byzantium's fate. Securing Ottoman control of Asia Minor in order to avoid distraction, Mehmed then (1452) built Rümeli Ḥiṣār, a great fortress on the European side of the Bosporus, to guarantee his grip on the Straits. His preparations completed, Mehmed moved his vast forces, including formidable new cannon, before the walls of Constantinople in early April 1453 and began his epic siege.

The city's defenders were few, demoralized, and badly divided. Token papal aid and contributions by some Venetians and Genoese were the only Western help. The city's once-great fortifications were in weak condition, unequal to the new challenge of artillery. Despite disadvantages, the defenders held out for nearly two months, regularly foiling the sultan's frantic determination and the desperate ingenuity of his subordinates. Raising the siege was considered, but Mehmed insisted on one last assault. Launched before dawn on 29 May 1453, it overwhelmed the final resistance and carried the Turks into the city for an orgy of looting and slaughter. Constantine XI, who had led the defense with devotion and dignity, perished in the last onslaught.

Byzantium was dead as a state, and its little remaining territory, notably in the Morea, was absorbed over the next eight years. Yet, Byzantine culture and energy were too vital to be extinguished even by such a catastrophe. While Byzantine influences survived strongly in neighboring regions or cultures, the spirit of later Byzantium's resurgent Hellenism lived on under Turkish rule, partly sublimated in the life of the Orthodox church, to find new realization in the latter-day world of secular nationalism with the creation of the modern nation of Greece in the nineteenth century.

BIBLIOGRAPHY

General works. Donald M. Nicol, *The Last Centuries of Byzantium, 1261–1453* (1972); George Ostrogorsky, *History of the Byzantine State,* Joan M. Hussey, trans., 2nd ed. (1969); Apostolos E. Vacalopoulos, *Origins of the Greek Nation, 1204–1461,* Ian N. Moles, trans. (1970).

Specialized works. Franz Babinger, *Mehmed the Conqueror and His Time,* William C. Hickman, ed., Ralph Manheim, trans. (1978); John W. Barker, *Manuel II Palaeologus (1391–1425): A Study in Late Byzantine Statesmanship* (1969); Ursula K. Bosch, *Kaiser Andronikos III. Palaiologos, Versuch einer Darstellung der byzantinischen Geschichte in den Jahren 1321–1341* (1965); George T. Dennis, *The Reign of Manuel II Palaeologus in Thesalonica, 1382–1387* (1960); Alice Gardner, *The Lascarids of Nicaea: The Story of an Empire in Exile* (1912); Deno J. Geanakoplos, *Emperor Michael Palaeologus and the West, 1258–1282* (1959); Joseph Gill, *The Council of Florence* (1959); Oscar Halecki, *Un empereur de Byzance à Rome: Vingt ans de travail pour l'union des églises et pour la défense de l'Empire d'Orient, 1355–1375* (1930); Nicolae Iorga, *Byzance après Byzance* (1935); Angeliki E. Laiou, *Constantinople and the Latins: The Foreign Policy of Andronicus II, 1282–1328* (1972); Alfonso Lowe, *The Catalan Vengeance* (1972); Chedomil Mijatovich, *Constantine, the Last Emperor of the Greeks, or the Conquest of Constantinople by the Turks (A.D. 1453)* (1892); Donald M. Nicol, *The Byzantine Family of Kantakouzenos (Cantacuzenus) ca. 1100–1460. A Genealogical and Prosopographical Study* (1968); Edwin Pears, *The Destruction of the Greek Empire and the Story of the Capture of Constantinople by the Turks* (1903, repr. 1969); Léon Pierre Raybaud, *Le gouvernement et l'administration centrale de l'empire byzantin sous les premiers Paléologues (1258–1354)* (1968); Steven Runciman, *The Fall of Constantinople 1453* (1969); Günter Weiss, *Johannes Kantakuzenos—Aristokrat, Staatsmann, Kaiser und Mönch—in der Gesellschaftsentwicklung von Byzanz in 14. Jahrhundert* (1969).

JOHN W. BARKER

[See also **Almogávares; Andronikos II Palaiologos; Andronikos III Palaiologos; Bayazid I; Bulgaria; Catalan Company; Constantine XI Palaiologos; Constantinople; Epiros, Despotate of; Ferrara-Florence, Council of; John III Vatatzes; John V Palaiologos; John VI Kantakouzenos; John VIII Palaiologos; Komnenoi; Laskarids; Latin Empire of Constantinople; Manuel II Palaiologos; Mehmed (Muḥammad) I; Mehmed (Muḥammad) II; Michael I of Epiros; Michael II of Epiros; Michael VIII Palaiologos; Murad I; Murad II; Nicaea, Empire of; Nicopolis; Serbs and Serbia; Palaiologues; Theodore I Laskaris; Trebizond; Varna; Zealots.**]

BYZANTINE LITERATURE. This topic is covered in three separate articles: **Byzantine Literature; Byzantine Literature: Popular;** and **Byzantine Poetic Forms.**

BYZANTINE LITERATURE. By "Byzantine literature" is meant the Greek literature of the Middle Ages from the late fifth century to the fifteenth century. The literature of the age of the church fathers of the fourth and the earlier fifth century belongs to the ancient rather than to the medieval world. And the literature written in the Byzantine Empire, or in areas under Byzantine influence, in languages other than Greek—Latin, Syriac, Coptic, Armenian, Georgian, Old Church Slavonic—is generally held to belong with these other literatures and not to form a part of Byzantine literature. This is not an entirely happy convention, particularly for the early Byzantine period, when Byzantine society was polyethnic and multicultural; but it will be followed in the present article.

By the late fifth century much of the literature of ancient Greece that was still available had become "classic"; its language and style were studied and imitated, but its thought was often imperfectly understood. Some literary genres had become obsolete. This is true especially of choral lyric poetry and of drama, both tragic and comic. There were few opportunities for political speeches, and not many more for genuine forensic oratory. But rhetoric was far from obsolete. It formed the basis of the higher education of the upper classes of society, and there were endless occasions for encomiastic speeches addressed to emperors or dignitaries, and for displays of technical virtuosity. Indeed, rhetoric tended to invade other genres. The panegyric or the descriptive set piece tended to replace genuine narrative or argument, the elegantly turned or striking phrase to replace spontaneous expression of feeling. History, poetry, and epistolography all became in some degree branches of rhetoric.

At the same time, the spread of Christianity and its new place as the official religion brought new literary genres to the fore. The sermon became a branch of applied rhetoric. By the fifth century the sermons of the great fourth-century church fathers were being studied for their style as much as for their message. The life of the holy man, the aim of which was the edification of readers and hearers and the glorification of God, could not so easily be fitted into a traditional framework. Beginning with Athanasius' *Life of Antony* in the mid fourth century, the saint's life displayed features of its own and soon became an accepted genre, with new principles of construction and style. Liturgical poetry had since the earliest times formed part of Christian worship. And in the early Byzantine period liturgical poetry of high quality appeared, the composition and style of which owed little or nothing to classical Greek models.

Phonetic changes, which had been slowly and almost imperceptibly occurring, led by the early Byzantine period to difficulties both for the poet who used traditional poetic forms and for his audience. The old distinction between long and short syllables, which formed the basis of ancient Greek meter, gradually vanished. And a new distinction between stressed and unstressed syllables gave rise to a new rhythmic organization of speech, of which traditional meter took no account. Poets still composed in the old quantitative meters. But they composed more for the eye than for the ear, and became less and less sure of the distinctions of quantity, which they no longer made in their own speech.

The composition of poetry in the traditional forms became a matter of study and technique rather than of inspiration or feeling. The complex dactylic meter of epic and other narrative poetry, which often required the use of archaic or unusual linguistic forms, offered special difficulties. There was therefore a tendency to replace the traditional dactylic meter with the simpler iambic meter, which had been used in the dialogue of classical tragedy and comedy. This meter could be more easily reorganized on the basis of the new stress rhythm, and it became the passe-partout twelve-syllable meter of Byzantine poetry. It used the language of prose, and it could do all that prose could do. The distinction between prose and poetry came to depend less on the subject matter and the mode of treatment, and more on personal choice.

Because of a long and continuous literary tradition, reinforced by the teaching of grammar and rhetoric, almost all Byzantine literature is composed in an archaizing learned language, which grew more and more distinct from the Greek used by all classes in everyday intercourse. Within the learned language there were distinctions of rigor, but all writers practiced archaism to some degree. Although the bilingualism of the medieval Greek world was all-pervasive, it did not have the political and social overtones of modern Greek diglossy. The situation was more comparable to that of some parts of Switzerland, where everyone talks Swiss German but all writing—even private letters—and all formal speech is in standard German.

SECULAR POETRY IN THE LEARNED LANGUAGE

In the fifth century the epic tradition was revived by Nonnos of Panopolis in Egypt, whose gigantic *Dionysiaca* (21,771 lines) is, in spite of its narrative form, really a panegyric of the god whose exploits it celebrates. Short narrative poems on mythological subjects were also written, such as *The Fall of Troy* by Tryphiodoros, *Hero and Leander* by Musaios, and *The Rape of Helen* by Kolluthos. The language and meter of Homer were used for panegyric or descriptive purposes, as in the description of the Church of Hagia Sophia by Paul the Silentiary (*ca.* 550) or in the encomiums in Homeric verse of the Egyptian poetaster Dioskoros.

There was also much short occasional poetry in traditional meter and style, particularly during the age of Justinian. The poets imitated in theme and treatment the epigrammatists of the Hellenistic and Augustan ages, composing erotic, dedicatory, sepulchral, and other types of poems. They also occasionally wrote on personal or contemporary themes. The prestige that this classicizing poetry, mainly in elegiac couplets, enjoyed is borne out by the number of public inscriptions in poetic form. In particular many of the churches built in Palestine during the sixth century had inscriptions Christian in content but Homeric in language and style.

However, Homeric meter and language presented difficulties to both poet and audience. About A.D. 500 Marianos "rewrote" the poems of Theokritos, Apollonios Rhodios, Aratos, and Nikandros—in all, many tens of thousands of lines—in iambic trimeters. This "rewriting" did not involve only a change in meter; it meant the abandonment of the traditional language and style of hexameter verse. Homer's wings had been clipped.

It was in iambic trimeters that George of Pisidia in the early seventh century wrote his long poems on the wars of Emperor Heraklios against the Persians and Avars and on the six days of the Creation. In these poems narrative and panegyric are inextricably intermixed. At his best George of Pisidia is a vigorous and inventive poet, with a fertile gift for striking imagery. At his worst he is long-winded and flat. His language is that of rhetorical prose, with few echoes of classical literature but many biblical allusions. Nevertheless, he responded to the taste of his time and was much appreciated throughout the Byzantine period. George of Pisidia set a pattern that was followed, with greater or less success, by later writers of narrative poetry. Theodosius the Deacon, who in the second half of the tenth century wrote a long poem on the recapture of Crete from the Arabs, clearly modeled himself on George. So too did Theodore Prodromos in the middle of the twelfth century in his numerous historical poems, in which panegyric tends to prevail over narrative.

In the short occasional poem, too, the hexameter and the dactylic couplet gave place to the iambic trimeter. Little such poetry—indeed, little secular poetry of any kind—survives from the two and a half centuries following the brief Indian summer of the sixth century. The long struggle for survival against Arabs, Avars, Slavs, and Bulgars, and the accompanying breakdown of high urban culture, did not favor the cultivation of elegant belles-lettres. When occasional poems or epigrams again began to be written and appreciated in the early ninth century, they were mainly in iambic trimeter. Theodore, abbot of the monastery of Studios in Constantinople, wrote neat little poems on the various duties of the monks of his community. John Geometres in the tenth century was the author of an extensive collection of short poems on historical, literary, artistic, mythological, and personal themes. Most are in iambic trimeter, but he also composed in hexameter and elegiac couplets. His purity of language, clarity, sureness of touch, and personal involvement are evidence of his study of classical epigrammatic poetry. It was during his lifetime that a great collection was made of Greek occasional poetry from the earliest times to the ninth century, of which the surviving *Anthologia Palatina* is an epitome.

In poetry, as in other domains, the Byzantines were returning after a long interval to the study, appreciation, and imitation of their Hellenic heritage. Contemporaries of John Geometres included the diplomat Leo Choirosphaktes and the imperial official Constantine the Rhodian, whose descriptive poems are marked by rhetorical striving after effect. From then on, the short occasional poem was one of the most cultivated literary genres. The variety of themes was virtually inexhaustible: epitaphs, dedications in churches, descriptions of works of art, the feasts and saints of the ecclesiastical calendar, expressions of thanks to benefactors, praise of friends, invective against enemies, historical events, religious dogma, personal adventures. Most of the poems are in iambic trimeter. The best of them are elegant, striking, and sometimes witty. But the Byzantine delight in technical virtuosity and in repeated variations on a theme often led to long-windedness and looseness of construction. Many poets lacked a sense of what was enough. Most, but not all, of them were short on imagination and feeling, for which they tried to compensate by exaggeration and rhetorical emphasis. They competently versified what might as well have been said in prose.

Among the most noteworthy epigrammatists of the eleventh century were John Mauropous, metropolitan of Euchaita, and the imperial secretary Christopher of Mytilene. Both wrote many poems on events of their own time, Mauropous with classical restraint, Christopher with Byzantine long-windedness and linguistic exhibitionism. The distinction between the epigram and the longer narrative, didactic, or descriptive poem was beginning to disappear.

There were few men of letters in the twelfth century—the age of the Komnenoi—who did not turn their hand to occasional verse. Their output ranged from single-line epigrams on saints or church feasts to long panegyrics on rulers, statesmen, or prelates that sometimes merge into the category of narrative poetry. Among the leading poets of the period were the doctor Nikolaos Kallikles; Theophylact Hephaistos, archbishop of Bulgaria (1090–1108); the ecclesiastical lawyer Theodore Balsamon, who excelled in descriptions of works of art; and Theodore Prodromos, who, in addition to longer panegyric and historical poems, composed many short epigrams on religious themes. These epigrams are distinguished by their elegance, technical perfection, and good taste rather than by any deep religious feeling. At the end of the century Nikephoros Chrysoberges wrote tolerable poems on a variety of topics, and Constantine Stilbes included among his undistinguished epigrams a striking long poem on a great fire at Constantinople that is marked by vivid imagery and descriptive power.

Only two fourteenth-century poets are worthy of mention. Manuel Philes wrote countless poems on all kinds of topics: his own poverty, historical events and personalities, works of art, all the traditional religious and secular themes. His fluency, his firm control of his medium, and his fertile imagination make him a distinguished versifier if not a great poet. Theodore Metochites, grand logothete to Emperor Andronikos II and a notable man of letters, revived the tradition of personal hexameter poetry in Homeric language. His twenty poems range in length from 229 to 1,355 lines. Some are banal amplifications of commonplaces, but many show great originality and capacity for self-revelation. The most interesting are a very long autobiographical poem (no. 1); a description of the Chora monastery, which he had rebuilt and decorated with mosaics and frescoes (no. 2); and his literary testament, addressed to his pupil Nikephoros Gregoras (no. 4). Metochites, for all his learning, flounders helplessly amid the technicalities of Homeric language and meter. His poems convey the impression of a powerful and original mind imprisoned by the archaizing taste of his age.

The eleventh and twelfth centuries were particularly fruitful in poetry and in other literature, as thinkers and men of letters imitated and critically examined the heritage of Hellenism so laboriously reconstructed in the later ninth and tenth centuries after the long hiatus of the "Dark Age." Several significant innovations were made in poetry. The first was the development of a new metrical form that had no classical antecedents and was therefore unconstrained by classical theories and rules. This was the fifteen-syllable accentual verse. Its origin is disputed. The earliest known literary use is in some short tenth-century poems. By the eleventh century it was being used by Michael Psellos and others for didactic poems on law, grammar, and the like, for ease of memorizing. Somewhat earlier in the same century the monk and mystic Symeon chose this meter for his contemplative and ascetic poems, partly for ease of memorizing, partly because of the freedom from pagan and classical associations.

By the twelfth century the new meter was widely used for subliterary purposes. John Tzetzes (*ca.* 1110–1185) chose it both for the simple, allegorical interpretations of Homer that he wrote for the German bride of Manuel I and for his interminable grammatical, mythological, and historical commentary on his own collection of letters. By contrast, his summary of the whole Trojan legend, written for educated readers, was composed in Homeric meter and language. Theodore Prodromos chose the fifteen-syllable accentual meter for panegyric and other poems that he composed to be chanted or declaimed at the imperial court. The first large-scale employment of this meter for narrative purposes was by Constantine Manasses (*d.* 1187) in his long, versified world chronicle and in his romance *Aristandros and Kallithea.* The fifteen-syllable accentual meter is particularly adapted to the natural rhythm of the Greek language, and in subsequent centuries it became more and more the meter par excellence. It was the commonest vehicle for popular poetry and folk song.

Another innovation of the intellectually fertile twelfth century concerns content rather than form. The Greek romances of the Hellenistic and Roman age generally treated the separation of a pair of lovers and their eventual reunion after a series of colorful and improbable adventures. They enabled their readers to enjoy a wide range of emotions without the inconvenience of experiencing them in their own lives, and to feel the strangeness of remote and dangerous lands without actually going there. Though neglected by ancient literary theory, they were widely read and appreciated in late antiquity and the Byzantine world.

In the mid twelfth century several writers composed entirely new works of fiction, modeled closely in plot and incident on the ancient Greek romances—and like them situated in a timelessly classical and pagan world. Most of these, unlike their ancient exemplars, were written in verse. Constantine Manasses' *Aristandros and Kallithea* survives only in fragments. Theodore Prodromos' *Rhodanthe and Dosikles,* Niketas Eugenianos' *Drosilla and Charikles,* and Eustathios Makrembolites' *Hysmine and Hysminias* (in prose) are preserved entire. Long-winded, inflated, remote from life, these works can easily be stigmatized as rhetorical and escapist. Yet they are among the earliest examples of pure invented fiction in modern European literature. They provide an insight into Byzantine erotic ideas and imagery, which are firmly excluded from most Byzantine literature. And they sometimes show startlingly modern psychological insight.

Akin to the Byzantine verse romance but of different origin was the romantic epic *Digenis Akritas* (The twain-born borderer), of which the earliest surviving version probably dates from the twelfth century. It is a fusion of two story lines: the first recounts the adventures of a Muslim emir, his love for a Byzantine girl (which leads him to cross to Byzantine territory and embrace Christianity), his battles in the Byzantine cause, and the eventual defection to Byzantium of all his family; the second recounts the life of his son Digenis, who shows precocious prowess, fights against Amazons, cattle rustlers, and dragons, wins his bride in battle, builds a splendid palace in the borderland, and eventually, like Alexander, dies at the age of thirty-two. Both stories are probably literary imitations of narrative folk-poems composed and circulating during the ninth and tenth centuries in the wild borderlands of Cappadocia and Armenia, where Christians and Muslims lived together in a mixture of hostility and friendship. This epic contains far too much literary allusion and reference to be a genuine folk poem. Its different versions all present the same narrative line and the same episodes. But they differ in their linguistic level, some showing many features of the spoken language. The relation between the variant versions is not yet clear. *Digenis Akritas* is a Byzantine parallel to the Old French chansons de geste and the Spanish *Cantar de mío Cid.*

Though some late versions of the *Digenis Akritas* are in something approaching the spoken Greek of the late Middle Ages, extensive use in poetry of the spoken language—in a somewhat adulterated form—did not occur until the early fourteenth century, after the hiatus of the Fourth Crusade and the Latin Empire. There were, however, some forerunners in the inventive twelfth century. The "Ptochoprodromic" poems belong to the mid century. In one of these a certain Ptochoprodromos ("Poor Prodromos") complains of poverty and a nagging wife. In another he dwells on the difficulties of bringing up a numerous family. A third poem satirizes abbots, contrasting their luxurious living with the wretched fare they allow to the brethren. The last is a complaint against the poor rewards of learning. All four are written in a language approaching spoken Greek. Whether the poems are by Theodore Prodromos or another is an open question. Their intent is satirical, and in their pastiche of everyday speech they show much wit and humor. But they are scarcely a serious attempt at literature in the vernacular.

The same can be said of the *Spaneas,* in which an elderly courtier gives advice on etiquette and morals to a younger colleague. About 1160 Michael Glykas, historian and theologian, wrote an appeal for release from prison to Manuel I Komnenos in a mixture of literary and demotic Greek. These poems all perhaps reflect the taste of the Komnenian court for pastiche and pseudovulgarity. But the prestige of the literary language and the educational system that supported it remained unshaken.

At the very end of the thirteenth century and in the first half of the fourteenth there was a sudden burst of poetry in demotic Greek. The influence of the learned language—and the difficulty of writing a hitherto unwritten vernacular—ensured that none of these poems is in pure vernacular; all show a macaronic mixture of vernacular and learned words and forms. The largest category of these demotic poems is romances of chivalry: *Kallimachos and Chrysorrhoe, Lybistros and Rhodamne, Belthandros and Chrysantza, Imberios and Margarona, Phlorios and Platziaphlora.* All display a complex plot, a flowing narrative style, a mixture of realism with legendary and fairy-tale motifs, and a taste for elaborate descriptions. Some give a larger place to the marvelous than do others—*Kallimachos and Chrysorrhoe* is much concerned with dragons, magic castles, witches, and enchanted maidens. All show some influence of Western romances of chivalry, both in plot and in incident. Two—*Imberios and Margarona* and *Phlorios and Platziaphlora*—are direct adaptations of Western models. All reflect, although not in a naturalistic mode, the confused world of late Byzantine society, in which traditional Byzantine ideas and beliefs mingled both with those of western Europe and those of the Muslim or Christian Near East. All are written in fifteen-syllable lines, without the Western innovation of rhyme.

The next category comprises "historical" poems. The longest of these is the *Chronicle of the Morea,* recounting in some 10,000 fifteen-syllable lines the occupation of the Peloponnese by the Franks and events there up to 1292. It is written from the point of view of the conquerors, anti-Byzantine, anti-Orthodox, and anti-Greek. There exists an Old French version of the *Chronicle,* and it is not yet settled which of the two is the original. The poem appears to be the work of a Hellenized Frank or of a Gasmul (the son of a Frank by a Greek woman) writing about the end of the thirteenth century.

The remaining historical poems deal with events of the remote past, often as transformed by popular tradition and imagination. They include two versions of Pseudo-Callisthenes' Alexander romance; a poem on Justinian's general Belisarios, which has no connection with actual historical events; and several poems dealing with the Trojan War: one in 1,166 fifteen-syllable lines, one written in Epiros about 1330 by Constantine Hermoniakos in eight-syllable lines, and one, still unpublished, that is an interminable translation of the Old French *Roman de Troie* of Benoît de Ste. Maure. All are reflections not of Homer but of the romanticized Hellenistic stories of the Trojan War that are preserved in the Latin works attributed to Dictys of Crete and Dares the Phrygian. There were also satiric poems in which Byzantine society was caricatured in the guise of animals or birds, allegorical poems, and poems of moral edification.

It was often supposed that this vernacular poetry originated in regions under Latin occupation and that it was a kind of folk poetry, composed by and for strata in society that had no share in the dominant culture. Both these propositions are now challenged. Many of the poems are clearly metropolitan rather than provincial, and *Kallimachos and Chrysorrhoe* is probably the work of a member of the imperial family. There is no sign of provincial dialect in these poems. No doubt this sudden flourishing of poetry in the vernacular is a sign of cultural breakdown and change. But it may well be a change initiated among the literate and educated, who sought a more flexible vehicle both for self-expression and for communication with the mass of their fellow citizens. The discussion continues.

It should be noted that the use of the vernacular in the late Byzantine period was virtually confined to poetry and to works of fiction. All "serious" writing made use of literary Greek. Only "frivolous" works could be composed in the language of everyday intercourse. This was in part due to the prestige of literary tradition and the values it embodied. Another factor was that literary Greek and spoken Greek were varieties or registers of the same language, and not different languages as were Latin and the west European vernaculars. Works composed in the literary language were accessible to many readers, who might not appreicate all their nuances. Thus the conditions were not yet ripe for a general development of literature in the vulgar tongue. There could be no Greek Dante in the Middle Ages.

Lyric poetry and songs in vulgar Greek doubtless existed, but the only direct evidence comes from peripheral areas under Latin rule. A collection of love poems, describing various stages in the pursuit of a girl by a young man, was probably put together about 1400 in Rhodes. And in Cyprus an unknown poet or poets composed a group of love poems, in Cypriot dialect and strongly influenced by Petrarch and his school.

Poetry both in the vernacular and in the learned language continued to be written in the last generations of the Byzantine Empire, but none is of great note. Moralizing poems and confessions of sin, often with alphabetic acrostics, are among the commonest vernacular poems of the period. More interesting are the poems on exile that express the passionate longings of those who had to abandon their homeland. Last, there are a number of poetic laments on the capture of cities by the Ottoman Turks, culminating in those for the fall of Constantinople.

In the learned language there was versification on a great variety of topics. George Lapithes and David Dishypatos wrote theological tracts. Allegorical dialogues of moralizing tone were composed by several authors. Panegyrics, epitaphs, and the like were produced as occasion demanded. The monk Matthew wrote a description of the Genoese colony of Caffa in the Crimea. Perhaps the most noteworthy poem of the period is the long (3,060 lines) allegorical poem of Theodore Meliteniotes (also author of a vast manual of astronomy), *On Temperance,* with its many personifications and learned catalogs. Almost all these works might as well have been in prose. The Muse had long abandoned the learned language and bestowed her favors, albeit grudgingly, on those who wrote in the tongue of the people.

LITURGICAL POETRY

From the earliest times song formed a part of the liturgy of the church (see Eph. 5:18–19), which was modeled largely on that of the synagogue. Besides chanted psalms and canticles, there were rhythmical responses by the congregation and hymns composed for liturgical use (see proceedings of the synod of A.D. 269, in *Patrologia graeca,* XXX, 709). Few examples of these early compositions survive. Many Christian writers composed religious poetry in classical meters—for instance, Clement of Alexandria (*d. ca.* 215), Methodios of Olympus (*d.* 311), Gregory of Nazianzus (*d.* 390), Synesios of Cyrene (*d. ca.* 413/414), and Sophronios of Jerusalem (*d.* 638)—but these poems do not appear to have found liturgical use. Short stanzas in accentual rhythm developed out of the responses after psalms and lessons; they were known as troparia, and they were generally expressions of prayer or glorification.

In the mid sixth century a more elaborate composition, the kontakion, began to replace the troparia. In form this was a series of up to twenty similar stanzas, composed of short phrases that were units of meter, of sense, and of music. Each stanza of the kontakion ended with a line or lines of refrain. The initial letters of the stanzas often formed an acrostic giving the name of the hymnographer or of the feast for which the kontakion was composed, in order to aid the memory of the singers. In content the kontakion was a narrative homily, recounting some event of biblical history or the life of a saint or martyr. The origin of the kontakion was partly in Syria, where short homilies in verse had long been in liturgical use. But the Syriac verse homilies had a simple rhythmical structure. The formal elaboration of the kontakion owes much to Greek poetic and liturgical tradition. In its developed form the kontakion had something of the richness, complexity, and infinite variation of the choral lyric of ancient Greece. And like the choral lyric it was a combination of words and music forming part of a ritual.

The first and greatest composer of kontakia was Romanos Melodos, a native of Emesa in Syria, possibly of Jewish origin, who came to Constantinople in the early years of the sixth century. He is said to have composed more than a thousand kontakia. Eighty-five attributed to him survive, not all of certain authenticity. Most of them contain a large element of dialogue, and it is in these dramatic passages that Romanos is at his best, re-creating with sympathetic imagination the changing thoughts and feelings of his characters. His language is strongly influenced by the Septuagint and the New Testament. There are scarcely any echoes of classical literature. His style is lucid and uncomplicated. His imagery is simple and never developed into allegory, his rhythmical—and musical—inventiveness boundless. Many of his poems are reworkings of narratives from saints' lives or the church fathers, freely developed in dramatic and descriptive form. Though no theologian, he expresses deep and occasionally passionate religious feeling. The music of Romanos' hymns, as of all early Byzantine liturgical poetry, is lost to us. But even without the music Romanos is worthy of a place among the greatest of Greek poets.

Kontakia continued to be composed until the early ninth century, but none had the dramatic power and brilliance of Romanos'. Changes in the liturgy often led to the abandonment of the kontakion in the congregational service, and its restriction to the monastic liturgy. This encouraged a reduction of the narrative and dramatic element in favor of ascetic and doctrinal themes. The last composer of kontakia of any note was Theodore, abbot of Studios (759–826).

A liturgical poem of the sixth century that is unique in form, and still holds a special place in the life of the Orthodox church, reminds us that the kontakion was not the only type of hymn then current. It is the *Akathistos Hymn,* consisting of twenty-four stanzas. The first twelve form a normal kontakion, recounting the story of Christ from the Annunciation to the flight into Egypt. The second half dwells on the mystery of the Incarnation. Each odd-numbered stanza has, in place of the normal refrain, a long series of salutations to the Virgin, enumerating her attributes in a kind of litany. The hymn was originally composed for the feast of the Annunciation but is now sung during Lent. It is said to have been sung during the siege of Constantinople by Avars and Persians in 626, and one of the surviving prefaces to it was composed for that occasion. Its authorship is unknown. It is now generally agreed that it is a work of the age of Romanos; beyond this the evidence does not permit us to go.

Toward the end of the seventh century the reintroduction of the sermon caused considerable restructuring of the liturgy. In consequence a new type of liturgical poem, the *kanōn,* appeared in the morning service. The *kanōn* was a series of nine odes, each with a different rhythmical pattern and melody, and consisting of several stanzas. But, unlike the kontakion, the *kanōn* was concerned not with narrative but with praise. Furthermore, each of its nine sections alluded to and echoed one of the nine biblical canticles (Exodus 15:1–18, Deuteronomy 32:1–43, 1 Samuel 2:1–10, Habakkuk 3:2–19, Isaiah 26:1–21, Jonah 2:2–9, Song of the Three Children (Apocrypha) 3–22 and 52–88, Luke 1:46–55). The music played a more prominent role in the *kanōn* than in the kontakion both because nine separate melodies were required and because a more ornate, melismatic style of singing developed, in which a single syllable could be prolonged over several notes. As in the kontakion, dialogue was prominent in the *kanōn.* The language tended to be more inflated, and easily drifted into repetitiousness and verbosity.

The first great composer of *kanōnes* was Andrew, bishop of Crete (*ca.* 660–*ca.* 740), a native of Damascus. His *Great* or *Penitential Kanōn,* of 250 stanzas, is still in liturgical use. He was familiar with the hymns of Romanos, on which he often elaborated. Other notable composers of *kanōnes* were the brothers John of Damascus and Kosmas of Maiuma (first half of the eighth century), Theodore of Studios, Theophanes Graptos (*d. ca.* 845), Kasia or Ikasia (mid ninth century), Joseph the Hymnographer (*d.* 886), Metrophanes of Smyrna (second half of the ninth century), Emperor Leo VI (*d.* 912), and John Mauropous (*d. ca.* 1055). No new hymns were added to the Constantinopolitan liturgy after the eleventh century. *Kanōnes* continued to be written as literary exercises or for local use during the late Byzantine period. Many are still unpublished. Some *kanōnes* may have preserved their original melodies in early manuscripts. Later melodies reflect the reform of church music introduced in the early fourteenth century by the Bulgarian John Kukuzelis and his school, involving elaborate ornamentation and coloratura, which sometimes rendered the words unintelligible.

HISTORY

The Byzantines were conscious both of the long and continuous literary tradition of Greece, going back to Homer, and of the almost equally long political tradition of the Roman Empire, which could be traced back to the conquest of the Hellenistic East by Rome in the second century B.C. or, with a little imagination, to the foundation of the city by Romulus. They were equally aware of the privileged position accorded in Christian thought to the Byzantine Empire, which would last until the end of things, and would in due course come to embrace the whole of the inhabited world. Their pride in their own traditions and in their providential mission led them to value history as a peculiarly Greek activity.

Byzantine historiography, like so much else in Byzantine culture, had two roots. One lay in classical Greek and Roman historiography, with its study of causes and its interest in the influence of characters upon events. Byzantine historians took from their classical and postclassical predecessors the use of elevated language and a solemn, sometimes moralizing, tone, rhetorical speeches, descriptive set pieces, and learned excursuses. The other source of Byzantine historiography was the Christian world chronicle. The earliest Christian chronicles had been primarily studies of chronology, aiming at fitting together biblical and profane history in such a way as to demonstrate the priority of the former. But they soon took on the further task of displaying to believers and nonbelievers alike the working of providence in history. This necessarily involved a theological view of historical causation; men and nations prospered because they did the will of God, or met with disaster because they opposed his will. Characterization, where present at all, was black and white. Such writing was relatively free from the influence of rhetoric, with its elevated language and its allusive manner.

All Byzantine historiography was influenced to some degree by both these traditions. But at most periods there was a fairly clear distinction between them. In the early Byzantine period a series of historians writing in conscious imitation of classical and Hellenistic predecessors dealt with the history of their own time or the immediately preceding generation. Procopius (*d. ca.* 562) wrote of Justinian's wars and of his building activity, and in his *Secret History,* which cannot have been widely circulated in the author's lifetime, provided a critical and often malicious commentary on his own published work. Agathias (*d.* 583) took up the history of the empire in 552, where Procopius left off, and continued it to 558. Menander Protector (whose history survives only in excerpts) continued the work of Agathias up to 582. Theophylact Symokattes (first half of the seventh century) continued that of Menander Protector up to 602, the year of Phokas' accession. In spite of differences in style and approach, all four historians share an imperial rather than a local point of view; a serious interest in the causes of major events and the characters of the actors in them; an elevated style; a narrative mode punctuated by set speeches, descriptions, and geographical and ethnographical excursuses; and a detached and objective literary persona. Though dealing with a Christian society, they all avoid the technical language of Christianity and direct allusion to Christian matters.

At the same time as these historians were writing their studies of short periods, others were composing world histories of a very different kind. Two of these survive. The *Chronicle* of John Malalas of Antioch (*ca.* 491–578) covers the period from the Creation to the end of the reign of Justinian (565). It follows a strictly annalistic arrangement; gives much space to the anecdotal and the remarkable, and to events of local Antiochene importance; often attributes the cause of events to the favor or wrath of God; and is generally uninterested in the character of men. There are no rhetorical set speeches, no descriptive passages, no learned excursuses, and the language is unpretentious and close to spoken Greek. But Malalas is not an incompetent writer; his *Chronicle* is attractive and entertaining, and was popular in later centuries.

At the same time Theophylact Symokattes was writing his history, an unknown clergyman composed the *Paschal* or *Easter Chronicle,* recounting world history from the Creation to 627. The arrangement is similar to that of Malalas, the tone more theological, and the interests of the author more limited. Both chronicles are by their nature works of selection and compilation, rather than of original writing. Edification was certainly a motive of the authors, but entertainment was also an aim. It is misleading to think of these and similar works as composed by and for monks; they appealed to a much wider public that looked for a simple explanation of how things came to be as they were. A similar chronicle, now preserved only in a few excerpts, was written by John of Antioch in the early seventh century.

Other types of historical writing were practiced in the early Byzantine period. Short, antiquarian studies of particular institutions, places, or problems belonged to the domain of technical writing. Examples are the studies of the Roman and Byzantine magistracies, the Roman calendar, and the Roman art of divination by the civil servant John the Lydian (*ca.* 490–*ca.* 560); the treatises on the antiquities of Constantinople preserved in the tenth-century compilation *Patria Constantinopoleos;* and the account by Nonnosos of his diplomatic missions on behalf of Justinian to Saracens, Ethiopians, and Himyarites, of which only excerpts survive. Other historians wrote accounts of particular wars or campaigns, such as the history of the long war of 571–591 between Byzantium and Persia by John of Epiphaneia (excerpts only).

A third and more important variety of historiography is ecclesiastical history, the pattern of which had been established in the fourth and fifth centuries by Eusebius, Socrates Scholasticus, Sozomenos, and Theodoret. In the early Byzantine period ecclesiastical histories were composed by Zacharias Scholasticus (Zacharias of Mytilene, *d.* 553) (surviving only in Syriac translation) and Evagrios, who continued the work of Socrates, Sozomenos, and Theodoret for the years 431–594 and devoted much attention to secular matters. Church histories by Theodore Anagnostes for 323–527 and by John Diakrinomenos from 429 to the reign of Anastasios are known only in fragments.

The writing of contemporary history in the classical manner came to an end in the early seventh century. No one wrote a continuation of the history of Theophylact Symokattes. The harsh conditions of the two centuries following the Arab conquests did not encourage so sophisticated a literary genre. In a sense the successor of Theophylact was George of Pisidia. But George wrote in verse, his work was as much panegyric as history, and it was deeply imbued with Christian thought and expression. A last outlier of classical Greek historiography is the history of the reign of Heraklios written in Armenian by Sebēos in the 670's.

World chronicles continued to be written in the Dark Age, though few survive. Some were no doubt suppressed because they praised iconoclast rulers. Bishop John of Nikiu in Egypt composed a chronicle about 700 that contains valuable information on the Arab conquest of Egypt and the early years of Arab rule. The original was probably in Coptic; what survives is an Ethiopic translation of an Arabic translation. A text incorporated in the tenth-century *Patria Constantinopoleos* and entitled *Brief Chronological Expositions* appears to be an excerpt from a chronicle written in the 740's. Marginal notes in the unique manuscript of the *Paschal Chronicle* and agreements between later chronographers point to a lost chronicle composed near the end of the eighth century. An account of the struggles against the Bulgarians in the early ninth century is probably an excerpt from a chronicle written shortly after those events.

With the world chronicle of George Synkellos (*d.* 810–811), which extends as far as the accession of Diocletian, and its continuation by Theophanes Confessor (*d.* 818), we once again have complete texts. Synkellos' work is a mere compilation from ancient sources that largely survive. That of Theophanes draws on a great variety of Byzantine sources, many of which are now lost. Both chronicles are arranged annalistically, and frequently date events wrongly through misunderstanding of the chronology of their sources. Both are written in a language less popular in syntax and morphology than that of Malalas or the *Paschal Chronicle,* and varying according to the source used. Theophanes' understanding of historical causation is theological, and his characterization does not go beyond epithets of praise or condemnation. In spite of his many shortcomings he is a valuable source for the period from the death of Justinian to his own day.

Theophanes' contemporary, Patriarch Nikephoros (806–815; *d.* 829), composed a history *(Breviarum)* of the period 602–769. His intention was clearly to continue the *History* of Theophylact Symokattes. But he neglected political history in favor of a theological explanation of events: the fatal illness of Heraklios was the consequence of his marriage to his niece, the volcanic eruption at Thera in 726 was connected with the iconoclastic doctrines professed by Leo III, and so on. Nikephoros' language is more classicizing than that of Theophanes, but his debt to classical Greek historiography goes no further than language. In the middle of the ninth century George the Monk composed a chronicle extending from the Creation to 842. His work has independent value only for the years 813–842. Even in this portion abuse of theological adversaries bulks larger than historical narrative. George's chronicle was continued to the year 948 by an unknown adherent of Romanos Lekapenos. The continuation is less theological in tone than the original, and more concerned with military and political events. Its annalistic structure and popular language are those traditional in Byzantine chronicles.

In the middle of the tenth century two historical works were written that were intended as continuations of the *Chronography* of Theophanes. Both were composed at the behest of Constantine VII. They are probably to be connected with a historical enterprise directly sponsored by the emperor. This was a series of lengthy excerpts from Greek historians from Herodotus to the ninth century, arranged according to subject matter. As Constantine observes in his preface, the bulk of historical writing was so great that no one could read it all; therefore, he had decided to save his subjects the vain effort by making comparable passages readily available. The original compilation consisted of fifty-three volumes. Surviving are *On Embassies* in its entirety, about half of *On Virtues and Vices,* and shorter sections of other volumes. Side by side with this compilation from past historians Constantine was anxious to have a continuous narrative history written to follow on that of Theophanes and continue to his own time. He was animated in part by the desire to glorify the Macedonian dynasty and to whitewash the assassination of Michael III, to which that dynasty owed its origin.

Two attempts were made to provide such a history. One was by Joseph Genesios, a high officer of state under Constantine VII. It covers the period 813 to the death of Basil I in 886. The other, known as *Scriptores post Theophanem* or *Theophanes continuatus,* was the work of several hands and dealt with the period from 813 to 961. The last portion seems to have been a later addition. The section recounting the reign of Basil I (book 5) is alleged to be the work of Constantine VII himself; the authorship of the other sections is uncertain.

Though expressly described as continuations of the *Chronography* of Theophanes, these two works differ entirely from it in historical conception, in arrangement, and in language and style. An interest in character and a capacity to describe it, a political rather than a theological view of historical causation, an objective attitude to their subject matter, the abandonment of rigid annalistic structure, a complex and sophisticated narrative style, and elevated, classicizing language mark these works as inaugurating a new era in Byzantine historiography.

Since the mid ninth century, scholars had been seeking out, copying, and reading half-forgotten works of classical and postclassical Greek literature. Higher education in the capital had been encouraged and organized by a series of emperors. Commentaries and lexica had been compiled to facilitate the understanding of older literature. A conscious attempt was being made by rulers and many of their subjects to set aside the ignorance of two and a half centuries and to re-create the world of Christian late antiquity. Genesios and the authors of the continuation of Theophanes, like their readers, had learned from classical models how to interpret and depict the recent past. Polybius and Plutarch had provided them with a new approach to narrative and description, causation and character. Though biased and in some respects dishonest, both works signaled a return to the classical tradition of historiography.

From the mid tenth century to the Fourth Crusade, there was no generation without historians. Some wrote world chronicles. Others dealt with the history of their own times. All were in greater or lesser degree working within the restored classical tradition, striving for at least the appearance of detachment and objectivity, and employing sophisticated narrative technique and classicizing language and style. Most had held high office in state or church and had access to sources of information. Together they provide a continuous, detailed narrative account of two and a half centuries of Byzantine history.

Still in the tenth century Symeon Logothete composed a chronicle from the Creation to the death of Romanos Lekapenos in 948. This work exists in different redactions and is attributed to different authors, and its many problems still await solution. The writer displays a strong sympathy for Romanos Lekapenos. Toward the end of the century Leo the Deacon narrated the course of events from 959 to 976 with some independence of judgment. It was as a continuation of Leo's history that Michael Psellos composed his *Chronography,* covering the period from 976 to 1078. The latter part of the *Chronography,* dealing with the years when Psellos himself held high office, is biased and apologetic in character, and the author's personality and point of view are everywhere present. The brilliance of Psellos' descriptions and the subtlety with which he delineates character hardly compensate for his lack of objectivity.

A younger contemporary of Psellos, the high government official Michael Attaleiates, composed a history covering the years 1034–1079/1080. Less brilliant than Psellos, Attaleiates is no more impartial; the latter part of his history is a panegyric of the emperor Nikephoros Botaneiates. About the same time the courtier John Skylitzes wrote a history of the years 811–1057, evidently intended as a continuation of the narrative of Theophanes. In his prologue Skylitzes mentions many historians of the period whose works are now lost. Along with a mass of military and political information Skylitzes includes sensational items of all kinds, designed to entertain the reader. He became a valuable mine of information for later historians.

The life and times of Alexios Komnenos form the subject of two historical works, one by his son-in-law, the other by his daughter. The modestly entitled *Material for History* of Nikephoros Bryennios, covering the years 1070–1079, is a combination of family memoir and critique of other historians. Nikephoros was well placed to know the truth of events, and in many domains he is a sober and reliable narrator. But where Alexios and his family are concerned, a romanticized and pseudo-heroic account is given.

The *Alexiad* of Anna Komnena deals with the

years 1069–1118. It is a passionate panegyric of the writer's father Alexios, written many years after his death. At the same time it is a recall in the imagination of Anna's own youth, when all the rewards and temptations of power were hers, and often reveals as much about the author as about her subject. Intelligent and singularly well-informed, Anna was a woman of strong feelings and violent prejudices, and the objectivity for which she sincerely strove was beyond her. Alexios was for her beyond criticism; the Crusaders were barbarians and scoundrels (though she was not insensitive to the charm of the dashing Norman leader Bohemond). Her brother John, whom she tried to oust from the succession, is treated with remarkable coldness. Anna was both a social and an intellectual snob. She is proud of her classical learning and misses no opportunity to display it. Her stilted classicizing language is sometimes more of a hindrance than a help to communication. But she has a natural talent for narration and description, and a good subject. She is without question one of the greatest historians of the Middle Ages.

Anna Komnena's *Alexiad* was continued by the imperial secretary John Kinnamos, who covered the years 1118–1176. Sober and well-informed, Kinnamos expresses the values of the military aristocracy that he served, yet he recounts with some objectivity the decline of Byzantine military and naval power. He has a talent for vivid and concrete description. But the great changes in the world situation that he witnessed were beyond his powers of analysis.

The task of continuing Anna Komnena was taken up a generation later, after the capture of Constantinople by the Latins and the breakup of the Byzantine Empire, by a former high officer of state, Niketas Choniates. Choniates began his account with the accession of John II in 1118 and carried it down to 1206. He probably knew the history of Kinnamos, and certainly drew on the extensive occasional literature of poems, panegyrics, and the like that flourished in the twelfth century. For the period from 1180 on, he was an eyewitness of much of what he recounts. His interest ranges from foreign affairs to court intrigues, from battles and sieges to details of everyday life. He has little understanding of the social changes and discontents of the period.

But Choniates knew that he was living in a period of catastrophic decline, the causes of which he tried to discover. Among these was the rapid deterioration of relations between Byzantium and the Latins, which he analyzes with pitiless penetration and few illusions. Another was the caliber of the rulers of the empire after Manuel's death, which he depicts with objectivity. His narrative style is complex, varying in pace, punctuated with vivid descriptions, ironic character studies, and carefully observed genre scenes. His language is learned and classicizing, but at the same time versatile. Like his friend and teacher Eustathios, he realizes that creative innovation is a part of classicism. His habit of throwing an oblique light on an event or a personality by means of a fleeting classical allusion makes him a difficult but rewarding writer, in whom Byzantine historiography perhaps reached its highest point.

Universal history was not neglected in the twelfth century, and several world chronicles were composed. All were written by men of letters who also practiced other literary genres. As a result they were less isolated from classical historiography in narrative method, concepts, and style than were the earlier chronicles. John Zonaras, lawyer and head of the imperial chancellery in the first half of the twelfth century, and author of a variety of other works, wrote a world chronicle from the Creation to 1118. His copious excerpts, sometimes in résumé, sometimes almost verbatim, from numerous earlier historians make his chronicle a valuable source for all periods. Zonaras shows great learning and judgment in his choice of sources, and has some capacity for historical criticism. His chronicle was much drawn on by later Byzantine historians.

The *World Chronicle* of Constantine Manasses, extending from the Creation to 1081, is in fifteen-syllable verse. Written about 1150 at the request of the Sebastocratorissa Irene, sister-in-law of Manuel I, it is full of decorative detail, appeals to emotion, and rhetorical commonplaces, but displays little historical judgment either in the selection or in the utilization of sources. Yet it is agreeable and interesting light reading, which is what its author intended it to be. If Zonaras aimed at edification, Manasses aimed at entertainment.

The third of the twelfth-century chronicles is that of Michael Glykas (or Sikidites), who was also the author of theological treatises and poems. Composed in the second half of the century, it covers the period from the Creation (which is treated at great length and in detail) to 1118. Roman and Byzantine history are dealt with rather briefly. Glykas offers little new information or evaluation, and often adopts a strongly moralizing tone. His language is less rigidly classicizing than that of most twelfth-century writers, and he readily admits demotic words and place-names.

Sometimes forms other than the world chronicle or the history of the author's time were adopted. An eyewitness account of the capture of Thessaloniki by the Arabs in 904 is attributed to one John Kameniates. It has recently been suggested that the work is a fifteenth-century forgery; the question is still open. Eustathios Kataphloros, Homeric commentator and metropolitan of Thessaloniki, wrote a graphic and moving account of the capture of the city by the Normans in 1185, set against the background of the history of the period. Another variety of historiography is represented by some of the antiquarian compilations prepared under the direction of Constantine VII in the tenth century. The *Book of Ceremonies* gives directions in great detail for the various ceremonies of the imperial court and includes many archival documents, notably the contingency plan for a mobilization of the army on the eastern front and the movement order for the unsuccessful campaign against Arab-held Crete in 911. There is little system or order in the presentation of the material. The work *On Themes* is a geographical account of the Byzantine Empire, province (theme) by province, often based on out-of-date sources.

The treatise *On the Government of the Empire*, addressed to Constantine's son Romanos, is a systematic discussion of the relation of the empire with the surrounding peoples: Pechenegs, Khazars, Rus, Bulgarians, Magyars, Franks, Arabs, Italians, Croats, Serbs. It incorporates many documents and excerpts from older texts, such as the description of the river route from Kiev to the Black Sea and the local history of Cherson in late antiquity. In the proem and elsewhere tenth-century Byzantine imperial ideology and the methods of Byzantine diplomacy are set out.

All these works lack linguistic and stylistic homogeneity, and often adopt a very unclassical, popular linguistic form. In the eyes of their sponsor and his collaborators they were not literature, but confidential state papers.

After the restoration of the Byzantine Empire in 1261, the tradition of historiography was eagerly taken up again. George Akropolites (1217–1282), teacher of Theodore II Laskaris, statesman, and diplomat, picked up the story of Byzantium where Niketas Choniates had left it, and narrated the history of the Nicaean Empire and its ousting of all rivals, including ultimately the Latin rulers of Constantinople. His history covers the years 1203–1261. Succinct, clear, and reliable, with an eye for historical connections, Akropolites slips into unobjective panegyric when he comes to deal with Michael VIII. And behind his careful analysis of historical causes there lurks a belief in the providential mission of the empire. His language is classical, but he avoids rhetorical inflation or bombast.

Akropolites had a continuator in the clergyman George Pachymeres (*d. ca.* 1310), rhetorician, philosopher, poet, statesman, and opponent of the union of the churches in 1274. His history covers the years 1255–1308. Objective, skeptical, and free from malice, Pachymeres has been called a Byzantine humanist. His narrative includes fictitious speeches and is more rhetorically keyed up than that of Akropolites. His language is strictly classicizing, full of rare and obsolete words and classical allusions.

The middle of the fourteenth century produced two notable Byzantine historians. Nikephoros Gregoras (1290/1291–1360) had an uneven career, oscillating between high office and disgrace. Although a layman, he was deeply involved in the theological disputes of the age. He wrote rhetorical and philosophical works, speeches, letters, and poems. His *Roman History* covers the years 1204–1359. Well-informed, critical, serious, aware of economic and social matters as well as of politics and war, Gregoras is an informative and reliable source until he reaches the hesychast dispute in the 1340's. Then his own involvement leads him to include some of his speeches and writings at length. This is an extreme example of the diffuseness and lack of structure that mars this remarkable history. Emperor John VI Kantakouzenos (1347–1354) spent the years from his abdication until his death at the age of ninety-one (1383) as a monk in monasteries in Constantinople and on Mount Athos. It was during this period that he wrote his history, which covers the period 1320–1356 but includes occasional references to later events. It is in essence an apologetic work, but not narrowly partisan. It is filled with a sense of the vanity of human endeavor, as the author discerns behind his own personal tragedy the greater tragedy of the Byzantine state and people. Clearly structured composition and smooth, even narrative give a sometimes misleading air of objectivity to this personal memoir. Kantakouzenos is evasive in his many replies to the charges that he unlawfully assumed imperial power and that he brought the Ottoman Turks into Europe. Classicizing language and allusion, and direct imitation of passages of Thucydides, go side by side with readiness to admit everyday technical terms and neologisms.

Both Gregoras and Kantakouzenos use the traditional form of classical historiography to answer new needs, which were the result of the rapidly deteriorating situation of state and people. For nearly a century after them no one took up the challenge of writing the history of his own time. The times were too disjointed and discouraging. And it may be that the urbane, leisured, cultured readership for which historians wrote no longer existed.

World chronicles continued to be written, though none could vie with that of Zonaras as history or with that of Manasses as entertainment. That of Joel is little more than a list of names and dates. Theodore Skutariotes included much detailed information on the age of the Komnenoi and the Nicaean Empire. The verse chronicle of Ephraim, in nearly 10,000 lines, covers the years from Caligula to 1261. It is a mechanical and uncritical compilation. Also surviving are a number of local chronicles, mostly very short, of which the most noteworthy are the history of the Empire of Trebizond by Michael Panaretos, the account by John Kananos of the attack on Constantinople by Sultan Murad in 1422, and that by Theodore Anagnostes of the capture of Thessaloniki in 1430. These brief chronicles point to a survival of the annalistic tradition in Byzantine society. The voluminous church history of Nikephoros Kallistos Xanthopoulos, composed about 1315 and reaching to 610, was compiled entirely from the ecclesiastical historians of late antiquity.

It took the shock of the capture of Constantinople by the Ottoman Turks in 1453 and the end of the Byzantine Empire to arouse the sleeping muse of history. Four men answered the challenge, each in his own way. George Sphrantzes (Phrantzes), friend and minister of the Emperor Constantine XI, was taken prisoner by the Turks in 1453, and after many adventures withdrew to Corfu, where he died as a monk about 1478. His history of the fall of the Byzantine Empire covers the years 1413–1477, and is a kind of expanded diary. He was an eyewitness of much of what he relates. Written in unpretentious language and style, without learned digressions or rhetorical flourishes, Sphrantzes' history has a direct, autobiographical character. A courtier, he saw things from the viewpoint of the imperial court, but was critical of much that went on there. In the sixteenth century Makarios Melissenos, metropolitan of Monembasia, incorporated the whole of Sphrantzes' history (the *Chronicon minus*) into his own history of Byzantium under the Palaiologoi (the *Chronicon maius*), which long passed as a work of Sphrantzes.

Doukas (his forename is unknown) spent most of his life in Genoese service in the Aegean and traveled widely in lands under Ottoman rule. His chronicle begins with a summary of events from Adam to the Palaiologoi, and recounts Byzantine and eastern Mediterranean affairs in detail from 1341 to 1462. It is thus a kind of continuation of the histories of Nikephoros Gregoras and John Kantakouzenos. In spite of his Latin connections and sympathies, Doukas' standpoint is that of a Byzantine. Clear and reliable, and with few illusions or prejudices, he is capable of lively narrative and vivid description, and sometimes writes with passion. His language is a strange mixture of learned forms and spoken Greek.

Laonikos Chalkokondyles (*ca.* 1425–*ca.* 1490) was a member of a distinguished Athenian family and cousin of Demetrios Chalkokondyles, professor of Greek in Padua and Florence and editor of the *editiones principes* of Homer and Isocrates. His history covers the years 1298–1463. Beginning as a conventional history of the Byzantine Empire, it gradually becomes a history of the Ottoman Empire. Chalkokondyles' true theme is the expansion of the Ottoman state to fill the power vacuum created by the decline of Byzantium. He clearly models himself on Herodotus and Thucydides, but his analysis of power owes more to Polybius. His wide-ranging study marks a break with conventional Byzantine history, which had a Constantinopolitan viewpoint and providential overtones.

Michael Kritobulos of Imbros (*ca.* 1405–*ca.* 1470) was appointed governor of his native island by Sultan Mehmed II, whose confidence he long enjoyed. His history, which covers the years 1451–1467, is written from a Turkish standpoint. His hero is Sultan Mehmed, to whom he applies the traditional terms of Byzantine imperial panegyric. His theme is the expansion of the Ottoman Empire. His information is derived from personal observation or oral communication. Kritobulos writes in classicizing Greek and in a style overloaded with antiquarian allusions. The political realism that prompted his interest in Turkish affairs did not diminish his appreciation for Greek culture.

BIOGRAPHY

In classical antiquity biography was a literary genre distinct from history in its aims and methods (see Plutarch, *Vita Alexandri* 1). The biographer's purpose was to reveal character, not to narrate events. In late antiquity, an age of striking and powerful personalities, there was much biographical writing: Eunapios' *Lives of the Philosophers and Sophists,* Marinos' *Life of Proklos,* Eusebius' *Life of Constantine,* Palladius' *Life of John Chrysostom,* Athanasius' *Life of Antony.* The Byzantine world may or may not have been rich in personalities, but it certainly attached less importance to individual character than did the ancient world.

Secular biography was virtually nonexistent. Only after the Fourth Crusade, when the prestige of Byzantine tradition had been diminished, do we find a few brief biographies of members of the imperial family. The lack of interest in the character of individuals is borne out by the poverty of biographical detail in the many funeral or commemorative orations that survive. Even autobiographies are few in number and late. The monk and scholar Nikephoros Blemmydes (*ca.* 1197–*ca.* 1272) wrote his autobiography late in life, as did a younger contemporary, Patriarch Gregory of Cyprus (*ca.* 1241–1290). Michael VIII included a short and tendentious autobiography in the *typikon* of a monastery that he founded. Theodore Metochites wrote a long autobiographical poem. And John Kantakouzenos' *History* is essentially an autobiographical account of his times.

In contrast with secular biography, religious biography flourished throughout the Byzantine period. The personality of the holy man was of absorbing interest both as a model to follow and as a guarantee of salvation. Hagiography has several roots. The early church preserved, expanded, and sometimes forged the official records of the trials and deaths of its martyrs. A brief account of the martyr's life was often added by way of preface. As the age of martyrdom passed, the life of the holy man replaced his death as an object of interest. Ancient biographical tradition contributed both structural features and topics to early hagiography. And one type of ancient biography, the aretalogy, or account of the development and revelation of the powers of the pagan wonder-worker (such as Philostratos' *Life of Apollonius of Tyana*), provided a model from which much was copied. Athanasius' mid-fourth-century *Life of Antony* (*ca.* 250–*ca.* 356) gave a literary form to the saint's life that was influential throughout the Byzantine period.

Many thousands of Byzantine hagiographical texts survive, from all epochs. In the early and middle Byzantine periods a useful distinction may be made between "low-level" and "high-level" saints' lives. The former are generally provincial, sometimes rural, in origin; they celebrate the superhuman and even supernatural endurance, virtue, and power of one who has turned his back on the society into which he was born and lives as an outsider within it, a kind of bridge between heaven and earth; miraculous healing, sometimes including resurrection of the dead, is prominent in these stories, which are usually written in subliterary Greek. "High-level" lives are more often of metropolitan origin, and recount the exploits and proofs of holiness of a man high in the church hierarchy; persecution at the hands of heretics and confutation of their doctrines are major topics, as are problems of administration and church discipline; such lives are usually written in literary Greek.

Good examples of the former category are the series of lives of stylites beginning with the fifth-century *Life of Symeon the Stylite* and the seventh-century *Life of Theodore of Sykeon.* Typical examples of the latter category are the *Life of the Patriarch Eutychios* (late sixth century) and those of the patriarchs Nikephoros and Ignatios (ninth century). But the distinction is not a clear-cut one.

In addition to narratives of the lives of holy men, hagiographical texts included accounts of their posthumous miracles (particularly in the case of "dead" saints, of whose lives little or nothing was known), panegyrics and encomiums recited at their festivals, and *acoluthiae* or hymns in their honor. They also contained collections of stories of hermits and monks and their sayings—for instance, Theodoret of Cyrus' *Religious History* of the holy men of Syria (fifth century), Palladios' *Lausiac History* (fifth century), John Moschos' *Spiritual Meadow* (seventh century), and the various collections entitled *Sayings of the Fathers.*

The life and death of a holy man were often celebrated on the anniversary of his death. In this way hagiographical texts found their way into the liturgy. To facilitate liturgical use, collections were made of hagiographical texts arranged according to the ecclesiastical calendar. Menologies contained extensive lives as well as *acoluthiae* and other texts. Shorter lives were collected in menaia and synaxaria; panegyrics and encomiums, in *homilaria* and *panegyrica.* There were also special collections for use by monks and, occasionally, collections of lives of female saints for use by nuns.

The revived classicism of the tenth century led to a stylistic revision of many of the earlier saints' lives. Symeon Logothete, known as Symeon Metaphrastes, composed a revised menology in the second half of the tenth century, in which texts written in subliterary Greek were "improved" in language and style. In the course of this revision much of the concrete and picturesque detail of those early lives was replaced by pious reflections or pronouncements of unimpeachable theological orthodoxy. The Metaphrastic Lives gradually replaced the earlier texts in liturgical usage, and served as models for subsequent hagiographers.

By the eleventh century the liturgy was virtually fixed, except for local variations. The composition of saints' lives now became a literary activity divorced from liturgical practice. These literary lives, both of traditional holy men and of such examples as their own age offered, were written by very many men of letters up to and beyond the fall of Constantinople. Literary elegance, doctrinal orthodoxy, and moral edification were the aims of these hagiographers, rather than truth or historical plausibility. Examples of this literary hagiography are the *Life of Meletios the Younger* by Nikolaos of Methone in the twelfth century, the many *Lives* composed by Constantine Akropolites and by Theodore Metochites in the early fourteenth century, the four *Lives* of Maximos Kausokalybes in the later fourteenth century, and the various *Lives* of "dead" saints attributed to George the Rhetor in the fifteenth century.

Acta sanctorum, a critical corpus of all hagiographical texts, Oriental and Western as well as Byzantine, was begun by the Bollandists in 1643. Arranged in accordance with the Greek liturgical calendar, beginning on 1 September, it had reached December by 1982.

The lives of saints are of importance not only for the historical, topographical, economic, social, and other information that they contain, but also for the way in which they reflect the ideals, desires, and fantasies of the society in which they were composed and written. This is particularly true of the "low-level" saints' lives. But in interpreting them it must be borne in mind that the holy man did not provide the only model that ordinary Byzantines sought to imitate, though it was no doubt one of the most attractive. In a literature in which there was virtually no fiction until the twelfth century, the lives of the saints, as well as fulfilling their primary aim of glorification and edification, provided something of the aesthetic and emotional satisfaction that readers of later epochs sought in works of pure fiction.

EPISTOLOGRAPHY

The letter was already a recognized literary genre in antiquity. Teachers of rhetoric formulated rules for the composition of letters—clarity, brevity, and middle-level language and style were prescribed—sets of model letters (Demetrios, Pseudo-Libanius, and Pseudo-Proclus) were used in teaching, and writers collected and published their own letters. Such literary letters were rarely the vehicles of an informatory message, which often was conveyed verbally by the bearer, but were intended, rather, to reflect a state of mind and to give aesthetic pleasure. A number of stock topics were developed in infinite variety: friendship as a mystical union of souls, the letter as a means of surmounting the barrier of distance, the letter as a consolation for absence, the letter as a love charm, the longing for wings.

The literary letter, like many other art forms, appears to have been largely neglected during the "dark age" between the seventh and ninth centuries. It was revived in the late ninth and tenth centuries as part of the deliberate re-creation of the culture of the Christian Roman Empire of late antiquity. From then on, there were few Byzantine men of letters whose correspondence was not somehow collected and preserved. Though many of these letters appear to be almost totally devoid of content, their elegant variations on emotionally important themes and their often subtle allusiveness enabled them not only to establish and maintain personal relationships but also to serve as affirmations and indications of the status of writer and addressee in a hierarchical and deferential society. Michael Psellos declared that a carefully constructed letter communicates more than the random exchanges of direct conversation. These rhetorical letters were public documents, since the recipient was expected to read them aloud to an appreciative audience who might in turn make copies of them; indeed, correspondents often speak of the audience of a letter, and many appear to be writing as much for the expected audience as for the addressee.

The Byzantines inherited from antiquity another tradition of epistolography, that of the didactic or dogmatic letter. This form of composition was first used by Hellenistic philosophers and men of science such as Epicurus and Archimedes. The use of the letter for didactic purposes by St. Paul and other early

Christian writers, as well as by the church fathers, gave great prestige, in the eyes of the Byzantines, to this type of epistolography. The letters of such church leaders as Maximus the Confessor (*ca.* 580–662), Patriarch Germanos I (deposed 730), Patriarch Tarasios (*d.* 806), Theodore of Studios (759–826), Patriarch Photios (*d.* after 886), and Gregory Palamas (fourteenth century) were appreciated both for their content and for their style. Such letters were of course not subject to the requirement of brevity.

Much Byzantine epistolography occupies a middle ground between the purely rhetorical and the didactic, inasmuch as it both conveys a message and gives elegant expression to an attitude of mind. In general, the longer a letter is, the more likely it is to strike an informatory or argumentative note. But many writers display a remarkable ability to spin out variations on a commonplace theme almost ad infinitum, while others occasionally choose to convey a message or make a point briefly, with little care for literary form. Among the more noteworthy collections of letters, in addition to those mentioned, are those of Arethas of Caesarea, Leon Choirosphaktes, and Patriarch Nicholas I (tenth century); John Mauropous, Michael Psellos, and Theophylact Hephaistos (eleventh century); Michael Italicus, George Tornikes, John Tzetzes, Theodore Prodromos, Eustathios, and Michael Choniates (twelfth century); Theodore II Doukas Laskaris, Nikephoros Blemmydes, and Demetrios Chomatianos (thirteenth century); Maximos Planudes, Patriarch Athanasios I, Theodore Metochites, Joseph the Philosopher, Nikephoros Gregoras, Nikephoros Chumnos, Michael Gabras, and Demetrios Kydones (fourteenth century); and Manuel Kalekas, Manuel Chrysoloras, Manuel II Palaiologos, John and Mark Eugenikos, Patriarch Gennadios II, Theodore Agallianos, and Bessarion (fifteenth century).

Whatever their content and whatever the intention of their writers, Byzantine letters were composed in the light of a strict—and sometimes restrictive—literary tradition going back to antiquity. They are never ingenuous effusions. The alert reader not only can appreciate their virtuosity but also can learn from them much about the ideals and values of authors and readers, and the society to which they belonged.

BIBLIOGRAPHY

General Works. S. A. Averintsev, ed., *Vizantiskaya literatura* (1974); and *Poetika ranne-vizantiskoy literatury* (1977); Hans-Georg Beck, *Kirche und theologische Literatur im byzantinischen Reich* (1959); and *Geschichte der byzantinischen Volksliteratur* (1971). Robert Browning, "Byzantine Literature," in D. R. Dudley and D. M. Lang, eds., *The Penguin Companion to Literature,* IV (1969); L. A. Freiberg, ed., *Antičnost i Vizantia* (1975); L. A. Freiberg and T. V. Popova, *Vizantiskaya literatura epokhi rastveta IX–XV vv.* (1978); Herbert Hunger, *Die hochsprachliche profane Literatur der Byzantiner,* 2 vols. (1978); Silvio Impellizzeri, *La letteratura bizantina da Costantino agli iconoclasti* (1965); Karl Krumbacher, *Geschichte der byzantinischen Literatur,* 2 vols. (1897; 2nd ed., 1970); Konstantinos Trypanes, *Greek Poetry from Homer to Seferis* (1981), 381–530.

Secular Poetry. A. D. Aleksidze, *Mir grečeskogo rytsarskogo romana XIII–XIV vv.* (1979); Raffaele Cantarella, *Poeti bizantini,* 2 vols. (1948); Franz Dölger, "Die byzantinische Dichtung in der Reinsprache," 2nd ed., in Εὐχαριστήριον, *Franz Dölger zum 70. Geburtstag* (1961); Henri Grégoire, Ὁ *Διγενὴς Ἀκρίτας* (1942); A. D. Komines, Τὸ *βυζαντινὸν ἱερὸν ἐπίγραμμα καὶ οἱ ἐπίγραμμα τὸ ποιοί* (1966); Otto Mazal, "Der griechische und der byzantinische Roman in der Forschung von 1945 bis 1960," in *Jahrbuch der oesterreichischen byzantinischen Gesellschaft* **11–12** (1962–1963), **13** (1964), **14** (1965); Th. Nissen, "Historisches Epos und Panegyrikos in Spätantike," in *Hermes,* **75** (1940); S. V. Poliakova, *Iz istorii vizantiskogo romana* (1979); K. A. Trypanes, ed., *Mediaeval and Modern Greek Poetry* (1951).

Liturgical Poetry. José Grosdidier de Matons, *Romanos le Mélode et les origines de la poésie religieuse à Byzance* (1977); K. Mitsakes, *βυζαντινὴ ὑμνογραφία*, I, *Ἀπὸ τὴν καινὴ Αἰαθὴκη ἕως τὴν εἰκονομαχία* (1971); N. V. Tomadakes, Ἡ *βυζαντινὴ ὑμνογραφία καὶ ποίησις*, 3rd ed. (1965); Egon Wellesz, *A History of Byzantine Music and Hymnography,* 2nd ed. (1961); Th. Xydes, *βυζαντινὴ ὑμνογραφία* (1978).

History. M. E. Colonna, *Gli storici bizantini dal IV al XV secolo,* I, *Storici profani* (1956); P. Dostalova, "Vizantyskaya istorografia," in *Vizantysky Vremennik,* **43** (1982); I. E. Karagiannopulos, Πηγαὶ *τῆς βυζαντινῆς ἱστορίας* (1970); G. Moravcsik, *Byzantinoturcica,* I, *Die byzantinischen Quellen der Geschichte der Türkvölker,* 2nd ed. (1958); F. H. Tinnefeld, *Kategorien der Kaiserkritik in der byzantinischen Historiographie von Prokop bis Niketas Choniates* (1971).

Biography. René Aigrain, *L'hagiographie* (1953); Sofia Boesch Gajano, ed., *Agiografia altomedievale* (1976); Pierre Canivet, *Le monachisme syrien selon Théodoret de Cyr* (1977); Hippolyte Delehaye, *Les légendes grecques des saints militaires* (1909, repr. 1975); *Les saints stylites* (1923); and *The Legends of the Saints* (1962); Hippolyte Delehaye, ed., *Synaxarium ecclesiae Constantinopolitanae, propylaeum ad Acta sanctorum nov.* (1902); Albert Ehrhard, *Überlieferung und Bestand der hagiographischen und homiletischen Literatur der griechischen*

Kirche von den Anfängen bis zum Ende des XVI. Jahrhunderts, 3 vols. (1937–1952); François Halkin, ed., *Bibliotheca hagiographica graeca,* 3rd ed., 3 vols. (1957).

Epistolography. Jean Darrouzès, *Épistoliers byzantins du Xe siècle* (1960); A. R. Littlewood, "An 'Ikon of the Soul': The Byzantine Letter," in *Visible Language,* **10**, no. 3 (1976); Gustav Karlsson, *Idéologie et cérémonial dans l'épistolographie byzantine,* 2nd ed. (1962); Louis Robert, "Les Kordakia de Nicée, le combustible de Synnada et les poissons-scies: Sur des lettres d'un métropolite de Phrygie au Xe siècle, philologie et réalites," in *Journal des savants* (1961) and (1962); V. A. Smetanin, *Epistolografia* (1970); Ioannes Sykoutres, "Probleme der byzantinischen Epistolographie," in *IIIe Congrès international des études byzantines, comptes-rendus* (1932); Klaus Thraede, *Grundzüge griechisch-römischer Brieftopik* (1970); N. B. Tomadakes, *βυζαντινὴ ἐπιστολογραφία,* 3rd ed. (1969).

ROBERT BROWNING

[See also **Agathias; Akathistos; Anna Komnena; Byzantine Poetry; Byzantine Popular Literature; Chronicles; Digenis Akritas; Genesios, Joseph; George of Pisidia; George the Monk; Historiography, Byzantine; John Kinnamos; John of Nikiu; John VI Kantakouzenos; Kanôn; Kontakion; Liturgy, Byzantine Church; Michael Attaleiates; Morea, Chronicle of; Nikephoros, Patriarch; Nikephoros Bryennios; Nikephoros Gregoras; Niketas Choniates; Paschale Chronicon; Procopius; Psellos, Michael; Rhetoric, Byzantine; Romanos Melodos; Sebêos; Skylitzes, John; Symeon Logothete; Synaxary; Theodore Balsamon; Theodore Metochites; Theodore of Studios; Theodore Prodromos; Theophanes Confessor; Theophanes Continuatus; Theophylact Symokattes; Zonaras, John.**]

BYZANTINE POETIC FORMS. Byzantine poetry is part of the continuing tradition of Greek poetry, defined only by the arbitrary dates of the Byzantine period. There is little unity of form, subject matter, or even language, for some early Byzantine poems are in Latin; and the range of Greek used is comparable to the range of language between the time of Vergil—perhaps even of Ennius—and that of the *Divina Commedia.* Within this diversity one may distinguish three major poetic strands—classicizing, liturgical, and popular—each with characteristics of language, form, and subject which evolve, decline, renew themselves, and influence each other.

Classicizing poetry was modeled on classical Greek poets, by the theory that Attic Greek language and literature had reached a perfection from which every change meant decline. This, the ideology of the Atticist movement, dominated Byzantine education. Increasingly, however, students lost touch with the beguiling pagans themselves, learning only the Atticists' rules of language and form, with references and quotations from florilegia. Since most Byzantine writers suffered these limitations, new literary forms and language did evolve, though slowly, often influenced by the postclassical Greek of the Bible. But in times of reform writers returned to the Atticists' sources with direct imitation of the ancients: such periods were the Justinianic (sixth century), the Macedonian (tenth and early eleventh centuries), the Komnenian (twelfth century), and the Palaiologan (late thirteenth and early fourteenth centuries).

These pressures are well illustrated by metrical developments. Before Justinian's day the difference between long and short syllables had disappeared in pronunciation, and classical meters had consequently lost all meaning save that of intellectual exercises. Yet of the four ancient meters widely used in early Byzantine poetry, the hexameter and pentameter remained vigorous in the sixth century and were used spasmodically later, while the iambic trimeter and the anacreontic were common till the end of Byzantium, though steadily losing their classical form. The distinctions between long and short syllables were gradually blurred or ignored. The avoidance of metrical resolution soon stabilized syllable numbers at twelve for the trimeter and eight for the anacreontic. Rules governing the position of stress-accents in the line were increasingly observed, particularly at line endings and before regular caesuras, following usual Indo-European patterns. Perhaps the stress-accent, the only metrical fact immediately appreciated by a Byzantine ear, was being used to indicate metrical divisions, marking the difference between verse and prose. Thus ancient trimeters and anacreontics seemed to survive by turning into accentual twelve-syllable and eight-syllable forms.

The hexameter was widely used in fifth- and sixth-century epic, in the *Posthomerica* of Quintus of Smyrna, in the *Dionysiaca* of Nonnos, and also in poems of Nonnos' school, including the *ekphraseis* of buildings by Paul the Silentiary and John of Gaza. Epigrams of this period in elegiac distichs of alternate hexameter and pentameter are preserved in the Palatine and Planudean Anthologies. Later poets, however, rarely used these meters, probably because they demanded variations in syllable numbers: the best later attempts were those of the twelfth-century Theodore Prodromos. The iambic trimeter took over the hexameter's functions, for example in the seventh-century epic description of the campaigns of Heraklios by George of Pisidia and the tenth-century *ekphrasis* of the Church of the Holy Apostles by Constantine of Rhodes. Between the ninth and eleventh centuries iambic trimeter was the major medium for the epigrams of Theodore of Studios, John Geometres, Christopher of Mytilene, and John Mavropous, four varied writers of considerable sensitivity and talent. Manuel Philes, the most prolific poet of the Palaiologan renaissance, also made wide use of the trimeter in a flexible and completely accentual form. The anacreontic was preeminently the meter of the lament, and was used for this purpose by a wide range of authors.

Liturgical verse was originally confined to the Psalms and biblical canticles. Religious poetry, like the hexameters of Gregory of Nazianzus (fourth century) and the hymns of Synesius of Cyrene (early fifth century, the last poems in a range of classical lyric meters), was not intended for liturgical use. The church was thus at a disadvantage against heretical sects that used contemporary hymns in worship. Eventually it adopted, from Syriac poetry, the kontakion, a kind of rhythmical sermon divided into successive strophes of the same rhythmical shape, developed primarily in the fourth century by Ephraem the Syrian and introduced to Constantinople in the fifth. In the sixth century it reached a climax in the anonymous *Akathistos Hymn* and the kontakia of Romanos the Melode, poems of complex technique and subtlety of thought and expression which establish Romanos as a major figure in religious literature. In the seventh century, after two centuries of dominance, the kontakion gave place to the *kanōn*, a longer and still more complex ninefold form based on similar metrical principles. It was introduced by Andrew of Crete and developed by John of Damascus, and still dominates Orthodox worship today.

Byzantine popular poetry is nearly all in accentual fifteen-syllable "political" verse. The earliest surviving examples date from the twelfth century, including the "Ptochoprodromos" poems and, probably, a formal version of the epic romance *Digenis Akritas.* After a break, popular romances, chronicles, and other poems survive from the fourteenth century—the beginnings of Modern Greek literature. But political verse was used in formal Greek before Ptochoprodromos. It first appears in tenth-century imperial laments, then in hymns by Symeon the New Theologian, didactic poetry by Michael Psellos, John Tzetzes, and Constantine Manasses, and ceremonial poems by Theodore Prodromos.

Was political verse then created and used only by the learned before breaking into popular use with Ptochoprodromos? Or have surviving texts been influenced by popular oral poetry before the twelfth century, in political verse and perhaps in other meters? It would be rash at present to make such an assumption, in view of the lack of direct evidence; yet there are indirect indications to support it. First, learned users of political verse do not claim to be innovators. They seem to have chosen it to please patrons or to be clearly understood, as if forced to use a despised but popular oral form. Second, some fourteenth-century popular poems show stylistic similarities to oral traditions in other languages, suggesting the existence, by then at least, of Greek oral poetry in political verse. More suggestive still, the three rhythmical forms of late Byzantine poetry (fifteen, twelve, and eight syllables respectively) are remarkably similar to the most common rhythms in medieval Latin. It is possible that there was some connection, perhaps at an oral level, but meter in both languages may have collapsed independently into similar rhythmic patterns.

BIBLIOGRAPHY

Bibliographical works. Hans-Georg Beck, *Kirche und theologische Literatur im byzantinischen Reich* (1959), and *Geschichte der byzantinischen Volksliteratur* (1971); Herbert Hunger, *Die hochsprachliche profane Literatur der Byzantiner,* 2 vols. (1978–1979).

Anthology. Constantine A. Trypanis, ed., *Medieval and Modern Greek Poetry* (1951).

General surveys. Robert Browning, *Medieval and Modern Greek* (1969); Franz Dölger, "Die byzantinische Dichtung in der Reinsprache," in *Eucharisterion. Franz Dölger zum 70. Geburtstage* (1961), 1–63, and "Byzantine Literature," in *The Cambridge Medieval History,* IV, 2 (1967); M. J. Jeffreys, "The Nature and Origins of the Political Verse," in *Dumbarton Oaks Papers,* 27 (1973); F. H. Marshall, "Byzantine Literature," in *Byzantium,* Norman H. Baynes and H. St. L. B. Moss, eds. (1948).

MICHAEL JEFFREYS

[See also **Classical Literary Studies in the Middle Ages; Greek, Byzantine; Kanōn; Kontakion;** and individual poets.]

BYZANTINE LITERATURE: POPULAR. Throughout the Byzantine period scattered literary works were written for a broad popular audience, in a language and style less archaic and artificial than the Byzantine norm. They are particularly concentrated in the areas of hagiography and chronicles. But the term "popular literature" is usually confined to works in a language containing substantial defining elements of modern spoken Greek. The first surviving examples date from the mid twelfth century. After a gap, there are others from the fourteenth century up to and beyond the fall of Constantinople.

Nearly all are in verse, almost invariably the fifteen-syllable *dekapentasyllabos,* or "political" verse, predominant even now in Greek folk song. Their language includes elements of the everyday speech of the time, but covers an amazing morphological range: modern Greek variants making their first appearance in surviving literature share lines with ancient forms already unstable in the New Testament. It has been suggested by some that political verse had formed its own traditional style and language for oral use before the writing of any surviving popular literature, so that popular poems preserved from the twelfth century on represent the written extension of an oral tradition. Others point out the extensive use of the meter from the tenth century on by some of the most learned men in Byzantium, and describe popular literature, political verse, and mixed language as experiments by the learned to reach a popular audience.

Surviving popular works of the twelfth century are all connected with the Komnenian imperial court. The best are four poems written by an unidentified Ptochoprodromos ("Penniless Prodromos"), a name referring to the many-talented literary figure Theodore Prodromos—though metrical features preclude attribution to him. Three of these poems are requests to patrons for support, including a lively description of the author's suffering at the hands of his dominant wife and an essay on the commercial worthlessness of education; the fourth is a satire on monastic life ostensibly written by a young monk. The other twelfth-century examples are moralizing advice from a Komnenian prince to a young relative (the *Spaneas* poem), a plea for release from prison addressed to Manuel I Komnenos by Michael Glykas, and an address to welcome an imperial bride arriving from France (the *Eisiterioi* for Agnes of France). The epic romance *Digenis Akritas* may also be datable to the twelfth century. The work survives in rather formal language in later manuscripts, but recent studies have suggested that it was compiled in the twelfth century from older material, at least some of it of popular origin.

The end of the twelfth century brought civil war and administrative collapse, ending in the capture of Constantinople by the Fourth Crusade (1204). The fragmented Greek states that survived to challenge the new Latin Empire were predisposed against vernacular experiments. Stress was put on archaic language and the study of ancient literature, to emphasize the unbroken cultural tradition that, it was hoped, would bridge the temporary political interruption of the Latin Empire. The desire to reestablish legitimacy continued these pressures even beyond the recapture of Constantinople (1261).

The Fourth Crusade marks a definitive break in Greek literary history. The Komnenian court had shown clear signs that imperial taste and patronage were pressing for simplicity of style and language. Obvious examples are the popular poems already listed; one may add numerous works for state ceremonial and even verse for educational purposes, both written in political verse at a simple level of the formal language, designed to be understood by the half-educated and even the uneducated. Circumstances seemed propitious for the development of a Greek vernacular literature to rival that of the West. By 1204, though, this line of progress was blocked, leaving the thirteenth century bare of surviving popular literature. When it reappears in the fourteenth century, popular literature rarely expresses popularizing forces within the Constantinopolitan aristocracy, but becomes a largely peripheral phenomenon. Though it is hard to ascribe authors, dates, and areas of the Greek world, available evidence often points to Westerners ruling Greek-speaking regions. Feeling, one suspects, little need to prove descent from the Romano-Greek imperial past, they sponsored literary works at the level of Greek best understood by themselves and their subjects.

The principal genre among these fourteenth- and fifteenth-century works is the romance. The romance had been in eclipse in Greek literature from around A.D. 300 until the mid twelfth centruy, from which there survive four romances in formal Greek: Theodore Prodromos' *Rhodanthe and Dosikles,* Constantine Manasses' fragmentary *Aristandros and Kallithea,* Eustathios Makrembolites' *Hysmine and Hysminias,* and Niketas Eugenianos' *Drosilla and Charikles.* These arose from the milieu discussed above, which produced works in fairly intelligible form, often for imperial commissions. These romances coincide in date with the first western European romances, immediately raising the question of whether Byzantine romances are primarily a genuine Byzantine development or an imitation of Western forms. It may be significant that two Greek romances probably were written before the Second Crusade (1147), while the major Western flowering follows it and may result from it.

Fourteenth-century Byzantine romances fall into two groups: some have discernible Western originals and some do not. Of the apparently independent Greek creations three—*Kallimachos and Chrysorrhoe, Belthandros and Chrysantza,* and *Lybistros and Rhodamne*—center on the separation, adventures, and eventual marriage of hero and heroine, with conventional ecphrases of gardens, castles, beautiful princesses, and the god of love. Yet these features, familiar to readers of Western romances, do not prove Western influence; they are equally explicable from the Greek tradition. Numerous details arise from Greek folk-song motifs, while increasing use of Western feudal trappings suggests that the last two above were written by Greeks under Western rule. *Kallimachos* is attributed (inconclusively) to Emperor Andronikos II's cousin, and may be the only popular Byzantine work written after 1204 by one of the Constantinopolitan elite.

Other seemingly original Greek romances include a rather formal version of the ubiquitous Greek Alexander Romance, and two poems on Homeric heroes: *Troas* bases its narrative on the stories of Paris and Achilles, however inaccurately and indirectly, on ancient mythological tradition, while the *Achilleis* (apart from the inserted conclusion) knows nothing about its hero but includes such names as Patroklos and the Myrmidons. Achilles is portrayed as a knightly medieval prince.

The romances based on Western originals make concessions to their new Greek form, giving the hero a precocious childhood or moral advice from his father, or omitting episodes unacceptable to Byzantine taste, together with numerous smaller changes. The works adapted are *Apollonius of Tyre,* the Trojan romance of Benoît de Sainte-Maure (the *Roman de Troie*), part of the Arthurian compilation of Rusticiano da Pisa *(Gyron le courtois), Blancheflour et Florence (Phlorios and Platziaphlora), Pierre de Provence et la belle Maguelonne (Imberios and Margarona),* and Boccaccio's *Teseida.*

Another important genre is the chronicle. The *Chronicle of the Morea* records in verse the history of the Crusader states of Greece down to 1292. Its style and language have been variously interpreted as a Frenchman's inadequate Greek or as Greek oral tradition with a Gallic tinge. It is an international text, with versions in Greek, French, Italian, and Aragonese of disputed priority. A similar verse chronicle describes the later conquests of the Tocco family. Quite different are the Cypriot chronicles of Leontios Machairas and Boustronios, which owe much of their considerable charm to their prose form, which permits more personal observation than did traditional verse.

An instructive example of a Western patron is a member of the Orsini family who ruled Epiros from 1323 to 1335 as John II Komnenos Angelos-Doukas. To support this Byzantine pose he commissioned Constantine Hermoniakos to paraphrase Homer in vernacular Greek. The result is so badly written and dependent on secondary sources that it is surprising to find a text of Homer employed in some passages. Octosyllables are used instead of the usual political verse.

Equally idiosyncratic is *Belisarios,* which projects onto Justinian's great general a millennium of varied examples of the destructive power of envy in Byzantine history. One has the impression of a kind of urban folk song, composed from the perspective of Constantinople with a unique antiaristocratic bias.

The animal fable and the lament are well represented in Byzantine popular literature. The *Story of the Animals,* the *Poulologos* (on birds), and two linked donkey stories are in verse, and there are prose fables about fruits and fish. They have largely resisted ascription to particular historical situations. The laments follow the defeats and sieges of the Byzantine decline, culminating in a series bewailing the capture of Constantinople (1453).

Vernacular personal poetry, which had vanished with Ptochoprodromos, reappears in Venetian Crete. Leonardo Dellaportas and Stephanos Sachlikis provide lively comment on personal and social problems—particularly, in Sachlikis' case, the seamier side of society. This development points to the future: Venetian Crete in the sixteenth and seventeenth centuries continued Byzantine popular literature and brought its tradition to a climax in the Cretan Renaissance theater and the *Erotokritos.*

Surviving remains of Byzantine popular literature probably represent a small proportion of what was written and a minute fraction of what was sung or chanted. It is likely that some of these texts are special written developments of extensive oral and traditional forms that may have flourished for centuries in Byzantine society without leaving other evidence of their existence. This dimension of Byzantine popular literature should not be ignored. Some of these oral forms (though probably not all that once existed) are preserved in modern Greek folk songs, which in some cases are as valid as the texts discussed above in reflecting the popular Byzantine cultural experience. The conclusions to be drawn from them, however, are severely limited, given the fluidity of oral tradition.

BIBLIOGRAPHY

Bibliographical works. Hans-Georg Beck, *Geschichte der byzantinischen Volksliteratur* (1971); Margaret Alexiou and D. Holton, "The Origins and Development of 'Politikos Stichos,'" in *Mandatoforos,* **9** (1976); E. M. Jeffreys, "The Popular Byzantine Verse Romances of Chivalry: Work Since 1971," in *Mandatoforos,* **14** (1979).

General surveys. Robert Browning, *Medieval and Modern Greek* (1969); M. J. Jeffreys, "The Literary Emergence of Vernacular Greek," in *Mosaic* (Manitoba), **8** (1974).

Recent editions. David Holton, ed., *Diegesis tou Alexandrou: The Rhymed Version* (1974); [*Ignoti auctoris*] *Chronica Toccorum Cephallensium,* J. Schirò, ed. (1975).

MICHAEL JEFFREYS

[See also **Alexander Romances; Byzantine Literature; Byzantine Poetry; Digenis Akritas; Fables; Morea, Chronicle of; Theodore Prodromos; Troy Story.**]